Programming
Microsoft® SQL Server™ 2005

twentysix
GROUP

PUBLISHED BY
Microsoft Press
A Division of Microsoft Corporation
One Microsoft Way
Redmond, Washington 98052-6399

Library of Congress Control Number 2006924467
978-0-7356-1923-4
0-7356-1923-9

Printed and bound in the United States of America.

1 2 3 4 5 6 7 8 9   QWT   1 0 9 8 7 6

Distributed in Canada by H.B. Fenn and Company Ltd.

A CIP catalogue record for this book is available from the British Library.

Microsoft Press books are available through booksellers and distributors worldwide. For further information about international editions, contact your local Microsoft Corporation office or contact Microsoft Press International directly at fax (425) 936-7329. Visit our Web site at www.microsoft.com/mspress. Send comments to *mspinput@microsoft.com*.

Acquisitions Editor: Ben Ryan
Project Editor: Lynn Finnel
Technical Editors: Lin Joyner, Tim Clewes, and Jim O'Brien from Content Master, a member of
    CM Group, Ltd., Jim Causey, Mike Wachal, Laurentiu Cristofor, and Raul Garcia
Copy Editor: Ina Chang
Indexer: Brenda Miller
Photographer: Jay Brady

Body Part No. X11-74980

To my wife, Lauren and my son, Miles. Thank you for your love,
your support and most of all, your patience.

— Andrew Brust

To CPT James M. Gurbisz: Your sacrifice
will not be forgotten.

— Stephen Forte

Contents at a Glance

Table of Contents

Part III ## Reporting and Business Intelligence

Acknowledgments

A number of people contributed to this book, both as technical experts and as providers of moral and logistical support. It's impossible to declare one category more important than the other, and so I'd like to thank people in both.

Several people, some of them now alumni, from the SQL Server Analysis Services team at Microsoft were extremely helpful. They provided information, code samples, and quick answers to last-minute questions that helped make a number of chapters in this book much stronger. Sometimes they thought they were just helping with conference presentations, but their assistance was invaluable in the completion of this book as well. Among them are T. K. Anand, Amir Netz, Ariel Netz, Mosha Pasumansky, Jamie MacLennan, and Matt Carroll. Thanks also to Matt Nunn, Alex Payne, and Francois Ajenstat for helping me connect with so many people on the team, and to Steve Lasker of the Visual Studio Data team for teaching me lots of the cool data binding tips in Chapter 8.

I would also like to thank a number of people at my company, twentysix New York, for their patience and flexibility as I worked on "the book." Phil Eames, Dave Mittereder, and Jay Rabin were unbelievably tolerant of my erratic schedule and lent much needed moral support when things got really hectic. Lawrence De Voe pitched in numerous times to pick up things that would otherwise have fallen through the cracks. Elizabeth Donsky, although no longer with the company, helped me keep my life and my business in order for almost a decade; the very idea of the book would not have existed without her. On the technical side, Brian Schmitt helped me understand the realities of deploying OLAP into production and managing the process of near-real-time BI. Mark Frawley not only helped me better understand MDX, but he helped me explain it more simply and more precisely in Chapter 19. And all the cool stuff in Chapter 9 on remote debugging is there only because of the assistance and instruction provided by Zach Plevritis.

Other "twentysixers" to be thanked are Elsie Pan and Kent Brown, for lending their expertise to this book and each writing a stellar chapter. It's a thrill and an honor to have them as co-authors on this book. And while we're on the topic of coauthors, Sahil Malik, Bill Wolff, and especially Rob Walters have my deep gratitude for coming in late in the project and writing chapters of their own that were crucial to the effort of getting things *done*. Steven Forte gets double thanks: he worked hard on the book, and he worked even harder to hold our friendship sacred when the work got tough.

A number of people at Microsoft Press deserve many thanks, specifically Lynn Finnel, Ben Ryan, and Ina Chang for their editorial leadership as well as Jim Causey, Lin Joyner, and Tim Clewes for their tech editing expertise. I have lost count of the number of times I wrote "good catch" in the margins of this book's manuscript in response to their suggestions.

And while they were not directly involved in this project, I feel it important to recognize all the good people at Fawcette Technical Publications (FTP) who gave me my "first break" as a technical author for *Visual Basic Programmer's Journal* (now *Visual Studio Magazine*) all the way back in 1994. The positive impact FTP has had on my career is immense, and it continues today. Jim Fawcette, Jeff Hadfield, Patrick Meader, and alumni Frank Moncrief, Lee Thé, and Matt Carter deserve very special thanks. It is rather fitting that Matt Carter, my first-ever editor, is now with Microsoft Press; I guess I need to thank him twice.

Most of all, I'd like to thank my family, on both sides, for encouraging me to soldier on through one of the longest projects I've ever worked on. Paula, David, Michael, Jessica, Valerie, Jill, Norman (Dad), and especially Sallee (Mom), thank you for your support and for dealing with me as a mostly absentee son or brother (in-law). And, to reiterate my overall dedication of the book, thanks to my wife Lauren and my now 19-month-old son Miles. We finally have our weekends back!

—Andrew Brust

It's nice to have your name on the cover of a book, but without help from various people, this book never would have happened. I'll start with Andrew, since it was all his fault. He recruited me and, with the help of Eileen Crain, brokered the deal with Microsoft Press. He also went above and beyond the call of duty when some coauthors quit or went missing and deadlines loomed

Thanks to my girlfriend Kathleen for putting up with my sometimes very harsh writing schedule and all of my complaints about the work involved.

I would not have been able to take on this project if I did not have the support of the folks at my company, Corzen. I would like to give special thanks to our CEO Bruce Murray, Director of Indicator Services Bob Plummer, Director of IT Michael Coakley, and my entire development staff, led by Al Cadalzo.

We have also had tons of great reviewers. I was blessed to have folks like Kimberly Tripp, Peter DeBetta, and Roman Rehak help out with reading my chapters, as well as Richard Campbell, Goksin Bakir, Malek Kemmou, Jason Gideon, and Julie Lerman.

A lot of folks at Microsoft helped in a meaningful way. So a special thanks to all of them, including: on the Mobility team, Kevin Collins, Durga Gudipati, Glenn Gailey, and Steve Lasker; on the SQL Server Integration Services team, Kirk Haselden, Ted Lee, and Sergei Ivanov; and on the SQL Server Management Studio team, Bill Ramos.

Lastly, all of the coauthors made this project so much smoother, but two took time out to write chapters that were my responsibility: thanks to Patrick O'Toole for Chapter 5 on SQL Server Management Studio, and to Ted Lee and Sergei Ivanov for Chapter 16 on SQL Server Integration Services.

—Stephen Forte

Introduction

When we started out with the idea of writing a book about the new version of Microsoft SQL Server, the notion seemed relatively straightforward. Our goal was to write a book that would provide exhaustive, comprehensive coverage of the product, and that goal seemed practical, for a number of reasons.

All of us involved with this book at its inception had worked with SQL Server for the better part of a decade and had been involved with Microsoft .NET since its early pre-release days. We knew that the next release of SQL Server, then code named "Yukon," would achieve a marriage of sorts between the database server and the .NET common language runtime (CLR).

We knew that the scalability story, which was already working out well with SQL Server 2000, would get better. We knew that post-release pieces of SQL Server 2000, such as Notification Services (and, later, Reporting Services) would be more integrated and feature-laden. We knew that Analysis Services would grow in importance and capability. We greeted these developments with great anticipation. This release of SQL Server would be cheered by database specialists and developer generalists alike; that made it unique and exciting.

With these assumptions, we knew we wanted to immerse ourselves in the product and write a book about it for Microsoft. We knew it would be hard work, but we wanted to understand the product at the level necessary to write the book, and we wanted to impart what we learned to the Microsoft developer community, for which we had been writing since the early 1990s. This seemed like a natural project—a "no brainer" in colloquial terms.

The truth is, we had no idea what we were in for. Bear with us here, because the outcome has been excellent and has given us an important vantage point on SQL Server 2005. But we must be honest: The journey we took in writing this book revealed some very important facts about SQL Server 2005 that we hadn't fully appreciated at the beginning of the project. That changed our approach to writing about SQL Server 2005, and we think it will affect the approach *you* take to learning it.

SQL Server 2005 is a huge release, and, to be truthful, SQL Server is now formidably vast and complex. It is no longer just a phenomenal enterprise relational database management system. It is now a *bona fide* middleware, service-oriented, message-based programming platform; an XML document repository; a desktop and mobile device database engine; a market-leading business intelligence (BI) platform; and a real-time alerting system all rolled into one. In fact, SQL Server isn't one product. It's a collection of products and technologies that, although related, should each be considered separately. How can such a massive product be covered comprehensively in a single book?

To understand our approach, we ask that you consider likening SQL Server 2005 to, of all things, a Sunday newspaper. A Sunday newspaper is made up of multiple sections, each of which is written separately and appeals to a distinct audience. The sections do have overlapping content and share some readership, of course, but most people don't read the whole paper, and they don't need to. Meanwhile, the entire paper is considered a single publication and those who read it think of themselves as readers of the paper rather than of one or more of its sections. Likewise, SQL Server has many pieces to it; few people will use them all, and people will need to learn about them gradually, over time, as their business needs dictate.

Our book reflects this reality and in many ways replicates the structure of a Sunday newspaper. For one thing, a great number of authors have been involved in producing the book, drawing on their expertise in their chapters' specific subject matter. For another, the context and style of certain chapters differ markedly from those of other chapters. Some chapters cover specific subject matter deeply. Others cover a broader range of material, and do so at a higher level. That's an approach we didn't anticipate when we started the book. But it's the approach we found most effective by the time we finished. We think it makes an otherwise overwhelming set of technologies much more approachable and makes the learning process much more modular.

Make no mistake, though, the overall vision for the book is a cohesive one—to explore the numerous programmability points of SQL Server 2005 and, in so doing, provide widespread coverage of the great majority of the product's features, in a voice that caters to developers' interests.

Whether you read every chapter in the book or just some of them, whether you read the book in or out of order, our goal has been to provide you with practical information, numerous useful samples, and a combination of high-level coverage and detailed discussion, depending on how deep we thought developers would want to go.

Just as the Sunday newspaper doesn't cover everything that's going on in the world, this book won't teach you everything about SQL Server. For example, we don't cover high-availability/ fault tolerance features such as replication, clustering, or database mirroring. We don't discuss query plans and optimization, nor do we provide extensive detail on SQL Server Profiler, SQL Trace, or the new Database Engine Tuning Advisor.

We discovered as we wrote the book that covering everything in the product would result in a book unwieldy in size and unapproachable in style. We hope we struck the right balance, providing a *digestible* amount of information with enough developer detail and enough pointers to other material to help you become a seasoned SQL Server professional.

Who This Book Is For

Now that we have established *what* the book does and does not cover, we'd like to clarify just *who* we believe will be most interested in it and best served by it. In a nutshell, this book is for

.NET and SQL Server developers who work with databases and data access, at the business logic/middle-tier layer as well as the application level.

In our perhaps self-centered view of the development world, we think this actually describes *most* .NET developers, but clearly some developers are more interested in database programming in general, and SQL Server specifically, than others, and it is this more interested group we want to reach.

We assume you have basic, working knowledge of .NET programming in C# on the client and Transact-SQL (T-SQL) on the server. We also assume you are comfortable with the basics of creating tables, views, and stored procedures on the server and working with ADO.NET *Connection, Command, DataReader*, and *DataSet* objects on the client using the *SqlClient* ADO.NET provider. On the tools side, we assume you are familiar with the prior generation of SQL Server and .NET tools—specifically, SQL Server Enterprise Manager, SQL Query Analyzer, and Visual Studio .NET 2002 or 2003. Having knowledge of these tools will better equip you to learn about their successors: SQL Server Management Studio and Visual Studio 2005.

Having said all that, we have a fairly liberal policy regarding these prerequisites. For example, if you've only dabbled with T-SQL or you're more comfortable with Visual Basic .NET than C#, that's OK, as long as you're willing to try and pick up on things as you read along. Most of our code samples are not that complex. However, our explanations assume some basic knowledge on your part, and you might need to do a little research if you lack the experience.

In addition to covering the SQL Server core relational engine and its ancillary services, this book also provides in-depth coverage of SQL Server's BI features, including Integration Services, Reporting Services, and the OLAP and Data Mining components of Analysis Services. Although ours is not a BI book per se, it is a database developer's book, and we feel strongly that all these features should be understood by mainstream database developers. BI is really one of the cornerstone features of SQL Server 2005, so the time is right for traditional database developers to "cross over" to the world of BI.

Realizing that these technologies, especially OLAP and data mining, will be new territory for many readers, we assume no knowledge of them on your part. Any reader who meets the prerequisites already discussed should feel comfortable reading about these BI features and, more than likely, feel ready and excited to start working with BI after reading the BI-focused chapters.

How This Book Is Organized

This book is broken down into three parts. Each part follows a specific SQL Server "theme," if you will.

Part I covers topics relevant to work on the database server, including the creation, management, and maintenance of entities you will design into your databases. We cover topics relating to database design (including the new XML data type); T-SQL programming of views, stored procedures, triggers, and functions (including new XQuery extensions); and security-related entities. We also introduce you to SQL Server's new .NET CLR integration features, which cut across our discussions of data types and server-side programming.

In Part II, we move away from the server and discuss concepts relating to actual database software development, be it in the middle tier or at the application level. We also cover various topics relevant to extending your databases' reach with technologies such as HTTP endpoints, SQL Server Service Broker, SQL Server Notification Services, SQL Server Express Edition, and SQL Server Everywhere Edition.

Part III is our BI section. In it, we provide efficient, practical coverage of SQL Server Integration Services, Analysis Services, and Reporting Services. We are particularly proud of this section because we assume virtually no BI knowledge on your part and yet provide truly deep coverage of SQL Server BI concepts, features, and programming.

Together, the three parts of the book provide you with a broad inventory of a slew of SQL Server 2005 developer-relevant features and the conceptual material necessary to understand them. We don't cover everything in SQL Server 2005, but we will arm you with a significant amount of core knowledge and give you the frame of reference necessary to research the product further and learn even more.

System Requirements

To follow along with the book's text and run its code samples successfully, we recommend that you install the Developer Edition of SQL Server 2005, which is available to a great number of developers through Microsoft's MSDN Premium subscription, on your PC. You will also need Visual Studio 2005; we recommend that you use the Professional Edition or one of the Team Edition releases, each of which is also available with the corresponding edition of the MSDN Premium subscription product.

Important   To cover the widest range of features, this book is based on the Developer Edition of SQL Server 2005. The Developer Edition possesses the same feature set as the Enterprise Edition of the product, although Developer Edition licensing terms preclude production use. Both editions offer a superset of the features available in other editions (Standard, Workgroup, and Express). We believe it is in the best interest of developers for us cover the full range of developer features in SQL Server 2005, including those available only in the Enterprise and Developer editions.

Most programmability features covered in this book are available in every edition of SQL Server 2005. Notable exceptions include the lack of Notification Services and Analysis Services support in the Express and Workgroup editions. Users of production editions other than the Enterprise Edition should consult the SQL Server 2005 Features Comparison page at *http://www.microsoft.com/sql/prodinfo/features/compare-features.mspx* for a comprehensive list of features available in each edition, in order to understand which features covered in the book are available to them in production.

To run these editions of SQL Server and Visual Studio, and thus the samples in this book, you'll need the following 32-bit hardware and software. (The 64-bit hardware and software requirements are not listed here but are very similar.)

■ 600-MHz Pentium III–compatible or faster processor (1-GHz or faster processor recommended).

■ Microsoft Windows 2000 Server with Service Pack (SP) 4 or later; Windows 2000 Professional Edition with SP4 or later; Windows XP with SP2 or later; Windows Server 2003 Standard Edition, Enterprise Edition, or Datacenter Edition with SP1 or later; or Windows Small Business Server 2003 with SP1 or later.

■ For SQL Server, at least 512 MB of RAM (1 GB or more recommended).

■ For Visual Studio, 192 MB (256 MB recommended).

■ For SQL Server 2005, approximately 350 MB of available hard disk space for the recommended installation. Approximately 425 MB of additional available hard disk space for SQL Server Books Online, SQL Server Mobile Everywhere Books Online, and sample databases.

■ For Visual Studio 2005 without MSDN Library, 1 GB of available space required on system drive, 2 GB of available space required on installation drive. For Visual Studio 2005 with MSDN Library: 1 GB of available space required on system drive; 3.8 GB of available space required on installation drive with a full installation of MSDN; 2.8 GB of available space required on installation drive with a default installation of MSDN.

■ CD-ROM or DVD-ROM drive.

■ Super VGA (1024 × 768) or higher resolution video adapter and monitor.

■ Microsoft Mouse or compatible pointing device.

■ Microsoft Internet Explorer 6.0 SP1 or later.

■ For SQL Server Reporting Services, Microsoft Internet Information Services (IIS) 5.0 or later and ASP.NET 2.0 or later.

Using the Samples

All the code samples discussed in this book can be downloaded from the book's companion content page at the following address:

http://www.microsoft.com/mspress/companion/0-7356-1923-9/

The companion materials are supplied in the form of a single MSI file that you can run directly from the preceding URL or download and run later. The MSI allows you to install the companion materials in a folder of your own choosing.

Important   This book and its sample code were written for, and tested against, the initial Release To Manufacturing (RTM) version of SQL Server 2005 Developer Edition. At press time, Microsoft had just released Service Pack 1 (SP1) of SQL Server 2005. Some of the book's sample code has been tested against SP1 and some of the text has been explicitly verified against it, but an exhaustive check of the book and its code was not feasible, given the near simultaneous release of SP1 and this book.

SP1 consists primarily of a combination of bug fixes to the RTM version of SQL Server 2005, as well as the commercial release of the SQL Server 2005 database mirroring functionality, which is not covered in this book. As such, we expect that very little, if any, content or sample code in the book will be incompatible with SP1.

If and when we discover any such incompatibilities, however, our intent is to update the sample code and post errata notes into the book's companion materials, available at *http://www.microsoft.com/mspress/companion/0-7356-1923-9/*. Please monitor that site for new code updates and errata postings. You might also want to visit *http://spaces .msn.com/PSS2005CUpdt*, where we will post, in blog form, announcements about any such updates. For those of you who use RSS readers, you can subscribe to this blog's RSS feed at *http://spaces.msn.com/PSS2005CUpdt/feed.rss*. SP1, its documentation, and a corresponding update to SQL Server 2005 Books Online can be downloaded from *http://www.microsoft.com/sql/sp1.mspx*.

Because this is a developer book, we often include one or more Visual Studio projects as part of the sample code, in addition to SQL Server Management Studio projects containing T-SQL or Analysis Services script files. Within the companion materials parent folder is a child folder for each chapter. Each chapter's folder, in turn, contains either or both of the following two folders: SSMS and VS. The former typically contains a SQL Server Management Studio solution file with the filename Chapter*XX*.ssmssln; the latter typically contains a Visual Studio solution file with the filename Chapter*XX*.sln. After you've installed the companion files, double-click either solution file, or both, to open the sample scripts or code in the appropriate IDE.

The solution files might contain multiple projects. In such cases, each project, and usually each file within it, is referred to in the chapter that the code accompanies. Occasionally, multiple solution files, each in a separate folder, are included with the sample code. When this is the case, the text explains the differences between each solution or the project(s) it contains.

Because most of the code is explicated in the text, you might prefer to create it from scratch rather than open the finished version supplied in the companion sample code. However, the finished version will still prove useful if you make a small error along the way or if you want to run the code quickly before reading through the narrative that describes it.

Some of the SQL Server Management Studio projects contain embedded connections that are configured to point to a default instance of SQL Server running on your local machine. Some of the Visual Studio source code contains connections or default connection strings (sometimes in code, sometimes in settings or config files, other times in the *Text* property of controls on the forms in the sample projects) that are configured likewise. If you have SQL Server 2005 installed as a default instance on your local machine, with the AdventureWorks sample database, the majority of the sample code should run without modification. If not, you'll need to modify the server name, add an instance name, or both. You'll also need to install Adventure-Works if you have not already done so.

Some chapters rely on the Northwind sample database, the AdventureWorksDW sample data warehouse database, and/or the Adventure Works DW Analysis Services sample database. Chapter 17 contains explicit directions on how to install the Northwind database. To install the AdventureWorksDW data warehouse database and the Adventure Works DW Analysis Services database, you must explicitly select the AdventureWorksDW Sample Data Warehouse and AdventureWorks Sample OLAP options in an advanced SQL Server install (these options appear under the Documentation, Samples, and Databases install option).

Support for This Book

Every effort has been made to ensure the accuracy of this book and the companion content. As corrections or changes are collected, they will be added to a Microsoft Knowledge Base article.

Microsoft Press provides support for books and companion content at the following Web site:

http://www.microsoft.com/learning/support/books/

Questions and Comments

If you have comments, questions, or ideas regarding the book or the companion content, or questions that are not answered by visiting the preceding sites, please send them to Microsoft Press via e-mail to

mspinput@microsoft.com

Or send them via postal mail to

Microsoft Press

Attn: *Programming Microsoft SQL Server 2005* Editor

One Microsoft Way

Redmond, WA 98052-6399

Please note that Microsoft software product support is not offered through the preceding addresses.

Part I
Design Fundamentals and Core Technologies

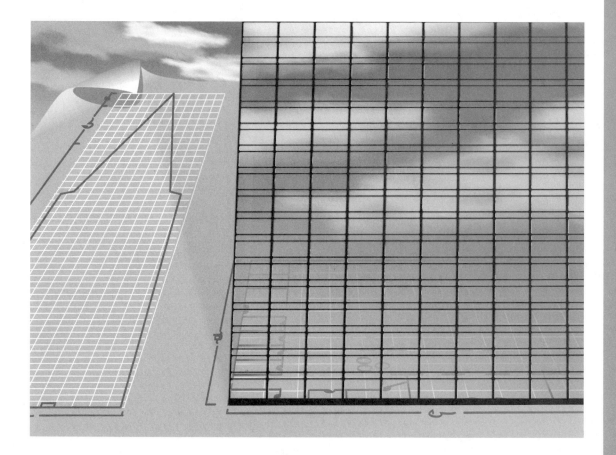

Chapter 1
Overview

–Andrew Brust

In this chapter:

This book is all about Microsoft SQL Server 2005 and specifically how to program it. We believe that virtually all custom-developed business software, whether on the server itself, in client applications or middle-tier code, or even within reports or data extraction and loading routines, hinges on database programming. We also believe that the Microsoft .NET programming platform is the best in the world and that SQL Server is the best database to work with. That's why we wanted to write a book that focuses on the newest version of SQL Server and how to program it, both natively and from .NET.

A Tough Act to Follow

SQL Server 2005 is the first new version of the SQL Server product in almost six years. But frankly, we were very happy with its predecessor. Although all the versions before SQL Server 2000 left us hungry for more features and better performance, SQL Server 2000 to this day remains an amazingly fast and feature-rich product. It has served us so well over the last six years because it is a rock-solid, complete product and because core relational database technology has evolved to only a modest degree since its release.

So why a new database? Why now? Is there more to this new version than, well, just a new version? The answer is that this release is enormously significant. It is, in fact, a watershed release. But how? Why? If relational technology has reached such maturity, what innovation in the database space could possibly be left for Microsoft to deliver? The answer lies not in the database market per se, but rather in the software development world where, in marked contrast to the database market, changes during the last six years have been nothing short of phenomenal.

The Software Industry and Disruptive Change

The advent and universal adoption of Extensible Markup Language (XML) and Web services technology have changed the way we write code, exchange data, and connect applications. The service-oriented architecture (SOA) approach to software development and the rising importance of middleware and the enterprise service bus (ESB) have radically altered application integration and business-to-business (B2B) communications.

The market for business intelligence (BI), including online analytical processing (OLAP); data mining; extraction, transformation, and loading (ETL) technology; and enterprise reporting has grown immensely, allowing organizations to use their data for strategic and competitive advantage. BI is becoming an indispensable part of doing business in a growing number of industries.

Mobile devices, and mobile connectivity, have increased geometrically since the release of SQL Server 2000. More and more people are using their phones and PDAs as true computers, to run applications locally, to run mobile Web applications over the Internet, or to receive text messages and e-mail. Faster and cheaper data connections, more sophisticated hardware, and support for Web services are making mobile devices a highly viable platform for all sorts of data-enabled applications.

Microsoft's introduction of .NET, including the .NET Framework and .NET versions of Visual Studio, has brought with it a complete rebuild of Microsoft-centric developer tools, application programming interfaces (APIs), and the general approach to application development. It has also brought a great (though not total) shift in momentum to the Microsoft platform and away from the Java platform championed by IBM, BEA, Oracle, and others.

So how does all this impact the database world? Simple: SQL Server 2005 is, more than all previous versions combined, *the* developer-oriented release of the product, and it offers a host of new features to accommodate the latest developer trends and technologies.

Industry Trends, SQL Server Features, and a Book to Show You the Way

Our goal with this book was to cover a potentially dizzying array of new developer-oriented features in this version of SQL Server, in the context of software development trends and innovations. In many ways, SQL Server 2005 mirrors each of the changes that have taken place in the software world since the release of SQL Server 2000. In planning the structure and content of this book, we decided to follow suit.

Programming the Server

In Part I of this book, we focus on the creation, management, and maintenance of entities you will design in your databases. These include tables (and the special data types of their columns); programmatic entities such as views, stored procedures, triggers, and functions; and security-related entities and features such as logins, users, roles, credentials, and key-based encryption.

In Chapter 2, we explore the significant enhancements to Transact-SQL (T-SQL). Whatever you might have read or heard, T-SQL isn't going away; in fact, it remains the best programming tool for exploiting new and old SQL Server features alike. We'll show you how to use T-SQL to create non-persistent views, and we'll cover the ins and outs of writing recursive queries with new common table expressions (CTEs). We'll cover new scalar functions that provide the basis of ranking, and we'll show you cool new ways to perform crosstab queries.

Chapter 3 provides thorough coverage of SQL common language runtime (CLR) programming—which lets you run compiled .NET code on SQL Server—as well as guidance on when and where you should put it to use. We go beyond mere stored procedures, triggers, and functions to explain and demonstrate the creation of CLR types and aggregates—entities that cannot be created *at all* in T-SQL. We also cover the different methods of creating SQL CLR objects in Microsoft Visual Studio 2005 and how to manage their deployment, both from Visual Studio and from T-SQL scripts in SQL Server Management Studio and elsewhere.

Moving on to your data itself, you'll be interested to know that SQL Server now supports XML as a native data type. Far from simply storing XML as text in the database, SQL Server 2005 supports validation through server-side XML schema collections and sophisticated querying using the new XQuery extensions to T-SQL. SQL Server 2005 can use XML in tables, variables, triggers, views, stored procedures, and functions. It can even index XML columns. We cover all this in depth in Chapter 4.

SQL Server 2005 offers so many new features that it is now imperative to have one centralized tool for managing them. The new SQL Server Management Studio application provides this management capability, subsuming the functionality previously supplied not just in SQL Server Enterprise Manager and SQL Query Analyzer, but in numerous other tools as well. The tool also rides on the same "chassis" as does Visual Studio, allowing you to organize your scripts into projects and solutions that can, in turn, be managed under source control. Essentially, SQL Server Management Studio is a cross between an administrative tool and a genuine team-friendly integrated development environment (IDE) for your servers and databases. Chapter 5 is dedicated to covering this formidable new application and the changes in approach to data management that it brings about.

Showing you how to manage your SQL Server databases in a GUI tool is all well and good, but lest we forget, this is a developer's book. So after we show you how to perform management tasks interactively in Chapter 5, we show you how to conduct them *programmatically*, using SQL Server Management Objects (SMO), in Chapter 6. You'll learn how to perform database backups and restores, execute DBCC runs, and more, all from your own code.

SQL Server 2005 has a slew of new security features as well. Whether it be key-based encryption, extended permissions, or turning on and off various features to reduce the surface area for attack, your choices for keeping your data safe and secure from prying eyes are now quite vast. With so many choices, you'll need a good overview of the new features and some guidance on when and how to use them. We provide that in Chapter 7.

Application Code and SQL Server: Extending Your Database's Reach

After we've covered so much material about what you can do on the server and in your database, we move to Part II of the book, where we cover technologies and techniques more relevant to building applications that work with your databases and extend their reach.

We start with Chapter 8, which covers ADO.NET 2.0, data binding in .NET Windows Forms and ASP.NET, and the data access features of Visual Studio, including typed *DataSet* objects. We provide a significant amount of coverage on consuming the SQL CLR objects you created on the server in Chapter 3, both in ADO.NET code and typed *DataSet* objects. And we show you how to take advantage of exciting new SQL Server and ADO.NET features such as query notifications (also known as "cache sync"), asynchronous queries, and client-side bulk copy.

With both client- and server-side development techniques under your belt (including T-SQL and CLR code on the server), you'll need to understand how to put them together and perform integrated debugging on all your code. In Chapter 9, we show you how to debug T-SQL and .NET code from Visual Studio, across languages and across tiers. We discuss debugging code on local SQL Server instances as well as on remote servers over your network. Remote debugger monitoring, authentication, and firewall configurations can be tricky; we'll guide you through the various dialog boxes, wizards, and Visual Studio settings necessary to make everything work together.

SQL Server 2005 scores big points in the SOA department, both with its support for XML as a native data type (which is great for storing passed messages in their native form) and its ability to expose stored procedures and functions as bona fide Web services. Given that these Web services can be implemented without even requiring the Microsoft Internet Information Services (IIS) Web server, SQL Server becomes a real Web services contender, capable of replacing ASP.NET for certain Web services tasks. In Chapter 10, we show you how to expose your SQL Server logic via Web services, how to manage security and authentication around these "HTTP endpoints," and how to consume the Web services from an application. Perhaps more importantly, we'll tell you when and why you would, or would not, want to do this.

No matter how you write and package your code—whether it be in T-SQL or a .NET language; exposed as a conventional stored procedure, function, or Web service; or deployed to the client or the server—you must keep your data consistent to ensure its integrity. The key to consistency is transactions, and as with other SQL Server programmability features, transactions can be managed from a variety of places. If you're writing T-SQL code or you're writing client code using the ADO.NET *SqlClient* provider or *System.Transactions*, you need to be aware of the various transaction isolation levels supported by SQL Server, the appropriate scope of your transactions, and best practices for writing transactional code. In Chapter 11, we get you there.

To round out both the middleware story and the guarantee of transactional operations, SQL Server programmers need infrastructure and an API for executing logic asynchronously and across servers that ensures the order and integrity of execution, even when some of those servers are unavailable for a period of time. Until the release of SQL Server 2005, such distributed, asynchronous, guaranteed execution of logic could be delivered only from queuing technology such as Microsoft Message Queue (MSMQ) or Enterprise Service Bus (ESB) products such as Microsoft BizTalk Server. But SQL Server 2005 brings with it SQL Server

Service Broker, a true middleware solution for delivering federated, guaranteed-delivery queu-ing functionality, based totally within the database. We tell you all about it in Chapter 12.

Information-rich databases, even those that are efficiently programmed, transactionally pro-tected, available through Web services, and queued asynchronous programming interfaces, can be made more useful through various "reach" technologies. Dissemination of real-time alerts—via e-mail, text messaging, and other channels—based on the data in your databases radically enhances the data's usefulness and business relevance. Such alerting functionality is available to SQL Server programmers via the product's Notification Services facility. In Chap-ter 13, we show you how easy it is to put this technology to work for your organization and the betterment of its operational agility.

Enterprises do not live by servers alone! The reliability, scalability, and processing power of big servers are the backbone of any successful database implementation. But extending the reach of an enterprise database to its full potential often requires that the data and database applications be available on distributed, sometimes disconnected, workstations and desktop systems. SQL Server Express Edition, designed for these platforms, offers an amazingly full implementation of the "up-level" SQL Server 2005 editions, including XML capabilities, encryption and security features, Service Broker integration, and full T-SQL and CLR pro-grammability. This edition of SQL Server also supports XCOPY and .NET ClickOnce deploy-ment, running in a reduced user permissions environment, and on-the-fly attachment to SQL Server database files. Best of all, the product is free to own and free to distribute. Learn all about it in Chapter 14.

We couldn't round out the reach story without a version of SQL Server that runs natively on the ever-increasing number of Windows-based mobile devices. These devices are used not just by consumers, but also by the mobile workforce—people who need ready access to their data no matter where they are, in both wireless online and offline settings. SQL Server Everywhere Edition is Microsoft's third-generation mobile database, offering advanced database capabilities on mobile devices and the ability to sync those devices, and their data, to conventional SQL Server databases using SQL Server Merge Replication. Learn how to deploy your data to the full spectrum of today's Windows Mobile devices with SQL Server Everywhere in Chapter 15.

It's the Strategy, Stupid

In Part III of the book, we help you take your broad-based but tactical database management and programming knowledge and extend it to the realm of strategic analysis. Specifically, we introduce you to the realm of building a true data warehouse through ETL and capitalizing on your data warehouse through OLAP, data mining, and reporting.

In Chapter 16, we show you the ropes of SQL Server Integration Services, the successor to the Data Transformation Services component of SQL Server 7.0 and SQL Server 2000. We show you how Microsoft's new ETL platform provides unprecedented reliability and scalability, as well as elegant integration with Visual Studio 2005. We'll take you from beginner-level proficiency to Integration Services expert in one chapter, facilitating your ability to build powerful data warehouses and data marts.

In Chapters 17 through 20, we show you how to take these transformed data repositories and use them as the basis for sophisticated SQL Server Analysis Services databases that support cutting-edge BI features. Many books on SQL Server exclude coverage of Analysis Services on the grounds that it is a "specialized" subject, but we respectfully disagree. The very premise of this release of Analysis Services and its unified dimensional model paradigm is the *mainstream* appeal and accessibility of BI. We hope to do our part in this crusade by showing you how easy BI programming can be, and how powerfully it complements conventional databases and conventional database programming.

In Chapter 17, we take you through the basics of designing OLAP cubes using the Analysis Services project designers in Visual Studio. We show you how to build, deploy, and query OLAP cubes that support actionable, drill-down analysis of your data. We kept Chapter 17 fairly short to provide a sort of "quick start" approach to BI for busy developers.

In Chapter 18, we take the basic cube we built in Chapter 17 and use Visual Studio designers to implement an array of new OLAP features brought to you by Analysis Services 2005. By the end of the chapter, your cube will have a number of the features underlying Microsoft's unified dimensional model. The chapter is long, but you can read it at your own pace, immediately mastering new features as you read each section.

Lest you think we have somehow digressed from our developer-centric approach, Chapter 19 provides comprehensive coverage of a host of OLAP application development techniques. We cover customization of Microsoft Excel PivotTables—not just from Excel but, through the magic of Office Web Components, from Web pages designed in Microsoft FrontPage as well as from Windows Forms and ASP.NET applications you can build in Visual Studio.

We provide a basic tutorial on Multidimensional Expressions (MDX) queries, showing you how to run them from SQL Server Management Studio's MDX query window, as well as your own applications through API-level programming with ADO MD.NET. We cover management of Analysis Services databases, both interactively using SQL Server Management Studio and programmatically using Analysis Management Objects (AMO). We introduce you to the Web services–based XML for Analysis (XMLA) standard on which both ADO MD.NET and AMO are built, showing you how to create XMLA scripts in Management Studio and manipulate XMLA programmatically in .NET code. We also introduce you to Analysis Services' own .NET CLR integration, and we show you how to create managed stored procedures in .NET using AMO and server-side ADO MD.NET.

Chapter 20 is all about data mining, and it provides a self-contained, end-to-end treatment of the topic. We start with a conceptual introduction, and then we provide a tutorial on designing, training, browsing, and deploying your mining structures and models in Visual Studio.

We then switch back to SQL Server Management Studio, showing you how to manage your mining structures and models interactively, using the GUI tools provided, and programmatically through SQL Data Mining Extensions (DMX) scripts. We then head back to .NET programming, showing you how to embed the Analysis Services Data Mining Model Browsers into your applications; how to use DMX, ADO.NET, and data binding together to build compelling Windows Forms and ASP.NET data mining applications; and how to use server-side ADO MD.NET to build DMX stored procedures. We finish by showing you how to use SQL Server Reporting Services to create special data mining prediction query reports.

After that small preview of using Reporting Services for data mining, we swing back in Chapter 21 and provide broader coverage of the SQL Server 2005 version of Reporting Services. We show you how to use Reporting Services to build sophisticated reports against relational databases, quickly and easily. We then teach you how to embed those reports into your .NET applications, allowing you to develop full-scale reporting information systems that expose all the information in the feature-packed databases you've learned to build, maintain, extend, and develop against in the rest of the book. This last chapter, in focusing on the raw relational data in your databases, in effect takes us full circle from the T-SQL programming covered at the beginning of the book.

A Collaborative Effort for, and by, Developers

Like SQL Server itself, this book is the result of many years of work and many authors' efforts. Our Web services and data mining chapters were written by experts on those subjects, and we were fortunate enough to have our chapters on database security, SQL Server Integration Services, and SQL Server Express Edition written by product managers from the Microsoft SQL Server product team. We are especially proud of the credentials of the book's extended team.

Still, even with the duration of the effort, the participation of so many people, and the book's rather high page count, there was no way to cover every aspect of SQL Server 2005 in this book. SQL Server 2005 is a massive product, and it would take thousands of pages to provide a comprehensive reference on the product. And besides, SQL Server Books Online already does that.

Our approach has been to add value to the product's documentation by providing a developer-oriented investigation of the new and improved features and services in SQL Server 2005. As such, this book features an abundance of sample code, including a library of Visual Studio and SQL Server Management Studio sample projects that you can download from the Web. (See the Introduction for details on downloading and using the sample code.)

You might find the text of this book most useful, using the sample code as mere supporting collateral. Or you might find the sample code most valuable, with the text serving more as documentation. Perhaps you'll feel differently at different times, depending on your mood, your research goals, or the requirements of a production project.

In the end, it doesn't really matter. If this book, its sample code, or some combination of the two makes a subject more approachable, a project easier to tackle, a deadline less intimidating, or your job a little easier, then we have met our goal. Everyone who has worked on this book has built a career on the noble pursuit of writing code, especially database code. We love building applications that update, process, and share data, and we think most other programmers do as well.

That's why we think you'll love this new version of SQL Server—because it is *so* programmable. With that in mind, we hope this book helps you program SQL Server 2005 adeptly and efficiently. Above all, we hope it makes programming SQL Server 2005 more fun.

Chapter 2

Exploring the T-SQL Enhancements in SQL Server 2005

–Stephen Forte

By now you must have heard that you can write Microsoft SQL Server 2005 stored procedures in any language that uses the common language runtime (CLR), such as Microsoft Visual C# or Microsoft Visual Basic .NET. This is great news if you've never mastered Transact-SQL (T-SQL), right? I hate to be the bearer of bad news, but CLR stored procedures are not a cure-all for all your programming challenges. As you'll see in Chapter 3, writing a stored procedure in a language that uses the CLR is useful for a number of database programming dilemmas; for instance, CLR stored procedures are often a good replacement for extended stored procedures in previous versions of SQL Server. For almost everything else, you will want to use T-SQL.

In fact, reports of T-SQL's death have been greatly exaggerated. In most cases, using T-SQL for your queries and stored procedures in SQL Server 2005 is more efficient than writing CLR stored procedures.

Given that T-SQL is alive and well, let's look at how it's changed in SQL Server 2005. T-SQL has been improved in many ways. In this chapter, we'll briefly introduce SQL Server Management Studio. (Look for a more thorough discussion of SQL Server Management Studio in Chapter 5.) Here, we'll also explore the most notable changes in T-SQL, including:

- Common table expressions and hierarchical queries
- *PIVOT* and *UNPIVOT*
- *APPLY*
- *TOP* enhancements
- Ranking functions
- Exception handling in transactions
- New data types
- *WAITFOR*
- Data definition language (DDL) triggers and notifications
- SNAPSHOT isolation
- Statement-level recompile

Introducing SQL Server Management Studio

With SQL Server 2005, you can write your T-SQL queries and stored procedures and manage your database using a single tool: SQL Server Management Studio (Figure 2-1). With SQL Server 2000, developers generally used two separate tools—Enterprise Manager for management tasks and Query Analyzer for writing T-SQL. Many developers had both tools open on their desktops all day long. SQL Server Management Studio provides one-stop shopping for all your SQL Server tasks. It replaces SQL Server 2000 Enterprise Manager, Query Analyzer, and Analysis Manager, and it also houses much more functionality, such as the ability to manage your SQL Server Everywhere databases, write XQuery documents, and build reporting services and notification services applications.

SQL Server Management Studio has a similar look and feel to Visual Studio, but it's not the same. It is a new application written in Visual C# and based on Visual Studio. Once you get up and running with SQL Server Management Studio, you can customize it in the same ways you can customize Visual Studio, with dockable windows, line numbering, keyboard shortcuts, and so on. SQL Server Management Studio also supports source control integration.

Just as in SQL Server 2000 Enterprise Manager, in SQL Server Management Studio you have to register your servers. SQL Server Management Studio lets you register SQL Servers, SQL Server Everywhere databases, Analysis Servers, and Reporting Servers. Although SQL Server

2005 and SQL Server Management Studio offer many new developer and administrative features, in this chapter we'll concentrate only on the developer features related to T-SQL.

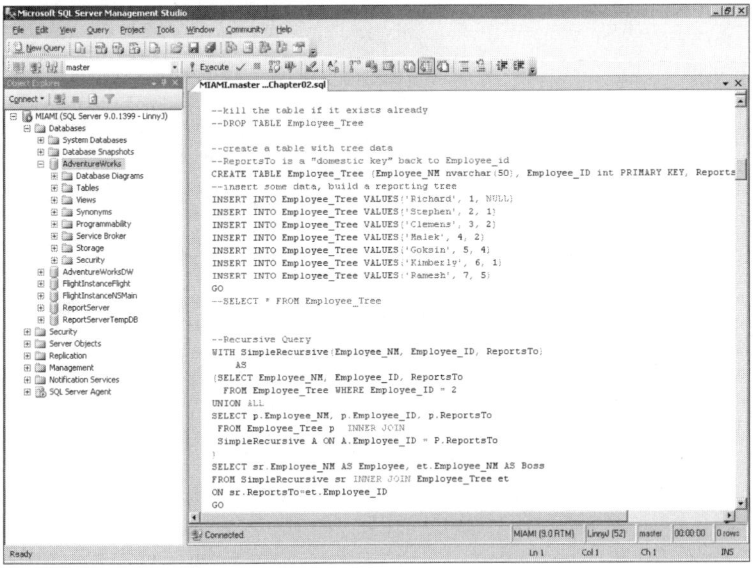

Figure 2-1   SQL Server Management Studio

Common Table Expressions

A common table expression (CTE) closely resembles a nonpersistent view. It is a temporary named result set that you define in your query that will be used by the *FROM* clause of the query. Each CTE is defined only once (but can be referred to as many times as it is in scope) and lives for as long as the query lives. You can use CTEs to perform recursive operations. Here is the syntax to create a CTE:

```
WITH <name of your CTE>(<column names>)
AS
(
<actual query>
)

SELECT * FROM <name of your CTE>
```

> **Note**   SQL Server 2005 also ships with a new database called AdventureWorks, which is like a Northwind database on steroids. Most of our examples will use AdventureWorks, which has much more functionality than Northwind. We will call out anything new and exciting about it as we bump into the features, but for most of this book all you have to know is that it is a basic order-entry system.

An example of a simple CTE using AdventureWorks is shown here:

Listing 2-1   A simple CTE

```
WITH AllMRContacts
AS
(SELECT * FROM Person.Contact WHERE Title='Mr.')

SELECT LastName + ', ' + FirstName AS Contact
FROM AllMRContacts
ORDER BY LastName
```

The results are shown here:

```
Contact
-------
Abbas, Syed
Achong, Gustavo
Adams, Jay
Adams, Ben
Adina, Ronald
Agcaoili, Samuel
[more rows]
```

The following example gets a count of all the sales a salesperson made in the AdventureWorks orders system as a CTE and then executes a simple inner join with the SalesPerson table to return more information about the salesperson, such as his quota. This demonstrates how a CTE is joined to your calling query. You can do this without a CTE, but think about all the times you have created a temp table or a throwaway view and joined back to it—now you can use a CTE instead and keep the complexity of aggregating in the CTE only, thereby simplifying your code. The code is shown here:

Listing 2-2   CTE-to-query join

```
USE AdventureWorks
GO

WITH OrderCountCTE(SalesPersonID, OrderCount)
AS
(
    SELECT SalesPersonID, COUNT(*)
    FROM  Sales.SalesOrderHeader
    WHERE SalesPersonID IS NOT NULL
    GROUP BY SalesPersonID
)
SELECT sp.SalesPersonID, oc.OrderCount, sp.SalesYTD
FROM Sales.SalesPerson sp
INNER JOIN OrderCountCTE oc ON oc.SalesPersonID=sp.SalesPersonID
ORDER BY oc.OrderCount
```

The results look like this:

```
SalesPersonID    OrderCount     SalesYTD
-----------------------------------------
288              16             219088.8836
284              39             636440.251
268              48             677558.4653
280              60             0.00
290              109            1758385.926
289              130            2241204.0424
287              140            1931620.1835
[more rows]
```

CTEs can also eliminate self-joins in some of your queries. Take a look at this example. We will create a table called Products and insert duplicates into the Product Name field.

Listing 2-3   Inserting duplicates into AdventureWorks' *Product_Name*

```
CREATE TABLE Products (
   Product_ID int NOT NULL,
   Product_Name varchar (25),
   Price money NULL,
CONSTRAINT PK_Products PRIMARY KEY NONCLUSTERED (Product_ID)
)
GO
INSERT INTO Products (Product_ID, Product_Name, Price) VALUES (1, 'widgets', 25)
INSERT INTO Products (Product_ID, Product_Name, Price) VALUES (2, 'Gadgets', 50)
INSERT INTO Products (Product_ID, Product_Name, Price) VALUES (3, 'Thingies', 75)
INSERT INTO Products (Product_ID, Product_Name, Price) VALUES (4, 'whoozits', 90)
INSERT INTO Products (Product_ID, Product_Name, Price) VALUES (5, 'whatzits', 5)
INSERT INTO Products (Product_ID, Product_Name, Price) VALUES (6, 'Gizmos', 15)
INSERT INTO Products (Product_ID, Product_Name, Price) VALUES (7, 'widgets', 24)
INSERT INTO Products (Product_ID, Product_Name, Price) VALUES (8, 'Gizmos', 36)
INSERT INTO Products (Product_ID, Product_Name, Price) VALUES (9, 'Gizmos', 36)
GO
```

One common problem found in databases is having duplicate product names with different product IDs. If you run a duplicate-finding query, that query will return all the records (the duplicates and the good values). This increases the difficulty of automatically deleting duplicates. If you want to find the Product Name duplicates without also including the first instance of the name in the table, you can use a self-join like this:

Listing 2-4   Self-join without CTE

```
SELECT * FROM Products WHERE Product_ID NOT IN
(SELECT MIN(Product_ID) FROM Products AS P
 WHERE Products.Product_Name = P.Product_Name)
```

The self-join returns data like this:

```
Product_ID        Product_Name        Price
----------------------------------------------
8                 Gizmos              36.00
9                 Gizmos              36.00
7                 Widgets             24.00
```

You can also rewrite your query using a CTE to eliminate the confusing-looking self-join and get the same results. This technique does not offer a performance gain over self-joins; it is just a convenience for code maintainability. The previous self-join example is rewritten here as a CTE and yields the same results:

Listing 2-5   Self-join as a CTE

```
WITH CTEMinProductRecords AS (
  SELECT MIN(Product_ID) AS Product_ID, Product_Name
  FROM Products
  GROUP BY Product_Name
  HAVING COUNT(*) > 1)
SELECT *
FROM Products JOIN CTEMinProductRecords ON
  Products.Product_Name = CTEMinProductRecords.Product_Name
  AND Products.Product_ID > CTEMinProductRecords.Product_ID
```

After you investigate your duplicates using the preceding CTE, you might want to delete the duplicate data. You might also want to update any foreign keys in related tables to use the original *Product_ID* value. If your duplicate data does not have any related child rows in another table, or if you have updated them to the correct *Product_ID*, you can delete the duplicate data by just rewriting the CTE like this, replacing the *SELECT* * with a *DELETE*:

Listing 2-6   Deleting duplicates in a CTE

```
WITH CTEMinProductRecords AS (
  SELECT MIN(Product_ID) AS Product_ID, Product_Name
  FROM Products
  GROUP BY Product_Name
  HAVING COUNT(*) > 1)
DELETE Products
FROM Products JOIN CTEMinProductRecords ON
  Products.Product_Name = CTEMinProductRecords.Product_Name
  AND Products.Product_ID > CTEMinProductRecords.Product_ID
```

Recursive Queries with CTEs

The true power of CTEs emerges when you use them recursively to perform hierarchical queries on tree-structured data. In fact, this was a major reason that Microsoft built CTEs, in addition to SQL-92 compliance. A recursive CTE is constructed from a minimum of two queries. The first, the anchor member (AM), is a nonrecursive query; the second, the recursive member (RM), is the recursive query. Within your CTE's parentheses (after the *AS* clause), you define queries that are independent or refer back to the same CTE. The AM and RM are separated by a *UNION ALL* statement. AMs are invoked only once; RMs are invoked repeatedly until the query returns no rows. You can append multiple AMs to each other using a *UNION* or *UNION ALL* operator, depending on whether you want to eliminate duplicates. (You must append recursive members using a *UNION ALL* operator.) Here is the syntax:

```
WITH SimpleRecursive(field names)
AS
(
    <Select Statement for the Anchor Member>

    UNION ALL

    <Select Statement for the Recursive Member>
)

SELECT * FROM SimpleRecursive
```

The following example demonstrates this feature. We'll create a table of employees and a self-referencing field back to *Employee_ID* called *ReportsTo*. We'll then write a query that returns all the employees who report to Stephen (*Employee_ID=2*) and all the employees who report to Stephen's subordinates.

Listing 2-7   Example table for recursive CTE queries

```
--create a table with tree data
CREATE TABLE Employee_Tree (Employee_NM nvarchar(50), Employee_ID int PRIMARY KEY, Repor
tsTo int)
--insert some data, build a reporting tree
INSERT INTO Employee_Tree VALUES('Richard', 1, NULL)
INSERT INTO Employee_Tree VALUES('Stephen', 2, 1)
INSERT INTO Employee_Tree VALUES('Clemens', 3, 2)
INSERT INTO Employee_Tree VALUES('Malek', 4, 2)
INSERT INTO Employee_Tree VALUES('Goksin', 5, 4)
INSERT INTO Employee_Tree VALUES('Kimberly', 6, 1)
INSERT INTO Employee_Tree VALUES('Ramesh', 7, 5)
```

Our table looks like this:

Employee_NM	Employee_ID	ReportsTo
Richard	1	Null
Stephen	2	1
Clemens	3	2
Malek	4	2
Goksin	5	4
Kimberly	6	1
Ramesh	7	5

Here's the recursive query to determine which employees report to Stephen:

Listing 2-8 Recursive CTE query

```
--Recursive Query
WITH SimpleRecursive(Employee_NM, Employee_ID, ReportsTo)
   AS
(SELECT Employee_NM, Employee_ID, ReportsTo
  FROM Employee_Tree WHERE Employee_ID = 2
UNION ALL
SELECT p.Employee_NM, p.Employee_ID, p.ReportsTo
  FROM Employee_Tree p  INNER JOIN
  SimpleRecursive A ON A.Employee_ID = P.ReportsTo
)
SELECT sr.Employee_NM AS Employee, et.Employee_NM AS Boss
FROM SimpleRecursive sr INNER JOIN Employee_Tree et
ON sr.ReportsTo = et.Employee_ID
```

Here are the results:

```
Employee      Boss
------------------
Stephen       Richard
Clemens       Stephen
Malek         Stephen
Goksin        Malek
Ramesh        Goskin
```

This recursion starts where *Employee_ID* = 2 (the *Anchor Member* or the first *SELECT*). It picks up that record and then, using the *Recursive Member* (the *SELECT* after the *UNION ALL*), picks up all the records that report to Stephen and that record's children. (Goksin reports to Malek, and Malek reports to Stephen.) Each subsequent recursion tries to find more children that have as parents the employees found by the previous recursion. Eventually the recursion returns no results, and that is what causes the recursion to stop (the reason why Kimberly is not returned). If the anchor member is changed to *Employee_ID = 1*, then Kimberly will also be returned in the results.

By design, the recursive member keeps looking for children and can cycle on indefinitely. If you suspect many cycles will occur and want to limit the number of recursive invocations, you can specify the *MAXRECURSION* option right after the outer query using the *OPTION* clause:

```
OPTION(MAXRECURSION 25)
```

This option causes SQL Server 2005 to raise an error when the CTE exceeds the specified limit. By default, the limit is 100 (if you've omitted the option). To specify no option, you must set *MAXRECURSION* to 0. You can also run the same query to find direct reports and subordinates only one level deep (including direct reports Clemens and Malek and Malek's subordinate Goksin but skipping Ramesh, which is three levels deep).

Listing 2-9   Recursive query with *MAXRECURSION*

```
--Recursive Query with MAXRECURSION
WITH SimpleRecursive(Employee_NM, Employee_ID, ReportsTo)
   AS
(SELECT Employee_NM, Employee_ID, ReportsTo
  FROM Employee_Tree WHERE Employee_ID = 2
UNION ALL
SELECT p.Employee_NM, p.Employee_ID, p.ReportsTo
 FROM Employee_Tree p  INNER JOIN
 SimpleRecursive A ON A.Employee_ID = p.ReportsTo
)
SELECT sr.Employee_NM AS Employee, et.Employee_NM AS Boss
FROM SimpleRecursive sr INNER JOIN Employee_Tree et
ON sr.ReportsTo = et.Employee_ID
OPTION(MAXRECURSION 2)
```

Here are the results:

```
Employee      Boss
------------------
Stephen       Richard
Clemens       Stephen
Malek         Stephen
Goksin        Malek
```

You will also see that the query raises the following error message:

```
Msg 530, Level 16, State 1, Line 2
The statement terminated. The maximum recursion 2 has been exhausted before statement completion.
```

One way to avoid the exception is to use a generated column to keep track of the level you are on and include that in the *WHERE* clause instead of *MAXRECURSION*. The following example returns the same data as the previous example but without the error.

Listing 2-10   Controlling recursion without *MAXRECURSION*

```
WITH SimpleRecursive(Employee_NM, Employee_ID, ReportsTo, SubLevel)
   AS
(SELECT Employee_NM, Employee_ID, ReportsTo, 0
  FROM Employee_Tree WHERE Employee_ID = 2
UNION ALL
SELECT p.Employee_NM, p.Employee_ID, p.ReportsTo, SubLevel + 1
 FROM Employee_Tree p  INNER JOIN
 SimpleRecursive A ON A.Employee_ID = p.ReportsTo
)
SELECT sr.Employee_NM AS Employee, et.Employee_NM AS Boss
FROM SimpleRecursive sr INNER JOIN Employee_Tree et
ON sr.ReportsTo = et.Employee_ID
WHERE SubLevel <=2
```

The *PIVOT* and *UNPIVOT* Operators

Let's face it: Users usually want to see data in tabular format, which is a bit of a challenge given that data in SQL Server is most often stored in a highly relational form. *PIVOT* is a new T-SQL operator that you can specify in your *FROM* clause to rotate rows into columns and create a traditional crosstab query.

Using *PIVOT* is easy. In your *SELECT* statement, you specify the values you want to pivot on. The following example using the AdventureWorks database uses the order years (calculated using the *DatePart* function) as the columns. The *FROM* clause looks normal except for the *PIVOT* statement. This statement creates the value you want to show in the rows of the newly created columns. This example uses the aggregate *SUM* of *TotalDue* (a calculated field in the *FROM* clause). Then we use the *FOR* operator to list the values we want to pivot on in the OrderYear column. The example is shown here:

Listing 2-11   Creating tabular results with the *PIVOT* operator

```
SELECT CustomerID, [2001] AS Y2001, [2002] AS Y2002, [2003] AS Y2003, [2004] AS Y2004
FROM
(
SELECT CustomerID, DATEPART(yyyy, OrderDate) as OrderYear, TotalDue
FROM Sales.SalesOrderHeader
) piv
PIVOT
(
SUM (TotalDue)
FOR OrderYear IN
([2001], [2002], [2003], [2004])
) AS chld
ORDER BY CustomerID
```

Here are the results:

```
CustomerID   Y2001        Y2002        Y2003         Y2004
-----------------------------------------------------------------
1            40732.6067   72366.1284   NULL          NULL
2            NULL1        5653.6715    12118.0275    4962.2705
3            39752.8421   168393.7021  219434.4265   51925.3549
4            NULL         263025.3113  373484.299    143525.6018
5            NULL         33370.6901   60206.9999    20641.1106
6            NULL         NULL         668.4861      2979.3473
7            NULL         6651.036     3718.7804     NULL
8            NULL         NULL         19439.2466    10900.0347
9            NULL         320.6283     11401.5975    5282.8652
10           NULL         96701.7401   291472.2172   204525.9634
[more rows]
```

That's all there is to it. Of course, this example is simplified to show you the new concept; other, more sophisticated aggregates are possible, and you can even use CTEs in the *FROM* clause. In any case, using *PIVOT* is simple.

Listing 2-12 shows *PIVOT* in an SQL statement and the corresponding Visual C# code to fill the *DataGrid*.

Listing 2-12   Using *PIVOT* in Visual C#

```
private void Page_Load(object sender, System.EventArgs e)
{
//Set up the connection string to SQL Server 2005.
//If using integrated security, you have to grant permission to the
//ASP.NET worker process.

SqlConnection conn =new SqlConnection("server=KILIMANJARO;integrated security=SSPI;
database=AdventureWorks");
//Open the connection to SQL Server (SQL Server 2005)
conn.Open();

//Create a new SQL string using the new T-SQL keyword PIVOT.
//You have to know something about your data.
string strSQL= @" SELECT CustomerID, [2001] AS Y2001, [2002] AS Y2002, [2003] AS Y2003,
[2004] AS Y2004
FROM
(
SELECT CustomerID, datepart(yyyy, OrderDate) AS OrderYear, TotalDue
FROM Sales.SalesOrderHeader
) piv
PIVOT
(
SUM (TotalDue)
FOR OrderYear IN
([2001], [2002], [2003], [2004])
) AS chld
ORDER BY CustomerID";

//Can set a command to a SQL text and connection
SqlCommand cmd = new SqlCommand(strSQL, conn);
SqlDataReader dr;

//Open a data reader.
dr = cmd.ExecuteReader(CommandBehavior.CloseConnection);
//Do the data binding to a simple data grid.
//Using a data grid for code simplicity to avoid complex data binding.
DataGrid1.DataSource = dr;
DataGrid1.DataBind();
}
```

Using *UNPIVOT*

You can use the new *UNPIVOT* operator to normalize data that is already pivoted. For example, suppose you have a table in your database that looks like this:

VendorID	Emp1	Emp2	Emp3	Emp4	Emp5
1	4	3	5	4	4
2	4	1	5	5	5

VendorID	Emp1	Emp2	Emp3	Emp4	Emp5
3	4	3	5	4	4
4	4	2	5	4	4
5	5	1	5	5	5

You might want to unpivot the data to display columns for VendorID, Employee, and Number of Orders. Listing 2-13 shows how to use the *UNPIVOT* operator to achieve this goal.

Listing 2-13   Using the *UNPIVOT* operator

```
SELECT VendorID, Employee, Orders AS NumberOfOrders
FROM
    (SELECT VendorID, Emp1, Emp2, Emp3, Emp4, Emp5
    FROM pvt) p
UNPIVOT
    (Orders FOR Employee IN
        (Emp1, Emp2, Emp3, Emp4, Emp5)
)AS unpvt
GO
```

Here are the results:

```
VendorID    Employee      NumberOfOrders
----------------------------------------
1           Emp           14
1           Emp           23
1           Emp           35
1           Emp           44
2           Emp           14
[more rows]
```

Dynamically Pivoting Columns

The problem with *PIVOT* is the same problem with *CASE* and other methods: You have to specify the columns. Consider this code.

Listing 2-14   Statically driven *PIVOT*

```
SELECT *
FROM (SELECT CustomerID, YEAR(OrderDate) AS orderyear, TotalDue
    FROM Sales.SalesOrderHeader) as Header
PIVOT(SUM(TotalDue) FOR orderyear IN([2002],[2003],[2004])) as Piv
```

The results show us a nice crosstab query with the years displayed as columns:

```
CustomerID    2002      2003          2004
----------------------------------------------------------
14324         NULL      2264.2536     3394.9247
22814         NULL      5.514         NULL
11407         NULL      59.659        NULL
```

```
28387            NULL            NULL            645.2869
19897            NULL            NULL            659.6408
15675            2699.9018       2682.9953       2580.1529
24165            NULL            2699.9018       666.8565
[more rows]
```

Because this data only goes up to 2004, what happens when you add 2005 to the data? Do you want to go into all your queries and add the current year to the *IN* clause? We can accommodate new years in the data by dynamically building the *IN* clause and then programmatically writing the entire SQL statement. Once you have dynamically written the SQL statement, you can execute it using *sp_executesql*, as shown in Listing 2-15. The results are exactly the same as those shown following Listing 2-14, except that as new yearly data is added to the table, the query dynamically adds the column for it.

Listing 2-15   Dynamically driven *PIVOT*

```
--Dynamic Pivot
DECLARE @tblOrderDate AS TABLE(y int NOT NULL PRIMARY KEY)
INSERT INTO @tblOrderDate SELECT DISTINCT YEAR(OrderDate) FROM Sales.SalesOrderHeader
-- Construct the column list for the IN clause
-- e.g., [2002],[2003],[2004]
DECLARE @cols AS nvarchar(MAX), @years AS int
SET @years = (SELECT MIN(y) FROM @tblOrderDate)
SET @cols = N''
WHILE @years IS NOT NULL
BEGIN
  SET @cols = @cols + N',['+CAST(@years AS nvarchar(10))+N']'
  SET @years = (SELECT MIN(y) FROM @tblOrderDate WHERE y > @years)
END
SET @cols = SUBSTRING(@cols, 2, LEN(@cols))
-- Construct the full T-SQL statement and execute it dynamically.
DECLARE @sql AS nvarchar(MAX)
SET @sql = N'SELECT *
FROM (SELECT CustomerID, YEAR(OrderDate) AS orderyear, TotalDue
      FROM Sales.SalesOrderHeader) as Header
  PIVOT(SUM(TotalDue) FOR orderyear IN(' + @cols + N')) AS Piv'
--PRINT @sql -- for debugging
EXEC sp_executesql @sql
```

You can accomplish the same results using the new CTE syntax instead of using the *TABLE* variable:

Listing 2-16   Dynamic CTE *PIVOT*

```
--Dynamic Pivot with CTE and "SELECT @cols = ..." syntax
-- Construct the column list for the IN clause
-- e.g., [2002],[2003],[2004]
DECLARE @cols AS nvarchar(MAX)
;
WITH YearsCTE
AS
(SELECT DISTINCT YEAR(OrderDate) as [Year] FROM Sales.SalesOrderHeader)
```

```
SELECT @cols = ISNULL(@cols + ',[', '[') + CAST([YEAR] AS nvarchar(10)) + ']'
FROM YearsCTE
ORDER BY [YEAR]

-- Construct the full T-SQL statement and execute it dynamically.
DECLARE @sql AS nvarchar(MAX)
SET @sql = N'SELECT *
FROM (SELECT CustomerID, YEAR(OrderDate) AS orderyear, TotalDue
        FROM Sales.SalesOrderHeader) as Header
  PIVOT(SUM(TotalDue) FOR orderyear IN(' + @cols + N')) AS Piv'
PRINT @sql -- for debugging
EXEC sp_executesql @sql
```

The *APPLY* Operator

APPLY is a new operator that you specify in the *FROM* clause of a query. It enables you to invoke a table-valued function for each row of an outer table. The flexibility of *APPLY* is evident when you use the outer table's columns as your function's arguments. The *APPLY* operator has two forms: *CROSS APPLY* and *OUTER APPLY*. *CROSS APPLY* doesn't return the outer table's row if the table-valued function returns an empty set for it; the *OUTER APPLY* returns a row with *NULL* values instead of the function's columns.

To see how *APPLY* works, we'll first create a *FUNCTION* that returns a *TABLE*. Here is a simple function that returns as a *TABLE* the top *n* rows from the SalesOrderHeader table:

Listing 2-17   Returning a TABLE

```
USE AdventureWorks
  GO
CREATE FUNCTION fn_getcustomerorders(@CustomerID int, @TopRecords bigint)
RETURNS TABLE
  AS RETURN
    SELECT TOP (@TopRecords) *
    FROM Sales.SalesOrderHeader
    WHERE CustomerID = @CustomerID
    ORDER BY OrderDate DESC
```

After creating the *TABLE* returning function *fn_getcustomerorders*, we call it from the query:

Listing 2-18   Executing query with *APPLY*

```
SELECT * FROM Sales.Customer cust
CROSS APPLY fn_getcustomerorders(cust.CustomerID, 647)
```

This query returns all the records from the Customers table and then, as additional fields, the records from the Orders table (by way of the *fn_getcustomerorders* function) that match for the customer ID because that's what's being passed in dynamically as an argument.

TOP Enhancements

In earlier versions of SQL Server, *TOP* allows you to limit the number of rows returned as a number or a percentage in *SELECT* queries. With SQL Server 2005, you can use *TOP* in *DELETE*, *UPDATE*, and *INSERT* queries and can also specify the number of rows (or percent) by using variables or any valid numeric returning expression (such as a subquery). The main reason for allowing *TOP* with *DELETE*, *UPDATE*, and *INSERT* was to replace the *SET ROW-COUNT* option, which SQL Server traditionally didn't optimize very well.

You can specify the *TOP* limit as a literal number or an expression. If you're using an expression, you must enclose it in parentheses. The expression should be of the *bigint* data type when you are not using the *PERCENT* option and a *float* value in the range 0 through 100 when you are using the *PERCENT* option. You might find it useful to create an expression for *TOP* and make it a parameter you pass in to a stored procedure, as shown here:

Listing 2-19   Using *TOP* enhancements in a stored procedure

```
USE AdventureWorks
GO

CREATE PROCEDURE usp_SEL_ReturnTopOrders
@NumberofRows bigint
AS
SELECT TOP (@NumberofRows) SalesOrderID
FROM Sales.SalesOrderHeader
ORDER BY SalesOrderID
```

Executing the stored procedure is easy. Just pass in the number of records you want (in this case, 100):

```
EXEC usp_SEL_ReturnTopOrders @NumberofRows = 100
```

Here are the results:

```
SalesOrderID
------------
43659
43660
43661
43662
43663
[more rows]
```

Using a subquery can be powerful when you're doing things on the fly. The following example shows how to get the *TOP* n orders based on how many records are in the SalesPerson table:

```
SELECT TOP (SELECT COUNT(*) FROM Sales.SalesPerson)
SalesOrderID, RevisionNumber, OrderDate
FROM Sales.SalesOrderHeader
ORDER BY SalesOrderID
```

The results look like this:

SalesOrderID	Revision	NumberOrderDate
43659	1	2001-07-01 00:00:00.000
43660	1	2001-07-01 00:00:00.000
43661	1	2001-07-01 00:00:00.000
43662	1	2001-07-01 00:00:00.000
43663	1	2001-07-01 00:00:00.000
43664	1	2001-07-01 00:00:00.000
43665	1	2001-07-01 00:00:00.000
43666	1	2001-07-01 00:00:00.000
43667	1	2001-07-01 00:00:00.000
43668	1	2001-07-01 00:00:00.000
43669	1	2001-07-01 00:00:00.000
43670	1	2001-07-01 00:00:00.000
43671	1	2001-07-01 00:00:00.000
43672	1	2001-07-01 00:00:00.000
43673	1	2001-07-01 00:00:00.000
43674	1	2001-07-01 00:00:00.000
43675	1	2001-07-01 00:00:00.000

Using the *PERCENT* option is just as easy. Just add the *PERCENT* keyword, and make sure your variable is a *float*. In this example, we're asking for the top 10 percent, so we'll get back 3147 records because the AdventureWorks SalesOrderHeader table has approximately 31,465 records in it.

Listing 2-20   Returning TOP percentages

```
DECLARE @NumberOfRows AS FLOAT
SET @NumberOfRows = 10

SELECT TOP (@NumberOfRows) PERCENT *
FROM  Sales.SalesOrderHeader
ORDER BY OrderDate
```

Ranking Functions

Databases hold data. Users sometimes want to perform simple calculations or algorithms on that data to rank the results in a specific order—like gold, silver, and bronze medals in the Olympics or the top 10 customers by region. SQL Server 2005 introduces functionality for using ranking expressions with your result set. You can select a number of ranking algorithms, which are then applied to a column that you specify. This comes in handy in .NET Framework applications for paging and sorting in a grid, as well as in many other scenarios.

ROW_NUMBER()

The most basic ranking function is *ROW_NUMBER()*. It returns a column as an expression that contains the row's number in the result set. This number is used only in the context of the result set; if the result changes, the *ROW_NUMBER()* changes. The *ROW_NUMBER()*

expression takes an *ORDER BY* statement with the column you want to use for the row count and the new *OVER* operator, which links the *ORDER BY* to the specific ranking function you are using. The *ORDER BY* in the *OVER* clause replaces an *ORDER BY* at the end of the SQL statement.

The following simple example gives a row number to each row in the result set, ordering by SalesOrderID:

Listing 2-21   Row number ranking

```
USE AdventureWorks
GO
SELECT SalesOrderID, CustomerID,
    ROW_NUMBER() OVER (ORDER BY SalesOrderID) AS RunningCount
FROM Sales.SalesOrderHeader
WHERE SalesOrderID>10000
```

Results are shown here:

```
SalesOrderID       CustomerID        RunningCount
------------------------------------------------
43659              676               1
43660              117               2
43661              442               3
43662              227               4
43663              510               5
43664              397               6
43665              146               7
43666              511               8
43667              646               9
[more rows]
```

ORDER BY Options

The ranking functions order your result set by the fields specified in the *ORDER BY* statement contained in the *OVER* clause. Alternatively, you can include an additional *ORDER BY* statement in your result set; this optional statement is distinct from the *ORDER BY* clause in the *OVER* expression. SQL Server 2005 allows this, but if you choose this option, the *ROW_NUMBER()* function's results are displayed in the order they are determined by in the additional *ORDER BY* statement, *not* by the *ORDER BY* statement contained within the *OVER* clause. The results can, therefore, be confusing, as in this example:

```
--Row_Number using a unique value, different order by
SELECT SalesOrderID, CustomerID,
    ROW_NUMBER() OVER (ORDER BY SalesOrderID) AS RunningCount
FROM Sales.SalesOrderHeader
WHERE SalesOrderID>10000
ORDER BY CustomerID --Different ORDER BY than in Row_Number
```

Here are the results:

```
SalesOrderID    CustomerID    RunningCount
--------------------------------------------
43860           1             202
44501           1             843
45283           1             1625
46042           1             2384
46976           2             3318
47997           2             4339
49054           2             5396
50216           2             6558
51728           2             8070
57044           2             13386
63198           2             19540
69488           2             25830
65310           3             21652
71889           3             28231
53616           3             9958
[more rows]
```

As you can see, if you expect the results to be sorted by the *OVER* clause's *ORDER BY* statement, you'd expect results ranked by SalesOrderID, when in fact they're ordered by CustomerID.

If you choose the *ROW_NUMBER()* function to run against a non-unique column that contains multiple copies of the same value (also known as "ties," such as the same amount of items sold and the same time in a race), *ROW_NUMBER( )* breaks the tie and still produces a running count so that no rows have the same number. For example, *CustomerID* can repeat in this example, which will generate several ties; SQL Server simply increases the running count for each row, regardless of how many ties exist:

Listing 2-22   Row number ranking with ties

```
SELECT SalesOrderID, CustomerID,
    ROW_NUMBER() OVER (ORDER BY CustomerID) AS RunningCount
FROM Sales.SalesOrderHeader
WHERE SalesOrderID>10000
```

The results are shown here:

```
SalesOrderID        CustomerID        RunningCount
---------------------------------------------------
43860               1                 1
44501               1                 2
45283               1                 3
46042               1                 4
46976               2                 5
47997               2                 6
49054               2                 7
```

```
50216              2              8
51728              2              9
57044              2              10
63198              2              11
69488              2              12
44124              3              13
[more rows]
```

Grouping and Filtering with a *Row_Number*

When you want to include a *GROUP BY* function in your query, ranking functions do not work. The easy way around this limitation is to create your *GROUP BY* in a CTE and then perform your ranking on the results, as shown here:

Listing 2-23   Grouping by row number

```
USE AdventureWorks
GO
--rank by totaldue, summed
--need a CTE to do the sum
--so this example will have a
--customerID summed with all of
--their orders
WITH CustomerSum
AS
(
SELECT CustomerID, SUM(totaldue) AS totalamt
FROM Sales.SalesOrderHeader
GROUP BY CustomerID
)
--this appends a row_number to the end of the resultset
SELECT *,
    ROW_NUMBER() OVER (ORDER BY totalamt DESC) AS RowNumber
FROM CustomerSum
```

Here are the results:

```
CustomerID      totalamt        RowNumber
----------------------------------------
678             1179857.4657    1
697             1179475.8399    2
170             1134747.4413    3
328             1084439.0265    4
514             1074154.3035    5
155             1045197.0498    6
72              1005539.7181    7
[more rows]
```

To filter by a *ROW_NUMBER*, you have to put the *ROW_NUMBER* function in a CTE.

Listing 2-24   Filtering by row number

```
USE AdventureWorks
GO
--use a common table expression if you want
--to filter by one of the rows that contain a
--ranking function since ranking functions
--are not allowed in where or having clauses
WITH NumberRows
AS
(
SELECT SalesOrderID, CustomerID,
    ROW_NUMBER() OVER (ORDER BY SalesOrderID) AS RowNumber
FROM Sales.SalesOrderHeader
)

SELECT * FROM NumberRows
WHERE RowNumber BETWEEN 100 AND 200
```

Here are the results:

```
SalesOrderID      CustomerID       RowNumber
------------------------------------------------
43759             13257            100
43760             16352            101
43761             16493            102
43762             27578            103
[more rows]
```

RANK()

The ranking function you will probably use the most is *RANK()*. *RANK()* ranks the data in the *ORDER BY* clause in the order you specify. *RANK()* is syntactically exactly like *ROW_NUMBER()* but with true ranking results. It works just like in the Olympics, when two people tie for the gold medal—the next rank is bronze. Similarly, with the RANK() function, if four rows are tied with the value '1', the next row value for the rank column will be '5'. Consider this code:

Listing 2-25   The *RANK()* function

```
USE AdventureWorks
GO
SELECT SalesOrderID, CustomerID,
    RANK() OVER (ORDER BY CustomerID) AS RunningCount
FROM Sales.SalesOrderHeader
WHERE SalesOrderID > 10000
```

Here are the results:

```
SalesOrderID    CustomerID      RunningCount
---------------------------------------------
43860           1               1
44501           1               1
45283           1               1
46042           1               1
46976           2               5
47997           2               5
49054           2               5
50216           2               5
51728           2               5
57044           2               5
63198           2               5
69488           2               5
44124           3               13
[more rows]
```

Just like with the other ranking functions, *RANK()* needs the aid of a CTE to work with aggregates. Consider this query that ranks the customers from highest to lowest by total sales. We have to use a CTE to perform the aggregate first and then rank over the newly created aggregate expression:

Listing 2-26   Ranked aggregates

```
USE AdventureWorks
GO
--rank by totaldue, summed
--need a CTE to do a sum
--so this example will have a
--customerID summed with all of
--their orders
WITH CustomerSum
AS
(
SELECT CustomerID, SUM(totaldue) AS totalamt
FROM Sales.SalesOrderHeader
GROUP BY CustomerID
)
SELECT *,
    RANK() OVER (ORDER BY totalamt DESC) AS Rank
FROM CustomerSum
```

The results are shown here. Notice that customer 697 is in first place:

```
CustomerID      totalamt        Rank
------------------------------------
697             1179475.8399    1
678             1164761.0209    2
170             1134747.4413    3
328             1084439.0265    4
514             1074154.3035    5
[more rows]
```

It is important to remember that the ranking functions provided by SQL Server 2005 are valid only for the scope of the running query. If the underlying data changes and then you run the same query again, you will get different results. For example, let's modify a record from customer 678:

Listing 2-27 *RANK()* results change with underlying data changes

```
USE AdventureWorks
GO
UPDATE Sales.SalesOrderDetail
SET OrderQty = 13 --3 is the orig amt
WHERE SalesOrderID = 44086 AND SalesOrderDetailID = 1542
```

The results are shown here. Notice that customer 678 is now the top customer:

```
CustomerID      totalamt        Rank
----------------------------------------
678             1185160.9609    1
697             1179475.8399    2
170             1134747.4413    3
328             1084439.0265    4
514             1074154.3035    5
```

DENSE_RANK() and NTILE(n)

The last two ranking functions we will cover are *DENSE_RANK()* and *NTILE(n)*. *DENSE_RANK()* works exactly like *RANK()*, except it increments only on distinct rank changes.

Listing 2-28 Ranking with *DENSE_RANK()*

```
USE AdventureWorks
GO
SELECT SalesOrderID, CustomerID,
    DENSE_RANK() OVER (ORDER BY CustomerID) AS RunningCount
FROM Sales.SalesOrderHeader
WHERE SalesOrderID > 10000
```

The results are shown here:

```
SalesOrderID    CustomerID      RunningCount
----------------------------------------------
43860           1               1
44501           1               1
45283           1               1
46042           1               1
46976           2               2
47997           2               2
49054           2               2
50216           2               2
```

```
51728            2              2
57044            2              2
63198            2              2
69488            2              2
44124            3              3
[more rows]
```

The following example shows the difference between *RANK()* and *DENSE_RANK()*. We will round the customers' sales to the nearest hundred (because managers always like to look at whole numbers in their reports!) and look at the difference when we run into a tie. The code is here:

Listing 2-29   *RANK()* versus *DENSE_RANK()*

```
USE AdventureWorks
GO
WITH CustomerSum
AS
(
SELECT CustomerID, ROUND(CONVERT(int, SUM(totaldue))/100,8) *100 as totalamt
FROM Sales.SalesOrderHeader
GROUP BY CustomerID
)
SELECT *,
    RANK() OVER (ORDER BY totalamt DESC) AS Rank,
    DENSE_RANK() OVER (ORDER BY totalamt DESC) AS DenseRank
FROM CustomerSum
```

And here are the results:

```
CustomerID       totalamt       Rank      DenseRank
---------------------------------------------------
678              1185100        1         1
697              1179400        2         2
170              1134700        3         3
328              1084400        4         4
[more rows]
87               213300         170       170
667              210600         171       171
196              207700         172       172
451              206100         173       173
672              206100         173       173
272              05200          175       174
687              205200         175       174
163              204000         177       175
102              203900         178       176
[more rows]
```

Notice that customers 451 and 672 are tied, with the same total sales amount. They are ranked 173 by both the *RANK()* and *DENSE_RANK()* functions. What happens next is what's important. Customers 27 and 687 are tied for the next position, and they are both assigned

175 by *RANK()* and 174 by *DENSE_RANK()*. Customer 163 is the next non-tie, and it is assigned 177 by *RANK()* and 175 by *DENSE_RANK()*.

NTILE(n) divides the returned rows into approximately evenly sized groups, the number of which you specify as a parameter to the function. It assigns each member of a group the same number in the result set. A perfect example of this is the percentile ranking in a college examination or a road race.

Listing 2-30   Ranking with *NTILE()*

```
SELECT SalesOrderID, CustomerID,
    NTILE(10000) OVER (ORDER BY CustomerID) AS RunningCount
FROM Sales.SalesOrderHeader
WHERE SalesOrderID > 10000
```

The results are shown here:

```
SalesOrderID    CustomerID      RunningCount
--------------------------------------------------
43860           1               1
44501           1               1
45283           1               1
46042           1               1
46976           2               2
47997           2               2
49054           2               2
50216           2               2
51728           2               3
57044           2               3
63198           2               3
69488           2               3
44124           3               4
[more rows]
```

Using All the Ranking Functions Together

So far we have looked at the ranking functions in isolation. The ranking functions are just regular SQL Server expressions, so you can have as many of them as you want in a single *SELECT* statement. We'll look at one last example that brings these all together into one SQL statement and shows the differences between the four ranking functions.

Listing 2-31   Contrasting SQL Server 2005 ranking functions

```
--Ranking All
USE AdventureWorks
GO
SELECT SalesOrderID AS OrderID, CustomerID,
    ROW_NUMBER() OVER(ORDER BY CustomerID) AS RowNum,
    RANK() OVER (ORDER BY CustomerID) AS Rank,
    DENSE_RANK() OVER (ORDER BY CustomerID) as DRank,
    NTILE(10000) OVER (ORDER BY CustomerID) as NTile
```

```
FROM Sales.SalesOrderHeader
WHERE SalesOrderID>10000
ORDER BY CustomerID
```

The results are shown here:

OrderID	CustomerID	RowNum	Rank	Drank	NTile
43860	1	1	1	1	1
44501	1	2	1	1	1
45283	1	3	1	1	1
46042	1	4	1	1	1
46976	2	5	5	2	2
47997	2	6	5	2	2
49054	2	7	5	2	2
50216	2	8	5	2	2
51728	2	9	5	2	3
57044	2	10	5	2	3
63198	2	11	5	2	3
69488	2	12	5	2	3
44124	3	13	13	3	4
44791	3	14	13	3	4

[more rows]

Ranking over Groups: *PARTITION BY*

The ranking functions can also be combined with windowing functions. A windowing function divides a result set into equal partitions based on the values of your *PARTITION BY* statement in conjunction with the *OVER* clause in your ranking function. This is like applying a *GROUP BY* to your ranking function—you get a separate ranking for each partition. The following example uses *ROW_NUMBER* with *PARTITION BY* to count the number of orders by order date by salesperson. We do this by using *PARTITION BY SalesPersonID OVER OrderDate*. You can do this with any of the four ranking functions.

Listing 2-32   Ranking over groups with *PARTITION BY*

```
USE AdventureWorks
GO
SELECT SalesOrderID, SalesPersonID, OrderDate,
ROW_NUMBER() OVER (PARTITION BY SalesPersonID ORDER BY OrderDate) AS OrderRank
FROM Sales.SalesOrderHeader
WHERE SalesPersonID is not null
```

The results are shown here. You might find that the order of your rows varies slightly from the results shown.

SalesOrderID	SalesPersonID	OrderDate	OrderRank
[more rows]			
43659	279	2001-07-01 00:00:00.000	1
43660	279	2001-07-01 00:00:00.000	2
43681	279	2001-07-01 00:00:00.000	3

43684	279	2001-07-01 00:00:00.000	4
43685	279	2001-07-01 00:00:00.000	5
43694	279	2001-07-01 00:00:00.000	6
43695	279	2001-07-01 00:00:00.000	7
43696	279	2001-07-01 00:00:00.000	8
43845	279	2001-08-01 00:00:00.000	9
43861	279	2001-08-01 00:00:00.000	10
[more rows]			
48079	287	2002-11-01 00:00:00.000	1
48064	287	2002-11-01 00:00:00.000	2
48057	287	2002-11-01 00:00:00.000	3
47998	287	2002-11-01 00:00:00.000	4
48001	287	2002-11-01 00:00:00.000	5
48014	287	2002-11-01 00:00:00.000	6
47982	287	2002-11-01 00:00:00.000	7
47992	287	2002-11-01 00:00:00.000	8
48390	287	2002-12-01 00:00:00.000	9
48308	287	2002-12-01 00:00:00.000	10
[more rows]			

Let's partition our ranking function by country. We'll create a CTE to aggregate the sales by customer and by country. Then we will apply the ranking function over the TotalAmt field and the Customer ID field, partitioned by the CountryName.

Listing 2-33   Aggregates with *PARTITION BY*

```
USE AdventureWorks
GO
WITH CTETerritory
AS
(
SELECT cr.Name AS CountryName, CustomerID, SUM(TotalDue) AS TotalAmt
FROM Sales.SalesOrderHeader soh
    INNER JOIN Sales.SalesTerritory ter
        ON soh.TerritoryID=ter.TerritoryID
    INNER JOIN Person.CountryRegion cr
        ON cr.CountryRegionCode=ter.CountryRegionCode
GROUP BY cr.Name, CustomerID
)
SELECT *, RANK() OVER(PARTITION BY CountryName ORDER BY TotalAmt, CustomerID DESC)
As Rank
FROM CTETerritory
```

The results look like this:

CountryName	CustomerID	TotalAmt	Rank
Australia	29083	4.409	1
Australia	29061	4.409	2
Australia	29290	5.514	3
Australia	29287	5.514	4
Australia	28924	5.514	5
[more rows]			

```
Canada           29267            5.514            1
Canada           29230            5.514            2
Canada           28248            5.514            3
Canada           27628            5.514            4
Canada           27414            5.514            5
[more rows]
France           24538            4.409            1
France           24535            4.409            2
France           23623            4.409            3
France           23611            4.409            4
France           20961            4.409            5
[more rows]
```

PARTITION BY supports other SQL Server aggregate functions, including *MIN* and *MAX* as well as your own scalar functions. You can apply your aggregate function in the same way that you apply the ranking functions, with a *PARTITION BY* statement. Let's apply this technique to the current sample by adding a column to our results set using the *AVG* function. We will get the same results but with an additional column showing the average by country:

Listing 2-34   Using *AVG* with *PARTITION BY*

```
USE AdventureWorks
GO
WITH CTETerritory
AS
(
SELECT cr.Name AS CountryName, CustomerID, SUM(TotalDue) AS TotalAmt
FROM Sales.SalesOrderHeader soh
   INNER JOIN Sales.SalesTerritory ter
      ON soh.TerritoryID=ter.TerritoryID
   INNER JOIN Person.CountryRegion cr
      ON cr.CountryRegionCode=ter.CountryRegionCode
GROUP BY cr.Name, CustomerID
)
SELECT *, RANK() OVER(PARTITION BY CountryName ORDER BY TotalAmt, CustomerID DESC)
AS Rank,
AVG(TotalAmt) OVER(PARTITION BY CountryName) AS Average
FROM CTETerritory
```

Here are the results:

```
CountryName      CustomerID       TotalAmt      Rank       Average
----------------------------------------------------------------------
Australia        29083            4.409          1         3364.8318
Australia        29061            4.409          2         3364.8318
Australia        29290            5.514          3         3364.8318
[more rows]
Canada           29267            5.514          1         12824.756
Canada           29230            5.514          2         12824.756
Canada           28248            5.514          3         12824.756
[more rows]
```

Exception Handling in Transactions

SQL Server 2005 offers major improvements in error handling inside T-SQL transactions. You can now catch T-SQL and transaction abort errors using the *TRY/CATCH* model without any loss of the transaction context. The only types of errors that the *TRY/CATCH* construct can't handle are those that cause the termination of your session (usually errors with severity 21 and above, such as hardware errors). The syntax is shown here:

```
BEGIN TRY
sql statement
END TRY
BEGIN CATCH TRAN_ABORT
    --sql statement for catching your errors
END CATCH
```

If an error within an explicit transaction occurs inside a *TRY* block, control is passed to the *CATCH* block that immediately follows. If no error occurs, the *CATCH* block is completely skipped.

You can investigate the type of error that was raised and react accordingly. To do so, you can use the new *ERROR* functions to return error information in the *CATCH* block, as shown here:

Listing 2-35   T-SQL exception handling example

```
BEGIN TRY
   SELECT 5/0
END TRY
BEGIN CATCH
    SELECT
        ERROR_NUMBER() AS ErrorNumber,
        ERROR_SEVERITY() AS ErrorSeverity,
        ERROR_STATE() AS ErrorState,
        ERROR_PROCEDURE() AS ErrorProcedure,
        ERROR_LINE() AS ErrorLine,
        ERROR_MESSAGE() AS ErrorMessage;
END CATCH
```

You can examine the value of the *ERROR* functions to decide what to do with the control flow of your procedure and whether to abort any transactions. When you experience a transaction abort error inside a transaction located in the *TRY* block, control is passed to the *CATCH* block. The transaction then enters a failed state in which locks are not released and persisted work is not reversed until you explicitly issue a *ROLLBACK* statement. You're not allowed to initiate any activity that requires opening an implicit or explicit transaction until you issue a *ROLLBACK*.

Sometimes certain types of errors are not detected by the *TRY/CATCH* block, and you end up with an unhandled exception even though the error occurred inside your *TRY* block. If this happens, the *CATCH* block is not executed. This is because *CATCH* blocks are invoked by errors that take place in actual executing code, not by compile or syntax errors. Two examples of such errors are syntax errors and statement-level recompile errors (for example, selecting from a nonexistent table). These errors are not caught at the same execution level as the *TRY* block, but at the lower level of execution—when you execute dynamic SQL or when you call a stored procedure from the *TRY* block. For example, if you have a syntax error inside a *TRY* block, you get a compile error and your *CATCH* block will not run:

```
-- Syntax error doesn't get caught
BEGIN TRY
    SELECT * * FROM XYX
END TRY
BEGIN CATCH
    PRINT 'Error'
END CATCH
GO
```

The result is an error from SQL Server, not from your *CATCH* block:

```
Msg 102, Level 15, State 1, Line 2
Incorrect syntax near '*'.
```

Statement-level recompilation errors don't get caught by *CATCH* blocks, either. For example, using a nonexistent object in a *SELECT* statement in the *TRY* block forces an error from SQL Server, but your *CATCH* block will not execute:

```
-- Statement level recompilation doesn't get caught
-- Example - nonexistent object
BEGIN TRY
    SELECT * FROM XYX
END TRY
BEGIN CATCH
    PRINT 'Error'
END CATCH
GO
```

The result is an error from SQL Server:

```
Msg 208, Level 16, State 1, Line 4
Invalid object name 'XYX'.
```

When you use dynamic SQL or a stored procedure, these types of compile errors are caught because they are part of the current level of execution. Each of the following SQL blocks will execute the *CATCH* block.

Listing 2-36   Catching syntax and recompilation errors in dynamic SQL with exception handlers

```
-- Dynamic SQL Example
BEGIN TRY
    EXEC sp_executesql 'SELECT * * FROM XYX'
END TRY
```

```
BEGIN CATCH
    PRINT 'Error'
END CATCH
GO

-- Stored Procedure Example
CREATE PROCEDURE MyErrorProc
AS
    SELECT * FROM XYX
GO

BEGIN TRY
    EXEC MyErrorProc
END TRY
BEGIN CATCH
    PRINT 'Error'
END CATCH
GO
```

New Data Types

SQL Server 2005 has several cool new data types. The most useful are *varchar(max)* and *xml*.

varchar(max) Data Type

varchar(max), *nvarchar(max)*, and *varbinary(max)* are extensions of the *varchar*, *nvarchar*, and *varbinary* data types that can store up to 2 gigabytes (GB) of data. They are alternatives to *text*, *ntext*, and *image* and use the *MAX* size specifier. Using one of these data types is easy—you just specify it in your *CREATE TABLE* statement with a *(max)* identifier, as shown here:

```
CREATE TABLE TablewithMaxColumn
(Customer_Id int, CustomerLifeStory varbinary(max))
```

All the standard T-SQL string functions operate on *varchar(max),* including concatenation functions *SUBSTRING, LEN, and CONVERT*. For example, you can use the T-SQL *SUBSTRING* function to read parts of the string (*chunks*), and the *UPDATE* statement has also been enhanced to support the updating of chunks.

This is a vast improvement over the limitations in SQL Server 2000, where TEXT and IMAGE fields are used to store this type of data. These data types are not allowed as stored procedure variables and cannot be updated directly, and many of the string manipulation functions don't work on the *TEXT* data type.

xml Data Type

To accommodate the growing importance of XML, SQL Server 2005 includes an *xml* data type. In the past, developers stored XML in a *varchar* or *text/ntext* field. That wasn't optimal because the XML wasn't in its native format and you couldn't query its contents efficiently.

The new data type allows you to store XML in its native format (actually, in a BLOB field) and gives you the ability, using XQuery, to query parts of the XML field.

The *xml* data type is a full-blown T-SQL citizen—it can be used as a type for table columns and variables, and it can participate in a *CAST* or *CONVERT* statement. You can even use the *FOR XML* statement to convert tabular data into XML from an SQL query, as shown here:

Listing 2-37   Converting data into XML

```
USE AdventureWorks
GO
DECLARE @xmlData AS xml
SET @xmlData = (SELECT * FROM HumanResources.Employee FOR XML AUTO, TYPE)
SELECT @xmlData
```

As expected, the results of a row look like this:

```
<HumanResources.Employee EmployeeID="1" NationalIDNumber="14417807"
ContactID="1209" LoginID="adventure-works\guy1" DepartmentID="7"
ManagerID="16" ShiftID="1" Title="Production Technician - WC60"
EmergencyContactID="1498" AddressID="61" BirthDate="1972-05-
15T00:00:00" MaritalStatus="M" Gender="M" HireDate="1996-07-
31T00:00:00" SalariedFlag="0" BaseRate="12.4500" PayFrequency="1"
VacationHours="21" SickLeaveHours="30" CurrentFlag="1"
rowguid="AAE1D04A-C237-4974-B4D5-935247737718" ModifiedDate="1996-07-
24T00:00:00" />
[more elements]
```

> **More Info**   For much more on the *xml* data type, see Chapter 4.

The *WAITFOR* Command

The *WAITFOR* command has also been enhanced in SQL Server 2005. In the past, *WAITFOR* waited for a specified duration or a supplied *datetime* value. Now, as with the *TOP* enhancements, you can use *WAITFOR* with an SQL expression. You can essentially use the *WAITFOR* function to wait for a T-SQL statement to affect at least one row. (You can also set a timeout on that SQL expression.) You can now specify *WAITFOR* to wait not only in *SELECT* statements, but also in *INSERT*, *UPDATE*, *DELETE*, and *RECEIVE* statements. In essence, *SELECT* statements won't complete until at least one row is produced, and *DML* statements won't complete until at least one row is affected.

Here is the syntax:

```
WAITFOR(<statement>) [,TIMEOUT <timeout_value>]
```

This feature creates a new alternative to polling. For example, you can use *WAITFOR* to select all the records in a log or a queue table:

```
WAITFOR (SELECT * FROM myQ)
```

> **More Info**   *WAITFOR* is useful when you're working with the SQL Server Service Broker. See Chapter 12 for more on SQL Server Service Broker.

DDL Triggers and Notifications

SQL Server 2005 supports data definition language (DDL) triggers, allowing you to trap DDL operations and react to them. You can thus roll back the DDL activity. DDL triggers work synchronously, immediately after the triggering event, similar to the way that DML triggers in previous versions of SQL Server work. SQL Server 2005 also has an asynchronous event consumption mechanism that uses notifications and allows you to be notified when certain events, such as DDL events, occur. (See Chapter 13.) DDL triggers can be database-wide and can react to certain types of DDLs or all DDLs.

The cool thing about DDL triggers is that you can get context information from querying the *EVENTDATA()* method. Event data is an XML payload of data about what was happening when your DDL trigger ran, including information about the time, connection, and user; the type of event that was fired; and other useful data. To get at *EVENTDATA()* data, you have to use the *EVENTDATA()* function in your trigger code. If you issue a *ROLLBACK* statement in the trigger, the *EVENTDATA()* function will no longer return information. In this situation, you must store the information in a variable before issuing the *ROLLBACK* statement to be accessed later.

The following AdventureWorks trigger, created at the database level, will capture *DROP TABLE* attempts. First we'll create a log table to log all our event data using an XML column, and then we'll create a dummy table that we will delete and test our trigger on. Our trigger will then write the event data to this table.

Listing 2-38   Catching *DROP TABLE* attempts with a trigger

```
USE Adventureworks
GO
--create a log table
CREATE TABLE tblDDLTriggerLog (LogInfo xml)
--create a dummy table to delete later on
CREATE TABLE toDelete (ID int primary key)
--add some dummy data in just for fun
INSERT INTO toDelete VALUES(1)
--create a trigger that will disallow any table
--drops and log the event data into our log table
CREATE TRIGGER StopDropAnyTable ON DATABASE AFTER DROP_TABLE
AS
DECLARE @eventData AS xml
SET @eventData = EVENTDATA()
ROLLBACK
-- For results window!
PRINT 'DROP TABLE attempt in database ' + DB_NAME() + '.'
INSERT INTO tblDDLTriggerLog VALUES(@eventData)
```

The following example will also attempt to drop a table and will query the tblDDLTriggerLog table:

```
--now see this trigger in action
DROP TABLE toDelete
SELECT * FROM tblDDLTriggerLog
```

The results look like this:

```
DROP TABLE attempt in database AdventureWorks.
 [1 row affected]
Msg 3609, Level 16, State 2, Line 1
Transaction ended in trigger. Batch has been aborted.
```

The *EventData()* XML stored in *tblDDLTriggerLog* looks like this:

```
<EVENT_INSTANCE>
  <EventType>DROP_TABLE</EventType>
  <PostTime>2004-12-07T20:40:58.597</PostTime>
  <SPID>53</SPID>
  <ServerName>KILIMANJARO</ServerName>
  <LoginName>KILIMANJARO\Stephen Forte</LoginName>
  <UserName>KILIMANJARO\Stephen Forte</UserName>
  <DatabaseName>AdventureWorks</DatabaseName>
  <SchemaName>dbo</SchemaName>
  <ObjectName>toDelete</ObjectName>
  <ObjectType>TABLE</ObjectType>
  <TSQLCommand>
    <SetOptions ANSI_NULLS="ON" ANSI_NULL_DEFAULT="ON" ANSI_PADDING="ON" QUOTED_
IDENTIFIER="ON" ENCRYPTED="FALSE" />
    <CommandText>DROP TABLE toDelete</CommandText>
  </TSQLCommand>
</EVENT_INSTANCE>
```

SNAPSHOT Isolation

For working with transactions in T-SQL, SQL Server 2005 offers a new isolation level called SNAPSHOT that allows you to work in a mode in which writers don't block readers. Readers thus read from a previously committed version of the data they request, rather than being blocked during write transactions. SNAPSHOT isolation works by SQL Server 2005 maintaining a linked list in tempdb that tracks changes to rows and constructs an older, committed version of data for readers to access. This isolation level is useful for optimistic locking, in which *UPDATE* conflicts are uncommon. For example, if process 1 retrieves data and later attempts to modify it, and if process 2 has modified the same data between the retrieval and modification, SQL Server produces an error when process 1 attempts to modify data because of the conflict. Process 1 can then try to reissue the transaction. This mode can be efficient in situations in which *UPDATE* conflicts are not common.

Look for a more thorough discussion of SQL Server isolation levels in Chapter 11.

Statement-Level Recompile

SQL Server 2005 introduces a major change in the way queries are compiled. SQL Server 2000 vastly improved its query plan architecture by having two plans: a compiled plan and an executable plan. The compiled plan (with a maximum of two plans per query, one for a serialized run and one for a parallel run) can be used by any user; an executable plan creates a data structure for each user who is running the query concurrently. Most database administrators and developers who get bogged down by the performance issues of stored procedure recompilation know that this system is a vast improvement over previous versions of SQL Server. But it isn't perfect: Schema changes and threshold changes in rows as well as some *SET* options cause a stored procedure to recompile, even if you have a large stored procedure and only a tiny portion would be affected by the schema or threshold change.

SQL Server 2005 has changed this architecture to perform statement-level recompiles. Each stored procedure is compiled on a module level, but recompiles are performed only at the statement level and do not affect the whole batch. Also note that a recompile does not invalidate the execution context, further enhancing performance.

Summary

We covered a lot of new ground in this chapter. SQL Server 2005 introduces many great enhancements to its T-SQL engine. You can see that Microsoft has continued its investment in T-SQL and that it offers many powerful new ways to query complex data using T-SQL, including *PIVOT*, *APPLY*, ranking functions, and recursive operations through common table expressions (CTEs). New data types have been added for your programming use, including the powerful *xml* data type, which is discussed in detail in Chapter 4. T-SQL is still the main way you will interact with data. When your operations require you to interact with the operating system or use the .NET Framework, you can use the CLR to write your queries. In the next chapter, we'll look at writing procedures in Visual Basic .NET or Visual C# via in-poc ADO, an exciting new feature.

An Overview of SQL CLR

–Andrew Brust

The banner headline for Microsoft SQL Server 2005 is its integration of the Microsoft .NET common language runtime (CLR). This architectural enhancement means that SQL Server can use certain .NET classes as basic data types and can accommodate the use of .NET languages for the creation of stored procedures, triggers, and functions, and even user-defined aggregates.

Note Throughout this chapter, we will refer to the CLR integration in SQL Server as SQL CLR features, functionality, or integration, and we will refer to stored procedures, triggers, functions, aggregates, and user-defined types as the five basic SQL CLR entities.

Let's face facts: Transact SQL (T-SQL) is essentially a hack. Back when SQL Server was first developed, Microsoft and Sybase took SQL—a declarative, set-based language—and added variable declaration, conditional branching, looping, and parameterized subroutine logic to make it into a quasi-procedural language. Although extremely clever and useful, T-SQL lacked, and still lacks, many of the niceties of a full-fledged procedural programming language.

This shortcoming has forced some people to write T-SQL stored procedures that are overly complex and difficult to read. It has forced others to put logic in their middle-tier code that they would prefer to implement on the database. And it's even forced some people to abandon stored procedures altogether and use dynamic SQL in their applications, a practice that we do not endorse. Because of these workarounds to address T-SQL's procedural limitations, CLR integration is a welcome new feature in SQL Server, and it has caught the market's attention.

Meanwhile, T-SQL—and, one might argue, SQL itself—is vastly superior to procedural languages for querying and manipulating data. Its set-based syntax and implementation simply transcend the approach of procedurally iterating through rows of data. This is no less true in SQL Server 2005 than in previous versions of the product, and T-SQL has been greatly enhanced in this release (as detailed in Chapter 2), making it more valuable still.

So this places database application developers at a crossroads. We must simultaneously learn how the SQL CLR features work and develop a sophisticated, judicious sense of when to use T-SQL instead of the SQL CLR feature set. We must resist the temptation to completely ".NET-ify" our databases but learn to take advantage of the SQL CLR feature set where and when prudent. This chapter aims to help you learn to use SQL CLR features and to develop an instinct for their appropriate application.

In this chapter, you will learn:

- How to enable (or disable) SQL CLR integration on your SQL Server

- How SQL Server accommodates CLR code, through the loading of .NET assemblies

- How to use SQL Server 2005 and Visual Studio 2005 together to write SQL CLR code and deploy it, simply and quickly

- How to deploy SQL CLR code independently of Visual Studio, using T-SQL commands, with or without the help of SQL Server Management Studio

- How to create simple CLR stored procedures, triggers, functions, aggregates, and user-defined types, use them in your databases, and utilize them from T-SQL

- How both the standard SQL Server client provider and the new server-side library can be combined to implement SQL CLR functionality

- How SQL CLR security works and how to configure security permissions for your assemblies

- When to use SQL CLR functionality, and when to opt to use T-SQL instead

Getting Started: Enabling CLR Integration

Before you can learn how to use SQL CLR features, you need to know how to enable them. As with many new products in the Microsoft Windows Server System family, many advanced features of SQL Server 2005 are disabled by default. The reasoning behind this is sound: Each additional feature that is enabled provides extra "surface area" for attacks on security or integrity of the product, and the added exposure is inexcusable if the feature goes unused.

The SQL CLR features of SQL Server 2005 are sophisticated and can be very useful, but they are also, technically, nonessential. It is possible to build high-performance databases and server-side programming logic without SQL CLR integration, so it is turned off by default.

Don't be discouraged, though: Turning on the feature is easy. Microsoft provides both a user-friendly GUI tool (aptly named the SQL Server Surface Area Configuration tool) and a system stored procedure for enabling or disabling SQL CLR integration. We'll cover both approaches.

To use the Surface Area Configuration tool, simply start it from the Configuration Tools subgroup in the Microsoft SQL Server 2005 programs group on the Windows start menu. Figure 3-1 shows the tool as it appears upon startup.

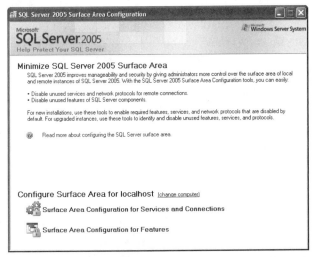

Figure 3-1   The SQL Server 2005 Surface Area Configuration tool

To configure CLR integration, click the Surface Area Configuration For Features link at the bottom of the form. After a short pause, the Surface Area Configuration For Features dialog box appears; a tree view-style list of features appears on the left, and the Ad Hoc Remote Queries feature is preselected. Click the CLR Integration node immediately below it, and you will see an Enable CLR Integration check box on the right of the form. (This is shown in Figure 3-2.) To enable SQL CLR features, make sure that the check box is checked, and click OK to close the Surface Area Configuration For Features window. (You can also clear the check box to disable SQL CLR integration.) Close the Surface Area Configuration tool by clicking its close box in the upper-right corner of the window.

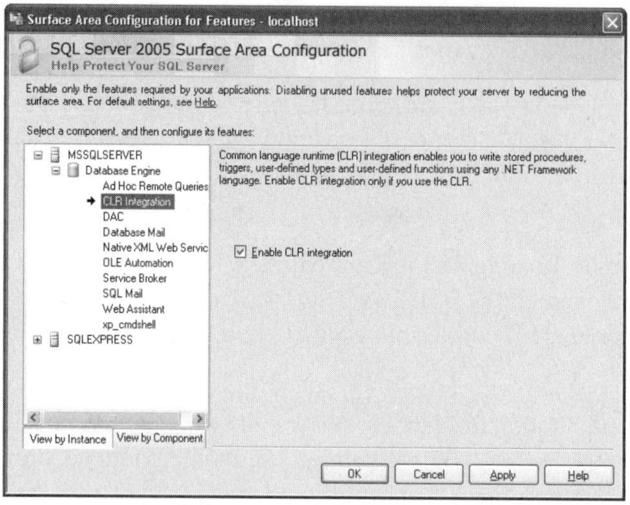

Figure 3-2   The Surface Area Configuration For Features window

If you'd prefer a command-line method for enabling or disabling SQL CLR functionality, open up SQL Server Management Studio and connect to the server you'd like to configure. Then, from a query window, type the following commands, and click the Execute button on the Management Studio SQL Editor toolbar.

```
sp_configure 'clr enabled', 1
GO
RECONFIGURE
GO
```

That's all there is to it! To disable SQL CLR integration, just use a value of 0, instead of 1, as the second parameter value in the *sp_configure* call.

Tip   Don't forget that this will work from any tool that can connect to SQL Server, not just Management Studio. In fact, you could issue the previous command text from your own code using the ADO.NET *SqlCommand* object's *ExecuteNonQuery* method as long as your code can connect to your server and your sever can authenticate as a user in the sysadmin server role.

With SQL CLR integration enabled, you're ready to get started writing SQL CLR code. Before we dive in, we need to discuss Visual Studio/SQL Server integration and when to use it.

Visual Studio/SQL Server Integration

Visual Studio 2005 and SQL Server 2005 integrate tightly in a number of ways. It's important to realize, however, that the use of Visual Studio integration is completely optional and the use of T-SQL is a sufficient substitute. T-SQL has been enhanced with new DDL commands for maintaining CLR assemblies, types, and aggregates, and its existing commands for stored procedures, triggers, and functions have been enhanced to recognize code within deployed assemblies. Visual Studio can execute those commands on your behalf. It can also make writing individual SQL CLR classes and functions easier.

Ultimately, we think all developers should be aware of both Visual Studio–assisted and more manual coding and deployment methods. You might decide to use one method most of the time, but in some situations you'll probably need the other, so we want to prepare you. As we cover each major area of SQL CLR programming, we will discuss deployment from both points of view. We'll cover some general points about Visual Studio integration now, and then we'll move on to cover SQL CLR development.

SQL Server Projects in Visual Studio

The combination of Visual Studio 2005 and SQL Server 2005 on the same development machine provides a special SQL Server Project type in Visual Studio and, within projects of that type, defined templates for the five basic SQL CLR entities. These templates inject specific code attributes and function stubs that allow you to create SQL CLR code easily. The attributes are used by Visual Studio to deploy your assembly and its stored procedures, triggers, and so on to your database. Some of them are also used by SQL Server to acknowledge and properly use your functions, user-defined types (UDTs), and aggregates.

To test out the new project type and templates, start Visual Studio 2005 and create a new project by using the File/New/Project... main menu option, the New Project toolbar button, the Ctrl+Shift+N keyboard accelerator, or the Create Project... hyperlink on the Visual Studio Start Page. In the New Project dialog box (Figure 3-3), select Database from the Project types tree view on the left (the Database node appears under the parent node for your programming language of choice; in Figure 3-3, the language is C#), and click the SQL Server Project icon in the Templates list on the right. Enter your own project name if you'd like, and click OK.

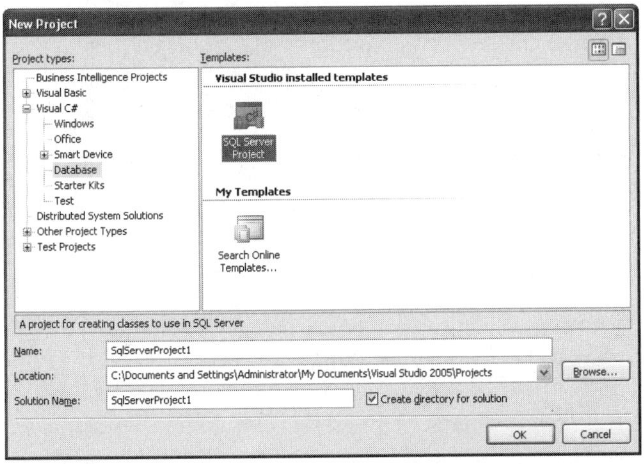

Figure 3-3   The Visual Studio 2005 New Project dialog box with the SQL Server project type selected

Next, the Add Database Reference dialog box appears (Figure 3-4).

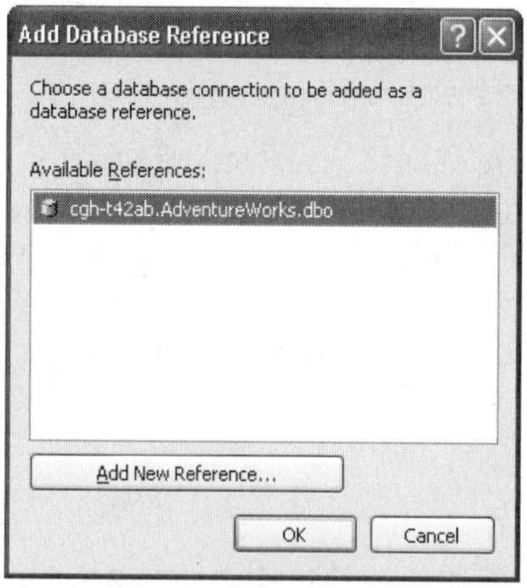

Figure 3-4   The Add Database Reference dialog box

Because Visual Studio provides automated deployment of your SQL CLR code, it must associate your project with a specific server and database via a database reference (connection). Any database connections that have already been defined in the Server Explorer window appear in this window, as does an Add New Reference button that allows you to define a new connection, if necessary. Pick an existing connection or define a new one, and then click OK. The project opens.

> **Note**   If no data connections have already been defined in the Server Explorer window, the New Database Reference dialog box will appear in place of the Add Database Reference dialog box. In the New Database Reference dialog box, you may specify server, login, and database details for a new database connection that will be used by your project as its database reference and added to the Server Explorer as a new data connection.

You can easily add preconfigured classes for the five basic SQL CLR entities to your project. You can do this in a number of ways: directly from the Project menu or from the Add submenu on the Server Explorer's project node shortcut menu (Figure 3-5).

You can also add the preconfigured classes from the Add New Item dialog box (Figure 3-6), which is available from the Project/Add New Item... option on the main menu, or the Add/New Item... option on the Solution Explorer project node's shortcut menu.

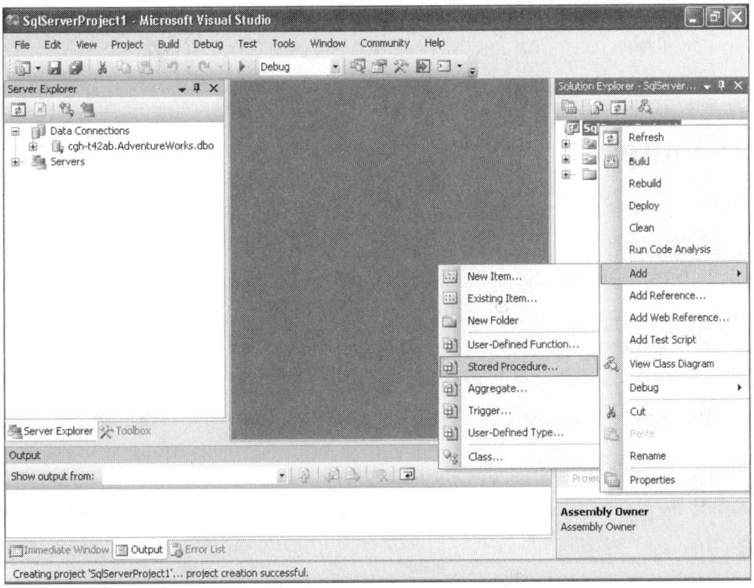

Figure 3-5   The Server Explorer project node shortcut menu and its Add submenu

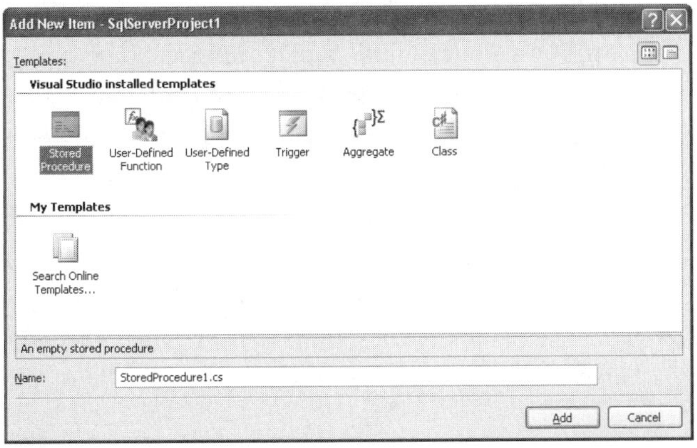

Figure 3-6   The Visual Studio SQL Server project Add New Item dialog box

Automated Deployment

Once opened, SQL Server projects add a Deploy option to the Visual Studio Build menu.
In addition, the Play (Start Debugging) button and the Start Debugging, Start Without
Debugging, and Step Over options on the Debug menu (and their keyboard shortcuts F5,
Ctrl+F5, and F10, respectively) all deploy the project assembly in addition to performing their
listed function.

Visual Studio can do a lot of deployment work for you. But as you'll learn, you can do so on your own and, in certain circumstances, have more precise control over the deployment process when you do so.

SQL CLR Code Attributes

A number of .NET code attributes are provided for SQL CLR developers; these are contained in the *Microsoft.SqlServer.Server* namespace. Many of them are inserted in your code when you use the various templates in the SQL Server project type, as is a *using* statement for the *Microsoft.SqlServer.Server* namespace itself. If you choose to develop code without these templates, you must add the appropriate attributes, and optionally the *using* statement, yourself. Although all these attributes are provided in the same namespace, some are used exclusively by Visual Studio and others are used by both Visual Studio and SQL Server.

Covering all SQL CLR attributes and their parameters would itself require an entire chapter, so our coverage will be intentionally selective. Specifically, we will provide coverage of the *SqlProcedure, SqlFunction, SqlTrigger, SqlUserDefinedAggregate*, and *SqlUserDefinedType* attributes. We will not cover the *SqlFacet* and *SqlMethod* attributes.

Just as certain attributes are not covered here, we cover only some of the parameters accepted by the attributes that we do cover. And in some cases, we cover only certain of the possible values that can be passed to these attributes. For example, *SqlFunction* accepts several parameters but the only ones we will cover are *Name, FillRowMethodName*, and *TableDefinition*. For *SqlUserDefinedAggregate* and *SqlUserDefinedType*, we will cover only a single value setting for the *Format* parameter, and will not cover the several other parameters those two attributes accept.

The coverage we provide will be more than sufficient for you to implement basic, intermediate, and certain advanced functionality with all the basic five SQL CLR entities. The attributes and parameters that we won't cover are useful mostly for optimizing your SQL CLR code, and they are well documented in SQL Server Books Online and articles on MSDN.

About the Sample Code

The sample .NET code for this chapter is provided in two versions. The primary material is supplied as a Visual Studio SQL Server project, accessible by opening the solution file Chapter03.sln in the Chapter03 subfolder of this chapter's VS sample code folder. We also supply the code as a standard Class Library project, accessible by opening the solution file Chapter03Manual.sln in the Chapter03Manual subfolder. The code in each project is virtually identical, although the Class Library project does not autodeploy when the various Build and Debug options are invoked in Visual Studio 2005. As we cover each SQL CLR feature, we'll discuss how automated deployment takes place from the SQL Server project and how command-driven deployment should be performed for the Class Library project.

We'll also discuss executing test scripts from within Visual Studio for the SQL Server project and from SQL Server Management Studio for the Class Library project. As a companion to those discussions, we also provide a Management Studio project, accessible by opening Chapter03.ssmssln in this chapter's SSMS folder. This project consists of a number of SQL scripts used for testing the sample SQL CLR code and a script for cleaning up everything in the database created by the sample code and tests. The project also contains a script file called CreateObjects.sql, which deploys the Class Library assembly and the SQL CLR entities within it.

Your First SQL CLR Stored Procedure

Although SQL CLR programming can get quite complex and involved, it offers in reality a simple model that any .NET developer can use with high productivity in relatively short order. That's because the crux of SQL CLR functionality is nothing more than the ability of SQL Server 2005 to load .NET assemblies into your database and then to allow you to use the procedures, functions, and types within the assembly as you define your columns, views, stored procedures, triggers, and functions.

To give you a good understanding of SQL CLR integration, we must go through its features and techniques carefully. Before doing so, however, let's quickly go through an end-to-end scenario for creating and executing a SQL CLR stored procedure. This will make it easier for you to understand the individual features as we describe them.

Strictly speaking, any .NET class library assembly (in certain cases using appropriate .NET code attributes in its classes and functions) can be loaded into your database with a simple T-SQL command. To see how easily this works, start up Management Studio and open a query window using a connection to the AdventureWorks sample database. In the sample code folder for this chapter, confirm that the file Chapter03.dll is located in the VS\Chapter03Manual\Chapter03\bin\Debug subfolder. If the parent folder were C:\ProgrammingSQL2005\Chapter03, you would load the assembly into the Adventure-Works database with the following T-SQL command:

```
CREATE ASSEMBLY Chapter03
FROM 'C:\ProgrammingSQL2005\Chapter03\VS\Chapter03Manual\Chapter03\bin\Debug\Chapter03.dll'
```

There are other syntax options for the *CREATE ASSEMBLY* command, but for now we'll focus on the previous limited usage.

Functions in an assembly that reside within a class and perform local computational tasks and/or certain types of data access can be easily exposed as SQL Server stored procedures, triggers, or functions. As with conventional stored procedures, triggers, and functions, all it takes is a simple T-SQL *CREATE PROCEDURE*, *CREATE TRIGGER*, or *CREATE FUNCTION* command to make this happen. We'll go through each of these options in this chapter, but let's cut to the chase and create a simple CLR stored procedure right now.

You can view the source code for the Chapter03 assembly by opening the solution file VS\Chapter03Manual\Chapter03Manual.sln in this chapter's sample code folder. Within the project, the file Sprocs.cs contains the following code:

```
using System.Data.SqlClient;
using Microsoft.SqlServer.Server;

public partial class Sprocs
{
    public static void spContactsQuick()
    {
        SqlContext.Pipe.ExecuteAndSend(new SqlCommand("Select * from Person.Contact"));
    }
};
```

The code within the procedure is designed to connect to the database in which its assembly has been loaded (AdventureWorks), perform a *SELECT* * against the Person.Contact table, and use special server-side objects to send the data back to the client application. To make this CLR code available via SQL Server as a stored procedure, also called *spContactsQuick*, you simply execute the following command from the Management Studio query window you opened previously.

```
CREATE PROCEDURE spContactsQuick
AS EXTERNAL NAME
Chapter03.Sprocs.spContactsQuick
```

Important   Be sure to enter the *Sprocs.spContactsQuick* portion of the command verbatim. This phrase is case-sensitive.

To test the SQL CLR stored procedure, run it from a Management Studio query window as you would any conventional stored procedure:

```
EXEC spContactsQuick
```

Or simply:

```
spContactsQuick
```

Management Studio should respond by displaying the contents of the Person.Contact table in the Results tab of the query window.

As you can see from this rather trivial example, writing a CLR stored procedure can be very easy and is a lot like writing client-side or middle-tier code that performs data access using

ADO.NET. The biggest differences involve the provision of a database connection and the fact that the data must be "piped" back to the client rather than loaded into a *SqlDataReader* and returned, manipulated, or displayed through a UI. In addition, the presence of the *SqlContext* object differentiates SQL CLR code from conventional .NET data access code. We'll cover the use of the *SqlContext* object and its *Pipe* property in the next section.

The bits of T-SQL and C# code just shown certainly don't tell the whole SQL CLR story. The use of the *ExecuteAndSend* method allowed us to skip over a number of otherwise important concepts. There are three ways to deploy assemblies, and you've seen only a simplified version of one of those ways. Security considerations must be taken into account, and we haven't even begun to look at triggers, functions, aggregates, or UDTs. So although the example showed how easy SQL CLR programming can be, we'll now take our time and show you the nooks and crannies.

CLR Stored Procedures and Server-Side Data Access

Our previous "quick and dirty" sample looked at CLR stored procedure development, but we need to cover that topic more thoroughly now. We've already covered the mechanics of writing and deploying a stored procedure, but let's back up a bit and try and understand how CLR stored procedures work from a conceptual standpoint.

SQL CLR stored procedure code runs in an instance of the .NET CLR that is hosted by SQL Server itself; it is not called as an external process, as COM-based extended stored procedures (XPs) would be. Because SQL CLR code runs in the context of the server, it treats objects in the database as native, *local* objects, more or less. Likewise, it must treat the client that calls it as *remote*. This contextual environment is, in effect, the opposite of that under which client and middle-tier ADO.NET code runs. This takes a little getting used to, but once you've mastered thinking about things this way, SQL CLR code becomes easy to write and understand.

Meanwhile, as .NET has no intrinsic way of accessing local objects on the server or transmitting data and messages to the client, you must use a special set of classes to perform these tasks. These classes are contained in the *Microsoft.SqlServer.Server* namespace.

> **Note**   As an aside, it is interesting and important to note that the *Microsoft.SqlServer.Server* namespace is actually supplied by the *System.Data* Framework assembly. This means that you don't need to worry about adding a reference to your project to use this namespace. The namespace's location within *System.Data* also further emphasizes the tight integration between .NET and SQL Server.

If you'd like, you can think of *Microsoft.SqlServer.Server* as a helper library for *System.Data.Sql-Client*. It supplies the SQL CLR code attributes we already mentioned, a few enumerations, an exception class, an interface, and five classes: *SqlContext*, *SqlPipe*, *SqlTriggerContext*, *SqlMeta-Data*, and *SqlDataRecord*. We'll cover *SqlMetaData* and *SqlDataRecord* at the end of this section, and we'll cover *SqlTriggerContext* when we discuss CLR triggers. We'll cover the *Sql-Context* and *SqlPipe* objects right now.

At a high level, the *SqlContext* object, which is *static*, provides a handle to the server-side context in which your code runs. It also has a channel to the client through which you can return data and text: its *Pipe* property, which in turn provides access to a properly initiated *SqlPipe* object.

A *SqlPipe* object can send data and messages to the calling client though several methods: *Send*, *SendResultsStart*, *SendResultsRow*, *SendResultsEnd*, and *ExecuteAndSend*. In the previous code sample, we used the *SqlPipe* object's *ExecuteAndSend* method to implicitly open a connection, call *ExecuteReader* on an *SqlCommand* object that uses that connection, and transmit the contents of the resulting *SqlDataReader* back to the client. Although the implicit work done by *ExecuteAndSend* might have been convenient, it's important to avoid such shortcuts in our detailed discussion on SQL CLR programming.

In general, SQL CLR stored procedure code that queries tables in the database must open a connection to that database, use the *SqlCommand* object's *ExecuteReader* method to query the data, and then use one or a combination of the *Send* methods to send it back. The *Send* methods do not accept *DataSet* objects; they accept only *SqlDataReader* objects, strings, and/or special *SqlDataRecord* objects. Listing 3-1, which shows the implementation of the function *spContacts* from spTest.cs in the sample project, is a representative example of how this is done.

Listing 3-1 *spContacts* from spTest.cs

```
[SqlProcedure]
public static void spContacts()
{
    SqlConnection conn = new SqlConnection("context connection=true");
    SqlCommand cm = new SqlCommand("Select * from Person.Contact", conn);

    conn.Open();
    SqlDataReader dr = cm.ExecuteReader();
    SqlContext.Pipe.Send("Starting data dump");
    SqlContext.Pipe.Send(dr);
    SqlContext.Pipe.Send("Data dump complete");
    dr.Close();
    conn.Close();
}
```

For this code to work, we need to use both the *Microsoft.SqlServer.Server* and *System.Data.SqlClient* namespaces (and if you look in the sample project rather than Listing 3-1, you'll see that we have). This is because any conventional ADO.NET objects we might use, such as *SqlConnection*, *SqlCommand*, and *SqlDataReader*, are supplied to us from *System.Data.SqlClient*, just as they would be in a conventional client application or middle-tier assembly. As already discussed, we need the *Microsoft.SqlServer.Server* namespace in order to use objects such as *SqlContext* and

SqlPipe. The stored procedure template in Visual Studio SQL Server projects includes the *using* statement for *Microsoft.SqlServer.Server* and *System.Data.SqlClient* automatically.

> **Note**   Readers who worked with early beta versions of SQL Server 2005 might recall a *System.Data.SqlServer* library, which in effect supplied all conventional and server-side ADO.NET objects necessary to write SQL CLR code. This hybrid library was eliminated and replaced with the dual-library approach later in the beta process.

Although server-side code uses *SqlClient* objects, it does so in a specialized way. For example, notice that the *context connection=true* connection string passed to the *SqlConnection* object's constructor. This essentially instructs ADO.NET to open a new connection to the database in which the CLR assembly resides. Notice also the second call to the *SqlContext.Pipe* object's *Send* method. Here, the *SqlDataReader* parameter overload of the *SqlPipe* object's *Send* method is used to push the contents of the *SqlDataReader* back to the client. You can think of this method as performing a *while (dr.Read())* loop through the *SqlDataReader* and echoing out the values of each column for each iteration of the loop, but instead of having to do that work yourself, the *Send* method does it for you.

Before and after the *SqlDataReader* is piped, we use the *String* parameter overload of the *Send* method to send status messages to the client. When this stored procedure is run in Management Studio, the piped text appears on the Results tab of the query window when you use the Management Studio Results To Text option and on the Messages tab when you use the Results To Grid option.

The rest of the listing contains typical ADO.NET code, all of it using objects from the *SqlClient* provider. And that illustrates well the overall theme of SQL CLR programming: Do what you'd normally do from the client or middle tier, and use a few special helper objects to work within the context of SQL Server as you do so.

Piping Data with *SqlDataRecord* and *SqlMetaData*

We mentioned that the *SqlPipe* object's *Send* method can accept an object of type *SqlDataRecord*, and we mentioned previously that *Microsoft.SqlServer.Server* provides this object as well as an object called *SqlMetaData*. You can use these two objects together in a CLR stored procedure to return a result set one row at a time, instead of having to supply the *SqlPipe* object's *Send* method with an *SqlDataReader*. This allows (but does not require) you to inspect the data before sending it back to the client. Sending *SqlDataReader* objects prevents inspection of the data within the stored procedure because *SqlDataReader* objects are forward-only result set structures. Using the *ExecuteAndSend* method and an *SqlCommand* object has the same limitation.

The *SqlDataRecord* object permits .NET code to create an individual record/row to be returned to the calling client. Its constructor accepts an array of *SqlMetaData* objects, which in turn describe the metadata for each field/column in the record/row.

Listing 3-2, which shows the implementation of function *spContactCount* from spTest.cs in the sample project, illustrates how to use *SqlPipe.Send* together with *SqlDataRecord* and *SqlMetaData* objects to return a single-column, single-row result set from a stored procedure.

Listing 3-2   *spContactCount* from spTest.cs

```
[SqlProcedure()]
public static void spContactCount()
{
    SqlConnection conn = new SqlConnection("context connection=true");
    SqlCommand cm = new SqlCommand("Select Count(*) from Person.Contact", conn);
    SqlDataRecord drc = new SqlDataRecord(new SqlMetaData("ContactCount", SqlDbType.Int));

    conn.Open();
    drc.SetInt32(0, (Int32)cm.ExecuteScalar());
    SqlContext.Pipe.Send(drc);
    conn.Close();
}
```

The code declares variable *drc* as a *SqlDataRecord* object and passes its constructor a single *Sql-MetaData* object. (Passing a single object rather than an array is permissible if the *SqlDataRecord* object will only have a single field/column.) The *SqlMetaData* object describes a column called *ContactCount* of type *SqlDbType.Int*.

> **Note**   The *SqlDbType* enumeration is contained within the *System.Data.SqlTypes* namespace. The SQL Server Stored Procedure template inserts a *using* statement for this namespace. If you are creating SQL CLR code without using this template, you should add the *using* statement yourself.

The rest of the code is rather straightforward. First, a context connection and command are opened and a *SELECT COUNT(*)* query is performed against the AdventureWorks Person.Contact table. Because the query returns a single scalar value, it is run using the *SqlCommand* object's *ExecuteScalar* method. Next, the value returned by *ExecuteScalar* is casted into an integer and that value is loaded into field/column 0 (the only one) of the *SqlDataRecord* object using its *SetInt32* method. The *SqlDataRecord* is then piped back to the client using the *SqlContext* object's *Send* method.

> **Note**   If we wanted to send back multiple *SqlDataRecord* objects, we would send the first one using the *SqlContext* object's *SendResultsStart* method and then send all subsequent *SqlDataRecord* objects using the *SendResultsRow* method. We would call the *SendResultEnd* method after all *SqlDataRecords* had been sent.

Once the stored procedure has been deployed (the techniques for which we will discuss shortly), you can execute it from SQL Server Management Studio as you would any other stored procedure. Although the result is a single value, it is presented as a column and the column name ContactCount is shown on the Results tab of the query window. Keep in mind that this *COUNT(*)* query result could have been returned without using the *SqlMetaData* and *SqlDataRecord* objects; the sample is provided to demonstrate the use of these objects as an alternative to piping *SqlDataReader* objects and text to the client.

CLR Stored Procedure Usage Guidelines

It's important to understand how to perform data access and retrieval in CLR stored procedures. As a .NET developer, you already know how to do more computational tasks within your code, so our samples illustrate server-side data access more than anything else. As proof-of-concept code, these samples are completely adequate.

Meanwhile, you should avoid writing CLR stored procedures that merely perform simple "CRUD" (Create, Retrieve, Update, and Delete) operations. Such tasks are better left to conventional T-SQL stored procedures, which typically perform these operations more efficiently than ADO.NET can. CLR stored procedures work well when you need to perform computation on your data and you need the expressiveness of a .NET language to do so (where such expressiveness is missing from T-SQL).

For example, implementing a "fuzzy search" using business logic embedded in .NET assemblies to determine which data has an affinity to other data is a good use of SQL CLR stored procedures. Regular-expression-based data validation in an update or insert stored procedure is another good application of SQL CLR integration. As a general rule, straight data access should be left to T-SQL. "Higher-valued" computations are good candidates for SQL CLR integration. We'll revisit the SQL CLR usage question at various points in this chapter.

Deployment

Before you can test your SQL CLR code, you must deploy the assembly containing it and register the individual functions that you want recognized as stored procedures. A number of deployment methods are at your disposal; we will pause to cover them now, before discussing testing of your stored procedures and the other four basic SQL CLR entities.

Deploying Your Assembly

As mentioned earlier, Visual Studio deploys the SQL Server project version of the sample code when you build, start, or step through the project or use the Build/Deploy function on Visual Studio's main menu. If you're working with the SQL Server project version of the samples, go ahead and use the Deploy option or one of the Start or Build options in Visual Studio now.

For deploying the Class Library project version, assuming C:\ProgrammingSQL2005\ Chapter03 as this chapter's sample code parent directory, you can execute the following T-SQL command from within Management Studio:

```
CREATE ASSEMBLY Chapter03
AUTHORIZATION dbo
FROM 'C:\ProgrammingSQL2005\Chapter03\VS\Chapter03Manual\Chapter03\bin\Debug\Chapter03.dll'
WITH PERMISSION_SET = SAFE
GO
```

The *AUTHORIZATION* clause allows you to specify a name or role to which ownership of the assembly is assigned. The default authorization is that of the current user, and because you are most likely logged in as dbo for AdventureWorks, in this case the clause is unnecessary (which is why we omitted it from our previous example).

The meaning and effect of the *WITH PERMISSION_SET* clause are discussed at the end of this chapter. For now, just note that this clause allows you to specify the security permissions with which your assembly runs. As with the *AUTHORIZATION* clause, in this case the *WITH PERMISSION_SET* clause is technically unnecessary because *SAFE* is the default *PERMISSION_SET* value used when a *CREATE ASSEMBLY* command is executed.

If your assembly has dependencies on other assemblies, SQL Server looks to see if those assemblies have already been loaded into the database and, if so, confirms that their ownership is the same as that of the specified assembly. If the dependent assemblies have not yet been loaded into the database, SQL Server looks for them in the same folder as the specified assembly. If it finds all dependent assemblies in that location, it loads them and assigns them the same ownership as the primary assembly. If it does not find the dependent assemblies in that folder, the *CREATE ASSEMBLY* command will fail.

You can supply a string expression instead of a literal in the *FROM* clause, allowing for some interesting data-driven possibilities. For example, you could fetch an assembly path reference from a table in your database. It is also possible to supply a bitstream in the *FROM* clause instead of a file specification. You do this by specifying a varbinary literal value or expression (or a comma-delimited list of varbinary values or expressions, when dependent assemblies must be specified) that contains the actual binary content of your assembly (or assemblies). This allows the creation of a database, including any CLR assemblies it contains, to be completely scripted, without requiring distribution of actual assembly files. The binary stream can be embedded in the script itself or, using an expression, it can be fetched from a table in a database.

More Info   See SQL Server Books Online for more information on this option.

In addition to using Visual Studio deployment and the *T-SQL CREATE ASSEMBLY* command, you can upload the assembly into your database interactively from Management Studio. Simply right-click the *servername*/AdventureWorks/Programmability/Assemblies node in the Object Explorer (where *servername* is the name of your server) and choose New Assembly... from the shortcut menu. The New Assembly dialog box, shown in Figure 3-7, appears.

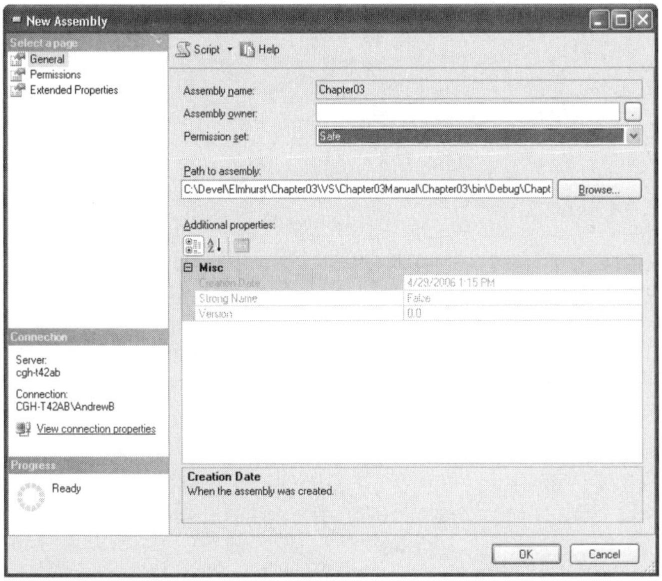

Figure 3-7   The Management Studio New Assembly dialog box

Type the assembly path and file name in the Path To Assembly text box, or use the Browse... button to specify it interactively. You can specify *AUTHORIZATION* and *WITH PERMISSION_SET* details in the Assembly Owner text box (using the ellipsis button, if necessary) and the Permission Set combo box, respectively.

Regardless of the deployment method you use, once your assembly has been added to your database, it becomes an integral part of that database and its underlying MDF file. This means if your database is backed up and restored, or xcopy deployed, any assemblies within it move along with the data itself and need not be manually added as a subsequent step.

Deploying Your Stored Procedures

In the SQL Server project version of the sample code, deployment of all the stored procedures is handled by Visual Studio when the assembly itself is deployed. This is due to the application of the *SqlProcedure* attribute to the functions in class *StoredProcedures* (found in file spTest.cs). The *SqlProcedure* attribute accepts an optional *Name* parameter, the value of which is the actual callable stored procedure name. If you do not supply a value for the *Name* parameter, the name of the .NET function is used as the stored procedure name.

The *SqlProcedure* attribute is used only by Visual Studio in SQL Server projects. Therefore, it has been removed from the source code in the Class Library project. Deploying the stored procedures from that version of the source code requires issuing a *CREATE PROCEDURE* T-SQL command using the new *EXTERNAL NAME* clause to specify the assembly, fully qualified class name specifier, and function name. For example, to load the Class Library version of *spContacts*, you would issue the following command.

```
CREATE PROCEDURE spContacts
AS EXTERNAL NAME Chapter03.StoredProcedures.spContacts
```

The preceding command specifies that function *spContacts*, in class *StoredProcedures*, in the loaded assembly with T-SQL name *Chapter03*, should be registered as a CLR stored procedure callable under the name *spContacts*.

> **Note**   All necessary *CREATE PROCEDURE* commands for the Class Library project version of the sample code are contained in the CreateObjects.sql script in the Management Studio project supplied with the sample code. You will need to run that script in order to execute the various SQL CLR entities implemented in the Class Library project.

Note that had the CLR stored procedure been written in Visual Basic .NET rather than C#, the class name specifier would change to *Chapter03.StoredProcedures*. This would necessitate a change to the deployment T-SQL code as follows:

```
CREATE PROCEDURE spContacts
AS EXTERNAL NAME Chapter03.[Chapter03.StoredProcedures].spContacts
```

In Visual Basic projects, the default namespace for a project itself defaults to the project name, as does the assembly name. The class within the project must be referenced using the default namespace as a prefix. Because the class specifier is a multipart dot-separated name, it must be enclosed within square brackets so that SQL Server can identify it as a single indivisible name. Because C# projects handle the default namespace setting a little differently, the namespace prefix is not used in the class specifier for C# assemblies.

One last point before we discuss how to test your now-deployed CLR stored procedures. It is important to realize that the class specifier and function name in the *EXTERNAL NAME* clause are *case-sensitive* and that this is true *even for assemblies developed in Visual Basic .NET*. Although this point perplexed us quite a bit at first, it does make sense in hindsight. SQL Server searches for your subs/functions within your assemblies, not within your source code. In other words, it's looking within Microsoft Intermediate Language (MSIL) code, not Visual Basic .NET or C# source code. Because MSIL is case-sensitive (it has to be, to support case-sensitive languages like C#), SQL Server must be as well as it searches for a specific class and sub/function.

The fact that SQL Server is not case sensitive by default (even though it once was) and that Visual Basic .NET is not a case-sensitive language is of no import! If you attempt to register a sub/function and you receive an error that it cannot be found within the assembly, double-check that the case usage in your command matches that of your source code.

Testing Your Stored Procedures

With your assembly and stored procedures now deployed, you're ready to run and test them. Typically, you should do this from Management Studio; however, Visual Studio SQL Server projects allow you to test your SQL CLR code from Visual Studio itself. When you create a Visual Studio SQL Server project, a folder called Test Scripts is created as a subdirectory in your source code directory. Within that subdirectory, Visual Studio creates a script file called Test.sql. If you look at that file, you will see that it contains commented instructions as well as commented sample T-SQL code for testing stored procedures, functions, and UDTs. It also contains an uncommented generic *SELECT* command that echoes a text literal to the caller.

Visual Studio connects to your database and runs this script immediately after your assembly is deployed, and the output from the script appears in Visual Studio's Output window. This allows you to execute any number of T-SQL commands directly from Visual Studio without having to switch to another tool. Although this approach is much less interactive than a Management Studio query window, it allows you to run quick tests against your code. It is especially useful for regression testing—that is, confirming that a new version of your assembly does not break older, critical functionality.

The file extension of the script must be .sql, but otherwise the name of the file is inconsequential. You can have multiple script files in the Test Scripts folder. To add a new one, right-click the Test Scripts folder node or the project node in the Solution Explorer window and select the Add Test Script option from the shortcut menu. Only one script can be active at one time, and as soon as you have more than one script, you must specify which one is active. To make a script active, simply right-click its node in the Solution Explorer window and select the Set As Default Debug Script option from its shortcut menu. When you do so, the node is displayed in bold. You may run or debug a script even if it is not the active script. To do so, right-click its node in the Solution Explorer window and select the Debug Script option from its shortcut menu.

Warning   At press time, there appears to be an anomaly in the working of the test script facility and the Output window in Visual Studio 2005. Simply put, if your test script executes a query (whether it be a T-SQL *SELECT* command or a call to a stored procedure) that returns a column of type uniqueidentifier (GUID), the query's result set will not appear in the Output window, and execution of the test script might hang Visual Studio. For this reason, you should avoid calling the sample code CLR stored procedures *spContactsQuick* and *spContacts* (both of which perform a *SELECT * FROM Person.Contact* query and thus retrieve the rowguid column, which is of type uniqueidentifier) from your test script and instead test these procedures from SQL Server Management Studio, where the anomaly does not occur. You can safely call *spContactCount*, which simply performs a *SELECT COUNT(*) FROM Person.Contact* query, from your Visual Studio test script. Alternatively, you can modify *spContactsQuick* and/or *spContacts* to select specific columns from the Person.Contact table, making sure that *rowguid* is not one of them.

If you're working with the Class Library version of the sample code, you must test the stored procedures from Management Studio or another SQL Server query tool. Even if you are working with the SQL Server project version, you'll find that testing your SQL CLR code in Management Studio provides a richer experience and more flexibility.

The script file TestStoredProcs.sql in the Management Studio project supplied with the sample code will run both of our CLR stored procedures (*spContactCount* and *spContacts*). Open the file in Management Studio, and click the Execute button on the SQL Editor toolbar, choose the Query/Execute option on the main menu, or press F5. (You can also right-click the query window and select Execute from the shortcut menu.)

When the script runs, you should see the single-valued result of the *spContactCount* stored procedure appear first, as shown in Figure 3-8. Note that the column name ContactCount appears on the Results tab and recall that this is a direct result of your using the *SqlMetaData* object in the CLR code. Below the *spContactCount* result, you will see the results from the *spContacts* stored procedure come in. Because the Person.Contact table has almost 20,000 rows, these results might take some time to flow in.

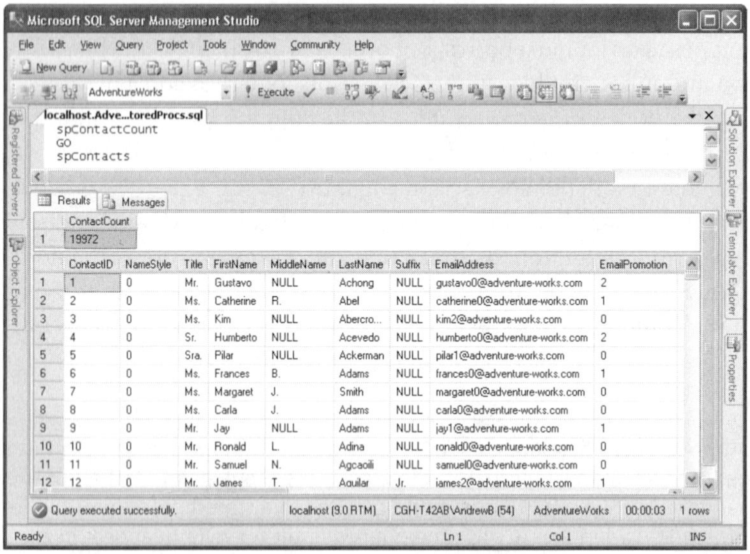

Figure 3-8   TestStoredProcs.sql script code and results

Even while the results are coming in, the "Starting data dump" status message should be visible on the Messages tab (or on the Results tab if you're using Management Studio's Results To Text option). Once all rows have been fetched, you should see the "Data dump complete" message appear as well. If you get impatient and want to abort the query before all rows have been fetched, you can use the Cancel Executing Query button on the SQL Editor toolbar or the Query/Cancel Executing Query option on the main menu; you can also use the Alt+Break keyboard shortcut.

We have yet to cover CLR functions, triggers, aggregates, and UDTs, but you have already learned most of the skills you need to develop SQL CLR code. You have learned how to create Visual Studio SQL Server projects and use its autodeployment and test script features. You have also learned how to develop SQL CLR code in standard Class Library projects and to use T-SQL commands and Management Studio to deploy the code for you. You've learned about the subtle differences between deploying C# code and Visual Basic .NET code, and we've covered the case-sensitive requirements of T-SQL-based deployment.

With all this under your belt, we can cover the remaining four basic SQL CLR entities relatively quickly.

CLR Functions

Let's take everything we've discussed about CLR stored procedures and deployment and apply it to CLR functions. As any programmer knows, a function is a lot like a procedure, except that it returns a value (or an object). Mainstream .NET functions typically return .NET types. SQL CLR functions, on the other hand, must return a *SqlType*. So to start with, we need to make sure our classes that implement SQL CLR functions import/use the *System.Data.SqlTypes* namespace. The SQL Server Project template for User Defined Functions contains the appropriate *using* code by default; you must add the code manually to standard Class Library class code.

Once the namespace is imported, you can write the functions themselves. In Visual Studio SQL Server Projects, they should be decorated with the *SqlFunction* attribute; this attribute accepts an optional name parameter that works identically to its *SqlProcedure* counterpart. In our sample code, we will not supply a value for this parameter. *SqlFunction* is used by Visual Studio SQL Server projects for deployment of your SQL CLR functions, but for scalar-valued functions in Class Library projects it is optional, so it appears in the Class Library sample code only for our table-valued function (described later).

Listing 3-3, which shows the code for function *fnHelloWorld* from fnTest.cs in the sample project, implements a simple "Hello World" function that returns a value of type *SqlString*.

Listing 3-3 *fnHelloWorld* from fnTest.cs

```
[SqlFunction()]
public static SqlString fnHelloWorld()
{
    return new SqlString("Hello World");
}
```

Notice that *SqlType* objects require explicit instantiation and constructor value passing; you cannot simply declare and assign values to them. The code in Listing 3-3 instantiates a *SqlString* object inline within the *return* statement to avoid variable declaration.

A function that returns a hardcoded value is of little practical use. Typically, functions are passed values and perform calculations on them, and they are often used from within T-SQL statements, in effect as extensions to the functions built into the T-SQL language itself. Listing 3-4, which shows the code for function *fnToCelsius* in fnTest.cs in the sample project, implements a Fahrenheit-to-Celsius conversion function.

Listing 3-4   *fnToCelsius* from fnTest.cs

```
[SqlFunction()]
public static SqlDecimal fnToCelsius(SqlInt16 Fahrenheit)
{
    return new SqlDecimal((((Int16)Fahrenheit) - 32) / 1.8);
}
```

The function accepts a Fahrenheit temperature (as a *SqlInt16*), converts it to Celsius, and returns it (as a *SqlDecimal*). Notice that the code casts the input parameter from a *SqlInt16* to a .NET *Int16*, applies a Fahrenheit-to-Celsius conversion formula, and passes the result to the constructor of a new *SqlDecimal* object.

Deployment of these functions is automatic in the Visual Studio SQL Server project version of our sample code. For the Class Library version, use the T-SQL *CREATE FUNCTION* command in a similar fashion to our use of the *CREATE PROCEDURE* command in the previous section, but include a data type specification for the return value. For example, to deploy the *fnHelloWorld* function, you would use this command:

```
CREATE FUNCTION fnHelloWorld()
RETURNS NVARCHAR(4000) WITH EXECUTE AS CALLER
AS EXTERNAL NAME Chapter03.UserDefinedFunctions.fnHelloWorld
```

Notice the use of data type *NVARCHAR(4000)* to correspond with the *SqlString* type used in the function's implementation. The *WITH EXECUTE AS CALLER* clause specifies that the SQL CLR function should execute under the caller's identity.

> **Tip**   You can enter the *CREATE FUNCTION* command yourself, but all such necessary commands for the sample code SQL CLR functions are contained in the CreateObjects.sql script file in the Management Studio project supplied with the sample code.

You can test these functions using the Visual Studio SQL Server project test script or in Management Studio. Use the following query in your test script or a Management Studio query window to test the two functions. (You can also run the TestScalarFunctions.sql script file in the Management Studio sample project.)

```
SELECT
  dbo.fnHelloWorld() AS HelloWorld,
  dbo.fnToCelsius(212) AS CelsiusTemp
```

T-SQL functions can return result sets as well as scalar values. Such functions are called *table-valued functions* (TVFs). Writing SQL CLR TVFs is possible, although you do so differently than you would CLR scalar-valued functions or CLR stored procedures. CLR TVFs must return a type that implements the .NET interface *IEnumerable*, and they must declare a "*FillRow*" method that interprets that type and converts an instance of the type to a table row.

Listing 3-5, which shows the code for functions *fnPortfolioTable* and *FillTickerRow* in fnTest.cs in the sample project, implements a TVF called *fnPortfolioTable*.

Listing 3-5 *fnPortfolioTable* and *FillTickerRow* from fnTest.cs

```
[SqlFunction(
    FillRowMethodName="FillTickerRow",
    TableDefinition="TickerSymbol nvarchar(5), Value decimal")]
public static System.Collections.IEnumerable fnPortfolioTable(SqlString TickersPacked)
{
    string[] TickerSymbols;
    object[] RowArr = new object[2];
    object[] CompoundArray = new object[3];
    char[] parms = new char[1];

    parms[0] = ';';
    TickerSymbols = TickersPacked.Value.Split(parms);

    RowArr[0] = TickerSymbols[0];
    RowArr[1] = 1;
    CompoundArray[0] = RowArr;

    RowArr = new object[2];
    RowArr[0] = TickerSymbols[1];
    RowArr[1] = 2;
    CompoundArray[1] = RowArr;

    RowArr = new object[2];
    RowArr[0] = TickerSymbols[2];
    RowArr[1] = 3;
    CompoundArray[2] = RowArr;

    return CompoundArray;
}

public static void FillTickerRow(object row, ref SqlString TickerSymbol, ref SqlDecimal
Value)
{
    object[] rowarr = (object[])row;
    TickerSymbol = new SqlString((string)rowarr[0]);
    Value = new SqlDecimal(decimal.Parse(rowarr[1].ToString()));
}
```

Rather than implementing its own *IEnumerable*-compatible type, *fnPortfolioTable* uses an array. This is perfectly legal because arrays implement *IEnumerable*. Function *fnPortfolioTable* accepts a semicolon-delimited list of stock ticker symbols and returns a table with each ticker symbol appearing in a separate row as column TickerSymbol and a value for the ticker as column Value. The structure of the returned table is declared in the *TableDefinition* parameter of the *SqlFunction* attribute in SQL Server projects and in the *CREATE FUNCTION* T-SQL command for Class Library projects. The assigned values are hardcoded, and only three rows are returned, regardless of how many ticker symbols are passed in. As with our other samples, this one is more useful as a teaching tool than as a practical application of TVFs.

Arrays are the name of the game here. First the *String.Split* method is used to crack the delimited ticker list into an array of single ticker strings. Then the TVF structures the data so that each element in the return value array (*CompoundArray*) is itself a two-element array storing a single ticker symbol and its value. The function code itself needs only to return *CompoundArray*. Next, the *FillTickerRow* function (named in the *FillRowMethodName* parameter of the *SqlFunction* attribute) takes each two-element array and converts its members to individual scalars that correspond positionally to the columns in the *TableDefinition* argument of the *SqlFunction* attribute.

Because the *FillRowMethodName* parameter of the *SqlFunction* attribute is required by SQL Server, we have decorated the Class Library version of function *fnPortfolioTable* with that attribute, supplying a value for that one parameter. In the SQL Server project version, we also supply a value for the *TableDefinition* parameter to enable autodeployment of the TVF.

As with the other functions, deployment of this function is performed by Visual Studio in the SQL Server project sample code. For the Class Library version, you can deploy the function using the following T-SQL command (also contained in the CreateObjects.sql script file):

```
CREATE FUNCTION fnPortfolioTable(@TickersPacked [NVARCHAR](4000))
RETURNS TABLE (
    TickerSymbol NVARCHAR(5),
    VALUE DECIMAL
)
WITH EXECUTE AS CALLER
AS EXTERNAL NAME Chapter03.UserDefinedFunctions.fnPortfolioTable
```

As with *fnHelloWorld*, we have mapped the *SqlString* data type to an *NVARCHAR(4000)*, this time for one of the input parameters. Because *fnPortfolioTable* is a TVF, its return type is declared as *TABLE*, with inline specifications for the table's definition.

Use the following query in your Visual Studio test script or a Management Studio query window to test the TVF (or run the TestTableValuedFunction.sql script file in the Management Studio sample project):

```
SELECT * FROM fnPortfolioTable('IBM;MSFT;SUN')
```

The following data should be returned:

```
TickerSymbol Value
------------ ------
IBM          1
MSFT         2
SUN          3
```

CLR Triggers

T-SQL triggers are really just stored procedures that are called by SQL Server at specific times and query values in the "inserted" and "deleted" pseudo-tables. SQL CLR triggers are similar to SQL CLR stored procedures, and they can be created for all data manipulation language (DML) actions (updates, inserts, and deletes).

SQL Server 2005 introduces the concept of data definition language (DDL) triggers, which handle actions such as *CREATE TABLE* and *ALTER PROCEDURE*. Like DML triggers, DDL triggers can be implemented in T-SQL or SQL CLR code. We will cover SQL CLR DML and DDL triggers in this section.

SQL CLR DML triggers, like their T-SQL counterparts, have access to the "inserted" and "deleted" pseudo-tables and must be declared as handling one or more specific events for a specific table or, under certain circumstances, a specific view. Also, they can make use of the *SqlTriggerContext* object (through the *SqlContext* object's *TriggerContext* property) to deter-mine which particular event (update, insert, or delete) caused them to fire and which columns were updated.

Once you latch on to these concepts, writing SQL CLR DML triggers is really quite simple. Listing 3-6, which shows the code for function *trgUpdateContact* from trgTest.cs in the sample project, shows the SQL CLR code for DML trigger *trgUpdateContact*, which is designed to function as a *FOR UPDATE* trigger on the Person.Contact table in the AdventureWorks database.

Listing 3-6   *trgUpdateContact* from trgTest.cs

```
//[SqlTrigger(Target="Person.Contact", Event="for UPDATE")]
public static void trgUpdateContact()
{
    SqlTriggerContext TriggerContext = SqlContext.TriggerContext;
    String OldName = String.Empty;
    String NewName = String.Empty;
    String OldDate = String.Empty;
    String NewDate = String.Empty;
    SqlConnection conn = new SqlConnection("context connection=true");
    SqlCommand cmOld = new SqlCommand("SELECT FirstName, ModifiedDate from DELETED", conn);
    SqlCommand cmNew = new SqlCommand("SELECT FirstName, ModifiedDate from INSERTED", conn);
    conn.Open();
    SqlDataReader drOld = cmOld.ExecuteReader();
    if (drOld.Read())
```

```
    {
        OldName = (string)drOld[0];
        OldDate = drOld[1].ToString();
    }
    drOld.Close();
    SqlDataReader drNew = cmNew.ExecuteReader();
    if (drNew.Read())
    {
        NewName = (string)drNew[0];
        NewDate = drNew[1].ToString();
    }
    drNew.Close();
    conn.Close();
    SqlContext.Pipe.Send("Old Value of FirstName:" + OldName);
    SqlContext.Pipe.Send("New Value of FirstName:" + NewName);
    SqlContext.Pipe.Send("Old Value of ModifiedDate:" + OldDate);
    SqlContext.Pipe.Send("New Value of ModifiedDate:" + NewDate);
    for (int i = 0; i <= TriggerContext.ColumnCount - 1; i++)
    {
        SqlContext.Pipe.Send("Column " + i.ToString() + ": " + TriggerContext
.IsUpdatedColumn(i).ToString());
    }

}
```

This CLR DML trigger queries the "deleted" and "inserted" tables and echoes back the "before and after" values for the FirstName and ModifiedDate columns when a row is updated. It does so not by piping back *SqlDataReader* objects but by fetching values from them and echoing back the values as text using the *SqlPipe* object's *Send* method. The trigger code also uses the *TriggerContext.IsUpdatedColumn* method to echo back a list of all columns in the Person.Contact table and whether each was updated.

To deploy the trigger automatically, you would normally configure a *SqlTrigger* attribute and apply it to the .NET function that implements the trigger. Because DML triggers are applied to a target object (a table or a view) and an event (for example, "for update" or "instead of insert"), the *SqlTrigger* attribute has parameters for each of these pieces of information and you must supply values for both. The *SqlTrigger* attribute deploys only a single copy of the trigger, but you can use T-SQL to deploy the same code as a separate trigger for a different event and/ or table. Each separate deployment of the same code is assigned a unique trigger name.

Unfortunately, a bug in Visual Studio prevents the *SqlTrigger* attribute from being used for target objects not in the dbo schema. (For example, our table, Person.Contact, is in the Person schema rather than the dbo schema.) This is because the value for the *Target* parameter is surrounded by square brackets when Visual Studio generates its T-SQL code (generating, for example, *[Person.Contact]*, which will cause an error). It is for this reason that the *SqlTrigger* attribute code is commented out in Listing 3-6. A workaround to this problem is available through the use of pre-deployment and post-deployment scripts, which we will discuss shortly.

> **Important**   Although you might be tempted to work around the Visual Studio schema bug by supplying a *Target* value of *Person].[Contact* instead of *Person.Contact*, rest assured that this will not work. You may initiate a trace in SQL Server Profiler to observe the erroneous T-SQL generated by Visual Studio in either scenario.

Although Listing 3-6 does not demonstrate it, you can create a single piece of code that functions as both the update and insert trigger for a given table. You can then use the *TriggerContext* object's *TriggerAction* property to determine exactly what event caused the trigger to fire, and you can execute slightly different code accordingly. Should you wish to deploy such a CLR trigger using the *SqlTrigger* attribute, you would set its *Event* parameter to "FOR UPDATE, INSERT".

The T-SQL command to register a .NET function as a SQL CLR trigger for the update event only is as follows:

```
CREATE TRIGGER trgUpdateContact
ON Person.Contact
FOR UPDATE
AS EXTERNAL NAME Chapter03.Triggers.trgUpdateContact
```

> **Note**   All necessary *CREATE TRIGGER* commands for the Class Library project version of the sample code are contained in the CreateObjects.sql script in the Management Studio project supplied with the sample code.

Beyond using such T-SQL code in Management Studio, there is a way to execute this T-SQL command from Visual Studio, and thus work around the *SqlTrigger* non-dbo schema bug. An essentially undocumented feature of Visual Studio SQL Server projects is that they allow you to create two special T-SQL scripts that will run immediately before and immediately after the deployment of your assembly. To use this feature, simply create two scripts, named PreDeployScript.sql and PostDeployScript.sql, in the root folder (not the Test Scripts folder) of your project. Although not case-sensitive, the names must match verbatim.

> **Tip**   You can create the PreDeployScript.sql and PostDeployScript.sql scripts outside of Visual Studio and then add them to your project using Visual Studio's Add Existing Item... feature. You can also add them directly by right-clicking the project node or Test Scripts folder node in the Solution Explorer, choosing the Add Test Script option from the shortcut menu, renaming the new scripts, and dragging them out of the Test Scripts folder into the root folder of your project.

To use this feature to work around the *SqlTrigger* non-dbo schema bug, insert the preceding *CREATE TRIGGER* code in your PostDeployScript.sql file and insert the following T-SQL code into your PreDeployScript.sql:

```
IF EXISTS (SELECT * FROM sys.triggers WHERE object_id = OBJECT_ID(N'[Person].[trgUpdateC
ontact]'))
DROP TRIGGER Person.trgUpdateContact
```

Regardless of deployment technique, you can use the following query in your Visual Studio test script or a Management Studio query window to test the trigger (this T-SQL code can be found in the TestTriggers.sql script file in the Management Studio project):

```
UPDATE Person.Contact
SET    FirstName = 'Gustavoo'
WHERE  ContactId = 1
```

When you run the preceding query, you will notice that the trigger is actually run twice. This is because the AdventureWorks Person.Contact table already has a T-SQL update trigger, called *uContact*. Because *uContact* itself performs an update on the ModifiedDate column of Person.Contact, it implicitly invokes a second execution of *trgUpdateContact*. By looking at the output of *trgUpdateContact*, you can confirm that the FirstName column is updated on the first execution (by the test query) and the ModifiedDate column is modified on the second execution (by trigger *uContact*). The two executions' output might appear out of order, but the values of *ModifiedDate* will make the actual sequence clear.

If you place the *TriggerContext* object's *TriggerAction* property in a comparison statement, IntelliSense will show you that there is a wide array of enumerated constants that the property can be equal to, and that a majority of these values correspond to DDL triggers. This demonstrates clearly that SQL CLR code can be used for DDL and DML triggers alike.

In the case of DDL triggers, a wide array of environmental information might be desirable to determine exactly what event caused the trigger to fire, what system process ID (SPID) invoked it, what time the event fired, and other information specific to the event type such as the T-SQL command that caused the event. The *SqlTriggerContext* object's *EventData* property can be queried to fetch this information. The *EventData* property is of type *SqlXml*; therefore it, in turn, has a *CreateReader* method and a *Value* property that you can use to fetch the XML-formatted event data as an *XmlReader* object or a string, respectively.

The code in Listing 3-7, taken from function *trgCreateTable* in trgTest.cs in the sample project, shows the SQL CLR code for the DDL trigger *trgCreateTable* registered to fire for any *CREATE TABLE* command executed on the AdventureWorks database.

Listing 3-7   *trgCreateTable* from trgTest.cs

```
[SqlTrigger(Target = "DATABASE", Event = "FOR CREATE_TABLE")]
public static void trgCreateTable()
{
    SqlTriggerContext TriggerContext = SqlContext.TriggerContext;
    if (!(TriggerContext.EventData == null))
    {
        SqlContext.Pipe.Send("Event Data: " + TriggerContext.EventData.Value.ToString());
    }
}
```

The code interrogates the *Value* property of *SqlContext.TriggerContext.EventData*, casts it to a string, and pipes that string back to the client. Note that the *SqlTrigger* attribute is not commented out in this case because a schema prefix is not used in the *Target* parameter value. Thus, you can use attribute-based deployment in the SQL Server project or the following command for the Class Library version:

```
CREATE TRIGGER trgCreateTable
ON DATABASE
FOR CREATE_TABLE
AS EXTERNAL NAME Chapter03.Triggers.trgCreateTable
```

Use the following T-SQL DDL command in your Visual Studio test script or a Management Studio query window to test the DDL trigger. (You can find this code in the TestTriggers.sql script file in the sample Management Studio project.)

```
CREATE TABLE Test (low INT, high INT)
DROP TABLE Test
```

Your result should appear similar to the following:

```
<EVENT_INSTANCE>
  <EventType>CREATE_TABLE</EventType>
  <PostTime>2006-04-29T16:37:50.690</PostTime>
  <SPID>54</SPID>
  <ServerName>CGH-T42AB</ServerName>
  <LoginName>CGH-T42AB\AndrewB</LoginName>
  <UserName>dbo</UserName>
  <DatabaseName>AdventureWorks</DatabaseName>
  <SchemaName>dbo</SchemaName>
  <ObjectName>Test</ObjectName>
  <ObjectType>TABLE</ObjectType>
  <TSQLCommand>
      <SetOptions ANSI_NULLS="ON" ANSI_NULL_DEFAULT="ON" ANSI_PADDING="ON" QUOTED_IDENTIFIER=
"ON" ENCRYPTED="FALSE" />
    <CommandText>CREATE TABLE Test (low INT, high INT)</CommandText>
  </TSQLCommand>
</EVENT_INSTANCE>
```

> **Note**   The actual output would consist of continuous, unformatted text. We added the line breaks and indentation to make the *EventData* XML easier to read.

CLR Aggregates

T-SQL has a number of built-in aggregates, such as *SUM()*, *AVG()*, and *MAX()*, but that set of built-in functions is not always sufficient. Luckily, the SQL CLR features in SQL Server 2005 allow us to implement user-defined aggregates in .NET code and use them from T-SQL. User-defined aggregates can be implemented only in SQL CLR code; they have no T-SQL equivalent. Because aggregates tend to perform computation only, they provide an excellent use case for SQL CLR code. As it turns out, they are also quite easy to build.

At first, aggregates feel and look like functions because they accept and return values. In fact, if you use an aggregate in a non-data-querying T-SQL call (for example, *SELECT SUM(8)*), you are in fact treating the aggregate as if it were a function. The thing to remember is that the argument passed to an aggregate is typically a column, and so each discrete value for that column, for whichever *WHERE*, *HAVING*, *ORDER BY*, and/or *GROUP BY* scope applies, gets passed into the aggregate. It is the aggregate's job to update a variable, which eventually will be the return value, as each discrete value is passed to it.

CLR aggregates require you to apply the *SqlUserDefinedAggregate* attribute to them. The *SqlUserDefinedAggregate* attribute accepts a number of parameters, but all of them are optional except *Format*. In our example, we will use the value *Format.Native* for the *Format* parameter. For more advanced scenarios, you might want to study SQL Server Books Online to acquaint yourself with the other parameters this attribute accepts. Sticking with *Format.Native* for the *Format* parameter is sufficient for many scenarios.

Unlike the *SqlProcedure*, *SqlFunction*, and *SqlTrigger* attributes, the *SqlUserDefinedAggregate* attribute is required by SQL Server for your class to be eligible for use as an aggregate. Visual Studio SQL Server projects do use this attribute for deployment, and the attribute is included in the aggregate template, but it also must be used in generic Class Library project code in order for T-SQL registration of the aggregate to succeed.

Aggregate classes must have four methods: *Init*, *Accumulate*, *Merge*, and *Terminate*. The *Accumulate* method accepts a SQL type, the *Terminate* method returns one, and the *Merge* method accepts an object typed as the aggregate class itself.

The *Accumulate* method handles the processing of a discrete value into the aggregate value, and the *Terminate* method returns the final aggregated value after all discrete values have been processed. The *Init* method provides startup code, typically initializing a class-level private variable that will be used by the *Accumulate* method. The *Merge* method is called in a specific multi-threading scenario, which we will describe later on.

Just to be perfectly clear, your aggregate class will not implement an interface to supply these methods; you must create them to meet what we might term the "conventions" that are expected of SQL CLR aggregate classes (as opposed to a "contract" with which they must comply). When you develop your code in a Visual Studio 2005 SQL Server project, the Aggregate template includes stubs for these four methods as well as the proper application of the *SqlUserDefinedAggregate* attribute.

Creating your own aggregates is fairly straightforward, but thinking through aggregation logic can be a bit confusing at first. Imagine you want to create a special aggregate called *Bakers-Dozen* that increments its accumulated value by 1 for every 12 units accumulated (much as a baker, in simpler times, would throw in a free 13th donut when you ordered 12). By using what you now know about CLR aggregates and combining that with integer division, you can implement a *BakersDozen* aggregate quite easily. Listing 3-8, the code from struct *BakersDozen* in aggTest.cs in the sample project, contains the entire implementation of the aggregate *BakersDozen*.

Listing 3-8   struct *BakersDozen* from aggTest.cs

```
[Serializable]
[Microsoft.SqlServer.Server.SqlUserDefinedAggregate(Format.Native)]
public struct BakersDozen
{
    private SqlInt32 DonutCount;

    public void Init()
    {
        DonutCount = 0;
    }

    public void Accumulate(SqlInt32 Value)
    {
        DonutCount += Value + ((Int32)Value) / 12;
    }

    public void Merge(BakersDozen Group)
    {
        DonutCount += Group.DonutCount;
    }

    public SqlInt32 Terminate()
    {
        return DonutCount;
    }
}
```

The code here is fairly straightforward. The private variable *DonutCount* is used to track the *BakersDozen*-adjusted sum of items ordered, adding the actual items- ordered value and incrementing the running total by the integer quotient of the ordered value divided by 12. By this logic, bonus items are added only when an individual value equals or exceeds a multiple of 12. Twelve includes a full dozen, and so would 13. Twenty-four includes two dozen, and so would 27. Two individual orders of 6 items each would not generate any bonus items because a minimum of 12 items must be ordered in a line item to qualify for a bonus.

To deploy the aggregate, use attribute-based deployment in the SQL Server project or the following command for the Class Library version:

```
CREATE AGGREGATE BakersDozen
       (@input int)
RETURNS int
EXTERNAL NAME Chapter03.BakersDozen
```

Notice that no method name is specified because the aggregate is implemented by an entire class rather than an individual function. Notice also that the return value data type must be declared as the data type of the values this aggregate function will process. The *@input* parameter acts as a placeholder, and its name is inconsequential. Note that aggregates can be built on SQL CLR types (covered in the next section) as well as SQL scalar types.

Note The preceding *CREATE AGGREGATE* command for the Class Library project version of the sample code is contained in the CreateObjects.sql script in the Management Studio project supplied with the sample code.

To see the aggregate work, first run the CreateTblAggregateTest.sql script file in the Management Studio sample project to create a table called AggregateTest with columns OrderItemId, OrderId, and ItemsOrdered and several rows of data, as shown here:

```
CREATE TABLE tblAggregateTest(
    [OrderItemId] [int] IDENTITY(1,1) NOT NULL,
    [OrderId] [int] NULL,
    [ItemsOrdered] [int] NOT NULL
)
GO

INSERT INTO tblAggregateTest VALUES (1,2)
INSERT INTO tblAggregateTest VALUES (1,4)
INSERT INTO tblAggregateTest VALUES (2,1)
INSERT INTO tblAggregateTest VALUES (2,12)
INSERT INTO tblAggregateTest VALUES (3,3)
INSERT INTO tblAggregateTest VALUES (3,2)
```

With such a table built, use the following T-SQL DDL command in your Visual Studio test script or a Management Studio query window to test the aggregate function:

```
SELECT
  OrderId,
  SUM(ItemsOrdered) AS SUM,
  dbo.BakersDozen(ItemsOrdered) AS BakersDozen
FROM tblAggregateTest
GROUP BY OrderId
```

For each distinct value in the OrderId column, this query effectively uses our CLR code under the following algorithm:

- Call *Init()*.

- Call *Accumulate* once for each row with the same *OrderId* value, passing it that row's value of the *ItemsOrdered* column.

- Call *Terminate* upon a change in the *OrderId* value to retrieve the aggregated value that the query will pipe to the client.

The results should be as follows:

```
OrderId     SUM          BakersDozen
----------- ------------ -----------
1           6            6
2           13           14
3           5            5
```

By including the built-in T-SQL aggregate *SUM* in our query, we can see how many bonus items were added. In this case, for OrderId 2, a single bonus item was added, due to one row in the table with the following values:

```
OrderItemId OrderId     ItemsOrdered
----------- ----------- ------------
4           2           12
```

All the other rows contain *ItemsOrdered* values of less than 12, so no bonus items were added for them.

Because SQL Server sometimes segments the work required to satisfy a query over multiple threads, the query processor might need to execute your aggregate function multiple times for a single query and then merge the results together. For your aggregate to work properly in this scenario, you must implement a *Merge* method.

The *Merge* method takes the result of one thread's aggregation and merges it into the current thread's aggregation. The calculation required to do this could be complicated for some aggregates; in our case, we simply added the *DonutCount* value from the secondary thread's aggregate (accessible via the *Group* input parameter) to our own. There is no need to add bonus items because they would have been added in the individual *Accumulate* calls on the secondary thread. Simple addition is all that's required. An aggregate that calculated some type of average, or tracked the largest value in the data series supplied, for example, would require more complex merge code.

Don't forget that aggregates can be passed scalar values and can be used from T-SQL without referencing a table. Your aggregate must accommodate this scenario, even if it seems impractical. In the case of *BakersDozen*, single scalar values are easily handled. To see for yourself, try executing the following table-less T-SQL query:

```
SELECT dbo.BakersDozen(13)
```

You will see that it returns the value 14.

> **Note**   The TestAggregate.sql script file in the Management Studio project contains both aggregate-testing queries.

Aggregates are an excellent use of SQL CLR programming. Because they are passed data values to be processed, they typically perform only computational tasks and no data access of their own. They consist of compiled CLR code, so they perform well, and unlike stored procedures, triggers, and functions, they cannot be implemented at all in T-SQL. That said, you must still make your aggregate code, especially in the *Accumulate* method, as "lean and mean" as possible. Injecting your own code into the query processor's stream of work is an honor, a privilege, and a significant responsibility. Take that responsibility seriously, and make sure that your code is as low-impact as possible.

CLR Types

The last SQL CLR feature for us to explore is user-defined types (UDTs). This feature is perhaps the most interesting, yet also the most controversial. It's interesting because, technically, it allows for storage of objects in the database. It's controversial because it's prone to abuse. CLR types were not implemented to allow developers to create object-oriented databases; they were created to allow multi-value or multi-behavior data types to be stored, retrieved, and easily manipulated.

CLR types have an 8 KB size limit. They also have certain indexing limitations, and their entire value must be updated when any of their individual property/field values is updated.

> **Note**   More information on CLR user-defined types is available in the MSDN article "Using CLR Integration in SQL Server 2005" by Rathakrishnan, Kleinerman, et al. You can find this article online at *http://msdn.microsoft.com/library/default.asp?url=/library/en-us/dnsql90/html/ sqlclrguidance.asp.*

CLR type methods must be static. You cannot, therefore, call methods from T-SQL as instance methods; instead, you must use a special *TypeName::MethodName()* syntax. You can implement properties as you would in any conventional class and read from them or write to them from T-SQL using a standard variable.property/column.property dot-separated syntax.

Listing 3-9, the code from struct *typPoint* in typTest.cs in the sample project, shows the implementation of *typPoint*, a CLR type that can be used to store Cartesian coordinates in the database.

Listing 3-9   struct *typPoint* from typTest.cs

```
[Serializable]
[SqlUserDefinedType(Format.Native)]
public struct typPoint : INullable
{
    private bool m_Null;
    private double m_x;
    private double m_y;

    public override string ToString()
    {
        if (this.IsNull)
            return "NULL";
        else
            return this.m_x + ":" + this.m_y;
    }

    public bool IsNull
    {
        get
        {
            return m_Null;
        }
    }

    public static typPoint Null
    {
        get
        {
            typPoint pt = new typPoint();
            pt.m_Null = true;
            return pt;
        }
    }

    public static typPoint Parse(SqlString s)
    {
        if (s.IsNull)
            return Null;
        else
```

```
        {
                typPoint pt = new typPoint();
                char[] parms = new char[1];
                parms[0] = ':';
                string str = (string)s;
                string[] xy = str.Split(parms);
                pt.X = double.Parse(xy[0]);
                pt.Y = double.Parse(xy[1]);
                return pt;
        }
    }

    public static double Sum(typPoint p )
    {
        return p.X + p.Y;
    }

    public double X
    {
        get { return m_x; }
        set { m_x = value; }
    }

    public double Y
    {
        get { return m_y; }
        set { m_y = value; }
    }

}
```

Through the class's *X* and *Y* properties, you can process coordinates in a single database column or variable. You can assign coordinate values to an instance of the type as a colon-delimited string (for example, *3:4*, by using the *Parse* method [implicitly]); you can read them back in the same format by using the *ToString* method. Once a value has been assigned, you can individually read or modify its X or Y portion by using the separate *X* and *Y* properties. The class implements the *INullable* interface and its *IsNull* property. The *Sum* method demonstrates how to expose a static member and allow it to access instance properties by accepting an instance of the CLR type of which it is a member.

Notice that the class is a struct and that the *Serializable* and *SqlUserDefinedType* attributes have been applied to it. As with the *SqlUserDefinedAggregate* attribute, *SqlUserDefinedType* is required by SQL Server and appears in the Class Library sample code as well as the SQL Server project version. As with the *SqlUserDefinedAggregate*, we simply assign a value of *Format.Native* to the *Format* parameter and leave the other parameters unused.

More Info   You might want to study SQL Server Books Online for information on using other parameters for this attribute.

Listing 3-10, the code from struct *typBakersDozen* in typTest.cs in the sample project, re-implements the BakersDozen logic we used in our aggregate example, this time in a UDT.

Listing 3-10   struct *typBakersDozen* from typTest.cs

```
[Serializable]
[SqlUserDefinedType(Format.Native)]
public struct typBakersDozen : INullable
{
    private bool m_Null;
    private double m_RealQty;

    public override string ToString()
    {
        return (m_RealQty + (long)m_RealQty / 12).ToString();
    }

    public bool IsNull
    {
        get
        {
            return m_Null;
        }
    }

    public static typBakersDozen Null
    {
        get
        {
            typBakersDozen h = new typBakersDozen();
            h.m_Null = true;
            return h;
        }
    }

    public static typBakersDozen Parse(SqlString s)
    {
        if (s.IsNull)
            return Null;
        else
        {
            typBakersDozen u = new typBakersDozen();
            u.RealQty = double.Parse((string)s);
            return u;
        }
    }

    public static typBakersDozen ParseDouble(SqlDouble d)
    {
        if (d.IsNull)
            return Null;
        else
```

```
        {
            typBakersDozen u = new typBakersDozen();
            u.RealQty = (double)d;
            return u;
        }
    }

    public double RealQty
    {
        get { return m_RealQty; }
        set { m_RealQty = value; }
    }

    public double AdjustedQty
    {
        get
        {
            return (m_RealQty + (long)m_RealQty / 12);
        }
        set
        {
            if (value % 12 == 0)
                m_RealQty = value;
            else
                m_RealQty = value - (long)value / 13;
        }
    }
}
```

The *RealQty* and *AdjustedQty* properties allow the ordered quantity to be assigned a value and the adjusted quantity to be automatically calculated, or vice versa. The real quantity is the default "input" value, the adjusted quantity is the default "output" value of the type, and the *Parse* and *ToString* methods work accordingly. If the *AdjustedQty* property is assigned a value that is an even multiple of 12 (which would be invalid), that value is assigned to the *RealQty* property, forcing the *AdjustedQty* to be set to its passed value plus its integer quotient when divided by 12.

To deploy the UDTs, use attribute-based deployment for the SQL Server project. The script file CreateObjects.sql in the Management Studio project supplied with the sample code contains the T-SQL code necessary to deploy the Class Library versions of the UDTs. Here's the command that deploys typPoint:

```
CREATE TYPE typPoint
EXTERNAL NAME Chapter03.typPoint
```

The script file TestTypPoint.sql in the Management Studio project contains T-SQL code that tests *typPoint*. Run it and examine the results for an intimate understanding of how to work with the type. The script file CreateTblPoint.sql creates a table with a column that is typed based on *typPoint*. Run it, and then run the script file TestTblPoint.sql to see how to manipulate tables that use SQL CLR UDTs.

The script file TestTypBakersDozen.sql contains T-SQL code that tests *typBakersDozen*. The *ParseDouble* method demonstrates how to implement a non-*SqlString* parse method. We named it *ParseDouble* because the *Parse* method itself cannot be overloaded. You must call *ParseDouble* explicitly as follows:

```
DECLARE @t AS dbo.typBakersDozen
SET @t = typBakersDozen::ParseDouble(12)
```

This is equivalent to using the default *Parse* method (implicitly) and assigning the string *12* as follows:

```
DECLARE @t AS dbo.typBakersDozen
SET @t = '12'
```

Notice that *typBakersDozen* essentially stores a value for the real quantity, and its properties are really just functions that accept or express that value in its native form or as an adjusted quantity. There is no backing variable for the *AdjustedQty* property; the *get* block of the *AdjustedQty* property merely applies a formula to the backing variable for *RealQty* and returns the result.

So *typBakersDozen* is not really an object with distinct properties, as *typPoint* is (with its admittedly simple ones). Because it merely implements a *SqlDouble* and adds some specialized functionality to it, *typBakersDozen* is a more appropriate implementation of CLR UDTs than is *typPoint*. In this vein, other good candidates for CLR UDTs include date-related types (for example, a type that stores a single underlying value for an annual quarter and accepts/presents its value as a calendar quarter or a fiscal quarter) and currency types (especially those with fixed rates of exchange between their native and converted values).

In general, you can think of CLR UDTs as "super scalars"—classes that wrap a scalar value and provide services and conversion functions for manipulating that scalar value and converting it among different interpretive formats or numbering systems. Do not think of SQL CLR UDTs as object-relational entities. This might seem counterintuitive, but consider the use of (de)serialization and the XML data type as more appropriate vehicles for storing objects in the database.

We have now investigated all five SQL CLR entities. Before we finish up, we need to discuss assembly security and ongoing maintenance of SQL CLR objects in your databases.

Security

Depending on the deployment method, you have numerous ways to specify what security level to grant a CLR assembly. All of them demand that you specify one of three permission sets:

- *Safe*   Assembly can perform local data access and computational tasks only.

- *External_Access*   Assembly can perform local data access and computational tasks and also access the network, the file system, the registry, and environment variables. Although *External_Access* is less restrictive than *Safe*, it still safeguards server stability.

- *Unsafe*   Assembly has unrestricted permissions and can even call unmanaged code. This setting can significantly compromise SQL Server security; only members of the sysadmin role can create (load) unsafe assemblies.

When you deploy an assembly from Visual Studio, its security level is set to Safe by default. To change it, you can select the project node in the Solution Explorer window and set the Permission Level property in the Properties window by selecting Safe, External, or Unsafe from the combo box provided (Figure 3-9).

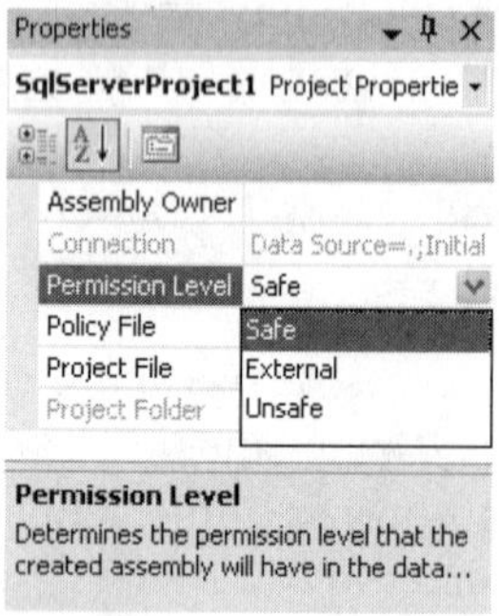

Figure 3-9   The Permission Level property and its options in the Visual Studio 2005 Properties window

Alternatively, you can right-click the project node in the Solution Explorer window and select Properties from the shortcut menu. You can also double-click the Properties node (or the My Project node in Visual Basic projects). Either action opens up the project properties designer. Select the designer's Database tab and then select a permission set from the Permission Level combo box (Figure 3-10). (The same three options are available here as in the Properties window.)

To specify an assembly's permission set using T-SQL, simply specify *SAFE*, *EXTERNAL_ACCESS*, or *UNSAFE* within the "*WITH PERMISSION_SET*" clause of the *CREATE ASSEMBLY* statement covered earlier in this chapter. Recall that our example used the default *SAFE* setting in this clause.

Finally, in the Management Studio New Assembly dialog box (shown earlier in Figure 3-7), you can select Safe, External Access, or Unsafe from the Permission Set combo box.

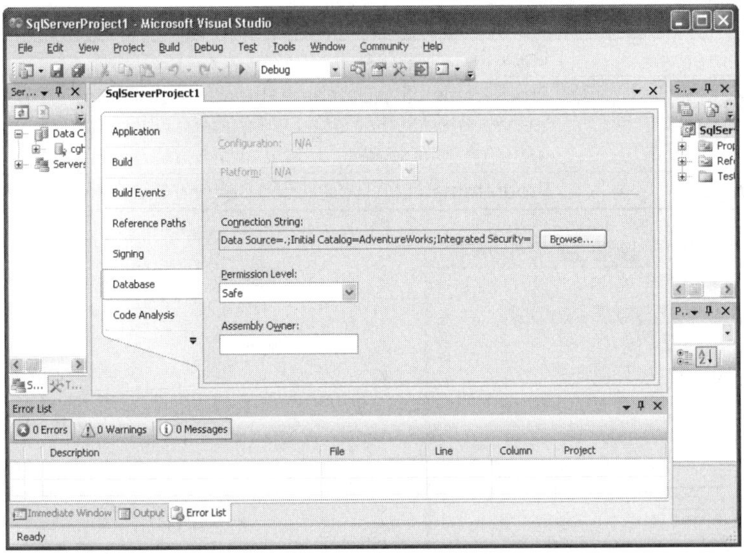

Figure 3-10   The Database tab of the Visual Studio project properties designer

Examining and Managing CLR Types in a Database

Once deployed, your SQL CLR stored procedures, functions, triggers, aggregates, and user-defined types and their dependencies might become difficult to keep track of in your head. Luckily, you can easily perform discovery on deployed CLR entities using the Management Studio UI. All CLR objects in a database can be found in Management Studio's Object Explorer window. To find them within the Object Explorer window's tree view, first navigate to the *servername*\Databases*databasename* node (where *servername* and *databasename* are the names of your server and database, respectively). Refer to Table 3-1 for the subnodes of this node that contain each CLR entity.

Table 3-1   Finding CLR Objects in Object Explorer

To view...	Look in...
Parent node for SQL CLR stored procedures, DDL triggers, functions, aggregates, and UDTs	Programmability (see Figure 3-11)
Assemblies	Programmability\Assemblies (see Figure 3-12)
Stored procedures	Programmability\Stored Procedures (see Figure 3-13)
Functions	Programmability\Functions\Scalar-Valued Functions and Programmability\Functions\Table-Valued Functions (see Figure 3-14)
Aggregates	Programmability\Functions\Aggregate Functions (see Figure 3-14)
DML triggers	Tables*tablename*\Triggers, where *tablename* is the name of the database table, including schema name, on which the trigger is defined (see Figure 3-15)

Table 3-1   **Finding CLR Objects in Object Explorer**

To view...	Look in...
DDL triggers	Programmability\Database Triggers (see Figure 3-16) (also *servername*\Server Objects\Triggers, where *servername* is the name of your server)
User-defined types	Programmability\Types\User-Defined Types (see Figure 3-17)

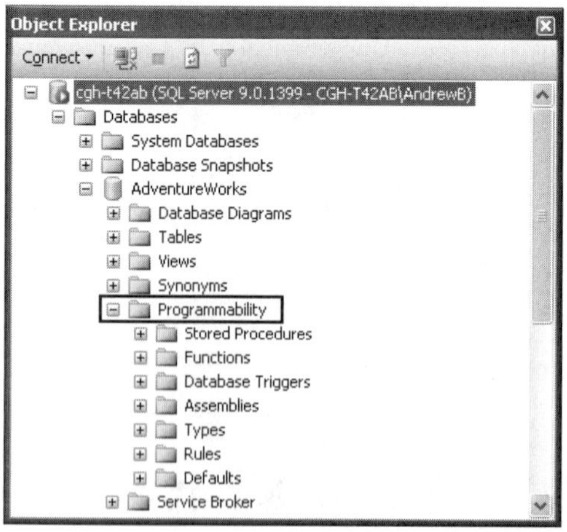

Figure 3-11   The SQL Server Management Studio Object Explorer window, with Programmability node highlighted

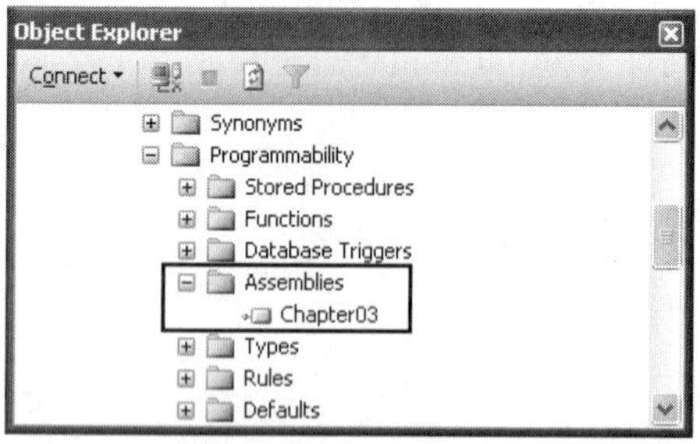

Figure 3-12   The Object Explorer window, with Assemblies node highlighted

Figure 3-13   The Object Explorer window, with CLR stored procedures highlighted

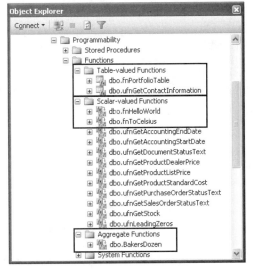

Figure 3-14   The Object Explorer window, with CLR table-valued, scalar-valued, and aggregate functions highlighted

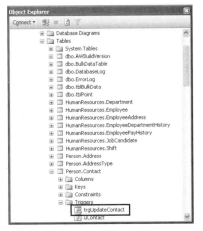

Figure 3-15   The Object Explorer window, with CLR DML trigger highlighted

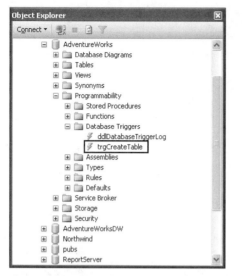

Figure 3-16   The Object Explorer window, with CLR DDL trigger highlighted

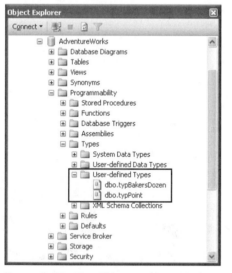

Figure 3-17   The Object Explorer window, with CLR UDTs highlighted

Bear in mind that you might need to use the Refresh shortcut menu option on the nodes listed in the table to see your CLR objects. If you've deployed or deleted any SQL CLR objects (as discussed shortly) since opening the Object Explorer's connection to your database, the tree view will be out of date and will have to be refreshed. Notice that the tree view icons for CLR stored procedures and CLR DML triggers differ slightly from their T-SQL counterparts; they have a small yellow padlock on the lower-right corner.

Once you've located a CLR entity in the Object Explorer window, you can right-click its tree view node and generate CREATE, DROP, and in some cases ALTER scripts for it by selecting the Script *object type* As option from the shortcut menu (where *object type* is the SQL CLR object type selected). The script text can be inserted into a new query window, a file, or the clipboard.

For stored procedures, you can also generate *EXECUTE* scripts or, by selecting Execute Stored Procedure from the shortcut menu, execute it interactively and generate the corresponding script via Management Studio's Execute Procedure dialog box. This dialog box explicitly prompts you for all input parameters defined for the stored procedure.

In addition to generating scripts for your CLR entities, you can view their dependencies (either objects that are dependent on them or objects on which they depend). Just right-click the object and choose the View Dependencies option from the shortcut menu.

To remove your CLR objects, either in preparation for loading a new version of your assembly or to delete the objects permanently, you have several options. For Visual Studio SQL Server projects, redeploying your assembly causes Visual Studio to drop it and any SQL CLR objects within it that were previously deployed by Visual Studio. This means that new versions can be deployed from Visual Studio without any preparatory steps.

For Class Library projects, you must issue T-SQL *DROP* commands for each of your SQL CLR objects and then for the assembly itself. You must drop any dependent objects before you drop the SQL CLR entity. For example, you must drop tblPoint before dropping typPoint. You can write these *DROP* scripts by hand or generate them by using the Script *object type* As/ DROP To shortcut menu options in the Management Studio Object Explorer window.

You can also use the Delete shortcut menu option on any SQL CLR object in the Management Studio Object Explorer window to drop an object. This option brings up the Delete Object dialog box (Figure 3-18).

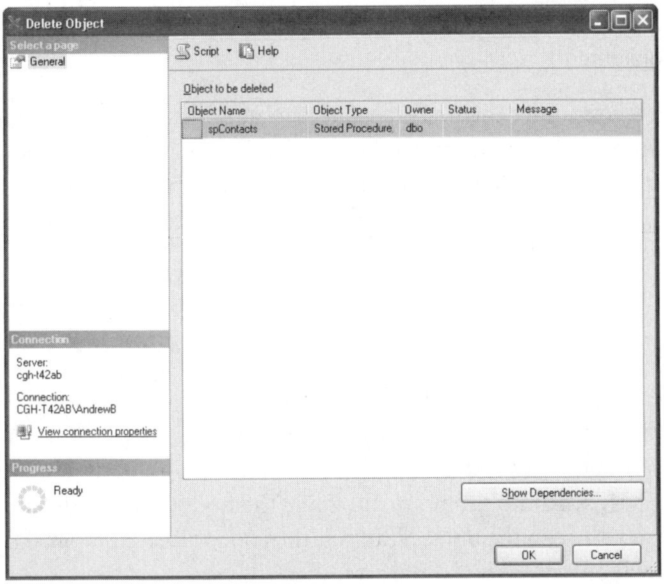

Figure 3-18   The Management Studio Delete Object dialog box

The script file Cleanup.sql in the Management Studio project provided with the sample code contains all the necessary *DROP* commands, in the proper order, for removing all traces of our Visual Studio SQL Server project or Class Library project from the AdventureWorks database. For the SQL Server project, run this script only if you want to permanently remove these objects. For the Class Library project, run it before you deploy an updated version of your assembly or if you want to permanently remove these objects.

SQL CLR objects, with the exception of DDL triggers, can also be viewed in Visual Studio 2005's Server Explorer window, as shown in Figure 3-19.

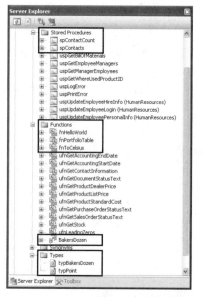

Figure 3-19   The Visual Studio Server Explorer window, with CLR stored procedures, functions, aggregates, and UDTs highlighted

You'll find most of the objects under their appropriate parent nodes within the data connection parent node: CLR stored procedures appear under the Stored Procedures node; scalar and table-valued functions, as well as aggregates, appear under the Functions node; the Types and Assemblies nodes contain their namesake objects; and DML triggers appear under the node of the table to which they belong.

You may also drill down on a particular assembly node and view a list of all its SQL CLR objects, as well as the source code files that make it up (see Figure 3-20).

For assemblies created from Visual Studio 2005 SQL Server projects, you may double-click on any SQL CLR object in the Server Explorer window to view its source code. (You may also do this by selecting the Open option from the SQL CLR object node's shortcut menu or the Data/Open option from Visual Studio's main menu while the node is selected.) If the assembly's project is open when you open the object's source, the code will be editable; if the project is not open, the source will be read-only.

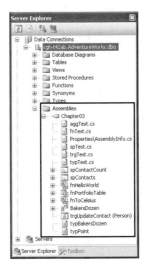

Figure 3-20   The Server Explorer window, with the Assemblies node and its child nodes highlighted

> **Caution**   Because *trgUpdateContact*, our SQL CLR DML trigger, was deployed via T-SQL
> in the PostDeployScript.sql script and not via the *SqlTrigger* attribute, its source cannot be
> browsed through the Server Explorer window connection's Tables\Contact (Person)\trgUp-
> dateContact node or its Assemblies\Chapter03\trgUpdateContact (Person) node. You can,
> however, view its source through the Assemblies\Chapter03\trgTest.cs node.

Best Practices for SQL CLR Usage

Before we close this chapter, we'd like to summarize certain best practices for the appropriate
use of SQL CLR programming.

The CLR integration in SQL Server 2005 is a powerful technology. In some cases, it allows you
to do things you can't do practically in T-SQL (such as apply complex business logic in stored
procedures or triggers), and in other cases it allows you to do things you can't do at all in
T-SQL (such as create your own aggregate functions).

The fact remains, however, that set-based data selection and modification is much better handled by the declarative constructs in T-SQL than in the procedural constructs of .NET and the
ADO.NET object model. SQL CLR functionality should be reserved for specific situations
when the power of .NET as a calculation engine is required.

In general, functions and aggregates are great uses of SQL CLR integration. UDTs, if used as
"super scalars" rather than objects per se, make good use of SQL CLR integration as well.

For stored procedures and triggers, we recommend that you start with the assumption that
these should be written in T-SQL and write them using SQL CLR code only if a case can be
made that they cannot be reasonably written otherwise. And before you make such a case,

consider that SQL CLR functions, aggregates, and UDTs can be used from within T-SQL
stored procedures and triggers.

Summary

In this chapter, you've been exposed to the "mechanics" of developing the five basic SQL CLR
entities and using them from T-SQL. You've seen how to take advantage of SQL Server 2005/
Visual Studio 2005 integration as well as how to develop SQL CLR code in conventional Class
Library assemblies and deploy them using T-SQL and SQL Server Management Studio. You've
also been exposed to most of the SQL CLR .NET code attributes and their use in SQL Server
projects and standard Class Library projects. You've gotten a sense of how to use Management
Studio and the Visual Studio 2005 Server Explorer window as management tools for your
SQL CLR objects, and we've discussed scenarios in which using SQL CLR integration is a
good choice as well as scenarios in which T-SQL is the better choice.

This first part of the book essentially covers building databases, so in this chapter we intentionally kept our focus on using SQL CLR objects from T-SQL and Management Studio. In the
previous chapter, we highlighted a number of enhancements to T-SQL that you can use in
your database development process. The second part of the book covers developing applications that use your databases. In Chapter 8, we'll look at how to consume your SQL CLR
objects in .NET applications by using ADO.NET, including within strongly typed *DataSet*
objects, and optionally using Windows Forms and ASP.NET data binding. And in Chapter 9,
we'll show you how to perform end-to-end debugging of client-side and SQL CLR code, as
well as T-SQL code, in Visual Studio 2005. The sum total of the material from Chapters 3, 8,
and 9 provides a rich resource for diving into SQL CLR development.

Chapter 4
XML and the Relational Database

–Stephen Forte

Since it appeared on the world scene in 1998, eXtensible Markup Language (XML) has become quite a useful standard for exchanging data and documents between different systems. XML is a markup language (derived from Standard Generalized Markup Language, or SGML) for documents that contain structured information.

You might be wondering why you would want to store and work with XML in the database. Isn't that what XML parsers and applications are for? Until now, XML was usually derived from database tables and queries and then programmatically placed into a transport format (such as a physical document or a Web service), parsed, read on the receiving end, and then placed into another database.

Database purists might insist that you should never store XML in the database because it is a transfer mechanism, not a storage mechanism. They would argue that you should always use XML to transport data from one database or application to another, deconstruct the XML on import and store it in relational tables, and reconstruct it on export from the relational tables back to XML for transport. On the other end of the spectrum, XML junkies (especially bloggers) might argue that the database is dead—that you don't need databases anymore because XML provides a nice data storage mechanism with data integrity (XML Schema or XML Schema Definition [XSD]) and a query engine (XQuery). They view the world as just a bunch of XML files—they rarely use relational databases and instead use XML technologies to store and manipulate their data.

As with the most extreme viewpoints in any dispute, however, both camps are wrong. Each has a good argument and valid points. A relational database has features such as primary keys, indexes, and referential integrity that make it a far superior storage and querying mechanism for raw data. Some applications, or even databases themselves, shred XML data into relational data to store it in the database and compose XML when data is retrieved. At other times, the XML data is simply persisted as (unstructured) text in the database. Microsoft SQL Server 2000 offers both of these options, yet neither is necessarily the desirable solution. It would be much better if XML could be stored in a relational database in its native format.

So which do you use, a "pure" relational approach or a hybrid approach where you store XML in the database and work with it there? The answer, as with so much in SQL Server, is "it depends." When you are architecting a highly transactional application system (traditionally referred to as an Online Transaction Processing, or OLTP, system) where many simultaneous reads and writes are made by users, the most suitable choice is a full relational database technology that includes features such as primary keys, referential integrity, and transactions. If you have a massive data warehouse and want to provide users with access to trend analysis and data mining algorithms, you should probably use the traditional relational model in conjunction with the Online Analytical Processing (OLAP) technology. When you have a lot of simultaneous database reads and writes by many users, you should use the traditional relational approach.

We will not try to convince you to convert all of your data to XML just for the sake of using a new technology, but sometimes you should definitely consider using XML in your database. One situation in which you might want to store and use XML in a relational database is when you are transforming data out of an OLTP database to another, "flatter" (less relational) database that is used for simple queries and for display on Web pages. For example, let's say you have a highly transactional real-time database with many users and the data is stored in fifth normal form. This data also powers your Web site, but the Web site can tolerate a level of latency in terms of the data being refreshed from the real-time application. (An example is a traditional banking application, which usually takes from 2 minutes to 1 day for an ATM transaction to appear on your online banking site, depending on the bank.) A good architecture choice is to transform on a regular basis (as your business needs require) the OLTP data to a more denormalized or flat model used for Web access and reports. Your data model is then tailored to the Web page access and queries that power the pages, and you can build an index strategy around this process. At this point, you might want to store some data for XML because you can easily transform it, bind it, or do whatever you want to it on the client side.

One such example from our experience involved architecting a large consumer destination Web site during the dot-com boom. This site was a well-known "brand name" and traffic was huge—more than a billion unique page views a month. We "published" a version of the OLTP database every four hours from production to the flat Web database. A few of the tables were for user search result functionality and contained all the detail of a record's data from our core business data in XML format in a *TEXT* column. The XML data was hierarchical and contained data from several sources, so it was a convenience to the Web developer to represent and store it as XML directly in the database. This approach was also advantageous because we had to support multiple clients: Netscape, Microsoft Internet Explorer, and WML (this was pre-ASP.NET). Our client ASP page transformed the XML field based on what browser was detected, so different HTML was sent down for Internet Explorer and Netscape, and WML was created with the same page for mobile browsers.

A negative result of this approach was that we could not use a lot of the XML technologies inside the database and we had to rely heavily on XSLT on the client tier. SQL Server 2000 does not support XML as much as we would have liked.

XML in SQL Server 2000

As mentioned in the previous section, SQL Server 2000 has two options for working with XML data: shred and compose or store as text. Let's assume a developer decides to store XML data in a text data type in an SQL Server 2000 database. The first issue is validating the XML that is persisted. SQL Server 2000 has no means of doing such a validation, so the XML data can't be validated except by an outside application (a risky proposition–the true power of a RDBMS is applying rules at the server level).

The second issue is querying the data. Sure, you could look for data using character and pattern matching using functions such as *CharIndex* or *PatIndex*, but these functions cannot efficiently find specific data in a structured XML document. In the consumer Web site in the previous example, we had to put the search elements in the XML data's TEXT column in regular SQL Server fields for querying. The developer could also implement full-text search, which could also index the text data, but this solution would make things only a little better. It would still be difficult to extract data from a specific attribute in a specific subelement in the XML, and it wouldn't be very efficient. You would not be able to write a query that said "Show me all data where the 'Author' attribute is set to 'John Smith'."

The third issue is modifying the XML data. The developer could simply replace the entire XML contents–which is not at all efficient–or use the *UpdateText* function to do in-place changes. However, *UpdateText* requires that you know the exact locations and length of data you are going to replace, which, as we just stated, would be difficult to do and slow.

Unless the XML is being persisted in the database as is and is being replaced as needed, it is difficult to implement an XML storage solution using text. Therefore, developers have taken the other route and have shredded and composed XML data as it is put in and retrieved from the database. SQL Server 2000 offers two features to facilitate these options: the *OPENXML* function for shredding XML data and the *FOR XML* clause of the *SELECT* statement for composing XML. However, *OPENXML* is not the most efficient mechanism for shredding XML data and *FOR XML* has its own limitations that in moderately complex scenarios require the use of the *EXPLICIT* option. (As any developer who has used this option will tell you, it is not a pretty sight.) Consequently, developers would instead shred and compose XML outside the database and pass relational data to and from SQL Server.

The natural evolution of persisting native XML data in the database has been realized in SQL Server 2005, which allows XML to be stored in its native format in the database. Not only can it persist native XML data in the database, but it can index it, query it using XPath and XQuery, and even modify it efficiently.

The *XML* Data Type

SQL Server 2005 introduces a new data type for working with XML data: the *XML* data type. Using this new data type, you can store XML in its native format, query the data within the XML, efficiently and easily modify data within the XML without having to replace the entire contents, and index the data in the XML. You can use it as any of the following:

- A variable
- A parameter in a stored procedure or a user-defined function (UDF)
- A return value from a UDF
- A column in a table

There are some limitations of the *XML* data type that you should be aware of. Although this data type can contain and be checked for null values, unlike other native types, you cannot directly compare an instance of an *XML* data type to another instance of an *XML* data type. Any such equality comparisons require first casting the *XML* type to a character type. This limitation also means that you cannot use *ORDER BY* or *GROUP BY* with an *XML* data type. There are several other restrictions, which we will discuss in more detail later.

These might seem like pretty severe restrictions, but they don't really affect the *XML* data type when it is used appropriately. The *XML* data type also has a rich feature set that more than compensates for these limitations.

Working with the *XML* Data Type as a Variable

Let's start by writing some code that uses the new *XML* data type as a variable. As with any other T-SQL variable, you simply declare it and assign data to it, as in the following example, which uses a generic piece of XML to represent a sales representative's data as XML:

```
DECLARE @xmlData AS XML
 Set @xmlData='
 <Customers>
   <CustomerID>CORZN</CustomerID>
   <CompanyName>Corzen, Inc</CompanyName>
   <ContactName>Stephen Forte</ContactName>
   <ContactTitle>Sales Representative</ContactTitle>
   <Address>5-9 Union Square West</Address>
   <City>New York</City>
   <PostalCode>10028</PostalCode>
   <Country>USA</Country>
   <Phone>030-0074321</Phone>
   <Fax>030-0076545</Fax>
   </Customers>
 '
 Select @xmlData
```

This basic example shows an XML variable being declared like any other native SQL Server data type by using the *DECLARE* statement. Then the variable is assigned a value. Oddly enough, a string of XML data is assigned to the *XML* data type and the type parses it into XML. (Coincidentally, CLR-based user-defined types also support and require this same parsing functionality.) The example also checks that the XML is well formed, such as by validating that an element's start and end tags match not only in name but also in case.

> **More Info** For more details on how to create well-formed XML, see Michael J. Young's book *XML Step by Step, Second Edition* (Microsoft Press, 2002).

The last statement returns the XML to the caller via a *SELECT* statement, and the results appear with the XML in a single column in a single row of data. Another benefit of having the database recognize that you are working with XML and not raw text that happens to be XML is that XML results in SQL Management Studio are displayed as a hyperlink, which when clicked opens a new window displaying nicely formatted XML (using the Microsoft Internet Explorer XML Template), as shown in Figure 4-1. But that's not all: If you right-click on the XML results window's title bar, you get a shortcut menu (Figure 4-2) with some useful options, such as the ability to save the XML to a file or to copy the full XML path.

```
<Customer CustomerID="1">
    <OrderDetail SalesOrderID="43860" OrderDate="2001-08-01T00:00:00" />
    <OrderDetail SalesOrderID="44501" OrderDate="2001-11-01T00:00:00" />
    <OrderDetail SalesOrderID="45283" OrderDate="2002-02-01T00:00:00" />
    <OrderDetail SalesOrderID="46042" OrderDate="2002-05-01T00:00:00" />
</Customer>
<Customer CustomerID="2">
    <OrderDetail SalesOrderID="46976" OrderDate="2002-08-01T00:00:00" />
    <OrderDetail SalesOrderID="47997" OrderDate="2002-11-01T00:00:00" />
    <OrderDetail SalesOrderID="49054" OrderDate="2003-02-01T00:00:00" />
    <OrderDetail SalesOrderID="50216" OrderDate="2003-05-01T00:00:00" />
    <OrderDetail SalesOrderID="51728" OrderDate="2003-08-01T00:00:00" />
    <OrderDetail SalesOrderID="57044" OrderDate="2003-11-01T00:00:00" />
    <OrderDetail SalesOrderID="63198" OrderDate="2004-02-01T00:00:00" />
    <OrderDetail SalesOrderID="69488" OrderDate="2004-05-01T00:00:00" />
</Customer>
```

Figure 4-1 SQL Server Management Studio and the Internet Explorer XML template

```
Save XML_F52E2B61-18A1-11d1-B105-00805F49916B1.xml
Close
Copy Full Path
New Horizontal Tab Group
New Vertical Tab Group
```

Figure 4-2 SQL Server Management Studio can save the XML results.

Working with XML in Tables

As we stated earlier, you can also define a column in a table as XML, as shown in the following example:

```
USE AdventureWorks
GO
--create the table with the XML Datatype
CREATE TABLE OrdersXML
  (OrderDocID INT PRIMARY KEY,
   xOrders XML NOT NULL)
```

As we also stated earlier, the *XML* data type has a few other restrictions, in this case when used as a column in a table:

- It cannot be used as a primary key.

- It cannot be used as a foreign key.

- It cannot be declared with a *UNIQUE* constraint.

- It cannot be declared with the *COLLATE* keyword.

We stated earlier that you can't compare two instances of the *XML* data type. Primary keys, foreign keys, and unique constraints all require that you must be able to compare any included data types; therefore, XML cannot be used in any of those situations. The SQL Server *COLLATE* statement is meaningless with the *XML* data type because SQL Server does not store the XML as text; rather, it uses a distinct type of encoding particular to XML.

Now let's get some data into the column. This example takes some simple static XML and inserts it into the OrdersXML table we just created, using the *XML* data type as a variable.

```
USE AdventureWorks
GO
--Insert Static XML via a variable
DECLARE @xmlData AS XML
SET @xmlData = '
<Orders>
    <Order>
    <OrderID>5</OrderID>
    <CustomerID>65</CustomerID>
    <OrderAmount>25</OrderAmount>
    </Order>
</Orders>'
--insert into the table
INSERT INTO OrdersXML (OrderDocID, xOrders) Values (1, @xmlData)
```

You can insert XML into these columns in a variety of other ways: XML bulk load (which we will discuss later in the chapter), loading from an XML variable (as shown here), or loading from a *SELECT* statement using the *FOR XML TYPE* feature, which we will discuss shortly.

Only well-formed XML (including fragments) can be inserted; any attempt to insert malformed XML will result in an exception, as shown in this fragment:

```
--Fails because of the malformed XML
INSERT INTO OrdersXML (OrderDocID, xOrders) VALUES (3, '<nm>steve</NM>')
```

The results produce the following error from SQL Server:

```
Msg 9436, Level 16, State 1, Line 1
XML parsing: line 1, character 14, end tag does not match start tag
```

Defaults and Constraints

The *XML* data type can, like other data types, conform to nullability, defaults, and constraints. If you want to make a field required (*NOT NULL*) and provide a default value on your XML column, just specify this as you would for any other column.

```
USE AdventureWorks
GO
CREATE TABLE OrdersXML
    (OrderDocID INT PRIMARY KEY,
    xOrders XML NOT NULL DEFAULT '<Orders/>'
```

The following insert works because it relies on the default:

```
INSERT INTO OrdersXML (OrderDocID, xOrders) VALUES (2, DEFAULT)
```

Adding a default does not enforce just *<Orders>* from being added. For example, we have specified an Orders node as the default but have not yet indicated any way to enforce that. The following insert works even if we only want *<Orders>* in our table because we have not declared a constraint on the column.

```
Insert Into OrdersXML (OrderDocID, xOrders) Values (3, '<blah>steve</blah>')
```

XML Schemas

One powerful feature of XML is its ability to strongly type the data in an XML document. XML Schema Definition (XSD) defines a standard set of data types that must be supported in all XML documents. You can use XSD to create an XML schema for your data, requiring that your data conform to a set of rules that you specify. This gives XML an advantage over just about all other data transfer/data description methods and is a major contributing factor to the success of the XML standard.

Without XML Schema, XML would just be a more modern, more verbose text-delimited format. An XML schema defines what your data should look like, what elements are required, and of what data types those elements will be. Analogous to how a table definition in SQL Server provides structure and type validation for relational data, an XML schema provides structure and type validation for the XML data.

We won't fully describe all the features of XML Schema here—that would require a book of its own. You can find the XSD specifications at the W3C at *http://www.w3.org/2001/XMLSchema*. Several popular XSDs are publicly available, including Really Simple Syndication (RSS), the protocol that powers weblogs, blogcasts, and other forms of binary and text syndication.

You can choose how to structure your XSD. XSD can create required elements and set limits on what data types and ranges are allowed. It can even allow document fragments.

SQL Server Schema Collections

SQL Server 2005 allows you to create your own schemas and store them in the database as database objects. For example, you can create the following simple and common XSD and add it to the *schemas* collection in AdventureWorks:

```
USE AdventureWorks
GO
--new syntax for adding a schema
--schema can disallow fragments if you say so
CREATE XML SCHEMA COLLECTION dbo.customer_xsd
AS
'<xsd:schema xmlns:xsd="http://www.w3.org/2001/XMLSchema"
            xmlns:tns="http://corzen.com/customer"
            targetNamespace="http://corzen.com/customer" >
   <xsd:simpleType name="customerAge" >
     <xsd:restriction base="xsd:int" >
        <xsd:maxInclusive value="65" />
        <xsd:minExclusive value="18" />
     </xsd:restriction>
   </xsd:simpleType>
   <xsd:element name="custage" type="tns:customerAge" />
</xsd:schema>'
GO
```

This schema is named customer_xsd, and you can use it on any XML type, including variables, parameters, return values, and especially columns in tables. This schema defines an element named *custage* that uses the *customerAge* type, which is defined as an *int* data type whose minimum value is anything greater than (but not including) 18 and whose maximum value is 65 inclusive. Next create a simple table and apply the schema to the XML column by referring to the schema name in parentheses after your *XML* data type in the *CREATE TABLE* statement shown here:

```
USE AdventureWorks
GO
--create table with xml column
--and use schema as a rule for
--a particular column
CREATE TABLE xml_schematest (
   Customer_ID int primary key,
   CustomerAge_XML XML(customer_xsd) --XML Schema Name
)
GO
```

As you can see in this example, the CustomerAge_XML column is defined not as simply *XML* but as *XML(customer_xsd)*. The *XML* data type has an optional parameter that allows you to specify the bound schema. This same usage also applies if you want to bind a schema to another use of an *XML* data type, such as a variable or a parameter. SQL Server now allows only a strongly typed XML document in the CustomerAge_XML column. This is much better than our *CHECK* constraint (which you can still add to this column). An advantage of using an XML schema is that your data is validated against it and you can enforce both data types (at the XML level) and make sure that only valid data is allowed into the particular elements. If you were using a *CHECK* constraint, for example, you would need a separate *CHECK* constraint for each validation you wanted to perform. This example requires a few *CHECK* constraints just to enforce the minimum and maximum ages. You need a constraint requiring the element and then another constraint to verify the allowed low end of the range (18) and another one to verify the high end of the allowed range (65).

> **Note**   When you create an XML column, any defaults you define must be valid for and not conflict with the bound XML schema; otherwise, the default value will always fail. Also, be sure that any defined constraints are valid for and do not conflict with the bound XML schema; otherwise, all attempts to insert or update data will likely fail.

Let's take a look at the schema in action.

```
USE AdventureWorks
GO
-- works
INSERT INTO xml_schematest VALUES(1,
 '<p:custage xmlns:p="http://corzen.com/customer">55</p:custage>')
GO
--works
INSERT INTO xml_schematest VALUES(2,
 '<p:custage xmlns:p="http://corzen.com/customer">45</p:custage>')
GO
```

SQL Server enforces the schema on insert and updates, ensuring data integrity. The data we provided conforms to the schema, so the inserts work smoothly. If you attempt to insert or update an invalid piece of data, you will receive an error:

```
USE AdventureWorks
GO
-- fails, age > 65
INSERT INTO xml_schematest VALUES(3,
 '<p:custage xmlns:p="http://corzen.com/customer">105</p:custage>')
GO
```

SQL Server reports back the following error:

```
Msg 6926, Level 16, State 1, Line 1
XML Validation: Invalid simple type value: '105'. Location: /*:custage[1]
```

We have only touched the surface with using XML schemas in SQL Server 2005. These schemas can get quite complex, and further discussion is beyond the scope of this book. You can easily enforce sophisticated XML schemas in your database once you master the syntax. We believe that you should always use an XML schema with your XML data to guarantee consistency in your XML data.

> **More Info**   See SQL Server 2005 Books Online and Michael J. Young's *XML Step by Step, Second Edition* (Microsoft Press, 2002) for more information on schemas.

The same error is reported back when you try to update already valid data with an invalid piece of XML:

```
-- fails
--column is validated on update also
UPDATE xml_schematest
  SET CustomerAge_XML = '
<p:custage xmlns:p="http://corzen.com/customer">105</p:custage>'
  WHERE Customer_id = 1
```

XML Indexes

You can create an XML index on an XML column using almost the same syntax as for a standard SQL Server index. There are four types of XML indexes: a single "primary XML index" that must be created and three types of optional "secondary XML index" that are created over the primary index. An XML index is a little different than a standard SQL index; it is a clustered index on an internal table used by SQL Server to store XML data. This table is called the *node table* and cannot be accessed by programmers.

To get started with an XML index, you must first create the *primary index* of all the nodes. The primary index is a clustered index (over the node table, not the base table) that associates each node of your XML column with the SQL Primary Key column. It does this by indexing one row in its B+tree structure for each node in your XML column, generating an index usually about three times as large as your XML data. For your XML data to work properly, your table must have an ordinary clustered Primary Key column defined. That primary key is used in a join of the XQuery results with the base table. (XQuery is discussed later in the chapter.) To create a primary XML index, you first create a table with a primary key and an XML column, as shown here:

```
--XML index Examples
USE AdventureWorks--but can be any DB
--Drop the table since we used it before
Drop Table OrdersXML

--Create the table with a PK
--and an XML column
CREATE TABLE OrdersXML
   (OrderDocID INT PRIMARY KEY,
   xOrders XML NOT NULL)
```

Next we insert some data into our new table:

```
--Insert some data into our new table
INSERT INTO OrdersXML
Values (1, '
<Orders>
    <Order>
    <OrderID>5</OrderID>
    <CustomerName>Stephen Forte</CustomerName>
    <OrderAmount>25</OrderAmount>
    </Order>
</Orders>')

INSERT INTO OrdersXML
Values (2, '
<Orders>
    <Order>
    <OrderID>7</OrderID>
    <CustomerName>Andrew Brust</CustomerName>
    <OrderAmount>45</OrderAmount>
    </Order>
</Orders>')

INSERT INTO OrdersXML
Values (3, '
<Orders>
    <Order>
    <OrderID>2</OrderID>
    <CustomerName>Bill Zack</CustomerName>
    <OrderAmount>65</OrderAmount>
    </Order>
</Orders>')
```

To create a primary XML index, we use the *CREATE Primary XML INDEX* syntax on the table:

```
CREATE Primary XML INDEX idx_1
    ON OrdersXML (xOrders)
```

We have successfully created a new primary XML index called idx_1 on the OrdersXML table's xOrders column. The primary XML index, idx_1, now has the node table populated. If you want to look at the node table's columns, run this piece of T-SQL:

```
-- display the columns in the node table
SELECT col.column_id, col.object_id,
    col.name, col.system_type_id
FROM sys.columns col
    inner JOIN sys.indexes idx
    ON idx.object_id = col.object_id
WHERE idx.name = 'idx_1'
 AND idx.type = 1
ORDER BY column_id
```

The results are shown in Table 4-1.

Table 4-1   Columns in a Typical Node Table

column_id	object_id	name	System_type_id
1	855674096	id	165
2	855674096	nid	56
3	855674096	tagname	231
4	855674096	taguri	231
5	855674096	tid	56
6	855674096	value	98
7	855674096	lvalue	231
8	855674096	lvaluebin	165
9	855674096	hid	167
10	855674096	xsinil	104
11	855674096	xsitype	104
12	855674096	pk1	56

The three secondary XML indexes are Path, Value, and Property. You can implement a secondary XML index only after you have created a primary XML index because they are both actually indexes over the node table. These indexes further optimize XQuery statements made against the XML data.

A path index creates an index on the Path ID (HID in Table 4-1) and Value columns of the primary XML index, using the *FOR PATH* keyword. This type of index is best when you have a fairly complex document type and want to speed up XQuery XPath expressions that reference a particular node in your XML data with an explicit value (as explained in the later discussion of XQuery). If you are more concerned about the values of the nodes queried with wildcards, you can create a value index using the *FOR VALUE* XML index. The *VALUE* index contains the same index columns as the *PATH* index, Value, and Path ID (HID), but in the reverse order (as shown in Table 4-1). Using the property type index with the *PROPERTY* keyword optimizes hierarchies of elements or attributes that are name/value pairs. The *PROPERTY* index contains the primary key of the base table, Path ID (HID), and Value, in that order. The syntax to create these indexes is shown here; you must specify that you are using the primary XML index by using the *USING XML INDEX* syntax, as shown here:

```
--structural (Path)
CREATE XML INDEX idx_a ON OrdersXML (xOrders)
USING XML INDEX idx_1 FOR PATH
--value
CREATE XML INDEX idx_b ON OrdersXML (xOrders)
USING XML INDEX idx_1 FOR VALUE
--property
CREATE XML INDEX idx_c ON OrdersXML (xOrders)
USING XML INDEX idx_1 FOR PROPERTY
```

There are some additional restrictions that you must be aware of:

- An XML index can contain only one XML column, so you cannot create a composite XML index (an index on more than one XML column).

- Using XML indexes requires that the primary key be clustered, and because you can have only one clustered index per table, you cannot create a clustered XML index.

SQL Server 2005 Management Studio allows you to view the indexes on a table by drilling down from the Database node to the table name and down to the Indexes node, as shown in Figure 4-3. Using this dialog box, you can also create a new primary XML index by right-clicking on the Indexes node and clicking New Index.

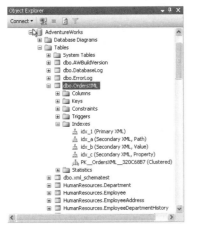

Figure 4-3 SQL Server Management Studio's Object Explorer showing the XML indexes

Armed with this new index type, you can write some very efficient queries using XQuery. Before we get to XQuery, however, let's take a look at some other XML features that will help you get XML data in and out of the database.

FOR XML Commands

SQL Server 2000 introduced an enhancement to the T-SQL syntax that enables normal relational queries to output their result set as XML, using any of these three approaches:

- *FOR XML RAW*
- *FOR XML AUTO*
- *FOR XML EXPLICIT*

As you probably expected, these three features are also in SQL Server 2005. We'll first discuss the features common to both versions and then look closely at the new and enhanced features available in SQL Server 2005.

FOR XML RAW

FOR XML RAW produces what we call *attribute-based XML. FOR XML RAW* essentially creates a flat representation of the data where each row returned becomes an element and the returned columns become the attributes of each element. *FOR XML RAW* also doesn't interpret joins in any special way. (Joins become relevant in *FOR XML AUTO*.) Listing 4-1 is an example of a simple query that retrieves customer and order header data.

Listing 4-1   Customer and Order Header Data with *FOR XML RAW*

```
USE AdventureWorks
GO

SELECT TOP 10 -- limits the result rows for demo purposes
    Customer.CustomerID, OrderHeader.SalesOrderID, OrderHeader.OrderDate
FROM Sales.Customer Customer
INNER JOIN Sales.SalesOrderHeader OrderHeader
    ON OrderHeader.CustomerID = Customer.CustomerID
ORDER BY Customer.CustomerID
FOR XML RAW
```

If you are using SQL Server 2000, this will be output as a stream of text to Query Analyzer. However, we will assume that you are working with SQL Server 2005, so you can click on the XML hyperlink in the returned results to see the results shown here:

```
<row CustomerID="1" SalesOrderID="43860" OrderDate="2001-08-01T00:00:00" />
<row CustomerID="1" SalesOrderID="44501" OrderDate="2001-11-01T00:00:00" />
<row CustomerID="1" SalesOrderID="45283" OrderDate="2002-02-01T00:00:00" />
<row CustomerID="1" SalesOrderID="46042" OrderDate="2002-05-01T00:00:00" />
<row CustomerID="2" SalesOrderID="46976" OrderDate="2002-08-01T00:00:00" />
<row CustomerID="2" SalesOrderID="47997" OrderDate="2002-11-01T00:00:00" />
<row CustomerID="2" SalesOrderID="49054" OrderDate="2003-02-01T00:00:00" />
<row CustomerID="2" SalesOrderID="50216" OrderDate="2003-05-01T00:00:00" />
<row CustomerID="2" SalesOrderID="51728" OrderDate="2003-08-01T00:00:00" />
<row CustomerID="2" SalesOrderID="57044" OrderDate="2003-11-01T00:00:00" />
```

As promised, you get flat results where each row returned from the query becomes a single element named *row* and where all columns are output as attributes of that element. Odds are, however, that you will want more structured XML output, which leads us to the next topic, *FOR XML AUTO.*

FOR XML AUTO

FOR XML AUTO produces attribute-based XML by default and can create nested results based on the tables in the query's join clause. For example, using the same query just demonstrated, you can simply change the *FOR XML* clause to *FOR XML AUTO*, as shown here.

Listing 4-2   Customer and Order Header Data with *FOR XML AUTO*

```
USE AdventureWorks
GO

SELECT TOP 10 -- limits the result rows for demo purposes
    Customer.CustomerID, OrderHeader.SalesOrderID, OrderHeader.OrderDate
FROM Sales.Customer Customer
INNER JOIN Sales.SalesOrderHeader OrderHeader
    ON OrderHeader.CustomerID = Customer.CustomerID
ORDER BY Customer.CustomerID
FOR XML AUTO
```

Execute and click the XML hyperlink in the results, and you will see the following output:

```
<Customer CustomerID="1">
  <OrderHeader SalesOrderID="43860" OrderDate="2001-08-01T00:00:00" />
  <OrderHeader SalesOrderID="44501" OrderDate="2001-11-01T00:00:00" />
  <OrderHeader SalesOrderID="45283" OrderDate="2002-02-01T00:00:00" />
  <OrderHeader SalesOrderID="46042" OrderDate="2002-05-01T00:00:00" />
</Customer>
<Customer CustomerID="2">
  <OrderHeader SalesOrderID="46976" OrderDate="2002-08-01T00:00:00" />
  <OrderHeader SalesOrderID="47997" OrderDate="2002-11-01T00:00:00" />
  <OrderHeader SalesOrderID="49054" OrderDate="2003-02-01T00:00:00" />
  <OrderHeader SalesOrderID="50216" OrderDate="2003-05-01T00:00:00" />
  <OrderHeader SalesOrderID="51728" OrderDate="2003-08-01T00:00:00" />
  <OrderHeader SalesOrderID="57044" OrderDate="2003-11-01T00:00:00" />
</Customer>
```

As you can see, the XML data has main elements named *Customer* (based on the alias assigned in the query) and subelements named *OrderHeader* (again from the alias). Note that *FOR XML AUTO* determines the element nesting order based on the order of the columns in the *SELECT* clause. You can rewrite the *SELECT* clause so an OrderHeader column comes before a Customer Column, as shown here:

```
SELECT TOP 10 -- limits the result rows for demo purposes
    OrderHeader.SalesOrderID, OrderHeader.OrderDate, Customer.CustomerID
```

The output (as viewed in the XML viewer) now looks like this:

```
<OrderHeader SalesOrderID="43860" OrderDate="2001-08-01T00:00:00">
  <Customer CustomerID="1" />
</OrderHeader>
<OrderHeader SalesOrderID="44501" OrderDate="2001-11-01T00:00:00">
  <Customer CustomerID="1" />
</OrderHeader>
<OrderHeader SalesOrderID="45283" OrderDate="2002-02-01T00:00:00">
  <Customer CustomerID="1" />
</OrderHeader>
```

```
<OrderHeader SalesOrderID="46042" OrderDate="2002-05-01T00:00:00">
  <Customer CustomerID="1" />
</OrderHeader>
<OrderHeader SalesOrderID="46976" OrderDate="2002-08-01T00:00:00">
  <Customer CustomerID="2" />
</OrderHeader>
<OrderHeader SalesOrderID="47997" OrderDate="2002-11-01T00:00:00">
  <Customer CustomerID="2" />
</OrderHeader>
<OrderHeader SalesOrderID="49054" OrderDate="2003-02-01T00:00:00">
  <Customer CustomerID="2" />
</OrderHeader>
<OrderHeader SalesOrderID="50216" OrderDate="2003-05-01T00:00:00">
  <Customer CustomerID="2" />
</OrderHeader>
<OrderHeader SalesOrderID="51728" OrderDate="2003-08-01T00:00:00">
  <Customer CustomerID="2" />
</OrderHeader>
<OrderHeader SalesOrderID="57044" OrderDate="2003-11-01T00:00:00">
  <Customer CustomerID="2" />
</OrderHeader>
```

These results are probably not the results you wanted. To keep the XML hierarchy matching the table hierarchy, you must list at least one column from the parent table before any column from a child table. If there are three levels of tables, at least one other column from the child table must come before any from the grandchild table, and so on.

FOR XML EXPLICIT

FOR XML EXPLICIT is the most complex but also the most useful and flexible of the three options. It produces XML by constructing a UNION query of the various levels of output elements. So, if again you have the Customer and SalesOrderHeader tables and you want to produce XML output, you must have two SELECT statements with a UNION. If you add the SalesOrderDetail table, you must add another UNION statement and SELECT statement.

As we said, FOR XML EXPLICIT is more complex than its predecessors. For starters, you are responsible for defining two additional columns that establish the hierarchical relationship of the XML: a Tag column that acts as a row's identifier and a Parent column that links child records to the parent record's Tag value (similar to EmployeeID and ManagerID). You must also alias all columns to indicate the element, Tag, and display name for the XML output, as shown here. Keep in mind that only the first SELECT statement must enforce these rules because aliases in subsequent SELECT statements in a UNION query are ignored.

Listing 4-3   Customer and Order Header Data with *FOR XML EXPLICIT*

```
USE AdventureWorks
GO

SELECT TOP 2 -- limits the result rows for demo purposes
    1 AS Tag,
    NULL AS Parent,
    CustomerID AS [Customer!1!CustomerID],
```

```
      NULL AS [SalesOrder!2!SalesOrderID],
      NULL AS [SalesOrder!2!OrderDate]
FROM Sales.Customer AS Customer

UNION ALL

SELECT TOP 10 -- limits the result rows for demo purposes
    2,
    1,
    Customer.CustomerID,
    OrderHeader.SalesOrderID,
    OrderHeader.OrderDate
FROM Sales.Customer AS Customer
INNER JOIN Sales.SalesOrderHeader AS OrderHeader
    ON OrderHeader.CustomerID = Customer.CustomerID

ORDER BY [Customer!1!CustomerID], [SalesOrder!2!SalesOrderID]
FOR XML EXPLICIT
```

Execute and click the XML hyperlink to see the following results:

```
<Customer CustomerID="1">
  <SalesOrder SalesOrderID="43860" OrderDate="2001-08-01T00:00:00" />
  <SalesOrder SalesOrderID="44501" OrderDate="2001-11-01T00:00:00" />
  <SalesOrder SalesOrderID="45283" OrderDate="2002-02-01T00:00:00" />
  <SalesOrder SalesOrderID="46042" OrderDate="2002-05-01T00:00:00" />
</Customer>
<Customer CustomerID="2">
  <SalesOrder SalesOrderID="46976" OrderDate="2002-08-01T00:00:00" />
  <SalesOrder SalesOrderID="47997" OrderDate="2002-11-01T00:00:00" />
  <SalesOrder SalesOrderID="49054" OrderDate="2003-02-01T00:00:00" />
  <SalesOrder SalesOrderID="50216" OrderDate="2003-05-01T00:00:00" />
  <SalesOrder SalesOrderID="51728" OrderDate="2003-08-01T00:00:00" />
  <SalesOrder SalesOrderID="57044" OrderDate="2003-11-01T00:00:00" />
</Customer>
```

This output happens to resemble the output from Listing 4-2.

FOR XML EXPLICIT allows for some alternative outputs that are not achievable using *RAW*. For example, you can specify that certain values be composed as elements instead of attributes by including *!ELEMENT* on the end of the aliased column. Listing 4-4 demonstrates this usage.

Listing 4-4   Using *FOR XML EXPLICIT*

```
USE AdventureWorks
GO
--XML EXPLICIT
SELECT TOP 2 -- limits the result rows for demo purposes
    1 AS Tag,
    NULL AS Parent,
    CustomerID AS [Customer!1!CustomerID],
    NULL AS [SalesOrder!2!SalesOrderID],
    NULL AS [SalesOrder!2!OrderDate!ELEMENT] --Render as an element
FROM Sales.Customer AS Customer
```

```
UNION ALL

SELECT TOP 10 -- limits the result rows for demo purposes
  2,
  1,
  Customer.CustomerID,
  OrderHeader.SalesOrderID,
  OrderHeader.OrderDate
FROM Sales.Customer AS Customer
INNER JOIN Sales.SalesOrderHeader AS OrderHeader
  ON OrderHeader.CustomerID = Customer.CustomerID

ORDER BY [Customer!1!CustomerID], [SalesOrder!2!SalesOrderID]
FOR XML EXPLICIT
```

Only one minor change was made (as indicated by the comment). However, this change has a major effect on the final output, as shown here:

```
<Customer CustomerID="1">
  <SalesOrder SalesOrderID="43860">
    <OrderDate>2001-08-01T00:00:00</OrderDate>
  </SalesOrder>
  <SalesOrder SalesOrderID="44501">
    <OrderDate>2001-11-01T00:00:00</OrderDate>
  </SalesOrder>
  <SalesOrder SalesOrderID="45283">
    <OrderDate>2002-02-01T00:00:00</OrderDate>
  </SalesOrder>
  <SalesOrder SalesOrderID="46042">
    <OrderDate>2002-05-01T00:00:00</OrderDate>
  </SalesOrder>
</Customer>
<Customer CustomerID="2">
  <SalesOrder SalesOrderID="46976">
    <OrderDate>2002-08-01T00:00:00</OrderDate>
  </SalesOrder>
  <SalesOrder SalesOrderID="47997">
    <OrderDate>2002-11-01T00:00:00</OrderDate>
  </SalesOrder>
  <SalesOrder SalesOrderID="49054">
    <OrderDate>2003-02-01T00:00:00</OrderDate>
  </SalesOrder>
  <SalesOrder SalesOrderID="50216">
    <OrderDate>2003-05-01T00:00:00</OrderDate>
  </SalesOrder>
  <SalesOrder SalesOrderID="51728">
    <OrderDate>2003-08-01T00:00:00</OrderDate>
  </SalesOrder>
  <SalesOrder SalesOrderID="57044">
    <OrderDate>2003-11-01T00:00:00</OrderDate>
  </SalesOrder>
</Customer>
```

Notice that the *OrderDate* is rendered as a child element of the SalesOrder element. Although *EXPLICIT* mode could create robust results, it also requires creating even more complex queries to get such results. For example, to add a few more fields from OrderHeader and to add some additional fields from OrderDetail, you would have to write the query shown in Listing 4-5 using *FOR XML EXPLICIT*.

Listing 4-5   Using *FOR XML EXPLICIT* with added fields

```
USE AdventureWorks
GO
--XML EXPLICIT
SELECT --TOP 2 -- limits the result rows for demo purposes
    1 AS Tag,
    NULL AS Parent,
    CustomerID AS [Customer!1!CustomerID],
    NULL AS [SalesOrder!2!SalesOrderID],
    NULL AS [SalesOrder!2!TotalDue],
    NULL AS [SalesOrder!2!OrderDate!ELEMENT],
    NULL AS [SalesOrder!2!ShipDate!ELEMENT],
    NULL AS [SalesDetail!3!ProductID],
    NULL AS [SalesDetail!3!OrderQty],
    NULL AS [SalesDetail!3!LineTotal]
FROM Sales.Customer AS Customer
WHERE Customer.CustomerID IN (1, 2)

UNION ALL

SELECT
    2,
    1,
    Customer.CustomerID,
    OrderHeader.SalesOrderID,
    OrderHeader.TotalDue,
    OrderHeader.OrderDate,
    OrderHeader.ShipDate,
    NULL,
    NULL,
    NULL
FROM Sales.Customer AS Customer
INNER JOIN Sales.SalesOrderHeader AS OrderHeader
    ON OrderHeader.CustomerID = Customer.CustomerID
WHERE Customer.CustomerID IN (1, 2)

UNION ALL

SELECT
    3,
    2,
    Customer.CustomerID,
    OrderHeader.SalesOrderID,
    OrderHeader.TotalDue,
    OrderHeader.OrderDate,
    OrderHeader.ShipDate,
    OrderDetail.ProductID,
    OrderDetail.OrderQty,
    OrderDetail.LineTotal
FROM Sales.Customer AS Customer
```

```
INNER JOIN Sales.SalesOrderHeader AS OrderHeader
   ON OrderHeader.CustomerID = Customer.CustomerID
INNER JOIN Sales.SalesOrderDetail AS OrderDetail
   ON OrderDetail.SalesOrderID = OrderHeader.SalesOrderID
WHERE Customer.CustomerID IN (1, 2)

ORDER BY [Customer!1!CustomerID], [SalesOrder!2!SalesOrderID]
FOR XML EXPLICIT
```

As you can see, the code has become quite complex and will become increasingly complex as you add additional data to the output. Although this query is perfectly valid in SQL Server 2005, this solution is unacceptable, which leads us to the new and improved *FOR XML* statement.

FOR XML Enhancements in SQL Server 2005

As you can see, SQL Server 2000 has a lot of XML features, even some not mentioned here (such as viewing the results over HTTP). Just about all of the SQL Server 2000 XML features revolve around *FOR XML*, a feature that appears to be much underused by developers. Following are a few ways SQL Server 2005 enhances the *FOR XML* feature:

- Using the *TYPE* option, *FOR XML* can output XML (as opposed to streamed results) from a *SELECT* statement using *FOR XML*, which in turn allows you to nest the results of *SELECT...FOR XML* into another *SELECT* statement.

- The new option, *FOR XML PATH*, allows you to more easily shape data and produce element-based XML than with the *EXPLICIT* option.

- You can explicitly specify a *ROOT* element for your output.

- You can produce element-based XML with *XML AUTO*.

- *FOR XML* can produce XML using an XSD Schema that uses a namespace you specify.

- Nesting, whitespace, and null handling have been improved.

FOR XML's TYPE Option

XML is an intrinsic data type of SQL Server 2005, so we can now automatically cast the XML output from the *FOR XML* query into an *XML* data type instance, as opposed to streamed results. You accomplish this by using the *TYPE* keyword after your *FOR XML* statement, like this:

```
USE AdventureWorks
DECLARE @xmlData AS XML

SET @xmlData =
(Select Customer.CustomerID, OrderDetail.SalesOrderID,
   OrderDetail.OrderDate
```

```
From Sales.Customer Customer
    inner join Sales.SalesOrderHeader OrderDetail
    on OrderDetail.customerid=Customer.customerid
WHERE Customer.CustomerID<3
ORDER BY Customer.CustomerID
For XML AUTO, TYPE)--Casts to XML type
SELECT @xmlData
```

This example declares a variable of XML and then sets that variable to a casted result of a *FOR XML* query using the *TYPE* statement. The results of this query are shown here for demonstration purposes, but you can use this new XML variable as part of an *INSERT* statement (to an XML column) or pass it to a stored procedure, as a couple of examples.

```
<Customer CustomerID="1">
   <OrderDetail SalesOrderID="43860" OrderDate="2001-08-01T00:00:00" />
   <OrderDetail SalesOrderID="44501" OrderDate="2001-11-01T00:00:00" />
   <OrderDetail SalesOrderID="45283" OrderDate="2002-02-01T00:00:00" />
   <OrderDetail SalesOrderID="46042" OrderDate="2002-05-01T00:00:00" />
</Customer>
<Customer CustomerID="2">
   <OrderDetail SalesOrderID="46976" OrderDate="2002-08-01T00:00:00" />
   <OrderDetail SalesOrderID="47997" OrderDate="2002-11-01T00:00:00" />
   <OrderDetail SalesOrderID="49054" OrderDate="2003-02-01T00:00:00" />
   <OrderDetail SalesOrderID="50216" OrderDate="2003-05-01T00:00:00" />
   <OrderDetail SalesOrderID="51728" OrderDate="2003-08-01T00:00:00" />
   <OrderDetail SalesOrderID="57044" OrderDate="2003-11-01T00:00:00" />
   <OrderDetail SalesOrderID="63198" OrderDate="2004-02-01T00:00:00" />
   <OrderDetail SalesOrderID="69488" OrderDate="2004-05-01T00:00:00" />
</Customer>
```

You can use *FOR XML, TYPE* in any valid SQL expression. The next example uses the *FOR XML, TYPE* syntax as an expression in the *SELECT* statement.

```
USE AdventureWorks
GO

SELECT
    CustomerID,
    (SELECT SalesOrderID,
                TotalDue,
                OrderDate,
                ShipDate
    FROM Sales.SalesOrderHeader AS OrderHeader
    WHERE CustomerID = Customer.CustomerID
    FOR XML AUTO, TYPE) AS OrderHeaders
FROM Sales.Customer AS Customer
WHERE CustomerID IN (1, 2)
FOR XML AUTO
```

The results are shown here:

```
1 <OrderHeader SalesOrderID="43860" TotalDue="14603.7393" OrderDate="2001-08-
01T00:00:00" ShipDate="2001-08-08T00:00:00" />
<OrderHeader SalesOrderID="44501" TotalDue="26128.8674" OrderDate="2001-11-
01T00:00:00" ShipDate="2001-11-08T00:00:00" />
<OrderHeader SalesOrderID="45283" TotalDue="37643.1378" OrderDate="2002-02-
01T00:00:00" ShipDate="2002-02-08T00:00:00" />
<OrderHeader SalesOrderID="46042" TotalDue="34722.9906" OrderDate="2002-05-
01T00:00:00" ShipDate="2002-05-08T00:00:00" />
2 <OrderHeader SalesOrderID="46976" TotalDue="10184.0774" OrderDate="2002-08-
01T00:00:00" ShipDate="2002-08-08T00:00:00" />
<OrderHeader SalesOrderID="47997" TotalDue="5469.5941" OrderDate="2002-11-
01T00:00:00" ShipDate="2002-11-08T00:00:00" />
<OrderHeader SalesOrderID="49054" TotalDue="1739.4078" OrderDate="2003-02-
01T00:00:00" ShipDate="2003-02-08T00:00:00" />
<OrderHeader SalesOrderID="50216" TotalDue="1935.5166" OrderDate="2003-05-
01T00:00:00" ShipDate="2003-05-08T00:00:00" />
<OrderHeader SalesOrderID="51728" TotalDue="3905.2547" OrderDate="2003-08-
01T00:00:00" ShipDate="2003-08-08T00:00:00" />
<OrderHeader SalesOrderID="57044" TotalDue="4537.8484" OrderDate="2003-11-
01T00:00:00" ShipDate="2003-11-08T00:00:00" />
<OrderHeader SalesOrderID="63198" TotalDue="4053.9506" OrderDate="2004-02-
01T00:00:00" ShipDate="2004-02-08T00:00:00" />
<OrderHeader SalesOrderID="69488" TotalDue="908.3199" OrderDate="2004-05-
01T00:00:00" ShipDate="2004-05-08T00:00:00" />
```

FOR XML PATH

If you want to create element-based XML, you can use *FOR XML PATH* to specify column aliases that contain valid XPath expressions that will shape your XML output.

```
USE AdventureWorks
GO
--XML FOR PATH
SELECT TOP 2 --limits result rows for demo purposes
ContactID AS [@Contact_ID],
FirstName AS [ContactName/First],
LastName AS [ContactName/Last],
Phone AS [ContactPhone/Phone1]
FROM Person.Contact FOR XML PATH
```

The output looks like this:

```
<row Contact_ID="1">
  <ContactName>
    <First>Gustavo</First>
    <Last>Achong</Last>
  </ContactName>
  <ContactPhone>
    <Phone1>398-555-0132</Phone1>
  </ContactPhone>
</row>
```

```
<row Contact_ID="2">
  <ContactName>
    <First>Catherine</First>
    <Last>Abel</Last>
  </ContactName>
  <ContactPhone>
    <Phone1>747-555-0171</Phone1>
  </ContactPhone>
</row>
```

Now let's revisit the last example shown in Listing 4-3: *FOR XML EXPLICIT*. Using the *TYPE* option in conjunction with *FOR XML PATH*, you can reproduce that awful and complex query with a much simpler version, as shown here:

```
USE AdventureWorks
GO

SELECT
    CustomerID AS [@CustomerID],
    (SELECT SalesOrderID AS [@SalesOrderID],
            TotalDue AS [@TotalDue],
            OrderDate,
            ShipDate,
            (SELECT ProductID AS [@ProductID],
                    OrderQty AS [@OrderQty],
                    LineTotal AS [@LineTotal]
             FROM Sales.SalesOrderDetail
             WHERE SalesOrderID = OrderHeader.SalesOrderID
             FOR XML PATH('OrderDetail'), TYPE)
     FROM Sales.SalesOrderHeader AS OrderHeader
     WHERE CustomerID = Customer.CustomerID
     FOR XML PATH('OrderHeader'), TYPE)
FROM Sales.Customer AS Customer
WHERE CustomerID IN (1, 2)
FOR XML PATH ('Customer')
```

Isn't that much better? This query uses a subselect using the *XML PATH* statement in conjunction with *TYPE* to produce element-based XML nested inside a much larger *FOR XML PATH* statement. This returns each separate Order for the customer as a new child node of the Customer ID node; you can see this in the results of the following query:

```
<Customer CustomerID="1">
  <OrderHeader SalesOrderID="43860" TotalDue="14603.7393">
    <OrderDate>2001-08-01T00:00:00</OrderDate>
    <ShipDate>2001-08-08T00:00:00</ShipDate>
    <OrderDetail ProductID="761" OrderQty="2" LineTotal="838.917800" />
    <OrderDetail ProductID="770" OrderQty="1" LineTotal="419.458900" />
More…
  </OrderHeader>
  <OrderHeader SalesOrderID="44501" TotalDue="26128.8674">
    <OrderDate>2001-11-01T00:00:00</OrderDate>
```

```
            <ShipDate>2001-11-08T00:00:00</ShipDate>
            <OrderDetail ProductID="761" OrderQty="1" LineTotal="419.458900" />
            <OrderDetail ProductID="768" OrderQty="3" LineTotal="1258.376700" />
More...
         </OrderHeader>
         <OrderHeader SalesOrderID="45283" TotalDue="37643.1378">
            <OrderDate>2002-02-01T00:00:00</OrderDate>
            <ShipDate>2002-02-08T00:00:00</ShipDate>
            <OrderDetail ProductID="759" OrderQty="1" LineTotal="419.458900" />
            <OrderDetail ProductID="758" OrderQty="3" LineTotal="2624.382000" />
            <OrderDetail ProductID="750" OrderQty="2" LineTotal="4293.924000" />
More...
         </OrderHeader>
         <OrderHeader SalesOrderID="46042" TotalDue="34722.9906">
            <OrderDate>2002-05-01T00:00:00</OrderDate>
            <ShipDate>2002-05-08T00:00:00</ShipDate>
            <OrderDetail ProductID="763" OrderQty="2" LineTotal="838.917800" />
            <OrderDetail ProductID="757" OrderQty="4" LineTotal="3499.176000" />
More...
         </OrderHeader>
      </Customer>
More...
```

If you are familiar and comfortable with XPath, you might like some additional *XML PATH* features. You can use the following XPath node test functions to further control the shape of your XML output:

- *data*

- *comment*

- *node*

- *text*

- *processing-instruction*

The following example uses the *data* and *comment* methods of XPath. The *data* method takes the results of the underlying query and places them all inside one element. The *comment* method takes data and transforms it into an XML comment, as shown in this example:

```
SELECT
    Customer.CustomerID AS [@CustomerID],
    Contact.FirstName + ' ' + Contact.LastName AS [comment()],
    (SELECT SalesOrderID AS [@SalesOrderID],
        TotalDue AS [@TotalDue],
        OrderDate,
        ShipDate,
        (SELECT ProductID AS [data()]
        FROM Sales.SalesOrderDetail
        WHERE SalesOrderID = OrderHeader.SalesOrderID
        FOR XML PATH('')) AS [ProductIDs]
    FROM Sales.SalesOrderHeader AS OrderHeader
```

```
      WHERE CustomerID = Customer.CustomerID
      FOR XML PATH('OrderHeader'), TYPE)
  FROM Sales.Customer AS Customer
  INNER JOIN Sales.Individual AS Individual
      ON Customer.CustomerID = Individual.CustomerID
  INNER JOIN Person.Contact AS Contact
      ON Contact.ContactID = Individual.ContactID
  WHERE Customer.CustomerID IN (11000, 11001)
  FOR XML PATH ('Customer')
```

The results are as follows; as you can see, the concatenated contact name becomes an XML comment, and the subquery of Product IDs is transformed into one element:

```
<Customer CustomerID="11000">
  <!--Jon Yang-->
  <OrderHeader SalesOrderID="43793" TotalDue="3756.9890">
    <OrderDate>2001-07-22T00:00:00</OrderDate>
    <ShipDate>2001-07-29T00:00:00</ShipDate>
    <ProductIDs> 966 934 923 707 881</ProductIDs>
  </OrderHeader>
More...
</Customer>
<Customer CustomerID="11001">
  <!--Eugene Huang-->
  <OrderHeader SalesOrderID="43767" TotalDue="3729.3640">
    <OrderDate>2001-07-18T00:00:00</OrderDate>
    <ShipDate>2001-07-25T00:00:00</ShipDate>
    <ProductIDs> 779 878 870 871 884 712</ProductIDs>
  </OrderHeader>
More...
</Customer>
```

Specifying a *ROOT* Element

The *ROOT* option allows you to add a main, or root, element to your *FOR XML* output. You can combine this with other *FOR XML* keywords, as shown here:

```
USE AdventureWorks
GO
--Root
SELECT Customer.CustomerID,
    OrderDetail.SalesOrderID, OrderDetail.OrderDate
FROM Sales.Customer AS Customer
INNER JOIN Sales.SalesOrderHeader OrderDetail
       ON OrderDetail.customerid=Customer.customerid
WHERE Customer.CustomerID<20
ORDER BY Customer.CustomerID
FOR XML AUTO, ROOT ('Orders')
```

The output looks like this:

```
<Orders>
  <Customer CustomerID="1">
    <OrderDetail SalesOrderID="43860" OrderDate="2001-08-01T00:00:00" />
```

```
      <OrderDetail SalesOrderID="44501" OrderDate="2001-11-01T00:00:00" />
      <OrderDetail SalesOrderID="45283" OrderDate="2002-02-01T00:00:00" />
      <OrderDetail SalesOrderID="46042" OrderDate="2002-05-01T00:00:00" />
   </Customer>
...more...
</Orders>
```

The code output here is the same as any *FOR XML AUTO* output for this query, except that the *XML ROOT* we specified with the *ROOT* keyword now surrounds the data. In this example, we used *ROOT ('Orders')*, so our output is surrounded with an *<Orders>* XML element.

Producing an Inline XSD Schema

As mentioned earlier, XML Schema Definition (XSD) provides an enforceable structure for your XML data. When you export data using the *FOR XML* syntax, you might want to include an inline XML schema for the recipient so that the recipient can enforce the rules on her end as well. Internet Explorer is an example of a recipient that enforces an XML schema if one is provided. When you use the *RAW* and *AUTO* modes, you can produce an inline XSD Schema as part of the output, as shown here:

```
USE AdventureWorks
GO
SELECT Customer.CustomerID,
    OrderDetail.SalesOrderID, OrderDetail.OrderDate
FROM Sales.Customer AS Customer
INNER JOIN Sales.SalesOrderHeader AS OrderDetail
    ON OrderDetail.CustomerID = Customer.CustomerID
WHERE Customer.CustomerID < 20
ORDER BY Customer.CustomerID
FOR XML AUTO, XMLSCHEMA
```

The output looks like this:

```
<xsd:schema targetNamespace="urn:schemas-microsoft-
com:sql:SqlRowSet1" xmlns:schema="urn:schemas-microsoft-
com:sql:SqlRowSet1" xmlns:xsd="http://www.w3.org/2001/XMLSchema" xmlns:sqltypes="http://
schemas.microsoft.com/sqlserver/2004/sqltypes" elementFormDefault="qualified">
  <xsd:import namespace="http://schemas.microsoft.com/sqlserver/2004/
sqltypes" schemaLocation="http://schemas.microsoft.com/sqlserver/2004/sqltypes/
sqltypes.xsd" />
  <xsd:element name="Customer">
    <xsd:complexType>
      <xsd:sequence>
        <xsd:element ref="schema:OrderDetail" minOccurs="0" maxOccurs="unbounded" />
      </xsd:sequence>
      <xsd:attribute name="CustomerID" type="sqltypes:int" use="required" />
    </xsd:complexType>
  </xsd:element>
  <xsd:element name="OrderDetail">
    <xsd:complexType>
      <xsd:attribute name="SalesOrderID" type="sqltypes:int" use="required" />
```

```
        <xsd:attribute name="OrderDate" type="sqltypes:datetime" use="required" />
      </xsd:complexType>
    </xsd:element>
  </xsd:schema>
  <Customer xmlns="urn:schemas-microsoft-com:sql:SqlRowSet1" CustomerID="1">
    <OrderDetail SalesOrderID="43860" OrderDate="2001-08-01T00:00:00" />
    <OrderDetail SalesOrderID="44501" OrderDate="2001-11-01T00:00:00" />
    <OrderDetail SalesOrderID="45283" OrderDate="2002-02-01T00:00:00" />
    <OrderDetail SalesOrderID="46042" OrderDate="2002-05-01T00:00:00" />
  </Customer>
```

SQL Server infers the schema based on the underlying data types of the result set. For example, the SalesOrderID field is set to an *int* and is a required field (as per the inline Schema based on the properties of the field in the underlying SQL table).

Producing Element-Based XML

Many developers prefer element-based XML over attribute-based XML. Element-based XML presents its data as individual elements, as opposed to individual attributes, for each data point. A welcome enhancement to *RAW* and *AUTO* is the ability to specify element-based XML as a result by using the *ELEMENTS* keyword:

```
Select Customer.CustomerID, OrderDetail.SalesOrderID,OrderDetail.OrderDate
From Sales.Customer Customer
inner join Sales.SalesOrderHeader OrderDetail
      on OrderDetail.customerid=Customer.customerid
where Customer.CustomerID=1
Order by Customer.CustomerID
For XML AUTO, ELEMENTS
```

The results look like this:

```
<Customer>
  <CustomerID>1</CustomerID>
  <OrderDetail>
    <SalesOrderID>43860</SalesOrderID>
    <OrderDate>2001-08-01T00:00:00</OrderDate>
  </OrderDetail>
  <OrderDetail>
    <SalesOrderID>44501</SalesOrderID>
    <OrderDate>2001-11-01T00:00:00</OrderDate>
  </OrderDetail>
  <OrderDetail>
    <SalesOrderID>45283</SalesOrderID>
    <OrderDate>2002-02-01T00:00:00</OrderDate>
  </OrderDetail>
  <OrderDetail>
    <SalesOrderID>46042</SalesOrderID>
    <OrderDate>2002-05-01T00:00:00</OrderDate>
  </OrderDetail>
</Customer>
```

As you can see, each column of the query becomes an element in the resulting XML, as opposed to an attribute of one row.

The *ELEMENTS* keyword used in conjunction with the *FOR XML* statement converts each column from your result set to an individual XML element; using *AUTO*, it also converts each row from a joined table to a new XML element. Note that element-based XML is more verbose than attribute-based XML but is usually easier to view and work with.

OPENXML Enhancements in SQL Server 2005

Up until now, we have been composing XML from rows of data, but what if we already have XML data and we want to shred it back into relational data? Well, SQL Server 2000 introduced a feature for this purpose called *OPENXML*. *OPENXML* is a system function that allows an XML document to be shredded into T-SQL rows. SQL Server 2005 also has the *OPENXML* function—with some enhancements, of course.

To shred data into relational rows using *OPENXML*, you must first create an XML document handle using the system stored procedure *sp_xml_preparedocument*. This system stored procedure takes an XML document and creates a representation that is referenced via a handle, which it returns via an *OUTPUT* parameter. *OPENXML* uses this handle along with a specified path and behaves like a database view to the XML data, so you simply choose *SELECT* from the *OPENXML* function just as you would *SELECT* from a table or a view. The following code shows an example of *OPENXML* in action.

```
USE AdventureWorks

DECLARE @int int
DECLARE @xmlORDER varchar(1000)
SET @xmlORDER ='
<ROOT>
<Customer CustomerID="BRU" ContactName="Andrew Brust">
   <Order CustomerID="BRU" EmployeeID="5" OrderDate="2005-11-04">
      <OrderDetail OrderID="10248" ProductID="16" Quantity="12"/>
      <OrderDetail OrderID="10248" ProductID="32" Quantity="10"/>
   </Order>
</Customer>
<Customer CustomerID="ZAC" ContactName="Bill Zack">
   <Order CustomerID="ZAC" EmployeeID="3" OrderDate="2005-11-16">
      <OrderDetail OrderID="10283" ProductID="99" Quantity="3"/>
   </Order>
</Customer>
</ROOT>'
--Create an internal representation of the XML doc
EXEC sp_xml_preparedocument @int OUTPUT, @xmlORDER
-- OPENXML rowset provider.
SELECT    *
FROM OPENXML (@int, '/ROOT/Customer',1)
WITH (CustomerID  varchar(10),ContactName varchar(20))
```

The code here takes the XML text and allows you to query and work with it as if it were relational data. The output looks like this:

```
CustomerID      ContactName
---------------------------
BRU             Andrew Brust
ZAC             Bill Zack
(2 row(s) affected)
```

You can optionally specify if you want *OPENXML* to use element-based or attribute-based XML relational mapping between the rowset columns and the XML nodes. There are two ways to control the mapping. The first is to use the *flags* parameter, which assumes that the XML nodes will map to corresponding rowset columns with exactly the same name. You can also use the *ColPattern* parameter, an XPath expression that allows you to use a schema to perform the mapping as part of *SchemaDeclaration* in the *WITH* clause. The mapping specified in *ColPattern* overwrites the mapping specified by the *flags* parameter.

SQL Server 2005 introduces two enhancements to *OPENXML*, both involving the new XML data type. First, the *XML* data type is supported as an output column or an overflow column with the *OPENXML* statement. Second, you can pass an *XML* data type variable directly into *sp_xml_preparedocument*. Both of these enhancements enable you to more easily work with existing XML data in an XML column or created data using *FOR XML TYPE*.

XML Bulk Load

SQL Server 2000 XML Bulk Load allows users to load large XML documents on the client side. It works by reading the XML and producing SQL *INSERT* statements that run on the client in batch. SQL Server 2005 greatly enhances XML Bulk Load by allowing it to run on the server as well as to load directly into an *XML* data type column.

Using the new XML Bulk Load requires using the system rowset provider function *OPENROWSET* and specifying the *BULK* provider:

```
Use AdventureWorks
--create a table with an xml column
create table tblxmlcustomers
(customer_id int primary key identity,
    customer_xml xml not null)

--this file will load 1 record in (SINGLE_CLOB)
--for more records use a format file
insert into tblxmlcustomers
Select * from OPENROWSET
(Bulk 'C:\customer_01.xml',
    SINGLE_CLOB) as xmldata
```

This example works by first creating a table that has an XML column and a primary key value. Then we use an *INSERT* statement that selects all of the data from the XML file using *OPEN-ROWSET. OPENROWSET* uses the *BULK* provider and loads into the XML column of the tblxmlcustomers table the entire contents of the customer_01.xml file.

Querying XML Data Using XQuery

Storing XML in the database is one thing; querying it efficiently is another. With SQL Server 2000, which has no *XML* data type, you have to deconstruct the XML and move element and attribute data into relational columns to perform a query on the XML data residing in the text column, or else you must use some other searching mechanism, such as full-text search.

XQuery Defined

XQuery is a language used to query and process XML data. It is a W3C standard whose specification is located at *http://www.w3.org/TR/xquery/*. The XQuery specification contains several descriptions of requirements, use cases, and data models. We encourage you to go to the specification and read "XQuery 1.0, an XML Query Language" and "XQuery 1.0 and XPath 2.0 Functions and Operators" to get a full understanding of what XQuery is all about. However, we will explain enough here for you to get the basics done. After reading this section, you will be able to select, filter, and update XML data using XQuery.

Understanding XQuery Expressions and XPath

The first thing to remember is that XQuery is an XML language, so all the rules of XML apply: It is case sensitive and its keywords are all in lowercase. While XQuery has some powerful formatting and processing commands, it is primarily a query language (as its name suggests), so we will focus on writing queries. The body of a query consists of two parts: an XPath expression and a *FLWOR* expression. Let's start by discussing XPath expressions.

XPath 2.0   XPath, another W3C standard (*http://www.w3.org/TR/xpath*), uses path expressions to identify specific nodes in an XML document. These path expressions are similar to the syntax you see when you work with a computer file system (for example, c:\folder\myfile.doc). Take a look at the following XML document:

```
<catalog>
  <book category="ITPro">
    <title>Windows Step By Step</title>
    <author>Bill Zack</author>
    <price>49.99</price>
  </book>
  <book category="Developer">
    <title>Developing ADO .NET</title>
    <author>Andrew Brust</author>
    <price>39.93</price>
  </book>
```

```
   <book category="ITPro">
     <title>Windows Cluster Server</title>
     <author>Stephen Forte</author>
     <price>59.99</price>
   </book>
 </catalog>
```

The following XPath expression selects the root element catalog:

```
/catalog
```

The following XPath expression selects all the book elements of the catalog root element:

```
/catalog/book
```

And this XPath expression selects all the author elements of all the book elements of the catalog root element:

```
/catalog/book/author
```

One additional note: If the path starts with a slash (/), it represents an absolute path to an element. To sum up, XPath enables you to specify a subset of data within the XML (via its location within the XML structure) with which you want to work. Using XPath gets you to the data you want to process, and it is essentially a very basic form of querying against XML data because it allows you to select a subset of data. XQuery is more robust and allows you to perform more complex queries against the XML data via *FLOWR* expressions.

Selection Logic: *FLWOR* Expressions   Just as *SELECT, FROM, WHERE, GROUP BY,* and *ORDER BY* form the basis of SQL's selection logic, the *for, let, where, order by,* and *return* (*FLWOR*) keywords form the basis of every XQuery query you write. You use the *for* and *let* keywords to assign variables and iterate through the data within the context of the XQuery. (The *let* keyword is not supported in the SQL Server 2005 implementation of XQuery.) The *where* keyword works as a restriction and outputs the value of the variable. For example, the following basic XQuery uses the XPath expression */catalog/book* to obtain a reference to all the <book> nodes, and the *for* keyword initiates a loop, but only of elements where the *category* attribute is equal to "*ITPro*". This simple code snippet iterates through each /catalog/ book node using the *$b* variable with the *for* statement only where the category attribute is "*ITPro*" and returns as output the resulting information ordered by the author's name using the *order* keyword.

```
for $b in /catalog/book
where $b/@category="ITPro"
   order by $b/author[1] descending
   return ($b)
```

Armed with this basic knowledge of XQuery expressions, you are ready to see it in action. Here is a simple example that uses this XQuery expression on an *XML* data type variable. We assign the XML to the variable and then use the preceding XQuery expression in the *query()* method (explained in the next section) of the *XML* data type.

```
DECLARE @XML xml
Set @XML='<catalog>
  <book category="ITPro">
    <title>Windows Step By Step</title>
    <author>Bill Zack</author>
    <price>49.99</price>
  </book>
  <book category="Developer">
    <title>Developing ADO .NET</title>
    <author>Andrew Brust</author>
    <price>39.93</price>
  </book>
  <book category="ITPro">
    <title>Windows Cluster Server</title>
    <author>Stephen Forte</author>
    <price>59.99</price>
  </book>
</catalog>
'
Select @XML.query('for $b in /catalog/book
  where $b/@category="ITPro"
  order by $b/author[1] descending
  return ($b)')
```

The results are as follows. Notice that Stephen's record is first because our order is descending by the author element. Andrew's record is not in the output because we are restricting only for "*ITPro*" in the category element.

```
<book category="ITPro">
  <title>Windows Cluster Server</title>
  <author>Stephen Forte</author>
  <price>59.99</price>
</book>
<book category="ITPro">
  <title>Windows Step By Step</title>
  <author>Bill Zack</author>
  <price>49.99</price>
</book>
```

Now that you have seen the basics, let's look at using XQuery with our SQL Server data.

SQL Server 2005 XQuery in Action

SQL Server 2005 has a standards-based implementation of XQuery that directly supports XQuery functions on the *XML* data type. It supports XQuery by using five methods of the *XML* data type:

- **xml.exist()**   Uses XQuery input to return 0, 1, or NULL, depending on the result of the query. It returns 0 if no elements match, 1 if there is a match, and NULL if there is no XML data on which to query. This method is often used for query predicates.

- **xml.value()**   Accepts an XQuery as input and returns an SQL Server scalar type.

- **xml.query()**   Accepts an XQuery as input and returns an *XML* data type stream as output.

- **xml.nodes()**   Accepts an XQuery as input and returns a single-column rowset from the XML document. In essence, it shreds XML into multiple smaller XML results.

- **xml.modify()**   Allows you to insert, delete, or modify nodes or sequences of nodes in an *XML* data type instance using XQuery Data Manipulation Language.

We will discuss the methods of the *XML* data type shortly. But first we must create some sample data. We will create a simple table that contains speakers at a software developers conference and the corresponding classes they will teach. Usually you normalize the data and have a one-to-many relationship between a speakers table and the classes table. Instead of using an additional normalized table, we will model this as one table with the speaker's information and one XML column with the speaker's classes. In the real world, you might encounter this scenario when in a back-office database you have the speaker and his classes represented in a series of one-to-many tables. Then for the Web database, you might "publish" a database on a frequent time interval (like a reporting database) or transform normalized data and use the XML column for easy HTML display (or XSLT transformations).

We first create an XSD schema (for reasons that will soon become clear) for our XML column. This schema will define the type of XML allowed in the column, including the *XML* data types and required properties for particular XML elements:

```
use AdventureWorks
go

CREATE xml schema collection dbo.classes_xsd
As
 '<?xml version="1.0" encoding="UTF-8" ?>
  <xs:schema xmlns:xs="http://www.w3.org/2001/XMLSchema">
  <xs:element name="class">
  <xs:complexType>
  <xs:attribute name="name" type="xs:string" use="required" />
  </xs:complexType>
  </xs:element>
```

```
<xs:element name="classes">
<xs:complexType>
<xs:sequence>
<xs:element ref="class" maxOccurs="unbounded" />
</xs:sequence>
</xs:complexType>
</xs:element>
</xs:schema>'
```

Next we create our table, tblSpeakers. Notice that the XML column, Speaker_XML, uses the *classes_xsd* XSD schema described earlier.

```
Create Table tblSpeakers
(
Speaker_ID Integer Primary Key Identity,
Speaker_NM nVarChar(50),
Speaker_Country nVarChar(25),
Speaker_XML XML (classes_xsd) Not Null)
```

XQuery runs more efficiently when there is an XML index on the XML column. As you learned earlier, an XML index works only if there is a primary key constraint on the table (which we have). The code here creates a primary and then a structural (*PATH*) index because our examples do a lot of *where* restrictions on the values of particular elements.

```
--XML Index: Primary
CREATE Primary XML INDEX idx_1
   ON tblSpeakers (Speaker_XML)
--PATH
CREATE XML INDEX idx_a
   ON tblSpeakers (Speaker_XML)
USING XML INDEX idx_1 FOR PATH
```

Now that we have our index, remember that XQuery works more efficiently if it is strongly typed, so you should always use an XSD schema on your XML column for the best performance. Without an XSD schema, the SQL Server 2005 XQuery engine assumes that everything is untyped and treats it as string data.

Lastly, we need to get some data into the table by using some T-SQL *INSERT* statements. The last *INSERT*, 'Bad Speaker', will fail because it violates the *classes_xsd* schema and does not contain a *<classes>* element:

```
Insert into tblSpeakers Values('Stephen Forte', 'USA',
'
<classes>
   <class name="Writing Secure Code for ASP .NET "/>
   <class name="Using XQuery to Query and Manipulate XML Data in SQL Server 2005"/>
   <class name="SQL Server and Oracle Working Together"/>
```

```
      <class name="Protecting against SQL Injection Attacks "/>
      </classes>
'
)

Insert into tblSpeakers Values('Richard Campbell', 'Canada',
'
<classes>
   <class name="SQL Server Profiler"/>
   <class name="Advanced SQL Querying Techniques"/>
   <class name="SQL Server and Oracle Working Together"/>
   <class name="T-SQL Error Handling in Yukon"/>
</classes>
'
)

Insert into tblSpeakers Values('Tim Huckaby', 'USA',
'
<classes>
   <class name="Smart Client Stuff"/>
   <class name="More Smart Client Stuff"/>
</classes>
'
)

Insert into tblSpeakers Values('Malek Kemmou', 'Morocco',
'
<classes>
   <class name="SmartPhone 2005"/>
   <class name="Office System 2003"/>
</classes>
'
)

Insert into tblSpeakers Values('Goksin Bakir', 'Turkey',
'
<classes>
   <class name="SmartPhone 2005"/>
   <class name="Office System 2003"/>
</classes>
'
)

Insert into tblSpeakers Values('Clemens F. Vasters', 'Germany',
'
<classes>
   <class name="SOA"/>
   <class name="FABRIQ"/>
</classes>
'
)

Insert into tblSpeakers Values('Kimberly L. Tripp', 'USA',
'
```

```
<classes>
    <class name="SQL Server Index"/>
    <class name="SQL Precon"/>
</classes>
'
)

Insert into tblSpeakers Values('Bad Speaker', 'France',
'
<CLASSES>
    <class name="SQL Server Index"/>
    <class name="SQL Precon"/>
</CLASSES>
'
)
```

Now that we have our data, it is time to start writing some XQuery expressions in SQL Server 2005. To do this, we will use the aforementioned methods of the *XML* data type inside a regular T-SQL query.

xml.exist()

Having XML in the database is almost useless unless you can query the elements and attributes of the XML data natively. XQuery becomes very useful when you can use it to search based on the values of a particular element or attribute. The *xml.exist()* function accepts an XQuery as input and returns 0, 1, or NULL, depending on the result of the query; 0 is returned if no elements match, 1 is returned if there is a match, and NULL is returned if there is no data to query on. For example, we will see if a node exists in this particular XML string of classes.

```
DECLARE @XML xml
Set @XML='
<classes>
    <class name="SQL Server Index"/>
    <class name="SQL Precon"/>
</classes>
'
Select @XML.exist('/classes')
```

The code returns 1 because the "classes" element exists in the XML variable. If you change the XQuery expression to search for an XML node that does not exist (*Select @XML.exist ('/dogs)*, for example), it will return 0. You can see this in action as part of a *CHECK CON-STRAINT*. SQL Server does not allow you to use an *xml.exist* as part of a *CHECK CON-STRAINT*. You have to first create a user-defined function (UDF) to perform the action.

This UDF accepts an XML field and returns the value of an *xml.exist()* method looking for an instance of *<Orders>*:

```
USE AdventureWorks
GO
CREATE FUNCTION dbo.DoesOrderXMLDataExist
(@XML XML)
RETURNS bit
AS
BEGIN
RETURN @XML.exist('/Orders')
END;
GO
```

To use this UDF as a *CHECK CONSTRAINT*, just create a table and pass to the UDF you just created the column you want to apply the constraint to.

```
--create the table using the function
CREATE TABLE OrdersXMLCheck
    (OrderDocID INT PRIMARY KEY,
    xOrders XML NOT NULL Default '<Orders/>'
 CONSTRAINT xml_orderconstraint
  CHECK(dbo.DoesOrderXMLDataExist(xOrders)=1))
```

You will most likely use the return value of *xml.exist()* (0, 1, or NULL) as part of a T-SQL *WHERE* clause. Think about it: You can run a T-SQL query and restrict the query on a value of a particular XML element! Going back to our main example, let's look for the value of *'SQL Server and Oracle Working Together'* in the *<class>* element. Here is the XQuery expression to do this:

```
/classes/class[@name="SQL Server and Oracle Working Together"]
```

This is how you put it to work:

```
Select * From tblSpeakers
Where Speaker_XML.exist('/classes/
class[@name="SQL Server and Oracle Working Together"]')=1
```

The results look like this:

```
1   Stephen Forte   USA      < classes>data</classes>
2   Richard Campbell Canada   <classes/>data</classes>
```

The XML returned in these results look like this for Stephen:

```
<classes>
  <class name="Writing Secure Code for ASP .NET " />
  <class name="Using XQuery to Query and Manipulate XML Data in SQL Server 2005" />
  <class name="SQL Server and Oracle Working Together" />
  <class name="Protecting against SQL Injection Attacks " />
</classes>
```

xml.value()

The *xml.value()* function takes a valid XQuery expression and returns an SQL Server scalar value that you specify. For example, let's say you have an XML column and inside of a T-SQL query you want to return some data from the XML as an intrinsic SQL data type. You call the *xml.value()* function on that column by passing in the XQuery expression and the data type you want to convert the output to. This requires you to know and understand the data in your XML column. Here's an example of the syntax against our current XML document in the database:

```
xml.value('/classes[1]/class[1]/@name', 'varchar(40)')
```

This XQuery contains an XPath expression that navigates the first class's name attribute and a cast to *varchar(40)*.

You must perform an XQuery expression on an XML column as part of a regular T-SQL query, as shown here. What is cool is that SQL Server combines both relational queries and XQuery in one query because in this example we use a traditional T-SQL *WHERE* clause to show only speakers from the USA.

```
USE AdventureWorks
select Speaker_ID, Speaker_NM,
Speaker_Country,
    Speaker_XML.value('/classes[1]/class[1]/@name', 'varchar(40)') as Sessions
From tblSpeakers
where speaker_country ='USA'
```

The results are shown here:

```
Speaker_ID     Speaker_NM        Speaker_Country     Session
-----------------------------------------------------------------------------------
1              Stephen Forte     USA                 Writing Secure Code for ASP .NET
3              Tim Davis         USA                 Smart Client Stuff
7              Kimberly Smith    USA                 SQL Server Index

(3 row(s) affected)
```

Let's dissect the XQuery expression. As you'll recall from our earlier listing, the XML for Stephen looks like this:

```
<classes>
    <class name="Writing Secure Code for ASP .NET "/>
    <class name="Using XQuery to Query and Manipulate XML Data in SQL Server 2005"/>
    <class name="SQL Server and Oracle Working Together"/>
    <class name="Protecting against SQL Injection Attacks "/>
</classes>
```

The following XQuery path expression returns the value of the first class's name attribute (*Writing Secure Code for ASP.NET*) as a *varchar(40)*. So in the preceding query, the XQuery expression is placed in the *value()* method of the XML column (Speaker_XML in our T-SQL query). The following XQuery expression does all the work of getting the first class's name:

```
/classes[1]/class[1]/@name
```

This approach is useful when you want to pull standard data out of the XML column and display it as regular scalar SQL Server data.

xml.query()

The *xml.query()* function works much like the *xml.value()* function, except it returns an *XML* data type value, so you have a lot more flexibility. It is useful only if you want the end result of the column in the query to be XML; if you want scalar data, use *xml.value()*.

If you want to return the same data as in the previous example, but you want to present the summary column in XML format, run the exact same query except with the *xml.query()*:

```
--xml.query
--returns XML data type
--same as previous example but returns XML
select Speaker_ID, Speaker_NM,
Speaker_Country,
    Speaker_XML.query('/classes[1]/class[1]') as Sessions
From tblSpeakers
where speaker_country ='USA'
```

XML.query() works by passing in an XQuery expression that will result in XML output. The XQuery expression can return a single element, all the elements, or use a *RETURN* (the R in *FLOWR*) expression to completely transform the results. In this example, the first instance of the class element is returned. The results of the "sessions" column for Stephen's records are the same as in the previous example except that the Sessions column is now formatted in XML:

```
<class name="Writing Secure Code for ASP .NET " />
```

Instead of using *xml.value()*, you can return a larger XML result of many nodes by leaving out the *[1]* ordinal position indicators in your path expression.

```
--same as previous but returns all
select Speaker_ID, Speaker_NM,
Speaker_Country,
    Speaker_XML.query('/classes/class') as Sessions
From tblSpeakers
where speaker_country ='USA'
```

The results are the same except for Stephen's classes; we get all of the XML results as an XML column:

```
<class name="Writing Secure Code for ASP .NET " />
<class name="Using XQuery to Query and Manipulate XML Data in SQL Server 2005" />
<class name="SQL Server and Oracle Working Together" />
<class name="Protecting Against SQL Injection Attacks" />
```

You can gain further control over your XQuery path expression by using the *FLOWR* expressions. For example, you can write an expression like this:

```
for $b in /classes/class
return ($b)
```

The expression uses the *for* and *return* keywords to loop through all of the class elements and return the values, and it yields the same results as the preceding example, which has *'/classes/ class'* as its XQuery expression. (Of course, you can come up with much more interesting examples.) You can incorporate this expression into your T-SQL query:

```
Select Speaker_ID, Speaker_NM, Speaker_Country, Speaker_XML.query('
    for $b in /classes/class
    return ($b)
    ') As Sessions
From tblSpeakers
```

Let's say you want to have more control over the XML output using *xml.query()* or *xml.value()* as well as combining the XQuery and a traditional T-SQL *WHERE* clause to show only the speakers in the United States. You can use an XML method in both the *SELECT* and *WHERE* clauses of a single query:

```
Select Speaker_ID, Speaker_NM, Speaker_Country, Speaker_XML.query('/classes/
class') As Sessions
From tblSpeakers
Where Speaker_Country='USA'
and Speaker_XML.exist('/classes/
class[@name="SQL Server and Oracle Working Together"]')=1
```

The T-SQL *WHERE* clause restricts on the Speaker_Country column, and our XQuery expression filters only for the *<class>* element we are interested in.

```
<class name="Writing Secure Code for ASP .NET " />
<class name="Using XQuery to Query and Manipulate XML Data in SQL Server 2005" />
<class name="SQL Server and Oracle Working Together" />
<class name="Protecting against SQL Injection Attacks " />
```

xml.nodes()

The *xml.nodes()* method takes an XQuery expression just like *exist()*, *value()*, and *query()*. *xml.nodes()* then returns instances of a special *XML* data type, each of which has its context set to a different node that the XQuery expression you supplied evaluates to. The special XML data type is used for subqueries of XML data in your result set.

SQL Server 2005 XQuery Extensions

Microsoft has made some extensions to the XQuery specification that are implemented in SQL Server 2005 to aid the developer in tasks such as referencing SQL data inside of your XQuery expression to XML DML statements.

Sql:column()

The *sql:column()* function, which is specific to SQL Server 2005 XQuery, allows the XQuery expression to refer to a column in the current row of the dataset. The syntax is *{sql:column("Column Name")}*, as shown here:

```
for $b in /classes/class
where $b/@name="SQL Server and Oracle Working Together"
return (<Sessions>{$b}<Speaker id="{sql:column("Speaker_ID")}">
   {sql:column("Speaker_NM")}</Speaker></Sessions>)
```

Bringing it all together, let's create an attribute called *Speaker id* with the value from the Speaker_ID column for the current row. The <Sessions> node is a node constructor, which means you can create a node as part of your *return* in your *for* expression:

```
Select Speaker_ID, Speaker_NM, Speaker_Country, Speaker_XML.query('
   for $b in /classes/class
   where $b/@name="SQL Server and Oracle Working Together"
   return (<Sessions>{$b}<Speaker id="{sql:column("Speaker_ID")}">
      {sql:column("Speaker_NM")}</Speaker></Sessions>)
   ') As Sessions
   From tblSpeakers
Where Speaker_XML.exist('/classes/
class[@name="SQL Server and Oracle Working Together"]')=1
```

In the XML result for Stephen's record, shown next, notice that our *xml.query* expression in our *SELECT* is in tune with our T-SQL XQuery *WHERE* clause, and we limit our results to show the same element as in our *WHERE* clause:

```
<Sessions>
  <class name="SQL Server and Oracle Working Together" />
  <Speaker id="1">Stephen Forte</Speaker>
</Sessions>
```

Sql:variable()

The *sql:variable()* function, which is unique to the SQL Server implementation of XQuery, works exactly like *sql:column()* but refers to a variable, not a value of a column in a row. You only have a single value for the current query.

```
Declare @Conf varchar(20)
Set @Conf= 'NYC .NET User Group'

Select Speaker_ID, Speaker_NM, Speaker_XML.query('
   for $b in /classes/class
   where $b/@name="SQL Server and Oracle Working Together"
      return (<Sessions
      conference="{sql:variable("@Conf")}">
      {$b}<Speaker id="{sql:column("Speaker_ID")}">
         {sql:column("Speaker_NM")}</Speaker></Sessions>)
   ') As Sessions
From tblSpeakers
Where  Speaker_XML.exist('/classes/
class[@name="SQL Server and Oracle Working Together"]')=1
```

The results look like this:

```
<Sessions conference="NYC .NET User Group">
  <class name="SQL Server and Oracle Working Together" />
  <Speaker id="1">Stephen Forte</Speaker>
</Sessions>
```

XML DML

The XQuery specification does not provide a way for you to modify data, as you would have with the *INSERT*, *UPDATE*, and *DELETE* keywords in T-SQL. The W3C has a working draft, but it might be a few years before it becomes a standard, so Microsoft has created its own XML data manipulation language, XML DML, which is included in its XQuery implementation. The Microsoft version conforms to the W3C working draft, but by no means do we know the final standard's look and feel.

XML DML gives you three ways to manipulate the XML data of a column via the *xml.modify()* function:

- **xml.modify(insert)** Allows you to insert a node or sequence of nodes into the *XML* data type instance you are working with

- *xml.modify(delete)* Allows you to delete zero or more nodes that are the result of the output sequence of the XQuery expression you specify
- *xml.modify(replace)* Modifies the value of a single node

xml.modify(insert)

The *xml.modify(insert)* function allows you to insert a node or sequence of nodes into the *XML* data type instance you are working with. You use the *xml.modify()* function in conjunction with a T-SQL *UPDATE* statement and, if necessary, a T-SQL or XQuery *where* clause (or both). You can also specify the keyword *first* or *last* beside an ordinal position.

```
--insert an XML node
Update tblSpeakers
Set Speaker_XML.modify(
'insert
<class name="Ranking and Windowing Functions in SQL Server 2005"/>
into /classes[1]'
)
Where Speaker_ID=1
```

xml.modify(delete)

The *xml.modify(delete)* function deletes zero or more nodes based on the criteria you specify. The following example deletes a specific node based on its ordinal position; you can also combine this with a T-SQL or XQuery *WHERE* clause.

```
Update tblSpeakers
Set Speaker_XML.modify('delete /classes/class[3]')
Where Speaker_ID=1
```

xml.modify(replace)

```
--modify a value
Update tblSpeakers
Set Speaker_XML.modify('
   replace value of
    /classes/class[3]
   to "Protecting against SQL Injection Attacks-Hackers must die"')
Where Speaker_ID=1
```

Converting a Column to XML

If you have existing text or *varchar()* columns in SQL Server 2000 that contain XML data, you're probably excited about using the *XML* data type and XQuery. Because you can use the T-SQL *CONVERT* and *CAST* functions to convert those columns into full-fledged XML data, you can write a simple upgrade script.

```
First we need a table. For this example, we'll create a simple table:
Create table tblXMLUpgradeTest
(Field_ID int Primary Key Identity,
 Field_XMLData nvarchar(4000))
```

Next we insert some data, but remember that it is stored as text, not XML.

```
--insert some data as txt but is XML
--remember no cool XQuery or anything allowed!
DECLARE @xmlData AS varchar(8000)
SET @xmlData = (Select Customer.CustomerID,
OrderDetail.SalesOrderID,OrderDetail.OrderDate
From Sales.Customer Customer
inner join Sales.SalesOrderHeader OrderDetail
   on OrderDetail.customerid=Customer.customerid
where Customer.CustomerID<5
Order by Customer.CustomerID
For XML AUTO, Root ('Orders'))
--first insert into the table
Insert Into tblXMLUpgradeTest (Field_XMLData) Values (@xmlData)
```

You can now convert your XML data from text to an XML column in a series of six steps:

1. In the table containing the text field holding the XML data, add a *varchar(8000)* or *text* field, depending on what your original column is.

2. Append the data in your current production text-based column into the new XML-based column.

3. Drop your text-based column.

4. Add the original column name back in, but with an *XML* data type.

5. Insert the data from the temporary column, using the *CONVERT* statement to convert the data to an *XML* data type.

6. Drop the temporary column.

   A code example of all six steps is shown here.

```
--first alter the table
ALTER TABLE tblXMLUpgradeTest ADD Field_XMLData_Temp varchar(8000)
go
--second update the Field_XMLData_Temp column
Update tblXMLUpgradeTest set Field_XMLData_Temp=Field_XMLData
go
--third drop the original text column (Field_XMLData)
ALTER TABLE tblXMLUpgradeTest Drop Column Field_XMLData
go
--fourth add the same column(Field_XMLData) but as XML
ALTER TABLE tblXMLUpgradeTest ADD Field_XMLData XML
```

```
go
--fifth insert the XML into Field_XMLData and convert to XML data type
Update tblXMLUpgradeTest set Field_XMLData=Convert(XML, Field_XMLData_Temp)
go
--sixth drop the Field_XMLData_Temp column since it has text, not XML
ALTER TABLE tblXMLUpgradeTest Drop Column Field_XMLData_Temp
go
```

Summary

We have taken a fairly extensive tour of the new *XML* data type and its data manipulation mechanisms, XQuery and XML DML. As you have seen, SQL Server 2005 provides a rich feature set of XML technologies. At times you will want to store XML in the database, and the new data type and query method allow you to work with XML natively—a vast improvement over SQL Sever 2000. Armed with this new data type and the ability to query it via XQuery, you can fully exploit the power of XML inside the database and build smart, XML-aware applications.

Chapter 5

Introducing SQL Server Management Studio

–Patrick O'Toole

In this chapter:

In Microsoft Visual Studio .NET, which was released in 2002, the integrated development environment (IDE) advanced to a new level. Now you'll find that same power, consistency, and integration in the Microsoft SQL Server management tools. SQL Server Management Studio, an entirely new application built on the Microsoft .NET platform, integrates the database programming and administration tasks that were previously carried out in Enterprise Manager and Query Analyzer into a powerful and flexible IDE with many new features. These features include:

- Fully customizable docking windows
- Integrated solution and project support
- Tabbed windows
- Extensive right-click shortcut menus
- Bookmarks
- Customizable toolbars
- Extensive template library and the ability to create custom templates
- Syntax highlighting
- Change tracking in edit windows
- GUI designers for all the common database objects
- Complete support for generating scripts for database objects

We'll start this chapter with an overview of the new Management Studio interface.

The New Management Studio Interface

Management Studio is installed as part of SQL Server 2005. To launch the application, click Start, point to All Programs, point to Microsoft SQL Server 2005, and then click SQL Server Management Studio. The first thing you'll notice is the totally revised interface. Anyone familiar with Visual Studio will feel right at home. If it's all new to you, you should find it powerful and easy to use; the tools you need are just a mouse click away.

Overview of New Features

Let's start with a quick tour of the interface. Figure 5-1 shows a customized version of the interface to highlight a few of the many new features. Most of the windows in Management Studio can be positioned anywhere on the screen, including being docked along the interface edge. Because windows must share space on the screen, multiple windows can share a frame with each window appearing as a tab within the frame. (See the Template Explorer and Properties tabs at the bottom of the image.) They can also be set to auto-hide when they don't have focus.

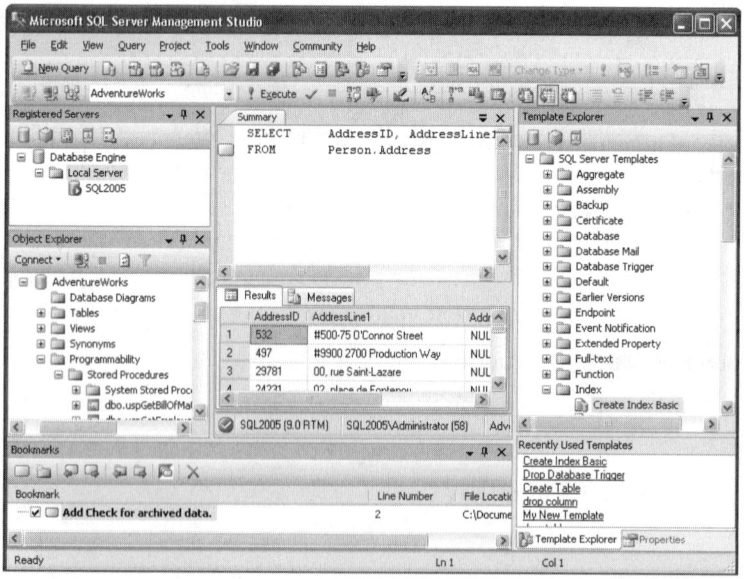

Figure 5-1 SQL Server Management Studio

The figure also shows the new Bookmarks window docked to the bottom of the screen along with the unique toolbar associated with that window. Bookmarks are shortcuts to locations in code and text files.

At the top of the image are some of the expanded and fully customizable tool bars.

Window Types

The IDE uses two types of windows, component windows and document windows. Component windows are used to display such things as the Solution Explorer, Properties, and Bookmarks. These windows are listed under the View menu and are used to display all the IDE components that aren't documents. One of the most welcome features of the new interface is the ability to dock these various component windows. You can reposition any of these windows to suit your taste. Component windows are displayed in one of three styles: floating, docked, or tabbed (as shown in Figure 5-2).

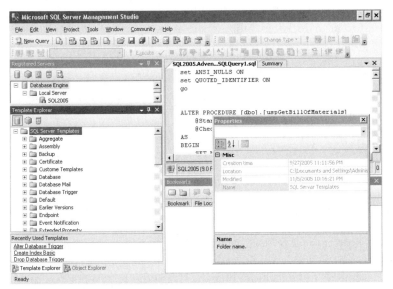

Figure 5-2 Management Studio's windows

Floating windows are just that—free-floating windows that can be positioned anywhere on the screen (the Properties window in Figure 5-2). Docked windows are anchored in a frame along at least one interface edge (Registered Servers and Template Explorer in Figure 5-2). You can also position docked windows so they share the same space on screen with other windows, for example, Template Explorer and Object Explorer. These windows appear in the same frame, with a tab for each window.

Document windows are used to view and edit scripts, XML, or any other type of text document. Document windows can be positioned to share the same area of the screen with other documents, but they always appear in the main part of the interface. This is the area normally used for text editing. A tab appears along the top of the document window, enabling access to each document. (See Figure 5-3.) If you prefer to work without tabs on the document windows, you can change to MDI mode. To change this option, select Options from the Tools menu and change the setting under the Environment General node.

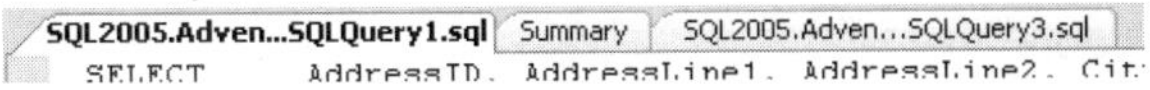

SQL2005.Adven...SQLQuery1.sql | Summary | SQL2005.Adven...SQLQuery3.sql

SELECT   AddressID, AddressLine1, AddressLine2, Cit

Figure 5-3 Document window tabs in SQL Server Management Studio

Any window in the interface except script and text edit windows can be switched between the three component window styles. Edit windows can appear only as document windows with tabs when in tabbed mode, or without tabs when in MDI mode.

You can change the type and configuration of component windows in several ways:

- Double-click on a docked window's title bar to toggle it from docked to floating mode.

- Double-click on a floating window's title bar to dock the window in its previous position.

- Drag a window's tab or title bar away from its docked position to make the window a floating window or to dock it in another part of the interface.

- Right-click on a window's tab or title bar, and select the desired state of the window from the shortcut menu. (See Figure 5-4.)

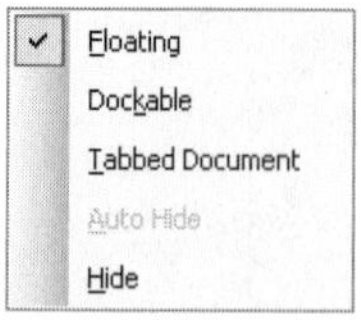

Figure 5-4   Management Studio's docking window menu

Positioning a Docking Window

You can position a floating window near the edge of the interface to dock it on that edge. This can be tricky when several windows are already docked. To help you position a window where you want it, Management Studio includes blue docking indicators. When you drag a floating window near a dockable part of the screen, docking indicators become visible to help you guide the window into position. (See Figure 5-5.)

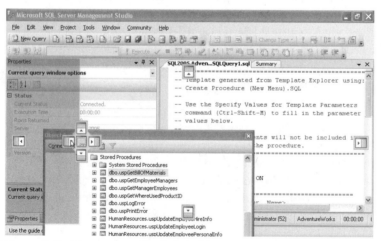

Figure 5-5   Management Studio's docking windows

> **Tip** To prevent a floating window from docking, hold down the CTRL key when you position it.

Window Customization Options

Management Studio also includes a large number of options for customizing a window, as shown in Figure 5-6. Here are several of the categories:

- **Font and Colors** The font and color of most of the interface text elements can be changed to suit your personal tastes. This includes the text editor window, where you can customize the different elements used in syntax highlighting. You can also change the options for text sent to the printer.

- **Text Editor** Under this category you can specify which code editor Management Studio should associate with a given file extension.

  You can also enable virtual space and word wrap behaviors and display line numbers. These options can be set for all languages, plain text, or XML.

- **Query Execution** In this category are query execution options for SQL Server and Analysis Server. The options for SQL Server include the maximum number of rows or the maximum size of the text returned by a query. Advanced options include transaction isolation level, deadlock priority, and lock time-out. The SQL Server and Analysis Server options both include a setting for execution time-out.

- **Query Results** Options in this category configure how results are generated. The default destination for results can be set to text, grid, or file. You can also change the default location for query results.

> **Note** Management Studio has shortcuts for just about everything, but unfortunately it doesn't allow you to edit them as you can in Visual Studio. You can, however, still assign tasks to Ctrl+F1, Alt+F1, and Ctrl+0 to Ctrl+9. You can find these under Environment/Keyboard in the Options dialog box. (Choose Tools, Options.)

Figure 5-6 The Options dialog box in Management Studio

Connecting to a Database Server

Generally when working in Management Studio, you will want to be connected to a server. You can work in a disconnected mode, which will be explained later. To establish a connection with a database server in SQL Server Management Studio, follow these steps:

1. Choose Connect Object Explorer from the File menu. This opens the Connect to Server dialog box.

2. As shown in Figure 5-7, select the server type from the drop-down list.

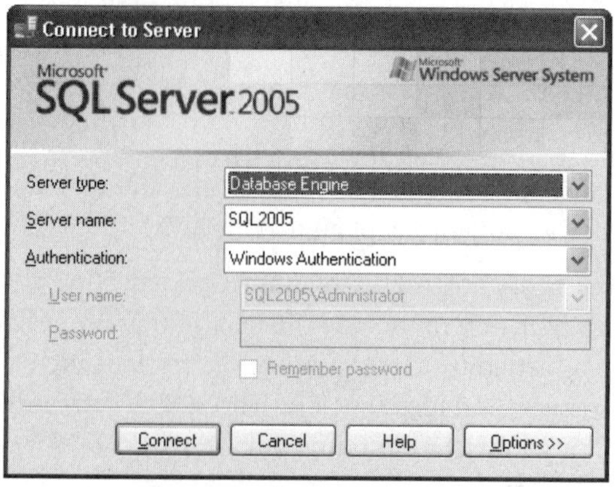

Figure 5-7   Management Studio's Connect to Server dialog box

> **Tip**   If the Object Explorer window is open, you can select the server type and open the Connect to Server dialog box by using the Object Explorer's Connect menu.

3. Use the Server name field drop-down list to select the server you want. If the name does not appear in the list, you can type in a server name, or select Browse for more... to open the Browse for Servers dialog box, where you can browse for local or network servers.

    Then, select the authentication method for the connection you are establishing.

4. Clicking on the Options button at the bottom of the Connect to Server dialog box reveals the Connections Properties tab. (See Figure 5-8.) On this tab, you can select a database, set network options (such as protocol and packet size), and set connection properties for connection time-out and execution time-out. Selecting the <default> value for the database option will connect you to the database that is the default for the user you are connecting as.

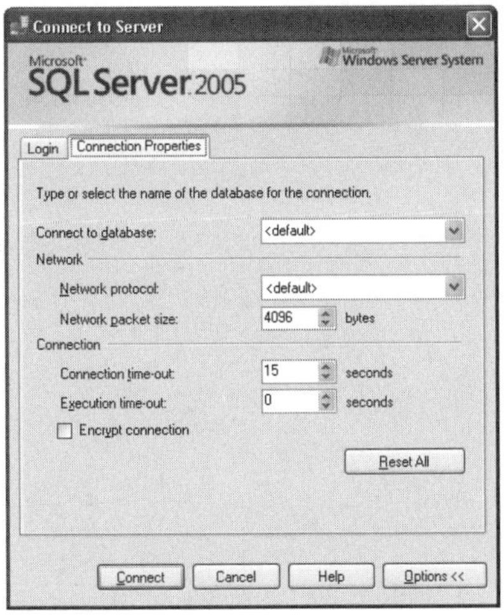

Figure 5-8   Connect to Server dialog box after clicking the Options button

5. After a connection is established, Management Studio populates the Object Explorer window with a tree structure containing folders of components available in the server instance. If the Object Explorer window is not already open, select Object Explorer from the View menu.

> **Note**   Management Studio is designed to work seamlessly with Database Engines, Analysis Services, Reporting Services, SQL Server Mobile, and Integration Services. The focus of this chapter is limited to database servers, but because of the consistent interface of Management Studio many of the features that apply to database servers apply to other kinds of servers as well.

Using Object Explorer

Object Explorer (Figure 5-9) provides a tree view of all the components in the connected SQL Server instance that can be managed using Management Studio. The default folders include:

- Databases, including system databases, database snapshots, and user databases.

- Security objects, such as logins, server roles, and credentials.

- Server objects, including backup devices, endpoints (SOAP and T-SQL), linked servers, and triggers.

- Replication components, including local publications and local subscriptions.

- Management components, including maintenance plans, SQL Server logs, activity monitor, database mail, distributed transaction coordinator, and full-text search.

- Notification Services component, listing the instances you have created.

Figure 5-9   Object Explorer in Management Studio

Object Explorer Filters

Management Studio includes a lot of productivity enhancements over previous versions of Enterprise Manager and Query Analyzer. The first one we'll look at is the ability to filter items in the Object Explorer window.

In a real-world application, the number of objects in a database can easily reach the hundreds of thousands. Searching through these objects to find a particular one can be time consuming. Developers and database administrators often use naming conventions to help speed up the search. In Management Studio, you now have the ability to add filter criteria to an object folder in Object Explorer.

You can add different filter criteria for each of the various object types. This means you can set up one set of criteria for tables and another for stored procedures. You can add filter criteria to most of the object types, but not all of them. For example, you can add a filter to the Security/Users folder but not the Security/Roles folder. Fortunately, you can add a filter to object types that need it most.

Creating a filter is simple. (See Figure 5-10.) Right-click on the object type for which you want to add a filter, and choose Filter. Below this are two submenu options, Remove Filter, which removes the current filter (this option is enabled only if a filter exists), and Filter Settings, which allows you to add a new filter or change the criteria of the current filter.

> **Note**   The Remove Filter command does not display a confirmation dialog box. If you select Remove Filter, the filter is deleted and Object Explorer is refreshed. This isn't a major concern because you can easily re-create an accidentally deleted filter, but it can be annoying if you click the wrong command because you have to wait for the server to refresh Object Explorer and then click again to add the filter back and wait while the filter is applied.

Figure 5-10   Adding a filter in Object Explorer

Filter Properties

You can set filter criteria for one or all of three predefined properties: Name, Schema, and Creation Date. (See Figure 5-11.) The Name and Creation Date properties appear for all object types, but Schema appears only for data-related items such as tables and stored procedures. For example, the Schema field does not appear when you add a filter to the User folder because items in this folder are not attached to schemas.

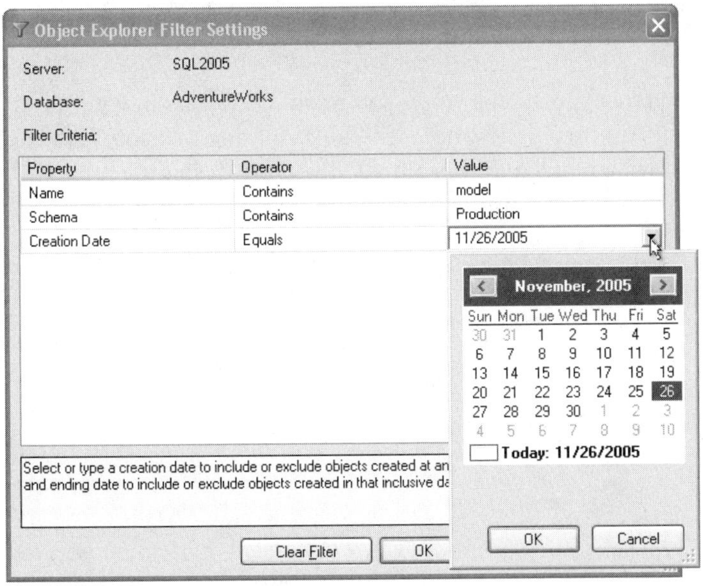

Figure 5-11   Object Explorer filter settings

Filter Operators

The Operator list contains basic comparison operators and is limited to appropriate comparisons for the relevant property. Table 5-1 shows the operators available for each property.

Table 5-1 Available Filter Operators

Operator	Name	Schema	Date
Equals	X	X	X
Contains	X	X	
Does not contain	X	X	
Less than			X
Less than or equal			X
Greater than			X
Greater than or equal			X
Between			X
Not between			X

Filter Values

The value used in the filter depends on the property. For example, the Name and Schema properties allow you to enter a string. The Creation Date property requires that you enter a date. For convenience, a popup calendar control allows you to select the date field. (See Figure 5-11.)

Filters can help you narrow your focus when you work on objects in your database. (See Figure 5-12.) Instead of trying to find a few tables among possibly hundreds, you can quickly find the ones you need. For example, if you are designing tables related to order processing, you can create a filter in which the Name property contains the word *order*.

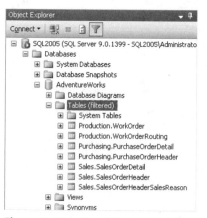

Figure 5-12 Object Explorer list filtered by the word *order*

Management Studio Solutions, Projects, and Files

When using the previous versions of the SQL Server tools, keeping track of the many SQL script files that comprised a real-world database was pretty much a do-it-yourself operation. In SQL Server 2005, Management Studio provides solution and project support that provides integrated file management.

A *project* is a container that holds related connections and SQL script files. A *solution* is a container that holds related project files. There is also a Miscellaneous folder in each project for miscellaneous files. You can add any file to this folder to keep it associated with the project. For example, if you have an SQL script that generates output to a file, you can add the output file to the Miscellaneous folder to store it in the project for future reference.

By default, when you create a new query file a solution is created for you. To create a project, go to the File menu, point to New, and then click Project. In the New Project dialog box that appears, you can specify the project type, the project name and location, and whether this project should be added to the current solution or a new solution created.

To create a new connection or query in a project, choose New Connection or New Query from the Project menu. To add an existing file to a project, choose Add Existing Item from the Project menu (Figure 5-13). In the Add Existing Item dialog box, locate and select the file, and then click Add. Management Studio automatically places the file in the appropriate folder according to the file type.

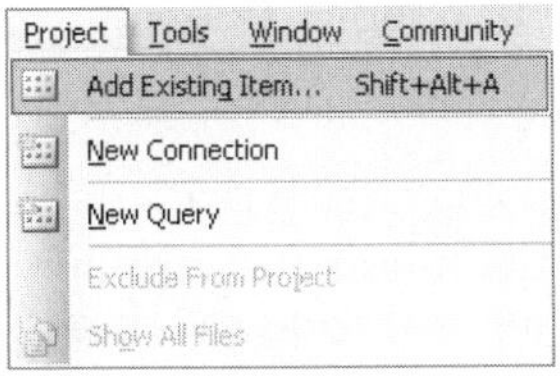

Figure 5-13   Add Existing Item menu option

It is important to note that projects are a way of organizing files, not database objects. The items associated with a project are stored in a folder on the hard drive just like any other file. If you create a stored procedure, that stored procedure is kept in the database as it always has been. But if you save the SQL script used to create that stored procedure to a file, you can group that file, stored on the hard drive, with other related files by adding them to a project.

This structure provides you with an easy way to group the scripts needed to re-create your database if required.

Code and Text Editor

The Code and Text Editor, which encompasses the features that were previously part of Query Analyzer, is a feature-rich text and script editor with color syntax highlighting, change tracking indicators, and customizable templates. The Code and Text Editor can edit any text file. If the text is source code the Editor is called the Query Editor. The Query Editor is more than a text editor, however; it also integrates features for designing, executing, and analyzing queries and stored procedures.

You can access the integrated design features of the Query Editor by using the right-click shortcut menu or the Query menu.

These menus include a lot of basic items such as cut, paste, and execute, which will be familiar to you. In this section, we'll focus on the items that help with design and development tasks.

Connection

In Query Analyzer, an open query window had to be connected to a server. Thankfully, this has been changed in SQL Server Management Studio. A query window can be connected to an SQL Server instance or entirely disconnected. This is useful for editing queries when you are offsite or unable to connect to the server. You can also disconnect a query window from an SQL Server instance and connect it to a different instance. For example, you can test your scripts against a development server and then use them against a production server without having to close and then reopen the script files.

The Connection submenu of the Query Editor menu has four options: Connect, Disconnect, Disconnect All Queries, and Change Connection.

You can choose Connect to select a server to connect to. If the current window is already connected, this option is grayed out. The Disconnect option disconnects the current window from the server it is connected to; Disconnect All Queries does the same for all open query windows. The Change Connection option allows you to select a different server or alter connection or authentication options.

Open Server in Object Explorer

This option acts as a shortcut for quickly finding the current server in Object Explorer. This option is disabled if the query window is disconnected.

Execute, Display Estimated Execution Plan, and Analyze Query in Database Engine Tuning Advisor

These options are all related to query execution. The actions are performed using the current query window. If the query window is disconnected, selecting one of these options opens the Connect to Database Engine dialog box and, when connected, performs the action.

Execute simply executes the query and displays the results. Display Estimated Execution Plan analyzes the current query but does not execute it. Below the query window, an execution plan window displays the plan that the database engine will use if the query is executed. Analyze Query in Database Engine Tuning Advisor launches the Database Engine Tuning Advisor, which you can use to help you improve the performance of your queries.

Design Query in Editor

This menu item opens the Query Designer, a new SQL Server development tool that is covered in more detail later in the chapter.

Include Actual Execution Plan and Include Client Statistics

These menu items toggle on and off for the current query window. Include Actual Execution Plan displays the execution plan that the database uses when the query is executed. Include Client Statistics shows profile information, such as the number and type of statements executed, network statistics, and execution time. (See Figure 5-14.) Client Statistics are cumulative while the query window is open. They can be reset by closing the window or by clicking Reset Client Statistics on the Query menu.

Results	Execution plan	Client Statistics					
		Trial 4	Trial 3	Trial 2	Trial 1	Average	
Client Execution Time		13:22:02	13:21:56	13:21:48	13:18:44		
Query Profile Statistics							
Number of INSERT, DELETE and UPDATE stateme...		0	→ 0	→ 0	→ 0	→ 0.0000	
Rows affected by INSERT, DELETE, or UPDATE st...		0	→ 0	→ 0	→ 0	→ 0.0000	
Number of SELECT statements		3	→ 3	→ 3	↑ 2	→ 2.7500	
Rows returned by SELECT statements		1	→ 1	→ 1	→ 1	→ 1.0000	
Number of transactions		0	→ 0	→ 0	→ 0	→ 0.0000	
Network Statistics							
Number of server roundtrips		4	→ 4	→ 4	↑ 2	→ 3.5000	
TDS packets sent from client		4	→ 4	→ 4	↑ 2	→ 3.5000	
TDS packets received from server		18	→ 18	→ 18	↑ 2	→ 14.0000	
Bytes sent from client		546	↑ 544	↓ 546	↑ 400	→ 509.0000	
Bytes received from server		60668	↓ 60806	↓ 60866	↑ 768	→ 45777.0000	
Time Statistics							
Client processing time		0	0	0	0	0.0000	

Figure 5-14   Client Statistics window

Results To

This menu item lets you select where the output from the query window will be sent. The choices are Results to Text, Results to Grid, and Results to File. These are the same as in Query Analyzer in previous versions of SQL Server.

Properties Windows

This option opens the Properties window (Figure 5-15) and makes it the active window. For a Transact-SQL (T-SQL) query, the Properties window displays general, read-only information about the current query such as execution time, rows returned, and database name.

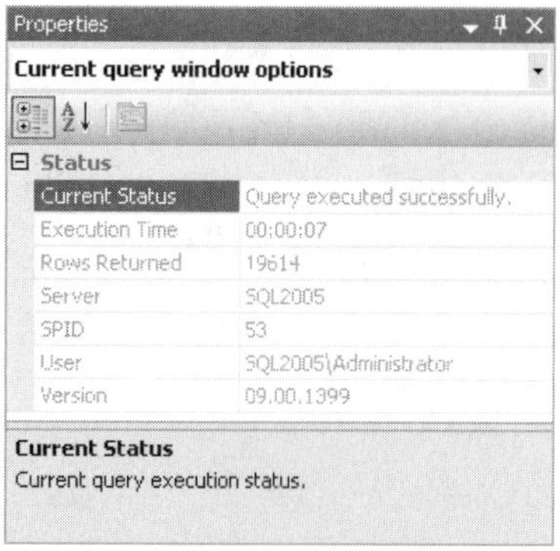

Figure 5-15   Query Properties window

Query Options

The Query Options item opens the Query Options dialog box (Figure 5-16), where you can set various Execution and Results options.

The options here are identical to those in the main Query Options dialog box on the Tools, Options menu. However, the options set with this dialog box only affect the active query window while it's open. When the window is closed, any changes to the options are not saved.

One important new option on the Results page is, "Include column headers when copying or saving the results." This option allows you to quickly copy the query results, including the headings, and paste them into a document or spreadsheet.

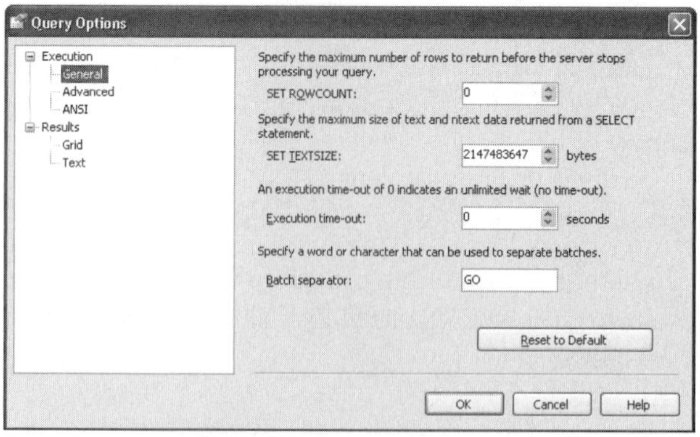

Figure 5-16   Query Options dialog box

Track Changes Indicator

One of the new features in the Editor is an indicator showing which lines of the script have changed. The Track Changes indicator shows up as a narrow colored bar on the left edge of the edit window.

In the example in Figure 5-17, you can see the location of the indicator (the dark gray and light gray bar to the left of the ALTER PROCEDURE statement) but unfortunately not the color. The dark gray and light gray correspond to green and yellow in the actual IDE. A green bar indicates an earlier change that has been saved to a file. A yellow bar indicates a recent change that has not been saved to a file.

```
SQL2005.Adven...LQuery16.sql*   SQL2005.Adve...QLQuery15.sql   SQL2
    set ANSI_NULLS ON
    set QUOTED_IDENTIFIER ON
    go


    ALTER PROCEDURE [dbo].[uspGetBillOfMaterial]
        @CheckDate [datetime],
        @StartProductID [int]

    AS
    BEGIN
        SET NOCOUNT ON;
```

Figure 5-17   Track Changes indicator

Important   The Track Changes indicator persists only while the script window is open. If a script is saved and the windows are closed, change tracking is lost. When the script is opened again from the saved file, it is considered the original and only new changes will be indicated.

Bookmarks

Another new productivity feature in Management Studio is the ability to create bookmarks. A bookmark is a shortcut to any line in any file in a project.

You can add a bookmark by choosing Bookmarks, Toggle Bookmark from the Edit menu. The bookmark is automatically added to the Bookmarks window, which displays all bookmarks in the current solution. Bookmarks can be renamed, and they are saved as part of the project file.

Because bookmarks can be renamed, you can use them as reminders about code you want to review or continue working on. They link directly to a line in a project, so you can quickly return to the code you're working on. For example, let's say it's late on a Friday afternoon and you are working on a complicated stored procedure. You want to leave work at a reasonable time, but you need to check the performance of the index your stored procedure uses and you need to include some additional validation code. Instead of scribbling on a Post-It note and sticking it to your monitor to help you find your place in the code on Monday, you can just add a bookmark. When you are ready to work on the code again, you just open the Bookmarks window (Figure 5-18) and double-click on the bookmark.

Bookmark	Line Number	File Location
Compare performance using alternate index	12	C:\Documents and Setting...
Add data validation code	32	C:\Documents and Setting...

Figure 5-18   Bookmarks window

Creating Objects

When we talk about developing databases, we are really talking about creating database objects: tables, stored procedures, indexes, users, and queries, to name just a few. In this section, we'll step through creating objects in Management Studio and look at some of the features the new environment offers.

> **Note** This section focuses on creating objects using the development environment's designers and dialog boxes. As always, you can create these same objects using SQL scripts.

Creating Tables

Creating a table in Management Studio is fairly easy. As in Enterprise Manager in previous versions of SQL Server, you create tables using the Table Designer (Figure 5-19). To open the designer, go to the Object Explorer window and expand the database node you want to create the table in. Right-click the Table node and then click New Table. You will notice that the designer uses the familiar Column Name/Data Type/Allows Nulls grid.

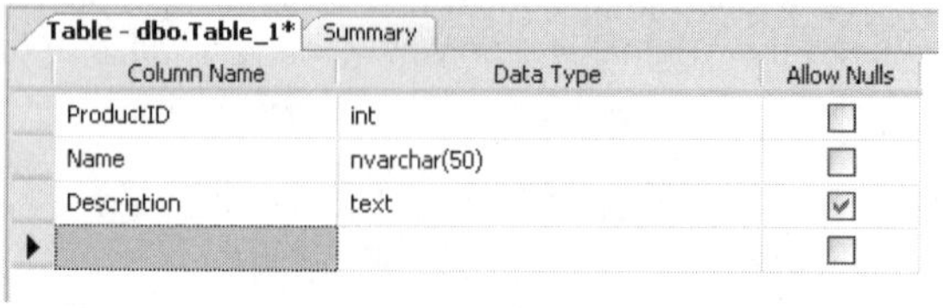

Column Name	Data Type	Allow Nulls
ProductID	int	☐
Name	nvarchar(50)	☐
Description	text	☑
		☐

Table - dbo.Table_1* / Summary

Figure 5-19 The Table Designer in Management Studio

If you are familiar with Enterprise Manager, you'll notice that the designer no longer has a separate column for length. Instead, the Data Type drop-down list (Figure 5-20) has multiple items for some data types, with common lengths already entered.

Data Type

```
int
varbinary(50)
─────────────
varbinary(50)
varbinary(MAX)
varchar(50)
varchar(MAX)
xml
AccountNumber:nvarcha...
Flag:bit
NameStyle:bit
```

Figure 5-20 The Data Type drop-down list

To change the length of variable length data types, you can enter a new value directly in the Data Type field or change the length in the Column Properties section below the grid.

Figure 5-21 shows two nvarchar fields with custom lengths of 75 and 9999, respectively. You will also notice some new data types in this list (which are described in Chapter 2 and Chapter 4).

Figure 5-21   The nvarchar data types

The Table Designer also includes a right-click shortcut menu (Figure 5-22) that provides easy access to create a primary key, table relationships (foreign keys), indexes, and constraints.

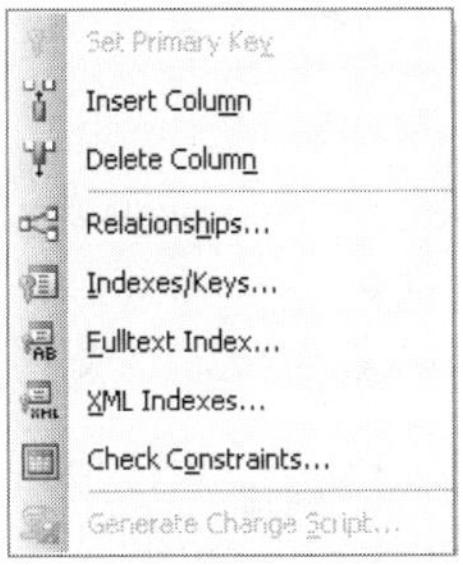

Figure 5-22   The Table Designer shortcut menu

Each menu item opens a corresponding designer. Although each designer presents different properties, they are all similar to the Foreign Key Relationships dialog box shown in Figure 5-23. They have an Add button to create a new object of the specific type and you can then use the properties list on the right to configure the object. Use the Delete button to delete the selected object.

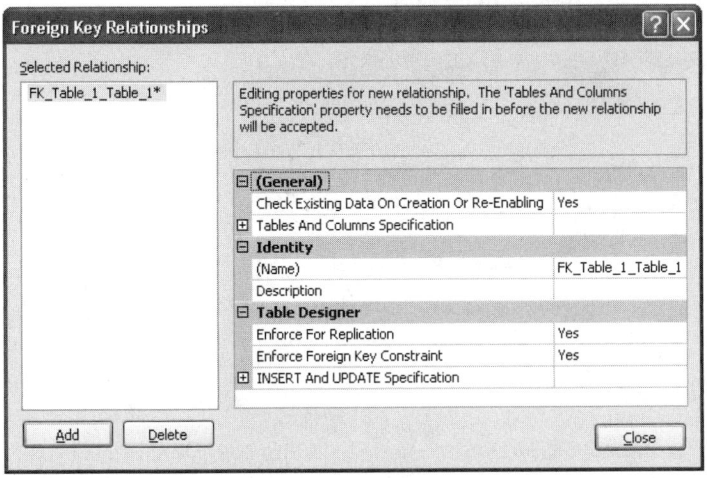

Figure 5-23   Foreign Key Relationships dialog box

Creating Table-Related Objects

If you expand a table node in Object Explorer, you see a list of table-related objects. Each of these has a shortcut menu that allows you to create an item of that type (Figure 5-24).

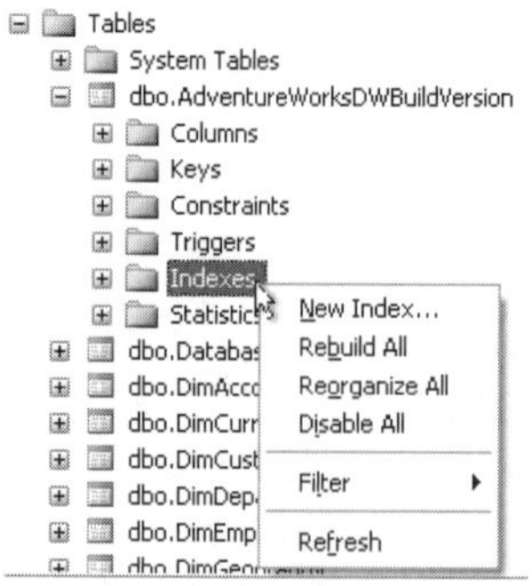

Figure 5-24   Table Indexes shortcut menu

Choosing the New <object> menu item for the Columns, Keys, and Constraints objects launches the Table Designer, and in the case of the Keys and Constraints objects also launches the corresponding object designer (previously discussed).

The New Trigger item behaves a little differently; it opens a script window with a template for a new trigger. Script editing and templates will be discussed in more detail later in this chapter.

Creating Indexes

To create a new index for a table, the table designer must be closed. Selecting New Index from the Indexes folder shortcut menu opens the New Index dialog box (Figure 5-25). You can create clustered, nonclustered, and primary XML indexes. The New Index dialog box includes General settings, Options, Included Columns, and Storage pages.

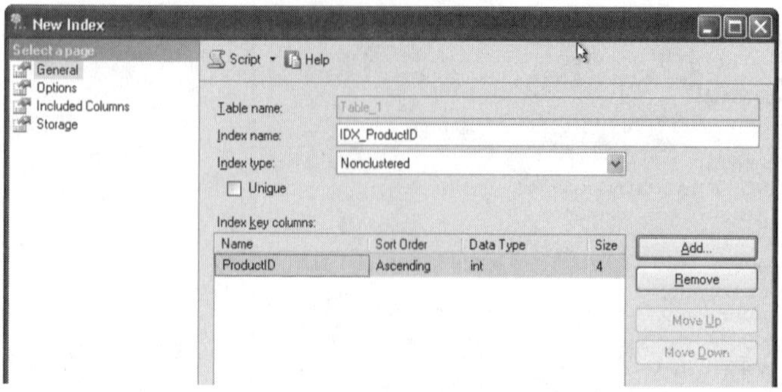

Figure 5-25   New Index dialog box

To create an index, type a name in the Index name field and select the index type. (XML Indexes are new and are available only when connecting to an instance of SQL Server 2005.) Each table can have only one clustered index.

Selecting the Unique check box means that no two rows in the index can have the same values in the indexed columns. If an indexed column allows NULL values, only one NULL is permitted per column.

To add columns to the index, click the Add button to display the Select Columns from <table name> dialog box (Figure 5-26). 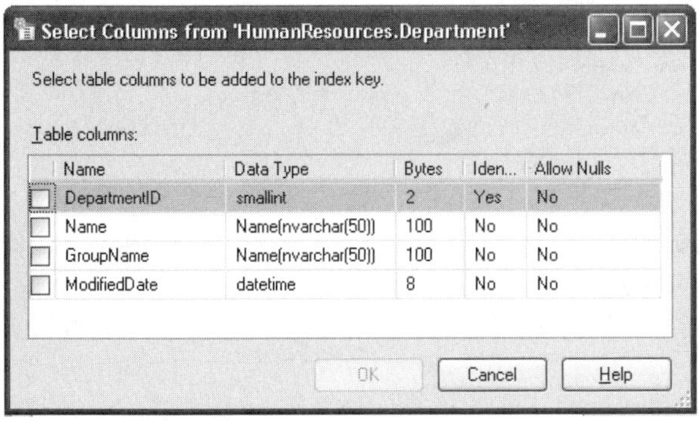

Figure 5-26   Adding existing columns to an index

Setting Properties for New Users

Creating most other objects in SQL Server 2005 is similar to creating indexes. Each object has its own designer. Some designers appear as tabbed windows in the main window, and others, such as the New User designer, appear in dialog boxes. In the New User dialog box (Figure 5-27), you can set all the properties for a user. 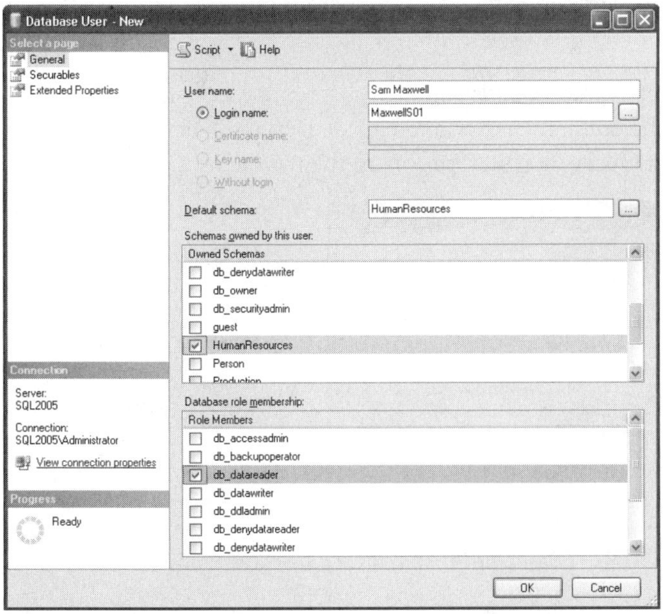

Figure 5-27   New User dialog box

Generating Scripts from Objects

At the top of many of the new and modify object dialog boxes, for example, the New Index dialog box, you'll notice a Script menu (Figure 5-28). This is just one of the many ways to generate an SQL script from an object.

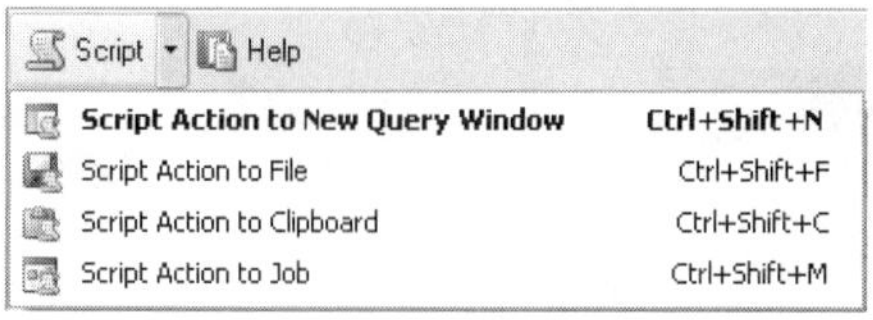

Figure 5-28   The Script menu

The Script menu allows you to script the current object to a new query window, file, clipboard, or job. This can be useful for keeping a backup copy of the scripts used to generate all the objects in your database or to generate the same object on a production server after testing it on a development server.

Creating Queries

A lot of SQL Server purists looked on their Microsoft Access counterparts with disdain when the latter used Access Query Designer—that is, until they actually tried it themselves and found out how convenient and powerful a tool it was for simple queries. Now even the purists will have a chance to try an updated and enhanced Query Designer that is part of SQL Server Management Studio (Figure 5-29).

You can create a new query by choosing New Query from the main toolbar or by pressing Ctrl+N.

By default, the New Query option opens a new SQL script window for editing. To get to the designer, right-click in the editing window and choose Design Query in Editor. Alternatively, you can click the Design Query in Editor button on the toolbar.

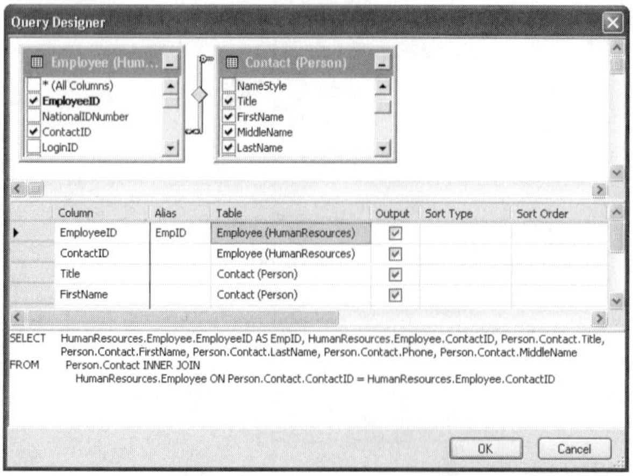

Figure 5-29   The Query Designer

Once in the Query Designer, you can select tables, views, functions, and synonyms from the current connection and add them to the query, as shown in Figure 5-30.

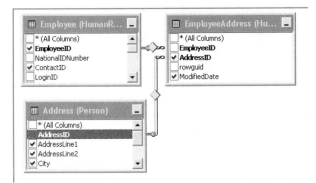

Figure 5-30   The Add Table dialog box

The Query Designer displays a list of available fields in the objects you added to the query (Figure 5-31).

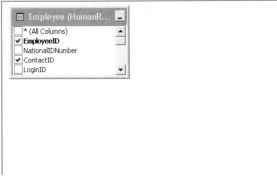

Figure 5-31   Table in the Query Designer

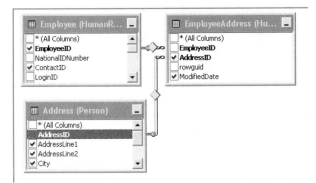

Figure 5-32   Relationships between tables

You'll notice in Figure 5-32 that the Query Designer also shows the relationship between the selected tables. These relationships establish the type of joins needed between the tables. You can modify the links to create the necessary type of join by right-clicking the join and selecting Properties from the menu.

You can add a field to the query by selecting the check box next to the field name, as shown in Figure 5-32. To add all the available fields, click the * (All Columns) check box at the top of the list.

When a field is added to the query, the designer adds it to a grid control and also updates a raw SQL view, as shown in Figure 5-33. In the grid, you can add a field alias, change the sort order, and add filter criteria. The grid and the SQL text box are linked, so changing the contents of one updates the other.

Column	Alias	Table	Output	Sort Type	Sort Order	Filter	(▲
EmployeeID	EmpID	Employee (…	☑			< 10000	
ContactID		Employee (…	☑				
LoginID		Employee (…	☑				
Title	Expr1	Contact (P…	☑			NOT IS NULL	
FirstName		Contact (P…	☑				
LastName		Contact (P…	☑	Ascending	1		▼

```
SELECT   HumanResources.Employee.EmployeeID AS EmpID, HumanResources.Employee.ContactID, HumanResources.Employee.
         Person.Contact.Title AS Expr1, Person.Contact.FirstName, Person.Contact.LastName, Person.Contact.Phone
FROM     HumanResources.Employee INNER JOIN
         Person.Contact ON HumanResources.Employee.ContactID = Person.Contact.ContactID
WHERE    (HumanResources.Employee.EmployeeID < 10000) AND (NOT (Person.Contact.Title IS NULL))
ORDER BY Person.Contact.LastName
```

Figure 5-33   Query Designer grid

After clicking OK, the Query Designer inserts the SQL text into a query window, where you can further edit the query or save it.

Executing Queries

When you write a query, it is important to know how the SQL Engine will execute that query. With this information, you can identify any potential bottlenecks and redesign the query if necessary. To assist you in this, Management Studio includes two query plan options: Display Estimated Execution Plan and Include Actual Execution Plan.

As the names imply, both options show the execution plan for the current query. The Display Estimated Execution Plan option parses the query and shows you the estimated plan, whereas the Include Actual Execution Plan executes the query and shows you the actual plan used.

Clicking the Display Estimated Execution Plan icon on the toolbar displays a diagram on the Execution Plan tab, as shown in Figure 5-34. This diagram uses icons to represent each stage of the query. Below each icon is a percentage estimation of the cost for that stage relative to the whole query.

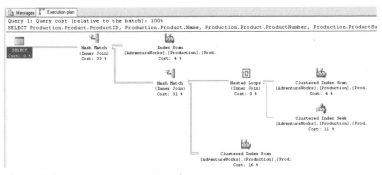

Figure 5-34   A query execution plan

To see the actual execution plan, you must click the Include Actual Execution Plan icon on the toolbar and execute the query. After the query executes, the execution plan will be displayed on the Execution plan tab in the results pane.

Using Templates

One of the best enhanced features in Management Studio is templates. Templates are fill-in-the-blank boilerplate scripts that you can use to create your own SQL scripts.

Management Studio offers hundreds of prewritten templates, covering many of the common scripts needed for creating and maintaining a database. They cover everything from the simple Drop User queries to the impressive-sounding Create Database on Multiple File Groups (Figure 5-35).

Figure 5-35   Templates listed in Template Explorer

You can access the templates by displaying the Template Explorer window. Table 5-2 lists some of the template categories included in Management Studio.

Table 5-2   Template Categories

Aggregate	Backup
Certificate	Database
Database Mail	Database Trigger
Default	Earlier Versions
Endpoint	Event Notification
Functions	Index
Restore	Rule
SQL Trace	Stored Procedure
Table	Trigger
User	View

These templates are more then just prewritten script libraries. You also get support for template parameters and the ability to create your own templates—a powerful addition to a database administrator's toolbox.

Double-clicking on any template node opens a Query Edit window. The window contains a template with the corresponding SQL code. Here is the code generated for the Create Index Basic template:

```
-- Create index basic template
USE <database_name, sysname, AdventureWorks>
GO

CREATE INDEX <index_name, sysname, ind_test>
ON <schema_name, sysname, Person>.<table_name, sysname, Address>
(
    <column_name1, sysname, PostalCode>
)
GO
```

Notice that the generated code includes bracketed (<>) parameter declaration tags. These tags have the following simple format:

```
<parameter_name, data_type, value>
```

These parameter tags are used by a special Specify Values dialog box that provides fill-in-the-blank simplicity (Figure 5-36). Choose Specify Values for Template Parameters from the Query menu, press Ctrl+Shift+M, or click the corresponding icon on the toolbar.

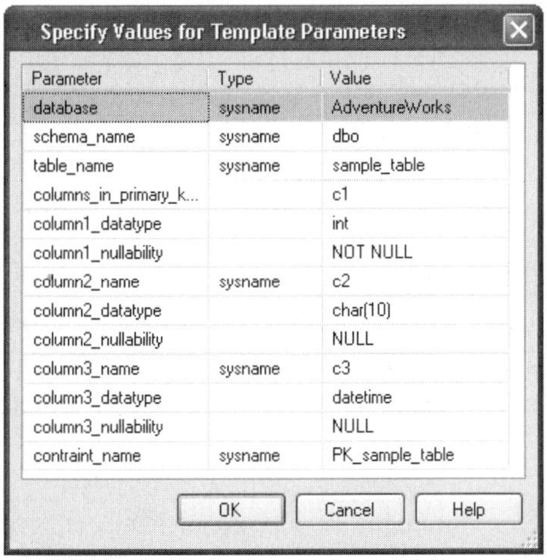

Specify Values for Template Parameters

Parameter	Type	Value
database	sysname	AdventureWorks
schema_name	sysname	dbo
table_name	sysname	sample_table
columns_in_primary_k...		c1
column1_datatype		int
column1_nullability		NOT NULL
column2_name	sysname	c2
column2_datatype		char(10)
column2_nullability		NULL
column3_name	sysname	c3
column3_datatype		datetime
column3_nullability		NULL
contraint_name	sysname	PK_sample_table

OK Cancel Help

Figure 5-36 Specify Values for Template Parameters dialog box

To fill in values for these parameters, simply type the appropriate data in the Value field for each parameter.

A few things to note about this dialog box:

- A template parameter of type SysName is expected to be the name of an object from the database, such as a field, table, or index.

- Template parameters are guidelines; they're not strongly typed or rigidly enforced.

- The fields are only guides for filling in the template. You can enter completely meaningless data and the dialog box won't complain; it will gladly generate useless SQL code.

Important The Type field is the template parameter type, not a stored procedure parameter type. It is only a helper to indicate the type of data the template parameter expects. No type checking is done on the value you enter.

Note that all three sections of the Template Parameter are required, but data type and value can be left blank.

Although the syntax isn't rigid, templates are very useful. If used correctly and with care, they can help speed up the writing of SQL code.

Maintenance Features

In this section, we'll look at some of the maintenance features in SQL Server Management Studio.

Using a Maintenance Plan

The day-to-day work of a database administrator often includes maintenance tasks that can be automated. For example, before running a backup of the database each night, you might want to run some statements that update inventories, delete old backup files, and rebuild some key indexes. In this situation, you want to be notified if an error occurs and when the process completes successfully.

To do this in Management Studio, you can use maintenance plans to organize and automate these database maintenance tasks (see Table 5-3). The following tasks can be added to a plan and saved as a single unit. Then, the plan can be run on demand or set to run on a regular schedule.

Table 5-3 Maintenance Tasks

Back Up Database	Backup type can be full or differential. The source can be any server to which you can establish a valid connection.
Check Database Integrity	Checks the integrity of user and system tables, and optionally indexes in the database.
Execute SQL Server Agent Job	Executes an existing Microsoft SQL Server Agent job as part of the maintenance plan.
Execute T-SQL Statement	Adds customized T-SQL statements to the maintenance plan.
History Cleanup	Deletes old historical information from tables in the msdb database. Cleanup can be done on backup and restore history, Microsoft SQL Server Agent Job history, and maintenance plan history.
Maintenance Cleanup	Deletes old files related to either maintenance plans or database backups.
Notify Operator	Sends a message to a Microsoft SQL Server operator using database mail. The operator must have a valid e-mail address.
Rebuild Index	Re-creates the indexes on the tables and/or views in the database.
Reorganize Index	Reorganizes the index on tables and/or views in one or more databases to improve efficiency.
Shrink Database	Shrinks the unused space in a database to a specified percentage of the data in the database.
Update Statistics	Updates the index and/or column statistics of tables and/or views in a database. SQL Server uses these statistics to optimize query plans.

To create a new maintenance plan, right-click on the Maintenance Plan node in the Object Explorer window and choose New Maintenance Plan.

In the Maintenance Plan Designer (Figure 5-37), the top portion shows the name of the plan and provides a space for entering a description. Below that, you can set a schedule for the plan to run on and add tasks to the plan.

The main part of the window is a drag-and-drop surface where you can place maintenance task icons from the Maintenance Plan Tasks toolbar.

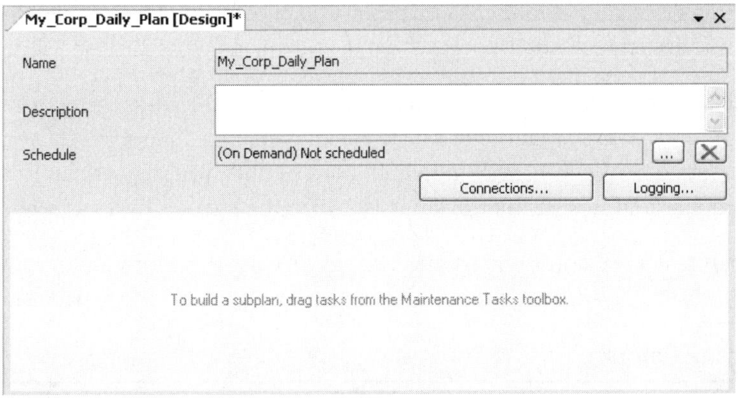

My_Corp_Daily_Plan [Design]*	▾ ×
Name	My_Corp_Daily_Plan
Description	
Schedule	(On Demand) Not scheduled [...] [×]
	Connections... Logging...

To build a subplan, drag tasks from the Maintenance Tasks toolbox.

Figure 5-37   Maintenance Plan Designer

You just drag an icon from the toolbox and drop it in the editor. Each task is represented in the designer by a placeholder. (See Figure 5-38.)

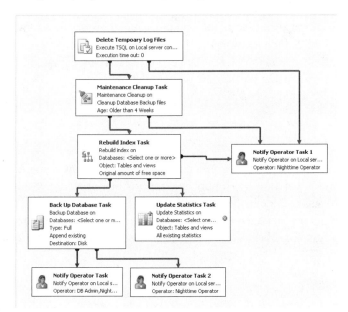

Figure 5-38   Maintenance Plan Designer with tasks

Each placeholder contains a task-specific icon, the name of the task at the top in bold, and some task-specific properties. Each task has many properties associated with it. Some properties are common among all tasks—these are related to such things as execution and error handling—and other properties are task specific, such as BackupDeviceType for the Back Up Database task.

You can modify properties for each task by using the Properties Window (press F4) or by right-clicking on the task and choosing Edit from the shortcut menu.

The Maintenance Plan Designer is, in itself, a nice tool. The information on each placeholder is easy to read and provides enough description for you to understand what the task will accomplish.

A maintenance plan allows you to execute tasks in sequence and to change the plan's execution path depending on the success or failure of a task. Each task can be linked to other tasks using one of three criteria: success, failure, or completion. For example, you might want to notify an operator if a backup task fails or shrink the database when the indexes have been rebuilt.

The links between tasks are color coded and are easy to attach and reposition. They are described in Table 5-4. An Auto Layout feature is also available on the Format menu.

Table 5-4   Task Link Colors

Link Color	Task Status
Green	Success
Red	Failure
Blue	Completion

There is also a Maintenance Plan Wizard available in Management Studio that allows you to select tasks and create a schedule for a maintenance plan. You can access this by right-clicking the Maintenance Plans node and clicking Maintenance Plan Wizard. By default, the wizard links the tasks to run in the order that you specify on completion of each task. You can then use the Maintenance Plan Designer to customize the links as required.

Performance Tools

Even with today's high-performance servers, efficient database processing is a function of good database design. Architects and developers are responsible for understanding how their database design processes data and identifying where improvements can be made. To help in this task, SQL Server Management Studio includes two tools: SQL Profiler and Database Engine Tuning Advisor. Both of these tools can be accessed from the Tools menu.

SQL Server Profiler

SQL Server Profiler, an extension of SQL Trace, allows you to capture and save data about the processes in the database engine as they occur. You can save this information and examine it later for bottlenecks, resource contention, security problems, and other performance-related information.

Database Engine Tuning Advisor

The Database Engine Tuning Advisor takes a predefined workload and executes it against a database. It then examines the performance effects of the workload and offers tips for creating or modifying indexes, indexed views, and partitions. The goal of the tool is to help you improve query performance and reduce execution time. Note that designing a workload that accurately reflects normal database operation is crucial to getting good recommendations from the Database Engine Tuning Advisor.

Summary

Management Studio is a major upgrade to the SQL Server development environment. The highly configurable interface and the new or expanded features such as syntax highlighting, Object Explorer, and bookmarks will enhance your productivity. Automated maintenance tasks help streamline the day-to-day tasks of a production environment.

There is a lot to explore in the new Management Studio interface; this chapter provides a good introduction to some of the most notable features.

Chapter 6

Using SQL Server Management Objects (SMO)

—Stephen Forte

Working with Microsoft SQL Server requires that you perform many different management tasks. As a developer, you might think that management is the realm of the database administrator (DBA) and that you only have to worry about building applications by writing code. This is not always the case. You sometimes have to perform simple maintenance tasks such as attaching a database as part of an application or setup program. For example, when you deploy an application, you might have to include an auxiliary program that attaches the application's database to an existing SQL Server installation. You might also make simple database security management part of your application. A contract developer or independent software vendor (ISV) might be required to supply some automated backup-and-restore functionality that sits outside the realm of the SQL Server agent technology. A corporate developer might need to perform some simple administrative functions programmatically to verify that certain administrative tasks are completed or automate simple tasks such as performing a group of database attaches and detaches.

In the past, you performed these tasks using SQL Distributed Management Objects (SQL-DMO). You created an application, perhaps in Microsoft Visual Basic, that performed some basic routine maintenance or administrative tasks based on user input. If your customers or users did not have a full-time DBA, you might have used SQL-DMO to create an easy-to-use administrative tool that performed more advanced administrative functions behind the scenes.

With the advent of Microsoft SQL Server 2005, we have a new object model called SQL Server Management Objects (SMO). SMO allows you to do all the things you did with SQL-DMO, including managing SQL Server 2000 and SQL Server 2005 database servers.

What Is SMO?

SMO is a new Microsoft .NET–based object model that ships with the SQL Server 2005 client tools in an assembly called *Microsoft.SqlServer.Smo.dll*. Other, supporting assemblies are located in the Program Files\Microsoft SQL Server\90\SDK\Assemblies folder, as shown in Table 6-1.

Table 6-1   SMO Namespace Map

Class	Function
Microsoft.SqlServer.Management.Smo	The core assembly of SMO, which contains instance classes, utility classes, and enumerations that are used to programmatically manipulate SQL Server
Microsoft.SqlServer.Management.Common	Classes that are common to Replication Management Objects (RMO) and SMO
Microsoft.SqlServer.Management.Smo.Agent	Classes for SQL Server Agent
Microsoft.SqlServer.Management.Smo.Wmi	Classes for the WMI Provider
Microsoft.SqlServer.Management.Smo .RegisteredServers	Classes for Registered Server
Microsoft.SqlServer.Management.Smo.Mail	Classes for Database Mail
Microsoft.SqlServer.Management.Smo.Broker	Classes for SQL Server Service Broker
Microsoft.SqlServer.Management.Smo .NotificationServices	Classes for SQL Server Notification Services

SMO allows you to programmatically manipulate SQL Server versions 2005, 2000, and 7.0. All the functionality in SQL Server Management Studio is available using SMO, but features available only in SQL Server 2005 (such as DDL [data definition language] triggers) will not function on earlier versions of SQL Server. Actually, SMO offers several more features than Management Studio, and 99 percent of all the features and functionality of SQL Server can be manipulated from SMO—a much larger percentage than with Management Studio. If you want, you can even create a more feature-complete version of Management Studio using Windows Forms and SMO.

Developers who are accustomed to programmatically running Transact-SQL (T-SQL) scripts during setup or on behalf of a user might never have looked at SQL-DMO and might wonder why SMO would be of any use to them. One reason is security. Executing T-SQL scripts results in a vulnerability to SQL injection attacks. SMO greatly reduces the attack surface because the developer explicitly defines what functions to expose. A user cannot inject malicious code into your *Backup* function using SMO and compiled C# code.

What About SQL-DMO?

Developers previously had to use the COM-based SQL-DMO to perform programmatic administrative tasks. SMO is the logical evolution of SQL-DMO. SMO has feature parity with

SQL-DMO and even many of the same objects, but it has a number of additional features that supersede SQL-DMO. To account for new SQL Server 2005 features and achieve maximum DDL and administrative support for SQL Server 2005, SMO adds more than 150 new classes. SQL Server 2005 Books Online has a complete listing of the SQL-DMO–to–SMO object and functionality mapping as well as a rich SMO object model description.

The primary advantages of SMO are that it is a native .NET object model and that it provides increased performance and scalability over SQL-DMO. SMO has a cached object model, which allows you to change several properties of an object before applying the changes to SQL Server. This offers a huge performance benefit because SMO makes fewer round-trips to the server. SMO also has optimized instantiation, which means you can partially or fully instantiate objects. You can load many objects quickly by not instantiating all the properties of the objects. Compare this with SQL-DMO, which must load all the properties of the object when you load the object, thereby increasing network traffic and use of server resources.

With its new object model, SMO is now the preferred API for programmatically managing and manipulating instances of SQL Server. SQL-DMO is shipped with SQL Server to provide backward compatibility. Because SQL-DMO is depreciated it is better to use SMO with COM Interop in COM applications than to use SQL-DMO to reduce migration issues in the future and to guarantee future support from Microsoft. If you need to use SQL-DMO for any reason, keep in mind that SQL-DMO has a managed object that simplifies the interface to WMI to support WMI monitoring and server configuration through the SMO object interface. If you are considering a move to SMO, Table 6-2 shows SQL-DMO-to-SMO mapping.

Table 6-2   SQL-DMO-to-SMO Mapping

SQL-DMO Object(s)	SMO Equivalent
Alert and *AlertSystem*	*Microsoft.SqlServer.Management.Agent* namespace
Application	Removed
BackupDevice, *Backup*, and *Backup2*	*Backup* and *BackupRestoreBase* objects
BulkCopy and *BulkCopy2*	Replaced by *Transfer* object
Category	Moved to *Microsoft.SqlServer.Management.Agent* namespace; replaced by *AlertCategory*, *OperatorCategory*, and *JobCategory* objects
Check	*Check* object
Column and *Column2*	*Column* object
Configuration	*Configuration* and *ConfigurationBase* objects
ConfigValue	*ConfigProperty* object
Database and *Database2*	*Database* object
DatabaseRole and *DatabaseRole2*	*DatabaseRole* object
DBFile object	*DataFile* object
DBOption and *DBOption2*	Moved into the *DatabaseOptions* object
Default and *Default2*	*Default* object

Table 6-2   SQL-DMO-to-SMO Mapping

SQL-DMO Object(s)	SMO Equivalent
DistributionArticle and *DistributionArticle2*, *DistributionDatabase* and *DistributionDatabase2*, *DistributionPublication* and *DistributionPublication2*, *DistributionSubscription* and *DistributionSubscription2*, *Distributor* and *Distributor2*	Part of RMO: *Microsoft.SqlServer.Replication* namespace
DRIDefault	Moved to *ScriptingOptions* object
FileGroup and *FileGroup2*	*FileGroup* object
FullTextCatalog and *FullTextCatalog2*	*FullTextCatalog* and *FullTextIndex* objects
Index and *Index2*	*Index* object
IntegratedSecurity	Functionality moved to *ServerConnection* object in *Microsoft.SqlServer.Management.Common* namespace
Job, JobFilter, JobHistoryFilter, JobSchedule, JobStep, JobServer and *JobServer2*, and *Operator*	Moved to *Microsoft.SqlServer.Management.Smo.Agent* namespace
Key	*ForeignKey* and *Index* objects
LinkedServer and *LinkedServer2*	*LinkedServer* object
LinkedServerLogin	*LinkedServerLogin* object
LogFile	*LogFile* object
Login and *Login2*	*Login* object
MergeArticle and *MergeArticle2*	*MergeArticle* object; moved to *Microsoft.SqlServer.Replication* namespace
MergeDynamicSnapshotJob	*Microsoft.SqlServer.Replication* namespace
MergePublication and *MergePublication2*	*MergePublication* object; moved to *Microsoft.SqlServer.Replication* namespace
MergePullSubscription and *MergePullSubscription2*	*MergePullSubscription* object; moved to *Microsoft.SqlServer.Replication* namespace
MergeSubscription	*MergeSubscription* object; moved to *Microsoft.SqlServer.Replication* namespace
MergeSubsetFilter	Moved to *Microsoft.SqlServer.Replication* namespace
NameList	Removed; similar functionality in *Scripter* object
Permission and *Permission2*	*ServerPermission, DatabasePermission, ApplicationRole,* and *ObjectPermission* objects
Property	*Property* object
Publisher and *Publisher2*	*ReplicationServer* object; moved to *Microsoft.SqlServer.Replication* namespace
QueryResults and *QueryResults2*	Replaced by *DataTable* or *DataSet* system object
RegisteredServer and *RegisteredSubscriber*	Moved to *Microsoft.SqlServer.Replication* namespace

Table 6-2   SQL-DMO-to-SMO Mapping

SQL-DMO Object(s)	SMO Equivalent
Registry and *Registry2*	Removed
RemoteLogin	*ServerConnection* object; moved to *Common* namespace
RemoteServer and *RemoteServer2*	*ServerConnection* object; moved to *Microsoft.SqlServer .Management.Common* namespace
Replication, ReplicationDatabase, and *ReplicationDatabase2*	Moved to *Microsoft.SqlServer.Replication* namespace
ReplicationSecurity	*ServerConnection* object; moved to *Microsoft.SqlServer .Management.Common* namespace
ReplicationStoredProcedure and *ReplicationStoredProcedure2*	*ReplicationStoredProcedure* object; moved to *Microsoft.SqlServer.Replication* namespace
ReplicationTable and *ReplicationTable2*	*ReplicationTable* object; moved to *Microsoft.SqlServer .Replication* namespace
Restore and *Restore2*	*Restore* and *BackupRestoreBase* objects
Rule and *Rule2*	*Rule* object
Schedule	Moved to *Microsoft.SqlServer.Replication* namespace
ServerGroup	Removed
ServerRole	*ServerRole* object
SQLObjectList	*SqlSmoObject* array
SQLServer and *SQLServer2*	*Server* object
StoredProcedure and *StoredProcedure2*	*StoredProcedure* and *StoredProcedureParameter* objects
Subscriber and *Subscriber2*	*Subscriber* object; moved to *Microsoft.SqlServer .Replication* namespace
SystemDatatype and *SystemDataType2*	*DataType* object
Table and *Table2*	*Table* object
TargetServer and *TargetServerGroup*	Moved to *Microsoft.SqlServer.Management.Smo.Agent* namespace
TransactionLog	Functionality moved into the *Database* object
TransArticle and *TransArticle2*	*TransArticle* object; moved to *Microsoft.SqlServer.Replication* namespace
Transfer method and *Transfer2* object	*Transfer* object
TransPublication and *TransPublication2*	*TransPublication* object; moved to *Microsoft.SqlServer .Replication* namespace
TransPullSubscription and *TransPullSubscription2*	*TransPullSubscription* object; moved to *Microsoft .SqlServer.Replication* namespace
Trigger and *Trigger2*	*Trigger* object
User and *User2*	*User* object
UserDefinedDatatype and *UserDefinedDataType2*	*UserDefinedType* object
UserDefinedFunction	*UserDefinedFunction* and *UserDefinedFunction-Parameter* objects
View and *View2*	*View* object

New Features in SMO

To account for the new features in SQL Server 2005, SMO includes the following functionality:

- Captures and batches the execution of T-SQL statements. Statements can be captured and sent as a batch to improve network performance.

- Manages SQL services using the WMI Provider. This means that SQL services can be started, stopped, and paused programmatically.

- Includes advanced scripting capabilities. T-SQL scripts can be generated to re-create SQL Server objects that describe relationships to other objects on the SQL Server instance.

- Data transfer leverages SQL Server Integration Services (SSIS).

- Uses unique resource names (URNs) for resolution of remote servers.

- Includes rich event handling model that allows you to insert code that will execute when a specific event occurs.

SMO also has a number of new objects and properties that correspond to new components in SQL Server 2005. These include:

- Support for snapshot isolation and row-level versioning for increased concurrency

- Table and index partitioning for storage of data on a partition scheme

- HTTP endpoints for managing Web service requests

- Full support for XML technologies, including the XML data type, XML schema collection, and XML indexes

- The ability to create read-only copies of databases using view point databases

- Full support for SQL Server Service Broker

- Facilitates management of Database Mail

- Allows programmatic management of registered servers

- Programmatic replay of SQL Server events and manipulation of SQL Trace

- Support for Notification Services

- Support for DDL triggers

Working with SMO in Visual Studio

To get started working with SMO, you must first set a reference in the Visual Studio project to the SMO assembly by choosing Project, Add Reference and selecting the *Microsoft.SqlServer.Smo* and *Microsoft.SqlServer.ConnectionInfo* components, as shown in Figure 6-1.

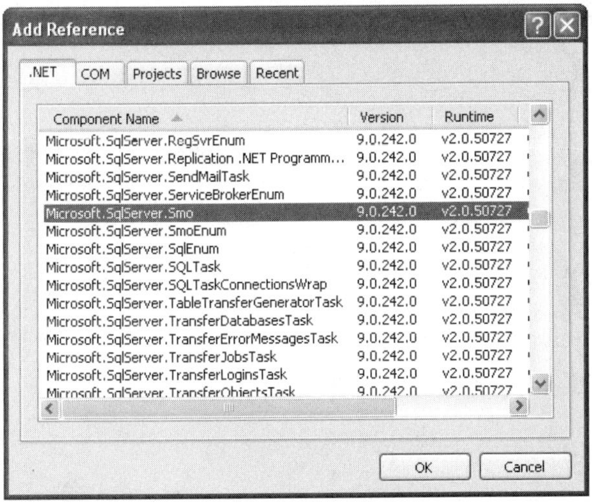

Figure 6-1 Setting a reference to SMO

You then add two *using* statements for the two namespaces that you will use most often. In C#, it looks like this:

```
using Microsoft.SqlServer.Management.Common;
using Microsoft.SqlServer.Management.Smo;
```

In Visual Basic, it looks like this:

```
Imports Microsoft.SqlServer.Management.Common
Imports Microsoft.SqlServer.Management.Smo
```

Next you will want to work with SMO objects, the first being the *ServerConnection* object. This object represents a connection to an SQL Server instance. It lets you connect to a server and assign that connection to an SMO *Server* object. The *Server* object represents an actual SQL Server instance. The object allows you to retrieve the database server's properties and perform tasks such as attaching a database. To help you understand how to use these objects, we will create a simple application to connect to an SQL Server instance using the *ServerConnection* object and then use a *Server* object to retrieve the SQL Server version, edition, and name of the instance. This application will ask the user for a user ID and password or allow the use of integrated security (as shown in Figure 6-2).

The code in Listing 6-1 shows how to connect to an SQL Server instance using either integrated security or SQL Server security. The results are shown in Figure 6-3.

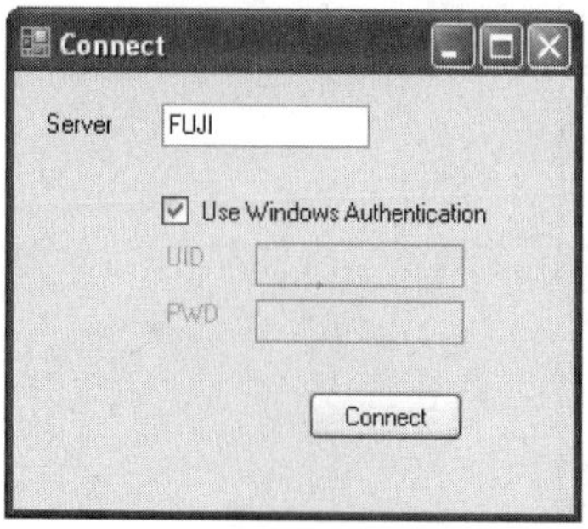

Figure 6-2   Simple SMO application

Listing 6-1   Connecting to an SQL Server database via SMO

```
private void btnConnect_Click(object sender, EventArgs e)
{
    //ServerConnection object used to connect
    ServerConnection conn = new ServerConnection();
    //pass in the name of the server/instance
    conn.ServerInstance = txtServer.Text.ToString();

    //determine if integrated security is set
    if (chkSSPI.Checked == false)
    {
        //using sql security
        conn.LoginSecure = false;
        conn.Login = txtUID.Text.ToString();
        conn.Password = txtPwd.Text.ToString();
    }

    //try to connect and return server information
    try
    {
        Server svrLocal = new Server(conn);
        //pop up the message box to the user here
        //get the info via the Information property
        MessageBox.Show("You are not connected to: " + svrLocal.Name +
System.Environment.NewLine +
            " Edition Info: " + svrLocal.Information.Edition +
System.Environment.NewLine +
            " Version Info: " + svrLocal.Information.Version,"SMO Demos");
    }

    catch (SmoException exSMO)
    {
        //catch SMO specific exceptions
        MessageBox.Show(exSMO.ToString());

    }
    catch (Exception ex)
    {
        MessageBox.Show(ex.ToString());
    }
}
```

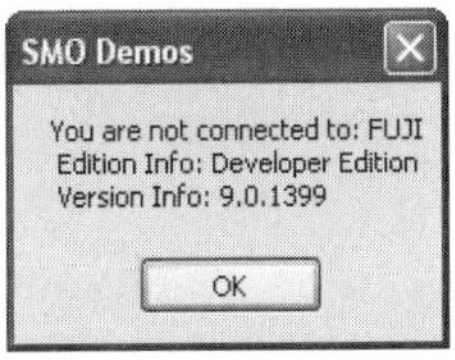

SMO Demos ☒

You are not connected to: FUJI
Edition Info: Developer Edition
Version Info: 9.0.1399

OK

Figure 6-3   Results of the simple SMO application

Tip   When you reference a local server with an instance name, you can use the syntax *(local)\instance_name* instead of the less flexible *server_name\instance_name*.

Iterating Through Available Servers

Depending on the type of functionality you need when performing your administrative tasks, you might have to programmatically enumerate a list of or iterate through available SQL Server instances. To perform this task in SMO, you can use the *SmoApplication* object's *EnumAvailableSqlServers* method, passing in a Boolean value to tell SMO whether to look only locally. The *EnumAvailableSqlServers* method returns a *DataTable* with the results of the enumeration filled with lots of properties. The following code calls a reusable method in a helper class called *ListAllKnownInstances*, as shown in Listing 6-2. *ListAllKnownInstances* searches the network for all the SQL Server instances it can "see" by using *EnumAvailableSqlServers* and returns the resulting *DataTable*. Our code then takes that *DataTable* and binds it to a *DataGridView*.

```
private void button1_Click(object sender, EventArgs e)
  {
    DataTable dtList = SMOUtilities.ListAllKnownInstances();
    dataGridView1.DataSource = dtList;
  }
```

Listing 6-2 makes a call to the *EnumAvailableSqlServers* method and displays the results in a *DataGrid*.

Warning   Be aware that the code in Listing 6-2 will sometimes take a long time to process. Microsoft uses similar code in the SQL Server Import and Export Wizard, and it takes a while to process the available servers. Books Online says, "The computer running the instance SQL Server might not receive responses to the *EnumAvailableSqlServers* method in a timely manner. The returned list might not show all the available instances of SQL Server on the network. However, by trying a second time or more, more servers might become visible."

Listing 6-2   Enumerating available servers

```
public static DataTable ListAllKnownInstances()
{
    //this method will return a DataTable
    //based on all of the servers available
    //this method can take some time depending on your network
    //will connect to SQL Server 2000 machines too
    DataTable dtServers = new DataTable();
    try
    {


        //Obtain a list of all SQL Server available
        //this method returns a DataTable
        dtServers = SmoApplication.EnumAvailableSqlServers(false);
    }

    catch (SmoException exSMO)
    {
        MessageBox.Show(exSMO.ToString());

    }
    catch (Exception ex)
    {
        MessageBox.Show(ex.ToString());
    }

    return dtServers;
}
```

Figure 6-4 shows the results of running the code in Listing 6-2.

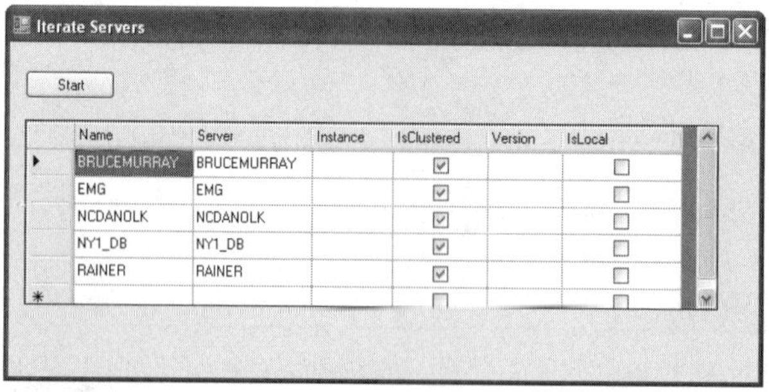

Figure 6-4   Simple enumeration of available servers

Retrieving Server Settings

A task you might find yourself performing often with SMO is retrieving server settings of a particular SQL Server instance. You might have to create a Windows application like the one shown in Figure 6-5 or create a Web-based application to retrieve server settings and allow your users to modify SQL Server settings. You can choose which settings to allow users to change by simply deciding whether to show those settings in the application.

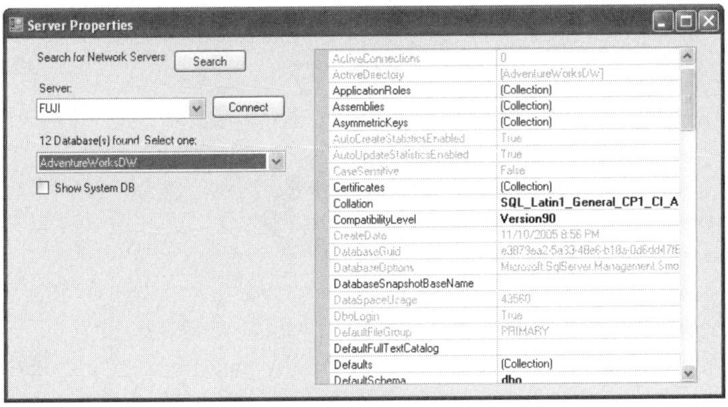

Figure 6-5   Retrieving server settings

The application in Figure 6-5 is really simple and builds on what you have learned so far. It allows you to iterate through all the available servers, select a server, and then select a database and display the server's settings.

We can list all the servers available to our application by reusing the *ListAllKnownInstances* method (which is part of the custom code shown previously in Listing 6-2). *ListAllKnown-Instances* returns a *DataTable* of all the servers that are available and visible to you. As shown in Listing 6-3, we then iterate through the *DataRow* collection for each row in the *DataTable*, verifying that the value is not null or blank and adding it to the combo box named *cboServers* using the *Items.Add* method. Lastly, after we have filled the combo box with all the available servers, we can select as the default value in the combo box the local SQL Server instance's name using the *LocalServer.Name* property.

Listing 6-3   Enumerating available servers and filling the combo box

```
private void btnSearch_Click(object sender, EventArgs e)
{
    Cursor = Cursors.WaitCursor;
    //get a DataTable of the servers
   DataTable dtList = SMOUtilities.ListAllKnownInstances();

    foreach (DataRow dr in dtList.Rows)
    {
        String ServerName;
        ServerName = dr["Server"].ToString();

        if (dr["Instance"] != null && dr["Instance"].ToString().Length > 0)
            ServerName += @"\" + dr["Instance"].ToString();

        if (cboServers.Items.IndexOf(ServerName) < 0)
            cboServers.Items.Add(ServerName);
    }

    //  By default select the local server
    Server LocalServer = new Server();
    String LocalServerName = LocalServer.Name;
```

```
if (LocalServer.InstanceName != null && LocalServer.InstanceName.Length > 0)
    LocalServerName += @"\" + LocalServer.InstanceName;

int intCboIndex = cboServers.FindStringExact(LocalServerName);
if (intCboIndex >= 0)
    cboServers.SelectedIndex = intCboIndex;

Cursor = Cursors.Default;
}
```

Next we need to connect to the selected server. We can do this by calling the *ConnectSMO* custom method described in Listing 6-4. You call this method by passing in the name of the SQL Server instance you want to connect to and a Boolean value indicating whether you want to include system databases in the returned list of available databases. The applications form has a check box to indicate whether you want to include system databases. We can call *ConnectSMO* like this:

```
private void btnConnect_Click(object sender, EventArgs e)
{
    ConnectSMO(cboServers.Text, chkSystemDB.Checked);
}
```

The *ConnectSMO* method is responsible for adding each database to the *cboDatabase* combo box. It first calls a generic method called *FillComboWithDatabases*, which is located in the *SMOUtilities* class. Listing 6-4 shows the *ConnectSMO* method that calls *FillComboWithDatabases*. After the *FillComboWithDatabases* method is called, *ConnectSMO* cleans up the user interface and returns control to the user.

Listing 6-4 The *ConnectSMO* custom method

```
private void ConnectSMO(string strServerName, bool blnIncludeSystemDB)
{
    try
    {
        //use an hourglass
        Cursor = Cursors.WaitCursor;
        //clear out the items, if you don't do this then
        //the combo box will have dupes when you click on
        //the show system database box
        cboDatabase.Items.Clear();

        //this is a reusable function that fills the
        //combo box with the available databases on a
        //particular server, passing in the cbo by reg
        //we will reuse this in a later example
        SMOUtilities.FillComboWithDatabases(strServerName, blnIncludeSystemDB, ref
cboDatabase);

        //now that the cbo is processed we
        //will manipulate the UI
```

```
        if (cboDatabase.Items.Count > 0)
        {
            lblDatabase.Text = cboDatabase.Items.Count.ToString() + " Database(s) found.
Select one:";
            cboDatabase.Enabled = true;
        }
        else
            lblDatabase.Text = "No Results";

        chkSystemDB.Enabled = true;
    }
    catch (SmoException exSMO)
    {
        MessageBox.Show(exSMO.Message.ToString());
        SetFormErrorParms();
    }
    catch (Exception ex)
    {
        MessageBox.Show(ex.ToString());
        SetFormErrorParms();
    }
    finally
    {
        Cursor = Cursors.Default;
    }

}
```

FillComboWithDatabases, shown in Listing 6-5, accepts a *ComboBox* object as well as the server name and a flag to indicate whether you should include system databases. *FillComboWithDatabases* obtains a reference to the SQL Server instance you want by using the *Server* object and then iterating through the *Databases* collection and adding each database to the *cboDatabase* combo box.

Listing 6-5   Filling the combo box with the databases using the *FillComboWithDatabases* custom method

```
public static void FillComboWithDatabases(string strServerName, bool blnIncludeSystemDB,
ref ComboBox cbo)
    {
        int intDBCount = 0;
        // Fill the db combo
        Server svr = new Server(strServerName);

        foreach (Database db in svr.Databases)
        {
            //determine if the system database
            //flag is set and include/exclude
            if (blnIncludeSystemDB || !db.IsSystemObject)
            {
                intDBCount++;
                cbo.Items.Add(db.Name);
            }
        }
    }
```

Now that we have our SQL Server instance selected, it's time to select the database and then display all its properties. In this application, we will bind the properties of the database to a Windows Forms *PropertyGrid*. We'll do this in the combo box's *SelectedIndexChanged* event, which is shown in Listing 6-6. If you want to show only certain properties, you can iterate through the properties collection and display only the properties you want the user to be able to see.

Listing 6-6   Reacting to the *SelectedIndexChanged* event

```
private void comboDB_SelectedIndexChanged(object sender, EventArgs e)
{
    try
    {
        //This function will get the database properties
        //for selected database in the combobox
        Cursor = Cursors.WaitCursor;

        Server SelectedServer = new Server(cboServers.Text);
        Database SelectedDatabase = SelectedServer.Databases[cboDatabase.Text];

        propertyGrid1.SelectedObject =SelectedDatabase;

    }
    catch (SmoException exSMO)
    {
        DBPropLabel.Text = "";
        MessageBox.Show(exSMO.ToString());
    }
    catch (Exception ex)
    {
        DBPropLabel.Text = "";
        MessageBox.Show(ex.ToString());
    }
    finally
    {
        this.Cursor = Cursors.Default;
    }
}
```

Creating Backup-and-Restore Applications

The most common application that developers created with SQL-DMO over the years was a backup-and-restore application—sometimes for customers who do not have security access to the database and cannot use Enterprise Manager and sometimes for customers who need remote administration and verification. These backup-and-restore applications eventually led to the creation of Web-based tools monitoring. SMO makes it easy to create an application for backup, verification, and restore. To demonstrate those capabilities, we will work with a simple backup-and-restore application created entirely in SMO, as shown in Figure 6-6.

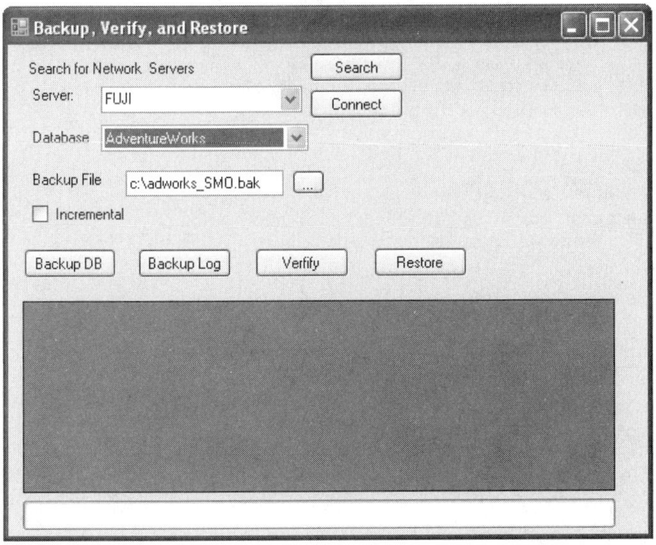

Figure 6-6   Backup-and-restore application

Backup

This application allows you to search for servers by reusing the code from prior examples. To obtain the list of servers, we will use our reusable *ListAllKnownInstances()* method as well as the *FillComboWithDatabases()* method to list all the databases on the server. The application then allows you to select a backup file–c:\adventureworksbackup.bak, for example. As shown in Figure 6-6, we also have a button in the user interface for the user to run the backup. Alternatively, this process could be automated in a console application and a .config file or easily be used from an ASP .NET Web page.

Once you have a server and a database selected, the code that runs the backup can be run. This code creates a *Server* and a *Backup* object and then assigns the *Action* property to *BackupActionType.Database* as the action to take for the backup. (We will look at log files next.) You have to add the device where you want to back up to (most likely a file), but you can back up to tape and other standard SQL devices as well. You can use an Incremental Boolean property to indicate whether to make only a differential backup, as shown in the following code. You perform the backup by executing the *SqlBackup* method, as shown in Listing 6-7.

Listing 6-7   Performing a backup programmatically using SMO

```
private void btnBackup_Click(object sender, EventArgs e)
{
    //use the server selected in the Server combo box
        //this server can be typed in as well to the Cbo
        Server svr = new Server(cboServers.Text.ToString());
    Backup bkp = new Backup();

    Cursor = Cursors.WaitCursor;
    dataGridView1.DataSource = "";
```

```
                    //attempt the backup and show a progress meter
                    //a lot can go wrong here, from file access
                    //to DBCC issues, so it is important to handle all
                    //errors that may arise
                        try
              {
                    string strFileName = txtFileName.Text.ToString();
                    string strDatabaseName = cboDatabase.Text.ToString();

                    bkp.Action = BackupActionType.Database;
                    bkp.Database = strDatabaseName;

                    //set the device: File, Tape, etc.
                    bkp.Devices.AddDevice(strFileName, DeviceType.File);
                    //set this when you want to do Incremental
                    bkp.Incremental = chkIncremental.Checked;

                    //progress meter stuff
                    progressBar1.Value = 0;
                    progressBar1.Maximum = 100;
                    progressBar1.Value = 10;

                    //this gives us the % complete by handling the event
                    //provided by SMO on the percent complete; we will
                    //update the progress meter in the event handler

                    //set the progress meter to 10% by default
                    bkp.PercentCompleteNotification = 10;
                    //call to the event handler to increment the progress meter

bkp.PercentComplete += new PercentCompleteEventHandler(ProgressEventHandler);
                    //this does the backup
                    bkp.SqlBackup(svr);
            //alert the user when it is all done
            MessageBox.Show("Database Backed Up To: " + strFileName, "SMO Demos");


              }
            catch (SmoException exSMO)
            {
                MessageBox.Show(exSMO.ToString());

            }
            catch (Exception ex)
            {
                MessageBox.Show(ex.ToString());
            }

            finally
            {
                Cursor = Cursors.Default;
                progressBar1.Value = 0;
            }
        }
```

Progress Meter

You might notice the progress meter on the bottom of the screen in the previous example, which displays the progress of the backup being performed. You can implement this quite easily. The following code shows the event handler for the backup with the *PercentComplete-EventArgs* parameter, which contains the percent complete value as an integer between 0 and 100. We set the progress bar's *Value* property equal to that value.

```
public void ProgressEventHandler(object sender, PercentCompleteEventArgs e)
{
   //increase the progress bar up by the percent
   progressBar1.Value = e.Percent;
}
```

To get this delegate working, just pass it to the *PercentCompleteEventHandler* object, as shown in the following code. By default, you can set the *PercentCompleteNotification* value to any value you want; we set it to 10 percent. This is the starting value of your progress meter, so 10 will represent 10 percent of the progress meter getting filled.

```
//this gives us the % complete by handling the event
//provided by SMO on the percent complete; we will
//update the progress meter in the event handler

//set the progress meter to 10% by default
bkp.PercentCompleteNotification = 10;
//call to the event handler to increment the progress meter

bkp.PercentComplete += new PercentCompleteEventHandler(ProgressEventHandler);
```

Tip   For larger databases, you might want to set the percentage to a lower value because 10 percent of a large backup might take a long time. You also want the user to see that the application is still functioning correctly. Using a smaller value will cause the progress meter to change more frequently.

Log Backup

You do back up your log files, don't you? Backing up a log file requires exactly the same code shown in Listing 6-3 for backing up your database, except that you set the *Action* property to *Log* instead of to *Database*:

```
bkp.Action = BackupActionType.Log;
```

Verify

After you perform a backup, you might want to verify that the backup was performed properly and that your backup device is not corrupt. (Or you might want to verify that your backup device is not corrupt before you perform the backup.) You can do this by using the *Restore* object's *SqlVerify* method, as shown in Listing 6-8. What's really cool is that SMO gives you back a *DataTable* filled with all the properties of the backup, and you can bind it to a *DataGrid*, as shown in Figure 6-7. This is quite useful if you want to build a Web page to show the results of a backup (which you can even check using your cell phone).

Listing 6-8   Verifying a backup via SMO

```
private void btnVerify_Click(object sender, EventArgs e)
{
    Server svr = new Server();
    Restore rest = new Restore();
    bool blnVerify;
    DataTable dt=new DataTable();


    Cursor = Cursors.WaitCursor;
    dataGridView1.DataSource = "";

    try
    {
        string strFileName = txtFileName.Text.ToString();

        rest.Devices.AddDevice(strFileName, DeviceType.File);
        blnVerify = rest.SqlVerify(svr);

        if (blnVerify == true)
        {
            MessageBox.Show("Backup Verified!", "SMO Demos");
            dt = rest.ReadFileList(svr);
            dataGridView1.DataSource = dt;
        }
        else
        {
            MessageBox.Show("Backup NOT Verified!", "SMO Demos");
        }
    }
    catch (SmoException exSMO)
    {
        MessageBox.Show(exSMO.ToString());

    }
    catch (Exception ex)
    {
        MessageBox.Show(ex.ToString());
    }

    finally
    {
        Cursor = Cursors.Default;
    }
}
```

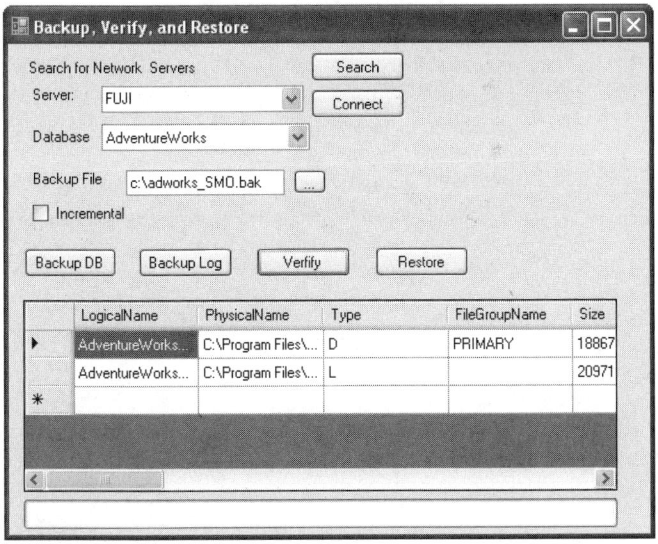

Figure 6-7 Backup verification

Restore

What good is a backup without a restore? As shown in Listing 6-9, you must instantiate a
Server and a *Restore* object and provide the name of the backup file (or device) and the name
of the database you are restoring to. Be sure to set the *Action* property of the *Restore* object to
RestoreActionType.Database to restore your database. If you are going to restore the log, set the
Action property of the *Restore* object to *RestoreActionType.Log*. Notice that we are using the
same event handler for the Progress meter as in the backup example, reusing as much code as
possible.

Listing 6-9 Performing a restore with SMO

```
private void btnRestore_Click(object sender, EventArgs e)
{
    Server svr = new Server(cboServers.Text.ToString());
    Restore res = new Restore();

    Cursor = Cursors.WaitCursor;
    dataGridView1.DataSource = "";

    try
    {
        string strFileName = txtFileName.Text.ToString();
        string strDatabaseName = cboDatabase.SelectedValue.ToString();

        res.Database = strDatabaseName;
        res.Action = RestoreActionType.Database;
        //use for restore of the log
        //res.Action = RestoreActionType.Log;
        res.Devices.AddDevice(strFileName, DeviceType.File);
```

```
        //progress meter stuff
        progressBar1.Value = 0;
        progressBar1.Maximum = 100;
        progressBar1.Value = 10;

        res.PercentCompleteNotification = 10;
        res.ReplaceDatabase = true;
        res.PercentComplete += new PercentCompleteEventHandler(ProgressEventHandler);

        //use below if you want to relocate the mdf files
        //res.RelocateFiles.Add(new RelocateFile("aw_data", @"c:\aw_dat.mdf"));

        //preform the restore
        res.SqlRestore(svr);

        MessageBox.Show("Restore of " + strDatabaseName + " Complete!", "SMO Demos");
    }
    catch (SmoException exSMO)
    {
        MessageBox.Show(exSMO.ToString());

    }
    catch (Exception ex)
    {
        MessageBox.Show(ex.ToString());
    }

    finally
    {
        Cursor = Cursors.Default;
        progressBar1.Value = 0;
    }
}
```

Restoring to a Different Location

The SMO backup and restore functionality has many other features, for example, changing the file location of your restore. SMO allows you to do this by simply using the *RelocateFiles* *.Add* method of the *Restore* object, as shown here:

```
res.RelocateFiles.Add(new RelocateFile("adventureworks1_data",
@"c:\adventureworks1_dat.mdf"));
```

Performing Programmatic DBCC Commands with SMO

Another feature worth exploring in SMO is database integrity checks. You can perform just about all the Database Consistency Check (DBCC) functions using SMO; Table 6-3 shows a subset of what is available. (DBCC can do many administrative checks besides integrity checks.)

Table 6-3 Integrity Checks with SMO

SMO Method	DBCC Function
CheckAllocations()	DBCC CHECKALLOC
CheckAllocationsDataOnly()	DBCC CHECKALLOC('databasename', NOINDEX)
CheckCatalog()	DBCC CHECKCATALOG
CheckTables()	DBCC CHECKDB
CheckTablesDataOnly()	DBCC CHECKDB('databasename', NOINDEX)

The following simple application uses the DBCC commands shown in Figure 6-8. The application allows you to search for servers reusing code from prior examples and then list all the databases on that server. To obtain the list of servers, we will use our reusable *ListAllKnownInstances()* method as well as the *FillComboWithDatabases()* method to list all the databases on the server. The code hardcodes the *CheckCatalog* SMO method (which is the DBCC command); however, you can use any of the DBCC commands listed in Table 6-3 with the exact same code.

> **Note** Books Online states that *CheckCatalog* performs various consistency checks between system metadata tables. In reality, if DBCC CHECKCATALOG reports back any errors, it means that someone manually added data to the system tables or edited or deleted data. I regularly perform this check on my Web site's database because a hole in your security and modified system tables are among the top symptoms of an SQL injection attack. You can run the code here every few hours programmatically and have the results e-mailed to you, or you can place the code in this section on a private administrative Web page that you can check anytime.

The *CheckCatalog()* method, like all integrity-checking SMO methods, returns a *StringCollection* object filled with the results. As the code in Listing 6-10 shows, you must iterate through the results and then take the appropriate actions. If all is fine in your database, as it is here, you get the ubiquitous message from DBCC: "DBCC execution completed. If DBCC printed error messages, contact your system administrator."

> **Note** The problem with running a DBCC check is that if you are not an SQL Server DBA, you most likely won't know what to do about an error. The administrative functions of DBCC are beyond the scope of the book, but you can consult a DBA for corrective action. If you are the developer and the DBA, this is an area where you should invest in some learning cycles.

Listing 6-10 Performing a Database Consistency Check (DBCC) with SMO

```
private void button1_Click(object sender, EventArgs e)
{
    Server svr = new Server(cboServers.Text.ToString());
    Database db = svr.Databases[cboDatabase.Text.ToString()];  StringCollection strCol;
    strCol = db.CheckCatalog();//can also do most DBCC commands
```

```
    for (int intCount = 0; intCount < strCol.Count; intCount++)
    {
        if (strCol[intCount].Length > 0)
        label1.Text+=System.Convert.ToString((strCol[intCount]));
    }
}
```

Figure 6-8   DBCC application via SMO

You can run many other DBCC functions. The code is exactly the same, but sometimes you have to pass in a table name or index name. See Table 6-3 or Books Online for more examples.

Summary

We only scratched the surface of SMO in this chapter because SMO is a purely administrative feature. That said, SMO is an exciting new object model that covers everything SQL Server does—even more than SQL Server Management Studio covers. As a developer, you might find yourself constantly performing the same task over and over again in Management Studio. If you find yourself doing that, think about writing an application in SMO and C# or Visual Basic. SMO is more feature-complete and performs better than the legacy SQL-DMO, and it can fulfill many of your administrative needs. As shown in this chapter, with very little code you can perform a variety of administrative tasks, including automation of backups and restores, as well as running consistency checks.

Chapter 7
SQL Server 2005 Security

–Rob Walters

In this chapter:

With the growing concern about personal data protection and the proliferation of computer viruses, developing a methodology for secure computing has been a vital task for Microsoft. Back in 2003, Microsoft created the Trustworthy Computing initiative, which described the advances that needed to be made in order for people to feel more comfortable using devices powered by computers and software. (The initiative can be found at *http://www.microsoft.com/mscorp/twc/twc_whitepaper.mspx.*) From this initiative, Microsoft SQL Server 2005 has leveraged what is known as the Security Framework (Figure 7-1).

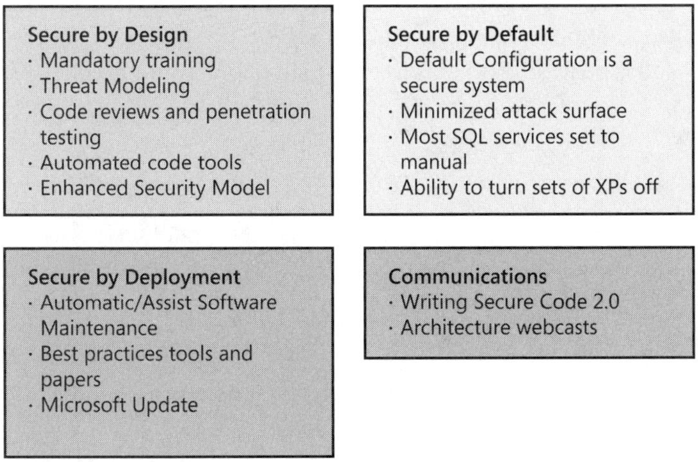
Secure by Design
· Mandatory training
· Threat Modeling
· Code reviews and penetration testing
· Automated code tools
· Enhanced Security Model
Secure by Default
· Default Configuration is a secure system
· Minimized attack surface
· Most SQL services set to manual
· Ability to turn sets of XPs off
Secure by Deployment
· Automatic/Assist Software Maintenance
· Best practices tools and papers
· Microsoft Update
Communications
· Writing Secure Code 2.0
· Architecture webcasts

Figure 7-1 Security Framework in SQL Server 2005

Four Themes of the Security Framework

SQL Server 2005 security is organized around four themes: Secure by Design, Secure by Default, Secure by Deployment, and Communications.

Secure by Design

Security has been a design consideration in all previous versions of SQL Server. With SQL Server 2005, the product development group made sure that everyone was on the same page when it came to security. The entire product team went through mandatory security training, and threat models were written and reviewed for all components of all the features within the product. In addition, a massive effort was carried out to review code with respect to security for the entire product. Microsoft takes security very seriously, and designers of features within SQL Server have made security a top consideration in the final design.

Secure by Default

The Secure by Default effort is one of the most notable areas of the Security Framework that SQL Server users will experience. You can experience it by simply installing SQL Server with the default options. Users of previous SQL Server versions will notice that services such as SQL Server Agent are off by default. In addition, certain features such as *xp_cmdshell* and OPENROWSET queries are disabled. This "off by default" effort attempts to minimize the surface area for attack, and the effects of this can be seen throughout the product.

Secure by Deployment

Perhaps one of the most challenging issues with SQL Server is effective deployment in a production environment. With so many different configurations and features, it can be difficult for administrators to keep on top of the latest patches and best practices. SQL Server 2005 is now a part of Microsoft Update to help alleviate the pain of determining the latest patch to apply.

Communications

Even before SQL Server 2005 was released to the public, a plethora of technical information was already available in various forms. White papers, Webcasts, and active newsgroups educated and assisted beta customers with the product. Today, most of these Webcasts and white papers have been updated and provide rich educational content.

All editions of SQL Server 2005 include security features that help users protect their data. This chapter will cover the following aspects of SQL Server security:

- Overview of security, including authentication and authorization
- User-schema separation

■ Encrypting data within the database and while in transit

■ Protecting SQL Server 2005

SQL Server 2005 Security Overview

If you are already familiar with the concepts of *users* and *roles* and SQL Server logins, you can probably skip ahead to the next section of this chapter. But for those who aren't, we'll provide a quick explanation. The concepts of users and roles exist both in the Microsoft Windows world and in SQL Server. In an abstract sense, they are referred to as *principals*. Principals are entities that can request resources from the application or an operating system. In the case of Windows, principals are entities such as Domain Users and Groups, and Local Users and Groups. In SQL Server, these entities are logins and server roles. Within a database, these entities are database users, database roles, and application roles, to name a few.

So what can we do with entities? Chances are, you have an object such as a file or a database table that you want to allow access to. These objects, or *securables*, are the resources to which the authorization system regulates access. Some securables can be contained within other securables, creating nested hierarchies called *scopes* that can themselves be secured. The securable scopes in the SQL Server Database Engine are *server*, *database*, and *schema*. Every securable in SQL Server has an associated permission that can be granted to a principal. Figure 7-2 shows a graphical representation of the principal-securable-permission model.

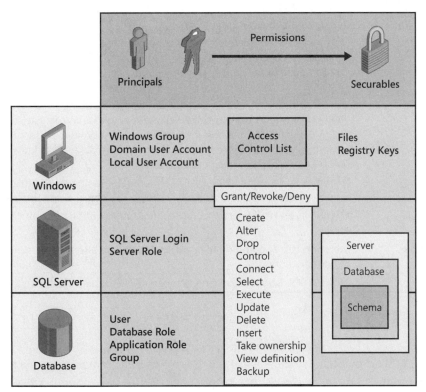

Figure 7-2   Principal-securable-permission model

SQL Server Logins

Now that we have discussed the big picture of SQL Server security and how it relates to Windows security, it is time to get into SQL Server–specific areas. To connect to SQL Server, you need a login. This login can be a combination of a custom user name (such as *Login1*) and a complex password. Alternatively, you can add an existing Windows account as a login to SQL Server and forgo the creation of a separate username and password. Thus, SQL Server supports two kinds of logins: Windows logins and SQL Server logins, respectively.

Logins themselves have no access to any specific database within SQL Server; they basically allow for connection to SQL Server. In addition, logins are the entities that can be granted server-wide permissions to perform certain actions. These actions are bundled into server roles such as sysadmin, diskadmin, and dbcreator (to name a few). Table 7-1 shows the list of server roles and their corresponding functions.

Table 7-1 SQL Server 2005 Fixed Server Roles

Server Role	Description
sysadmin	Members can perform any activity in the server. By default, all members of the Windows BUILTIN\Administrators group, the local administrator's group, are members of the sysadmin fixed server role. The SQL Server service account is also a member of this role.
dbcreator	Members can create, alter, drop, and restore any database.
diskadmin	This role is used for managing disk files. Most of the capabilities relate to adding and removing backup devices.
Processadmin	Members can terminate processes that are running in an instance of SQL Server. This role is useful if you want to give someone the ability to kill a long-running query or an orphaned connection.
securityadmin	Members can manage logins and their properties. They can GRANT, DENY, and REVOKE server-level permissions as well as database-level permissions. They can also reset passwords for SQL Server logins. This role has no rights to assign database permissions. If you want securityadmin members to be able to do this, you must make their logins part of the db_accessadmin fixed database role for the specific database.
Bulkadmin	Members can run the BULK INSERT statement. Membership in this role still requires that non-sysadmins have access to the object being updated.
serveradmin	Members can change server-wide configuration options and shut down the server.
setupadmin	Members can add and remove linked servers and also execute some system stored procedures.
public	All valid SQL Server logins are members of the public role.

Database Users

Logins can be created using SQL Server Management Studio or via the T-SQL statement *CREATE LOGIN*. After you create a login, the natural desire is to then grant it access to a particular database. Databases themselves have their own set of roles that define specific access and actions that users of these roles can take. Before we can go ahead and give a login access to a database, we must create a database User for this login. Again, you can create a database user by using SQL Server Management Studio or via the T-SQL statement *CREATE USER*.

Once you create a database user, you can optionally include it in one of the database roles. Table 7-2 lists the roles that all databases have.

Table 7-2   SQL Server 2005 Fixed Database Roles

Database Role	Description
db_accessadmin	Members can add or remove access for Windows logins, Windows groups, and SQL Server logins.
db_backupoperator	Members can back up the database.
db_datareader	Members can read all data from all user tables.
db_datawriter	Members can add, delete, or change data in all user tables.
db_ddladmin	Members can run any Data Definition Language (DDL) command in a database.
db_denydatareader	Members cannot read any data in the user tables within a database.
db_denydatawriter	Members cannot add, modify, or delete any data in the user tables within a database.
db_owner	Members can perform all configuration and maintenance activities on the database, including dropping the database.
db_securityadmin	Members can modify role membership and manage permissions.

There is a special role that sysadmins cannot explicitly give users permissions to; it is known as the public role. All database users that are created are included in the public role. This role captures all default permissions for users in a particular database. It cannot have users, groups, or roles assigned to it because everyone belongs to this role by default. This role cannot be dropped. Thus, to protect against unauthorized data access, you should minimize the permissions granted to the public role. Instead, grant permissions to other database roles and to user accounts associated with logins.

The Guest User Account

On the topic of unauthorized data access, it is important to note a special user account available in SQL Server called guest. This account is created by default on new user-defined databases but does exist in master and tempdb. However, the guest account is disabled by default, which means it does not have any access within the database. The guest account allows a login without a user account to access a database. A login assumes the identity of the guest user when all of the following conditions are met:

- The login has access to an instance of SQL Server but does not have access to the database through his or her own user account or via a Windows group membership.

- The database contains a guest user account.

- The guest account is enabled in the database.

You can apply permissions to the guest user account just as you can any other user account. But you should avoid using the guest account because all logins without their own database permissions obtain the database permissions granted to this account. If you must use the guest account, grant minimum permissions.

Up to now, we have discussed the various aspects of server and database principals. A complete discussion of these topics is beyond the scope of this book; for in-depth information on user management within SQL Server, see SQL Server Books Online.

Authentication and Authorization

Before we dive into the concepts of authentication and authorization, it is important to discuss a new feature in SQL Server 2005 called Endpoints. In previous versions of SQL Server, clients could connect via TCP, Named Pipes, Shared Memory, and VIA. As long as one of these protocols was enabled on the server and the user had a valid login, the connection was accepted. SQL Server 2005 introduces a separation of this behavior via Endpoints.

Endpoints can be considered a point of entry into SQL Server. Administrators can create an endpoint for not only TCP, Named Pipes, Shared Memory, and VIA, but also for HTTP. Once an endpoint is created, you can restrict access so users can connect only via a certain endpoint type. For example, you might create a login called Login1 and grant access to the HTTP endpoint and deny access to all other endpoints (TCP, Named Pipes, Shared Memory, and VIA). In this state, Login1 can access SQL Server only via the HTTP endpoint; it cannot directly connect to SQL Server via TCP or any other protocol. To see how this endpoint verification affects authentication, let's consider the process of making a client connection.

How Clients Establish a Connection

If a TCP client wants to make a connection to SQL Server, it must first know which port to connect to. In previous versions of SQL Server, there was always a thread waiting on UDP port 1434. Its purpose was to give back details on all of the instances of SQL Server that were running, as well as the port numbers of those instances. All a client had to do was make a connection to this port and determine which port it wanted to connect to, given a specific instance of SQL Server. This process generally worked until hackers found a way to launch a Denial of Service (DoS) attack on SQL Server by continuously sending packets to this port requesting the enumeration. Because this process of enumerating was part of the SQL Server service, the "SQL Slammer" worm virus created some headaches for SQL Server users. In SQL Server 2005, this functionality has been pulled out into a separate service called the SQL Server Browser service. Now you can turn this functionality on and off without touching the SQL Server service itself.

Note   You can mitigate the DoS issue with the browsing service if you block the 1434 port on your firewall. However, if you are concerned about intranet attacks, you might want to consider not running this service and instead explicitly passing the port numbers on the connections strings.

After the network connection request and pre-login handshake has been made, SQL Server must authenticate the user to make sure he has access to begin with. Figure 7-3 depicts the authentication process.

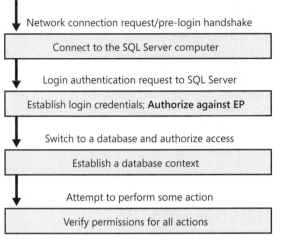

Figure 7-3   SQL Server 2005 authentication model

At this point, the service accepts the login credentials supplied by the user and attempts to validate them. If successful, the login is authorized against the endpoint corresponding to the type of connection made to SQL Server. In this example, the login is checked to see if it has been granted CONNECT permissions to the TCP endpoint. If this is true, the authentication process proceeds; otherwise, the connection fails at this point.

> **Note**   By default, new logins are automatically granted CONNECT permissions to the TCP endpoint.

Once the login has passed the endpoint check, SQL Server switches to a database context (the default database specified for the login or specified in the connection string). It then attempts to authenticate the login as a user of that database. If this is successful, the connection succeeds; otherwise, it fails. Now that a database context is established and the login has been authenticated, the user can perform his work against the server.

Password Policies

In the Windows world, administrators can set login expirations and enforce password policies (for example, requiring passwords to be a certain length and contain a mixture of special characters). Traditionally in SQL Server, SQL logins never respected these global policy settings. In SQL Server 2005, both Windows-authenticated and SQL logins obey the group policy settings defined in the Windows domain.

> **Note**   Password policy enforcement is available only in SQL Server running on Windows
> Server 2003 and later.

To help illustrate password policies, let's define a minimum password length using the Local
Security Settings applet located in the Administrative Tools folder of the Control Panel.
This tool is shown in Figure 7-4.

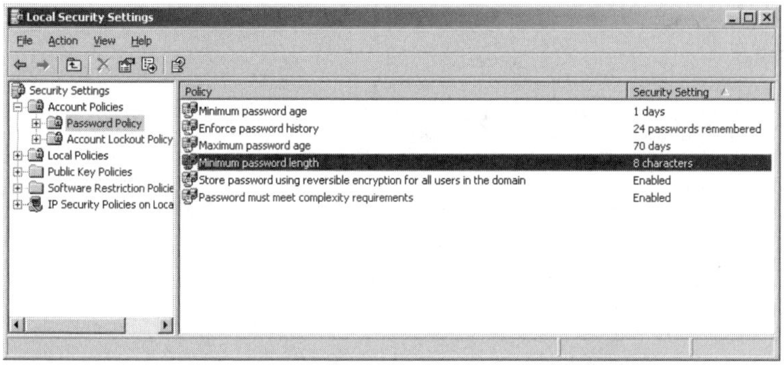

Figure 7-4   Password Policy node of Local Security Settings

Using this tool, we can change a variety of parameters. For this example, we will change the
minimum password length to eight characters. Once this change has been made, we can
proceed with creating our new login.

Instead of using sp_addlogin, as previous versions of SQL Server did, SQL Server 2005 has a
new DDL for creating logins: *CREATE LOGIN*.

```
CREATE LOGIN foo
WITH PASSWORD='123',
CHECK_POLICY=ON,
CHECK_EXPIRATION=ON
```

When this command is executed, it will fail because our password has only three characters
and we specified a minimum of eight.

```
Msg 15116, Level 16, State 1, Line 1
Password validation failed. The password does not meet
        policy requirements because it is too short.
```

The new system view sys.sql_logins returns information about the login such as whether the
policy and expiration are set, but if you want additional information regarding the login, such
as how many bad passwords for this login were submitted, you can use the *LOGINPROPERTY*
built-in function, as shown here.

```
DECLARE @name varchar(20)

SET @name='foo'
```

```
SELECT LOGINPROPERTY( @name, 'PasswordLastSetTime' ) AS PasswordLastSetTime,
LOGINPROPERTY( @name, 'IsExpired' ) AS IsExpired,
LOGINPROPERTY( @name, 'IsLocked' ) AS IsLocked,
LOGINPROPERTY( @name, 'IsMustChange' ) AS IsMustChange,
LOGINPROPERTY( @name, 'LockoutTime' ) AS LockoutTime,
LOGINPROPERTY( @name, 'BadPasswordCount' ) AS BadPasswordCount,
LOGINPROPERTY( @name, 'BadPasswordTime' ) AS BadPasswordTime,
LOGINPROPERTY( @name, 'HistoryLength' ) AS HistoryLength,
LOGINPROPERTY( @name, 'PasswordHash' ) AS PasswordHash
```

User-Schema Separation

Imagine an employee in an organization who is a heavy SQL Server user. She has created many tables and stored procedures, and then suddenly one day she is let go by the company. As a database administrator, your task is to reassign ownership of all the objects that she created and owned. In previous versions of SQL Server, this was a tedious task. In SQL Server 2005, the task is made a lot easier because of the schema feature.

SQL Server 2005 introduces a different concept of schemas than in previous versions of SQL Server. In SQL Server 2000, database users and schemas are equivalent. Every database user is the owner of a schema that has the same name as the user. An owner of an object is effectively identical to the owner of the schema that contains the object. This one-to-one mapping behavior is what makes ownership reassignment so tedious.

SQL Server 2005 separates users and schemas, and schemas are independent buckets that can contain zero or more objects. Users can own one or more schemas and can be assigned a default schema. If a default schema is not specified, the user is defaulted to the dbo schema of the database. This default schema is used to resolve the names of securables that are referred to without using their fully qualified name. In SQL Server 2000, the location that is checked first is the schema owned by the calling database user, followed by the schema owned by dbo. In SQL Server 2005, each user has a default schema, so when SQL Server resolves the names of securables, it checks the default schema.

You can thus transfer ownership of many securables, and a schema can contain securables owned by a database user other than the owner of the schema. This is important to note because if you leverage the old system views, such as *sysobjects*, the results returned in queries will not show up correctly. You must use a catalog view, such *sys.objects*, instead.

The *CREATE SCHEMA* DDL is used to create a new schema. It can also be used to create tables and views within the new schema, and to set *GRANT, DENY*, or *REVOKE* permissions on those objects, as shown in the following example:

```
CREATE SCHEMA Sales
AUTHORIZATION Rob
CREATE TABLE Leads (id int, name varchar(max),phone nvarchar(20))
```

```
GRANT SELECT ON Sales.Leads TO Tammie
DENY SELECT ON Sales.Leads TO Vince;
GO
```

This example creates the Sales schema and assigns it to Rob. A Leads table is created within the Sales schema, and Tammie is granted select access to the table while Vince is denied select access.

For Tammie to access the table in SQL 2000, she must use *Rob* for the schema name, as shown here:

```
SELECT * FROM Production.SalesReps.Rob.Leads
```

In SQL Server 2005, she can use the *Sales* schema name instead:

```
SELECT * FROM Production.SalesReps.Sales.Leads
```

If Rob ever quits or gets fired, all the sysadmin has to do to transfer ownership of the Sales schema to Tammie is the following:

```
ALTER AUTHORIZATION ON SCHEMA::Sales TO Tammie;
GO
```

The abstraction of database users from schemas provides many benefits to developers and administrators, including the following:

- Multiple users can own a single schema through membership in roles or Windows groups. This extends the familiar functionality and allows roles and groups to own objects.

- Dropping database users is greatly simplified.

- Dropping a database user does not require renaming objects that are contained by the schema of that user. Therefore, you do not have to revise and test applications that refer explicitly to schema-contained securables after dropping the user who created them.

- Multiple users can share one default schema for uniform name resolution.

- Shared default schemas allow developers to store shared objects in a schema that was created specifically for a specific application, instead of in the dbo schema.

- Permissions on schemas and schema-contained securables can be managed with a higher degree of detail than in earlier releases.

- Fully qualified object names have four parts: server.database.schema.object.

Execution Context

Granting and managing permissions to non-sysadmin users has always been an interesting challenge, especially when it comes to users who own stored procedures that use tables and other objects they do not own. In a typical example, suppose there are three users: User1, User2, and User3. User3 owns a table, CustomerInformation. User2 has written a stored procedure that enumerates only the customer name from this table. User1 needs to execute User2's stored procedure. With previous versions of SQL Server, User1 not only needs *EXECUTE* permission on User2's stored procedure, but she also needs access to the underlying CustomerInformation table owned by User3. Now multiply this requirement across an enterprise, and you can see the permission management nightmare that unfolds. With SQL Server 2005, User2 can change the execution context of the stored procedure to any of the following:

- **EXECUTE AS CALLER** Executes under the credentials of the caller. This is the same default behavior as in previous versions of SQL Server.

- **EXECUTE AS SELF** Executes under the credentials of the user who last modified the stored procedure.

- **EXECUTE AS <insert name of login>** Executes under the credentials of the login specified. For this to work, the user creating or modifying the stored procedure must have *IMPERSONATE* permission for the login specified.

> **Note**   *EXECUTE AS* also takes a database user name. If you use a login, the scope for the impersonation is server level. If you use a database user, the scope is for the database only.

- **EXECUTE AS OWNER** Executes under the credentials of the login who owns the stored procedure. If the owner changes after the object was created, the execution context is automatically mapped to the new owner.

Referring back to our example, let us write our original problem (Listing 7-1).

Listing 7-1 Execution context example

```
--Create our users
create login User1 with password='^*ahfn2@^(K'
go
create login User2 with password='*HABa7s7aas'
go
create login User3 with password='zxd837&^gqF'
go
create database ExampleDB
go
use ExampleDB
go
```

```
--User 3 will own a table
create user User3 with default_schema=User3
go
create schema User3 authorization User3
go
--User 2 will have SELECT access and write a proc to access
create user User2 with default_schema=User2
go
create schema User2 authorization User2
go

--User 1 will have the right to exec the proc
create user User1 with default_schema=User1
go
create schema User1 authorization User1
go

grant create table to User3
go
grant create proc to User2
go
execute as login='User3'
go
create table User3.CustomerInformation
(CustomerName nvarchar(50))
go
insert into CustomerInformation values ('Bryan''s Bowling Alley')
insert into CustomerInformation values ('Tammie''s Tavern')
insert into CustomerInformation values ('Frank''s Fresh Produce')
go
grant select on CustomerInformation to User2
go
revert
go
execute as login='User2'
--create a stored proc that will return the rows in our table
create proc ViewCustomerNames
AS
BEGIN
select * from User3.CustomerInformation
END
go
grant execute on ViewCustomerNames to User1
go
revert
go
```

Now that all of the users and objects are created, let's log in as User1 and try to directly access the table and stored procedure.

```
execute as login='User1'
--Notice User1 cannot access table directly
select * from User3.CustomerInformation
```

```
--User1 can execute the procedure but does not have permissions on the underlying table
exec User2.ViewCustomerNames
go
revert
go
```

At this point, in previous versions of SQL Server we would have to give User1 some type of
access against User3's table. In SQL Server 2005, User2 can change the execution context of
the stored procedure. In our example, User2 will change the execution context to *EXECUTE
AS OWNER*. This will cause the stored procedure to be executed as User2 because he is the
owner of the stored procedure.

```
execute as login='User2'
go
ALTER PROCEDURE ViewCustomerNames
WITH EXECUTE AS OWNER
AS
BEGIN
select * from User3.CustomerInformation
END
go
revert
go
```

Now when User1 executes User2's stored procedure, the stored procedure will be executing
under the credentials of User2 and thus have access to User3's table only within the context
of the stored procedure. This allows User1 to execute User2's stored procedure without having explicit access to the underlying table.

```
execute as login='User1'
--User1 still cannot access table directly
select * from User3.CustomerInformation
--User1 can execute a procedure that uses the CustomerInformation table
exec User2.ViewCustomerNames
go
revert
go
```

Another form of execution context switching is used within the previous example. In SQL
Server 2005 it is possible to change the execution context of the current connection without
having to close and reopen the connection. The user must either be a sysadmin or have
IMPERSONATE permission on the login for this to work. Alternatively, you can use this same
statement to switch context for a database user. When used for switching context on a database, the scope of impersonation is restricted to the current database. In a context switch to a
database user, the server-level permissions of that user are not inherited. In addition, a user
must either be a sysadmin or have *IMPERSONATE* permission on the user of the database.

Executing context switching is a powerful and efficient way to reduce the number of permissions to manage. For developers and sysadmins, it provides an easy way to test scripts and debug without having to log out and reconnect to SQL Server.

Encryption Support in SQL Server 2005

Let's face it: data that is stored in databases is interesting not only to us as users but to many others in the world whom we might not know. With the increased leverage of the power of relational databases by businesses and consumers, database vendors are under increasing pressure to provide more security-related features.

Other than locking down access to databases such as SQL Server, administrators and developers can provide another layer of protection against the bad guys, and that is encryption. At a high level, encryption takes the interesting information, such as your Social Security number, and translates it into a binary representation that can be understood only by authorized parties. Data can be encrypted for use in transit, such as when you are passing your password back to a Web server, or it can be stored in an encrypted format (on the file system or in a database, for example).

Data in SQL Server 2005 is encrypted by using the concept of *encryption keys*. These keys can be either symmetric or asymmetric, and there are pros and cons to using either one. In symmetric key encryption, both the sender and receiver of the data have the same key. The sender encrypts the data using the key and an encryption algorithm. When the data reaches the recipient, it is decrypted using the same encryption algorithm and key. The main benefit of this approach is the better performance of the encryption and decryption compared to using asymmetric keys. The problems with symmetric key encryption come into play when we consider what happens when someone else somehow gets a hold of our symmetric key. Because we are encrypting with just one key, anyone who has that key can decrypt the data.

Asymmetric key encryption uses two keys, a public key and a private key. The sender encrypts the data using the recipient's public key, which is freely obtainable by anyone. The security comes in when the recipient receives the data; the recipient decrypts it via her private key. The public key in this case cannot decrypt the data. Thus, the private key is the valuable asset when using asymmetric encryption.

The other concept that pops up in encryption discussions is certificates. Certificates are basically asymmetric keys that contain extra metadata. This metadata includes information such as an expiration period and the certificate authority that issued the certificate. Certificates can be created by anyone, and in some circumstances you want to make sure the sender or recipient of the data is who he says he is. This is where certificate authorities come into play. These companies act as a middleman between the sender and receiver. After you pay a nominal fee and they conduct an identity check, they can provide you with a certificate that they have signed. Now when you use this signed certificate to send data, the recipient can validate the certificate with the certificate authority, and because both of you trust the certificate authority, odds are the message was in fact signed by the sender.

There is another type of certificate call a *self-signed certificate,* which anyone can create. In some cases, it is acceptable to use a self-signed certificate. SQL Server 2005 automatically creates a self-signed certificate the first time it starts. This certificate is used to encrypt the connection during SQL Server authentication.

Encrypting Data on the Move

All connection login requests made to SQL Server 2005 are encrypted if the client is using the SQL Server Native Access Client APIs. This is a huge step forward because using previous versions, if a user wants to authenticate using SQL Server Authentication, the username and password are basically sent in clear text across the wire. SQL Server 2005 can automatically encrypt the login packet information via the self-signed certificate it created the first time the service started.

Login packets are not all that's encrypted in the connection. The whole connection itself can optionally be encrypted for the lifetime of the connection. The request for an encrypted channel can be forced by the server (so that all connections are encrypted by default) or requested by the client making the connection. It is recommended that administrators use a real certificate rather than the self-signed certification because of potential "man-in-the-middle" attacks.

To force encryption on the server, launch the SQL Server Configuration Manager tool (available in the Configuration Tools folder of the SQL Server 2005 Program Files menu item). This tool is used for managing the protocols and services of SQL Server. Select Properties from the Protocols for MSSQLSERVER shortcut menu to launch the Protocol Properties dialog box (Figure 7-5).

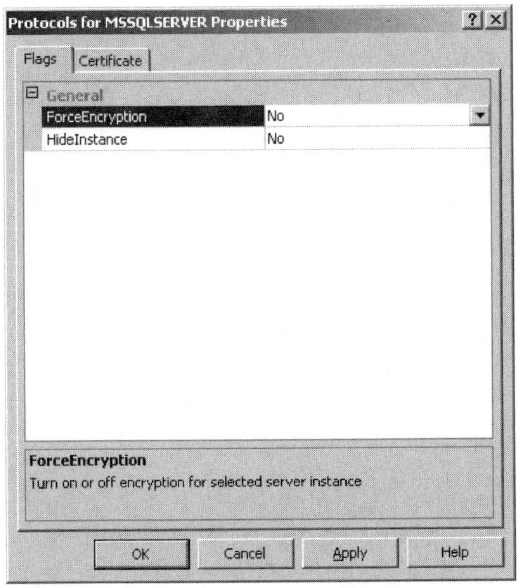

Figure 7-5   Protocol Properties dialog box

The dialog box has two tabs. The Flags tab allows you to force encryption on the server. The Certificate tab allows you to select a certificate that is already installed on the local machine to be used by SQL Server to encrypt the data. If you do not select a certificate and choose to force encryption, SQL Server uses its self-signed certificate to encrypt the data. Remember that SQL Server's self-signed certificate is not considered trusted by the client connections. For clients to be able to use SQL Server's self-signed certificate, they must set this option in the Properties dialog box of the SQL Native Client Configuration node in the same Configuration Manager tool. This dialog box is shown in Figure 7-6.

Figure 7-6   Protocol Properties dialog box for SQL Native Client Configuration

This dialog box offers two options. The Force Protocol Encryption option forces clients to always make encryption connections. The second option is what needs to be set if the client wants to make encryption connections to SQL Server and have it leverage SQL Server's self-signed certificate.

Encrypting Data at Rest

Social Security numbers, credit card numbers, salary information—the list of sensitive information just keeps going. Access to this information stored in the database has traditionally been secured by permissions. This is still the case, but another layer of protection is now available natively in SQL Server 2005. Sensitive data can now be encrypted using symmetric keys, asymmetric keys, or certificates.

Before we jump in and encrypt data in a column, it is important to define the building blocks of encryption support within SQL Server. The first time SQL Server starts, it creates a special symmetric key called the Service Master Key (SMK). This key is used to encrypt all database master keys (DMKs) as well as all server-level secrets such as credential secrets or linked server login passwords. The key itself is a 128-bit 3DES key. The 3DES algorithm is used because of its availability on all Windows platforms supported by SQL Server 2005.

> **Note** Encryption algorithm availability depends on the cryptographic service provider of the operating system that SQL Server 2005 is running on. For example, Windows XP SP2 supports DES, 3DES, RC2, RC4, and RSA, while Windows Server 2003 supports all those plus AES128, AES192, and AES256.

The SMK is encrypted using the Windows security API, DPAPI, and the credentials of the SQL Server service account. Because the SMK is used to encrypt all DMKs and other server-level secrets, it is very important and should be regularly backed up. You can back up and restore the SMK by using the *BACKUP SERVICE MASTER KEY* or *RESTORE SERVICE MASTER KEY* DDL. In the event of a compromise of the SMK, or if you want to change the SMK as part of implementing a normal security best practice, you can regenerate it using the *ALTER SERVICE MASTER KEY REGENERATE* DDL statement.

With respect to encrypting data, the SMK is used by SQL Server to decrypt the DMK so that the DMK can in turn decrypt the requested data for the client. There is only one DMK per database, and none are created by default because a DMK is used only for data encryption.

To create a DMK, we can use the new DDL statement as follows:

```
USE <<insert user-defined database>>
CREATE MASTER KEY
ENCRYPTION BY PASSWORD = '<<insert favorite password here>>'
```

When DMKs are created, they are encrypted by the SMK (so SQL Server can decrypt the data for the client) and by a password. It is possible to remove the SMK encryption, but the password of the DMK would need to be specified by the user every time she accesses this key.

Now that we have discussed the key components of encryption, let's consider an example. This example will include a table called SalaryInfo that contains the name, department, and salary of employees at our company. There is a user HR_User that needs to be able to insert and view data into this table.

Because a lot of steps are involved in setting up this example, it is best to walk through it line by line. (See Listing 7-2.) We have included in-line comments throughout the example that explain exactly what each T-SQL statement does and why.

Listing 7-2   Encryption_HR.sql

```sql
CREATE LOGIN HR_Login WITH PASSWORD='SomeComplexPassword'
GO
CREATE DATABASE ExampleDB
GO
use ExampleDB
GO
CREATE USER HR_User FOR LOGIN HR_Login
GO

--Create the database master key for the ExampleDB database
CREATE MASTER KEY ENCRYPTION BY PASSWORD='AComplexPassword'
GO

--Create the table that will store sensitive information
--Notice we use a varbinary for our salary information
--This is because the ciphertext (encrypted data) is binary
CREATE TABLE SalaryInfo
(employee nvarchar(50),
department nvarchar(50),
salary varbinary(60))
GO

--Give access to this table to HR_User so they can add data
GRANT SELECT,INSERT TO HR_User
GO

--Create a Symmetric Key
--Encrypt the key with a password
--Give access to the key to HR_User
CREATE SYMMETRIC KEY HR_User_Key
AUTHORIZATION HR_User
WITH ALGORITHM=TRIPLE_DES
ENCRYPTION BY PASSWORD='CompensationPlansRule'
GO

--Now, let's login as HR_User and encrypt some data
EXECUTE AS LOGIN='HR_Login'
GO

--First, we need to open the key that will be used to encrypt data
--Notice we have to pass the password for the key
OPEN SYMMETRIC KEY HR_User_Key DECRYPTION BY PASSWORD='CompensationPlansRule'
GO

--This system view shows open keys that can be used for encryption
select * from sys.openkeys

--Insert sensitive data into the table
--encryptByKey takes the GUID of the key and the text of the data
--Since remembering GUIDs is not easy, Key_GUID is a function
--that does the lookup for us
INSERT INTO SalaryInfo VALUES
('Bryan','Sales',encryptByKey(Key_GUID('HR_User_Key'),'125000'))
```

```
INSERT INTO SalaryInfo VALUES
('Tammie','Sales',encryptByKey(Key_GUID('HR_User_Key'),'122000'))
INSERT INTO SalaryInfo VALUES
('Frank','Development',encryptByKey(Key_GUID('HR_User_Key'),'97500'))
INSERT INTO SalaryInfo VALUES
('Fran','Marketing',encryptByKey(Key_GUID('HR_User_Key'),'99500'))

--When we are done, always close all keys
CLOSE ALL SYMMETRIC KEYS
GO

--View the table as it lives in the database, notice the binary
select * from SalaryInfo

--Now, let's decrypt and view the contents
--We use decryptByKey and pass the column name
--We don't have to specify a key GUID because SQL will look
--at all your open keys and use the appropriate one automatically
OPEN SYMMETRIC KEY HR_User_Key DECRYPTION BY PASSWORD='CompensationPlansRule'
GO

SELECT employee,department,
CONVERT(varchar,decryptByKey(salary))
FROM SalaryInfo
GO

CLOSE ALL SYMMETRIC KEYS
GO

--Revert back to sysadmin
REVERT
GO

--When encrypting by password, need to know the password
--and pass it every time you encrypt something.
--Alternatively you can create a certificate and give access to
--the HR User. With this, the user doesn't have to provide a password
--and you can easily revoke access to that encrypted data by simply
--removing the certificate for that user
CREATE CERTIFICATE HRCert1
AUTHORIZATION HR_User
WITH SUBJECT='Certificate used by the Human Resources person'

--Open the key so we can modify it
OPEN SYMMETRIC KEY HR_User_Key DECRYPTION BY PASSWORD='CompensationPlansRule'
GO

--We cannot remove the password because we would leave the key
--exposed without encryption so we need to add the certificate first
ALTER SYMMETRIC KEY HR_User_Key
ADD ENCRYPTION BY CERTIFICATE HRCert1
GO

--Now we can remove the password encryption from the key
ALTER SYMMETRIC KEY HR_User_Key
```

```
DROP ENCRYPTION BY PASSWORD= 'CompensationPlansRule'
GO
CLOSE ALL SYMMETRIC KEYS
GO


--Now change context to HR_Login to test our changes
EXECUTE AS LOGIN='HR_Login'
GO

--Notice we opened the key without a password!
--This is because we created the certificate and gave authorization
--on it explicitly to HR_User
OPEN SYMMETRIC KEY HR_User_Key DECRYPTION BY CERTIFICATE HRCert1
GO

SELECT employee,department,
CONVERT(varchar,decryptByKey(salary))
FROM SalaryInfo
GO
```

The preceding example described the basics of encrypting and decrypting in SQL Server 2005. The amount of data in this example is trivial to encrypt and decrypt, even for my three-year-old laptop. Performance for encryption depends on two factors other than how big of a box you are running on: size of the data to encrypt and the algorithm you use to encrypt the data. If you use RSA2048 to encrypt a larger file, this might take a bit longer than encrypting a Social Security number. It is difficult to give a nice graph of size versus time because it depends on so many factors. The best thing to do is set up a test environment that mimics your production environment and run some performance tests: encrypt and decrypt various data sizes in different algorithms or at least the algorithm you are planning to use.

Another interesting issue with encrypted columns is indexing and searching. To SQL Server itself, these are binary columns so there is no effective way to create an index on them because we cannot predict a random stream of bytes. The best thing to do in this case is to create or use another unencrypted column to index on. The problem with this is that you might inadvertently give information about the data that is encrypted. Imagine we want to index on salaries and create a column called range. Anyone who has *SELECT* permission on the table can guess what the employee makes. If you must index or search encrypted data, be creative about your unencrypted columns.

Encryption is not a trivial undertaking, and a thorough discussion is outside the scope of this book. Resources are available online to help you understand more about encryption in SQL Server security. Laurentiu Cristofor, one of the Microsoft developers behind encryption in SQL Server 2005, has a wealth of information on his blog site dedicated to encryption: *http://blogs.msdn.com/lcris*. Raul Garcia is also on the Microsoft Security team and has a blog of useful information: *http://blogs.msdn.com/raulga/*.

Protecting SQL Server 2005

It appears that hackers are always finding new ways to attempt to break into systems and applications. With the wealth of information available inside databases, these types of applications have become prime targets for mischievous users. In this section, we will cover how SQL Server addresses some of the issues around security as well as some of the things hackers do to try and exploit your system.

Reducing the Surface Area for Attack

The more doors you have in your house, the more opportunities an intruder has to break in. Even if those doors are made of solid steel, each with a nice shiny lock, they are still considered a surface area that is vulnerable for attack. One way to eliminate this vulnerability is to not have a door where you don't need one. The computer application equivalent is that if you are not using a particular feature, turn it off if possible.

Out of the box, SQL Server 2005 provides a reduced surface area for attack by automatically turning off features that are optional. These features include the SQL Server Agent service, SQL Server Browser service, and various server functions including *xp_cmdshell*, using the common language runtime within SQL Server, and others. The management tool that allows administrators to turn on and off these features is the SQL Server Surface Area Configuration tool. This tool is installed as part of a database engine installation, so you should have it regardless of which edition or components you install.

When the tool is launched, you get two options: Surface Area Configuration for Services and Connections, and Surface Area Configuration for Features.

The Services And Connections dialog box (Figure 7-7) shows a treeview list of sql components that are installed on the server.

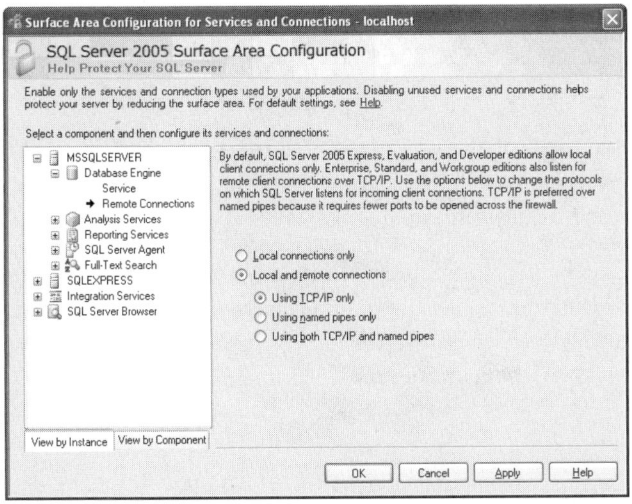

Figure 7-7   The Surface Area Configuration tool's Remote Connections panel

Under Database Engine are two panels. The first panel, Services, allows the user to start, stop, and change the automatic startup settings of the service. The other panel, Remote Connections, is perhaps one of the more important switches to remember. By default in Express, Evaluation, and Developer editions of SQL Server, remote connections are disabled. Thus, if you install Express Edition and try to connect to it from another client machine, the connection will fail. To enable remote connections, you must choose which kind of remote connections to allow.

Note   If you allow remote connections and have trouble connecting, check your firewall settings. You might have to add an exception for the Sqlsvr.exe process or open a specific port for SQL Server.

The other important feature of this tool is the ability to configure which features should be on or off. Clicking on Surface Area Configuration For Features launches the dialog box shown in Figure 7-8.

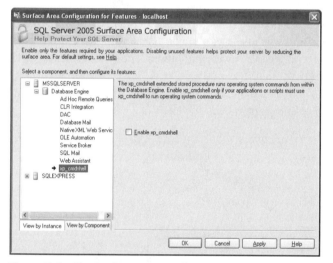

Figure 7-8   The Surface Area Configuration tool's Features panel

In the figure, you can see that the tool allows you to enable and disable the use of the *xp_cmdshell* extended stored procedure. Other features that can be turned on and off include the common language runtime, ad hoc remote queries, and Service Broker.

Each of these options can also be programmatically turned on and off via the *sp_configure* stored procedure. To view these options, set the *show advanced options* property on *sp_configure* first. There is also a new system view called *sys.configurations* that effectively shows the same information as *sp_configure* with *show advanced options* set.

How Hackers Attack SQL Server

To begin this section, we must start with a disclaimer. This section does not cover every possible way that hackers can attempt to compromise SQL Server. It is meant to introduce the various methods of exploitation and get you thinking about security when you design database applications and configure your system. Let's start the discussion with topics related to how SQL Server is configured.

Direct Connection to the Internet

Exposing any operating system or application directly to the Internet without the use of a firewall is a bad thing—no matter whether you are using Linux, UNIX, Windows, or any other operating system. It's rather like the carnival game where someone sits on a platform above a pool of water waiting for someone else to throw a ball and hit the bull's eye. When it happens, the person sitting on the platform is plunged into the water. Why expose your system, allowing anyone to take shots until they finally get you soaked? Microsoft has done a lot of work around protecting its operating systems and applications out of the box. When an exploit happens, they quickly address these problems and provide fixes.

This is only half of the battle, though. With all the switches and states of security for various products, it is not that difficult for an administrator or user to accidentally misconfigure something and expose the systems to exploits. To mitigate these issues, it is very important that users isolate their systems from the Internet via firewalls and use other isolation techniques.

Weak SA Passwords

One of the easiest ways to give someone the keys to SQL Server is by providing a weak password for the system administrator account. In previous versions of SQL Server, it was possible to give a blank password for the SA account without much complaint from SQL Server itself. SQL Server 2005 has a lot more functionality around password policies and enforcement. Previously in this chapter, we discussed this topic in regard to SQL Server authentication accounts obeying the group policies of the Windows domain. Configuring a strong password length and account lockout in your domain will ensure that all users of SQL Server are supplying passwords that are more difficult to crack.

SQL Server Browser Service

SQL Server uses UDP port 1434 to return SQL Server instance names and port numbers to the requesting client. A few years back, this enumeration was the key to the "SQL Slammer" DoS virus. By consistently hitting the server with requests for enumeration, the virus left the server too busy to process other requests. In SQL Server 2005, this enumeration functionality is in a separate service called the SQL Server Browser service. The functionality no longer runs in SQL Server's process space, and it can be turned on and off without affecting SQL Server. If you do not want to use the SQL Server Browser service, you can still connect to other instances on your server, but the connection string must contain additional information (such as a specific port number in the case of TCP connections). If you want to use the Browser service in your organization, you can mitigate additional attacks by blocking UDP port 1434 on your firewall.

SQL Injection

SQL injection is the process by which a malicious user enters SQL statements instead of valid input. For example, suppose a Web site is asking for a user name. Instead of actually typing in a user name, a malicious user might type *'blah'; DROP TABLE sales;*. The Web server will happily take the user input and pass it to its middle layer, where it is executed in code as follows:

```
SqlCommand cmd = new SqlCommand("SELECT * FROM sales WHERE name='" + s_Customername + "'
",myConnection)
```

To SQL Server, it looks like the following:

```
SELECT * FROM sales WHERE name='blah'; DROP TABLE sales;
```

When it is executed, the sales table will be erased. You can see how easy it can be for malicious users to cause problems and return potentially sensitive information via simple inputs to Web pages or applications that directly use user input. To mitigate this particular issue, you can add the user input as a parameter to the *SqlCommand*, as shown below:

```
Using (SqlCommand cmd = new SqlCommand("SELECT * FROM sales WHERE name= @s_CustomerName"
, myConnection));
{
cmd.Parameters.Add("@s_CustomerName",s_CustomerName);
…
```

To SQL Server, whatever the user types will be considered just the value of the name part of the *where* clause.

Intelligent Observation

With the advent of powerful search engines such as Google and MSN Search, finding things on the Web is relatively easy. Web crawlers from these search engines go off and fetch key words and place them into their own internal database. These key words are used within their own search algorithms so that when you type something to search on, the search engine can easily return a list of possible choices. These crawlers not only search for and store such things as Web sites for pizza places, but they also obtain various kinds of error information returned from Web servers. This information is very valuable to a hacker. For example, if a hacker types *invalid password access denied* into the search string in MSN, he'll get a list of various topics that are, in general, not that interesting. However, one item will show this string: *Warning: mysql_pconnect():* *Access denied for user 'root'@'localhost' (using password: YES) in /home/vhosts/<<removed for legal reasons>>/docs/citeheader.inc.php on line 2.* A hacker knows that this site is using MySQL and PHP and now knows some of the directory structure of the Web site */home/vhosts/<<removed for legal reasons>>/docs.* Now the hacker can try to query that individual directory path using his Internet browser to see if he can uncover any additional goodies—a script file, perhaps. If he finds a script file in this directory and the developer has hardcoded login credentials to the database, he is one connection away from compromising the database.

The moral of the story is that search engines are very good hacker tools. Never hardcode passwords in script files, and always provide Web page redirects for errors within your Web application. In addition, always pay extra attention to any Web application that receives input. Make sure these kinds of data are protected against SQL injection attacks.

Summary

Security is one of the most important considerations in any project, and the time you spend learning how to lock down SQL Server and your application is worthwhile in the long run. Microsoft has made efforts to increase the security of SQL Server 2005 out of the box by turning off features such as *xp_cmdshell*, the SQL Server Agent service, and many other optional features within the product. It has also extended the security feature set by adding the ability to easily encrypt data in transit and at rest within the database, by providing more granular permissions and allowing easy context switching, among other examples.

This chapter introduced some of the core concepts of security in SQL Server 2005. Many online resources (such as SQL Server Books Online) go through these and additional security topics in more detail. As you sit down to design your next application, never stop thinking how someone might try to illegally gain access to your data or application. In today's world, a simple lock on the door to keep honest people honest is not enough. Everyone from IT professionals to developers must be diligent and always think about security.

Part II
Application Development and Reach Technologies

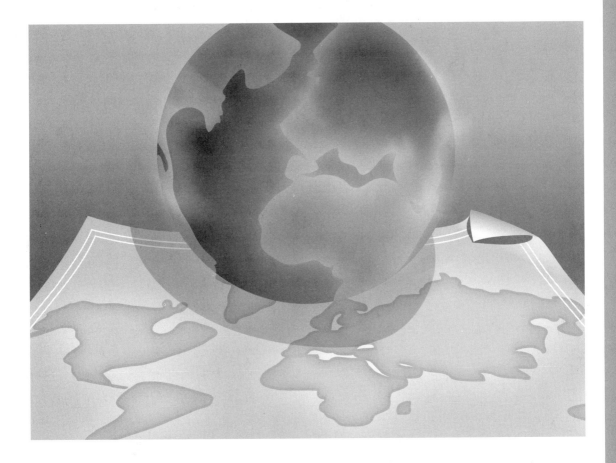

Chapter 8

ADO.NET 2.0, Typed *DataSet* Objects, and .NET Data Binding

—Andrew Brust

Now in its second major version, Microsoft ADO.NET continues to be the data access tool of choice for .NET developers. Whether you're writing SQL CLR code that runs on the server or writing client-side or middle-tier code that queries and manipulates SQL Server data, ADO.NET is key. ADO.NET 2.0 offers full support for the new features in SQL Server 2005 and introduces a few new features of its own. In addition, .NET typed *DataSet* objects and Visual Studio's typed DataSet designer have been greatly enriched, and the data binding technology within both ASP.NET and Windows Forms has been greatly enhanced to make getting at your data easier than ever.

The combination of ADO.NET 2.0 native features, typed *DataSet* objects, and .NET data binding forms an integrated suite of technologies that is valuable for anyone writing a .NET application with SQL Server as its database. This chapter will introduce you to the best parts of each of these technologies.

Before we dive into ADO.NET 2.0, its features, and its integration points with SQL Server, we need a brief data access library history lesson. Understanding what makes ADO.NET unique requires understanding what its predecessors did and how they did it.

A Brief History of Data Access Object Models

If you've been around Microsoft languages and database technology for a while, you know about the litany of data access object models through the years. Understanding the history of these object models and how each laid the foundation for its successors provides a context for understanding the initial feature set in ADO.NET and the new features in ADO.NET 2.0.

DAO: A Golden Oldie

In the early 1990s, we had Data Access Objects (DAO), which was designed to work against the Jet database engine used by Microsoft Access and Microsoft Visual Basic 3.0 and later. The DAO "Swiss Army knife" of data retrieval was the paradigm-setting *Recordset* object, which, although no longer with us, still provides Microsoft developers with a frame of reference for client- and middle-tier data access. DAO, through Jet's attached tables feature, also provided access to the world of ODBC-compatible databases, including version 4.2 of SQL Server.

Jet's ODBC (Open Database Connectivity) facility was implemented as a wrapper around the low-level ODBC API. But the API turned out to be easily accessible from Visual Basic code as well, and code that used the API directly offered performance far superior to Jet's ODBC access. Although *Recordset* objects were convenient and API programming was not, developers worked around this by creating their own function libraries for direct ODBC API data access, and usually the results were quite good.

RDO: A Thin API Wrapper

Microsoft realized that the road to SQL Server market penetration in the Visual Basic developer world was not through a secondary database engine (Jet) and that a thin object model layer around the ODBC API was the way to go. Out of this thinking came Remote Data Objects (RDO). RDO's API-specific but database-neutral architecture set a precedent for future data access object models. RDO lacked a *Recordset* object but offered a similar *Resultset* object (and rumor had it that this nomenclature was used as a courtesy to the Jet and DAO teams), so the familiar paradigm stuck.

Enter OLE DB and ADO "Classic"

Eventually, Microsoft decided to replace the API-oriented ODBC with the more COM-friendly Object Linking and Embedding Database library (OLE DB). This happened at about the same time that Active Server Pages (ASP) was released, so ASP was selected as the first vehicle for a new object model that wrapped OLE DB. The ASP data access object model was called ActiveX Data Objects (ADO). Initially, you had to do some work to get ADO to work from Visual Basic. But by the time Visual Basic 6.0 came out, ADO was the standard data access object model and OLE DB was the standard low-level data access library in the Microsoft world. ADO reintroduced *Recordset* as the name for its standard result set repository object.

ADO + .NET = ADO.NET

While .NET was still in beta, its data access object model was called ADO+. (Interestingly, its Web development technology was called ASP+.) Eventually, all the components of .NET with the + suffix were renamed with .NET suffixes, so ADO.NET became the name of the new .NET data access object model, and that name has stayed with us to this day.

ADO.NET 1.0 and Microsoft Visual Studio .NET introduced two radically new concepts. The first one, contributed by ADO.NET, was the replacement of the (usually) connected single-result-set–oriented *Recordset* object with a disconnected, multiple-result-set relational object called the *DataSet*. The second new concept, contributed by Visual Studio.NET and based on .NET native support for inheritance, was the ability to create strongly typed *DataSet* objects (also known, simply, as typed *DataSet* objects).

Typed *DataSet* objects are child classes that inherit from the *DataSet* base class but add schema-specific nested classes, methods, and properties to make data access from outside the database a more context-sensitive experience. One big benefit of typed *DataSet* objects is that their object models force column-level type fidelity in your code when you use their implemented properties. For example, a compiler error is generated if you try to store a string value into a column of a numeric data type. Likewise, the nested classes and properties, along with Visual Studio's IntelliSense, prevent you from misspelling table or column names. The benefits go on and on.

ADO.NET didn't forget the people who were less interested in persistent cursors and more interested in (quickly) retrieving or modifying data and using a "firehose" (forward-only, read-only) result set mechanism when data is queried. For this crowd, ADO.NET offered the *Command* and *DataReader* objects. *Command* objects, much like their ADO "classic" counterparts, offer a minimalist mechanism for direct execution of SQL commands or stored procedure calls against a database. *DataReader* objects are connected objects that handle a single result set and function much like an ADO *Recordset* when opened in forward-only, read-only mode.

This ends our history lesson of ADO.NET 1.0 and its predecessors. Now let's move on to ADO.NET 2.0.

What's New in ADO.NET 2.0?

ADO.NET 2.0 offers a number of enhancements and new objects that together support several new features in SQL Server 2005. Visual Studio 2005 and .NET 2.0, meanwhile, offer an array of improvements to typed *DataSet* objects, new data binding models for Windows Forms and ASP.NET environments, and a range of designers and wizards to make these all work together harmoniously.

New Typed *DataSet* Members

Typed *DataSet* objects have been enhanced in a number of ways in ADO.NET 2.0. Visual Studio features a dedicated DataSet designer (unlike Visual Studio .NET 2002 and 2003, which use the XML schema designer for typed *DataSet* objects) with its own wizards and data-oriented interface. Typed *DataSet* objects contain their own connections, *TableAdapter* objects (essentially, typed *DataAdapter* objects), and *Query* objects, which are visually designed methods on typed *DataSet* classes and the *TableAdapter* nested classes within them. *Column* objects, within *DataTable* objects belonging to a *DataSet*, are configurable objects whose properties are respected by the design-time data binding features offered by Visual Studio 2005.

Notably, typed *DataSet* objects have also been enhanced to be useful to developers who don't want to use *DataSet* objects per se. The DataSet designer can now generate "DBDirect" methods, which you can use to execute immediate updates, inserts, and deletes directly against the database, without caching those changes in the disconnected *DataSet*. In effect, this allows you to use the DataSet designer for generating the four "CRUD" (create, retrieve, update, and delete) *Command* objects, which would otherwise have to be created manually in code. This comes in handy, especially in ASP.NET applications, as we will see at the end of the chapter.

Other Enhancements

The core ADO.NET library has been enhanced to support asynchronous queries and new SQL Server 2005 features such as multiple active result sets (MARS), query notifications, and consumption of table columns that contain XML and CLR user-defined type (UDT) data. ADO.NET 2.0 even adds a new client-side bulk copy facility to its bag of tricks.

Storage of connection strings and avoidance of hardcoding them are major issues for .NET applications. To address this, .NET projects now support the concept of a dedicated config file section for storing connection strings. Visual Studio provides a designer for maintaining the connection string section of the config file (and dialog boxes for building the actual connection strings) for developers who do not want to edit the config file directly. Virtually all the data access facilities in Visual Studio, including the DataSet designer and its wizards, support direct reading and writing of connection strings from and to this dedicated config file section.

Data binding, within both the Windows Forms and the ASP.NET development environments, has been enhanced significantly as well. You can now use typed *DataSet* objects to create fully data-bound forms that are capable of displaying, updating, deleting, and creating data, and you can navigate through rows in a result set in Windows and Web applications without writing any code. Meanwhile, those who prefer to write their own code can interact with typed *DataSet* objects and these binding mechanisms without barriers or concerns that the otherwise-generated code cannot be implemented manually.

In this chapter, we will look at all these features and how you can incorporate them into your applications. We'll look at code-oriented techniques within Windows Forms as well as design-time techniques in both Windows Forms and ASP.NET applications. When you're done with the chapter, you should have a keen sense of how to expose all the exciting new SQL Server 2005 features in your applications.

It should be noted that ADO.NET also offers new features that are not specific to SQL Server. These include the ability to write provider-independent code using new ADO.NET base and factory classes and some new helper classes for building connection strings. We want you to be aware of these features, but we will not cover them because they are neither provided by, nor explicitly supportive of, SQL Server and its feature set.

Typed *DataSet* Enhancements

Whether you program in C# or Visual Basic .NET, typed *DataSet* objects can be a great tool for your applications and middle-tier objects. Whether or not you want to take advantage of data binding technology, typed *DataSet* objects provide an elegant encapsulation layer for your data, its schema, and various queries on that data.

In Visual Studio 2005, as with Visual Studio .NET 2002 and 2003 before it, typed *DataSet* objects consist of one or more *DataTable* objects and, optionally, relations between those *DataTable* objects.

In Visual Studio 2005 typed *DataSet* objects, you specify the structure of the *DataTable* objects visually, and you can do so by designing them from scratch, by using the TableAdapter Configuration Wizard, or by using drag-and-drop techniques in concert with the Server Explorer window in Visual Studio. You can add typed *DataSet* objects to your project in Visual Studio by using the Add New Item dialog box. You can call this dialog box up via the Add/New Item... option on the Solution Explorer window's project node shortcut menu, the Project/Add New Item... main menu option, or the Ctrl+Shift+A keyboard shortcut.

Note   You can also add a typed *DataSet* object using the new Data Sources window's toolbar; we discuss this option in a note in the data binding section of the chapter.

The Visual Studio sample solution for this chapter includes a C# Windows Application project called Chapter08. You can examine the typed *DataSet* objects and forms in that project as you read this section of the chapter, or you can create a new C# Windows Application project and execute the steps outlined here.

Using the keyboard, menu, or the Solution Explorer project node's shortcut menu options just discussed, open the Visual Studio Add New Item dialog box. Select DataSet from the list of objects, and name your typed *DataSet* **AdventureWorks.xsd**, as shown in Figure 8-1.

Figure 8-1   The Visual Studio Add New Item dialog box with the (typed) DataSet option selected

Click OK and observe that the *DataSet* opens in its own designer in the main tabbed document area of Visual Studio. For a new typed *DataSet*, the designer merely renders with an empty blue-and-white striped background and text that instructs you to add items using the DataSet tab of the Toolbox window (Figure 8-2) or Server Explorer window (Figure 8-3).

Figure 8-2   The Toolbox window's DataSet tab

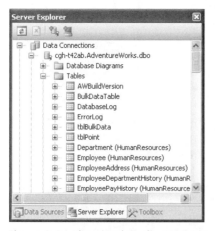

Figure 8-3   The Visual Studio 2005 Server Explorer, with Data Connections, the AdventureWorks database, and its Tables node expanded

To get started, let's add the HumanResources.Employee table to our new typed *DataSet*. First make sure you have defined a connection to the AdventureWorks database within the Server Explorer window. If you have defined a connection, a node should appear within the Server Explorer window's Data Connections node that is configured to point to the AdventureWorks database, as shown in Figure 8-3. If not, right-click the Database Connections node and choose the Add Connection... option from the shortcut menu. In the Add Connection dialog box, specify the server and login connection information, select the AdventureWorks database, and click OK. Expand the AdventureWorks database node, and then expand the Tables node within it. Finally, locate the Employee (HumanResources) node and drag and drop it onto the DataSet designer surface. Your *DataSet* should now contain fully specified *DataTable* and *TableAdapter* definitions for the Employee table (Figure 8-4).

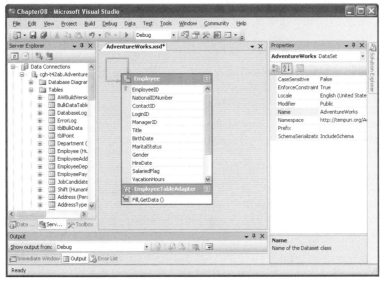

Figure 8-4   The typed DataSet designer with a *DataTable* and *TableAdapter* definition

We'll cover how to add queries to a *TableAdapter* and we'll add more tables to the typed *DataSet*, but first let's take an inventory of what we have added so far.

DataTable Objects in the Typed DataSet Designer

First notice that the large rectangle representing the HumanResources.Employee table is divided into two sections. The top section, labeled Employee, represents the actual ADO.NET *DataTable* within the *DataSet*. Click on one of the table's columns, and look at the Properties window. You'll see that the *Column* object, which is a visual representation of an ADO.NET *DataColumn* object, has a number of editable properties. Notable among these is the *Caption* property. Changing the *Caption* of a column causes all descriptive labels for any subsequent data-bound controls for that column to reflect the caption rather than the name of the physical column in the database. We'll see this in action when we cover data binding later in the chapter; to prepare for that now, change the *Caption* property of the *HireDate* column from HireDate to **Date of Hire**.

Other properties of interest include the *Expression* property, which allows you to configure the column to receive a computed value; the *ReadOnly* and *MaxLength* properties, which provide for declarative data validation rules independent of any constraints in the database; the *DefaultValue* property, which also operates independently of the physical table metadata; and the *AllowDBNull* and *NullValue* properties, which govern handling of Nulls, also in a database-independent fashion.

TableAdapter Objects

The lower part of the rectangle, labeled *EmployeeTableAdapter*, represents the strongly typed *DataAdapter*, which manages the population of, and modifications to, the data in the Employee *DataTable*. Select it, and look at the Properties window. Several, but not all, standard *DataAdapter* properties are exposed, and a *Connection* property is provided, allowing you to specify a single *Connection* that will be used by the *TableAdapter* object's *SelectCommand*, *InsertCommand*, *UpdateCommand*, and *DeleteCommand* child object properties.

Just as the *DataTable* segment contains *Column* objects within it, the *TableAdapter* object contains *Query* objects within it. The *EmployeeTableAdapter* contains a single item by default—the line labeled *Fill,GetData ()*. Select it, and examine its properties in the Properties window; you will notice that a *Query* object has many of the properties of a simple ADO.NET *Command* object. We will discuss *Query* objects in more detail shortly.

Moving back to the *TableAdapter* object, notice that the *Connection* property itself has a number of child properties that can be independently configured. Rather than having to edit each one, you can select a named connection string from a drop-down list in the value column of the parent *Connection* property, or you can enter it manually in the value column of the *Connection.ConnectionString* child property. You might wonder where these named connections come from and how to maintain the list of them. Explaining this requires a brief detour out of the DataSet designer and into the new Visual Studio 2005 Settings designer.

Connection String Management

To make the visual design of typed *DataSet* objects and both Windows Forms and Web data binding more straightforward than in the past, .NET provides a config file section explicitly for connection strings. You can thus reference connection strings by name and avoid the discouraged practice of hardcoding connection strings into application code. Visual Studio creates robust design-time support around this feature in several ways:

■ For Windows Application projects, a special Settings designer allows you to create connection string entries in the application config file without editing the file directly and to specify your connection string information using a Connection Properties dialog box.

■ As mentioned earlier, the Properties window, when used with *TableAdapter* objects inside the typed DataSet designer, permits selection of any config file–defined named connection string.

- The TableAdapter Configuration Wizard, which we will examine later in this chapter, allows selection of any config file–defined named connection string and saves any newly created connection strings into the config file if you ask it to.

- When you are writing code in Windows Forms projects, IntelliSense prompts you with a full list of connection string entries as soon as you type the period after the expression *[ProjectName].Properties.Settings.Default*, where *[ProjectName]* is the name of your project's root namespace.

To see connection string management in action, let's open the Settings designer. In C# projects, you can get to the Settings designer by expanding the Properties node in the Solution Explorer window and then double-clicking its Settings.settings child node. You can also reach the Settings designer through the Settings tab of the Properties designer, which you can bring up by double-clicking the Solution Explorer window's Properties node in C# projects (or the My Properties node in Visual Basic projects); by selecting the Properties option from the project node's shortcut menu; or by selecting the Project/*Projectname* Properties option from the main menu (where *Projectname* is the name of your project). Once in the Settings designer, you should see entries for any Server Explorer–derived connection strings.

To create a new connection string entry, just click in the blank row at the bottom of the grid, type a name for the entry, select *(Connection string)* as the type (this option is the next-to-last item in the drop-down list), leave the scope as Application (the scope will change to Application automatically when the Type cell loses focus), and then double-click your cursor within the Value cell. You should see an ellipsis (...) button at the right of the cell, as shown in Figure 8-5.

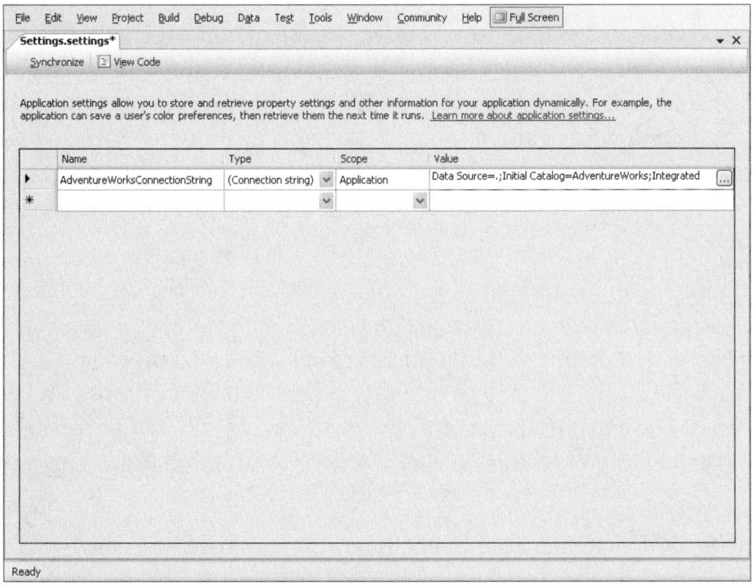

Figure 8-5   Adding a connection string entry in the Visual Studio Settings designer

Click the ellipsis button to invoke the Connection Properties dialog box and define your connection string interactively, or type the connection string manually. In the former case, the
connection string appears in the cell when you click OK in the Connection Properties dialog
box. Go ahead and create an entry called *AdventureWorksConnectionString* that points to the
AdventureWorks database on your SQL Server 2005 box. (If such an entry already exists, you
don't need to add anything.)

Close the Settings designer/Properties designer, go back to the DataSet designer, and select
the *EmployeeTableAdapter* object. In the Properties window, click the drop-down arrow next to
the *Connection* property. You should see all the connection string entries you created in the
Settings designer in the drop-down list; select *AdventureWorksConnectionString* from it for now.

Later in this chapter, you will encounter other contexts in which the connection string setting
entries are available. One of those is the TableAdapter Configuration Wizard, which we will
examine now.

Using the TableAdapter Configuration Wizard

So far we have used the Server Explorer drag-and-drop technique to place a table into a typed
DataSet. Another, perhaps more flexible, technique is to use the TableAdapter Configuration
Wizard (which we'll refer to simply as the TableAdapter Wizard).

1. Launch the wizard by right-clicking on a blank area of the DataSet designer surface and
    choosing the Add/TableAdapter... shortcut menu option. A blank *DataTable/Table-
    Adapter* pair is added to the designer surface and the TableAdapter Wizard appears after
    a brief pause.

2. On the first wizard page, the Choose Your Data Connection page, you specify a connec-
    tion for the *DataTable/TableAdapter* pair you want to add to the *DataSet*. You will notice
    right away that the wizard allows selection of any config file–based connection string.
    Just click the drop-down list, and if you'd like to know the underlying connection string,
    expand the Connection String node in the bottom half of the wizard page, as shown in
    Figure 8-6. Select the AdventureWorksConnectionString entry you just created, and
    then click Next.

3. On the Choose A Command Type page, you specify whether the *TableAdapter* object's
    underlying *SelectCommand*, *InsertCommand*, *UpdateCommand*, and *DeleteCommand*
    should be based on dynamic SQL statements or calls to stored procedures. In the latter
    case, you have the choice of using existing stored procedures or having the wizard gen-
    erate new ones. The existing stored procedures option actually allows you to select func-
    tions as well as stored procedures. Select the Create New Stored Procedures option, and
    click Next.

4. On the Enter A SQL Statement For The SELECT Stored Procedure page, you can enter a
    SQL query around which a stored procedure will be generated. If you embed parameters
    (named values prefixed with @) within your *WHERE* clause, the wizard builds the

stored procedure with corresponding Transact-SQL (T-SQL) parameters. You can click the Query Builder... button to design your query visually and generate the appropriate SQL, and you can turn off certain code generation defaults in the Advanced Options dialog box by clicking the Advanced Options... button. Type **SELECT * FROM Sales.Currency** as your query text, and then click Next. The wizard parses the *SELECT* statement you provide and generates a corresponding stored procedure. It also generates corresponding insert, update, and delete query-based stored procedures, unless you have explicitly requested otherwise in the Advanced Options dialog box.

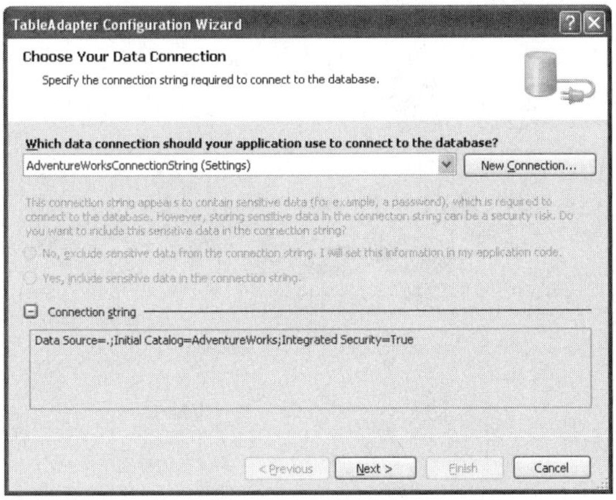

Figure 8-6   The TableAdapter Wizard's Choose Your Data Connection page

5. On the Create The Stored Procedures page, you supply a name(s) for your stored procedure(s) and can preview the T-SQL script for the *SELECT* stored procedure by clicking the Preview SQL Script... button. Enter the names **uspSelectCurrency**, **uspInsertCurrency**, **uspUpdateCurrency**, and **uspDeleteCurrency**, and then click Next.

6. On the Choose Methods To Generate page, simply accept the default names by clicking Next. Recall that a *TableAdapter* is a class to which *Query* objects can be added and that these *Query* objects offer methods on the *TableAdapter* class. In fact, each *Query* on a *TableAdapter* can be manifested in the *Fill* method, the *GetData* method, or both. (The methods are named or prefixed *Fill* and *GetData* by default.) The *Fill* method is a simple wrapper around the underlying *DataAdapter* class's *Fill* method; it is used to populate a *DataTable* passed to it as an argument. The *GetData* method is also a wrapper around *Fill*, but rather than populating a passed *DataTable* object, it fills a standalone *DataTable*, which it sends back as its return value/object.

7. On the Wizard Results page, you can review the tasks performed by the wizard and then click Finish to dismiss the wizard.

You should now see your *DataTable* and *TableAdapter* on the DataSet designer surface; the *DataTable* should be named *Currency*, and the *TableAdapter* should be named

CurrencyTableAdapter. Within the *TableAdapter* segment, you should see the *Fill* and *GetData* methods listed. Had you renamed these methods or chosen to generate only one of them, the method list would reflect your specific selections.

Before moving on, drag and drop the Contact (Person) table, the *uspGetBillOfMaterials* stored procedure, and the *vEmployeeDepartment* view from the Server Explorer window onto your typed *DataSet*. Your typed *DataSet* should now appear as shown in Figure 8-7.

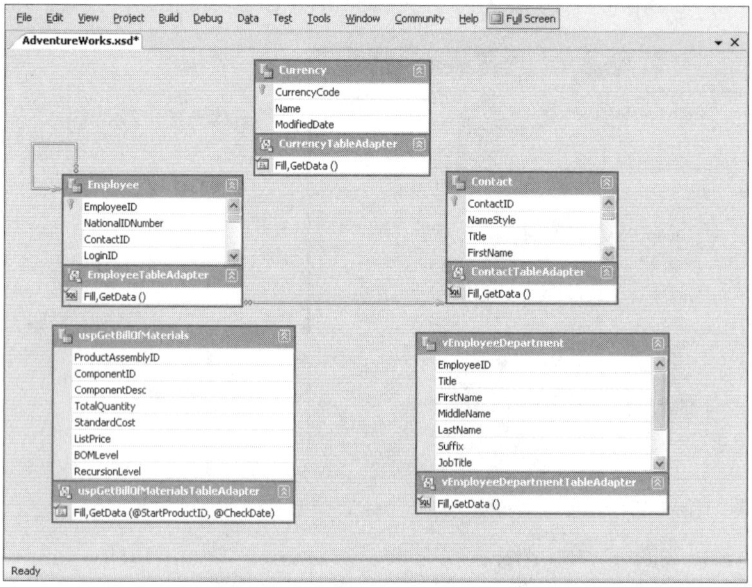

Figure 8-7   The typed DataSet designer with various *DataTable/TableAdapter* pairs defined

More on Queries and Parameters

Notice that the method list for the *Query* object within *uspGetBillOfMaterialsTableAdapter* includes parameters named *@StartProductId* and *@CheckDate*. These appear because the *uspGetBillOfMaterials* stored procedure itself has these parameters. Stored procedure or SQL query parameters are exposed as ADO.NET parameters on the individual *Command* objects managed by your *TableAdapter* objects, and they are exposed as code-level parameters in the *TableAdapter* object's *Fill* and *GetData* methods.

The parameter(s) from your query as well as a stock *@RETURN_VALUE* parameter are represented in the *Parameters* collection property of the *Query* object and of the *TableAdapter* object's *SelectCommand*. See this for yourself by clicking in the Properties window value cell of either *Parameters* property and clicking the ellipsis button. The wizard makes certain assumptions about the data type, scale, size, and direction of the parameters, as well as the existence of a return value; you can override any of these assumptions by changing the property values of individual parameters or by adding parameters to or deleting parameters from the collection properties.

Adding Query Objects

You can easily add queries to your existing *TableAdapter* objects; let's see this in action by adding one to the *ContactTableAdapter* object in the AdventureWorks typed *DataSet*. Just right-click on the *ContactTableAdapter* object in the DataSet designer and select the Add/Query... shortcut menu option. This action invokes the TableAdapter Query Configuration Wizard (hereafter referred to as the Query Wizard), which is essentially a simplified version of the TableAdapter Wizard.

The Query Wizard doesn't solicit connection information because it uses the *Connection* information from its parent *TableAdapter* object, so the Query Wizard's first page is the Choose A Command Type page. This page offers the choices of SQL, new stored procedure, and existing stored procedure, as the TableAdapter Wizard does; select the Use SQL Statements option. For the first two of these three choices, a Choose A Query Type page appears, allowing you to specify whether your query will select rows, select a scalar value, or perform an update, insert, or delete. These choices directly correspond to the *ExecuteAction* property of the *Query* object, and your selection determines whether an ADO.NET *ExecuteReader*, *ExecuteScalar*, or *ExecuteNonQuery* method call on the underlying *Command* object is generated within the *Query* object's implementation. Choose the SELECT Which Returns Rows option, and then click Next. On the Specify A SQL Select Statement page, type the following query:

```
SELECT * FROM Person.Contact WHERE (ContactID = @ContactId)
```

As you will see shortly, embedding the parameter *@ContactId* in the SQL query parameterizes the *Query* object you are adding to your *TableAdapter*. Click Next.

> **Note**   If you had selected the Use Existing Stored Procedure option on the Choose A Command Type page, the wizard would have asked you, on the Choose An Existing Stored Procedure page, to supply the name of an existing stored procedure. It would then provide you, on the Choose The Shape Of Data Returned By The Stored Procedure page, the choice of tabular, single value, or no value, which roughly corresponds to the options offered by the Choose A Query Type page previously described.

The wizard's next page, the Choose Methods To Generate page, is similar to its namesake in the TableAdapter Wizard. Accept the default method names (*FillBy* and *GetDataBy*) and click Next.

> **Note**   If you were to supply an SQL *UPDATE*, *INSERT*, or *DELETE* command, the Choose Function Name page would appear and would solicit the method name used to wrap the non-row-returning query.

On the Wizard Results page, click Finish. You should see your new *FillBy*, *GetDataBy* (*@ContactId*) query listed in the *TableAdapter* segment of your *DataTable/TableAdapter* pair.

In the Properties window, confirm that your Query object has an *@ContactId* item in its *Parameters* collection property. You can also test the query through its Preview Data... shortcut menu option; the resulting Preview Data dialog box prompts you for an *@ContactId* value; type **1001** in the Value column and click Preview to see the details for that contact record, as shown in Figure 8-8.

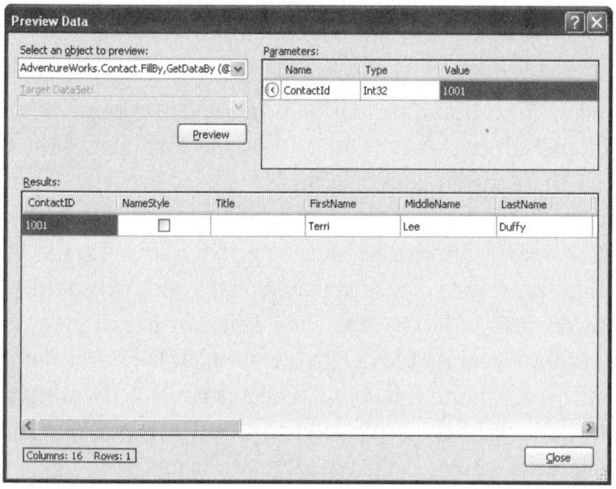

Figure 8-8   The DataSet designer's Preview Data dialog box, showing the results of a parameterized query on the Person.Contact table from the AdventureWorks database

You can modify an existing *TableAdapter* object through the TableAdapter Wizard by right-clicking it and choosing the Configure... option on the shortcut menu. You can do the same for an existing *Query* object through the Query Wizard by right-clicking it and choosing the Configure... option from its shortcut menu. You can add *Query* objects directly to a *DataSet*, rather than a *TableAdapter*, by right-clicking the DataSet designer surface and choosing the Add/Query... shortcut menu option. Doing so invokes the Query Wizard, but in such a way as to solicit connection string information from you, much as the TableAdapter Wizard does under normal circumstances.

DBDirect Methods and Connected Use of Typed *DataSet* Objects

TableAdapter objects act as strongly typed *DataAdapter* objects and are thus ideal disconnected data sources. But *TableAdapter* objects have a special property, *GenerateDBDirectMethods*, that enables them to function as connected data sources as well. The *GenerateDBDirectMethods* property, a Boolean property whose default value is *True*, provides for auto-generation of three special methods on the *TableAdapter* class that handle immediate updates, inserts, and deletes, respectively, on the *DataTable* object's underlying physical table.

By using these three methods (which are automatically named *Update*, *Insert*, and *Delete*) along with the *GetData* method, developers can use the schemas and queries within typed

DataSet objects without actually needing to store any data in their *DataTable* objects. Ironically, this allows you to use typed *DataSet* objects as if they were not *DataSet* objects at all. This usage is akin to setting up four separate ADO.NET *SqlCommand* objects and a *SqlConnection* object and using the *ExecuteReader* and *ExecuteNonQuery* methods of the *SqlCommand* objects to fetch and modify data, respectively.

The stored schemas that the *DataTable* objects contain facilitate design-time data binding, even when you use such connected techniques. As you will see later, ASP.NET's data binding framework relies heavily on this mechanism.

Standalone *DataTable* Objects

You can add a *DataTable* without a *TableAdapter* by right-clicking the DataSet designer surface and selecting the Add/DataTable shortcut menu option. This action does not invoke a wizard; rather, it inserts an empty *DataTable* object into the typed *DataSet*. You can rename the *DataTable* by selecting it and then slowly clicking on its title bar; by choosing the Rename option from its shortcut menu; or by editing its *Name* property in the Properties window. You can add *Column*, *Key*, and *Relation* objects from the Add submenu on the shortcut menu or from the Toolbox window. Once you add a *Column* object, you can configure it using the Properties window. At least one *Column* must exist before *Key* and *Relation* objects can be added.

If the ability to add your own *DataTable* objects and columns confuses you, remember that *DataSet* objects are disconnected data repositories and are completely database agnostic. *DataTable* objects are essentially just highly evolved arrays, and nothing prevents you from defining their name, structure, and contents on your own. The fact that *DataAdapter* objects (and *TableAdapter* objects) happen to move data between databases and *DataTable* objects, and that they can also create *DataTable* objects as they populate them with the result sets from database queries, is technically irrelevant.

Meanwhile, *DataTable* objects are first-class data sources for .NET data binding, and by composing your own *DataTable* objects within a typed *DataSet* you can build data-bound UIs for them using little or no code.

"Pure" ADO.NET: Working in Code

We have spent a lot of time covering the visual design features of typed *DataSet* objects. That information will help you to be a productive SQL Server 2005 developer, but many of the new features in ADO.NET 2.0 require at least some coding, without the use of Visual Studio designers. You can use coding techniques to manipulate or populate your typed *DataSet* objects, but for now let's get down to some pure code development techniques that don't use typed *DataSet* objects at all. (We'll come back to designer-oriented features later in the chapter when we cover data binding.)

We'll start with querying and displaying a simple result set from a table, and then we'll branch out to some of ADO.NET's most exciting new features. Specifically, we'll look at how to register a query notification that updates the displayed data when the underlying data is changed by another process, how to execute queries asynchronously, how to use the new ADO.NET client-side bulk copy features, and how to consume XML columns. We'll conclude by examining how to handle SQL CLR UDT columns and manipulate them as objects in our .NET code.

Querying 101

This chapter assumes that you have a basic familiarity with ADO.NET programming in C#. However, experienced developers without such knowledge should still be able to follow along, as long as they are comfortable learning from contextual examples. To assist such readers, we will first look at a simple query against the AdventureWorks Person.Contact table.

To implement this query, add a new form, called **frmCodeDemos.frm**, to the project; you can do this by using the Project/Add Windows Form... and Project/Add New Item... main menu option, as well as various shortcut menu equivalents in the Solution Explorer window. Next, drag a *DataGridView* control from the Toolbox window's Data tab onto the form, and name the control **dgvContacts**. Drag a *Button* control from the Toolbox's Common Controls tab onto the form, and name it **btnLoadNormal**. Set the *Anchor* property of *dgvContacts* to *Top, Bottom, Left, Right* and the *Anchor* property of *btnLoadNormal* to *Bottom, Right*.

Using ADO.NET against SQL Server requires the use of the *System.Data.SqlClient* ADO.NET provider, and it is a good idea to use that namespace in your code. So in the form's code-behind class, add the following line immediately after the existing lines of code that start with the *using* command:

```
using System.Data.SqlClient;
```

After you take care of the namespace housekeeping, you simply use a *SqlConnection*, a *SqlCommand*, and a *SqlDataAdapter*, along with a *DataSet* or *DataTable* object and a bound control, to query your database and display the result set.

It is possible to avoid creating and using the *SqlConnection* and *SqlCommand* objects because the *SqlDataAdapter* has a constructor overload that creates these objects for you implicitly. Nonetheless, we think it sensible to show you how to use the objects explicitly. The code in Listing 8-1, which contains the implementation of the *Click* event handler for the *btnLoadNormal Button* control, performs a simple query against the Person.Contact table, populates a *DataTable* with the results, and binds that *DataTable* to the *DataGridView* control.

Listing 8-1   Executing an SQL *SELECT* command and binding the results to a *DataGridView* control

```
private String ConnString = Properties.Settings.Default.AdventureWorksConnectionString;

private void btnLoadNormal_Click(object sender, EventArgs e)
{
    SqlConnection cn = new SqlConnection(ConnString);
    SqlCommand cm = new SqlCommand("Select LastName, EmailAddress from Person.Contact",
cn);
    SqlDataAdapter da = new SqlDataAdapter(cm);
    DataTable dt = new DataTable();
    da.Fill(dt);
    dgvContacts.DataSource = dt;
}
```

Notice that the connection string we added to the settings file earlier is stored into a class-level variable called *ConnString* which, in turn, is passed to the *SqlConnection* object's constructor; you can refer to the connection string by name using the *Properties.Settings* object's *Default* property. We could also pass a string literal, but the *Properties.Settings* technique is more sound because a change to the connection string in the settings file cascades out to this code without any additional effort on your part.

Passing a string literal or expression to the *SqlConnection* object's constructor has the effect of setting the object's *ConnectionString* property as the object is instantiated. Similar "constructor shortcuts" are used in the code listing: The *CommandText* and *Connection* properties of the *SqlCommand* object and the *SelectCommand* property of the *SqlData-Adapter* object are set by passing the corresponding string and objects to the constructors of objects *cm* and *da*. The *DataTable* object is instantiated using a default constructor and needs no specific initialization.

Once the objects are properly instantiated, we execute the query and populate our *DataTable* with its result set by simply calling the *SqlDataAdapter* object's *Fill* method and passing it our *DataTable* object. To display the results, we set our *DataGridView* control's *DataSource* property to *dt*—our *DataTable* object—and we're done. Make *frmCodeDemos* your startup form, and run the application to confirm that the *DataGridView* control is populated correctly.

Keeping Data Up to Date

Arguably, simple code like the code we just explored is all that's necessary to create applications that query and display data from your SQL Server 2005 databases. But ADO.NET 2.0 adds some interesting features to make your code more sophisticated. For example, only a small amount of code is required to take advantage of SQL Server 2005 query notifications, whereby the data displayed in the *DataGridView* control can be updated when data in the underlying result set is changed by another process.

Because SQL Server query notifications rely on the SQL Server 2005 Service Broker feature, you must first enable Service Broker on the AdventureWorks database before you can write any ADO.NET code that uses query notifications. Fortunately, this is very easy to do. Simply open up a query window in SQL Server Management Studio and connect to your SQL Server. Then enter the following T-SQL code and execute the query (or simply open and execute the script file EnableServiceBroker.sql in the Management Studio solution supplied with the sample code for this chapter):

```
ALTER DATABASE AdventureWorks SET ENABLE_BROKER
```

Wait until Management Studio displays the following message on the Messages tab of the query window's Results pane:

```
Command(s) completed successfully.
```

If the previous message is not displayed, and instead an "Executing Query..." message is displayed in the query window's status bar, make sure all connections to the server outside of your Management Studio session, including any opened from Visual Studio's Server Explorer window, are fully closed. (You might want to restart your SQL Server instance to clear any open connections.)

Add a new *Button* control to your form and name it **btnNotifications**; set its *Anchor* property to *Bottom, Right*, as you did with *btnLoadNormal* (and continue doing so with all other buttons added to the form). The ADO.NET side of query notifications is handled by the new *SqlDependency* object and the use of delegates in your code. The code required to implement query notification–aware logic is shown in Listing 8-2.

Listing 8-2   SQL query notification code for a bound *DataGridView* control

```
private delegate void RefreshData();

private void btnNotifications_Click(object sender, EventArgs e)
{
    LoadData();
}

private void LoadData()
{
    SqlConnection cn = new SqlConnection(ConnString);
    SqlCommand cm = new SqlCommand("Select LastName, EmailAddress from Person.Contact",
cn);
    SqlDataAdapter da = new SqlDataAdapter(cm);
    DataTable dt = new DataTable();

    SqlDependency sd = new SqlDependency(cm);
    sd.OnChange += new OnChangeEventHandler(ContactInfoChanged);
    SqlDependency.Start(ConnString);

    da.Fill(dt);
```

```
        dgvContacts.DataSource = dt;

}

private void ContactInfoChanged(object caller, SqlNotificationEventArgs e)
{
    Invoke(new RefreshData(LoadData));
}

private void frmBindingTest_FormClosing(object sender, FormClosingEventArgs e)
{
    SqlDependency.Stop(ConnString);
}
```

Notice that we declare a delegate called *RefreshData* at the top of the class definition. A *void* function called *LoadData* serves as our all-purpose data loader, and we call it from the *btnNotifications* control's *Click* event handler. Within *LoadData*, our command object, *cm*, is passed to a *SqlDependency* object's constructor, and a callback function, *ContactInfoChanged*, is registered as the handler for the object's *OnChange* event. We also call the static *SqlDependency.Start* method, passing it the connection string we are using to run our query. All the *SqlDependecy* object–related code is (and must be) placed before the *DataAdapter* object's *Fill* method is called. The callback function is called whenever a query notification takes place and it, in turn, calls *LoadData* again to refresh the data display, through the delegate we declared. Finally, to clean up our work, we call the static *SqlDependency.Stop* method from the form's *FormClosing* event handler.

With this code in place, everything should work beautifully. Try it and see: Run the sample project, click the button to load the data, and then open the Person.Contact table from Visual Studio's Server Explorer window or SQL Server Management Studio's Object Explorer window. In either case, make a small change to the *LastName* or *EmailAddress* field for one of the rows that's visible in the sample application's form, and then watch as that change is propagated and displayed by the sample application itself.

You might be wondering why *LoadData* had to be called through a delegate and the use of *Invoke*. The reason is simple: The code in the callback function executes on a secondary thread, and .NET 2.0 does not permit code on a secondary thread to modify the UI. Using a delegate and *Invoke* ensures that our *LoadData* code executes on the UI's thread, thus avoiding runtime exceptions. We will need to use this technique again for executing asynchronous queries—our next topic.

Responsive UIs: Executing Queries Asynchronously

Another powerful new feature in ADO.NET 2.0 is the ability to execute queries, and fetch their results, asynchronously. Unlike with our previous examples, async queries cannot be executed through the use of a *DataAdapter*; instead, a *DataReader* must be retrieved and traversed to obtain the result set. To make the async code easier to understand, let's first examine a synchronous query example that retrieves a *SqlDataReader* directly from a *SqlCommand* object. The code appears in Listing 8-3. (There is no need to implement this code. Just read through it for now; we will add an asynchronous version of it soon.)

Listing 8-3 Synchronous command execution and result set processing

```
SqlConnection cn = new SqlConnection(ConnString);
SqlCommand cm = new SqlCommand(
  "Select LastName, EmailAddress from Person.Contact", cn);
cn.Open();
SqlDataReader dr = cm.ExecuteReader(CommandBehavior.CloseConnection);

DataTable dt = new DataTable();
dt.Columns.Add("LastName", System.Type.GetType("System.String"));
dt.Columns.Add("EmailAddress", System.Type.GetType("System.String"));
while (dr.Read())
{
    DataRow drow = dt.NewRow();
    drow[0] = dr[0];
    drow[1] = dr[1];
    dt.Rows.Add(drow);
}
dr.Close();

dgvContacts.DataSource = dt;
```

Listing 8-3 uses the *SqlCommand* object's *ExecuteReader* method to retrieve a *SqlDataReader*. Because *DataReader* objects cannot be bound to Windows Forms controls, the code takes the unusual step of transferring the data in the *DataReader* to a *DataTable*, the structure of which has been programmatically configured to match the schema of the query's result set. Once the *DataTable* is populated, it is bound to the *DataGridView* control exactly as in our previous examples.

Having seen a synchronous sample, we can now move on with relative ease to discussing how to execute the query asynchronously.

Connection String Modifications

Before introducing the necessary code modifications, we must revisit the topic of connection string management. Asynchronous queries can be executed only on connections that have been configured to allow such operations. Specifically, the connection string must contain the *Asynchronous Processing=True* clause. If you're supplying a literal connection string or hand-coding your application's config file or settings file, you must manually create a connection string and insert this clause somewhere in it. If you're using the Settings designer to configure connection strings in your settings file, you must take special steps.

For our purposes, it will be convenient to have both a standard and an async-specific connection string in our settings file. We already have the standard one (AdventureWorksConnectionString), which we've been using, so we just need to add the async version.

To do this, get into the Settings designer using any of the techniques described previously and add a new connection string entry called **AdventureWorksConnectionStringAsync**, using the steps previously described. Click in the Value cell, and then click on the ellipsis (...) button to bring up the Connection Properties dialog box. As with the previous entry, type your server name and login information, and then select AdventureWorks as the database to connect to, but do not click OK yet.

We still need to specify that this connection is async-capable. To do this, click the Advanced... button in the bottom right of the Connection Properties dialog box to bring up the Advanced Properties dialog box, which consists of a property browser and OK and Cancel buttons. Locate the *Asynchronous Processing* property, which is the first one under the *Initialization* category, and set its value to *True*, as shown in Figure 8-9.

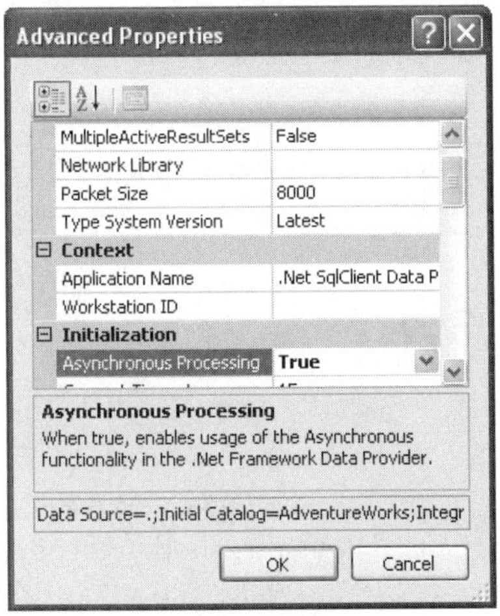

Figure 8-9 Setting the *Asynchronous Processing* property in the Advanced Properties dialog box for connection properties

To save this value into the connection string, click OK. This returns you to the Connection Properties dialog box, where you might want to click the Test Connection button before clicking OK again. Once you're back in the Settings designer, click in the Name cell for your new entry and then hover the mouse over the Value cell. A ToolTip should appear showing the fully generated connection string (unless your resolution is high enough that the whole connection string is visible within the Settings grid). The connection string should contain the *Asynchronous Processing=True* clause. You can now click Save on the Visual Studio Standard toolbar and close the Settings designer.

With this new connection string setting entry in place, we are ready to convert our *DataReader* code to work asynchronously. We'll cover the necessary modifications one by one.

Doing the Two-Step

The crux of asynchronous query operations is using the *BeginExecuteReader* and *EndExecuteReader* methods of the *SqlCommand* object rather than the object's *ExecuteReader* method. The *BeginExecuteReader* method has several overloads, but the one we will use accepts an *AsyncCallback* object, a state object, and a *CommandBehavior* enumerated constant. In our code, the *AsyncCallback* object references a function called *Callback* in which we will perform the *EndExecuteReader* method call. Because *BeginExecuteReader* and *EndExecuteReader* must be called on the same *SqlCommand* object and *EndExecuteReader* is called in a separate callback function, our *SqlCommand* object must be declared as a private, class-level variable rather than as a local variable. Our *SqlConnection* object can be a local variable, but its constructor must be passed (or its *ConnectionString* property set to) our new connection string Settings entry, *AdventureWorksConnectionStringAsync*. With all this taken into account, our revised data loading code is shown in Listing 8-4.

Listing 8-4   Asynchronous command execution processing

```
private SqlCommand _cm;
private void LoadDataAsync()
{
    SqlConnection cn = new
SqlConnection(Properties.Settings.Default.AdventureWorksConnectionStringAsync);

    _cm = new SqlCommand("Select LastName, EmailAddress from Person.Contact", cn);
    cn.Open();

    _cm.BeginExecuteReader(new AsyncCallback(Callback), new Object(),
CommandBehavior.CloseConnection);
}
```

We still need to supply the callback function. In this function, we will call the *SqlCommand* object's *EndExecuteReader* method, which, like the *ExecuteReader* method, returns an *SqlDataReader* object. We must then copy the contents of the *SqlDataReader* into a *DataTable* (which will eventually be bound to our *DataGridView* control) and close the *DataReader* object. The callback code is shown in Listing 8-5.

Listing 8-5   Asynchronous command callback

```
private void Callback(System.IAsyncResult oResult)
{
    SqlDataReader dr = _cm.EndExecuteReader(oResult);
    DataTable dt = new DataTable();
    dt.Columns.Add("LastName", System.Type.GetType("System.String"));
    dt.Columns.Add("EmailAddress", System.Type.GetType("System.String"));

    while (dr.Read())
    {
        DataRow drow = dt.NewRow();
        drow[0] = dr[0];
```

```
        drow[1] = dr[1];
        dt.Rows.Add(drow);
    }
    dr.Close();

    Invoke(new DataBind(DataBindProc), dt);
}
```

Notice that the callback must be structured to accept an object of type *System.IAsyncResult* and that this object must be passed to the *EndExecuteReader* method of our class-level *SqlCommand* object, on which *BeginExecuteReader* was originally called. Most of the remaining code in the callback function is identical to the result-set processing code in our synchronous example, with the exception of the last line. The last line uses the form's *Invoke* method to call a delegate function to which our *DataTable* is passed. The delegate function simply binds the *DataTable* to our *DataGridView* control, but, as with the query notification example, it will (and must) do so on the UI's own thread. The delegate declaration and the delegate function code are shown in Listing 8-6.

Listing 8-6   Delegate declaration and implementation for UI display of the asynchronous query's result set

```
private delegate void DataBind(DataTable dt);
private void DataBindProc(DataTable dt)
{
    dgvContacts.DataSource = dt;
}
```

To test everything out, add a new button to the form and name it **btnLoadAsync**. Implement its *Click* event handler code as shown in Listing 8-7.

Listing 8-7   Click event handler code for *btnLoadAsync* Button control

```
private void btnLoadAsync_Click(object sender, EventArgs e)
{
    LoadDataAsync();
    MessageBox.Show("Data is loading...");
}
```

Now run the application and click the new *btnLoadAsync Button* control. Because the data is being loaded asynchronously, you should see the message box pop up with the "Data is loading..." message *before* the *DataGridView* control is populated with data. (Change the code to call *LoadData* instead of *LoadDataAsync*, and you will see that the data loading blocks the UI, forcing the message box to come up only after the data has loaded.) This behavior is somewhat dependent on your hardware and other tasks running on your development PC and server, so results might vary, but rest assured that the data will be fetched from your database asynchronously.

Important Earlier we mentioned another new SQL Server 2005 feature supported by ADO.NET 2.0: multiple active result sets (MARS). We don't specifically cover this feature in this book because its use is more or less implicit. To take advantage of MARS, you first add the clause *MultipleActiveResultSets=True* to your connection string, using the same technique you used earlier to add the *Asycnhronous Processing=True* clause.

With that connection string change in place, simply create multiple data-returning ADO.NET *SqlCommand* objects on a single *SqlConnection* object. Call the *ExecuteReader* method on one of the *SqlCommand* objects, and then call it on the second object before all rows on the first one have been fetched (using the *Read* method). By opening a second result set before the first one has been fetched and closed, you are using the MARS feature. Doing this with earlier versions of SQL Server required each *SqlCommand* object to have its own connection. You can combine MARS techniques with many of the features discussed in this section of the chapter.

Not for Servers Only: Client-Side Bulk Copy

SQL Server has had a bulk copy feature for high-efficiency data imports since the early 1990s, but programmatic client access provided only the SQL *INSERT* and *SELECT ... INTO* commands for this type of operation (unless special APIs were used). ADO.NET 2.0's *SqlClient* provider changes all that with the introduction of the new *SqlBulkCopy* object. This object can copy the contents of a *SqlDataReader*, a *DataTable*, or an array of *DataRow* objects to a developer-specified table. The table must exist in a database pointed to either by a *SqlConnection* object or by a connection string, one of which must be passed to the *SqlBulkCopy* object's constructor.

This feature is quite easy to demonstrate, but to do so we need a table into which the *SqlBulkCopy* object can load its data. In this chapter's Management Studio sample solution, open and run the CreateTblBulkData.sql script file to create a table called tblBulkCopy with LastName and EmailAddress columns. Next, run the CreateUspGetNamesAndEmails.sql script to create a stored procedure—*uspGetNamesAndEmails*—that will return the data we want to bulk load. Add a new button to the form and name it **btnBulkCopy**, and then implement its *Click* event handler using the code shown in Listing 8-8.

Listing 8-8 ADO.NET bulk copy coding

```
private void btnBulkCopy_Click(object sender, EventArgs e)
{
    this.Cursor = Cursors.WaitCursor;

    SqlConnection cn = new SqlConnection(ConnString);
    SqlCommand cm = new SqlCommand("uspGetNamesAndEmails", cn);
    cm.CommandType = CommandType.StoredProcedure;
    SqlDataAdapter da = new SqlDataAdapter(cm);
    DataTable dt = new DataTable();

    da.Fill(dt);
```

```
    cn.Open();
    SqlCommand cmDelete = new SqlCommand("Delete from tblBulkData", cn);
    cmDelete.ExecuteNonQuery();

    SqlBulkCopy bdQueryData = new SqlBulkCopy(cn);
    bdQueryData.DestinationTableName = "tblBulkData";
    bdQueryData.WriteToServer(dt);

    bdQueryData.Close();
    cn.Close();

    this.Cursor = Cursors.Default;
    MessageBox.Show("Bulk copy complete!");
}
```

Don't run the code just yet—although it is fairly straightforward, it still merits some discussion before you test it. First, you should realize that the premise is a bit contrived: Using the ADO.NET Bulk Copy feature to copy data from one table to another in the same database is hardly a real-world scenario. Typically, the source data would come from another database, a text file, or some other non–SQL Server data source, and it would be your job to load that data into a *DataTable*, *SqlDataReader*, or *DataRow* array. For convenience, we made our data source identical to the result set we processed in all the previous examples in this section.

While we were at it, we decided to call a stored procedure to get the data rather than perform a dynamic SQL *SELECT* query in our code. We did this mostly to demonstrate how easy it is to call stored procedures from code and how doing so is almost identical to executing SQL queries. The only differences are that we must pass the stored procedure name in place of the SQL string to the *SqlCommand* object's constructor (or as the value of its *CommandText* property) and we must set the *SqlCommand* object's *CommandType* property to *CommandType.StoredProcedure* rather than using its default value setting of *CommandType.Text*. This technique works equally well with SQL CLR or T-SQL stored procedures.

You'll also notice that, as a matter of course, we ran a delete query against tblBulkData to empty it before populating it with the bulk copy operation. Running queries that do not return data is performed with the *Command* object's *ExecuteNonQuery* method rather than with *ExecuteReader*. Although we do not provide an async example for executing non-data-returning queries, it is possible to do so using the *SqlCommand* object's *BeginExecuteNonQuery* and *EndExecuteNonQuery* methods.

Run the application and click the new button to perform the bulk copy operation. After the message box appears alerting you to completion of the bulk copy process, open tblBulkData in Management Studio (from the Object Explorer window) or Visual Studio (from the Server Explorer window) to confirm that it was properly loaded.

You now know how to retrieve and display data synchronously, asynchronously, and with query notifications, and to bulk copy data into your databases. You know how to do this with dynamic SQL and with stored procedures, and you also know how to execute non-data-returning queries that might, for example, execute SQL *UPDATE*, *INSERT*, or *DELETE* commands or stored procedures.

The fact remains, however, that we've only covered processing of result sets with scalar data columns; we haven't shown you how to process XML or SQL CLR UDT columns. We will do so now.

It's Not Just Text: Processing XML Columns with ADO.NET and the *System.Xml* Namespace

SQL Server 2005 offers native support for XML data, as we discussed extensively in Chapter 4. In earlier versions of SQL Server, nothing was there to stop you from storing XML data in long *varchar* or *text* columns; it was always possible to store and retrieve XML data from the database, essentially as large strings. In fact, even native XML data in SQL Server 2005 databases are treated by ADO.NET as string data unless you handle your data retrieval very carefully.

Given the richness of the .NET Framework's *System.Xml* namespace, it seems highly preferable to read native XML data as *XmlReader* objects rather than as strings, and ADO.NET permits this. The trick is to retrieve your result set as a *SqlDataReader* and to use the *SqlDataReader* object's *GetSqlXml* method to retrieve the data as a *System.Data.SqlTypes.SqlXml* object. Finally, you can use the *System.Data.SqlTypes.SqlXml* object's *CreateReader* method to read the data as a *System.Xml.XmlReader* object.

To put this technique to work for you, add a new button to the form and name it **btnXML**, then implement its *Click* event handler using the code shown in Listing 8-9.

Listing 8-9   Processing SQL Server 2005 native XML data in ADO.NET 2.0

```
private void btnXML_Click(object sender, EventArgs e)
{
    SqlConnection cn = new SqlConnection(ConnString);
    SqlCommand cm = new SqlCommand("Select AdditionalContactInfo from Person.Contact
where ContactID = 1", cn);
    cn.Open();
    SqlDataReader dr = cm.ExecuteReader(CommandBehavior.CloseConnection);

    if (dr.Read())
    {
        System.Xml.XmlReader xrContactInfo = dr.GetSqlXml(0).CreateReader();

        System.Xml.XmlDocument xdcContactInfo = new System.Xml.XmlDocument();
        xdcContactInfo.Load(xrContactInfo);
        MessageBox.Show(xdcContactInfo.InnerText);
    }
    dr.Close();
}
```

The code queries the Person.Contact table's AdditionalContactInfo XML column to demonstrate the XML data fetching technique we just discussed. For demonstration purposes, the code loads the *XmlReader* into an *XmlDocument* object whose *InnerText* property value is then displayed in a message box. The *InnerText* property strips out the XML tags, making the data somewhat more readable for quick visual inspection.

It should be pointed out that loading the *XmlReader* object's contents into an *XmlDocument* object is not an especially efficient use of the *XmlReader* object we so carefully extracted from the result set. An *XmlDocument* object can be created from the string representation of the XML data in the first place. A more realistic use of the *XmlReader* is to leverage its *Read...* and *MoveTo...* methods to avoid loading the whole XML document into memory (which is exactly what the *XmlDocument.Load* call does).

Nothing but .NET: Consuming SQL CLR UDT Data as Native .NET Objects

In Chapter 3, we showed you how to embed public structs in .NET assemblies, load those assemblies into your SQL Server 2005 databases, and use those structs as native UDTs. This feature allows you to type columns in tables with these UDTs, essentially making each row's value for that column a bona fide instance of those structs.

In Chapter 3, we also showed you how to manipulate UDT columns in T-SQL, allowing you to access individual property values or read the entire UDT as a specially formulated string. All these T-SQL techniques can be used from ADO.NET, allowing you to have the same property-level and object-level access available in Management Studio. But given that these UDT columns began life as .NET structs, it seems wasteful for actual .NET code to have to consume UDT column values as string values. It stands to reason that if these UDT data are instances of .NET structs, .NET code should be able to consume them as such.

As it turns out, this precise scenario is supported by SQL Server 2005 and by the .NET Framework. As long as your application contains a reference to the same assembly loaded into your database, you can cast CLR UDT values into instances of the structs on which they are based. You can do this in the sample application by adding a reference to the Chapter03.dll assembly, which is the compiled version of the sample application in Chapter 3.

Important   Before the CLR-related code in this chapter can execute properly, you must (if you haven't already) open and run (compile and deploy) the Chapter03 Visual Studio solution included with the sample code for Chapter 3. Also be sure to open the Chapter 3 Management Studio sample solution and execute the CreateTblAggregateTest.sql script within it.

Recall that Chapter03.dll defines a UDT called *typPoint* and that the sample Management Studio project contains scripts to create and populate a table called tblPoint, whose column

ThePoint is of type *dbo.typPoint*. With all this in place, add a new button to the form and name it **btnUDT**, and then implement its *Click* event handler using the code shown in Listing 8-10 to consume the type in its native form.

Listing 8-10   Processing SQL CLR UDTs, with casting, for type fidelity

```
private void btnUDT_Click(object sender, EventArgs e)
{
    SqlConnection cn = new SqlConnection(ConnString);
    SqlCommand cm = new SqlCommand("SELECT ID, ThePoint FROM tblPoint", cn);
    cn.Open();
    SqlDataReader dr = cm.ExecuteReader();

    while (dr.Read())
    {
        MessageBox.Show(String.Format("ID={0}, X={1}, Y={2}", dr[0], ((typPoint)dr[1]).X
, ((typPoint)dr[1]).Y));
        MessageBox.Show(typPoint.Sum((typPoint)dr[1]).ToString());
    }

    dr.Close();
    cn.Close();
}
```

Because the query selects both columns—ID and ThePoint—from tblPoint, in that order, the resulting *SqlDataReader* object's column 1 (the second column) contains the UDT data. Thus the expression *dr[1]* can be cast to the type *typPoint* and when the entire cast expression is parenthesized, the *X* and *Y* properties can be interrogated directly. When you type this code, you get full IntelliSense support once you type the period after the closing parenthesis surrounding the cast expression. Although not demonstrated in the code, you can also declare a local variable of type *typPoint*, assign *(typPoint)dr[1]* directly into it, and then use the local variable rather than using the cast expression each time.

The second line of code in the *While* loop calls the static method *Sum* and displays the results in a message box. The *Sum* method requires that a valid *typPoint* instance be passed as a parameter, so the *typPoint*-cast *dr[1]* is supplied as a parameter value and the *System.Double* return value's *ToString* method is called to supply the *MessageBox.Show* method with a valid string.

Back to the Drawing Board

We have now covered all the "pure-code" ADO.NET features and techniques we need to cover. But we need to discuss numerous additional design-time techniques, including embedding SQL CLR objects into typed *DataSet* objects and then leveraging all our typed *DataSet* assets through data binding, in both Windows Forms and ASP.NET environments.

Embedding SQL CLR Objects in Typed *DataSet* Objects

We have already discussed how to work with stored procedures, including CLR stored procedures and CLR UDTs, in code. Now we'll turn back to typed *DataSet* objects and see how to embed CLR objects, including aggregates and user-defined functions as well as stored procedures and UDTs, within them. By doing so, we can use the data binding techniques covered in the next section as an alternative to the code-based SQL CLR access techniques covered in the previous section.

The DataSet designer does not offer full support for SQL CLR stored procedures or SQL Server tables that use SQL CLR UDTs. There are, however, workarounds for this shortcoming. Some work by "tweaking" the DataSet designer's drag-and-drop behaviors, and others work by using the TableAdapter Wizard. Pursuing these workarounds is worthwhile. They might require special effort in the DataSet designer, but later on they make short work of building data-bound forms and application code that consume your SQL CLR objects. We'll cover these workarounds quickly now and then show you how to consume the objects in the next section of the chapter.

First, in fairness, we must point out that it *is* possible to drag and drop SQL CLR stored procedures onto the DataSet designer surface. Doing so has the effect of adding *Query* objects to your typed *DataSet* without creating any underlying *DataTable* objects. Such query objects are made available to developers as methods of a specially created *TableAdapter* class (called *QueriesTableAdapter*), but only SQL CLR objects that return a single value or return no data at all can be used in this way. This might be sufficient for some needs, but it does not support data binding scenarios; it is therefore worthwhile to understand how to add SQL CLR object-derived *DataTable* objects to your typed *DataSet* objects.

We'll now cover some specific examples of embedding SQL CLR objects in typed *DataSet* objects. Keep in mind that the biggest stumbling block to making this work is that the designer has trouble properly reading SQL CLR objects' schemas. We will solve this by manually configuring the *DataTable* object's *Columns* collection and/or the *TableAdapter* object's various *Command* properties and their *Parameters* collections.

Adding a CLR Stored Procedure to a Typed *DataSet*

Let's start by adding a CLR stored procedure from Chapter 3 to a new typed *DataSet*. First add a new *DataSet* to the project and name it **CLRDS.xsd**. Because the Server Explorer window's drag-and-drop operations do not generate *DataTable* objects for SQL CLR stored procedures or functions, you must use the TableAdapter Wizard to do so. Right-click the designer surface and select the Add/TableAdapter... option from the shortcut menu. On the Choose Your Data Connection page, select AdventureWorksConnectionString (Settings)—make sure not to select AdventureWorksConnectionStringAsync—and click Next. On the Choose A Command Type page, select the Use SQL Statements option (we'll change the *TableAdapter* object's

CommandType property to *StoredProcedure* afterwards, through the Properties window) and click Next. On the Enter A SQL Statement page, type the following query:

```
SELECT * FROM Person.Contact
```

Click the Advanced Options... button. In the Advanced Options dialog box, clear the Generate Insert, Update And Delete statements check box and then click OK. Back in the TableAdapter Wizard, click Next. On the Choose Methods To Generate page, clear the last check box—the one labeled "Create methods to send updates directly to the database (GenerateDBDirect-Methods)." Click Next. Be sure the Wizard Results page appears exactly as shown in Figure 8-10 (if not, click Previous and check that all previous pages were completed properly) and then click Finish.

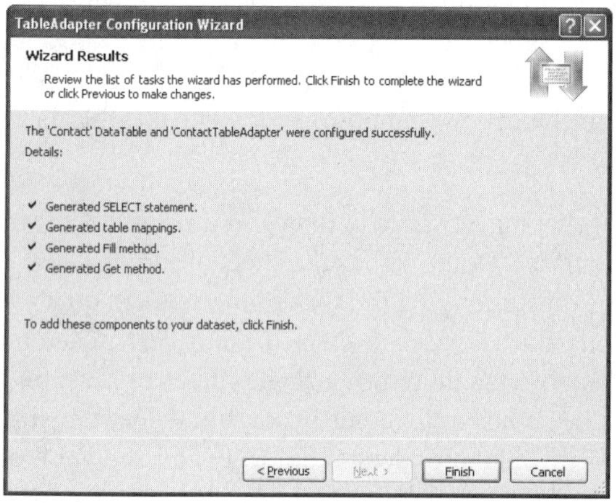

Figure 8-10   The TableAdapter Wizard's Wizard Results page

You should see the *DataTable* and *TableAdapter* appear in the designer. Just for clarity, change the *DataTable* object's name from *Contact* to *spContacts* by using the Properties window or the *DataTable* object's shortcut menu, or by selecting the *DataTable* and either clicking its title bar slowly or pressing F2 to enter in-place edit mode. Renaming the *DataTable* renames its *TableAdapter* as well.

What you have just done is add a select-only *TableAdapter* and *DataTable* for the Person.Contact table. We did this because this table and the *spContacts* CLR stored procedure we built in Chapter 3 have identical schemas. We thus have the necessary schema without having to add the *Column* objects to the *DataTable* ourselves. Now we must change the *TableAdapter* object's *SelectCommand* to execute the CLR stored procedure instead of the dynamic SQL query we typed on the TableAdapter Wizard's Enter A SQL Statement page.

To do this, we must change the *TableAdapter* object's *SelectCommand* object's *CommandText* and *CommandType* properties. This is especially easy to do. First select the *TableAdapter* by clicking on its title bar (the blue background area labeled spContactsTableAdapter). Next, locate the *SelectCommand* property in the Properties window, and click on its drill-down + sign. Change the *SelectCommand* object's child *CommandText* property value to:

```
spContacts
```

At this point, the DataSet designer will get a little confused. It will first display a message box asking if you'd like to regenerate updating commands. Click No. Next you'll see another message box displaying a "Failed to update CommandText" message. This is simply a symptom of the designer's inability to read the CLR stored procedure's schema. Don't let it faze you; just click OK, and then change the *CommandType* property's value to *StoredProcedure*.

You're done! To prove that everything is working correctly, right-click the *DataTable* or *TableAdapter* and choose the Preview Data... option from the shortcut menu to bring up the Preview Data dialog box. In the dialog box, click the Preview button, and after a brief pause you should see the data come back from the CLR stored procedure, as shown in Figure 8-11.

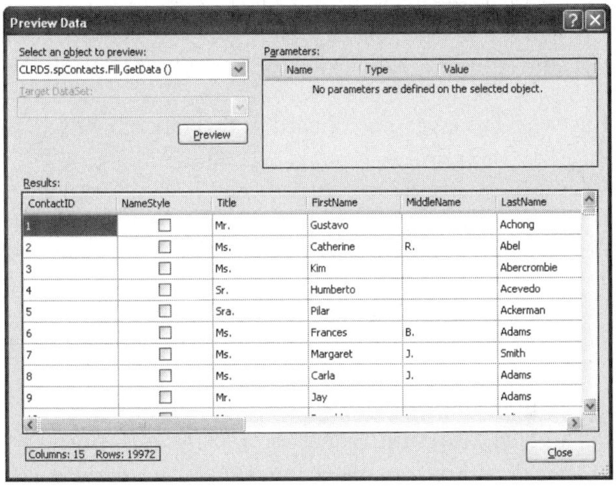

Figure 8-11   The DataSet designer's Preview Data dialog box, with data from a CLR stored procedure displayed

Now we're cooking with gas! Let's quickly add our CLR table-valued function (TVF) and then a couple of *DataTable/TableAdapter* pairs that will expose our CLR aggregate and our UDT.

TVFs: Easy Living

For the CLR TVF, it turns out that no workarounds are necessary. Simply drag and drop the *fnPortfolioTable* function from the Server Explorer window onto the typed *DataSet* object's design surface. This creates the *DataTable/TableAdapter* pair without any additional effort. One small adjustment is prudent, however. Select the *TableAdapter* object's *Query* object (by clicking on the line labeled *Fill, GetData()*), and in the Properties window, click the ellipsis button in the value column for the *Parameters* property to bring up the Parameters Collection Editor dialog box. In the dialog box, change the *Size* property of the *@TickersPacked* parameter from 1024 to 50. Click OK.

The TVF *DataTable/TableAdapter* is now complete. Test it by choosing the Preview Data... option from the *TableAdapter*'s shortcut menu. In the Preview Data dialog box, be sure to enter a parameter value (such as **IBM;MSFT;SUN**) for the *TickersPacked* parameter, and then click Preview and make sure the data is being returned properly. Once you're done testing the TVF, click Close.

Aggregates and UDTs

To test our CLR aggregate function, create *DataTable/TableAdapter* pairs using the Table-Adapter Wizard *exactly* as we did in our previous *spContacts* example (be sure to reread, and follow, each step carefully), but type the following query text entry on the Enter A SQL State-ment page:

```
SELECT OrderId, SUM(ItemsOrdered) AS SUM, dbo.BakersDozen(ItemsOrdered) AS BakersDozen
FROM tblAggregateTest GROUP BY OrderId
```

No post-wizard property modifications are necessary! Preview the data to confirm this.

To test our CLR UDT, we will use the TableAdapter Wizard in the same fashion, once again, but we will simply type *x* as the query text on the Enter A SQL Statement page.

Note The Enter A SQL Statement page requires at least one character to be entered in its text box, so we entered *x* to satisfy that data validation requirement. After the wizard finishes, we will manually enter the real *CommandText* using the Properties window.

On the Wizard Results page, you will get an error message. Simply ignore it and click Finish. In the designer, rename the *DataTable* as **tblPoint**. Select the *TableAdapter* object's *Query* object, and set the *CommandText* property to an empty string (that is, delete the *x*). Next, using the *DataTable* object's Add/Column shortcut menu option, add *Column* objects called *ID* and *ThePoint* to it, and, in the Properties window, set the *ID Column* object's *DataType* property value to *System.Int32*. Finally, go back and reset the *Query* object's *CommandText* property to the following:

```
SELECT ID, CONVERT(nvarchar, ThePoint) AS ThePoint FROM tblPoint
```

After entering the previous query, Visual Studio displays an error message. Click OK on the message box and rest assured that the query you typed has in fact been assigned to the *Com-mandText* property.

Preview the data to confirm that everything was built properly. To save your work, click the Save All button (third from the left) on the Visual Studio Standard toolbar or choose the File/ Save All option on the main menu.

We now have a typed *DataSet* with embedded *DataTable/TableAdapter* pairs that make use of the CLR stored procedure, TVF, UDT, and user-defined aggregate objects that we created in Chapter 3. Along with the first typed *DataSet* we created in this chapter, we now have a wide range of conventional and SQL CLR data sources suitable for data binding. Our final tasks are to build Windows Forms and ASP.NET front ends that bind to these data sources.

Windows Forms Data Binding

With our typed *DataSet* objects solidly in place, we can cover Windows Forms data binding relatively quickly. The work we did to build these typed *DataSet* objects, including the extra work we did to embed SQL CLR objects, will now pay off handsomely because we can build data-bound forms against all our *DataTable* objects without writing a bit of code.

What's more, the Visual Studio design-time data binding tools easily handle all of the following scenarios:

- Simple binding of a *DataTable* to a *DataGridView* control.

- "Details view" binding wherein one row of a *DataTable* is displayed at a time and each field is bound to an individual control. A toolbar that handles navigation and basic maintenance operations is automatically created.

- Master-detail binding where, for example, the master row is displayed in a details view and all its child rows appear in a *DataGridView* control.

- Binding *ComboBox* controls to a foreign key field in the main *DataTable* and populating it with values from a related *DataTable*. The field's lookup value can then be displayed instead of its underlying foreign key value.

- Parameter binding handled by a special toolbar, generated to supply parameter values for *TableAdapter* objects whose *SelectCommand* objects are parameterized. This works well with our CLR TVF (*fnPortfolioTable*), T-SQL stored procedure (*uspGetBillOf Materials*), and the *FillBy/GetDataBy* Query object on the *ContactTableAdapter* object in the AdventureWorks typed *DataSet*.

All these scenarios are handled via simple drag-and-drop operations from Visual Studio's new Data Sources window onto the Windows Forms designer. The Data Sources window is typically docked along the left side of the Visual Studio window, in the same tabbed window group as the Server Explorer window and the Toolbox window. If the Data Sources window is not visible, activate it by selecting the Data/Show Data Sources option from the Visual Studio main menu. When the window comes up, both the AdventureWorks and CLRDS typed *DataSet* objects should be visible within it. If you drill down on each of them, all their *Data-Table* objects should be displayed, as shown in Figure 8-12. Each of these tables can be dragged and dropped onto a Windows Form.

Figure 8-12   The Data Sources window lists all your typed *DataSet* objects and their constituent *DataTable* objects.

> **Note**   The Data Sources window has its own toolbar buttons, two of which (Add New Data Source and Configure DataSet With Wizard) invoke the Data Source Configuration Wizard. You can use this wizard to create a new typed *DataSet* or change which objects are contained in existing ones. We do not cover the Data Source Configuration Wizard because the *DataSet* creation techniques that we do cover provide much more granular control over the configuration of the typed *DataSet* object's *DataTable*, *TableAdapter*, *Query*, and *Column* objects. At the end of the chapter, we will briefly cover the ASP.NET version of the Data Source Configuration Wizard. You might want to explore the Windows Forms version on your own.

DataGridView Binding

To test *DataGridView* control binding, add a new form to your project and then drag and drop the AdventureWorks *DataSet* object's Employee table onto it. After a brief pause, Visual Studio generates and injects the following controls and components onto your form:

- Instances of the AdventureWorks typed *DataSet* and the *EmployeeTableAdapter* object. (These appear in the form's "component tray" below its main designer surface.)

- A *BindingSource* object connected to the Employee *DataTable* (also in the component tray).

- A *BindingNavigator* object for the Employee *DataTable*. The *BindingNavigator* consists of an object in the component tray and a special *ToolStrip* control on the top of the form itself. The *ToolStrip* includes various controls for navigating through and editing the *DataTable* object's rows.

- A *DataGridView* control that is bound to the *BindingSource* object.

To see the fruits of your (rather modest) labor, make this form your startup form, and run the project. You should see the form appear with the Employee table's data displayed. You can also edit, insert, and delete data simply by making modifications within the *DataGridView* control and clicking the Save button (at the far right) on the form's *ToolStrip*.

Details View Binding

Admittedly, the navigation and data maintenance buttons on the form (with the exception of the Save button) are somewhat superfluous, given that the *DataGridView* handles most of these operations natively. On the other hand, this toolbar would be very useful for a details view version of the form. Creating a details view form is almost as simple as creating a Data-GridView version, so let's create one now.

Start by adding another new form to your project. With the new form open in its designer, click the Employee table within the Data Sources window, and then click the drop-down arrow to the right of it. You should see the following options listed: DataGridView, Details, [None], and Customize..., as shown in Figure 8-13.

Figure 8-13   The Data Sources Window with the Employee table's drop-down mode menu

Select Details, and then drag and drop the Employee table onto your new form.

Visual Studio generates and injects most of the same controls and components as before, but this time it generates labels and individual controls for each column in the Employee table rather than a single *DataGridView* control for the entire result set. Make this form your startup form, and run the project. You should have all the same capabilities you had in the *DataGrid-View* version of the form, but this time the *ToolStrip*'s navigation controls, as well as its Add New and Delete buttons, should prove useful and intuitive.

Smart Defaults

Close the form at run time to get back into design mode in Visual Studio, and note that the control names for the field-level bound controls and labels are mnemonically named based on the *Column* objects to which they are bound. Also notice that the labels' *Text* property values are spaced wherever intercapping is used in the *Column* object's name. (For example, the column named *FirstName* generates a label whose text property value is First Name.)

Technically speaking, it is not the *Column* object's *Name* property that governs the Labels' *Text* property values, but rather its *Caption* property. By default, *Name* and *Caption* have the same value, but recall that at the beginning of this chapter we changed the *Caption* property of the

Employee *DataTable* object's *HireDate Column* object to *Date of Hire*. If you look carefully at your data-bound form, you will see that the *Text* property value of the label corresponding to the *HireDate* field is *Date of Hire* even though the names of the *Column* object's *Label* and *DateTimePicker* controls are derived form the column's name (*HireDate*).

Binding to Stored Procedures and Views

The techniques we just described work identically for tables, stored procedures, and views. To see this yourself, build data-bound forms against the AdventureWorks view-derived *vEmployeeDepartment DataTable* and the stored procedure–derived *Currency DataTable* in the AdventureWorks typed *DataSet*. Bear in mind that the *Currency DataTable* supports data display as well as updates, inserts, and deletes because its *TableAdapter* is bound to four separate stored procedures, each supporting a specific CRUD operation. For tables, the TableAdapter Wizard generates the appropriate SQL *UPDATE*, *INSERT*, and *DELETE* commands by parsing the *SELECT* command you supply it with. For views, the data-bound forms will select only data unless you manually specify values for the *UpdateCommand*, *InsertCommand*, and *DeleteCommand* properties of the view's *TableAdapter Query* object.

SQL CLR Binding

Because of the work we put in designing the CLRDS typed *DataSet*, you can also use the techniques we've described against SQL CLR objects. Try doing so against the spContacts, tblAggregateTest, and tblPoint *DataTable* objects. Bear in mind that these *DataTable* objects do not support updates, inserts, and deletes—not because SQL CLR objects can't support these operations, but because extra work is required for them to do so.

For example, with *spContacts*, we did not define an *UpdateCommand*, *InsertCommand*, or *DeleteCommand* for its *TableAdapter* because we did not develop corresponding SQL CLR (or T-SQL) stored procedures for these operations. Had we done so, we could have used them in the *DataSet* and could have supported all four CRUD operations against the *spContacts DataTable*.

The *TableAdapter* for the tblAggregateTest *DataTable* also has only a *SelectCommand* defined for it, and the query underlying it is inherently not updatable because it contains a *GROUP BY* clause and an aggregate function in its *SELECT* clause (which was the whole point!). For the tblPoint *TableAdapter*, creating an *UpdateCommand*, *InsertCommand*, and *DeleteCommand* would require manually determining the corresponding SQL commands.

Master-Detail and Lookup Binding

Binding to single result sets is fine for many application requirements, but most real-world scenarios require you to accommodate hierarchical/master-detail data and lookup values. For example, binding to the Employee table as we did earlier is fine as far as it goes, but for a production-ready system, it is better to show all the employee's direct reports and to show the name of the employee rather than the value of his or her *ContactId* column. Furthermore, if we want to allow edits to the *ContactId* column, we need a way to select a contact by name because we can no longer enter the *ContactId* value directly (because we're showing the name instead).

Previous data binding models got us only part way to this level of functionality. In general, they let us bind to a simple result set and then customize the data-bound form with our own code—or manual property settings, if we were lucky. But the Data Sources window and its drag-and-drop binding support this functionality as a matter of course. Let's explore how to take advantage of these features.

First let's go back to the AdventureWorks typed *DataSet* and make some changes. We'll add a computed column to the *Contact DataTable* that we can use to display the contact's full name. Do this by adding a new *Column* object using the *DataTable* object's shortcut menu; name it **FullName**, and set its *Expression* property value to the following SQL expression. (Note that the quoted strings between the plus signs each contain a single space, whereas those within the *ISNULL* function calls have no spaces.)

```
ISNULL(FirstName, '') + ' ' + ISNULL(MiddleName, '') + ' ' + ISNULL(LastName, '')
```

Next, edit the *ContactTableAdapter* object's *SelectCommand.CommandText* property, and append the following *ORDER BY* clause to it:

```
ORDER BY LastName, FirstName, MiddleName
```

When asked if you'd like to regenerate the updating commands and whether you'd like to update other queries, click the No button each time. These two changes allow us to populate a combo box with all the employees' full names, in alphabetical order. Be sure to save your changes before proceeding to the next step.

Next, add another new form to your project, show the Data Sources window, and carefully perform the following steps:

1. Drill down on the AdventureWorks *DataSet*, put the Employee *DataTable* into Details mode, and then drill down on it (if it's not already drilled down).

2. Click the drop-down arrow next to the *ContactId* column, and change its control type from *TextBox* to *ComboBox*. Change the *rowguid* column's control type to *[None]*.

3. Drag and drop the Employee table from the Data Sources Window onto the form.

4. Go to the end of the column list under the Employee table and note that the Employee table itself appears as the last "field" (because the Employee table is constrained in the AdventureWorks database to have a self-join between its *ManagerId* and *EmployeeId* columns). Click the drop-down arrow of this "child" Employee table and change its mode to *DataGridView*. Then drag and drop it onto the form, to the right of all the fields already on the form.

5. Drag the Contact table from the DataSources window and drop it *on top of* the *contactIdComboBox* control in your form. You should see a shortcut icon appear just before you release the mouse button.

6. Select the *contactIdComboBox* control, and then click its SmartTag triangle (which should appear at the upper-right corner of the control). In the ComboBox Tasks Smart-Tag property dialog box that appears, change *Display Member* from *Title* to *FullName*.

7. Change the *Text* property value of the *contactIDLabel* control from *Contact Id:* to *Employee Name:*, and change the *DropDownStyle* property of the *contactIdComboBox* control from *DropDown* to *DropDownList*.

8. Make this new form the project's startup form, and run the project. Navigate to the third record (with an *EmployeeId* field value of 3). Your form should appear exactly as shown in Figure 8-14.

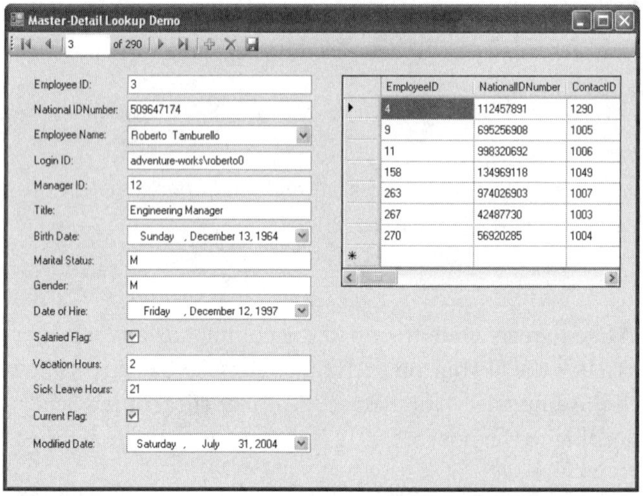

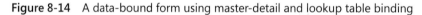

Figure 8-14 A data-bound form using master-detail and lookup table binding

In this short series of steps, we have demonstrated how to do the following:

■ Customize control type mapping (by changing the *ContactID* column's control type from *TextBox* to *ComboBox*).

■ Perform lookup binding (by performing a "second pass" drag-and-drop of the Contact table onto the *contactIDComboBox* control).

■ Customize default data-bound property values (using the SmartTag ComboBox Tasks property dialog box of the *contactIDComboBox* control).

■ Perform master-detail binding (by dragging and dropping the "child" Employee table onto the form).

Space restrictions prevent us from going into detail about all this, but it is important to observe what objects, property settings, and code the drag-and-drop operations generated.

Notice that our form has three *BindingSource* objects (one each for the master employee data, the child employee data, and the contact data). Because two of these *BindingSource* objects point to the same *DataTable*, only two *TableAdapter* objects are needed (one each for Employee and Contact).

Now look at the *DataSource* and *DataMember* properties of the *BindingSource* objects. The contact *BindingSource* and the master employee *BindingSource* point to *DataTable* objects within the typed *DataSet* instance, but the *child* employee *BindingSource* points to the foreign key relation within the *master* employee *BindingSource*. Understanding this unlocks the whole secret of Windows Forms 2.0 master-detail data binding.

Review the event handler code in the form's code-behind. You don't have to write any code to perform design-time data binding, but some code is generated for you. Note that the *Fill* method of each *TableAdapter* is called in the form's *Load* event and *employeeTableAdapter.Update* is called in the Save button's *Click* event.

Parameterized Query Data Binding

The topic of generated code provides an excellent segue into a quick investigation of parameterized data binding, while also incorporating our SQL CLR TVF. Demonstrating how all this works is incredibly simple: Add another form to the project, and then drag and drop the CLRDS typed *DataSet* object's *fnPortfolioTable* object onto it (in either DataGridView or Details mode). Recall from Chapter 3 that this TVF requires a semicolon-delimited list of three ticker symbols and returns a three-row result set with each of those ticker symbols and manufactured values for them. Now take a look at your form; you should see that the drag-and-drop operation inserted a special *ToolStrip* control at the top of the form with a *TextBox* control that solicits the delimited ticker list input parameter and a button labeled *Fill* that executes the parameterized query.

A look at the form's code-behind class reveals no code in the form's load event. Because we don't have a parameter value initially, we can't call the *TableAdapter* object's *Fill* method upon loading the form. Instead, the *Fill* method is called in the Fill button's *Click* event handler. Notice that no code is generated to configure a parameter object. Instead, the parameter value is passed as the second argument to the *Fill* method! The typed DataSet designer generates a specially formulated version of the *TableAdapter* object's *Fill* method that accepts the parameter value and loads it into a *SqlParameter* object.

You can check out this generated code if you'd like. Just drill down on the CLRDS.xsd file in the Solution Explorer window and double-click the CLRDS.designer.cs file. In the source code editor, search for *Fill(CLRDS.fnPortfolioTable*, and examine the code immediately after the resulting cursor position. Do not change the code—or, if you do, close the file without saving changes.

Make this new form your startup form, and run the project. In the top *ToolStrip,* type a three ticker symbol list (such as *IBM;MSFT;SUN*) in the TickersPacked *TextBox* and click Fill. Your results should be similar to those shown in Figure 8-15.

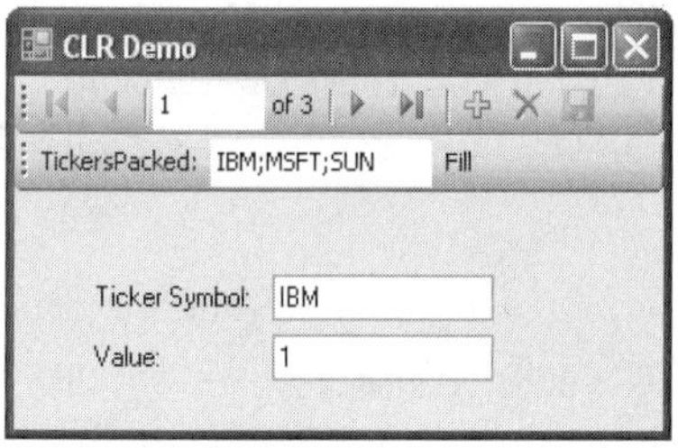

Figure 8-15   A data-bound form supporting entry of input parameters

Data Binding on the Web

Before we close this chapter, we'd like to show you that much of what we've discussed about the Windows Forms environment works nicely on the Web, in the ASP.NET environment. Our coverage here will be brief because the typed *DataSet* skills you've picked up can already be applied handily in an ASP.NET Web application. Furthermore, the ASP.NET data binding model, although differing significantly from the Windows Forms model, is largely a code-free model. Essentially, you need only combine a typed *DataSet* with an ASP.NET form that has some of the new data-bound controls and the new *ObjectDataSource* control, and you have a fully functional data-bound form.

The sample Visual Studio solution for this chapter includes an ASP.NET site called Chapter08Web. You can examine the typed *DataSet* and forms in that project, or you can create a new ASP.NET Web site in Visual Studio and follow along with the steps outlined next.

Typed *DataSet* Objects and the Web.config File

Create a new Web site using the File/New Web Site... main menu option. Add a new *DataSet* to the site using the Web Site/Add New Item... main menu option or the Add New Item... option on the Web site node's shortcut menu in the Solution Explorer window. Click Yes when asked if you want to create the *DataSet* within a new App_Code folder.

After a brief pause, the TableAdapter Wizard starts. ASP.NET projects do not contain settings files or a Settings designer, but the ASP.NET Web.config file has a dedicated section for storing connection strings, just as the App.config file does in a Windows Forms project. The Table-Adapter Wizard can write connection strings to the Web.config file in much the same way that it does with a Windows Forms project settings file, and it creates the Web.config file for you if one does not already exist within your site.

On the wizard's Choose Your Data Connection page, select an existing data connection to the AdventureWorks database if one exists. (If not, click New Connection..., in the Add Connection dialog box, configure the connection to point to the AdventureWorks database, and then click OK.) Click Next to advance to the Save Your Connection String To The Application Configuration File page. Make sure the page's check box is checked and that the connection string entry name is one you're happy with, and then click Next. The TableAdapter Wizard creates a new Web.config file in your site and creates an entry there for your AdventureWorks connection string.

On the Choose A Command Type page, select the Use SQL Statements option and click Next. On the Enter a SQL Statement page, enter the following query:

```
SELECT * FROM HumanResources.Employee
```

Click Next twice, click Finish, and then save your work. A Web.config file should now be added to your Web site; open it to view your connection string encoded within it.

The Data Source Configuration Wizard, the *ObjectDataSource* Control, and the New Data-Bound Controls

In the Solution Explorer window, delete the Default.aspx page, and then add a new Web form via the Add New Item... main menu or shortcut menu option. Name the new form **GridView.aspx**. With the new form open in its designer, from the Data section of the toolbox, drag and drop a *GridView* control onto the form; the control's GridView Tasks SmartTag property dialog box opens. In the Choose Data Source combo box, select New Data Source. The Data Source Configuration Wizard launches. On the wizard's Choose A Data Source Type page, select the Object option and change the name in the Specify An ID For The Data Source text box to **odsEmployee**. The wizard and the proper selection are shown in Figure 8-16.

Click OK to advance to the Choose A Business Object page, and select *AdventureWorksTableAdapters.EmployeeTableAdapter* from the combo box. Note that you can use this dialog box to select any class that adheres to a certain set of requirements, not just *TableAdapter* classes.

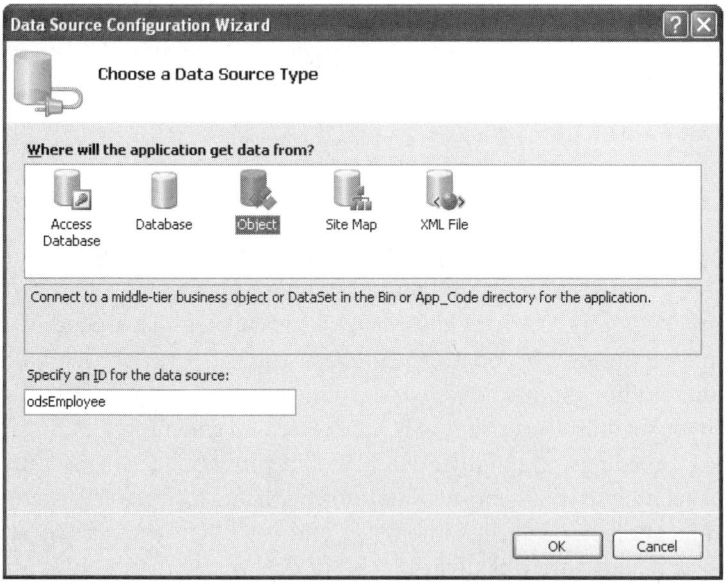

Figure 8-16   The ASP.NET Data Source Configuration Wizard allows binding to a number of data source types, each corresponding to a specific ASP.NET data source control.

Click Next to advance to the Define Data Methods page. Here you define which methods of your class can be used for each of the four CRUD operations. Recall that the *GetData* method and the three *DBDirect* methods meet this requirement exactly; on each tab, make sure that the appropriate method is selected. (The proper methods should be selected by default: the *GetData* method on the SELECT tab and the *Update*, *Insert*, and *Delete* methods on their respective namesake tabs.) Click Finish, and you will be back in the Web Forms designer, with an expanded GridView Tasks SmartTag Property menu visible. Select the first three of the four check boxes (all but the Enable Selection check box), and then click the Auto Format link. In the Auto Format dialog box, select a scheme you find pleasing and click OK. Now run your project; when asked if you'd like to enable debugging, click OK.

When the form is rendered in your browser, you should be able to page, sort, edit, and delete your data. You can do all this without writing any .NET code because of the declarative nature of ASP.NET data binding. We recommend examining the property settings of the *ObjectData-Source* and *GridView* controls, and their corresponding HTML attributes and subelements, to get a better sense of how this all works.

Repeat this process using the new *DetailsView* and *FormsView* controls in place of the *Grid-View*. In the Properties window, set the *AllowPaging* property of each control to *True*, and set the *PagerSettings.Mode* property to *NextPreviousFirstLast*. Each of these controls provides a record-at-a-time UI that allows you to insert new rows as well as update and delete existing ones. The layout of the *DetailsView* control is fixed, with column names on the left and data-bound controls on the right. The *FormsView* control is templated, and the UI for each of its modes (*ReadOnly*, *Edit*, and *Insert*) is completely customizable. Default templates are generated for you when you create the control so that you do not need to create them from scratch. If you do want to edit the templates, you can do so through the control's Edit Template shortcut menu option or the Edit Templates hyperlink in the FormView Tasks SmartTag property dialog box.

Summary

SQL Server 2005 is arguably the first version of the product to explicitly target the developer. Its hosting of the .NET CLR, its XML features, and its extensions to T-SQL provide multiple channels for delivery of your data. As you have seen in this chapter, Visual Studio 2005, ADO.NET 2.0, Windows Forms 2.0, and ASP.NET 2.0 provide an array of programmable objects, controls, and binding models as well as deep integration with a greatly enhanced typed *DataSet* facility that faithfully carries the SQL Server 2005 data programming torch. The diversity of choices for reading and modifying data within your applications is immense, so you should pick the technique you're most comfortable with and learn it well. From there, all the other tools and technologies will click into place, and you'll find yourself working in an extremely tight, efficient, and powerful environment for data access development.

Chapter 9
Debugging

–Andrew Brust

This is a book about programming and the many ways you can "program" Microsoft SQL Server 2005. As you have already seen (and will continue to see), this release of SQL Server is the most programmable ever. Whether it be through T-SQL, ADO.NET and the SQL Client provider, or the new SQL CLR programming model, SQL Server developers have numerous programming tools at their disposal to facilitate data access, data manipulation, and data management.

Historically, the job of debugging database code on the server has involved the use of different tools and a different outlook than has debugging code on the client. For example, while it's been possible to debug T-SQL code from Microsoft Visual Studio for some time, the setup work involved has been non-trivial and consistency with the client code debugging experience has been lacking. What SQL Server developers have long needed is a straightforward and seamless way to debug all their code, with minimal disruption, as they jump between languages and tiers.

SQL Server 2005 and Visual Studio 2005 together do an excellent job of addressing this need. You can now easily debug T-SQL and SQL CLR code separately or together, on your local machine or a remote server. You can do all of this on an ad hoc basis or from within an application debugging session. You can even debug some server-side code when it is called by an application other than your own.

You know that Visual Studio lets you set breakpoints in your application code from within the code editor. It also provides the Debug branch of the main menu and the Debug toolbar for helping you navigate through your code, and it provides special windows such as the Autos, Locals, Watch, Call Stack, and Command windows to help you get your bearings as you do so.

> **Note** Visual Studio provides up to four separate Watch windows (labeled Watch 1, Watch 2, Watch 3, and Watch 4). By default, Visual Studio shows the Watch 1 window and allows you to show or hide it and the other Watch windows using the Debug/Windows/Watch submenu, which is available when Visual Studio is in Debugging mode or Running mode. Throughout this chapter, we will refer to the collection of Watch windows generically as "Watch" or "the Watch window."

All of these facilities are available to you not just for debugging application code but also for debugging server-side SQL CLR code. Merely by selecting the Allow SQL/CLR Debugging shortcut menu option on a specific connection node in the Server Explorer window and calling your SQL CLR code from your project's test script, you can easily debug that code. Your T-SQL test script itself can be debugged as well.

You can also debug server-side code in a number of other ways. For example, you can use the Server Explorer window to debug your stored procedures and functions, without even having any source projects open in Visual Studio. Interestingly, this technique works for T-SQL code as well as it does for SQL CLR code. It is also possible to step into your server-side code while debugging client-side ADO.NET code that calls into it. It is even possible to step into T-SQL code from SQL CLR code, and vice-versa.

Various combinations of client-side and server-side .NET code (be it in C# or Visual Basic .NET), along with T-SQL code, can be debugged together or separately using common IDE tools. While you can do this kind of cross-tier, mixed-language debugging with relative ease, you need to be aware of the many menu and dialog box settings required to make everything work together correctly. There are also IDE tools and techniques important for debugging that are less than obvious and thus bear special mention. And for remote debugging, you must be aware of some special setup requirements.

We think that if you consider all types of Visual Studio debugging together, as a unified suite of tools, you can more easily perform any specific debugging task. It is the goal of this chapter to point out various debugging settings, tools, and techniques, make you comfortable with SQL Server debugging in general, and thus heighten your efficiency and productivity as a SQL Server developer.

About the Sample Code

As with other chapters in this book, sample code for this chapter is provided in the form of a Visual Studio 2005 solution (Chapter09.sln in the VS subfolder) and a SQL Server Management Studio solution (Chapter09.ssmssln in the SSMS subfolder). The Visual Studio solution contains a SQL Server project called Chapter09SQLCLR and a Windows Forms application called Chapter09 that we will use as a debugging test harness. The startup project for the solution is set to Current Selection. This means that when the Windows Forms project (or one of its child nodes) is selected in the Solution Explorer window, Visual Studio's Start Debugging option will run that application. When the SQL Server project is selected, Visual Studio's Start Debugging option will instead run that project's test script. Bear this in mind as you read the chapter because you will be instructed to run each of these at different times.

Note   You must set the Chapter 09SQLCLR project's database reference to point to the AdventureWorks database on your local SQL Server Instance. Do so by right-clicking the project's node in the Solution Explorer window and selecting Properties from the shortcut menu, and then click the Browse... button on the Database tab of the resulting property sheet. In the Chapter09 project's form, the *Text* property of the *TextBox* control *txtConnectionString* contains a similarly configured connection string. Modify it through the Properties window as necessary.

The Visual Studio solution has also been configured in such a way that the Chapter09 SQLCLR assembly will *not* automatically deploy when the Start Debugging option is invoked. Had we not configured the solution in this way, the assembly would be deployed to the database every time you invoked the Start Debugging option from *either* project. To deploy the assembly from Visual Studio, you need to select the Deploy option from the Chapter09-SQLCLR project node's shortcut menu in the Solution Explorer window. Open the Visual Studio solution and deploy the Chapter09SQLCLR assembly now.

The SQL Server Management Studio solution contains three scripts; the first two (spTSQL.sql and spTSQLAndCLR.sql) create simple T-SQL stored procedures that we will use in several of our debugging scenarios. Go ahead and open the solution, and then execute these two scripts against the AdventureWorks database on your development SQL Server. We'll use the third script toward the end of the chapter to demonstrate how to debug SQL CLR code invoked from SQL Server Management Studio; don't execute this script yet.

Note   The connection in the Management Studio project also assumes that the development SQL Server is available as the default instance on your local machine. For now, the server must be local (we will cover debugging on remote servers at the end of the chapter) but need not be installed as the default instance. Delete and re-create the connection to change the instance name, if necessary. If you do re-create the connection, make certain to configure the connection to point to the AdventureWorks database and to configure each script to use the connection.

With the preliminaries behind us, let's start debugging! We will start with the simplest scenarios, looking carefully at the options available within them and then branching out into increasingly complex situations.

Ad Hoc Debugging

The simplest way to debug SQL Server code is to use the Server Explorer window's Step Into... feature. Using this tool, you can debug a stored procedure or function, written in T-SQL or a CLR language, and do so without having to open a project in Visual Studio (although we happen to have a solution open already). Because this is the simplest and easiest debugging scenario, let's start by examining it and using it as our portal into understanding the tools available to us while code is being debugged.

Creating Database Connections

Before you can do any debugging, you must add a database connection to the Server Explorer window in Visual Studio. You have likely already done this as a byproduct of the work we did in Chapter 3, but let's create a database connection from scratch anyway to understand database connections more fully and to create a connection that is independent of any SQL Server project in Visual Studio.

In Visual Studio, show the Server Explorer window, if it's not already visible, using the View/ Server Explorer main menu option or its Ctrl+Alt+S keyboard shortcut. Next, right-click the Database Connections node in the window's tree view, and select the Add Connection... option from the shortcut menu. Depending on your Visual Studio configuration, this action will either invoke the Choose Data Source dialog box (Figure 9-1) or the Add Connection dialog box (Figure 9-2).

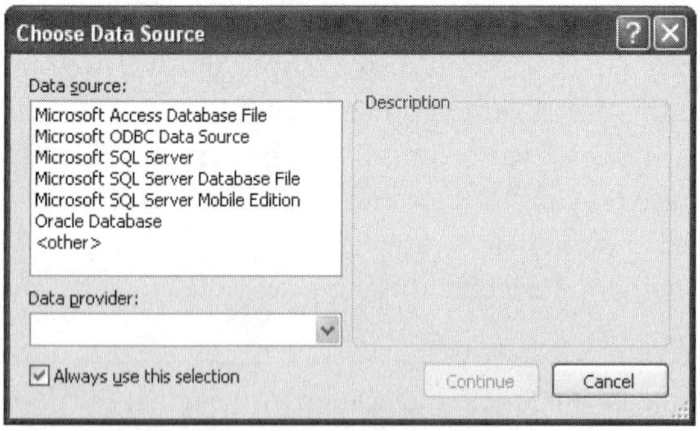

Figure 9-1   The Choose Data Source dialog box

If the Choose Data Source dialog box appears, select Microsoft SQL Server from the Data Source list box and .NET Data Provider For SQL Server from the Data Provider drop-down list. We recommend that you select the Always Use This Selection check box; doing so ensures that subsequent use of the Server Explorer window's Add Connection... shortcut menu option will take you directly to the Add Connection dialog box, with the SQL Server .NET provider selected by default. (You can always change this default by clicking the Add Connection dialog box's Change... button.) Click OK to advance to the Add Connection dialog box.

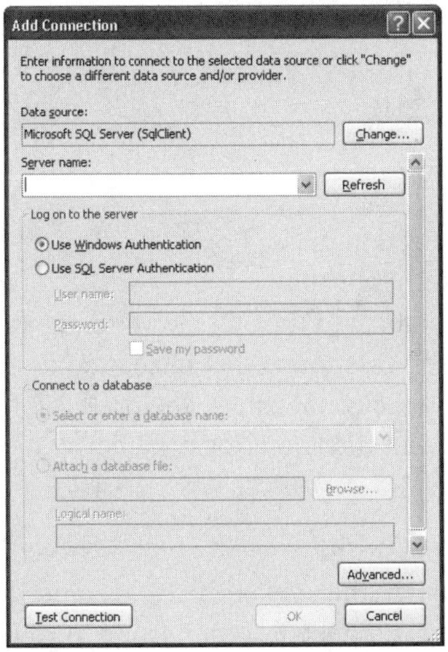

Figure 9-2   The Add Connection dialog box

You can use the Add Connection dialog box as a simple tool for connecting to a specific SQL Server instance and database quickly and easily. You can also use it as a tool for learning about sophisticated connection options and configuring them. The easiest way to use the dialog box is to specify a server, an instance name, and a database name, and then click OK.

You can specify these options manually or by selecting them from drop-down lists. Using the Server Name drop-down list can be time consuming because it invokes the SQL Server browser to look for servers on your network. We recommend that you enter server information by typing the server's name (or IP address) and, if applicable, following it with a back-slash character (\) and an instance name. If you're connecting to a SQL instance running on your local machine, you can enter (*local*), *localhost*, or "." as the server name (enter only the period, not the quotes).

Once you have entered or selected a valid server name and optional instance name, you should be able to accept the default Use Windows Authentication setting and click the drop-down arrow for the Select Or Enter A Database Name drop-down list. From here, you can select a database on the server and then click OK. This should add a new connection node to the Server Explorer window's tree view; expand this node now. If you further expand the Stored Procedures or Functions child nodes, you will see a full list of the corresponding object types. You can then right-click any individual stored procedure or function node representing a T-SQL object and, provided certain security requirements are met, select the Step Into Stored Procedure or Step Into Function shortcut menu option to debug the corresponding stored procedure or function.

Before you do that, however, let's go back into the connection dialog box to understand it a bit better. To do this, right-click the connection's node in the Server Explorer window and select the Modify Connection... shortcut menu option. This will bring up the Modify Connection dialog box, which is identical to the Add Connection dialog box, except that it initially displays settings stored within the selected connection.

Log On Options

Consider the options available in the Modify Connection dialog box's Log On To The Server group box. Accepting the default Use Windows Authentication option tells the Server Explorer window to use *your* Windows identity to attach to the SQL Server database. If you want, you can instead use SQL Server authentication (assuming that mixed mode authentication is enabled on the server/instance to which you are connecting). You do this by selecting the Use SQL Server Authentication option button and then entering a valid user name and password in the corresponding text boxes.

If you click the Save My Password check box, the password you enter will be stored and retrieved in later Visual Studio sessions. This gives you the convenience of not needing to enter the password each time you run Visual Studio and open the connection. If you leave the check box unchecked, attempts to open this Server Explorer connection in subsequent Visual Studio sessions will result in the Connect to SQL Server dialog box appearing to solicit the necessary password (Figure 9-3).

Figure 9-3   The Connect To SQL Server dialog box

Selecting the Save My Password check box adds the security risk of storing your password persistently. Assuming that your Windows account is sufficiently credentialed on your SQL Server, we recommend accepting the Windows Authentication option.

Advanced Properties

As we discussed in Chapter 8, if you click the Advanced... button, the Advanced Properties dialog box appears. This dialog box allows for precise configuration of the connection string your Server Explorer window will use. Rather than force you to enter that connection string manually, the dialog box prompts you for each connection string name/value pair that the selected database provider (the .NET SQL Server provider, in our case) supports.

As you supply values for specific connection string properties, help text for the one currently selected will appear below the property grid, and the full connection string, as configured at that moment, will be displayed in a read-only text box at the bottom of the dialog box. Although the connection string might appear truncated, you can resize the dialog box to view more of the connection string at once, and you can also select the entire connection string with your mouse, copy it to the clipboard, and then paste it somewhere (such as Microsoft Word or Notepad) to read it in its entirety.

> **Tip**   Most of these advanced connection string properties have little impact on the usage of the connection from the Server Explorer window for debugging purposes. However, if the database connection's objects are later used in the DataSet designer for a typed *DataSet* that is subsequently used in an application, these settings might have great impact. For example, if you set the Asynchronous Processing property to True, then *Query* objects within any typed *DataSet* objects that use the connection could be executed asynchronously.

T-SQL "Step Into" Debugging

Once you have added a connection to the Server Explorer window and successfully configured it, you're ready to do some debugging. For example, you can add a connection to the AdventureWorks sample database, and then drill down to its Stored Procedures node. Expand the Stored Procedures node, locate the node for the *spTSQL* stored procedure, and right-click it; then select the Step Into Stored Procedure shortcut menu option.

The stored procedure *spTSQL* is shown in Listing 9-1.

Listing 9-1   T-SQL stored procedure *spTSQL*

```
CREATE PROCEDURE dbo.spTSQL
    (
    @VendorId int
    )
AS

    SET NOCOUNT ON

    SELECT      ProductID, VendorID, AverageLeadTime, StandardPrice, LastReceiptCost,
    LastReceiptDate, MinOrderQty, MaxOrderQty, OnOrderQty, UnitMeasureCode, ModifiedDate
    FROM        Purchasing.ProductVendor
    WHERE       (VendorID = @VendorId)
```

The stored procedure selects data from the ProductVendor table and uses the parameter value as a selection criterion on the table's VendorID column. Because the stored procedure is parameterized, the Run Stored Procedure dialog box (Figure 9-4) appears after you select the Step Into Stored Procedure shortcut menu option.

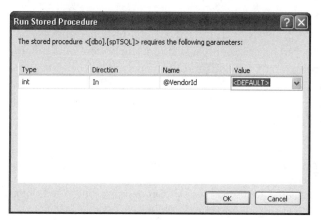

Figure 9-4   The Run Stored Procedure dialog box

Enter a value of **54** for the parameter *@VendorId*, and then click OK.

At this point, Visual Studio enters Debugging mode, the stored procedure's T-SQL code appears in a code editor window, and a yellow instruction pointer arrow appears to the left of the stored procedure's first executable line of code (the one immediately following the *AS* keyword). This is shown in Figure 9-5.

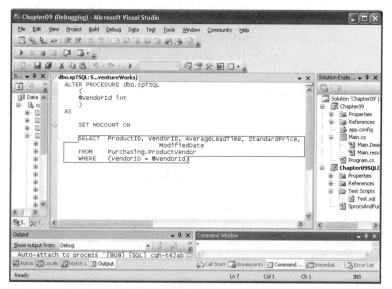

Figure 9-5   Debugging T-SQL code in Visual Studio

Without even executing this line of code, you can take advantage of a number of debugging features immediately. Let's explore a few of these now.

Debugging Tools at Your Service

The Output window (Figure 9-6) displays some thread information and reports the name of the stored procedure you are running, along with its input parameter names and values.

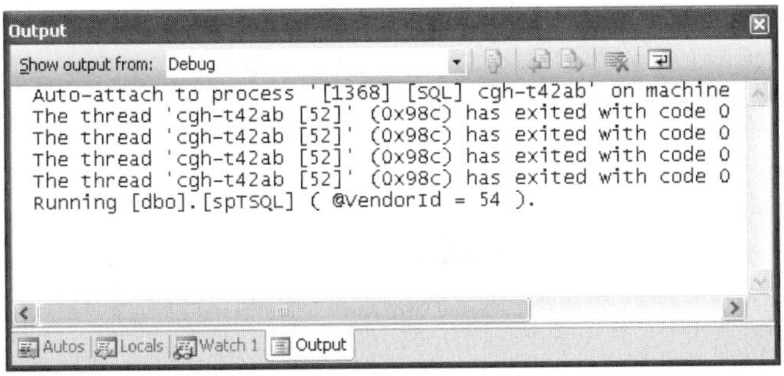

Figure 9-6 The Output window during an ad hoc T-SQL debugging session

The Call Stack window (Figure 9-7) displays the same stored procedure information and reports the current line number pointed to by the instruction pointer.

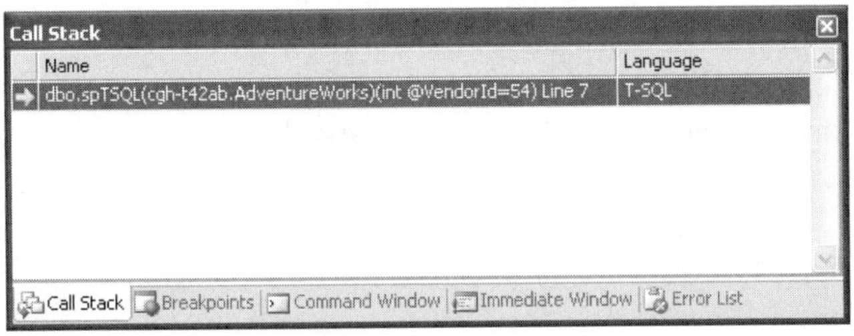

Figure 9-7 The Call Stack window during an ad hoc T-SQL debugging session

When you debug a stored procedure or function directly through the Server Explorer window, the Call Stack window might appear to offer little value. However, as we will see later, if your stored procedure or function calls into *other* server-side code, the Call Stack window helps you keep track of where you are and how you got there, and it allows you to view the source of any server code within the call stack itself. If you are looking at source code one or more layers down in the call stack, you can use the Show Next Statement shortcut menu option to return immediately to the line of code currently pointed to by the instruction pointer.

Note that the Locals window (Figure 9-8) displays the input parameter and its current value; the latter is *editable* in this window.

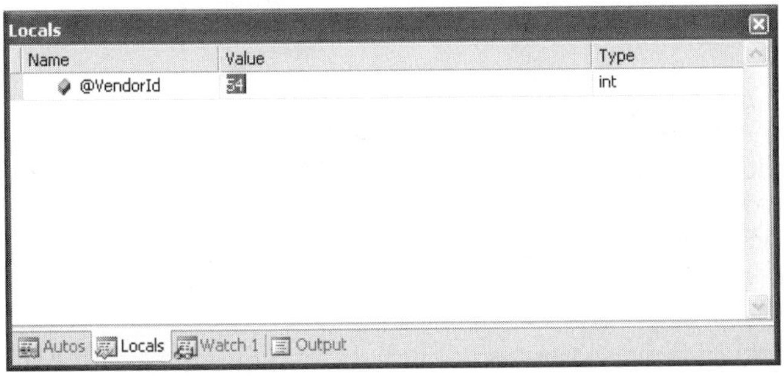

Figure 9-8 The Locals window during an ad hoc T-SQL debugging session, with the parameter value being edited

To edit the value, just double-click the cell in the Values column or right-click it and choose the Edit Value shortcut menu option. Next, type in a new value and then either click away from the cell or press the Enter key on your keyboard.

The value is immediately updated, its text color changes to red, indicating that you have changed it, and the new value is updated dynamically in the Call Stack window. You can also hover your mouse over the parameter's name anywhere within the source code, view its value in a ToolTip, and edit the value in-place, if you'd prefer. (Make sure to press Enter when you're done editing the value, or the new value will not be saved.)

> **Tip**   When you update a parameter value through its ToolTip, the new value will not be displayed in the Call Stack window, although it will in fact be properly assigned.

Another useful diagnostic tool is the Visual Studio Command Window. Although, when used in a T-SQL debugging session, it lacks the full feature set offered during .NET code debugging sessions, it is very handy for interrogating parameter and variable values. For example, you can type the following command to determine the value of the *@VendorId* input parameter:

```
? @VendorId
```

When you press the Enter key on your keyboard, the parameter value appears on the next line. You can also interrogate SQL Server system variables such as *@@version* or *@@spid* to determine those environmental values. Unfortunately, you cannot assign values to variables/parameters, execute ad hoc T-SQL commands, or even evaluate mathematical expressions in the Command Window during a T-SQL debugging session.

A close cousin of the Command Window is the Immediate Window. While you are debugging T-SQL code, it can evaluate the same T-SQL parameter and variable expressions as the Command Window. But the Immediate Window also allows you to evaluate expressions or call .NET base class library functions while debugging .NET code or even at design time when .NET code or forms are opened. You can show the Immediate Window using the Debug/Windows/Immediate main menu option. When you are debugging .NET code, the Immediate Window provides full IntelliSense support for interactive expression evaluation. The Immediate Window is therefore extremely useful when you are debugging application code or SQL CLR code.

> **Tip**   If the Debug/Windows/Immediate option is not available on the menu in your copy of Visual Studio, you can add it by selecting the Tools/Customize... main menu option and then selecting the Debug option in the Categories list in the resulting Customize dialog box. From there, you can drag and drop the Immediate option from the Commands list to the toolbar or menu of your choice.

Now let's discuss the debugging features of the code editor itself, where the options available are remarkably similar to those available during .NET debugging sessions. For example, using the Debug toolbar or the Debug branch of the main menu, you can stop debugging, continue execution (without further debugging), or step through your code line by line. You can also edit your code and invoke an in-place SQL designer (either for editing exiting SQL blocks or for inserting new ones). However, edit and continue is not available in T-SQL debugging sessions, so any changes you make will not take effect until you reexecute the modified code.

Breakpoints

The code editor also allows you to set breakpoints or use the Run To Cursor option (which is similar to setting a breakpoint, continuing execution, and then deleting the breakpoint). As with .NET code, any breakpoints you set are persisted for use in future Visual Studio sessions. As you will see later, setting breakpoints in your T-SQL code is required when you want to debug that code while debugging application code that calls it (as opposed to debugging the T-SQL code using the Server Explorer window's Step Into... options).

You set a breakpoint by moving your cursor to the line of code on which you want to place the breakpoint and then doing one of the following: (1) selecting the Debug/Toggle Breakpoint option from the main menu, (2) pressing the F9 key on your keyboard, (3) clicking in the gray margin area to the left of the line of code, or (4) right-clicking the line of code and selecting the Breakpoint/Insert Breakpoint shortcut menu option. Once you set the breakpoint, a small red sphere appears in the gray margin area to the left of the line of code on which the breakpoint was set (Figure 9-9).

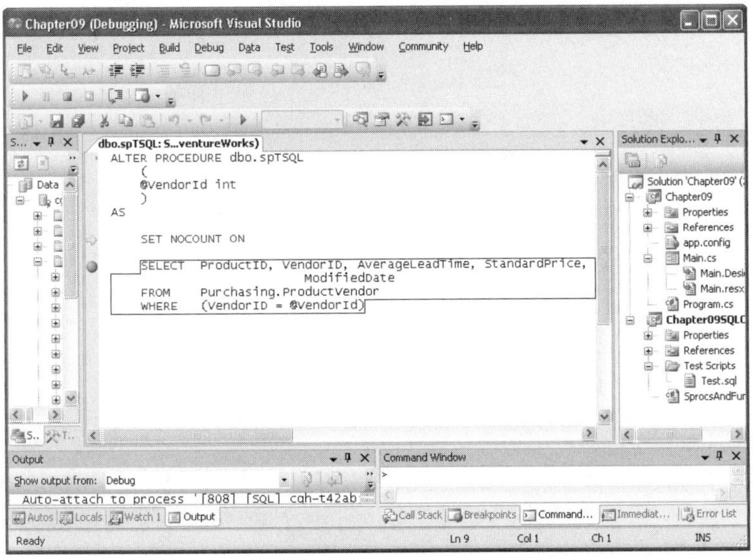

Figure 9-9   T-SQL debugging session with breakpoint set

Try setting a breakpoint now: place your cursor at the beginning of the *SELECT* statement in the *spTSQL* stored procedure (i.e., on the line following the *SET NOCOUNT ON* command), and use one of the techniques just described to set a breakpoint there. Since we were already debugging this stored procedure, you can now select the Debug/Continue option from the main menu, click the Continue button on the Debug or Standard toolbar, or press the F5 key on your keyboard. This should advance the instruction pointer to the breakpoint line, and the gray margin area should display a yellow arrow superimposed on the breakpoint's red sphere. Also, the breakpoint should appear within Visual Studio's Breakpoints window (Figure 9-10).

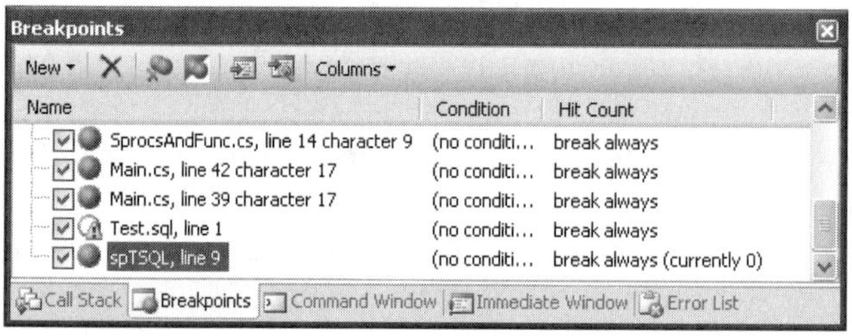

Figure 9-10 The Breakpoints window

You can now *delete* the breakpoint by using any of the techniques described earlier for *setting* one (except for the Breakpoint/Insert Breakpoint shortcut menu option, of course; use the Breakpoint/Delete Breakpoint shortcut menu option instead). You can also use the code editor shortcut menu's Breakpoint/Disable Breakpoint option to disable the breakpoint without removing it.

When a breakpoint is removed, the red sphere disappears from the gray margin area to the left of the line of code. If you merely disable the breakpoint, the red sphere changes to a thin, hollow, red circle (Figure 9-11).

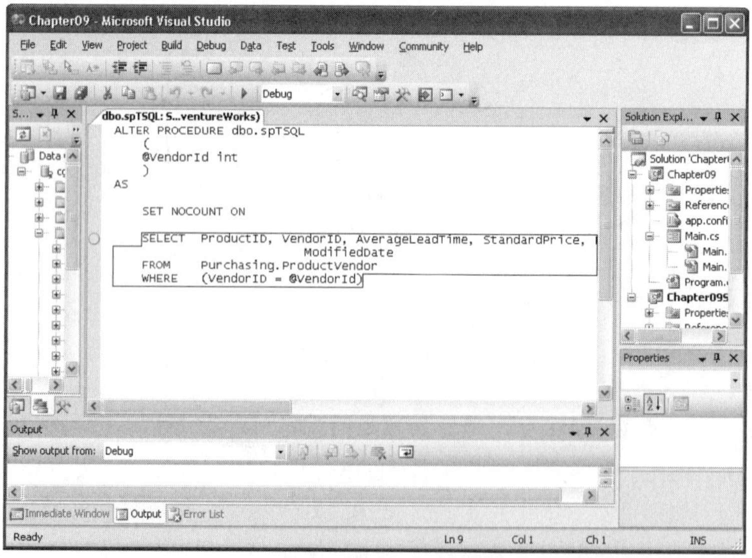

Figure 9-11 T-SQL code with a disabled breakpoint on the *SELECT* line

Clear the breakpoint, and then continue execution again so the stored procedure executes in its entirety.

Tracepoints

Along with breakpoints, the T-SQL editor allows you to set Visual Studio tracepoints. Tracepoints tell Visual Studio to perform certain tasks when a line of code is encountered and certain conditions are met. Specifically, you can display custom text messages (to the Output window) based on a certain logical condition and/or an expression based on the number of times the line of code has been encountered. You can also, optionally, run a Visual Studio macro and then either continue or suspend code execution. As it turns out, breakpoints *are* tracepoints. In effect, a breakpoint is a tracepoint that is triggered by a "hit count" of 1 (i.e., the first time the code line is hit), without any other conditions; it displays no text, executes no macros, and simply suspends execution.

You set a tracepoint using the Breakpoint/Insert Tracepoint shortcut menu option in the code editor. Selecting this option brings up the When Breakpoint Is Hit dialog box (Figure 9-12), which allows you to specify the output text, Visual Studio macro to be executed, and whether execution should continue.

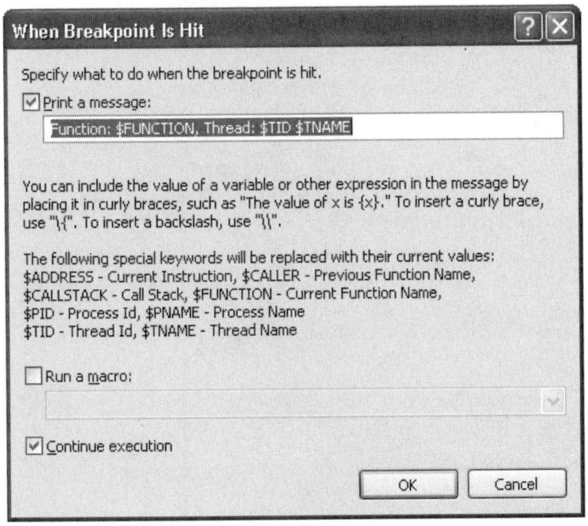

Figure 9-12   The When Breakpoint Is Hit dialog box

Notice that the custom text output can contain special variable names that allow you to display the current address, caller, call stack, and function name, as well as the current process or thread's ID or name. Once the tracepoint is set, a small red diamond appears in the gray margin area to the left of the line of code (Figure 9-13).

Visual Studio recognizes tracepoints as breakpoints, so the various disable and delete breakpoint menu options work with tracepoints as well. If you disable a tracepoint, the solid red diamond in the gray margin area changes to a thin, hollow one (Figure 9-14).

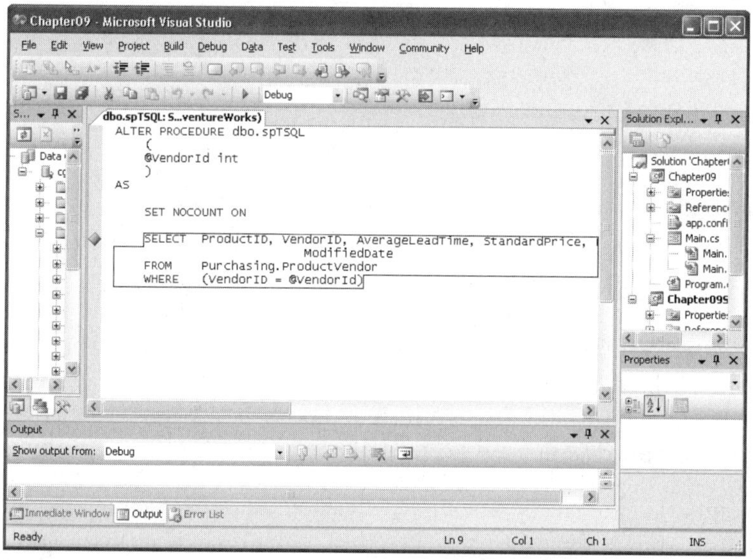

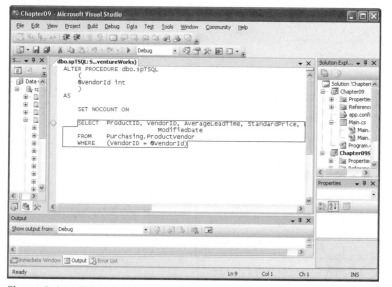

Figure 9-13 T-SQL code with a tracepoint set on the *SELECT* line

Figure 9-14 T-SQL code with a disabled tracepoint on the *SELECT* line

You can modify tracepoints using the shortcut menu available by right-clicking the tracepoint's red diamond. You can display the same options on a submenu by right-clicking the tracepoint line of code and selecting the Breakpoint option from the initial shortcut menu.

The shortcut menu options are as follows:

- **Delete Breakpoint**   Deletes the tracepoint

- **Disable Breakpoint**   Disables the tracepoint

- **Location...**   Opens the File Breakpoint dialog box, where you can specify the tracepoint location (i.e., the specific source code file, line number, and character position)

- **Condition...**   Not supported by the T-SQL editor

- **Hit Count...**   Opens the Breakpoint Hit Count dialog box, where you can specify a numerical constant or expression that dictates how many times the tracepoint should be encountered before its actions are triggered

- **Filter...**   Opens the Breakpoint Filter dialog box, where you can specify a logical expression (involving the machine name and process or thread's name or ID) that must be satisfied for the tracepoint to trigger

- **When Hit...**   Reopens the When Breakpoint Is Hit dialog box (discussed earlier)

These same shortcut menu options are available for conventional breakpoints as well as tracepoints, further underscoring the fact that breakpoints are merely a type of tracepoint. In fact, if you select the When Hit... shortcut menu option on a conventional breakpoint and select the Print A Message and/or Run A Macro check box, as well as the Continue Execution check box, in the When Breakpoint Is Hit dialog box, you change the breakpoint to a true tracepoint. The former breakpoint's sphere then changes to a diamond.

This works in reverse as well: if you select the When Hit... shortcut menu option on a tracepoint and clear at least the Continue Execution check box in the When Breakpoint Is Hit dialog box, you change the tracepoint to a conventional breakpoint and change the former tracepoint's diamond to a sphere.

> **Note**   If you set a hit count on a breakpoint or a tracepoint, a plus sign (+) appears within its sphere or diamond.

To try out tracepoints for yourself, go back to the *SELECT* line in stored procedure *spTSQL*. Set a tracepoint on that line using one of the techniques discussed previously. In the When Breakpoint Is Hit dialog box, make sure the Print A Message check box is checked and then enter the following text in the text box immediately below it:

```
Tracepoint point hit in stored procedure $FUNCTION
```

Make sure the Run A Macro check box is cleared and the Continue Execution check box is selected, and then click OK. A solid red diamond should appear in the gray margin to the left of the *SELECT* command. Once again, right-click the spTSQL node in the Server Explorer window and select the Step Into Stored Procedure shortcut menu option. In the Run Stored Procedure dialog box, the previous parameter value of 54 should appear as the default value for the input parameter *@VendorId*; if it doesn't, enter the value yourself.

Click OK in the Run Stored Procedure dialog box to bring up the T-SQL source code in debugging mode, and then continue execution to run the stored procedure. The stored procedure's output data should appear in Visual Studio's Output window, with the tracepoint text appearing in the third-to-last line, as shown in Figure 9-15.

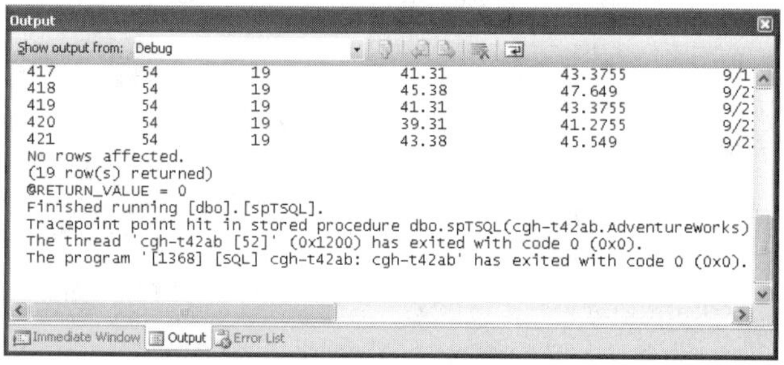

Figure 9-15 Output window displaying tracepoint text (on the third line from the bottom)

Application Debugging

So far we have covered a lot of details pertinent to debugging T-SQL stored procedures. Many of the features and special windows we have examined are relevant to a collection of other debugging scenarios we will need to discuss, so a lot of the necessary exploration for this chapter is already done. Arguably, though, the real power of debugging server-side code comes into play when you run an *application* that actually calls the server-side code in the first place. It turns out that this more integrated debugging scenario is not much harder to accommodate than the Server Explorer window–based debugging we have so far considered.

To demonstrate this, let's now focus on this chapter's sample Visual Studio solution. As we mentioned previously, the solution contains a simple SQL Server project (Chapter09SQLCLR) as well as a Windows Forms client application (Chapter09) that is used as a test harness suitable for running and debugging server-side SQL code (both SQL CLR and T-SQL).

Right-click the Chapter09 project node in the Solution Explorer window and choose the Properties shortcut menu option, then click the resulting property designer's Debug tab. Notice that the Enable SQL Server debugging check box (the second-to-last UI element on the tab) is checked, as shown in Figure 9-16.

Now, within the Server Explorer window, right-click the node for the connection you created earlier and make sure the Application Debugging option is selected, as shown in Figure 9-17.

With both of these options selected, Visual Studio allows you to debug your T-SQL code from within a client code debugging session. In other words, you can jump from debugging client-side .NET code that *calls* your server-side T-SQL code to debugging the T-SQL code itself, and then jump back to debugging your client code when the T-SQL code completes its execution.

(For this type of heterogeneous debugging session to work, you must also have set a break-point in your T-SQL code.)

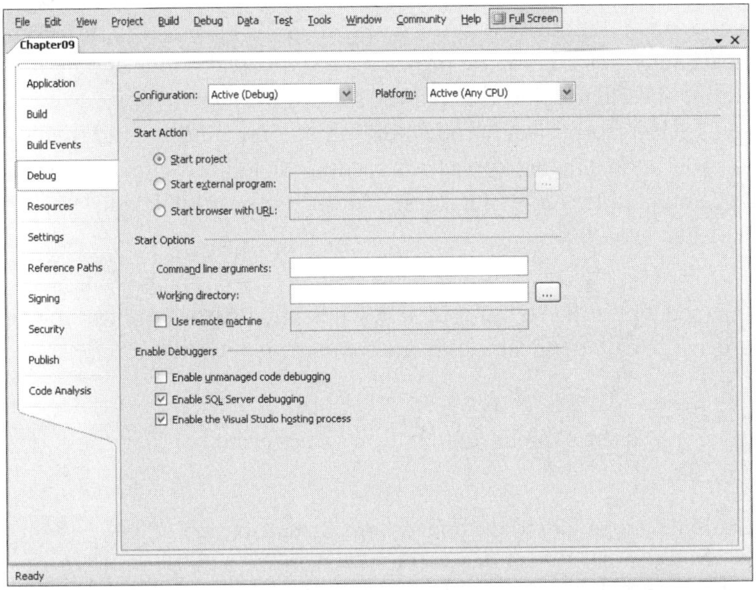

Figure 9-16   The Windows application property sheet Debug tab, with the Enable SQL Server Debugging option set

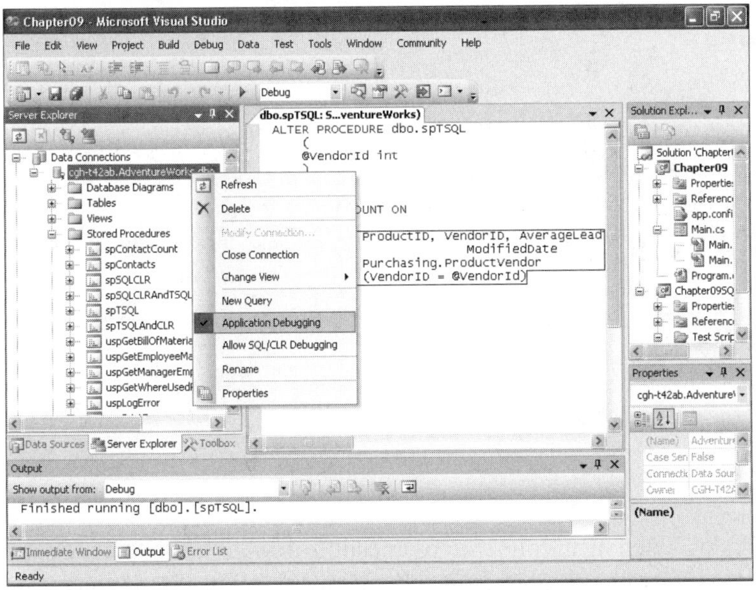

Figure 9-17   Enabling the Application Debugging option on a database connection in the Server Explorer window

To see all of this in action, start by once again adding a conventional breakpoint into the *spTSQL* stored procedure, on the line of code containing the *SELECT* query. (Delete the old tracepoint first if it's still there.) Next, confirm that breakpoints are already set on the third and fourth lines of executable code within the *try* block in the *btnExecute_Click* event handler in *frmMain* in the Chapter09 sample code project. (The two breakpoints should be set on the code lines containing the *Fill* method call and the start of the *foreach* loop.) Now run the Chapter09 project. (Select the project in the Solution Explorer window, and then start debugging.) When the application's main form appears, enter the following text into the form's T-SQL Query Or Command text box (if it doesn't already appear by default):

```
EXEC spTSQL 54
```

Do not click the Execute button yet, but note that when you do, the application code will make a stored procedure call identical to the one we made iteratively via the Server Explorer window.

Before we continue, let's discuss the Execute button's *Click* event handler, the code for which is shown in Listing 9-2.

Listing 9-2   Click event handler for sample application's Execute button

```
private void btnExecute_Click(object sender, EventArgs e)
{
    cboResultSets.Items.Clear();
    dgvResults.DataSource = null;
    ds = new DataSet();

    try
    {
        SqlDataAdapter da = new SqlDataAdapter(txtQuery.Text, txtConnectionString.Text);
        da.SelectCommand.CommandTimeout = 300;
        da.Fill(ds);
        foreach (DataTable dtCurr in ds.Tables)
        {
            cboResultSets.Items.Add(dtCurr.TableName);
        }
        cboResultSets.SelectedIndex = 0;
    }
    catch (Exception ex)
    {
        MessageBox.Show(ex.Message);
    }
}
```

Before we debug this function and the stored procedure it will call, a couple of coding techniques used in it merit some brief discussion. First, notice the line of code that sets the *CommandTimeout* property of the *SqlCommand* object pointed to by our *SqlDataAdapter* object's *SelectCommand* property. We intentionally set this timeout to 300 seconds (5 minutes) because we expect to debug the server-side code behind that *SqlDataAdapter* object's query execution. By allowing such a long timeout, we can reasonably ensure that we'll have sufficient time to do our debugging without generating an exception on the line of code that calls the object's *Fill* method.

Next, notice the *foreach* loop that follows the *Fill* method call. In this loop, we allow for the possibility that our query might return multiple result sets. In such a case, our *DataSet* object (*ds*) will have multiple members in its *Tables* collection. We simply loop though the collection, stuffing the name of each *DataTable* object into the *Items* collection of *cboResultSets* (a *ComboBox* control). When the loop completes execution, we set the *SelectedIndex* property of the *ComboBox* control to 0, forcing the control's *SelectedIndexChanged* event to fire and the first result set to be loaded into the *dgvResults* (a *DataGridView* control). As a user, you can display a different result set (if others are available) by selecting the appropriate *DataTable* name from the Result Set combo box.

Entering Debugging Mode

Click on the running form's Execute button. You should now hit the first breakpoint in the event handler's code, on the line that calls the *SqlDataAdapter* object's *Fill* method. Observe the objects and values displayed in the Autos, Locals, and Call Stack windows. Now step through your code once by selecting the Debug/Step Over main menu option or by pressing the F10 or F11 key on your keyboard; this causes the *Fill* method to execute and triggers the underlying stored procedure call. As a result, the debugger should switch context over to your T-SQL code.

At this point, the debugging environment should be virtually identical to the one encountered when we called the stored procedure via the Server Explorer window. The Autos, Locals and Call Stack windows should now appear as they did earlier and, as before, you can hover your mouse pointer over the *@VendorId* parameter in the code editor to determine (or set) its value.

However, there are a couple of subtle differences between debugging T-SQL code from an application and from the Server Explorer window. For example, if you show the Call Stack window, you will see that the stored procedure appears above a sort of pseudo-code entry, denoted by the text "Dynamic T-SQL() Line 1" (Figure 9-18).

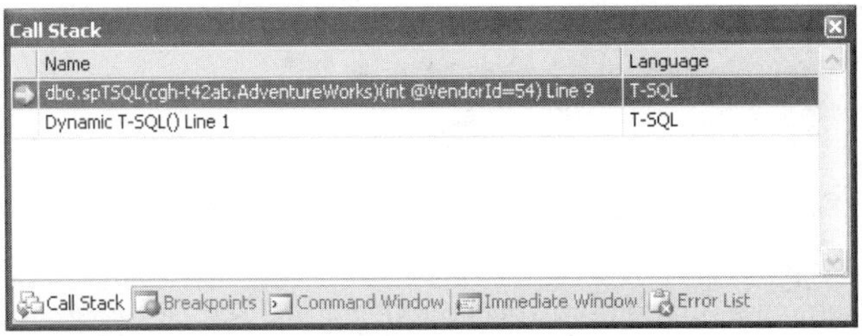

Figure 9-18   The Call Stack window, while debugging T-SQL code from within an application debugging session

If you double-click that line, a code editor window opens, displaying the stored procedure call invoked by the .NET client code.

Another difference is in how execution continuation is handled. To see this, execute a single line of code or continue execution (the two are equivalent because everything in the stored procedure after the *SET NOCOUNT ON* executes as a single statement); you return to the .NET code, hitting the second breakpoint. The Autos, Locals, and Call Stack windows revert back to their .NET states, as if the T-SQL debugging session had never occurred. Now continue execution again, and you will see the results of the stored procedure displayed in the sample application form's *DataGridView* control (Figure 9-19).

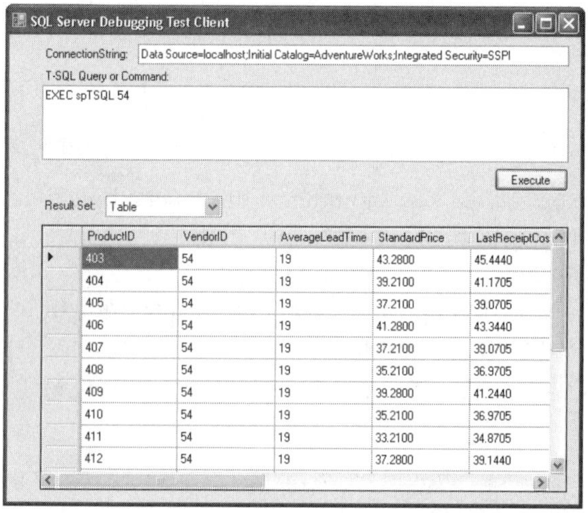

Figure 9-19   Sample application displaying results from stored procedure *spTSQL*

Close the application's form to return Visual Studio to design mode.

Debugging SQL CLR Code

Now let's shift gears a little by debugging *SQL CLR* code on the server instead of T-SQL code. First, right-click the AdventureWorks database connection's node in the Server Explorer window and select the Allow SQL/CLR Debugging option from the shortcut menu. You might be prompted with the message box shown in Figure 9-20. If so, click Yes.

Figure 9-20   Thread stop warning resulting from selecting the Allow SQL/CLR Debugging option in the Server Explorer window

Now run the Chapter09 application again. This time, when the application's form appears, enter the following text into the form's Query text box:

```
EXEC spSQLCLR
```

The code for *spSQLCLR* is shown in Listing 9-3.

Listing 9-3   SQL CLR stored procedure *spSQLCLR*

```
[SqlProcedure()]
public static void spSQLCLR()
{
    SqlConnection conn = new SqlConnection("context connection=true");
    SqlCommand cm = new SqlCommand("Select Count(*) from Person.Contact", conn);
    SqlDataRecord drc = new SqlDataRecord(new SqlMetaData("ContactCount", SqlDbType.Int));
    conn.Open();
    drc.SetInt32(0, (Int32)cm.ExecuteScalar());
    SqlContext.Pipe.Send(drc);
    conn.Close();
}
```

The code from the Chapter09SQLCLR project implements, of course, a SQL CLR stored procedure (modeled after the *spContactCount* stored procedure from Chapter 3); as such, the line of code in our client application that calls the *Fill* method of the *SqlDataAdapter* object this time triggers an underlying stored procedure call to SQL CLR code, rather than T-SQL code. To help you debug that SQL CLR code, we have set a breakpoint on the first executable line of the function (the one where the *SqlConnection* object *conn* is declared and initialized). If for any reason the breakpoint is not set already, please set it on your own.

More Info   You can set breakpoints in Visual Studio SQL Server projects by opening their source code files from the Server Explorer window or the Solution Explorer window, or from disk. Code developed within Visual Studio Class Library projects can be opened only from the Solution Explorer window or from disk; the ability to open SQL CLR source code from the Server Explorer window is not possible with Class Library projects.

Click the test application form's Execute button, and then single-step once through the code (for example, by pressing the F10 key or F11 key once). You should now find yourself debugging the SQL CLR stored procedure, with the instruction pointer set to the line of code in *spSQLCLR* where we set the breakpoint.

Important   As the Visual Studio debugger shifts context from your application code to your SQL CLR code, you might experience a prolonged pause, and your machine might become very sluggish in general, until the context switch is complete. This pause might occur in other tier-context switches encountered later in this chapter as well.

Notice that the debugging environment for the SQL CLR code is very similar to that provided for T-SQL code. As shown in Figure 9-21, the Call Stack window displays lines only for the stored procedure and for Dynamic T-SQL (although there is an additional *[External Code]* call in between them).

Figure 9-21   The Call Stack window, while debugging SQL CLR code from within an application debugging session

The Language column within the Call Stack window indicates that the Dynamic T-SQL call is in T-SQL and that the *spSQLCLR* code is written in C#.

The debugging environment provides the full set of features accorded any .NET debugged code. For example, step through the first two lines of code in the SQL CLR stored procedure, show the Locals window, and then drill down on *cm* (our ADO.NET *SqlCommand* object). Now you can edit the Value column's contents for the *CommandText* property and change the query in place (Figure 9-22).

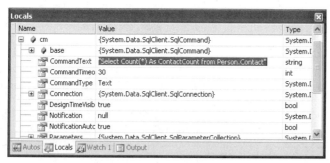

Figure 9-22   Changing a property's value in the Locals window while debugging SQL CLR code

When you're done, press the Enter key on your keyboard and the new value will turn red, indicating that it has changed. Now you can click the magnifying glass icon at the right edge of the cell to view the query text in the Visual Studio Text Visualizer (Figure 9-23).

Close the Text Visualizer window and continue stepping through your code. As you step through the line of code that calls the ADO.NET *ExecuteScalar* method, a Dynamic T-SQL window opens. We will discuss the mechanics of this later in the chapter. For now, just step through the T-SQL code line in that window and you will pass back into the SQL CLR source code.

Figure 9-23   The Text Visualizer window, opened while debugging SQL CLR code

As you step past the last line in the *spSQLCLR* stored procedure, the context should switch back to your application code—specifically, to the start of the *foreach* loop. At this point, continue execution. You should see the *spSQLCLR* stored procedure's result set displayed in the sample application's form (Figure 9-24).

Figure 9-24   Sample application displaying results from stored procedure *spSQLCLR*

Close the application's form to return Visual Studio to design mode.

Breakpoints and Context Switching

Before proceeding with the discussion, we have a confession to make. The specific breakpoints we set in the application code and the server-side code made the whole premise of debugging and context switching seem easier than it in fact is. It might seem logical that stepping through a line of application code that implicitly calls T-SQL or SQL CLR code would automatically load the server-side source code. Likewise, it would seem only natural for the debugger to flow back to your application code after you have stepped through the last line of code on the server.

The fact remains, however, that this apparently seamless context switching works only if breakpoints are set at the lines of code in which the context switching takes place. For example, when we stepped through the line of code in the client application that calls the ADO.NET *Fill* method, we could step through the implicitly called code in *spTSQL* and *spSQLCLR* only because we set breakpoints in those stored procedures' source code. Conversely, we were able to flow back from the server code to the application code only because we had set a second breakpoint in the application's *btnExecute_Click* event handler, at the beginning of the *foreach* loop. Try removing one of those breakpoints, and you will see that a switch from client code to server code (or vice-versa) causes code execution to continue, even if you merely step through the last line of code before the context change.

Under specific circumstances, such strategically placed breakpoints are not, however, required when you jump from one piece of server-side code to another, even if you are calling a T-SQL stored procedure from SQL CLR code. We'll discuss such a server-side mixed-language scenario next.

> **Tip**   If you want to debug server-side code called from a client application but do *not* want to debug the client-side code itself, Visual Studio can accommodate you. Simply set a breakpoint in the server code (T-SQL or SQL CLR) and remove or disable any client-side breakpoints, and you'll be able to debug your server-side code directly, providing that your client code calls it.

Mixing SQL CLR and T-SQL Code

So far, we've seen how to debug T-SQL code using the Server Explorer window and how to debug T-SQL or SQL CLR code from a client application debugging session. In so doing, we've covered enough scenarios to allow you to meet most of your SQL Server debugging needs.

We have a few more scenarios to cover, however. These include debugging calls made from SQL Server Management Studio (or any other application that is not your own) and the special steps necessary to debug code running on an instance of SQL Server that is *not* installed on your own development machine. Before we cover those techniques, however, let us first consider debugging a *combination* of T-SQL and SQL CLR code. Our discussion will be relevant to the Server Explorer window and application debugging scenarios we have already discussed, as well as debugging from a SQL Server project test script (a technique we covered in depth in Chapter 3).

When you debug a combination of T-SQL and SQL CLR code, it is important to realize that because all of the code is running on the same tier, the client/server context switch we just discussed does not come in to play. When you debug a piece of code on the server by single-stepping through it, and that code calls into another server-side routine, you automatically step into the second routine, even if you have not set a breakpoint within its source. This is the case for pure T-SQL and pure SQL CLR scenarios, as well as for a mixture of the two.

> **Caution** The handoff from T-SQL code to SQL CLR code (or vice-versa) works the first time code is debugged within an application debugging session. On subsequent executions, the handoff can fail. For this reason, you may wish to set additional breakpoints to ensure a smooth transition between T-SQL and SQL CLR code. In the scenarios described below, however, it is not necessary to do so.

To see this in action, we will now run two new stored procedures. The first of these, *spSQLCLRAndTSQL*, is shown in Listing 9-4.

Listing 9-4 SQL CLR stored procedure *spSQLCLRAndTSQL*, which calls *spTSQL* internally

```
[SqlProcedure()]
public static void spSQLCLRAndTSQL()
{
    // ADO.NET variables for SQL CLR operations:
    SqlConnection conn = new SqlConnection("context connection=true");
    SqlCommand cm = new SqlCommand("Select Count(*) from Person.Contact", conn);
    SqlDataRecord drc = new SqlDataRecord(new SqlMetaData("ContactCount", SqlDbType.Int));

    // Call out to a T-SQL stored procedure:
    SqlDataAdapter da = new SqlDataAdapter("EXEC spTSQL 54", conn);
    DataTable dt = new DataTable();
    da.Fill(dt);

    // Execute Select Count(*) query and return result:
    conn.Open();
    drc.SetInt32(0, (Int32)cm.ExecuteScalar());
    SqlContext.Pipe.Send(drc);
    conn.Close();
}
```

This SQL CLR stored procedure performs the same work as *spSQLCLR*, but it also calls through to *spTSQL*, the T-SQL stored procedure that we looked at earlier. The call to *spTSQL* is benign because the result set returned is placed in a *DataTable* object, which is not used in any way. This is done simply to force a switch from SQL CLR code to T-SQL code and back again, for demonstration purposes.

The second new stored procedure, *spTSQLAndCLR*, is shown in Listing 9-5.

Listing 9-5   T-SQL stored procedure *spTSQLAndCLR*, which calls *spSQLCLR* and *fnHelloWorldCh9* internally

```
CREATE PROCEDURE dbo.spTSQLAndCLR
   (
   @VendorId int
   )
AS
   SET NOCOUNT ON
   DECLARE       @ContactCount int
   SELECT        ProductID, VendorID, AverageLeadTime, StandardPrice, LastReceiptCost,
LastReceiptDate, MinOrderQty, MaxOrderQty, OnOrderQty, UnitMeasureCode, ModifiedDate
   FROM          Purchasing.ProductVendor
   WHERE         (VendorID = @VendorId)
   EXEC spSQLCLR
   SELECT dbo.fnHelloWorldCh9() As HelloWorld
```

This stored procedure is identical to *spTSQL* except that it also calls through to *spSQLCLR* and the rather simplistic SQL CLR function *fnHelloWorldCh9*, shown in Listing 9-6.

Listing 9-6   SQL CLR function *fnHelloWorldCh9*

```
[SqlFunction()]
public static SqlString fnHelloWorldCh9()
{
    return new SqlString("Hello World");
}
```

Let's start by right-clicking the *spSQLCLRAndTSQL* stored procedure node in the Solution Explorer window and selecting the Step Into Stored Procedure option from the shortcut menu. After a pause, a debugging session should begin, with the SQL CLR source code for *spSQLCLRAndTSQL* appearing in a code window and the instruction pointer set to the line containing the function's opening brace.

Now right-click on the line of code within *spSQLCLRAndTSQL* that calls the ADO.NET *Fill* method (it's the sixth executable line after the function's opening brace) and select the Run To Cursor shortcut menu option to advance the instruction pointer to that line. Now single-step through the code *once*. This causes the underlying call to *spTSQL* to execute. Notice that you are now placed in a Dynamic T-SQL editor window containing the actual T-SQL call that your CLR code is making (Figure 9-25).

We have discussed this window in some depth already, but did so in the context of running a stored procedure from application code. In that context, we could see the Dynamic T-SQL window only by double-clicking the Dynamic T-SQL line in the Call Stack window. But in the case of CLR code calling T-SQL code, this window is opened for us as we debug and the instruction pointer points to the only line of T-SQL code within it.

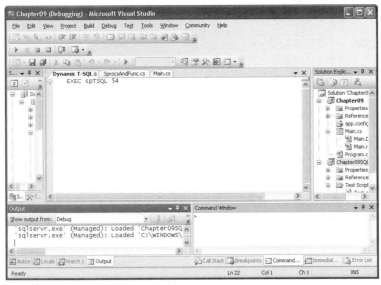

Figure 9-25   The Dynamic T-SQL window, resulting from debugging an internal T-SQL call within SQL CLR code

Single-step through the code one more time, and you will be placed within the T-SQL source code for *spTSQL*. Show the Call Stack window. In it, you will see that the entire call stack, including the *spSQLCLRAndTSQL* code, the Dynamic T-SQL code, and the *spTSQL* code, is shown (Figure 9-26).

Figure 9-26   The Call Stack window, displayed while debugging T-SQL code called from within SQL CLR code

Notice that the language details are properly shown (indicating that *spSQLCLRAndTSQL* is written in C# and the other two modules are in T-SQL), the parameter information is shown for *spTSQL*, and the full assembly and class prefix appear for *spSQLCLRAndTSQL*.

If you'd like, you can double-click on any row in the Call Stack window (other than the *[External Code]* lines) to go to the corresponding source code. Otherwise, you can continue stepping through the code. After you step past the last line of *spTSQL*, debugging flows back to *spSQLCLRAndTSQL* without requiring any special effort (or breakpoints). If you continue to single-step to and step through the line of code that calls the ADO.NET *ExecuteScalar* method (the third-to-last line of code in *spSQLCLRAndTSQL*), you will see that yet another Dynamic

T-SQL window opens up. Step four more times, and the entire execution will complete. Among other status information, the Output window should contain the *spSQLCLRAndTSQL* stored procedure's result set:

```
ContactCount
------------
19972
```

Now let's repeat this process but work the other way around: let's trace through the T-SQL stored procedure *spTSQLAndCLR*. Take a look again at the code in Listing 9-5. As a reminder, the stored procedure performs three tasks: (1) it executes a query; (2) it calls the SQL CLR stored procedure *spSQLCLR*; and (3) from within an additional *SELECT* query, it calls the SQL CLR function *fnHelloWorldCh9*, returning the result in a column called HelloWorld. Each of these three steps returns its own result set.

Right-click the Server Explorer node for *spTSQLAndCLR* and select Step Into Stored Procedure from the shortcut menu. When prompted, supply a value of **54** for the *@VendorId* parameter and click OK. You will be placed within the T-SQL editor window with the source code for *spTSQLAndCLR* loaded and the instruction pointer set to the T-SQL *SET NOCOUNT ON* command within the stored procedure. Single-step through twice to arrive at the line that executes the CLR stored procedure *spSQLCLR*. Step through your code once more to start debugging the CLR code. Once you are inside the CLR code, continue execution (skipping past any breakpoints, as necessary) to return Visual Studio to design mode.

By now, you should be getting the picture: as far as Visual Studio is concerned, server code is server code. In these scenarios, the debugger can pass through SQL CLR and T-SQL code, essentially without incident, and the debugging experience remains remarkably consistent. Breakpoints are not needed to accommodate the handoff between blocks of code in different languages, although you can set them anywhere you want them.

You can carry out this same experiment from within an application debugging session as well. To see this, simply set a breakpoint at the first executable lines of code in both *spSQL-CLRAndTSQL* and *spTSQLAndSQLCLR*, clear any breakpoints in the Windows project's form, and then run the Windows Forms project. When the application's form appears, enter the following query in the form's Query text box:

```
EXEC spTSQLAndCLR 54
```

Click the form's Execute button. When you hit the T-SQL breakpoint, step through the code as you did before and note that the experience is virtually the same. Recall that this stored procedure returns multiple result sets, and that we have special code in the Execute button's event handler for just such an occasion. When you are done debugging your code, the application will display the first result set (the results of the stored procedure's *SELECT* query from the *Product-Vendor* table) in the *DataGridView* control. Try selecting the Table1 and Table2 options from the Result Sets *ComboBox* control to see results of the calls to *spSQLCLR* and *fnHelloWorldCh9*.

You can test the SQL CLR–to–T-SQL scenario by stopping and restarting the sample application, and then entering the following query in the form's text box:

```
EXEC spSQLCLRAndTSQL
```

Click Execute, and debug the code as you see fit. When you're done, close the form to return Visual Studio to design mode.

Test Script Debugging

To be fully versed in SQL Server debugging, you need to learn about a few other configurations under which to debug these stored procedures. The first is from the test script in the Chapter09SQLCLR SQL Server project. Open Test.sql from the Solution Explorer window. The two T-SQL commands you just used (the ones you entered into the Windows application's Query text box) should appear, with a breakpoint on the first line in the script; if this is not the case, edit the script to fit this description. Clear or disable all breakpoints you might have set in your T-SQL and SQL CLR stored procedures.

Now start debugging on the Chapter09SQLCLR project (i.e., run the test script). When you hit the breakpoint in your test script, single-step through its first line of code to advance to the code for the stored procedure *spTSQLAndCLR*. Continue stepping until you advance to the source code pertaining to the inner stored procedure call (i.e., the source code for *spSQLCLR*). Show the Call Stack window again. You should see rows for your test script and each of your stored procedures. Continue stepping though your code until you land back on the second line of the test script's code. Continue stepping until all code has finished executing.

Debugging Queries External to Visual Studio

As we have seen, Visual Studio gives you a wide array of debugging "launch points": the Server Explorer window, your own application's code, and SQL Server project test scripts. With all of these options at your disposal, you might feel that your debugging needs are well taken care of. But what if you need to debug server-side code in the context of it being called from an application *other* than Visual Studio? Suppose, for example, that you want to call your stored procedure from SQL Server Management Studio but still be able to debug it in Visual Studio.

The good news is that this type of debugging *is* possible if your debugging target is SQL CLR code. Look quickly at the DebugCLRFromSSMS.sql script in the sample code's SQL Server Management Studio solution. It's a simple one-line script that calls our second SQL CLR stored procedure, *spSQLCLRAndTSQL*:

```
EXEC spSQLCLRAndTSQL
```

In a moment, we'll show you how to set a breakpoint in your SQL CLR code, execute this script in SQL Server Management Studio, and debug the SQL CLR code in Visual Studio. Before we do so, however, we want to call out one detail of this scenario. The stored procedure *spSQLCLRAndTSQL*, as you will recall, is a SQL CLR stored procedure that executes a query against the Person.Contact table in the AdventureWorks database and also makes an internal call to the T-SQL stored procedure *spTSQL*. In the Visual Studio–initiated debugging scenarios we've seen so far, stepping through the SQL CLR code allowed us to step seamlessly into the T-SQL code and back again.

This CLR–to–T-SQL handoff happened at two points: The first was when the internal call to *spTSQL* was encountered (from the ADO.NET *Fill* method call). The second was when the SQL *SELECT* query was executed (from the ADO.NET *ExecuteScalar* method call), resulting in the opening of a Dynamic T-SQL window. It will be interesting to see how a SQL Server Management Studio–initiated debugging session will handle these mixed-language handoffs.

Let's start the debugging session now; doing so is surprisingly easy. First place a breakpoint on the first line of code in the *spSQLCLRAndTSQL* function. Next, select the Debug/Attach to Process... main menu option in Visual Studio; this invokes the Attach To Process dialog box (Figure 9-27).

Attach to Process						? X
Transport:	Default					∨
Qualifier:	CGH-T42AB				∨	Browse...

Transport Information
The default transport lets you select processes on this computer or a remote computer running the Microsoft Visual Studio Remote Debugging Monitor (MSVSMON.EXE).

Attach to:	Managed code, T-SQL code				Select...

Available Processes

Process	ID	Title	Type	User Name	Session	
rrpcsb.exe	508		x86	SYSTEM	0	
rundll32.exe	1564		x86	CGH-T42AB\Andr...	0	
rundll32.exe	4008		x86	CGH-T42AB\Andr...	0	
S24EvMon.exe	1688		x86	SYSTEM	0	
services.exe	1096		x86	SYSTEM	0	
SMAgent.exe	432		x86	SYSTEM	0	
SMax4PNP.exe	4184		x86	CGH-T42AB\Andr...	0	
smss.exe	868		x86	SYSTEM	0	
spoolsv.exe	404		x86	SYSTEM	0	
SpriteService.exe	4940		x86	CGH-T42AB\Andr...	0	
sqlbrowser.exe	1596		x86	NETWORK SERVICE	0	
sqlservr.exe	1368		T-SQL, Ma...	CGH-T42AB\Andr...	0	

☑ Show processes from all users   ☐ Show processes in all sessions   Refresh

Attach   Cancel

Figure 9-27   The Attach To Process dialog box

Select the Show Processes From All Users check box, if it's not already selected. Next, scroll down to and select the Sqlservr.exe process. The process list is sorted alphabetically; you can type the name of the process (or just the first few characters) to move the selection to it without scrolling.

Tip   You may see more than one Sqlserver.exe process listed because each distinct instance of SQL Server—including instances of SQL Server Express Edition—runs as its own process. It may take a little trial-and-error work to determine the correct process to select. You may wish to stop other instances of SQL Server to remove them from the Available Processes list. You can stop other instances from Management Studio or the Services applet from the Windows Administrative Tools menu. After the instances have been stopped, click the Refresh button in the Attach To Process dialog box.

Once the Sqlservr.exe process is selected, click the Attach button. Visual Studio should now be in Running mode, and you are ready to conduct an externally-initiated debug session. Switch over to SQL Server Management Studio, and execute the DebugCLRFromSSMS.sql script. You should hit your breakpoint immediately (in Visual Studio). Carefully step through your code five times, until you get to the line containing the *Fill* method call. Step once more to execute the *Fill* and, implicitly, the internal call to *spTSQL*.

Take note of how the debugging session behaved. The T-SQL code was completely stepped over. Continue stepping through the code up until, and then just past, the *ExecuteScalar* call, and you will see that it is handled the same way. Now continue code execution via the F5 key (or the various menu or toolbar equivalents). Focus is returned to SQL Server Management Studio, and the results of the CLR stored procedure are displayed in the query window's results pane (Figure 9-28).

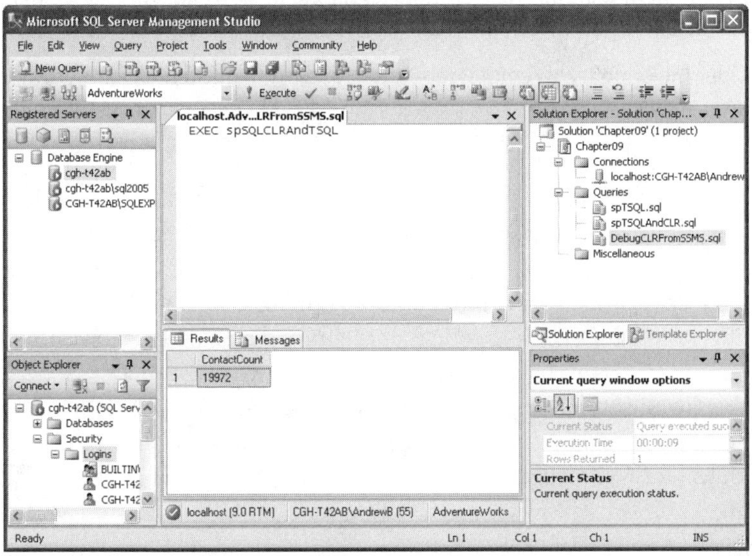

Figure 9-28   Viewing results in Management Studio from a debugged SQL CLR stored procedure

As you can see, externally-initiated debugging sessions allow us to debug SQL CLR code, but not T-SQL code, even if there is an explicit call to T-SQL code from the SQL CLR code being debugged. To see this from a different perspective, set a breakpoint within the T-SQL stored procedure *spTSQLAndCLR* and an additional one in *spSQLCLR* (recall that the latter is called internally by the former), and then execute *spTSQLAndCLR* from SQL Server Management Studio with this line of code:

```
EXEC spTSQLAndCLR 54
```

You will see that even in the case where SQL Server Management Studio is calling a T-SQL stored procedure, we *can't* debug the T-SQL code, but we *can* debug any SQL CLR code the T-SQL code itself calls!

When you're done with your external debugging work, release Visual Studio from Running mode via the Debug/Stop Debugging main menu option, its Shift+F5 keyboard equivalent, or the Stop Debugging button the Debug toolbar.

Remote Debugging

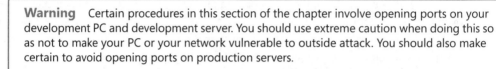

> **Warning**   Certain procedures in this section of the chapter involve opening ports on your development PC and development server. You should use extreme caution when doing this so as not to make your PC or your network vulnerable to outside attack. You should also make certain to avoid opening ports on production servers.
>
> In our discussion, we specifically advise you to set the scope of any port openings as narrowly as possible (for example, to your local subnet only rather than to the entire Internet). Even here, you should be cautious: if your machine is connected directly to a cable or DSL modem, your local subnet will include other customers' PCs.
>
> You must consider the benefits of remote debugging against the potential dangers of modifying your software firewall settings.

We have now explored a variety of debugging scenarios, each providing a great deal of capability and flexibility. However, each scenario has required that SQL Server 2005, our database, and our server-side code (be it T-SQL- or SQL CLR-based) be installed locally on our development machine. Such environmental requirements are not unreasonable for a developer, but in some instances it is necessary to debug code that is running on a true remote server. Luckily, all of the debugging scenarios we have reviewed thus far can work remotely, as long as you can meet a manageable list of setup requirements. In this final section of our debugging chapter, we will enumerate these remote debugging setup prerequisites. We'll also cover a few trouble-shooting techniques that will help you get past some common roadblocks to successful remote debugging.

Server Configuration

First and foremost, to prepare for remote debugging, you must establish a connection to the remote server in Visual Studio's Server Explorer window. (Don't do this just yet, however.) This connection *must* use integrated security (Windows authentication); therefore, the Windows login you are using on your development machine must be a valid login on the remote SQL Server instance to which you are trying to connect. In addition, remote debugging capability will be granted to you only if your login is also a member of the sysadmin server role. Use SQL Server Management Studio on the remote server to authorize your Windows login and grant it membership to the sysadmin role.

Next on the list of requirements is to make certain the remote server will accept external connections. This might seem obvious, but the Developer Edition of SQL Server 2005 is configured by default to allow local client connections only. You can use the SQL Server Surface Area Configuration tool—which we discussed in Chapter 3—to enable remote connections. Run the tool (on the remote server, not on your development machine), and click the Surface Area Configuration For Services And Connections hyperlink at the bottom of the tool's main window. In the resulting Surface Area Configuration For Services And Connections dialog box, select the appropriate instance's Database Engine\Remote Connections child node from the tree view on the left of the window, and then select the Local And Remote Connections option button to the right (as shown in Figure 9-29) and click OK.

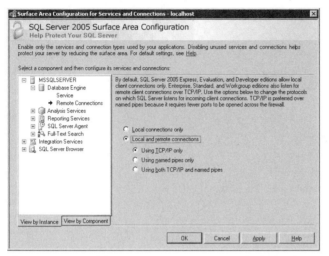

Figure 9-29   Enabling remote connections with the Surface Area Configuration tool

> **Note**   Indented underneath the Local And Remote Connections option button are three more option buttons that allow you to authorize connections using TCP/IP, Named Pipes, or both protocols. Remote debugging can work over either protocol.

A message box appears telling you to restart the SQL Server service in order for the change to take effect. Click OK to return to the configuration tool's main window. The tool might lose focus after you click OK; if this happens, simply switch back to it using the Windows task bar or the Alt+Tab task shortcut menu. Don't restart the SQL Server service just yet because we have a few more prerequisites to deal with first.

If you want to debug (or just execute) SQL CLR code on the server, make sure that CLR integration is enabled. As we discussed in Chapter 3, you can do this by clicking the Surface Area Configuration tool's Surface Area Configuration For Features link. In the resulting Surface Area Configuration For Features dialog box, select the appropriate instance's Database Engine\CLR Integration child node in the left-hand tree view, and then select the Enable CLR Integration check box to the right (or confirm that it is selected already), and click OK. Close the Surface Area Configuration tool when you're done.

Remote debugging uses DCOM to establish a remote procedure call connection between the SQL Server instance and its debugging client. As such, the SQL Server service on the remote server machine must run under the identity of a Windows account with sufficient permissions to establish a DCOM connection. Use the Services applet from Windows Administrative Tools (again, on the remote server) to edit the Log On properties of the SQL Server service (Figure 9-30) to make sure this requirement is met.

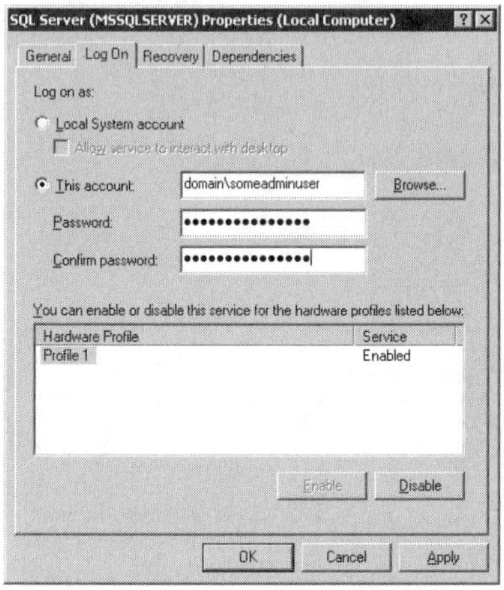

Figure 9-30   Assigning a domain account to the SQL Server service

If you have more than one instance of the SQL Server service running on your server, make certain you modify the Log On properties of the service(s) corresponding to the instance(s) you want to debug.

> **More Info**   For more details on configuring login properties/accounts for SQL Server services, see the "Setting Up Windows Service Accounts" topic in SQL Server Books Online.

When you are done configuring your remote SQL Server instance and modifying its service properties, restart the service using the Services applet's Restart Service toolbar button (the right-most button on the toolbar), the Action/Restart menu option, or the Restart shortcut menu option. You can also use the Action/All Tasks/Restart menu option, the All Tasks/Restart shortcut menu option, or the Restart The Service hyperlink.

Server Firewall Considerations

While your service configuration requirements should now be met, you must still consider some potential firewall issues. Because remote debugging uses DCOM to make a connection between client and server, you must make certain your firewall software will not prevent a DCOM connection from being established. Specifically, you must allow communication over TCP port 135 and UDP ports 4500 and 500 between the client and the server.

Be judicious here by opening these ports in the context of the *most limited* network scope that includes both the client and server. Very often this scope will be defined by your TCP/IP sub-net. If you are running firewall software on your server, you'll want to open these ports as explicit exceptions in your firewall's rules. On the client, opening these ports is a little easier.

That's because Visual Studio is aware of the Windows Firewall's default blocking of these ports and can open them on your behalf. We'll cover the mechanics of this shortly.

Back to the Client

At this point, you should be done configuring your server and ready to configure Visual Studio on your client PC. Start by adding a connection to your remote server, using integrated security, in the Server Explorer window. If the connection cannot be established, go back over the server requirements we've discussed and double-check that your Windows login is properly authorized on the server.

Next, to test remote debugging, drill down on the remote server connection to a T-SQL stored procedure and select the Step Into Stored Procedure shortcut menu option. If the stored procedure requires input parameters, you should be prompted for their values. If not, the debugging session should start and the stored procedure's code should load in a code editor window. You might first, however, encounter a message box or two alerting you to certain server- or client-side configuration changes that are still required.

For example, if your Windows login has not been assigned to the sysadmin server role, you will likely see a message box similar to the one in Figure 9-31 when you initiate a debugging session.

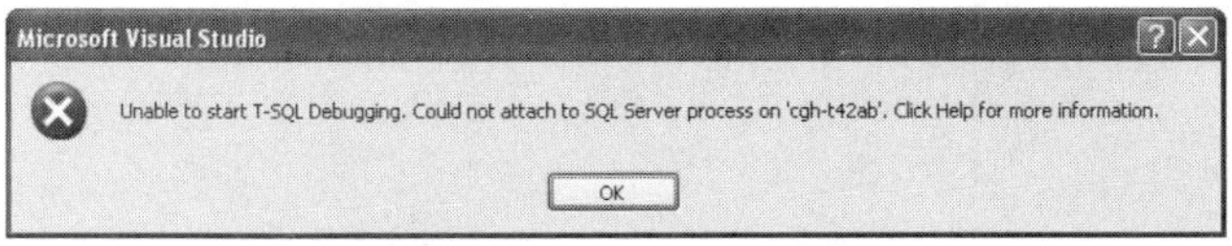

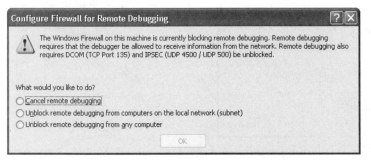

Figure 9-31   Remote process attachment failure message box

If this happens, go back to the server and assign your login the correct role membership, and then reestablish the connection on the client and try debugging the stored procedure again.

Client Firewall Configuration

Another message box you might see pertains to the firewall issues we discussed. In the case of the ports being closed, for users of the Windows Firewall, the Configure Firewall For Remote Debugging dialog box, shown in Figure 9-32, is displayed.

Figure 9-32   The Configure Firewall For Remote Debugging dialog box

If you select the Unblock Remote Debugging From Computers On The Local Network (Subnet) option button (the second option button in the list) and click OK, Visual Studio opens the ports for you on the Windows Firewall and your debugging session should initiate properly.

Visual Studio opens the ports by adding the appropriate items to the Windows Firewall's list of exceptions. To see the results of Visual Studio's work, open the Windows Firewall applet in Windows Control Panel. When the applet opens, click on its Exceptions tab; among the exceptions listed should be two items specifically for IPsec and one for RPC Endpoint Mapper and DCOM Infrastructure, as shown in Figure 9-33.

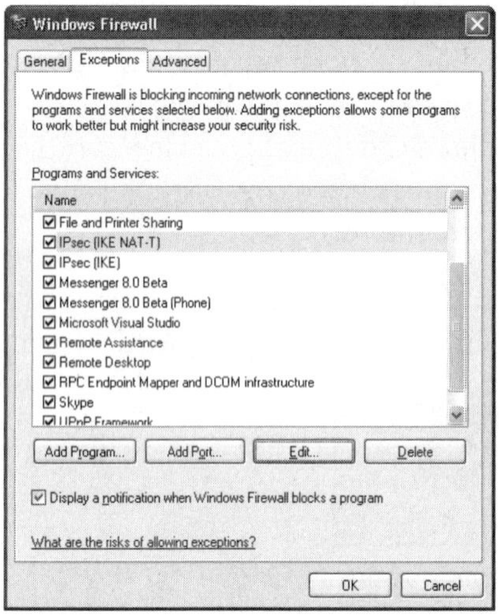

Figure 9-33   The Windows Firewall Exceptions tab

You can double-click any one of these exceptions to open the Edit A Port dialog box to view or change the actual port setting that the exception allows. The settings for one of the IPsec exceptions is shown in Figure 9-34.

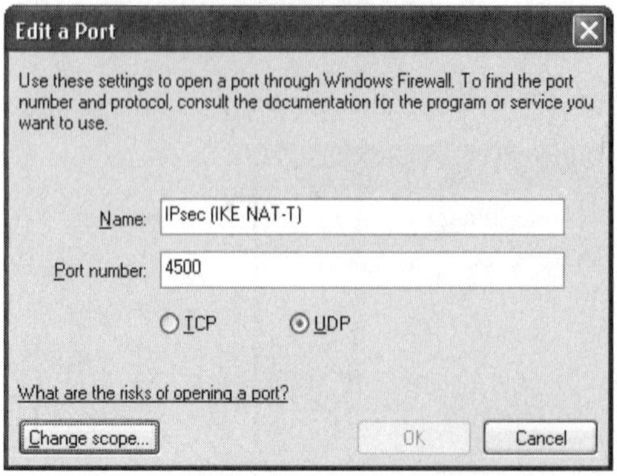

Figure 9-34   The Edit A Port dialog box

You can click the Change Scope... button to open the Change Scope dialog box and view or edit the network scope of the firewall exception, as shown in Figure 9-35.

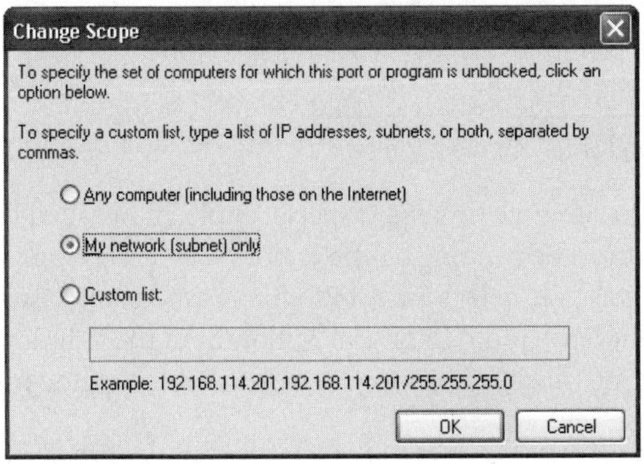

Figure 9-35 The Change Scope dialog box

Depending on your network configuration, you may wish to use this dialog box to narrow the firewall exception's scope from your entire subnet to a specific computer (or set of computers) by selecting the Custom List option button and specifying a single IP address, or a list of comma-separated IP addresses, in the text box below it.

If you are using third-party firewall software, your dialog boxes will look different, and you must open the ports yourself. Make sure inbound connections are permitted on TCP port 135 and UDP ports 4500 and 500 between your PC and the remote server with which you want to conduct remote debugging sessions.

Attaching to a Remote Process

Once the configuration work is done, the debugging experience for each of the Visual Studio–initiated scenarios we have discussed in this chapter should be enabled, with the identical behavior to their local debugging equivalents. In the case of externally-initiated debugging sessions (such as executing SQL CLR code from within SQL Server Management Studio), meanwhile, some extra steps are required. You must attach to the Sqlservr.exe process running on the *remote server*. This can be somewhat complex but is still quite manageable.

To attach to the remote server's SQL Server process, as you did for local service attachment, select the Debug/Attach To Process... main menu option. In the Attach To Process dialog box, enter the machine name of the remote server in the Qualifier text box (or use the Browse... button and the Browse For Computer dialog box to select the remote server instead). After you specify your remote server, you might see an error message box such as that shown in Figure 9-36.

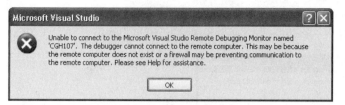

Figure 9-36   Remote debugging monitor failure message box

In order for Visual Studio to attach to a remote process, a special application called the Visual Studio Remote Debugging Monitor must be running on the remote server. There are two ways to get the monitor to run. The first way is to select the All Programs\Microsoft Visual Studio 2005\Visual Studio Tools\Visual Studio Remote Debugger option from the Windows Start menu (on the remote server). Selecting this menu option launches the debugging monitor in interactive mode, as shown in Figure 9-37.

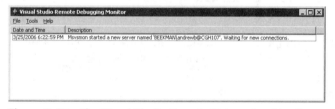

Figure 9-37   The Visual Studio Remote Debugging Monitor, running in interactive mode

Alternatively, you can select the All Programs\Microsoft Visual Studio 2005\Visual Studio Tools\Visual Studio Remote Debugger Configuration Wizard option from the Windows Start menu (also on the remote server). This shortcut launches a special wizard that allows you to configure the debugging monitor to run as a service on the remote machine. On the wizard's Configure The Visual Studio 2005 Remote Debugger Service page, you can select the Run The "Visual Studio 2005 Remote Debugger" Service check box and supply a properly authorized Windows user name and password. (The wizard recommends using an account in the Administrators group.) This is shown in Figure 9-38.

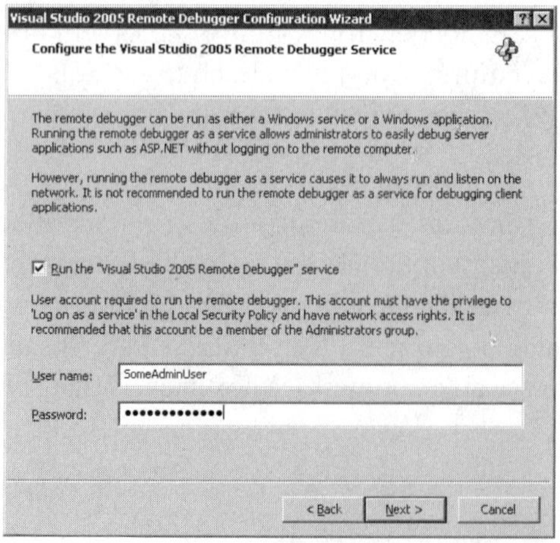

Figure 9-38   The Visual Studio Remote Debugger Configuration Wizard

Click Next, and then, assuming the wizard notifies you that it was successful, click Finish.

Once you have started the debugging monitor on the remote server, either interactively or as a service, you should be able to attach to the Sqlservr.exe process on that machine and then proceed to debug your SQL CLR code by invoking that code from outside Visual Studio, as we did previously against our local SQL Server process.

Summary

In this chapter, we covered a variety of scenarios for debugging SQL Server code. Whether your code is written in T-SQL or a CLR language, or even if you have a combination of T-SQL and CLR code, Visual Studio can debug it. The Server Explorer window provides an easy entry point into debugging stored procedures and functions, but you can also initiate debugging sessions from SQL Server project test scripts or from within a .NET application debugging session. You can even debug SQL CLR code in Visual Studio if that code is executed by an external application, including SQL Server Management Studio.

You saw how the debugging experience is impressively consistent across languages and tiers. You learned how to use breakpoints and tracepoints and tools such as the Locals, Watch, and Call Stack windows in each debugging context to hone in on your code's inner workings. You also saw how each SQL Server debugging technique can be used as effectively with a remote server as it can with a local instance of SQL Server, provided certain Windows security, firewall, and remote debugging monitor requirements are adhered to.

This book is all about programming SQL Server. Even great programmers have bugs in their code. The best programmers know how to minimize bugs in their code *and* know the fastest, easiest, and most efficient methods to identify, isolate, and remove the bugs that do slip through. In other words, they understand how to use debuggers to maximum advantage. While advanced debugging tools for server-side code in SQL Server have previously been hard to configure and harness, Visual Studio 2005 and SQL Server 2005 together provide an innovative debugging solution. With the techniques you've learned in this chapter, you're now ready to exploit this technology to full advantage and get your applications written faster and working more reliably.

Chapter 10

SQL Server 2005 Native XML Web Services

–Kent Brown

Now that XML and service-oriented architecture (SOA) have taken over the hearts and minds of software developers and architects everywhere, it should come as no surprise that Microsoft SQL Server 2005 has the ability to expose data over Web services. As a matter of fact, using XML over HTTP is old hat for SQL Server–SQLXML 1.0 for SQL Server 2000 provided this functionality way back in 2001. SQLXML 3.0 SP3, the latest version before the release of SQL Server 2005, provided SOAP 1.1 support and removed the dependency on the SOAP Toolkit.

So what is new about Native XML Web Services, and how is it an improvement over previous SQLXML functionality? SQLXML is still available in SQL Server 2005 as SQLXML 4.0, but the Web services portion has been pulled out into Native XML Web Services. This represents a significant upgrade of the SOAP support that was available in SQLXML 3.0, providing better performance, better security, simpler configuration, and better support for the latest Web services specifications. Simply put, Native XML Web Services is a built-in mechanism within SQL Server 2005 that provides simple, direct, secure, standards-compliant access to SQL Server programmability as Web services.

In this chapter, you will learn:

- How Native XML Web Services handles SOAP communication without reliance on Microsoft Internet Information Services (IIS).

- How to expose stored procedures and user-defined functions as Web service endpoints using Native XML Web Services.

- How to configure security access to your exposed Native XML Web Services endpoints.

- How to program client applications to consume your exposed Native XML Web Services endpoints.

- Security and performance best practices for Native XML Web Services endpoints.

- When to use Native XML Web Services.

Understanding Native XML Web Services

How exactly does SQL Server expose Web services without a dependency on IIS? The answer is Http.sys, the kernel-mode networking component that is baked into the base operating system of Windows Server 2003 and Windows XP SP2. Http.sys is the same component that makes it possible to host Web sites in Visual Studio .NET 2005 outside of IIS. Http.sys acts as sort of a dispatcher, receiving HTTP requests and passing them off to the registered handler for each URL. IIS is still the default handler for most HTTP requests, but now with Http.sys you have a configurable mechanism to redirect requests to the handler of your choice.

Native XML Web Services in SQL Server 2005 allows you to register endpoints with Http.sys through the use of data definition language (DDL) commands, such as *CREATE ENDPOINT*. Because Http.sys handles requests even before IIS is invoked, it can pass requests to registered URLs on to SQL Server to be handled without IIS being involved in any way. The SQL Server Native XML Web Services handler supports the acceptance of SOAP request messages and the sending of SOAP response messages, as well as the returning of WSDL that describes the service to support developer tools.

Comparing Native XML Web Services and SQLXML

A natural question to ask is how Native XML Web Services differs from the previous SQLXML support in SQL Server 2000. Here are the differences:

- SQLXML 3.0:
    - Supports SOAP 1.1.
    - Relies on IIS and an ISAPI Filter DLL.
    - Can act as a Web application—using templates on the database server, you can return data as HTML ready for presentation in the browser.
    - Uses UpdateGrams.
    - Supports XML bulk load.
- SQLXML 4.0:
    - Does not support SOAP access as SQLXML 3.0 does; SOAP access has been factored out into Native XML Web Services.

- Native XML Web Services:
  - ❑ True Web services with fully standards-compliant support for SOAP 1.1, SOAP 1.2, and WSDL.
  - ❑ Does not rely on IIS.
  - ❑ Supports most Transact-SQL (T-SQL) data types—does not require that data be returned using *FOR XML*.
  - ❑ Security is controlled inside of SQL Server—you must explicitly publish endpoints to allow access.
  - ❑ Does not support the XML templates in SQLXML. The client application consumes the Web service directly and can apply XSLT templates or use other available means to format the data for the user interface.
  - ❑ Does not support XML Bulk Load.
  - ❑ Supports ad hoc T-SQL batch statements.

Exposing SQL Programmability as Web Services

Native XML Web Services provides two types of Web services access to data: exposing specific stored procedures or user-defined functions (UDFs) as Web methods, and batch mode access.

Stored Procedures and User-Defined Functions

Native XML Web Services allows virtually any stored procedure or UDF to be exposed as a Web method. There are a few minor limitations (discussed later in the chapter), such as restrictions on stored procedure parameter names and lack of support for UDFs that return tables. However, in general you can choose to expose any existing stored procedure as a Web service, allowing it to do double duty as a normal stored procedure in your applications and as a Web service.

SQL Batch

In addition to exposing individual stored procedures and UDFs, Native XML Web Services also supports exposing T-SQL batch statements. Because of the wide-ranging power of this level of access, SQL batch is disabled by default.

Reserving URLs with Http.sys

It is not strictly necessary to register a URL with Http.sys in order to expose an endpoint. The *CREATE ENDPOINT* statement implicitly registers the URL defined by its *PORTS*, *SITE*, and *PATH* arguments. However, this registration takes place only when the endpoint is running, so it is possible for another application to register the same URL before your service starts up, causing a conflict. Therefore, it is usually a good idea to reserve the specific URL for your endpoints.

To register a URL to be handled by SQL Server, you call the *sp_reserve_http_namespace* stored procedure:

```
EXEC sp_reserve_http_namespace N'http://localhost:80/sql'
```

or

```
EXEC sp_reserve_http_namespace N'https://localhost:443/sql'
```

The registration of namespaces with Http.sys is hierarchical, which means any sub URLs, such as *http://localhost:80/sql/AdventureSales*, are also handled by SQL Server.

> **Note**   You must be logged on to SQL Server with an account that has Windows Administrator privileges on the computer where the instance of SQL Server 2005 is installed in order to reserve an HTTP namespace with the kernel-mode HTTP driver (Http.sys).

Creating and Managing Endpoints

For obvious security reasons, Native XML Web Services does not expose any Web services by default—you must explicitly expose them by creating endpoints. Only system administrators can create endpoints or grant rights to other users to create them. However, if you have the correct permissions, creating endpoints is easy—you simply execute the *CREATE ENDPOINT* statement.

CREATE ENDPOINT

The *CREATE ENDPOINT* statement has a lot of options, but here we'll simplify it and look only at the most commonly used options for creating Web service endpoints.

```
CREATE ENDPOINT endPointName
STATE = { STARTED | STOPPED | DISABLED }
AS HTTP (
PORTS = ( { CLEAR | SSL} [ ,... n ] ),
SITE = {'*' | '+' | 'webSite' },
PATH = 'url',
AUTHENTICATION =({ BASIC | DIGEST | INTEGRATED | NTLM | KERBEROS } [ ,...n ] )
)
FOR SOAP(
[ WEBMETHOD [ 'namespace' .] 'method_alias'
    NAME = 'database.owner.name',
```

```
    SCHEMA = { NONE | STANDARD | DEFAULT } ,
    FORMAT = { ALL_RESULTS | ROWSETS_ONLY | NONE} ] [ ,...n ]
BATCHES = { ENABLED | DISABLED },
WSDL = { NONE | DEFAULT | 'sp_name' },
SESSIONS = { ENABLED | DISABLED },
LOGIN_TYPE = { MIXED | WINDOWS },
DATABASE = { 'database_name' | DEFAULT },
NAMESPACE = { 'namespace' | DEFAULT },
SCHEMA = { NONE | STANDARD }
)
```

STATE

The *STATE* argument specifies the state of the endpoint after it is created. By default, an endpoint is created in the *STOPPED* state and you must then use the *ALTER ENDPOINT* statement to activate it. If you want the endpoint to be activated immediately upon creation, you specify *STARTED* for this argument. When an endpoint is in the *STOPPED* state, the server listens for and handles requests to the port but returns an error to clients indicating that the port is not active. When an endpoint is in the *DISABLED* state, the server does not listen on the port and will not respond to any client requests.

PORTS, SITE, and PATH

You specify the full URL address for the endpoint in three parts: *[protocol]://[host name]* + *[path]*, defined by the *PORTS, SITE,* and *PATH* arguments, respectively. The *PORTS* argument determines whether the URL begins with *http://* (for CLEAR) or *https://* (for SSL). Note that it is possible to listen on both ports. The *SITE* argument defines the host name used. The *PATH* argument defines the rest of the URL after the server name. For example, you would use the following options to define the URL as *http://localhost/sql/AdventureSales.*

```
PORTS = ( CLEAR ),
SITE = 'localhost'
PATH = '/sql/AdventureSales'
```

The following options result in the URL *https://myserver/NXWSEndpoints/MyEndpoint.*

```
PORTS = ( SSL ),
SITE = 'MyServer'
PATH = '/NXWSEndpoints/MyEndpoint'
```

Note   Although the use of *sql* as the base of the *PATH* argument seems to be common usage, this is by no means required. You can put any value (that results in a valid URL string) in the *PATH* argument to define the URL.

AUTHENTICATION

The *AUTHENTICATION* argument defines the types of authentication supported by the endpoint. These options should be familiar to you because they are the common options available under IIS for authenticating Web sites and Web services. However, conspicuously missing from the list is an option for anonymous access. This is by design; the caller must be authenticated as a Windows account or an SQL Server account to invoke a Web service on an endpoint.

You should pay attention to a few details regarding the authentication options. Because Basic authentication passes the username and password in clear text, you are required to choose the SSL value for *PORTS* when you specify Basic authentication. If the *INTEGRATED* value is specified, the server will use Kerberos or NTLM authentication, depending on how the client initiates authentication. Before you can use Kerberos authentication, the SQL Server must associate a Service Principal Name (SPN) with the account it will be running on. You can do this using the Windows SetSPN.exe support tool in Windows 2003.

More Info   See the "Registering Kerberos Service Principal Names by Using Http.sys" topic in SQL Server Books Online for more information about configuring the Http.sys kernel driver to support Kerberos for Native XML Web Services.

WEBMETHOD

You must enter a *WEBMETHOD* clause for each stored procedure or UDF that you want to expose. The *method_alias* argument allows you to assign the public name for the Web method, which can differ from the actual name of the stored procedure or function it maps to. The optional *namespace* argument allows you to override, for this particular Web method, the namespace defined at the endpoint level. You set *NAME* to the actual database name for the stored procedure or function, fully qualified as *[database].[owner].[name]*.

The *SCHEMA* argument controls whether an XML Schema Definition (XSD) is included inline with the SOAP response. There is also a *SCHEMA* option at the endpoint level, so at the *WEBMETHOD* level we can specify *DEFAULT* to use the value set at the endpoint level or override it for a particular Web method. If this option is set to *STANDARD*, the XSD schema is included in the response; if it is set to *NONE*, it is not.

Note   If you want to receive the result set as a *DataSet* on the client side, you must set *SCHEMA* to *STANDARD* because the schema is required by the client proxy to create the *DataSet*.

The final option for the *WEBMETHOD* clause is *FORMAT,* which is used to control whether row count, error messages, and warnings are returned with the result set. The default,

ALL_RESULTS, causes all of these results to be passed back to the client. In addition to controlling what is passed back from the server, the *FORMAT* argument also affects the interface of the generated proxy when you add a Web reference in Visual Studio .NET. The *ALL_RESULTS* value causes the proxy to return an *object* array to the client application. Although it is useful to have access to the row count, error messages, and warnings, receiving an *object* array requires the client code to do a little more work to get at the desired *DataSet*. See the section titled "Calling Native XML Web Service Endpoints from Client Applications" later in the chapter for client-side programming details. Setting *FORMAT* to *ROWSETS_ONLY* changes the Web method signature on the proxy to return a single *DataSet*, which is simpler for the client code to consume.

BATCHES

The *BATCHES* option, if set to *ENABLED*, creates an extra Web method called *sqlbatch* that allows you to pass a string containing T-SQL commands. Because this gives you broader access to data—for example, enabling you to execute ad hoc SQL queries—the default is *DISABLED*. Keep in mind that even with *BATCHES* set to *ENABLED*, the authenticated user must have rights to the underlying database objects. So if you protect access to all tables in a database and only give rights to stored procedures, turning on *BATCHES* will allow the user only to invoke multiple stored procedures in a single call— not to execute SQL statements directly against the tables.

DATABASE

The *DATABASE* argument defines the database the endpoint will be run against. If this argument is not set, it defaults to the *DEFAULT* database for the login.

NAMESPACE

You can define the default SOAP *namespace* for all of the exposed Web methods in an endpoint by including the *NAMESPACE* argument. Individual Web method entries can override this default by specifying the namespace in the *WEBMETHOD* clause.

SCHEMA

The *SCHEMA* argument at the endpoint level controls the default value for the *SCHEMA* argument in contained *WEBMETHOD* clauses. It defines whether an XSD schema is included inline with the SOAP response. If this option is set to *STANDARD*, the XSD schema is included in the response; if it is set to *NONE*, it is not.

> **Note** The *SCHEMA* setting is not related to the *XMLSCHEMA* option in a *SELECT* query that uses the *FOR XML* option. If you want the XML returned by a stored procedure to contain a schema, you must specify the *XMLSCHEMA* option in the T-SQL statement, regardless of the *SCHEMA* setting here.

WSDL

The *WSDL* argument allows you to control how the endpoint generates WSDL to support client applications. If you set this value to *NONE*, there will be no support for WSDL. If you need to support a custom WSDL format, you can set the *WSDL* argument to the name of a stored procedure that generates the WSDL and returns it. Due to the complexity of WSDL, implementing the code to return custom WSDL is not a trivial task. You will rarely need to generate custom WSDL, but it's nice to know the option is there if you need it.

> **More Info**   You can find more information about generating custom WSDL for your endpoints in the SQL Server Books Online section titled "Implementing Custom WSDL Support."

The default value, and most common choice, for the *WSDL* argument is *DEFAULT*, which instructs SQL Server to generate WSDL for the endpoint. The WSDL generation actually supports two versions of WSDL for the endpoint. The first is called default WSDL and is returned when you put *?wsdl* at the end of the URL (for example, *http://MyServer/sql/MyEndpoint?wsdl*). This default version of WSDL provides mappings from SQL Server data types to corresponding data types in the .NET Framework 2.0. For example, a number of types in the *System.Data.SqlTypes* namespace are better suited than the normal .NET primitive types to holding data from SQL Server.

The data type mappings provided in the default WSDL format are useful for client applications built with Visual Studio 2005, but clients written with other technologies might not be able to parse this form of the WSDL. For example, clients written with the SOAP Toolkit cannot understand all of the XSD types in the default WSDL. To support these clients, Native XML Web Services provides the simple WSDL format, which you can obtain by adding the word *simple* to the end of the Web service URL, as shown here: *http://MyServer/sql/MyEndpoint?simple*. The simple WSDL format uses only simple XSD types, so it has better backward compatibility with older Web services clients and with non-Microsoft Web services client technologies.

Let's look at a simple example:

```
CREATE ENDPOINT my_sql_endpoint
    STATE = STOPPED
AS HTTP(
    PATH = '/sql/HelloWorld',
    AUTHENTICATION = (INTEGRATED),
    PORTS = (CLEAR),
    SITE = 'localhost'
)
FOR SOAP (
    BATCHES = ENABLED,
    SCHEMA = STANDARD,
```

```
    WSDL = DEFAULT,
    DATABASE = 'AdventureWorks',
    NAMESPACE = 'http://HelloWorld/'
)
```

Here we create the endpoint named *my_sql_endpoint*. It runs in clear HTTP, and the URL is *http://localhost/sql/HelloWorld*. It starts out in the *STOPPED* state. The only Web method exposed is the *sqlbatch* Web method because *BATCHES* is enabled. It runs against the *AdventureWorks* database.

ALTER ENDPOINT

The syntax for *ALTER ENDPOINT* is pretty much the same as for *CREATE ENDPOINT*, except you only need to specify the parts that should be changed. You can use *ALTER ENDPOINT* to add, modify, or drop an existing Web method in the endpoint and to change the properties of the endpoint. For example, you might want to add a new Web method to the endpoint:

```
ALTER ENDPOINT my_sql_endpoint
FOR SOAP ( ADD WEBMETHOD 'SayHello' (name='AdventureWorks.dbo.SayHello') )
```

If you created the endpoint with *STATE* set to *STOPPED*, you can start the endpoint like this:

```
ALTER ENDPOINT my_sql_endpoint
STATE = STARTED
```

Later, you might decide to remove that Web method from the endpoint:

```
ALTER ENDPOINT my_sql_endpoint
FOR SOAP ( DROP WEBMETHOD 'SayHello')
```

DROP ENDPOINT

DROP ENDPOINT is used to remove an endpoint definition. The syntax is simple, as you would expect:

```
DROP ENDPOINT my_sql_endpoint
```

Granting Endpoint Permissions

By default, only the creator has access to an endpoint. Access for other users must be explicitly granted using the *GRANT ON ENDPOINT* statement:

```
GRANT permission ON ENDPOINT :: endpoint_name TO < server_principal >
```

The permissions that can be set are ALTER, CONNECT, CONTROL, TAKE OWNERSHIP, and VIEW DEFINITION.

Calling Native XML Web Service Endpoints from Client Applications

Because Native XML Web Services fully supports SOAP 1.1 and SOAP 1.2 and returns WSDL, programming against an endpoint is pretty much the same as programming against any Web service. If you are programming from Visual Studio .NET, you take the following steps:

1. Add a Web reference to the project. The wizard allows you to enter the URL for the Web service, and it then downloads the WSDL and creates a proxy class in your project for calling the Web service.

2. Create an instance of the proxy class.

3. Invoke a Web method on the proxy class.

4. If the Web method is configured to use the *ALL_RESULTS FORMAT*, you must loop through the returned *object* array, checking the types of each entry and casting them to the appropriate .NET type.

Listing 10-1 demonstrates how to invoke a Web method and consume the returned *object* array, in this case simply displaying a *MessageBox* for each type to show the returned value(s). When the Web method is configured to use the *ALL_RESULTS FORMAT*, six primary types can be returned by the server in the *object* array, which we need to be prepared to handle in the client code:

- **Primitive Scalar value**   For scalar UDFs, the return value can be consumed directly. In the upcoming code, it is converted to a string and displayed.

- *System.Data.DataSet*   The expected return from a stored procedure that returns a row set.

- *NativeSOAPApp1.server.SqlRowCount*   Returns the row count of the returned row set.

- *System.Xml.XmlElement*   The return type for a stored procedure that uses XML AUTO to format the return data as XML.

- *NativeSOAPApp1.server.SqlMessage*   If any errors occurred during execution of the stored procedure or UDF, the error is returned as an *SQLMessage*.

- *NativeSOAPApp1.server.SqlParameter*   If there is an *out* parameter, it is returned as an *SQLParameter*.

Note   Notice that the types used for *SqlRowCount, SqlMessage,* and *SqlParameter* are defined as classes within the namespace of the generated client-side Web service proxy, rather than the corresponding types defined in the *System.Data.SQLClient* namespace. The reason for this is that one of the goals of Native XML Web Services is for client applications not to have any dependency on the SQL Server client software. To accomplish this, the WSDL defines types that match the corresponding types in the *System.Data.SQLClient* namespace, which causes these classes to be generated in the proxy.

Listing 10-1   Sample client code

```
private void invokeWebMethod(string inParam) {

System.Data.SqlTypes.SqlString outParam = "";
server.sql_endpoint proxy = new server.sql_endpoint();
proxy.Credentials = System.Net.CredentialCache.DefaultCredentials;
object[] results;
results = proxy.GetCustomerInfo(inParam, ref outParam);
for (int j = 0; j < results.Length; j++)
   {
     object r;
     server.SqlMessage errorMessage;
     System.Xml.XmlElement xmlResult;
     System.Data.DataSet resultDS;

     r = results[j];

     //return value from SP is an int
     if (r.GetType().IsPrimitive)
     {
       MessageBox.Show(r.ToString());
     }

     switch (r.ToString())
     {
        case "System.Data.DataSet":
            resultDS = (System.Data.DataSet)r;
            MessageBox.Show(resultDS.GetXml());
            break;

        case "NativeSOAPApp1.server.SqlRowCount":
            MessageBox.Show(((NativeSOAPApp1.server.SqlRowCount)r).Count);
            break;

        case "System.Xml.XmlElement":
            xmlResult = (System.Xml.XmlElement)r;
            MessageBox.Show(xmlResult.OuterXml);
            break;

        case "NativeSOAPApp1.server.SqlMessage":
          errorMessage = (server.SqlMessage)r;
            MessageBox.Show(errorMessage.Message + ", " + errorMessage.Source);
            break;

        case "NativeSOAPApp1.server.SqlParameter":
            string outParamMsg= "Outparam name is :" +
                            ((server.SqlParameter)r).name + ", " +
                            "Outparam value is :" +
                            ((server.SqlParameter)r).Value;
            MessageBox.Show(outParamMsg);
            break;
   }
 }
}
```

```
    // output param value
    MessageBox.Show("Output Param: " + outParam.ToString());
}
```

Example Native XML Web Services Project

Having examined the basics of exposing Native XML Web Services, let's look at a sample application. For our example, we will use the fictitious Adventure Works Cycles, a small bicycle company that is the basis for the samples that ship with SQL Server 2005. In our scenario, Adventure Works Cycles has just hired a new sales manager who is responsible for increasing revenue. He has decided that the sales representatives need mobile access to customer information while they are on the road visiting client stores. He has named this application *Adventure Sales* and has written up a list of what the application must allow sales representatives to do:

1. Search for client stores by name or location (to help minimize travel time by scheduling visits to multiple stores in a locality).

2. View address and contact information for stores (to facilitate making appointments and getting directions to the stores).

3. View the status of orders recently placed by the store (to be able to field questions about orders during a visit).

Our detail-oriented sales manager ordered smartphone PDAs for the sales force and announced his new initiative to the senior executives and the sales team before consulting with the IT manager.

The IT department at Adventure Works Cycles is small and extremely busy. The only person available to work on the project is a junior developer who does not have the time or expertise to develop a full-blown n-tier system. However, after analyzing the requirements, the savvy IT manager realizes that because the company's data is stored on SQL Server 2005, they can complete this project in a few days using a simple Windows Forms application to run under Windows Mobile 5.0 and to access the data via Native XML Web Services.

 Note   Although our scenario demands a Windows Mobile solution, the sample code is implemented as a standard C# Windows Forms project. This allows you to open the project and work with the code without needing additional setup to support Windows Mobile 5.0. Because Windows Mobile 5.0 supports invoking Web services, this application can quite easily be rewritten as a mobile application.

Creating the SQL Server Functionality

We'll be creating three new stored procedures and a UDF to implement the required SQL Server functionality for our application. The SQL scripts for creating these are in the SQL Server Management Studio sample project for this chapter called Chapter10 SQL Server

Scripts. You can open this project and run the scripts in the order they are discussed in this section. This way, you'll be ready to expose them as Web methods in the Native XML Web Services endpoint we will be creating later in the section.

To demonstrate returning data as XML and consuming it on the client side, the first stored procedure, *GetStoreInfo*, shown in Listing 10-2, takes a store *CustomerID* and returns the store name and address as XML.

Listing 10-2   *GetStoreInfo* from GetStoreInfo.sql

```
USE AdventureWorks;
GO
IF OBJECT_ID ( 'dbo.GetStoreInfo', 'P' ) IS NOT NULL
    DROP PROCEDURE [dbo].[GetStoreInfo];
GO
CREATE PROCEDURE [dbo].[GetStoreInfo]
   @CustomerID [int]
AS
BEGIN

SELECT Store.Name, Address.AddressLine1, Address.City, Address.PostalCode,
   StateProvince.StateProvinceCode as State
FROM   Sales.Store
   INNER JOIN Sales.CustomerAddress
   ON Store.CustomerID = CustomerAddress.CustomerID
   INNER JOIN Person.Address
   ON CustomerAddress.AddressID = Address.AddressID
   INNER JOIN Person.StateProvince
   ON Address.StateProvinceID = StateProvince.StateProvinceID
   AND Address.StateProvinceID = StateProvince.StateProvinceID
WHEREStore.CustomerID=@CustomerID
FOR XML AUTO, ELEMENTS

END;
GO
```

The other two stored procedures simply return the results of an SQL query without using the *FOR XML* functionality. We will use the *DEFAULT* choice for the *WSDL* option when we create the endpoint so that the data will be returned to the client application as a *DataSet*.

> **Note**   We can safely return a *DataSet* in our example because we know the client application is using the .NET Framework 2.0. If you need to support non-Microsoft clients, you should use the simple WSDL when setting up the client proxy to ensure compatibility, and you should avoid .NET-specific types.

The *GetStoreContacts* stored procedure shown in Listing 10-3 returns all of the contacts associated with the store identified by the passed *CustomerID*.

Listing 10-3 *GetStoreContacts* from GetStoreContacts.sql

```
USE AdventureWorks;
GO
IF OBJECT_ID ( 'dbo.GetStoreContacts', 'P' ) IS NOT NULL
    DROP PROCEDURE [dbo].[GetStoreContacts];
GO
CREATE PROCEDURE [dbo].[GetStoreContacts]
   @CustomerID [int]
AS
BEGIN

   SET NOCOUNT ON;

   SELECT  Contact.FirstName, Contact.LastName,
              Contact.EmailAddress, Contact.Phone
   FROM      Person.Contact
              INNER JOIN Sales.StoreContact
              ON Contact.ContactID = StoreContact.ContactID
              INNER JOIN Sales.Store
              ON StoreContact.CustomerID = Store.CustomerID
   WHERE     (Store.CustomerID = @CustomerID)

END;
GO
```

The *GetStoreRecentOrders* stored procedure is shown in Listing 10-4. It returns orders that are less than two months old or are still open.

Listing 10-4 *GetStoreRecentOrders* from GetStoreRecentOrders.sql

```
USE AdventureWorks;
GO
IF OBJECT_ID ( 'dbo.GetStoreRecentOrders', 'P' ) IS NOT NULL
    DROP PROCEDURE [dbo].[GetStoreRecentOrders];
GO
CREATE PROCEDURE [dbo].[GetStoreRecentOrders]
   @CustomerID [int]
AS
BEGIN

DECLARE @TwoMonthsAgo DATETIME

SELECT @TwoMonthsAgo = DATEADD(Month, -26, GETDATE())
SELECT      SalesOrderHeader.OrderDate, SalesOrderHeader.DueDate, SalesOrderHeader
            .ShipDate, dbo.ufnGetSalesOrderStatusText(Sales.SalesOrderHeader.Status)
              AS OrderStatus
FROM        Sales.Store
              INNER JOIN Sales.SalesOrderHeader
                ON Sales.Store.CustomerID = Sales.SalesOrderHeader.CustomerID
WHERE((Sales.SalesOrderHeader.OrderDate>@TwoMonthsAgo
              OR Sales.SalesOrderHeader.DueDate>@TwoMonthsAgo)
```

```
    OR (Sales.SalesOrderHeader.Status<>5 AND Sales.SalesOrderHeader.Status<>6)
)
              AND (Sales.Store.CustomerID = @CustomerID)
ORDER BY Sales.Store.CustomerID, OrderDate DESC
END;
GO
```

> **Note**   Because all the sample data in the *AdventureWorks* database is dated before 2005, we cheated a bit in the *GetStoreRecentOrders* stored procedure in Listing 10-4 and subtracted 26 months from the current date instead of 2 months, as the requirements for the scenario demand. Depending on when you run the example, you might need to tweak this value or add new data to the *AdventureWorks* database to get recent orders to show up in the application.

The *ufnGetStoreSalesYTD* user-defined function is shown in Listing 10-5. It returns the sum of the sales orders placed by the store in the current year.

Listing 10-5   *ufnGetStoreSalesYTD* from ufnGetStoreSalesYTD.sql

```
USE AdventureWorks;
GO
IF OBJECT_ID ( 'dbo.ufnGetStoreSalesYTD', 'FN' ) IS NOT NULL
    DROP FUNCTION [dbo].[ufnGetStoreSalesYTD];
GO
CREATE FUNCTION [dbo].[ufnGetStoreSalesYTD](@CustomerID Int)
RETURNS [decimal]
AS
BEGIN
   DECLARE @ThisYear Int
   SELECT @ThisYear = DATEPART(year, GETDATE())-2
   DECLARE @YTDSale decimal

   SELECT @YTDSale = SUM(SubTotal)
   FROM Sales.SalesOrderHeader
   WHERE CustomerID=@CustomerID AND DATEPART(year, OrderDate)=@ThisYear

RETURN @YTDSale
END;
GO
```

> **Note**   As with the *GetStoreRecentOrders* stored procedure, we had to cheat a bit in the *ufnGetStoreSalesYTD* user-defined function shown in Listing 10-5 to get non-zero values. We did this by subtracting two years from the current year to get back to where AdventureWorks data exists. Depending on when you run the example, you might need to tweak this value or add new data to the *AdventureWorks* database to get recent orders to show up in the application.

Registering the URL with Http.sys

To register a URL to be handled by SQL Server, execute the following T-SQL:

```
USE AdventureWorks
GO
EXEC sp_reserve_http_namespace N'http://localhost:80/sql'
GO
```

Exposing the Endpoints

Now that the stored procedures and functions are created and the main URL namespace is registered with Http.sys, the next step is to create the endpoint that exposes the stored procedures as Web services, as shown in Listing 10-6.

Listing 10-6   Script to create the AdventureWorks endpoint from CreateEndPoints.sql

```
USE AdventureWorks
GO
CREATE ENDPOINT AdventureWorks
    STATE = STARTED
AS HTTP(
    PATH = '/sql/AdventureSales',
    AUTHENTICATION = (INTEGRATED),
    PORTS = (CLEAR),
    SITE = 'localhost'
)
FOR SOAP (
    WEBMETHOD 'http://Adventure-Works/'.'GetStoreInfo'
            (NAME='AdventureWorks.dbo.GetStoreInfo',
             SCHEMA=NONE),
    WEBMETHOD 'http://Adventure-Works/'.'GetStoreContacts'
            (NAME='AdventureWorks.dbo.GetStoreContacts',
             SCHEMA=STANDARD),
    WEBMETHOD 'http://Adventure-Works/'.'GetStoreRecentOrders'
            (NAME='AdventureWorks.dbo.GetStoreRecentOrders',
             SCHEMA=STANDARD, FORMAT=ROWSETS_ONLY),
    WEBMETHOD 'GetStoreSalesYTD'
            (name='AdventureWorks.dbo.ufnGetStoreSalesYTD'),
    BATCHES = ENABLED,
    SCHEMA = STANDARD,
    WSDL = DEFAULT,
    DATABASE = 'AdventureWorks',
    NAMESPACE = 'http://Adventure-Works/'
)
GO
```

Let's take a look at some of the options we chose for the *CREATE ENDPOINT* statement in Listing 10-6. We chose to use integrated security over HTTP on port 80 because we will expose this endpoint over the Internet, but only to employees of Adventure Works Cycles who have Windows accounts. We have a *WEBMETHOD* entry for each of our stored procedures and for the user-defined function. For the *ufnGetStoreSalesYTD* function, we provided a different name for the Web method than the actual name of the function in the database, for readability. For the stored procedures, we supplied the namespace prefix, but for the function we left it off, taking the default specified in the *NAMESPACE* attribute. (We did this simply to demonstrate the ability to define a default namespace prefix at the endpoint level and to override it at the Web method level. In this case, the result is the same because the default namespace prefix is the same as the one used for the first three *WEBMETHOD* entries.)

To allow our client to make ad hoc SQL queries against the database (to support the searching functionality), we set the *BATCHES* option to *ENABLED*. Because we know that the client is a Windows Forms application using the .NET Framework 2.0, we used the default *WSDL* option. (See the section titled "WSDL" earlier in the chapter for the *WSDL* options available.)

Granting Security Access to the Endpoints

To make it easy to control access to our endpoint and add new users later as needed, we'll create a Windows Security Group with the name AdventureWorksSalesTeam, as shown in Figure 10-1. In this figure, we have added the *JSmith* user to this group. When you create this group on your server, you should add the user you will use to run this application.

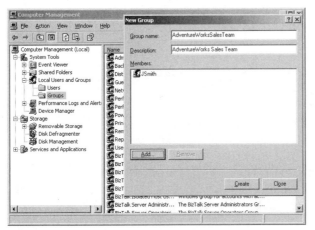

Figure 10-1   Setting up the AdventureWorksSalesTeam security group

 Note   In our example, we use a local security group because this is probably how you will want to set up your development environment to run the example. However, in a real environment this should probably be a domain group.

Even though we will grant access to the endpoint to members of the AdventureWorksSalesTeam group, we must also grant access to the stored procedures and functions themselves, just as we would for any application. Listing 10-7 shows the T-SQL statements necessary to grant the AdventureWorksSalesTeam security group access to our stored procedures, function, and endpoint.

Listing 10-7   Script to grant rights to stored procedures, UDF, and the endpoint from GrantSecurity.sql

```
USE master
GO
EXEC sp_grantlogin @loginame='DataServer\AdventureworksSalesTeam'
EXEC sp_grantdbaccess @loginame='DataServer\AdventureWorksSalesTeam'
GO
USE [Adventureworks]
GO
GRANT EXECUTE ON [dbo].[GetStoreContacts] TO [DataServer\AdventureworksSalesTeam]
GRANT EXECUTE ON [dbo].[GetStoreInfo] TO [DataServer\AdventureworksSalesTeam]
GRANT EXECUTE ON [dbo].[GetStoreRecentOrders] TO [DataServer\AdventureworksSalesTeam]
GRANT EXECUTE ON [dbo].[ufnGetStoreSalesYTD] TO [DataServer\AdventureworksSalesTeam]
GO
USE master
GO
GRANT CONNECT ON ENDPOINT::Adventureworks TO [DataServer\AdventureworksSalesTeam]
GO
```

> **Note**   In this script, we use the fictional server name *DataServer*. You should replace all references to *DataServer* with the name of your server when you set up the sample application to run in your environment.

That's all there is to it. With just a few extra T-SQL commands, we've exposed all of the functionality we need for the Adventure Sales application as a Web service! Let's go ahead and test the endpoint to make sure everything is working before we start building the client application. We can't easily test the Web methods without a client application, but we can point to the URL and see that it generates WSDL as it should. See Figure 10-2 for the result we get when we browse to *http://localhost/sql/AdventureSales?wsdl*.

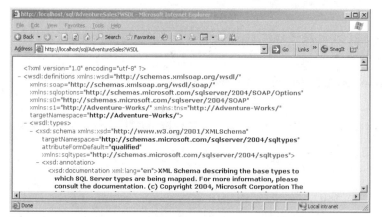

Figure 10-2   The WSDL generated by our endpoint

Creating the Client Application

For the client portion of our example, we created a simple Windows Forms application, called AdventureSales, that calls the Native XML Web Service endpoint we created and provides the user interface for searching and viewing data related to the Adventure Works Cycles customer stores. We will explain some of the important steps for creating this application in Visual Studio and examine some of the interesting parts of the code, but we will not provide step-by-step instructions to create this application. You'll find a complete solution–the AdventureSales Visual Studio solution–in the sample code for this chapter. You can open this solution to look at the code and run the application, as long as you have completed the preceding steps to create the endpoint.

In Visual Studio .NET, we start by creating a new C# Windows Application project and creating a simple form with two tabs–one for searching the *AdventureWorks* database for a store and one for viewing the detailed information for a particular store. Figure 10-3 shows the Search page of the Adventure Works Sales form of our application.

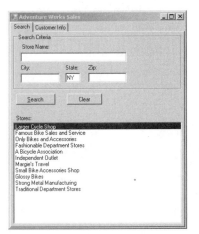

Figure 10-3   The Search page of the Adventure Works Sales form

To enable our application to invoke the Native XML Web Services endpoint we have exposed, we add a Web reference in the project to the AdventureSales Web service. To add a Web reference, you right-click the project in Visual Studio and choose Add Web Reference. This starts the Add Web Reference Wizard. To point to our endpoint, enter *http://localhost/sql/AdventureSales?wsdl* for the URL and click Go. The wizard downloads the WSDL for the endpoint and displays the available Web methods. To give our proxy object a meaningful name, type **AdventureSalesWebService** in the Web Reference Name text box, and click Add Reference. The wizard generates a proxy object that handles all the complexity of invoking Web services over SOAP. Figure 10-4 shows the page from the Add Web Reference Wizard where we specify the URL and set the class name for the Web reference proxy.

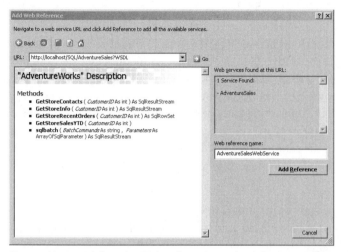

Figure 10-4   Adding the Web reference to the AdventureSales Web service

As a programming convenience, we set up a property called *Proxy* (see Listing 10-8) that returns an instance of the proxy object with the security credentials already attached.

Listing 10-8   *Proxy* property from AdventureSalesForm.cs

```
private AdventureSalesWebService.AdventureWorks Proxy
{
    get
    {
        if (_proxy == null)
        {
            _proxy = new AdventureSalesWebService.AdventureWorks();
            _proxy.Credentials = System.Net.CredentialCache.DefaultCredentials;
        }
        return _proxy;
    }
}
private AdventureSalesWebService.AdventureWorks _proxy;
```

When the user clicks the Search button on the Search tab, the code shown in Listing 10-9 is executed. The *GetSearchSQL* method, which is called by *searchButton_Click*, dynamically builds an SQL string based on the values the user enters in the search criteria text boxes. The *AddToWhereClause* method is called by *GetSearchSQL* to add the optional sections to the *WHERE* clause.

Listing 10-9   *searchButton_Click* and supporting methods from AdventureSalesForm.cs

```
private void searchButton_Click(object sender, EventArgs e)
{
    string searchSQL = GetSearchSQL();
    _CustomerId = 0;
    AdventureSalesWebService.SqlParameter[] p = null;
    DataSet ds = GetDataSet(Proxy.sqlbatch(searchSQL, ref p));
```

```
    if (!(ds == null))
    {
        storesListBox.DataSource = ds.Tables[0];
        storesListBox.DisplayMember = "Name";
        storesListBox.ValueMember = "CustomerID";
    }
    else
    {
        storesListBox.DataSource = null;
    }
}

private string GetSearchSQL()
{
    string searchSQL =
    "SELECT  Store.CustomerID, Store.Name, Address.City, " +
    "         Address.PostalCode as Zip, " +
    "         StateProvince.StateProvinceCode as State " +
    "   FROM Sales.Store " +
    "   INNER JOIN Sales.CustomerAddress " +
    "    ON Store.CustomerID = CustomerAddress.CustomerID " +
    "   INNER JOIN Person.Address " +
    "    ON CustomerAddress.AddressID = Address.AddressID " +
    "   INNER JOIN Person.StateProvince " +
    "    ON Address.StateProvinceID = StateProvince.StateProvinceID " +
    "AND Address.StateProvinceID = StateProvince.StateProvinceID ";

    string whereClause = "";
    if (!String.IsNullOrEmpty(this.searchStoreNameTextBox.Text))
        whereClause = AddToWhereClause(whereClause, "Store.Name Like '"
                                      + searchStoreNameTextBox.Text + "%'");

    if (!String.IsNullOrEmpty(this.searchCityTextBox.Text))
        whereClause = AddToWhereClause(whereClause, "Address.City Like '" + this.search
CityTextBox.Text + "%'");

    if (!String.IsNullOrEmpty(this.searchStateTextBox.Text))
        whereClause = AddToWhereClause(whereClause, "StateProvince.StateProvinceCode = '
" + this.searchStateTextBox.Text) + "'";

    if (!String.IsNullOrEmpty(this.searchZipTextBox.Text))
        whereClause = AddToWhereClause(whereClause, "Address.PostalCode Like '" + this.s
earchZipTextBox.Text + "%'");

    return searchSQL + whereClause;
}

private string AddToWhereClause(string whereClause, string newSection)
{
    if (String.IsNullOrEmpty(whereClause))
        return " WHERE " + newSection;
    else
        return whereClause + " AND " + newSection;
}
```

As mentioned earlier, the client-side programming challenge when you invoke Native XML Web Services is that the results are returned as an array of type *object*. For this sample, we have created a helper function, shown in Listing 10-10, to loop through the array and extract the expected *DataSet*.

Listing 10-10 *GetDataSet* from AdventureSalesForm.cs

```
private DataSet GetDataSet(Object[] results)
{
    DataSet data = null;
    for (int j = 0; j < results.Length; j++)
    {
        object result;
        result = results[j];
        if (result.ToString() == "System.Data.DataSet")
        {
            data = (System.Data.DataSet)results[j];
            break;
        }
    }
    return data;
}
```

After the user has searched for and identified a store, she can double-click the row in the list box to activate the Customer Info tab. Listing 10-11 shows the *storesListBox_DoubleClick* method that handles this event. This method calls on the *LoadStoreInfo*, *LoadStoreContacts*, *LoadStoreRecentOrders*, and *LoadStoreSalesYTD* methods to retrieve the various pieces of information from the database using the proxy and to bind the data to the appropriate controls in the user interface.

Listing 10-11 *storesListBox_DoubleClick* and supporting methods from AdventureSalesForm.cs

```
private void storesListBox_DoubleClick(object sender, EventArgs e)
{
    if ((storesListBox.SelectedIndex == -1) || (storesListBox.Items.Count==0))
        return;
    _CustomerId = (int)storesListBox.SelectedValue;
    LoadStoreInfo();
    LoadStoreContacts();
    LoadStoreRecentOrders();
    LoadStoreSalesYTD();
    this.CustomerTabControl.SelectedIndex = 1;
}

private void LoadStoreInfo() {
    System.Xml.XmlElement xmlData = GetXMLElement(Proxy.GetStoreInfo(this._CustomerId));
    if (!(xmlData == null))
    {
        this.nameTextBox.Text = xmlData.SelectSingleNode("//Name").InnerText;
```

```
            this.address1TextBox.Text = xmlData.SelectSingleNode
("//AddressLine1").InnerText;
            this.cityStateZipTextBox.Text = xmlData.SelectSingleNode
("//City").InnerText + ", " +
                            xmlData.SelectSingleNode
("//State").InnerText + ", " +
                            xmlData.SelectSingleNode
("//PostalCode").InnerText;
        }
        else
        {
            this.nameTextBox.Text = "";
            this.address1TextBox.Text = "";
            this.cityStateZipTextBox.Text = "";
        }
    }

    private void LoadStoreContacts() {
        DataSet ds = GetDataSet(Proxy.GetStoreContacts(this._CustomerId));
        if (!(ds == null))
            this.contactsDataGridView.DataSource = ds.Tables[0];
        else
            this.contactsDataGridView.DataSource = null;
    }

    private void LoadStoreRecentOrders() {
        DataSet ds = Proxy.GetStoreRecentOrders(this._CustomerId);
        if (!(ds == null))
            this.recentOrdersDataGridView.DataSource = ds.Tables[0];
        else
            this.recentOrdersDataGridView.DataSource = null;
    }

    private void LoadStoreSalesYTD() {
        System.Data.SqlTypes.SqlDecimal yTDSales =      Proxy.GetStoreSalesYTD
(this._CustomerId);
        if (!yTDSales.IsNull)
            this.salesYTDTextBox.Text = String.Format("{0:C}", (Decimal)yTDSales);
        else
            this.salesYTDTextBox.Text = String.Format("{0:C}", 0.0D) ;
    }
```

For *LoadStoreContacts* and *LoadStoreRecentOrders*, we simply bind the returned *DataSet* to the appropriate *DataGridView* control. Because the *GetStoreRecentOrders WEB METHOD* clause specifies *ROWSET_ONLY* for the *FORMAT* option, we don't have to use the *GetDataSet* helper function (shown earlier in Listing 10-10). The *GetStoreRecentOrders* Web method returns a *DataSet* directly. Because *LoadStoreSalesYTD* returns a simple scalar value, we format it as a string using the Currency standard format.

The *LoadStoreInfo* method in Listing 10-11 shows the result coming back as an *XmlElement*. In this case, we take advantage of the *SelectSingleNode* method of the *XMLElement*, using *XPATH* expressions to pull out the desired values and populate the controls. A helper method,

GetXMLElement, shown in Listing 10-12, is used to pull back the *XMLElement* returned by the Web method.

Listing 10-12 *GetXMLElement* helper method from AdventureSalesForm.cs

```
private System.Xml.XmlElement GetXMLElement(Object[] results)
{
    System.Xml.XmlElement data=null;
    for (int j = 0; j < results.Length; j++)
    {
        object e1;
        e1 = results[j];
        if (e1.ToString() == "System.Xml.XmlElement")
        {
            data = (System.Xml.XmlElement)results[j];
            break;
        }
    }
    return data;
}
```

Figure 10-5 shows the final result, with the Customer Info tab populated with data. We've done it! The sales representatives can now get the data they need to be more effective on the road, the sales manager is happy, and of course the IT manager and the junior developer get well-deserved pay raises.

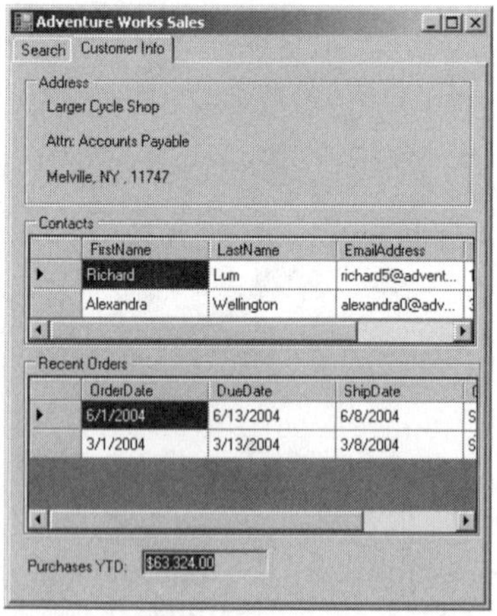

Figure 10-5 The final result—viewing information for the selected store on the Customer Info tab

Best Practices for Using Native XML Web Services

The ability to expose Web services directly from the database opens up some interesting architectural possibilities and questions. In many situations, the ability to eliminate the middle tier makes it much simpler to build, test, deploy, and manage an application. However, as with any exciting new programming option, you must be careful not to misuse it, and you should evaluate its appropriateness for the business problem at hand. In this section, we will look at some of the strengths and limitations of using Native XML Web Services and offer some advice about where to appropriately apply it and how to avoid potential security and performance pitfalls.

Advantages of Native XML Web Services

Before we talk about the limitations, let's summarize the advantages of using Native XML Web Services:

- Allows "zero-footprint clients." Native XML Web Services eliminates the need to deploy the MDAC stack to client machines.

- Provides a simple means to expose SQL Server data to non-Microsoft clients. If the client application can understand WSDL and communicate using SOAP, it can consume the data. Visual Studio .NET projects can just add a Web reference, and there are Java tools available with similar capabilities.

- Simpler to construct than a full-blown three-tier architecture for simple applications. Eliminates the need to build a middle tier because the client application connects directly to stored procedures on the server.

- Can be used as an alternative to JDBC for Java-based clients.

Limitations of Native XML Web Services

Native XML Web Services has a few limitations that you should be aware of:

- It must be run on an operating system that supports Http.sys, which currently means Windows 2003 or Windows XP SP2. When using Windows XP, you must make sure that the World Wide Web service is shut down before you run the *CREATE ENDPOINT* T-SQL statement because the *CREATE ENDPOINT* statement will fail if IIS is running. Once you have exposed your endpoint(s), you can restart the World Wide Web service and both IIS and Native XML Web Services will work.

- Although you can configure an endpoint to use multiple ports, a particular endpoint can listen only on one port of each type (CLEAR/SSL).

- It does not support table-valued user-defined functions.

- Some deprecated parameter-naming conventions that are still supported in stored procedures for backward compatibility cannot be used in stored procedures exposed as Native XML Web Services Web methods. These naming conventions are @, @@, and *@@param*; they must be changed to the *@param* convention.

- Some system stored procedures do not have the necessary metadata information to allow Native XML Web Services to generate correct WSDL. The solution for exposing these system stored procedures is to wrap the system stored procedure in your own stored procedure or open up the *sqlbatch* Web method.

Security Recommendations

Native XML Web Services closes some potential security holes by disallowing anonymous authentication and by requiring SSL when Basic authentication is used. However, you should still take care to protect your database and your transmitted data from security threats. We suggest you take the following precautions:

- Always run SQL Server behind a firewall. If possible, open up access only to specific known IP addresses.

- Use Kerberos authentication if possible because it supports mutual authentication, which protects client applications from imposter "man-in-the-middle" servers.

- Use well-defined Windows Security groups to grant access to endpoints. Granting rights to an endpoint to the Public role makes it easy to give all users access, but we strongly discourage this. The "principle of least privilege" dictates that you should give users only the access they require and expose each endpoint only to users who require it.

- Use SSL to protect visibility of any sensitive data being exposed over Native XML Web Services.

- Don't enable *sqlBatch* unless it is necessary. Ideally, *sqlBatch* should be enabled only when the underlying tables are protected and the users have access only to specific stored procedures.

Performance Recommendations

Keep in mind that SOAP will never be as efficient as the Tabular Data Stream (TDS) protocol. Returning data as XML requires more CPU power and memory on the server and returns a larger amount of data over the network. According to tests that returned large XML documents, Native XML Web Services results in a 20 to 30 percent performance degradation compared with TDS. We offer the following performance guidelines:

- Avoid returning very large result sets. This is always true, but it is especially important when you use Native XML Web Services.

- Avoid returning BLOBs. Binary data does not transfer efficiently in a SOAP call.

- When optimal performance is required, avoid Native XML Web Services altogether.

When to Avoid Native XML Web Services

One situation in which Native XML Web Services is not an appropriate solution is when a significant amount of business logic must be enforced. The motivation for a three-tiered architecture is to separate the business logic into a middle tier that can be coded, deployed, and scaled independently from the user interface logic running in the client application and from the database logic on the server. When you use Native XML Web Services, you bypass the middle tier, effectively creating a two-tiered architecture. If you need to enforce business logic, you must do so in the client application (fat client) or in the database stored procedures (fat server). There is not necessarily anything wrong with either of these architectures, as long as you understand the trade-offs. As mentioned earlier, a two-tiered architecture can simplify the coding and deployment of your application.

However, if you choose to enforce the business logic in the client application, you leave the database somewhat vulnerable—the logic must be enforced in all client applications because an application that doesn't abide by the rules can corrupt the integrity of your data. On the other hand, if you choose to enforce business logic in the stored procedures in the database, you end up writing this logic in T-SQL (unless you choose to use SQL CLR), which is generally less expressive than C# or Visual Basic. In addition, when you put business logic in the database, you put a load on the database server that could be offloaded to middle-tier servers, which are easier to scale.

Scalability is probably the main reason to be cautious about using Native XML Web Services extensively in large applications. In a highly scalable system, the ultimate bottleneck for achieving higher levels of throughput is usually the database. The reason for this is that unlike middle-tier servers, which can be deployed in a farm with network load balancing, a database is difficult to scale out. Because of the overhead of replication, putting a database on multiple servers usually does not yield a performance increase proportional to the investment. So in general, the scaling option for the database tier is to scale up—to buy more RAM, more CPUs, and larger, faster disk storage for the database server. Scaling up can get you quite far, but you ultimately hit a maximum. Of course, with the latest advancements in hardware and operating systems, you can scale up to 64 CPUs and use the 64-bit version of Windows 2003, which allows you to vastly increase memory, but the hardware to support this level of scalability is quite expensive.

Native XML Web Services adds a load to the database server because of both the extra processor work and the memory required to format the data as XML and any business logic that is run in the database stored procedures. If you have a large application and you are concerned that you might reach the capacity limit of your database server, avoid extensive use of Native XML Web Services.

When to Use Native XML Web Services

Native XML Web Services is likely to be the right solution when one or more of the following is true:

- Your application is fairly simple and the business logic is minimal.
- You do not expect the load on the SQL Server to be high.
- You need to provide access to your data to non-Microsoft clients.
- You want to avoid installing database drivers on the client.
- You don't have the developer resources to implement a full-blown n-tier architecture.

Native XML Web Services works well for these purposes:

- Administrative scripts that execute batch statements to manage the database. These scripts can be integrated into a single solution for managing all databases in your enterprise and can be written in Perl or run on Linux.

- Mobile clients. With the latest Windows Mobile releases, you can invoke Web services directly from a mobile device. By using Native XML Web Services, you can avoid having to install SQL Mobile Edition on the device.

- Small, simple applications. As demonstrated by the example earlier in the chapter, you can get a lot done with limited programming staff and expertise.

- Enterprise integration solutions. BizTalk Server can invoke Web services, and Native XML Web Services might be the simplest way to expose database functionality to BizTalk Orchestrations.

Summary

In this chapter, we took a detailed look at Native XML Web Services. You saw that it provides standards-compliant SOAP access to data, and you learned how to configure SQL Server 2005 to expose and secure Web services. We also looked at a sample application that shows how to program against Native XML Web Services from a .NET Framework application. Finally, we discussed best practices and recommendations for using Native XML Web Services appropriately and looked at some common scenarios in which it is often used.

Chapter 11
Transactions

—Sahil Malik

Have you ever developed an application with the intention of writing unreliable code? We doubt it. It would be equally absurd for a customer to hug you and shed tears of joy because the system you wrote completely corrupted his data. Likewise, we assume you have little patience when a customer service representative cannot help you because his computer tells him something that might not be correct.

As absurd and exaggerated as these scenarios may be, the fact remains that many software professionals treat the idea of writing reliable software too casually. They concentrate most of their effort on getting the logic right and pay too little attention to making sure that the logic behaves correctly under all circumstances. At the same time, more and more tasks are becoming automated, which is the result of increasingly complex software, which in turn is made possible by increasingly powerful hardware. Just as the desktop machine you work on today is thousands of times more powerful than the microprocessors of 20 years ago, software has grown dramatically more complex. This increase in complexity demands much more reliability in our code, not less.

Despite this, most programmers continue to write unreliable software. Think of the last paycheck you received—the multitude of computer systems it went through and all the programmers who worked on that software. How would you feel if careless programming or inadequate testing resulted in a $100 reduction in your paycheck? Or what if a computer bug accidentally wiped out your retirement account, your Social Security number, or your identity? What if the airplane you see outside your window flew into your home because of a computer bug?

Many programmers expect every careless mistake to be caught in testing. But testing environments can barely load-test applications appropriately and are for the most part incapable of reproducing various concurrent scenarios. The reality is that most software issues manifest themselves in the production environment, not in development or testing. Therefore, as developers, we must focus on getting the logic right and making sure that the logic behaves consistently in all scenarios. Logical operations must conform to the *ACID* properties: *atomicity*, *consistency*, *isolation*, and *durability*. Generally, you ensure this by wrapping logical operations in transactions. So we'll begin this chapter by exploring what a transaction is.

What Is a Transaction?

A *transaction* is a single operation or set of operations that succeed or fail together, thereby ensuring consistency of data should unforeseen circumstances arise. An example might be a financial transaction. For example, let's say you buy a car. The single transaction of buying a car consists of three distinct operations:

1. You select a car.

2. You pay for it.

3. You drive the car off the lot.

Skipping any of these steps could cause major angst to one or more of the parties involved. This is a simple example of a set of steps that must always occur together in a consistent manner.

Transactions allow us to ensure consistency in our data through four basic principles. These principles provide a set of rules that must be followed in order for our transaction to succeed. The four principles help ensure that the state of our data is atomic, consistent, isolated, and durable regardless of the success or failure of the transaction. These properties are covered in the next topic.

Understanding the ACID Properties

Consider the transaction of going to an ATM and withdrawing $100 from your bank account. The data for this transaction can be easily represented in a database as a table with two columns, one holding your AccountID and the other holding your AccountBalance.

To begin with, your account balance is $100, so after withdrawing $100, your updated balance should be zero. Also, it makes logical sense that before the money can be disbursed, the system must ensure that you have the funds available in your account. What this means in database terms is that two database queries must be run in this transaction. The first query checks the account balance.

```
SELECT AccountBalance FROM Account WHERE AccountID = @AccountID
```

If the query returns an *AccountBalance* value greater than or equal to the requested withdrawal, you can perform the operation of withdrawing cash.

After withdrawing the cash, you must update the account record with the updated balance. To do so, you run an *UPDATE* query.

```
UPDATE Account
SET AccountBalance = AccountBalance - 100
WHERE AccountID = @AccountID
```

The three distinct operations in this transaction are two database queries and one operation of withdrawing cash. All three must succeed or fail together in an *atomic* manner, or the transaction should not be considered complete. **Atomicity** is the first ACID property.

Now let's change the nature of the transaction a bit. Let's say the original account balance is $150 and that within the same transaction, the user requests to withdraw $100 and to transfer another $75 to a second account. The first update query will succeed, changing the account balance to $150 − $100 = $50. But the second operation will fail because there won't be enough money left in the account to transfer the $75. You therefore need a way to undo the cash transfer and withdrawal steps and return the database to its original state. You cannot leave the database midway through a transaction because it may be in an inconsistent state. In a real-world scenario, you would not normally wrap a withdrawal and a transfer in the same transaction in the event that you want at least one of the operations to be successful. The point here is to show how the data can end up in an inconsistent state between two operations. Rolling back operations that cannot be completed in this manner demonstrates the second ACID property, **consistency**.

Let's say the two operations—cash withdrawal and cash transfer—are broken up into two distinct transactions instead of one but that they happen to run simultaneously, or concurrently. Each transaction will have to check the current balance. They will do this by attempting to execute a query like this:

```
SELECT AccountBalance FROM Account WHERE AccountID = @AccountID
```

Unless your system has explicit checks blocking concurrent reads, both transactions will get the same result: $150. Thus they will both assume that the account has enough funds for the transaction. One transaction will disburse $100, and the other will transfer $75. But this will result in an overall deduction of $100 + $75 = $175, even though the account actually has only $150. In a well-designed system, the transactions must be isolated from each other to prevent what is known as "dirty reads." A dirty read happens when data is read at one point in a transition state and the "read" doesn't reflect the data's true state at the end of the current operation. This brings us to the third ACID property, **isolation**.

Isolation means that other transactions attempting to request a common resource will be blocked. Blocking, in turn, seriously affects the response times of your application. As it turns out, you'll often want to relax this blocking behavior to suit your application architecture. This involves using isolation levels, which we'll discuss later in the chapter.

Finally, when you have successfully completed all your operations within a transaction, you don't want to lose the changes made. In other words, system failures must not affect the transactional integrity of your operations. This brings us to the fourth ACID property, **durability**.

Let's review the four ACID properties again before we continue:

- **Atomicity**   Operations succeed or fail together. Unless all steps succeed, the transaction cannot be considered complete.

- **Consistency**   Operations leave the database in a consistent state. The transaction takes the underlying database from one stable state to another, with no rules violated before the beginning or after the end of the transaction.

- **Isolation**   Every transaction is an independent entity. One transaction will not affect any other transaction that is running concurrently.

- **Durability**   Every transaction is persisted on a reliable medium that cannot be undone by system failures. Also, if a system failure occurs in the middle of a transaction, the completed steps must be undone by the system or the uncompleted steps must be executed to finish the transaction. This typically happens by use of a log that can be played back to return the system to a consistent state.

> **Important**   Besides ACID, there are two other important points that we brushed over. The first refers to the actual process of disbursing cash as a part of the transaction. This alludes to the fact that transactions are not necessarily limited to only database entities. We will be looking at that later in this chapter when we discuss a new namespace in the .NET Framework 2.0 called *System.Transactions*. The second refers to isolation levels that allow you to tweak the isolation behavior of a transaction to your specific needs.

A transaction can work with a single resource, such as a database, or multiple resources, such as multiple databases or message queues. Transactions limited to a single resource are referred to as *local transactions*, and transactions that span multiple resources are called *distributed transactions*. We'll first concentrate on local transaction support in Microsoft SQL Server 2005, and we'll talk about distributed transactions later in the chapter.

Local Transactions Support in SQL Server 2005

SQL Server 2005, like any leading database engine, provides built-in transaction support that enables you to wrap one or more queries inside a transaction. Local transactions (transactions that deal with only one physical database) operate in one of four transaction modes:

- Autocommit

- Explicit

- Implicit
- Batch-scoped

Let us explore each of these in turn.

Autocommit Transaction Mode

The autocommit transaction mode is the default transaction mode. Under this mode, whether or not you requested a transaction, SQL Server ensures data sanctity across the lifetime of the query execution. For example, if you execute a *SELECT* query, the data will not change over the execution lifetime of the query. On the other hand, if you execute a data manipulation language (DML) query (*UPDATE*, *INSERT*, or *DELETE*), the data will be committed if no errors occur or if the operation is rolled back in the case of errors. Over the execution of a single DML query, you should never end up with only a partial modification of records. The two notable exceptions to this rule are recursive common table expressions (CTEs), for which all of the returned data is not locked in advance, and situations where you explicitly request no transactional sanctity.

Explicit Transaction Mode

Under the explicit transaction mode, you explicitly request the boundaries of a transaction. In other words, you explicitly control when the transaction begins and when it ends. The autocommit transaction mode enables you to run single queries in a transactional manner, but frequently you'll want a batch of queries to operate in a single transaction, which is where you will want to use explicit transactions. SQL Server continues to work under the autocommit transaction mode until you request an exception to the rule, so if you want to execute a number of Transact-SQL (T-SQL) statements as a single batch, use the explicit transaction mode instead.

You can request when the transaction starts by using the *BEGIN TRANSACTION* T-SQL statement. After you call *BEGIN TRANSACTION* on a database connection, the database engine attempts to enlist all ensuing operations within the same transaction. The *BEGIN TRANSACTION* T-SQL statement uses the following syntax:

```
BEGIN { TRAN | TRANSACTION }
    [ { transaction_name | @tran_name_variable }
    [ WITH MARK [ 'description' ] ]
    ]
```

In the statement, you can specify a name for the transaction by using *transaction_name* or *@tran_name_variable*. You can also mark a transaction in the transaction log by specifying a description. This is useful if you want to restore the database to a named mark. For more information on this feature, refer to SQL Server Books Online.

Let's say you have called *BEGIN TRANSACTION* and have been merrily executing a number of T-SQL commands. After a while, you will want to end your transaction by saving (committing) your changes or undoing (rolling back) them in the event of an error. To end a transaction, you have two choices. First, if you want to make the changes permanent, you call the *COMMIT TRANSACTION* T-SQL statement. It uses the following syntax:

```
COMMIT { TRAN | TRANSACTION } [ transaction_name | @tran_name_variable ] ]
```

Thus the following is a valid transactional block.

```
BEGIN TRANSACTION
  UPDATE Table1 SET Column1 = 'One'
  INSERT INTO Table2 (Column2) VALUES ('Two')
COMMIT
```

Note that SQL Server maintains the transaction count, which you can access by using the *@@TRANCOUNT* function. This function returns the number of active transactions for the current connection. The default value is 0. Every time you call *BEGIN TRANSACTION*, *@@TRANCOUNT* is incremented by 1. You can also call *BEGIN TRANSACTION* inside another *BEGIN TRANSACTION* block, which will increase the *@@TRANCOUNT* as well. Also, every time you call *COMMIT TRANSACTION*, SQL Server decrements *@@TRANCOUNT* by 1. But as long as *@@TRANCOUNT* is not zero, the transaction is considered active. When you call *BEGIN TRANSACTION* within a transaction block, you effectively create a *nested transaction*. But it isn't quite as simple as that. Before you can understand the nature of nested transactions in SQL Server 2005, we must also consider the second scenario, in which you want the changes to be undone (not saved permanently) in the event of failure of a statement within the transaction.

If you do not want the changes to be permanent and want to restore the database to its previous state, you can roll back the changes by calling the *ROLLBACK TRANSACTION* T-SQL statement. *ROLLBACK* uses the following syntax:

```
ROLLBACK { TRAN | TRANSACTION }
    [ transaction_name | @tran_name_variable
    | savepoint_name | @savepoint_variable ]
```

ROLLBACK is the opposite of *COMMIT*. Instead of saving, it undoes all changes made in the transaction. It is important to realize that SQL Server never assumes *COMMIT*. If you disconnect from SQL Server without explicitly issuing a *COMMIT*, SQL Server assumes a *ROLLBACK*. However, as a best practice, you should never leave that decision to SQL Server. You should explicitly tell SQL Server which of the two options you want. The reason for this is that due to connection pooling implemented at various levels in any common data access API, even if you close a connection, it might take a while before an API such as ADO.NET physically closes the connection. SQL Server might have to keep the transaction running and hence block valuable resources for longer than expected.

Another important difference between *COMMIT* and *ROLLBACK* is that if a severe error occurs during the execution of a transaction, SQL Server rolls back the transaction. Unfortunately, SQL Server doesn't make clear its definition of a severe error. A severity level of 19 or higher generally aborts the connection, stops the execution of the current batch, and rolls back the transaction. Because of this ambiguity, it is a good idea to explicitly call *ROLLBACK* if an error occurs.

> **Tip** Always call *ROLLBACK* explicitly, and never rely on the API or SQL Server to issue a rollback for you.

There is another important, yet subtle, difference between *COMMIT* and *ROLLBACK*. *COMMIT TRANSACTION* decrements *@@TRANCOUNT* by 1, but *ROLLBACK TRANSACTION* always reduces *@@TRANCOUNT* to 0. What does this mean in terms of nested transactions? We'll explore this topic next.

Nested Transactions

What does all this talk of *@@TRANCOUNT* and nested transactions mean in practical terms? Let's look at the following code snippet:

```
BEGIN TRANSACTION OUTERTRAN
 INSERT INTO TEST (TESTCOLUMN) VALUES (1)
  BEGIN TRANSACTION INNERTRAN
   INSERT INTO TEST (TESTCOLUMN) VALUES (2)
  COMMIT TRANSACTION INNERTRAN
ROLLBACK
```

Interestingly, when you run this code (assuming that the Test table exists), no rows are inserted into the database. This is because the *ROLLBACK* statement automatically rolls back the entire transaction to the outermost *BEGIN TRANSACTION* statement, reducing *@@TRANCOUNT* to 0. So the *ROLLBACK* nullifies *COMMIT*, even though *COMMIT* was called before *ROLLBACK*. This is a subtle but important point that is specific to SQL Server.

Savepoints

Another important concept related to transactions is savepoints. Savepoints are defined using a *SAVE TRANSACTION* T-SQL statement. It uses the following syntax:

```
SAVE { TRAN | TRANSACTION } { savepoint_name | @savepoint_variable }
```

By calling *SAVE TRANSACTION* during a transaction, you mark a point within a transaction to which you can roll back without losing everything. Consider the following code:

```
BEGIN TRANSACTION
 INSERT INTO TEST (TESTCOLUMN) VALUES (1)
 SAVE TRANSACTION SAVEPOINT1
  INSERT INTO TEST (TESTCOLUMN) VALUES (2)
 ROLLBACK TRANSACTION SAVEPOINT1
 COMMIT
```

This code inserts a row and sets a savepoint with the name *SAVEPOINT1*. It then performs another insert, but because you set a savepoint prior to this insert, you can roll back to the savepoint without losing your first insert. As you might have guessed, at the end of the code block only one row is inserted with *TestColumn = 1*.

To get a better feel for how these features of transactions work, we suggest working with different permutations and combinations of *BEGIN TRANSACTION*, *SAVE*, *COMMIT*, *ROLLBACK*, and *@@TRANCOUNT* on a test table in your SQL Server 2005 database.

Implicit Transaction Mode

When you connect to a database using SQL Server Management Studio and execute a DML query, the changes are automatically saved. This occurs because, by default, the connection is in autocommit transaction mode. If you want the opposite behavior—no changes committed unless you explicitly ask them to be committed—you set the connection to implicit transaction mode.

You can set the database connection to implicit transaction mode or unset it by calling the *SET IMPLICIT_TRANSACTIONS* T-SQL statement.

```
SET IMPLICIT_TRANSACTIONS {ON | OFF}
```

When a connection is set in the implicit transaction mode and the connection is not currently in a transaction, a transaction is automatically started for you when you issue one of the following statements: *ALTER TABLE*, *CREATE*, *DELETE*, *DROP*, *FETCH*, *GRANT*, *INSERT*, *OPEN*, *REVOKE*, *SELECT*, *TRUNCATE TABLE*, or *UPDATE*.

The big difference, however, is that the transaction is not committed or rolled back unless you explicitly request to do so. This means that if you issue an *UPDATE* statement, SQL Server will maintain a lock on the affected data until you issue a *COMMIT* or *ROLLBACK*. If you do not issue a *COMMIT* or *ROLLBACK* statement, the transaction is rolled back when the user disconnects.

In practical terms, you should try to avoid setting a connection to use implicit transaction mode on a highly concurrent database. This is because you will implicitly start transactions by issuing queries in an interactive mode through SQL Server Management Studio and might end up locking database resources, thus seriously affecting the performance of the system as a whole. An example of appropriate use of implicit transaction mode is on a data warehouse where the reports need only read-only access to the data and can be run under the Read-Uncommitted or Snapshot isolation level (levels that avoid blocking, as discussed shortly), and you want to be very careful not to inadvertently modify the data.

Batch-Scoped Transaction Mode

SQL Server 2005 connections can support multiple active result sets (MARS) on the same connection. Note that we said multiple active results, not parallel execution of commands. The command execution is still interleaved with strict rules that govern which statements can overstep which other statements.

Connections using MARS have an associated batch execution environment. The batch execution environment contains various components—such as SET options, security context, database context, and execution state variables—that define the environment under which commands execute. When MARS is enabled, you can have multiple interleaved batches executing at the same time, so all changes made to the execution environment are scoped to the specific batch until the execution of that batch is complete. Once the execution of the batch completes, the execution settings are copied to the default environment.

Thus, a connection is said to be using batch-scoped transaction mode if it is running a transaction, has MARS enabled on it, and has multiple interleaved batches running at the same time.

MARS and Transactions

MARS lets you execute multiple interleaved batches of commands. However, MARS does not let you have multiple transactions on the same connection, only multiple active result sets. Transactions and MARS are an interesting mix, but to understand how transactions work in MARS, you must first understand what the command interleaving rules are.

In MARS, a command that reads results (such as *SELECT*, *FETCH*, or *READTEXT*) can, generally speaking, be interleaved freely or interrupted by a command that attempts to modify data (such as *UPDATE* or *INSERT*). Thus, write can block read, but read cannot block write. Read ensues once the write has finished. Also, if two writes show up together, they are serialized in the order of execution. Remember that command execution in SQL Server is always sequential, never parallel, even in multithreaded environments. Finally, *BULK INSERT* statements block all other read and write operations.

So theoretically, *BULK INSERT* will block *UPDATE/INSERT/DELETE*, which in turn will block all read operations. The problem, however, is that in most practical scenarios you cannot accurately predict which command actually blocks which other command. This is because your read might have finished before the write interjected. You also cannot predict exactly when the read finished and the write started because the read depends on a number of factors—CPU speeds, network speeds, packet size, network traffic, and so on. It is thus impossible to predict whether the read data was "put on the wire" before the write was requested.

What this means in terms of transactions is that if you are running a transaction that inserts a row, which fires a trigger, and there is a *SELECT* statement in the trigger, the MARS interleaving rules will dictate that your trigger's *SELECT* statement be blocked by the original *INSERT* statement. Also, because of different command execution times, this behavior is impossible to predict reliably. If it ever happens, the SQL Server 2005 deadlock monitor will detect this scenario and fail the *SELECT* statement. You might end up with a system that will work on a low-load developer's machine but fail in production where the load is greater. Thus, when you use MARS, you must consider interleaving rules and multiple batches in your design.

MARS and Savepoints

Because you have multiple interleaved commands all working in the same transaction, the commands that issue savepoints can easily confuse each other's logic. Imagine a situation in which two interleaved batches issue a rollback to a named savepoint, and it just happens that the savepoint name is the same in both batches. You cannot predict which rollback occurred first, so which savepoint should SQL Server roll back to? In addition, because you cannot accurately predict which statement ended up interleaving which statement, you can't really be sure if the savepoint was ever created before you issued a rollback to it.

For these reasons, if multiple serialized commands are executing, MARS allows you to set a savepoint, but as soon as commands begin to get interleaved, any request to *BEGIN TRANS-ACTION* will fail. Because you cannot accurately predict the exact interleaving order of commands, you cannot accurately predict whether your *BEGIN TRANSACTION* statement will succeed or fail.

Considering this unpredictable behavior, it is best to stay away from savepoints on a MARS connection.

Using Local Transactions in ADO.NET

In ADO.NET, commands can be executed against a data source using a class that inherits from *DbCommand*. For instance, to execute commands on an SQL Server database, you use *SqlCommand*, which inherits from *DbCommand*. Let's say you have a table defined using the following T-SQL:

```
CREATE TABLE TestTable
(
    TestID INT IDENTITY PRIMARY KEY,
    TestColumn INT
)
```

Further, you need to execute a simple *INSERT* command on the table shown in this code:

```
INSERT INTO TestTable (TestColumn) VALUES (100)
```

You can easily wrap this T-SQL command inside a *SqlCommand* instance, as shown in Listing 11-1.

Listing 11-1   Using *SqlCommand* to execute a simple T-SQL command

```
using (SqlConnection dbConn = new SqlConnection(connectionString))
{
    SqlCommand dbCmd = dbConn.CreateCommand();
    dbCmd.CommandText = "INSERT INTO TestTable (TestColumn) VALUES (100)";
    try
    {
        dbConn.Open();
        dbCmd.ExecuteNonQuery();
    }
    catch (Exception ex)
    {
        Throw ex;
    }
    finally
    {
        dbConn.Close();
    }
}
```

The *SqlCommand.ExecuteNonQuery* method executes the command specified in the *dbCmd .CommandText* property against the database specified in the connection string property. (To learn about the other *Execute* methods, see *Microsoft ADO.NET 2.0*, by David Sceppa [Microsoft Press, 2006].)

Now consider the following T-SQL code block, which includes two database queries in one transaction:

```
BEGIN TRANSACTION
   INSERT INTO TestTable (TestColumn) VALUES (100)
   INSERT INTO TestTable (TestColumn) VALUES (200)
COMMIT
```

The code block is actually made up of four distinct T-SQL commands. One straightforward approach would be to simply call the four lines of code as different command texts on an *SqlCommand* object. But that is hardly an elegant solution. It is good practice to ensure that a transaction be executed by wrapping the entire statement within one *SqlCommand* object. There are no guarantees that the same *SqlCommand* object will be available to your code when executing later commands. A much better implementation of the transactional code is to use two instances of the *SqlCommand* object and bind both of them in the same transaction, as shown in Listing 11-2.

Listing 11-2   Binding two *SqlCommand* objects into one transaction

```
using (SqlConnection dbConn = new SqlConnection(connectionString))
{
    SqlCommand dbCmd1 = dbConn.CreateCommand();
    dbCmd1.CommandText = "INSERT INTO TestTable (TestColumn) VALUES (100)";
    SqlCommand dbCmd2 = dbConn.CreateCommand();
    dbCmd2.CommandText = "INSERT INTO TestTable (TestColumn) VALUES (200)";

    SqlTransaction dbTran = null;
    try
    {
        dbConn.Open();
        dbTran = dbConn.BeginTransaction();
        dbCmd1.Transaction = dbTran;
        dbCmd2.Transaction = dbTran;

        dbCmd1.ExecuteNonQuery();
        dbCmd2.ExecuteNonQuery();
        dbTran.Commit();
    }
    catch (Exception ex)
    {
        dbTran.Rollback();
        throw ex;
    }
    finally
    {
        dbConn.Close();
    }
}
```

As you can see, the code in Listing 11-2 is remarkably similar to the nontransactional code you saw earlier. The big difference, however, is that as soon as we open the connection, we begin the transaction on the connection using the *SqlConnection.BeginTransaction* method. That method returns a variable of data type *SqlTransaction*, which is assigned to the *Transaction* property of all *SqlCommand* objects that are intended to be run in the same transaction on the same connection. In addition, we use the *try/catch/finally* construct to ensure a commit in the event of success or a rollback in the event of failure.

It is worth noting, however, that you need the connection to be open before you can call *BeginTransaction*, and once you have called *BeginTransaction* on a connection, all subsequent commands until a commit or rollback must lie within the same transaction. This is a bit of discipline that ADO.NET forces on you to keep your code clean.

Transaction Terminology

Before we go beyond the basics of transactions, let's go over some terminology that is commonly used when talking about transactions.

- **Beginning a transaction**   Defines that all subsequent operations that occur after a transaction begins are assumed to lie within the transaction.

- **Rolling back a transaction**   Undoing operations that have occurred since a transaction began, thus restoring the affected data to its original state. This is done in the event of failure.

- **Committing a transaction**   Making permanent all operations that have occurred since a transaction began. A transaction is committed in the event of success.

- **Dirty read**   The operation of reading data that is yet to be committed. This occurs, for example, when transaction B is being blocked by transaction A, but because you have tweaked the isolation behavior, transaction B ends up reading transaction A's changes even though they have not been committed.

- **Nonrepeatable read**   A condition where transaction B modifies the data transaction A was working with, during the lifetime of transaction A. As a result, transaction A reads modified data, and the original read cannot be repeated.

- **Phantom read**   Like a nonrepeatable read, except that the number of rows changes between two reads within the same transaction. The rows that differ between the two reads are referred to as *phantom rows*.

Isolation Levels

As mentioned earlier in this chapter, the isolation behavior of a transaction can be tweaked to your application's needs. This is generally done by setting the isolation level of a transaction. Put simply, isolation levels determine how concurrent transactions behave. Do they block each other? Do they let each other step over themselves? Or do they present a snapshot of a previous stable state of data in the event of an overstepping?

You might find a slight mismatch between the isolation levels defined in ADO.NET compared with the isolation levels in SQL Server 2005 because ADO.NET was not written exclusively for SQL Server. We'll begin by looking at the isolation-level support in SQL Server 2005.

Isolation Levels in SQL Server 2005

You can set isolation levels in SQL Server 2005 by using the *SET TRANSACTION ISOLATION LEVEL* T-SQL command, which uses the following syntax:

```
SET TRANSACTION ISOLATION LEVEL
    { READ UNCOMMITTED
    | READ COMMITTED
    | REPEATABLE READ
    | SNAPSHOT
    | SERIALIZABLE
    }
```

A sample usage of this command with the *BEGIN TRANSACTION* command is shown here:

```
SET TRANSACTION ISOLATION LEVEL READ UNCOMMITTED
BEGIN TRANSACTION
 SELECT TestColumn FROM TestTable
COMMIT
```

As you can see from the syntax, SQL Server 2005 supports five isolation levels:

- Read uncommitted
- Read committed
- Repeatable read
- Snapshot
- Serializable

Read Uncommitted Isolation Level

By specifying the read uncommitted isolation level, you essentially tell the database to violate all locks and read the current immediate state of data. But by doing so, you might end up with a dirty read—reading data that is not yet committed. You should therefore avoid this isolation level because it can return logically corrupt data.

Let's explore this isolation level by using an example.

1. Create a table called Test with the following data in it.

   ```
   TestID   TestColumn
   -------------------
   1        100
   ```

2. Open two instances of SQL Server Management Studio. In each instance, use the database that contains the Test table. These two instances will be used to simulate two users running two concurrent transactions.

3. In instance 1, execute an *UPDATE* on the row of data by executing the following code block:

   ```
   BEGIN TRANSACTION
   UPDATE Test SET TestColumn = 200 WHERE TestId = 1
   ```

4. In instance 2 of Management Studio, execute the following query:

   ```
   SELECT TestColumn FROM Test WHERE TestId = 1
   ```

You will notice that your *SELECT* query is blocked. This makes sense because you are trying to read the same data that instance 1 is busy modifying. Unless instance 1 issues a *COMMIT* or a *ROLLBACK*, your query will remain blocked or will simply time out.

5. Cancel your blocked *SELECT* query by pressing Alt+Break or clicking the Cancel button on the toolbar. Execute the following T-SQL command to set the isolation level of your *SELECT* query to read uncommitted on the connection held by instance 2.

```
SET TRANSACTION ISOLATION LEVEL READ UNCOMMITTED
```

6. Execute the *SELECT* query again.

```
SELECT TestColumn FROM Test WHERE TestId = 1
```

You will find that the query isn't blocked; it produces *200* as a result.

7. Go back to instance 1 and issue a *ROLLBACK*.

8. Back in instance 2, execute the same *SELECT* query again. You should get *100* as the result.

As you might have noticed, instance 2 returned different results for the same query at different times. As a matter of fact, the value *200* was never committed to the database, but because you explicitly requested a dirty read by specifying the *READ UNCOMMITTED* isolation level, you ended up reading data that was never meant to be final. So the downside is that you ended up reading logically incorrect data. On the upside, however, your query did not get blocked.

Read Committed Isolation Level

Read committed is the default isolation level in both SQL Server and Oracle databases. As you will see shortly, this isolation level is the default because it represents the best compromise between data integrity and performance. This isolation level respects locks and prevents dirty reads from occurring. In the example you saw earlier, until we explicitly requested that the isolation level be changed to read uncommitted, the connection worked at the read committed isolation level. Therefore, our second transaction (the autocommit mode transaction in the *SELECT* query) was blocked by the transaction executing the *UPDATE* query.

Read committed prevents dirty reads, but phantom reads and nonrepeatable reads are still possible when using this isolation level. This is because the read committed isolation level does not prevent one transaction from changing the same data at the same time as another transaction is reading from it.

A phantom read can occur in the following type of situation:

1. Transaction 1 begins.

2. Transaction 1 reads a row.

3. Transaction 2 begins.

4. Transaction 2 deletes the row that was read by transaction 1.

5. Transaction 2 commits. Transaction 1 can no longer repeat its initial read because the row no longer exists, resulting in a phantom row.

A nonrepeatable read can occur in the following type of situation:

1. Transaction 1 begins.

2. Transaction 1 reads a row.

3. Transaction 2 begins.

4. Transaction 2 changes the value of the same row read by transaction 1.

5. Transaction 2 commits.

6. Transaction 1 reads the row again. Transaction 1 has inconsistent data because the row now contains different values from the previous read, all within the scope of transaction 1.

Repeatable Read Isolation Level

As the name suggests, the repeatable read isolation level prevents nonrepeatable reads. It does so by placing locks on the data that was used in a query within a transaction. As you might expect, you pay a higher price in terms of concurrent transactions blocking each other, so you should use this isolation level only when necessary. The good news, however, is that a concurrent transaction can add new data that matches the *WHERE* clause of the original transaction. This is because the first transaction will place a lock only on the rows it originally read into its result set. In other words, a transaction using this isolation level acquires read locks on all retrieved data but does not acquire range locks.

If you examine this pattern closely, you'll see that although nonrepeatable reads are avoided when using this isolation level, phantom reads can still occur. They can occur under the following circumstances:

1. Transaction 1 begins.

2. Transaction 1 reads all rows with, say, *TestColumn = 100*.

3. Transaction 2 begins.

4. Transaction 2 inserts a new row with *TestID = 2, TestColumn = 100*.

5. Transaction 2 commits.

6. Transaction 1 runs an *UPDATE* query and modifies *TestColumn* for the rows with *TestColumn = 100*. This also ends up updating the row that transaction 2 inserted.

7. Transaction 1 commits.

Because shared locks are not released until the end of the transaction, concurrency is lower than when using the read committed isolation level, so care must be taken to avoid unexpected results.

Serializable Isolation Level

A transaction running at the serializable isolation level will not permit dirty reads, phantom reads, or nonrepeatable reads. This isolation level places the most restrictive locks on the data being read or modified, keeping your data perfectly clean. This might sound like an isolation level that gives you perfect isolation behavior, but there is a good reason why you should seldom use this isolation level. This places the most restrictive locks on the data being read, or modified. In a sense, this is the perfect transaction, but transactions will block other running transactions, thereby affecting concurrent performance or even creating deadlocks. Thus even if this transaction will keep your data perfectly clean, it will severely affect system performance. In most practical situations, you can get away with a lower isolation level.

Snapshot Isolation Level

In all isolation levels previously presented, we seem to be trading concurrent performance for logical sanctity of data. Because a transaction locks the data it is working on, other transactions that attempt to work with the same data are blocked until the first transaction commits or rolls back. Of course, the traditional way of getting around this problem is to allow dirty reads (and hence corrupt data) or simply reduce the duration of transactions. But neither of these solutions allows you to read logically consistent data while offering nonblocking concurrent behavior.

Application architectures frequently present circumstances in which even the smallest transactions become a problem or transactions end up modifying so much data that their duration cannot be kept small. To get around this issue, SQL Server 2005 introduces a new isolation level: the snapshot isolation level. This isolation level gives you consistent reads without blocking.

Transactions running under the snapshot isolation level do not create shared locks on the rows being read. In addition, repeated requests for the same data within a snapshot transaction guarantee the same results, thus ensuring repeatable reads without any blocking. This sounds like the best of both worlds—the responsiveness of read uncommitted combined with the consistency of repeatable read. However, you pay a price.

This nonblocking, repeatable read behavior is made possible by storing previously committed versions of rows in the tempdb database. As a result, other transactions that were started before the write in the current transaction and that have already read the previous version will continue to read that version. Because the previous version is being read from tempdb, the write can occur in a nonblocking fashion and other transactions will see the new version. The obvious problem, of course, is the increased overhead on the tempdb database. For this reason, SQL Server requires you to enable the snapshot isolation level before you can use it. You shouldn't arbitrarily enable snapshot isolation on databases. But after testing, if you decide that your database needs this isolation level, you can enable it by using the following T-SQL commands:

```
ALTER DATABASE Test
SET ALLOW_SNAPSHOT_ISOLATION ON
```

As with all isolation levels, once you enable snapshot isolation for a database, you can use it on individual connections by using the following T-SQL statement:

```
SET TRANSACTION ISOLATION LEVEL SNAPSHOT
```

Read Committed Snapshot Isolation Level   Snapshot isolation prevents readers from being blocked by writers by providing readers with data from a previously committed version. Over the duration of the transaction, you are thus assured of repeatable reads. However, this method of ensuring a repeatable read incurs additional overhead and bookkeeping for the database engine that might not be necessary in all situations. Thus, SQL Server 2005 offers a slight modification to the read committed isolation level that provides nonrepeatable reads over the duration of the transaction that are not blocked by transactions writers. It is called the read committed snapshot isolation level. This isolation level guarantees consistency of the data over the duration of a read query within a transaction but not over the entire transaction that holds the reader. The obvious advantage over read committed snapshot as compared to read committed is that your readers do not get blocked. When they request data, they are offered either a previous state of data (before any write operations) or the new state of data (after write operations), depending on the state of other concurrently running transactions, but they are never required to wait until other concurrent transactions release their locks on the data being requested.

To use the read committed snapshot isolation level, you must first enable it at the database level by using the following T-SQL command:

```
ALTER DATABASE Test
SET READ_COMMITTED_SNAPSHOT ON
```

Once you have enabled the read committed snapshot isolation level on a database, all queries using the read committed isolation level will exhibit snapshot-like behavior. Although this isolation level will give you snapshot-like behavior, you will not be able to do repeatable reads over the duration of a transaction.

Isolation Levels in ADO.NET

As mentioned earlier, isolation levels in ADO.NET are slightly different than those for SQL Server. This is because ADO.NET is designed as a generic data access technology that supports other databases, as well SQL Server. The isolation levels defined in ADO.NET 2.0 under the *System.Data.IsolationLevel* enumeration are as follows:

- **Chaos**   Pending changes from more highly isolated transactions cannot be overwritten. This setting is not supported in SQL Server or Oracle.

- **ReadUncommitted**   Similar to read uncommitted in SQL Server, this level means that no shared locks are placed and no exclusive locks are honored.

- **ReadCommitted**   Similar to read committed in SQL Server, shared locks are held while the data is being read by the transaction. This avoids dirty reads, but you might still get nonrepeatable reads and phantom reads.

- **RepeatableRead**   Shared locks are placed on all data that is used in the predicate (criterion) of the query. Again, as with repeatable read in SQL Server, dirty reads and nonrepeatable reads are not possible, but phantom reads are.

- **Snapshot**   Similar to the snapshot isolation level in SQL Server, this isolation level provides a snapshot of earlier data while offering repeatable reads with nonblocking selects. Do not confuse this level with the read committed snapshot isolation level in SQL Server 2005, which must be enabled at the database level.

- **Serializable**   This can be considered an ideal transaction type to use, in which exclusive locks are placed on data. This prevents other users from reading or modifying the data. Keep in mind there are always tradeoffs, and exclusive locks should not be held for long periods of time.

- **Unspecified**   This is a catch-all isolation level for databases that support isolation levels not covered by the other choices or for scenarios in which the isolation level cannot be accurately determined.

You can specify an isolation level for a transaction as a parameter to the *SqlConnection.Begin-Transaction* method. For instance, in the following code snippet, we begin a transaction with the ReadUncommitted isolation level.

```
SqlTransaction myTransaction =
    dbConnection.BeginTransaction(IsolationLevel.ReadUncommitted) ;
```

In this example, any *SqlCommand* with its *Transaction* property set to *myTransaction* will not honor any exclusive locks and will let you perform dirty reads on data being held by other transactions.

Distributed Transactions

So far, our discussion in this chapter has been limited to transactions on a single database. What if more than one database is involved? What if more than one database server is involved? What if a non-database operation, such as modifying an in-memory cache, is involved? Can you use *BEGIN TRANSACTION* or *SqlTransaction.BeginTransation* to bind other such operations within a single transaction? Unfortunately you can not. *BEGIN TRANSACTION* and *SqlTransaction.BeginTransation* work only on local transactions dealing with data in a database. These transactions do not apply to in-memory cache due to the lack of a transaction logging mechanism being available.

The term *distributed transaction* is a bit of a misnomer because here we will learn about transactions involving more than one resource. In this section, we will look at a deeper theory of transactions and explore a new namespace in the Microsoft .NET Framework 2.0 called *System.Transactions*. We will also see why a transaction that is inherently expensive due to the overhead of dealing with the transaction itself becomes even more expensive because it is now being managed by an external entity—a transaction coordinator. This discussion addresses a scope broader than only database transactions.

Distributed Transaction Terminology

You will frequently encounter these terms in discussions about distributed transactions.

Resource Manager

Transactions (database or otherwise) manage a resource. Any operation that needs to be made transactional is managed by a logical entity—a subroutine, a function, a DLL, an executable, a machine, or anything else. Any such logical entity that is eventually responsible for managing the resource in a transactional manner is called a *resource manager* (RM).

Thus, a resource manager has the ability and responsibility to enlist itself in a current running transaction and offer transactional capabilities.

Transaction Manager or Transaction Coordinator

If you have a resource manager that manages its resources in a transactional manner by enlisting in a current running transaction, by definition you need an external entity that manages the transaction itself. This external entity is responsible for listening to and coordinating between several resource managers that are all enlisted within the same transaction. It acknowledges requests for new transactions and listens for and sends notifications in the event of success and failure. This entity is referred to as a *transaction manager* (TM), *transaction coordinator* (TC), or *distributed transaction coordinator* (DTC). Two common transaction coordinators that ship with Windows are the Lightweight Transaction Manager (LTM) and Microsoft Distributed Transaction Coordinator (MS DTC).

Do note that a transaction coordinator is not necessarily a distributed transaction coordinator. In fact, if the resource manager itself has transactional capabilities built in, it might not need a transaction coordinator at all. For instance, in the case of SQL Server, if a transaction is limited to a single database, SQL Server is fully capable of managing the transaction on its own. Thus, for local transactions, SQL Server 2005 chooses not to consult the MS DTC. There are good reasons for this, which will become evident once you read about the typical implementation of a distributed transaction, namely the two-phase commit process.

Two-Phase Commit

A distributed transaction can be implemented in a number of ways. One of the most common ways is through the two-phase commit process. Here is the typical flow of a two-phase transaction involving two RMs and a DTC.

1. The transaction initiator requests a transaction from the DTC. This transaction initiator can be the application that interacts with the two resource managers or it can be one of the resource managers itself.

2. The transaction initiator requests that the resource managers to do their work as a part of the same transaction. The resource managers register themselves with the DTC as a part of the same transaction, thus expressing an interest in receiving notifications about success or failure of the transaction as a whole. This process is referred to as "enlisting within a transaction."

3. The resource managers go ahead and do their work and notify the DTC of a success, while keeping a rollback mechanism in place. This is the first phase of a two-phase commit process, also called the *prepare phase*.

4. Once the DTC receives a success notification for the prepare phases from each of the enlisted resource managers, the DTC issues a notification to go ahead and make the changes permanent. Upon receiving such a notification, all resource managers make their changes permanent by committing their transient states. This is also known as the *commit phase*. The system has now gone from one stable state to another. Thus the distributed transaction is complete.

Rules and Methods of Enlistment

As you might have noticed, the distributed transaction coordinator on a Windows machine, MS DTC, engages in a lot of chatty communication with the various RMs involved in a transaction. Due to the network roundtrips involved, this chatting affects the performance of the application in general and might also be blocked by a firewall. In addition, resource managers that enlist themselves in a distributed transaction often use the serializable isolation level. This architecture is the easiest to implement because when using the serializable isolation level, you have a perfect transaction—no dirty reads, no phantom reads, and no nonrepeatable reads. Of course, the downside is a serious hit on performance.

But SQL Server 2005 itself is capable of managing transactions, so why should it have to escalate the isolation level to serializable in every circumstance? After all, depending upon your logic, you may want to take advantage of an MS DTC–based transaction *if and only if* your transaction ends up involving more than one resource manager. But as long as only one database connection is involved, you shouldn't have to pay the extra cost of involving the DTC. As it turns out, the brilliant Microsoft engineers thought of this situation before we did. And in order to rectify this situation, there happens to be different ways a resource manager can enlist within a transaction.

Volatile Enlistment

A resource manager that deals with resources that are volatile (not permanent) is a good candidate for volatile enlistment. Typically, in a volatile enlistment scenario, if the resource manager cannot perform the second (commit) phase of a distributed transaction for any reason, it doesn't explicitly need to recover the first (prepare) phase. This means that if a resource manager crashes in the middle of a transaction or fails, the resource manager doesn't need to provide an explicit recovery contract to the transaction coordinator. Volatile enlistment doesn't need the implementation of MS DTC, so it is usually managed by the Lightweight Transaction Manager (LTM), which is a much lighter weight transaction coordinator designed to work with volatile enlistment scenarios.

Durable Enlistment

Durable enlistment is necessary if the RM has permanent (durable) data that depends on the transaction for consistency. A good example is a transaction that involves disk I/O. Say you are writing to a file on disk. If the transaction fails, or if the resource manager crashes, the file that was written as a part of the prepare phase will need to be deleted. Thus the resource manager will need to prepare a transaction log and record the history of changes since the transaction was begun. In the event of a requested recovery, the resource manager needs sufficient information to perform a graceful rollback.

Promotable Single-Phase Enlistment

In many situations the nature of a transaction can change as new resource managers continue to enlist. For instance, an SQL Server 2005 database is perfectly capable of managing a transaction on its own, as long as the transaction is limited to one database. Or say, for instance, that a resource manager that manages an in-memory cache doesn't need the implementation of MS DTC because the cache by nature is unreliable anyway. But if there is a transaction containing an in-memory cache resource manager or an SQL Server 2005 connection being managed by the LTM, and a second SQL Server 2005 connection enlists itself in the same transaction, the transaction will be promoted to MS DTC because the resource managers are no longer capable of managing the transaction on their own.

It is important to note that along with the promotion comes the various disadvantages of MS DTC—a higher isolation level and a more expensive and chatty transaction in general. Promotable single-phase enlistment (PSPE) offers a huge advantage in that as long as you don't really need MS DTC, you don't use it, so you don't pay the penalty for it.

In fact, there are well-defined rules for the promotion of a transaction from LTM to MS DTC. A transaction is escalated from LTM to MS DTC if any of the following happens:

- A durable resource that doesn't support single-phase notifications is enlisted in the transaction.

- Two durable resources that support single-phase notification enlist in the same transaction.

- The transaction coordinator receives a request to marshal a transaction to a different appdomain or process.

> **Note** SQL Server 2000 connections are always promoted to MS DTC, and SQL CLR connections inside a *System.Transactions.TransactionScope* are promoted to MS DTC even if only one of them is enlisted in the transaction scope.

With a good theory and a common terminology on our side, next we'll look at the support for distributed transactions in SQL Server 2005 and the .NET Framework in general.

Distributed Transactions in SQL Server 2005

SQL Server 2005 supports distributed transactions using the *BEGIN DISTRIBUTED TRANSACTION* T-SQL statement. This statement requests the start of a T-SQL distributed transaction managed by the MS DTC. It uses the following syntax:

```
BEGIN DISTRIBUTED { TRAN | TRANSACTION }
    [ transaction_name | @tran_name_variable ]
```

The easiest way to enlist remote instances of the database engine in a distributed transaction is to execute a distributed query that references a linked server. For instance, you can link ServerB and execute a query that looks like this:

```
DELETE FROM ServerB.TestDB.TestTable Where TestID = 1
```

Enlisting the previous query in a distributed transaction is rather simple:

```
BEGIN DISTRIBUTED TRANSACTION
  DELETE TestDB.TestTable WHERE TestID = 1
  DELETE ServerB.TestDB.TestTable WHERE TestID = 1
COMMIT
```

The obvious shortcoming of this implementation is that the second query has no way to explicitly enlist. This might seem trivial, but if the second query is a stored procedure that calls ServerC, which in turn calls ServerD, all of them will be tied up in one really expensive transaction, all managed by the one MS DTC on the initiating server.

You can get around this issue by configuring the default behavior to not promote linked server queries to MS DTC. You can do this in two ways. First, you can do it at the server level, by using the following T-SQL command:

```
sp_configure remote proc trans 0
```

Or you can do it at the connection level, by using the following syntax:

```
SET REMOTE_PROC_TRANSACTIONS OFF
```

You can then use *BEGIN TRANSACTION* and have the database engine manage the transactions for you. Conversely, if you use a setting of *1* or *ON*, a *BEGIN TRANSACTION* statement involving linked servers will then involve MS DTC—but this is an all-or-nothing approach.

Distributed Transactions in the .NET Framework

The concept of distributed transactions was not introduced with the .NET Framework. Prior to the .NET Framework, you could enlist in distributed transactions using third-party transactions coordinators such as COMTI or solutions such as COM+ or MTS (Microsoft Transaction Server) to enlist in distributed transactions. Starting with the .NET Framework 1.0, you could use the *System.EnterpriseServices* namespace to enlist within a distributed transaction.

The problem with *EnterpriseServices*-based solutions was that you had to implement your operation as a class library, decorate it with the *TransactionOption* attribute, strongly name it, and register it in the global assembly cache (GAC). This made debugging and deployment difficult. Also, the *TransactionOption* attribute hardcoded the transactional behavior of your operation to one of the following values:

- **Disabled** Does not participate in transactions. This is the default value.
- **NotSupported** Runs outside of the context of a transaction.
- **Supported** Participates in a transaction if one exists. If one doesn't exist, the operation will not request or create one.
- **Required** Requires a transaction. If no transaction exists, one is created. If one exists, the operation enlists itself in the transaction.
- **RequiresNew** Requires a transaction and creates a new transaction for itself.

You really couldn't enlist on demand in the .NET Framework 1.0, and debugging and deployment were difficult. .NET Framework 1.1 offered a slightly better solution, which was made possible by the *ServiceConfig* class, as shown in Listing 11-3.

Listing 11-3 Using the *ServiceConfig* class

```
ServiceConfig config = new ServiceConfig();
config.Transaction = TransactionOption.Required;
ServiceDomain.Enter(config);
```

```
try
{
    // SqlConnections will auto enlist in the transaction.
}
catch
{
    ContextUtil.SetAbort();
}
finally
{
    ServiceDomain.Leave();
}
```

This solution did not require you to register your assembly in the GAC or even strongly name it, but unfortunately it was limited to Windows 2003 and Windows XP with Service Pack 2. In addition, you couldn't use concepts such as promotable enlistment. Thus, the .NET Framework 2.0 introduced a new namespace called *System.Transactions* to address all of these issues.

Let's look at the behavior of a *System.Transactions*-based transaction by creating an example. We will set up two databases and execute one query on each. (You can find this example in the companion content under the DistributedTrans example.)

1. Set up two databases, Test1 and Test2. Create a table called FromTable in Test1 and a table called ToTable in Test2, both of them with one column called Amount (INT). Insert a row in the FromTable table with the value 100 and a row in the ToTable table with the value 0. The following T-SQL script sets up the databases for you.

   ```sql
   CREATE DATABASE Test1
   GO
   USE Test1
   GO
   CREATE TABLE FromTable (Amount INT)
   GO
   INSERT INTO FromTable(Amount) VALUES (100)
   GO

   CREATE DATABASE Test2
   GO
   USE Test2
   GO
   CREATE TABLE ToTable (Amount INT)
   GO
   INSERT INTO ToTable(Amount) VALUES (0)
   GO
   ```

2. Create a Console Application and name it DistributedTrans. Add the necessary references to *System.Data* (if necessary) and *System.Transactions*. Add the necessary *using*

statements to reference *System.Data*, *System.Data.SqlClient*, and *System.Transactions*, as shown here:

```
using System;
using System.Data;
using System.Data.SqlClient;
using System.Transactions;
```

3. The aim of this example is to execute two queries, one on each database. One query will subtract 50 from the Test1 FromTable, and the other will add 50 to the Test2 ToTable. Both operations must be bound within the same transaction. We can do this easily by using the following code snippet. (Don't worry if you don't understand it just yet—we will slice and dice the code shortly.) Note that in the code we are using the *connStr1*, *connStr2*, *cmdText1*, and *cmdText2* string variables to hold the necessary connection strings and commands. This helps us keep the code presentable and clean. You can find the actual values of these variables in the companion content, which you can download from *http://www.microsoft.com/mspress/companion/0-7356-1923-9/*.

```
using (TransactionScope tsc = new TransactionScope())
{
    using (SqlConnection conn1 = new SqlConnection(connStr1))
    {
        SqlCommand cmd1 = conn1.CreateCommand();
        cmd1.CommandText = cmdText1;
        conn1.Open();
        cmd1.ExecuteNonQuery();
    }

    // Operation #1 is done, going to Operation #2

    using (SqlConnection conn2 = new SqlConnection(connStr2))
    {
        SqlCommand cmd2 = conn2.CreateCommand();
        cmd2.CommandText = cmdText2;
        conn2.Open();
        cmd2.ExecuteNonQuery();
    }
    tsc.Complete();
}
```

4. Run the code. Notice that *cmd1* and *cmd2*, which hold command texts *cmdText1* and *cmdText2*, respectively, run in a distributed transaction. If the second query fails, the first one will automatically roll back.

It's really that simple. Of course, more complicated implementations are possible, but the basic process of implementing a distributed transaction using *System.Transaction* is really that easy. Now let's take a closer look at the code we just wrote.

At the beginning of the code snippet is a *using* block:

```
using (TransactionScope tsc = new TransactionScope())
{
  // ...Do transactional operations here...
}
```

The *using* block ensures that a dispose is always called on the *TransactionScope* instance *tsc*. The instantiation of a *TransactionScope* starts a new transaction; *Dispose* is called when the distributed transaction is committed. Thus, within the *using* block, any RM will attempt to enlist itself in the current running transaction.

Also, as you might have noticed, the process of executing a query on the database is implemented in regular ADO.NET code.

```
using (SqlConnection conn1 = new SqlConnection(connStr1))
{
    SqlCommand cmd1 = conn1.CreateCommand();
    cmd1.CommandText = cmdText1;
    conn1.Open();
    cmd1.ExecuteNonQuery();
}
```

The magic here is that the *SqlConnection* instance *conn1* knows that it is working inside a *TransactionScope*. Therefore, it enlists itself with the appropriate transaction manager.

Notice that we said *appropriate transaction manager*, not MS DTC. This is because when an *SqlConnection* instance is connected with an SQL Server 2005 database, it exhibits PSPE–that is, the transaction is managed by LTM and not MS DTC until the *conn2.Open* statement is called.

In the code snippet, right at *conn2.Open*, set a breakpoint and run the application again. When the breakpoint is reached, check for the following value:

```
Transaction.Current.TransactionInformation.DistributedIdentifier.ToString()
```

While still in debug mode, execute the *conn2.Open* statement and check this value again. What do you see? You will see that right before *conn2* is opened, the value is a null GUID:

```
"00000000-0000-0000-0000-000000000000"
```

Right after *conn2.Open* is executed, this value changes to a not null GUID, similar to the following:

```
"d9534b03-f9b7-4d3f-812e-dc6272e184ff "
```

If right now you went to Control Panel, under Administrative Tools, Component Services, and looked up the Transaction List, you would notice the very same GUID in the current running transaction list (Figure 11-1).

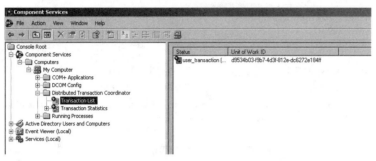

Figure 11-1   The current active transaction being managed by MS DTC

What this tells you is that right before *conn2.Open* was executed, the transaction was being managed by the LTM and hence didn't have a valid *DistributedIdentifier*. But as soon as the second RM enlisted in the transaction, the transaction was bumped up to MS DTC and got a valid *DistributedIdentifier*. If you were to run this same code sample against an SQL Server 2000 database, the *DistributedIdentifier* would have a valid value right after *conn1.Open* executes, thus proving that *SqlConnection* enlists durably when connecting with an SQL Server 2000 database and exhibits PSPE when connecting with an SQL Server 2005 database.

However, it could be argued that why do we have a whole new namespace when you could easily achieve the same thing through the T-SQL statement *BEGIN DISTRIBUTED TRANSACTION*? It is important to realize that *System.Transactions* gives a much more flexible architecture in which you can logically choose to enlist or not, and it deals with more than just database transactions. You can theoretically write an RM that encapsulates any operation in a transactional manner. Next we'll look at an example to understand that better.

Writing Your Own Resource Manager

It is only reasonable to expect that because databases are the most critical part of the architecture, they have had fantastic transactional support for a long time. But don't you want your other, non-database operations to be transactional as well?

Let's consider the simple operation of setting a value to an integer, and wrapping that as a part of a transaction. The first question is, how do you set a value for an integer?

```
int myInt;
myInt = 10;
```

Unfortunately, wrapping the previous code in a *TransactionScope* won't make it transactional. This is because *System.Int32* is not smart enough to understand that it is being wrapped inside a *TransactionScope* and that it should auto-enlist within a running transaction. This is probably a good thing because in the event of a rollback, to perform a graceful recovery *System.Int32* would have to maintain a previous version. You probably wouldn't want to pay this overhead in every circumstance. So we need to write a class that allows us to maintain enough history in the event of a rollback. This class should also be able to interact with a transaction manager and listen for various two-phase commit notifications. To do so, this class, or the RM you are writing, must implement the *IEnlistmentNotification* interface. This interface requires you to implement certain methods that are called at the appropriate moments by the transaction coordinator during the two phases of a two-phase commit process.

Here are the methods that *IEnlistmentNotification* requires you to implement:

- **Commit**   Notifies the RM that the transaction has been committed. The RM then makes the changes permanent.

- **Rollback**   Notifies the RM that the transaction has been rolled back. The RM then reverts to the previous stable state.

- **Prepare**   Called during the first (prepare) phase of a distributed transaction—when the transaction manager asks the participants whether they are ready to commit. If the TM receives a successful notification from each participating RM, it calls the *Commit* methods.

- **InDoubt**   Notifies the RMs if the TM loses contact with one or more participants in the transaction. In this situation, the status of the transaction is unknown and the application logic must decide whether to revert to the previous consistent state or remain in an inconsistent state.

Listing 11-4 puts all of these concepts into actual code. It shows a full implementation of a volatile RM. You can also find this code in the YourOwnRM solution in the companion content.

Listing 11-4   Implementing your own resource manager

```
public class VolatileRM : IEnlistmentNotification
{
    private string whoAmI = "";
    public VolatileRM(string WhoAmI)
    {
        whoAmI = WhoAmI;
    }

    private int memberValue = 0;
    private int oldMemberValue = 0;
    public int MemberValue
    {
        get { return memberValue; }
        set
        {
            Transaction currentTx = Transaction.Current;
            if (currentTx != null)
```

```
            {
                Console.WriteLine(
                    whoAmI + ": MemberValue setter - EnlistVolatile");
                currentTx.EnlistVolatile(this, EnlistmentOptions.None);
            }
            oldMemberValue = memberValue;
            memberValue = value;
        }
    }

    #region IEnlistmentNotification Members
    public void Commit(Enlistment enlistment)
    {
        Console.WriteLine(whoAmI + ": Commit");
        // Clear out oldMemberValue
        oldMemberValue = 0;
        enlistment.Done();
    }

    public void InDoubt(Enlistment enlistment)
    {
        Console.WriteLine(whoAmI + ": InDoubt");
        enlistment.Done();
    }

    public void Prepare(PreparingEnlistment preparingEnlistment)
    {
        Console.WriteLine(whoAmI + ": Prepare");
        preparingEnlistment.Prepared();
    }

    public void Rollback(Enlistment enlistment)
    {
        Console.WriteLine(whoAmI + ": Rollback");
        // Restore previous state
        memberValue = oldMemberValue;
        oldMemberValue = 0;
        enlistment.Done();
    }
    #endregion
}
```

Let's examine this code more closely. At the very top, we define a class that implements *IEnlistmentNotification*.

```
public class VolatileRM : IEnlistmentNotification
{
    private string whoAmI = "";
    public VolatileRM(string WhoAmI)
    {
        whoAmI = WhoAmI;
    }
    ...
}
```

This signifies that our RM will receive notifications from the current transaction manager. Note that we are also passing in a variable called *whoAmI* to the RM's constructor. This will be incredibly valuable for our understanding of the chain of events via the trace, when we have more than one RM involved.

Next we have a member variable by the name of *memberValue*.

```
private int memberValue = 0;
private int oldMemberValue = 0;
public int MemberValue
{
    get { return memberValue; }
    set
    { ... }
}
```

Note another variable called *oldMemberValue*. The whole point of writing this class is because *System.Int32* is unable to interact with an RM or maintain historical values in the event of a rollback. The *oldMemberValue* variable holds the historical value that we would use in the event of a rollback.

With the class and its data set up, the rest of the details involve hooking up implementation so that we can enlist in a current running transaction with the RM and perform the appropriate actions based on the notifications received.

The set clause of the *MemberValue* property enlists in the currently running transaction.

```
private int memberValue = 0;
private int oldMemberValue = 0;
public int MemberValue
{
    get { return memberValue; }
    set
    {
        Transaction currentTx = Transaction.Current;
        if (currentTx != null)
        {
            Console.WriteLine(
                whoAmI + ": MemberValue setter - EnlistVolatile");
            currentTx.EnlistVolatile(this, EnlistmentOptions.None);
        }
        oldMemberValue = memberValue;
        memberValue = value;
    }
}
```

As you can see, we first try to find the current transaction in the *Transaction.Current* variable, and then we use the *EnlistVolatile* method to enlist in the current transaction in a volatile manner. Volatile enlistment is sufficient for this example. If we were working with a durable resource, we would call the *EnlistDurable* method instead. Finally, in this method we perform the actual business logic of assigning the new value and preserving the older value.

The second important part of receiving appropriate notifications from the TM and notifying the TM of the current status is implemented in the four methods that the *IEnlistmentNotification* interface requires you to implement. The TM calls the appropriate methods (*Commit*, *Rollback*, *Prepare*, and *InDoubt*) for you and passes in a *System.Transactions.Enlistment* variable as a parameter. After successfully performing each step, you should call the *enlistment.Done()* method to indicate that this step has done its work.

The only exception to this rule is the *Prepare* method, which receives a special kind of *Enlistment*, a *System.Transactions.PreparingEnlistment* variable, as a parameter, which inherits from the *System.Transactions.Enlistment* class. *PreparingEnlistment* adds a few methods to *Enlistment*:

- **ForceRollBack() or ForceRollBack(Exception)**   Notifies the TM that an error has occurred and that the current participating RM wants to issue a rollback. You can specify your own exception if you want.

- **Prepared**   Notifies the transaction manager that this RM has successfully finished doing its part of the transaction (the prepare phase of the two-phase commit process).

- **byte[] RecoveryInformation**   Used to specify information to the TM in the event of reenlistment to perform a graceful recovery (in situations such as the RM crashing). Alternatively, you can call the base class method *Done* so you can act as an innocent bystander and observe the transaction but not really participate in it. If you call *Done* in the prepare phase, the TM skips notifying the RM of the second (commit) phase of a two-phase notification process.

With our business operation wrapped inside an RM, using the RM in a transaction becomes really simple. This RM can participate in transactional code in a number of ways, as we'll discuss next.

Using a Resource Manager in a Successful Transaction

Using the resource manager in transactional code is rather simple. You just wrap it in a *TransactionScope*, as shown here:

```
VolatileRM vrm = new VolatileRM("RM1");
Console.WriteLine("Member Value:" + vrm.MemberValue);

using (TransactionScope tsc = new TransactionScope())
{
    vrm.MemberValue = 3;
    tsc.Complete();
}
Console.WriteLine("Member Value:" + vrm.MemberValue);
```

When you run this code, you should see the output shown in Figure 11-2.

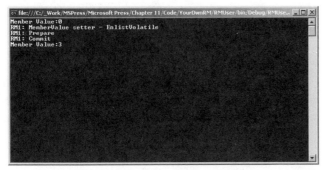

Figure 11-2 Our resource manager participating in a successful transaction

As you can see, our resource manager enlists in the prepare and commit phases of the two-phase commit process.

Using the Resource Manager When the Caller Issues a Rollback

Now we'll modify the code and comment out the *tsc.Complete()* statement and then run the application again. You should see the output shown in Figure 11-3.

Figure 11-3 Our resource manager participating in a transaction when the caller issues a rollback

By commenting out the *tsc.Complete()* statement, we are simulating a circumstance in which the application that uses the resource managers enforces a rollback. Instead of calling the prepare and commit phases, the code calls the rollback phase, and the final value of the member variable is unchanged from the original value.

Using the Resource Manager When It Issues a Rollback

Now we'll go ahead and put *tsc.Complete* back in the code and modify the *Prepare* method of the resource manager.

```
public void Prepare(PreparingEnlistment preparingEnlistment)
{
    Console.WriteLine(whoAmI + ": Prepare");
    // preparingEnlistment.Prepared();
    preparingEnlistment.ForceRollback();
}
```

Comment out the *Prepare* method call and put in a *ForceRollBack* call instead. The resource manager now issues a rollback. When we execute the application with *tsc.Complete* in place, we should see an exception, as shown in Figure 11-4.

Figure 11-4   An exception caused because the resource manager itself issued a rollback

Using the Resource Manager with Another Resource Manager

Now we'll change the *Prepare* method of our resource manager back to its original state so that a rollback isn't issued. Back in the caller application, we'll modify the original code to include a second resource manager participating in the same transaction, as shown here:

```
VolatileRM vrm = new VolatileRM("RM1");
VolatileRM vrm2 = new VolatileRM("RM2");
Console.WriteLine("Member Value 1:" + vrm.MemberValue);
Console.WriteLine("Member Value 2:" + vrm2.MemberValue);

using (TransactionScope tsc = new TransactionScope())
{
    ...
    vrm.MemberValue = 3;
    vrm2.MemberValue = 5;
    tsc.Complete();
}

Console.WriteLine("Member Value 1:" + vrm.MemberValue);
Console.WriteLine("Member Value 2:" + vrm2.MemberValue);
```

As you can see, the code simply enlists another instance of the resource manager we wrote in the same transaction. When this code is executed, we get the output shown in Figure 11-5.

Figure 11-5   Two instances of our resource manager in a single transaction

As you can see, when multiple resource managers are involved in the transaction, the appropriate prepare, commit, or rollback phases are called for each resource manager in succession. As an exercise, you could modify the resource manager code to include a *ForceRollBack* and see the succession of events if one of the resource managers issues a *RollBack* to the entire transaction.

We've saved the best part for last. Remember that *SqlConnection* is nothing but an RM, so you can retry this experiment with an instance of *SqlConnection*, a *SqlCommand*, and a database query executed within the same transaction that *VolatileRM* is enlisted in. To do so, modify the code to match this:

```
VolatileRM vrm = new VolatileRM("RM1");
Console.WriteLine("Member Value:" + vrm.MemberValue);

using (TransactionScope tsc = new TransactionScope())
{
    vrm.MemberValue = 3;

    using (SqlConnection conn1 = new SqlConnection(connStr))
    {
        SqlCommand cmd1 = conn1.CreateCommand();
        cmd1.CommandText = cmdText;
        conn1.Open();
        cmd1.ExecuteNonQuery();
    }
    tsc.Complete();
}

Console.WriteLine("Member Value:" + vrm.MemberValue);
```

By doing so, you would note that our *VolatileRM* now participates in the same transaction that a database query has enlisted itself in. This is something that *BEGIN DISTRIBUTED TRANSCTION* cannot do because by its very nature it talks to database queries, which cannot perform non-database operations (unless, of course, you are using SQL CLR, where things get a bit blurry).

Transactions in SQL CLR (CLR Integration)

No chapter on transactions is complete without a discussion of transactions in SQL CLR. Transactions behave so differently in the SQL CLR that this topic warrants its own section.

So far we have discussed local transactions in SQL Server and ADO.NET, as well as distributed transactions in ADO.NET, SQL Server, and the .NET Framework in general. We noted that in PSPE a distributed transaction might not be distributed. Thus, the boundaries of what is distributed and what is not are already blurry. Well, in SQL CLR they are not only blurry, they are downright indistinct.

In Chapter 3, you learned about the basics of SQL CLR. We will build on the same concepts here, and we will write a simple SQL CLR stored procedure to demonstrate the behavior of SQL CLR objects in a surrounding transaction. The stored procedure we will use is simplistic. It will accept no parameters and will simply insert a row in the TestTable table. The code for this stored procedure is shown here:

```
[Microsoft.SqlServer.Server.SqlProcedure]
public static void InsertRow()
{
    using (SqlConnection contextConn =
        new SqlConnection("context connection = true"))
    {
        SqlCommand insertCmd = contextConn.CreateCommand();
        insertCmd.CommandText =
            "INSERT INTO TestTable(TestColumn) VALUES(100)";
        contextConn.Open();
        insertCmd.ExecuteNonQuery();
        contextConn.Close();
    }
}
```

As you can see, the code uses a context connection to execute an *SqlCommand*. The *SqlCommand* inserts a row in TestTable using a simple *INSERT* command. This SQL CLR stored procedure, once registered with SQL Server 2005, can be executed using the following T-SQL command:

```
EXEC InsertRow
```

As you can see, if you have a matching TestTable in the appropriate database, executing the stored procedure will indeed insert a row.

But what if we wrap this line of T-SQL code inside a *BEGIN TRANSACTION/ROLLBACK* block?

```
BEGIN TRANSACTION
  INSERT INTO TestTable(TestColumn) VALUES (200)
  EXEC InsertRow
ROLLBACK
```

Interestingly, the row that the *InsertRow* stored procedure would have inserted is rolled back. Thus, the *InsertRow* stored procedure can successfully enlist within a calling transaction.

Important An SQL CLR object automatically enlists within a current running transaction.

You can easily issue a rollback from T-SQL by using the *ROLLBACK* command. Can you do the same from an SQL CLR stored procedure? Luckily, due to the fantastic integration of *System .Transactions* with SQL Server transactions, you can access the current running transaction from right within SQL CLR and issue a rollback. You do this by simply modifying the SQL CLR stored procedure, as shown here:

```
[Microsoft.SqlServer.Server.SqlProcedure]
public static void InsertRow()
{
    using (SqlConnection contextConn =
        new SqlConnection("context connection = true"))
    {
        SqlCommand insertCmd = contextConn.CreateCommand();
        insertCmd.CommandText =
            "INSERT INTO TestTable(TestColumn) VALUES(100)";
        contextConn.Open();
        insertCmd.ExecuteNonQuery();
        contextConn.Close();
    }
    Transaction.Current.Rollback();
}
```

Now we'll modify the T-SQL block so it will attempt to commit, not roll back.

```
BEGIN TRANSACTION
    INSERT INTO TestTable(TestColumn) VALUES (200)
    EXEC InsertRow
COMMIT
```

Now when we attempt to execute this T-SQL code block, we'll see an exception message, albeit an ambiguous one, something along the lines of "Transaction is not allowed to roll back inside a user defined routine...." However, the overall effect is that the transaction is rolled back. It would be nice if Microsoft would provide a better error message in this circumstance, but either way the job gets accomplished. You would probably want to wrap such an error in a custom *BEGIN TRY...CATCH* or *try/catch/finally* block and throw a better error message.

Important An SQL CLR object is able to roll back a current running transaction with the help of *System.Transactions* integration.

So far, we have been using a context connection to insert a row in the database. Instead, let's change the connection string to the one shown here:

```
Data Source=RemoteMachine;Initial Catalog=OtherDB;Integrated Security=SSPI;
```

A subtle difference is introduced in the previous connection string. The T-SQL code we were executing connected to the Test database. In contrast, the new connection string connects to an entirely different database on an entirely different server. Now let's remove the *ROLLBACK* from the SQL CLR stored procedure and build and deploy it in the original database. Then we'll execute the following T-SQL code block:

```
BEGIN TRANSACTION
    INSERT INTO TestTable(TestColumn) VALUES (200)
    EXEC InsertRow
COMMIT
```

The transaction now spans two databases. In other words, SQL CLR was smart enough not only to understand that we were calling the SQL CLR object within a transaction, but also to promote that transaction to a distributed transaction because an external resource is involved. In fact, if we tried connecting to an Oracle database, it would still be enlisted within the same transaction. If you want to change this default behavior to not enlist within the same transaction, you can add *enlist=false* to the fully qualified connection string.

> **Important**   SQL CLR will attempt to enlist any external connections within the same transaction.

So far, we have been using *System.Transactions.Transaction.Current* to obtain a handle to the current transaction. The obvious question here is, what else could we use? Could we use *SqlTransaction*? Yes, we could definitely use *SqlTransaction*, and in that case we would use *SqlConnection.BeginTransaction* in a manner identical to non–SQL CLR ADO.NET. (We therefore won't cover it in depth here.)

The other approach, of course, is to use *System.Transactions.TransactionScope*. In fact, in most scenarios you probably don't want to deal with the current transaction using *Transaction.Current* directly. The only situations in which you'll want a direct handle on the transaction are the following:

- You want to roll back the external transaction by calling *Transaction.Current.Rollback*.

- You want to enlist resources that for some reason didn't auto-enlist. You can do so by using *Transaction.Current.EnlistVolatile* or *EnlistDurable*.

- You want to manually enlist in the current running transaction or modify the default behavior by explicitly listening for various callbacks in the two-phase commit process.

In all other cases, you probably want a more transparent method of writing transactional code, such as wrapping it in a *using* block so that everything is handled automatically, or using *TransactionScope*. This is easy to do by modifying your SQL CLR stored procedure code, as shown here:

```
[Microsoft.SqlServer.Server.SqlProcedure]
public static void InsertRow()
{
    using (TransactionScope tsc = new TransactionScope())
    {
        using (SqlConnection contextConn =
            new SqlConnection("context connection = true"))
        {
            SqlCommand insertCmd = contextConn.CreateCommand();
            insertCmd.CommandText =
                "INSERT INTO TestTable(TestColumn) VALUES(100)";
            contextConn.Open();
            insertCmd.ExecuteNonQuery();
            contextConn.Close();
        }
        tsc.Complete();
    }
}
```

Note that we are wrapping a context connection inside a *TransactionScope*. This is usually a bad practice, as you will find out soon. But if you have more than one database or RM involved in the transaction, *TransactionScope* will take care of enlisting everything in one transaction. The good part of this programming paradigm is that if there is already an active transaction, *TransactionScope* will take advantage of that transaction. If there is no active transaction, it will simply start a new transaction. This level of transparency helps you write more understandable and more manageable code.

Now let's comment out the *tsc.Complete()* statement from our SQL CLR stored procedure code, and then build and deploy the stored procedure on the SQL Server 2005 database again. Then we'll try running it in the transactional T-SQL code. We'll get the following error:

```
Msg 8520, Level 16, State 1, Line 4
Internal Microsoft Distributed Transaction Coordinator (MS DTC) transaction failed to
commit: 0x8004d019(XACT_E_ABORTED).
```

This is as expected; we didn't mark the *TransactionScope* as complete, and the transaction aborted. What is surprising here, though, is that the message is coming from MS DTC. We had only one database connection, the context connection, and yet the transaction was promoted. This brings us to the next important point about SQL CLR transactions.

> **Important**   When working inside SQL CLR in SQL Server 2005, the *TransactionScope* object will always cause the transaction to promote to MS DTC, even if you are using only context connections.

Therefore, if you're only going to use context connections, you should avoid using *Transaction-Scope* and stick with *SqlTransaction* or *System.Transactions.Transaction.Current*.

Putting It All Together

Let us end this chapter with one example that sums it all up. We'll take the SQL CLR stored procedure we wrote and call it from a console application. Inside the console application we will wrap the SQL CLR stored procedure and the resource manager we wrote earlier in the chapter in a single transaction, bound together with a single *System.Transactions.TransactionScope*.

Because we are using only a context connection in our SQL CLR stored procedure, let's follow the best practice of not using *TransactionScope* inside the SQL CLR stored procedure. The SQL CLR stored procedure should look like this:

```
[Microsoft.SqlServer.Server.SqlProcedure]
public static void InsertRow()
{
    using (SqlConnection contextConn =
        new SqlConnection("context connection = true"))
    {
        SqlCommand insertCmd = contextConn.CreateCommand();
        insertCmd.CommandText =
            "INSERT INTO TestTable(TestColumn) VALUES(100)";
        contextConn.Open();
        insertCmd.ExecuteNonQuery();
        contextConn.Close();
    }
}
```

Build and deploy the stored procedure to a SQL Server 2005 database. Create a console application called BigBang (you can find it in the companion content), and add references to *System.Transactions* and the the resource manager project from the YourOwnRM solution we wrote earlier in the chapter.

Now modify the code of the BigBang console application's entry-point *Main* method, as shown here:

```
static void Main(string[] args)
{
    string connStr =
        "Data Source=(local);Initial Catalog=Test1;Integrated Security=SSPI;";
    string cmdText = "InsertRow";
```

```
VolatileRM vrm = new VolatileRM("RM1");
Console.WriteLine("Member Value:" + vrm.MemberValue);

using (TransactionScope tsc = new TransactionScope())
{
    using (SqlConnection conn1 = new SqlConnection(connStr))
    {
        SqlCommand cmd1 = conn1.CreateCommand();
        cmd1.CommandText = cmdText;
        cmd1.CommandType = CommandType.StoredProcedure;
        conn1.Open();
        cmd1.ExecuteNonQuery();
    }
    vrm.MemberValue = 3;

    tsc.Complete();
}

Console.WriteLine("Member Value:" + vrm.MemberValue);
}
```

When we execute this application, we'll see output similar to that shown in Figure 11-6.

Figure 11-6   The BigBang example running

Also note that our transaction is not promoted to MS DTC. As an exercise, you should try add-ing more resource managers (say, another *SqlConnection*) or a non-context connection inside the SQL CLR stored procedure, try to run the procedure, and see the behavior of the code. *System.Transactions* transparently integrates all your operations between T-SQL, ADO.NET, and SQL CLR, and it promotes your transaction to MS DTC as necessary.

Summary

In this chapter, we covered the basic theory of transactions, which is probably one of the most important topics related to application architecture. You learned about transaction support in SQL Server 2005 and the supported isolation levels and their behavior. You also saw a side-by-side comparison with ADO.NET.

We also covered implementation of distributed transactions and the new support for writing transactional code that might have nothing to do with a database except that it might enlist in the same transaction as the database.

Finally, you learned about the transaction support and implementation in SQL CLR. You saw how the *SqlConnection* object takes advantage of both local transaction implementation and distributed transaction implementation as well as PSPE behavior when necessary.

Chapter 12

SQL Server Service Broker: The New Middleware

—William H. Zack

The new features in Microsoft SQL Server 2005 have generated a lot of excited chatter. One powerful enhancement, SQL Server Service Broker, has been all but eclipsed by the excitement over common language runtime (CLR) integration (which makes it possible to write stored procedures in languages such as Microsoft C# and Microsoft Visual Basic .NET) and the new Reporting Services. Service Broker is a new extension to SQL Server in the core SQL Server engine. It provides a great new way to implement database-oriented middleware and distributed database applications.

In this chapter, you will learn what the SQL Server Service Broker is and where it fits in the world of middleware. You will also learn how to define the database objects that support Service Broker and how to use Service Broker to implement distributed database applications.

What Is Middleware?

Middleware is a communications plumbing layer that allows applications to interact across a network. It connects applications that normally run on separate, possibly heterogeneous platforms, and passes data between them. These applications are normally free-running processes that execute independently such that the requesting application does not wait synchronously for a reply to be returned. Every middleware product has its own distinct application programming interface (API) that you use to take advantage of its services. For instance, in the Microsoft Windows world, we have message queuing middleware in the form of Microsoft Message Queuing Services (MSMQ), which is part of COM+, .NET Remoting, Web services, and Enterprise Services. In the IBM world, we have MQSeries, and other vendors have equivalent offerings. And now, as you will see in this chapter, we also have SQL Server Service Broker, which provides database-oriented middleware.

As we mentioned, each of these middleware products has its own API. Windows Communications Foundation (formerly called Indigo), which will be released in the next version of Microsoft .NET, will unify these APIs and allow you to change the underlying middleware transport by changing a configuration file (rather than having to modify the calling code). This will be a major improvement.

What Is SQL Server Service Broker?

Service Broker is a database application framework that lets internal or external database-related processes send and receive messages to each other. Service Broker uses extensions to Transact-SQL (T-SQL) and standard .NET programming languages to provide guaranteed, reliable asynchronous message delivery and confirmation between database endpoints.

Service Broker uses the SQL Server 2005 core engine and extensions to SQL Server triggers to implement this service. It also uses message queues that are defined by the developer and housed in the databases themselves. Using database-resident message queues provides quite a few advantages, such as transactional integrity.

Comparing Service Broker and MSMQ

MSMQ and Service Broker are often compared to each other. MSMQ is a part of Windows and comes free of charge. Service Broker requires SQL Server licenses at each endpoint. In MSMQ, message ordering is not guaranteed. It is the responsibility of application logic to keep track of the arrival sequence of messages and sort them out if the sequence is important.

MSMQ also requires the use of a two-phase commit protocol to perform distributed transactions. Because Service Broker is built into the SQL Server database, it performs transactional messaging faster and more efficiently than MSMQ. This is especially true in a message routing scenario involving encrypted messages, where MSMQ has to decrypt an entire message to route it on the next endpoint.

Furthermore, when you build an application that uses MSMQ, your processing logic and the data to be transferred are separate. With Service Broker, they are both inside of the database and protected by the standard database protection features, such as backup/recovery, mirroring, and failover. With MSMQ, this is an application responsibility.

One company that we know of has spent years implementing a middleware solution that allows automatic collection of external spreadsheet data that is used to update their distributed corporate databases. Service Broker eliminates much of this kind of work, or at least makes it a lot easier. It allows you to define messages, data queues, and dialogs between instances of SQL Server. Because these definitions reside within instances of SQL Server databases, Service Broker can take advantage of SQL Server's inherent transactional nature. Also, having everything implemented inside distributed SQL Server databases solves one of the more difficult problems in messaging—guaranteeing that a message sent from one endpoint to another is delivered to the receiving endpoint once and only once. Service Broker guarantees ordered, one-time, asynchronous delivery of messages. Few other messaging systems (including MSMQ) can make this claim.

What Is a SQL Server Service Broker Application?

SQL Server Service Broker supports the development of distributed database application programs. These programs are called *service programs*. In the context of Service Broker, a service program can be either a SQL Server stored procedure defined in the target database or an external program started by some event outside of SQL Server, such as a scheduled task. From here on in this chapter, we will use the term *service program* unless it is necessary to distinguish between a stored procedure and an externally activated program.

Any program that can communicate with SQL Server can originate a Service Broker request. This can be a stored procedure written using T-SQL or a .NET language. It can also be an external application program communicating with the database using ADO.NET. When a program wants to send a message to a service program, the program at the originating location simply invokes a local stored procedure that is defined by the database administrator (DBA). The stored procedure then issues a send request containing the message to be sent. The originating Service Broker subsequently puts this message in a local database queue for sending and returns control to the sending program. Later, the sending Service Broker retrieves the message from the queue and sends it to the Service Broker at the receiving location.

At the receiving location, several things happen. First the receiving Service Broker places the message in a queue at that site. If the service program is a stored procedure and that procedure is actively waiting for incoming messages, it can dequeue the message, process it, and optionally send a reply to the originator. If the stored procedure is not active, an incoming message can start it. If the rate of message arrival is higher than a single instance of the stored procedure can handle, multiple instances of the stored procedure are started to handle the backlog of messages that need processing. These additional message-processing procedures can be written to terminate after a program-determined interval during which no new messages have arrived. This automatic startup and termination provides a high level of scalability. Now let's take a look at the architecture that makes this possible.

Service Broker Architecture

A set of new data definition language (DDL) and data manipulation language (DML) statements have been added to T-SQL to define and manage Service Broker's messaging process. Figure 12-1 shows the Service Broker architecture. Service Broker includes several new terms and entities that define and manage the message-brokering process. All of these entities are objects in the database and as such are subject to all the security and protection features of other database objects.

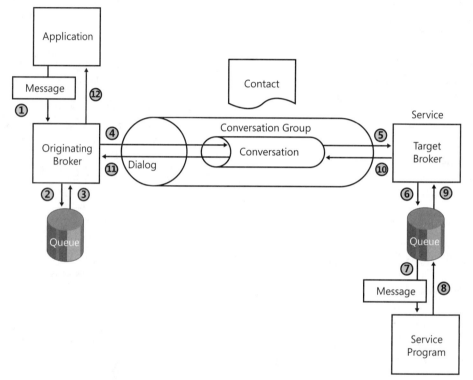

Figure 12-1   Service Broker architecture

The Service Broker objects are listed below.

 Note   We will be accepting a lot of defaults in the examples in this chapter. Each one of the Service Broker DDL statements has a large number of options, which you should investigate using for any real application. For a complete listing of all the options, you can refer to SQL Server Books Online, which covers every DML and DDL statement and option in great detail.

- **Contract**   Defines the types of messages that can be sent and received. It also specifies the specific messages that each endpoint can use. A contract is defined in T-SQL as in the following example:

```
CREATE CONTRACT [PickListContract]
  (
     [PickListRequest] SENT BY INITIATOR,
     [PickListResponse] SENT BY TARGET);
```

A contract includes references to the message types that can be sent and received between the initiating and sending Service Broker instances.

- **Message type**   A message type defines the data that a program can send and receive. A message type definition includes a unique message type identifier as well as a description of the data to be transferred in the body of the message. Messages can contain binary data, valid XML, and even XML that adheres to a specific XML schema. In the latter case, one helpful feature of the Service Broker architecture is that Service Broker will throw an error if the XML in the message does not match the referenced schema or is otherwise invalid in any way.

A message type is defined in T-SQL using the following statement:

```
CREATE MESSAGE TYPE [PicklistRequest]
    VALIDATION = NONE;
```

The *VALIDATION = NONE* clause is the simplest of formats. When used, it simply tells Service Broker to treat the message data as a binary stream and not to apply any validation rules to that data.

- **Dialog**   A dialog is a one-way or two-way message interaction that involves data sent between two endpoints. These endpoints can be located in multiple SQL Server databases in any accessible SQL Server instance.

A dialog lasts from the time the sending Service Broker receives the request and creates the dialog until no more messages remain for the receiving Service Broker to process or until an error occurs. Dialogs can be long-lived, lasting days, hours, or even years, or they can be short-lived and measured in seconds.

One of the difficult problems in messaging is guaranteeing that a message sent from one endpoint to another is delivered to the receiving endpoint once and only once. Service Broker guarantees ordered, one-time, asynchronous delivery of messages. Other messaging systems that operate outside of SQL Server cannot make this claim.

A dialog also supports *atomic* failure semantics. Service Broker transactions across multiple endpoints are atomic in that a failure at any point causes both endpoints to be notified of the failure and the entire transaction to be rolled back. The net result of this process is that when an error occurs, Service Broker puts messages that have been removed for processing back in the queue for later processing.

The following statement shows how to create a dialog.

```
DECLARE @ConversationHandle uniqueidentifier;
  BEGIN DIALOG CONVERSATION @ConversationHandle
    FROM SERVICE [SalesOfficeService]
    TO SERVICE 'WarehouseService'
    ON CONTRACT [PicklistContract]
  WITH ENCRYPTION = OFF;
  SEND ON CONVERSATION @ConversationHandle
    MESSAGE TYPE  [PicklistRequest] (@Message);
```

> **Note** A dialog ties together the conversation, contract, service program identifier, and the initiating message type to be used in the dialog. Also note that *@Message* in the statement defines the procedure variable that will receive the actual message data.

Unlike the DDL statements covered so far, this is a DML statement, and as such it is executed at run time. A dialog is created during processing using a T-SQL statement that ties together a conversation ID with information about all the services, contracts, and message types involved in the dialog. Dialogs are also very lightweight and persistent.

■ **Conversation** A conversation is a long-running, reliable, asynchronous exchange of messages between two endpoints. A conversation can involve multiple dialogs. Just as messages are the building blocks of dialogs, multiple dialogs can be grouped together into conversations when they are defined. *BEGIN DIALOG* always returns a conversation handle that can be used in subsequent requests.

■ **Conversation group** A conversation group is a related group of dialogs that perform some set of related tasks, normally implementing a business function. An example is the order fulfillment process after an order is accepted by an order entry application. Every conversation is part of a conversation group. A conversation group can contain conversations with multiple Service Broker instances. This allows the developer to create applications with a high degree of parallelism.

The originating Service Broker assigns each conversation group a conversation group ID (CGID). This CGID is a globally unique ID (GUID) that can be used by the receiving procedure as a database table key if it needs to maintain any kind of application state related to the processing of multiple messages. If maintaining state is a requirement, the database is the natural place to store this state information.

From the standpoint of the database, a conversation group defines a grouping of conversations that, in turn, define a logical unit of work that can be completed or rolled back by Service Broker as a unit. Our order entry example has three separate subsystems: order entry, order billing, and order shipping. Using the Service Broker architecture, you can accept and validate an order with the customer on the phone. Then you can engage in a dialog with both the Billing and the Shipping subsystems in parallel and asynchronously. When each of these processes is completed, you can send response messages back to the order entry subsystem indicating that the whole transaction is complete and that it can be committed by SQL Server.

■ **Queue** Service Broker uses both send and receive queues to protect the end-to-end integrity of messages and ensure one-time, in-order delivery of messages. Queues store messages at the originating site before transmission and at the destination site before they are read by the target service program.

The following example shows the minimum DDL that can be used to create a queue.

```
CREATE QUEUE [WarehouseQueue];
```

The *CREATE QUEUE* definition can also specify whether the service program is to be automatically initiated when messages arrive and how many instances will be started to handle peak loads.

■ **Service program** Service programs are responsible for writing and/or reading messages in the queue. Service programs run under control of a Service Broker that runs in each SQL Server 2005 instance. As we discussed earlier, a service program can be either a stored procedure in the target database or an external program. An incoming message can activate a service program, or the program can be started by some event external to SQL Server.

In T-SQL, you can define a service program as shown in the following example. Note that a service program is associated with a queue and a contract.

```
CREATE SERVICE [WarehouseService]
   ON QUEUE [WarehouseQueue]
   (PickListContract);
```

Integrated Management and Operation

One of the major benefits of the Service Broker architecture is that the management and operation of the messaging system is integrated within the database. Thus, when you are backing up and or recovering the database or you are transporting the database to another system, the state of the queues and the application automatically travels with the database. The same procedures that protect the integrity of the database can protect the queues. This means that the queues are backed up, recovered, and restarted along with the database data. This integration with the database automatically takes advantage of advanced database features such as log shipping, database mirroring, and failover. Note that this feature is not natively present in other middleware such as MSMQ, where you have to implement your own failover and mirroring features. With Service Broker, you get this essentially for free.

Routing and Load Balancing

Although conversations and dialogs move messages between two Service Broker instances, this does not mean that there cannot be one or more intermediate Service Broker instances involved in the process. For example, the originating Service Broker (SB1) in Figure 12-2 sends a message to the receiving Service Broker (SB4). This message can actually pass through one or more intermediate Service Broker instances before reaching the target Service Broker.

Figure 12-2   Service Broker routing

Figure 12-2 illustrates an originating and target Service Broker that are separated by intermediate Service Broker instances. Each Service Broker instance contains routing logic to determine the next Service Broker location to be used to route the message to its final destination.

The advantage of this architecture over classic message-handling architectures is that the Service Broker instances can route encrypted data to the next Service Broker in a chain without having to fully decrypt and re-encrypt the data in transit. An external messaging system such as MSMQ, in contrast, must decrypt, analyze, and re-encrypt the message before forwarding it at each intermediate point. The ability to route encrypted data through intermediate Service Broker instances without decryption and re-encryption makes the Service Broker solution efficient and improves performance.

You can also use Service Broker to improve scalability by implementing load balancing. You can define multiple target service programs and spread the load across them.

The diagram in Figure 12-3 represents an originating Service Broker (SB1) and three target Service Broker instances (SB2 through SB4) that can all process the same messages. The originating program does not need to know anything about the physical location of the target service programs because all location dependencies are defined in the respective database instances. The originator simply engages in logical conversations between endpoints. Service Broker and the defined Service Broker objects take care of the details.

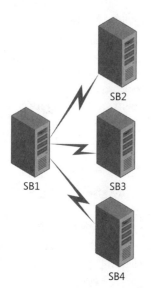

Figure 12-3   Service Broker load balancing

Service Broker Programming in T-SQL

A short programming example will help to illustrate how the messaging process works. Our example is an order entry application. To keep things as simple as possible, we will focus on the entry of an order in the order entry subsystem and the printing of a picklist at the warehouse as part of the order fulfillment process. (A *picklist* is a list of the order products and quantities sorted in warehouse location order so that they can be efficiently retrieved and packed for shipment.) Figure 12-4 illustrates the configuration of this application.

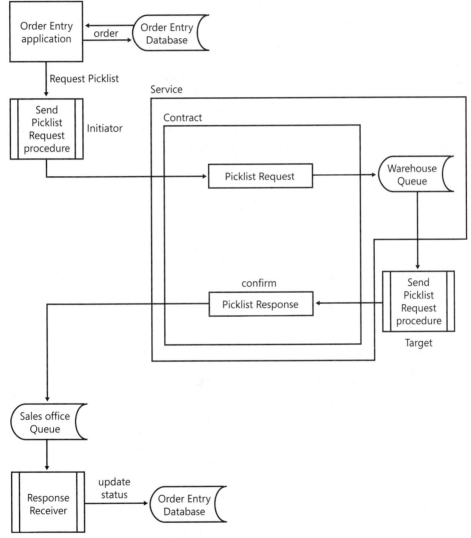

Figure 12-4   Order entry application

Our order entry application running at the sales office accepts orders and checks inventory interactively while a customer is still on the phone with an order entry clerk. When the order entry process is completed, the order must be sent to the warehouse for fulfillment processing. At the warehouse, a picklist is printed so that warehouse personnel can pick and pack the merchandise for shipment. After the picklist is printed, a confirming message is returned to the sales office to confirm that the picklist has been printed. This confirmation message is processed by another application participating in the process and is used to update the order status in the database.

A Word About Programming Languages

One of the most interesting new features implemented in SQL Server 2005 is the ability to host the .NET common language runtime. This makes it possible to code database stored procedures in high-level .NET languages such as C# and Visual Basic .NET in addition to T-SQL. In this part of the chapter, we decided to use T-SQL so you would not have to learn two new concepts at once. Bear in mind that you can also use .NET languages such as Visual Basic .NET and C# to develop Service Broker objects. If you are doing mostly data manipulation in your procedures, you will probably want to stick to using T-SQL anyway. If you are doing large amounts of complex calculations or making use of external non-database resources, you might want to use a .NET language instead.

Enabling Service Broker

Before you can use a Service Broker application, message delivery must be enabled for the database you are using. To do this, execute an *ALTER DATABASE* statement using the *ENABLE_BROKER* option as shown below.

```
ALTER DATABASE AdventureWorks SET ENABLE_BROKER
```

Defining Service Broker Objects

Before invoking any application code, you have to write the service programs, and a developer or database administrator has to set up database objects to define messages, dialogs, conversations, and conversation groups. These definitions have to be added to the SQL Server databases at the sending and receiving Service Broker locations.

All Service Broker–related objects must be defined in the databases at all endpoints that participate in the messaging application. You do this by using new DDL statements, in the same way that you define databases, tables, and other database objects. For instance, there are new *CREATE*, *MODIFY*, and *DROP* DDL statements for contracts, message types, queues, and other Service Broker–related objects.

The definition DDL for our application is shown in Listing 12-1. There are a large number of options you can specify in each DDL statement when you define your Service Broker objects.

In this chapter, we will talk about only a few of the most significant ones. Again, for a complete listing of all the options, you can refer to SQL Server Books Online, which covers every DML and DDL statement and option in great detail. The following should, however, be enough to give you a feel for how to define these objects.

Listing 12-1   Object creation DDL

```
-- Create Message Types
CREATE MESSAGE TYPE [PicklistRequest]
    VALIDATION = NONE;
CREATE MESSAGE TYPE [PicklistResponse]
    VALIDATION = NONE;

-- Create Contract
CREATE CONTRACT [PicklistContract]
    (
        [PicklistRequest] SENT BY INITIATOR,
        [PicklistResponse] SENT BY TARGET
    );

-- Create Queues
CREATE QUEUE [WarehouseQueue];
CREATE QUEUE [SalesOfficeQueue];

-- Create Services
CREATE SERVICE [WarehouseService]
    ON QUEUE [WarehouseQueue]
    (PicklistContract);
CREATE SERVICE [SalesOfficeService]
    ON QUEUE [SalesOfficeQueue];
```

This listing shows the DDL used to create the required Service Broker objects. It begins with a definition of the message types that will be used in the application. In our application, we have two message types, one for the picklist request message to be sent to the warehouse and one for a confirming picklist response message to be sent back to the sales office.

The *VALIDATION = NONE* clause in the *CREATE MESSAGE* statement used in Listing 12-1 is the simplest form that we can code when defining message types. We can use other forms to request that the queue accept only valid XML in the body of a message or even to validate the XML against a predefined XML schema. If the message data is not in the defined appropriate format, the Service Broker will throw an exception.

After defining the message types, we grouped them into a contract using the *CREATE CONTRACT* statement. The contract defines the message types that our application will use. These are, of course, the two message types we just defined.

The direction of message flow was defined by the *INITIATOR* and *TARGET* clauses in the *CREATE CONTRACT* statement. In our example, the picklist request message flows from the sales office to the warehouse, and the corresponding picklist response message flows from the warehouse back to the sales office.

To allow asynchronous processing of messages at the initiating and target sites, we needed to define two queues, a warehouse queue to accept the request messages at the warehouse and a sales office queue to receive the reply. We used two instances of the *CREATE QUEUE* statement to accomplish this.

> **Note**   In a real application, we would probably define our queues using an *Activation* clause so the appropriate service procedures (to be defined next) are activated automatically upon receipt of an incoming message. In our case, we will not do that because we want to be able to see the messages in the respective queues before we process them. With activation enabled, the messages in the warehouse queue would probably be processed and removed before we could see them in the queue.

Finally, we created the service program descriptions using the *CREATE SERVICE* statement to define the service programs at each endpoint. These service program descriptions defined the service name, queue name, and the contract to be used.

The Sending Service Program

At the sales office, our order entry application calls into a stored procedure to send the picklist request to the warehouse. At the warehouse, another stored procedure receives the request, processes it, and sends a response to the sales office. Because these are stored procedures, they must first be defined in the database. Listing 12-2 shows the sending procedure, and Listing 12-3 shows the receiving procedure.

Listing 12-2   Sending procedure

```
CREATE PROCEDURE SendPicklistRequest
   @Message NVARCHAR(MAX)
AS
SET NOCOUNT ON;
DECLARE @ConversationHandle UNIQUEIDENTIFIER
BEGIN TRANSACTION
BEGIN DIALOG CONVERSATION @ConversationHandle
   FROM SERVICE [SalesOfficeService]
   TO SERVICE 'WarehouseService'
   ON CONTRACT [PicklistContract]
WITH ENCRYPTION = OFF;
SEND ON CONVERSATION @ConversationHandle
    MESSAGE TYPE  [PicklistRequest] (@Message);
COMMIT TRANSACTION;
```

> **Note**   In the example above, the data type *NVARCHAR(MAX)* is one of the new data types defined in SQL Server 2005. You can read about these new data types in Chapter 2.

We will assume that the sending stored procedure is invoked from the order entry application. (For testing purposes, however, we will just invoke it with an *EXEC* T-SQL call and pass it a simple message to process; this is sufficient to show the messages as they move from queue to queue and procedure to procedure.)

The sending procedure started with the declaration of a conversation handle using a *DECLARE* statement. This is the conversation handle that will uniquely identify the conversation. Next it began a transaction (with *BEGIN TRANSACTION*) and then opened the dialog with the warehouse service using *BEGIN DIALOG* to specify the originating and target service program and the predefined contract.

Following the start of the dialog, the sending procedure sent the picklist request message to the warehouse service via Service Broker using the *SEND ON CONVERSATION* statement.

Finally, the sending procedure committed the transaction and ended. All subsequent processing of the message occurred asynchronously, leaving the originating program to continue with other processing. Of course, if a response is expected eventually, it is up to the application to receive and process the response message at a later time as appropriate.

The Receiving Service Program

The warehouse picklist printing procedure is a bit more complex, as shown in Listing 12-3.

Listing 12-3   Receiving procedure

```
CREATE PROCEDURE ReceivePicklistRequest
AS
SET NOCOUNT ON;
DECLARE @ConversationHandle UNIQUEIDENTIFIER,
      @ConversationGroupID UNIQUEIDENTIFIER,
      @MessageBody NVARCHAR(2000),
      @MessageTypeName NVARCHAR(128);
BEGIN TRANSACTION;
RECEIVE TOP(1)
   @MessageTypeName = message_type_name,
   @ConversationHandle = conversation_handle,
   @MessageBody = message_body
      FROM WarehouseQueue;
DECLARE @Message AS NVARCHAR(MAX);
SET @Message = 'Message received: ' + @MessageBody;

-- Print Picklist, etc...

SEND ON CONVERSATION @ConversationHandle
   MESSAGE TYPE [PicklistResponse] (@Message);
END CONVERSATION @ConversationHandle;
COMMIT TRANSACTION;
```

At the receiving location, this service procedure was defined to process the picklist request and send back the response. In a real application, we would most likely define our queues to automatically activate the appropriate service procedure when a message arrives for that procedure in the appropriate queue. Our simple example defines our queues without activation so we can actually look into the warehouse and sales office queues at each step to see the messages being sent and received. The syntax of a queue definition with activation follows this format:

```
CREATE QUEUE <queue>
WITH
ACTIVATION (
            STATUS = ON,
              PROCEDURE_NAME = <procedure>,
              MAX_QUEUE_READERS = <max_readers>
);
```

You can see that the *CREATE QUEUE* statement allows us to specify activation information such as the activation status, the name of the procedure to be activated automatically, and the maximum number of queue readers that can be started to handle incoming message requests. It also allows some additional parameters that we do not have time to cover here.

In our example, the warehouse procedure began with a declaration of variables to hold the conversation handle, conversation group ID, message type name, and the message body itself.

Upon activation, the warehouse procedure attempted to receive a message from the input queue. In our example, we will activate this procedure manually. If the queue had been defined with activation enabled, the service program would know that at least one message was waiting for it in the queue and that message would be processed and then removed from the queue. The *RECEIVE TOP(1)* statement will receive the first message in the queue and return the conversation handle, conversation group ID, message type name, and message body. (As with all statements, there are additional optional parameters, such as a timeout limit, that you can also code.)

After processing the input message and formulating a reply, the warehouse service sends it back on the same conversation. Then it ends the conversation and commits the transaction. When it ends the conversation, a special Service Broker end-of-conversation message is sent to the queue at the other endpoint along with the reply message. This message has a message type name of *http://schemas.microsoft.com/SQL/ServiceBroker/EndDialog*. (Service Broker defines common messages with a URI. When you learn about Notification Services, you will see that Notification Services messages are also defined by URIs.)

Running the Application

To run our simple application, we will simply invoke the sending procedure with the statement *EXEC SendPicklistRequest @Message='Picklist Request'*. This sends the message to the warehouse queue. We can prove this by looking in the warehouse queue using the following *SELECT* statement:

```
SELECT conversation_handle, conversation_group_id, service_name, service_contract_name,
message_type_name
   FROM WarehouseQueue;
```

You can see that the warehouse queue has received a message, and you can also see some interesting columns in the queue record for the message. The results of this query are shown in Figure 12-5.

	conversation_handle	conversation_group_id	service_name	service_contract_name	message_type_name
	464e2b98-d1bb-4411-...	9251da6f-1ad2-47d5-9c...	WarehouseServi...	PicklistContract	PicklistRequest

Figure 12-5 A picklist request message in the warehouse queue

To see the actual message, issue the following query:

```
SELECT CAST(message_body AS NVARCHAR(MAX)) FROM WarehouseQueue;
```

The result of this query is shown in Figure 12-6. As you can see, the request message is clearly in the warehouse queue.

	(No column name)
1	Picklist Request

Figure 12-6 Picklist request message data

Next we want to receive and process the message at the warehouse and send a reply to the sales office. In our simple case, we will issue an *EXEC ReceivePicklistRequest* to invoke the receiving stored procedure. Then we can again look in the warehouse queue and see that the request message is gone. To look at the warehouse queue, we can issue the following query:

```
SELECT conversation_handle, conversation_group_id, service_name, service_contract_name,
message_type_name
   FROM WarehouseQueue;
```

The result of this query is shown in Figure 12-7. The queue is indeed empty.

	conversation_handle	conversation_group_id	service_name	service_contract_name	message_type_name

Figure 12-7 The warehouse queue after message processing

To look in the sales office queue, we can use the following query:

```
SELECT conversation_handle, conversation_group_id, service_name,
    service_contract_name, message_type_name
    FROM SalesOfficeQueue;
```

Figure 12-8 shows the message in the sales office queue.

	conversation_handle	conversation_group_id	service_name	service_contract_name	message_type_name
1	462759a2-ad54-4dad-8682-368785046514	8f7c409e-ebe5-43d3-b1...	SalesOfficeServi...	PicklistContract	PicklistResponse
2	462759a2-ad54-4dad-8682-368785046514	8f7c409e-ebe5-43d3-b1...	SalesOfficeServi...	PicklistContract	http://schemas.microsoft.com/SQL/ServiceBroker/EndDialog

Figure 12-8   The sales office queue after message receipt

We now see the confirmation message in the queue, and we can retrieve the value of the message body as we did before, with the following query:

```
SELECT CAST(message_body AS NVARCHAR(MAX)) FROM SalesOfficeQueue;
```

The results of this query are shown in Figure 12-9.

	(No column name)
1	Message received: Picklist Request
2	NULL

Figure 12-9   The sales office picklist confirmation message

Note that there is also an end-of-dialog message in the queue, which indicates that the other endpoint has ended the dialog.

A More Robust, Real-World Application

Our simple "hand-activated" application is useful for illustrating how Service Broker works and how messages flow between endpoints. In a more robust, real-world application, the queues would be defined with activation enabled so the appropriate service programs would be started automatically as messages arrive. In addition, the service programs would also be designed to process multiple messages with one execution. This can be accomplished by either receiving more than the *TOP(1)* message in the queue or by looping and waiting for new messages to arrive. Service Broker provides the *WAITFOR* statement to allow the program to wait for incoming messages or for a time limit to be reached. Service Broker also supports a very useful capability to have the expiration of a timer put a message in a Service Broker queue. This can be used to notify a target service program that some time-dependent event has occurred.

This Windows message processing loop-like architecture is depicted in Figure 12-10.

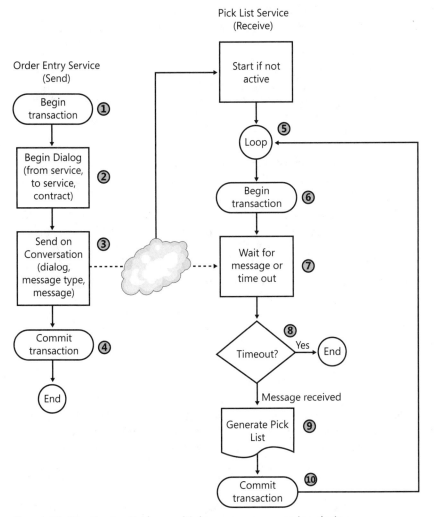

Figure 12-10   Service Broker multiple-message processing design

Service Broker and Query Notification

One of the most useful features in SQL Server 2005 is the ability of an ASP.NET or Windows Forms application using ADO.NET to be notified when the data in a database table or view that the program is depending on changes. This feature is mainly useful for data that is normally used as reference data in list boxes or data grids. This type of data generally changes infrequently, if at all. When used in conjunction with caching of database data in ASP.NET or Windows Forms smart client applications, this feature allows the developer to have the best of both worlds—fast, cached access to data that is also up-to-date at all times. The technology that makes this work is called *query notification*. The reason for including a query notification example in this chapter is that query notification provides an excellent example of the use of Service Broker. SQL Server 2005 uses Service Broker internally to implement this service.

> **Note** Service Broker must be enabled in the database, and the user must have permission to subscribe to query notifications given with *GRANT SUBSCRIBE QUERY NOTIFICATIONS TO username*. (We have been using Service Broker in this chapter, so we can assume that Service Broker is already enabled.)

The SQL Server native provider for ADO.NET 2.0 provides two levels of support for query notification: SqlDependency and SqlNotification. In this chapter, we will discuss the simpler and more automated of the two features, SqlDependency. To be notified of changes in underlying table or view data using SqlDependency, you must create a dependency object and associate it with your ADO command object. The steps required to make use of this facility are:

1. Create a dependency object and associate it with your command object.

2. Associate your change handler with the dependency so you will be notified if the depended-upon data changes.

3. Open the database, and issue the command that retrieves the data.

4. Make use of the data returned.

5. When a change notification causes the handler to be invoked, get the updated data.

> **Note** There are quite a few restrictions on the T-SQL statements that you can monitor using query notifications. For instance, your queries must not contain derived tables, rowset functions, *UNION*, subqueries, or outer or self joins. For a complete accounting, you should check out SQL Server Books Online.

The following example is based on an example posted by Sushili Chordia in his blog. (See *http://blogs.msdn.com/dataaccess/archive/2005/09/27/474447.aspx.*)

Listing 12-4 Query notification application

```
using System;
using System.Data;
using System.Data.SqlClient;
class QuikExe
{
    public static string connectionstring =
"Data Source=.;Initial Catalog=AdventureWorks;Integrated Security=True";
    public void DoDependency()
    {
        using (SqlConnection conn = new SqlConnection(connectionstring))
        {
            conn.Open();
            Console.WriteLine("Connection Opened...");
```

```
            SqlCommand cmd = conn.CreateCommand();
            cmd.CommandText = "Select ShiftID, Name from HumanResources.Shift";

            //Notification specific code
            SqlDependency dep = new SqlDependency(cmd);
            dep.OnChange += delegate(Object o, SqlNotificationEventArgs args)
            {
                Console.WriteLine("Event Recd");
                Console.WriteLine("Info:" + args.Info);
                Console.WriteLine("Source:" + args.Source);
                Console.WriteLine("Type:" + args.Type);
            };

            SqlDataReader r = cmd.ExecuteReader();
            //Read the data here and close the reader
            while (r.Read())
            {
                Console.WriteLine(r[0].ToString());
            }
            r.Close();
            Console.WriteLine("DataReader Read...");
        }
    }

    public static void Main()
    {
        try
        {
            //Start the listener infrastructure on the client
            SqlDependency.Start(connectionstring);
            QuikExe q = new QuikExe();
            q.DoDependency();
            Console.WriteLine("Wait for Notification Event...");
            Console.Read();
        }
        finally
        {
            //Optional step to clean up dependency else it will fallback
            // to automatic cleanup
            SqlDependency.Stop(connectionstring);
        }
    }
}
```

This example illustrates how to set up a query notification that will fire when the underlying table is changed for any reason.

The *Main* procedure sets up a query notification dependency on the connection using the line *SqlDependency.Start(connectionstring);*. This line starts the change listener. Note that it will listen on a separate connection from the one used to retrieve data from the database. Then it instantiates QuikExe and calls its *DoDependency* method. This is where the database will be read.

In QuikExe, we first create the new connection, protecting the scope of database operations with a *using* statement (which, you will recall, is a best practice for enforcing the *finally/dispose* pattern). Next we open the connection and create the command object that specifies the command text to use for the request. So far this has all been standard ADO.NET stuff. The next lines define a dependency object and link it to the command. Then they define an anonymous delegate to be registered and called when a table change notification occurs.

```
SqlDependency dep = new SqlDependency(cmd);
dep.OnChange += delegate(Object o, SqlNotificationEventArgs args)
{
    Console.WriteLine("Event Recd");
    Console.WriteLine("Info:" + args.Info);
    Console.WriteLine("Source:" + args.Source);
    Console.WriteLine("Type:" + args.Type);
};
```

Note   You must follow certain rules when you deal with query notifications. The database must have Service Broker enabled for query notifications to work. Also, the SQL statement used in the command must specify field names and cannot just use "*." The table name used must also be fully qualified, as shown in the example.

After you set up the anonymous delegate, you use a standard ADO.NET *DataReader* to retrieve and display the data to the console. The result of this is shown in Figure 12-11.

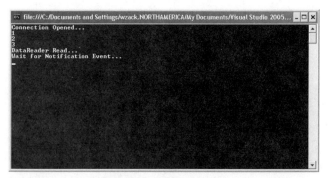

Figure 12-11   Waiting for a notification

This remains the status quo until the data in the table is changed. Figure 12-12 shows what happens in the application if we go into SQL Server Management Studio and update a row in the table.

Figure 12-12   After the change notification

> **Note**   The event indicates that the table was changed by an update. The notification tells you only that a change was made to a row in the table, it does not tell you which row was changed.

It is fairly easy to see from this example that you could create a static cache object of your own and save the data read from the database in that object. Then you could use the cached data whenever it was required. A change to the underlying table would then notify you to get the data from the database the next time you need it and not to take it from the cache (probably by clearing all objects of that type from your cache).

Service Broker's Place in the Middleware World

Now that you see how Service Broker works, one natural question is, how does Service Broker compare with other middleware products, such as MSMQ? Microsoft's answer to this frequently asked question is that Service Broker deals with transactional delivery of messages between multiple databases. MSMQ, on the other hand, lets applications send messages between distributed programs when a database might not be involved. You should use Service Broker whenever you have distributed, multi-database SQL Server applications that perform tasks such as the following, in addition to many other types of distributed database applications:

- Data collection and database update

- Application deserialization (e.g., parallel stored procedure execution)

- SQL Server farming (e.g., distributing requests to multiple servers)

- Deferred processing (e.g., time-shifting workload to off-peak hours)

Summary

In this chapter, we showed you what SQL Server Service Broker is and how you can use it to build highly effective, scalable, mission-critical distributed database applications. We introduced you to the new database objects and DDL/DML statements that you can use to create Service Broker applications. We also developed and analyzed a simple Service Broker application in T-SQL to show you how easy it is to develop Service Broker applications.

There is a lot more to SQL Server Service Broker than you have read about in this chapter, and in fact we only scratched the surface. Service Broker supports strong security features and also comes with performance monitoring and troubleshooting functionality and many other capabilities. We hope that this short introduction will motivate you to dig deeper into the capabilities that SQL Server Service Broker provides and what Service Broker can do for you and for your organization.

Chapter 13
Using SQL Server 2005 Notification Services

—Stephen Forte

People receive notifications all the time. When your cable or credit card bill is due, you are notified, usually in the form of a paper bill or e-mail. In today's wired, fast-paced world, we get notifications all the time on a variety of different platforms, including e-mail, short message service (SMS), and voicemail. Microsoft SQL Server has a built-in way to create notifications, which makes SQL Server an important player among multi-tier, service-based application architectures.

What Is a Notification Application?

Quite simply, a notification application is an application that alerts or notifies you when an event you are interested in takes place. As shown in Figure 13-1, it is a new class of application that delivers personalized and timely information to a variety of devices. For example, a classic notification application could allow a user to subscribe to an airline flight notification event. The user subscribes only to the flight that she is taking. If the flight details change, such as a delay or a gate change, the user receives a notification of this event on her cell phone using SMS.

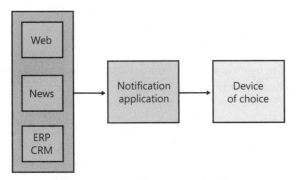

Figure 13-1 Typical notification applications

You could, of course, build these applications on your own, but it would require a lot of work, and therefore a lot of time and money. To relieve you of this task, Microsoft in 2002 introduced SQL Server Notification Services as an add-on for SQL Server 2000. Notification Services is a separate executable process (NSService.exe) and is a platform built on SQL Server, XML, and the .NET Framework that provides a scalable architecture for developing applications that deliver notifications to users who request them. This Notification Services framework allows you to model a notification system in the real world using configuration files. When the application is compiled, SQL Server 2005 creates the database schemas and catalogs for you and models the events that happen in the real world.

Notification Services Components

SQL Server 2005 Notification Services is what you would call "middleware," or part of an application server. SQL Server is traditionally a "back end" or an infrastructure component of your architecture. Traditionally, Microsoft has not provided a lot of middleware, but because of the success of Microsoft Transaction Server (MTS), the company has been providing more and more reliable and scalable middleware (such as Microsoft Internet Information Services [IIS] and BizTalk). Unlike SQL Server 2000, Notification Services is provided as part of the SQL Server 2005 package; however, it is not part of the core database engine. It has a separate setup option that is turned off by default when you initially install your SQL Server 2005 server. You must either select Notification Services to install it at initial setup or rerun the setup program and add Notification Services when it's needed.

If you choose to install SQL Server 2005 Notification Services, all its components and support files are installed in a separate subdirectory. (The default installation directory is \Program Files\Microsoft SQL Server\90\NotificationServices.) If you explore this folder and its subfolders, you can see that Notification Services is made up of a few components. Here are the important ones:

- **microsoft.sqlserver.notificationservices.dll** The actual guts of Notification Services. This is a managed .NET assembly that contains the core code for Notification Services and the built-in providers for retrieving data and creating notifications and subscriptions.

- **nsService.exe** The executable shell of microsoft.sqlserver.notificationservices.dll, which runs as a Windows service. Each instance of nsService.exe runs as a Windows service and can be managed by SQL Server Management Studio. Instances of nsService.exe are independent of SQL Server 2005 instances.

- **ncontrol.exe** A utility that you use when you compile your application. It generates the SQL Server database and objects that the Windows service application uses to retrieve data and create notifications.

- **XML schemas** When you generate a Notification Services application, you use XML-based configuration files. The schemas provided as part of the framework validate those documents.

- **Sample applications**   These are installed at C:\Program Files\Microsoft SQL Server\ 90\Samples\Notification Services by default. They fully demonstrate the power of Notification Services. We will explore them in this chapter because they provide an end-to-end Notification Services solution and are easily accessible.

One component that is not readily visible in the Notification Services directory structure is the provider. Providers are part of the extensible Notification Services framework that offers extension of three features—event notification, content formatting, and the delivery mechanism. We'll look at each provider type to see what it is made of.

Event Providers

Event providers are used when an event in the real world happens that might cause a notification, such as a flight gate change, stock price change, or a credit card bill that is past its due date. A notification begins as a change in data, which exists in a database *external* to your notification application. You use the event provider to bring the changed data into your application. The type of event provider you use depends on the type of access you have to the external data. Out-of-the-box Notification Services has the event providers listed here:

- **File Watcher event provider**   One of the most commonly used event providers, the File Watcher event provider, does just what its name implies: It watches the file system for a new file to appear in a particular (configurable) directory. A third-party system or another system that you have developed typically provides the event data. That system is responsible for sending the event data to your notification application. The files that come in must be in an XSD-enforced XML format so that Notification Services can use the SQLXML bulk loader (which is part of SQLXML 3.0).

- **SQL Server event provider**   This provider runs an SQL statement of your choosing to query a table in another SQL Server database to determine whether rows have changed or have been added and whether an event should be submitted to Notification Services. You can use SQL Server linked servers to query non–SQL Server or remote SQL Server databases.

- **Analysis Services event provider**   This provider does the same as the SQL Server event provider, except that it runs Multidimensional Expressions (MDX) against Online Analytical Processing (OLAP) data.

- **IEventProvider and IScheduledEventProvider**   These are interfaces that allow you to write your own providers.

Content Formatters

Content formatters transform data contained in the database tables and format it for delivery. Only one content formatter is provided: the XSLT formatter. This provider formats your notification into XML and then applies an XSLT transformation that you provide. If, for example, you want to output the data as HTML, you can simply use an XLST stylesheet that transforms the data to the HTML format that you require.

For developers seeking more flexibility, there is also the *IContentFormatter* interface, which allows you to write your own custom content format provider.

Delivery Protocol Providers

After your notification is fired and formatted, Notification Services must deliver it to the user's preferred device. Notification Services can send data only to a device that it knows how to deliver it to. Notification Services ships with several useful delivery protocol providers:

- **SMTP**   Facilitates sending notifications by e-mail. This is the most basic and most popular provider.

- **File**   Writes notifications to a file on the file system. It is typically used for application testing and debugging.

- **HTTP**   Sends the notification using HTTP with a Web service.

- **Microsoft Alerts provider**   Allows you to send notifications to the .NET Alerts Service. This provider is part of the .NET Alerts toolkit. The NET Alerts Service needs a specific format for its inputs and sends the alert to IM, SMS, or other platforms that you know about. All you need to do is send the data to the Alerts Service. (.NET Alerts Service is built on top of Notification Services.)

- **SMS providers**   Providers that send notifications to the major mobile phone services that have commercial SMS aggregators. Microsoft just provides the plumbing because each SMS partner might be different.

- **Third-party products**   Architectures for delivering to third-party products (such as a Blackberry server). These are used in conjunction with the *IDeliveryProtocol* interface, which allows you to create your own providers.

Notification Services Deployment Strategies

Before moving on, we want to bring up a few points about middleware and its deployment strategies. Depending on the size of your application and its importance to your business, you might choose to run all components on a single server or spread them across several servers for performance and failover reasons. As you will see later in this chapter, a Notification Services application is comprised of several distinct parts, each of which can live on its own server. How you choose to deploy those parts will depend on your needs.

A notification application is deployed in an instance of Notification Services. Each instance of Notification Services has its own instance database in an SQL Server. A single instance (of NSService.exe) can run one or multiple applications. Each Notification Services instance, separate from SQL Server instances, has its own set of subscribers because subscribers and their delivery devices are stored in the instance database. Each application has its own separate application database that holds the event information. It is important to remember that the source data for your events—usually an online transaction processing (OLTP) system—and the actual event/notification application data are two separate entities that will in all likelihood exist on different physical servers.

Lastly, the generator and distribution sections of your application can be spread out across multiple machines. Each machine requires its own instance of Notification Services, but you can easily scale up your processing. You can even get as sophisticated as to send only certain types of messages (e-mail, for example) from different machines, allowing you to scale your application to handle extremely large loads. For example, you can have a deployment strategy like this:

- Server 1,n—Instance database containing event and subscription data

- Server 2—Back-end OLTP system

- Server 3—Web server containing Subscriber application

- Server 4, n—Generator and Distributor services

Notification Services can scale out as large as you need it to. For example, the Notification Services instance can be on one server and its actual database storage can be on another server or multiple servers. In addition, the Notification Services engine components and databases can run on a failover cluster, allowing you to significantly scale your application.

Working with Notification Services

Notification Services in SQL Server 2005 offers some new and enhanced features compared to the version in SQL Server 2000.

- SQL Server Management Studio now has a management interface for Notification Services administrative functions (*NSControl*), as shown in Figure 13-2. Using Object Explorer in Notification Services, you can perform most nscontrol command prompt utility tasks, as well as start and stop instances of Notification Services. If you have worked with Notification Services before, you will see that this by itself makes the upgrade worthwhile because in the past all Notification Services (*NSControl*) functions were performed at the command line.

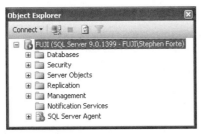

Figure 13-2   The new Notification Services Administration tool in SQL Server Management Studio

- Notification Services now supports both 32-bit and 64-bit platforms. (SQL Server 2000 Notification Services supported only a 32-bit platform.) This is important because more large-scale Web sites and applications are moving to the 64-bit platform.

- Notification Services now provides integration with business intelligence (BI) functions using the new Analysis Services event provider. The Analysis Services event provider allows you to monitor changes to an existing Analysis Services cube. You can use the Analysis Services event provider to submit Notification Services events based on MDX queries.

- Minor changes to the object model reflect enhancements in the subscription objects API. For example, Notification Services supports a new type of action called a *condition action*, which allows subscribers to define their own query clauses over a predefined data set. This gives you more flexibility, but it can also lead to a proliferation of custom views of data, so be careful what you allow your users to do!

- Notification Services has a new management namespace (*Microsoft.SqlServer.Management .Nmo*) that allows you to develop and manage Notification Services instances and applications.

- Notification Services offers performance improvements. General performance was a major focus in this version of Notification Services. Notification Services has made performance improvements in the data removal process, which is called "vacuuming." According to Microsoft, and generally confirmed by our own personal observations, you can expect a performance improvement of approximately 150 percent over the previous version of Notification Services, depending on the application and the hardware configuration.

- Notification Services uses the Transact-SQL (T-SQL) INSERT INTO...SELECT syntax to improve performance and security (in lieu of the old *Notify()* function). The *Notify()* function in the previous version of Notification Services generates notifications and uses three extended stored procedures that are detrimental to performance and add deployment steps.

- Notification Services now offers Windows Clustering improvements. Notification Services has supported Windows Clustering technology since its initial release. This is our favorite feature of Notification Services—the ability to scale using clustering technology. To provide better support for clustering in this release, you can now configure a separate cluster resource group for Notification Services, which can fail over separately from other cluster resource groups.

Creating Notification Applications

After you have installed Notification Services, you can start writing a notification application right away. When you begin your planning, you must think about the four types of components that make up all notification applications. These are described in Table 13-1.

Table 13-1 Components of an SQL Server Notification Application

Component	Description
Subscriber	A user (or service) that receives notifications.
Subscription	Represents a request for a notification. Subscriptions are created using the Notification Services API in an application coded by the developer.
Event	Data coming into your database of interest to particular subscriptions (flight delays, for example).
Notification	Sends the registered subscriber the data using a predefined delivery channel.

A notification application does the following:

■ Uses two configuration files, one for the instance of Notification Services and the other for application-specific data. We will discuss these later in the chapter.

■ Manages subscriptions (adding users and their device and delivery preferences).

■ Loads event data (such as flight status) from an event provider.

■ Matches subscribers (T-SQL join).

■ Renders the content for delivery (XSLT).

■ Delivers a notification using the distribution engine.

Users (subscribers) create subscriptions with a subscription management application created by the developer using ASP.NET or Windows Forms as a front end. Developers generate subscriptions using a managed API. This is a pretty straightforward process, but you must provide the necessary functionality to allow users to select the data they want notifications on as well as the preferences for delivery and the format and address of delivery. After the subscriptions are entered into the database, the data that will form the basis of your notifications is loaded in using event providers.

The following happens when Notification Services gets data from an event provider:

1. The notification application collects events by loading data into the database.

2. Using T-SQL *JOIN* statements, Notification Services matches events to the subscriptions.

3. If a match is found, Notification Services generates new notifications.

4. Using XSLT, a formatter formats the notification and Notification Services delivers it through the delivery channel to the registered target device of the subscriber.

Next we'll get to work on a sample application that demonstrates these steps.

A Sample Notification Application

We will use the sample notification application that ships with SQL Server 2005 Notification Services. The rest of the chapter will dissect one of the samples as a step-by-step tutorial. To get the sample and follow along with the chapter, you must install the SQL Server samples. If you choose to install them when you install SQL Server, you must choose Start, All Programs, Microsoft SQL Server 2005, Documentation and Tutorials, Samples, Microsoft SQL Server 2005 Samples. This brings up the InstallShield Wizard (Figure 13-3). Step through the wizard to install the SQL Server Notification Services sample applications. The Flight example will be installed at C:\Program Files\Microsoft SQL Server\90\ Samples\Notification Services\Flight.

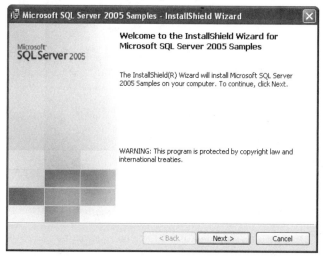

Figure 13-3   The InstallShield Wizard

Flight Price Notification Sample Application

We will use the Flight sample, which is an event-driven Notification Services application that produces notifications about flight prices for subscribers. In the scenario for this example, users are customers who subscribe to flight price notifications. The users are searching for bargains and want to be notified when a particular type of flight meets their criteria. For example, a user might want to be notified when a trip to Cancun or Paris becomes available at a certain price so he can take a last-minute vacation. In each subscription, the user indicates a departure and arrival city, a target price, and optionally an airline.

The fictitious company running the Flight application submits flight price event data to the application by dropping XML data into a watched folder. Notification Services then picks up this data and generates notifications for subscribers with matching subscriptions. Notifications are generated when all of the following conditions are met:

- The event ticket price is less than the subscription ticket price.

- The event departure airport equals the subscription departure airport.

- The event arrival airport equals the subscription arrival airport.

- The event airline equals the subscription airline (if specified).

If multiple notifications are destined for one subscriber at the same time, Notification Services uses digest delivery to combine the notifications. Notification Services then formats the notification using an XSLT content formatter and uses the specified delivery channel (e-mail or file) to distribute the notification. We will look at this example in C#, but Microsoft provides both a C# and a Visual Basic .NET example for the same application.

To build the instance, you create the instance of Notification Services, register it, and grant SQL Server, database, and folder permissions to the account you are using.

Creating the Notification Services Instance

We'll start by creating the instance of Notification Services.

1. Open SQL Server Management Studio and connect to the instance of SQL Server that will host your application.

2. In Object Explorer, right-click the Notification Services folder and select New Notification Services Instance, as shown in Figure 13-4.

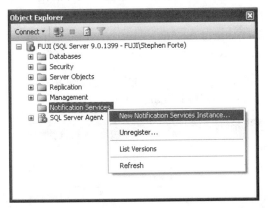

Figure 13-4   Adding a new Notification Services instance

3. In the New Notification Services Instance dialog box (Figure 13-5), click the Browse button and select the InstanceConfig.xml file in the Flight sample's root folder. (The default is C:\Program Files\Microsoft SQL Server\90\Samples\Notification Services\ Flight\InstanceConfig.xml.)

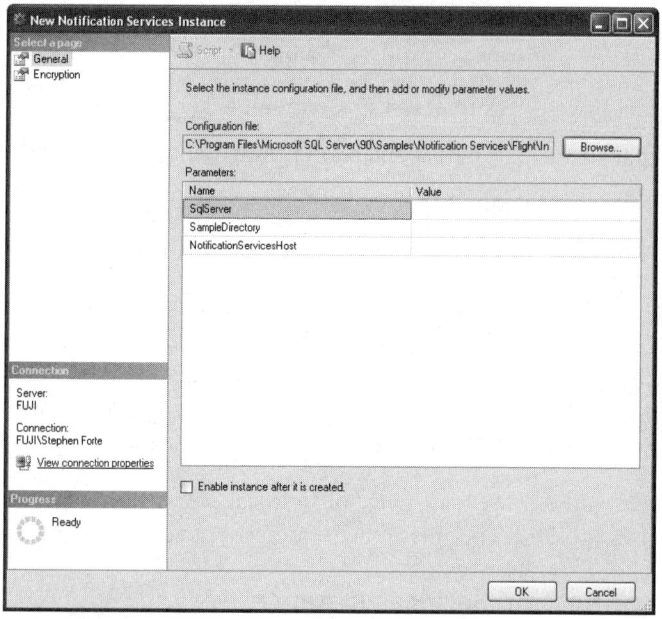

Figure 13-5   The New Notification Services Instance dialog box

4. In the Parameters box, enter values for the three parameters:

    ■ **SampleDirectory**   This is the path of the Flight sample's root folder. The default path is C:\Program Files\Microsoft SQL Server\90\Samples\Notification Services\Flight.

    ■ **NotificationServicesHost**   This is the name of the Notification Services server. It should have the same name as the database server running the instance of Notification Services.

    ■ **SQLServer**   This is the name of the SQL Server instance. It should be the same as the database server instance containing your data.

5. Select the Enable instance after it is created check box. Click OK. Notification Services creates the instance for you, as shown in Figure 13-6.

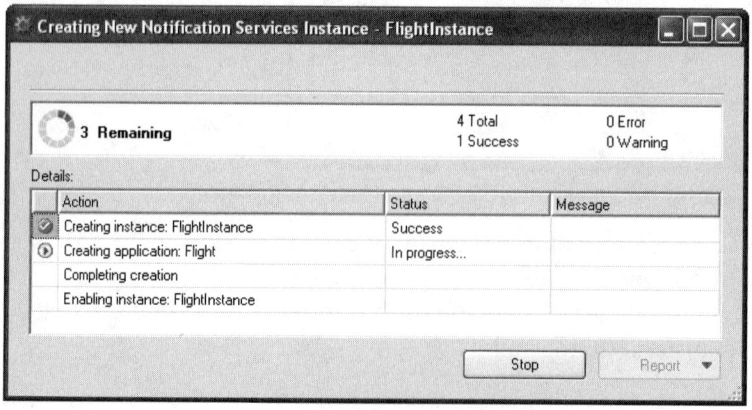

Figure 13-6   Creating a Notification Services instance

Listing 13-1 has the complete instance configuration file that comes with the sample. An instance configuration file is an XML document that describes a single instance of Notification Services. It contains all the metadata for applications that the particular instance hosts. In this case, we have one instance, and it is named FlightInstance. It will host only one application–the Flight application we are working on.

Besides metadata about the instance, the instance configuration file contains the name of the database server, delivery protocols, and delivery channels. Information about the application is also stored, including the application name, base directory path, and, most important, the name of the application configuration file (more on this later). You will also notice in Listing 13-1 that configuration files in Notification Services can use parameters or symbolic names that appear as name/value pairs (indicated by percent sign delimiters, as in *%SqlServer%*), so you do not have to hardcode server, path, and file information into the file.

Listing 13-1   The instance configuration file for the flight notification application

```xml
<?xml version="1.0" encoding="utf-8"?>
<NotificationServicesInstance xmlns:xsd="http://www.w3.org/2001/
XMLSchema" xmlns:xsi="http://www.w3.org/2001/XMLSchema-instance"
xmlns="http://www.microsoft.com/MicrosoftNotificationServices/ConfigurationFileSchema">
<InstanceName>FlightInstance</InstanceName>
<SqlServerSystem>%SqlServer%</SqlServerSystem>
<Applications>
   <Application>
   <ApplicationName>Flight</ApplicationName>
   <BaseDirectoryPath>%SampleDirectory%\AppDefinition</BaseDirectoryPath>
   <ApplicationDefinitionFilePath>appADF.xml</ApplicationDefinitionFilePath>
      <Parameters>
      <!-- These parameters are defined as environment variables or
      as command line arguments.  They are passed to the ADF file. -->
      <Parameter>
         <Name>_DBSystem_</Name>
         <Value>%SqlServer%</Value>
      </Parameter>
      <Parameter>
         <Name>_NSSystem_</Name>
         <Value>%NotificationServicesHost%</Value>
      </Parameter>
      <Parameter>
         <Name>_BaseDirectoryPath_</Name>
         <Value>%SampleDirectory%</Value>
      </Parameter>
      <Parameter>
         <Name>_EventsDir_</Name>
         <Value>%SampleDirectory%\Events</Value>
      </Parameter>
      </Parameters>
      </Application>
   </Applications>
   <DeliveryChannels>
      <DeliveryChannel>
         <DeliveryChannelName>FileChannel</DeliveryChannelName>
```

```
        <ProtocolName>File</ProtocolName>
        <Arguments>
          <Argument>
          <Name>FileName</Name>
          <Value>%SampleDirectory%\Notifications\FileNotifications.txt</Value>
          </Argument>
        </Arguments>
      </DeliveryChannel>
      <DeliveryChannel>
        <DeliveryChannelName>EmailChannel</DeliveryChannelName>
        <ProtocolName>SMTP</ProtocolName>
      </DeliveryChannel>
    </DeliveryChannels>
  </NotificationServicesInstance>
```

Registering the Notification Services Instance

Now let's register the instance of Notification Services.

1. In SQL Server Management Studio, open the Notification Services folder, right-click FlightInstance, point to Tasks, and then click Register, as shown in Figure 13-7.

Figure 13-7   Registering a Notification Services instance

2. In the Register dialog box (Figure 13-8), select the Create Windows Service check box. The Windows service will run the instance of Notification Services on this computer.

3. Under Service Logon, enter a Windows logon account and password. This is the Windows account under which the service will run, so be sure to use an account that can access the resources your application will use (such as the folder that the event data will be dropped into). If you use Windows Authentication to access SQL Server, the Windows service will also use this account to connect to SQL Server. If you don't use Windows Authentication to access SQL Server, enter the SQL Server authentication credentials and click OK. SQL Server will then register the instance of Notification Services.

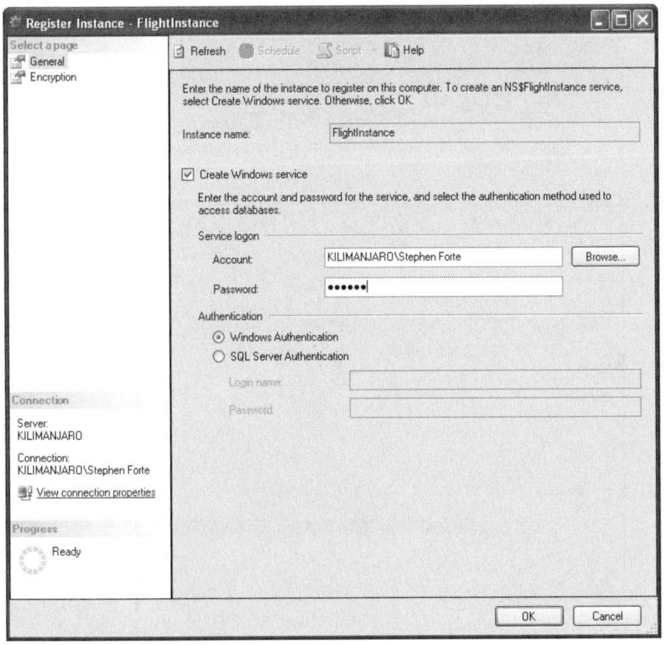

Figure 13-8   The Register Instance dialog box

Granting SQL Server Permissions

Before we start using the sample application, we have to grant SQL Server permissions to the database for the account we are using.

1. In Object Explorer, expand the Security folder and find the account that you assigned to the instance of Notification Services. If the login used by the Windows service already has access to SQL Server, right-click the login and select Properties. In the left pane of the Login Properties dialog box, select Database Access, as shown in Figure 13-9. Grant permissions for the FlightInstanceNSMain database; in the Databases Accessible By This Login box and in the Database roles for FlightInstanceNSMain, select NSRunService. Then grant permissions for the FlightInstanceFlight database, and in the Database roles for FlightInstanceFlight, select NSRunService.

2. Now we must grant the correct permissions on the folders used in the sample. In Windows Explorer, navigate to the sample's Events folder (the default is: C:\Program Files\Microsoft SQL Server\90\Samples\Notification Services\Flight\Events) and configure security for it by right-clicking the folder, selecting Sharing And Security, and then selecting the Security tab. (If you do not see the Security tab, you must enable it via Tools, Folder Options, View, and uncheck Use Simple File Sharing [Recommended], as shown in Figure 13-10.)

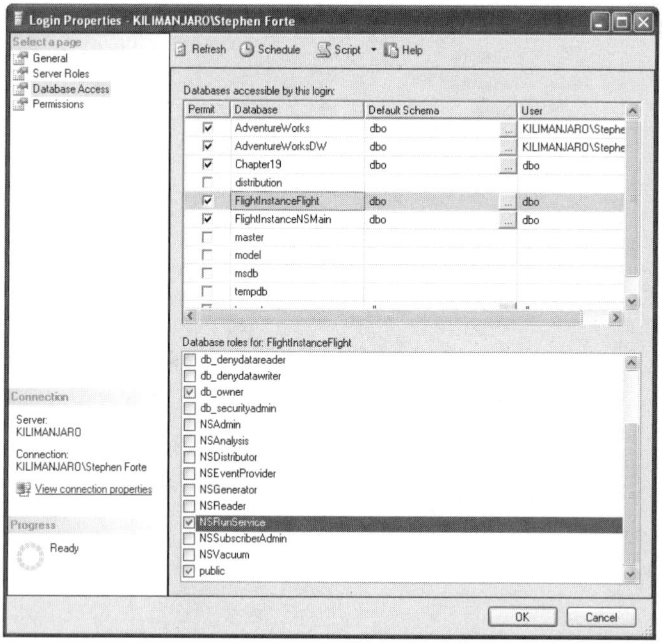

Figure 13-9   Grant Permissions dialog box

3.   Select or add the account used by the Windows service. In the Permissions box, select both the Read and Modify permissions. Navigate to the Flight sample's Notification folder, and select or add the account used by the Windows service. In the Permissions box, select Write permissions.

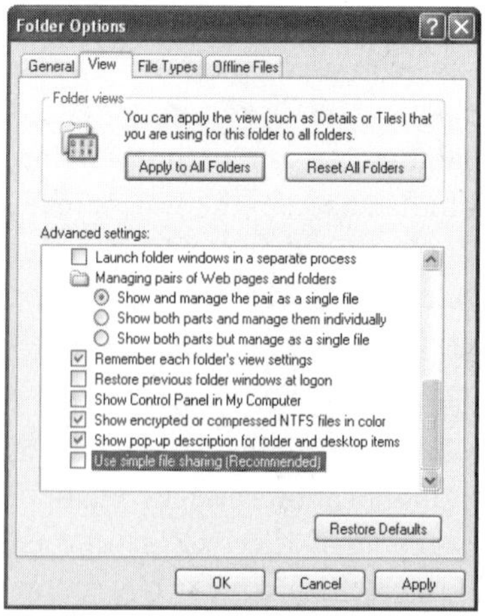

Figure 13-10   Simple file sharing

Application Definition File

The most important configuration file for your application is the application definition file, or ADF. The ADF stores all the metadata about your Notification Services application. When you "code" your notification application, the ADF is what you are coding and creating. It is an XML file that tells Notification Services what do to. Here is an example of a bare-bones application configuration file:

```xml
<?xml version="1.0" encoding="utf-8" ?>
<Application xmlns:xsd="http://www.w3.org/2001/XMLSchema" xmlns:xsi="http://www.w3.org/
2001/XMLSchema-instance" xmlns="http://www.microsoft.com/MicrosoftNotificationServices/
ApplicationDefinitionFileSchema">
    <SubscriptionClasses>
        <SubscriptionClass>
            <SubscriptionClassName>My Name</SubscriptionClassName>
            <Schema>
                <Field>
                    <FieldName>MyField</FieldName>
                    <FieldType>nvarchar(255)</FieldType>
                </Field>
            </Schema>
        </SubscriptionClass>
    </SubscriptionClasses>
    <NotificationClasses>
        <NotificationClass>
            <NotificationClassName>My Name</NotificationClassName>
            <Schema>
                <Fields>
                    <Field>
                        <FieldName>MyField</FieldName>
                        <FieldType>nvarchar(6)</FieldType>
                    </Field>
                <Fields>
            </Schema>
            <ContentFormatter>
                <ClassName>XsltFormatter</ClassName>
            </ContentFormatter>
        </NotificationClass>
    </NotificationClasses>
    <Generator><SystemName>%_NSSystem_%</SystemName></Generator>
    <Distributors>
        <Distributor>
            <SystemName>%_NSSystem_%</SystemName>
        </Distributor>
    </Distributors>
</Application>
```

The ADF of any application must have each of the following four required nodes (as defined by its XSD, which is located at *http://www.microsoft.com/MicrosoftNotificationServices/ApplicationDefinitionFileSchema*)

- **SubscriptionClasses** Defines the subscription classes used in your application. As you can see from the <SubscriptionClass> node in Listing 13-2, the classes are defined by both a name and a schema. The schema indicates the fields and their SQL Server data types representing the data you want to store. You can also specify the SQL Server field attributes as attributes of the node (such as nullability and default values). You do not create these tables using TSQL or SQL Server Management Studio; you create them here in the ADF. Notification Services creates these objects for you and the T-SQL appears in the ADF. Because the ADF is XML, the T-SQL must be encoded (for example, you must use < instead of <).

- **NotificationClasses**   Defines the classes that your application needs for actual notifications. As with the subscription classes, you enter a name and SQL Server schema information. You must also define the formatter that is used to format the content of your notification, such as sending a stock quote using e-mail.

- **Generator**   Manages the rule processing for the entire application by specifying which system runs the rules process. This is where you can tweak the settings and distribute parts of the application to other systems (servers) and even specify such things as how many threads the generator can use.

- **Distributor**   Manages the formatting and delivery of your notifications. As with the Generator node, you can tweak the settings and specify which system will run the distributor and how many threads will be used.

As you can see, no events are actually required in the schema for an ADF. However, events will probably be important in your application because they can trigger a notification. Events are processed by event providers (for example, the file watcher event provider). These providers send the event data to your application, which inserts the data into the event table. That event table is defined in the ADF and is built automatically when you compile your application. The syntax of an event table is shown here from the ADF. Notice that, as with the subscription class, the basic syntax includes the name and the schema.

```xml
<EventClasses>
   <EventClass>
      <EventClassName>My Event</EventClassName>
      <Schema>
         <Field>
            <FieldName>My Field</FieldName>
            <FieldType>nvarchar(6)</FieldType>
         </Field>
      </Schema>
   </EventClass>
</EventClasses>
```

The Flight sample application has an ADF in the subfolder .\AppDefinition. Listing 13-2 shows the important parts of the appADF.xml file.

Listing 13-2   Flight notification ADF

```xml
<?xml version="1.0" encoding="utf-8" ?>
<Application xmlns:xsd="http://www.w3.org/2001/XMLSchema" xmlns:xsi=
"http://www.w3.org/2001/XMLSchema-instance" xmlns="http://www.microsoft.com/
MicrosoftNotificationServices/ApplicationDefinitionFileSchema">
```

```xml
<EventClasses>
    <EventClass>
        <EventClassName>FlightEvents</EventClassName>
        <Schema>
            <Field>
                <FieldName>LeavingFrom</FieldName>
                <FieldType>nvarchar(6)</FieldType>
            </Field>
            <Field>
                <FieldName>GoingTo</FieldName>
                <FieldType>nvarchar(6)</FieldType>
            </Field>
            <Field>
                <FieldName>Carrier</FieldName>
                <FieldType>nvarchar(255)</FieldType>
            </Field>
            <Field>
                <FieldName>Price</FieldName>
                <FieldType>float</FieldType>
            </Field>
        </Schema>
    </EventClass>
</EventClasses>
<SubscriptionClasses>
    <SubscriptionClass>
        <SubscriptionClassName>
        FlightSubscriptions
      </SubscriptionClassName>
        <Schema>
            <Field>
                <FieldName>DeviceName</FieldName>
                <FieldType>nvarchar(255)</FieldType>
            </Field>
            <Field>
                <FieldName>LeavingFrom</FieldName>
                <FieldType>nvarchar(6)</FieldType>
            </Field>
            <Field>
                <FieldName>GoingTo</FieldName>
                <FieldType>nvarchar(6)</FieldType>
            </Field>
            <Field>
                <FieldName>Carrier</FieldName>
                <FieldType>nvarchar(255)</FieldType>
            </Field>
            <Field>
                <FieldName>Price</FieldName>
                <FieldType>float</FieldType>
            </Field>
        </Schema>
        <EventRules>
            <EventRule>
                <RuleName>FlightSubscriptionsEventRule</RuleName>
```

```
          <Action>
              INSERT INTO FlightNotifications
              (SubscriberId, DeviceName, SubscriberLocale,
              Carrier, LeavingFrom, GoingTo, Price,
              Conditions)
              SELECT S.SubscriberId, S.DeviceName,
              S.SubscriberLocale, E.Carrier, E.LeavingFrom,
              E.GoingTo, E.Price, E.Conditions
              FROM FlightEvents E, FlightSubscriptions S
              WHERE E.LeavingFrom = S.LeavingFrom
              AND    E.GoingTo = S.GoingTo
              AND    ((E.Carrier = S.Carrier)
              OR    (S.Carrier = '*'))
              AND    E.Price &lt; S.Price
          </Action>
          <EventClassName>FlightEvents</EventClassName>
        </EventRule>
      </EventRules>
    </SubscriptionClass>
</SubscriptionClasses>
<NotificationClasses>
    <NotificationClass>
<NotificationClassName>
    FlightNotifications
</NotificationClassName>
        <Schema>
          <Fields>
            <Field>
              <FieldName>Carrier</FieldName>
              <FieldType>nvarchar(6)</FieldType>
            </Field>
            <Field>
              <FieldName>LeavingFrom</FieldName>
              <FieldType>nvarchar(6)</FieldType>
            </Field>
            <Field>
              <FieldName>GoingTo</FieldName>
              <FieldType>nvarchar(6)</FieldType>
            </Field>
            <Field>
              <FieldName>Price</FieldName>
              <FieldType>float</FieldType>
            </Field>
            <Field>
              <FieldName>Conditions</FieldName>
              <FieldType>nvarchar(3500)</FieldType>
            </Field>
          </Fields>
        </Schema>
        <ContentFormatter>
          <ClassName>XsltFormatter</ClassName>
          <Arguments>
            <Argument>
              <Name>XsltBaseDirectoryPath</Name>
              <Value>%_BaseDirectoryPath_%\AppDefinition</Value>
            </Argument>
```

```xml
                    <Argument>
                        <Name>XsltFileName</Name>
                        <Value>NoOp.xslt</Value>
                    </Argument>
                </Arguments>
            </ContentFormatter>
            <DigestDelivery>true</DigestDelivery>
            <Protocols>
                <Protocol>
                    <ProtocolName>SMTP</ProtocolName>
                    <Fields>
                        <Field>
                            <FieldName>Subject</FieldName>
                            <SqlExpression>
                            'Flight notification: '+CONVERT (NVARCHAR(30), GETDATE())
                                        </SqlExpression>
                        </Field>
                        <Field>
                            <FieldName>BodyFormat</FieldName>
                            <SqlExpression>'html'</SqlExpression>
                        </Field>
                        <Field>
                            <FieldName>From</FieldName>
                            <SqlExpression>
                                            'sender@adventure-works.com'
                                        </SqlExpression>
                        </Field>
                        <Field>
                            <FieldName>Priority</FieldName>
                            <SqlExpression>'Normal'</SqlExpression>
                        </Field>
                        <Field>
                            <FieldName>To</FieldName>
                            <SqlExpression>
                                            DeviceAddress
                                        </SqlExpression>
                        </Field>
                    </Fields>
                </Protocol>
            </Protocols>
        </NotificationClass>
    </NotificationClasses>
    <Providers>
        <HostedProvider>
            <ProviderName>FlightEP</ProviderName>
            <ClassName>FileSystemWatcherProvider</ClassName>
            <SystemName>%_NSSystem_%</SystemName>
            <Arguments>
                <Argument>
                    <Name>WatchDirectory</Name>
                    <Value>%_EventsDir_%</Value>
                </Argument>
                <Argument>
                    <Name>SchemaFile</Name>
                    <Value>%_BaseDirectoryPath_%\AppDefinition\EventsSchema.xsd</Value>
                </Argument>
```

```
            <Argument>
                <Name>EventClassName</Name>
                <Value>FlightEvents</Value>
            </Argument>
        </Arguments>
    </HostedProvider>
</Providers>
<Generator>
    <SystemName>%_NSSystem_%</SystemName>
</Generator>
<Distributors>
    <Distributor>
        <SystemName>%_NSSystem_%</SystemName>
    </Distributor>
</Distributors>
</Application>
```

Starting the Instance

When you create a Notification Services application, you need an instance configuration file and an ADF, as shown previously in Listings 13-1 and 13-2. You can compile them manually to start the service on the command line by using the NSControl.exe file, or you can do it using SQL Server Management Studio by right-clicking on the FlightInstance instance in the Object Browser and selecting Start from the shortcut menu, as shown in Figure 13-11.

Note   You will be asked to confirm starting the service. This is a major enhancement in SQL Server 2005. Prior to SQL Server 2005, there was only the command line option. We can't tell you how many times we typed in a wrong parameter on the command line tool!

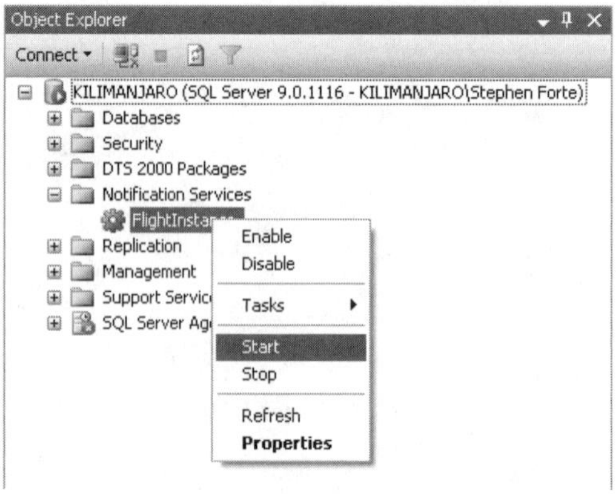

Figure 13-11   Starting an instance

Adding Subscribers and Subscriptions

To add subscription capabilities to our application, you can create a separate ASP.NET application or Windows-based application that accesses the Notification Services service (the

Notification Services instance database) and adds subscribers, subscriber devices, and subscription information. Or, as will often be the case, you can incorporate the functionality of adding subscribers, subscriber devices, and subscriptions into an existing ASP.NET or Windows-based application. For example, a travel Web site might want to allow users to select flights and see fares on a flight-by-flight basis. You can add this "subscription" capability as a new feature of the existing Web site.

Note that this application lives outside the realm of your Notification Services application, and that its architecture and design are entirely up to you. As you will soon see, you use a Notification Services API to add subscribers to the Notification Services instance database that powers your application. It is possible to directly manipulate this database with ADO.NET, but it is preferable to use the API because it takes care of several Notification Services nuances and also guarantees consistency. If you are deploying a lot of Notification Services applications in your organization, you might consider writing a wrapper class for the Notification Services API and giving that class to developers to use.

Subscriber information is usually stored in the form of a unique ID, and device information includes the delivery device type (SMS or e-mail) and device address (such as a cell phone number or an e-mail address). Subscription data depends on the type of Notification Services application you have built. For a stock notification application, subscription data might include the stock symbol for the company and the current stock price. In our example, subscription data consists of the airlines the users are interested in, the cities they want to fly to and from, and the fares. The *Microsoft.SqlServer.NotificationServices* namespace includes a set of objects (called Subscription Management Objects, not to be confused with SQL Server Management Objects) for adding this metadata.

Our sample application has a simple console application that performs this task. All you have to do is run it in debug mode to dissect it and understand the concepts. Let's open Visual Studio 2005 and open the Flight.sln or Flight_VB.sln solution (located in the C:\Program Files\Microsoft SQL Server\90\Samples\Notification Services\Flight folder by default when you install the SQL Server 2005 Samples). The solution, shown in Figure 13-12, contains the AddSubscribers and AddSubscriptions projects, which are used to add Subscribers and Subscriptions, respectively, as well as the ADF and configuration files and some event data in XML.

Expand the AddSubscribers project in Solution Explorer to make sure you can see all the objects in the project. You must create a new strong name key (SNK) file before running the application. You can do this by using the Signing Properties dialog box for the project—a new feature in Visual Studio 2005 that makes signing assemblies much more user friendly. Right-click on the project in Solution Explorer (Figure 13-13), and click Properties. Sign the assembly, and create an SNK file by clicking on the Signing tab of the property pages and selecting <New...> from the Choose a strong name key file section, as shown in Figure 13-13. In the dialog box that appears (Figure 13-14), enter a name for the SNK file and optionally enter a password (which we strongly recommend). Enter the same name as the assembly, which we have named **AddSubscribers**.

Figure 13-12   The Flight solution open in Visual Studio 2005

Figure 13-13   The AddSubscribers project's properties in Visual Studio 2005

Figure 13-14   The AddSubscribers project's SNK file generation

The project hardcodes some subscribers and uses Subscription Management Objects to load them in. Let's investigate how this works. Listing 13-3 (and Listing 13-4 in Visual Basic) shows

the private subscriber class. The subscriber class is a wrapper for an individual subscriber and contains properties for all the information. The class holds the Subscriber ID, along with a device type, an address for the device, and the delivery channel. For example, this class can contain a Subscriber ID of 123456, with a device type of SMS and the device address of a cell phone number with an SMS delivery channel name.

Listing 13-3   The subscriber class in C#

```csharp
public class Subscriber
{
    private string _id;
    private string _deviceTypeName;
    private string _deviceAddress;
    private string _deliveryChannelName;

    public Subscriber(string id, string deviceTypeName, string deviceAddress,
string deliveryChannelName)
    {
        this._id = id;
        this._deviceTypeName = deviceTypeName;
        this._deviceAddress = deviceAddress;
        this._deliveryChannelName = deliveryChannelName;
    }

    public string Id
    {
        get
        {
            return this._id;
        }
    }
    public string DeviceTypeName
    {
        get
        {
            return this._deviceTypeName;
        }
    }
    public string DeviceAddress
    {
        get
        {
            return this._deviceAddress;
        }
    }
    public string DeliveryChannelName
    {
        get
        {
            return this._deliveryChannelName;
        }
    }
}
```

Listing 13-4   The subscriber class in Visual Basic

```vb
Public Class Subscriber
    Private _id As String
    Private _deviceTypeName As String
    Private _deviceAddress As String
    Private _deliveryChannelName As String


    Public Sub New(ByVal id As String, ByVal deviceTypeName As String, ByVal
deviceAddress As String, ByVal deliveryChannelName As String)
        Me._id = id
        Me._deviceTypeName = deviceTypeName
        Me._deviceAddress = deviceAddress
        Me._deliveryChannelName = deliveryChannelName
    End Sub


    Public ReadOnly Property Id() As String
        Get
            Return Me._id
        End Get
    End Property

    Public ReadOnly Property DeviceTypeName() As String
        Get
            Return Me._deviceTypeName
        End Get
    End Property

    Public ReadOnly Property DeviceAddress() As String
        Get
            Return Me._deviceAddress
        End Get
    End Property

    Public ReadOnly Property DeliveryChannelName() As String
        Get
            Return Me._deliveryChannelName
        End Get
    End Property
End Class
```

When you run the application, the *AddSubscribers* method is the first code to run, as shown in Listing 13-5 (and Listing 13-6 in Visual Basic). This method does all the work in adding new subscribers to the instance database. It first passes in an array of new subscribers to the *AddSubscribers* method—this is the hardcoded list of subscribers created in the module's declarations section. In a real-world scenario, you would create these subscribers based on the data the user added to your application. The array, *sampleSubscribers*, is shown here:

```
private Array sampleSubscribers = new Subscriber[]
  {
  new   Subscriber("Stephanie", "File", "stephanie@adventure-works.com", "FileChannel"),
  new   Subscriber("David", "Email", "david@adventure-works.com", "EmailChannel"),
  new   Subscriber("Richard", "File", "richard@adventure-works.com", "FileChannel"),
  new   Subscriber("Scott", "File", "scott@adventure-works.com", "FileChannel")
  };
```

Next the code loops through the array and actually adds each subscriber in the list to the database using the Subscription Management Objects object model. A separate method, *AddSubscriberDeviceInfo*, facilitates adding the device data. (We'll discuss it later in Listing 13-7 [and Listing 13-8 in Visual Basic].) The result of this operation is the addition of the subscribers into the instance database, along with their device info.

Listing 13-5   The *AddSubscribers* method in C#

```
private void AddSubscribers(Array subscribersArray)
    {
        //Create a new Subscriber
        ns.Subscriber nsSubscriber = new ns.Subscriber();

        try
        {
            //Try initializing the subscriber.
            //An exception is thrown if the service is disabled.
            nsSubscriber.Initialize(nsInstance);

            foreach (Subscriber s in subscribersArray)
            {
                //How-to: Add subscriber
                //Assign subscriber ID and add subscriber
                try
                {
                    nsSubscriber.SubscriberId = s.Id;
                    nsSubscriber.Add();

                    Console.WriteLine(s.Id + " Subscriber Added");

                    this.AddSubscriberDeviceInfo(s);

                }
                catch (ns.NSException ex)
                {
                    //Subscriber could not be added,
                    //do not add device info
                    //Output a message then try the next subscriber.
```

```
                            //You could also log the error
                            Console.WriteLine(ex.Message + "\n");
                    }
                }
            }
            catch (ns.NSException ex)
            {
                Console.WriteLine(ex.Message + "\n");
            }
            finally
            {
                nsSubscriber = null;
            }
        }
```

Listing 13-6   The *AddSubscribers* method in Visual Basic

```
    Private Sub AddSubscribers(ByVal subscribers As Array)
        'Create a new Subscriber
        Dim nsSubscriber As New ns.Subscriber()

    'Try initializing the subscriber. An exception is thrown if the service is 'disabled.
        nsSubscriber.Initialize(nsInstance)

        Dim s As Subscriber
        For Each s In subscribers
            'How-to: Add subscriber
            'Assign subscriber ID and add subscriber
            Try
                nsSubscriber.SubscriberId = s.Id
                nsSubscriber.Add()

                Console.WriteLine(s.Id + " Subscriber Added")

                Me.AddSubscriberDeviceInfo(s)

            Catch ex As ns.NSException
                'Subscriber could not be added, do not add device info
                'Output a message then try the next subscriber.
                'You could also log the error
                Console.WriteLine(ex.Message + vbLf)
            End Try
        Next s
    End Sub
```

Adding a device is just as straightforward. Using Subscription Management Objects, you can add a device and its proper type, as well as the method of getting to it (such as a phone number), as shown in Listing 13-7 (and Listing 13-8 in Visual Basic). The individual subscriber object (shown previously in Listings 13-3 and 13-4) is passed into the *AddSubscriberDeviceInfo* method that uses the Subscription Management Objects object model to add the device information for the subscriber. The result of this operation is that the instance database is updated. As we said earlier, you can alter this database on your own using ADO.NET, but using this object model is more straightforward and also helps prevent errors.

Listing 13-7   The *AddSubscriberDeviceInfo* method in C#

```csharp
private void AddSubscriberDeviceInfo(Subscriber subscriber)
    {
        //Create a new Subscriber Device
        ns.SubscriberDevice nsSubscriberDevice = new ns.SubscriberDevice();
        nsSubscriberDevice.Initialize(nsInstance);
            //Populate SubscriberDevice properties
        nsSubscriberDevice.DeviceName = "myDevice";
            nsSubscriberDevice.SubscriberId = subscriber.Id;
            nsSubscriberDevice.DeviceTypeName = subscriber.DeviceTypeName;
            nsSubscriberDevice.DeviceAddress = subscriber.DeviceAddress;
            nsSubscriberDevice.DeliveryChannelName = subscriber.DeliveryChannelName;

        try
        {
            //Add SubcriberDevice from Subscriber
            nsSubscriberDevice.Add();

            Console.WriteLine(subscriber.Id + " Device Info added\n");
        }
        catch (ns.NSException ex)
        {
            //How-to: Catch an exception adding SubscriberDevice info to maintain
subscriber data integrity
            //You could remove the subscriber if there is an error adding device info
            //You could log the error
            Console.WriteLine(ex.Message);
        }
        finally
        {
            nsSubscriberDevice = null;
        }
    }
```

Listing 13-8   The *AddSubscriberDeviceInfo* method in Visual Basic

```vb
Private Sub AddSubscriberDeviceInfo(ByVal subscriber As Subscriber)
        'Create a new Subscriber Device
        Dim nsSubscriberDevice As New ns.SubscriberDevice()
        nsSubscriberDevice.Initialize(nsInstance)
        'Populate SubscriberDevice properties
        nsSubscriberDevice.DeviceName = "myDevice"
        nsSubscriberDevice.SubscriberId = subscriber.Id
        nsSubscriberDevice.DeviceTypeName = subscriber.DeviceTypeName
        nsSubscriberDevice.DeviceAddress = subscriber.DeviceAddress
        nsSubscriberDevice.DeliveryChannelName = subscriber.DeliveryChannelName

        Try
            'Add SubcriberDevice from Subscriber
            nsSubscriberDevice.Add()

            Console.WriteLine(subscriber.Id + " Device Info added" + vbLf)
        Catch ex As ns.NSException
```

```
        'How-to: Catch an exception adding SubscriberDevice info to maintain
            subscriber data integrity
        'You could remove the subscriber if there is an error adding device info
        'You could log the error
        Console.WriteLine(ex.Message)
    End Try

    nsSubscriberDevice = Nothing
End Sub
```

After you compile the AddSubscribers example, you can run the application and look at the subscribers in the application database to see if they are there. Once again, you could have inserted the subscribers and their device data using T-SQL or ADO.NET, but using the Subscription Management Objects API is much simpler. Now that we have subscribers in the database, the last thing we have to do is run the AddSubscriptions project to add subscriptions. This is the data associated with each subscriber, and it is specific to the application. In this application, we are concerned with flights, locations, and prices.

Be sure you still have the Flights solution (or Flights_VB solution) open in Visual Studio 2005. Expand the AddSubscriptions project in Visual Studio to make sure you can see the application's files, and add an AddSubscriptions.snk file, as we did for the AddSubscribers project earlier. AddSubscriptions is a console application that will use Subscription Management Objects to add subscriptions.

> **Warning** If you open your project and get an ugly error that looks like the following, it simply means that you forgot to add the SNK file to your project or have accidentally put it in the wrong location.
>
> ```
> Cryptographic failure while signing assembly 'C:\Program Files\Microsoft SQL
> Server\90\Samples\Notification Services\Flight\AddSubscriptions\cs\
> AddSubscriptions\obj\Debug\AddSubscriptions.exe' -- 'Error reading key file
> 'c:\Program Files\Microsoft SQL Server\90\Samples\Notification Services\
> Flight\samplekey.snk' -- The system cannot find the file specified.
> 'AddSubscriptions
> ```

The AddSubscription code is structured much like the previous AddSubscribers example. Listing 13-9 (and Listing 13-10 in Visual Basic) first defines a private *Subscription* class, which is used to hold the subscription name and the data the subscription will contain. Because a subscription is always tied to a Subscriber ID, the code also includes a holding property.

Listing 13-9 The *Subscription* class in C#

```
public class Subscription
{
    private string _subscriberId;
    private Hashtable _subscriptionData;

    //Create a new subscription for subscriberId
    public Subscription(string subscriberId)
```

```
{
    this._subscriberId = subscriberId;
}

public void AddSubscriptionData(string name, string value)
{
    if (this._subscriptionData == null)
        this._subscriptionData = new Hashtable();

    this._subscriptionData.Add(name, value);
}

public Hashtable SubscriptionData
{
    get
    {
        return _subscriptionData;
    }
}

public string SubscriberId
{
    get
    {
        return _subscriberId;
    }
}
}
```

Listing 13-10   The *Subscription* class in Visual Basic

```
Public Class Subscription
    Private _subscriberId As String
    Private _subscriptionData As Hashtable
    'Create a new subscription for subscriberId
    Public Sub New(ByVal subscriberId As String)
        Me._subscriberId = subscriberId
    End Sub
    Public Sub AddSubscriptionData(name As String, value As String)
        If Me._subscriptionData Is Nothing Then
            Me._subscriptionData = New Hashtable()
        End If
        Me._subscriptionData.Add(name, value)
    End Sub
    Public ReadOnly Property SubscriptionData() As Hashtable
        Get
            Return _subscriptionData
        End Get
    End Property
    Public ReadOnly Property SubscriberId() As String
        Get
            Return _subscriberId
        End Get
    End Property
End Class
```

Now that you've seen the *Subscription* class, let's look at the *AddSubscription* method shown in Listing 13-11 (and Listing 13-12 in Visual Basic). When the application is first run, it adds the subscription data to the *Subscription* object and then calls the *AddSubscription* method (but not in a loop, as in the previous example). The code that adds the subscription information is shown here. Remember that in your application you will fill the *Subscription* object with data that the user has entered into a Web form or some other data entry screen. In this example, it is just hardcoded.

```
s = new Subscription("Stephanie");
s.AddSubscriptionData("LeavingFrom", "SEA");
s.AddSubscriptionData("GoingTo", "CUN");
s.AddSubscriptionData("Carrier", "*");
s.AddSubscriptionData("Price", "800");
this.AddSubscription(s);

s = new Subscription("David");
s.AddSubscriptionData("LeavingFrom", "SEA");
s.AddSubscriptionData("GoingTo", "CUN");
s.AddSubscriptionData("Carrier", "*");
s.AddSubscriptionData("Price", "800");
this.AddSubscription(s);
```

The *AddSubscription* method uses the Subscription Management Objects API to create a new subscription and pass in all the data from the custom *Subscription* class that contains all the user information. You then have subscriptions associated with your subscribers. (An individual subscriber can have multiple subscriptions.) The last thing we need to do now is load in some event data and watch our notifications go out to any matching subscriptions!

Listing 13-11   The *AddSubscription* method in C#

```
private void AddSubscription(Subscription subscription)
    {
        //Create a new subscription
        string result = String.Empty;

        ns.Subscription nsSubscription = new ns.Subscription();

        //Try initializing the subscription. An exception is thrown if the service
is disabled.
        nsSubscription.Initialize(nsApplication, subscriptionClassName);
        nsSubscription.SetFieldValue("DeviceName", "myDevice");
        nsSubscription.SetFieldValue("SubscriberLocale", "en-us");

        nsSubscription.SubscriberId = subscription.SubscriberId;

        foreach (DictionaryEntry s in subscription.SubscriptionData)
        {
            nsSubscription.SetFieldValue(s.Key.ToString(), s.Value.ToString());
        }
```

```
    try
    {
        result = nsSubscription.Add();

        Console.WriteLine("Subscription ID " + result + " created for "
+ subscription.SubscriberId + "\n");
    }

    catch (ns.NSException ex)
    {
        //How-to: Catch subscription add exception to test for subscriber
        //Notification Services failed to insert the new subscription.
        //Most likely the subscriber does not exist
        Console.WriteLine(ex.InnerException.Message + "\n");
    }
}
```

Listing 13-12   The *AddSubscription* method in Visual Basic

```
Private Sub AddSubscription(ByVal subscription As Subscription)
    'Create a new subscription
    Dim result As String = String.Empty
    Dim nsSubscription As New ns.Subscription()
    'Try initializing the subscription.
    nsSubscription.Initialize(nsApplication, subscriptionClassName)
    nsSubscription.SetFieldValue("DeviceName", "myDevice")
    nsSubscription.SetFieldValue("SubscriberLocale", "en-us")
    nsSubscription.SubscriberId = subscription.SubscriberId
    Dim s As DictionaryEntry
    For Each s In subscription.SubscriptionData
        nsSubscription.SetFieldValue(s.Key.ToString(), s.Value.ToString())
    Next s
    Try
        result = nsSubscription.Add()
        Console.WriteLine("Subscription ID " + result + " created for "
+ subscription.SubscriberId + vbLf)
    Catch ex As ns.NSException
        'How-to: Catch subscription add exception to test for subscriber
        'Notification Services failed to insert the new subscription.
        'Most likely the subscriber does not exist
        Console.WriteLine(ex.InnerException.Message + vbLf)
    End Try
End Sub
```

Loading in Events and Receiving Notifications

Now it's time to see the application in action! Event data is loaded into the system in XML format. A file watcher (as defined by the ADF) looks for the event data in a particular folder (for this application, the /Events subdirectory). To trigger some events in this application, in Windows Explorer, navigate to the Flight sample's root folder, and copy the EventData.xml file (shown in the following code) to the Events subfolder. When you drop the file, the file system watcher event provider reads the data from the file, submits it to the application, and then changes the file extension to .done. (If an error occurs when the data is read or submitted, the event provider will change the file extension to .err.)

```xml
<eventData>
   <event>
        <LeavingFrom>SEA</LeavingFrom>
        <GoingTo>CUN</GoingTo>
        <Carrier>MA</Carrier>
        <Price>765</Price>
        <Conditions>Purchase no later than: December 28.
Complete your travel no later than: June 7.
Off-peak flights: For U.S. destinations, you need to fly Tuesdays,
Wednesdays, or Saturdays. If you're flying to Mexico, you need to fly Sundays through
Wednesdays. If you're flying from Mexico, you need to fly Tuesdays through Fridays.
Blackout dates: Vary by destination. Check fare rules for details.
Minimum stay: Two nights, for travel in the U.S. and Canada.
Maximum stay: 30 days, for travel to Mexico.
Note: Tickets are nonrefundable. </Conditions>
   </event>
   <event>
        <LeavingFrom>SEA</LeavingFrom>
        <GoingTo>LHR</GoingTo>
        <Carrier>EA</Carrier>
        <Price>1235</Price>
        <Conditions>Purchase no later than: December 23.
Complete your travel no later than: June 7.
Off-peak flights: You need to fly Tuesdays, Wednesdays, or Saturdays.
Blackout dates: Dec-31 to Jan-5
Minimum stay: Two nights.
Maximum stay: 30 days.
Note: Tickets are nonrefundable. </Conditions>
   </event>
   <event>
        <LeavingFrom>SEA</LeavingFrom>
        <GoingTo>LAX</GoingTo>
        <Carrier>RA</Carrier>
        <Price>99</Price>
        <Conditions>Purchase no later than: December 28. Note: Tickets are
nonrefundable. </Conditions>
   </event>
</eventData>
```

That's it! Your notification should appear in the /Notifications folder. In the real world, you would configure Notification Services to send an e-mail or SMS, but that's hard to debug at first.

Summary

SQL Server 2005 Notification Services is a powerful middleware platform that allows you to create robust notification applications with great ease. SQL Server has changed the rules of middleware, and SQL Server Notification Services leads the way. With the new version of SQL

Server 2005, Notification Services is now fully integrated into SQL Server and you can easily manage and administer your notification applications in the familiar environment of SQL Server Management Studio. Notification Services has matured into a nice development platform for your applications, one that is easily scalable—you can scale out using Windows Clustering technology and scale up with 64-bit processor technology.

Chapter 14

Developing Desktop Applications with SQL Server Express Edition

—Rob Walters

As time passes, database engines that perform basic relational database actions are becoming more of a commodity. With the advent of MySQL, Postgres, and a number of other open source database vendors, more options exist today for developers then ever before. The impact of these disruptive technologies can be seen in the free database offerings not only from Microsoft but also from Oracle (Oracle Express) and IBM (DB2 Express). Each of these relational database vendors wants you, the developer, to use their product so that one day your application might grow enough that you actually need to buy a license for an "upper-level" edition. Although these marketing tactics might be of little interest to us as developers, in reality we benefit tremendously from this competitive environment. Could you ever have imagined 10 years ago that companies like Microsoft would essentially give away a powerful developer tool like Visual Studio Express? Bundled with a rock-solid database like SQL Server, it solves a lot of development needs for a reasonable price: free.

This chapter covers SQL Server Express Edition. It goes into depth about installation, configuration, and management, and it explores Express Edition's features. It also compares and contrasts Express Edition with the Microsoft SQL Server Desktop Engine (MSDE). Finally, you will learn how Express Edition fits into the overall SQL Server product lineup.

What Is SQL Server Express Edition?

Express Edition is one of four SQL Server editions. The others are Workgroup, Standard, and Enterprise. Figure 14-1 shows the progression of editions from Express to Enterprise.

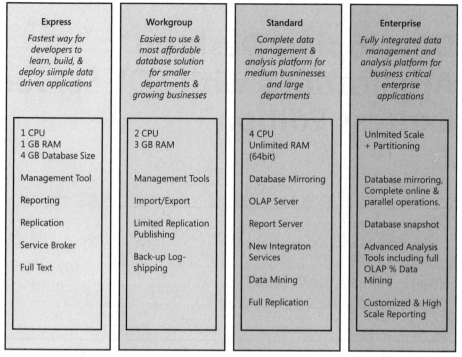

Figure 14-1   The four editions of SQL Server 2005

Some people might be wondering, "Where is Developer Edition?" The Developer and Evaluation editions are actually the same as Enterprise Edition, but with some licensing restrictions. Each SQL Server edition builds on the previous one's functionality. So Standard Edition, for example, has the same functionality as Express Edition and Workgroup Edition (such as management tools, the ability to import and export, and so on).

Note that the Express database engine itself is the same as those of the other editions. It differs only in the restrictions imposed on its use: 1 CPU, 1 GB of RAM, and 4 GB database file size. There are some interesting things to note about these restrictions. If you have a multi-core CPU, Express Edition will leverage all the cores. (After all, to the SQL engine it's still just one CPU.) If you exceed the database file size limit, you will get an error on the command that caused the size to exceed the limit and any transactions in that session will be rolled back. This is the same behavior you would see if you set a fixed size for a database, the database almost reached that size, and then you tried to insert one more row, causing it to exceed the limit. One of the restrictions that existed previously in MSDE was the workload governor. This "feature" intentionally decreased performance as the workload increased. You can forget about this in Express Edition—there is no such thing, so you can throw as much work at Express Edition as your box can handle (and as the CPU, RAM, and database size restrictions allow). Express Edition truly is the same database engine as all the other editions.

Licensing

Some in the developer community might be thinking about deploying Express Edition with their own applications. This is possible, legal, and royalty-free as long as you do not change any parts of the shipped bits of Express Edition. You must also register on Microsoft's Web site if you want to redistribute Express Edition. The URL is *http://go.microsoft.com/fwlink/?LinkId=64062*.

Later in this chapter, we will cover how to silently install Express Edition—this is the most likely way you will deploy Express Edition with your application. In addition to the database engine, Express Edition contains a few extra components such as SQL Server Management Studio Express and SQLCMD. All these tools are also redistributable as long as you don't change them. You cannot redistribute the tools alone, however—you must redistribute Express Edition in addition to the tools. You can, however, redistribute just the SQL Server Express Edition engine.

Feature Review

With the exception of the memory, database size, and CPU restrictions, SQL Server Express Edition contains all the basic relational database features seen in the other editions. For example, you can create common language runtime (CLR) stored procedures, store data as XML, and encrypt your data using symmetric keys. However, Microsoft did not give away the farm in this edition—if you want to use more "enterprise-like" features such as database mirroring or partitioning, you have to pay for the upper-level edition. The business intelligence tools (such as SQL Server Analysis Services) and extract, transform, and load (ETL) tools (such as SQL Server Integration Services, known as Data Transformation Services in SQL 2000) are also not available in Express Edition.

The lack of Integration Services in Express Edition causes some minor pain. For one thing, there is no Import And Export Wizard for moving a database nor any relatively easy alternative. The easiest workaround is to perform a detach, file copy, and attach. Alternatively, you can back up and then restore a database on the destination server. If you need just specific tables within a database, you might consider using the Bulk Copy Program (BCP), which ships with Express Edition as well as all the other editions of SQL Server.

Now let us focus on the database engine–specific features that are significant to SQL Server Express Edition users. Table 14-1 shows key database administration features for the SQL Server product as described by the folks in SQL Server marketing. This table includes a column that describes the availability of the feature in Express Edition.

Table 14-1   SQL Server Database Engine Features

Feature	Available in Express Edition?
Database Mirroring	No
Online Restore	No
Online Indexing Operations	Yes
Fast Recovery	Yes

Table 14-1 **SQL Server Database Engine Features**

Feature	Available in Express Edition?
Security Enhancements	Yes
New SQL Server Management Studio	Available as a scaled-down version called SQL Server Management Studio Express.
Dedicated Administrator Connection	Yes, but it is not enabled by default. To use it in Express Edition, you must start the service using the trace flag 7806. You do not need to specify this trace flag if you are using any other edition of SQL Server.
Snapshot Isolation	No
Data Partitioning	No
Replication Enhancements	Available but scaled down. Later in this chapter, see the "Replication in Express Edition" section for additional details.
SQL Server Agent	No. The workaround is to create Transact-SQL (T-SQL) scripts that are executed via SQLCMD through the Windows Task Scheduler.
SQL Mail and Database Mail	No
Mirrored Media Sets	No
Address Windowing Extensions (AWE)	No
Hot-add memory	No
Failover clustering	No
VIA Protocol support	No

Table 14-2 shows the key development features of SQL Server as well as their availability in Express Edition.

Table 14-2 **SQL Server Database Development Features**

Feature	Available in Express Edition?
.NET Framework Hosting	Yes. This feature is off by default in all SQL Server editions, so you must enable the CLR by selecting the Enable CLR check box in the SQL Server Surface Area Configuration tool.
XML Technologies	Yes
ADO.NET 2.0	Yes
T-SQL Enhancements	Yes
SQL Service Broker	Available but scaled down. Later in this chapter, see the "Service Broker in Express Edition" section for additional details.
Notification Services	No
Web Services	No. You cannot create HTTP endpoints in Express Edition, but it is still possible to create a Web service and use Express Edition—you just can't make Express Edition an HTTP listener.
Reporting Services	Yes. Later in this chapter, see the "Reporting Services in Express Edition" section for additional details.
Full-Text Search Enhancements	Yes. Later in this chapter, see the "Full Text in Express Edition" section for additional details.

Replication in Express Edition

Express Edition can serve as a Subscriber for all types of replication, providing a convenient way to distribute data to client applications that use SQL Server Express Edition. Note that this is a change in behavior from MSDE. If you are using MSDE for replication, MSDE can be either a Snapshot Publisher or a Merge Publisher. If you want to continue to use this functionality, you must upgrade to at least Workgroup Edition.

SQL Server Express Edition does not include the SQL Server Agent, which is typically used to run replication agents. If you use push subscription, replication agents run at the Distributor, which will be an instance of SQL Server 2005, so options are available for synchronizing. But if you use a pull subscription, in which agents run at the Subscriber, you must synchronize the subscription by using the Windows Synchronization Manager tool or do it programmatically using Replication Management Objects (RMO).

Windows Synchronization Manager is available with Microsoft Windows 2000 and later. If SQL Server is running on the same computer as Synchronization Manager, you can do the following:

- Synchronize a subscription.
- Reinitialize a subscription.
- Change the update mode of an updatable transactional subscription.

Service Broker in Express Edition

Service Broker is a new technology in SQL Server 2005 that helps developers create distributed applications that provide support for queuing and reliable messaging. Developers can compose applications from independent, self-contained components called services. Applications can then use messages to interact with these services and access their functionality. Service Broker uses TCP/IP to exchange messages between SQL Server instances, and it includes features to help prevent unauthorized access from the network and to encrypt messages sent over the network.

The SQL Server Express Edition database engine supports Service Broker only as a client. Express Edition can participate in a Service Broker messaging application only when a paid edition of SQL Server (Workgroup, Standard, or Enterprise) is part of the message chain. Express Edition can also send Service Broker messages to itself.

SQL Server 2005 Express Edition with Advanced Services

At the time SQL Server 2005 Express Edition shipped, Microsoft promised that it would soon release a version of Reporting Services as well as Full-Text Search capabilities for Express Edition. The time has come—with the release of Service Pack 1 (SP1) also comes the release of SQL Server Express Edition with Advanced Services, SQL Server Express Edition Toolkit, and SQL Server Management Studio Express.

> **Express Edition Download Page**
>
> SQL Server 2005 Express Edition with Advanced Services is available for download
> from the main SQL Server Express Edition page. The URL is *http://
> msdn.microsoft.com/vstudio/express/sql/download/*.

On the download page for Express Edition, you have a number of options, depending on
exactly what features you need. The following are the available downloads:

- **SQL Server Express Edition with SP1 (SQLEXPR.exe)**   This download gives you just the
  Express Edition database engine and connectivity tools. It does not include any
  management tools or any of the advanced services such as Full-Text Search or Reporting
  Services.

- **SQL Server Express Edition with Advanced Services (SQLEXPR_ADV.exe)**   This download
  gives you the Express Edition database engine plus additional components that include
  SQL Server Management Studio Express, support for full-text catalogs, and support
  for viewing reports via Report Server. SQL Server Express Edition with Advanced
  Services also includes SP1. It's a bit tricky if you already have Express Edition installed
  from RTM: Installing this component is just like installing another instance of Express
  Edition. During the setup of Express Edition with Advances Services, if you choose not
  to upgrade your current Express Edition installation, you will end up with two
  installations of Express Edition on your box.

- **SQL Server Express Edition Toolkit (SQLEXPR_TOOLKIT.exe)**   SQL Server 2005 Express
  Edition Toolkit provides tools and resources to manage SQL Server Express Edition and
  SQL Server Express Edition with Advanced Services. It also allows you to create reports
  using SQL Server 2005 Business Intelligence Development Studio. This download does
  not include the database engine; it includes only the management tools.

- **SQL Server Management Studio Express (SQLServer2005_SSMSEE.msi)**   SQL Server
  Management Studio Express provides a graphical management tool for managing SQL
  Server 2005 Express Edition and SQL Server 2005 Express Edition with Advanced
  Services instances. Management Studio Express can also manage relational engine
  instances created by any edition of SQL Server 2005. It cannot manage Analysis
  Services, Integration Services, SQL Server 2005 Mobile Edition, Notification Services,
  Reporting Services, or SQL Server Agent. This download is just for the Management
  Studio Express tool; it does not contain the database engine or the reporting services
  designer.

In summary, if you want to install Express Edition with all the bells and whistles, just download and install SQL Server Express Edition with Advanced Services (SQLEXPR_ADV.exe)
followed by SQL Server Express Edition Toolkit (SQLEXPR_TOOLKIT.exe). This will get you
all the components that Express Edition has to offer.

Reporting Services in Express Edition

Reporting Services in SQL Server Express Edition is a server-based solution that enables the creation and management of reports derived from data stored in Express Edition. The full version of Reporting Services found in other editions provides many more features—such as the ability to schedule deployment of reports and create subscriptions—but even without these advanced features, Express Edition users have a powerful enough database engine and toolset to conquer many scenarios.

To use Reporting Services within Express Edition, you must have Microsoft Internet Information tion Services (IIS) installed before you install Express Edition.

> **Note** If you installed the Microsoft .NET Framework before installing IIS, you might receive an error in the Express Edition setup program asking you to reinstall the .NET Framework. To avoid rolling back and reinstalling the .NET Framework, run the following on the command line and then click the Retry button.
>
> Aspreg_iis.exe –i This .exe file is located in the .NET Framework folder under <installation drive>:\WINDOWS\Microsoft.NET\Framework\v2.0.50727.

Reporting Services can be considered a two-part installation. The Reporting Server service and Web-based administration page can be installed as an option with SQL Server Express Edition with Advanced Services (SQLEXPR_ADV.exe). If you want to actually create reports and do not want to modify XML using Notepad, you might want to also install BI Development Studio from the SQL Server Express Edition Toolkit (SQLEXPR_TOOLKIT.exe). BI Development Studio is a Visual Studio application that allows you to create reports using a full-featured wizard or by manually building reports using a designer surface (Figure 14-2).

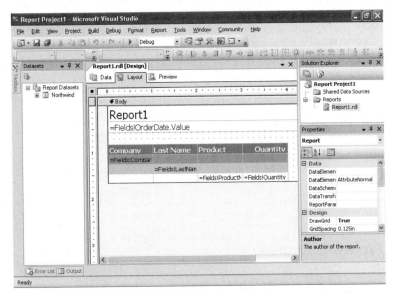

Figure 14-2 Report designer in SQL Server BI Development Studio

During the setup of SQL Server Express Edition with Advanced Services, if you opt to include Report Server, you are presented with some additional forms asking whether you want to configure the Report Server now or later. If you install the report server without configuring it, you can use the Reporting Services Configuration Manager to perform the same configuration work. You must configure the Report Server before you can deploy any reports (Figure 14-3).

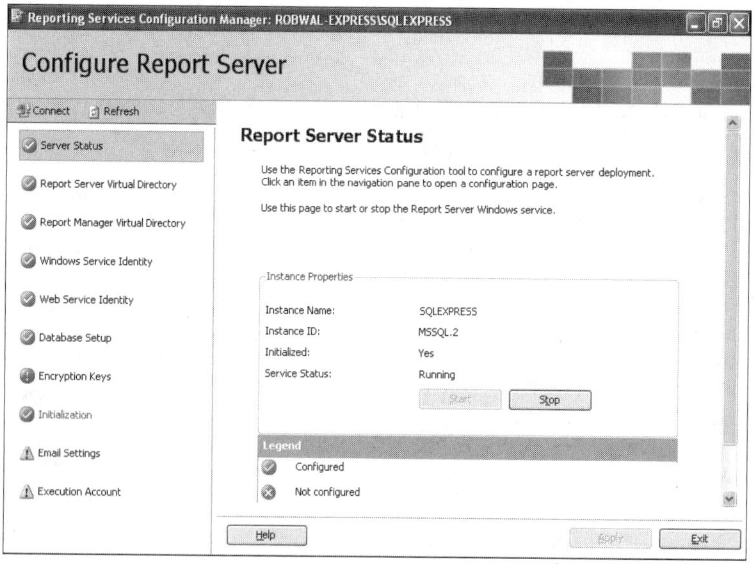

![Configure Report Server tool]

Figure 14-3   Configure Report Server tool

Note   If you instructed setup to automatically configure Report Server, you should know that it creates the Report Server Virtual Directory as ReportServer$SQLEXPRESS and it creates the Report Manager Virtual Directory as Reports$SQLEXPRESS. This is important because when you are deploying your report using the Report Designer, you must tell the designer to use ReportServer$SQLEXPRESS, not ReportServer, which is the default. This property is called the *TargetServerURL*, and you can change it by going to the Properties dialog box reached via the Project menu.

An in-depth discussion of Reporting Services is beyond the scope of this book, but a plethora of resources are available online, including free Report Packs to help you get started writing reports. Report Packs can be found at *http://www.microsoft.com/downloads/ details .aspx?FamilyId=D81722CE-408C-4FB6-A429-2A7ECD62F674&displaylang=en.*

MSDN provides tutorials on Reporting Services as well as Webcasts and many other types of information. Go to this URL: *http://msdn.microsoft.com/sql/bi/reporting/.*

Full Text in Express Edition

The full-text feature within SQL Server Express Edition is no different than in any other edition of SQL Server. The main issue with full text in Express Edition is that the SQL Server

Management Studio Express tool does not have any fancy user interface to manage the full-text catalogs or anything related to full text. Thus, to use full text within Express Edition, you must brush up on your T-SQL skills. Luckily, Template Explorer within Management Studio Express helps you by providing templates for creating a full-text catalog, creating a full-text index, populating an index, and stopping population of an index.

To start playing with full text in Express Edition, we'll walk through creating a full-text index on the ProductName of the Products table in the Northwind database. First we must create our full-text catalog as shown here:

```
USE Northwind
GO
CREATE FULLTEXT CATALOG MyNorthwindCatalog AS DEFAULT
```

In SQL Server 2005, all user-defined databases are enabled for full text by default, so there is no need to explicitly call *sp_fulltext_database 'enable'*, as you do in previous versions of SQL Server. Next we will create the actual index:

```
CREATE FULLTEXT INDEX ON dbo.Products(ProductName) KEY INDEX PK_Products
```

Now we can use this index and query the Products table. Because I love gumbo, I can now quickly return all the gumbo products using the *CONTAINS* keyword, as shown here:

```
SELECT ProductName from Products where CONTAINS(ProductName,'Gumbo')
```

The result is as follows:

```
ProductName
---------------------
Chef Anton's Gumbo Mix
```

In SQL Server 2005, only columns of type *char, varchar, nchar, nvarchar, text, ntext, image, xml,* and *varbinary* can be indexed for full-text search. The previous example shows how to quickly get an index up and running. However, as with most multi-generational features in SQL Server, the capabilities of full text go far beyond what was discussed here. If you are interested in learning more about full-text searching within SQL Server 2005, go to *http:// msdn2.microsoft.com/en-us/library/ms142547(SQL.90).aspx*.

Configuration

Every new database version seems to have even more features, more knobs to turn, and other things that users must learn about. SQL Server 2005 reflects a lot of effort put into improving the security of the product. One aspect of this effort was an "off by default" initiative, which basically required all nonessential features of SQL Server to be turned off. For example, on a default installation of SQL Server, the Browser service and Full-Text service are not running. Turning these features off reduces the surface area available for a malicious user.

The SQL Server Surface Area Configuration tool allows you to turn on and off these various features. This tool is installed as part of a database engine installation, so you have it regardless of which edition or components you install.

When the Surface Area Configuration tool is launched, you get two options: Surface Area Configuration for Services and Connections, and Surface Area Configuration for Features.

The Services and Connections dialog box, shown in Figure 14-4, shows a tree view list of SQL Server components installed on the server.

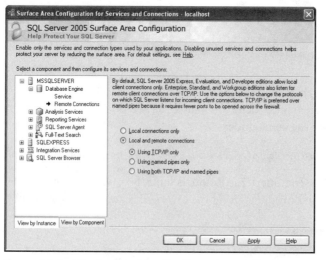

Figure 14-4   The Surface Area Configuration tool's remote connections panel

Under Database Engine you'll find two panels: Services allows the user to start, stop, and change the automatic startup settings of the service, and Remote Connections is perhaps one of the more important switches to remember. By default, in the Express, Evaluation, and Developer editions of SQL Server, remote connections are disabled. Thus, if you installed Express Edition and try to connect to it from another client machine, the connection will fail. To enable remote connections, you must choose which kind of remote connections to allow.

> **Note**   If you allow remote connections and are still having trouble connecting, check your firewall settings. You might have to add an exception for the sqlsvr.exe process or open a specific port for SQL Server.

The other important feature of this tool is the ability to configure which features should be on or off. Clicking on Surface Area Configuration for Features launches the dialog box shown in Figure 14-5.

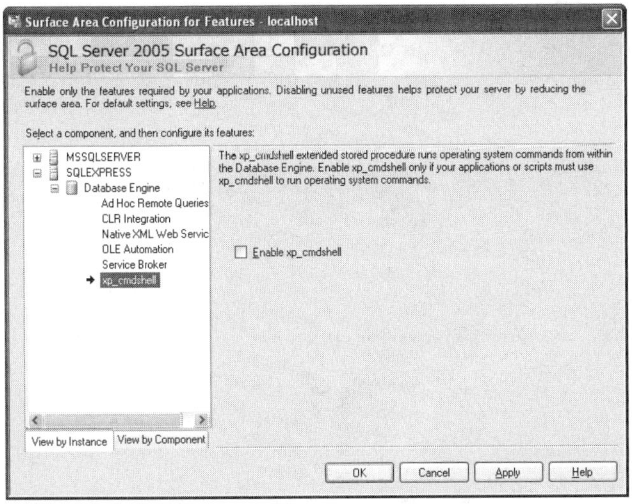

Figure 14-5   The Surface Area Configuration tool's features panel

Express Edition has a reduced set of features to enable or disable compared to other versions of SQL Server. This is because Express Edition doesn't have features such as SQL Mail, Database Mail, and SQL Server Agent. In Figure 14-5, you can see that the Surface Area Configuration tool allows you to enable and disable the use of the *xp_cmdshell* extended stored procedure. Other features that you can turn on and off include the CLR, ad hoc remote queries, and Service Broker.

You can programmatically turn on and off each of these options via the *sp_configure* stored procedure. To view these options, set the Show Advanced property on *sp_configure* first. There is also a new system view called *sys.configurations* that effectively shows the same information as *sp_configure* with the Show Advanced option set.

Working with SQL Server Express Edition

SQL Server Management Studio Express is a graphical user interface tool for managing SQL Server. It is a stripped-down version of its parent SQL Server Management Studio. The full version, which ships with all other editions of SQL Server, includes support for managing Analysis Services and Integration Services and offers much more functionality. This isn't to say that Management Studio Express is not useful; on the contrary, it supports all the basic administration functions, such as backup and restore, and it provides a rich text editor for creating and executing queries.

You can launch Management Studio Express from the Start menu. You first see a Connection dialog box. The default *SQLEXPRESS* instance name is automatically provided for you, so to connect to your Express Edition instance on your local machine, simply click the Connect button.

The GUI has three main parts: the toolbar, the Object Explorer tree view, and the document window, as shown in Figure 14-6. Visual Studio users will be most familiar with how the GUI works—in fact, SQL Server Management Studio is technically a Visual Studio application.

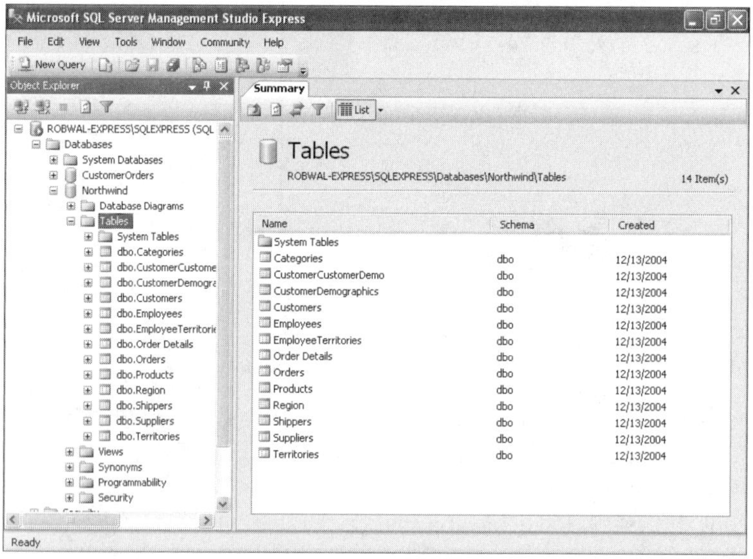

Figure 14-6   The SQL Server Management Studio Express tool

Figure 14-6 shows Management Studio Express connected to a server. The Object Explorer tree enumerates the Tables node of the Northwind database. One issue to note is that multi-select is not supported in Object Explorer in either Management Studio or Management Studio Express. To perform an action such as deleting multiple objects, you must use the Summary panel. By default, this panel shows information that depends on which object is selected in Object Explorer. You can close this panel without closing Management Studio Express. If this panel is not visible, you can always enable it by choosing Summary from the View menu or by pressing F7.

On the subject of multi-select, you can hold down the Ctrl key and select multiple objects in the grid and then right-click on the grid to see a shortcut menu of available options. This is the same behavior you would expect from any other Windows application. Another thing you will notice with shortcut menus and multi-select is that a lot more options are available when you select only one object. Because Object Explorer only supports selecting one item at a time, you get the same shortcut menu for both Object Explorer and the Summary grid if you have only one object selected.

You can use Management Studio Express to manage other editions of SQL Server, but the functionality is limited to what is available for Express Edition. (For example, when you connect to Workgroup Edition or Enterprise Edition, there is no way to manage Agent jobs.)

At this point, we are ready to discuss some of the more useful features within Management Studio Express. For this example, we will create a new database called CustomerOrders. Connect to your Express Edition server and select New Database from the shortcut menu of the Database Node in Object Explorer. This brings up the New Database dialog box (Figure 14-7).

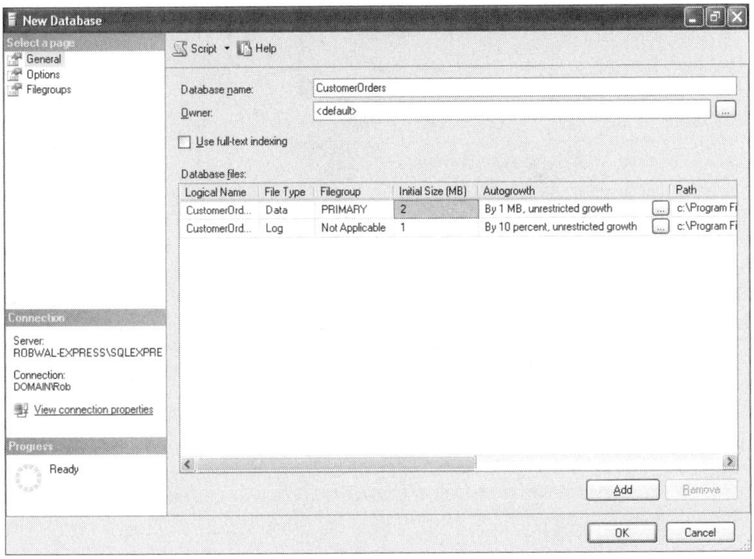

Figure 14-7   The New Database dialog box in Management Studio Express

Using this dialog box, we can specify the most common parameters, such as data and log file location, autogrowth parameters, and other database attributes. Almost all dialog boxes in Management Studio Express (including those in the full version of Management Studio) allow you to script the action instead of actually executing the action against the server. This is useful in a variety of ways—for example, if we want to know exactly what will be executed against our server without actually executing any commands. All you do is click the Script button in the dialog box and choose where to dump the script.

Once we have specified the name of the database—in our case, CustomerOrders—we can click OK, and we will see the new CustomerOrders node in Object Explorer. Now it's time to create a table for our new database. We could open a new query window and type the *CREATE TABLE* syntax with all the interesting columns we want, but there is a much simpler way to use Management Studio Express.

Management Studio Express provides a table designer for creating and modifying tables, as well as a view designer. To launch the table designer, right-click on the Tables node under our new database and choose New Table. This launches the table designer in another document window, as shown in Figure 14-8. This modeless approach allows users to go back and forth between document windows without having to close down each one first. Every dialog box used in Management Studio Express is modeless, so you do not have to launch another instance of Management Studio Express to do other work while another task (such as restoring a database) is taking a long time.

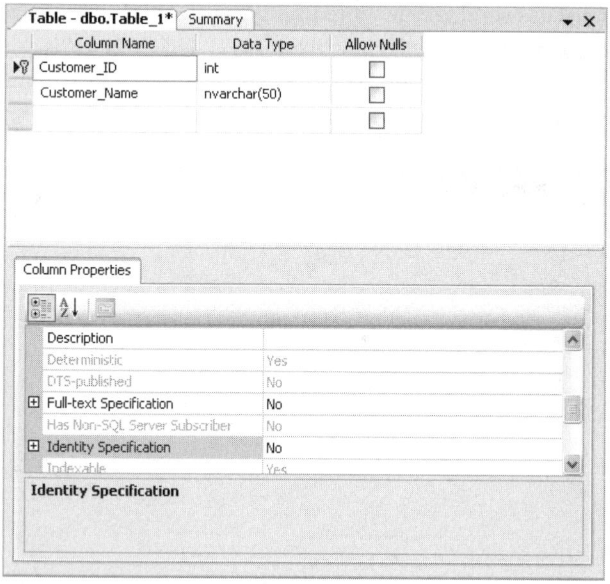

Table - dbo.Table_1*	Summary		▼ ✕

Column Name	Data Type	Allow Nulls
▶🔑 Customer_ID	int	☐
Customer_Name	nvarchar(50)	☐
		☐

Column Properties

Description	
Deterministic	Yes
DTS-published	No
⊞ Full-text Specification	No
Has Non-SQL Server Subscriber	No
⊞ Identity Specification	No
Indexable	Yes

Identity Specification

Figure 14-8   The table designer in Management Studio Express

The table designer has two main sections, the column definition grid and the column properties panel at the bottom of the window. The grid allows you to simply type the name of the column, select a data type from the combo box, and specify whether the column will allow null values. You can set the primary key, create an index, and create check constraints—among other things—by right-clicking a row in the grid. The power of the table designer and its ease of use make it a valuable asset in Management Studio Express.

The View designer in Management Studio Express provides a feature-rich environment for creating and modifying views. This designer has four panes: Diagram, Criteria, SQL, and Results. You can enable all panes at once (which results in a busy user interface, but if you have a big enough monitor this might be OK). For a clearer demonstration, Figure 14-9 shows the designer with the Diagram and Criteria panes, and Figure 14-10 shows the SQL and Results panes. These figures show data from the Northwind database because it offers a more complex relationship than the single table we have built so far in this chapter.

The Diagram pane shows an entity relationship among the various tables within the view.

> **Note**   To diagram the database, you can use a separate Diagram node in Object Explorer, which produces a user interface that is similar to the designers previously described.

The boxes indicate a table; you can resize and move them by clicking and dragging with the mouse. This view is not read-only; it's interactive—you can modify the contents of the tables and add or remove tables. For example, if you selected the Description check box in the Categories table, this would add Description to the criteria pane and you can add this to your view.

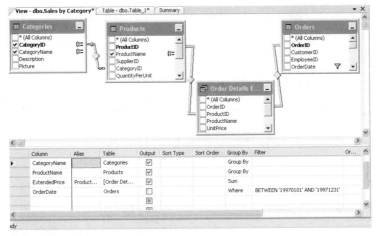

Figure 14-9   The View designer with the Diagram and Criteria panes

Figure 14-10   The View designer with the SQL and Results panes

If you want to tweak the T-SQL in the view, you can do so through the SQL pane. Any changes made in the SQL pane are carried over to all the other panes, and vice-versa. So if you checked the Description check box in the Categories table, this information is automatically added to the Criteria pane and the T-SQL within the SQL pane.

To conclude our discussion of Management Studio Express, we'll look at the ability to create and manage ad hoc queries. To create a new query, you simply click the New Query button. This creates a new document window and allows you to free-type T-SQL or load or save a script file. The query editor (as it is called) does not have IntelliSense (which offers autocompletion based on the first few characters of an object name that are typed), but it does have some other helpful features, such as line numbering and displaying the execution plan. Figure 14-11 shows the execution plan of the Invoices view in the Northwind database.

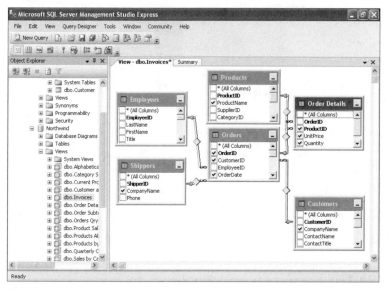

Figure 14-11   Invoices view

Notice the three tabs in the bottom section of the document window: Results, Messages, and Execution Plan. The Results tab normally shows up by default, displaying the results of whatever we submitted to SQL Server. In this example, to get the Execution Plan tab to show up, we had to first choose Include Actual Execution Plan from the Query menu.

Management Studio Express goes far beyond any management tool provided with MSDE—which is, basically, nothing. Most important, its tools are free and can be freely distributed with any custom application as long as the SQL Server Express Edition engine is shipped in the same application.

SQLCMD Command-Line Tool

Traditionally, command-line tools have always been available for executing script or ad hoc queries against SQL Server. These have included iSQL and oSQL, which each use a different technology, such as Open Database Connectivity (ODBC), to connect to the server instance and have different features. In SQL Server 2005, a new command-line tool replaces both oSQL and iSQL. SQLCMD is not just a replacement—it extends the functionality of the current tools in a variety of ways. Some of the new features include the following:

- Scripting variables

- Ability to include multiple in-line scripts

- Ability to dynamically change connections

- Support for Dedicated Administrator Connection (DAC)

- Support for the new SQL Server 2005 data types: *xml* and *nvarchar(max)*

Suppose you need to create a maintenance script that performs a DBCC *CHECKDB*, performs a database backup, and then copies the backup file to another location. Here is an example T-SQL script:

```
DBCC CHECKDB ('Northwind') WITH NO_INFOMSGS
GO
BACKUP DATABASE [Northwind] TO DISK='C:\Backups\Northwind\Northwind.bak'
GO
Exec xp_cmdshell 'copy C:\Backups\Northwind\*.bak D:\TapeBackupDropFolder\Northwind'
GO
```

Life with this single script file goes well, and eventually you are tasked with doing this for another database. Fine—you copy and paste the code and change the Northwind entries to pubs entries, and now you have the script shown in Listing 14-1.

Listing 14-1   T-SQL script

```
DBCC CHECKDB ('Northwind') WITH NO_INFOMSGS
GO
BACKUP DATABASE [Northwind] TO DISK='C:\Backups\Northwind\Northwind.bak'
GO
Exec xp_cmdshell 'copy C:\Backups\Northwind\*.bak D:\TapeBackupDropFolder\Northwind'
GO
DBCC CHECKDB ('Pubs') WITH NO_INFOMSGS
GO
BACKUP DATABASE [Pubs] TO DISK='C:\Backups\Pubs\Pubs.bak'
GO
Exec xp_cmdshell 'copy C:\Backups\Pubs\*.bak D:\TapeBackupDropFolder\Pubs'
GO
```

Time passes, and you are asked to do this for another three databases, and the location of the drop folder has changed. You can imagine that every time you want to add databases to this script, another copy and paste will be required, which introduces the possibility of bugs within the script. Wouldn't it be great if we could use variables within the script instead? SQLCMD in SQL Server 2005 supports the use of variables for this type of scenario. To create a variable, we use *:SETVAR*, as shown in the modified script in Listing 14-2.

Listing 14-2   T-SQL script (modified)

```
:SETVAR DatabaseName Northwind
DBCC CHECKDB ($(DatabaseName)) WITH NO_INFOMSGS
GO
BACKUP DATABASE $(DatabaseName) TO DISK='C:\Backups\$(DatabaseName)\$(DatabaseName).bak'
GO
Exec xp_cmdshell 'copy C:\Backups\$(DatabaseName)\*.bak D:\TapeBackupDropFolder\
$(DatabaseName)'
GO

:SETVAR DatabaseName Pubs
```

```
DBCC CHECKDB ($(DatabaseName)) WITH NO_INFOMSGS
GO
BACKUP DATABASE $(DatabaseName) TO DISK='C:\Backups\$(DatabaseName)\$(DatabaseName).bak'
GO
Exec xp_cmdshell 'copy C:\Backups\$(DatabaseName)\*.bak
D:\TapeBackupDropFolder\$(DatabaseName)'
GO
```

Before we optimize this example, we should mention a few key points. You can create and change variables throughout the script. You can also place the value of the variable by typing the name of the variable preceded by $(and followed by). The replacement happens at run time for the script, and as you can see in this example, it dynamically places the backup in the folder whose name is defined in the variable. In addition, a list of environment variables are available to use within your script. They are listed in Table 14-3.

Table 14-3   SQLCMD Environment Variables

Variable	Related Switch	Read/Write
SQLCMDUSER	U	R
SQLCMDPASSWORD	P	N/A
SQLCMDSERVER	S	R
SQLCMDWORKSTATION	H	R
SQLCMDDBNAM	d	R
SQLCMDLOGINTIMEOUT	l	R/W
SQLCMDSTATTIMEOUT	t	R/W
SQLCMDHEADERS	h	R/W
SQLCMDCOLSEP	s	R/W
SQLCMDCOLWIDTH	w	R/W
SQLCMDPACKETSIZE	a	R
SQLCMDERRORLEVEL	m	R/W
SQLCMDMAXVARTYPEWIDTH	y	R/W
SQLCMDMAXFIXEDTYPEWIDTH	Y	R/W

Using these special variables is the same as using a custom variable. For example, if we want to print out the name of the workstation executing the script, we can do the following:

```
Print "$(SQLCMDWORKSTATION)"
```

Returning to our example, if we simply left the script as is, our managers and colleagues might question our programming skills. To make this script more efficient, let's just write the process once and define the variables on the command line. So our script, which we will call BackupMyDatabase.sql, becomes that shown in Listing 14-3.

Listing 14-3   BackupMyDatabase.sql

```
DBCC CHECKDB ($(DatabaseName)) WITH NO_INFOMSGS
GO
BACKUP DATABASE $(DatabaseName) TO DISK='C:\Backups\$(DatabaseName)\$(DatabaseName).bak'
GO
Exec xp_cmdshell 'copy C:\Backups\$(DatabaseName)\*.bak D:\TapeBackupDropFolder\
$(DatabaseName)'
GO
```

To back up each database, we can use SQLCMD as follows:

```
SQLCMD -E -S.\SQLEXPRESS -i "C:\MaintenanceScripts\BackupMyDatabase.sql" -
v DatabaseName="Northwind"
```

Notice that the parameters are case sensitive. A *-v* tells SQLCMD that the subsequent value is a variable name, not a severity level (as in the case of a capital *V*). In this example, we tell SQL-CMD to connect to the *SQLEXPRESS* instance, execute the .sql script file BackupMyData-base.sql, and define the *DatabaseName* variable to be *Northwind*. Now all we have to do is repeat this for pubs, and we are all set. However, we can leverage yet another feature to make this even more efficient. We can include a script within an existing script and still keep our variable values. Expanding on this example, let's create a new script called LaunchBackup.sql, as defined in Listing 14-4.

Listing 14-4   LaunchBackup.sql

```
:SETVAR DatabaseName Northwind
:R "BackupMyDatabase.sql"
:SETVAR DatabaseName Pubs
:R "BackupMyDatabase.sql"
```

The *:R* tells SQLCMD to load the .sql script in-line at run time, before execution. Now it's quite easy to add another database to our process of backing up the database.

> **Note**   To run this script, all we have to do is tell SQLCMD to launch the script file. We don't have to pass variables because they are defined in the script file itself.
>
> ```
> SQLCMD -E -S.\SQLEXPRESS -i "LaunchBackup.sql"
> ```

What if we want to perform this operation on multiple servers or multiple instances of SQL Server? SQLCMD has yet another feature that allows the script to make connections from within the script using the *:CONNECT* command. Expanding on our example, say we want to connect to our test server and perform this operation. We can do this with the code in Listing 14-5.

Listing 14-5   LaunchBackup.sql connecting to multiple servers

```
--Connect to my local express machine
:CONNECT .\SQLEXPRESS
:SETVAR DatabaseName Northwind
:R "BackupMyDatabase.sql"
--Now connect to my test server and backup Northwind
:CONNECT TESTSERVER1\SQLEXPRESS
:SETVAR DatabaseName Northwind
:R "BackupMyDatabase.sql"
```

Combining the powerful functionality of connecting to different servers and variables gives us the ability to do a plethora of tasks within our database scripts. One additional key feature of SQLCMD is worth mentioning here. In the SQL Server 2005 engine there is a special thread that basically waits just for a connection from an SQLCMD client with a -A parameter. This special connection is called the Dedicated Administrator Connection (DAC), and its purpose is to provide administrators with a way to connect to SQL Server if, for whatever reason, the server becomes unresponsive. The DAC is available only when you connect to SQL Server via SQLCMD with the special -A parameter. You cannot make this connection from any other client software (such as SQL Server Management Studio). In addition, only one connection of this type is allowed per instance of SQL Server because this feature is designed to be used only in the event that administrators cannot gain access through a normal network connection.

There is one more important point about the DAC: In Express Edition, the DAC is disabled. To use the DAC, you must start the service running a trace flag of 7806. If you have trouble connecting to the DAC once you restart the service with this trace flag, make sure the SQL Server Browser service is running.

> **Note**   To set a trace flag in SQL Server, use -T# as a startup parameter, where # is the trace flag number. If you view the SQL Server service properties from the Service control panel, you will see a Start Parameters text box. To experiment with the DAC, you can place -T7806 (no space between the T and 7) there.

SQLCMD can connect to the Express Edition–only feature called User Instances. However, there is another tool called SSEUTIL (available for download on MSDN) that looks and feels like SQLCMD but is used primarily to manage Express Edition user instances. Before we go into the details of SSEUTIL and how it compares with SQLCMD, we should first provide an overview of User Instances.

User Instances

SQL Server 2005 Express Edition supports a new feature called User Instances that is available only when you use the .NET Framework data provider for SQL Server (SqlClient). This feature is available only with Express Edition. A user instance is basically a separate instance of the Express Edition database engine that is generated by a parent instance. For example, as a Windows administrator, I can install Express Edition on my client machine. I can then take an application that will connect to Express Edition and create a separate instance of Express Edition for each client user of the application. When connected to this user instance, the client is the sysadmin for that instance but does not have any special privileges on the parent Express Edition instance. This is important because software executing on a user instance with limited permissions cannot make system-wide changes. This is because the instance of Express Edition is running under the non-administrator Windows account of the user, not as a service. Each user instance is isolated from its parent instance and from any other user instances running on the same computer. Databases running on a user instance are opened in single-user mode only, and multiple users cannot connect to databases running on a user instance. Replication, distributed queries, and remote connections are also disabled for user instances.

When you install Express Edition, one of the setup wizard pages asks if you want to enable User Instances. This is one way to enable them; the other is to toggle the setting using *sp_configure*, as follows:

```
-- Enable user instances.
sp_configure 'user instances enabled','1'
-- Disable user instances.
sp_configure 'user instances enabled','0'
```

There are a couple more restrictions on user instances. For one thing, the only way to connect to them is through Named Pipes. In addition, SQL Server logins are not supported on User Instances; connections to the User Instance must be made using Windows Authentication.

Now that we have discussed User Instances and some of the restrictions on them, take a look at the example connection string shown here:

```
Data Source=.\\SQLExpress;Integrated Security=true;
User Instance=true;AttachDBFilename=|DataDirectory|\InstanceDB.mdf;
Initial Catalog=InstanceDB;
```

Note the following:

- The *Data Source* keyword refers to the parent instance of Express Edition that is generating the user instance. The default instance is *.\sqlexpress*.

- *Integrated Security* is set to *true*. To connect to a user instance, you must use Windows Authentication; SQL Server logins are not supported.

- *User Instance* is set to *true*, which invokes a user instance. (The default is *false*.)

- *AttachDBFilename* indicates the location of the InstanceDB database.

- The *DataDirectory* substitution string enclosed in the pipe symbols refers to the data directory of the application opening the connection and provides a relative path indicating the location of the .mdf and .ldf database and log files. If you want to locate these files elsewhere, you must provide the full path to the files.

When the *SqlConnection* is opened, it is redirected from the default Express Edition instance to a run-time-initiated instance running under the caller's account.

Unlike with versions of SQL Server that run as a service, SQL Server Express Edition user instances do not need to be manually started and stopped. Each time a user logs in and connects to a user instance, the user instance is started if it is not already running. User instance databases have the *AutoClose* option set so that the database is automatically shut down after a period of inactivity. The Sqlservr.exe process that is started is kept running for a limited timeout period after the last connection to the instance is closed, so it does not need to be restarted if another connection is opened before the timeout has expired. The user instance automatically shuts down if no new connection opens before that timeout period has expired. A system administrator on the parent instance can set the duration of the timeout period for a user instance by using *sp_configure* to change the user instance timeout option. The default is 60 minutes.

The first time a user instance is generated for each user, the master and msdb system databases are copied from the Template Data folder to a path under the user's local application data repository directory for exclusive use by the user instance. This path is typically C:\Documents and Settings\<UserName>\Local Settings\Application Data\Microsoft\Microsoft SQL Server Data\SQLEXPRESS. When a user instance starts up, the tempdb, log, and trace files are also written to this directory. A name is generated for the instance, which is guaranteed to be unique for each user.

By default, all members of the Windows Builtin\Users group are granted permissions to connect on the local instance as well as read and execute permissions on the SQL Server binaries. Once the credentials of the calling user hosting the user instance have been verified, that user becomes the sysadmin on that instance. Only shared memory is enabled for user instances, which means that only operations on the local machine are possible.

Note that users must be granted both read and write permissions on the .mdf and .ldf files specified in the connection string. These files represent the database and log files, respectively, and are a matched set. The main database file will not open if it is coupled with the wrong log file.

To prevent data corruption, a database in the user instance is opened with exclusive access. If two different user instances share the same database on the same computer, the user on the first instance must close the database before it can be opened in a second instance. User instances are given a globally unique ID (GUID) as a name. This makes them a bit more challenging to manage. The SSEUTIL command-line tool makes managing user instances easier.

SSEUTIL

SSEUTIL is available as a free download from MSDN at *http://www.microsoft.com/downloads/ details.aspx?FamilyID=fa87e828-173f-472e-a85c-27ed01cf6b02&DisplayLang=en*. The tool lets you easily interact with SQL Server. Among other things, it allows you to:

- Connect to the main instance or user instance of SQL Server

- Create, attach, detach, and list databases on the server

- Upgrade database files to match the version of the server

- Execute SQL statements via the console (similar to SQLCMD)

- Retrieve the version of SQL Server that is running

- Enable and disable trace flags (for example, to trace SQL statements sent to the server by any client application)

- List the instances of SQL Server on the local machine or on remote machines

- Checkpoint and shrink a database

- Measure the performance of executing specific queries

- Create and play back lists of SQL commands for the server to execute

- Log all input and output

Although SSEUTIL might appear to be very similar to SQLCMD, it uses different command-line switches to connect to SQL Server. Once you connect to SQL Server Express Edition using SSEUTIL, you can either use a command prompt (which resembles the SQLCMD behavior) or you can request a graphical console window. Either way, you must specify either *-c* for a command prompt or *-consolewnd* to use the graphical user interface, as shown here:

```
c:\>sseutil -s .\sqlexpress -c
```

The default in Express Edition is to call the named instance, *SQLEXPRESS*. SSEUTIL does not require you to specify the *-s* (*servername*) parameter; if you omit it, SSEUTIL assumes that you want to connect to the *SQLEXPRESS* instance on your local box.

Another important point about SSEUTIL and defaults is worth noting. From the preceding information, you might think that we are connecting to the default parent instance of Express Edition. In reality, we are connecting to the server instance, *.\sqlexpress*, but our connection is then redirected to the user instance of the user who is logged in. If we specifically want to connect to the Express Edition parent instance, we must pass the *-m* parameter, as shown here:

```
c:\>sseutil -s .\sqlexpress -m
```

If you do not specify *-m*, SSEUTIL uses the *-child* parameter, which tells SSEUTIL to connect to the user instance of the user who is currently logged in to the box. You can append a different user name to this parameter if you want to connect to another user instance. To obtain a list of active user instances, you can use the *-childlist* parameter, as shown here:

```
C:\>sseutil -childlist
User            Pipe                                        ProcessId   Status
-------------------------------------------------------------------------------
DOMAIN\robwal   \\.\pipe\07EB27D8-877E-4F\tsql\query        2168        alive
```

Now that we have discussed how to connect to both the parent and child instances using SSEUTIL, it's time to do something useful with SSEUTIL. Suppose we want to attach the Northwind database to our user instance. We can enumerate the databases that are attached to our instance by using the *-l* parameter:

```
C:\>sseutil -child DOMAIN\robwal -l
Using instance '\\.\pipe\07EB27D8-877E-4F\tsql\query'.

1. master
2. tempdb
3. model
4. msdb
```

SSEUTIL lets you attach or detach a database from both the parent instance and any user instance on your box. Let's attach Northwind, whose database files we'll assume are located in a directory called C:\databases.

```
C:\>sseutil -child DOMAIN\robwal -a "C:\databases\northwnd.mdf" Northwind
Using instance '\\.\pipe\07EB27D8-877E-4F\tsql\query'.

Command completed successfully.
```

For completeness, we specified the *-child* parameter, but it does not actually need to be there because it's the default. The *-a* attach parameter takes two values. The first is the location of the .mdf file to be attached. The second parameter, which is optional, is the name of the database. Once attached, the database exists on the instance but not on the parent instance, again reinforcing our belief that user instances are truly a separate instance of SQL Server.

Here is a list of databases on the parent Express Edition instance:

```
C:\>sseutil -m -l master
2. tempdb
3. model
4. msdb
5. CustomerOrders
```

Here is a list of databases on the user instance of the logged-in user:

```
C:\>sseutil -child DOMAIN\robwal -l
Using instance '\\.\pipe\07EB27D8-877E-4F\tsql\query'.

1. master
2. tempdb
3. model
4. msdb
5. Northwind
```

If you develop an application that uses user instances, you will find that SSEUTIL is a useful tool for quickly obtaining information and performing tasks against the instance. Alternatively, you can use SQL Server Management Studio Express against a user instance. To do this, you simply obtain the pipename of the user instance. One way to get the pipename is to use the *-childlist* parameter. In the examples in this section, our pipename was \\.*pipe**07EB27D8-877E-4F**tsql**query*. Open Management Studio Express and, in the Connection dialog box, paste the pipename into the Server Name text box.

Installing SQL Server Express Edition

Express Edition offers three ways to perform an installation or upgrade: via the Setup Wizard, silently through the use of command-line parameters, or via a configuration file. Using the wizard to quickly get your development or test environment set up is useful if you don't already have Express Edition on your box. When bundling Express Edition with your application, you might find that installing Express Edition via a configuration file provides the best user experience.

> **Note**   You might already have Express Edition installed if you already have Visual Studio installed on your box. You can check to see whether Express Edition is installed by going to the Services applet in Control Panel and looking for "SQL Server (SQLEXPRESS)." Note that if you installed Express Edition and gave it a different instance name from the default SQLEXPRESS, the name shown in Control Panel might be different.

You can also run the Express Edition setup to install another instance of Express Edition. Express Edition supports up to 50 instances on a single computer.

Existing Beta Versions of SQL Server 2005

If your box contains previously released versions of SQL Server, you might run into problems if you attempt to upgrade to the released version by simply executing the setup program of the released version. To ensure a successful installation, manually remove all pre-release versions of SQL 2005, Visual Studio 2005, and the .NET

Framework 2.0. If you are lucky enough to be in this situation, it will be beneficial to read through the MSDN article "Uninstalling Previous Versions of Visual Studio 2005," which can be found at *http://msdn.microsoft.com/vstudio/express/support/uninstall*.

If you want to download SQL Server 2005 Express Edition from the Microsoft Web site, you can go to *http://go.microsoft.com/fwlink/?LinkId=64064*. On this Web page, you will see the prerequisites for installing Express Edition. You need Windows Installer 3.0 and the .NET Framework 2.0. The Web page includes links for downloading these—you must install them before you can run setup for Express Edition, which is the file on this Web page called SQLEXPR.exe. If you simply run this executable, it self-extracts and runs through the Setup Wizard. To perform a silent installation or an installation using the configuration file, you can download this file and run SQLEXPR.exe /X with the /X attribute; this extracts the files without running the Setup Wizard. If you do not want to extract all the Express Edition installation files, you can also pass installation parameters to SQLEXPR.exe.

After we have the Express Edition setup bits on our box, we can either run through the wizard to install or upgrade to SQL Server 2005 Express Edition or we can use a configuration file called Template.ini to silently perform an installation. We will first cover installing Express Edition using the Setup Wizard.

Using the Setup Wizard to Manually Install Express Edition

Once you have the .NET Framework 2.0 and at least version 3.0 of the Windows Installer, you are ready to run the Setup Wizard for Express Edition. In this example, we'll use the setup for SQL Server Express Edition with Advanced Services (SQLEXPR_ADV.exe).

Setup first installs the SQL Native Client and some additional setup support files. The SQL Native Client is a standalone data access API that is used for both the Object Linking and Embedding Database (OLE DB) and ODBC. It combines the SQL OLE DB provider and the SQL ODBC driver into one native dynamic link library (DLL). It also provides new functionality beyond that supplied by the Microsoft Data Access Components (MDAC).

Next, the familiar Welcome screen appears. Continuing through the wizard brings us to the System Configuration Check page. This page does some rudimentary checks to see whether your operating system is appropriate for Express Edition and whether you have any pending reboot requests from another application, and it looks at a number of other issues that could prevent setup from working correctly.

The next page in the wizard is for registration (Figure 14-12).

Notice the Hide Advanced Configuration Options check box at the bottom of the page. This is selected by default; if we uncheck it, we can change the name of the instance and database collation, as well as specify some of the service settings for the SQL Server and SQL Server Browser service.

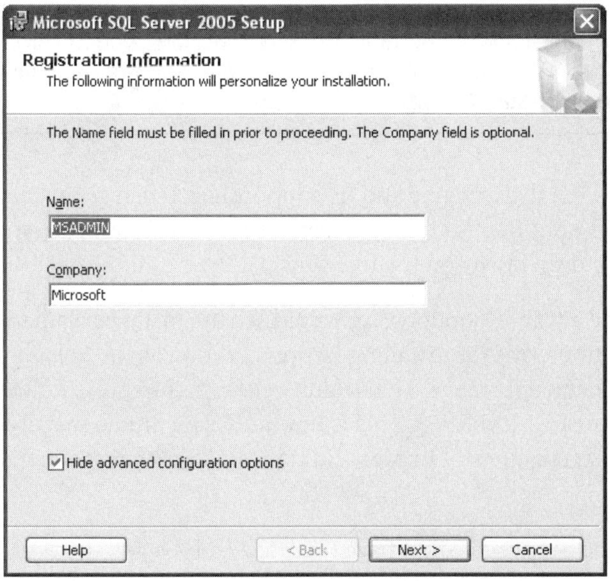

Figure 14-12   Registration Information page of the Setup Wizard

If we uncheck the box and continue with the wizard, we are presented with the Feature Selection page. This page is not an advanced option; users see it whether or not they chose to hide the advanced options. Figure 14-13 shows this page.

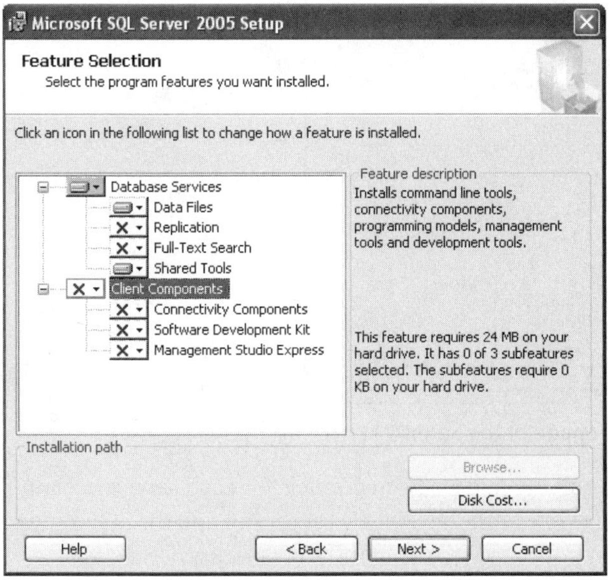

Figure 14-13   Feature Selection page of the Setup Wizard

> **Note**   If you are running the Advanced Services setup and have IIS installed, you will see an option for installing Reporting Services. Choosing to install Reporting Services leads to a few other dialog boxes not listed here. If you choose to install Reporting Services, the wizard will ask if you want to configure Report Server now or later. If you select later, you can always configure it through the Report configuration tool, which is one of the tools provided under the Microsoft SQL Server node on the Start Menu.

Note that by default, only the database engine and its support files (such as the master database) are installed. If you want Replication, Full-Text, or Management Tools, you must explicitly add them using the drop-downs in the tree view.

If we had requested to see the advanced options, we would see the Instance Name page next. This page has two option buttons, one for installing Express Edition as the default instance and one for installing it as a named instance. The default is to install Express Edition as a named instance with the name SQLEXPRESS. This is how all Visual Studio installations of Express Edition create their installations of Express Edition, and it is the recommended installation.

The next advanced page is the Service Account page (Figure 14-14).

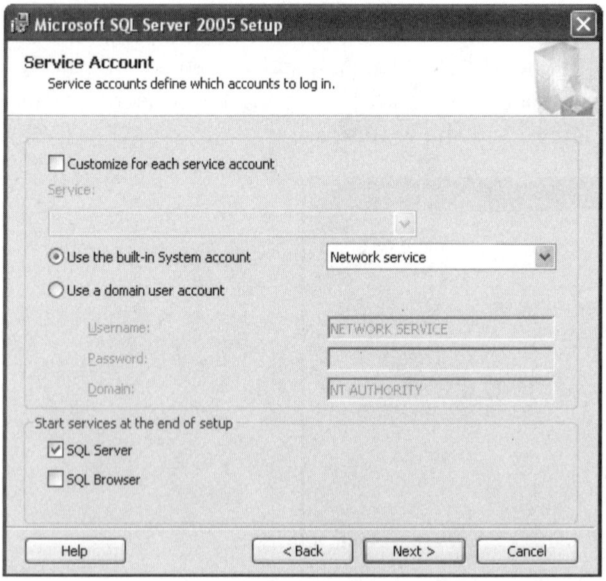

Figure 14-14   Service Account page of the Setup Wizard

The first option you see is the ability to specify credentials for each service account. This is applicable if you are planning to use both the SQL Server service and the SQL Browser service. Most of the time, you can run both services using the Network service account.

Most developers can probably intuit what the "SQL Server" service is. But some of us might not be so sure about the SQL Browser service. In previous versions of SQL Server that supported the idea of "instances," there needed to be a way for client machines to connect to SQL and ask, "What are all your available instances and their corresponding port numbers?" Traditionally, UDP port 1434 was used for this. As you can imagine, having this inside the server process was not only taxing but there was no way to effectively turn it off. In SQL Server 2005, this functionality has been separated out into a new service called the SQL Browser service.

The next page is the Authentication Mode page. Here you can set Express Edition to support only Windows Authentication or both SQL Authentication and Windows Authentication. If you choose Windows Authentication, you will still have an "sa" account, but that account will be disabled and have a random complex password.

Continuing on with the wizard, if you elected to show advanced pages, you will see the Collation Settings page. This page allows you to specify whether databases should be case sensitive or case insensitive, as well as what kind of sort order the database should use.

The next page asks you if you want to enable User Instances. User Instances is an Express Edition–specific feature—it is not available on any other edition of SQL Server. (User Instances were covered in the earlier section titled "Working with SQL Server Express Edition.")

At this point, we are almost done with the wizard. The last page that requires us to make some sort of decision is the Error And Usage Report Settings page. This page asks two questions: "Can SQL automatically send error reports to either a central server in your organization or directly to Microsoft?" and "Can SQL send data on feature usage to Microsoft?" Both of these options enable Microsoft to compile a lot of information about the use of SQL Server and common errors. With the second option, no personally identifiable information is sent, so if you are in the mood to contribute to future products, you might want to select this box.

The next page shows a summary of the actions the wizard will perform. After this page, the wizard proceeds and installs Express Edition, including whatever options you have selected. The final page (Figure 14-15) displays some information about the installation, as well as two hyperlinks.

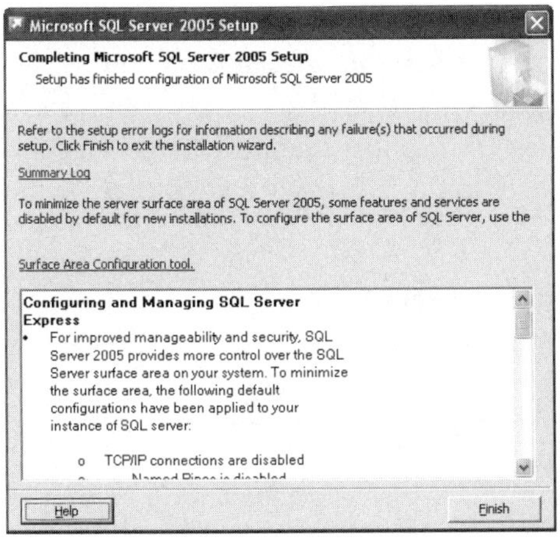

Figure 14-15   The final page of the Setup Wizard

The Summary Log link loads the installation log into Notepad for your reading or trouble-shooting enjoyment. The other link launches the Surface Area Configuration tool (described previously in this chapter). If you do not run this tool now, you can always launch it from the Start menu later.

At this point, you are ready to start working with Express Edition.

Installing via Command-Line Parameters or a Configuration File

There are two ways to programmatically install, modify, and remove SQL Server Express Edition components. First, you can call Setup.exe and pass a series of parameters on the command line. Alternatively, you can configure all the parameters within a single file and pass that file as a command-line parameter to Setup.exe. This file is called Template.ini, and it is located in the root directory of SQL Server Express Edition. An example of launching Setup and passing the configuration file is as follows:

```
start /wait setup.exe /qb /settings c:\template.ini
```

For those not familiar with the Windows command line, *start* is an application that opens a new console window. The */wait* parameter tells the console window to wait until the program finishes execution before terminating itself. A complete list of parameters for the *start* command can be obtained by passing */?* as a parameter. The next parameter in the line of code is *setup.exe*. This is the name of the application to launch; in this case, it's SQL Server Express Edition Setup. The rest of the parameters are arguments for the setup program. The Setup.exe argument */qb* tells Setup to run in quiet mode, which requires no user interaction. This mode does provide some visual indicators about the status of the installation.

> **Note**   Alternatively, you can specify */qn*. The only difference between */qb* and */qn* is that when you use */qn*, there is no visual status indicator.

All errors from Setup in SQL Server are recorded in the setup log files. If you call Microsoft for support on a setup-related issue, the Product Support specialist will probably want you to find these files. By default, the setup log files are located at C:\Program Files\Microsoft SQL Server\90\Setup Bootstrap\LOG\Files. If you encounter problems when developing a custom SQL Server Express Edition installation, these files are a good place to start debugging.

The */settings* parameter in the command-line code tells Setup to obtain all installation information from the file that is defined in the next parameter. In the code example, the Template.ini file is stored in the root of the C drive.

> **Important**   If you have downloaded SQL Server Express Edition from the Web, you might not see the Setup.exe application if you downloaded a single SQLEXPR.exe file. If this is the case, you need to call Setup.exe from the command line to extract the Express Edition files from this compressed executable. To perform this extraction, run *SQLEXPR /X* from the command line. A dialog box appears, prompting you for a location to extract the files to. The Express Edition files are copied to the location that you specify. These files include Setup.exe and Template.ini, among many other files and folders.

The Template.ini file is a plain-text file that can be opened by using a text editor such as Notepad. When you open this file, you see a long commented introduction citing examples of how to use the file. The file itself is well documented, and a lot of the options are explained in great detail within the file itself. For that reason, this chapter will not cover all the options. Instead, here are just a few parameters of interest.

- *PIDKEY*   This parameter is required for all SQL Server editions except Express Edition.

- *ADDLOCAL*   This parameter specifies which components to install. If *ADDLOCAL* is not specified, Setup will fail. You can specify *ADDLOCAL=ALL*, which installs all components. There are some rules around this parameter:

1. Feature names are case sensitive.

2. To use *ADDLOCAL*, you must provide a comma-delimited list of features to install, with no spaces between them.

3. Selecting a parent feature installs only the parent feature, not the child features. Installing a child feature installs the parent and the child. Removing the parent feature removes both the parent and the child.

4. You can also use *ADDLOCAL* to add components in maintenance mode.

Confused yet? We will give a few examples to demonstrate various installation combinations. First we must explain the possible valid feature names for each edition of SQL Server. Tables 14-4, 14-5, and 14-6 list the feature names unique to Express Edition, Express Edition with Advanced Services, and the Express Edition Toolkit, respectively.

Table 14-4   Valid *ADDLOCAL* Parameters for Express Edition

Feature	Parent Feature Name	Child Feature Name
SQL Server Database Services	SQL_Engine	
Data Files		SQL_Data_Files
Replication		SQL_Replication
Client Components	Client_Components	
Connectivity Components		Connectivity
Software Development Kit		SDK

Table 14-5   Valid *ADDLOCAL* Parameters for Express Edition with Advanced Services

Feature	Parent Feature Name	Child Feature Name
SQL Server Database Services	SQL_Engine	
Data Files		SQL_Data_Files
Replication		SQL_Replication
Full-Text Search Engine		SQL_FullText
Reporting Services	RS_Server	
Report Manager		RS_Web_Interface
Client Components	Client_Components	
Connectivity Components		Connectivity
Software Development Kit		SDK
Management Studio Express		SQL_SSMSE

Table 14-6   Valid *ADDLOCAL* Parameters for Express Edition Toolkit

Feature	Parent Feature Name	Child Feature Name
Client Components	Client_Components	
Connectivity Components		Connectivity
Software Development Kit		SDK
BI Development Studio		SQL_WarehouseDevWorkbench
Management Studio Express		SQL_SSMSE

Even though some of these feature names are self-descriptive, Table 14-7 provides a description of each feature, for completeness of our discussion.

Table 14-7   Feature Descriptions

Feature	Description
SQL_Engine	Installs the SQL Server database, including the SQL Server and SQL Browser services.
SQL_Data_Files	Installs core SQL Server databases, including master, the resource database, and tempdb.
SQL_Replication	Installs files necessary for replication support in SQL Server Express Edition.

Table 14-7 Feature Descriptions

Feature	Description
SQL_FullText	Installs files necessary for Full-Text Search support in SQL Server Express Edition.
RS_Server	Installs the Report Server service, which manages, executes, and renders reports.
RS_Web_Interface	Installs a Web-based tool used for managing a report server.
Client_Components	Installs components for communication between clients and servers, including network libraries for ODBC and OLE DB. Also installs applications such as the sqlcmd utility (oSQL replacement), SQL Server Configuration Manager, and the Surface Area Configuration tool.
Connectivity	Installs components for communication between clients and servers, including network libraries for ODBC and OLE DB.
SDK	Installs software development kits containing resources for model designers and programmers. This includes SQL Server Management Objects (SMO) and Replication Management Objects (RMO).
SQL_SSMSE	Installs SQL Server Management Studio Express.
SQL_WarehouseDevWork bench	Installs BI Development Studio. It also installs Visual Studio Premier Partner Edition if no other edition of Visual Studio is installed on the computer.

With this many options, quite a number of installation combinations are possible. The following are examples of common installation configurations.

- **Install everything**
  `ADDLOCAL=All`

- **Install just the database engine**
  `ADDLOCAL=SQL_Engine,SQL_Data_Files,Connectivity`

- **Install just the management tool**
  `ADDLOCAL=SQL_SSMSE`

- **REMOVE** This parameter is similar to *ADDLOCAL*, but instead of adding components, it either removes a specific component or completely uninstalls SQL Server Express Edition if you use *REMOVE=ALL*. The following example removes the client components of an existing Express Edition installation:

  `REMOVE=Client_Components.`

You do not have to specify an instance name because the *Client_Components* are not instance-specific. If you were removing *SQL_Replication* support, you would also need to add the following parameter:

  `INSTANCENAME=<<name of the SQL Server Express Instance>>`

The *INSTANCENAME* parameter is needed whenever the feature is instance-specific.

■ **UPGRADE**   This parameter is used for upgrading from MSDE to SQL Server 2005 Express Edition. When you use *UPGRADE*, you must also specify the same instance name as the name of the MSDE instance you want to upgrade. This is because it is possible to have up to 16 MSDE instances on a single computer. Here is an example upgrade parameter:

```
UPGRADE=SQL_Engine INSTANCENAME=<<name of the MSDE instance>>
```

When you write custom installation applications, it can be difficult to remember these parameter names for all your projects. To make things easier, you can write a custom wrapper class to encapsulate setting the parameters and to provide a reusable stub for your custom applications. The wrapper class does not expose every option available, but it should give enough direction to suit your own custom installation needs.

Deploying Express Edition Applications Using a Wrapper

As a custom application developer, you have three options for including SQL Server Express Edition within your application:

■ Install Express Edition and then install the custom application.

■ Install the custom application and then install Express Edition.

■ Create a wrapper that combines the two-step process into a single step.

> **Note**   An SQL Server Express Edition wrapper cannot be MSI–based because Windows Installer does not support multiple instantiation of the Windows Installer service.

The remainder of this section focuses on creating a wrapper for your custom application. In the example code (Listing 14-6), the wrapper is a simple class that exposes three public methods: *IsExpressInstalled*, *EnumSQLInstances*, and *InstallExpress*. Ideally, you would not need to know if Express Edition or any other instance of SQL Server is already installed on the local computer. This example includes this information in case you want to give the user the flexibility of selecting an existing instance of Express Edition to install your application against instead of always creating a new instance.

The first step is to create a simple class. This class will contain local variables of most of the command-line switches supported by the SQLEXP.exe installation executable. These switches will be exposed as properties of the class object.

> **Important**   The following code is only a guideline for installing SQL Server Express Edition with your custom application. It is not complete and does not contain robust error-handling routines.

Listing 14-6   *EmbeddedInstall* class definition

```
public class EmbeddedInstall
    {
        #region Internal variables

        //Variables for setup.exe command line
        private string instanceName = "SQLEXPRESS";
        private string installSqlDir = "";
        private string installSqlSharedDir = "";
        private string installSqlDataDir = "";
        private string addLocal = "All";
        private bool sqlAutoStart = true;
        private bool sqlBrowserAutoStart = false;
        private string sqlBrowserAccount = "";
        private string sqlBrowserPassword = "";
        private string sqlAccount = "";
        private string sqlPassword = "";
        private bool sqlSecurityMode = false;
        private string saPassword = "";
        private string sqlCollation = "";
        private bool disableNetworkProtocols = true;
        private bool errorReporting = true;
        private string sqlExpressSetupFileLocation =
System.Environment.GetEnvironmentVariable("TEMP") + "\\sqlexpr.exe";

        #endregion
        #region Properties
        public string InstanceName
        {
            get
            {
                return instanceName;
            }
            set
            {
                instanceName = value;
            }
        }

        public string SetupFileLocation
        {
            get
            {
                return sqlExpressSetupFileLocation;
            }
            set
            {
                sqlExpressSetupFileLocation = value;
            }
        }

        public string SqlInstallSharedDirectory
        {
            get
```

```
        {
            return installSqlSharedDir;
        }
        set
        {
            installSqlSharedDir = value;
        }
    }
    public string SqlDataDirectory
    {
        get
        {
            return installSqlDataDir;
        }
        set
        {
            installSqlDataDir = value;
        }
    }
    public bool AutostartSQLService
    {
        get
        {
            return sqlAutoStart;
        }
        set
        {
            sqlAutoStart = value;
        }
    }
    public bool AutostartSQLBrowserService
    {
        get
        {
            return sqlBrowserAutoStart;
        }
        set
        {
            sqlBrowserAutoStart = value;
        }
    }
    public string SqlBrowserAccountName
    {
        get
        {
            return sqlBrowserAccount;
        }
        set
        {
            sqlBrowserAccount = value;
        }
    }
    public string SqlBrowserPassword
    {
        get
```

```csharp
        {
            return sqlBrowserPassword;
        }
        set
        {
            sqlBrowserPassword = value;
        }
    }
    //Defaults to LocalSystem
    public string SqlServiceAccountName
    {
        get
        {
            return sqlAccount;
        }
        set
        {
            sqlAccount = value;
        }
    }
    public string SqlServicePassword
    {
        get
        {
            return sqlPassword;
        }
        set
        {
            sqlPassword = value;
        }
    }
    public bool UseSQLSecurityMode
    {
        get
        {
            return sqlSecurityMode;
        }
        set
        {
            sqlSecurityMode = value;
        }
    }
    public string SysadminPassword
    {
        set
        {
            saPassword = value;
        }
    }
    public string Collation
    {
        get
        {
            return sqlCollation;
        }
```

```
                    set
                    {
                        sqlCollation = value;
                    }
                }
                public bool DisableNetworkProtocols
                {
                    get
                    {
                        return disableNetworkProtocols;
                    }
                    set
                    {
                        disableNetworkProtocols = value;
                    }
                }
                public bool ReportErrors
                {
                    get
                    {
                        return errorReporting;
                    }
                    set
                    {
                        errorReporting = value;
                    }
                }
                public string SqlInstallDirectory
                {
                    get
                    {
                        return installSqlDir;
                    }
                    set
                    {
                        installSqlDir = value;
                    }
                }
            }

            #endregion
```

Now that you have set up the local variables and properties for the class object, you can work on the public methods *IsExpressInstalled*, *EnumSQLInstances*, and *InstallExpress*.

Assuming a local server installation, you can simply look to the local registry to see if Express Edition or any other instance of SQL Server is installed. The method in Listing 14-7 enumerates and checks the *Edition* value for keys under this location, where *X* is an instance of SQL Server:

```
HKEY_LOCAL_MACHINE\Software\Microsoft\Microsoft SQL Server\MSSQL.X
```

Listing 14-7   *IsExpressInstalled* method

```
public bool IsExpressInstalled()
        {
              using (RegistryKey Key =
Registry.LocalMachine.OpenSubKey("Software\\Microsoft\\Microsoft SQL
Server\\", false))
              {
                    if (Key == null) return false;
                    string[] strNames;
                    strNames = Key.GetSubKeyNames();

                    //If we cannot find a SQL Server registry key, we
don't have SQL Server Express installed
                    if (strNames.Length == 0) return false;

                    foreach (string s in strNames)
                    {
                        if (s.StartsWith("MSSQL."))
                        {
                            //Check to see if the edition is "Express Edition"
                            using (RegistryKey KeyEdition =
Key.OpenSubKey(s.ToString() + "\\Setup\\", false))
                            {
                                if ((string)KeyEdition.GetValue("Edition") ==
"Express Edition")
                                {
                                    //If there is at least one instance of
SQL Server Express installed, return true
                                    return true;
                                }
                            }
                        }
                    }
              }
              return false;
        }
```

By using the local registry, you can determine more information about all the SQL Server instances, regardless of edition, that are installed on the local server. Having this information is useful if you want to provide a better installation experience. The method in Listing 14-8 takes a reference and populates a string array for instances, editions, and versions. It returns the number of instances of SQL Server that are installed on the local computer.

Listing 14-8   *EnumSQLInstances* method

```
public int EnumSQLInstances(ref string[] strInstanceArray, ref string[] strEditionArray,
  ref string[] strVersionArray)
        {
              using (RegistryKey Key = Registry.LocalMachine.OpenSubKey("Software\\
Microsoft\\Microsoft SQL Server\\", false))
              {
```

```
                    if (Key == null) return 0;
                    string[] strNames;
                    strNames = Key.GetSubKeyNames();

                    //If we can not find a SQL Server registry key, we return 0 for none
                    if (strNames.Length == 0) return 0;

                    //How many instances do we have?
                    int iNumberOfInstances = 0;

                    foreach (string s in strNames)
                    {
                        if (s.StartsWith("MSSQL."))
                            iNumberOfInstances++;
                    }

                    //Reallocate the string arrays to the new number of instances
                    strInstanceArray = new string[iNumberOfInstances];
                    strVersionArray = new string[iNumberOfInstances];
                    strEditionArray = new string[iNumberOfInstances];
                    int iCounter = 0;

                    foreach (string s in strNames)
                    {
                        if (s.StartsWith("MSSQL."))
                        {
                            //Get Instance name
                            using (RegistryKey KeyInstanceName =
Key.OpenSubKey(s.ToString(), false))
                            {
                                strInstanceArray[iCounter] =
(string)KeyInstanceName.GetValue("");
                            }

                            //Get Edition
                            using (RegistryKey KeySetup =
Key.OpenSubKey(s.ToString() + "\\Setup\\", false))
                            {
                                strEditionArray[iCounter] =
(string)KeySetup.GetValue("Edition");
                                strVersionArray[iCounter] =
(string)KeySetup.GetValue("Version");
                            }

                            iCounter++;
                        }
                    }
                    return iCounter;
                }
            }
```

Now you can install SQL Server Express Edition. First convert the properties of the class into a command-line argument that can be passed to the SQLEXPR.exe installation application. The *BuildCommandLine* method performs this task, as shown in Listing 14-9.

Listing 14-9   *BuildCommandLine* method

```
private string BuildCommandLine()
        {
            StringBuilder strCommandLine = new StringBuilder();

            if (!string.IsNullOrEmpty(installSqlDir))
            {
                strCommandLine.Append("INSTALLSQLDIR=\"").Append(installSqlDir)
                    .Append("\"");
            }

            if (!string.IsNullOrEmpty(installSqlSharedDir))
            {
                strCommandLine.Append("INSTALLSQLSHAREDDIR=\"")
                    .Append(installSqlSharedDir).Append("\"");
            }

            if (!string.IsNullOrEmpty(installSqlDataDir))
            {
                strCommandLine.Append("INSTALLSQLDATADIR=\"")
                    .Append(installSqlDataDir).Append("\"");
            }

            if (!string.IsNullOrEmpty(addLocal))
            {
                strCommandLine.Append(" ADDLOCAL=\"").Append(addLocal).Append("\"");
            }

            if (sqlAutoStart)
            {
                strCommandLine.Append(" SQLAUTOSTART=1");
            }
            else
            {
                strCommandLine.Append(" SQLAUTOSTART=0");
            }

            if (sqlBrowserAutoStart)
            {
                strCommandLine.Append(" SQLBROWSERAUTOSTART=1");
            }
            else
            {
                strCommandLine.Append(" SQLBROWSERAUTOSTART=0");
            }

            if (!string.IsNullOrEmpty(sqlBrowserAccount))
            {
                strCommandLine.Append("SQLBROWSERACCOUNT=\"")
                    .Append(sqlBrowserAccount).Append("\"");
            }

            if (!string.IsNullOrEmpty(sqlBrowserPassword))
```

```
    {
        strCommandLine.Append("SQLBROWSERPASSWORD=\"")
            .Append(sqlBrowserPassword).Append("\"");
    }

    if (!string.IsNullOrEmpty(sqlAccount))
    {
        strCommandLine.Append(" SQLACCOUNT=\"").Append(sqlAccount)
            .Append("\"");
    }

    if (!string.IsNullOrEmpty(sqlPassword))
    {
        strCommandLine.Append(" SQLPASSWORD=\"").Append(sqlPassword)
            .Append("\"");
    }

    if (sqlSecurityMode == true)
    {
        strCommandLine.Append(" SECURITYMODE=SQL");
    }

    if (!string.IsNullOrEmpty(saPassword))
    {
        strCommandLine.Append(" SAPWD=\"").Append(saPassword).Append("\"");
    }

    if (!string.IsNullOrEmpty(sqlCollation))
    {
        strCommandLine.Append(" SQLCOLLATION=\"").Append(sqlCollation)
            .Append("\"");
    }

    if (disableNetworkProtocols == true)
    {
        strCommandLine.Append(" DISABLENETWORKPROTOCOLS=1");
    }
    else
    {
        strCommandLine.Append(" DISABLENETWORKPROTOCOLS=0");
    }

    if (errorReporting == true)
    {
        strCommandLine.Append(" ERRORREPORTING=1");
    }
    else
    {
        strCommandLine.Append(" ERRORREPORTING=0");
    }

    return strCommandLine.ToString();
}
```

Now you can create the *InstallExpress* method, as shown in Listing 14-10.

Listing 14-10 *InstallExpress* method

```
public bool InstallExpress()
    {

        //In both cases, we run Setup because we have the file.
        Process myProcess = new Process();
        myProcess.StartInfo.FileName = sqlExpressSetupFileLocation;
        myProcess.StartInfo.Arguments = "/qb " + BuildCommandLine();
        /*      /qn -- Specifies that setup run with no user interface.
                /qb -- Specifies that setup show only the basic
user interface. Only dialog boxes displaying progress information are
displayed. Other dialog boxes, such as the dialog box that asks users if
they want to restart at the end of the setup process, are not displayed.
        */
        myProcess.StartInfo.UseShellExecute = false;

        return myProcess.Start();

    }
```

Finally, we can create the sample application that calls the wrapper class and installs Express Edition, as shown in Listing 14-11.

Listing 14-11 Main application

```
class Program
    {
        static void Main(string[] args)
        {
            EmbeddedInstall EI = new EmbeddedInstall();

            if (args.Length > 0)
            {
                int i = 0;
                while (i < args.Length)
                {
                    if ((string)args[i].ToUpper() == "-V")
                    {
                        string[] strInstanceArray = new string[0];
                        string[] strVersionArray = new string[0];
                        string[] strEditionArray = new string[0];

                        int iInstances = EI.EnumSQLInstances(ref strInstanceArray,
                          ref strEditionArray, ref strVersionArray);
                        if (iInstances > 0)
                        {
                            for (int j = 0; j <= iInstances - 1; j++)
                            {
                                Console.WriteLine("SQL Server Instance:
                                  \"" + strInstanceArray[j].ToString() + "\" -- " +
```

```
strEditionArray[j].ToString() + "   (" + strVersionArray[j].ToString() +
")");
                    }

                }
                else
                {
                    Console.WriteLine("No instance of SQL Server
                        Express found on local server.\n\n");
                }

                return;
            }

            if ((string)args[i].ToUpper() == "-I")
            {
                if (EI.IsExpressInstalled())
                {
                    Console.WriteLine("An instance of SQL Server
                        Express is installed.\n\n");
                }
                else
                {
                    Console.WriteLine("There are no SQL Server
                        Express instances installed.\n\n");
                }

                return;
            }

            i++;
        }
    }

    Console.WriteLine("\nInstalling SQL Server 2005 Express Edition\n");

    EI.AutostartSQLBrowserService = false;
    EI.AutostartSQLService = true;
    EI.Collation = "SQL_Latin1_General_Cp1_CS_AS";
    EI.DisableNetworkProtocols = false;
    EI.InstanceName = "SQLEXPRESS";
    EI.ReportErrors = true;
    EI.SetupFileLocation = "C:\\Downloads\\sqlexpr.exe";
      //Provide location for the Express setup file
    EI.SqlBrowserAccountName = ""; //Blank means LocalSystem
    EI.SqlBrowserPassword = ""; // N/A
    EI.SqlDataDirectory = "C:\\Program Files\\Microsoft SQL Server\\";
    EI.SqlInstallDirectory = "C:\\Program Files\\";
    EI.SqlInstallSharedDirectory = "C:\\Program Files\\";
    EI.SqlServiceAccountName = ""; //Blank means LocalSystem
    EI.SqlServicePassword = ""; // N/A
    EI.SysadminPassword = "ThIsIsALoNgPaSswoRd1234!!"; //<<Supply
      a secure sysadmin password>>
    EI.UseSQLSecurityMode = true;
```

```
        EI.InstallExpress();

        Console.WriteLine("\nInstalling custom application\n");


        //
If you need to run another MSI install, remove the following comment lines
        //and fill in information about your MSI

        /*Process myProcess = new Process();
        myProcess.StartInfo.FileName = "";//
<<Insert the path to your MSI file here>>
        myProcess.StartInfo.Arguments = ""; //
<<Insert any command line parameters here>>
        myProcess.StartInfo.UseShellExecute = false;
        myProcess.Start();*/


    }
```

Deploying Express Edition Applications Using ClickOnce

ClickOnce is a new feature that is part of the .NET Framework 2.0. ClickOnce lets you deploy Windows-based client applications to a computer by placing the application files on a Web or file server that is accessible to the client, and then providing the user with a link. This lets users download and run applications from centrally managed servers without requiring administrator privileges on the client machine.

In this section, we will illustrate the ClickOnce/SQL Server Express Edition experience by developing a simple Windows Forms application. This application uses the AdventureWorks sample database, which can be downloaded from *http://go.microsoft.com/fwlink/ ?linkid=65209.*

This example demonstrates how to create a single WinForm for viewing the departments in the HumanResources.Department table in the AdventureWorks database.

To create a Windows Form that displays the Department table:

1. Launch Visual Studio.

2. Create a new Windows Application project.

3. When the Form1 Designer opens, add a reference to the AdventureWorks database.

4. Right-click the Project node in the Solution Explorer pane, and then select both Add and Existing Item. Navigate to the AdventureWorks database and click OK.

5. In the Data Source Configuration Wizard, under the Tables node, select the Department table, and then continue with the wizard.

6. When the wizard finishes, you will notice the AdventureWorks.mdf database icon in the Solution Explorer pane and a new AdventureWorks connection in Database Explorer.

Database Explorer lets you perform database operations such as creating new tables, querying and modifying existing data, and other database development functions.

7.   Add the *DataGridView* control to the WinForm. This grid control is located in the toolbox. When you drag the grid control onto the design surface, you have the option of selecting the AdventureWorks dataset that you created when you ran the Data Source Configuration Wizard. This dialog box is shown in Figure 14-16.

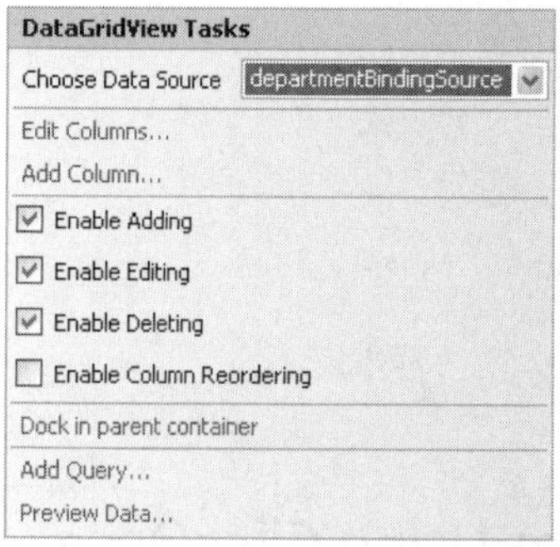

DataGridView Tasks

Choose Data Source `departmentBindingSource`

Edit Columns...
Add Column...

☑ Enable Adding
☑ Enable Editing
☑ Enable Deleting
☐ Enable Column Reordering

Dock in parent container
Add Query...
Preview Data...

Figure 14-16   *DataGridView* task properties

When a data source is configured, you should be able to run the application and have the grid control display the values for the Department table, as shown in Figure 14-17.

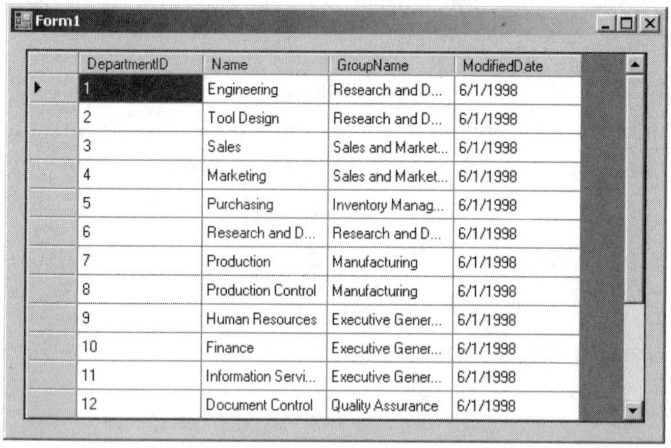

	DepartmentID	Name	GroupName	ModifiedDate	
▶	1	Engineering	Research and D...	6/1/1998	
	2	Tool Design	Research and D...	6/1/1998	
	3	Sales	Sales and Market...	6/1/1998	
	4	Marketing	Sales and Market...	6/1/1998	
	5	Purchasing	Inventory Manag...	6/1/1998	
	6	Research and D...	Research and D...	6/1/1998	
	7	Production	Manufacturing	6/1/1998	
	8	Production Control	Manufacturing	6/1/1998	
	9	Human Resources	Executive Gener...	6/1/1998	
	10	Finance	Executive Gener...	6/1/1998	
	11	Information Servi...	Executive Gener...	6/1/1998	
	12	Document Control	Quality Assurance	6/1/1998	

Figure 14-17   Department table enumerated using the *DataGridView* control

You can now deploy this application using ClickOnce.

To deploy the application by using ClickOnce:

1.   To publish the application, select Publish from the Build menu. The Publish Wizard opens, as shown in Figure 14-18.

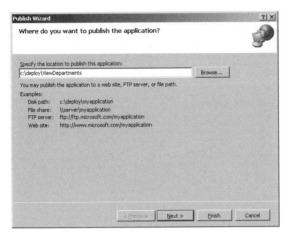

Figure 14-18   The Publish Wizard's Where Do You Want To Publish The Application? page

2. On the first page of the wizard, you specify where the compiled bits should physically be placed. In the Specify The Location To Publish This Application box, enter **C:\deploy\ViewDepartments**. Click Next.

3. On the next page of the wizard (Figure 14-19), you specify the location from which users will install the application. Select From A CD-ROM Or DVD-ROM. Click Next.

Figure 14-19   The Publish Wizard's How Will Users Install The Application? page

4. On the next page of the wizard (Figure 14-20), you specify whether the application will check for updates.

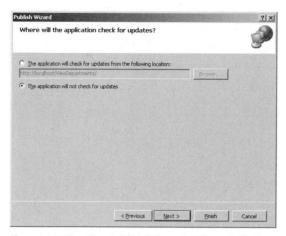

Figure 14-20   The Publish Wizard's Where Will The Application Check For Updates? page

5. ClickOnce gives applications the ability to look for updates at certain times, such as when the application starts or whenever the application developer chooses to call the appropriate update APIs. (There are some issues when you use this feature with a database, which we will discuss later in this chapter.) For this example, select The Application Will Not Check For Updates. Click Next.

6. The last page of the wizard (Figure 14-21) displays summary information and notifies you that, because you are writing to a CD or DVD-ROM, Setup will install a shortcut and entry in Add Or Remove Programs for your application. Click Finish.

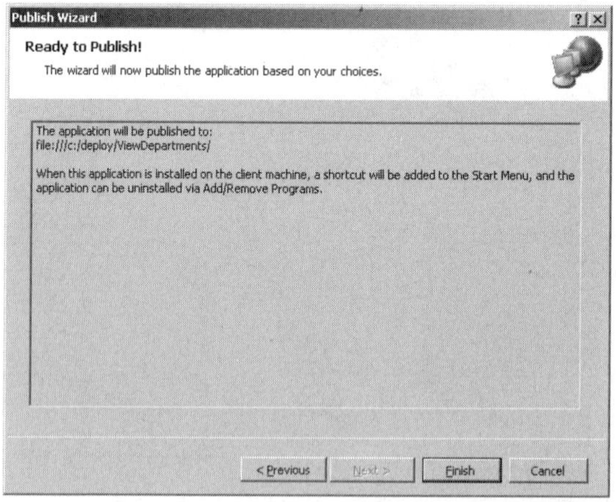

Figure 14-21   The last page of the Publish Wizard

You can write an application that will live on the application server only and will never be installed on the client machine. Regardless, ClickOnce will prompt the user to install any missing prerequisites, such as the .NET Framework 2.0 or SQL Server Express Edition, as shown in Figure 14-22.

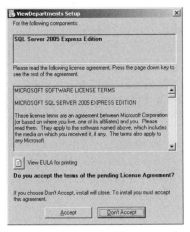

Figure 14-22 Prerequisites not installed when user launches application

> **Note** Whether the application itself is designed to be run on demand from an application server or to be installed locally, SQL Server Express Edition is always installed on the local machine if the custom application requires it.

When the Publish Wizard finishes, new files are placed in the deployment directory. These files include the compressed data files and the setup installer application. You might want to copy these files to a CD and distribute them to your users, to provide them with the necessary information about applications that use SQL Server Express Edition.

> **Important** A user who is not an administrator on the local machine cannot install the .NET Framework or SQL Server Express Edition. In this case, system administrators should deploy these components first. They can do this manually or by using a distributed software management system such as Microsoft Systems Management Server.

Updating ClickOnce Deployments That Use Express Edition

Let's say the user has successfully installed your application. The user had all necessary prerequisites installed, and the application is running successfully.

The user has entered data into version 1.0 of the database and now the developers have come out with version 2.0. This new version has an additional column named Location in the Departments table. This new column stores the geographical location of the department. When the developer deploys version 2.0, the new version of the database is pushed down to the client, and the previous version is automatically moved to a separate folder named Pre. The developer must now write a database migration script to move all the data from the 1.0 version in the Pre folder to the new database. Because Visual Studio does not have any tools to support this migration, it is completely up to the developer to perform the migration.

Otherwise, none of the data that was entered in version 1.0 will be accessible to the application. Additionally, if the developer publishes an interim version (for example, 2.1) to reconcile this migration problem, or if the developer accesses the .mdf file by simply viewing the structure in Server Explorer, ClickOnce will see that the date and time stamp has changed and deploy version 2.1 of the database. This moves version 2.0 of the database to the Pre folder and deletes version 1.0 of the database. This results in complete data loss and a poor customer experience.

To avoid this, Visual Studio should not include the database files when the application is deployed. Instead, it should provide installation scripts to create the database. Also, when you perform a ClickOnce update, you must write and call a separate update script. The ViewDepartments example from the previous section is used in this section to help clarify the workaround solution.

ViewDepartments is a single WinForm application that connects to the AdventureWorks database and enumerates the Departments table. When you developed this application, you pointed Visual Studio to the AdventureWorks .mdf file, which created a new data source. As the application functions now, if you were to use ClickOnce to deploy the application, the application would always include the AdventureWorks .mdf file and cause the overwrite problems mentioned previously.

To avoid unwanted data loss in your application:

1. In the Solution Explorer pane, click the AdventureWorks database icon, as shown in Figure 14-23. In the Properties pane, select Do Not Copy for the Copy To Output Directory property.

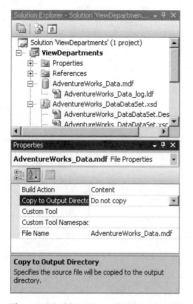

Figure 14-23   Copy To Output Directory property for the AdventureWorks database

2. Choose Properties from the Project menu to open the Project Properties panel. On the Publish tab, click Application Files. This launches a dialog box that contains a list of all the files in the solution. Change the Publish Status to Exclude for the .MDF and .LDF files of the AdventureWorks database, as shown in Figure 14-24.

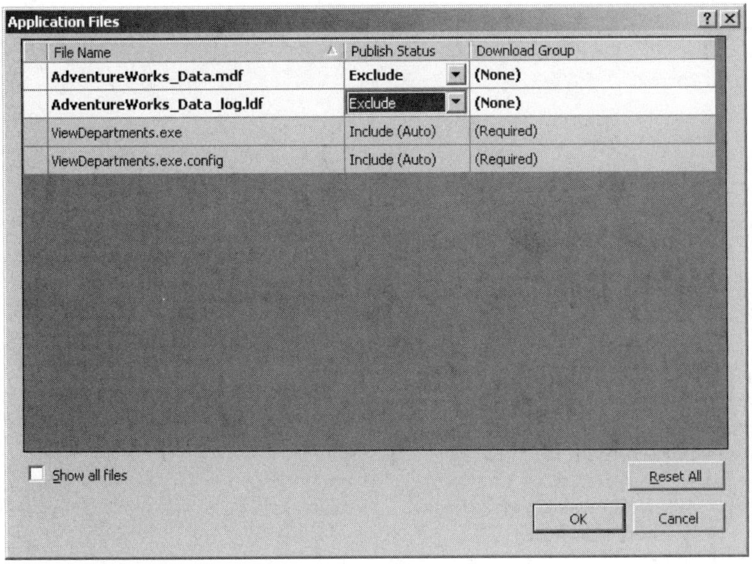

File Name	∧	Publish Status	Download Group
AdventureWorks_Data.mdf		Exclude ▼	(None)
AdventureWorks_Data_log.ldf		Exclude ▼	(None)
ViewDepartments.exe		Include (Auto)	(Required)
ViewDepartments.exe.config		Include (Auto)	(Required)

☐ Show all files   Reset All

                                        OK   Cancel

Figure 14-24   Excluding database files

Next you script the creation of the AdventureWorks database. You can script a database in many ways. In SQL Server Management Studio, you can right-click the database in Object Explorer and create the entire script there. Or you can use the Generate SQL Server Scripts Wizard for more scripting options. If you do not have a license for this tool or any other scripting tool, you can easily create a small program that uses the SQL Server Management Objects (SMO) object model to create a script by using the *Scripter* class.

> **Note**   If you installed SQL Server Express Edition with the developer components, the SMO DLLs are located by default in C:\Program Files\Microsoft SQL Server\90\SDK\Assemblies.

Listing 14-12 shows a modified AdventureWorks creation script that creates and populates the Departments table.

Listing 14-12   AdventureWorks creation script

```
USE [master]
GO
CREATE DATABASE [AdventureWorks] ON  PRIMARY
( NAME = N'AdventureWorks_Data', FILENAME = N'C:\Program Files\Microsoft
 SQL Server\MSSQL.1\MSSQL\Data\AdventureWorks_Data.mdf' , SIZE = 167936KB
, MAXSIZE = UNLIMITED, FILEGROWTH = 16384KB )
```

```
  LOG ON
( NAME = N'AdventureWorks_Log', FILENAME = N'C:\Program Files\Microsoft
SQL Server\MSSQL.1\MSSQL\Data\AdventureWorks_Log.ldf' , SIZE = 2048KB ,
MAXSIZE = 2048GB , FILEGROWTH = 16384KB )
  COLLATE SQL_Latin1_General_CP1_CI_AS
GO
EXEC dbo.sp_dbcmptlevel @dbname=N'AdventureWorks', @new_cmptlevel=90
GO
USE [AdventureWorks]
GO
SET ANSI_NULLS ON
GO
SET QUOTED_IDENTIFIER ON
GO
CREATE TYPE [dbo].[Name] FROM [nvarchar](50) NULL
GO
EXEC sys.sp_executesql N'CREATE SCHEMA [HumanResources] AUTHORIZATION [dbo]'
GO
CREATE TABLE [HumanResources].[Department](
    [DepartmentID] [smallint] IDENTITY(1,1) NOT NULL,
    [Name] [dbo].[Name] NOT NULL,
    [GroupName] [dbo].[Name] NOT NULL,
    [ModifiedDate] [datetime] NOT NULL CONSTRAINT
[DF_Department_ModifiedDate]  DEFAULT (getdate()),
 CONSTRAINT [PK_Department_DepartmentID] PRIMARY KEY CLUSTERED
(
    [DepartmentID] ASC
)WITH (IGNORE_DUP_KEY = OFF) ON [PRIMARY]
) ON [PRIMARY]
GO
insert into [HumanResources].[Department](Name,Groupname)
values('Engineering','Research and Development')
GO
insert into [HumanResources].[Department](Name,Groupname) values('Tool
Design','Research and Development')
GO
insert into [HumanResources].[Department](Name,Groupname)
values('Sales','Sales and Marketing')
GO
insert into [HumanResources].[Department](Name,Groupname)
values('Marketing','Sales and Marketing')
GO
insert into [HumanResources].[Department](Name,Groupname)
values('Purchasing','Inventory Management')
GO
insert into [HumanResources].[Department](Name,Groupname) values('Research
and Development','Research and Development')
GO
insert into [HumanResources].[Department](Name,Groupname)
values('Production','Manufacturing')
GO
insert into [HumanResources].[Department](Name,Groupname)
values('Production Control','Manufacturing')
```

```
GO
insert into [HumanResources].[Department](Name,Groupname) values('Human
Resources','Executive General and Administration')
GO
insert into [HumanResources].[Department](Name,Groupname)
values('Finance','Executive General and Administration')
GO
insert into [HumanResources].[Department](Name,Groupname)
values('Information Services','Executive General and Administration')
GO
insert into [HumanResources].[Department](Name,Groupname) values('Document
 Control','Quality Assurance')
GO
insert into [HumanResources].[Department](Name,Groupname) values('Quality
Assurance','Quality Assurance')
GO
insert into [HumanResources].[Department](Name,Groupname)
values('Facilities and Maintenance','Executive General and
Administration')
GO
insert into [HumanResources].[Department](Name,Groupname) values('Shipping
and Receiving','Inventory Management')
GO
insert into [HumanResources].[Department](Name,Groupname)
values('Executive','Executive General and Administration')
GO
--This next table is used to identify the version of the database
CREATE TABLE AdventureWorks..AppInfo
(Property nvarchar(255) NOT NULL,
Value nvarchar(255))
GO
INSERT INTO AdventureWorks..AppInfo Values('Version','1.0.0.0')
GO
```

Because the actual .mdf file is not included in this solution, you must define and synchronize versions of the database that the application is connected to. An easy workaround is to add the AppInfo table to the AdventureWorks database. When you start the application, it should first check to see if the versions match. If they don't, the application should either run an upgrade script or fail. This is explained in more detail next.

To implement a version check, you add a resource file to your project and then store the script as an embedded resource within the application:

1. Right-click the project in the Solution Explorer pane and select Add, and then select New Item. Select Resource File, and then click Add. This launches the Resource File document window shown in Figure 14-25.

2. You can add the SQL scripts as separate strings or as text files; for simplicity, we'll store the Create and Update scripts as separate files within this resource. From the Add Resource drop-down menu, select Add Existing File. Locate the creation script we produced earlier and add this file.

Figure 14-25 Resource document window showing our creation script

3. Next we'll create an upgrade script for the AdventureWorks database. Although you might not have to upgrade your application right away, you should also include the upgrade script to upgrade your database to version 1.0.0.3.

```
USE [AdventureWorks]
GO
ALTER TABLE [HumanResources].[Department]
ADD Location char(2)
GO
UPDATE AdventureWorks..AppInfo set Value='1.0.0.3' where
Property='Version'
GO
```

4. Save this script as UpgradeAdventureWorks.sql. Add it to the resource file, as described earlier.

5. Modify the application to check versions and run any necessary scripts.

> **Note** In the previous example, the *Form_Load* method contains code that was autogenerated when we assigned the AdventureWorks dataset via the UI: *this.departmentTableAdapter.Fill(this.adventureWorks_DataDataSet.Department);* You should remove or comment out this code because you want to perform the database version check first.

You should also set the *DataSource* property (which was pre-populated in the grid control when you used the UI to bind the grid to the data source) to *None* (Figure 14-26).

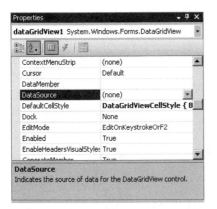

Figure 14-26 *DataSource* property autogenerated by Visual Studio

Listing 14-13 shows the complete code for the *Form1* class:

Listing 14-13 Form1.cs

```
using System;
using System.Collections.Generic;
using System.ComponentModel;
using System.Data;
using System.Drawing;
using System.Text;
using System.Windows.Forms;
using System.Data.SqlClient;
using System.Text.RegularExpressions;


namespace ViewDepartments
{

    public partial class Form1 : Form
    {

        enum VersionCheck { Failed = 0, Equal, DatabaseIsMoreNew,
          DatabaseIsOlder, DatabaseNotFound };

        private SqlConnection sqlCon = new SqlConnection();
        private SqlCommand sqlCmd = new SqlCommand();

        public Form1()
        {
            InitializeComponent();

            if (SetupDatabase() == false)
            {
                return;
            }

            PopulateGrid();
        }
```

```csharp
public bool SetupDatabase()
{
    bool bContinue = false;

    //Create a connection to SQL Server
    try
    {
        sqlCon.ConnectionString = "Server=
          .\\sqlexpress;Integrated Security=true";
        sqlCon.Open();
    }
    catch (SqlException sql_ex)
    {
        MessageBox.Show("Fail to connect to SQL Server Express\n"
+ sql_ex.Number.ToString() + " " + sql_ex.Message.ToString());
        return bContinue;
    }

    //Now that you are connected to Express, check the database versions

    switch (CheckVersion())
    {
        case (int)VersionCheck.Equal:
            {
                bContinue = true;
                break;
            }
        case (int)VersionCheck.Failed:
            {
                bContinue = false;
                break;
            }
        case (int)VersionCheck.DatabaseIsOlder:
            {
                //Run the upgrade script
                bContinue = RunScript(Resource1.UpdateAdventureWorks.ToString());
                break;
            }
        case (int)VersionCheck.DatabaseIsMoreNew:
            {
                bContinue = false;
                break;
            }
        case (int)VersionCheck.DatabaseNotFound:
            {
                //Run the creation script
                bContinue = RunScript(Resource1.CreateAdventureWorks.ToString());
                break;
            }
        default:
            {
                bContinue = false;
                break;
```

```csharp
            }

        }


        return bContinue;


    }
    public bool RunScript(string strFile)
    {
        string[] strCommands;
        strCommands = ParseScriptToCommands(strFile);
        try
        {
            if (sqlCon.State != ConnectionState.Open) sqlCon.Open();

            sqlCmd.Connection = sqlCon;

            foreach (string strCmd in strCommands)
            {
                if (strCmd.Length > 0)
                {
                    sqlCmd.CommandText = strCmd;
                    sqlCmd.ExecuteNonQuery();
                }
            }
        }
        catch (SqlException sql_ex)
        {
            MessageBox.Show(sql_ex.Number.ToString() + " " +
                sql_ex.Message.ToString());
            return false;
        }

        return true;
    }
    public int CheckVersion()
    {
        //Get Version information from application
        Version v=new Version(Application.ProductVersion.ToString());

        try
        {

            string strResult;

            //Verify that the AdventureWorks Database exists
            sqlCmd = new SqlCommand("select count(*) from
                master..sysdatabases where name='AdventureWorks'",sqlCon);
            strResult = sqlCmd.ExecuteScalar().ToString();
            if (strResult == "0")
            {
                sqlCon.Close();
                return (int)VersionCheck.DatabaseNotFound;
```

```
                }

                sqlCmd = new SqlCommand("SELECT value from
    AdventureWorks..AppInfo where property='version'", sqlCon);
                strResult=(string)sqlCmd.ExecuteScalar();

                Version vDb = new Version(strResult);

                sqlCon.Close();

                if (vDb == v)
                    return (int)VersionCheck.Equal;

                if (vDb > v)
                    return (int)VersionCheck.DatabaseIsMoreNew;

                if (vDb < v)
                    return (int)VersionCheck.DatabaseIsOlder;

            }
            catch (SqlException sql_ex)
            {
                MessageBox.Show(sql_ex.Number.ToString() + " " +
                  sql_ex.Message.ToString());
                return (int)VersionCheck.Failed;
            }
            catch (Exception system_ex)
            {
                MessageBox.Show(system_ex.Message.ToString());
                return (int)VersionCheck.Failed;
            }

            return (int)VersionCheck.Failed;

        }

        public string[] ParseScriptToCommands(string strScript)
        {
            string[] commands;
            commands = Regex.Split(strScript, "GO\r\n", RegexOptions.IgnoreCase);
            return commands;
        }

        public void PopulateGrid()
        {

            String strCmd = "Select * from [Adventureworks].[HumanResources].[Department
    ]";

            SqlDataAdapter da;

            da = new SqlDataAdapter(strCmd, sqlCon);
            DataSet ds = new DataSet();
            da.Fill(ds, "Departments");
            dataGridView1.DataSource = ds;
            dataGridView1.DataMember = "Departments";
```

```
        }

        private void Form1_Load(object sender, EventArgs e)
        {
            // TODO: This line of code loads data into the
  'adventureWorks_DataDataSet.Department' table. You can move or remove this
  line as necessary.
            //this.departmentTableAdapter.Fill(this.adventureWorks_DataDataSet.
  Department);
        }
    }
}
```

In the code for Form1.cs, a call is made to *SetDatabase()*. This function first attempts to make a connection to SQL Server Express Edition. When that call succeeds, it calls into the *Check-Version()* method, which checks to see if the AdventureWorks database exists. If it does, the method obtains the version number from the AppInfo table. If the AdventureWorks database does not exist, the creation script located in the resource file is executed. If the database version is earlier than the application version, the upgrade script is run.

Note   The version that is compared against the database comes from the *File Version* property of the project. This property can be set within the Assembly Information dialog box (which is accessible from the Application tab in Project Properties).

When you first execute this application against a blank SQL Server Express Edition database, it creates the AdventureWorks database, and you see the four columns of the Departments table. The next time you execute this application, it will be upgraded to include another column in the table named Location.

Summary

SQL Server Express Edition uses the same database engine as all the other editions of SQL Server, but with memory, disk, and some feature restrictions. Even with these restrictions, it is possible to develop and deploy a variety of Express Edition applications.

SQL Server Express Edition with Advanced Services, which was released simultaneously with Service Pack 1, allows users to develop reports and issue full-text queries against Express Edition databases. This upgrade comes with a stripped-down version of SQL Server Management Studio. The Advanced Services Toolkit also includes a graphical report designer used to create reports for Report Server. With all these features and functionality, SQL Server Express Edition provides users with a powerful relational database engine—for free.

Chapter 15

Developing Applications with SQL Server 2005 Everywhere Edition and SQL Server Merge Replication

–Stephen Forte

As technology evolves, the way we interact with data changes. With the advent of wireless data transfer technologies such as Wi-Fi and General Packet Radio Service (GPRS), mobile users now expect to have access to data anywhere and anytime, uninterrupted. The world has clearly gone digital, mobile, virtual, and personal. Applications in this new environment require connectivity as well as persistent storage for when a connection is just not possible. You have all this with SQL Server 2005 Everywhere Edition (SQL Everywhere), a scaled-down version of SQL Server that runs on small embedded devices, including the Pocket PC, Smart-Phone, and Windows CE devices as well as the Win32 platform (XP, Vista, and Tablet PC).

SQL Everywhere, which is the next release after SQL Server CE Edition, is a mobile database platform for writing applications that target Microsoft Windows mobile-based devices as well as Windows applications. SQL Everywhere is fully integrated with SQL Server 2005 and supports bidirectional replication to a back-end server running SQL Server. New features and enhancements in SQL Everywhere focus on the following:

- Integration with SQL Server 2005 and its management tools (in SQL Server Management Studio)

- Increased reliability and performance

- Faster development of mobile applications

- Integration with Microsoft Visual Studio 2005

- Deployment with ClickOnce

SQL Everywhere Integration with SQL Server 2005

Compared with what came before it, SQL Everywhere is light years ahead in terms of integration with the SQL Server tools and product line. This tighter integration with SQL Server 2005 allows mobile database administrators and developers to take advantage of SQL Server Management Studio. You can use Management Studio to manage an SQL Everywhere database on a desktop computer or a connected mobile device! You can create and design tables, write queries, and prepare and test your database locally before you deploy to a device. You can use graphical query plans to easily see query plans and modify query hints to quickly achieve performance-tuning results.

Comparing SQL Express and SQL Everywhere

SQL Server Express Edition, covered in Chapter 14, is a free version of SQL Server that runs on the Win32 platform and is intended for developing small client applications. Then why is there SQL Everywhere and when should a developer use SQL Everywhere? SQL Express is a service and requires Admin rights to install. It is the same engine as SQL Server, supporting all multi-user features, merge replication, and Transact-SQL (T-SQL). It also leaves a large footprint, over 50 megs. SQL Everywhere is a lightweight engine, runs in-proc, has an updatable resultset, supports merge replication, and can be deployed via ClickOnce technology without Admin rights. Also, it has a tiny 1.4 meg footprint. We'll let you decide which database to use in which situation, but some very simple guidance is that if you need to build multi-user applications, use SQL Express. If you're deploying a local, single-user database, SQL Everywhere is your best bet. Lastly, on a mobile device, SQL Everywhere is your only option; SQL Express will not run on a PocketPC, SmartPhone, or CE device.

One great new feature of SQL Server 2005 and SQL Everywhere Edition is SQL Server Integration Services. Integration Services enables developers to import and export data to an SQL Everywhere database from a variety of data sources, including flat files, XML, SQL Server, Microsoft Access, Oracle, and IBM DB2. Transferring data is also made easy with bulk copy program (BCP) file consumption. Developers can improve scalability for initial synchronization and increase performance for dynamically filtered publications by using snapshots that contain pre-created BCP files.

Replication Terminology

If you are not that familiar with SQL Server replication terminology or replication in general, you should check out SQL Server Books Online for specific details and tutorials that go beyond the basics covered in this chapter. This chapter introduces the underlying technology and assumes that you know the basics of SQL Server replication. We'll review some of the terminology here, however.

For starters, SQL Server uses the publisher/subscriber model of replication topology. An SQL Server database that makes its data available for replication is referred to as the *publisher*. SQL Server supports replicating tables, views, stored procedures, and user-defined functions. A group of one or more supported database objects that are enabled for replication is called a *publication*.

An SQL Server database (SQL Server 2000, SQL Server 2005, or SQL Server 2005 Everywhere Edition) that gets data from the publisher is called a *subscriber*. Replication, which is managed by the system database, is called *distribution*. As you will learn later in this chapter, a distribution database (which can reside on the publisher, subscriber, or a completely separate server) is created when you go through the wizards. In a high-end enterprise environment, it usually makes sense to separate the publisher from the distribution. The server that hosts the distribution database is referred to as the *distributor*.

Most mobile applications use SQL Server merge replication to push a replica (or, more likely, a filtered, or partial, replica) of an SQL Server database in the enterprise down to a device. SQL Everywhere includes a New Subscription Wizard that makes it easy to create and then synchronize a subscription database.

SQL Everywhere also offers support for download-only *articles* (replicated tables). This feature reduces both the amount of metadata transferred during synchronization and the processing time on SQL Server for subsequent synchronizations.

Support for filtered articles is another improved feature of SQL Everywhere 2005. Many mobile applications (such as delivery routes for drivers) filter data in such a way that users do not share data across devices. With support for filtered articles, developers can significantly reduce synchronization time and increase scalability. This feature is especially useful for large deployments of mobile devices.

Working with SQL Everywhere Databases in Management Studio

A major problem with earlier versions of SQL Server Everywhere was that you could only administer or work with the database on the physical device. The only way to create tables and query data was to write SQL commands as part of an ADO command object in code running on the device. Typical deployment of an application involved creating the database and tables on the device via code on the first run. SQL Everywhere removes this impediment.

In SQL Server 2005 Management Studio, choose File, and then Connect Object Explorer from the main menu. Next select SQL Everywhere from the Server Type drop-down menu to either connect to or create a new SQL Everywhere database, as shown in Figure 15-1.

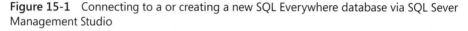

Figure 15-1   Connecting to a or creating a new SQL Everywhere database via SQL Sever Management Studio

The dialog box shown in the figure allows you to connect to an SQL Everywhere database on a device or on your local hard drive. SQL Everywhere databases exist in an .sdf file on the file system, so you either have to navigate to one or create a new one.

Let's create a new database to connect to and get working with SQL Everywhere. Later in the chapter, we will create a new database to be used with SQL Server 2005 replication, but for now let's get started with the basics. As previously demonstrated, in SQL Server 2005 Management Studio, choose File and then Connect Object Explorer from the main menu. Next select SQL Everywhere from the Server Type drop-down menu and <New Database...> in the Database File section. In the Create New Database dialog box, create an SQLMobileTest1.sdf file and connect to it (as shown in Figure 15-2). You have the option to encrypt the database as well as set a password and default sort order type. It is okay to accept the defaults, but you should set a database password. Now that the database is created, we are ready to code.

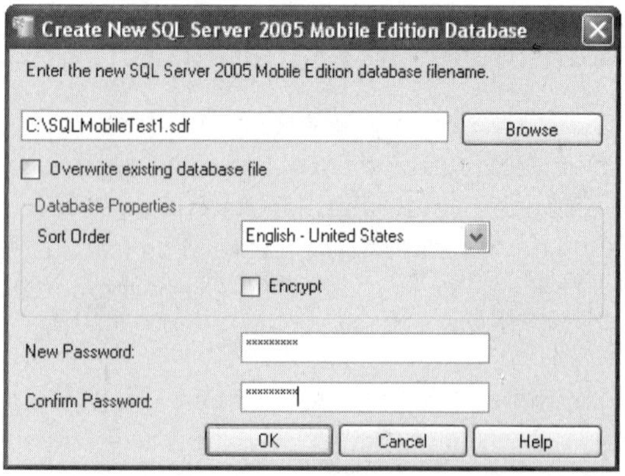

Figure 15-2   Create New Database dialog for SQL Everywhere

Creating a Table in Management Studio

You can create a table in SQL Everywhere in two ways: using SQL Server Management Studio or using code. We will try the code approach first. Now that we are connected to the database in SQL Server Management Studio, open a new query window; this is a query window to your SQL Server Everywhere Edition database, a database currently on your local hard drive, not a device yet. Typing the following code into Management Studio's query windows and executing it against the mobile database you are connected to creates a new table in your database.

```
Create Table Customers (Customer_ID INTEGER IDENTITY(1,1) CONSTRAINT pkCustId PRIMARY KEY,
CustomerName nvarchar(50),Region_ID int)
```

If you browse the database using Object Explorer in Management Studio (Figure 15-3), you'll see the new database we just created as well as the index created by the primary key constraint in our SQL code.

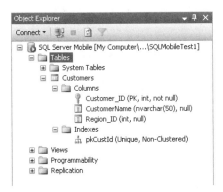

Figure 15-3 SQL Mobile's Object Explorer in Management Studio showing an SQL Everywhere database

SQL Everywhere Data Types You are probably realizing that SQL Everywhere is slightly different from SQL Server 2005 when it comes to data types and syntax. Table 15-1 lists all the data types supported by SQL Server SQL Everywhere 2005.

Table 15-1 SQL Server 2005 Data Types

Data Type	Description
bigint	Integer (whole number) data from -2^{63} ($-9,223,372,036,854,775,808$) to $2^{63}-1$ ($9,223,372,036,854,775,807$). Storage size is 8 bytes.
integer	Integer (whole number) data from -2^{31} ($-2,147,483,648$) to $2^{31}-1$ ($2,147,483,647$). Storage size is 4 bytes.
smallint	Integer data from $-32,768$ to $32,767$. Storage size is 2 bytes.
tinyint	Integer data from 0 to 255. Storage size is 1 byte.
bit	Integer data with a value of 1 or 0. Storage size is 1 bit.

Table 15-1 SQL Server 2005 Data Types

Data Type	Description
numeric (p, s)	Fixed-precision and scale-numeric data from $-10^{38}+1$ to $10^{38}-1$. The *p* variable specifies precision and can range from 1 to 38. The *s* variable specifies scale and can vary between 0 and *p*. Storage size is 19 bytes.
money	Monetary data values from $(-2^{63}/10000)$ ($-922,337,203,685,477.5808$) to $2^{63}-1$ ($922,337,203,685,477.5807$), with accuracy to a ten-thousandth of a monetary unit. Storage size is 8 bytes.
float	Floating point number data from $-1.79E+308$ to $1.79E+308$. Storage size is 8 bytes.
real	Floating precision number data from $-3.40E+38$ to $3.40E+38$. Storage size is 4 bytes.
datetime	Date and time data from January 1, 1753, to December 31, 9999, with an accuracy of one three-hundredth of a second, or 3.33 milliseconds. Values are rounded to increments of .000, .003, or .007 milliseconds. Stored as two 4-byte integers. The first 4 bytes store the number of days before or after the *base date*, January 1, 1900. The base date is the system's reference date. Values for *datetime* earlier than January 1, 1753, are not permitted. The other 4 bytes store the time of day represented as the number of milliseconds after midnight. Seconds have a valid range of 0 to 59.
national character(n) *Synonym:nchar(n)*	Fixed-length Unicode data with a maximum length of 4000 characters. Default length is 1. Storage size, in bytes, is two times the number of characters entered.
national character varying(n) *Synonym:nvarchar(n)*	Variable-length Unicode data with a length of 1 to 4000 characters. Default length is 1. Storage size, in bytes, is two times the number of characters entered.
ntext	Variable-length Unicode data with a maximum length of $(2^{30}-2)/2$ (536,870,911) characters. Storage size, in bytes, is two times the number of characters entered.
binary(n)	Fixed-length binary data with a maximum length of 8000 bytes. Default length is 1. Storage size is fixed, which is the length in bytes declared in the type.
varbinary(n)	Variable-length binary data with a maximum length of 8000 bytes. Default length is 1. Storage size varies. It is the length of the value in bytes.
image	Variable-length binary data with a maximum length of $2^{30}-1$ (1,073,741,823) bytes. Storage is the length of the value in bytes.
uniqueidentifier	A globally unique identifier (GUID). Storage size is 16 bytes.
IDENTITY [(s, i)]	A property of a data column, not a distinct data type. Only data columns of the *integer* data type can be used for identity columns. A table can have only one identity column. You can specify a seed (*s*) and an increment (*i*); the column cannot be updated. *s* = starting value *i* = increment value
ROWGUIDCOL	A property of a data column, not a distinct data type. It is a column in a table that is defined by using the *uniqueidentifier* data type. A table can have only one *ROWGUIDCOL* column.

Visually Creating a Table in Management Studio

Creating database objects is much easier using a tool. SQL Server CE has no visual tools for creating an object, and you cannot work with the database on the physical device. With SQL Everywhere, SQL Server Management Studio offers the Create New Table dialog box (Figure 15-4), which works much like the Create Table dialog box in SQL Server. Using the dialog box is easy—you define the table name and its columns, data types, and properties.

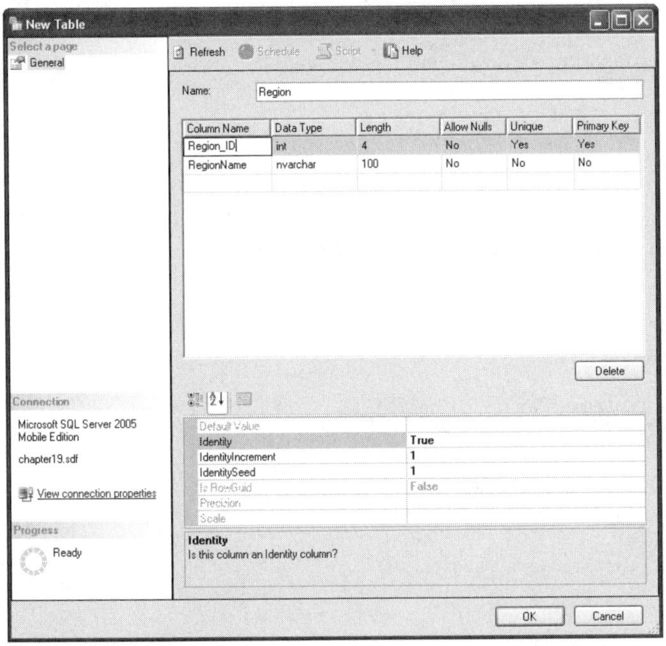

Figure 15-4   SQL Everywhere's Create New Table dialog box

Working with SQL Everywhere Data in Management Studio

We'll start by inserting data the old-fashioned way, using SQL *INSERT* statements. Now that we can work with databases on our hard drive, we can prepare the database before shipping it to the device. Other ways to get data into your tables include:

- Using Integration Services to import data from another data source
- Using SQL Server replication
- Using data entry from a custom application on the device
- Running SQL *INSERT* statements on the device

Adding data is easy. Listing 15-1 contains a create table statement and some simple *INSERT* statements that get the job done. (You can't leave out the *GO* statement, as you can in SQL Server.)

Listing 15-1 Creating an SQL Everywhere table and inserting data

```
Create Table Region (Region_ID INTEGER IDENTITY(1,1)
CONSTRAINT pkRegId PRIMARY KEY, RegionName nvarchar(50) NOT NULL)
Go
Insert Into Region (RegionName) values( 'USA')
Go
Insert Into Region (RegionName) values('Europe')
Go
Insert Into Region (RegionName) values('Asia')
Go
Insert Into Region (RegionName) values('South American')
Go
Into Region (RegionName) values('Africa')
Go
Insert Into Customers (CustomerName, Region_ID)
   values ('Stephen', 1)
Go
Insert Into Customers (CustomerName, Region_ID)
   values ('Goksin', 2)
Go
Insert Into Customers (CustomerName, Region_ID)
   values ('Malek', 3)
Go
Insert Into Customers (CustomerName, Region_ID)
   values ('Kimberly', 4)
Go
Insert Into Customers (CustomerName, Region_ID)
   values ('Clemens', 5)
Go
Insert Into Customers (CustomerName, Region_ID)
   values ('Richard', 1)
Go
```

Querying an SQL Everywhere Database Using Management Studio

Now that we have added data to the database, it is time to query it. Let's start with the basics:

```
Select * From Customers
```

The code produces the results shown in Figure 15-5. If you have been using SQL Server CE, you might have just fallen out of your seat—we just queried an SQL Everywhere database from SQL Server Management Studio!

But wait, there's more! Turn on Show Actual Execution Plan in Management Studio by selecting Query, and then Display Estimated Query Plan from the main menu and run this query:

```
Select RegionName, Count(*) as CountofRegions
From Customers inner join Region
   on Customers.Region_ID=Region.Region_ID
Group By RegionName, Customers.Region_ID
```

```
FUJI.master - ...ryDatabase.sql   C:\...\SQLMobi...xamples.sqlce*
  --Example 3: Simple Select
Select * From Customers
```

	Customer_ID	CustomerName	Region_ID
1	1	Stephen	1
2	2	Goksin	2
3	3	Malek	3
4	4	Kimberly	4
5	5	Clemens	5
6	6	Richard	1

Figure 15-5   Querying SQL Everywhere data using Management Studio

SQL Everywhere sends Management Studio its query plan for you to analyze, as shown in Figure 15-6. Notice that a table scan was performed. A table scan usually sets off alarm bells, so to facilitate the join we'll use the Add New Index dialog box (Figure 15-7) to add an index to the Region_ID column in the Customers table. To add the index, right-click Indexes under the table in SQL Management Studio's Object Explorer for the Customer table and enter an Index name in the dialog box and add the Region_ID column as shown in Figure 15-7.

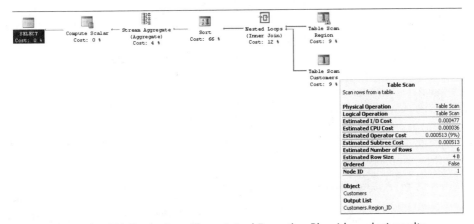

Figure 15-6   The SQL Everywhere Show Actual Execution Plan (showplan) results window

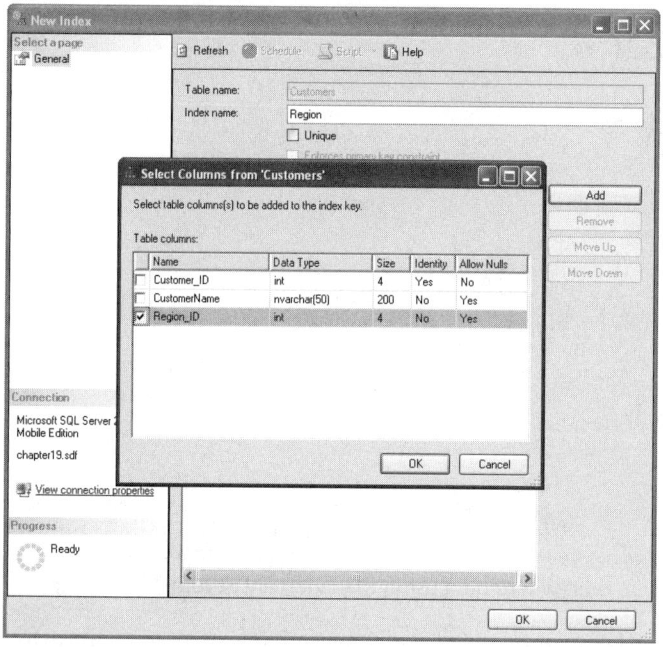

Figure 15-7   The Create New Index dialog box

Creating a SQL Everywhere Application with SQL Server Replication and Visual Studio 2005

Let's explore the features of SQL Everywhere by exploiting its strengths. We'll create a SQL Server 2005 replica on a mobile device such as a Pocket PC. The first step is to create a database in SQL Server (not SQL Everywhere) that we will synchronize to a SQL Everywhere database on our Pocket PC or other device. We will create a simple database in SQL Server Management Studio to keep track of a delivery company's drivers and their deliveries. This database will exist on your SQL Server machine and then it will be replicated down to an SQL Everywhere database, so we will move back to "normal" SQL Server for a few minutes. We will have basic Customers, Drivers, and Delivery tables in our database. (Of course, there should be many more fields in this database, but we're keeping it simple for the example.) To create the database, use SQL Management Studio, connect to your local SQL Server, and install and run the script shown in Listing 15-2.

Listing 15-2   Creating a database and tables to use for Merge Replication

```
Create Database Chapter15
Go
Use Chapter15
Go
SET ANSI_NULLS ON
GO
```

```
SET QUOTED_IDENTIFIER ON
GO
CREATE TABLE [dbo].[Customers](
   [Customer_ID] [int] IDENTITY(1,1) NOT NULL,
   [CustomerName] [varchar](50) NOT NULL,
 CONSTRAINT [PK_Customers] PRIMARY KEY CLUSTERED
(
   [Customer_ID] ASC
) ON [PRIMARY]
) ON [PRIMARY]
GO

CREATE TABLE [dbo].[Drivers](
   [Driver_ID] [int] IDENTITY(1,1) NOT NULL,
   [DriverName] [varchar](50) NOT NULL,
 CONSTRAINT [PK_Drivers] PRIMARY KEY CLUSTERED
(
   [Driver_ID] ASC
) ON [PRIMARY]
) ON [PRIMARY]

GO
CREATE TABLE [dbo].[Delivery](
   [Delivery_ID] [int] IDENTITY(1,1) NOT NULL,
   [DeliveryDate] [datetime] ,
   [Address] [varchar](50) NOT NULL,
   [Customer_ID] [int] NOT NULL,
   [Driver_ID] [int] NOT NULL,
 CONSTRAINT [PK_Delivery] PRIMARY KEY CLUSTERED
(
   [Delivery_ID] ASC
) ON [PRIMARY]
) ON [PRIMARY]
GO
SET ANSI_NULLS OFF
GO
SET QUOTED_IDENTIFIER OFF
GO
IF NOT EXISTS (SELECT * FROM sys.foreign_keys WHERE object_id = OBJECT_ID(N'FK_Delivery_
Customers') AND parent_object_id = OBJECT_ID(N'[dbo].[Delivery]'))
ALTER TABLE [dbo].[Delivery] WITH CHECK ADD  CONSTRAINT [FK_Delivery_Customers] FOREIGN
 KEY([Customer_ID])
REFERENCES [dbo].[Customers] ([Customer_ID])
GO
IF NOT EXISTS (SELECT * FROM sys.foreign_keys WHERE object_id = OBJECT_ID(N'FK_Delivery_
Drivers') AND parent_object_id = OBJECT_ID(N'[dbo].[Delivery]'))
ALTER TABLE [dbo].[Delivery] WITH CHECK ADD  CONSTRAINT [FK_Delivery_Drivers] FOREIGN K
EY([Driver_ID])
REFERENCES [dbo].[Drivers] ([Driver_ID])
```

Next let's add some customer, driver, and delivery data. A *NULL* value in the Delivery Date field in the Delivery table means that the delivery has not been made. The goal is for data entry staff (or a system) to fill this data and for drivers to use a handheld device to record when the delivery is made (*see* Listing 15-3).

Listing 15-3   Adding data to the SQL Server database tables

```
Use chapter15
go
Insert into Customers values('George')
Insert into Customers values('John')
Insert into Customers values('Tom')
Insert into Customers values('James')
Insert into Customers values('Jose')
Insert into Customers values('Sally')
Insert into Customers values('Bill')
Insert into Customers values('Kathleen')
Insert into Customers values('Lynn')

Insert into Drivers values('Andrew')
Insert into Drivers values('Bill')
Insert into Drivers values('Steve')

Insert into Delivery values(22/01/2006, '123 Main Street', 1,1)
Insert into Delivery values(20/01/2006, '123 Main Street', 2,2)
Insert into Delivery values(19/01/2006, '123 Main Street', 3,3)
Insert into Delivery values(18/01/2006, '123 Main Street', 4,1)
Insert into Delivery values(null, '123 Main Street', 5,2)
Insert into Delivery values(null, '123 Main Street', 1,3)
Insert into Delivery values(null, '123 Main Street', 2,1)
Insert into Delivery values(null, '123 Main Street', 3,2)
Insert into Delivery values(null, '123 Main Street', 4,3)
Insert into Delivery values(null, '123 Main Street', 5,1)
```

Creating a Publication

We now need to create a publication to enable bi-directional synchronization with the SQL Everywhere device. Follow these steps:

1. Use SQL Management Studio and connect to the Chapter15 database that we just created in Listing 15-2 and Listing 15-3.

2. In Object Explorer, drill down to the Replication folder and expand the tree that lists Local Publications. Select the Local Publications folder, right-click it, and then select New Publication (Figure 15-8).

3. In the New Publication Wizard, click Next on the Welcome page.

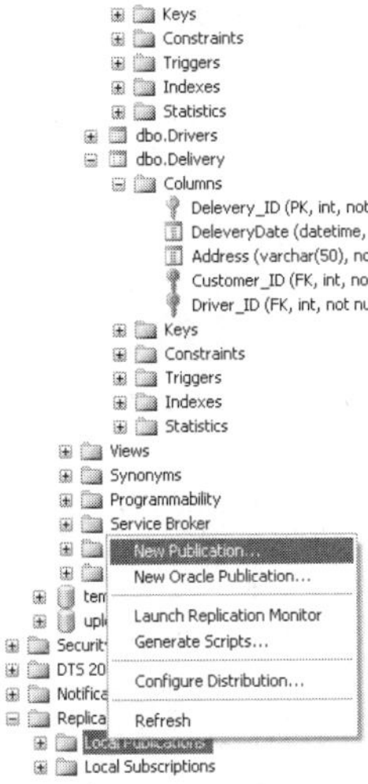

Figure 15-8   Object Explorer in Management Studio

4. On the Replication Distributor page (Figure 15-9), you should not see any publications if you are working with a new installation. If there are no publications on the server, you must configure the distribution server. You do this only once. When the Distributor page appears, choose the option to have your machine be its own distributor, and then click Next.

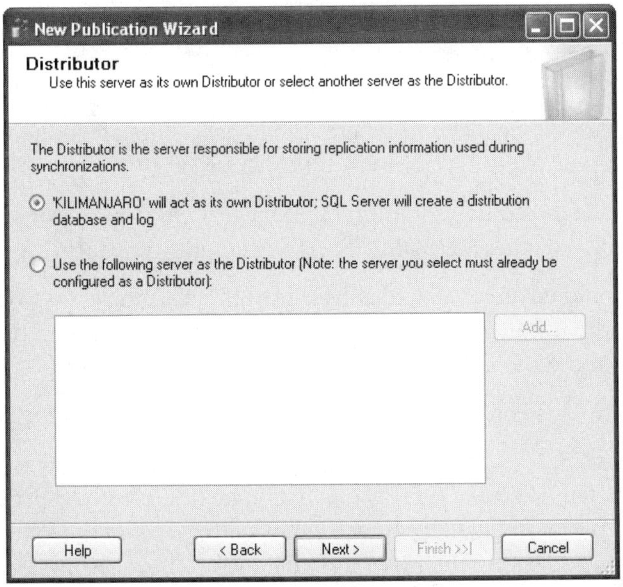

Figure 15-9   Replication Distributor page of the New Publication Wizard

5. If you do not have SQL Server Agent configured to start when you start your computer, you will see the Start SQL Server Agent page. Click Next.

On the Snapshot Folder page (Figure 15-10), we will create a share to allow another machine to read the snapshot data. This is where the snapshot file and schema files will be placed for subscribers to retrieve and synchronize with the subscription databases. In a production environment, we'll want to have Microsoft Internet Information Services (IIS) and SQL Server on separate machines. The IIS machine will need the SQL Everywhere replication components installed. Do *not* click Next yet. We'll read the data from the share we created.

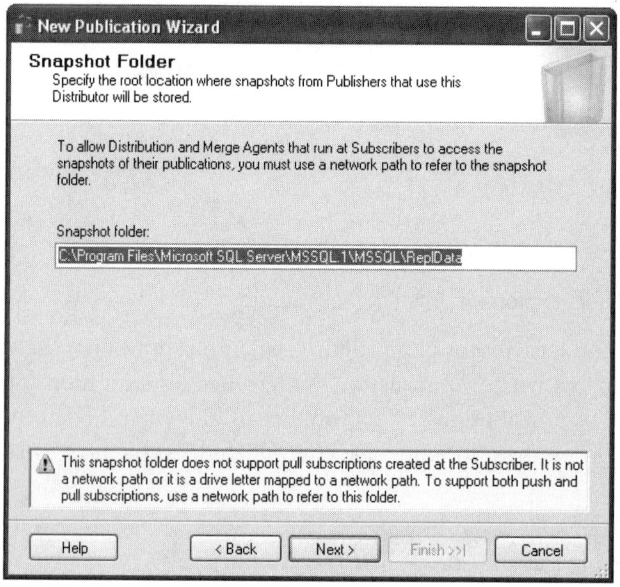

Figure 15-10   Snapshot Folder page

We'll create a share on the machine where the snapshot files are located by default, and we'll assign FULL ACCESS permissions to EVERYONE.

6. To do this, go back to Windows Explorer and navigate to the C:\Program Files\Microsoft SQL Server\MSSQL.1\MSSQL\repldata directory.

7. Right-click the repldata directory and choose the Sharing And Security option. Note that in a production environment, for security reasons, you should assign particular users READ ACCESS to the share where the snapshot directory is created.

8. Choose the Share This Folder option, and leave the default name of *repldata* for the share name.

    Different versions of Windows display this dialog box differently, especially depending on what service packs are installed. Once you have configured the folder to be shared, click Permissions and choose FULL CONTROL in the Allow Permissions section of the dialog box.

9. Return to the wizard and type **\\ComputerName\repldata** (for example, on my computer it's *Kilimanjaro**repldata*) in the Snapshot Folder text box. Click Next. You can find the computer name by right-clicking My Computer and looking at properties.

10. On the Choose Database page (Figure 15-11), we'll choose the database to make a publication from. Choose the Chapter15 database that you previously created, and then click Next.

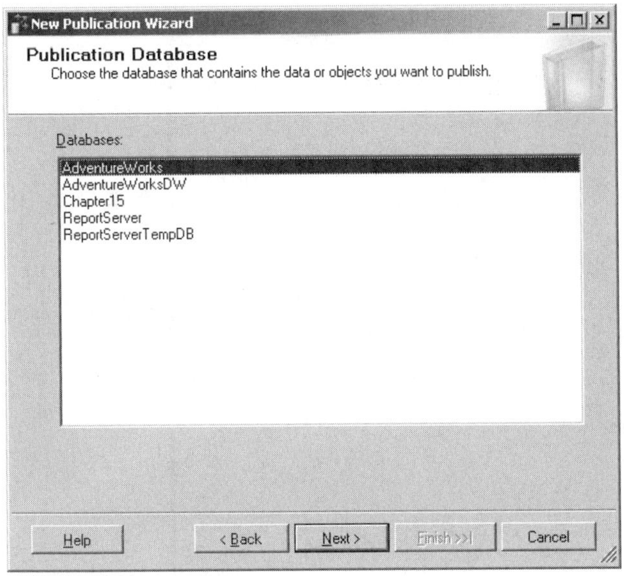

Figure 15-11   Choose Database page

11. On the Choose Replication Type page, we'll choose the type of publication to create (Figure 15-12). SQL Everywhere can work only with publications that are of the merge replication type. This means that for this example, we must select Merge Publication. Click Next.

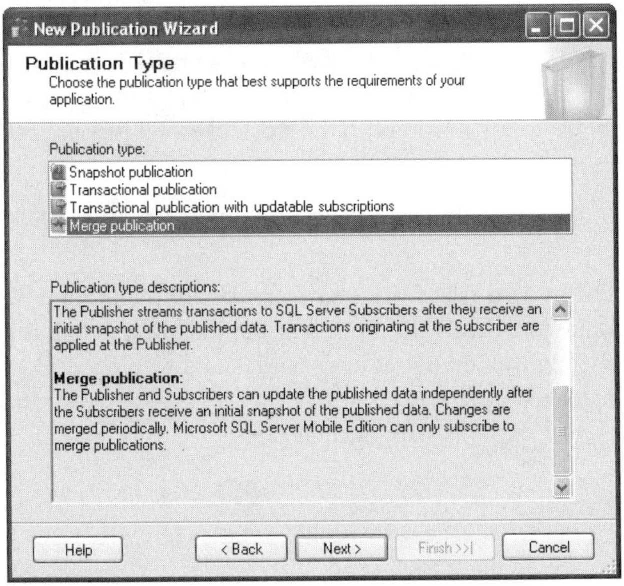

Figure 15-12   Choose Replication Type page

12.   On the Subscriber Types page (Figure 15-13), we'll choose SQL Everywhere Edition
(as well as any other editions we want to replicate to, but for this example we'll use
SQL Everywhere). Click Next. We are almost there—just a few more wizard pages.

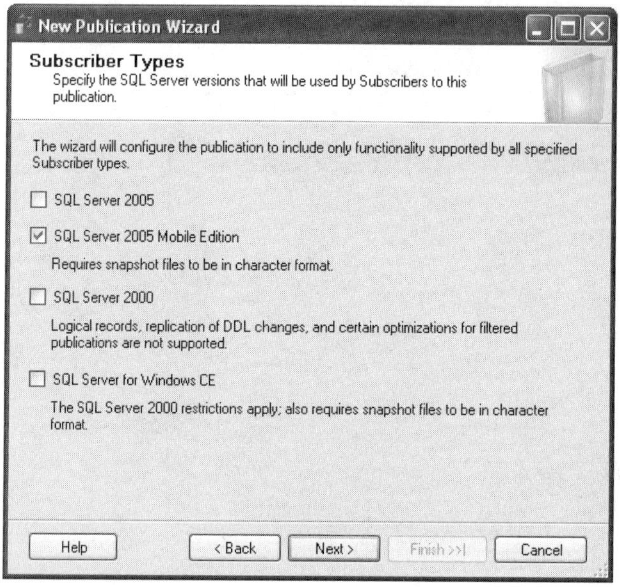

Figure 15-13   Choose Subscriber Type page

13.   On the Articles page (Figure 15-14), we'll choose which database tables to mark for
replication. We'll choose the tables that will synchronize down to the SQL Everywhere subscription database on the mobile device and that will be tracked for all
changes (including schema changes). All DML changes that occur on the SQL
Everywhere subscription database will also be tracked and propagated back to the
SQL Server database. You can also select what columns are replicated (keeping one
only in the master database, for example). There are a lot of settings here that you can
use to alter the behavior of your replica, but for now we'll just use the defaults.
Click Next.

You will be informed that the wizard will create a uniqueidentifier column. Accept that,
and click Next.

The next page of the wizard asks if you want to filter your publication. You can filter out
certain views of data from the publication—for example, you can publish data only from
Europe. This is useful if you do not want to send data down to a device if the user will
never have reason to view it; this speeds up the data transfer as well as increases security.
For our example, we'll skip this step, so click Next

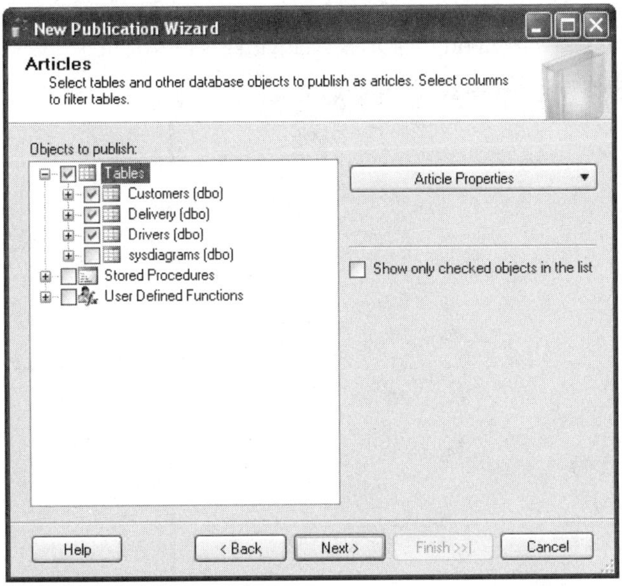

Figure 15-14   Choose Database Tables To Replicate page

14. On the Snapshot Agent page (Figure 15-15), we can choose to run the agent immediately and set up a schedule. Let's run it each day after any batch processes might run. Click Next.

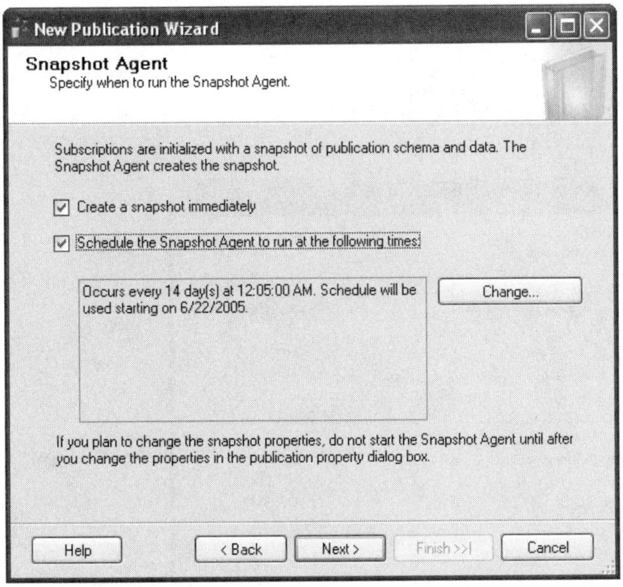

Figure 15-15   Snapshot Agent page

15. On the Snapshot Security page (Figure 15-16), we'll assign the security rights for the snapshot agent. The snapshot agent is responsible for creating snapshot files that are used in the sync process. Click Security Settings to assign the necessary rights for the snapshot agent to

run. You can configure a user account for the snapshot agent, but for our example, we'll use whatever account you logged on to SQL Server with (as long as it is not SA!). Click Next.

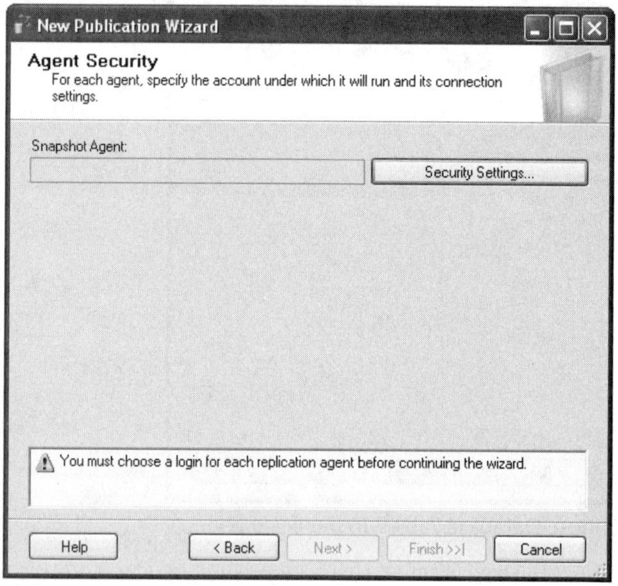

Figure 15-16   Snapshot Security page

16. The next page asks whether you want to create the publication now or script out all the options you just selected. Select the Immediate option, and click Next.

17. On the final page of the wizard, we'll name the publication. Choose Chapter15_Mobile, and click Finish. The wizard runs through all the steps (Figure 15-17). We are now ready to begin setting up synchronization.

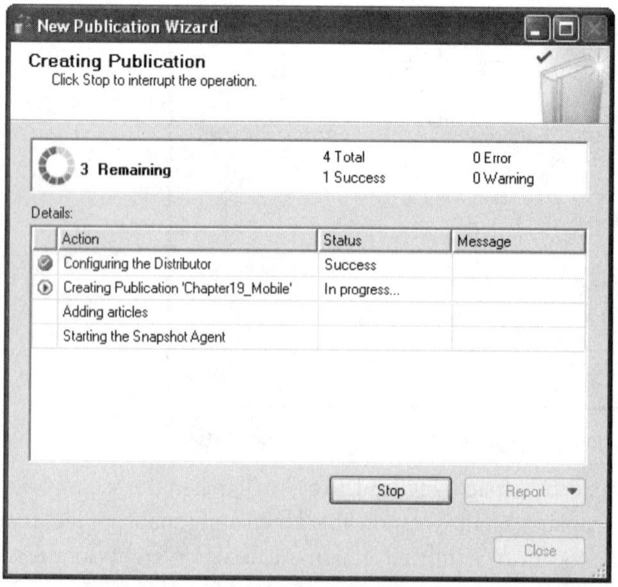

Figure 15-17   Creating Publication page

Installing and Configuring SQL Everywhere Server Components for IIS

Now we need to configure the components that will allow the SQL Everywhere database to communicate with the back-end SQL Server. A machine with IIS installed that has access to the Internet and your SQL Server is required. Our example uses a Windows XP Service Pack 2 laptop machine installed with IIS, Visual Studio, and SQL Server—an easy way to prototype this application. Having IIS and SQL Server on the same machine in a production environment is not recommended, however, due to security and scaling concerns.

Follow these steps to set up the SQL Everywhere server-side components by using the Microsoft SQL Server 2005 Everywhere Edition Server Tools Setup Wizard.

1. In Windows Explorer, navigate to the C:\Program Files\Microsoft SQL Server\90 \Tools\Binn\VSShell\Common7\IDE directory. Double-click the setup file called SQLCE30SetupEn.msi.

> **Note** In the same directory as the wizard's setup file, you'll find an SQL Everywhere setup help file named setupsqlmobile.chm that can be very useful if you run into any unexpected problems.

2. On the Welcome page, click Next. On the License page, accept the license.

3. On the Configuration Check page, all the items should have a status of "success" except the last item, which is for synchronizing to an SQL Server 2000 database. We will be synchronizing only to an SQL Server 2005 database, so we can ignore the warning. Click Next.

4. On the next page (Figure 15-18), we must select synchronizing SQL Mobile With A SQL Server 2005 database because we are installing only the components on the IIS machine that relate to an SQL Server 2005 server. Accept the defaults, and click Next.

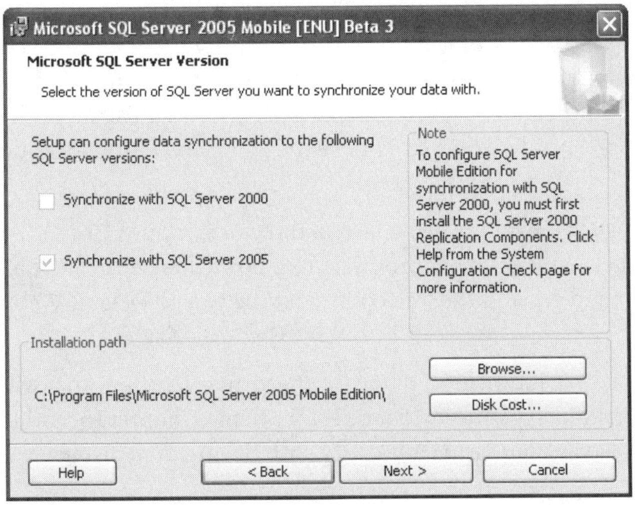

![Microsoft SQL Server 2005 Mobile [ENU] Beta 3 setup window. Microsoft SQL Server Version. Select the version of SQL Server you want to synchronize your data with. Setup can configure data synchronization to the following SQL Server versions: Synchronize with SQL Server 2000 (unchecked); Synchronize with SQL Server 2005 (checked). Note: To configure SQL Server Mobile Edition for synchronization with SQL Server 2000, you must first install the SQL Server 2000 Replication Components. Click Help from the System Configuration Check page for more information. Installation path: C:\Program Files\Microsoft SQL Server 2005 Mobile Edition\. Browse... Disk Cost... Help, < Back, Next >, Cancel buttons.]

Figure 15-18   SQL Server Version page

5. The wizard asks you to begin the installation. Click Install. This installation must be done on the server that will run IIS and allow your users to communicate with the database.

At this point, we have installed the SQL Everywhere server components onto the machine. Now we need to run yet another wizard to configure IIS with the necessary parameters to allow SQL Everywhere to sync with SQL Server.

1. Return to SQL Server Management Studio and double-click the Replication node in Object Explorer. Drill down to Local Publications, right-click your publication (Chapter15 in our example), and select Configure Web Synchronization (Figure 15-19).

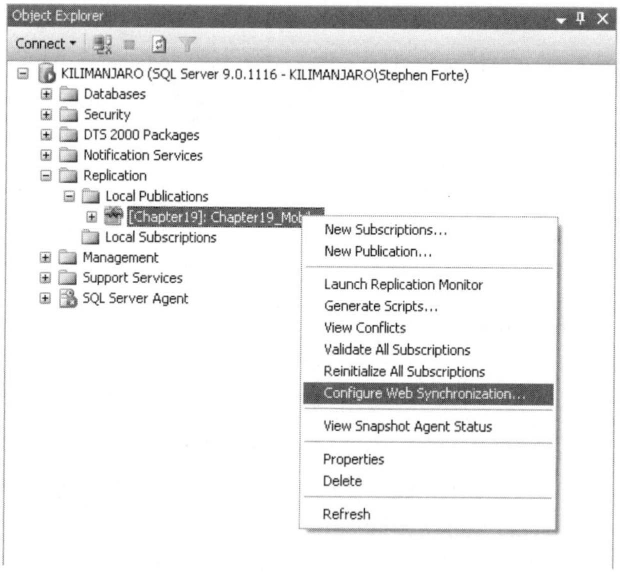

Figure 15-19   Selecting the Configure Web Synchronization option

2. The Configure Web Synchronization Wizard starts. On the Welcome page, click Next. This wizard is used both for SQL Server subscribers who want to perform synchronization over HTTP and SQL Everywhere subscribers, so we must choose what subscriber type to configure. For this example, choose the SQL Server Mobile Edition option. Click Next.

3. On the next page, we'll create a new virtual directory (Figure 15-20). Type the value of your computer name in the appropriate text box. Choose Create A New Virtual Directory, and then expand the tree control all the way to Default Web Site. Click Next.

4. On the next page, we'll provide a name for the virtual directory that will be created in IIS. For this example, type the virtual directory name **Chapter15**, and then click Next. You can also create a virtual directory with IIS and then just navigate to it from this page.

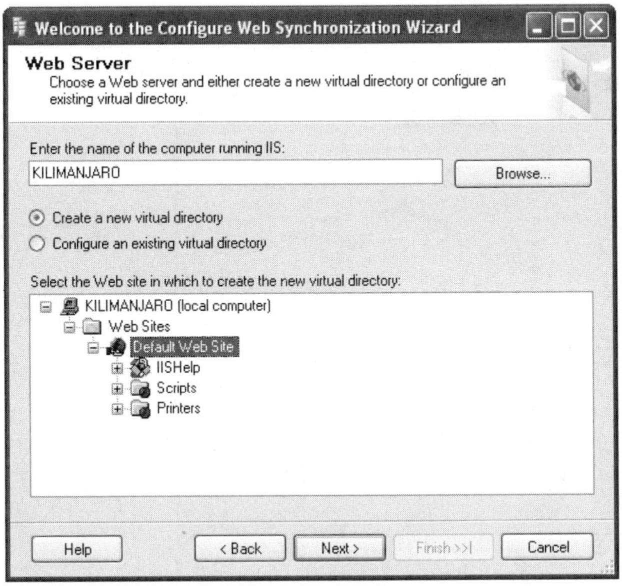

Figure 15-20   New Virtual Directory page

5.   The next page asks if you want SSL to be used. SSL is great for a production environment, but we won't require it for our example. SQL Server 2005 replication over HTTP requires SSL, but SQL Everywhere does not. When you go to production, it is important to revisit this issue and install a certificate and use SSL. (Note: If your Web server does not have a certificate installed, your only option is no SSL.) Click Next.

6.   On the next page, we'll specify what type of authentication to use. This is the authentication that the device running SQL Everywhere will use to authenticate with the IIS server. For simplicity, we will use Anonymous authentication, so choose the option labeled *Clients will connect anonymously. A user name and password will not be required.* (In production, you should use Basic authentication, and a user name and password will be required.) Click Next.

7.   The next page is for configuring security. In the production environment, this is where you configure a user account, but in this example we will use the default—the ASP.NET Worker process. Click Next.

8.   On the Share Information page (Figure 15-21), specify the share you created in the previous wizard (\\computername\repldata or, on my machine, \\Kilimanjaro\repldata). Click Next.

9.   On the Summary page, you can opt to run the wizard.

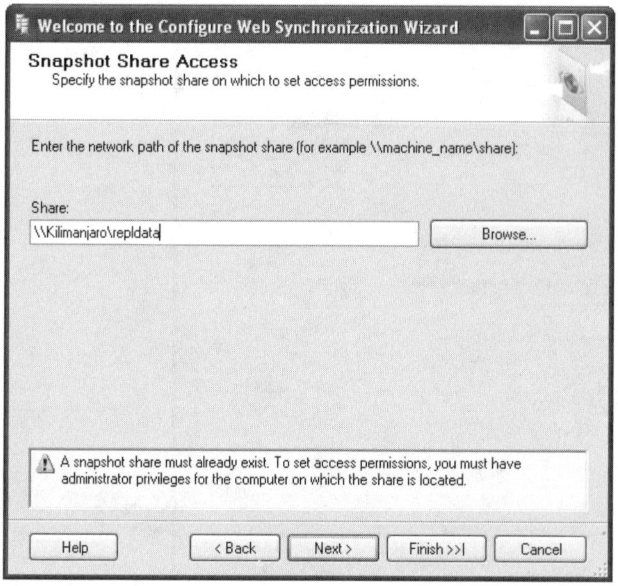

Figure 15-21   Share Information page

We have accomplished a lot at this point. We created the database in SQL Server and then created a publication, thus allowing us to send the database to a device as an SQL Everywhere subscription database and allowing for full bidirectional synchronization. We set up our IIS box to broker the communication between our device and the machine running SQL Server. Now we have to configure the subscription. Only one more wizard to go!

Creating a Subscription Using Management Studio

As we saw earlier, a new feature of SQL Everywhere and SQL Server 2005 is the ability to create, query, and manipulate an SQL Everywhere database on the desktop using Visual Studio 2005 or SQL Server 2005. When distributing a database out to the field, you might want to perform the initial synchronization to simplify setup. This is a major benefit of the new ability to work with a mobile database on your desktop. Let's get started and use SQL Server 2005 to create a subscription database on the desktop.

1. Create a new SQL Everywhere database on your desktop by opening Management Studio and choosing Connect, SQL Everywhere from the Object menu and connecting to SQL Mobile Everywhere (as shown earlier in Figure 15-1).

2. From the Database File drop-down list, select New Database. This brings up the Create New Database dialog box. We will create the Chapter15_ship.sdf database on our C drive and connect to it. The SQL Everywhere database we just created will appear as a database to be managed in Object Explorer.

3. Next we'll create a subscription database. Expand the tree control in Object Explorer for the SQL Mobile Everywhere object and then expand the Replication tree. Right-click the

Subscriptions node and choose New Subscriptions (Figure 15-22). This launches the New Subscription Wizard.

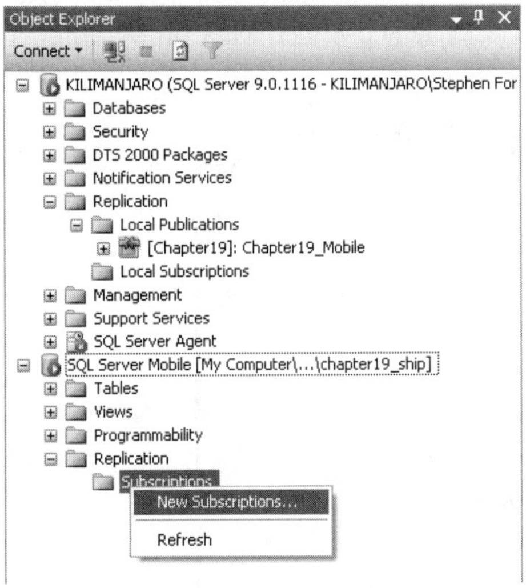

Figure 15-22   Choosing the New Subscriptions option

4. Navigate past the Welcome page to the next page. Select the Find SQL Server Publisher option in the Publisher drop-down list. The Connect To Server dialog box appears for logging on to your server. Select the publication we just created, Chapter15, and click Next.

5. Next we need to assign a name for the subscription (Figure 15-23). This can be any name that uniquely identifies the subscription. For this example, we'll use *Chapter15_sub*. (Note: If we had set up filtering when we created our publication, we could enter a value in the HOST_NAME text box. This would allow us to bring down a subset of data to the SQL Everywhere subscription database.) Click Next.

> **Note**   Although we will not cover filtered articles in this chapter, if you are using them in your applications, be aware of the following security note from SQL Server Books Online:
>
> The value for the HOST_NAME() function can be overridden; therefore, it is not possible to use filters that include HOST_NAME() to control access to partitions of data. To control access to partitions of data, use SUSER_SNAME(), SUSER_SNAME() in combination with HOST_NAME(), or use static row filters.

6. On the Web Server Authentication page (Figure 15-24), we'll provide information on accessing SQL Everywhere server-side components and the type of authentication to use.

The URL we'll use in our example is *http://kilimanjaro/Chapter19/sqlcesa30.dll*. The DLL file, which was placed there by the previous wizard, is the SQL Everywhere Agent, which brokers communication to the SQL Server publication. Under "How Will The Subscriber Connect To the Web Server?" select The Subscriber Will Connect Anonymously. In production, you must always configure a user name and password and use SSL.

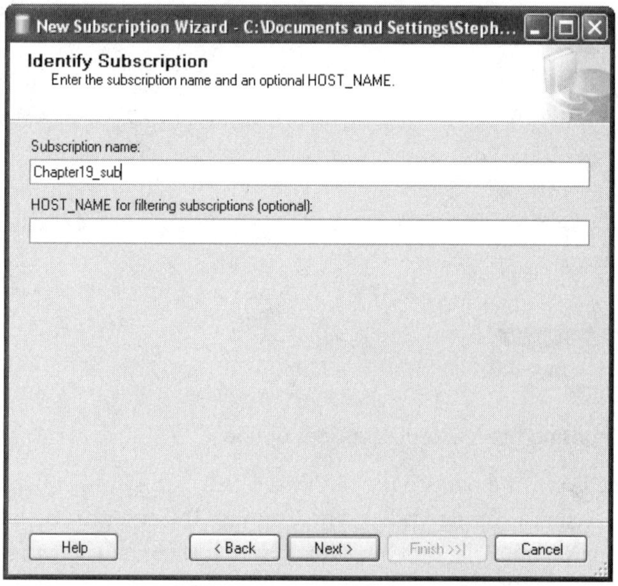

Figure 15-23 Specifying new subscription options

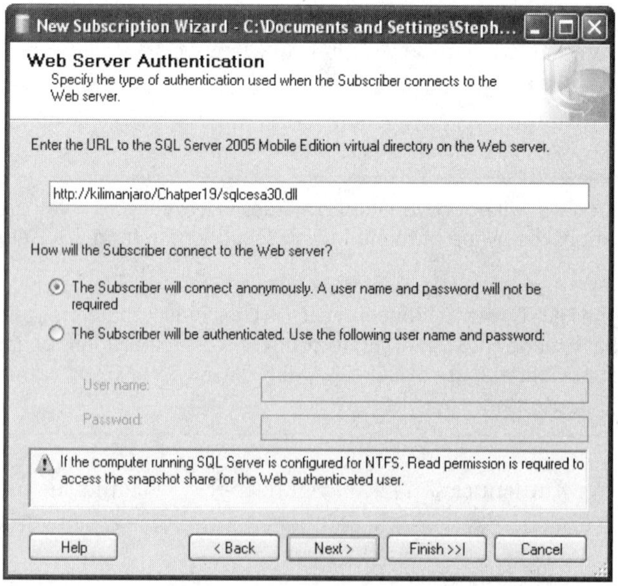

Figure 15-24 Web Server Authentication page

7. The next page allows you to choose Windows Authentication or SQL Server Authentication. Choose SQL Server Authentication so we do not have to assign permissions to the ASP.NET Worker Account for the SQL Server database. Click Next.

8. The last page creates code for use in your application. Copy and paste the code for C# shown in Listing 15-4 into Notepad for now. Click Finish to allow the wizard to synchronize the data.

Listing 15-4   Results of the New Subscription Wizard

```
Click Finish to create a new subscription with the following options:

Publisher: KILIMANJARO
PublisherDatabase: Chapter15
Publication: Chapter15_Mobile
Subscriber: Chapter15_sub
HostName:
InternetUrl: http://kilimanjaro/Chapter19/sqlcesa30.dll
Web Server Authentication: Anonymous
PublisherSecurityMode: SQL Server Authentication

Code Sample (C#):

//using System.Data.SqlServerCe;

SqlCeReplication repl = new SqlCeReplication();

repl.InternetUrl = @"http://kilimanjaro/Chapter19/sqlcesa30.dll";
repl.Publisher = @"KILIMANJARO";
repl.PublisherDatabase = @"Chapter15";
repl.PublisherSecurityMode = SecurityType.DBAuthentication;
repl.PublisherLogin = @"mobileuser1";
repl.PublisherPassword = @"<...>";
repl.Publication = @"Chapter15_Mobile";
repl.Subscriber = @"Chapter15_sub";
repl.SubscriberConnectionString = @"Data Source=""C:\data\Chapter15_ship.sdf"""";Max Datab
ase Size=128;Default Lock Escalation =100;";
try
{
    repl.AddSubscription(AddOption.ExistingDatabase);
    repl.Synchronize();
}
catch (SqlCeException e)
{
    MessageBox.Show(e.ToString());
}


Code Sample (Visual Basic .NET):

'imports System.Data.SqlServerCe

dim repl as new SqlCeReplication()
```

```
repl.InternetUrl = "http://kilimanjaro/Chapter19/sqlcesa30.dll"
repl.Publisher = "KILIMANJARO"
repl.PublisherDatabase = "Chapter15"
repl.PublisherSecurityMode = SecurityType.DBAuthentication
repl.PublisherLogin = " mobileuser1"
repl.PublisherPassword = "<...>"
repl.Publication = "Chapter15_Mobile"
repl.Subscriber = "Chapter15_sub"
repl.SubscriberConnectionString = "Data Source=""C:\data\Chapter15_ship.sdf"";
Max Database Size=128;Default Lock Escalation =100;"
try
    repl.AddSubscription(AddOption.ExistingDatabase)
    repl.Synchronize()
catch err as SqlCeException
    MessageBox.Show(err.ToString)
end try
```

We have successfully created an SQL Everywhere database on the desktop and have obtained the source code from the wizard in Visual Basic or C# to allow us to programmatically perform a synchronization.

Verifying the Subscription Using Management Studio

To verify that our database has been synchronized, all we do is connect to the mobile database (C:\Chapter15_ship.sdf) through Management Studio. Then we can see that the objects have been pushed down through replication to the mobile database (Figure 15-25) and query the database tables (Figure 15-26).

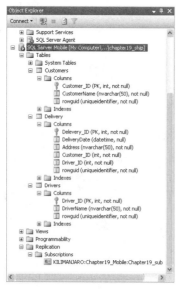

Figure 15-25   SQL Mobile in Object Explorer

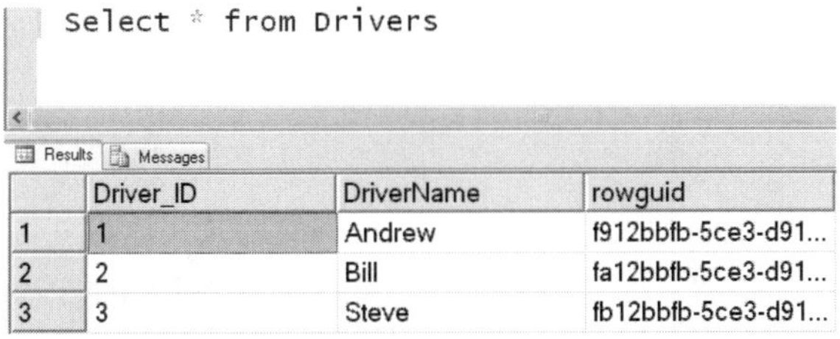
Select * from Drivers
Results
Messages
Driver_ID
DriverName
rowguid
1 1 Andrew f912bbfb-5ce3-d91...
2 2 Bill fa12bbfb-5ce3-d91...
3 3 Steve fb12bbfb-5ce3-d91...

Figure 15-26 Query results

Creating a Mobile Application Using Visual Studio 2005

Let's take the example a step further and create a new Visual Studio 2005 mobile application that will synchronize an SQL Everywhere database to the SQL Server publication we just created. Out of the box, Visual Studio 2005 can create a mobile application that runs on a Pocket PC, SmartPhone, or Windows CE device.

1. Open Visual Studio 2005. In the Server Explorer window, right-click the Data Connections object and choose Add Connection (Figure 15-27).

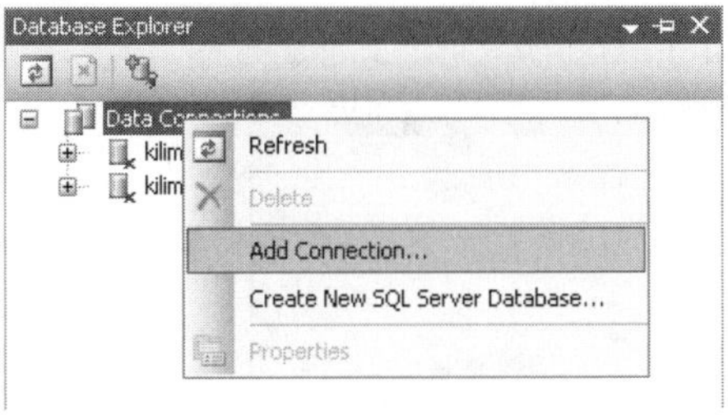
Database Explorer
Refresh
Delete
Add Connection...
Create New SQL Server Database...
Properties

Figure 15-27 The Add Connection dialog box

2. Change the provider to SQL Everywhere. The Add Connection For SQL Everywhere dialog box appears (Figure 15-28). Type the path to your .sdf file of the subscription database. In production, we will deploy that local database to the actual device, but for now we will just test with the Visual Studio device emulators.

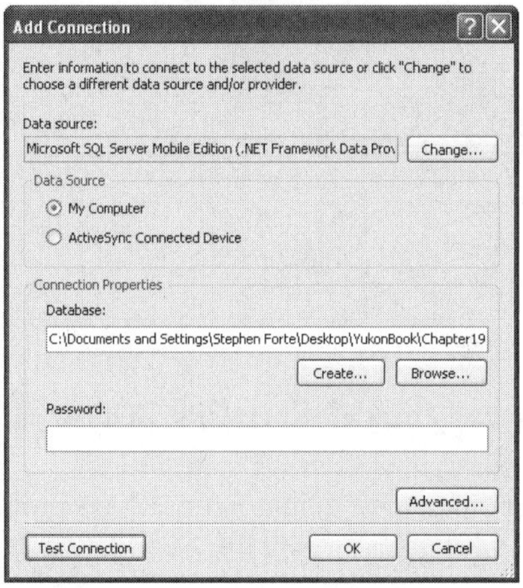

Figure 15-28   The Add Connection For SQL Everywhere dialog box

Next we'll create a Pocket PC project. You can create the same application for any device.

3. Choose File, New, and then click Project. On the New Project form (Figure 15-29), expand the C# (or Visual Basic) node and click the Smart Device node.

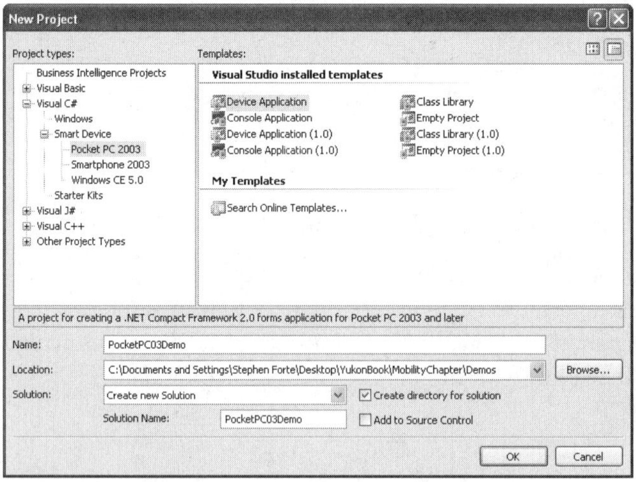

Figure 15-29   Visual Studio project types

This exposes a series of templates. Choose Pocket PC 2003 Application. We will give it the name **Pocket PCDemo** in the Name text box and place it in the C:\Chapter15 folder on our hard drive. You should have an empty environment, as shown in Figure 15-30.

Figure 15-30   Smartphone 2003 forms

Setting Up the Project

At this point, we will change some of the defaults of the project.

1. We will first change the form name to **Chapter 15**. Focus the project by clicking the edge of the device image. This brings up the properties for the form in the Properties window, just like for a Windows form or Web form. Change the form name to **Chapter 15**.

2. Next we'll change the default form behavior to close the application instead of minimizing it. (Pocket PC applications are minimized and kept in memory by default.) In the Properties window, scroll down to the MinimizeBox property. Change it from True (the default) to False. This changes the Minimize button's icon on the form from an X to OK.

3. Next we will create a DataSource so we can use new features in Visual Studio 2005 that allow you to drag and drop data to the form and create bound *DataGrid* objects to view data. Choose Data, Add New Data Source to launch the Data Source Configuration Wizard (Figure 15-31). Click Next.

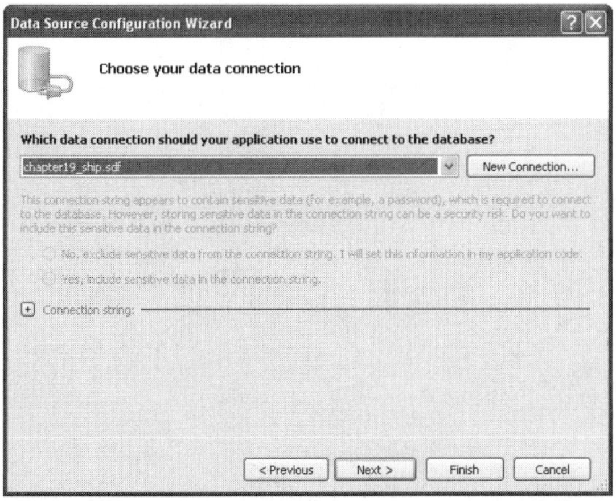

Figure 15-31   Data Source Configuration Wizard

4. Click the Database icon, and then click Next. If you have only one data source set up in Visual Studio (the mobile database we just connected to), by default the correct data connection should appear. If not, select the SQL Everywhere Chapter 15 database and click Next.

5. On the Choose Your Database Objects form (Figure 15-32), on the Tables node, expand both tables that are part of the Chapter 15 database. Uncheck the rowguid columns for all three tables. As you might have guessed, this is a field that SQL Server added to keep track of replication; it is not needed when displaying data to the user. Click Finish so that we can start working with the data.

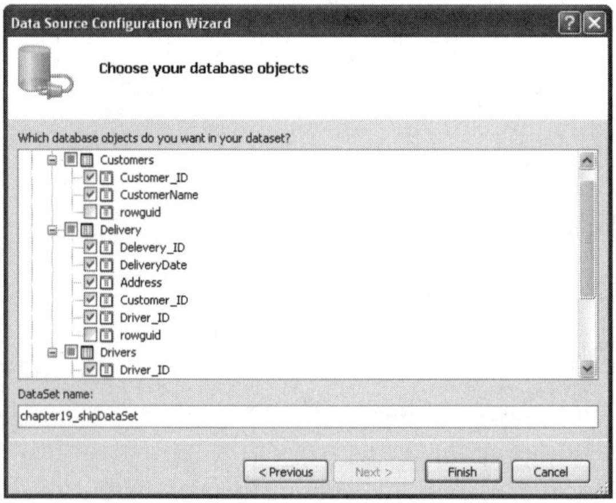

Figure 15-32   Selecting database objects and columns for replication

Binding SQL Mobile Data to a Pocket PC Form

As we did with Windows Forms in Chapter 8, we will now bind a *DataGrid* to a Pocket PC form. We will take advantage of the same data binding features we saw in Chapter 8.

1. Choose Data, Show DataSources. Drill down into the Driver table, and expand the node to see the fields and related tables. You should also see the Delivery table (Figure 15-33). Change the Customer_ID field to a ComboBox and the Driver_ID field to a ComboBox using the smart tag next to each field. Also set the Delivery field to show Details by using its smart tag.

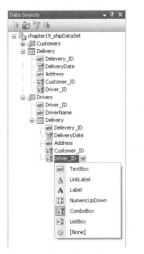

Figure 15-33   DataSource Configuration window

2. Drag the Driver table onto the form, and dock it in the upper-left corner of the form. Then drag the Delivery table from the Driver node (as shown in Figure 15-33), and place it under the grid. A details view should appear.

   Since we set our relationships, when we run this project we will see a one-to-many relationship. Go ahead and reposition your details view records and delete the Driver ID column—we already know who the driver is from the master records.

3. Drag the Customer table onto the Customer_ID drop-down box on the form, and use the smart tag shown in Figure 15-34 to verify that the combo box is set to the proper display and value properties. Your form is almost ready to go!

Figure 15-34   Bound form configuration

Programmatic Synchronization   At this point, without writing any code, we have created a data-bound grid and details form for a SQL Everywhere database. Now we need to hook up one more piece to this project that will allow the application to synchronize to SQL Server using merge replication. To do this, we need to copy the code that was generated by the SQL Everywhere Subscription Wizard earlier in this chapter.

Be sure the focus is on the form by clicking the skin of the device. Bring up the code window for the *Form Load* event by pressing F7. Notice that Visual Studio has written a few lines of code already that fills the Grid And Details form. We don't want to change that, so we'll create a new routine:

```
public void CreateSubscriptionandSync{}
```

Next we will add the synchronization code that we have on our clipboard and modify the connection string to have the database referenced in the \Program Files\Chapter15 directory. The code sample was taken from the SQL Everywhere subscription database that was created on the desktop, so we must modify it to point to a location on the actual device. The autogenerated code for the bound *DataGrid* objects references the database in the directory where the application is, so we must modify the *SubscriberConnectionString* property so that the location is \Program Files\SQLMobile\Chapter15_ship.SDF. This code will create a new subscription and perform the initial synchronization. You want to perform this action only once, so let's create a button for the application to call this code.

```
private void button1_Click(object sender, EventArgs e)
    {
        CreateSubscriptionandSync();
    }

public void CreateSubscriptionandSync
{
    SqlCeReplication repl = new SqlCeReplication();

    repl.InternetUrl = @"http://kilimanjaro/Chapter15/sqlcesa30.dll";
    repl.Publisher = @"KILIMANJARO";
    repl.PublisherDatabase = @"Chapter15";
    repl.PublisherSecurityMode = SecurityType.DBAuthentication;
    repl.PublisherLogin = @"mobileuser1";
    repl.PublisherPassword = @"<...>";
    repl.Publication = @"Chapter15_Mobile";
    repl.Subscriber = @"Chapter15_sub";
repl.SubscriberConnectionString = @"Data Source=""\Program Files\SQLMobile\
Chapter15_ship.SDF";
    try
    {
        repl.AddSubscription(AddOption.ExistingDatabase);
        repl.Synchronize();
```

```
    }
    catch (SqlCeException e)
    {
        MessageBox.Show(e.ToString());
    }
}
```

To create a synchronization routine, copy the preceding code and comment out the following line of code. Now we are ready to deploy to a device or emulator.

```
repl.AddSubscription(AddOption.ExistingDatabase);
```

Deploying the Mobile Application

Let's deploy the application! Deployment is easy—just press F5 as in a normal Visual Studio application. A Deploy dialog box will appear (Figure 15-35). You have the option to deploy to an actual device or an emulator. We always use an emulator to test our applications.

> **Note** If you are using a Virtual PC, the emulator will not work.

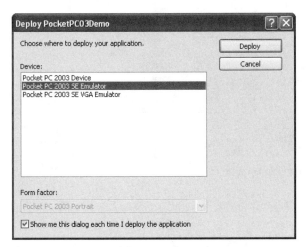

Figure 15-35   Bound form configuration

Once you have chosen your deployment target, your application will run on the device or emulator (Figure 15-36).

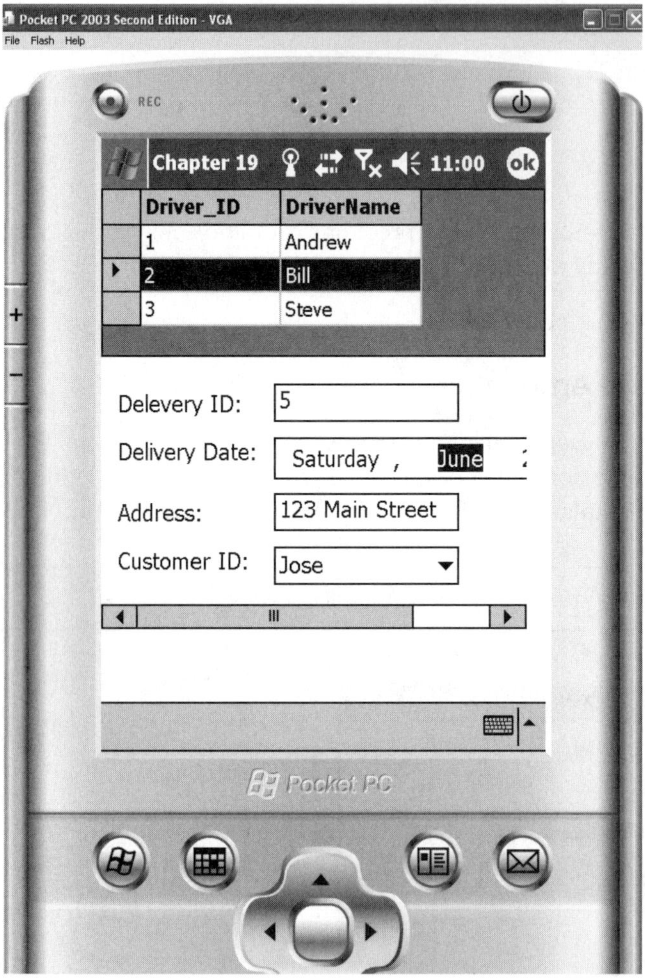

Figure 15-36   Our application working on a device emulator

Summary

With its integration with SQL Server 2005, SQL Everywhere has matured in the past few years. You saw how easy it is to create a database and start working with it using SQL Management Studio. If you want to learn more about SQL Everywhere, go to the following Web sites.

- The SQL Everywhere page on MSDN: *http://msdn.microsoft.com/mobility/sqlmobile/ default.aspx*

- SQL Everywhere page from SQL Server home: *http://www.microsoft.com/sql/editions/ sqlmobile/default.mspx*

- Newsgroups: microsoft.public.sqlserver.ce

- MSDN forums (you will find SQL Everywhere under SQL Server): *http:// forums.microsoft.com/msdn/default.aspx?forumgroupid=19&siteid=1*

Part III
Reporting and Business Intelligence

Chapter 16

Using SQL Server 2005 Integration Services

—Ted Lee and Sergei Ivanov

Without the ability to import data to and export it from a database, a database management system is merely a big repository of data. Since version 7.0, Microsoft SQL Server has had a good way of transforming and manipulating data using Data Transformation Services (DTS). SQL Server 2005 offers a new way of manipulating data, with the replacement for DTS: SQL Server Integration Services. This chapter focuses on Integration Services from a programmer's perspective. We introduce Integration Services concepts as well as the tools and techniques available for package creation and management. We then look at coding techniques and Integration Services internals so that you can understand how to create and extend packages programmatically.

History of Data Transfer in SQL Server

Before we jump right into Integration Services, it is important to review the historical context for the Integration Services design goals. Ten years ago in SQL Server 6.5, one of the few ways to import data to or export data from SQL Server outside of T-SQL and Bulk Insert was through the command-line bcp utility. Although bcp did the job, it exported in a simple text format by default and was difficult to automate. To master **bcp**, you had to go to the command line, set many parameters, and usually set up schema (format) files. In addition, **bcp** provided no easy way to manipulate data going into or out of SQL Server.

When SQL Server 7.0 shipped in 1998, we were first introduced to Data Transformation Services. DTS was a robust and easy-to-use replacement for **bcp** built on OLE DB technology.

(Of course, **bcp** still ships with SQL Server, as does DTS.) With DTS, you could easily import and export between SQL Server and any OLE DB data source. You could also move data from one non-SQL Server–based data source to another, so moving data from a text file to SQL Server or from Microsoft Access to Oracle was simple—all you had to do was use DTS on your local machine or remotely on a server. In addition, you could apply transformations to your data and save the functionality into one location called a DTS Package. DTS shipped with a wizard and interface that made the package creation process pretty straightforward. This opened a new door that **bcp** had kept nailed shut.

DTS Packages

DTS was a huge improvement over its predecessors and whatever else was available in the marketplace at the time, so millions of DTS packages were developed around the world. Developers set up packages to process sets of data in a succession of steps. SQL Server 2000 expanded on this methodology with performance and wizard improvements, but packages were still created in SQL Server Enterprise Manager. Developers now had many packages with several steps in them, but they quickly learned that logic and control flow was still far from perfect, and no form of debugging was available. Developers could make steps in a package dependent on each other and run simple ActiveX scripts as steps in a package, but other than that, they had to turn to third-party components or fancy T-SQL hacks to get the control flow that they desired.

Working with Integration Services Packages

SQL Server 2005 ships with SQL Server Integration Services. Integration Services is a replacement for DTS that extends the same metaphor of a package, but the designer has been radically changed to use Visual Studio and to focus on controlling the flow of the data, giving the developer more control over the design of the package. In this section, we introduce the concepts you must understand to work with Integration Services.

Control Flow

Control flow is the new model for representing the process embodied by the package. When you open a package in the Integration Services designer, the first thing you see is the control flow design surface. The visual representation of control flow is a flowchart. The shapes in the flowchart are called *tasks*. Tasks are the atomic units of execution in an Integration Services package. The lines connecting tasks are the *precedence constraints*, which govern the order in which tasks are executed.

In addition to tasks, the control flow can contain a special type of object called a *container*. You can think of containers as very tightly built-in tasks; they are internally integrated with the package execution engine and can provide some interesting features above and beyond what is possible for tasks. The Sequence container supports nesting of the control flow. When you add a Sequence container to your package, it is as if you have another package within the current package—you can add tasks and precedence constraints, all scoped within that container. In fact, the package itself is a top-level Sequence container. The For Loop container supports iterative execution of the control flow in the container until the loop expression remains true. The Foreach Loop container supports looping over a collection of objects supplied by the chosen Foreach Loop enumerator. Figure 16-1 shows a control flow containing a Sequence container and use of precedence constraints.

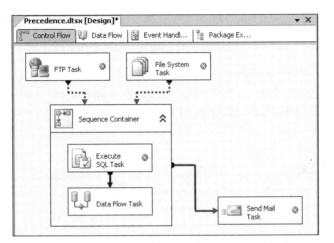

Figure 16-1   Containers and precedence constraints in a control flow

The control flow can also contain a few other things to help you control execution of your process. The first thing you need to do with almost any package is to define connections to be used by your tasks. Structurally, there is a *Connections* collection associated with the package, where you can define and manage all the connections that the package uses. When you have a complete package, which as experience shows often becomes large to handle the complex extract, transform, and load (ETL) processes that must be performed, you can appreciate the benefit of centrally controlling properties of your connections in one spot. Compare this to DTS, where DTS tasks must often be individually configured with connection information.

Variables are another important feature. For every Sequence container you have a collection of variables. You can set the data type, the initial value, and a few other properties on the variable. During execution, tasks can read and write variables. Precedence constraints that control ordering of execution of tasks can also refer to variables. Using variables, you can specify that a particular task be executed if the preceding task had succeeded and the value of a specific variable meets a certain condition.

Major Tasks

Integration Services comes with more than 20 items in the Control Flow toolbox. Let's take a look at some of the most significant and commonly used tasks.

- **Execute SQL task**   Runs queries against databases. This task is very flexible and supports many features, such as parameterized queries, input and output parameters for stored procedures, and multiple ways of returning results.

- **Execute Process task**   Executes a program. This is helpful for launching various command-line utilities from the package.

- **Execute Package task**   Executes another Integration Services package, either in the same or a different process space.

- **File System task**   Performs various file system operations.

- **FTP task**   Transfers files between systems using File Transfer Protocol (FTP).

- **Script task**   Executes custom scripts written in Microsoft Visual Basic .NET.

- **Data Flow task**   Transfers and transforms data between multiple sources and destinations. This is the biggest task in the product and is the subject of the next section.

Data Flow

One of the Integration Services tasks is the Data Flow task. Its function is to support ETL scenarios in which data enters into the data flow from one or more sources, is transformed in the middle of the flow, and is then consumed by destinations at the end of the flow. As the data goes through the flow, the flow itself can be split and merged, and the data can be conditionally routed through the multiple flow paths. The Data Flow task is such a powerful and flexible part of Integration Services that it has its own object model, and the Integration Services designer has a separate design surface area and toolbox to facilitate working visually with data flows. Figure 16-2 shows the data flow design surface.

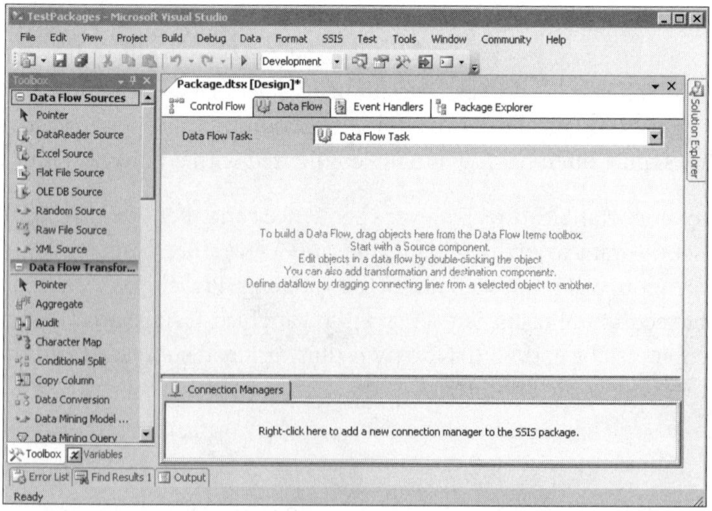

Figure 16-2   The data flow design surface and toolbox

Anatomy of a Data Flow

A data flow consists of components connected by paths. Each component is a point of operation on the data as the data flows from component to component. Components that operate on the data are called *transforms*. Components can also be sources that generate the data at the start of a flow, or destinations that consume the data at the end of a flow. Those components are called *source adapters* and *destination adapters*, respectively. Components have collections of inputs and outputs, and paths are used to connect the output of one component to the input of another. Inputs and outputs have collections of columns that describe the data flow from the output to the input. The data that flows through the components are held in memory buffers represented as rows of columns, just as data is represented in a table in a relational database.

Source Adapters

Source adapters are data flow components that generate data for the start of a flow. The data can be generated by reading from an external source, such as a database, or it can be created internally by the source adapter. Source adapters include:

- **OLE DB source adapter**   Works with the OLE DB Connection Manager to read data into the flow using an OLE DB provider.

- **XML source adapter**   Reads data into the flow from XML files. This adapter is unique in Integration Services because it is the only stock source adapter that supports multiple non-error outputs.

Destination Adapters

Destination adapters are data flow components that consume data at the end of a data flow. The components can insert the data into a database or simply end the data flow without doing anything with the data. Destination adapters include:

- **OLE DB destination adapter**   The counterpart to the OLE DB source adapter. This adapter inserts data from the flow into a database that can be accessed using an OLE DB provider.

- **Data Reader destination adapter**   Makes the data at the end of a flow available to other clients using Microsoft ADO.NET.

Transforms

Transforms are used within the data flow to perform operations on the data, direct data through the flow, or modify the flow itself. Operations can be row-based or set-based. For example, a transform that performs row-based operations is the Copy Column transform. Given a column in a row, the transform needs access to only one row at a time because it copies the data for that column into another column in the same row. An example of a transform that performs set-based operations is the Aggregate transform. To aggregate rows based on data in a column, this transform needs access to the entire set of rows. Transforms that perform row-based operations are called *synchronous* in Integration Services because the operation occurs on one row at a time such that the count and order of rows that flow out of the transforms are the same, or synchronous with, the rows that flow in. Likewise, transforms that perform set-based operations are called *asynchronous* because their operations generate rows that flow out of the transform independently of, or asynchronously with, the rows that flow in. It is worth noting that aynchronous transforms can generate rows based on either subsets or the entire set of input rows.

Synchronous, or row-based, transforms include:

■ **Derived Column transform**   Applies a user-defined expression to the data in a column.

■ **Character Mapping transform**   Applies a user-selected, string-related operation to the data in a column.

Asynchronous, or set-based, transforms include:

■ **Aggregate transform**   Aggregates data in a set of rows.

■ **Sort transform**   Sorts a set of rows based on columns that are designed as keys.

Some transforms are designed to affect the flow of the data by splitting or merging it. These transforms include:

■ **Conditional Split transform**   Applies a user-defined expression to the data and, based on the result, directs each row to one of multiple output flows. This transform is synchronous.

■ **Union All transform**   Combines data from multiple incoming flows into one outgoing flow. This transform is asynchronous. Figure 16-3 shows data flow containing multiple flow paths.

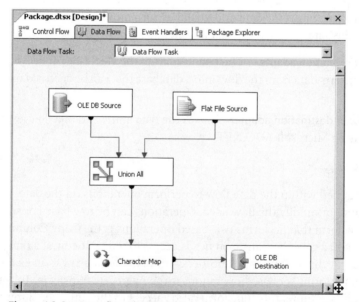

Figure 16-3   Data flow that combines two sources and is then transformed and loaded into a database table

Data Flow Layout

The Data Flow task does not need to know the operational details of its components for it to execute. To the data flow engine, each component is a black box. All that is needed from each component is the correct setting of its metadata, which includes the component's properties, inputs, outputs, and columns. For example, the Aggregate transform indicates to the data flow that its operation is asynchronous by setting its output's *SynchronousInputID* property to 0. How the component's metadata is set up and how the components are connected to each other is called the *data flow layout*.

> **More Info**   All objects in the layout—including components, inputs, outputs, paths, columns, and properties—are identified with an integer that is unique within that layout. These object IDs are used for identifying objects, and appear in parentheses in object identification strings (for example, *'Component "OLE DB Source" (34)'*).

Data Flow Validation

When you design a package or before you execute a data flow, validation takes place. Validation ensures that the data flow layout is correctly constructed and that its components are configured correctly. The layout validation is done by the data flow engine, and the component validation is done by the components. The data flow engine does not allow execution to start if any part of layout or component validation fails.

Data Flow Execution

Given the many possible layouts, how does the data flow engine know how to execute the flow? Before execution begins, the data flow task first analyzes the layout to construct execution trees.

Execution Trees   Each tree describes a segment of the layout for which only one buffer is needed. In general, the segment described by a tree has the following pattern: The segment starts at an asynchronous output, such as the output of a source adapter, where rows are added to the buffer. That segment continues on the path from the output and includes any synchronous components along the way before the segment ends. Finally, the segment ends at the first input that isn't synchronous with any output, such as the input of a destination adapter where the rows added to the buffer by the initial output that started the segment are consumed.

> **More Info**   Along with destination adapters, asynchronous components such as the Aggregate end execution trees with their inputs. However, they also start new trees with their asynchronous outputs.

Execution Plans   Once all the trees are constructed, they are used to generate an execution plan. This plan determines how the data buffers are queued and passed to the components, and how the data flow engine's worker threads are allocated across the layout. The execution trees and plan can be logged for analysis to help with debugging and improving performance, via the Logging dialog box in the designer (as shown in Figure 16-4).

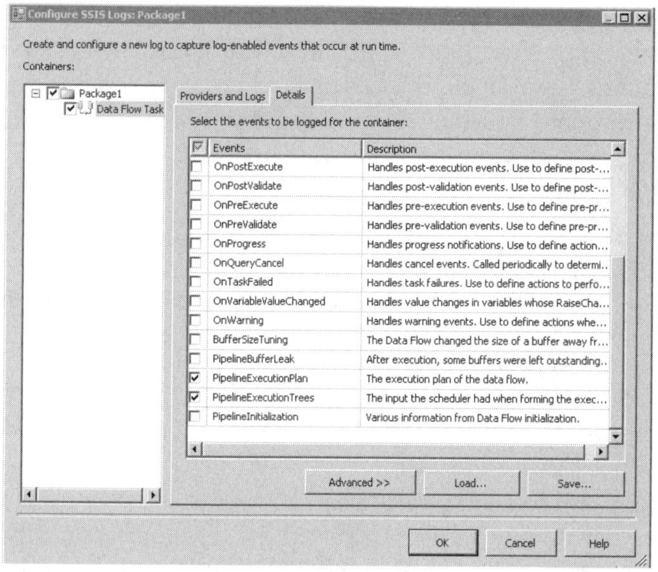

Figure 16-4 Configuring the data flow task to log its execution trees and execution plan

Execution Phases As the data flow is executed, components are given the chance to respond to different phases of execution. This gives the data flow engine and components a chance to perform any additional processing needed for the execution. Here, in order, are the execution phases.

- **PrepareForExecute** The data flow engine and components can perform any one-time preparation needed before execution starts.

- **PreExecute** As with *PrepareForExecute*, the data flow engine and components can perform any one-time preparation needed before execution starts. *PreExecute* occurs closer to the main execution of the data flow, so you should use *PreExecute* instead of *PrepareForExecute* to perform any work that requires acquiring and holding onto an expensive or shared resource to minimize the time the resource is needed. Also, any connections needed by components are acquired after *PrepareForExecute* and before *PreExecute*, so any preparation that requires connections should occur in *PreExecute* instead of *PrepareForExecute*.

- **PrimeOutput** Source adapters and asynchronous transforms are primed with data buffers via *PrimeOutput*. However, they handle the buffers differently. Source adapters immediately start adding data to those buffers. As those buffers become full, the data flow engine pushes them downstream to be consumed by other components. Asynchronous transforms do not add immediately data to their buffers. Instead, they hold onto the buffers and end their *PrimeOutput* phase. Because asynchronous components, like the Aggregate, add output data based on their input data, they must wait until they get enough input data to start adding rows to their cached buffers.

■ *ProcessInput*   Destination adapters and transforms are asked to process their input data via *ProcessInput*. For asynchronous components, whose output buffers are cached in *PrimeOutput*, data is added to those buffers when enough input data has been processed.

■ *PostExecute*   This phase counterbalances *PreExecute* and is used for any post-execution processing, usually releasing any resources acquired in *PreExecute*. Connections that were made before *PreExecute* are also released after *PostExecute*.

■ *Cleanup*   This phase counterbalances *PrepareForExecute* and is used for any necessary cleanup. Once the execution phases are complete, the data flow task signals to the Integration Services runtime that it has either succeeded or failed in its execution.

Viewing Data in the Flow During Execution

While the data flow task executes in the designer, you can see the data passing from one component to another by using data viewers, which is great for debugging if you need to see how the components transform the data. To do this, double-click on a path between the two components where you want to view the data, select Data Viewers, and then click Add. Four types of data viewers can be added to display the data in different forms, with the grid format being the most traditional because it displays the data in tabular form.

One thing to keep in mind when using the data viewers is that when they access the data flow buffers to display the data, they actually pause the data flow. To allow the flow to continue, you must click the Play button on the viewer. This means if the row in the data flow that you are trying to view is near the end of the flow, you might have to click through a lot of pauses before seeing the row. One solution, although not perfect, is to fast-forward through the data flow, hopefully pausing again closer to the row you want. You can do this by clicking the Detach button to detach the viewer to let more rows through. When enough rows have gone through, click the Attach button to attach the viewer again. Figure 16-5 shows the data viewer in action.

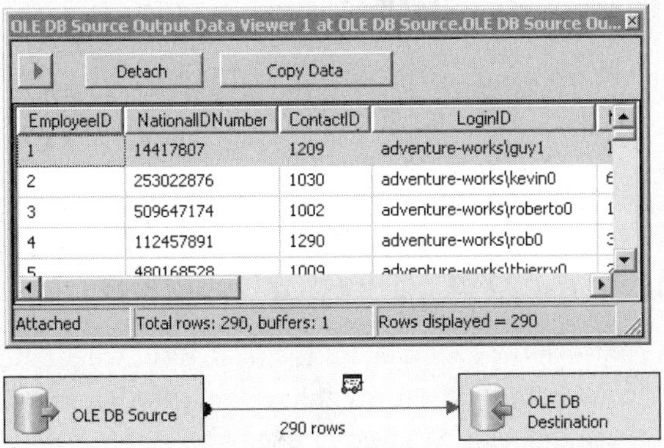

Figure 16-5   Data viewer showing the data during execution

Handling Component Errors Within the Data Flow

Some components support error outputs, which are represented by red outputs in the designer. The term *error output,* however, is misleading because what constitutes an error is component specific. In other words, these are outputs used by the component for pushing rows into the data flow that have not been successfully processed by the component. For example, the Lookup component might consider a failed lookup an error and then route that row to its error output. Component errors in Integration Services are divided into two groups: truncation errors and non-truncation errors. (An example of a truncation error is when some string data used by the component is too long and needs to be trimmed.) These two categories were created because in many business scenarios, truncations are either not considered errors or must be handled differently from other errors. Most components that support error outputs also have the option to fail on an error or truncation, ignore the error or truncation, or route the row with the error or truncation to their error outputs. You can set this option by modifying the component's error or truncation disposition on the column that the error or truncation can occur on. Figure 16-6 shows what a data flow can look like when error outputs are connected.

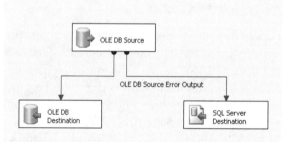

Figure 16-6   A source adapter with its error output connected

Using Integration Services Packages

Integration Services packages can be created using the Import And Export Wizard or in the SQL Server Business Intelligence Development Studio, maintained in Management Studio, and executed either individually or in a batch. This section describes the different ways of creating and managing Integration Services packages using the tools available in SQL Server 2005.

Creating Packages Using the Import And Export Wizard

The Import And Export Wizard is one of the easiest ways to create basic Integration Services packages for importing and exporting data. The wizard guides you through the available options and then generates a package that can be saved or executed. A package that is saved can be loaded into BI Development Studio to be further modified or used as a starting point for a package template.

Creating Packages Using BI Development Studio

BI Development Studio provides a designer that you can use to create and edit Integration Services packages. The designer is a visual environment for working with packages; it supports drag-and-drop, copy and paste, IntelliSense for editing scripts, and other conveniences. The UI elements of the designer, such as the task and component UIs, are designed to provide visual help in correcting mistakes made when working with packages. This, in turn, eases the learning curve and reduces the internal knowledge needed to use Integration Services. As a result, this chapter does not focus on using the designer to work with packages, which you can easily figure out, but on creating packages through non-UI programming. For users new to the designer, Chapter 20 includes a sample that walks through the process of creating an Integration Services package using the designer.

Managing Packages Using Management Studio

You can manage Integration Services packages in SQL Server Management Studio using Object Explorer. Object Explorer enumerates running packages and packages saved in the file and the database stores. Other management tasks you can do include stopping running packages and importing packages into the stores. The SQL Server Integration Services service is used; if the service is stopped, Object Explorer restarts it as needed. You can do some configuration for the service by modifying the MsDtsSrvr.ini.xml file in the 90\DTS\binn directory where SQL Server is installed. After making modifications, you must stop and restart the service for the modifications to take effect. Figure 16-7 shows the Object Explorer in Management Studio working with Integration Services.

Figure 16-7   Managing packages using Object Explorer in Management Studio

Using the Command Line to Execute and Manage Packages

You can execute packages in batch processing using the Microsoft SQL Server Execute Package utility, which is often referred to by its executable name, DTExec. The utility has many options for package execution using command-line parameters. To see the list of parameters and their usage, run *DTExec /Help* or *DTExec /?*. To get help with a specific parameter, run *DTExec /Help [parameter]*. The command line for DTExec can also be generated using a

GUI-based utility, DTExecUI. After specifying the execution options and generating the command line, you can choose to execute the package directly from DTExecUI. Figure 16-8 shows DTExecUI in use.

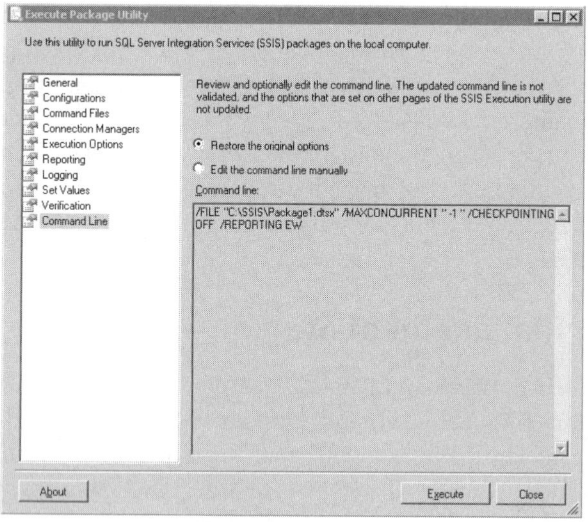

Figure 16-8 Using DTExecUI to generate the command line for DTExec

> **Tip** DTExec has an unsupported option, /z, which causes the utility to pause before and after executing a package. This is very useful for debugging. The first pause gives you time to attach the debugger to DTExec before the package starts executing. The second pause gives you a chance to review the package output in the console window between the end of package execution and the termination of DTExec. Keep in mind that because this option is unsupported, its behavior is not guaranteed and you should not use it if you must rely on its behavior.

The utility for managing packages in batch processing is the Microsoft SQL Server Integration Services Package Utilities, or DTUtil, which allows for management tasks such as copying and signing packages. The command-line parameters for this utility are specified in a similar manner as with DTExec. Use *DTUtil /Help* or *DTUtil /?* to see the list of options and functionality available. Unlike DTExec, which has the graphical counterpart DTExecUI, DTUtil has no graphical counterpart that ships with Integration Services.

Scheduling Packages Using SQL Server Agent

You can schedule execution of packages using SQL Server Agent. This is easily done with the new Integration Services subsystem built into Agent. First you create a job and then a job step. When you create a job step, you have the option of selecting a job type. One of the options is the SQL Server Integration Services Package.

To schedule a package, start SQL Server Management Studio, connect to your server, and right-click the SQL Server Agent node. If the service is not running, you will see a Start menu item. Click that if necessary. Click New Job to go to the Create New Job dialog box. Enter the name of the job, and proceed to the Steps page. There, click the New button, enter the name you want for this job step, and select SQL Server Integration Services Package as the job step type.

On the General tab, you can specify the location of your package, and you'll see several other tabs where you can specify other, more advanced options for running your package.

The rest of the process of scheduling a package is the same as for any other job type. Proceed to the Schedules page to specify scheduling parameters, set any other options you want, and then click OK to finish creating the job.

Configuring and Deploying Packages

Once you have built a package that works in the development environment, you must consider how to deploy it. Will it be run on different servers? Will you be the only one to run and maintain it, or will you release it to other people to own? To make a package that can work in any environment and is easy to maintain calls for use of configuration features.

Why do you need configurations? For example, suppose your package reads data from files on a network share that were placed there by some other process, and suppose the path to the share is hardcoded in the package. A few weeks after you deploy the package, the IT department decommissions that server and sets up a new server on better hardware. Your package now breaks. Even worse, if your package was deployed on several servers, it breaks on several systems at the same time and you have to update all these packages to resolve the problem. If you're not available, your successor has the big task of debugging and troubleshooting the package even to get to the point of understanding why the package failed, let alone how to fix it.

To prevent this, Integration Services offers configuration features. You can declare configurable attributes in your package using the Package Configurations Organizer. When you create a configuration, you can specify the property, variable, or connection that you configure, and you can specify where the value for the configured attribute should be read from. It can be read from an XML file, an environment variable, a registry entry, a parent package variable, or a SQL Server table.

Going back to our example, if you use configurations to read the property that specifies the path to your data files from an XML file, you can trivially update the configuration file to specify the path to the share on the new server without ever touching the package itself. In most packages, multiple attributes might need to be configured, and having all configurable parameters in one place—the configuration file—is very convenient. In some situations, the person who is authorized to modify a package configuration file is not authorized to modify the package itself—a setup that enforces separation between operators and package developers to ensure that packages are not accidentally modified in unforeseen (that is, "unsupported") ways.

To access the Package Configurations Organizer, right-click the design surface for the control flow in BI Development Studio and choose Package Configurations, as shown in Figure 16-9.

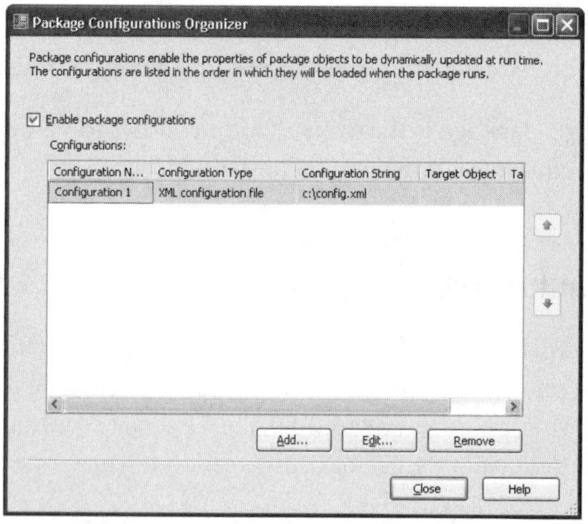

Figure 16-9   The Package Configuration Organizer

Overview of Programming Package Extension

Integration Services provides programmability interfaces to control flow, data flow, and other objects in the package. This enables custom applications to drive loading, creation, parameterization, and execution of packages. It also provides extensibility interfaces that enable custom components to be loaded into packages. You can think of this as building components underneath the package (extensibility objects) and on top of the package (custom applications).

Integration Services interfaces are exposed as .NET assemblies that you can reference in your application. The primary assemblies are:

- *Microsoft.SqlServer.ManagedDTS*
- *Microsoft.SqlServer.PipelineHost*
- *Microsoft.SqlServer.DTSRuntimeWrap*
- *Microsoft.SqlServer.DTSPipelineWrap*

Integration Services includes five types of extensibility objects:

- Tasks
- Connection managers
- Log providers

- Foreach enumerators
- Data flow components

To build an extensibility object, you use Microsoft Visual Studio to create a Class Library project and implement a class derived from the appropriate base class provided by Integration Services. Detailed steps are described later in the chapter.

Ivolva Digital provides free wizard plug-ins for Visual Studio to simplify creation of tasks and data flow components: *http://www.ivolva.com/ssis_wizards.html*.

Security

Because packages involve sensitive information such as passwords as well as data that needs to be protected, security is a major concern. One area in which Integration Services packages have greatly improved DTS is security.

Dealing with Sensitive Information and Assets

Packages often contain sensitive information or information that can be used to gain access to other assets. There are several types of sensitive information, and packages offer features you can use to protect each type of sensitive information. Let's look at the sort of sensitive information a package might contain:

- **Passwords**   This is by far the most common type of sensitive information. Because of the nature of ETL, the package must connect to multiple data sources and destinations and quite frequently a password is required to make a connection.

- **Properties and variables**   Less frequently, raw values of task properties might be sensitive. This is very much environment specific.

- **Control flow and data flow**   Sometimes the very process that is embodied in the package is sensitive. Or you might want to keep the package content out of reach so that no one is tempted to tweak any parameters. Often the package fails because somebody has changed something and it seemed like a good idea at the time.

Integration Services provides several protection levels for sensitive information in the package. You set the protection level by changing the *ProtectionLevel* property on the package. When you edit the package in the package designer, you can access this property using the Properties window. The options available are as follows:

- *DontSaveSensitive*   Offers the ultimate protection and sometimes, depending on the point of view, the ultimate ease of use. Sensitive information is not saved to storage. When the package is loaded from storage, sensitive fields are empty and the values must be reentered.

- *EncryptSensitiveWithUserKey*   Encrypts only the sensitive information in the package using the Data Protection API. This method allows the same user on the same machine to decrypt sensitive information without any prompts. If the package is transferred to another machine, sensitive information cannot be decrypted and is blanked out.

- *EncryptAllWithUserKey*   Applies the same technique as *EncryptSensitiveWithUserKey*, but to the entire package. If the package is transferred to another machine, the package cannot be decrypted.

- *EncryptSensitiveWithPassword*   Encrypts only the sensitive information in the package, using a password. The password should be entered in the *PackagePassword* property of the package. You are prompted for the password when you open the package.

- *EncryptAllWithPassword*   Applies the same technique as *EncryptSensitiveWithPassword*, but to the entire package.

- *ServerStorage*   A protection level you can use if the package is saved to SQL Server. No part of the package is encrypted, and the security configuration of SQL Server provides the protection. The network connection used to transfer the package from the client and to SQL Server is encrypted, however.

Considerations for Working on a Single Development Machine

When you work on a single development machine, you're likely to use the same account for both editing and executing the package. In this case, the most convenient method for protecting sensitive information is to use *EncryptSensitiveWithUserKey* (or *EncryptAllWithUserKey*).

Packages protected in this way are very secure and are convenient to use because no credential must be supplied. Your user account credential is used for encryption. The downside is that packages protected this way cannot be used on another machine. When transferred to another machine, packages protected with *EncryptSensitiveWithUserKey* have the sensitive information blanked out and packages protected with *EncryptAllWithUserKey* cannot be opened.

Considerations for Workgroups

When you have a workgroup situation, in which multiple people are expected to run and edit the same package that contains sensitive information, you can either use a shared password to protect the package (make sure this is not your user account password!) or use the *ServerStorage* protection level and store the package in SQL Server. The latter approach is generally recommended because access to SQL Server is centrally controlled. However, sharing the package password is sometimes convenient as a quick-and-dirty solution. If you do use a shared password, be vigilant about communicating it to your workgroup; sending it in e-mail is probably not a good idea. Also remember that Integration Services uses strong encryption, so if the package password is lost, the data cannot be recovered.

Integration Services does not have built-in version control features, so members of your workgroup must avoid making concurrent changes to packages stored in SQL Server because it is impossible to reconcile the changes.

Another advanced technique is to separate sensitive information from the package using a configuration file. You can create a configuration file using the Package Configurations Organizer and store it on an access-controlled file share. Enter all the sensitive information there. The package contains only a reference to the configuration file. You might be able to avoid having to secure the package—the package can be freely copied and shared, but only people with access to the file share will have the sensitive information loaded into the package when it opens.

Programming Integration Services

Using the concepts explained in this chapter so far, we are ready to discuss programming for Integration Services. The learning curve is considerably steeper than for creating packages using the Import And Export Wizard and the designer. We advise you to become familiar with using the wizard and the designer to create packages before you start working with package creation and extension programmatically. This helps you better understand the flow and design of the code samples presented later in this chapter.

Programming in Visual Studio

Programming Integration Services in the Visual Studio environment is easy to set up. Depending on whether you're building an extensibility object or a custom application, you can create either a Class Library project or an application project. Then you add references to the appropriate assembly and begin implementing your classes.

If you are building control flow extensibility object or a custom application that controls the Integration Service package, you must reference *Microsoft.SqlServer.ManagedDTS*. If you are building a data flow component, you must reference *Microsoft.SqlServer.PipelineHost*, *Microsoft.SqlServer.DTSRuntimeWrap*, and *Microsoft.SqlServer.DTSPipelineWrap*.

Loading and Executing Packages in Applications

You can load packages in applications by using the Integration Services *Application* object. This object returns information about the state of Integration Services (such as the data flow components that are installed) and performs other Integration Services–related tasks (such as determining which packages are running). One of the tasks supported by the object is the loading of packages. More than one method is available to do this—including *LoadPackage* and *LoadFromSqlServer*. The method you should use depends on how the package is stored. To create the *Application* object in managed code, you need to add a reference to *Microsoft.SQLServer.ManagedDTS* and use the namespace *Microsoft.SqlServer.Dts.Runtime*.

Listing 16-1 shows a managed code example that demonstrates package loading and execution.

Listing 16-1   Loading and executing a package

```
using Microsoft.SqlServer.Dts.Runtime;

class ApplicationDemo
{
    static void Main(string[] args)
    {
        Application application = new Application();
        Package package = application.LoadPackage("package.dtsx", null);
        package.Execute();
    }
}
```

Creating Packages Programmatically

In addition to loading and executing packages programmatically, you can also use the Integration Services object model to create packages programmatically. The package's control flow and data flow are conceptually different and therefore have different methods for their construction.

Control Flow

The programming model for control flow is rooted in the *Package* object. You create this object first and then create additional objects with the *Package* object's *Executables* collection. If the object you create is a task, you get a task and you can set properties on it. If the object you create is a container, you get a container and you can set properties on the container and create child objects in the container's *Executables* collection.

Once you have the executable objects in place, you can create precedence constraints by adding items to the *PrecedenceConstraints* collection.

Likewise, to create connections and variables, you add items to the *Connections* collection on the *Package* object and to the *Variables* collection on container objects.

Although you can create the entire package from scratch programmatically, one approach is to templatize the process as much as possible. Build most of the package interactively in SQL Server Business Intelligence Development Studio ahead of time, and then load the template package programmatically and modify it as needed until it has the correct composition. In this way, you minimize the amount of code you need to write and maximize ease of maintenance of your application because you can handle many types of changes simply by changing the template package; you don't have to change a single line of code. Later in this chapter, we show an example of constructing a package from scratch that contains a data flow.

Data Flow

The data flow has its own object model for programmatically setting up the layout that describes a flow. For our example, we programmatically construct a package in C# containing a data flow that uses an OLE DB source adapter to read in data from a SQL Server 2005 table and then inserts the data into a destination table using the OLE DB destination adapter. The flow of the program is similar to how the Import And Export Wizard constructs its packages. Along the way, we review and introduce some concepts that programmers working with the data flow must know. To run the sample, you must have the AdventureWorks database available and the destination table available in tempdb (as shown in Listing 16-2).

Listing 16-2   SQL statement for the destination table used in the data flow programming sample

```
use tempdb
create table Employee
(
EmployeeID int,
Title nvarchar(50)
)
```

Listing 16-3 shows a complete data flow programming sample. When you build the sample, you must add references to:

Microsoft.SqlServer.ManagedDTS, *Microsoft.SqlServer.DTSPipelineWrap*, and *Microsoft.SqlServer.DTSRuntimeWrap*

Listing 16-3   Complete data flow programming sample

```
using Microsoft.SqlServer.Dts.Runtime;
using Microsoft.SqlServer.Dts.Pipeline.Wrapper;

namespace Sample
{
    class DataFlowConstruction
    {
        static void Main(string[] args)
        {
            // Create a new package
            Package package = new Package();
            package.Name = "OLE DB Transfer";

            // Add a Data Flow task
            TaskHost taskHost = package.Executables.Add("DTS.Pipeline") as TaskHost;
            taskHost.Name = "Transfer Table";
            IDTSPipeline90 pipeline = taskHost.InnerObject as MainPipe;

            // Get the pipeline's component metadata collection
            IDTSComponentMetaDataCollection90 componentMetadataCollection = pipeline.Com
ponentMetaDataCollection;
```

```
                // Add a new component metadata object to the data flow
                IDTSComponentMetaData90 oledbSourceMetadata =
componentMetadataCollection.New();

                // Associate the component metadata object with the OLE DB Source Adapter
                oledbSourceMetadata.ComponentClassID = "DTSAdapter.OLEDBSource";

                // Instantiate the OLE DB Source adapter
                IDTSDesigntimeComponent90 oledbSourceComponent =
oledbSourceMetadata.Instantiate();

                // Ask the component to set up its component metadata object
                oledbSourceComponent.ProvideComponentProperties();

                // Add an OLE DB connection manager
                ConnectionManager connectionManagerSource = package.Connections.Add("OLEDB");
                connectionManagerSource.Name = "OLEDBSource";

                // Set the connection string
                connectionManagerSource.ConnectionString =
"provider=sqlncli;server=.;integrated security=sspi;database=AdventureWorks";
                // Set the connection manager as the OLE DB Source adapter's
runtime connection
                IDTSRuntimeConnection90 runtimeConnectionSource =
oledbSourceMetadata.RuntimeConnectionCollection["OleDbConnection"];
                runtimeConnectionSource.ConnectionManagerID = connectionManagerSource.ID;

                // Tell the OLE DB Source adapter to use the SQL Command access mode.
                oledbSourceComponent.SetComponentProperty("AccessMode", 2);

                // Set up the SQL command
                oledbSourceComponent.SetComponentProperty("SqlCommand", "select EmployeeID,
Title from HumanResources.Employee");

                // Set up the connection manager object
                runtimeConnectionSource.ConnectionManager = DtsConvert.ToConnectionManager90
(connectionManagerSource);

                // Establish the database connection
                oledbSourceComponent.AcquireConnections(null);

                // Set up the column metadata
                oledbSourceComponent.ReinitializeMetaData();

                // Release the database connection
                oledbSourceComponent.ReleaseConnections();

                // Release the connection manager
                runtimeConnectionSource.ReleaseConnectionManager();

                // Add a new component metadata object to the data flow
                IDTSComponentMetaData90 oledbDestinationMetadata =
componentMetadataCollection.New();
```

```
            //
 Associate the component metadata object with the OLE DB Destination Adapter
            oledbDestinationMetadata.ComponentClassID = "DTSAdapter.OLEDBDestination";

            // Instantiate the OLE DB Destination adapter
            IDTSDesigntimeComponent90 oledbDestinationComponent =
oledbDestinationMetadata.Instantiate();

            // Ask the component to set up its component metadata object
            oledbDestinationComponent.ProvideComponentProperties();

            // Add an OLE DB connection manager
            ConnectionManager connectionManagerDestination =
package.Connections.Add("OLEDB");
            connectionManagerDestination.Name = "OLEDBDestination";

            // Set the connection string
            connectionManagerDestination.ConnectionString =
"provider=sqlncli;server=.;integrated security=sspi;database=tempdb";

            // Set the connection manager as the OLE DB
Destination adapter's runtime connection
            IDTSRuntimeConnection90 runtimeConnectionDestination =
oledbDestinationMetadata.RuntimeConnectionCollection["OleDbConnection"];
            runtimeConnectionDestination.ConnectionManagerID =
connectionManagerDestination.ID;

            // Tell the OLE DB Destination adapter to use the SQL Command access mode.
            oledbDestinationComponent.SetComponentProperty("AccessMode", 2);

            // Set up the SQL command
            oledbDestinationComponent.SetComponentProperty("SqlCommand",
"select EmployeeID, Title from Employee");

            // Set up the connection manager object
            runtimeConnectionDestination.ConnectionManager =
DtsConvert.ToConnectionManager90(connectionManagerDestination);

            // Establish the database connection
            oledbDestinationComponent.AcquireConnections(null);

            // Set up the external metadata column
            oledbDestinationComponent.ReinitializeMetaData();

            // Release the database connection
            oledbDestinationComponent.ReleaseConnections();

            // Release the connection manager
            runtimeConnectionDestination.ReleaseConnectionManager();

            // Get the standard output of the OLE DB Source adapter
            IDTSOutput90 oledbSourceOutput =
oledbSourceMetadata.OutputCollection["OLE DB Source Output"];

            // Get the input of the OLE DB Destination adapter
```

```
              IDTSInput90 oledbDestinationInput = oledbDestinationMetadata.InputCollection
["OLE DB Destination Input"];

              // Create a new path object
              IDTSPath90 path = pipeline.PathCollection.New();

              // Connect the source and destination adapters
              path.AttachPathAndPropagateNotifications(oledbSourceOutput, oledbDestination
Input);

              // Get the output column collection for the OLE DB Source adapter
              IDTSOutputColumnCollection90 oledbSourceOutputColumns =
oledbSourceOutput.OutputColumnCollection;

              //
 Get the external metadata column collection for the OLE DB Destination adapter
              IDTSExternalMetadataColumnCollection90 externalMetadataColumns =
oledbDestinationInput.ExternalMetadataColumnCollection;

              // Get the virtual input for the OLE DB Destination adapter.
              IDTSVirtualInput90 virtualInput = oledbDestinationInput.GetVirtualInput();

              // Loop through our output columns
              foreach (IDTSOutputColumn90 outputColumn in oledbSourceOutputColumns)
              {
                  // Add a new input column
                  IDTSInputColumn90 inputColumn =
oledbDestinationComponent.SetUsageType(oledbDestinationInput.ID,
virtualInput, outputColumn.LineageID, DTSUsageType.UT_READONLY);

                  // Get the external metadata column from the OLE DB Destination
                  // using the output column's name
                  IDTSExternalMetadataColumn90 externalMetadataColumn =
externalMetadataColumns[outputColumn.Name];

                  // Map the new input column to its corresponding
external metadata column.
                      oledbDestinationComponent.MapInputColumn(oledbDestinationInput.ID,
inputColumn.ID, externalMetadataColumn.ID);
              }

              // Save the package
              Application application = new Application();
              application.SaveToXml(@"c:\OLEDBTransfer.dtsx", package, null);
          }
      }
}
```

Adding a Data Flow to the Package   The first step in working with a data flow after creating the package programmatically is to add a data flow task:

```
// Create a new package
Package package = new Package();
```

```
package.Name = "OLE DB Transfer";

// Add a Data Flow task.
TaskHost taskHost = package.Executables.Add("DTS.Pipeline") as TaskHost; taskHost.Name =
  "Transfer Table";
```

Use *DTS.Pipeline* as the moniker for the data flow task when you add a new task to the
package. It's good practice to give a name to the data flow if your package is opened in the
Integration Services designer. If you don't, the designer labels the data flow task with its
GUID, which is not very user friendly.

```
IDTSPipeline90 pipeline = taskHost.InnerObject as MainPipe;
```

IDTSPipeline90 is the top-level interface that provides access to the entire data flow object
model. It is retrieved as the inner object from the task host for the data flow task.

Setting Up Components and Component Metadata   After adding a data flow task and
getting the pipeline object, you can start adding members to the pipeline object's various
collections. Let's start by adding an OLE DB source adapter. Looking at the collections
available, you see that there is no component collection, but there is a component metadata
collection. The component metadata contains all the metadata that describes a component—
for example, the columns and properties used by the component. From the component
metadata, the component itself can be instantiated. Within this instantiated component is the
custom code that does the work based on how the component metadata is set up. For
example, for the OLE DB source adapter, its component metadata holds the SQL command as
a property and its component contains the OLE DB client code that uses that property to
retrieve data into the data flow.

```
// Get the pipeline's component metadata collection
IDTSComponentMetaDataCollection90 componentMetadataCollection =
pipeline.ComponentMetaDataCollection;

// Add a new component metadata object to the data flow
IDTSComponentMetaData90 oledbSourceMetadata = componentMetadataCollection.New();

// Associate the component metadata object with the OLE DB Source Adapter
oledbSourceMetadata.ComponentClassID = "DTSAdapter.OLEDBSource";
```

You associate the component metadata with a data flow component by setting its
ComponentClassID property. For unmanaged components, which are COM objects, the class
ID or prog ID is used. For managed components, the full assembly name is used.

> **Tip**   One way to determine what value to use for the *ComponentClassID* property for a component is to look in its property page after placing it onto the data flow design surface. The value needed to instantiate the component is shown under the *ComponentClassID* property if it's unmanaged and under the *UserComponentTypeName* if it's managed. This brings up an interesting point: if we are looking at the *UserComponentTypeName* property for managed components, what value is in its *ComponentClassID* property? It is the class ID for the managed component wrapper, which is an unmanaged component internal to the data flow that hosts the managed component. One of the main reasons for the use of a managed component wrapper is to marshal the data in the buffers from the unmanaged data flow execution engine to managed components.

```
// Instantiate the OLE DB Source adapter
IDTSDesigntimeComponent90 oledbSourceComponent = oledbSourceMetadata.Instantiate();
```

Calling the component metadata's *Instantiate* method instantiates the component that contains all the design-time and runtime custom code. The component has two interfaces: *IDTSDesigntimeComponent90* and *IDTSRuntimeComponent90*. As you can guess, the design-time interface contains methods for design-time functionality, such as setting properties and adding columns to its component metadata, and the runtime interface contains methods related to running the component in a data flow execution. To programmatically set up the data flow, we only need to use the methods on the design-time interface.

```
// Ask the component to set up its component metadata object
oledbSourceComponent.ProvideComponentProperties();
```

The *ProvideComponentProperties* method is usually the first method in the component that is called after a component is instantiated. This method tells the component to add any necessary properties, inputs, outputs, and other metadata needed to set up its component metadata from an empty state to a state that describes the component. In our sample, before we call *ProvideComponentProperties*, the component metadata will not have any metadata specific to the OLE DB source adapter. When the method is called, the component adds metadata, such as the *SqlCommand* and *CommandTimeout* properties, to the component metadata to make it specific to the OLE DB source adapter.

Setting Up Connection Managers   Some components use connection managers to access resources outside of the data flow. The OLE DB source adapter is one such component, and the connection manager it uses is the OLE DB Connection Manager. Components describe their association with connection managers by using a runtime connection collection in their component metadata. There is one runtime connection in that collection for each connection manager required by the component. We have already called *ProvideComponentProperties* on the OLE DB source adapter, which should have added one runtime connection to that collection because that adapter requires only one connection to do its work.

```
// Add an OLE DB connection manager
ConnectionManager connectionManagerSource = package.Connections.Add("OLEDB");
connectionManagerSource.Name = "OLEDBSource";

// Set the connection string
connectionManagerSource.ConnectionString = "provider=sqlncli;server=.;integrated
security=sspi;database=adventureworks";
```

As the data source for this example, we'll use a table in the AdventureWorks database on the local machine, logging on using Windows authentication. You can change the connection string as needed, depending on your own configuration.

```
// Set up the OLE DB Source adapter's runtime connection
IDTSRuntimeConnection90 runtimeConnectionSource =
oledbSourceMetadata.RuntimeConnectionCollection["OleDbConnection"];

runtimeConnectionSource.ConnectionManagerID = connectionManagerSource.ID;
```

The runtime connection is associated with the connection manager by the connection manager's ID. When a connection manager is made available to the component by the client or the data flow engine, the ID in the *ConnectionManagerID* property is used to determine which connection manager is needed.

> **Tip**   One way to find the name of the runtime connection is to look for it in the Connection Managers page in the component's Advanced Editor in the designer.

> **More Info**   Instead of using *OleDbConnection* as the index value into a component's runtime connection collection, we could also use 0 as the index because there is only one runtime connection in the collection. However, in general, if there is more than one object in a collection, using the object name instead of an integer as the index is less error-prone because the data flow does not guarantee the ordering of objects in its collections.

Setting Up Column Information   The source table for this example is HumanResources. Employee in the AdventureWorks database. We set up the OLE DB source adapter to use two columns from that table as its data source:

```
// Tell the OLE DB Source adapter to use the SQL Command access mode.
oledbSourceComponent.SetComponentProperty("AccessMode", 2);

// Set up the SQL command
oledbSourceComponent.SetComponentProperty("SqlCommand", "select EmployeeID, Title from
HumanResources.Employee");
```

Best Practices   We only need two columns from the table, so it is more effcient to bring only the two columns from the database into the data flow instead of using a SQL command such as *select * from HumanResources.Employee*, which would bring all the columns into the data flow.

The OLE DB source adapter can use one of several access modes to get its data. The mode we are using here is *SqlCommand*, which has an *AccessMode* enumeration value of 2. This access mode tells the adapter to execute a SQL statement to retrieve its data.

More Info   Other *AccessMode* values are available, such as a mode for retrieving the SQL command from an Integration Services variable. One way to get a list of access modes and their associated enumeration is to look in the type library for the OLE DB source adapter. For example, you can open Oledbsrc.dll in the Object Browser in Visual Studio.

Both *AccessMode* and *SqlCommand* are custom properties on the OLE DB source adapter, which means they are specific to the adapter and are added to its component metadata object when *ProvideComponentProperties* is called.

Best Practices   You might wonder why we call a method to set a property when we can just access the property directly in the component metadata's custom property collection. For example, we could have set the *AccessMode* property by using *oledbSourceMetadata. CustomPropertyCollection["AccessMode'].value = 2;*.

The reason is that when we use *SetComponentProperty*, we ask the component to update its component metadata for us, giving it a chance to reject or react to the new property value if it needs to. If a design-time method is available for modifying the component metadata, you should use it instead of working directly with the component metadata.

```
// Set up the connection manager object
// This needs a reference to Microsoft.SqlServer.DTSRuntimeWrap
runtimeConnectionSource.ConnectionManager =
DtsConvert.ToConnectionManager90(connectionManagerSource);
```

To retrieve the column information for the SQL command, the adapter must have access to the connection manager for its connection. You set this by assigning the connection manager to the *ConnectionManager* property on the adapter's runtime connection. Notice the use of *DtsConvert*, which is needed to convert the connection manager from the *ConnectionManager* to *IDTSConnectionManager90*. As mentioned at the beginning of this sample, for this code to compile, we'll need to add a reference to *Microsoft.SqlServer.DTSRuntimeWrap,* which is needed for *IDTSConnectionManager90* to be available.

Now that the connection manager is set up, we can establish the database connection and tell the component to set up its columns:

```
// Establish the database connection
oledbSourceComponent.AcquireConnections(null);

// Set up the column metadata
oledbSourceComponent.ReinitializeMetaData();

// Release the database connection
oledbSourceComponent.ReleaseConnections();

// Release the connection manager
runtimeConnectionSource.ReleaseConnectionManager();
```

The call to *AcquireConnections* tells the OLE DB source adapter to use the connection manager to establish access to the database. This is followed by the call to *ReinitializeMetaData,* which tells the adapter to query the database for the columns associated with the SQL command provided earlier, and then modify its component metadata to capture those columns. One of these modifications is the addition of output columns on the component metadata, which are needed for the data flow engine to construct its data buffers for execution. Another modification is the addition of external metadata columns, which are columns that describe metadata external to the component—in this case, the columns returned by the SQL command. At this point, the external metadata and output columns are the same, both describing the columns returned by the SQL command. However, the OLE DB source adapter allows its output columns to be customized by the user later but doesn't allow its external metadata columns to be customized. This means the adapter can always rely on its external metadata columns to be a snapshot of the columns returned by the SQL command if it needs to know anything about those columns. After the call to *ReinitializeMetaData,* the connection and connection manager are released.

> **More Info**   We have described how the OLE DB source adapter uses its external metadata columns and how it implements *ReinitializeMetaData,* but note that these are specific to that adapter; another component can use its external metadata columns for any purpose and have whatever logic is necessary in its *ReinitializeMetaData.*

Figure 16-10 shows the use of the Advanced Editor to access a component's external metadata and output column information.

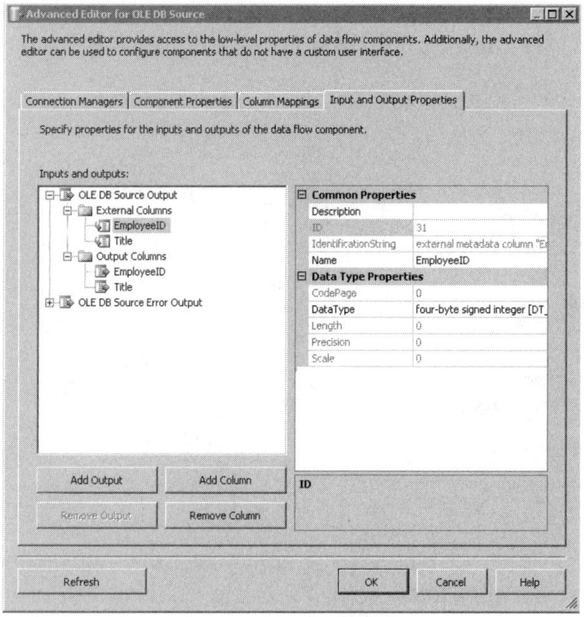

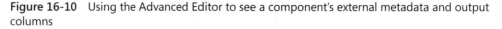

Figure 16-10   Using the Advanced Editor to see a component's external metadata and output columns

> **More Info**   What happens if we change the OLE DB source adapter's SQL command and call *ReinitializeMetaData* again? Some components might just delete all the output columns based on the old SQL command and create new output columns based on the new SQL command. However, the OLE DB source adapter tries to reuse as many of the old columns as possible. So why is it important for the adapter to try to avoid deleting and re-creating output columns? The reason is to minimize disruption to the components downstream of the adapter that have already established mappings to those output columns for their input columns.

Setting Up the OLE DB Destination Adapter   Now that we have the OLE DB source adapter set up to retrieve data into the data flow, we need to set up an OLE DB destination adapter to take the data out of the data flow and insert it into a destination table. Setting up the OLE DB destination adapter mostly follows the same process as setting up the source adapter, so we will skip a line-by-line analysis. However, one difference that needs explanation is the following:

```
// Set up the external metadata columns
oledbDestinationComponent.ReinitializeMetaData();
```

Here the OLE DB destination adapter creates only a snapshot of its destination using external metadata columns—it does not create any input columns. One reason for this is that you create input columns by specifying mappings from them to upstream output columns from where the data originates, and those output columns might not yet be available.

More Info   Input columns map to upstream output columns using a property called *LineageID*.

Connecting the Source and Destination Adapters with a Path   To connect the OLE DB source and destination adapters, we need to create a new path in the data flow:

```
// Create a new path object
IDTSPath90 path = pipeline.PathCollection.New();
```

Next we need to connect the standard output (that is, non-error output) of the source adapter with the input of the destination adapter:

```
// Get the standard output of the OLE DB Source adapter
IDTSOutput90 oledbSourceOutput = oledbSourceMetadata.OutputCollection["OLE DB Source Out
put"];

// Get the input of the OLE DB Destination adapter
IDTSInput90 oledbDestinationInput =
oledbDestinationMetadata.InputCollection["OLE DB Destination Input"];

// Connect the source and destination adapters
path.AttachPathAndPropagateNotifications(oledbSourceOutput, oledbDestinationInput);
```

More Info   Why are notifications needed when *AttachPathAndPropagateNotifications* is used? The answer is that some components must react to their input or output being attached or detached by updating their component metadata. For example, a component such as the Multicast that supports multiple outputs might start with only one output after *ProvideComponentProperties* is called. When the user indicates that he wants to use that output by attaching it, the component can respond by adding a new output to bring its number of outputs to two. If that output is attached as well, the component can respond by adding yet another output. This mechanism is one way for the user to interactively tell the component how many outputs the user wants the component to support. Components respond to *AttachPathAndPropagateNotifications* using methods on the design-time interface called *OnInputPathAttached* and *OnOutputPathAttached*.

Caution   As mentioned earlier regarding the runtime connection collection, instead of accessing the input and output collections using an integer index, we use the names of the input and output, which were set when the input and output were added by the adapters during *ProvideComponentProperties*. This is less susceptible to error for components with more than one input or output. For the OLE DB source adapter, which has a standard output for the data and an error output, we want to make sure that we don't attach a path from the error output instead of the standard output; if we use an index of 0 to get the standard output, we might get the error output instead.

Once the path has been set up and the two adapters attached, we can use the output columns of the source adapter to create the input columns of the destination adapter. In our sample, we do this as follows:

```
// Get the output column collection for the OLE DB Source adapter
IDTSOutputColumnCollection90 oledbSourceOutputColumns =
oledbSourceOutput.OutputColumnCollection;

// Get the external metadata column collection for the OLE DB Destination adapter
IDTSExternalMetadataColumnCollection90 externalMetadataColumns =
oledbDestinationInput.ExternalMetadataColumnCollection;

// Get the virtual input for the OLE DB Destination adapter.
IDTSVirtualInput90 virtualInput = oledbDestinationInput.GetVirtualInput();
```

The virtual input is used to access a component's virtual input column collection. This collection contains columns that are based on all the upstream columns that can be used to create the component's input columns. Many component UIs in the data flow designer also use virtual columns to show the possible columns that can be selected as input columns. In our sample, the virtual input column collection created with the OLE DB destination adapter's input will contain two columns, which are based on the two columns originating from the OLE DB source adapter.

```
// Loop through our output columns
foreach (IDTSOutputColumn90 outputColumn in oledbSourceOutputColumns)
{
    // Add a new input column
    IDTSInputColumn90 inputColumn =
oledbDestinationComponent.SetUsageType(oledbDestinationInput.ID,
virtualInput, outputColumn.LineageID, DTSUsageType.UT_READONLY);

    // Get the external metadata column from the OLE DB Destination
    // using the output column's name
    IDTSExternalMetadataColumn90 externalMetadataColumn = externalMetadataColumns[output
Column.Name];

    // Map the new input column to its corresponding external metadata column.
    oledbDestinationComponent.MapInputColumn(oledbDestinationInput.ID, inputColumn.ID,
externalMetadataColumn.ID);
}
```

Now we need to loop through the output columns from the OLE DB source adapter. For each output column, we first use its *LineageID* to set the usage type of a virtual input column to read-only, which effectively adds an input column to the OLE DB destination adapter and maps it to that output column. To understand how this works, we first need to understand what an input column's usage type is. Usage type is a property on input columns that indicates how the columns are used in the data buffer. By using *UT_READONLY*, we indicate to the data flow engine that the data for those input columns will be read but not modified by the component. If you use *UT_READWRITE* instead of *UT_READONLY*, our sample will still work. However, it is good practice to set the usage type correctly so the data flow engine can make the best optimization when planning its buffer usage for execution. Using the output column's lineage ID, the *SetUsageType* method can find the virtual input column associated with that output column. Then the method will create an input column for the component, set its usage type, and map it to the output column by setting its lineage ID property.

> **More Info** Once an input column has been created using *SetUsageType*, how can the column be removed? To remove the column, call *SetUsageType* with a usage type of *UT_IGNORED*.

> **More Info** For output columns, the *LineageID* is the same as its object ID because output columns are the source of their own data.

After calling *SetUsageType* to create the input columns, we now need to associate the input column columns with the external metadata columns that the OLE DB destination adapter created when its *ReinitializeMetaData* method was called. We do this by calling the *MapInput-Column* method, which sets the input column's *ExternalMetadataColumnID* property to the object ID of its associated external metadata column. That property is generally how both input and output columns are associated with external metadata columns.

With that last step, our data flow construction is complete. You can save the package programmatically and then open it in the Integration Services designer to view what we created:

```
// Save the package
Application application = new Application();
application.SaveToXml(@"c:\OLEDBTransfer.dtsx", package, null);
```

Although our sample uses only two components, we can construct other, more complex data flows containing more components by following this pattern. Figure 16-11 shows our package executed in the designer.

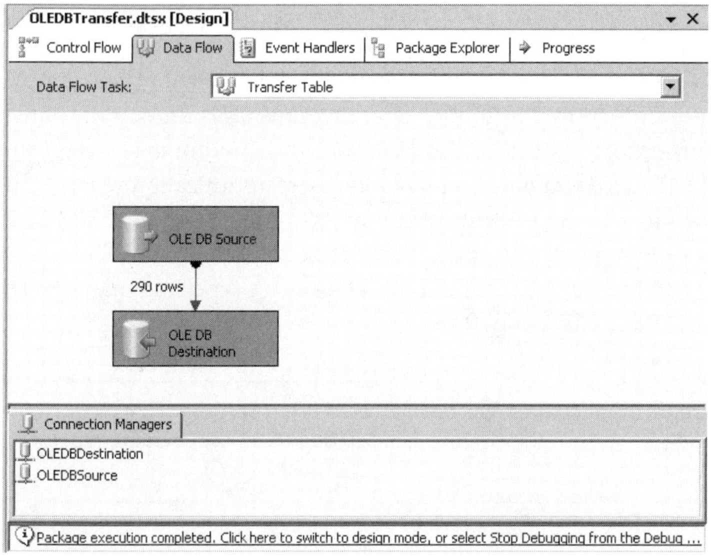

Figure 16-11   Loading and executing our programmatically constructed data flow in the designer

Extensibility

Integration Services provides a very valuable and feature-rich extensible model, which is useful when the tasks and components that come with Integration Services do not supply the functionality you need. Most of the extensibility is achieved by allowing you to write your own logic in scripts, custom tasks, and custom components.

Script Tasks

A Script Task is a very simple way to introduce custom code into the execution of a package. It does not require building separate components—the code for the Script Task is stored inside the package and compiled on demand before execution. After you add a Script Task to the control flow of your package, you can immediately edit it and start entering the code. When you execute the package in SQL Server Business Intelligence Development Studio, you can set breakpoints in your script code and debug the code interactively.

Performance of Script Tasks is very good because unlike the ActiveX Task in previous versions of SQL Server, the Script Task actually compiles the scripts. The source code is compiled to Microsoft intermediate language (MSIL), which is then translated to native code during execution by the common language runtime.

The advantage of the Script Task is ease of use. The disadvantage is that the source code is in the package and therefore can be seen by anyone who can edit it (although sometimes this can be an advantage). Figure 16-12 shows the Script Task development environment.

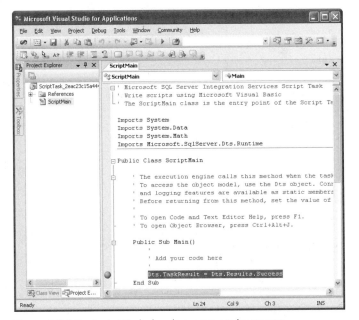

Figure 16-12   Script Task development environment

Custom Tasks

If you want to create a reusable task component that will be distributed as a compiled assembly, you can create a custom task project. To build a custom task, create a Class Library project in Visual Studio. Add a reference to the *Microsoft.SqlServer.ManagedDTS* assembly. In the project properties, go to the Signing tab and select the Sign The Assembly check box. Use a key file you already have or create a key file by clicking New.

Next, create a class derived from *Task* and add the *DtsTask* attribute to the class. Build the project, and add the compiled assembly to the global assembly cache (GAC). Also copy the assembly to %ProgramFiles%\Microsoft SQL Server\90\DTS\Tasks. Restart SQL Server Business Intelligence Development Studio, and you should see your custom connection manager in the list of available connection managers.

Listing 16-4 shows the default output from the free Custom Task Wizard from Ivolva Digital (*www.ivolva.com*). This is as simple a task as you can have.

Listing 16-4   Custom task example

```
using System;
using System.Collections.Generic;
using System.Text;
using Microsoft.SqlServer.Dts.Runtime;

namespace CustomTask
{
```

```
[ DtsTask(
DisplayName = "Custom Task",
Description = "Description of custom task",
IconResource = "CustomTask.TaskIcon.ico" ) ]
public class CustomTask : Task
{
private int _sleepPeriod = 3000;

// TODO: Implement task properties as needed. These properties will appear
// in Properties window when you select your task in the Control Flow.
public int SleepPeriod
{
get { return _sleepPeriod; }
set { _sleepPeriod = value; }
}

public override DTSExecResult Validate(Connections connections, VariableDispenser
variableDispenser, IDTSComponentEvents componentEvents, IDTSLogging log)
{
// TODO: Add your validation code here.
return DTSExecResult.Success;
}

public override DTSExecResult Execute(Connections connections, VariableDispenser
variableDispenser, IDTSComponentEvents componentEvents,
IDTSLogging log, object transaction)
{
// TODO: Add your execution code here. The following is an example.

bool fireAgain = false;
componentEvents.FireInformation(1, "", "Sleeping for " + _sleepPeriod.ToString() + " ms"
, "", 0, ref fireAgain);
System.Threading.Thread.Sleep(_sleepPeriod);
componentEvents.FireInformation(2, "", "Woke up", "", 0, ref fireAgain);

return DTSExecResult.Success;
}
}
}
```

Custom Components

Writing custom components is one way to extend the functionality of the data flow task. In a sense, all components are custom components, even the ones that ship with Integration Services, which shows how flexible and powerful custom components can be. However, writing components is often not a trivial matter. Here are some advantages and disadvantages to consider before deciding whether to write your own component.

The advantages include:

- Fewer restrictions on the functionality you can implement.

- More control over the code—for example, if you need to tune the code for performance.

- More language options for writing the component. This is important if the component needs to use another technology that's available only using certain languages.

- Can be reused easily in different packages once the component is installed.

The disadvantages include:

- Steep learning curve.

- Usually takes more time and effort than other ways of extending the data flow task.

- Less portability because the custom component must be available on the machine running the Integration Services package that uses it.

- Might require that a custom UI editor be written if the default UI editor available in Integration Services for custom components does not work well enough.

Custom components can be managed or unmanaged. Let's start with unmanaged components. Unmanaged components are COM objects that implement the two component interfaces, *IDTSDesigntimeComponent90* and *IDTSRuntimeComponent90*. The methods on *IDTSDesigntimeComponent90* support design-time functionality, such as setting property values. The methods on *IDTSRuntimeComponent90* support runtime functionality, such as processing the data in the data flow. In addition to installing the component in the registry as a COM object, you must also put other information about the component in the registry. Under the COM entry for the component, you must put in a section called DTSInfo that contains information about the component, such as whether it is a source, a transform, or a destination. Also, the component's registry entry must have an Implemented Categories key for registering it with the category for data flow components so it can be enumerated by Integration Services. For an example of a registry entry for an unmanaged component, use regedit on a machine with Integration Services installed to look for the OLE DB source adapter under HKEY_CLASSES_ROOT\CLSID\{2C0A8BE5-1EDC-4353-A0EF-B778599C65A0}. Unfortunately, Integration Services does not include a base class for writing unmanaged components.

In contrast to unmanaged components, managed components are written as classes deriving from the *PipelineComponent* base class, which has default implementations for the methods on *IDTSDesigntimeComponent90* and *IDTSRuntimeComponent90*. The same component information that unmanaged components must add to the registry is made available to Integration Services using the *DtsPipelineComponent* attribute on the managed component.

How do you decide whether to write a managed or unmanaged component? Here are some advantages to writing a managed component rather than an unmanaged component:

- Integration Services ships with a base class for writing managed components but no base class for writing unmanaged components.

- In general, managed code is more forgiving than unmanaged code and takes less time to write.

- A more moderate learning curve

Here are some advantages to writing an unmanaged component:

- All data flow functionality is available, including some direct data buffer access techniques.

- Possibly better performance during execution due to no interop cost because the data flow engine is unmanaged.

Most custom component authors write more managed components than unmanaged. Given that, we present a sample of a custom managed component that maps months from a numeric representation to a string representation. For example, 1 will be mapped into "Jan". The sample shows some of the fundamental techniques for writing custom components. Listing 16-5 shows the complete sample before we start.

Listing 16-5   Complete custom component sample

```
using Microsoft.SqlServer.Dts.Pipeline;
using Microsoft.SqlServer.Dts.Pipeline.Wrapper;
using Microsoft.SqlServer.Dts.Runtime.Wrapper;

namespace SSISComponent
{
    [
        DtsPipelineComponent(DisplayName = "Map Month", ComponentType =
            ComponentType.Transform)
    ]
    public class MapMonthComponent : PipelineComponent
    {
        private int inputColumnBufferIndex = -1;
        private int outputColumnBufferIndex = -1;
        private string[] monthNames = new string[12]{"Jan", "Feb", "Mar", "Apr", "May",
            "June", "July", "Aug", "Sept", "Oct", "Nov", "Dec"};

        public override void ProvideComponentProperties()
        {
            // Set the name
            ComponentMetaData.Name = "Map Month";

            // Support one input
            ComponentMetaData.InputCollection.RemoveAll();
            IDTSInput90 input = ComponentMetaData.InputCollection.New();
            input.Name = "MapMonthInput";

            // Support one output
            ComponentMetaData.OutputCollection.RemoveAll();
            IDTSOutput90 output = ComponentMetaData.OutputCollection.New();
            output.Name = "MapMonthOutput";
            output.SynchronousInputID = input.ID;

            // Add an output column
```

```
        IDTSOutputColumn90 outputColumn = output.OutputColumnCollection.New();
        outputColumn.Name = "Month";
        outputColumn.SetDataTypeProperties(DataType.DT_WSTR, 7, 0, 0, 0);
}

public override DTSValidationStatus Validate()
{
    DTSValidationStatus validationStatus = base.Validate();

    if (validationStatus != DTSValidationStatus.VS_ISVALID)
    {
        return validationStatus;
    }

    // Check the number of input
    IDTSInputCollection90 inputCollection = ComponentMetaData.InputCollection;
    if (inputCollection.Count != 1)
    {
        bool cancel = false;
        ComponentMetaData.FireError(-1, ComponentMetaData.IdentificationString,
          "One input is supported.", "", 0, out cancel);
          return DTSValidationStatus.VS_ISBROKEN;
    }

    // Check the number of input columns
    IDTSInputColumnCollection90 inputColumnCollection =
      ComponentMetaData.InputCollection[0].InputColumnCollection;
      if (inputColumnCollection.Count != 1)
    {
        bool cancel = false;
        ComponentMetaData.FireError(-2, ComponentMetaData.IdentificationString,
          "One input column is supported.", "", 0, out cancel);
          return DTSValidationStatus.VS_ISBROKEN;
    }

    // Check the data type of the input column.
    if (inputColumnCollection[0].DataType != DataType.DT_I4)
    {
        bool cancel = false;
        ComponentMetaData.FireError(-3, ComponentMetaData.IdentificationString,
          "The input column is not of data type DT_I4", "", 0, out cancel);
          return DTSValidationStatus.VS_ISBROKEN;
    }

    return DTSValidationStatus.VS_ISVALID;
}

public override void PreExecute()
{
    // Get the buffer column index for the input column
    IDTSInput90 input = ComponentMetaData.InputCollection[0];
    IDTSInputColumn90 inputColumn = input.InputColumnCollection[0];

    inputColumnBufferIndex = BufferManager.FindColumnByLineageID
      (input.Buffer, inputColumn.LineageID);
```

```
                // Get the buffer column index for the output column
                IDTSOutputColumn90 outputColumn = ComponentMetaData.OutputCollection
                  [0].OutputColumnCollection[0]; outputColumnBufferIndex =
                    BufferManager.FindColumnByLineageID
                      (input.Buffer, outputColumn.LineageID);
            }

        public override void ProcessInput(int inputID, PipelineBuffer buffer)
        {
            if (!buffer.EndOfRowset)
            {
                while (buffer.NextRow())
                {
                    // Get the month in the input column
                    int month = buffer.GetInt32(inputColumnBufferIndex);

                    // Transform the month and put it in the output column
                    if (month < 1 || month > 12)
                    {
                        buffer.SetString(outputColumnBufferIndex, "Invalid");
                    }
                    else
                    {
                        buffer.SetString(outputColumnBufferIndex, monthNames[month -
1]);
                    }
                }
            }
        }
    }
}
```

To begin, we must add references to the following:

- **Microsoft.SqlServer.PipelineHost**   For the *PipelineComponent* and other managed component support
- **Microsoft.SqlServer.DTSPipelineWrap**   For the data flow object model
- **Microsoft.SqlServer.DTSRuntimeWrap**   To access the Integration Services data type enumeration

Here are some of properties of the *DtsPipelineComponent* attribute we use:

```
DtsPipelineComponent(DisplayName = "Map Month", ComponentType = ComponentType.Transform)
```

There are other properties as well. The *CurrentVersion* property is worth mentioning because it is a part of the automatic upgrade system available to components. Here's an overview of how the upgrade system works: If the current version of the component installed on the machine on which an Integration Services package is executed is later than the version of the component within the package, the old version of the component in the package can be automatically updated to the new version by using its *PerformUpgrade* method.

The base class for managed components is the *PipelineComponent* class. The first method we override is *ProvideComponentProperties*. This method is called to allow a component to provide its properties and other metadata by modifying its component metadata, which is accessed by using the *ComponentMetaData* property.

```
public override void ProvideComponentProperties()
{
        // Set the name
        ComponentMetaData.Name = "Map Month";

        // Support one input
        ComponentMetaData.InputCollection.RemoveAll();
        IDTSInput90 input = ComponentMetaData.InputCollection.New();
        input.Name = "MapMonthInput";

        // Support one output
        ComponentMetaData.OutputCollection.RemoveAll();
        IDTSOutput90 output = ComponentMetaData.OutputCollection.New();
        output.Name = "MapMonthOutput";
        output.SynchronousInputID = input.ID;

        // Add an output column
        IDTSOutputColumn90 outputColumn = output.OutputColumnCollection.New();
        outputColumn.Name = "Month";
        outputColumn.SetDataTypeProperties(DataType.DT_WSTR, 7, 0, 0, 0);
}
```

We design our component to use one input and one column. The input contains one column of data type *integer*. The value of that integer is mapped to a month, which is set into an output column. So, in the method, our component adds one input and one output. To its output, it adds an output column called Month, and it sets its data type to a Unicode string type with a length of 7, which is sufficient for all the month-related data the component adds to the flow, including a string for handling invalid data. No input column is added in this method because you create input columns by mapping them to upstream output columns from where the data originates, and no upstream output columns are available in this method because the component's input was just created and therefore not yet attached to any other component. If you worked through the earlier section on constructing a data flow programmatically, you should see that the correct method for creating our component's input column is its *SetUsageType* method.

Best Practices   It's good practice to set the length of your output columns to be as small as possible so that less memory is needed, making each data row smaller. In turn, this allows more rows to fit into each data buffer, which should generally increase the performance of the data flow execution.

Note the setting of the *SynchronousInputID* property on the output. This property synchronizes the input and output of the component so the same data row flowing into the input will flow out of the output. If the input and output are not in sync, the component becomes asynchronous, like the Aggregate component, which means that it must generate its own output rows independently of the incoming input rows.

> **More Info**   Instead of setting up the input and output manually, you can have the component call *base.ProvideComponentProperties();* so the base class sets up the input and output. However, keep in mind that calling the base class for this method is not always correct because the base class always tries to set up the component as a synchronous transform, which is correct for our sample component but might not be for other components. For example, if your component doesn't have any inputs, as in a source adapter, you should not call the base class.

In addition to *ProvideComponentProperties*, custom components can implement other methods to control how they can be configured during design-time. For example, our sample component only needs one output column of data type *DT_WSTR* and a length of 7. To control whether the column's data type or length can be modified, the component can implement the design-time method *SetOutputColumnDataTypeProperties* to either accept or reject a change to the column's data type property.

Now we get to the *Validation* method:

```
public override DTSValidationStatus Validate()
{
    DTSValidationStatus validationStatus = base.Validate();

    if (validationStatus != DTSValidationStatus.VS_ISVALID)
    {
        return validationStatus;
    }

    // Check the number of input
    IDTSInputCollection90 inputCollection = ComponentMetaData.InputCollection;
    if (inputCollection.Count != 1)
    {
        bool cancel = false;
        ComponentMetaData.FireError(-1,
ComponentMetaData.IdentificationString, "One input is supported.", "", 0, out cancel);
        return DTSValidationStatus.VS_ISBROKEN;
    }

    // Check the number of input columns
    IDTSInputColumnCollection90 inputColumnCollection =
ComponentMetaData.InputCollection[0].InputColumnCollection;
    if (inputColumnCollection.Count != 1)
    {
        bool cancel = false;
```

```
        ComponentMetaData.FireError(-2,
ComponentMetaData.IdentificationString, "One input column is supported.", "", 0, out can
cel);
        return DTSValidationStatus.VS_ISBROKEN;
    }


    // Check the data type of the input column.
    if (inputColumnCollection[0].DataType != DataType.DT_I4)
    {
        bool cancel = false;
        ComponentMetaData.FireError(-3,
ComponentMetaData.IdentificationString, "The input column is not of data type DT_I4", ""
, 0, out cancel);
                return DTSValidationStatus.VS_ISBROKEN;
    }

    return DTSValidationStatus.VS_ISVALID;
}
```

Validation is called during package construction by the Integration Services designer and
before execution by the data flow engine. This method ensures that the component is in a
valid state and that the data flow engine does not start execution unless all components pass
validation. For example, our sample component requires one input column, so its validation
method should check for it. Validation should indicate that something is wrong by posting an
error and returning the appropriate validation status. This status is an enumeration with the
following possible values, listed here from the least to the most severe:

- *VS_ISVALID*   Indicates that everything is okay with the component.

- *VS_NEEDSNEWMETADATA*   Indicates that something is wrong but the component can
  fix the problem if its *ReinitializeMetaData* method is called. If you return this status,
  make sure the code in *ReinitializeMetaData* can fix the problem.

- *VS_ISBROKEN*   Indicates that something is wrong but the problem can be
  fixed manually by the user with the component's custom UI editor or the advanced
  UI editor.

- *VS_ISCORRUPT*   Indicates that something is wrong and the only way to correct the
  problem is to reset the component. One way to do this is to call the component's
  ProvideComponentProperties method.

> **Best Practices**   It is good practice to validate for the most severe problems first, if possible.
> For example, most users will be upset if they go out of their way to fix *VS_ISBROKEN*-related
> problems, only to be presented with a *VS_ISCORRUPT* problem that requires them to reset the
> component, thereby wiping out all the changes they made to fix the *VS_ISBROKEN*-related
> problems. Another good practice is to return the most severe status if multiple problems are
> found with different validation statuses.

The use of the *ComponentMetaData.FireError* method in *Validation* demonstrates how custom error messages are posted. That method takes a custom error code, which should be unique among all the error codes used by the component. The error text passed into the method should be the final version of the text, without any unfilled parameters, and already localized if needed. The *cancel* parameter is passed into the method but is not used. Its value can be set by the event sink that handles the error to tell the component to cancel processing.

> **Best Practices**   Every object in the data flow object model has an identification string with the following format: *object type "object name" (object ID)*. The object ID contained in the string is unique for each object within the same data flow, so using the identification string is less ambiguous than using just the object name in error messages.

The call to *base.Validate* validates the component generically, which includes a call to *ComponentMetaData.Validate* to have the data flow task validate the component in the context of the layout.

It is often impractical to have *Validate* be exhaustive—for example, when a certain portion of the validation requires a resource that is expensive to acquire. In those cases, the problem might surface during execution, in which case the component should attempt to fail gracefully. The validation of our sample component is not exhaustive, but other required validation steps, such as checking the output metadata, follow the same guidelines discussed so far for validation.

If a component in a data flow returns *VS_ISVALID*, it is in a valid state and can be executed. The component's runtime methods that support execution are *PrepareForExecute*, *PreExecute*, *PrimeOutput*, *ProcessInput*, *PostExecute*, and *Cleanup*. Our sample component implements *PreExecute* and *ProcessInput*:

```
public override void PreExecute()
{
    // Get the buffer column index for the input column
    IDTSInput90 input = ComponentMetaData.InputCollection[0];
    IDTSInputColumn90 inputColumn = input.InputColumnCollection[0];
    inputColumnBufferIndex = BufferManager.FindColumnByLineageID(input.Buffer,
inputColumn.LineageID);

    // Get the buffer column index for the output column
    IDTSOutputColumn90 outputColumn = ComponentMetaData.OutputCollection[0].OutputColumn
Collection[0];
    outputColumnBufferIndex = BufferManager.FindColumnByLineageID(input.Buffer,
outputColumn.LineageID);
}

public override void ProcessInput(int inputID, PipelineBuffer buffer)
{
    if (!buffer.EndOfRowset)
```

```
{
// Do any additional processing if needed,
    // Get the month in the input column
    while (buffer.NextRow())
        {
            // Get the month in the input column
            int month = buffer.GetInt32(inputColumnBufferIndex);

            // Transform the month and put it in the output column
            if (month < 1 || month > 12)
            {
                buffer.SetString(outputColumnBufferIndex, "Invalid");
            }
            else
            {
                buffer.SetString(outputColumnBufferIndex, monthNames[month - 1]);
            }
        }
    }
}
```

Our sample component's *PreExecute* method makes use of the *BufferManager*, whose methods are used to return information about the data buffers set up by the data flow engine. For the component to know which columns in the data buffer are mapped to its input and output columns, it uses the *FindColumnByLineageID* method of *BufferManager*. Given a column's *lineageID*, that method returns the index of the column in the data buffer.

> **More Info**   Notice that *input.Buffer* is used instead of *output.Buffer* to get the buffer column index for the component's output column. Why isn't *output.Buffer* used? The use of *output.Buffer* currently returns an error for synchronous components. The reason is that our sample's component output is synchronous with its input, so the same rows flowing into its input flow out of its output. For the rows to be the same flowing in and out, they must internally contain all the columns for the input and the output. So, *input.Buffer* and *output.Buffer* in this case point to the same internal buffer for those rows, and *input.Buffer* was chosen to be the handle for that internal buffer. Perhaps in a later version of Integration Services, *output.Buffer* will also return the correct buffer handle instead of an error.

In *ProcessInput*, our sample component processes its input by applying its transformation to the data. Each call to *ProcessInput* gives the component a new buffer full of rows to process. If a component supports more than one input, it can check the input ID passed into the method to determine which input the buffer is used for. The standard processing done in the method starts with checking whether the buffer has the end-of-rowset flag set. This flag is used to signal to the component to do any processing needed after receiving the last buffer of data. For example, an asynchronous transform such as the Sort can start adding the sorted rows to its output buffer. If the end of rowset has not been reached, the component accesses the correct columns in the buffer by using the column indexes it obtained in *PreExecute*. So, does our sample component need to set the end-of-rowset flag when it is done? The answer is no. The reason is that our sample component is synchronous and therefore does not generate new rows or remove existing rows from the buffer. This means our component does not have to deal with controlling the size of the rowset by setting the end-of-rowset flag. So who sets the flag? The flag is set by the component that adds the rows, such as a source component or an asynchronous transform, to indicate that it has no more rows to add.

> **Tip**   The *ProcessInput* method is where synchronous components spend most of their time during execution. This method should be the first to be optimized if good performance is critical for your custom component.

Once the sample component is built, it should be installed into the Integration Services data flow component directory under 90\DTS\PipelineComponents in the SQL Server directory. If the component is unmanaged, it should be registered in the registry. If it's managed, it should be added to the GAC. You can then add the component to the toolbox of the Integration Services designer and use it in a package. Figure 16-13 shows our custom transform in the middle of execution.

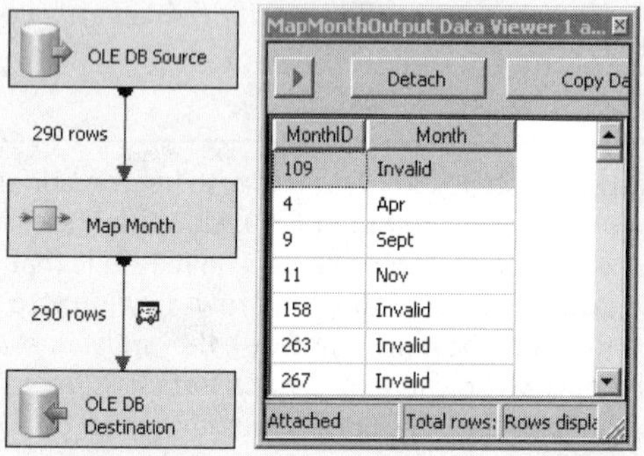

Figure 16-13   Our custom transform in action

Writing custom components can also involve other factors not demonstrated by our sample component—these include connection managers, error outputs, and asynchronous outputs. However, the information and guidelines presented in this section should make a good starting point for exploring those other topics on your own.

Script Components

The script component is one of the easiest ways to extend the functionality of the data flow. It allows access to the data flow using script written in Visual Basic .NET. When should you use a script component instead of a custom component? Here are some advantages to using the script component:

- Less component housekeeping required, allowing you to focus more on scripting the transformation logic.

- Gives guidance by providing script templates and classes that are generated based on how the component is set up in the data flow. This, in turn, improves the effectiveness of IntelliSense in the script editor.

The disadvantages include:

- It's harder to port scripts from one package to another than to install a custom component that can be used in any package.

- Scripts must be updated to use the latest component column metadata whenever the metadata has changed.

- Some data flow functionality, such as multiple inputs, is not available to the script component, due to the limitations of the component or its UI editor.

To compare a script component to a custom component further, let's walk through creating a script component that does the same transformation as the component we created earlier in the section about writing custom components. That is, the script component will take an input column of data type *integer* and map that integer to the name of a month. For example, 1 will be mapped to "Jan".

First create a data flow in the Integration Services designer, and then add a source adapter that contains at least one output column with a data type of *DT_I4* to be used as the input column to our script component. If you have the data flow from the section on constructing packages programmatically, you can load that package in the designer as your starting point.

Once the data flow with the source adapter is set up, place a script component onto the design surface. A dialog box appears asking if the script component is to be a source adapter, a transformation, or a destination adapter. Select the Transformation option, which initializes the component to be a synchronous transform with one input and one output. Internally in the component, this means the *SynchronousInputID* property of the output is set to the ID of the input. Next, connect the output of the source adapter to the input of the component. This makes the output columns from the adapter available as upstream columns for the component, which means those columns can be selected as input columns for the component.

Now we are ready to select which input column we want to use. Double-click on the script component to bring up its UI editor. Notice that this is the editor for the script component, which lets you modify the component's metadata, and is not the editor for modifying the script itself. Select the Input Columns page. Here the upstream columns originating from the source adapter should be displayed as available input columns. Select the column of data type *DT_I4* to be used as the input column for the script component. If you are using the data flow from the section on programmatic package construction, select the EmployeeID column from the HumanResources.Employee table, as shown in Figure 16-14. This adds an input column to the script component. Internally in the component, the *LineageID* of the input column is set to the *LineageID* of the upstream output column. Also notice that the usage type of the input column is set to *ReadOnly* by default, which is correct for our case because the script component will only be reading the value of the column and not writing into the column. Although EmployeeID is not the most likely set of data to be mapped to a month name, for the purposes of package reuse and sample continuity in this chapter, we will use it in this sample. Another option for users who do not want to use EmployeeID is to change the data source so that provides real month data—for example, *"select month(startdate)as MonthNumber from DimPromotion"* from the AdventureWorksDW database.

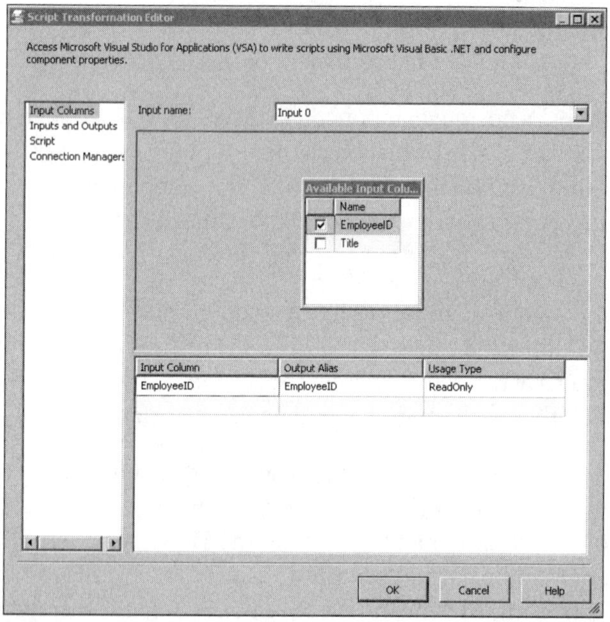

Figure 16-14 Selecting the input column from the list of upstream columns

After selecting the input column, we must add an output column to store the name of the month. In the script component UI editor, select the page for Inputs and Outputs, which displays the input and output of the script component in a tree view. Rename the input to **MapMonthInput** and the output to **MapMonthOutput**. Expand the output, and select Output Columns. Click Add Column, and then rename the new output column to **Month**. Select the new output column, and change its data type to *DT_WSTR*, with a length of 7, as shown in Figure 16-15.

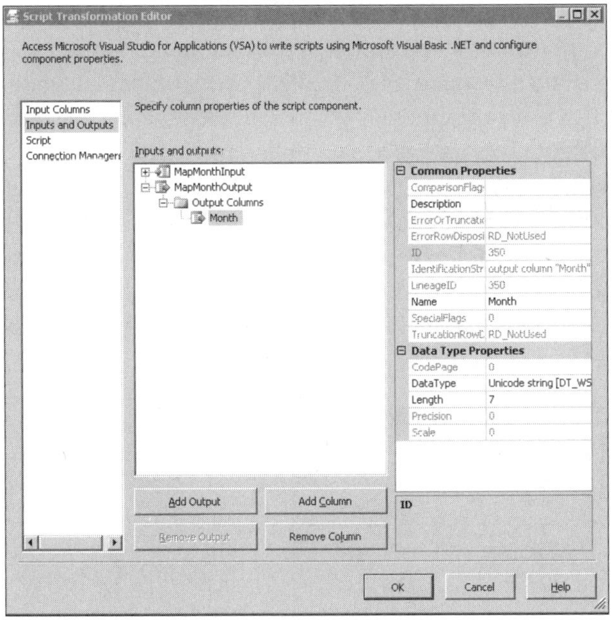

Figure 16-15 Adding an output column

With the input and output columns in place, we are ready to write the script for the component. In the editor, select the Script page and click Design Script to bring up Microsoft Visual Studio for Applications set up as the script editor for the component. Here you can open up the Project Explorer window to see the references that are set and the classes, such as *Buffer-Wrapper* and *ComponentWrapper*, that are needed to make the script execution in the data flow possible. The class we need to edit is the *ScriptMain* class, which contains a template for an overridden method called *MapMonthInput_ProcessInputRow*. This method will be called once for each row in the data buffer that flows through the component, with the row passed into the method as the *Row* parameter. Add the code shown in Listing 16-6 to the class.

Listing 16-6 Script component example

```
Public Class ScriptMain
    Inherits UserComponent

    Private Month() As String = New String() {"Invalid", "Jan", "Feb", "Mar", "Apr",
"May", "June", "July", "Aug", "Sept", "Oct", "Nov", "Dec"}

    Public Overrides Sub MapMonthInput_ProcessInputRow(ByVal Row As MapMonthInputBuffer)
        If Row.EmployeeID < 1 Or Row.EmployeeID > 12 Then
            Row.Month = Month(0)
        Else
            Row.Month = Month(Row.EmployeeID)
        End If
    End Sub

End Class
```

The *Row* object has been generated with properties that correspond to the input and output columns we added to the component, making access to the data in the buffer very easy. You can see the implementations of these properties in the *BufferWrapper* class. If you worked through the section on writing custom components, you will notice that the custom component's *ProcessInput* method takes an entire data buffer and iterates through the rows within the method. In contrast, our script component's *MapMonthInput_ProcessInputRow* method is passed a row at a time. What happened to the standard *ProcessInput* method for the script component? It is still there, but in the *ComponentWrapper* class. If you bring up the code for that class, you can see the *ProcessInput* method and how it iterates through the rows in the buffer, calling the *MapMonthInput_ProcessInputRow* method once per row. Figure 16-16 shows the script for the component being edited.

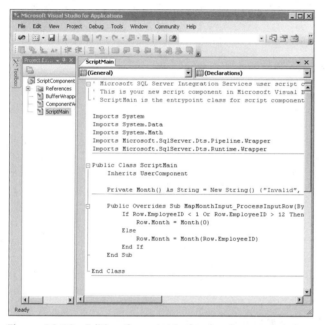

Figure 16-16   Editing the script in the development environment

Once our script has been added, close the script editor and then the script component editor. This completes the configuration of our script component; its output can be attached to the input of another transform or destination adapter that needs the Month output column generated by the component.

This example shows how to use the script component in the most common scenario: as a synchronous transform. However, if you need to implement more advanced functionality in the component, knowledge of data flow concepts becomes invaluable. For example, if you need the script component to be a transform with an asynchronous output instead of a synchronous output that the UI sets up initially, you need to know that you must adjust the configuration made by the UI by manually setting the *SynchronousInputID* property on the component's output to 0 using the script component's UI editor.

Custom Connection Managers

Integration Services supports the notion of pluggable connection manager components. If you build and register a connection manager component, it will appear in the list of available connection types when you right-click in the Connection Managers tray and choose New Connection.

To build a custom connection manager, create a Class Library project in Visual Studio. Add a reference to the *Microsoft.SqlServer.ManagedDTS* assembly. In the project properties, go to the Signing tab and select the Sign The Assembly check box. Use a key file you already have, or create a new key file by clicking New.

Next, create a class derived from *ConnectionManagerBase* and add the *DtsConnection* attribute to the class. Build the project, and add the compiled assembly to the GAC. Also copy the assembly to %ProgramFiles%\Microsoft SQL Server\90\DTS\Connections. Restart SQL Server Business Intelligence Development Studio, and you should see your custom connection manager in the list of available connection managers, as shown in Figure 16-17.

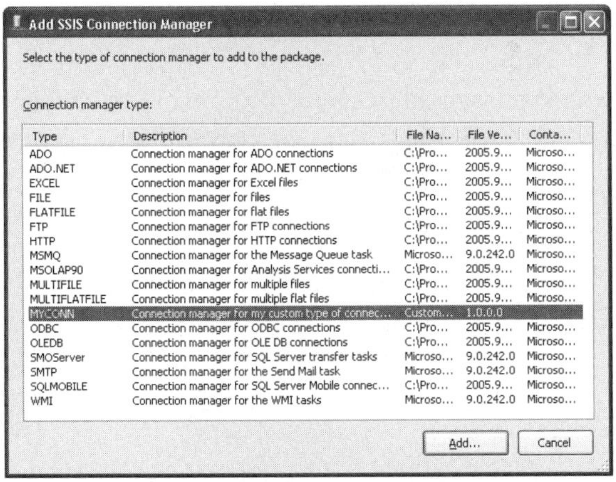

Figure 16-17   Add SSIS Connection Manager

Listing 16-7 shows sample code for a custom connection manager class.

Listing 16-7   An Example of a Custom Connection Manager Class

```
using System;
using Microsoft.SqlServer.Dts.Runtime;

namespace CustomConnectionManager
{
    public class MyConnection
    {
        // TODO: Implement your connection class
    }
```

```
[DtsConnection(
    ConnectionType = "MYCONN",
    DisplayName = "My Custom Connection",
    Description = "Connection manager for my custom type of connections")]
public class CustomConnectionManager : ConnectionManagerBase
{
    public override object AcquireConnection(object txn)
    {
        MyConnection myConnection = new MyConnection();
        // TODO: Add code to open your type of connection
        return (object) myConnection;
    }

    public override void ReleaseConnection(object connection)
    {
        MyConnection myConnection = (MyConnection)connection;
        // TODO: Add code to close your type of connection
    }
}
}
```

Log Providers

Custom log providers are useful when you want to integrate Integration Services logging with a system of logging you already have in place. The custom log provider sees the stream of log entries just as the built-in log providers do. What you do with these log entries is up to you.

To create a custom Log Provider component, you follow the steps given earlier for creating a custom connection manager except that your class should be derived from *LogProviderBase* and the attribute on that class should be *DtsLogProvider*. Copy the compiled assembly to %ProgramFiles%\Microsoft SQL Server\90\DTS\LogProviders.

Foreach Enumerator

You might want to create a custom Foreach Enumerator component to extend the Foreach Loop container so it can iterate over collections of items that the product doesn't know about. For example, if you read data using some kind of proprietary method, you can use a custom Foreach Enumerator component to execute some control flow in a loop over each data element.

To create a custom Foreach Enumerator component, you follow the steps given earlier for creating a custom connection manager except your class should be derived from *ForEachEnumerator-Base* and the attribute on that class should be *DtsForEachEnumerator*. Copy the compiled assembly to %ProgramFiles%\Microsoft SQL Server\90\DTS\ForEachEnumerators.Summary.

Summary

As you have seen, Integration Services delivers far more power for the developer than does DTS. By giving you the ability to create and debug packages in Visual Studio and take complete control over the flow of data, and by providing increased security, Integration Services offers a great environment for transforming data.

Chapter 17
Basic OLAP

—Andrew Brust

This chapter and the three that follow it focus very heavily on Analysis Services, the core business intelligence (BI) component of SQL Server 2005. SQL Server has had BI capabilities since the release of OLAP Services with SQL Server 7 in 1999. You might think that with such a significant history of BI components in the product, most SQL Server professionals would be well-versed in the technology.

However, as you probably know, this is not the case at all. For many SQL Server customers, the BI capabilities of the product have lain dormant, not well understood, and somewhat shrouded in mystery. To be certain, the core SQL Server relational database product is separate from Analysis Services, and it is quite feasible to be an expert in the former while being completely unschooled in the latter.

Wherefore BI?

To be frank, an organization that merely collects and manages its data, and perhaps reviews that data semi-regularly through basic and ad hoc reports, is losing out almost completely on the strategic value and the information that the data holds. Moreover, taking advantage of the basic features of Analysis Services isn't that hard, and the concepts aren't all that difficult for relational database experts to grasp.

If you look carefully at the entire suite of features and components in SQL Server 2005, you'll find that the biggest advances have come from the BI side. Don't get us wrong: New relational database features such as the Service Broker, native XML support, and the SQL CLR programming model are important in their own right. But their importance must be understood in the context of *incremental* change in a relational database engine that was already mature, sophisticated, scalable, and well understood by the market.

The advances in Analysis Services, meanwhile, are much more ground-breaking. The release of SQL Server 2005 Analysis Services marks the product's crossover into mainstream ease of use, programmability, interoperability, and integration with the rest of SQL Server and its toolset. Because of this, we feel strongly that coverage of Analysis Services in this book is of paramount importance. And, by extension, we feel that every SQL Server professional should have at least a basic understanding of this portion of the SQL Server product.

We believe strongly that understanding Analysis Services is totally within reach for anyone proficient in the relational side of SQL Server. Our goal is to provide coverage of Analysis Services that is approachable, practical, and fun. This chapter provides a relatively brief introduction to OLAP. When you finish this chapter, you'll be ready to build OLAP cubes, and you'll likely realize substantial benefits from doing so. You don't have to read any of the next three chapters before starting, and we encourage you to strike out on your own after reading this chapter and taste the victory of your new OLAP knowledge.

Once these practical achievements galvanize your interest in the technology (and, we presume, your self-confidence in being able to learn more about it), you will likely want to move on to Chapter 18, where we cover several advanced OLAP features, many of which are new to SQL Server 2005. Chapter 18 is much longer than this chapter, but you can read it in pieces and immediately put what you've read about to use. When you finish Chapter 18, you'll be able to build extremely sophisticated OLAP cubes.

You can stop there if you want, but as a developer you'll probably want to go on to Chapter 19, where we cover a variety of software development techniques you can use to integrate OLAP functionality into your own applications. You'll learn how to build OLAP front ends with Excel and with the Office Web Components–supplied PivotTable and Chart controls in your own .NET projects, be they Windows Forms applications, ASP.NET Web sites, or just plain HTML pages. You'll also learn how to use a number of APIs/object models, including ADO MD.NET, XMLA (XML for Analysis), and AMO (Analysis Management Objects). You'll even discover how to use Analysis Services' own CLR programming model to build server-side code in .NET languages. Chapter 19, like Chapter 18, is long, but it can be read and applied gradually.

Again, you can stop there if you want, but you'll probably want to move on to Chapter 20, where we cover Analysis Services' data mining capabilities. Data mining features were first introduced in the SQL Server 2000 version of Analysis Services, but they have matured and solidified in SQL Server 2005 to a very significant degree. In many ways, data mining development and design is easier to grasp than OLAP. As such, we cover the entirety of data mining in a single, albeit long, chapter. Many of the programming techniques discussed in Chapter 19 will be reprised in Chapter 20, allowing our coverage of them to be concise. As with Chapters 18 and 19, Chapter 20 lends itself well to gradual reading and application. We think you'll be impressed by the power of the product as you read Chapter 20.

OLAP 101

Let's begin our exploration of Analysis Services with a "quick hit" introduction to OLAP. In this chapter, you'll learn the fundamentals of OLAP, including general OLAP concepts and the basics of how to build, maintain, and query OLAP cubes in Microsoft SQL Server 2005. Specifically, we'll cover the following topics:

- Definitions of several terms, including cubes, measures, dimensions, attributes, hierarchies, levels, members, and axes

- Data warehousing concepts and the motivation behind so-called star and snowflake schemas

- The basics of Visual Studio Analysis Services projects, such as data sources, data source views, the cube and dimension designers, and various wizards

- Querying cubes in the cube designer's Browser tab

As we just mentioned, SQL Server first brought OLAP functionality to us in version 7 with OLAP Services, a product that was essentially separate from, though bundled with, SQL Server proper. SQL Server 2000 Analysis Services included better OLAP functionality and new data mining capabilities but offered only slightly better integration with the SQL Server relational database. Analysis Services in SQL Server 2005 brings huge improvements in functionality over its predecessor, much better integration into the product, an architectural "rethink," and impressive ease-of-use features. We'll begin to tackle this new functionality in this chapter, but let's start with some basic concepts first.

OLAP, which is an acronym for the rather vague moniker "**on**line **a**nalytical **p**rocessing," can be thought of as database technology optimized for drill-down analysis. That's it! Forget all the confusing explanations you may have heard—there's really no magic here, and it need not be confusing. OLAP allows users to perform drill-down queries incredibly quickly and does so in two ways:

- OLAP cubes store so much data that in many cases, both the high-level roll-ups and mid-level and low-level drilled-down figures needed for any given query are already calculated and need only be output.

- Even calculations that need to be done on the fly can be performed quickly because an OLAP engine is optimized for this task and doesn't need to concern itself with the complex tasks of a relational database, such as managing indexes, performing joins, or (except in specific circumstances) dealing with updates and concurrency. OLAP cubes essentially contain data at the lowest drilled-down levels, calculate some or all of the higher-level aggregations when a cube is built, and calculate the others at query time by aggregating the lower-level numbers already in the cube.

The result is a technology that lets users do an incredible amount of exploration through their data, allowing them to entertain a number of ad hoc, what-if scenarios without worrying about the time and resources it would take a relational engine to satisfy the same queries. If users don't have to be "afraid" to ask their questions, they'll ask a lot more of them, gain useful insight into their data, make better business decisions, and get a much higher return on investment on the relational systems that supply the cubes' data in the first place.

OLAP Vocabulary

A *cube*, which is the OLAP equivalent of a table in a relational database, consists of *measures*, which are the numeric data that users will analyze (for example, sales amount), and *dimensions*, which are the categories that the measures will be drilled down by (for example, Time, Geography, Shipper, or Promotion). Dimensions can be hierarchical. For example, a Geography dimension would likely be hierarchical and might consist of country, state/province, city, and postal code *levels*. The individual countries, states, and so on are called the *members* of their respective levels. Such a scheme allows users to break down sales by country, then drill down on a specific country (good to do if that country's sales are particularly high or low), then on a specific state or province within that country, then on specific cities in that state or province, and then even on postal codes in one or more of those cities. (This would allow a user to pinpoint quickly why a particular country's sales are so high or low.)

This all seems elementary and unsophisticated, doesn't it? Are you disillusioned? Don't be. Let's up the ante a bit: Imagine a spreadsheet where the columns contain the set of countries in which a company operates, the rows contain each of the four quarters of the last fiscal year, and each cell contains a sales figure for each corresponding combination of country and fiscal quarter. Imagine further that users can drill down on any quarter (to reveal the three months within it) and/or any country to reveal the sales numbers for those cross-sections of the cube. Imagine that the spreadsheet is replicated numerous times, once for each salesperson's sales data, where each of these spreadsheets offers the same drill-down capabilities, returning the specific results implied by the drill-down, quickly and easily.

This entire set of spreadsheets can be returned by an OLAP engine with one fairly simple query. Still not impressed? Imagine each of the sales numbers in each spreadsheet appearing next to the corresponding year-ago figure and that, even with this enhancement, the whole interactive drill-down report can *still* be produced with a single query. Hopefully, we've caught your attention and have given you some insight into the power and business value of OLAP.

Dimensions, Axes, Stars, and Snowflakes

Let's go back to some definitions. Because OLAP cubes and even OLAP query result sets can contain data along multiple physical dimensions, not just rows and columns, the term *multidimensional* is often used to refer to OLAP databases. In fact, the language you use to query SQL Server OLAP cubes is called MDX (which stands for "multidimensional expression language"). The object models used to write OLAP applications are called ADO MD (the COM-based object model) and ADO MD.NET (its .NET managed equivalent); in both cases, the *MD* stands for *multidimensional*. Thinking tangibly about multidimensional data can be visually and logically challenging. Be prepared for this so that you are not discouraged along the way; meanwhile, we'll do our best to get you through it.

OLAP cubes are created from a collection of special tables in a relational database: fact tables and dimension tables. To illustrate what's in each of these, imagine a simple cube containing unit sales, total sales, and discount as its only measures and supplier and geography as its only dimensions. Imagine that the supplier dimension is flat, that is, nonhierarchical, and that the geography dimension is hierarchical, with its lowest level being postal code. The fact table then needs to contain the sales data for products from each supplier in each postal code. Each row contains a postal code in one column, a key for a supplier in a second column, and the corresponding measures data in additional columns. Each possible combination of postal code and supplier corresponds to a separate row in the fact table (except for postal codes where specific shippers were not responsible for any sales).

We also need dimension tables. Let's start with a dimension table for the supplier. This is simply a lookup table containing the supplier key and name in separate columns. You can see how joining the fact table to this table on supplier ID will allow us to get the shipper's name for each shipper/postal code fact data row.

Because geography is hierarchical, the relationship between the fact table and the dimension table is more complex. The geography dimension's information can be captured in a single, denormalized table that corresponds to each unique postal code with a city, state/province, and country, or you can have separate, normalized lookup tables for each level in the hierarchy. (You can also have a combination of semi-denormalized tables, each combining a couple of hierarchical levels.) See Figure 17-1 for a sample representation of the data in the fact table and the two denormalized dimension tables. Notice that the fact table contains only measure data and foreign keys to the lowest level of each of the two dimensions.

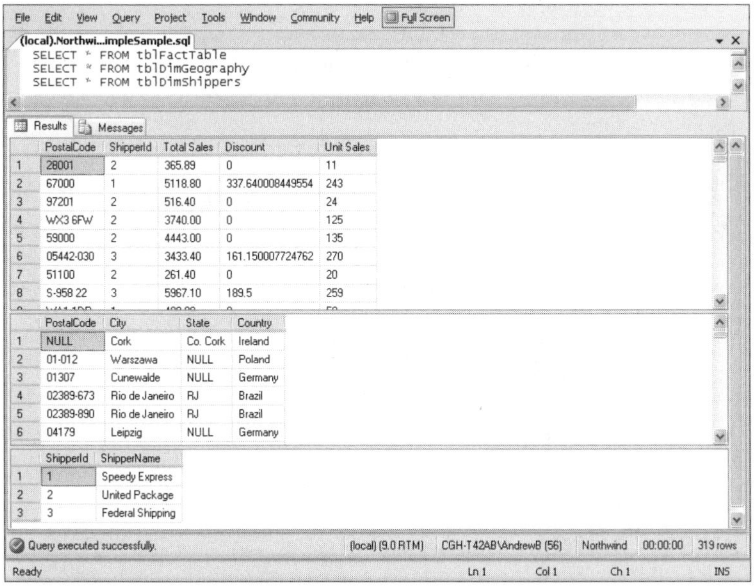

Figure 17-1   The data and structure of the two hypothetical dimension tables and a very simple fact table that references them

Once the cube is built, the normalized or denormalized basis of its dimensions matter very little, so your choice at cube design time is essentially one of convenience. In the case of fully denormalized dimension tables, the schema ends up consisting of a fact table in the center with "spokes" branching out to each dimension table, as shown in Figure 17-2. The geometry of this type of schema suggests a star, so it is often referred to as a *star schema*. Dimensions that involve multiple tables somewhat weaken the star-like analogy because the spokes have multiple nodes. Dimensions with multiple tables are therefore more commonly referred to as having a *snowflake* schema (a snowflake essentially resembling a more geometrically complex version of a star).

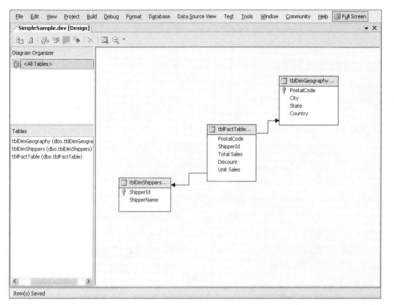

Figure 17-2   Although this schema contains only two dimension tables, you can begin to see where the name *star schema* comes from.

Typically, databases with star/snowflake schemas are created by taking normalized databases and running scripts, stored procedures, or ETL (extract, transform, and load) processes on them to create the transformed fact tables and dimension tables. These tables can be created in a new standalone database, and they in effect form the basis of a data warehouse. As such, they can serve as excellent data sources for running relational reports as well. Given that these tables have some degree of denormalization, they are easy to create reports against, and because they're in a separate database, or at least exist as separate tables in the main database, allowing users to run reports from them poses no strain on the production online transaction processing (OLTP) tables. If you find the physical transformation of the data inconvenient, remember that fact and also that dimension "tables" can, in fact, be views.

Building Your First Cube

Now that you can imagine the design and implementation of fact tables and dimension tables, how do you go about creating a cube? Let's go over the steps required to do this now.

Preparing Star Schema Objects

For the purposes of this chapter, rather than using the sample data warehouse and cubes based on the AdventureWorks database that comes with Analysis Services, we'd like to create our own from scratch. To do so, we'll base our sample on the older Northwind SQL Server sample database. The Management Studio solution in the sample code for this chapter contains several SQL scripts that create a fact table, a time dimension table, and several views suitable for use as dimension tables from the Northwind database.

> **Note** SQL Server 2005 does not ship with the Northwind database because the Adventure-Works database was designed to replace it. However, you may use the version of Northwind that came with SQL Server 2000, if you have it, and attach it to your SQL Server 2005 server. Microsoft has also published an MSI file that will install both Northwind and the older pubs sample databases on your server. The MSI provides both MDF/LDF files that can be directly attached, as well as T-SQL scripts, which can be executed to create the databases from scratch. At press time, the download page for this MSI is *http://www.microsoft.com/downloads/details.aspx?FamilyID= 06616212-0356-46a0-8da2-eebc53a68034&DisplayLang=en*. An Internet shortcut to this URL is included with this chapter's sample code. Should the link not work for you, try running a Web search on "Northwind and pubs Sample Databases for SQL Server 2000".

Once the Northwind database has been installed on your server, run each script in the Chapter20 Management Studio project against the Northwind database, making sure that tbl-Time.sql is run *before* tblFact.sql. (The order of execution for the other scripts is insignificant.) Once these steps are complete, your copy of Northwind should contain a new table called tblFact that will serve as the fact table, a new table called tblTime that will serve as the time dimension table, and the following views, which will serve as the other dimension tables: vwEmployees, vwGeography, vwProducts, vwShippers, and vwSuppliers. Each of these tables and views is created by its namesake SQL script. Once these tables and views are in place, you can proceed to design, build, and query your cube.

A Tool by Any Other Name

You're ready to build your cube now, and in order to do so, you'll need special design tools. Under SQL Server 2000 Analysis Services, cubes were designed and managed in a tool called Analysis Manager, a Microsoft Management Console (MMC) snap-in that was, in effect, the Analysis Services analog to SQL Server Enterprise Manager. Back in the late 1990s, MMC snap-ins were a popular vehicle for management and design tools. These days, Visual Studio, with its rich extensibility APIs, is a more popular choice.

The Analysis Services team decided to use Visual Studio 2005 as the host for a number of business intelligence (BI)–related designers, including those for Reporting Services, Integration Services, and, most pertinent to this chapter, Analysis Services. It turns out, as we will see in the next chapter, that SQL Server Management Studio can also be used as a management tool for Analysis Services databases; however, the Analysis Services *designers* are hosted inside Visual Studio.

Although most of you reading this book will have a copy of Visual Studio 2005 at your disposal, not all developers and administrators working with Analysis Services will. Microsoft realized this, of course, and knew they needed a workable solution to the problem. In effect, Microsoft needed a way to ship the bare-bones Visual Studio integrated development environment (IDE) with SQL Server 2005 so that the various designers and project types supported by the SQL Server BI components that use Visual Studio could be created and manipulated by users who do not have a license for the Visual Studio product itself.

When you install the BI components of SQL Server on a machine that does not have Visual Studio 2005 installed, the SQL Server installer will place just such a scaled-down version of Visual Studio on the target machine; if a copy of Visual Studio 2005 is already installed on the machine, the BI designers will use it instead.

> **Note**   The Express editions of Visual Studio are not sufficient to accommodate the various SQL Server BI designers. Machines with any of the Visual Studio Express Edition SKUs are treated by SQL Server identically to machines that have no Visual Studio 2005 bits on them at all.

So far, all of this seems reasonable, but there is one detail of nomenclature that can make this a bit confusing. The SQL Server 2005 installer will create a shortcut to Visual Studio on your machine (either the bare-bones copy it might have installed or the existing copy you otherwise already had). This shortcut's name is not "Microsoft Visual Studio 2005" but "SQL Server Business Intelligence Development Studio."

It is important to realize that this shortcut actually points to Visual Studio, be it the bare-bones version or the full product, and that there really is *no such thing* as Business Intelligence Development Studio. You may find this name useful to identify the bare-bones version of the Visual Studio IDE (and the BI designers) we have just discussed, but that explanation becomes inaccurate when you realize that the shortcut labeled "SQL Server Business Intelligence Development Studio" actually links to the *full* Visual Studio product on machines that have it.

In order to make things perfectly clear, in this book we will refer to the host environment of the Analysis Services and other BI designers as "Visual Studio." We make this point for more than just clarifying nomenclature. The real reason it is important to refer to the BI designers as being hosted in Visual Studio and not in Business Intelligence Development Studio is to make clear that a single Visual Studio solution can indeed contain a *mix* of SQL Server BI project types and more conventional Visual Studio .NET application project types.

For example, a single Visual Studio 2005 solution could contain an Analysis Services project, an Integration Services project, a Reporting Services project, *and* various C# or Visual Basic

.NET projects including a Windows Forms application, a Class Library project, and/or an ASP.NET Web site. This fact will allow us to maintain the standard used in other chapters of having a single Management Studio solution and a single Visual Studio solution contain *all* the sample code for a given chapter. This will be especially pertinent in Chapter 20, the sample code for which includes a Visual Studio solution containing one of each of the six BI and .NET project types enumerated previously.

Creating the Project

With our understanding of the toolset and its proper name now established, it's time to create an Analysis Services project and design our cube. Start Visual Studio and select the File/New/ Project... option from the main menu. In the New Project dialog box, select Business Intelligence Projects from the Project Types tree view on the left and select Analysis Services Project from the Templates pane on the right. Enter **Chapter17** as your project name, with a file path that works conveniently for you. (Figure 17-3 shows how the dialog box should appear.) You're now ready to click OK and create your project.

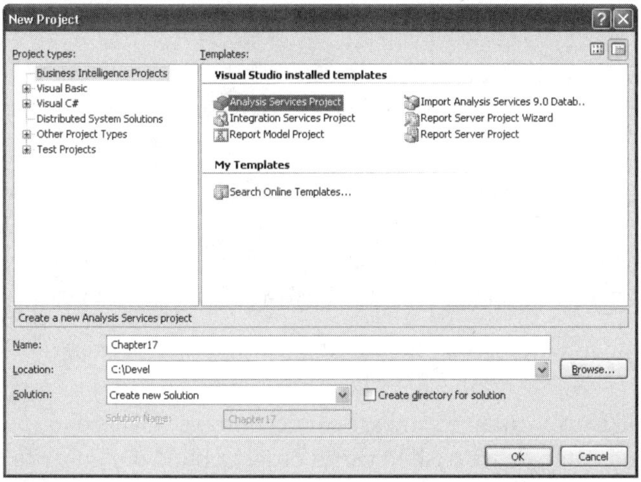

Figure 17-3   Creating a new Analysis Services project in the New Project dialog box

You'll notice that your new project is empty, unlike in .NET projects in Visual Studio, where a default object is created for you and you merely need to open it. In Analysis Services projects, you start from scratch. The best things to add right away are a data source and a data source view. Create a new data source by right-clicking on the Data Sources folder in Solution Explorer and selecting New Data Source... from the shortcut menu to bring up the Data Source Wizard.

Click Next on the wizard's Welcome page to advance to the Show How to Define the Connection page. Click the New... button to bring up the Connection Manager dialog box, and then for the provider, specify .Net Providers\SqlClient Data Provider. For the Server Name, enter the name of your server, supply your login credentials (Windows Authentication is likely your best choice here), and select Northwind as the database name. The dialog box should appear similarly to what is shown in Figure 17-4.

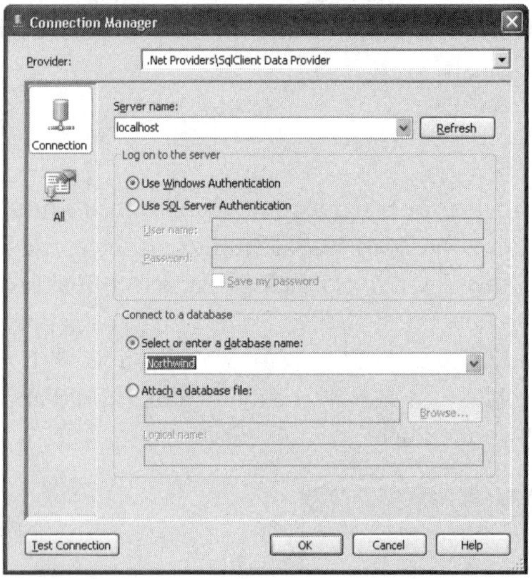

Figure 17-4   Filling out the Connection Manager dialog box to create an Analysis Services project data source

Click OK to dismiss the Connection Manager dialog box. Back in the Data Source Wizard, click Next to advance to the Impersonation Information page, where you should select the Default option button (that is, the last one in the list) and click Next again. In the Completing the Wizard page, set the name of the data source to **Northwind**, and click Finish.

Adding a Data Source View

What we've done so far is akin to creating a database connection; we still need to specify what objects from the Northwind database we wish to use in order to build our cube. To specify this information, we need to add a data source view to our project. To do this, right-click the Data Source Views folder in Solution Explorer and select New Data Source View... from the shortcut menu. This brings up the Data Source View Wizard.

Click Next on the Welcome page, and click Next again on the Select A Data Source page, making sure that the Northwind data source you just created is selected. On the Select Tables And Views page, select (that is, move from the Available Objects list to the Included Objects list) the tables tblFact and tblTime (tables are listed first in the Included Objects list) and the views vwShippers, vwProducts, vwGeography, vwEmployees, and vwSuppliers (which appear toward the bottom of the Included Objects list). Figure 17-5 shows how the lists should appear at this point.

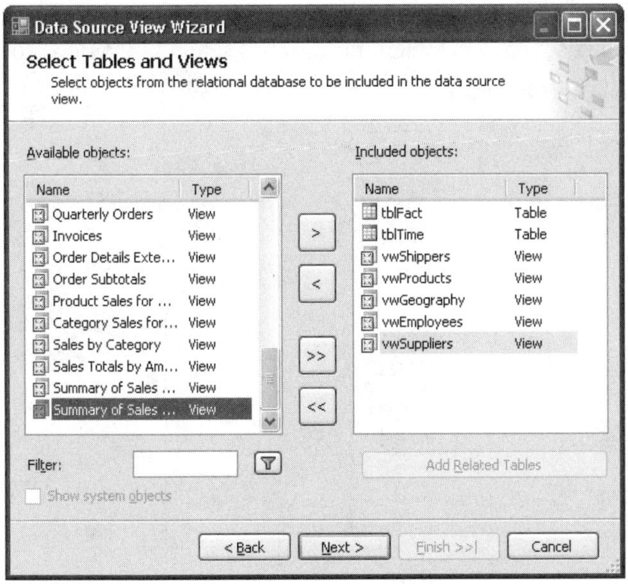

Figure 17-5 In the Data Source View Wizard, you can select fact tables and dimension tables (which can also include views) for your data source view and, eventually, your cube.

When you're building data source views, don't panic if you're not sure which tables to select. You can bring back this page later as the standalone Add/Remove Tables dialog box in the Data Source View designer when you're done with the wizard. We'll explain to you later in this chapter how to do that.

You can type a wildcard filter expression in the Filter text box to limit the tables and views that appear in the Available Objects list. For example, typing **vw** and then either pressing the Enter key on your keyboard or clicking the funnel icon button to the right of the text box filters the list to display only tables and views that begin with the letters *vw*.

Once you've moved at least one table into the Included Objects list, you can select a table (or multiple tables) and click the Add Related Tables button to instantly select all tables related to it (or them).

> **Tip** This can be a great shortcut: If you include the fact table first and then click Add Related Tables, you can often move over all the dimension tables at once, depending on the design of your star schema database. Because we're using views and an unrelated table for our dimension tables, this shortcut will not work in our particular case.

When you're done selecting your tables, click Next. On the Complete the Wizard page, accept the default name of "Northwind" assigned to your data source view and then click Finish.

After a brief pause, the wizard disappears and your data source view automatically opens in its designer. The tables in the data source view might need to be manually arranged so that they are all visible simultaneously with the fact table in the center (Figure 17-6).

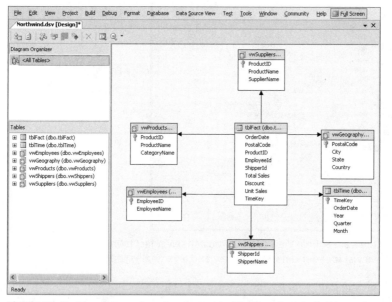

Figure 17-6   The data source view generated by the wizard after some layout tidying has been done

The designer is divided into three panes: On the upper left is the Diagram Organizer pane, on the bottom left is the Tables pane, and on the right is the diagram pane. The All Tables diagram that is displayed in the diagram pane shows all the tables you selected in the Wizard. It is possible to add additional diagrams to the data source view that contain only a subset of the tables/views in the data source view by selecting the Data Source View/New Diagram main menu option, right-clicking within the Diagram Organizer pane and selecting New Diagram from the shortcut menu, or clicking the New Diagram toolbar button (third from left). After taking any of these three actions, you can type a diagram name and then drag tables and views from the Tables pane onto the design surface in the diagram pane. If you accidentally drag a table or view that you don't want into the diagram, simply right-click it and choose Delete Table From DSV.

The set of tables and views that the data source view is based on, which you first specified in the Select Tables And Views page of the Data Source View Wizard, can be altered within the data source view designer. You may do so through the Add/Remove Tables dialog box, which can be brought up via the Data Source View/Add Remove Tables... main menu option, the Add Remove Tables... diagram pane shortcut menu option, or the Add/Remove Objects toolbar button (on the far left). Individual tables can be removed from the data source view by selecting them in the Tables or diagram pane and clicking the Delete toolbar button (third from right) or by right-clicking the tables in either pane and selecting the Delete Table From DSV shortcut menu option.

By default, all foreign key constraint relationships between tables are shown in the diagrams as the tables they relate to are added to a diagram. In our case, no pre-declared constraint relationships exist, so you must add relationships to the data source view diagram yourself. To do so, just click in the foreign key column in tblFact and drag the mouse to connect to the corresponding column in the corresponding dimension table.

For example, you can click the EmployeeId field in tblFact (to highlight it) and drag the mouse to the EmployeeId field in vwEmployees. Release the mouse button, and you should see an arrow-headed line joining the fact table to the view. Double-click it (or single-click it and select the Data Source View/Edit Relationship... main menu option, or right-click it and select the Edit Relationship... shortcut menu option) to bring up the Edit Relationship dialog box, where you can edit the properties of this relationship and confirm that you joined the correct columns (Figure 17-7).

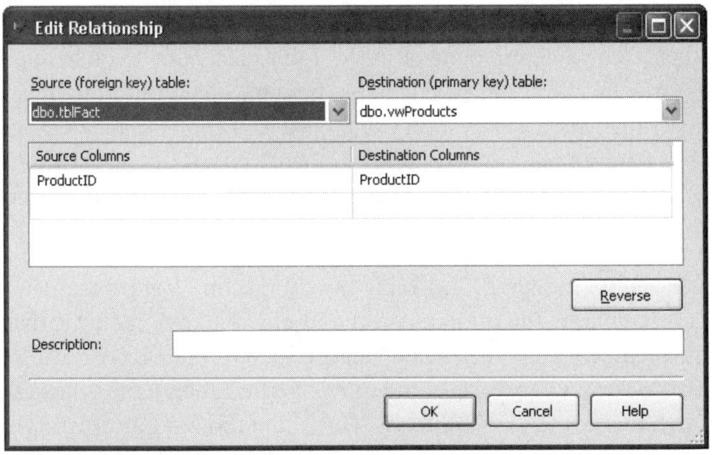

Figure 17-7   The Edit Relationship dialog box

The Edit Relationship dialog box is essentially a property sheet for the relationship between the fact table and the employee dimension "table" (which is actually the view called "vwEmployees"). A modified version of this dialog box, the Create Relationship dialog box, can be used to create relationships if the drag-and-drop method does not appeal to you. You can bring up the Create Relationship dialog box by selecting the Data Source View/New Relationship... main menu option, by selecting the New Relationship... diagram pane shortcut menu option, or by clicking the New Relationship toolbar button (fourth from right).

For our cube, we need to build relationships between tblFact and each of the dimension tables (views). Build the following additional relationships and then save your changes. (See the text following the table for special instructions on the relationships to vwGeography and tblTime.)

Source Table	Source Column	Destination Table	Destination Column
tblFact	ProductId	vwProducts	ProductId
tblFact	PostalCode	vwGeography	PostalCode
tblFact	ProductId	vwSuppliers	ProductId
tblFact	ShipperId	vwShippers	ShipperId
tblFact	TimeKey	tblTime	TimeKey

You'll notice that for vwGeography and tblTime, a logical primary key does not exist, and the designer will ask if you'd like to define one. The designer asks this question because no columns in either of these views are primary keys in the physical tables they are derived from. For now, select Yes; we'll cover logical primary keys again in the next chapter.

The data source view designer allows you to add and remove tables, relationships, and so-called named queries from diagrams. Named queries are much like database views, but they are persisted in your data source view and not in the star schema database. Right-clicking on a particular table, either in the diagram pane or in the Tables list, allows you to add a named calculation. This is essentially like adding a calculated field in a view, but again it is persisted in the data source view rather than in the source database. You can also browse the data within any table in your data source view and perform PivotTable, Chart, and PivotChart analysis on it by right-clicking it (again, in the diagram pane or the Tables list) and selecting Explore Data from the shortcut menu.

The data source view designer toolbar's Find Table button (second from right), the Data Source View/Find Table... main menu option, and the Find Table option on the diagram pane's shortcut menu all allow you to locate and select a specific table by choosing it from a list in the Find Table dialog box. (Merely selecting a table in the Tables pane achieves the same purpose, so this feature is somewhat superfluous.) The Zoom toolbar button/drop-down button (on the far right) allows you to zoom in and out in the diagram. The Refresh Data Source View button (second from the left), the Data Source View/Refresh... main menu option, and the Refresh... option on the diagram pane's shortcut menu let you refresh the data source view; this is a great way to update the schemas of all of a data source view's tables if they've been modified in the source database, without having to delete the data source view and rebuild it.

Creating a Cube with the Cube Wizard

Once you're done perfecting your data source view, close it and save your changes. You're now ready to build your cube! To do this, select the Project/New Cube... main menu option, or right-click the Cubes folder in Solution Explorer and select the New Cube... option from the shortcut menu to bring up the Cube Wizard.

On the Welcome page, click Next to advance to the Select Build Method page. For our purposes, you'll want to select the Build The Cube Using A Data Source option button. You can leave the Auto Build check box in a checked state if you'd like. If you do, make sure that the

Create Attributes And Hierarchies option is selected in the combo box right below it. By examining your data source view's schema, Analysis Services can detect which tables in it are fact tables and dimension tables and can sometimes determine which dimensional hierarchies should be created. Click Next to move to the Select Data Source View page. Confirm that the data source you created before is selected, and click Next again.

If you selected the Auto Build option, the Detecting Fact And Dimension Tables page will display a progress bar as the wizard analyzes your data source view and will display a message when it's complete, at which point you should click the Next button. In the Identify Fact And Dimension Tables page, you will be asked to identify your fact tables and dimension tables. You should leave both check boxes deselected for tblTime, select the Fact check box for tblFact, and select the Dimension check boxes for all of the other tables (views). If you selected the Auto Build option, default selections might already be made for you, but make sure that both check boxes are cleared for tblTime. You can configure each table from your data source view to be a fact table or dimension table through the Tables tab or the Diagram tab. (Actually, a table can be both a fact and a dimension table, though this would be the exception rather than the rule.)

When you have a time dimension and are building it using a dimension table (as opposed to using a date field in the fact table, a technique we'll cover in the next chapter), you can indicate which table you'll be using in the Time Dimension Table combo box. For now, leave this setting as <None> because we'll cover the creation of a time dimension using the Dimension Wizard later in the chapter. If you receive error messages on a yellow background at the bottom of the dialog box, you might want to click on the Diagram tab to determine why one or more tables are incorrectly configured. (These tables will appear in red.) Figure 17-8 shows the selections that should be made for this page. When you're done, click Next.

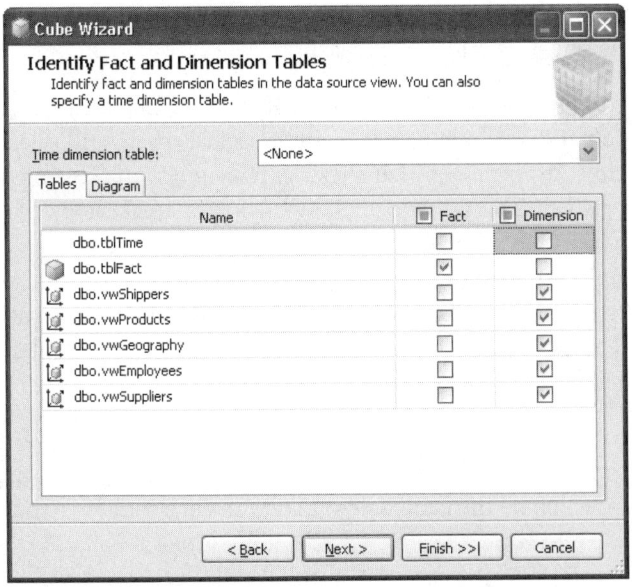

Figure 17-8   The Identify Fact And Dimension Tables page of the Cube Wizard, where you indicate which tables are fact tables and which are dimension tables

On the Select Measures page, you are asked to create your measures and measure groups. By default, one measure for each numeric field in your fact table(s) that is not a foreign key to a dimension table is listed here, and a default measure (called Tbl Fact Count, in our case), based on the record count, will be listed as well. The field-based measures will have the same name as the field names on which they are based, with spaces inserted where "intercap" characters exist. (For example, a field called UnitPrice will create a measure with a default name of Unit Price.)

You can browse the first 1000 rows of any of your fact tables by right-clicking any measure based on it (you can right-click anywhere on the measure's entire row) and choosing View Sample Data.... You can edit measure names by setting the focus on the cell containing the name (by using the mouse or the keyboard). Individual measures can also be deselected, preventing them from being added to the cube. For our example, deselect Tbl Fact Count because we will not need it.

One measure group is created for each fact table you specified in the Identify Fact And Dimension Tables page. Measure group names are editable—don't be fooled by the grey background that stays gray even when you click within the cell. For our example, change the name of the single measure group detected from tblFact to **Main**. When you're done configuring your measures and measure groups, click Next.

If you selected the Auto Build option, the wizard's Detecting Hierarchies page will display a progress bar as the wizard analyzes your data source view, and it will display a message when it's complete, at which point you should click Next. On the Review New Dimensions page, all default dimensions are listed (one per dimension table). Drill down on any dimension to reveal the Attributes node in the tree view, and then drill down on the attributes node to display all the suggested attributes (which can become levels in a hierarchy). The attributes are formulated based on the columns in the dimension table, and the wizard names them following a scheme identical to the one it uses to name measures.

As with measures, you can deselect any attribute to prevent it from being created. You can change the default dimension and attribute names by right-clicking them and selecting Rename Dimension or Rename Attribute or by left-clicking them and then pressing the F2 key on your keyboard. You can also enter edit mode on a dimension or attribute by clicking one, pausing, and clicking again. Use one of these techniques to remove the "Vw" prefix from the dimension names, for example, rename the Vw Products dimension as "Products", and make sure that you do this for each dimension. Each dimension contains a like-named attribute, which also features the undesired "Vw" prefix. We will rename these attributes later; you may accept the default attribute names for now.

When you're done configuring your dimensions and attributes, click Next. On the Completing The Wizard page, you can accept the default name for the cube or type a new name more to your liking (for this example, name the cube **Sales**) and then click Finish.

Using the Cube Designer

When the Cube Wizard finishes processing, your cube design will be generated and opened, placing you in the Cube Structure tab of the cube designer, as shown in Figure 17-9.

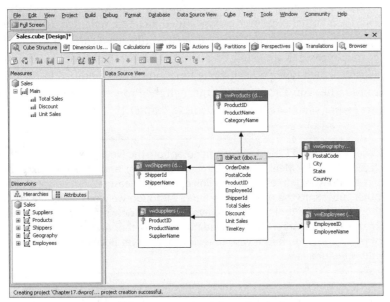

Figure 17-9   The Cube Structure tab of the cube designer

The cube designer has an array of tabs across the top, and the Cube Structure tab is divided into three panes: Measures on the upper left, Dimensions on the lower left, and Data Source View on the right. This Data Source View pane depicts a subset of the tables in the data source view upon which the cube is based; it contains only the tables and views selected in the Cube Wizard when we identified our fact and dimension tables.

Note   You can add any other table to the Data Source View pane that may be present in the base data source view simply by selecting the Data Source View/Show Tables... main menu option, choosing the Show Tables... option from the Data Source View pane's shortcut menu, or clicking the Show Table toolbar button (fifth from right).

You can also add tables related to a specific table in the Data Source View pane by left-clicking the table and selecting the Data Source View/Show Related Tables main menu option or right-clicking the table and selecting the Show Related Tables shortcut menu option. You can hide a table from the Data Source View pane by selecting the table, then clicking the Data Source View/Hide Table main menu option, choosing the Hide Table shortcut menu option or clicking the Hide Table toolbar button (fourth from right).

These actions have no effect on the base data source view itself because the Data Source View pane is simply a convenient filtered diagram based on the cube's underlying data source view.

By default, the Measures pane contains a tree view with the cube name at the root, measure groups appearing as the root's children, and individual measures listed as children of their measure groups. You can change the tree view to a grid view via the Show Measures option in the Cube menu, the Show Measures In option in the Measures pane's shortcut menus, or the Show Measures Grid/Show Measures Tree toolbar drop-down button (fifth from the left). Measure groups and individual measures can be added, deleted, renamed, or moved up and down through options on the shortcut menus. Even the cube itself can be renamed in this way. In grid view, only measures are listed; measure groups can be manipulated only in the tree view. The measure's data type and aggregate function can be modified in the grid view. These and other properties can also be edited through the Properties window. (We'll cover advanced property settings in more detail in the next chapter.)

> **Note**   The Cube/New Linked Object... main menu option, the New Linked Object... shortcut menu option (available in the Measures and Dimensions panes), and the New Linked Object toolbar button (seventh from left) allow you to link or import measures, dimensions, and other objects from other cubes into the one you're editing. Although we won't cover linked objects in this book, they are a useful tool to help you avoid building new physical cubes when you want to combine elements of other cubes (including those in other Analysis Services databases and even on other servers). You might wish to review SQL Server Books Online for more information on this feature.

The cube designer is the primary tool for designing and building cubes; the Cube Wizard simply provides a front end to the designer to help get you started. If you want to add new measures to the cube after running the wizard, you can easily do so within the designer. Simply select the New Measure... option from the Cube menu, the New Measure... option from the Measures pane's shortcut menus, or click the New Measure toolbar button (third from left) to bring up the New Measure dialog box, shown in Figure 17-10.

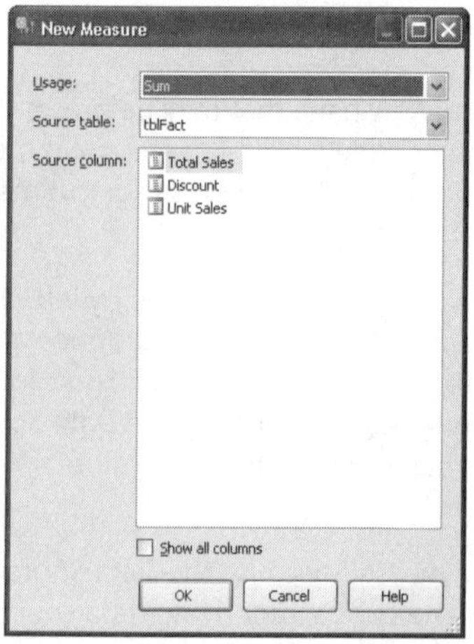

Figure 17-10   The New Measure dialog box allows you to add measures to your cube even after the Cube Wizard has completed its work.

From the Source column tree view that occupies most of the dialog box, you can select the fact table field from which you want to derive your measure and then click OK to create the measure. Only non–foreign key, numeric fields are displayed by default; the Show All Columns check box at the bottom left of the dialog box allows you to display (and select) other fields.

You can also add measure groups if fact tables exist that have not yet been assigned to an existing measure group. This is a more advanced scenario that we will not cover in this book.

The Dimensions pane allows you to inspect and maintain dimensions, attributes, and hierarchies. It offers two tabs: Hierarchies and Attributes. Both feature tree views of the dimensional structure of your cube, with the cube as the root node and dimensions listed as the cube's children. Sensibly, attributes of a dimension appear as its children on the Attributes tab; hierarchies of a dimension appear as its children on the Hierarchies tab. On either tab, you can edit a dimension's name, delete the dimension, or move it up or down. You can also create a new dimension through the Dimension Wizard or edit an existing dimension in the Dimension designer.

Using the Dimension Wizard

To invoke the Dimension Wizard and create a dimension (which we'll need to do because we haven't yet created our time dimension), choose the Cube/Add Cube Dimension... option, select the Add Cube Dimension... option from the Dimension pane's shortcut menus, or click the Add Cube Dimension toolbar button (sixth from left). Each of these actions brings up the Add Cube Dimension dialog box, shown in Figure 17-11.

Figure 17-11   The Add Cube Dimension dialog box allows you to add existing database-level dimensions to your cube or define new dimensions.

Click the New Dimension ... button to bring up the Dimension Wizard. You can also invoke the Dimension Wizard by right-clicking the Dimensions folder in the Solution Explorer window and choosing New Dimension. Invoking the Dimension Wizard using this technique adds the dimension to the Analysis Services *database* but not to the *cube*; to add the dimension to the cube itself, you must use the Add Cube Dimension dialog box and select your new dimension from the list of dimensions in the database.

On the Welcome page of the Dimension Wizard, click Next. On the Select Data Source View page, confirm that the Northwind data source view is selected and click Next again. On the Select The Dimension Type page, you can indicate whether you are creating a standard dimension (the default), a time dimension, or a server time dimension. In our case, we'll select the Time Dimension option.

For a standard dimension, you would need merely to accept the default option button selection and click Next. (Go ahead and try these next steps if you'd like, but when you're done, use the Back button to come back to the Select The Dimension Type page and select Time dimension again.)

On the Select The Main Dimension Table page, you can select the desired dimension table (from the top combo box) and its key column(s) (from the checked list box that takes up most of the page). You can also optionally select a name column (from the bottom combo box). Click Next to go to the Select Dimension Attributes page, where you can specify the name, key column, and name column of each of the dimension's attributes. Several attributes are suggested automatically, based on the columns in the table, and you can edit or deselect any of these.

Click Next to go to the Specify Dimension Type page. If you're experimenting with standard dimensions, you can stick with the Regular dimension type and click Next to go to the Define Parent-Child Relationship page. We'll describe parent-child relationships in the next chapter; for now, you can click Next to advance to the Detecting Hierarchies page. On this page, the wizard will attempt to detect, from the structure of your dimension table, possible hierarchies in your dimension. You should wait for the processing to complete and then click Next. On the Review New Hierarchies page, you can review the hierarchies, if any, generated by the wizard, deselect any of them (or any of their constituent levels) if you'd like, and then click Next.

If you followed the previous steps, click the Back button to get back to the Select The Dimension Type page (not the Specify Dimension Type page), and select the Time Dimension option button. If you didn't follow the previous steps, this should already be done. In the Time Dimension combo box, select tblTime (it will appear as dbo_tblTime) as the table that will serve as our time dimension table. Time dimension tables are specially configured to contain a key (which also appears as a foreign key in the fact table) and columns with corresponding year, month, or other time-related data. Figure 17-12 shows the structure and an abbreviated set of data for tblTime. (The four non-key columns *in that table* will each support a level in the time dimension.)

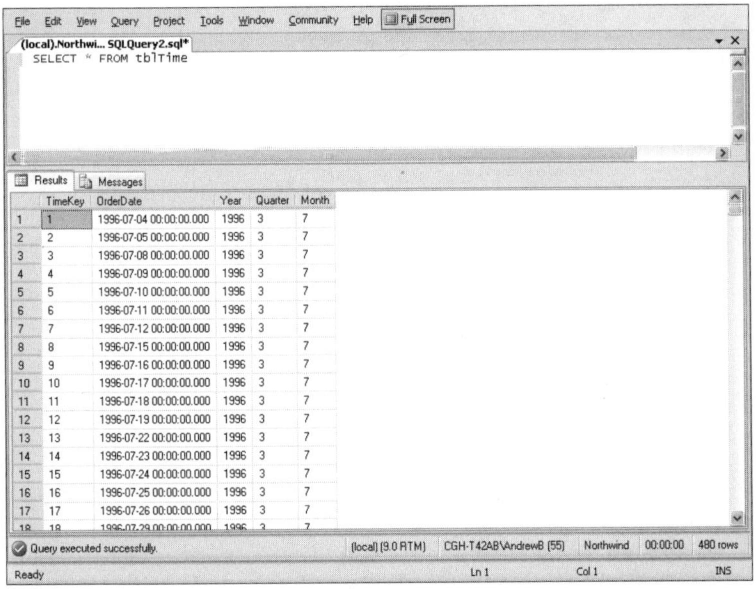

Figure 17-12   The structure and some data for tblTime, the time dimension table used in our example cube

Click Next to proceed to the Define Time Periods page, where you should select the columns in the Time Table Columns column that correspond to the items in the Time Property Name column. (See Figure 17-13 for the proper settings for tblTime.) The Time Intelligence feature in SQL Server 2005 Analysis Services allows this type of declarative identification of dimensional levels. Click Next to continue. On the Review New Hierarchies page, review and confirm the time hierarchy that the Dimension Wizard constructed for you, and then click Next again.

On the Completing The Wizard page, you can review the schema for your dimension, accept its default name or enter a name of your own (for our example, type **Time** as the dimension name), and then click Finish. Back in the Add Cube Dimension dialog box, make sure that the new Time dimension is selected, and then click OK to add it to the cube and return to the cube designer. Your new dimension should be displayed on the Dimensions pane of the Cube Structure tab, and the dimension table should be added to the Data Source View pane.

For the new time dimension, or any of the others on the Hierarchies tab or the Attributes tab, you can drill down and display child nodes. The first child node in either pane is a clickable hyperlink that opens the dimension designer and allows you to edit that dimension. (The nodes that follow enumerate the attributes or hierarchies and levels of the dimension, if any, depending on which tab you're on.) In addition to the hyperlink, you may open the dimension designer by selecting a dimension in the Dimensions pane and choosing the Edit Dimension option from the Cube menu, or you may right-click the Dimension and select the Edit Dimension option from its shortcut menu. Use one of these techniques to open the Geography dimension in the dimension designer now.

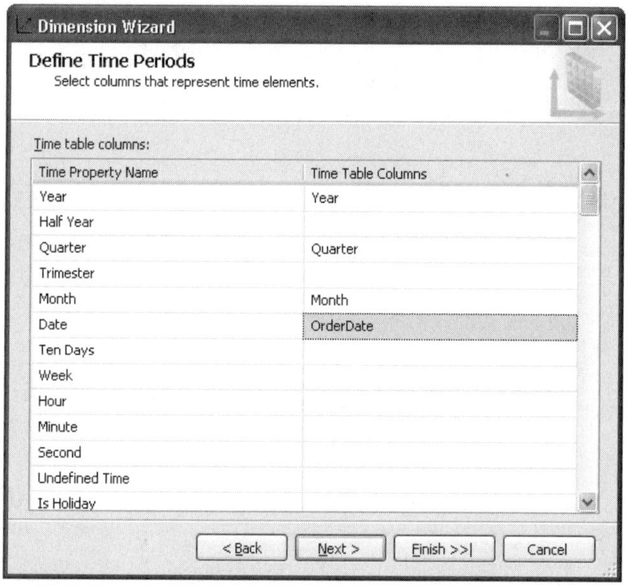

Figure 17-13   The Define Time Periods page allows you to tell the Dimension Wizard which columns represent which levels in the time dimension.

Using the Dimension Designer

The dimension designer, like the cube designer, has tabs across the top and a three-pane view in the rest of the window. Within the Dimension Structure tab, the Attributes pane is on the left, the Hierarchies And Levels pane is in the center, and the Data Source View pane is on the right.

Attributes can be displayed in a tree, grid, or list view. Cycle through the views by choosing the Show Attributes In option from the Dimension menu or the Show Attributes In option from the Attributes pane's shortcut menus. You can also use the third drop-down button from the left on the Dimension designer's toolbar. Note that when you enter the list or grid views, the Hierarchies And Levels pane pivots from the center to the upper left and the Attributes pane shifts to the lower left. Certain properties for attributes are available in the grid view, but all properties are accessible through the Properties window regardless of which view you're in. We'll discuss more on the Properties window later.

Attributes can also be renamed via their shortcut menus, the *Name* property in the Properties window, or by pressing the F2 key when the attribute is selected. Rename the Vw Geography attribute to **Postal Code** now. The attribute is in fact based on the Postal Code field, but its default name was set otherwise because it is the key attribute for the Geography dimension (which is based on the view Vw Geography). Renaming the attribute now will make things much more user-friendly when it comes time to query the cube.

The dimension designer makes it easy to create hierarchies from the universe of a dimension's attributes. Let's create a hierarchy for the Geography dimension now so that we can later query our cube data hierarchically by country, then state or province, then city, and then postal code. Start by dragging the Country attribute from the Attributes pane to the Hierarchies And Levels pane (you may also right-click the Country attribute and select the Start New Hierarchy option from its shortcut menu, or left-click the Country attribute and select the Dimension/Start New Hierarchy option from the main menu). This will create a new hierarchy with the default name of "Hierarchy" in its own rectangular block, with the Country attribute as the hierarchy's top (and only) level.

You can drag additional attributes onto this block to create additional levels (or select the hierarchy and then either right-click an attribute and select Create Level from the shortcut menu or left-click an attribute and select the Create Level option from the Dimension menu). You can reorder the levels within the hierarchy by using drag-and-drop, and you can delete and rename attributes and hierarchies in a manner similar to other UI scenarios already described. Also, instead of dragging attributes from the Attributes pane to create hierarchies or add levels to an existing hierarchy, you can drag columns from the Data Source View pane.

Using any of the techniques just discussed, add the State, City, and Postal Code attributes as the second, third, and fourth levels of the new hierarchy (leaving Country as the first level). Once you've added all the levels, rename the second level from State to **State-Province** and rename the hierarchy itself to **Country - State-Province - City - Postal Code**. The completed hierarchy design is shown in Figure 17-14.

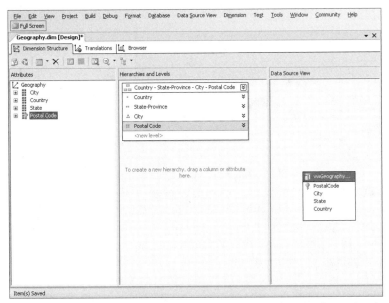

Figure 17-14   The dimension designer, with our Geography dimension, including its new hierarchy, fully designed and configured

The dimension designer has two other tabs: Translations and Browser. We'll cover the Translations tab in the next chapter. You can use the Browser tab to examine all of the dimension's levels and each level's members in a tree view, but only after the cube has been processed (a step we'll take you through shortly).

Working with the Properties Window and Solution Explorer

Some of the settings we've discussed, as well as others we'll discuss in the next chapter, can be set through the Properties window. To see how this works, return to the cube designer's Cube Structure tab, click on any measure in the Measures pane, and then look at the Properties window. (Press F4 or choose the View/Properties Window main menu option if it's not visible.) To make the Properties window easier to view, assuming it is docked, double-click its caption bar to undock it (you can double-click its caption bar again to redock it), center it within your screen, and resize it so its columns are wide and many rows are displayed without the need to scroll. Your Properties window should now look similar to Figure 17-15.

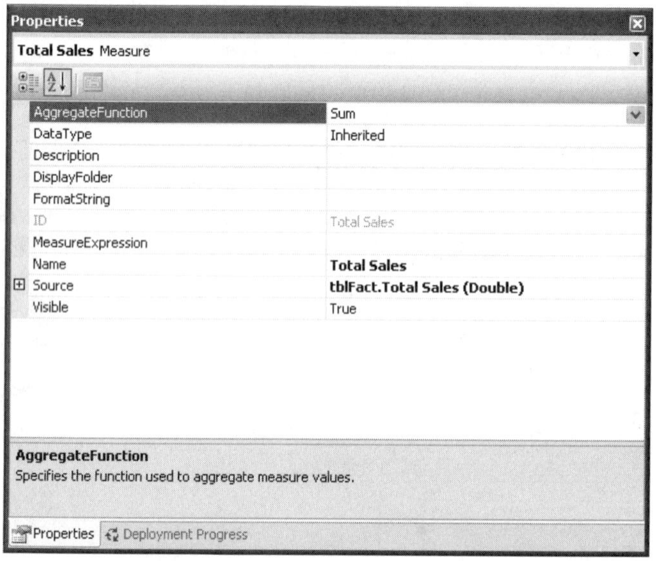

Properties		⊠
Total Sales Measure		▾
AggregateFunction	Sum	▾
DataType	Inherited	
Description		
DisplayFolder		
FormatString		
ID	Total Sales	
MeasureExpression		
Name	**Total Sales**	
⊞ Source	**tblFact.Total Sales (Double)**	
Visible	True	

AggregateFunction
Specifies the function used to aggregate measure values.

Properties | Deployment Progress

Figure 17-15   The Properties window allows advanced manipulation of measures, dimensions, cubes, and other objects.

Notice how *AggregateFunction* and *DataType* are visible and editable, as are several other properties. Click the drop-down arrow in the upper-right corner of the Properties window, and you should see all the measures in your cube displayed in the drop-down list. Double-click the Properties window's caption bar again to dock it, and then select a dimension in the Dimensions pane. Undock the Properties window a second time, and you'll see that this dimension's properties are now editable and that all dimensions in your cube are listed in the drop-down list at the top of the window. This technique works for virtually any class of object in your cube, in any pane, in any tab of the cube designer (except the Calculations and Browser tabs) or dimension designer. Experiment with this technique in different parts of the designers so that you can appreciate the breadth of power the Properties window has in the cube editing process.

Before we move on to processing and querying our cube, you should know that you can manipulate high-level objects such as data sources, data source views, dimensions, and the cube itself by opening them from Solution Explorer. For example, to edit a dimension in the dimension designer, instead of clicking its hyperlink in the Dimensions pane of the cube designer, you can double-click its node in the Dimensions folder of your project in the Solution Explorer window. Try this to see how easily it works. Also, if you right-click any editable object in the Solution Explorer window and choose View Code, you'll see that the basis for each object is a simple XML file. Imagine the cube design/generation possibilities this raises for third-party and custom-developed front ends.

> **Note**   The particular XML schema used by the designers is an established standard called XML for Analysis, or XMLA for short. We will examine the structure and use of XMLA in more depth in the next three chapters, especially in Chapter 19. We will also cover how XMLA can be manipulated in your own applications and how the various Analysis Services APIs use XMLA "behind the scenes."

Processing the Cube

You can process your dimension in the dimension designer by using the second toolbar button from the left or by choosing the Dimension/Process... option from the main menu, but for now just close the dimension designer and click Save when prompted. Back in the cube designer, you can process the entire cube by using the Database/Process... or Cube/Process... option, or by clicking the Process toolbar button (second from left). Processing the cube or database automatically processes any pending changes to dimensions they may contain.

Processing your cube requires that your Analysis Services project be built and deployed. When you choose to process your cube (do this now), if it hasn't already been built and deployed (which ours has not), you'll be notified that these steps are necessary and asked if you'd like them to be performed before building. Click Yes. (Alternatively, you could first execute the build and deploy operations from the Build branch of the main menu.)

You can watch the progress of the build and deploy processes in the Deployment Progress window. Once these steps are complete, you'll be prompted with the Process Cube - <cube-name> dialog box. The Remove, Impact Analysis..., and Change Settings... buttons in this dialog box provide precise control over how your cube is processed. We encourage you to explore the use of these tools in SQL Server Books Online. For the work we will do in this book, it is sufficient simply to click Run. This will process the cube and bring up the Process Progress dialog box. Once the processing has completed, click Close in both dialog boxes and your cube should be ready to query!

Running Queries

In Chapter 19, we'll cover how to write .NET code to query your cube in your own applications. For now, we'll just use the Browser tab within the cube designer to run some quick queries. Click the Browser tab now—it's the last one. Although this cube browser is really just an administrative tool and limited to result sets with two axes, it's a vast improvement over SQL Server 2000 Analysis Manager's Cube Browser and similar in functionality to Excel's PivotTable tool. (It actually uses the PivotTable control from version 11 of Office Web Components.)

Once the browser loads, drill down on the Measures node and then on the Main measure group node in the tree view on the upper left. Drag the Unit Sales measure into the Drop Totals Or Detail Fields Here area of the output region. Next, drag the Shipper Name attribute of the Shippers dimension (drill down on the dimension to display its attributes) onto the Drop Row Fields Here area. You'll see your unit sales for each of the various shippers in the Northwind database. Now drill down on the Geography dimension. Drag the entire Country – State-Province – City – Postal Code hierarchy onto the Drop Column Fields Here area. You should now see the same data but further correlated (on the columns axis) by the Country level in the Geography dimension's hierarchy (Figure 17-16). You can drill down on any country to see its data broken down further by state/province, and you can drill down even further to individual cities or postal codes. Notice how quickly the drill-downs complete.

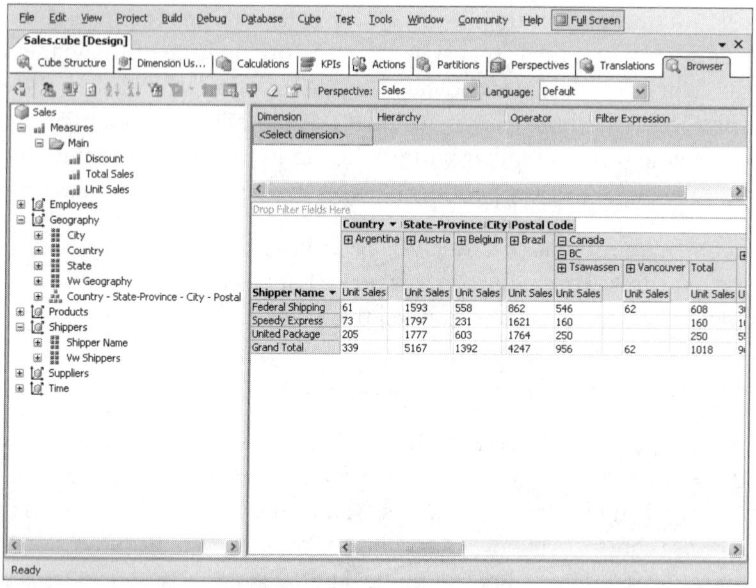

Figure 17-16   The cube designer's Browser tab allows for fairly sophisticated querying of OLAP cubes.

You can now drag even more dimensions onto either axis, optionally removing the old dimensions first. Putting two dimensions on one axis allows you to drill down on one dimension to reveal members of the other. It's a convenient way of projecting multiple logical axes onto a single physical axis. Executing queries that *truly* project onto three or more axes is possible, but not in the Browser tab of the cube designer.

You can also add filters to the query. You do this by dragging an attribute or hierarchy onto the Drop Filter Fields Here area and then clicking the drop-down arrow next to the entity's name and selecting or deselecting specific members to be counted or ignored in the data below. You can create expression-based filters in the area right above the Drop Filter Fields Here area. Here you can enter simple Boolean or complex MDX expressions for filtering the data below. We'll cover the creation of MDX expressions in the next chapter.

Third-party front-ends let you do even more in the way of queries, and you can also build your own applications that exceed the Browser tab's functionality. But considering that we're on our first OLAP chapter in this book, we've already done quite a lot.

Summary

We've covered quite a bit in this chapter. You've learned the basic premise and vocabulary of OLAP, including all the principles necessary to understand how to design a star/snowflake schema data warehouse and a cube based on it. In addition to all this theory, you've learned the practical skills of creating an Analysis Services project in the Visual Studio and adding a data source, a data source view, and a cube to your project. You've learned how to create and maintain measures and dimensions and how to process and query a cube.

In this one chapter alone, you have learned to use the Data Source Wizard, Data Source View Wizard, Cube Wizard, and Dimension Wizard as well as the cube designer (Cube Structure and Browser tabs) and dimension designer (Dimension Structure and Browser tabs). You now have enough knowledge to build basic but highly useful OLAP cubes on your transactional data. In the next two chapters, we'll investigate how to implement more advanced features in your cubes and then how to write .NET code to build OLAP querying functionality into your applications.

Chapter 18
Advanced OLAP

—Andrew Brust

In the previous chapter, you learned the basic concepts and vocabulary of online analytical processing (OLAP) and learned how to create your own cube, based on the Northwind database. Building a cube from scratch gives you an understanding of OLAP that would be hard to acquire by merely studying the *AdventureWorks* sample cube supplied with Microsoft SQL Server 2005. After going through the process of creating a fact table and dimension tables and then designing, creating, and querying a cube in the cube browser, you should have a sense of the relative ease and power of using OLAP. As a result, you should be able to dispense with the trepidation that many people experience when they approach OLAP.

Most of the features we covered in Chapter 17 were, in fact, available in SQL Server 2000 Analysis Services. The ability to create a dimensional version of your database using a fact table and several dimension tables, and then perform fast drill-down queries on it, has been around for quite a while. In fact, it's been possible to do this since the introduction of SQL Server 7.0 OLAP Services. But make no mistake: The user-friendliness of the Analysis Services 2005 environment, including the designers and wizards and the flexibility they offer when you design and build cubes, is entirely new.

Analysis Services 2005 also provides a variety of new OLAP features that we believe will revolutionize the business intelligence (BI) market. Together, these features make cubes easier to build, query, and keep up-to-date. They enable cubes to track information that is much more relevant to business users than was possible with earlier releases of the product. In this chapter, we'll cover some of these features.

> **More Info**   The book's sample code includes two Visual Studio solutions: Chapter18Begin.sln and Chapter18End.sln (both in this chapter's VS folder). Chapter18Begin.sln is essentially a clone of the Visual Studio sample code provided with Chapter 17, but with the project and databases renamed *Chapter18*. If you want to follow along with the steps described in this chapter, you should open Chapter18Begin.sln and do your work within it. Chapter18End.sln contains all enhancements from this chapter already implemented. Use this code if you do not want to implement this chapter's steps manually, or if you need to "borrow" from, or look at, the finished version of the code. A SQL Server Management Studio solution with the SQL and MDX scripts required or referenced in this chapter is available as Chapter18.smsssln in this chapter's SSMS folder.

What We'll Cover in This Chapter

Covering all of the new Analysis Services 2005 OLAP features would require an entire book. We believe strongly that all database developers should be well-acquainted with a subset of those features, however, and at least be aware of the others. So in this chapter we will extend our Northwind cube to take advantage of many of these features.

Specifically, we will extend our cube to use a parent-child dimension, fact dimensions, role-playing dimensions, advanced property settings for measures and dimensions, member grouping (discretization), display folders, calculated members, named sets, actions, key performance indicators, perspectives, and translations, and we'll also look at how security roles work. In the next chapter, we'll show you how to "expose" many of these features in your own applications using ADO MD.NET and other OLAP APIs.

We will also discuss partitioning, storage options, aggregation design, and proactive caching. The last of these features is perhaps the biggest breakthrough in Analysis Services 2005. It's hard to do it justice in just a portion of a chapter, but we'll make you comfortable with the concepts involved.

> **Note**   Some concepts and features that we will not cover here, but that you might want to explore on your own, include linked objects, ragged (unbalanced) hierarchies, advanced processing options, MDX templates in the cube designer, multiple fact tables (along with referenced and many-to-many dimensions), and the Analysis Services designers' Add Business Intelligence feature.

MDX in Context

At various points in this chapter, we will cover Analysis Services 2005 features that require the entry of expressions written in the multidimensional expression language (MDX). This poses a challenge because we provide only the most basic introduction to MDX in this book and that material is in the next chapter. However, the MDX code we will use in this chapter should be easy to understand in context, given the OLAP conceptual coverage we provide and your own background as a developer. That said, we will provide more top-down MDX coverage in the next chapter. After reading Chapter 19, you might want to refer back to the MDX code in this chapter to deepen your understanding of the examples provided here.

And Now a Word from Our Sponsor...

The Books Online documentation supplied with SQL Server 2005, including its Analysis Services component, is excellent. This book is meant to complement the Books Online material by easing you into things more comfortably and providing alternative examples to reinforce certain concepts. Likewise, our use of the Northwind database in our OLAP chapters is meant to augment, rather than compete with, the AdventureWorks samples supplied with SQL Server 2005.

We strongly recommend that you also study the Adventure Works DW sample Analysis Services database and that you go through the Analysis Services 2005 tutorial provided in Books Online. The tutorial provides impressive depth and breadth of coverage, and the Adventure Works sample cube goes even further, covering virtually every feature of Analysis Services 2005.

 Note   You'll find the Analysis Services 2005 tutorial in the Contents tree view in Books Online or in Visual Studio help under SQL Server 2005 Tutorials\Analysis Services Tutorials\ SQL Server 2005 Analysis Services Tutorial. You can also launch the tutorial directly from the Windows Start menu by selecting the Microsoft SQL Server 2005\Documentation and Tutorials\Tutorials program group, selecting the SQL Server Tutorials item, and then clicking the Analysis Services link.

Meanwhile, we recommend that you read this chapter first because it can help you get productive quickly. The Books Online tutorial and sample cube are more top-down and formal, so they will make more sense after you've read the discussion of advanced OLAP features in this chapter. We'll start that discussion by focusing on how to use the advanced dimension and measure features in Analysis Services 2005.

Advanced Dimensions and Measures

In the previous chapter, you learned how to use the Cube Wizard to build several dimensions for our Northwind *Sales* cube. The Cube Wizard offers the convenience of building several dimensions at once, but it does not provide access to all the features you can build into your dimensions.

You also learned in Chapter 17 how to go beyond the Cube Wizard and build your own hierarchy. (We did this by building a *Country - State-Province - City - Postal Code* hierarchy in the *Geography* dimension using the dimension designer.) But that was only a start—we could have done a lot more with that dimension and the others. Let's now refine what we have built.

Keys and Names

We'll start with the *Shippers* dimension. Recall that this dimension is flat (nonhierarchical); therefore, little refinement should be necessary. Meanwhile, this dimension contains two attributes while one is sufficient. We should remedy this right away. We're not doing this just to be elegant—by discussing how to clean this up, we will introduce some important concepts related to dimension attributes.

Open the Shippers dimension in the dimension designer. You'll notice that two attributes are defined for this dimension. One is named *ShipperName*, and the other is *Vw Shippers*, named after the SQL Server view that served as its dimension table. Both of these attributes allow us to drill down by shipper, but only one is named well and only the other one is properly keyed on shipper ID; we need to combine these two attributes into one.

Select the *Vw Shippers* attribute and make sure the Properties window is visible. (If it is not, press F4 to show it or select the View/Properties Window option from Visual Studio's main menu.) Look at the value settings for the attribute's *KeyColumns* and *NameColumn* properties; they are set to *vwShippers.ShipperId* and *(none)*, respectively. Look also at the *OrderBy* property, and you will see that the members of this attribute are configured to be sorted by their IDs. This attribute is about halfway toward being what we need; its name needs to be changed to *Shipper Name*, its *NameColumn* needs to be changed to *vwShippers.ShipperName*, and its *OrderBy* property needs to be changed from *Id* to *Name*. Bear in mind that because the *Shippers* dimension's other attribute is already called *Shipper Name*, we'll need to remove it before we rename *Vw Shippers*.

Before we delete the existing *Shipper Name* attribute and rename its companion, take a look at the property settings of the existing *Shipper Name* attribute. You'll see that its *KeyColumns* property is set to *ShipperName* and its *NameColumn* property is set to *(none)*. You'll also see that its *Usage* property is set to *Regular*, whereas the *Vw Shippers* attribute's *Usage* property is set to *Key*. The latter setting is important because every dimension must have a key attribute.

At this point, we need to delete the existing *Shipper Name* attribute and then rename the *Vw Shipper* attribute to *Shipper Name* to replace it. To perform the delete, simply right-click the *Shipper Name* attribute and choose Delete from the shortcut menu. Click the OK button in the message box that asks you to confirm the deletion. To rename the *Vw Shipper* attribute, you can modify its *Name* property in the Properties window or you can right-click the attribute and choose the Rename shortcut menu option (or select the attribute and press F2) and then edit the name in place.

After renaming the attribute in the Properties window, select the *NameColumn* property, click the drop-down arrow, and select the (new) option from the drop-down list (Figure 18-1).

Figure 18-1   Setting an attribute's *NameColumn* property through the Properties window

In the resulting Object Binding dialog box, select *ShipperName* from the Source Column list (Figure 18-2) and click OK.

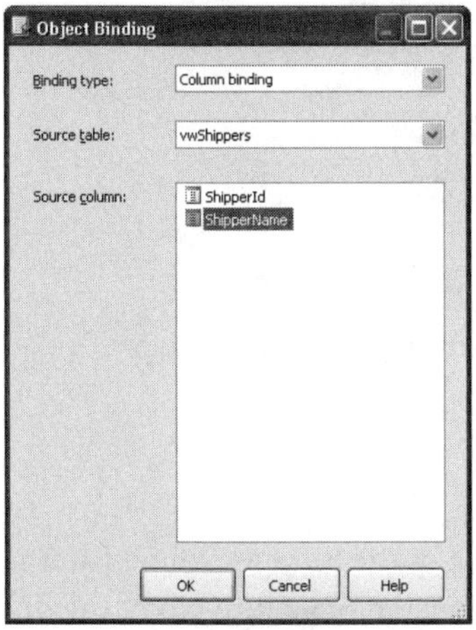

Figure 18-2   Selecting a specific column in the Object Binding dialog box

We're almost done adjusting our attribute. Before continuing, right-click the newly renamed *Shipper Name* attribute. On the shortcut menu's Set Attribute Usage submenu (an alternative interface to the attribute's *Usage* property), confirm that you see a check mark next to the Key option.

We're done with our attribute work, so now it's time to deploy our changes to the server and then use the dimension designer's Browser tab to make sure everything looks right. Click the Start Debugging toolbar button (ninth from the left, with the VCR play button icon), select the Debug/Start Debugging main menu option, or press F5 on your keyboard to save your changes and deploy them to the server.

> **Important**   You should follow this same procedure throughout this chapter each time we ask you to save and deploy your changes, unless otherwise instructed.

When deployment and processing has completed, click the dimension designer's Browser tab. Drill down on the All (root) node of the tab's tree view control; your screen should appear as shown in Figure 18-3.

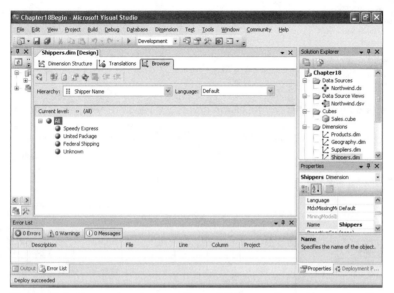

Figure 18-3   Inspecting the reconfigured Shippers dimension on the dimension designer's Browser tab

Changing the *All* Member

To neaten things up completely, let's change the name of the Shippers dimension's *All* member to *All Shippers*. To do this, return to the Dimension Structure tab of the dimension designer, select the root node in the Attributes tree view (that is, select the node representing the dimension itself), and in the Properties window change the value of the *AttributeAll-MemberName* property to *All Shippers*.

Save and deploy your changes. Then return to the Shippers dimension designer's Browser tab. (Visual Studio might place you there automatically.) Because the structure of the dimension and the cube has changed, the connection between the browser and the dimension is no longer valid. Reestablish this connection by clicking the Reconnect button (second from the left) on the designer's toolbar, choosing the Dimension/Reconnect option from the main menu, or clicking the Reconnect hyperlink in the yellow error panel at the bottom of the designer (Figure 18-4).

You should see *Shipper Name* appear as the default (and only) hierarchy in the Hierarchy drop-down list (on the Browser tab) and an *All Shippers* node appear in the browser's tree view instead of the *All* node that preceded it. (You might need to reconnect more than once for this to display properly.) If you drill down on *All Shippers*, you should see the three shipper names and an *Unknown* member, sorted alphabetically.

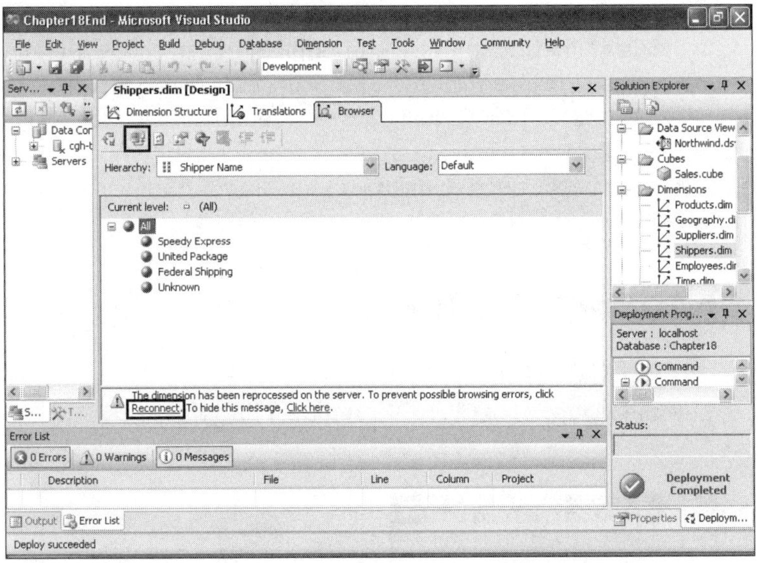

Figure 18-4   The dimension browser as it appears when a reconnect is necessary

> **Planning**   At some point, you might want to clean up the *Suppliers* and *Employees* dimensions using an approach similar to the one we just took with *Shippers*. The *Geography* dimension was refined in Chapter 17, the *Time* dimension does not need any cleanup, and we will tidy the *Products* dimension shortly. (Note that we will add a new employee-based dimension in the next section, but we will not be cleaning up the original *Employees* dimension.)

Adding a Named Query to a Data Source View

Now let's look at improving some of the other dimensions in the cube and creating a few new dimensions in the process. Let's start by looking at the *Employees* dimension. Open it by double-clicking its node in Solution Explorer. In the Data Source View pane of the dimension designer, take a look at the various fields in *vwEmployees*, the dimension "table" on which it's based. As with the *Shippers* and *Suppliers* dimensions, only two fields—a key and a name—appear in the view. Meanwhile, several other fields are available in the original table, one of which will be useful to add: the *ReportsTo* column. This column contains the ID of the employee's supervisor and thus serves as a self-join foreign key. Using this column will allow us to make a new employee-based parent-child dimension.

To start using the *ReportsTo* column, we could simply modify *vwEmployees* back in the relational database and refresh our data source view. Another approach would be to create a named query in the data source view itself. A named query, in essence, is a view, but creating one does not modify the relational database. Named queries can be a life saver if you have read-only access to the database. In our case, we created a view in the first place, so it would stand to reason that we could modify it subsequently. However, let's create a named query instead, just to see how it's done.

Start by opening the Northwind data source view by double-clicking its node in the Solution Explorer window. In the diagram pane, right-click an empty spot and choose the New Named Query shortcut menu option to invoke the Create Named Query dialog box. This dialog box is essentially a container for the same SQL query designer found in SQL Server Management Studio, along with a customized toolbar, text boxes for a name and description, and a drop-down list of data sources. Name the query *Employees*, and insert the following query text into the SQL pane (the multi-line text box on the bottom) of the query editor:

```
SELECT EmployeeID, LastName + ', ' + FirstName AS EmployeeName, ReportsTo FROM Employees
```

Click the mouse in one of the other panes to force them to update. The dialog box should now appear exactly as shown in Figure 18-5. Click OK, and then save the changes made to the data source view.

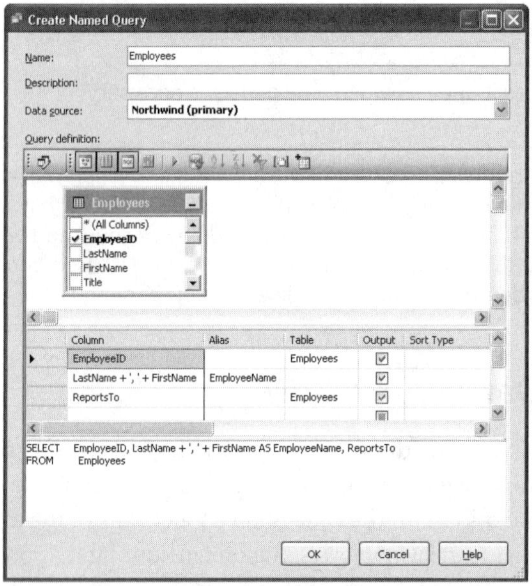

Figure 18-5 The Create Named Query dialog box

Before we can use this named query to create a new employee-based dimension, we need to create two relationships on it: one to codify the self-join from the *ReportsTo* column to the *EmployeeId* column and another from the *EmployeeId* column of *tblFact* to the like-named column in the named query. To do this, start by right-clicking the *EmployeeId* column of the *Employees* named query and choosing the Set Logical Primary Key shortcut menu option (or left-click the column and select the Data Source View/Set Logical Primary Key option from the main menu). Next, create the relationship between the fact table and the named query and the self-join just discussed by using the drag-and-drop procedure described in the previous chapter, the Data Source View/New Relationship... main menu option, or the New Relationship... main menu option on any of the various shortcut menus in the Diagram pane or the Tables pane. You can also use the New Relationship button (fourth from the right) on the data source view designer's toolbar. When you're done, your data source view should appear as shown in Figure 18-6. Save your changes before proceeding.

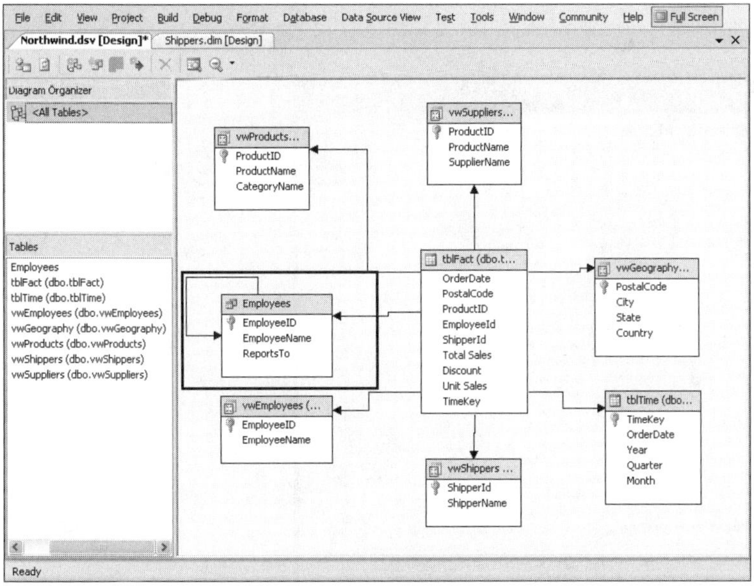

Figure 18-6   Our data source view, modified to include and join the *Employees* named query

Parent-Child Dimensions

Before we create a new employee-based dimension, right-click the *Employees* named query in the data source view designer and choose Explore Data. Examine the data shown. You will see that Suyama, King, and Dodsworth report to Buchanan, and that Buchanan and all other employees report to Fuller (except Fuller himself, of course). Our task will be to create a special dimension that represents these relationships, in a hierarchy, without transforming the structure of the dimension table itself. To do this, you invoke the Dimension Wizard.

> **Tip**   Adding a new dimension to a cube is a two-step process: You must first create a *database* dimension, and then you add it to the *cube*. To create the database dimension, you must invoke the Dimension Wizard. You can invoke the wizard by choosing the New Dimension... option on the Dimensions node shortcut menu in Solution Explorer or the Project/New Dimension... option on the main menu. However, the New Dimension option invokes the wizard directly and requires that you later add the database dimension to your cube as a separate step.
>
> You add an existing database dimension to a cube by using the Add Cube Dimension dialog box, which you invoke via the Cube/Add Cube Dimension... main menu option, which is available when the cube designer is open and its Cube Structure or Dimension Usage tab is active. You can also select the Add Cube Dimension... option on the shortcut menu in the Cube Structure tab's Dimensions pane or on the Dimension Usage tab. You can invoke the Dimension Wizard directly from the Add Cube Dimension dialog box itself; this allows you to compress the two steps into one.

Accept the default selections on the Select Build Method, Select Data Source View, and Select Dimension Type pages. On the Select The Main Dimension Table page, select the *Employees* named query from the Main Table drop-down list, select *EmployeeId* as the key column, and select *EmployeeName* as the member name column (Figure 18-7).

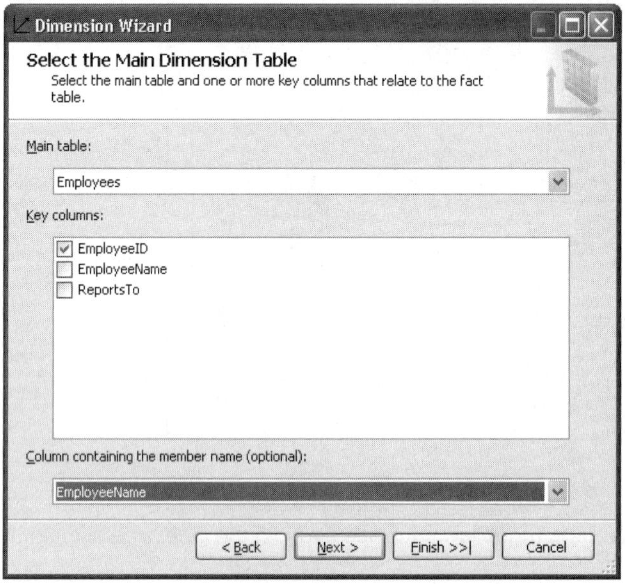

Figure 18-7   The Select The Main Dimension Table page of the Dimension Wizard

On the Select Dimension Attributes page, make sure the check box next to the *ReportsTo* column is checked. Accept the default setting of Regular on the Specify Dimension page.

On the Define Parent-Child Relationship page, confirm that the check box at the top of the page is selected and that the Reports To column is selected in the Identify Parent Attribute drop-down list, as shown in Figure 18-8.

The Dimension Wizard detects that our new dimension might contain a parent-child attribute and allows us to specify which field (*ReportsTo*, in this case) should serve as its basis. Note that the *ReportsTo* value for Andrew Fuller is NULL, indicating that he reports to no one but that several other employees report to him.

Click Next to advance to the Detecting Hierarchies page, and click Next again when the detection process has completed. On the Review New Hierarchies page, you will see that no hierarchies were detected; this is the expected result, so click Next to advance to the Completing The Wizard page. Notice the special parent-child icon displayed next to the *Reports To* attribute (Figure 18-9).

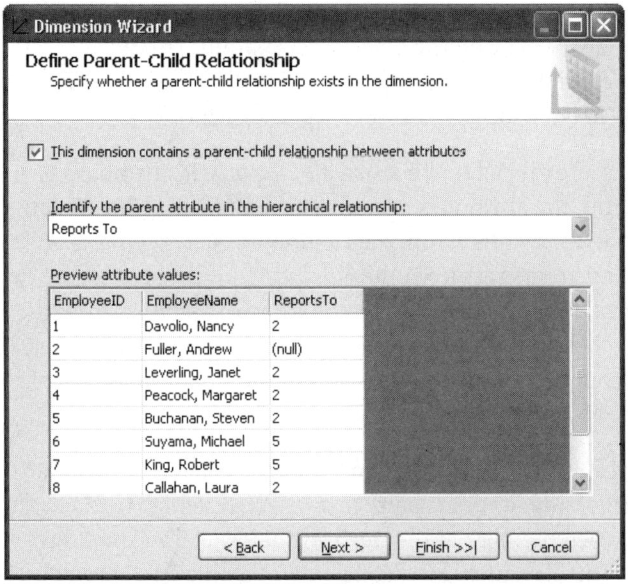

Figure 18-8   The Define Parent-Child Relationship page of the Dimension Wizard

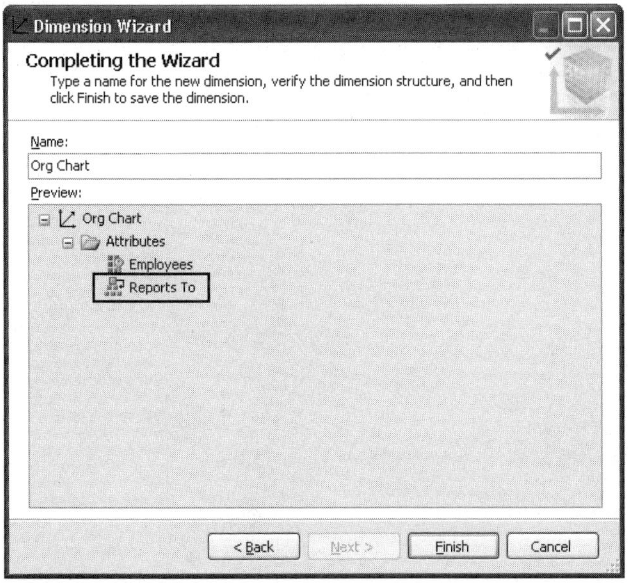

Figure 18-9   The dimension designer's Completing The Wizard page, with a parent-child dimension selected

Type *Org Chart* as the name of the new dimension, and then click Finish. Now open the new dimension in the dimension designer (you might be placed there automatically, depending on how you launched the Dimension Wizard).

The *Org Chart* dimension now contains an attribute called *Employees* that displays values from the *EmployeeName* column and is keyed on the *EmployeeId* column. This attribute will serve as the child level of our parent-child dimension. For clarity, rename this attribute *Employee Name* by using its shortcut menu (Rename option) or the Properties window (*Name* property).

The parent-child hierarchy is already defined because the *Reports To* attribute's usage is set to *Parent*. You can see this from the attribute's icon, its shortcut menu (the Set Attribute Usage/Parent option is checked), and the Properties window (the *Usage* property is set to *Parent*). But we still need a little refinement: Set the *NameColumn* property of the *Reports To* attribute to *(new)*, select *EmployeeName* in the Object Binding dialog box (from the Source Column list box), and then click OK. This ensures that, like the *Employee Name* attribute, *Reports To* will be properly configured to display the employee's name and be keyed on the employee's ID (stored in the *ReportsTo* column).

Save and deploy your changes, and then click the dimension designer's Browser tab (if you are not placed there automatically). Make sure *Reports To* is selected in the Hierarchy drop-down list, and then drill down on each member in the tree view below it. You should see the entire reporting hierarchy properly displayed, and the collection of employees at each level sorted alphabetically, as shown in Figure 18-10.

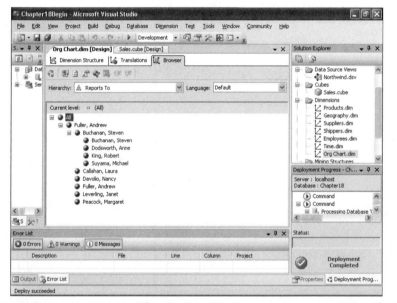

Figure 18-10   The dimension designer Browser tab with our parent-child attribute selected

The dimension browser confirms that our parent-child attribute has been correctly configured, for the most part. Note that Fuller and Buchanan are shown as reporting to themselves. We will address this anomaly shortly. Select *Employee Name* from the Hierarchy drop-down list, and you'll see all employees listed, alphabetically, in a nonhierarchical fashion.

> **Note**   If you want to eliminate the standalone *Employee Name* attribute hierarchy, you can do so by setting the *Employee Name* attribute's *AttributeHierarchyVisible* property to *False*. Doing this allows you to keep the attribute in the dimension's structure—which you must do because it is the key attribute—but hide the attribute from client applications.

Now reselect Reports To from the Hierarchy drop-down list, select the first Fuller, Andrew node in the tree view, and notice the name *Level 02* listed next to the Current Level label just above the tree view, as shown in Figure 18-11.

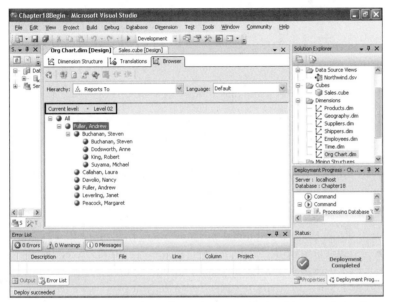

Figure 18-11   The dimension designer Browser tab with generic level name highlighted

Click the first Buchanan, Steven node and then the Dodsworth, Anne node and notice that their levels are named Level 03 and Level 04, respectively. These level names are generated by Analysis Services because the hierarchy is generated automatically and was not explicitly designed by you.

We can change these level names on the Dimension Structure tab by simply using the *NamingTemplate* property of the *ReportsTo* attribute. In the Properties window, click the property's ellipsis button to bring up the Level Naming Template dialog box. Fill out the dialog box as shown in Figure 18-12, and click OK.

The Level Naming Template dialog box allows entry of custom level names for parent-child attributes/hierarchies. By supplying names for levels 2, 3, and 4, we will override the Analysis Services–generated names *Level 02*, *Level 03*, and *Level 04*. Finally, to prevent employees with direct reports from being listed twice, set the *MembersWithData* property to *NonLeafDataHidden*.

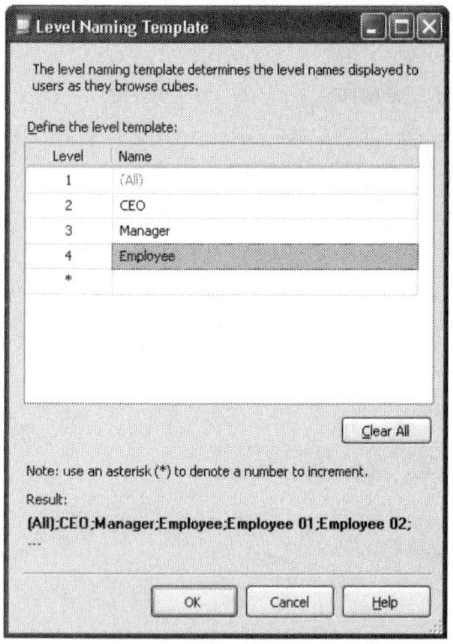

Figure 18-12   The Level Naming Template dialog box

Save and deploy your changes, and confirm on the Browser tab that the hierarchy is now structured properly and that its levels are intelligently named. (You might need to reconnect for the change to appear.) If you haven't already done so, add the *Org Chart* dimension to the *Sales* cube using the Add Cube Dimension dialog box in the cube designer, and then save and deploy your changes once more. Now query the new *Org Chart.Reports To* hierarchy and any measure of your choice on the cube's Browser tab (reconnecting first, if necessary).

Drill down through the levels to see that you can now query the cube data by CEO, Manager, and Employee. You might also notice that the some of the level totals exceed the sum of their members; this is because we have hidden all data associated with the non-leaf members of the hierarchy. Setting the *Reports To* attribute's *MembersWithData* property back to *NonLeafData-Visible* would eliminate the totaling problem, but it would cause those employees to be listed twice, as we saw earlier.

Member Grouping

Our next stop is the Products dimension. Start by renaming the *Vw Products* attribute to *Product Name* and then creating a hierarchy called Category - Product using the *Category Name* and *Product Name* attributes, in that order, as its levels. Save and deploy your changes and, on the dimension designer's Browser tab, select *Product Name* from the Hierarchy drop-down list. Drill down on the *All* member, and you will see that the number of products is rather large. Using the *Category - Product* hierarchy makes the product list more manageable, but you might not always want to break up products along category lines.

One solution to this problem is to use an Analysis Services feature called member grouping, or *discretization*. Essentially, this feature groups members of a particular attribute by creating a new attribute/level "above" it. Each member of the new level ends up containing a specific number of child members from the original attribute.

To implement member grouping for the Products dimension, return to the Dimension Structure tab. Drag the *ProductName* column from the Data Source View pane to the Attributes pane, and change its name from the default *Product Name 1* to **Product Group**. Next, set this new attribute's *DiscretizationBucketCount* property to *10* and its *DiscretizationMethod* property to *Automatic*. This creates 10 discrete parent members that can be used in a new hierarchy along with the *Product Name* attribute. Create a new hierarchy by dragging the *Product Group* attribute into the Hierarchies pane, and then drag the *Product Name* attribute underneath it into the new hierarchy. Name the new hierarchy **Group - Product**, and then save and deploy your changes.

Use the new hierarchy in the cube browser (first reconnecting, if necessary) to drill down on *Unit Sales By Product Group* (using the *Group - Product* hierarchy, rather than the *Product Group* attribute). When sales in a particular group look especially high or low, drill down on that group to see which product or products are responsible for the high or low sales. You'll find that looking through the limited number of members in the *Product Group* level is much easier than looking through the entire product list to find outlier data.

Server Time Dimensions

As we built our original Northwind *Sales* cube in the previous chapter, you might have thought that building a special dimension table for the *Time* dimension was a bit wasteful. After all, the concept of time is fairly universal, and there's a limited set of possible attributes and hierarchies that might be needed, any of which could be easily keyed off a date field in the fact table rather than an arbitrary time key.

In Analysis Services 2000, the concept of a date column–derived time dimension was very basic and easily implemented. Analysis Services 2005 has enhanced this facility, but its use is slightly less obvious. The new implementation of time dimensions is based on a server-generated pseudo-dimension table and an array of predefined attributes and hierarchies. In fact, time dimensions are implemented by creating a special dimension type called a *server time dimension*.

Let's add a server time dimension to our cube. Simply invoke the Dimension Wizard, and on the Select The Dimension Type page select the Server Time Dimension option button. On the Define Time Periods page, specify **January 1, 1996**, and **June 30, 1998**, as the first and last calendar days, respectively, and select Year, Quarter, Month, and Date from the Time Periods list box, as shown in Figure 18-13.

The Dimension Wizard's Define Time Periods page appears only for server time dimensions. It allows you to specify the (automatically built) levels of your server time dimension simply by selecting items from a list. It also lets you specify the beginning and end dates for the dimension, which should correlate to the fact table date columns' data, for which the dimension will be built.

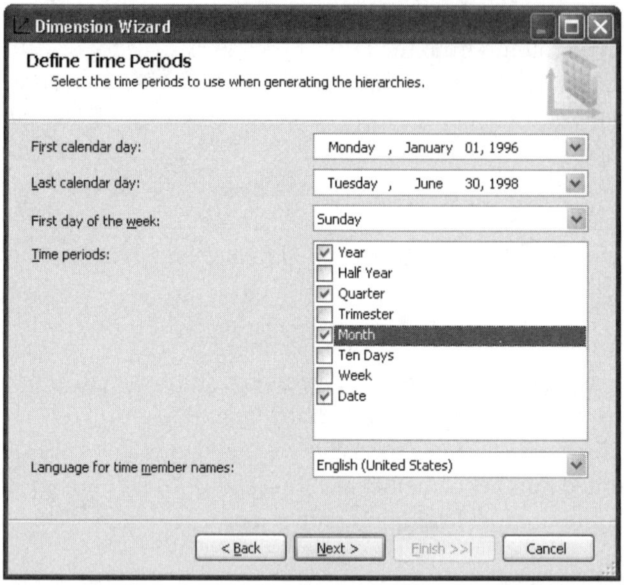

Figure 18-13 The Define Time Periods page of the Dimension Wizard

Accept the defaults for all other settings, and name your new dimension **ServerTime** before clicking Finish. Add the dimension to your cube as described earlier, and then click on the cube designer's Dimension Usage tab. This tab is where you configure dimensions that typically are not based on conventional relationships between fact and dimension tables.

Click in the cell at the intersection of the *ServerTime* dimension row and the *Main* measure group column, and then click the cell's ellipsis (...) button. In the Define Relationship dialog box, specify a Regular relationship, *Date* as the Granularity Attribute, and *OrderDate* as the Measure Group Column, as shown in Figure 18-14.

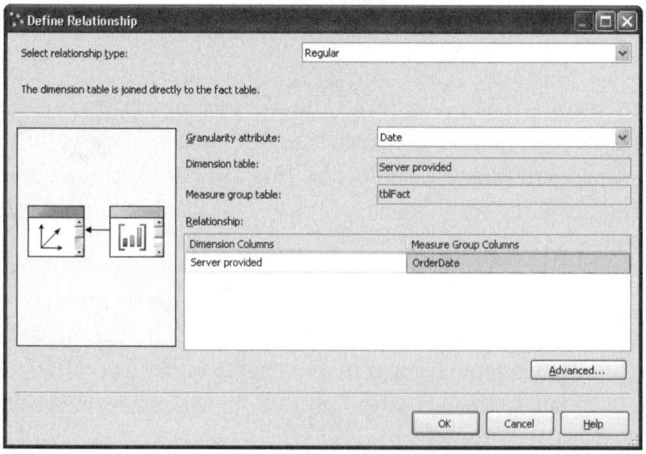

Figure 18-14 The Define Relationship dialog box, configured for a server time dimension

Notice the "Server provided" designation under the Dimension Columns header; this indicates that the dimension table is server-generated and therefore does not require you to specify a dimension column. Click OK, and note that the cell on the Dimension Usage tab now reads *Date*, indicating the granularity attribute of the server time dimension. Save and deploy your changes, and then inspect them in the cube browser (reconnecting first, as necessary).

> **More Info**   If you drill down on the *ServerTime* dimension in the cube browser's metadata tree view, you will see that *server time* dimensions offer an array of default attributes. If you open the *ServerTime* dimension in the dimension designer, you will see an even larger array of columns (from which new attributes can be created) in the Dimension Structure tab's Time Periods pane.

Fact Dimensions

One hallmark of Analysis Services 2005 is its ability to adapt to your database's structure rather than making you perform ETL (extract, transform, and load) gymnastics to satisfy Analysis Services requirements. Suppose, for example, that you want to create a dimension out of data that is stored in your fact table. With Analysis Services 2000, you would have to duplicate that data within the cube, and then relate that data back to your fact table to use it as a dimension. Analysis Services 2005, on the other hand, is much less rigid: You simply specify that your dimension data is in your fact table, and Analysis Services will accommodate you.

For example, the *Orders* table in the Northwind database contains geographic information pertaining to the shipping location that can be constructed into a useful dimension. Our current *Geography* dimension, derived from data in the *Customers* table, was easy to construct. But it is less obvious how to use fields such as *ShipCountry* and *ShipRegion* from our fact table (and derived from the Northwind database's *Orders* table) as levels in a new dimension.

It is less obvious, but it is still feasible to build this dimension with Analysis Services 2005. We'll show you how to build such a dimension, but first run the script tblFact.sql in the Management Studio solution included with the sample code for this project. (This script is different from the one of the same name in the Chapter 17 sample code.) This script drops *tblFact* and then re-creates it with a modified structure and repopulates it. After you run the script, open the Northwind Data Source View and click its Refresh toolbar button so that the new structure of *tblFact* is properly reflected. The Refresh Data Source View dialog box will appear, asking you to confirm the new changes to the structure of *tblFact*. Click OK.

Next, create a new standard, regular dimension called *Ship Geography*, making sure to identify *tblFact* as the dimension table, *Ship Region* as the key column, and *Ship Country* as the only attribute column. (Do not select any related tables.) Open the new dimension in its designer if it is not already open, and rename the *Tbl Fact* attribute to **Ship Region**. Create a user hierarchy called **Country - Region** using the *Ship Country* and *Ship Region* attributes, in order, as its levels, and then add the new dimension to your cube if you have not already done so.

Before you can save and deploy your changes, a little more work is required. You must explicitly tell Analysis Services that your new dimension is a fact dimension. You do this on the Dimension Usage tab of the cube designer. The adjustment is rather simple. On the tab, scroll down to the bottom of the list of dimensions and locate the cell where the *Ship Geography* dimension row intersects with the *Main* measure group column. The *Ship Region* field name is displayed in that cell. Everything appears to be normal, but an adjustment is indeed necessary.

Click within the *Ship Region* cell, and you should see an ellipsis button appear (as shown in Figure 18-15).

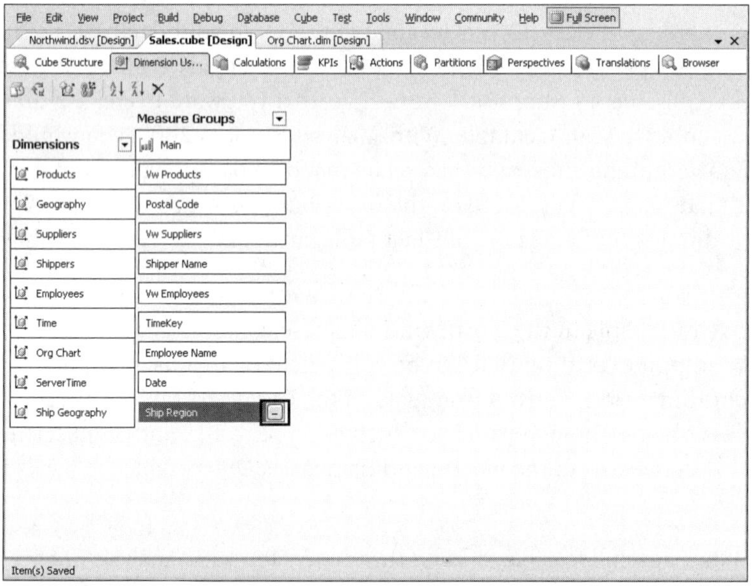

Figure 18-15   The Dimension Usage tab with the ellipsis button for the *Ship Geography/Main* measure group cell highlighted

Because *Ship Geography* is a fact dimension, you'll need to override its default usage and tell Analysis Services to establish a fact relationship as its basis. Click the ellipsis button to invoke the Define Relationship dialog box, change the relationship type from Regular to Fact, as shown in Figure 18-16, and then click OK.

Back on the Dimension Usage tab of the cube designer, note that the special fact dimension icon now appears in the dimension's cell, as shown in Figure 18-17.

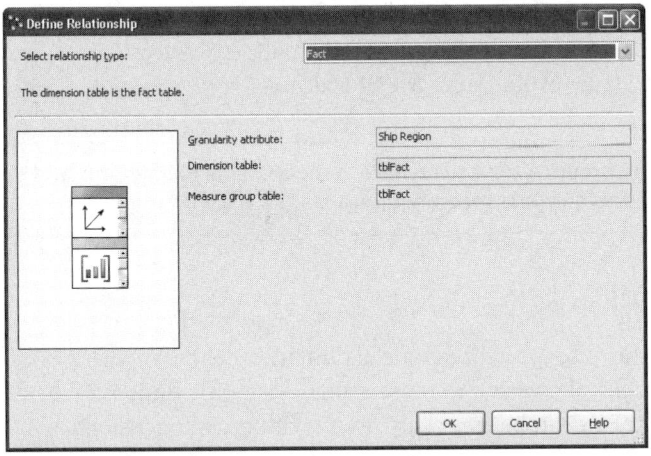

Figure 18-16   The Define Relationship dialog box with the Fact relationship type selected

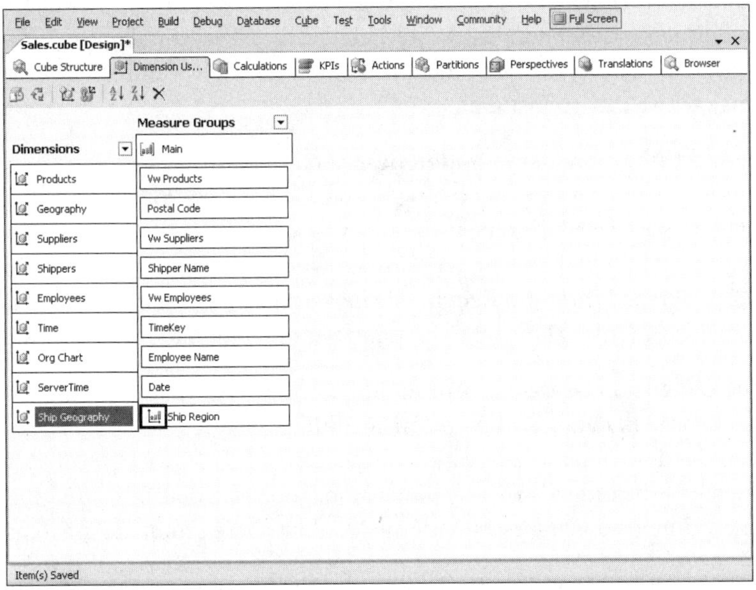

Figure 18-17   The Dimension Usage tab with the Ship Geography's fact dimension icon highlighted

Save and deploy your changes. On the Browser tab of the cube designer, reconnect if necessary, and you should be able to drill down on any measure by the *Ship Country* or *Ship Region* attributes or through the hierarchy that includes both. As you do so, consider how quickly you were able to create this dimension, add it to your cube, and start using it. We had to run a script to modify our fact table, but that's merely an artifact of how we built the fact table in the first place. In many real-world scenarios, adding a fact dimension involves simply using fields that were already there. No ETL is required, and you don't need to create a special dimension table, a view, or even a named query. This kind of flexibility—what we might call a *casual* ability to enhance a cube—simply didn't exist in Analysis Services 2000. That Analysis Services 2005 offers it is a true revolution in the BI space.

> **Caution**   Each measure group in a cube can have at most one fact dimension, and each fact dimension can be related to only one measure group.

Role-Playing Dimensions

Fact dimensions are not the only specialized type of dimension; there are many others. One of these, *role-playing dimensions*, allows you to reuse a single database dimension as multiple distinct cube dimensions. This can be especially useful with time dimensions, which usually have identical structures.

Our newly modified *tblFact* table now contains three date fields: *OrderDate* (which was there all along), *RequiredDate*, and *ShippedDate*. Wouldn't it be nice if we could reuse our *ServerTime* dimension twice more, relating the new "instances" to *RequiredDate* and *ShippedDate*, respectively? As it turns out, we can do just that.

Simply use the Add Cube Dimension option described previously, select the *ServerTime* dimension in the Add Cube Dimension dialog box, and click OK. You should see your new dimension added as *ServerTime 1*. Repeat the process to add dimension *ServerTime 2*. In the Dimensions pane of the cube designer's Cube Structure tab, rename *ServerTime 1* and *ServerTime 2* to **Shipped Date** and **Required Date**, respectively; finally, rename the original *ServerTime* dimension to **Order Date** to better identify it in relation to these new dimensions.

Now move to the Dimension Usage tab. You should see all three of the cube dimensions that are based on the *ServerTime* database dimension, including the original *ServerTime* (now *Order Date*) dimension, listed with names appearing in the format *ServerTime (cubedim)*, where *cubedim* is the name of the individual cube dimension. You should also see that the cells at which the two new dimensions intersect with the Main measure group are gray and empty.

Click in one of the empty cells, and then click the ellipsis button to invoke the Define Relationship dialog box. Select Regular from the Relationship Type drop-down list, select Date from the Granularity Attribute drop-down list, and select the appropriate fact table date column (*ShippedDate* or *RequiredDate*) under Measure Group Columns. These settings explicitly tell Analysis Services the foreign key in the fact table on which to join the server time pseudo-dimension table. Click OK, repeat this process for the remaining unconfigured dimension, save and deploy your changes, and then examine the changes in the cube browser.

In Analysis Services 2000, each distinct time dimension requires its own dimension table (or at least its own view). As with fact dimensions, Analysis Services handles things so that no ETL tasks, views, or named queries are required to implement the three different time dimensions. As you might have surmised, role-playing dimensions are so named because they allow a single database dimension to play the "role" of multiple distinct cube dimensions by linking to different columns in the measure group (fact table). This is similar to using the same table more than once in a SQL query and assigning it an alias: The various role-playing dimensions in the cube are essentially aliases of the one physical database dimension.

Advanced Measures

With all this work on our dimensions, we shouldn't forget measures. Shortly, we'll discuss how to create measures that are completely calculated by our cube, but for now let's just concentrate on tidying up the measures we have.

Measure Formatting

As you browsed the cube, you might have noticed that the dollar amounts stored in the measures are displayed as raw numbers and are not formatted as currency data. This can make the data difficult to read, but the problem is easily solved.

Open the *Sales* cube in the cube designer, click on the Cube Structure tab, and select the *Total Sales* measure in the Measures pane. Then, in the Properties window, set the *FormatString* property to *Currency* and do the same for the other two measures. Note the other formatting options available for use when you design cubes in the future. Analysis Services 2005 makes it easy to implement flexible server-side formatting of all your measures. In the next chapter, you'll see how easy it is to display formatted measure values in your applications.

Special Aggregates

The Properties window lets you do more than simply format your measures; it also lets you alter their formulaic definitions. The *Aggregate* property allows you to create measures whose aggregations are not simple sums.

For example, in addition to our *Total Sales* measure, we might want to have a measure that reflects average total sales for a given dimensional slice. Adding such a measure to our cube is easy. On the Cube Structure tab of the cube designer, click the New Measure toolbar button (third from the left), select Cube/New Measure... from the main menu, or select the New Measure... option on the Measures pane's shortcut menu. In the resulting New Measure dialog box, select Average Over Time from the Usage drop-down list, select the *Total Sales* item in the Source Column list box, and then click OK.

You'll see the new measure appear as *Total Sales − Main*. Using its shortcut menu, the F2 key, or the *Name* property in the Properties window, rename it to **Avg Total Sales**. In the Properties window, notice that the *AggregateFunction* property is set to *AverageOfChildren*; this is the result of selecting the Average Over Time option in the New Measure dialog box. As you did with the other measures, set the *FormatString* property of this new measure to *Currency*.

> **More Info**   Clicking the drop-down arrow in the *AggregateFunction* property value cell reveals numerous other aggregate functions that you can select for your measures. The *MeasureExpression* property allows you to enter an MDX expression that will determine the value of the leaf levels of your dimensions before the aggregate function is applied.

Display Folders

When your cube has a large number of measures, you might want to group related ones together, something Analysis Services 2005 lets you do with display folders. By simply entering a folder name into a measure's *DisplayFolder* property, you can segregate related sets of measures. The cube browser, embedded in the cube designer and in Management Studio, offers direct support for display folders. In the next chapter, we will cover how to support display folders in your own applications.

Once the display folder name is entered in the Properties window, it morphs into a drop-down list item. You can then easily assign the same display folder name to other measures in your cube without having to type it from scratch and risk entering it inconsistently. Enter the name **Non-Sum** as the *DisplayFolder* property value for the *Avg Total Sales* measure you previously created, and enter **Sum** as the *DisplayFolder* property value for the *Total Sales* measure. Then select one of the remaining measures, and notice that both *Sum* and *Non-Sum* appear in its *DisplayFolder* property drop-down list. Select *Sum* and do likewise for the remaining measure.

Save and deploy your changes, and then click on the cube designer's Browser tab. Reconnect and then browse your cube. The original three measures should appear under the *Sum* display folder, and the *Avg Total Sales* measure should appear under the *Non-Sum* display folder (both within the *Main* measure group). When browsed, each measure's data should be formatted as currency values, with dollar signs and decimals displayed.

> **Important**   User hierarchies within dimensions also have a *DisplayFolder* property that you can use in the same way as outlined here for measures. You can enter folder names using a filespec-like syntax (for example, *parent folder\child folder*), allowing you to create display folder hierarchies.

Calculations

There's a lot more to explore than these measure and dimension features. For instance, Analysis Services allows you to store calculated MDX expressions on the server that you can use in your queries. You can reference custom-built sets by name, create calculated measures or dimension attribute members, and more. The Calculations tab of the cube designer provides a nice front end for specifying named sets and calculated members, without requiring you to hand-code the MDX yourself. You can view the generated MDX if you're curious or if you want to learn more MDX through reverse engineering.

> **Note**   We'll examine MDX more carefully in the next chapter. If the syntax or expression content is confusing to you now, don't worry too much because it will become clearer later on.

Imagine that the Northwind Trading Company has defined Albuquerque, New Mexico; Boise, Idaho; and Kirkland, Washington, as test markets and often needs to view the sales in those three markets. By creating a named set containing those three cities, we can provide users with an easy way to query data for just those test markets. We might also like to see net sales rather than having to look at the *Total Sales* and *Discount* measures separately. By creating a calculated member defined as the difference between *Total Sales* and *Discount*, we can have an easy way to look at net sales without needing to embed that data in the fact table or embed expressions in our queries.

We might also want to define an additional calculated member that specifies our net sales growth for any time period, by comparing the period's net sales with that of the previous period and looking at the growth percentage (positive or negative) between the two. As you will see shortly, the Analysis Services 2005 calculations facility and MDX make this pretty easy.

Calculated Members

> **Note**   Because the calculated members created in this chapter belong to the MEASURES hierarchy, they can also be called calculated *measures*. Therefore, the terms *calculated member* and *calculated measure* are used interchangeably.

Let's start by creating the calculated measures we just described. Click on the cube designer's Calculations tab, shown in Figure 18-18.

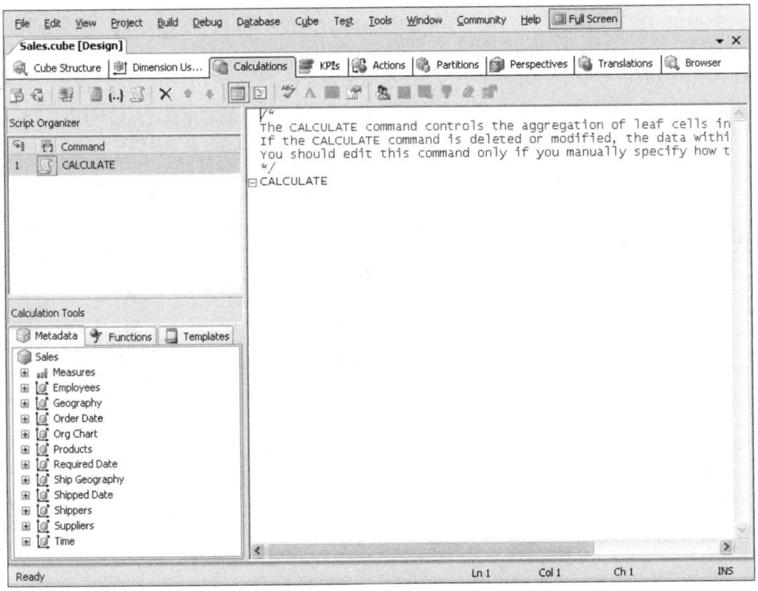

Figure 18-18   The cube designer's Calculations tab

A single calculation is already defined; leave that intact because the correct calculation of any new entries will depend on it. Next, click the New Calculated Member button (fourth from the left) on the designer's toolbar (or select the Cube/New Calculated Member option on the main menu or the New Calculated Member option on the Script Organizer pane's shortcut menu). This action adds a new calculated member to the cube, which you must now configure.

The main area of the designer window displays a form prompting you for various parameters of the calculated member (Figure 18-19).

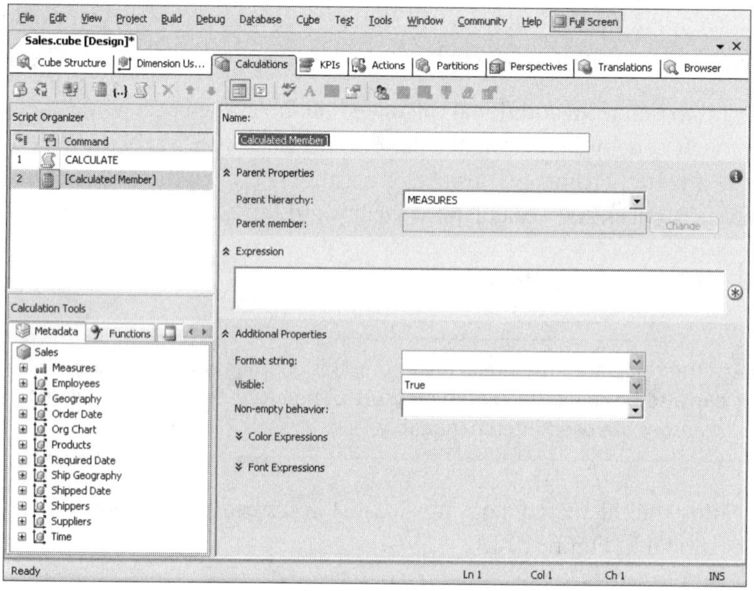

Figure 18-19   The cube designer's Calculations tab, in form view

Enter **[Adjusted Sales]** for the Name field (all calculated member names with embedded spaces must be contained within square brackets), confirm that MEASURES is selected from the Parent Hierarchy drop-down list, and enter the following MDX expression in the Expression text area:

```
[Measures].[Total Sales] - [Measures].[Discount]
```

Next, select *"Currency"* from the Format String drop-down list. The completed calculated member form for *[Adjusted Sales]* is shown in Figure 18-20.

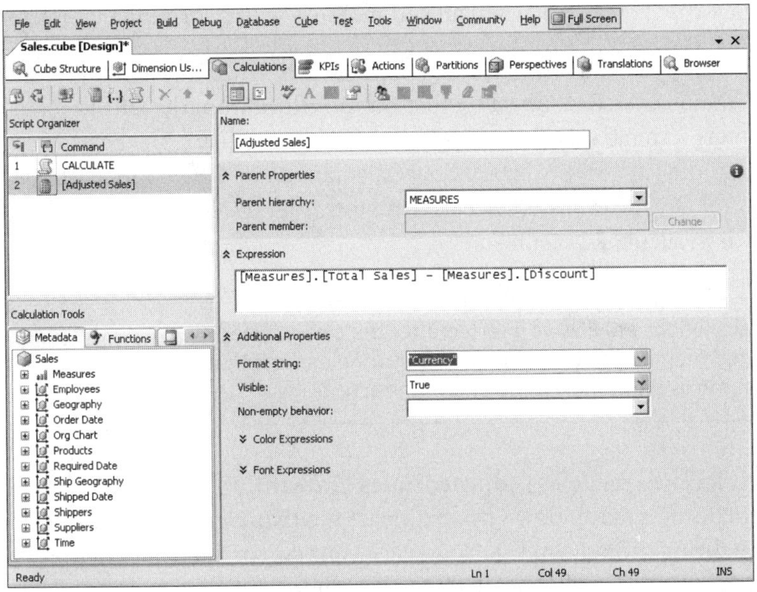

Figure 18-20   The Calculation tab in Form view for the Adjusted Sales calculated member

You have just defined a calculated measure called Adjusted Sales, which is the difference between the values for Total Sales and Discount. To see the MDX code that the designer generated, simply click the Script View toolbar button (11th button from the left or right) or choose the Cube/Show Calculations In/Script option from the main menu. Starting on the second line of the exposed MDX script (excluding comments), you should see the following MDX code, which represents the calculated measure you just created.

```
CREATE MEMBER CURRENTCUBE.[MEASURES].[Adjusted Sales]
  AS [Measures].[Total Sales] - [Measures].[Discount],
FORMAT_STRING = "Currency",
VISIBLE = 1;
```

As you can see, each field in the designer simply prompts you for a different clause of the MDX *CREATE MEMBER* command.

Complex Expressions

Calculation expressions can certainly be more complex than simple arithmetic formulas. The MDX query language is extremely rich and expressive, allowing you to embed powerful declarative analytic functionality within calculations. Although an in-depth look at MDX is beyond the scope of this chapter, let's build one more calculation and, in the process, sample the power of MDX.

First save and deploy your changes (this time by choosing the Build/Deploy Chapter18 main menu option) so that *[Adjusted Sales]* can be used within the expression for a new calculated measure (that is, we will create a *new* calculated measure with a formula that references *[Adjusted Sales]*).

Click the Calculations tab's Reconnect toolbar button (third from the left) to refresh the Calculation Tools pane's Metadata tab. Switch back to form view using the Form View toolbar button (10th from the left) or the Cube/Show Calculations In/Form option on the main menu. In the Script Organizer pane, select the *[Adjusted Sales]* calculated member you just created and add a new calculated member.

> **Tip** New calculations are always inserted after the one selected. Selecting the *[Adjusted Sales]* calculated member before adding the new one ensures that the latter will be added at the bottom of the list (and thus at the end of the script).

Name the new calculated member **[Adjusted Sales Growth]**, and then select MEASURES from the Parent Hierarchy drop-down list. Skip past the Expression field, and select Percent from the Format String drop-down list. Now place your cursor back in the Expression text area. The MDX expression for this calculation will be more complex than the last, so let's take it step by step.

First enter the following text:

```
CASE
    WHEN
```

Be sure to type a single space after the *WHEN* keyword. This allows you to insert code immediately afterward and ensures that a space will exist between the *WHEN* keyword and the inserted code.

Using Calculation Tools

The next section of code is prone to typographical errors if typed manually, so we will take advantage of the Calculations Tools pane to continue entering our MDX expression. You can think of the Calculations Tools pane and its Metadata, Functions, and Templates tabs as a sort of drag-and-drop IntelliSense feature: You can actually drag your cube's objects, MDX function call prototypes, or entire code templates into the Expression area, and code corresponding to the item you have dragged will be inserted for you.

> **Important** The Calculation Tools pane is a coder's tool. Therefore it is visible and usable not only when the cube designer's Calculations tab is in form view but also when it is in script view.

If the Metadata tab is not already selected within the Calculation Tools pane, click it to make it active. Next, drill down on the *Order Date* dimension and locate the *Year - Quarter - Month - Date* hierarchy, which should appear as the dimension node's last child node. Drag and drop this hierarchy object into the Expression area, positioning it at the end of the second line, one space to the right of the *WHEN* keyword. Your expression text should now appear as follows:

```
CASE
    WHEN [Order Date].[Year - Quarter - Month - Date]
```

If the code does not appear exactly as above, you can manually edit it to make it so.

You will continue by using a mixture of drag-and-drop and manual typing techniques, developing the MDX expression to contain the code shown here. (Don't type it just yet.)

```
CASE
    WHEN [Order Date].[Year - Quarter - Month -
  Date].CURRENTMEMBER.LEVEL.ORDINAL = 0 THEN
        NULL
    WHEN ISEMPTY(([Order Date].[Year - Quarter - Month -
  Date].PREVMEMBER, [Measures].[Adjusted Sales])) THEN
        "EMPTY"
    ELSE
        [Measures].[Adjusted Sales]/
        ([Order Date].[Year - Quarter - Month -
  Date].PREVMEMBER, [Measures].[Adjusted Sales]) - 1
END
```

In a moment, we'll discuss what this expression actually calculates; we'll first discuss whether and how to use the items on the various tabs of the Calculation Tools pane to build out parts of the code.

You will find that the *[Measures].[Adjusted Sales]* item can be dragged and dropped from the Metadata tab; simply expand the Measures node at the top of the Metadata tab's tree view, and then drag and drop the Adjusted Sales node into the Expression text area. The *CURRENT-MEMBER* and *PREVMEMBER* properties can be found in, and dragged from, the Navigation branch of the Functions tab's tree view. Doing so might be more trouble than it's worth, however. You might find it easier to use the List Members or Complete Word shortcut menu options from within the expression edit region. You can also use the like-named options available by selecting Edit/IntelliSense on the main menu. You might find the Ctrl+J (for List members), Ctrl+Space, or Alt+Right Arrow (for Complete Word) keyboard shortcuts even more convenient.

The *LEVEL* and *ORDINAL* property keywords can be found under the Metadata node of the Functions tab (not the Metadata tab). They can also be dragged and dropped, but, again, doing so offers little in the way of productivity increases and requires manual replacement of the generated <<*Member*>> and <<*Level*>> prefixes. Sometimes it's best to use the Calculation Tools pane simply as a reference tool to remind yourself of MDX syntax; at other times, the drag-and-drop functionality can be useful. Typically, complex expressions involving long dimension, hierarchy, and/or level and member names are better dragged than typed.

> **More Info**   The items on the Templates tab of the Calculation Tools pane offer skeletal versions of long code constructs and give you a great head start for digging deeper into MDX. Items from this tab must, by their very nature, be dragged and dropped.

Regardless of how you compose the expression code, you should perform a syntax check on it when you're done. To do so, use the Check Syntax toolbar button (10th from the right, with a spell check icon) or choose the Cube/Check Syntax option from the main menu. A message box should appear with the message "The syntax check was successful." If not, check the formula text or open the Chapter18End Visual Studio Analysis Services solution included in the sample code for this chapter, open the *Sales* cube in the cube designer, click on the Calculations tab, select the *[Adjusted Sales Growth]* calculated member, and copy and paste the expression text from there.

Deciphering the Code

Now let's discuss how the calculation expression we just entered actually works. The easiest way to understand the expression is to start at the bottom and work your way up. Start by looking at the formula within the *ELSE* clause of the expression:

```
[Measures].[Adjusted Sales]/
      ([Order Date].[Year -  Quarter -  Month -  Date].PREVMEMBER,
[Measures].[Adjusted Sales]) - 1
```

This parenthetical part of this formula calculates Adjusted Sales for the previous period within the *Year - Quarter - Month - Date* hierarchy of the *Order Date* dimension. Adjusted Sales for the *current* period is then divided by this number, and finally the number 1 is subtracted from the quotient. The resulting value is the period-over-period growth for the Adjusted Sales calculated measure.

The previous and current "periods" that the expression references are determined by the context set by the query calling this function. For example, if the expression is calculated for a member of the *Year* level, the expression will record annual growth in Adjusted Sales. If it is calculated for a member of the *Quarter* level, the expression will return quarter-over-quarter growth, and so on. We will see shortly how you can use this calculated member in the cube browser to see Adjusted Sales growth at several levels of the *Order Date* dimension's *Year - Quarter - Month - Date* hierarchy.

Once you understand the formula in the *ELSE* clause, the rest of the expression is easy because it just deals with invalid comparison scenarios. Moving upward through the code, if the expression is evaluated for the very first period in its level (for example, January 1996 in the *Month* level), *PREVMEMBER* will be empty and the formula will return the hardcoded string *EMPTY*. If the period passed to the formula is at level 0 of the hierarchy (that is, the *All* member), the formula will return *NULL* because the *All* member by definition can have no predecessor.

Named Sets

Before we deploy and test these new calculations, let's add a named set that references the three test-market cities we mentioned earlier. This is quite easy to do. Simply make sure the *[Adjusted Sales Growth]* calculated member is selected in the Script Organizer pane of the cube designer's Calculations tab, and then add a new named set using the Calculation tab's toolbar, the Script Organizer's shortcut menu, or the Cube branch of the main menu. Name the set **[Test Markets]**, and enter the following text in the Expression area:

```
{[Geography].[City].&[Albuquerque], [Geography].[City].&[Boise],
[Geography].[City].&[Kirkland]}
```

> **Tip** You might find it easiest to compose the expression by typing the (curly) braces, commas, and spaces yourself and generating the rest of the code by dragging and dropping the appropriate members of the *City* attribute of the *Geography* dimension from the Metadata tab of the Calculation Tools pane. Specifically, you would need to expand the Geography\City\ Members\All node and then drag and drop each of the three cities from the alphabetically sorted list to the appropriate insertion points in the Expression text box.

Using drag-and-drop techniques to specify members of a set results in rather formal syntax usage in the generated code—namely, the use of the ampersand (&) character and the square brackets around each name, which are technically not necessary. The brackets are superfluous because none of the names contains embedded spaces. The ampersand character is used to reference a member key rather than a member name. In our case, the name and the key are one and the same and the names are unique, so the ampersand is not strictly required. You might want to leave the brackets and ampersands in the expression code so subsequent name changes involving the use of embedded spaces or member keys can be accommodated without requiring major changes.

More on Script View

Save your changes now, but before deploying them, switch back to script view to look at the entire set of generated code. Note that each calculation you entered, as well as the *CALCU-LATE* script command that was there initially, simply form successive sections of a single MDX script. These snippets of code appear within that script in the same order in which they appear in the Script Organizer pane displayed in form view.

Script view does not contain .NET code, but the dichotomy between form view and script view provides the same experience as working in form view and code view in a Windows Forms project or an ASP.NET Web site in Visual Studio. There is no concept in MDX of events or "code behind," but the dynamic of designer-generated code is very much in effect, and changes in one view necessarily affect the other.

Furthermore, the code editor supports many of the same features as the code editor in .NET projects: Blocks of code can be expanded or contracted; word completion, member listing, and real-time "squiggle" syntax error prompting are supported; parameter information is supplied in ToolTips when you use MDX functions; and you can enter comments using either of the T-SQL comment syntax patterns (/*comment*/ and –comment) or the C-style (//comment). Comments entered in script view make your MDX code more readable and do not prevent form view from rendering properly.

> **Tip**   Even when you're *not* in script view, the Expression text region in form view supports many of the features just described.

Debug Mode

The similarities with .NET projects do not end there; they extend to the entire debugging experience. You can set and clear breakpoints, and you can choose the Debug/Step Over main menu option when a breakpoint is hit. This brings up an important point: Until now, we have spoken of choosing the Debug/Start Debugging main menu option and the Start Debugging toolbar button as being equivalent to deploying the project to an Analysis Services server. In fact, that's not quite true. Choosing Build/Deploy *projectname* from the main menu does perform that task (which is why we instructed you to use it before), but the Start Debugging toolbar/menu options deploy the project *and* step into your cube's calculation script if the cube designer is open and the Calculations tab is selected when the option is selected.

Try this yourself by clicking one of the Start Debugging toolbar or menu options with the Calculations tab open. After the project is built and deployed, Visual Studio places you in script view mode (even if you were in form view mode when you selected the Start Debugging option), and then the whole IDE goes into debug mode, just as it would for a .NET project. The Debug toolbar becomes visible, the Debug menu becomes fully enabled, and a special Debug pane opens up on the Calculations tab.

The Debug pane provides a Pivot Table tab (onto which you can drag and drop objects from the Metadata tab) and four interactive MDX tabs for diagnostic querying. The Debug pane can be hard to see; you might need to auto-hide any docked windows on the bottom edge of the Visual Studio parent window and then move the splitter bar immediately below the MDX code editor to make the debug pane readily visible. The Calculations tab debug mode is shown in Figure 18-21.

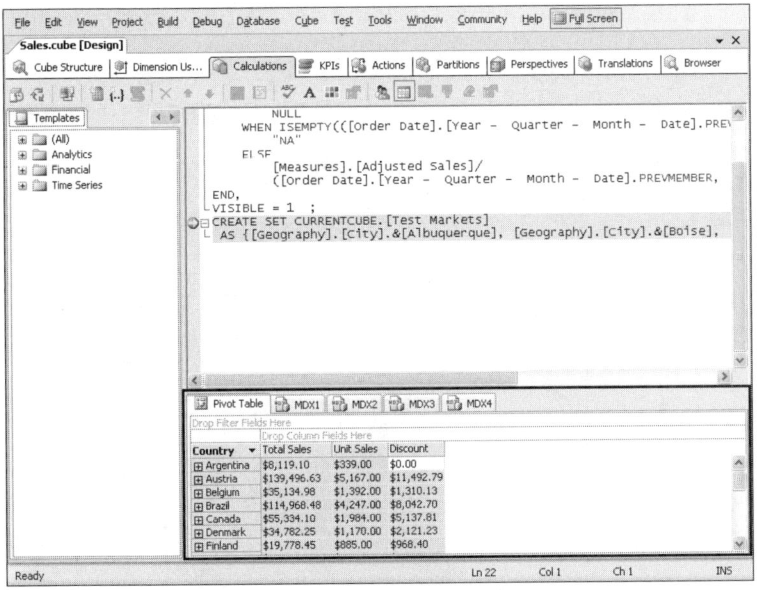

Figure 18-21   The Calculations tab in debug mode, with the Debug pane highlighted

Note, and consider the power of, the breakpoint set in the MDX code. This powerful debugger tool can save you hours of tedious debugging, tabbing back and forth between Visual Studio and SQL Server Management Studio.

Back to the Browser

Before we conclude our discussion of calculations, let's actually cover how to use them. If you're still in debug mode, select the Debug/Stop Debugging main menu option or click the Stop Debugging button on the Debug toolbar (third from the left, with a VCR stop button icon); you can also use the Shift+F5 keyboard shortcut. Click on the cube designer's Browser tab and reconnect. In the metadata tree view, drill down on the Measures and Geography nodes. Doing so will reveal your calculated measures and named set as children. Note that the calculated measures do not appear indented underneath either display folder or even our measure group. We will correct this shortly.

Now construct a query using your new calculations by performing the following steps:

1. Drag the *Order Date* dimension's *Year - Quarter - Month - Date* hierarchy to the Row Fields area.

2. Drag the *Adjusted Sales* and *Adjusted Sales Growth* calculated members to the Detail Fields area. (Be sure to drop *Adjusted Sales Growth* to the right of *Adjusted Sales*.)

3. Drag the *Test Markets* named set to the filter pane (*not* to the Drop Filter Fields Here area of the Pivot Table pane).

4. In the Rows Fields area, drill down on the Calendar 1997 node and then on the
    Quarter 1, 1997 node.

The results of these drag-and-drop steps are also displayed in Figure 18-22.

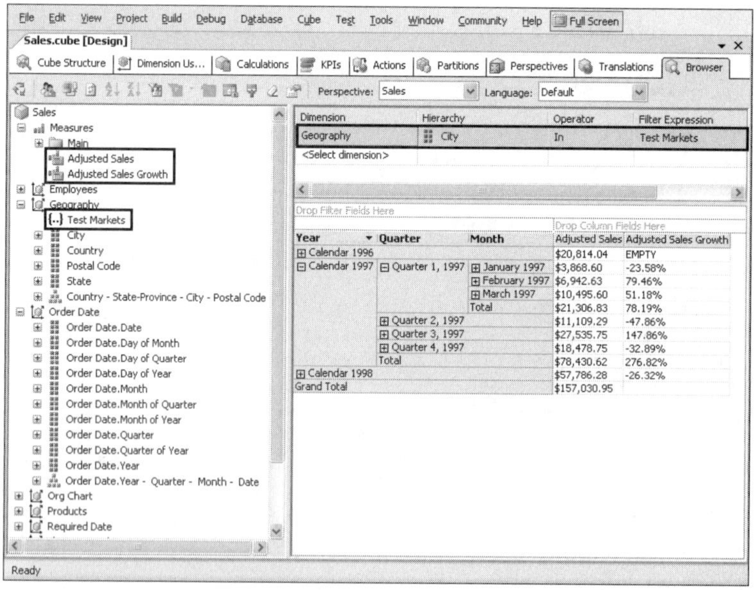

Figure 18-22   The cube browser with calculated measures and named set highlighted

Notice that the *Adjusted Sales Growth* figure is EMPTY for Calendar 1996 because there is no previous period from which to calculate growth. For other cells, you should see the proper growth figures (some of them negative) based on the *Adjusted Sales* number compared to its previous period.

In the previous figure, the data displayed is filtered to reflect sales for only our three test markets. If you want to see data for the entire cube, right-click the named set's line in the Filter pane and choose Delete from the shortcut menu (or select it and press the Delete key). You might want to then drill down on one of the displayed month's nodes in the Pivot Table pane to reveal the day-to-day *Adjusted Sales Growth* data. (Doing this while the Test Markets named set filter was in effect would have displayed many empty cells.)

As we mentioned earlier, our two calculated measures do not appear within the *Main* measure group, let alone its *Sum* display folder. We can remedy this by clicking on the cube designer's Calculations tab and then clicking the Calculation Properties toolbar button (seventh from the right) or choosing the Cube/Calculation Properties... option from the main menu. In the resulting Calculation Properties dialog box, you can add the two calculated measures and specify the measure group and/or display folder for each, as shown in Figure 18-23.

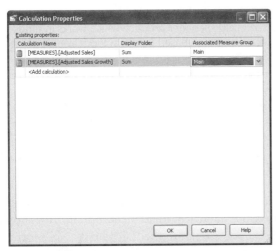

Figure 18-23   The Calculation Properties dialog box with display folder and measure group definitions for our calculated measures

If you skip ahead to Figure 18-38, you will see that the calculated measures are properly contained within the Sum display folder after these changes are deployed to the server.

Key Performance Indicators

Measures and dimensions define what a cube can show you, giving you insight into, for example, your business's performance, your site's Web traffic, or your clinical experiment's findings. You can run an MDX query and look at a measure's value over some slice of your cube, and because you're familiar with its measures and dimensions, you can decide if the values meet, exceed, or fall short of your goals or your expectations. With the help of key performance indicators (KPIs) in Analysis Services 2005, you can now embed that goal criteria in the cube rather than evaluate it in your head or in your application.

KPIs simply consist of a set of MDX-based conditional expressions, stored on the server, that return numeric values indicating the performance of a measure, a calculated measure, or a calculated expression over a slice of the cube and/or the relative performance of that value over a period of time. KPIs are associated with certain predefined icon sets, providing a visualization tool (even if a crude one) over your measures and an easy way for your users to get up to speed quickly on what the measures data are telling you.

Pay attention here because this is the stuff that's currently hot in the market: KPIs enable what are known in the BI and business performance management (BPM) worlds as *scorecards*, and they lend themselves extremely well to dashboard-type user interfaces. If you take what you learn from this chapter, and the programming techniques we'll cover in the next chapter, you'll have what it takes to build scorecard and dashboard applications with relative ease.

More Info   Microsoft's Business Scorecard Manager product, which works in tandem with Analysis Services, provides a Microsoft SharePoint–based platform for delivering scorecards and KPI data to end users.

Let's set up a KPI and then look at it in the special KPI browser view. Unfortunately, the cube's Browser tab will not display or allow querying of KPIs, but after building and browsing our KPI we'll address this shortcoming. We'll do so by making a short detour over to SQL Server Management Studio, where we will query our KPI values using that application's MDX Query window.

Click on the KPIs tab of the cube designer, and then click the New KPI toolbar button (fourth from the left) or choose the Cube/New KPI main menu option. You should see a new KPI open in form view, which is quite similar to the Calculations tab's form view. The main, right-hand area of the tab contains a field-oriented form for defining your KPI. A Calculation Tools pane, identical to that of the Calculations tab, appears at the lower left, and a KPI Organizer pane, similar to the Calculations tab's Script Organizer pane, appears at the upper left.

The form fields for a KPI include its name, the measure group it is associated with, and MDX expressions for the value to be tracked and a "goal" value for it. The KPI value and goal value are purely numeric indicators that alone offer little extra value over measures and calculated members.

KPI Visualization: Status and Trend

Extra value *is* provided, however, by MDX expressions for the KPI's *status* and its *trend*. The status expression returns a value, typically between −1 and +1, indicating the relative health of the KPI value; the trend expression returns a value, usually in the same range, indicating the increase or decrease in status value relative to a prior period of time. Along with the expressions themselves, you can also select associated indicator graphics (icon sets).

A status or trend value of +1 conveys a "good" state of affairs for whatever the KPI is meant to monitor. A value of −1 is a "bad" value, and a value of 0 is "neutral." The icon sets selected for your status and trend expressions contain several icons, each corresponding to a different discrete value returned by the expression.

At a minimum, these icons support the values of −1, 0, and 1. For example, a Traffic Light graphic displays a red, yellow, or green light, respectively. Others, such as a Gauge graphic, accommodate intermediate values, typically +.5 and −.5, which we might associate with "fair" and "substandard," respectively. These intermediate values (and the icons to which they correspond) are relevant only for status; trend, by definition (by the Analysis Services 2005 definition, anyway), is always positive, negative, or neutral.

A Concrete KPI

This is all rather abstract, but it will become clear once we've a built a KPI and put it to use. Our KPI will be based on our *Avg Total Sales* measure. Configure the KPI you added earlier as follows:

1. Set the Name to **Average Total Sales KPI** (no square brackets necessary).

2. Select Main for Associated Measure Group.

3. Set the Value Expression to **[Measures].[Avg Total Sales]**. (You might want to drag and drop the Measures\Main\Non-Sum\Avg Total Sales node from the Metadata tab of the Calculation Tools pane onto the Value Expression area rather than typing this manually.)

4. Set the Goal Expression to **1500**.

5. Set the Status Indicator graphic to Gauge, if it has not been done already.

6. Enter the MDX code in Listing 18-1 into the Status Expression area. (You might want to drag and drop items from the KPI folder of the Functions tab in the Calculation Tools pane to complete this step more easily.)

7. Set the Trend Indicator to Standard Arrow, if it has not been done already.

8. Set the Trend Expression to the contents of Listing 18-2 (using drag and drop from the Calculation Tools pane as appropriate).

Listing 18-1   Status expression MDX code for Average Total Sales KPI

```
CASE
    WHEN KPIVALUE("Average Total Sales KPI") /
  KPIGOAL("Average Total Sales KPI") >= .95 THEN
        1
    WHEN KPIVALUE("Average Total Sales KPI") / KPIGOAL("Average Total Sales KPI") <  .95
    AND
    KPIVALUE("Average Total Sales KPI") / KPIGOAL("Average Total Sales KPI") >= .85 THEN
        0
    ELSE
        -1
END
```

The MDX expression in Listing 18-1 determines actual average sales as a percentage of the Goal ($1500) and maps as positive (+1) values that are 95 percent and up. Average Sales greater or equal to 85 percent and less than 95 percent of goal are neutral (0), and those below 85 percent are negative (−1).

Listing 18-2   Trend MDX expression code for Average Total Sales KPI

```
CASE
    WHEN ISEMPTY(( [Measures].[Avg Total Sales],
    [Order Date].[Year -  Quarter -  Month -  Date].PREVMEMBER)) THEN
        NULL
    WHEN [Measures].[Avg Total Sales] < ([Measures].[Avg Total Sales],
    [Order Date].[Year -  Quarter -  Month -  Date].PREVMEMBER) THEN
        -1
    WHEN [Measures].[Avg Total Sales] = ([Measures].[Avg Total Sales],
    [Order Date].[Year -  Quarter -  Month -  Date].PREVMEMBER) THEN
        0
    ELSE
        1
END
```

The MDX expression in Listing 18-2 uses the *PREVMEMBER* property of our *Order Date* dimension's hierarchy to compare *Adjusted Sales Growth* for the period and level for which the KPI is being evaluated and compares it to the previous period's value. If the previous period's value is lower, growth is positive and the trend expression returns a value of +1; if the value is higher, growth is negative and a value of −1 is returned. If the two values are equal, growth is flat and a value of 0 is returned.

Note   In reality, comparing the difference between the two periods' values and returning 0 for a range of values from slightly below 0 to slightly above 0 might be a better determinant of flat growth, but for the purposes of this exercise, we'll stick with a difference of 0.

Click the down arrow icon next to the Additional Properties header to expand that section of the form. We won't enter values for all the fields here, but it's important to know the available options. Display folders for KPIs work similarly to the way they do for measures, calculations, and hierarchies, allowing you to group KPIs by category. You can enter multiple folder names, thus allowing your KPIs to appear under more than one folder, if you separate them with a semicolon.

A parent KPI allows you to organize your KPIs hierarchically and establishes a calculation relationship whereby the parent KPI's value is determined by that of its children. The relative contribution of each child KPI's value to that of its parent is determined by the value entered in the Weight field. In the Current Time Member field, you can specify an exclusive time period within which the KPI is valid. You must specify a member of a time dimension defined for the measure group with which the KPI is associated.

Note   When you enter values for a KPI's fields, remember that the Value Expression, Goal Expression, Status Expression, Trend Expression, Weight, and Current Time Member field values are full-fledged MDX expressions, supporting all MDX language constructs, word completion, member listing, "squiggle" syntax error prompting, and entry of comments.

Finally, the Description field allows you to document your KPI by storing a descriptive string of text about it in the cube itself. This text is retrievable by client applications, which, again, makes it easier for users to browse your cube. Go ahead and type **Monitors health of average total sales** in the Description field for our KPI and leave the other fields in the Additional Properties section blank.

Now that we have completed the definition of our KPI, it's time to test it, but our testing method will be different than for other elements in our cube. We'll cover those differences in a minute, but first save and deploy your changes and make sure you do so while the KPI's tab is visible. After the deployment, notice that the KPI tab has switched from form view to browser view.

Testing KPIs in Browser View

The Browser View toolbar button is now selected, and form fields have disappeared, giving way to a new window. In the upper pane of this window you can specify a slice of your cube for which to view the KPI data; the lower pane displays your KPI data. This data includes the value for the current slice, the goal value, graphical depictions of the status and trend values, and the weight value. An information icon also appears; you can hover your mouse pointer over it to display the KPI's description in a ToolTip.

The KPI browser view provides an easy way for you to view KPI values for specific dimensional subsections (slices) of your cube. However, by default, the browser displays aggregated KPI data for the entire cube, which is almost meaningless. Narrowing down that scope requires making specific selections in the filter pane. For example, we can look at the KPI data for Brazil in the fourth quarter of 1996 by making the following selections in the filter pane. (You might need to first reconnect in order to be allowed to make these selections.)

Dimension	Hierarchy	Operator	Filter Expression
Order Date	Year - Quarter - Month - Date	Equal	{Quarter 4, 1996}
Geography	Country	Equal	{Brazil}

For Filter Expression, you must click the drop-down arrow at the right edge of the column. Then, in the dimension browser popup window, drill down to the member you're interested in, click its check box, and then click OK. The necessary selection state for the {Quarter 4, 1996} member of the *Order Date* dimension is shown in Figure 18-24.

After you specify your cube slice, click off the selected cell in the filter expression table (for example, click anywhere in the lower pane) to force the new KPI data to load and display.

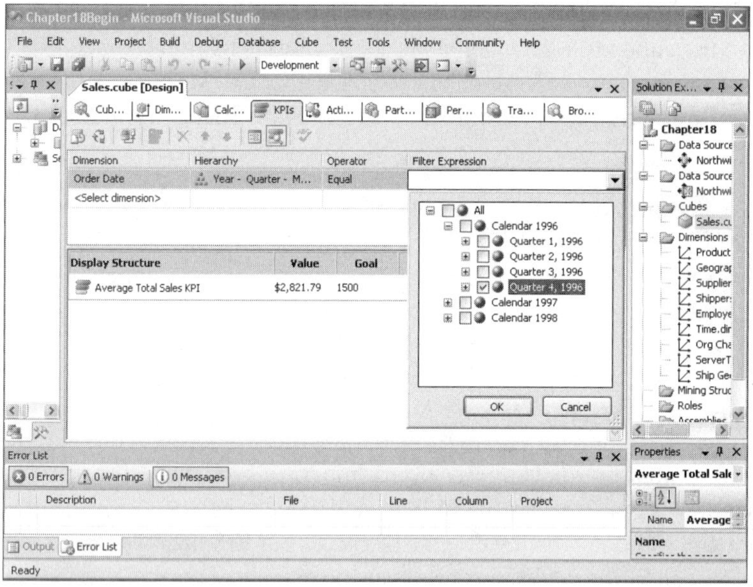

Figure 18-24   The KPI browser with the Filter Expression member selection popup window displayed

Interpreting Results and Modifying the Slicer

When you've completed the previous steps, the KPI browser view should appear as shown in Figure 18-25.

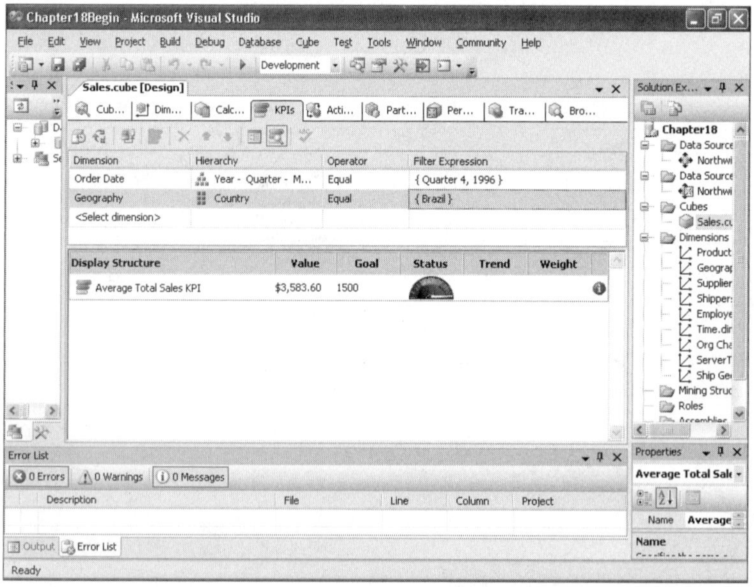

Figure 18-25   The KPI browser showing KPI data for a cube slice defined as Quarter 4, 1996, in Brazil

Notice that the Value column displays $3583.60, which is well above goal. Accordingly, the Status column's graphic displays a full green (indicating a status value of +1). The Trend column displays no graphic at all. This results from a value of *NULL* being returned by the trend formula because of an anomaly in the way the KPI browser filters its data. Shortly, we will bring back KPI data through an MDX query to obtain the correct value for the trend.

Now try changing the country to UK. (Remember to *uncheck* Brazil before clicking OK.) You should see the KPI value decrease to $1082.23 and the Status column graphic indicate red, which is correct given that this value is less than 85 percent of goal ($1500). Next, change the *Order Date* filter expression to *{Calendar 1997}* and the *Geography* filter expression to *{Brazil, Canada}*. (Again, remember to *uncheck* the old filter member—UK—before clicking OK.) You should see the KPI value increase to $1420.01 and the Status column graphic indicate yellow, which is correct given that this value is about 94.7 percent of goal and our range for yellow (status formula value of 0) is between greater than or equal to 85 percent and less than 95 percent.

KPI Queries in Management Studio

At this point, you should have a sense of the effectiveness of KPIs and the relative ease with which you can create them. The graphics might seem simplistic at first, but they make the data in your cube much more digestible and easier to understand.

To convey KPI data to your end users, though, you must use something other than the KPI browser, which is simply a technologist's tool. For example, access to KPIs from the cube browser might be more helpful. (The cube browser might seem to also be a technologist's tool, but it is actually the Excel PivotTable component, which is available to users through the 2003 versions of Office Web Components and Microsoft Excel itself.)

Unfortunately, KPIs are *not* available in the cube browser, so you must use a different end-user technology. To this end, we'll now explore how to write simple MDX queries that return KPI data. In the next chapter, we'll explain how to build your own UI around KPIs by generating and executing these queries. For now, we'll simply design and execute these queries interactively, and we'll do so not in Visual Studio but in Management Studio itself.

Management Studio Does BI

So far, we've used Management Studio mostly as a tool to manage relational databases. Management Studio is the successor to Enterprise Manager and Query Analyzer from SQL Server 2000, but it is also the successor to Analysis Manager and the MDX Sample Application, the Analysis Services 2000 management tools.

Using Management Studio, you can create and edit MDX queries for OLAP cubes, DMX queries for data mining models (which we'll cover in Chapter 20), and XML for Analysis (XMLA) scripts that you can use to create, modify, and drop virtually any Analysis Manager object, as well as to execute embedded MDX and DMX queries. Management Studio also supports the creation and maintenance of Analysis Services Scripts projects, which can contain a combination of MDX, DMX, and XMLA queries/scripts. You can combine Analysis Services Scripts projects and SQL Server Scripts projects into a single solution to manage the entire universe of objects in your data warehouse systems.

To see how all of this works, open Management Studio, and make sure the Registered Servers and Object Explorer windows are visible. If they're not, simply click the Registered Servers and Object Explorer buttons (fifth and third from the right, respectively) on the Standard toolbar or like-named options from the View branch of Management Studio's main menu. Now click the Analysis Services button on the Registered Servers window's toolbar (second from the left, with a cube icon) and then double-click the tree view node representing your server. (If it's not there, add it.) A node representing your Analysis Services server, as well as Databases and Assemblies child nodes, should now be displayed in the Object Explorer window. Expand the Databases node, and all databases on your Analysis Services server should be displayed, as shown in Figure 18-26.

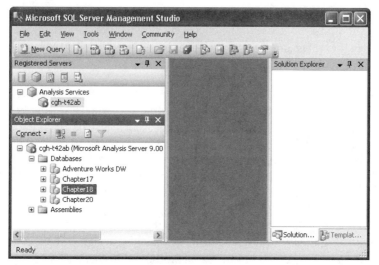

Figure 18-26   SQL Server Management Studio, with our Analysis Services server displayed in the Registered Servers and Object Explorer windows

The MDX Query Window

Select the Chapter18 node, and click the New Query button on the Standard toolbar. An MDX query window appears. On the left, the window has a tools pane, consisting of a drop-down list of cubes in the database; a Metadata tab that lists the measures, dimensions, *and* KPIs in the selected cube; and a Functions tab (equivalent to the one you've seen on the Calculations and KPIs tabs of the cube designer in Visual Studio). On the right side of the MDX query window is an MDX editor that supports color coding, squiggle syntax error prompting, and interspersing of comments and code. Member listing and word completion are available through the Edit/IntelliSense option on the main menu or via keyboard shortcuts.

> **Note** Clicking the New Query button is only one of several ways to open an MDX query window in Management Studio. For example, you can click the Analysis Services MDX Query button (third from the left) on the Standard toolbar or choose the File/New/Analysis Services MDX Query option from the main menu.
>
> Either action opens the Connect To Analysis Services dialog box, where you specify your Analysis Services server and database names. To specify the database name, click the Options button, click the Connection Properties tab that becomes visible, and then select or type the database name in the Connect To Database drop-down list. Then click Connect.
>
> You can avoid the entire Connect To Analysis Services dialog box step by using the New Query toolbar button when a specific Analysis Services database is selected in the Object Explorer window because the connection and database are implied. Another shortcut is to select the New Query/MDX option from the database node's shortcut menu in the Object Explorer window.
>
> You can change the connection parameters for an open MDX query window by choosing the Connection/Change Connection... option from its shortcut menu, the Query/Connection/Change Connection... option on the main menu, or by clicking the Change Connection button (third from the left) on the SQL Analysis Services Editors toolbar. The server and database you are currently connected to are displayed in the query window's status bar and in the Properties window when the query window is active.

If you expand the KPI's node on the Metadata tab, you should see a single node for our new KPI; if you expand that node, you should see one child node each for the KPI's value, goal, status, and trend, as shown in Figure 18-27.

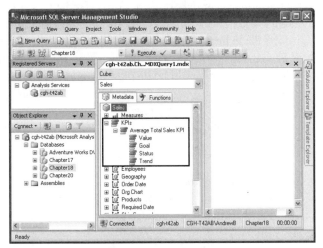

Figure 18-27 The Management Studio MDX query window with our sample cube loaded and its KPI displayed on the Metadata tab

You can drag and drop any of these child nodes into the query editor to generate expressions that can be used in an MDX *SELECT* statement. Using a combination of manual typing and drag-and-drop from the Metadata tab, enter the MDX code in Listing 18-3 into the editor pane of the MDX query window. (The query is in the file KPIQuery.mdx in the Management Studio solution included with the sample code.)

Listing 18-3   An MDX query suitable for execution from Management Studio

```
SELECT
  {
  KPIValue("Average Total Sales KPI"),
  KPIGoal("Average Total Sales KPI"),
  KPIStatus("Average Total Sales KPI"),
  KPITrend("Average Total Sales KPI")
  }
  ON COLUMNS
FROM [Sales]
WHERE
  (
  [Order Date].[Year - Quarter - Month -  Date].[Year].&[1997-01-01T00:00:00],
  {[Geography].[Country].&[Brazil],
  [Geography].[Country].&[Canada]}
  )
```

Tip   In Listing 18-3, the rather obscure expression involving the [Order Date] dimension (in the *WHERE* clause) actually represents the Calendar 1997 member of that dimension. Using drag-and-drop from the Metadata tab, you can avoid manually typing that entire expression.

The query selects the *Average Total Sales KPI* value, goal, status, and trend for data in 1997 from sales to Brazil and Canada (the same slicer data retrieved by our most recent KPI browser view query). You can run a syntax check on the query by choosing the Query/Parse main menu option or by clicking the Parse button (seventh from the right, with the check mark icon) on the SQL Analysis Services Editors toolbar. A Results pane appears with a Messages tab, on which the following output should be displayed:

```
Parsing the query ...
Obtained object of type: Microsoft.AnalysisServices.AdomdClient.CellSet
Parsing complete
```

Assuming you have passed your syntax check, go ahead and execute the query. You will find an Execute option on the query editor's shortcut menu, the Query branch of the menu, or the SQL Server Analysis Services Editors toolbar. You can also press the F5 key or Ctrl+E on your keyboard to execute the MDX query.

Tip   As with the Management Studio Database Engine Query (SQL query) window, the MDX query window executes as a query whatever text is selected, or it executes the entire editor's contents if no text is selected within it. The Parse option behaves this way as well. You should therefore make sure that no text (or all text) is selected in the MDX query editor when you parse or execute your query.

After you execute your query, the result is displayed on a new Results tab in the Results pane of the MDX query editor and should look similar to Figure 18-28.

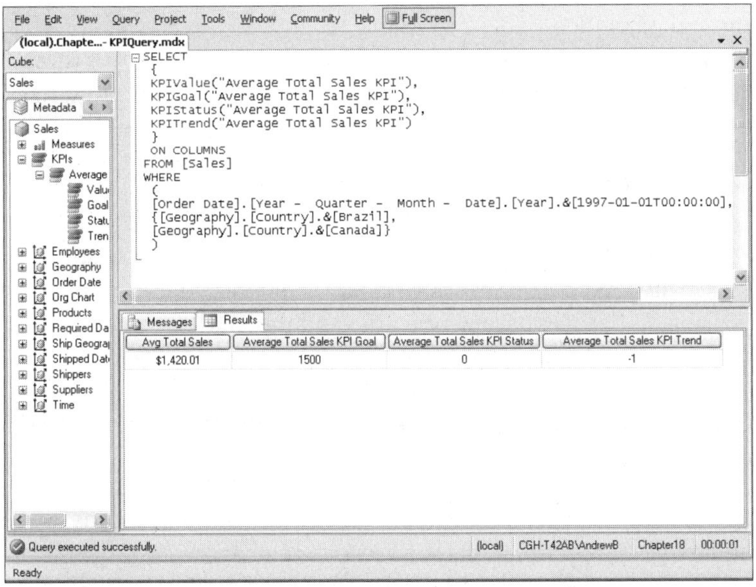

Figure 18-28   The MDX Query window with KPI-revealing MDX query text and results shown

Compare the output to the KPI browser view of the cube designer back in our Analysis Services project in Visual Studio, and you will see that they are essentially the same. One obvious exception is that the status value is displayed numerically rather than graphically. In your own application, you can write code to execute this MDX query and render the KPI status and trend data graphically through conditional interpretation of the KPI values.

> **More Info**   You'll notice that this query returns a non-*NULL* value for trend (specifically, a value of –1). If you run the same query for calendar 1996, you will see that the average total sales for that period was $1987.43. Therefore, the KPI value for calendar 1997 ($1420.01) is in fact a decrease over the prior period, and –1 is the correct trend result.
>
> If you run the query for calendar 1998, you will see that the KPI value rises to $1787.37 and the KPI trend formula correctly returns a value of 1. The trend returned for calendar 1996 is *NULL*, which is correct because we have no data in the cube for what would be the previous period (calendar 1995).
>
> The cube designer's KPI browser filters data in such a way that prior period data is not available, resulting in a *NULL* return value (and no graphic) for all filter conditions. MDX queries do not (and your own applications will not) exhibit this same defect.

Other BI Tricks in Management Studio

We still need to discuss adding actions, perspectives, translations, and roles to our cube, and how to manage their storage. Before we do so, however, let's examine what other OLAP-related tasks we can accomplish in Management Studio.

To start with, expand the Chapter18 database's node in the Object Explorer window. You should see child nodes appear for the database's data sources, data source views, cubes, dimensions, mining structures, roles, and assemblies. These are, of course, the same high-level nodes that appear in the Solution Explorer window for an Analysis Services project in Visual Studio. Although Management Studio does not offer full design control over these elements, you can enumerate each of them and view their properties in multi-page property sheets by right-clicking any of them and selecting the Properties shortcut menu option.

By using the objects' shortcut menus, you can browse dimensions and cubes in Management Studio just as if you were in Visual Studio (just as you can browse mining structures and mining models, which we'll cover in Chapter 20). You can also process objects and add and configure partitions. We will cover partitions shortly, but we mention these options now so you know they are available in both Management Studio and the Analysis Services designers in Visual Studio.

XMLA Scripts in Management Studio and Visual Studio Analysis Services Projects

You can also generate XMLA scripts for objects by using their shortcut menus. By generating scripts for individual objects, or entire Analysis Services databases, you can easily migrate your databases to other servers. You can then transmit the scripts to other developers and/or keep them in source control by organizing the scripts within Management Studio Analysis Services Scripts projects.

> **More Info**   Management Studio offers source control integration through the Source Control\Plug-in Selection tree view item in its Options dialog box. (Choose Tools/Options from the main menu.)

To get a feel for what XMLA scripts look like, drill down to the *Products* dimension in the Object Explorer window, right-click on it, and choose Script Dimension As/CREATE To/New Query Editor Window from the shortcut menu. The XMLA script for the dimension appears in a new XMLA query window. Notice that each facet of the dimension is meticulously described within the various XML elements in the body of the document.

Now return to our Visual Studio Analysis Services project and drill down to and select the Products.dim dimension node in the Solution Explorer window. Right-click this node and select the View Code option from its shortcut menu or choose View/Code from the main menu. You will see that nearly the same XML content is displayed. This similarity reveals that the Visual Studio Analysis Services project designers are merely GUI front ends to the XMLA scripts that are necessary to create the objects on an Analysis Services server. When you deploy your project from Visual Studio, you are essentially executing the scripts generated by the designers. XMLA scripts can also be executed in Management Studio; to do so you simply use one of the Execute menu or toolbar options from within the XMLA query editor window.

Actions

You might have noticed a pattern emerging in our study of calculations and KPIs: Analysis Services allows you to store a variety of things in your cube that you could, if called upon to do so, create within your own application or queries. Think about it: Your calculations simply represent a collection of commands that make up an MDX script, and each of your KPIs is, in effect, a collection of MDX expressions and literal values (description, status graphic name, trend graphic name) that you could store and evaluate on the client side.

But by that logic, views, functions, and stored procedures in relational databases could be handled by your applications as well. Of course, we use those server-side facilities because DBAs can design, secure, and provide them to a range of applications and users. Similarly, Analysis Services offers calculations and KPIs to put their management and security in the hands of DBAs and to make them available to anyone consuming your Analysis Services databases.

We will now quickly cover actions, which are yet another server-side, MDX-based object type.

Actions Simply Defined

You can think of actions as context-sensitive external commands. In other words, actions allow you to store an MDX-based template that, when evaluated, evaluates to a command string of one form or another. Actions are associated with objects in your cube, whether they be structural objects—such as measures, attributes, hierarchies, levels, or their members—or actual cells in the cube. The types of commands range from drillthrough queries that extract a cell's underlying data from the relational database, to URLs that embed a cell or member's value, to SQL or command-line strings that can also embed a cell or member's value.

Actions are defined on the Actions tab of the cube designer, and they appear in the cube browser on shortcut menus. From your own applications, you can enumerate actions and compute their values through programmatic techniques we will discuss in the next chapter.

Designing Actions

The cube designer's Actions tab, like its Calculations and KPIs tabs, consists of an Organizer pane (Actions Organizer, in this case), a Calculation Tools pane, and a form that you must complete in order to fully describe the action you are creating or editing. Unlike the Calculations and KPIs tabs, however, the Actions tab has only a form view; there is no script view or browser view. By now you should be familiar with the meaning and mechanics of editing the fields in form view, so we can proceed with creating a couple of actions without a lot of background discussion.

Start by creating a drillthrough action by selecting the Cube/New Drillthrough Action option on the main menu or clicking the New Drillthrough Action button (fourth from the right) on the Actions tab's toolbar. Enter **Total Sales Drillthrough** for the Name field (no brackets necessary), select Main from the Measure Group Members drop-down list, leave the Condition field blank and, in a new row in the Drillthrough Columns grid, select MEASURES in the Dimensions column and Total Sales in the Return Columns column. (You can do this by clicking the drop-down arrow, selecting the Total Sales item in the popup window, and then clicking its OK button.) The form should appear as shown in Figure 18-29.

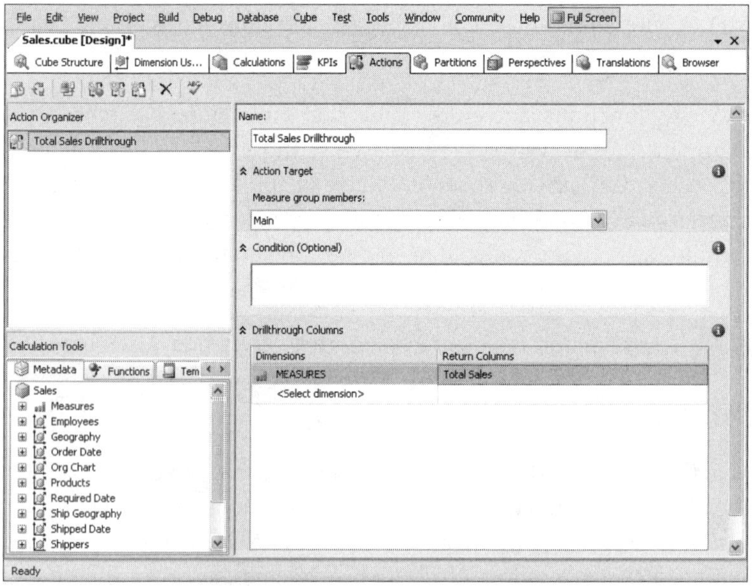

Figure 18-29   The cube designer's Actions tab, with a drillthrough action fully configured

This creates an action that allows you to right-click any cell in the cube browser and see in a popup window the Total Sales data for each row in the fact table that underlies it.

Next, add a (regular) action by selecting the Cube/New Action option on the main menu or clicking the New Action button (fourth from the left) on the Actions tab's toolbar. Enter **MSN Search** in the Name field, select Level Members from the Target Type drop-down list (if it is not already selected), and select Geography.Country - State-Province - City - Postal Code.City in the Target Object drop-down list. (Click the drop-down arrow, drill down to and select the appropriate node in the dimension browser popup window, and click OK.) Leave the condition expression blank, select URL from the Type drop-down list (if it is not already selected) in the Action Content section, and enter the following in the Action Expression field:

```
"http://search.msn.com/results.aspx?q=" + [Geography].[City].CURRENTMEMBER.NAME
```

The form should appear as shown in Figure 18-30.

This action generates a URL that navigates to the MSN Search Web site and performs a search on the selected city's name. By right-clicking any city in the row or column headers in the cube designer's Browser tab, you can select the action from the shortcut menu and bring up the corresponding URL in Microsoft Internet Explorer.

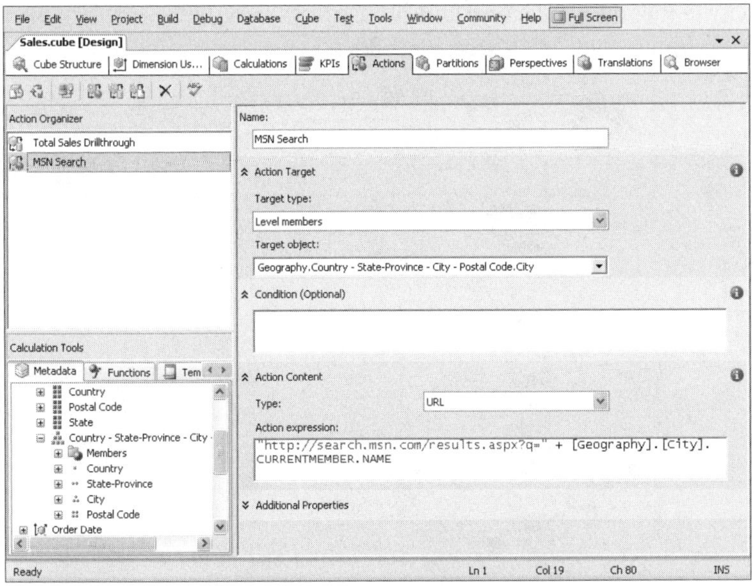

Figure 18-30   The cube designer's Actions tab, this time showing a fully configured URL action

Testing Actions

You can test your actions by saving and deploying your changes and then entering the Browser tab of the cube designer. Drag the Total Sales measure to the detail fields area, and drag the City level of the Country - State-Province - City - Postal Code hierarchy of the Geography dimension (*not* the City attribute of the *Geography* dimension) to the row fields area. Right-click any cell in the data area and choose Total Sales Drillthrough from the shortcut menu to view the drill-through query results for that cell in a popup window (as shown in Figure 18-31).

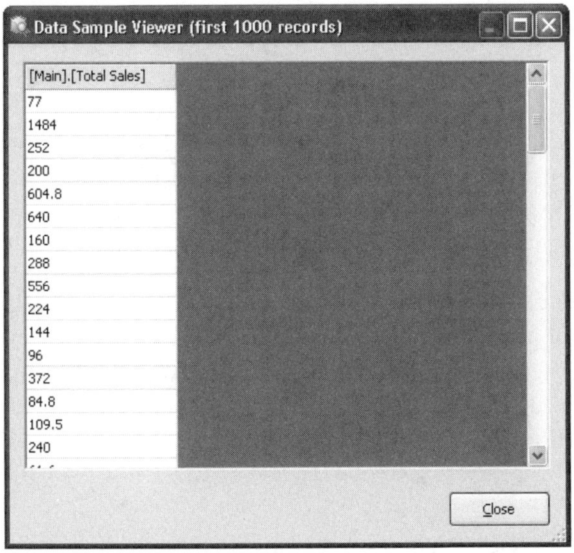

Figure 18-31   The Data Sample Viewer window, invoked from a drillthrough action on a cell in the cube browser

Right-click any city in the row header area and choose MSN Search (as shown in Figure 18-32) from the shortcut menu to view MSN search results for that city's name in Internet Explorer.

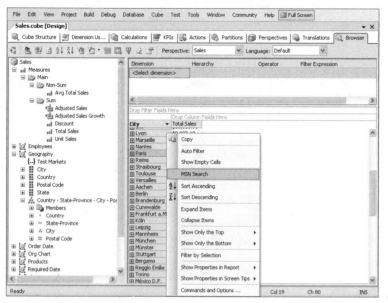

Figure 18-32   URL actions appear as shortcut menu options on their target objects (level members, in this case) in the cube browser.

Experiment with the other action types and consider using actions extensively in your cubes. OLAP is all about drill-down analysis, and what better drill-down functionality is there than providing your users with detailed information about cube data from other applications, databases, and the Web?

Partitions, Aggregation Design, Storage Settings, and Proactive Caching

Cubes are great, and having all that BI data in one place is convenient, but sometimes parts of your cube will have different demands placed on them than other parts. Analysis Services partitions allow you to slice your cube physically and use specific storage and aggregation settings that are appropriate to each subset of your cube's data and the unique demands placed on it.

For example, if users rarely need data older than a certain date, you might store that data on a slower (cheaper) disk, process it much less frequently, and perhaps precalculate many fewer aggregations than you would for recent data. You might also or instead want to implement such physical separation of your cube's storage along product lines, geography, or any combination of dimensional criteria. Partitions allow you to do just that.

Analysis Services 2005 partitions allow you to define their content (or "source") by specifying a fact table that the partition should be based on or a SQL query that selects only a subset of the rows from a fact table. You can then configure various aspects of the partition's processing and storage as well as its aggregation design.

Every cube consists of at least one partition (or, to be more precise, at least one partition per measure group), so you need to be familiar with partition configuration even if you don't want to "partition" your cube (in the ordinary sense of the word). In fact, we will concentrate on a single partition scenario using our Northwind *Sales* cube for the remainder of this section.

Editing and Creating Partitions

If you click the Partitions tab of the cube designer, you will find that a partition for the *Sales* cube has already been defined. The existing partition is built on our fact table, tblFact, without any filtering query defined for row selection. Storage and processing locations are set to the Analysis Services defaults; you can modify them in the Partition Type Selection dialog box (see Figure 18-33) by selecting the partition's row in the designer's grid and then selecting the *StorageLocation* property in the Properties window and clicking the ellipsis button in its value column.

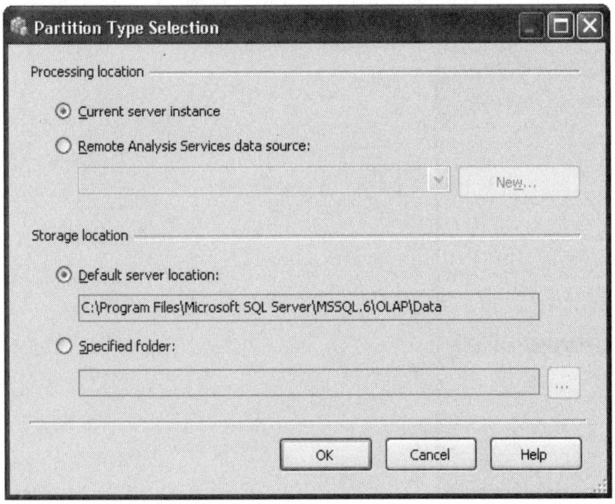

Figure 18-33   The Partition Type Selection dialog box

You can modify partition content by clicking in the partition's cell in the Source column of the designer's grid and clicking its ellipsis button or selecting the partition's *Source* property in the Properties window and clicking the ellipsis button in its Value column (Figure 18-34).

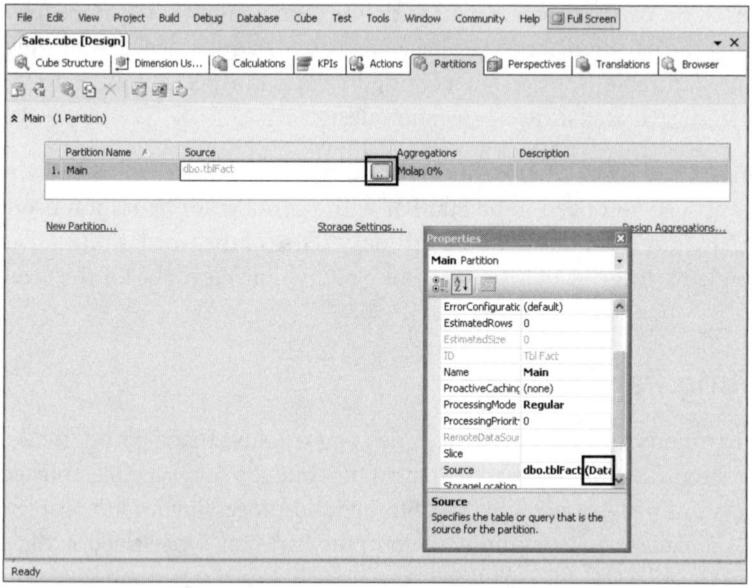

Figure 18-34   The cube designer Partitions tab, with the Partition Source dialog box ellipsis buttons highlighted

Either approach opens the Partition Source dialog box in table binding view (Figure 18-35).

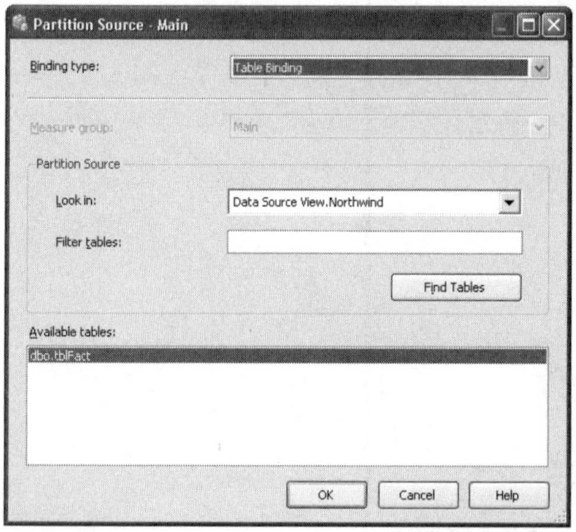

Figure 18-35   The Partition Source dialog box in table binding view

Select the Query Binding option from the Binding Type drop-down list to bring up the query binding view. The table binding view lets you define your partition based on the contents of an entire fact table, whereas the query binding view allows you to specify a SQL query that might select only a subset of rows. When you're done examining these options, click the dialog box's Cancel button because we don't want to modify our partition's source.

> **More Info**   You might also be interested in exploring the Partition Wizard, which provides an alternative interface for setting many of the properties mentioned here—but only for new partitions. You can do so by clicking the New Partition toolbar button (third from the left), the New Partition... hyperlink, the Cube/New Partition... main menu option, or the New Partition... shortcut menu option.
>
> You might not be able to fully explore each wizard page unless you delete the existing partition, thus freeing up the fact table to be used in a new partition. If you do this, be sure to close the cube designer after you delete the existing partition and then *discard* your changes. This will ensure that the existing partition is *not* actually deleted from the cube.

In addition to these partition properties, you can also modify storage settings and aggregation design, as we'll discuss next.

Aggregation Design

Aggregation design lets you specify a limit on the number of precalculated aggregations stored in your cube as a function of disk space or percentage performance gain. Alternatively, you can start building the aggregations manually and manually end the process; in this case, the aggregations are limited by processing time rather than by disk cost or performance gain.

You configure aggregation settings using the Aggregation Design Wizard, which you can invoke from the Design Aggregations toolbar button (third from the right), the Design Aggregations... hyperlink, the Cube/Design Aggregations... main menu option, or the Design Aggregations...shortcut menu option. You specify all aggregation design settings on the wizard's Set Aggregation Options page, which is the second-to-last page in the wizard.

Before you reach the Set Aggregation Options page, you must define the medium for your cube's storage and the way it is cached on the Specify Storage And Caching Options page, which appears immediately after the Welcome page. You can also set these options in the Partition Storage Settings dialog box (Figure 18-36).

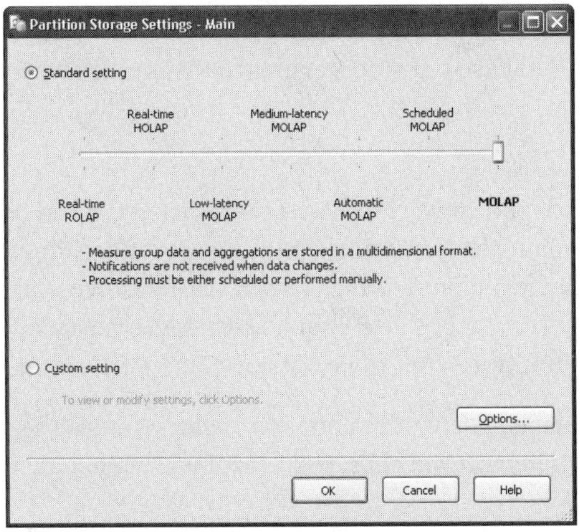

Figure 18-36   The Partition Storage Settings dialog box

You can open the Partition Storage Settings dialog box when a specific partition is selected by selecting the Storage Settings toolbar button (on the far right), the Storage Settings... hyperlink, the Cube/Storage Settings... main menu option, or the Storage Settings... shortcut menu option. You can also select the partition's *ProactiveCaching* property in the Properties window and then click the ellipsis button in its value column.

> **More Info**   You can also modify a partition's storage settings by editing the individual child properties of the *ProactiveCaching* property. However, the Partition Storage Settings dialog box and the Storage And Caching Options page of the Aggregation Design Wizard provide a much friendlier UI.

The fact that partition storage options are simply configured through a dialog box (or wizard page) can be misleading. The dialog box and wizard page actually offer an enormously rich set of options that can take a while to fully appreciate. The dialog box is also, in effect, a dashboard for controlling what is arguably the most important feature of Analysis Services: proactive caching.

It is impossible to do justice to the proactive caching feature in a book that does not focus exclusively on BI. What's more, you can leave these settings at their default values and still work productively with Analysis Services 2005 cubes. But we will attempt to convey a simple overview of what these settings control and how they work.

Partition Storage Options

In the SQL Server 7.0 OLAP Services and SQL Server 2000 Analysis Services days there were three types of storage: Multidimensional OLAP (MOLAP), Relational OLAP (ROLAP), and Hybrid OLAP (HOLAP). With MOLAP (the default), all fact and aggregation data are stored in the Analysis Services multidimensional store, which provides the fastest query response times. ROLAP, in which facts stay in the relational database's fact table and aggregations are stored in special relational tables of their own, provides for faster cube processing times (for obvious reasons) but slower query response times. HOLAP, a sort of compromise option, keeps the facts data in the relational database but stores aggregations multidimensionally.

Proactive Caching

MOLAP, ROLAP, and HOLAP have not gone away in Analysis Services 2005, but their limitations are mitigated by the proactive caching feature. For example, proactive caching allows you to use ROLAP as your underlying storage medium (which ensures faster processing time and thus accommodates real-time, or near-real-time, OLAP) but instructs Analysis Services to cache your cube in the MOLAP medium (for better query performance).

You choose how often the cache is flushed. Depending on your cache settings, the MOLAP cube can be immediately invalidated when certain changes to the underlying data warehouse are made. In this case, queries are fulfilled against the base ROLAP cube; the MOLAP version is reprocessed in the background, and then it's swapped back in when processing is complete. You can also configure things such that the outdated ("stale") MOLAP data continues to be used while updated MOLAP data is being rebuilt and processed. This enhances performance (because MOLAP storage continues to be used) but decreases freshness of data.

As you can see in the Partition Storage Settings dialog box, proactive caching allows for a "spectrum" of seven standard settings, ranging from Real-Time ROLAP on the left to pure, non-cached MOLAP on the right. All but the last option set a degree of caching and automatic processing of your partition. As you move the slider between the settings, you see new text appear in the dialog box, below the slider control, with a high-level description of the current setting. For an even more detailed view of these settings click the Options button, which brings up the Storage Options dialog box (Figure 18-37).

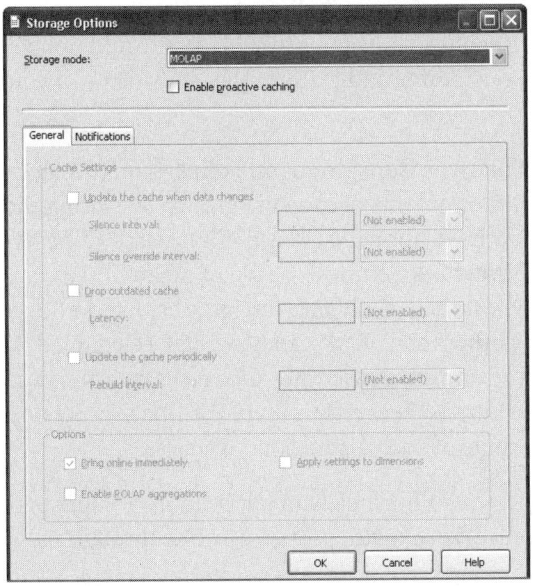

Figure 18-37   The Storage Options dialog box

On the General tab of the Storage Options dialog box you can view the specific cache update and latency intervals. The Notifications tab lets you specify particular tables or SQL queries to monitor for data changes. You get a huge amount of granular control in this dialog box. Take your time getting acquainted with it. These tuning options let you strike the perfect balance between performance, freshness of data, and real-time availability of data. If you get things right here, you will be a hero to your entire organization—no exaggeration.

If you modify any of the preconfigured settings in the Storage Options dialog box, you automatically shift from using one of the seven standard settings to using a custom setting (unless you happen to configure the individual settings to match exactly one of the other six standard settings). Try it yourself and see: Change one of the settings slightly, and then click OK. When you return to the Partition Storage Settings dialog box, you will see that the Custom Setting option button, rather than the Standard Setting option button, is selected and the slider control is disabled.

> **Note**   You can also configure storage settings at the cube, database dimension, and measure group level rather than at the partition level. You can edit cube-level or measure-group-level settings in the cube designer: Just select a cube or measure group node on a tab that has one (for example, the two root nodes of the Measures tree view in the Cube Structure tab) and click the ellipsis button in the Value column of the *ProactiveCaching* property in the Properties window. You can similarly configure dimension storage options through the Properties window, but in the dimension designer rather than in the cube designer.

Additional Features and Tips

Our coverage of partitions, proactive caching, and aggregation design would not be complete without mentioning a few miscellaneous points and features that are worthy of your further exploration, as time permits.

First, a word on writeback (write-enabled) measure groups and dimensions. Analysis Services permits users to modify their view of the contents of measure groups by storing those modifications in special writeback tables in the relational database. Choose the Cube/Writeback Settings... main menu option or the Writeback Settings... shortcut menu option to specify the data source and table for writeback storage. Only measure groups that do not contain special aggregates (that is, aggregates other than *SUM*) can be writeback-enabled. Our measure group, because it contains the non-sum-based *Avg Total Sales* measure, is not writeback-enabled; however, the *Sales Targets* measure group of the Analysis Services sample Adventure Works cube is a good example of such a partition.

You can also write-enable dimensions, thus allowing client applications to update their contents, by simply setting the dimension's *WriteEnabled* property to *True* through the Properties window in the dimension designer.

And one last tip: In Management Studio, you can create partitions and change storage/writeback settings at the dimension, partition, and cube level. Management Studio's property sheets let you modify these settings so you don't have to use Visual Studio to change them after deploying your cube.

Perspectives

As we mentioned previously, one hallmark of Analysis Services 2005 is its flexibility and accommodating nature. For example, the ability to have drillthrough actions, role-playing dimensions, and multiple fact tables allows you to use a single cube for a multitude of multidimensional *and* relational queries. With Analysis Services 2000, each fact table requires its own cube, role-playing dimensions do not exist, drillthrough functionality is much more limited, and the lack of proactive caching means that cube data cannot be as fresh as is sometimes necessary.

This notion of a single cube acting as a one-stop shop for all your dimensional data gives rise to an Analysis Services 2005 concept called the *unified dimensional model* (UDM). The UDM paradigm advocates softening the distinction between dimensional and relational data and promotes an outlook, if you will, that a cube is more than just a cube. The UDM philosophy sees a properly built Analysis Services 2005 cube as a comprehensive repository for all aggregated and fact-level data.

That's all well and good, but the UDM paradigm causes an issue of its own: If you jam too much stuff into a single cube, many of your users might become overwhelmed by the content of that cube and therefore find it less useful. For this reason, Analysis Services 2005 introduces the ability to create *perspectives* within your cubes.

Perspectives are simply filtered views of a cube's content. You define a perspective by picking a set of specific measure groups (or specific measures), dimensions (or individual attributes and hierarchies), calculations, KPIs, and actions for the perspective and assigning it a name. Client applications treat perspectives as if they are separate physical cubes. You can, for example, combine sales, inventory, and HR information into a single cube, and then publish each category of data as a separate perspective. This gives you the simplicity and power of the UDM paradigm without dispensing with the ability to deploy components of your dimensional data as discrete units that appear as cubes in their own right.

Creating a perspective is easy. Simply click on the Perspectives tab of the cube designer and click the New Perspective toolbar button (second from the right), the Cube/New Perspective main menu option, or the New Perspective shortcut menu option. Any of these actions creates a new column on the Perspective tab's grid. From there, you enter the name of your perspective and then select all of the cube objects you want to include. For now, create a new perspective called *Product Info* and assign it the entire *Main* measure group, the *Products* and *Suppliers* dimensions, the *Average Total Sales KPI* KPI, the *Total Sales Drillthrough* action, and the two calculated measures (*Adjusted Sales* and *Adjusted Sales Growth*).

Save and deploy your changes. In the cube browser, first reconnect (you might have to do this more than once to see the changes), and then notice that the Perspective drop-down list now contains two items: Sales (the physical cube) and Product Info (the perspective we just created). Select Product Info from the drop-down list, and notice that in the metadata tree view only the cube's measures (including the two calculated measures) and the two dimensions we selected when defining the perspective are listed, as shown in Figure 18-38.

Note also that the calculated measures are both listed under the Sum display folder because the Calculation Properties settings illustrated in Figure 18-23 were applied to the *Sales* cube, and they cascade through to the perspective as well.

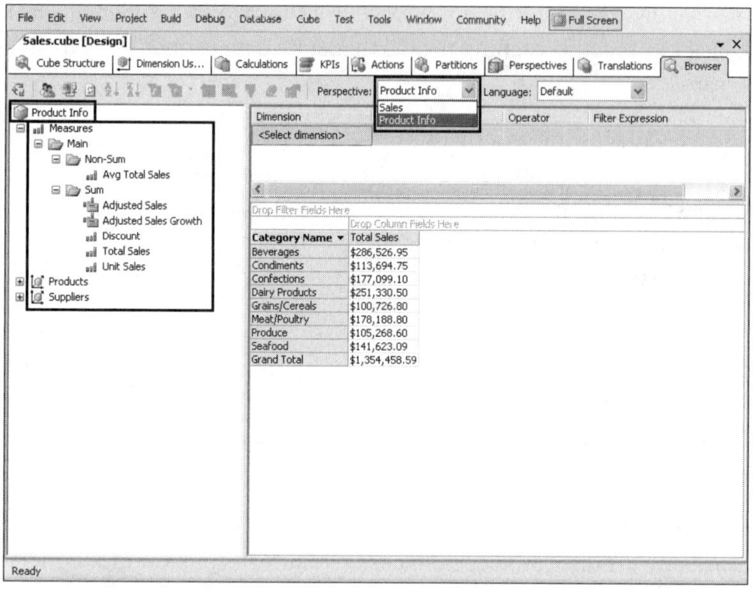

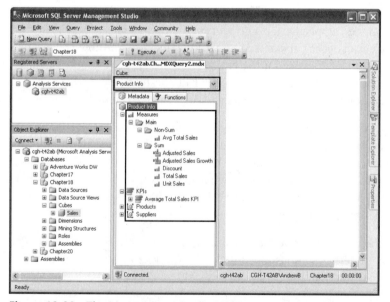

Figure 18-38   The cube browser with the Product Info perspective selected and highlighted

In Management Studio, the Object Explorer window enumerates only the physical cubes in an Analysis Services database. However, the MDX query window lists the perspectives in the Cubes drop-down list (and because the *Product Info* perspective precedes the *Sales* cube alphabetically, the former will be selected by default). The Metadata tab lists just the measures (including calculated measures), dimensions, and KPIs, if any, that belong to the selected perspective or cube, as shown in Figure 18-39.

Figure 18-39   The Management Studio MDX query window shown with the Product Info perspective selected and highlighted

Perspectives provide an audience-targeted experience for your cubes, and they do so through server-side configuration, easing the burden on application developers. This notion of a *server-enforced* customized view of a cube can be extended. For example, language localization of the names of your cube's objects and the cube's contents can be governed on the server as well. You can accomplish this by creating Analysis Services 2005 *translations*. Also, enforcement, in the true sense of the word, is made possible by creating security *roles* that include declaratively specified membership and cube object-level permissions. The remaining sections of this chapter will cover translations and roles.

Translations

Much like you do with perspectives, you define translations on their own tab in the cube designer, in a grid containing distinct rows for each object in the cube, with each translation occupying its own column in the grid. Rather than soliciting a name and providing check boxes next to each object, however, the Translations tab solicits a language and culture and provides an editable cell for the translated name of each object.

For our exercise, click on the Translations tab, and then click the New Translation toolbar button (*second from the right*), the Cube/New Translation... main menu option, or the New Translation... shortcut menu option. Select Spanish (Spain) in the Select Language dialog box, and then click OK. A translation should contain localized strings for each object in the cube, but we will translate just the *Time* dimension (the original, table-based one that we defined in Chapter 17, rather than any of the server time dimensions we added in this chapter) for this exercise. Type **Tiempo** in the cell at the intersection of the Spanish (Spain) translation's column and the Time dimension row, as shown in Figure 18-40.

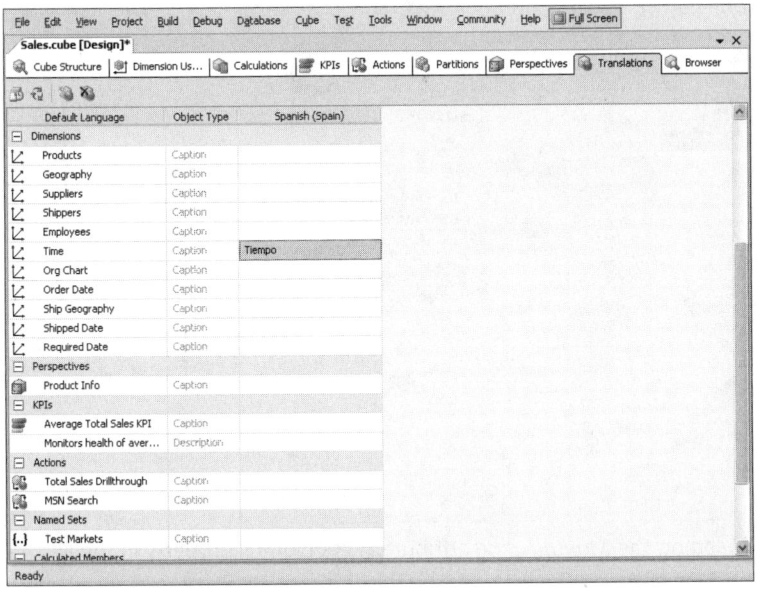

Figure 18-40 The Translations tab with the Time dimension translation entry for Spanish (Spain)

Our work on the Translations tab is finished, but our work in defining the translation is not. We still need to define translated names for each attribute and hierarchy, and we need to explore how to provide translations for members within the attributes. All attributes of our *Time* dimension happen to be numeric, so let's add a new attribute that displays the name of the month rather than its number. Then we can look at how to provide Spanish translations for each member of the new attribute.

To create the attribute, first run the script tblMonthNames.sql, which is contained in the Management Studio solution included with this chapter's sample code. This adds to the Northwind database a table called tblMonthNames that contains, in separate columns, English and Spanish names for each month of the year, as well as the corresponding month number. After the script has run, add the tblMonthNames table to the Northwind data source view with the data source view designer's Add/Remove Objects toolbar button (on the far left), the Data Source View/[Add/Remove Tables...] main menu option, or the Add/Remove Tables... shortcut menu option. Then create a relationship from tblTime.Month to tblMonthNames.MonthNumber. (Click Yes when asked if you'd like to create a logical primary key.) Save your changes and click OK when asked if you'd like to proceed in updating the *Sales* cube as well.

Next, open the *Time* dimension in its designer and show the tblMonthNames table in the Data Source View pane, using the Data Source View/Show Tables... main menu option, the Show Tables... option on the shortcut menu, or the Show Table toolbar button (fifth from the left). Now create a new attribute by dragging and dropping the English Month Name field from the tblMonthNames table in the Data Source View pane onto the Attributes pane. Rename the new attribute from *English Month Name* to **Month Name** and change its *OrderBy* property to *Key*. Change its *KeyColmns* property to *tblMonthNames.MonthNumber* by clicking the property's ellipsis button and changing the *Source.ColumnId* property in the DataItem Collection Editor dialog box (Figure 18-41) and clicking OK.

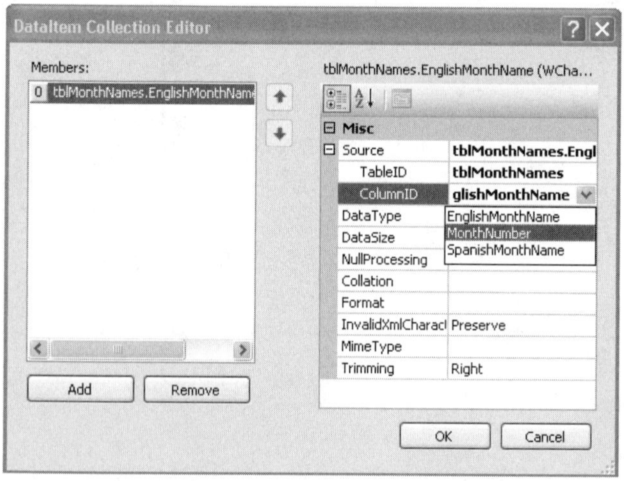

Figure 18-41   Changing the *Month Name* attribute's *KeyColumns* property in the DataItem Collection Editor dialog box

Finally, change the *Month Name* attribute's *NameColumn* property to *tblMonthNames.English-MonthName*.

Now onto the translations work. Click the *dimension designer's* Translations tab, and then add a new translation (using any of the options discussed earlier for adding the cube's translation). As in the cube designer, select Spanish (Spain) in the Select Language dialog box, and then click OK. Now enter the following Spanish strings for the dimension, each of its attributes, and its hierarchy:

Object	Translated Name
Time (dimension)	Tiempo
Year (attribute)	Año
Quarter (attribute)	Trimestre
Month (attribute)	Mes
OrderDate (attribute)	Fecha de la Orden
Time Key (attribute)	Llave de Tiempo
Month Name (attribute)	Nombre del Mes
Year - Quarter - Month - OrderDate (hierarchy)	Año - Cuarto - Mes - Fecha de la Orden

Tip   To type the *ñ* in *año*, open Notepad or Microsoft Word, and hold down the Alt key while entering the number 164 on your keyboard's numeric keypad. Then cut and paste the character from your document into the dimension designer's Translations tab.

Tip   Translation strings entered for attributes are automatically copied into the cells of any corresponding user hierarchy levels. You can manually overwrite these default level translations if you want.

We have entered a translated name for each attribute but have not yet specified the translated names for the *members* of the new *MonthName* attribute. Member names are not static; they are derived from data in the dimension table, so their translated names must be data-driven as well. We must, in effect, inform Analysis Services that the Spanish translation should use the tblMonthNames.SpanishMonthName column for the *Month Name* attribute in place of the EnglishMonthName column.

Doing so is quite easy: Simply click in the Nombre del Mes cell in the Translations tab grid, and then click the ellipsis button that becomes visible to open the Attribute Data Translation dialog box. In the Translation Columns tree view, select the SpanishMonthName column, as shown in Figure 18-42.

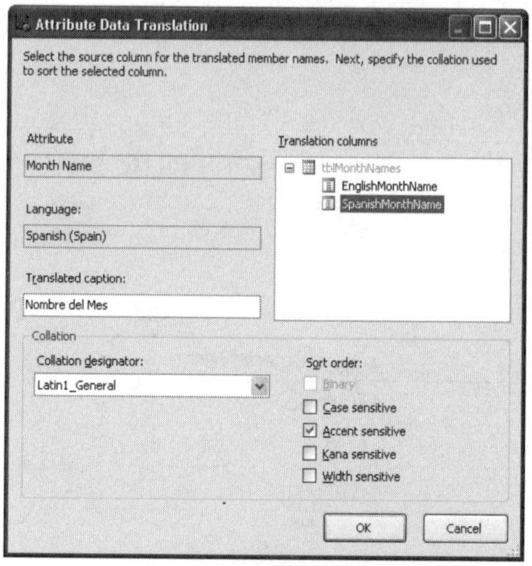

Figure 18-42 Configuring Nombre del Mes members in the Attribute Data Translation dialog box

Now click OK. A special table icon will appear at the left side of the Nombre del Mes cell, as shown in Figure 18-43.

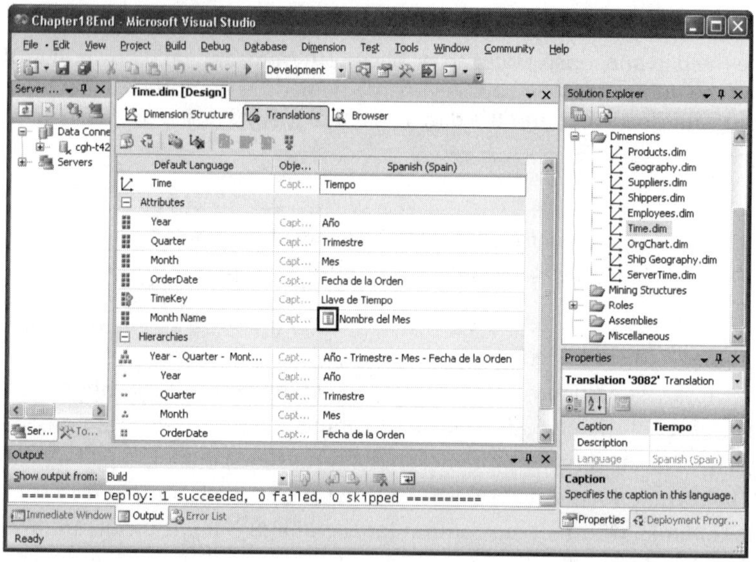

Figure 18-43 The Translations tab of the dimension designer with the attribute data translation icon highlighted

Save and deploy your changes, and then check them on the Browser tab of the dimension designer. (We'll also do this in the cube browser shortly.) Select Spanish (Spain) from the Languages drop-down list, and then click the drop-down arrow for the Hierarchy list. Before making a selection, notice that each attribute and hierarchy appears with its translated name. Select Nombre del Mes, and then drill down on the All node in the browser tree view. Notice that each month name appears in Spanish and that the months are sorted chronologically. Change Language back to Default to see each month name change to its corresponding name in English.

Now open the cube designer and click on the Browser tab. Reconnect, select Sales from the Perspectives drop-down list and, once again, select Spanish (Spain) from the Languages drop-down list. In the metadata tree view, notice that the Time dimension's name changes to *Tiempo*. Drill down on the dimension to reveal that all of the attribute names are displayed in Spanish. Drill down on the Nombre del Mes node and *its* Nombre del Mes child node to reveal that all member nodes are displayed in Spanish as well. Using the *Nombre del Mes* attribute in the query grid will demonstrate equally well that the Spanish names we've created are displayed in place of their English counterparts. All of this is illustrated in Figure 18-44.

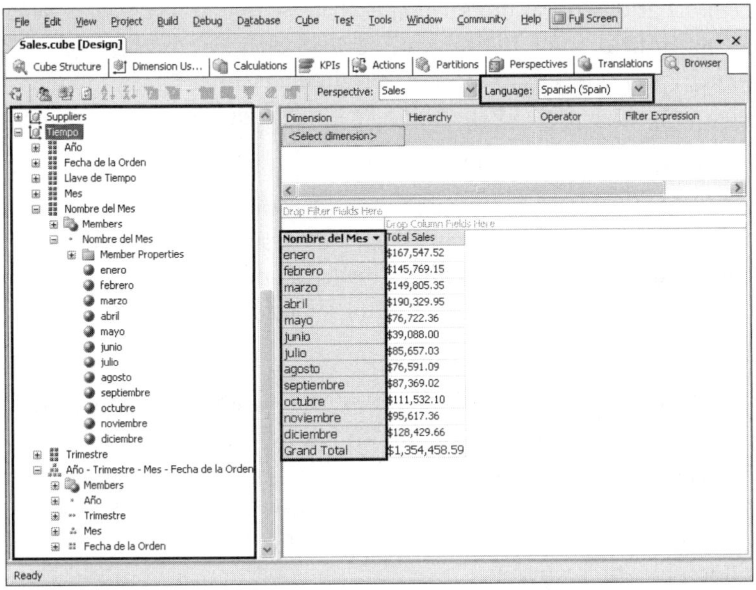

Figure 18-44   The cube browser, with the Language set to Spanish (Spain) and translated objects highlighted

Note that the *Total Sales* measure is displayed in the query grid in English because we provided no translation for it.

Another, perhaps better, way to test translations is by changing your workstation's local language and country settings. To do this, select the Regional and Language Options applet from the Windows Control Panel, change the Standards And Formats setting on the Regional Options tab to Spanish (Spain), and then click Apply. Close and reopen Visual Studio (and your project), and then enter the cube designer Browser tab (for the *Sales* cube). With Language set to Default—*not* to Spanish (Spain)—you should see the Time dimension appear as *Tiempo* and its child objects appear in Spanish as well.

This same technique will force the Metadata tab in the Management Studio MDX query window to display the dimension and its child objects in Spanish; in fact, this technique is the only way to do so. (To see this change, you must open a new MDX query window if one was open when you changed your workstation's regional settings, but you should not need to restart Management Studio itself.) When you're done experimenting, go back to the Regional And Language Options applet, switch back to your normal language and culture setting, and then click OK. Close and reopen the Management Studio MDX query window, as well as Visual Studio and your Analysis Services project, and everything should return to English.

Roles

Perspectives and translations allow specific groups of users to see customized views of your cubes, but only real security settings can prevent users from seeing specific items in your physical cubes. By defining one or more roles in your Analysis Services project, you can restrict the access that specific users or groups have to certain data sources, cubes, dimensions, attributes, members, and even individual cube cells in your Analysis Services database.

You can block access to objects completely or limit users' permissions to read-only access; you can also control whether users in the role can process the entire database, specific cubes, and/or specific dimensions. Finally, you can assign administrator rights within the database to certain roles, and you can grant read access to the definitions of the entire database, its data sources, or dimensions. (You can assign many of these permissions for data mining models and structures as well.)

The basics of the role designer are fairly simple to learn. You add a new role to your project by clicking the New Role option on the Roles node's shortcut menu in the Solution Explorer window or by choosing the Project/New Role option from the main menu. Your role will be assigned a default name (both at the object level and the filename level), which you should change by using the Properties window or the Rename option on the role node's shortcut menu in the Solution Explorer window.

The role designer consists of several tabs where you define permissions for various Analysis Services objects. The General tab allows you to enter a description for the role and assign its database-level permissions: Full Control (Administrator), Process, and/or Read Definition. The Membership tab lets you specify which users and groups belong to the role. You use the tab's Add... button to specify the role's membership by using a standard Windows Select Users Or Groups dialog box.

The remaining tabs allow you to configure specific permissions for your database's data sources, cubes, cells, dimensions, dimension data (attribute members), and mining structures. You can also test your role, using a sort of simulated impersonation, via the Cell Data tab's Test Cube Security hyperlink.

To test this feature for yourself, add a role to our cube and name it **NAmericaNoOrderDate** (because it will limit the *Geography* dimension to enumerate only North American countries and will hide all attributes of the *Order Date* dimension). On the General tab, enter a description if you like, and leave all check boxes unchecked. (We do not want to assign any database-level permissions to this role.) You can assign specific users and/or groups to this role on the Membership tab, but this is not strictly necessary because we will be testing this role only through the Test Cube Security facility (covered shortly). It is also unnecessary to make any adjustments on the Data Sources tab.

Skip to the Cell Data tab, and note that the Cube drop-down list is empty. To address this, select the Cubes tab and set the Access level for the *Sales* cube to Read, as shown in Figure 18-45.

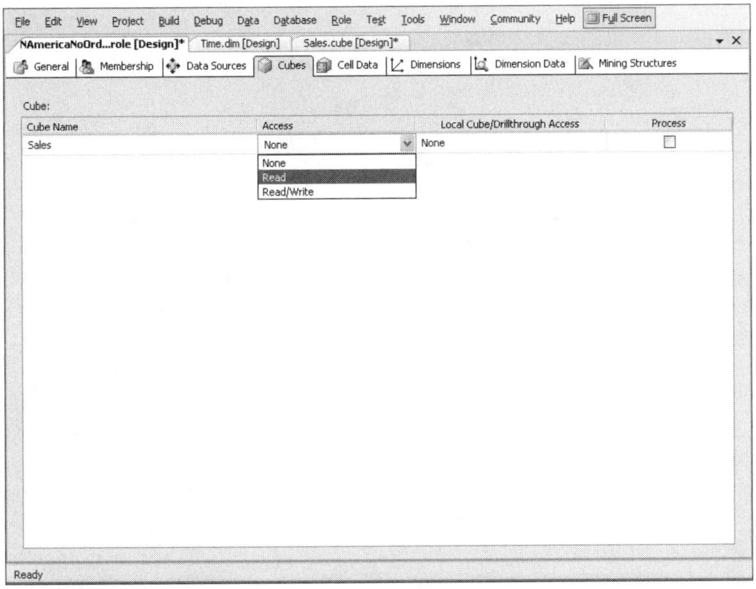

Figure 18-45   The Cubes tab of the role designer, showing Access for the *Sales* cube being set to Read

Reselect the Cell Data tab (Figure 18-46), and note that the *Sales* cube is now listed in the Cube drop-down list.

Now click on the Dimension Data tab. From the Dimension drop-down list, select the *Geography* dimension of the *Sales* cube (not the *Geography* dimension of the Chapter18 database). From the Attribute Hierarchy drop-down list, select the *Country* attribute. Click the Deselect All Members option button to clear the check boxes next to each country, and then manually select the check boxes next to Canada, Mexico, and USA, as shown in Figure 18-47.

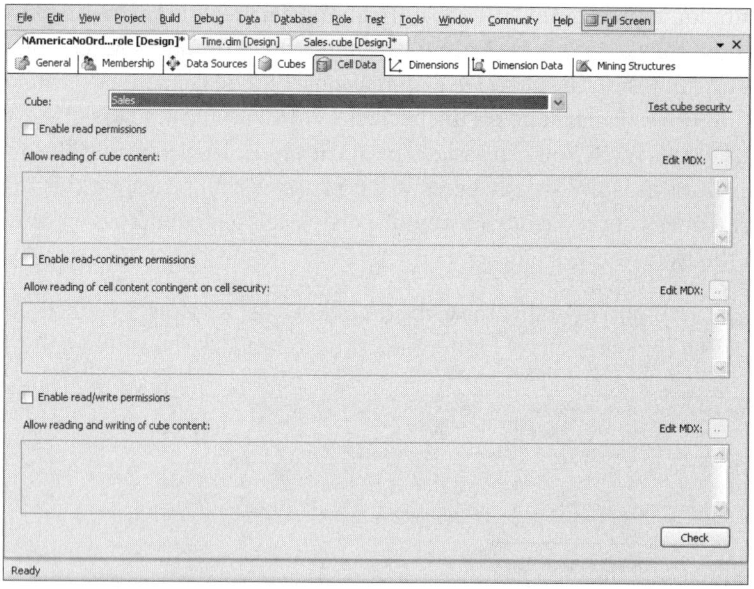

Figure 18-46   The Cell Data tab of the role designer, with the *Sales* cube selected

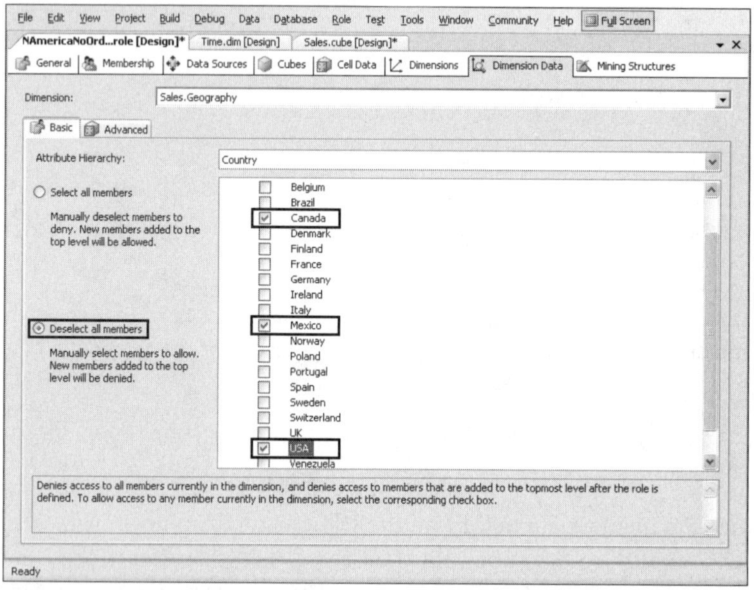

Figure 18-47   The Basic tab within the Dimension Data tab of the role designer, with attribute-level security for the *Sales* cube's *Geography.Country* attribute highlighted

Select the *Sales.Order Date* dimension (again, be sure to scroll down through the dimension list past the database dimensions to the cube dimensions), and then for *each* of its attributes (10 in all) click the Deselect All Members option button, and do not manually select any members. Click the Advanced tab, and note that it is possible to specify allowed (or denied) members by entering MDX expressions rather than manually selecting (or deselecting) each member on the Basic tab.

Save and deploy your changes, and then click back on the Cell Data tab, where you will notice that a set of three check boxes and MDX expressions are available to enable read, read contingent, and read/write permissions for the cells in the cube.

Click the Test Cube Security hyperlink in the upper right. This opens a new window within Visual Studio containing the cube browser that is connected to the database under a simulated login emulating that of members of the role. (An information icon and descriptive text at the top of the window remind you of these details.) In the metadata tree view, drill down on the Members node for the *Country - State-Province - City - Postal Code* hierarchy of the *Geography* dimension and everything under the *Order Date* dimension. Canada, Mexico, and USA are the only members that appear for *Geography.Country - State-Province - City - Postal Code.Country*, and no members appear under any of the *Order Date* attributes or its hierarchy, as partially shown in Figure 18-48.

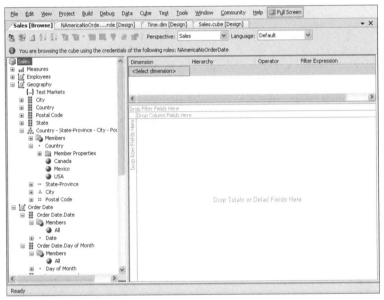

Figure 18-48 The cube browser as launched by the Test Cube Security hyperlink in the role designer's Cell Data tab

Summary

The advances in Analysis Services 2005 OLAP over the feature set in Analysis Services 2000 are nothing short of staggering. Numerous new dimension types, better drillthrough, and the addition of KPIs, perspectives, translations, and, most important, proactive caching make it far easier to build cubes and make those cubes more powerful and more relevant to business users. Combined with the new data mining features, these capabilities put Analysis Services 2005 on track to dominate the entire BI market and to expand that market to include many developers and users who have previously limited themselves to relational database technology.

You now know how to build sophisticated cubes. In the next chapter, we will show you how to develop applications that query cubes by using PivotTable components, ADO MD.NET, XML for Analysis (XMLA), and Analysis Management Objects (AMO). We'll also show you how to create server-side logic using the .NET CLR integration in Analysis Services.

Chapter 19
OLAP Application Development

—Andrew Brust

The previous two chapters introduced you to basic and more advanced Online Analytical Processing (OLAP) features in SQL Server Analysis Services 2005. Many of these features are truly groundbreaking; others are merely carryovers from earlier versions of the product, but even those are now more accessible. If you were planning to use end-user OLAP tools against your cubes, including the cube browser we worked with in each of the last two chapters, you'd be all set.

But the reality is that OLAP is most useful when its capabilities are integrated into your custom applications rather than delivered through special tools. So how *do* you work OLAP queries into your applications? What are the programming tools and APIs? What are the UI techniques? And how does the multidimensional expression language (MDX) work, anyway?

In this chapter, we'll give you the answers to these questions and more. Whether you want to query your cube from Microsoft Excel or write .NET code that queries your cube and its meta-data, this chapter has it covered. We'll show you how to connect Excel PivotTables to your cubes, introduce you to the MDX query language, and discuss the use of XML for Analysis (XMLA) as the native API in Analysis Services 2005. We'll show you how to program to XMLA directly and how to use ADO MD.NET (ADO.NET Multidimensional) and AMO (Analysis Management Objects) to build full-featured OLAP front ends in managed (.NET) code. We'll even show you how to write .NET code that runs on your Analysis Services server (which is similar to the SQL CLR programming we covered in Chapter 3).

This might seem like a lot for one chapter, but as you will see, all of these tools lie along a single continuum and build on each other. As you learn about each successive tool, your knowledge and understanding of the others will be enhanced.

About the Sample Code

The sample code for this chapter includes .NET code, MDX and XMLA scripts, a stand-alone HTML page (suitable for viewing in Microsoft Internet Explorer and editing in Microsoft FrontPage 2003), and even an Excel workbook file. The Chapter19 sample code folder consists of four subfolders called Excel, FrontPage-IE, SSMS, and VS. The Excel folder contains a single file (PivotTableChart.xls) containing a PivotTable and linked chart, each on a separate tab. The FrontPage-IE folder contains the file OWC.htm, which in turn contains Excel *PivotTable* and *ChartSpace* controls (both supplied by Office Web Components). The SSMS folder contains the solution file Chapter19.ssmssln, which in turn contains three separate Analysis Services projects (MDX Demos, XMLA Demos, and CLR Demos). The VS folder contains the solution file Chapter19.sln, which in turn contains a Windows Forms project (Chapter19), an ASP.NET project (Chapter19Web), and a Class Library project (Chapter19AdomdServer).

Throughout this chapter, we will examine development techniques using these code samples. You can build the samples from scratch or simply follow along using the sample spreadsheet, HTML page, and code. Almost all of the samples are ready to run (provided that the database built in the last chapter is available as Chapter18 on your localhost Analysis Services server). The MDX scripts in the CLR Demos project will run once the assembly in the Chapter19AdomdServer project is deployed to your Analysis Services server.

As we explain techniques in this chapter, we will reference the components of the sample code that best implement them. Some figures in the chapter are from the sample Windows Forms application and Management Studio scripts. In certain cases, the sample code explores techniques that go even deeper into the topics than does the chapter text. If you can, go through all the code carefully; you'll find it to be a valuable reference.

Using Excel

The number one OLAP client in the world today is Excel. For IT organizations, the ubiquity of Microsoft Office—and the resulting simplicity of deployment and low cost—make Excel quite popular. For users, the familiarity of the spreadsheet interface makes Excel a highly requested front end. As a result, Microsoft has gone out of its way to make the PivotTable and chart functions in Excel especially OLAP savvy.

This means that whether you prefer to use the full-blown Excel client application or the Office Web Components (OWC), connecting users to your Analysis Services 2005 cubes is really easy. And because OWC is deployed as a set of ActiveX controls, you can host PivotTables and charts in Web applications (including ASP.NET pages) or Windows Forms applications (using COM Interop). Best of all, because the Excel PivotTable and chart components feature drag-and-drop field lists, you (and your users) can use these tools to query your cubes without any knowledge of MDX.

In this section, we'll cover how to use Excel as a bona fide OLAP client. The techniques laid out here are for Excel 2003. If you're using Excel 2000 or Excel 2002 (the Office XP version), or if you're using "Excel 2007" (as the version after Excel 2003, still in beta at press time, will likely be called), the steps and screenshots in this section will not align precisely with what you experience. Regardless, you should be able to follow these steps as a general procedure for working with cubes from Excel.

Working Within Excel

> **Important**   The techniques described in this section require that MSQuery, an Excel instal-
> lation option, be installed on your PC. If it is not, Excel will ask you at a certain point if you want
> to install it. When asked, you should answer Yes and supply your Office installation media if
> prompted.

Before you venture into using Office Web Components from within your own applications, you should know how to connect PivotTables and charts to your cubes from within an Excel spreadsheet:

1. In Excel, choose Data/Import External Data/New Database Query....

2. The resulting Choose Data Source dialog box (which you might have used to import relational data into Excel) has three tabs: Databases, Queries, and OLAP Cubes. Use the OLAP Cubes tab (Figure 19-1) to attach a PivotTable to your cube.

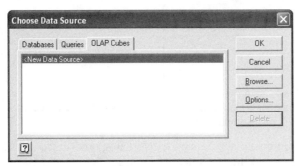

Figure 19-1   The Choose Data Source dialog box in Excel 2003, with the OLAP Cubes tab selected

Defining a Data Source

To define a data source, follow these steps:

1. If this is the first time you've imported OLAP data into Excel, the OLAP Cubes tab will display only an option to add a new data source. Double-click the <New Data Source> item in the list.

2. In the Create New Data Source dialog box (Figure 19-2), type a name for the data source in field 1. A drop-down list box will become enabled in field 2.

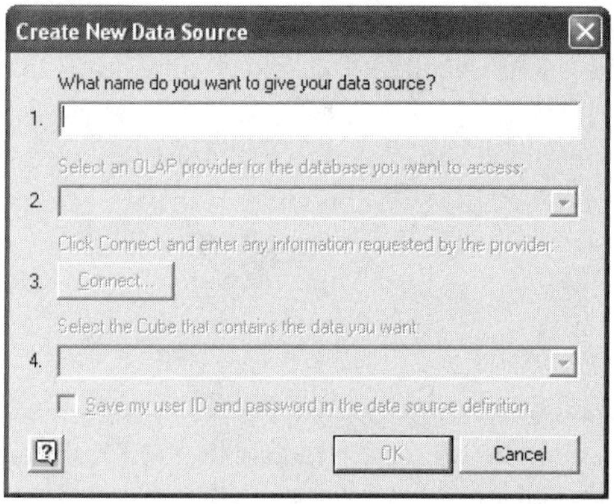

Figure 19-2   The Create New Data Source dialog box

3. Click the drop-down list's drop-down arrow, and you will see a list of all OLE DB for OLAP providers that might be installed on your system (Figure 19-3). Select Microsoft OLE DB Provider for Analysis Services 9.0 (the official version number of SQL Server 2005 is 9.0), and then click the Connect button in field 3.

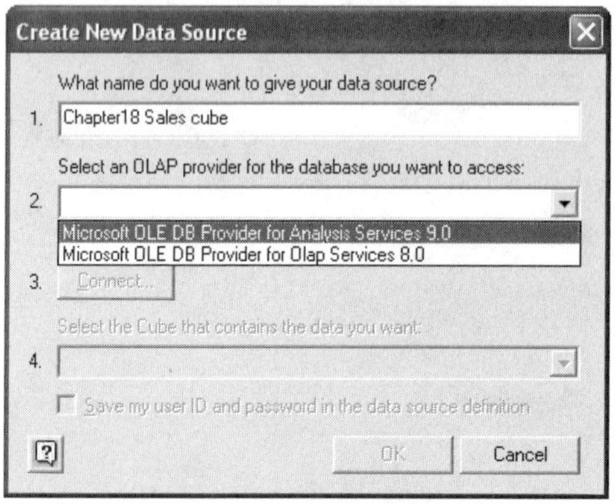

Figure 19-3   The Create New Data Source dialog box, with the data source name supplied and the OLAP providers drop-down list shown

4. In the special Multidimensional Connection 9.0 dialog box (Figure 19-4), be sure that the Analysis Server option button is selected, and then type the name of your server (which might be "localhost" or simply "."). Click Next. (Analysis Services uses integrated security, so you can leave the User ID and Password fields blank.)

5. The dialog box should now list all Analysis Services databases on your server. Select one and click Finish to return to the Create New Data Source dialog box.

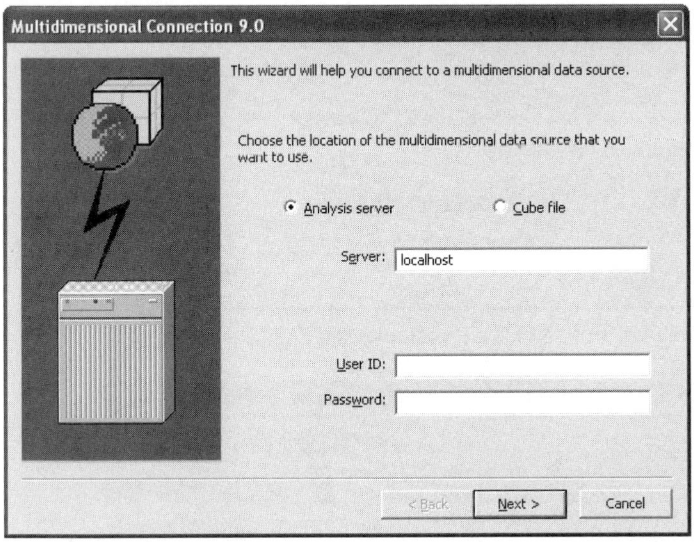

Figure 19-4   The Multidimensional Connection 9.0 dialog box

6. A drop-down list should now be enabled in field 4. Click the list's drop-down arrow to see a list of all cubes and perspectives in the Analysis Services database that you selected in the Multidimensional Connection 9.0 dialog box. Select a cube or perspective, and then click OK.

7. Your newly defined data source should now appear on the OLAP Cubes tab of the Choose Data Source dialog box. Double-click it.

Creating the PivotTable

The Step 3 page of the PivotTable And PivotChart Wizard (Figure 19-5) should now be displayed. This can be confusing because we never explicitly invoked this wizard, nor did we complete information on the Step 1 or Step 2 pages. Our advice to you is to ignore the title of this dialog box and simply make the appropriate selections.

Specifically, you must indicate whether you want to insert the new PivotTable in a specific existing worksheet or a new one, and at what cell location, and then you click Finish. You'll see a blank PivotTable on the left of your screen and a PivotTable Fields List window (either floating or docked) on the right containing all of your Attributes, Hierarchies, and Measures (Figure 19-6). The PivotTable tab of the file PivotTableChart.xls, supplied with this chapter's sample code, contains a fully built-out PivotTable bound to the *Sales* cube of our Chapter18 database.

Figure 19-5 The Step 3 page of the PivotTable And PivotChart Wizard

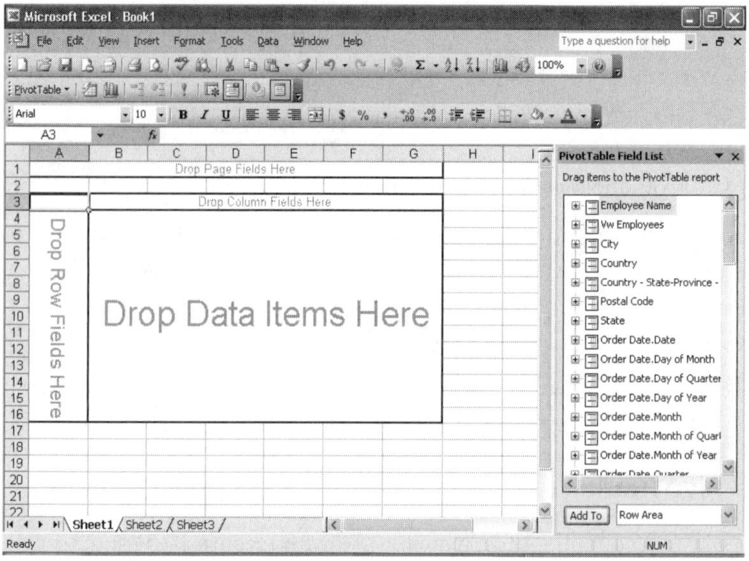

Figure 19-6 An empty PivotTable in a new Excel spreadsheet with hierarchies and attributes from our Chapter18 database displayed in the Field List window

Adding Fields   If the interface and environment you're now in seems familiar, it should: The cube browser hosted by both SQL Server Management Studio and the Visual Studio Analysis Services project cube designer uses a modified version of the Excel PivotTable. You can distinguish measures from both hierarchies and attributes by the measures' distinct icons (which depict zeroes and ones), as shown in Figure 19-7.

You can drag and drop hierarchies and attributes from the Field List to the Row Fields, Column Fields, and Page Fields areas, and you can drag and drop measures to the Data Items area in the PivotTable much as you can in the cube browser. You can also add an item by selecting it in the PivotTable Field List window, selecting a target drop area from the drop-down list at the bottom of the window, and then clicking the Add button to its left. Multiple items can be "stacked" in the same area, and you can remove items by dragging and dropping them outside the physical boundaries of the PivotTable.

Figure 19-7 Measures appear in the Field List window immediately after hierarchies and attributes.

Filtering and Drilling Down After dragging hierarchies or attributes into the Rows, Columns, or Pages areas, you can click the drop-down arrow next to the level or attribute name to reveal a list of members, any of which you can select or deselect (Figure 19-8). You can also double-click any member to drill down on it. Again, these features are similar to features offered by the cube browser. In fact, dragging items into the Page Fields area and picking a specific member in its drop-down list allows you to use this area within the PivotTable as you would use the cube browser's Filter Fields area.

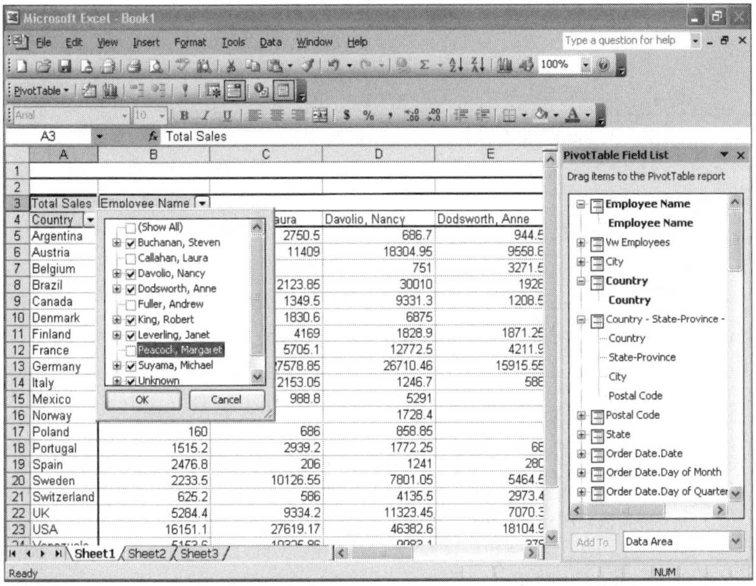

Figure 19-8 A member selection popup for the Employee Name attribute, with three names excluded

Offline Cube Files The PivotTable toolbar (which should appear automatically) provides a number of tools and options for customizing the look and content of your PivotTable. Of particular interest is the Offline OLAP option on the PivotTable drop-down button (the first toolbar button on the left). Selecting this option brings up the Offline OLAP Settings dialog box (Figure 19-9). You can click the Create Offline Data File... button in the dialog box to open the Create Cube File dialog box (which is actually a wizard; see Figure 19-10).

Figure 19-9 The Offline OLAP Settings dialog box

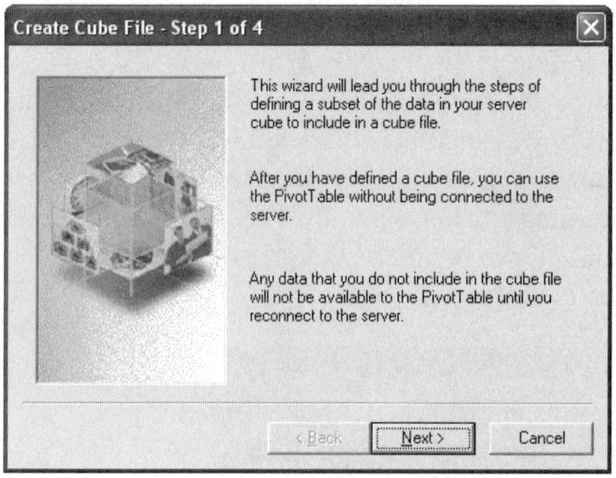

Figure 19-10 The Create Cube File dialog box/wizard

This wizard is an extremely important tool: On its Step 2 page, you can pick a subset of the cube's dimension objects (hierarchies, levels, or attributes), and on the Step 3 page you can select a subset of the cube's measures and members of the dimensions you chose on the Step 2 page. The Step 4 page lets you save the selected cube subset to an offline cube file (with a .cub extension). Offline cube files can be queried directly by PivotTables and by ADO MD .NET (just use the filespec in the data source= section of your connection string), allowing you to work with your OLAP data even when you're disconnected from Analysis Services.

> **Caution** When you connect to offline cube files from Excel, in the Multidimensional Connection 9.0 dialog box select Cube File instead of Analysis Server and *manually* supply the *full path* to your cube file. If you select the file using the ellipsis (...) button and the File Open dialog box, only the file name will be inserted and you will be unable to connect.

In addition to generating the .cub file, the Create Cube File dialog box places in the same folder a text file called SlicerDDL.txt, which contains the MDX query used to create the .cub file. Such queries can be executed directly from your own applications or from SQL Server Management Studio's MDX Query window, which means that Excel is not required to generate offline cube files (even though it *can* connect to offline files created outside Excel). See the OfflineFile.mdx file in the Management Studio sample solution's MDX Demos project for a sample of such a query.

Creating and Configuring Charts

After you've put some work into your PivotTable, you'll see that the numbers it presents and the format are quite usable. Still, with OLAP data, visualization is often key to users' immediate comprehension of the data presented. Luckily, Excel makes it uncannily easy to present a PivotTable's data graphically. To see this for yourself, start by right-clicking any cell in the PivotTable and selecting PivotChart from the shortcut menu. Excel immediately creates a stacked column chart, on its own tab, from the data displayed.

> **Tip**   To view a PivotTable's data graphically, you can also do any of the following: Click the ChartWizard button (the third button from the left) on the PivotTable toolbar; click the Pivot-Table drop-down button (far left) on the PivotTable toolbar and then select the PivotChart option from the drop-down menu; or choose Insert/Chart... from Excel's main menu.

The stacked column chart is useful, but a different chart type will likely be more helpful. To change the chart type, simply click the chart and choose Chart/Chart Type... from the Excel main menu or right-click on the chart and choose Chart Type... from the shortcut menu. Either action will invoke the Chart Type dialog box (Figure 19-11).

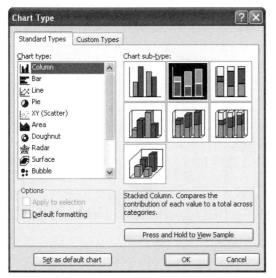

Figure 19-11   The Chart Type dialog box in Excel

For a more interesting chart, pick the Line option (third from the top) from the Chart Type list, and then choose 3-D Line (the last option) from the Subtype menu and click OK. You should see a chart similar to that shown in Figure 19-12.

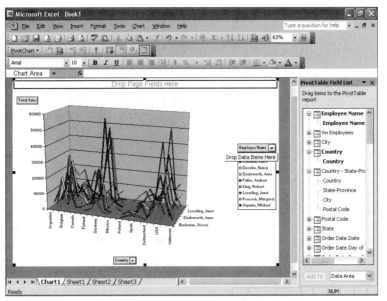

Figure 19-12   A PivotTable-linked 3-D line chart, with the Field List window showing

The Chart tab of the PivotTableChart.xls file, supplied with this chapter's sample code, contains a fully built-out 3-D line chart linked to the PivotTable on the file's other tab.

Charts provide impressive visual output, and they are as configurable as PivotTables. In other words, with the PivotTable Field list showing, you can drag and drop dimensions and measures onto and off your chart (to/from its Data Items, Series, and Category areas) instead of the PivotTable it is linked to. If you flip back to the PivotTable after making changes to the chart, you will see your changes reflected in the PivotTable. Experiment a bit more and you'll discover that the converse is true as well.

As you can see, PivotTables make Excel an able OLAP client. Virtually all the capabilities of the cube browser are available within it, which offers a familiar environment for many users. Those features, combined with the ubiquity of Excel, make Excel a tempting deployment vehicle for your OLAP needs.

Using PivotTables and Charts in Applications and Web Pages

Although the temptation to use Excel as your OLAP front end is compelling, such a client environment is a far cry from a true custom-developed application. Many developers will greatly prefer to host PivotTables within applications rather than ceding control of OLAP functionality to Excel. The good news for them is that PivotTables are available as programmable controls from Office Web Components (OWC), which ships with Office. PivotTables can therefore be used from .NET Windows Forms applications and from any HTML page (including pages in an ASP.NET or Active Server Pages application). In fact, the cube browser is an example of one such application.

> **Important**   For applications and Web pages that use OWC controls to execute correctly, the user must have Office or OWC installed.

One advantage of using the OWC *PivotTable* control in your own application is that you can provide your own front end. Rather than make the user select a server, database, cube/perspective, or even dimensions and measures, your application can configure some or all of these settings programmatically. You can programmatically show, hide, or format various parts of the PivotTable as well, giving users exactly what they need without overwhelming them with connection and metadata options.

Using PivotTables in Windows Forms Applications

To use the *PivotTable* control from a Windows Forms application, start by opening an existing Windows Forms project in Microsoft Visual Studio 2005 or creating a new one. Right-click the Visual Studio Toolbox window, and select Choose Items... from the shortcut menu (Figure 19-13).

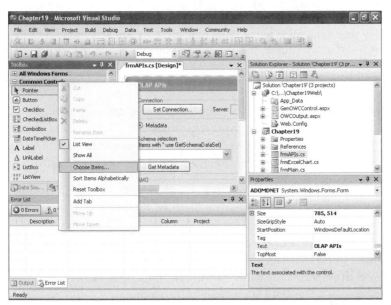

Figure 19-13   Invoking the Visual Studio 2005 Toolbox's Choose Items option

In the Choose Toolbox Items dialog box, on the COM Components tab, check the box next to the Microsoft Office PivotTable 11.0 object and click OK (Figure 19-14).

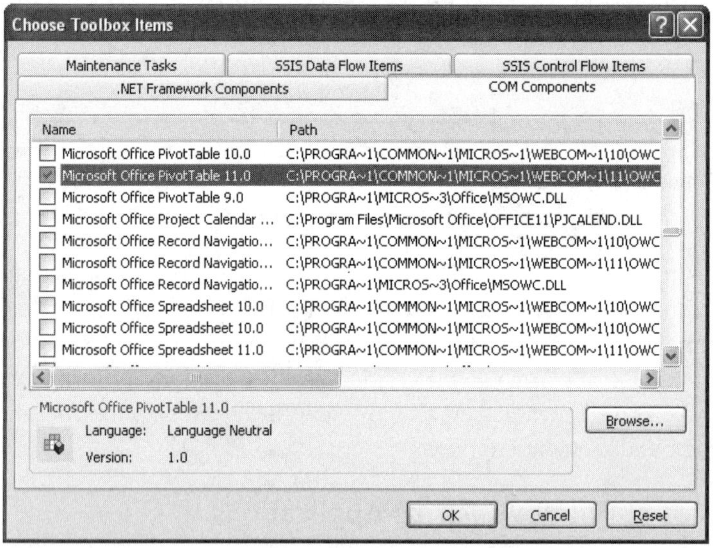

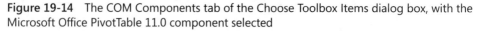

Figure 19-14   The COM Components tab of the Choose Toolbox Items dialog box, with the Microsoft Office PivotTable 11.0 component selected

> **More Info**   You might find earlier versions of the PivotTable component on your system. Version 10 was supplied with Office XP/Excel 2002, and version 9 was supplied with Office 2000/Excel 2000. You might want to experiment with these versions of the component if you intend to deploy your application to machines running those earlier versions of Office and Excel. However, this chapter assumes that you will be using version 11 of OWC, which is supplied with Office 2003.

After you add the PivotTable component to your toolbox, you can drag and drop an instance of it onto a form. Try to position it at the upper-left corner of the form's client area; if you have trouble doing this, set the control's *Location.X* and *Location.Y* properties to 0 in Visual Studio's Properties window. After you add and position the control, resize your form to accommodate the control's full width and height.

The control should now appear with a mostly disabled toolbar and its client area displaying the Microsoft Office Web Components logo in gray over a white background, with a hyperlink at the bottom center of the control labeled "Click here to connect to data." Click the Commands And Options toolbar button (third from the right) on the control. (You can also press the Control key while clicking the hyperlink, but you may need to click the link more than once.) The Data Source tab of the Commands And Options dialog box (Figure 19-15) appears.

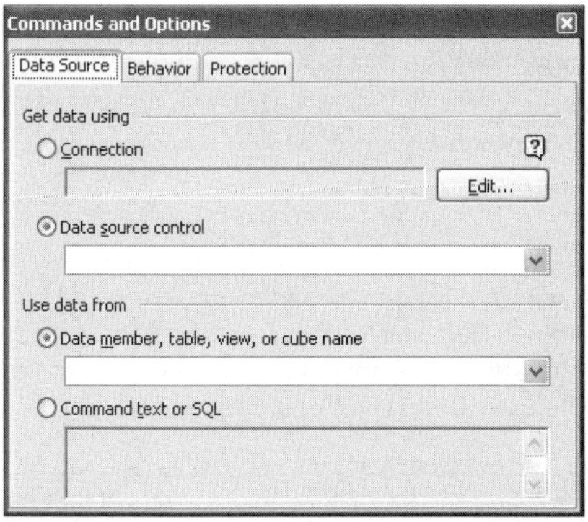

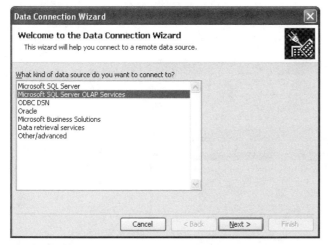

Figure 19-15   The Commands And Options dialog box as it first appears when the *PivotTable* control's Commands And Options toolbar button is clicked

Data Source Configuration   Click the Edit... button to display the Select Data Source dialog box (essentially, a standard File Open dialog box pointing to your My Data Sources folder). From here, you can select an existing Data Source file, but initially there will be none to select, so click the New Source... button on the bottom right to bring up the Data Connection Wizard (Figure 19-16).

Figure 19-16   The *PivotTable* control's Data Connection Wizard, with the Microsoft SQL Server OLAP Services (Analysis Services) data source option selected

On the Welcome page of the wizard, select Microsoft SQL Server OLAP Services from the data source list and click Next. On the Connect To Database Server page, type your server name, make sure the Windows Authentication option is selected, and click Next again. On the Select Database And Table page, select the desired Analysis Services database from the drop-down list at the top, make sure the Connect To A Specific Cube Or Table check box is selected, and select the desired cube or perspective from the list below it. Click Next.

On the Save Data Connection File And Finish page, supply a name and description for your data source file (or accept the defaults) and click Finish. This will put you back in the Select Data Source dialog box, where you should select the data source file you just created and click Open (or simply double-click on the data source file name). After a brief pause, the Commands And Options dialog box will reappear. You can close it.

> **More Info**   PivotTable data source files, which have an .odc extension, are saved by default in your My Documents\My Data Sources folder. Data source files have different icons depending on whether they connect to a particular database, connect to a specific cube within a database, or are merely designed to prompt the user for a server or a data source.
>
> If you open an .odc file in Notepad, you will see that it contains very specialized HTML. Search for the <odc:ConnectionString> tag, and you will find the OLE DB connection string that is necessary to connect to the server, database, and cube you specified when you built the data source.
>
> Perhaps more interestingly, if you open a cube-specific (or relational table/view-specific) data source file in Internet Explorer and choose to allow blocked content when prompted, you will see a Web page that hosts a *PivotTable* control that is already connected to the file's data source.

Configuring *PivotTable* Controls at Design Time   The *PivotTable* control should now appear, still empty, in your form. In place of the OWC logo and connection hyperlink, the PivotTable's Row, Column, and Filter and Detail Fields areas should be visible. The toolbar should appear with more of its buttons enabled, and a title area should appear between the toolbar and the Filter Fields area that reads "Microsoft Office PivotTable 11.0" (Figure 19-17).

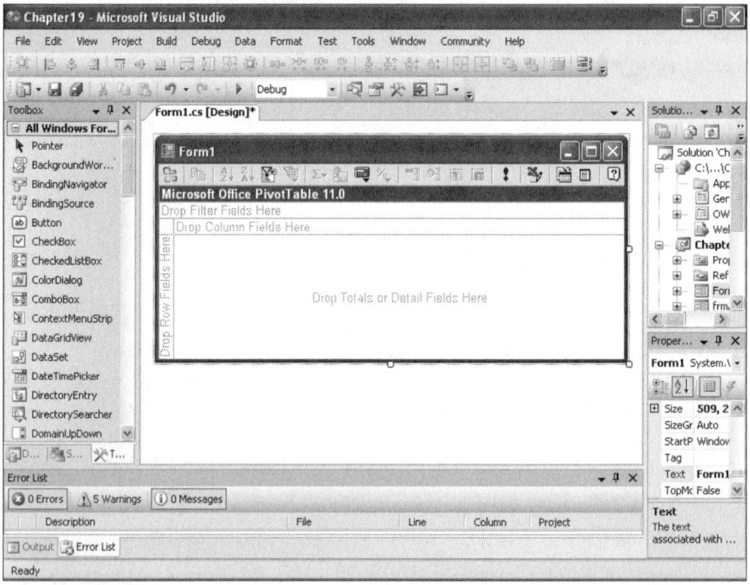

Figure 19-17   A connected but empty *PivotTable* control, shown at design time in the Visual Studio Windows Forms designer

Click the (now enabled) Field List button on the toolbar (second from the right) to show the PivotTable Field List window. Notice that a parent node for the cube appears at the top of the list, and immediately beneath it is a node labeled "Totals" that contains all the measures in the cube. In most other respects, the PivotTable Field List is the same one we saw earlier within Excel.

Although you are technically working with the control in the design-time environment (rather than using it at run time), the control itself is almost fully functional. You can add dimensions and measures in the Windows Forms designer at design time without writing code and without directly setting properties. To do so, select items from the Field List window (Figure 19-18) and add them to the PivotTable's areas using the area drop-down list and the Add To button at the bottom of the window. (Drag and drop will not work at design time.)

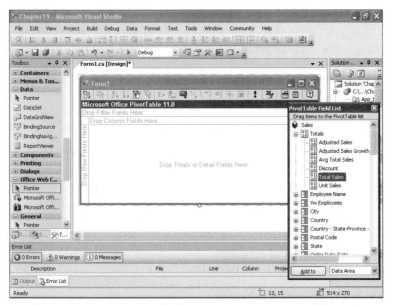

Figure 19-18   The Field List window, which you invoke by clicking the *PivotTable* control's Field List toolbar button

After you configure your PivotTable, you should be able to use it interactively, even within the designer. Run your application (using the Debug/Start Debugging main menu option or the Start Debugging toolbar button) to see that users can easily do likewise at run time.

The *frmPivotTable* form in the Chapter19 Windows Forms project (which is supplied with this chapter's sample code) contains a fully built-out form with a *PivotTable* control bound to the *Sales* cube of our Chapter18 database.

Setting Properties   Close your application and return to Visual Studio's design-time environment. Some properties of the PivotTable can be set through the Visual Studio Properties window; others must be set in the Commands And Options dialog box that we just discussed.

You can open this dialog box in three ways: by clicking the control's Commands And Options toolbar button (third from the right), by right-clicking the *PivotTable* control and choosing Commands And Options... from the shortcut menu, or by clicking the control's SmartTag and choosing the ActiveX –Commands And Options... option.

> **Note**   When launched through the SmartTag, the Commands And Options dialog box appears with a normal-sized title bar labeled "Properties" rather than a toolbox-sized title bar labeled "Commands And Options," but it is in fact the same dialog box.
>
> In addition to letting you set the PivotTable's connection and data member information on the Data Source tab, the dialog box lets you set a number of the PivotTable's appearance and formatting properties on the Format, Filter and Group, Captions, Report, Behavior, and Protection tabs. You might find setting the Report Title Bar caption to be especially useful because it lets you remove the default "Microsoft Office PivotTable 11.0" caption initially displayed on the control.
>
> The specific tabs available in the Commands And Options dialog box depend on exactly where you right-click the *PivotTable* control before selecting the Commands And Options shortcut menu option.

Using Charts in Windows Forms Applications

Most of what we've already covered about PivotTable integration into your Windows Forms applications also applies to charts, but a few differences are worth noting. We'll now quickly cover how to embed Excel charts in an application, in the context of what we've already described for PivotTables.

To start, right-click the toolbox and once again select the Choose Items... shortcut menu option. This time, you'll want to add the Microsoft Office Chart 11.0 object (on the COM Components tab). You can then add an instance of the object to a new form, following the same procedure you followed with the PivotTable control. The default size of the *ChartSpace* control is larger than that of the PivotTable, so you might want to put Visual Studio into full-screen mode (choose View/Full Screen from the main menu or press Shift+Alt+Enter), resize the form, and then exit full-screen mode (by clicking the Full Screen button to the right of the main menu or by using either of the techniques you used to enter full-screen mode).

Configuring the Data Connection   Once the control is on the form, it should display the Office Web Components logo in gray. To connect the chart with specific data, you right-click the control and choose Data... from the shortcut menu. This brings up the chart's Commands And Options dialog box. (You might need to right-click the control two or three times before the shortcut menu appears.) Although this dialog box shares a name with the PivotTable's Commands And Options dialog box, it is significantly different (Figure 19-19).

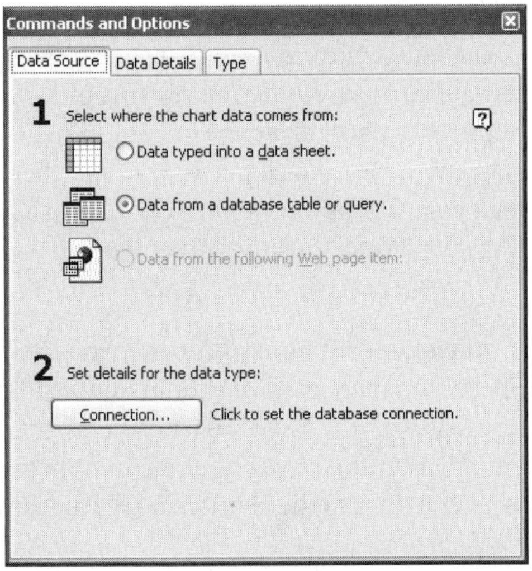

Figure 19-19   The Commands And Options dialog box for the *ChartSpace* control as it first appears after you choose Data… from the control's shortcut menu

Select the Data From A Database Table Or Query option. This causes the Data Details and Type tabs to appear and should also cause the caption of the button in the Data Source tab's "2" section to change from Data Sheet… to Connection… and enable the button. Click the Data Details tab or the Connection… button to activate the tab (Figure 19-20), and then click the Edit… button on the Data Details tab.

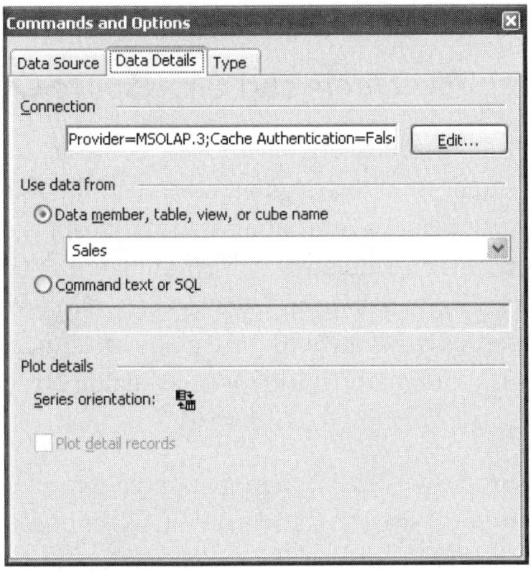

Figure 19-20   The Data Details tab of the *ChartSpace* control's Commands And Options dialog box, after the data source has been configured

You're now back in the Select Data Source dialog box we discussed earlier in the context of the *PivotTable* control. Select an existing .odc Data Source file (you can first click New Source... to create a new one, as described earlier). After a short pause, the Commands And Options dialog box will reappear. From here, you can select a particular cube or perspective by clicking the Data Member, Table, View, Or Cube Name radio button (if necessary) and then making a selection from the drop-down list right below it. If your data source pointed to a specific cube or perspective, the drop-down list selection should already reflect the data source's configuration.

Configuring Fields and the Chart Type   After you configure your data connection, close the Commands And Options dialog box. The *ChartSpace* control should now render with a partially enabled toolbar and empty chart area. As with the PivotTable Field List, you can show the Chart Field List using the appropriate toolbar button or shortcut menu option, and then add the appropriate measures, attributes, or hierarchies to the chart using the area drop-down list and Add To button at the bottom of the Chart Field List window.

The chart's default type is Clustered Column. To change the type, click the Chart Type toolbar button (first actual button from the left, just to the right of the Microsoft Office logo) to reopen the Commands And Options dialog box, and then click on the Type tab. You can also click the Show/Hide Legend toolbar button (fourth actual button from the left, not counting the Office logo) to show a legend for the Series data.

The *frmExcelChart* form in the Chapter19 Windows Forms project (supplied with this chapter's sample code) contains a fully built-out form with a *ChartSpace* control, displaying a 3-D line chart, bound to the *Sales* cube of our Chapter18 database.

Using the Properties Window with *PivotTable* and *ChartSpace* Controls

Although you can set properties for both the *PivotTable* and *ChartSpace* controls through the Commands And Options dialog box, you might want to assign values to certain of these properties directly in the Visual Studio Properties window. A number of useful properties are revealed there, and in many cases you can set their value through enumerated options in combo boxes. Noteworthy among them are *ConnectionString, DataMember, DisplayFieldList,* and *DisplayToolbar*. Using these four properties, you can configure many attributes of a *Pivot-Table* or *ChartSpace* control without using the Commands And Options dialog box (although you will still need the dialog box to change the default type of a chart).

Assigning a value to the *ConnectionString* property is easier than you might expect, and it avoids the need to build a data source. You simply use the standard OLE DB connection string format, using MSOLAP as the provider name. For example, if you want to connect to the Chapter18 database on your local machine, you can use this string entry:

```
Provider=MSOLAP;Data Source=localhost;Initial Catalog=Chapter18
```

To connect to the *Sales* cube within the database, you can then set the *DataMember* property to *Sales*.

If you leave the *DisplayFieldList* property set to the default value of *True*, the Field List window will appear when the application is run and the form is shown (although at design time, the Field List window will appear and then quickly become hidden again). Set the property to *False* if you don't want the Field List to appear initially when users execute your application.

For Charts Only   For a chart, you'll likely want to set both the *AllowPropertyToolbox* property (which allows the Commands And Properties dialog box to appear at run time) and *Display-Toolbar* properties to *True*. The latter is set to *True* automatically when you configure the data connection through the Commands And Options dialog box. However, the property's default value is actually *False*, and when you set the *ConnectionString* and *DataMember* properties though the Properties window, you must set *DisplayToolbar* to *True* explicitly. You might also want to change the chart's type from the default Clustered Column; to do so, you must use the Type tab of the Commands And Options dialog box.

Other useful *ChartSpace*-specific properties include *HasChartSpaceTitle* and *HasChartSpace-Legend*, which make the chart's title and legend visible, respectively. To change the chart's title from the default "Chart Workspace Title," click on the title itself, open the Commands And Options dialog box, and on the Format Tab edit the text in the Caption text box (near the bottom). Close the dialog box when you're done.

UI Niceties   For both PivotTables and charts, you'll likely want to set the *Anchor* property to *Top, Bottom, Left, Right* to ensure that the control will resize properly when the form is resized (for proper PivotTable resizing, you will also need to set the *AutoFit* property to *False*). For PivotTables, this will allow users with large, high-resolution monitors to see lots of data if they so choose; for charts, it will ensure that the series and category labels do not "crunch" together and overtype each other.

Setting *PivotTable* and *ChartSpace* Properties Programmatically

Most of the design-time property settings we've described can also be set in code. This gives you the opportunity to create your own UI, solicit from your users the particular cube or perspective they'd like to see, and then present them with an empty but connected PivotTable or chart, a displayed Field List, and the ability to drag and drop the data items of their choice onto the appropriate areas of the control.

The sample code for this chapter includes a .NET Windows Forms MDI application that includes child windows that display *PivotTable* and *ChartSpace* controls. That application references the Microsoft OLE DB Service Component 1.0 Type Library to allow programmatic invocation of the standard Data Link dialog box. This dialog box lets users specify their connection strings through a standard Windows UI rather than having to type them in. It then interrogates the *PivotTable* or *ChartSpace* object using special code to populate a combo box with a list of cubes and perspectives from the Analysis Services database indicated by the user's connection string.

The sample code demonstrates how a *PivotTable* or *ChartSpace* control's *ConnectionString*, *DataMember*, and other properties can be set through code by fetching the connection string from the Data Link dialog box and the desired cube or perspective name through the ComboBox. One nice thing about working in code is that several properties that are *not* available through the Properties window can be set programmatically. For example, you can set the chart type in a single line of code. If you want to set the chart type of a *ChartSpace* control named *echMain* to 3D Area, you can do so with the following line of code:

```
echMain.Charts[0].Type =
Microsoft.Office.Interop.Owc11.ChartChartTypeEnum.chChartTypeArea3D;
```

What About the Web?

In case you were wondering, both the *PivotTable* and *ChartSpace* controls can be used within Web pages as ActiveX controls. As long as blocked content is enabled in Internet Explorer or the page's site of origin is included in your list of trusted sites, both controls will render properly within Internet Explorer on any machine running an appropriate version of Office.

OWC and FrontPage   An easy way to begin Web development with Office Web Components is to compose your pages (or at least start composing them) using Microsoft FrontPage. In FrontPage, you can easily insert OWC controls onto a page, and you get a design-time experience similar to that of the Windows Forms designer in Visual Studio. FrontPage might not be everyone's Web development tool of choice, but it is good for generating the appropriate *<object>* tag HTML snippets. You can then insert these snippets into Web pages in other design tools, including ASP.NET pages in Web site projects with Visual Studio 2005. We'll quickly cover both Web development environments now.

To see the FrontPage OWC design-time support in action, start up FrontPage on your system, create a new HTML page (or use the default page created by FrontPage upon startup), and enter design mode by clicking the Design button at the far lower-left corner of the FrontPage window. Choose Insert/Web Component... from the main menu to open the Insert Web Component dialog box.

In the dialog box, scroll down to the end of the Component Type list (on the left) and select Advanced Controls (the last item in the list). From the Choose A Control list (on the right), select ActiveX Control. The dialog box should appear as shown in Figure 19-21.

Click Next and select Microsoft Office PivotTable 11.0 (or Microsoft Office Chart 11.0) from the Choose A Control list, and then click Finish.

At this point, you should see an instance of your selected control on your HTML page. If you inserted a *ChartSpace* control, the Commands And Options dialog box should be visible (Figure 19-22); if you inserted a *PivotTable* control, you must click the "Click here to connect to data" hyperlink or the Commands And Options toolbar button on the control to show the Commands And Options dialog box.

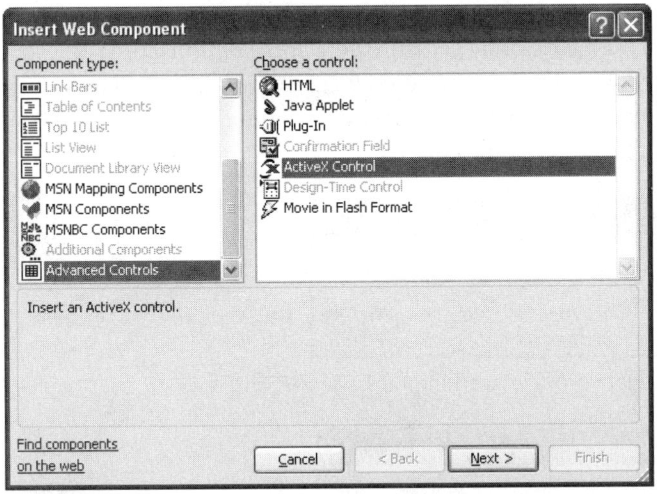

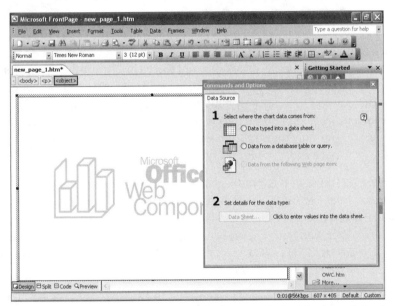

Figure 19-21 The Insert Web Component dialog box in FrontPage 2003, with the Advanced Controls component type and ActiveX Control control type selected

Figure 19-22 The *ChartSpace* control's Commands And Options dialog box, invoked in FrontPage design view

Under ideal conditions, you could configure the control's data connection and contents right away. Unfortunately, default safety settings on your PC will likely prevent you from making a cube selection in the Commands And Options dialog box; even if you type the cube name manually, these same settings will probably prevent you from viewing any of your cube's measures or dimensions in the Field List window.

To correct this, simply save your page and then refresh it by using the F5 key, by choosing View/Refresh from the main menu, or by clicking the Refresh button (fifth from the right) on the FrontPage Standard toolbar. FrontPage will then advise you that the page uses a data provider that might be unsafe and that the page is trying to connect to a data source under your login's identity (Figure 19-23 and Figure 19-24).

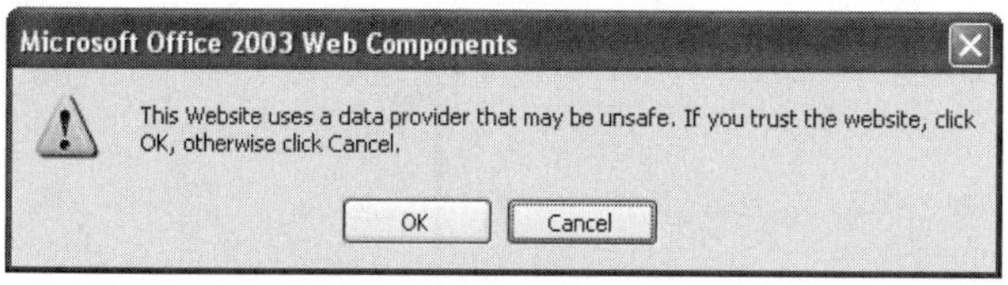

Figure 19-23 The unsafe data provider warning message in FrontPage

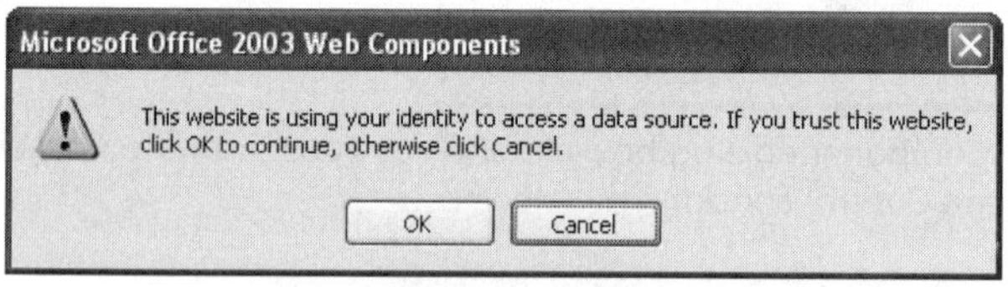

Figure 19-24 The identity impersonation warning message in FrontPage

Click OK in each message box. The page and the control will then render properly, and you can use the Commands And Options dialog box and the Field List window by clicking the appropriate buttons on the control's toolbar. From here, you can customize your control to configure it just the way you want. Bear in mind that FrontPage does not have a Properties window like the one in Visual Studio, so the Commands And Options dialog box and the Field List window are your only tools for customizing the control on the page. Once you're done, you can save the page and close FrontPage.

The Web page file OWC.htm, in the FrontPage-IE folder of this chapter's sample code, contains fully built-out *PivotTable* and *ChartSpace* controls, bound to the *Sales* cube of our Chapter18 database. You can open this file in FrontPage 2003 or Internet Explorer. If you open the file in FrontPage, you must click through the warning message boxes just described (there will be four warnings in all—two each for the *PivotTable* and *ChartSpace* controls). In Internet Explorer, you must follow the directions described next.

Blocked Content in Internet Explorer   At this point, the page can be viewed in Internet Explorer, either from the file system or through a Web server. However, the page will render properly upon initial display only if the page is served from a Web *server* (including your own IIS instance on your local PC) *and* that Web server has been entered into your list of trusted sites in Internet Explorer. If you open the file directly from the file system or from an untrusted Web site, both the *PivotTable* and *ChartSpace* controls will initially fail to render and will display warning messages, as shown in Figure 19-25.

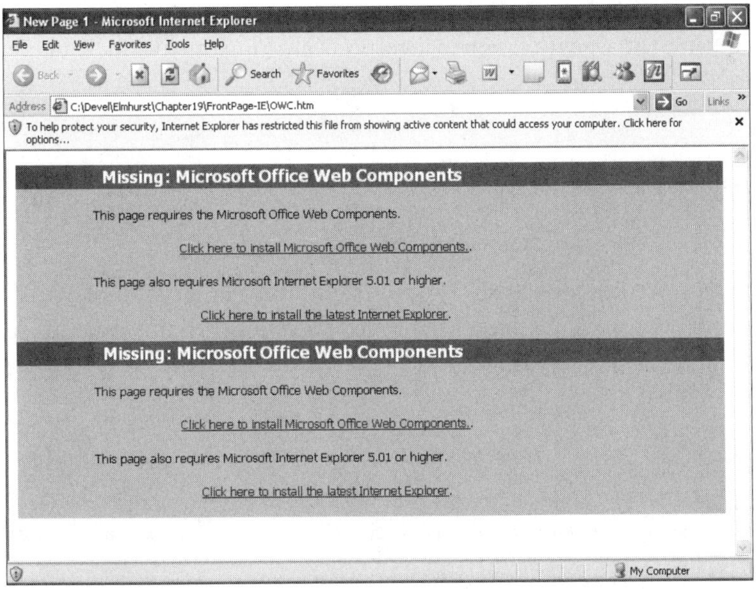

Figure 19-25   Our FrontPage-designed OWC Web page shown in Internet Explorer 6, with active content blocked

The error messages displayed are misleading because they suggest that the OWC controls are not properly installed. You can cause the page to render properly by simply clicking the yellow security bar at the top of the page, selecting the Allow Blocked Content... option on the shortcut menu, and clicking Yes in the subsequent Security Warning message box.

Programming OWC Controls in ASP.NET Applications   We've covered all you really need to know about *composing* Web pages using the OWC *PivotTable* and *ChartSpace* controls. Meanwhile, as a developer, especially as a .NET developer, you'd probably prefer not to use FrontPage as your *development* tool. For example, it might make a great deal of sense to develop an ASP.NET application that features its own UI through which your users indicate the server and cube they're interested in looking at. From there, you might dynamically generate a page containing OWC controls preconfigured according to the user's selections, with the Field List window displayed.

In trying to build such an application, you'll face two hurdles. First, the ASP.NET page designer in Visual Studio 2005 does not allow you to design an OWC-control-based page manually. Second, adapting a FrontPage-generated page is extremely difficult because all property values in the FrontPage-generated HTML are inserted into the control's *XMLData* property.

The solution is fairly easy: You simply need to know the basic HTML markup to emit for the PivotTable and chart controls, as well as the additional HTML required to pre-configure each control's properties. In general, the HTML you need for either control has the following structure, where *controlname* is the actual name of the control, *controlclassid* is the GUID that identifies the control, and *propertyname* and *propertyvalue* represent the name of a property you want to pre-configure and the value you want to assign to it, respectively. (You can include multiple property name/value pairs.)

```
<object classid="controlclassid" id="controlname">
    <param name="propertyname" value="propertyvalue" />
</object>
```

This might seem abstract, but it's actually quite straightforward. For example, the following HTML code, embedded in an ASPX page, will properly display a *PivotTable* control, connected to the *Sales* cube, in the Chapter18 Analysis Services database, on the local server, with its Field List window visible:

```
<object classid="clsid:0002E55A-0000-0000-C000-000000000046"
  id="PivotTable1">
    <param name="ConnectionString" value="Provider=MSOLAP;Data Source=.;Initial Catalog=
Chapter18" />
    <param name="DataMember" value="Sales" />
    <param name="DisplayFieldList" value="True" />
</object>
```

And the following code will do likewise for an OWC *ChartSpace* control:

```
<object classid="clsid:0002E55D-0000-0000-C000-000000000046"
  id="ChartSpace1">
    <param name="ConnectionString" value="Provider=MSOLAP;Data Source=.;Initial Catalog=
Chapter18" />
    <param name="DataMember" value="Sales" />
    <param name="DisplayToolbar" value="True" />
    <param name="AllowPropertyToolbox" value="True" />
    <param name="DisplayFieldList" value="True" />
</object>
```

With knowledge of this rather simple HTML, you can quite easily create an ASP.NET interface that requests server, database, cube, and control type (*PivotTable* or *ChartSpace*) from the user and then presents a page with the requested control connected to the requested cube. The ASP.NET project Chapter19Web, in the Visual Studio solution included with this chapter's sample code, includes ASP.NET sample code that demonstrates this technique.

More Info   Neither of the previous code snippets contains code to pre-configure the measures (data fields) or dimensions (row and column fields). It is possible to do this (in fact, we proved that when we designed the pages in FrontPage), but it requires rather complex programming of the controls' *XMLData* property. If you are interested in manipulating this property, you might want to reverse-engineer the FrontPage-generated HTML. You'll find that HTML much easier to read if you replace all occurrences of *<* and *>* with < and >, respectively.

Beyond OWC: Full-On OLAP Development

We have covered in great detail how to develop powerful front ends, both for Windows and the Web, using OWC. OWC front ends are a serious option for OLAP development, given the ubiquity of and business users' familiarity with Office. Moreover, using OWC controls enables you to create compelling front ends with minimal programming.

Although the OWC option lets you avoid the need for much programming, it also precludes the granular control that a more programmatic approach would offer. OWC controls also require that Office be installed on the user's machine if you want to offer the controls' full feature set and avoid tricky deployment issues. Furthermore, OWC controls all but require direct *intranet* access to an Analysis Services server from the *user's* machine. Even when run from a Web page, the controls run and connect to cubes locally rather than on the server.

If you want to write true Web applications, where the user needs only a browser and nothing else to run queries against your cube, you should avoid using OWC controls. If you want fine-grained control over the query—moving beyond mere selection of measures and dimensions—you'll once again want to steer clear of OWC. And if you're a .NET developer and want to use your ADO.NET and/or data binding skills in the context of an OLAP application, you'll absolutely want to steer clear of OWC.

MDX and Analysis Services APIs

In short, if you want to build highly customized OLAP applications, you'll almost definitely want to learn some basic multidimensional expression language (MDX) and understand how to execute MDX queries using ADO MD.NET (the Multidimensional ADO.NET data provider). We will discuss both of these technologies shortly and demonstrate how to apply them to Windows Forms applications.

> **More Info**   Management Studio relies upon, and therefore includes, ADO MD.NET. If your development machine does not have Management Studio installed, you can download ADO MD.NET (in the form of an installable MSI file) as part of the SQL Server 2005 "feature pack" page on microsoft.com. At the time of this book's publication, the SQL Server 2005 feature pack page was located at *http://www.microsoft.com/downloads/details.aspx?familyid= d09c1d60-a13c-4479-9b91-9e8b9d835cdc&displaylang=en*. An Internet shortcut to this URL, which will save you the trouble of typing it in manually, is provided with the sample code. If the link is broken when you attempt to navigate to it, try performing a Web search on "Feature Pack for Microsoft SQL Server 2005" or "ADOMD.NET 9.0 download."

As we cover MDX and ADO MD.NET, we will explain how to use SQL Server Management Studio as an MDX client. We will also investigate how to execute XML for Analysis (XMLA) queries from Management Studio. XMLA can be used as both a DML (data manipulation language) and DDL (data definition language) facility from Management Studio. ADO MD.NET acts as a wrapper around the DML side of XMLA. Another managed object model, Analysis

Management Objects (AMO), acts as a wrapper against its DDL side. We will examine programmatic use of XMLA in your code, and how to expose "raw" XMLA responses from ADO MD.NET.

To complete our coverage of OLAP development, we will show you how to take advantage of the CLR server-side programming features in Analysis Services. As we do this, you'll see how your client-side OLAP development skills can be migrated to the server to develop sophisticated logic that extends the innate capabilities of MDX from the client.

Moving to MDX

Whether you're programming on the client or the server, using ADO MD.NET, or just working with SQL Server Management Studio, you'll need at least a working knowledge of MDX. MDX is an extremely rich language, the complexity of which we can merely glimpse at this chapter. Luckily, using MDX for simple queries is itself simple and will be somewhat familiar to those with a grounding in SQL. A practical prototype of an MDX query is as follows:

```
SELECT [column members] ON COLUMNS,
       [row members] ON ROWS
FROM [cubename]
WHERE [measure]
```

This "schematic" code glosses over the details of specifying row and column members and oversimplifies the real purpose of the WHERE clause, but we will remedy these shortcomings soon. Let's start by looking at an actual query that selects from the *Sales* cube from our Chapter18 database, showing *Total Sales* broken shown by the *Shipper Name* attribute of the *Shippers* dimension (on the *COLUMNS* axis) and *Year* attribute of the *Time* dimension (on the *ROWS* axis):

```
SELECT Shippers.[Shipper Name].MEMBERS ON COLUMNS,
       Time.Year.MEMBERS ON ROWS
FROM Sales
WHERE Measures.[Total Sales]
```

Before we go any further in our discussion of this query or of MDX itself, let's discuss SQL Server Management Studio's use as a top-notch tool for running, designing, and learning how to write MDX queries.

Management Studio as an MDX Client

In Chapter 5, we covered SQL Server Management Studio in depth, but we did so essentially by documenting its capabilities as a management and query tool for relational databases. To augment this coverage, in Chapter 18 we looked at Management Studio's additional capabilities for managing Analysis Services databases and we provided brief coverage of its MDX and

XMLA Query window capabilities. We will now explore the MDX Query window's capabilities more fully.

As mentioned in Chapter 18, Management Studio is a replacement not only for SQL Enterprise Manager and SQL Query Analyzer but also for the SQL Server 2000 Analysis Services tools: Analysis Manager and the MDX Sample Application. The MDX Sample Application, shown in Figure 19-26, allows for execution of ad hoc MDX queries and saving and retrieving them to and from text files, and it includes a simple UI that allows for drag-and-drop visual composition of these queries. It's a useful tool, although it is completely separate from the other SQL Server 2000 tools, and it is provided, as its name implies, as a sample application (including its Visual Basic 6.0 source code) more than as a tool per se.

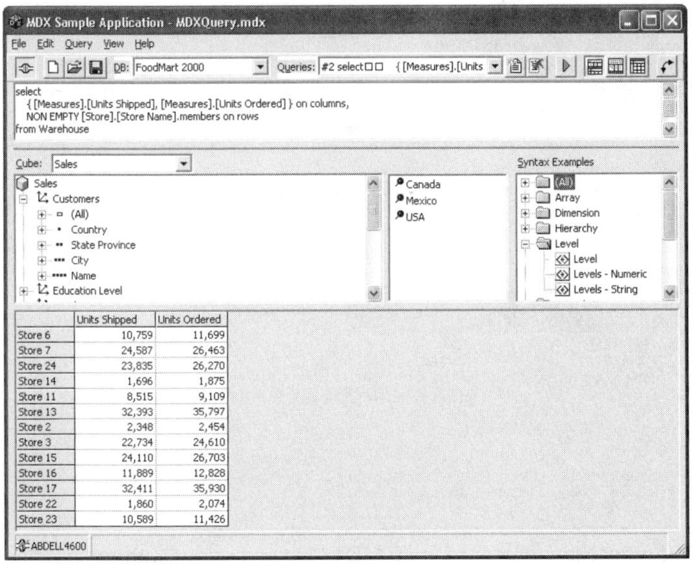

Figure 19-26   The MDX Sample Application (supplied with SQL Server 2000 Analysis Services)

As we saw in the previous chapter, Management Studio includes the functionality of the MDX Sample Application by providing MDX Query windows that work almost identically to its SQL Query windows. MDX query functionality is thus integrated with the rest of the Management Studio feature set, and Management Studio also provides some extra features, including IntelliSense. Analysis Services script projects, which can include MDX queries, can be created within Management Studio, allowing you to create solutions consisting of both SQL and Analysis Services projects with scripts for related tables and cubes.

> **Caution**   Although both the MDX Sample Application and Management Studio use the .mdx extension for their respective MDX query files, the two file formats are not compatible. The MDX Sample Application stores multiple queries per file and separates them using a quote delimiter scheme. Management Studio stores MDX query text without any additional formatting, much as it does with SQL text in .sql files.

The sample code for this chapter includes an SQL Server Management Studio solution, which can be opened via the file Chapter19\SSMS\Chapter19.ssmssln. The solution contains three Analysis Services projects, one of which (Chapter19\SSMS\Chapter19\MDX Demos.ssm-sasproj) consists of separate .mdx files for each query presented in the chapter, including the one discussed previously. Open the solution now, and double-click on the SimpleQuery.mdx query file to open the query in Management Studio. Click the Execute button on the SQL Server Analysis Services Editors toolbar (or use the keyboard, main menu, or shortcut menu equivalent) to see the results of the MDX query displayed in a grid on the Results tab, as shown in Figure 19-27.

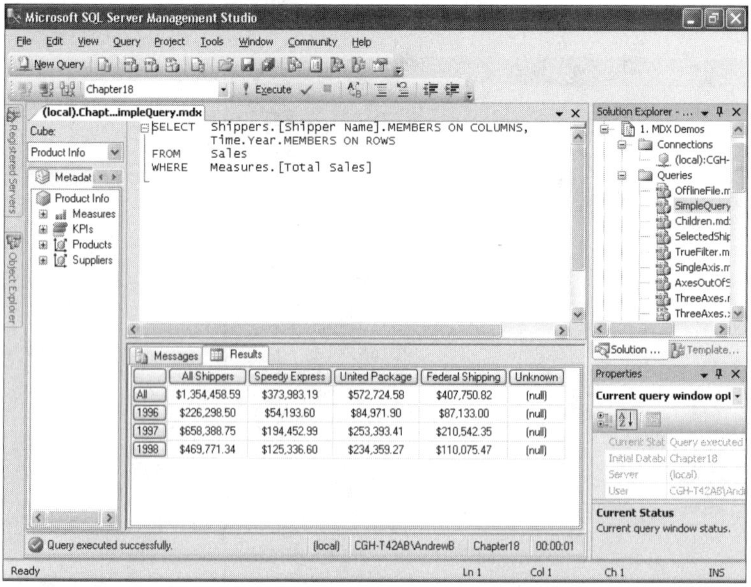

Figure 19-27   The SQL Server Management Studio MDX Query window, with the Results tab visible

Rich MDX Support

Besides being a convenient text editor for writing and testing your queries, Management Studio includes many features that make the creation of MDX queries easy for people who are new to MDX. In Chapter 18, we briefly covered the MDX Query window tools pane, and the MDX IntelliSense features provided by Management Studio. Let's explore Management Studio's MDX feature set in more depth now.

Making the Connection   First you should understand the various ways to open a new query. We covered some of these in Chapter 18, but include them here again for review and for thoroughness. These include the File/New/Analysis Services MDX Query main menu option, and the toolbar button of the same name (third from the left) on the Standard toolbar. Either option opens a new MDX Query window but first presents the Connect To Analysis Services dialog box, which requires you to connect or cancel before it places you in the MDX editor. Much like its Connect To Database Engine "cousin," this dialog box requires you to provide a server/instance name and allows you to enter optional connection properties by clicking the Options button and supplying information (such as the database to connect to) on the Connection Properties tab that appears.

To avoid the Connect To Analysis Services dialog box and go directly into an MDX Query window, select an Analysis Services server in the Registered Servers or Object Explorer windows, and then click the New Query button (first on the left) on the Standard toolbar. To view Analysis Services servers in the Registered Servers window, you must click the Analysis Services button (second from the left, with the cube icon) on the window's toolbar.

Other ways of "speed dialing" into the MDX Query window include double-clicking an Analysis Services connection in the Solution Explorer window; right-clicking a connection there and choosing New Query; right-clicking an Analysis Services server node in the Registered Servers window and choosing Connect/New Query from the shortcut menu; and right-clicking an Analysis Services server or database node in the Object Explorer window and choosing New Query/MDX. When you use the last of these techniques with a database node, your MDX Query window will select that database by default.

Once an MDX Query window is open, you can change the connection information by using the Change Connection button (third from the left) on the SQL Server Analysis Services Editors toolbar or choosing Query/Connection/Change Connection... from the main menu. Either approach opens the Connect To Analysis Services dialog box. If you did not connect successfully to begin with, you can accomplish the same thing by clicking the Connect button (first from the left) on the SQL Server Analysis Services Editors toolbar or choosing Query/Connection/Connect... from the main menu. The Query/Connection main menu options are also available from the Connection option on the MDX Query window's shortcut menu.

Once connected, you can use a different database on the same server by selecting that database from the databases drop-down list (just to the right of the Change Connection button) on the SQL Server Analysis Services Editors toolbar. You can intentionally return your MDX Query window to a disconnected state by clicking the Disconnect button (second from the left) on the SQL Server Analysis Services Editors toolbar or by choosing Query/Connection/Disconnect from the main menu (or Connection/Disconnect from the MDX Query window's shortcut menu).

After you open the MDX Query window and connect to the appropriate server and database, the Tools pane (the section to the left of the MDX edit region) will become enabled, its drop-down list of available cubes/perspectives will populate, and metadata for the selected cube/perspective will be displayed in the Metadata tab's tree view.

Building a Query   With all this in mind, open a new MDX Query window, making sure that you are connected to the *Sales* cube of the Chapter18 database. In this window, we will create a new query, similar to the previous one, but rather than typing it from scratch, we will use features of Management Studio to help us compose our MDX code.

One excellent way to learn MDX is through the use of the MDX templates supplied with Management Studio. To see these, you must show Template Explorer if it's not shown already. Use the Template Explorer button (second from the right) on the Standard toolbar, choose View/Template Explorer from the main menu, or press Ctrl+Alt+T. Next, click the Analysis Services button (second from the left or right) on the Template Explorer window's toolbar to display Analysis Services templates. Drill down on the MDX node and then on its child Expressions and Queries nodes to show all available MDX templates (Figure 19-28).

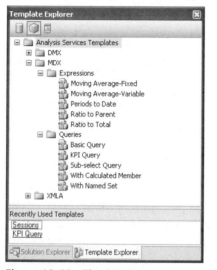

Figure 19-28   The SQL Server Management Studio Template Explorer, with Analysis Services MDX templates displayed

In all, SQL Server Management Studio includes 10 MDX templates to help you learn the language. Because we're writing simple queries, we'll start with the Basic Query template. Drag and drop the Basic Query node (under the Queries parent node) into the open MDX window, and then press the left arrow or Home key on your keyboard to deselect the MDX template text. Notice that the skeletal MDX provided is similar to the "schematic" MDX query we discussed earlier:

```
-- ============================================
-- Basic MDX Query
-- ============================================

Select <row_axis, mdx_set,> on Columns,
       <column_axis, mdx_set,> on Rows

From <from_clause, mdx_name,>
Where <where_clause, mdx_set,>
```

Important   Management Studio's Basic Query MDX template erroneously places a row_axis place holder in the on Columns clause and a column_axis placeholder in the on Rows clause. It should, of course, use the reverse arrangement. Nevertheless, if you follow our directions carefully, the query you will generate will be correct.

With this skeletal code in place, our next task is to fill out all the parameterized clauses that appear as angle-bracketed text. Choose Query/Specify Values For Template Parameters... from the main menu or click the Specify Values For Template Parameters button (fifth from the right) on the SQL Server Analysis Services Editors toolbar to open the Specify Values For Template Parameters dialog box (Figure 19-29).

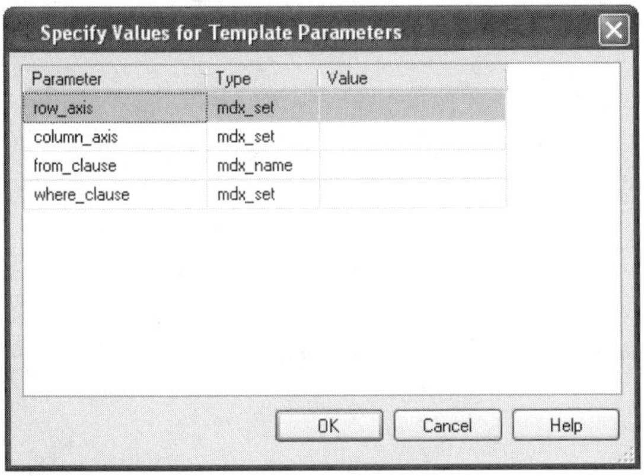

Figure 19-29   The Specify Values For Template Parameters dialog box in SQL Server Management Studio

This dialog box offers a single UI for specifying all query specifics, but it is designed for programmers who are already sufficiently experienced with MDX syntax such that typing the clauses without assistance is feasible and preferable. We are still getting acquainted with MDX, so we'll supply the parameterized clauses through different means. For now, click Cancel to dismiss the dialog box.

We will supply the four requested clauses (*ON ROWS*, *ON COLUMNS*, *FROM*, and *WHERE*) one at a time. Let's start with the *row_axis*: Select the entire *<row_axis, mdx_set,>* angle-bracketed clause and press the Delete key. Next, in the metadata tree view, drill down on the Geography dimension node and then drag its *Country* attribute child node into the MDX edit region, dropping it just to the left of the "on Columns" portion of the command (leaving a space to the right of the drop position). Press the right arrow key to deselect the dropped text. Next, type a period. Your query text should now appear as follows:

```
Select [Geography].[Country]. on Columns,
      <column_axis, mdx_set,> on Rows

From <from_clause, mdx_name,>
Where <where_clause, mdx_set,>
```

With the cursor just to the right of the period you typed, choose IntelliSense, List Members from the Edit menu or press Ctrl+J. An IntelliSense popup list should appear; type **members**, and the keyword MEMBERS should become selected. Press Enter or Tab to insert the entire word into your code.

Repeat this process for the *column_axis* clause, but this time use the *Beverages* member of the *Category - Product* hierarchy of the *Products* dimension as the base of the expression (that is, drill down to the Products\Category - Product\Members\All\Beverages node and drag it into the MDX editor). Next, after typing a period as you did for the *row_axis* clause, click on the Functions tab in the Tools pane, drill down to the Navigation\CHILDREN node, and drag it to the right of the period in the editor. After you drop the text, delete the *«Member»*. text (including the period) immediately to the left of the CHILDREN keyword.

Remove the bracketed *from_clause* text from the query, and then click the Metadata tab and drag the Sales (root) node to the cursor position. Finish by removing the *where_clause* parameter and dragging the Measures\Main\Sum\Total Sales node to take its place. Your query should appear as follows. (If not, you can find it in the file Children.mdx.)

```
Select [Geography].[Country].MEMBERS on Columns,
       [Products].[Category - Product].[Category Name].&[Beverages].CHILDREN on Rows

From [Sales]
Where [Measures].[Total Sales]
```

Execute the query. Figure 19-30 shows a partial view of the results you should receive.

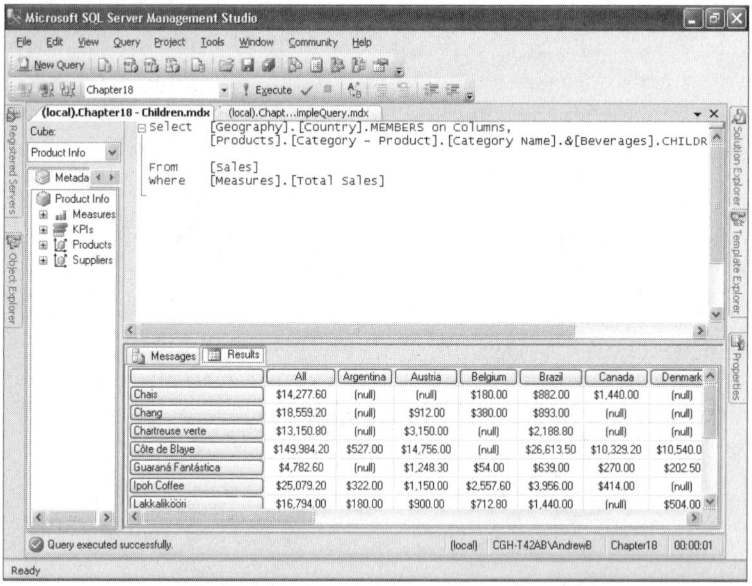

Figure 19-30   Our fully configured MDX query, with results displayed

Beyond Syntax

Although we have written only two queries so far, we have covered quite a lot. You've learned the basic MDX syntax and the use of the MDX Query window. You've learned how to use the

Registered Servers and Object Explorer windows with Analysis Services servers, including several shortcuts for opening MDX Query windows against specific connections and databases. In the MDX Query window, you learned how to use Template Explorer, MDX IntelliSense, and the Metadata and Functions tabs in the Tools pane to design your MDX queries step by step. However, although we've exposed you to the mechanics of MDX and the MDX features in Management Studio, we haven't really discussed the language itself in much depth. Let's remedy that now by focusing on some important MDX concepts.

Let's start with our first query. Notice that both the *ON COLUMNS* and *ON ROWS* clauses use a dot-separated syntax to specify the dimension and attribute. The name of our measure, Total Sales, is enclosed within square brackets; this is required syntax for any name that contains one or more embedded spaces. Names without embedded spaces can also be enclosed in square brackets, although we did not do so in this query. As you saw when you used the MDX-generating tools in SQL Server Management Studio, however, use of squared brackets for non-spaced names is encouraged.

Immediately following the attribute names in the *ON COLUMNS* and *ON ROWS* clauses, we used the MDX function keyword MEMBERS to request that each individual member of the attribute be included as a row or column. Axis specifiers (that is, the expressions preceding the ON ROWS or ON COLUMNS keywords) must always indicate a *set*—that is, a collection of items belonging to one or a combination of attributes or hierarchy levels. These items must either be listed explicitly or specified through the use of an MDX function, such as *MEMBERS*.

The proper MDX name for items in a set is *tuple*. A tuple, whose more formal syntax we will describe shortly, specifies a member in *every dimension* in the cube. In practice, however, a tuple need not explicitly specify members for more than one or perhaps a few dimensions. That's because each tuple implicitly references the default member of each dimension when a specific member is not given, and in most cases the default member is the *[All]* member. So even if we identify a tuple by, say, a shipper name and nothing else, that tuple will refer to the subset of the cube for that shipper in the *Shippers* dimension and the *[All]* member (that is, the entirety) of all other dimensions.

We must tell you now that this rather theoretical definition of a tuple makes sense to very few people at first. At this point, you need simply to acknowledge it and file it away for later, when you've had more OLAP experience and it will make more sense. In practice, you can think of sets as consisting of simply specified members, rather than cryptically defined tuples. To illustrate the set concept more directly, here is a variation on our first query in which we use an explicit set specifier for the *COLUMNS* axis:

```
SELECT {[Speedy Express], [Federal Shipping]} ON COLUMNS,
    Time.Year.MEMBERS ON ROWS
FROM Sales
WHERE Measures.[Total Sales]
```

This query (contained in the file SelectedShippers.mdx) allows us to request a limited, specific set of *Shippers* attribute members rather than having to show them all. Each shipper is technically a tuple, but you can feel free to think of each one as a member for now.

As you can see, explicitly specifying even members can be a bit tedious and the syntax requirements are quite stringent. That's why functions such as MEMBERS can be extremely useful— they allow you to specify large sets with relatively little typing and few curly braces. But OLAP developers do not live by the *MEMBERS* function alone! MDX contains a dizzying array of other set-generating functions.

For example, you can use the MDX keyword *CHILDREN* to list all of the child members of a specified node in a hierarchy. To understand how this works, refer back to our second query (in Children.mdx). The *ROWS* axis shows products in the Beverages category (the children of the *Beverages* member of the *Category Name* level of the *Category – Product* hierarchy of the *Products* dimension).

Grokking the *WHERE* Clause   Now let's discuss the *WHERE* clause of this query in more detail. We have been using the *WHERE* clause thus far as a mechanism to specify the measure we want to see in our result set. This is a valid and typical use of the *WHERE* clause in an MDX query, but it obfuscates the real purpose of the clause: to specify for the query a filter condition for each and every dimension in the cube.

On initial inspection, this seems counterintuitive on a number of fronts. For example, our *WHERE* clause specified our desired *measure* but it did not seem to specify any type of filter or filter condition, nor anything relating to *dimensions*. But it turns out that, technically speaking, our *WHERE* clause does indeed supply a dimension filter. Understanding why this is the case requires an appreciation of how MDX views measures and how it uses the default members of a dimension.

Simply put, MDX considers your cube to consist of dimensions and data only. Rather than viewing measures as distinct entities within your cube, it considers each measure to be a member of a flat hierarchy of a single dimension called Measures. For this reason, the expression *[Measures].[Total Sales]* in the *WHERE* clause *is* a filter condition: In effect, you are telling the MDX engine to limit the query to analysis of the *[Total Sales]* member of the *Measures* "dimension." For all other dimensions in the cube, no filter condition is specified, so the MDX query returns the entire contents of all the actual dimensions.

If you want to place a filter that seems more "real" in your query, you can do so by adding to the *WHERE* clause. For example, to limit our first query to sales of products in the Condiments category, you would modify the previous query to the following (which can be found in the script file TrueFilter.mdx):

```
SELECT Shippers.[Shipper Name].MEMBERS ON COLUMNS,
       Time.Year.MEMBERS ON ROWS
FROM Sales
WHERE (Measures.[Total Sales],
       Products.[Category Name].Condiments)
```

Notice that the filtering condition on the *Products* dimension is concatenated to the existing condition on the *Measures* "dimension" with a comma delimiter, and that the entire *WHERE* clause expression is enclosed in parentheses.

The parentheses are required for any tuple that is specified through two or more explicitly named members. Because in this case we are specifying a tuple with two members (*Measures.[Total Sales]* and *Products.[Category Name].Condiments*), we must supply them in a comma-delimited list and enclose the list in parentheses. The tuple in our *WHERE* clause is the subset of the cube consisting of *[Total Sales]* data for products within the Condiments product category and the entirety of all other dimensions in the cube. The rest of our query then breaks down this subset of the cube by shipper name and calendar year.

> **More Info**   It is important to remember that the *WHERE* expression in the previous query (which contained the simple expression *Measures.[Total Sales]*) was also a tuple in its own right. Even though it appeared to be a simple member specifier, its implicit reference to the *[All]* member of each dimension in the cube qualified it to be every bit as much a tuple expression as the more complex one used just now.

The Power of Axes   Let's take a step back and discuss the concept of axes. The queries we've looked at thus far have all returned results over two axes, namely *ROWS* and *COLUMNS*. Such two-dimensional result sets are convenient and often sufficient, but MDX can handle many more than two axes. Although the first five axes have names, you can also refer to them by number.

For example, consider the following query (which can be found in the file SingleAxis.mdx) that returns data along a single, numbered axis:

```
SELECT Geography.Country.MEMBERS ON 0
FROM Sales
WHERE Measures.[Total Sales]
```

Here we are specifying only a columns axis, using its axis number. Axis 0 is the *COLUMNS* axis, and axis 1 is the *ROWS* axis. Note that no gaps are allowed in the axis sequence, so a single-axis query must use the *COLUMNS* axis and not the *ROWS* axis. Axes can, however, be listed out of sequence, as in the following query (which can be found in the file AxesOutOfSequence.mdx) that returns data on two axes but specifies the *ROWS* axis before the *COLUMNS* axis and does not use a *WHERE* clause:

```
SELECT Products.[Category - Product].[Category Name].Beverages.CHILDREN ON 1,
        Measures.MEMBERS ON 0
FROM Sales
```

This query asks for the members of the Measures "dimension" to be listed along the *COLUMNS* axis, thus allowing us not to use a *WHERE* clause that would normally specify our selected measure.

What about queries with more than two axes? MDX permits queries to return a theoretically boundless number of axes (though available resources on the server and client hardware will impose some limit). You can name three axes past the *COLUMNS* and *ROWS* axes. The axes' names after *ROWS* are, in axis order, *PAGES*, *SECTIONS*, and *CHAPTERS*. These correspond numerically to axes 2, 3, and 4 (with *COLUMNS* and *ROWS* being 0 and 1, respectively). The names of these higher axes convey what it means to bring back data on more than two axes: Although it is difficult to imagine seeing data presented on more than two axes at once, it is relatively easy to imagine a series of two-axis result sets spread over several pages, sections, and chapters of a book.

Another way to think through axis management is to imagine an Excel workbook. In Excel, data is always shown one spreadsheet at a time, and each sheet has both columns and rows. But one workbook can contain multiple tabs (pages), several workbooks can be contained in a folder (section), and a collection of folders can be contained in a parent folder (chapter). You can easily imagine more "axes" by understanding that multiple drives can be managed by a single server, multiple servers can belong to a single farm, and so on. You can thus imagine writing queries with more axes than the five named ones.

With this understanding of the use of multiple axes, the following query (which can be found in the file ThreeAxes.mdx) should now seem quite sensible:

```
SELECT Shippers.[Shipper Name].MEMBERS ON COLUMNS,
       Geography.Country.MEMBERS ON ROWS,
       Time.Year.MEMBERS ON PAGES
FROM Sales
WHERE (Measures.[Total Sales],
    Products.[Category Name].Condiments)
```

When executed, the query returns total sales for all products in the Condiments category, broken down into shippers and country on the *ROWS* and *COLUMNS* axes, with the data for each distinct calendar year on a separate page.

However, if you execute this query in SQL Server Management Studio, the Results tab will be empty and the following text will be returned on the Messages tab of the results pane:

```
Executing the query ...
Obtained object of type: Microsoft.AnalysisServices.AdomdClient.CellSet
Formatting.
Results cannot be displayed for cellsets with more than two axes.
Execution complete
```

The second line of this message indicates that the query is valid and executed without error. However, the fourth line indicates that queries returning data over more than two axes cannot be displayed in the SQL Server Management Studio MDX Query window.

> **More Info**   Although we won't cover XMLA queries until later in this chapter, you might want to open and execute the query in the file ThreeAxes.xmla. It contains the same MDX query as does ThreeAxes.mdx, but it will execute without error because data is returned as XML rather than in a grid. If you scroll down toward the bottom of the XML returned on the Results tab, you will see the individual values for each cell on all three axes. How you can read and process this XML will become clear by the end of the chapter.

CROSSJOIN and *DRILLDOWNMEMBER*   How can we deal with this dilemma? Shortly, we'll explore how to execute MDX queries in .NET code and discuss two ways of handling queries that return more than two axes. For now, however, you can rewrite your query as follows:

```
SELECT Shippers.[Shipper Name].MEMBERS ON COLUMNS,
    CROSSJOIN([Time].[Year].MEMBERS,
        Geography.Country.MEMBERS) ON ROWS
FROM Sales
WHERE (Measures.[Total Sales],
    Products.[Category Name].Condiments)
```

The query (which can be found in the file CrossJoin.mdx) uses the MDX *CROSSJOIN* function to "stack" or "flatten" the members of *Time.Year* and *Geography.Country* together on the *ROWS* axis. This has the effect of creating a result set where each row "header" has two members within it: a country and a year.

> **Note**   In our crossjoin query, data is returned by year and then country. If the order of the sets in the *CROSSJOIN* function had been reversed, the data would have been returned by country and then year.

If you review the results data, you will see that the second row in the 1996 section of our result set (and the 25th row overall), which contains total sales data for all condiments sold in Argentina in 1996, contains nothing but *NULLs*. This indicates that no condiment products were sold in Argentina in 1996; likewise, the last column (for the *Unknown* product member) also consists of empty cells. MDX makes it easy to suppress these empty axis members with the use of the *NONEMPTYCROSSJOIN* and *NONEMPTY* functions. To see this in action, modify the query as follows. (This version can be found in the file NonEmpty.mdx.)

```
SELECT NON EMPTY(Shippers.[Shipper Name].MEMBERS) ON COLUMNS,
    NONEMPTYCROSSJOIN(Time.Year.MEMBERS, Geography.Country.MEMBERS) ON ROWS
FROM Sales
WHERE (Measures.[Total Sales],
    Products.[Category Name].Condiments)
```

When you execute the query, the columns and rows that were completely populated with *NULL*s will be gone and you will find the results much easier to read.

We can't hope to cover the comprehensive set of hierarchy-oriented functions in MDX, but we can give you a taste by showing another query (which can be found in the file DrillDownMember.mdx). This query returns the same data as the previous one but also returns the state/province-level data for Canada and the United States:

```
SELECT NONEMPTY(Shippers.[Shipper Name].MEMBERS) ON COLUMNS,
       NONEMPTYCROSSJOIN(Time.Year.MEMBERS,
       DRILLDOWNMEMBER(Geography.[Country - State-Province - City -
       Postal Code].Country.MEMBERS, {CANADA, USA})) ON ROWS
FROM Sales
WHERE (Measures.[Total Sales],
    Products.[Category Name].Condiments)
```

Note the use of the *DRILLDOWNMEMBER* function to obtain the *[Total Sales]* data for the states and provinces in Canada and the USA in addition to the country data. The *DRILLDOWNMEMBER* function accepts two sets and returns the union of the first with the children of any of its members contained in the second.

KPIs, Calculated Members, and Named Sets

We're almost done with the theoretical side of MDX, and you now have a good sense of its power (although we still have plenty to explain about how to execute MDX queries programmatically). But all the queries we've examined so far leverage only the simple components of our cube—specifically, dimensions and measures. Let's not forget, though, that in the previous chapter we implemented some more complex Analysis Services features, including the definition of calculated members, named sets, and Key Performance Indicators (KPIs). The question is, how can we use these from MDX?

First let's start with KPIs. Recall that a KPI, when applied to a slice of our cube, generates a value, a goal, a status, and a trend (the latter two usually returning a discrete value between −1 and +1, inclusive). Recall also that MDX functions exist for returning all four of these values. The following query (which can be found in the script file AverageTotalSalesKPI.mdx) returns all four values for the KPI we created in the previous chapter (*Average Total Sales KPI*). It does so for each calendar year for which the cube holds sales data in the United Kingdom.

```
SELECT {KPIValue("Average Total Sales KPI"),
       KPIGoal("Average Total Sales KPI"),
       KPIStatus("Average Total Sales KPI"),
       KPITrend("Average Total Sales KPI")} ON COLUMNS,
       [OrderDate].[Year - Quarter - Month - Date].Year.MEMBERS ON ROWS
FROM Sales
WHERE Geography.Country.UK
```

MDX cannot tell us the status and trend graphics we configured the KPI to use, but we can retrieve that information from the ADO MD.NET *Kpi* object, which we will focus on later in this chapter.

What about calculated members and named sets? The beauty of calculated members is that they can be referenced from an MDX query as if they were physically part of the cube, rather than calculated. You can use named sets as substitutes for explicitly stated sets, such as the one we examined earlier in the SelectedShippers.mdx query. All of this is much easier to understand when viewed in a query such as the following one (which can be found in Named-SetCalcMember.mdx):

```
SELECT Time.[Year -  Quarter -  Month -  OrderDate].Year.MEMBERS ON COLUMNS,
    [Test Markets] ON ROWS
FROM Sales
WHERE Measures.[Adjusted Sales]
```

This query returns values for the *[Adjusted Sales]* calculated measure, broken down by calendar year on the *COLUMNS* axis and by the three cities in our *[Test Markets]* named set on the *ROWS* axis.

The next query (which can be found in AdjustedGrowthByState.mdx), demonstrates how to query a calculated measure whose formula is based on a time series comparison. In this case, we are querying our *[Adjusted Sales Growth]* calculated measure, which measures year-on-year sales growth as a percentage. This calculated measure requires that the *Order Date* dimension, on which its formula is based, be used in one of the axis specifiers, which it is.

```
SELECT [Order Date].[Year].MEMBERS ON COLUMNS,
[Geography].[Country - State-Province - City Postal Code].[Country].USA.CHILDREN ON ROWS
FROM Sales
WHERE Measures.[Adjusted Sales Growth]
```

This query shows the growth numbers, for all years for which the cube holds data, on the *COLUMNS* axis, broken down by individual states in the United States on the *ROWS* axis.

At this point, we've studied enough MDX and it's time to start learning how to put it to use. Keep in mind that we've covered how to take advantage of a number of advanced cube features, including KPIs and calculations (named sets and calculated members). We haven't covered drillthrough-based or URL-based actions, even though these are all based on stored MDX expressions. We will cover these shortly; having some basic API knowledge under your belt first will make this easier. So let's set aside writing queries for now and learn how to put them to work in our applications.

OLAP Development with ADO MD.NET

Think about everything we've covered in the last two chapters and up to this point in this chapter. You've learned how to design a cube from scratch and extend it with calculations, KPIs, actions, and perspectives. You've also learned how to query the cube using Excel Pivot-Tables and charts, both in Excel itself and from your own Windows Forms and ASP.NET applications. And we just covered in great detail how to use MDX to query your cube in a variety of ways in SQL Server Management Studio, giving you extremely precise control over what results are returned.

What we haven't yet covered is how to execute MDX queries from within your own applications and display the results. It will be important to know how to execute queries that return data over two axes and display results quickly. It will also be important to understand how to execute more complex queries—those with three or more axes—and examine the results programmatically so that members of the third and higher axes can be enumerated in your own custom user interfaces.

With the introduction of SQL Server Analysis Services 2005, this kind of programming is almost as easy as data access programming against relational databases. That's because Microsoft has created an ADO.NET managed data provider called ADO MD.NET, which you can use against Analysis Services databases. In fact, ADO MD.NET was introduced in May 2004 for use with SQL Server Analysis Services 2000, but using it with that version of the product was tricky. ADO MD.NET is implemented as a wrapper around XML for Analysis (XMLA), which (as we saw in action in the last chapter) is the native protocol of Analysis Services 2005. Analysis Services 2000 did not use XMLA natively (it instead used a protocol called PivotTable Service, or PTS), so using ADO MD.NET against Analysis Services 2000 required the installation of an XMLA wrapper (the XMLA SDK) around PTS.

Using Your ADO.NET Skills

One of the great things about ADO MD.NET is that you can treat it like any other ADO.NET provider—using *Connection, Command, DataReader, DataAdapter, DataTable,* and *DataSet* objects to execute MDX queries and handle the results. But you can also use a wide array of OLAP-specific objects to explore a cube's metadata and carefully crawl through result sets (including those with more than two axes) axis by axis and cell by cell.

These OLAP-specific objects are essentially clones of the objects available in the old ADO MD object model (initially introduced with OLAP Services in SQL Server 7.0), which was effectively the native API for OLAP programming in SQL Server 2000 Analysis Services. ADO MD was a COM-based wrapper around OLE DB for OLAP (much as ADO was a COM wrapper around OLE DB). ADO MD.NET is thus the "fusion" of ADO MD and ADO.NET, and it is based on XMLA.

To use ADO MD.NET in your applications, simply set a reference to the *Microsoft.AnalysisServices.AdomdClient* managed assembly, which is listed on the .NET tab of Visual Studio's Add Reference dialog box. If you are working on a PC that has the older ADO MD.NET provider for SQL Server 2000 Analysis Services installed, be sure to select the new version (version 9.0) as shown in Figure 19-31. Once you set the reference, use the namespace of the same name in your code.

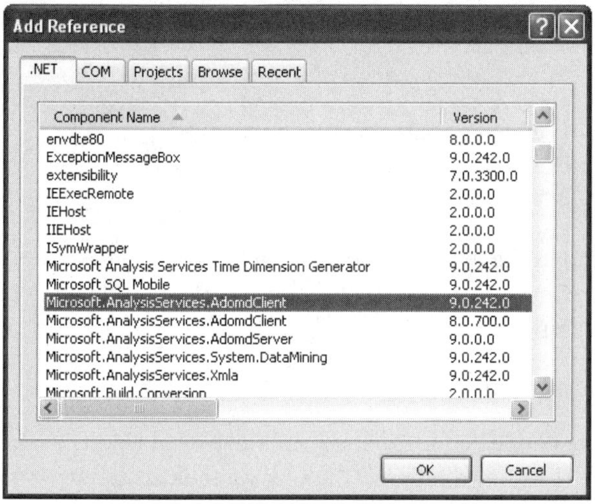

Figure 19-31   The Add Reference dialog box in Visual Studio, with the .NET tab active and the ADO MD.NET assembly (*Microsoft.AnalysisServices.AdomdClient*) selected

You now have direct access to all objects in the ADO MD.NET library, including *AdomdConnection*, *AdomdCommand*, and *AdomdDataAdapter*. Connection strings for the *AdomdConnection* simply require *Data Source* and *Initial Catalog* specifiers; the *CommandText* property of the *AdomdCommand* can then be set to any MDX query and can be used to return an *AdomdDataReader* (or, using the *AdomdDataAdapter.Fill* method, a *DataTable* or *DataSet*).

Beyond this standard ADO.NET functionality, you can also use the special *AdomdCommand .ExecuteCellSet* method to get back an OLAP-specific result set object called a *CellSet*. Under "classic" ADO MD, *CellSet* objects were the only OLAP result set vehicle available. Although *CellSet* objects are not as convenient to work with as *DataReader*, *DataTable*, and *DataSet* objects, they have *Axes* and *Cells* collections and thus allow for better programmatic manipulation of MDX result sets, especially when more than two axes are returned.

In addition to *CellSet* objects, ADO MD.NET offers other unique objects that make OLAP-oriented programming easier. ADO MD.NET makes it relatively easy to create .NET code that connects to OLAP cubes and then explores their metadata, executes MDX queries against them, and displays the results. We'll now show you how to use ADO MD.NET to write code that queries both a cube's data and its metadata.

Executing MDX Queries

Let's start on the data side. The following code connects to the Chapter18 database on a local-host Analysis Services host, executes a simple MDX query against the *Sales* cube, and then binds the results to a *DataGridView* control called *dgvResults*:

```
AdomdConnection conn = new AdomdConnection("DataSource=localhost;Initial
 Catalog=Chapter18");
AdomdDataAdapter da = new AdomdDataAdapter("SELECT
 Shippers.[Shipper Name].MEMBERS ON COLUMNS, Time.Year.MEMBERS ON ROWS FROM
 Sales WHERE Measures.[Total Sales]", conn);
DataTable dt = new DataTable();
da.Fill(dt);
dgvResults.DataSource = dt;
```

Code similar to this can be found in the function *ExecMDX* in the form *frmAPIs* in the sample code's Windows Forms project, Chapter19. Note that the previous code will work only if the following *using* directive has been placed at the top of the class file:

```
using Microsoft.AnalysisServices.AdomdClient;
```

In case you weren't counting, we connected to, queried, and displayed results using just five lines of code, not including the *using* directive. Granted, we took advantage of the *AdomdDataAdpater* object's ability to accept an MDX command string in its constructor and thus create an *AdomdCommand* object on our behalf. But the point still stands: Writing .NET OLAP code doesn't have to be hard.

Working with More Than Two Axes

Now let's consider a harder case: a query with three axes. In this case, we'll need to explicitly declare and initialize *AdomdConnection* and *AdomdCommand* objects, and we'll bring the results back as a *CellSet* object. We'll insert each member of the *PAGES* axis in a *ComboBox* control called *cboPages*, and we'll display all the rows and columns of the selected page (and their data) in a *ListView* control called *lvwResults* (the *View* property of which must be set to *Details*).

To start with, here's the code that declares and initializes our *AdomdConnection* and *Adomd-Command* objects:

```
AdomdConnection conn = new AdomdConnection("Data Source=localhost;Initial
 Catalog=Chapter18");
AdomdCommand cmd = new AdomdCommand("SELECT Shippers.[Shipper Name].MEMBERS
 ON COLUMNS, Geography.Country.MEMBERS ON ROWS, Time.Year.MEMBERS ON PAGES
 FROM Sales WHERE (Measures.[Total Sales],
 Products.[Category   Name].Condiments)", conn);
```

Next, the code grabs the results of the three-axis MDX query in an ADO MD.NET *CellSet* (assuming that *cs*, an object of type *CellSet*, has already been declared at the class level):

```
conn.Open();
cs = cmd.ExecuteCellSet();
conn.Close();
```

Once we have the *CellSet*, we can iterate through axis 2 (the *PAGES* axis) and populate our *ComboBox* control with the name of each page.

```
foreach (Position p in cs.Axes[2].Positions)
{
    cboPages.Items.Add(p.Members[0].Caption);
}
```

In almost the same fashion, we can loop through the axis 1 (*COLUMNS* axis) positions and add an item to the *ListView* object's *Columns* collection for each position on the axis (first adding a blank "dummy" column to accommodate the row headers that will appear):

```
lvwResults.Columns.Add(String.Empty);
foreach (Position p in cs.Axes[0].Positions)
{
    lvwResults.Columns.Add(p.Members[0].Caption);
}
```

Next we'll preselect PAGE 0 by setting the *SelectedIndex* property of *cboPages*:

```
cboPages.SelectedIndex = 0;
```

In the *SelectedIndexChanged* event handler of *cboPages*, we'll add a new item to the *ListView* control for each position in axis 1 (the *ROWS* axis), setting its text to the caption of the *ROW* axis. We'll then add one *SubItem* to that *ListViewItem* for every column, fetching the *FormattedValue* of the corresponding cell:

```
lvwResults.Items.Clear();
foreach (Position p in cs.Axes[1].Positions)
{
    ListViewItem newItem = lvwResults.Items.Add(p.Members[0].Caption);
    for (int i = 0; i < cs.Axes[0].Positions.Count; i++)
    {
        newItem.SubItems.Add(cs.Cells[i, newItem.Index,
        cboPages.SelectedIndex].FormattedValue);
    }
}
```

Notice that we fetch the correct cell using a three-level coordinate, in the (column, row, page) format, where the column is determined by the inner loop's counter value (the position in axis 0, the *COLUMNS* axis), the row is determined by the new *ListViewItem* object's index, and the page is determined by the *SelectedIndex* of *cboPages*.

Code that implements these techniques can be found in the *AdomdCommand.ExecuteCellSet* region in the source code of form *frmAPIs* in the sample code's Windows Forms project, Chapter19. Figure 19-32 shows the OLAP APIs form after that code has been executed.

	All Shippers	Speedy Express	United Package	Federal Shipping	Unknown
All	$113,694.75	$43,118.75	$40,876.70	$29,699.30	
Argentina	$907.00			$907.00	
Austria	$16,802.40	$8,193.85	$6,274.95	$2,333.60	
Belgium	$2,714.70	$816.00	$1,111.70	$787.00	
Brazil	$12,139.00	$7,056.15	$1,850.80	$3,232.05	
Canada	$5,010.60	$1,750.00	$318.50	$2,942.10	
Denmark	$4,455.40	$2,466.00	$585.00	$1,404.40	
Finland	$1,873.00	$950.00	$570.00	$353.00	
France	$7,148.40	$985.10	$3,420.30	$2,743.00	
Germany	$17,395.10	$6,026.90	$5,547.80	$5,820.40	
Ireland					
Italy	$1,448.25	$260.00	$648.00	$540.25	
Mexico	$1,235.45		$651.50	$583.95	
Norway	$234.00		$234.00		
Poland	$627.00		$199.50	$427.50	
Portugal	$3,869.45		$1,798.40	$2,071.05	
Spain	$1,789.45		$1,504.45	$285.00	
Sweden	$4,970.30	$3,069.00	$1,023.30	$878.00	

Figure 19-32   The sample application's OLAP APIs form, with a three-axis query executed and the *Time.Year = All PAGES* axis member displayed

Working with *CellSet* objects is harder than working with *DataReader*, *DataTable*, or *DatsSet* objects, but the results are often better. Because we grab the *Caption* property of each axis position/member, our column and row headers are more user friendly than the unique name-based column and row headers returned in *DataReader*, *DataTable*, and *DataSet* objects. Our data presentation is more user friendly as well because we're displaying the data fetched from the *FormattedValue* property of each cell (and recall that in Chapter 18 we configured each of our measures to use currency formatting).

> **Note**   The API programming techniques we cover in this chapter can be used in ASP.NET as well as Windows Forms applications. However, ASP.NET data binding does not work well with MDX result sets (be they in the form of *AdomdDataReader*, *DataTable* or *DataSet* objects). Therefore, you may wish to limit your ASP.NET/ADO MD.NET development to the programmatic manipulation of *CellSet* objects.

Cell References: Coordinate-Based vs. Ordinal

Speaking of cells, they are typically referenced from a *CellSet* object's *Cells* collection by coordinate reference. For two-axis queries, we use a (column, row) coordinate format; for three-axis coordinates, we use a (column, row, page) format. (The coordinate reference is determined by axis order.) But you can also reference cells ordinally, by supplying a single value as the index into the *Cells* collection. For a two-axis *CellSet*, the ordinal value is calculated as follows:

```
row number * column count + column number
```

Therefore, *Cells[5, 2]* in a *CellSet* with 10 columns can be also be referenced as *Cells[25]* (because 2 * 10 + 5 = 25). For a three-axis *CellSet*, the formula is as follows:

```
(page number * row count * column count) + (row number * column count) + (column number)
```

Cells[5, 2, 3] in a *CellSet* with 20 rows and 10 columns can also be referenced as *Cells[625]* (because 3 × 20 × 10 + 2 × 10 + 5 = 625). Understanding the formula for fetching cells ordinally allows you to write code that generically fetches cell values from a CellSet of any number of axes.

Cracking the Metadata

If you know how to fetch MDX result sets as *DataReader*, *DataTable*, *DataSet*, and *CellSet* objects, you can build applications that can query virtually any cube and return the results. Of course, to build these applications, you must have full knowledge of the cube's structure and embed the MDX queries into your application code. This tends to be how we write relational applications, but it does not always work well for OLAP applications.

The whole point of OLAP is to allow users to explore their data. Just as Excel PivotTables and charts offer a Field List window where users can change their queries on the fly, your own applications might benefit from offering users a list of measures, dimensions (and their attributes and hierarchies), and KPIs. You might even want to create a high-powered front end that presents the measure groups, display folders, and other advanced metadata you used when designing your cube.

We will now discuss three distinct methods for fetching metadata in your cubes: two that use ADO MD.NET and one that uses Analysis Management Objects (AMO). Although we don't have room here to provide explicit examples of enumerating every possible piece of metadata, we will provide representative code examples and you can refer to the sample code provided with this chapter for several more.

Getting Metadata from ADO MD.NET   The ADO MD.NET object model provides access to a full list of your database's cubes and much of their metadata. This is possible because the *AdomdConnection* object contains a *Cubes* collection whose child members, in turn, contain *Kpis*, *NamedSets*, *Measures*, and *Dimensions* collections. Each object in these collections contains important details. For example, each *Kpi* object in the *Kpis* collection contains *StatusGraphic* and

TrendGraphic properties that specify which graphics were selected when the KPI was designed. Combining this information with the data returned by the MDX *KPIStatus* and *KPITrend* functions allows you to present a rich UI for the KPI data in your cube.

Each *Dimension* object has a *Hierarchies* and an *AttributeHierarchies* collection (the latter containing attributes). *Hierarchy* objects have a *Levels* collection, and *Level* objects have a *GetMembers* method that returns a collection of *Member* objects. To get a sense of how this works, consider the following code. It opens a connection to our Chapter18 Analysis Services database and then populates *cboMeasures* (a *ComboBox* control) with a list of all measures in the *Sales* cube:

```
AdomdConnection conn = new AdomdConnection("Data Source=localhost;Initial
  Catalog=Chapter18");
conn.Open();
CubeDef cube = conn.Cubes["Sales"];
foreach (Measure m in cube.Measures)
{
    cboMeasures.Items.Add(m.Caption);
}
conn.Close();
```

Code that implements a similar technique can be found in the *Measures* region in the source code of form *frmAPIs* in the sample code's Windows Forms project, Chapter19.

> **Note**   As with the previous example (and later code examples in this chapter), the previous code will work only if the *Microsoft.AnalysisServices.AdomdClient* namespace is properly referenced in a *using* statement.

Schema *DataSet* Objects   The ADO MD.NET object model itself does not contain collections or objects for measure groups, calculated members, or actions. Instead, you can enumerate these objects by using the *AdomdConnection* object's *GetSchemaDataSet* method, which returns a one-table *DataSet* containing detailed metadata. The method has several overloads, the simplest of which accepts an enumerated constant indicating the type of metadata desired and a special restriction array used to filter the metadata returned.

For example, you can use *GetSchemaDataSet* to get a list of measure groups quite easily. The following five lines of code fetch a *DataSet* containing detailed metadata information for all measure groups in the *Sales* cube in the Chapter18 database and then display the metadata in *dgvResults*, a *DataGridView* control:

```
AdomdConnection conn = new AdomdConnection("Data Source=localhost;Initial
  Catalog=Chapter18");
conn.Open();
DataSet ds = conn.GetSchemaDataSet(AdomdSchemaGuid.MeasureGroups, new
  object[] { "", "", "Sales" });
dgvResults.DataSource = ds.Tables[0];
conn.Close();
```

Code that implements a similar technique can be found in the *Measure Groups* region in the source code of form *frmAPIs* in the sample code's Windows Forms project, Chapter19.

When you view the contents of the schema *DataSet* in the *DataGridView* control, you should take note of a few important things. First, notice that the third column (column 2, named *CUBE_NAME*) contains the cube name; this is precisely why we placed our desired cube name ("Sales") in the third element in the inline array passed to *GetSchemaDataSet*. The structure of restriction arrays aligns with the columns in the schema *DataSet* table that they filter. Had we not specified a cube name in the restrictions array, all measure groups in the entire database would have been returned. The results of such an unfiltered query are shown in Figure 19-33.

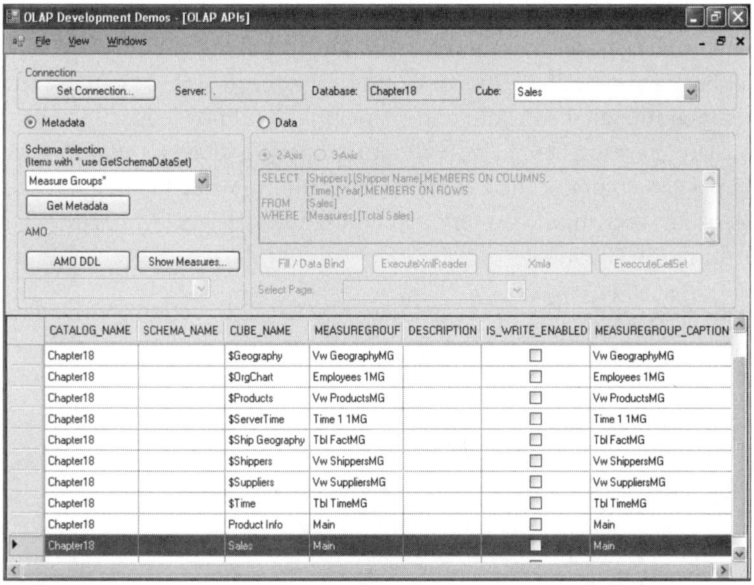

Figure 19-33 Contents of the *MeasureGroups* schema *DataSet* bound to, and displayed in, a *DataGridView* control

Next, notice that the seventh and final column (column 6, named *MEASUREGROUP_CAPTION*) contains the actual name of the measure group. You can therefore use the following code to populate a *ComboBox* control called *cboMeasureGroups* with the measure groups in the cube:

```
foreach (DataRow dr in ds.Tables[0].Rows)
{
    cboMeasureGroups.Items.Add(dr["MEASUREGROUP_CAPTION"]);
}
```

In addition to fetching measure groups, you can use schema *DataSet* objects to fetch lists of databases, calculated members, and actions (using the enumerated constants *AdomdSchema-Guid.Catalogs*, *AdomdSchemaGuid.Members*, and *AdomdSchemaGuid.Actions*, respectively) from a server. In fact, you can use schema *DataSet* objects to discover much of the same metadata that can be fetched from the ADO MD.NET object model itself. Just bear in mind that when you use ADO MD.NET, certain metadata can be fetched *only* using *GetSchema-DataSet*.

Executing Actions Using Schema *DataSet* Objects   *GetSchemaDataSet* technically returns only metadata, but sometimes this metadata is useful for more than determining a cube's structure and contents. Specifically, if you want your application to support any actions you created when you designed your cube, *GetSchemaDataSet* is indispensable. Recall that in Chapter 18 we created a URL action that performs an MSN search on cities and a drillthrough action to show fact data underlying cells in the cube.

The target of our URL is the members of the *City* level of the *Country – State-Province – City – Postal Code* hierarchy of the *Geography* dimension; the target of our drillthrough is the individual cells in our cube. To get specific URLs or drillthrough result sets, we can use the *Adomd-SchemaGuid.Actions* enumerated constant and then apply our knowledge of the actions' targets to the restriction arrays. Doing this will return specific schema *DataSet* objects, with tables that contain a text column called content. This column will contain a fully computed URL for the URL action and an MDX query containing the special *DRILLTHROUGH* command for the drillthrough action.

The following code determines the value generated by the URL action for the city of Vancouver and then navigates to that URL using a *WebBrowser* control.

```
object[] Restrictions = new object[7];
Restrictions[2] = "Sales";
Restrictions[5] = "Geography.[Country - State-Province - City -
 Postal Code].City.Vancouver";
Restrictions[6] = MDACTION_COORDINATE_MEMBER;

DataTable results = conn.GetSchemaDataSet(AdomdSchemaGuid.Actions, Restrictions).
Tables[0];
dgvResults.DataSource = results;
MessageBox.Show("Content = " + results.Rows[0]["Content"].ToString() + "\nClick OK to
navigate to action URL");

wbrMain.Navigate(results.Rows[0]["Content"].ToString());
```

This code relies on a few things:

- As before, that *conn* is a valid *AdomdConnection* object pointing to our Chapter 18 database and *dgvResults* is a *DataGridView* control.

- That *MDACTION_COORDINATE_MEMBER* has already been defined with its documented value of 4.

- That *wbrMain* is a *WebBrowser* control.

  Code that implements this technique can be found in the *Actions - URL* region in the source code of form *frmAPIs* in the sample code's Windows Forms project, Chapter 19.

The values we store in the restrictions array ensure that the schema *DataSet* returns only actions for the *Geography.[Country − State-Province − City − Postal Code].City.Vancouver*-level member of the *Sales* cube. We know that only one action has been defined for this member, so we can assume that row 0 of the *DataTable* object *results* contains that action info and that its *Content* column contains the specific URL for Vancouver (*http://search.msn.com/ results.aspx?q=Vancouver*). The URL is displayed in a message box; when the user clicks OK, the resulting page is displayed in the *WebBrowser* control.

The next snippet of code works similarly, but instead of retrieving a URL it retrieves a special MDX query whose results are the drillthrough data for the slice of the cube defined by sales of products in the Beverages category in Vancouver:

```
object[] Restrictions = new object[7];
Restrictions[2] = "Sales";
Restrictions[5] = "(Geography.[Country - State-Province - City -
 Postal Code].City.Vancouver, Products.[Category Name].Beverages)";
Restrictions[6] = MDACTION_COORDINATE_CELL;

DataTable results = conn.GetSchemaDataSet(AdomdSchemaGuid.Actions, Restrictions).
Tables[0];
dgvResults.DataSource = results;
MessageBox.Show("Content = " + results.Rows[0]["Content"].ToString() + "\nClick OK to
See Drillthrough Data");

txtMDX.Text = results.Rows[0]["Content"].ToString();
ExecMDX(conn);
```

The code assumes that *MDACTION_COORDINATE_CELL* has already been defined with its documented value of 6. It then fetches an entire MDX query from the *Content* column of the *DataTable* object *results*, inserts that MDX text into the *txtMDX TextBox* control, and calls the sample code's *ExecMDX* void function (mentioned earlier) to execute the query. Drill-through queries happen to return tabular result sets rather than multidimensional ones. Because *ExecMDX* uses an *AdomdDataAdapter* to execute the query, the tabular result set is handled gracefully and is easily bound to the *DataGridView* control in our application. Code that implements this technique can be found in the *Actions - Drillthrough* region in the source code of form *frmAPIs* in the sample code's Windows Forms project, Chapter19.

The drillthrough query, which is displayed in a message box before being executed, deserves some discussion before we move on. Here's the text of the query:

```
DRILLTHROUGH  Select
  (Geography.[Country - State-Province - City - Postal Code].City.Vancouver,
  [Products].[Category Name].&[Beverages]) on 0
From [Sales] RETURN [Main].[Total Sales]
```

If you want, you can enter the *DRILLTHROUGH* query text into an MDX query window in SQL Server Management Studio and execute it there. (The query can be found in, and executed from, the file Drillthrough.mdx in the MDX Demos project in the Chapter19.ssmssln sample code solution.)

Notice that the query has three parts:

- A *SELECT* query that consists of a single axis specifier that returns *exactly* one cell
- The *DRILLTHROUGH* keyword (at the beginning)
- A *RETURN* clause that indicates the measure(s) whose underlying fact data should be returned (at the end)

As long as you follow these syntax rules you can execute your own ad hoc drillthrough queries whenever you like, from your own applications or from Management Studio.

As you can see, drillthroughs are just special MDX queries; drillthrough actions do *not* have to be defined in order for drillthrough queries to be performed. Drillthrough actions generate *DRILLTHOURGH* MDX queries for you and let you define at the server which specific columns should be returned, but they are a convenience only and are not strictly necessary.

The combination of MDX and ADO MD.NET provide everything you need to create full-featured OLAP applications. But several other OLAP APIs can augment the baseline functionality provided by ADO MD.NET. We'll continue by examining another of these APIs.

Using Analysis Management Objects (AMO)   If you're left feeling frustrated that ADO MD.NET relies so heavily on schema *DataSet* objects because its native object model does not provide a full picture of Analysis Services databases, you might be interested in learning about its cousin, Analysis Management Objects (AMO). AMO allows you to discover all metadata and to modify and create Analysis Services objects as well. You can use it by simply setting a reference to its assembly, *Microsoft.AnalysisServices.dll*.

> **Caution**   The *Microsoft.AnalysisServices.dll* assembly does *not* appear on the .NET tab of the Add Reference dialog box in Visual Studio. You must use the Browse tab and reference the file directly. By default, the assembly is installed in the C:\Program Files\Microsoft SQL Server\90\SDK\Assemblies folder on your development PC.

Once you add the reference, you can import the AMO namespace into your code by using the following line of code at the top of your source code file:

```
using Microsoft.AnalysisServices;
```

The AMO library is rich with objects and methods that enable you to do virtually anything against an Analysis Services database that you can do within SQL Server Management Studio or the Analysis Services designers in Visual Studio. We cannot even begin to cover the full set of capabilities of AMO, but we'll present a few examples.

The following code populates a *ComboBox* control called *cboCatalogs* with a list of all databases on the localhost Analysis Services server:

```
Server s = new Server();
s.Connect("Data Source=localhost");
foreach (Database d in s.Databases)
{
    cboCatalogs.Items.Add(d.Name);
}
```

The following additional code adds a new (empty) database called NewDatabase:

```
Database dbNew = new Database("NewDatabase");
s.Databases.Add(dbNew);
dbNew.Update();
```

The code in Listing 19-1 is a bit more elaborate. It adds a new dimension called *NewDim*, with the attribute *NewAttr*, to the Adventure Works cube in the Adventure Works DW database. Notice that many of the properties manipulated are the same ones that appear in the Visual Studio Properties window when a dimension or attribute object is selected in one of the Analysis Services designers.

Listing 19-1   Creating Objects with AMO

```
// Create new dimension object NewDim:
Dimension dimNew;
dimNew = s.Databases.GetByName("Adventure Works
  DW").Dimensions.Add("NewDim");
dimNew.Type = DimensionType.Regular;
dimNew.UnknownMember = UnknownMemberBehavior.Visible;
dimNew.AttributeAllMemberName = "All";
dimNew.Source = new DataSourceViewBinding("Adventure Works DW");
dimNew.StorageMode = DimensionStorageMode.Molap;

// Create new dimension attribute NewAttr:
DimensionAttribute atrNew = new DimensionAttribute("NewAttr");
atrNew.KeyColumns.Add(new DataItem("dbo_DimPromotion",
  "EnglishPromotionCategory", System.Data.OleDb.OleDbType.WChar, 50));
atrNew.Usage = AttributeUsage.Key;
atrNew.OrderBy = OrderBy.Name;
atrNew.ID = "EnglishPromotionCategory";
atrNew.Type = AttributeType.Regular;

// Add the new attribute to the dimension:
dimNew.Attributes.Add(atrNew);
dimNew.Update();
```

Important   The Adventure Works sample Analysis Services project must be installed by explicitly including the AdventureWorks Sample OLAP item in an advanced SQL Server install (it appears three levels deep under the Documentation, Samples, and Sample Databases install option). After the install of SQL Server is complete, a second step is still required: You must run the special SQLServerSamples.msi file, which by default is installed in the C:\Program Files\ Microsoft SQL Server\90\Tools\Samples folder. A shortcut to the MSI file can be found in the All Programs\Microsoft SQL Server 2005\Documentation and Tutorials\Samples branch of the Windows Start menu. After running this MSI, the Analysis Services project will be installed by default within the C:\Program Files\Microsoft SQL Server\90\Tools\Samples\AdventureWorks Analysis Services Project folder. Open the project in Visual Studio and deploy it to your server in order to query or modify the Adventure Works sample cube.

You might want to remove the new database and the dimension (from the Adventure Works cube) in SQL Server Management Studio, after you execute the code in Listing 19-1 and the snippet preceding it.

More Info   Space limitations prevent us from discussing the code in *frmAPIs* in the Chapter19 Windows Forms application, which executes after you click the Show Measures... button, in detail. But take a look at the code contained in the *btnMeasureDetails_Click*, *lstMeasureGroups_SelectedIndexChanged*, and *lstDisplayFolders_SelectedIndexChanged* event handlers in the *AMO* source code region for an example of how AMO is more useful than ADO MD.NET.

In this particular instance, the *AdomdClient.Measure* object has a *DisplayFolder* property, but you must use *GetSchemaDataSet* with *AdomdSchemaGuid.Measures* to determine what measure group a given measure belongs to. In contrast, The AMO *Measure* object has a *Parent* property that provides this information right from the object model. This allows you to write code that iterates through a collection to determine the parent measure group of each measure, and avoids the need to extract that information from a *DataTable*.

These examples, although brief, should give you a sense of the power and the inner workings of AMO. Through AMO object properties and child collections, you can configure virtually every facet of an Analysis Services database. This includes not only major objects such as dimensions and measures and more esoteric ones such as scripts and translations, but also specific configuration settings for proactive caching, partitioning, and security roles.

XMLA at Your (Analysis) Service

Together, ADO MD.NET and AMO provide an almost overwhelmingly rich array of programming interfaces. Nothing is "hidden": Anything that Management Studio and Visual Studio can do against Analysis Services databases and cubes, you can do, too, by using these two libraries. But it's important to understand that underlying each of these libraries is nothing but XMLA.

In the previous chapter, you saw how the Analysis Services designers were, effectively, sophisticated front ends for generating XMLA scripts. You also saw how SQL Server Management

Studio innately supports the generation of XMLA scripts for virtually any Analysis Services entity and sports a dedicated XMLA query window for executing those scripts.

We'd like to take a moment now to explore XMLA a bit further, by showing you how to use it from Management Studio for more than DDL scripts, how to use XMLA programmatically, and how you can expose "raw" XMLA functionality from ADO MD.NET. This will provide you with only a high-level understanding of how XMLA works, but we think it's still extremely important. If you understand how to work with XMLA, you can potentially control Analysis Services from virtually any environment or platform that supports XML and Web services. Even if you do not plan to leave the .NET environment, understanding XMLA means understanding the native protocol of Analysis Services, and that has plenty of value in itself.

An API of Many Faces

You can understand XMLA from at least three different vantage points. First, you can see XMLA as a simple, programmable API. The core XMLA Web service provides just two methods: *Discover* (used to fetch metadata information from the server) and *Execute* (typically used to execute MDX queries and fetch the results). These methods accept and return information in the form of XML documents, which can be parsed or transformed to process or display the results.

Although XMLA can be used as a true Web service (and before the SQL Server 2005 release of Analysis Services, it had to be), its elevation to native API status changes things a bit. On the .NET platform, XMLA works over TCP/IP rather than HTTP, and a thin, managed assembly provides an API with certain enhancements over that provided by a Web reference proxy class. Specifically, if you want to use XMLA, you should set a reference to the *Microsoft.AnalysisServices.Xmla* library (listed on the .NET tab of the Add Reference dialog box in Visual Studio). Then you simply instantiate a *Microsoft.AnalysisServices.Xmla.XmlaClient* object to start writing XMLA code.

Before we look at an XMLA coding example, we will explore the second way to use XMLA: through the XMLA Query window in SQL Server Management Studio. You got a glimpse of how this works in Chapter 18, but we will explore that facility further here. As you will see, it is possible to create scripts that query your OLAP cubes as well as scripts that can create cubes, modify their structure, or perform an array of management tasks on them.

Finally, you can use ADO MD.NET to access the underlying XML payload returned by XMLA when MDX queries are executed. You get XML-formatted results from your MDX queries without having to submit your MDX queries in XML format or deal directly with XMLA as an API.

Using XMLA from SQL Server Management Studio

We'll start our tour of XMLA in the XMLA Query window in Management Studio. The best way to understand XMLA is to use it in conjunction with Template Explorer because the built-in XMLA templates give you an excellent jump start on understanding the syntax and variety of possible XMLA queries.

Start by opening up a new XMLA Query window against the Chapter18 database. (You can use the same techniques you use to open an MDX Query window: just select the XMLA option, where available, in place of the MDX option, from all relevant menus.) Show the Template Explorer window if it is not visible, click the Analysis Server button (second from the left) on the window's toolbar, and drill down on the XMLA node in the tree view. Drill down further on each of the three child nodes (Management, Schema Rowsets, and Server Status) to reveal the various XMLA templates available.

Using <*Discover*> for Metadata and Status Information   To see how easy it is to perform XMLA queries, drag the Sessions node (the third-to-last node under Server Status) into the XMLA Query window. Move the cursor left to deselect the text. You should see the following text in the window:

```
<Discover xmlns="urn:schemas-microsoft-com:xml-analysis">

  <RequestType>DISCOVER_SESSIONS</RequestType>

  <Restrictions>
    <RestrictionList>
    </RestrictionList>
  </Restrictions>

  <Properties><PropertyList></PropertyList></Properties>

</Discover>
```

The parent <*Discover*> element indicates that we will be calling the XMLA Web service's *Discover* method (rather than its *Execute* method). You can think of the <*RequestType*> and <*Restrictions*> elements in much the same way that you think of the *GetSchemaDataSet*'s enumerated constant and restrictions array. The former is set to *DISCOVER_SESSIONS*, and the latter is empty; this will result in a complete list of all active sessions for the server.

The <*Properties*> child element is required for all XMLA commands. Usually this element/parameter will contain connection and formatting information. But because we already supplied server-level connection information when the XMLA window was opened, all default settings are acceptable to us and we will leave this element empty.

To see the XML-formatted results of this command, press F5, Ctrl+E (or use the various Execute toolbar or menu commands). The results might look bewildering at first, but the XML results are easier to interpret if you scroll past the <*xsd:schema*> element to the first <*row*> element. That element's content format should look similar to the following:

```
<row>
  <SESSION_ID>12394A18-5CB8-4AD1-AEB1-88E151C0030B</SESSION_ID>
  <SESSION_SPID>2356</SESSION_SPID>
  <SESSION_CONNECTION_ID>27</SESSION_CONNECTION_ID>
```

```
      <SESSION_USER_NAME>MYMACHINE\UserName</SESSION_USER_NAME>
      <SESSION_CURRENT_DATABASE>Chapter18</SESSION_CURRENT_DATABASE>
      <SESSION_START_TIME>2005-12-25T20:52:56</SESSION_START_TIME>
      <SESSION_ELAPSED_TIME_MS>841</SESSION_ELAPSED_TIME_MS>
      <SESSION_LAST_COMMAND_START_TIME>2005-12-25T20:52:57</SESSION_LAST_COMMAND_START_TIME>
      <SESSION_LAST_COMMAND_END_TIME>2005-12-25T20:52:56</SESSION_LAST_COMMAND_END_TIME>
      <SESSION_LAST_COMMAND_ELAPSED_TIME_MS>0</SESSION_LAST_COMMAND_ELAPSED_TIME_MS>
      <SESSION_IDLE_TIME_MS>0</SESSION_IDLE_TIME_MS>
      <SESSION_CPU_TIME_MS>80</SESSION_CPU_TIME_MS>
      <SESSION_LAST_COMMAND>DISCOVER_SESSIONS</SESSION_LAST_COMMAND>
      <SESSION_LAST_COMMAND_CPU_TIME_MS>0</SESSION_LAST_COMMAND_CPU_TIME_MS>
    </row>
```

XMLA supports two response formats, tabular and multidimensional. Typically, as in this case, the *Discover* method returns tabular-formatted results, with each row contained in a separate <row> element, and each column contained in its own named child element. The *Execute* method, which we will examine shortly, typically uses the multidimensional format for its response content.

> **More Info**   The tabular XMLA response format is nearly identical to the XML format used by the ADO.NET *DataTable* object, which is used, in turn, by the *DataSet* object's *ReadXml* and *WriteXml* methods. Therefore, when you use XMLA programmatically, you can tweak tabular response content slightly and convert it to an ADO.NET *DataTable*, which is suitable for binding to Windows Forms or ASP.NET controls.

> **Note**   The content of the <*SESSION_USER_NAME*> element in the XML snippet just shown has been obfuscated to MYMACHINE\UserName; actual results would present the real domain name and user name of the user logged into the session.

Using <*Execute*> for DDL Tasks   Let's try another query. This time, we'll use XMLA to perform an administrative task—processing the Adventure Works cube in our Adventure Works DW database:

```
<Execute xmlns="urn:schemas-microsoft-com:xml-analysis">
<Command>
      <Process xmlns="http://schemas.microsoft.com/analysisservices/2003/engine">
            <Type>ProcessFull</Type>
            <Object>
              <DatabaseID>Adventure Works DW</DatabaseID>
              <CubeID>Adventure Works DW</CubeID>
            </Object>
          </Process>
</Command>
<Properties />
</Execute>
```

Notice that this command is contained in an *<Execute>* element instead of the *<Discover>* element used in our last query. That's because this query performs an action. The *<Execute>* element contains a child *<Command>* element and an empty *<Properties>* child element, as with the last query. Within the *<Command>* element, the *<Process>* child element (and its child *<Type>* and *<Object>* elements) tells Analysis Services to run a full process against the Adventure Works cube in the Adventure Works DW database.

> **Important**   The cube ID supplied is "Adventure Works DW," even though the cube itself is named "Adventure Works." XMLA, as it turns out, works with IDs rather than names. In the case of the Adventure Works cube, the ID and name do not match. To determine the ID of a cube, right-click on it in the Object Explorer window in Management Studio and choose Properties from the shortcut menu. The cube's ID will appear in the second row of the General page in the Cube Properties dialog box, as shown in Figure 19-34.

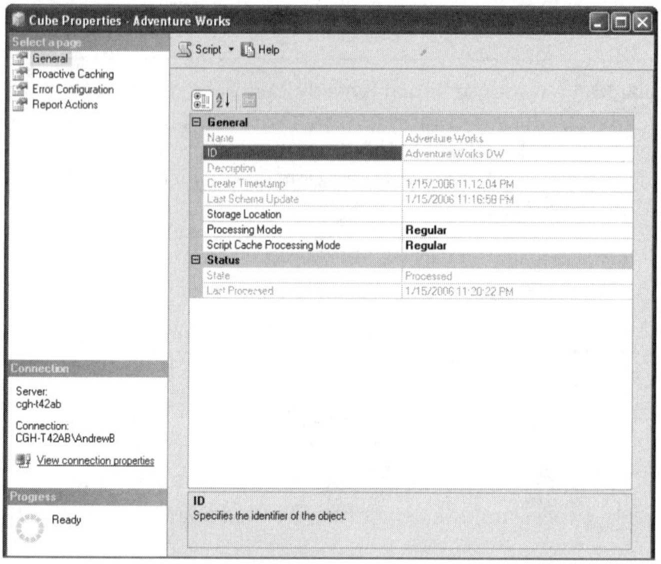

Figure 19-34   The Cube Properties dialog box in SQL Server Management Studio, with the General page and ID property selected

Press F5 to run the process task. During processing, you will see the "Executing query..." message and animated icon appear in the XMLA Query window's status bar and various status information on the Messages tab of the Results pane. When the processing is done, the Results tab will appear, displaying a standard "empty" XMLA message indicating that the process terminated successfully:

```
<return xmlns="urn:schemas-microsoft-com:xml-analysis">
  <root xmlns="urn:schemas-microsoft-com:xml-analysis:empty" />
</return>
```

It might seem counterintuitive for an empty response to indicate success, but consider that a failed process will always return an error message on the Messages tab. For example, if you were to intentionally change the <CubeID> element's contents from Adventure Works DW to Adventure Works (which is a valid cube *name* but an invalid cube *ID*) and re-execute the query, you would see the following text on the Messages tab:

```
Executing the query ...
Errors in the metadata manager. Either the cube with the ID of 'Adventure Works' does
 not exist in the database with the ID of 'Adventure Works DW', or the user does not
have permissions to access the object.
Execution complete
```

Using *<Execute>* to Run MDX Queries   To round out your understanding of XMLA you must understand that XMLA can also be used to execute MDX queries. It is a bit ironic that we are pointing this out *after* discussing XMLA's DDL scripting capabilities because XMLA was originally designed primarily for MDX query execution (and metadata discovery). As such, XMLA easily accommodates the notion of cell sets containing axes, positions, and a collection of cells. Each of these entities is neatly packaged in the multidimensional-formatted XML response payload.

Under most circumstances, you would let ADO MD.NET process this XML document and populate a *CellSet* (or *DataSet, DataTable*, or *DataReader*) object with its contents, but you can use the Management Studio XMLA window to examine the XML content directly. This is relatively easy to do because the XML content, though somewhat complex, is quite readable if you have an understanding of OLAP, MDX, and cell sets.

For example, to run a simple query against the *Sales* cube in our Chapter 18 database, consider the following script (which can be found in the QueryCubeChapter18.xmla file in the XMLA Demos project in the sample code SSMS solution):

```
<Execute xmlns="urn:schemas-microsoft-com:xml-analysis">
  <Command>
    <Statement>
      SELECT Shippers.[Shipper Name].MEMBERS ON COLUMNS,
             Time.Year.MEMBERS ON ROWS
      FROM Sales
      WHERE Measures.[Total Sales]
    </Statement>
  </Command>
  <Properties>
    <PropertyList>
      <Catalog>Chapter18</Catalog>
    </PropertyList>
  </Properties>
</Execute>
```

Note that we once again use *<Execute>* as our parent tag, indicating that we are calling XMLA's *Execute* method. The *<Execute>* element, as before, contains *<Command>* and *<Properties>* sub-elements. This time the *<Command>* element consists merely of a *<Statement>* element whose value is the MDX command we want to execute.

The *<Properties>* element, rather than being left empty as in our previous examples, consists of a *<PropertyList>* child element, which can in turn contain several child elements containing simple values. In the case of our query, we are only specifying the database name (in the *<Catalog>* element). For all other properties, we are using default values. Without a *<Catalog>* value, the query would run against the default database.

> **Note**   It might seem odd that we must specify a database name, since the connection information we supplied to the XMLA window already indicates the database we want to use, but XMLA connections effectively accommodate only server information. The fact that the XMLA Query window uses the standard Connection To Analysis Services dialog box (on whose Connection Properties tab you can specify a database after clicking the Options button) is an anomaly. The database selection made in the Connection To Analysis Services dialog box is ignored; therefore, when you create an XMLA query, you must explicitly specify your database within the XMLA query itself.

Execute the query now to fetch the multidimensional response. You will see that a large XML response is returned. To make this XML easier to read, copy and paste it into a new XMLA Query window. This will allow you to expand and contract elements within the XML using the outline nodes in the left margin of the XMLA editor.

Now contract the *xs:schema* node in the *return/root* element (it begins on the third line of the document), and then contract the *OlapInfo/CubeInfo* element two lines below it. Go down one line more and examine the *AxesInfo* element. Notice that each axis, as well as the "Slicer" axis (which represents the MDX command's *WHERE* clause), is described. Now contract the *OlapInfo* node (on line 4 of the document) and examine the *Axes* node immediately below it, looking at each *<Axis>* node within it. Notice that each tuple and member is enumerated, complete with *Caption*, *UniqueName* (*<UName>* element), and other property values.

For example, the entire *COLUMNS* axis (axis 0) is described in the XML response payload as follows, with one tuple per shipper (and one each for the *All* and *Unknown* members):

```
<Axis name="Axis0">
  <Tuples>
    <Tuple>
      <Member Hierarchy="[Shippers].[Shipper Name]">
        <UName>[Shippers].[Shipper Name].[All Shippers]</UName>
        <Caption>All Shippers</Caption>
        <LName>[Shippers].[Shipper Name].[(All)]</LName>
        <LNum>0</LNum>
        <DisplayInfo>66536</DisplayInfo>
      </Member>
    </Tuple>
```

```
      <Tuple>
        <Member Hierarchy="[Shippers].[Shipper Name]">
          <UName>[Shippers].[Shipper Name].&amp;[1]</UName>
          <Caption>Speedy Express</Caption>
          <LName>[Shippers].[Shipper Name].[Shipper Name]</LName>
          <LNum>1</LNum>
          <DisplayInfo>0</DisplayInfo>
        </Member>
      </Tuple>
      <Tuple>
        <Member Hierarchy="[Shippers].[Shipper Name]">
          <UName>[Shippers].[Shipper Name].&amp;[2]</UName>
          <Caption>United Package</Caption>
          <LName>[Shippers].[Shipper Name].[Shipper Name]</LName>
          <LNum>1</LNum>
          <DisplayInfo>131072</DisplayInfo>
        </Member>
      </Tuple>
      <Tuple>
        <Member Hierarchy="[Shippers].[Shipper Name]">
          <UName>[Shippers].[Shipper Name].&amp;[3]</UName>
          <Caption>Federal Shipping</Caption>
          <LName>[Shippers].[Shipper Name].[Shipper Name]</LName>
          <LNum>1</LNum>
          <DisplayInfo>131072</DisplayInfo>
        </Member>
      </Tuple>
      <Tuple>
        <Member Hierarchy="[Shippers].[Shipper Name]">
          <UName>[Shippers].[Shipper Name].[All Shippers].UNKNOWNMEMBER</UName>
          <Caption>Unknown</Caption>
          <LName>[Shippers].[Shipper Name].[Shipper Name]</LName>
          <LNum>1</LNum>
          <DisplayInfo>131072</DisplayInfo>
        </Member>
      </Tuple>
    </Tuples>
  </Axis>
```

For the Slicer axis, notice that the *Measures* tuple/member has a *UniqueName* of *[Measures].[Total Sales]*, which squares with the *WHERE* clause in our MDX query:

```
<Axis name="SlicerAxis">
  <Tuples>
<Tuple>
  <Member Hierarchy="[Measures]">
    <UName>[Measures].[Total Sales]</UName>
    <Caption>Total Sales</Caption>
    <LName>[Measures].[MeasuresLevel]</LName>
    <LNum>0</LNum>
    <DisplayInfo>0</DisplayInfo>
  </Member>
  ...
```

Now contract the *Axes* node and examine the *CellData* node immediately following it. Notice that each cell's *Value* and *FormattedValue* (*<FmtValue>* element) is provided, and that the cells are identified by the ordinal address we discussed earlier:

```
<CellData>
<Cell CellOrdinal="0">
   <Value xsi:type="xsd:double">1.35445859E6</Value>
   <FmtValue>$1,354,458.59</FmtValue>
</Cell>
<Cell CellOrdinal="1">
   <Value xsi:type="xsd:double">3.7398319E5</Value>
   <FmtValue>$373,983.19</FmtValue>
</Cell>
...
```

Calling *Execute* Programmatically from .NET

With this understanding of XMLA's encoding of *CellSet* objects, you can imagine how it would be possible to create an XSL stylesheet that transforms the data into a human-readable HTML page. In fact, Microsoft has created just such a stylesheet. It is called Xamd.xsl, and it is distributed as part of a sample application in the XMLA SDK 1.1 (which you can download for free from *http://msdn.microsoft.com*, and which is actually designed for SQL Server 2000). You can use the stylesheet to transform any two-axis XML cell set into well-formed HTML, with the results displayed in a table.

You can thus execute MDX queries via XMLA directly from .NET (using *Microsoft.AnalysisServices.Xmla*, as discussed earlier). You can then use the stylesheet, some *System.Xml* code, and a *WebBrowser* control to display the results. To do so, you'll first need to make sure you include the following namespaces in your code:

```
using System.Xml;
using System.Xml.Xsl;
using System.IO;
```

Once the namespaces are properly imported, you can use the code in Listing 19-2 (taken from the *Xmla* source code region in *frmAPIs* in the sample code's Chapter19 Windows Forms application), which performs the XSL transformation for the MDX query we just discussed. It assumes that the variable *ConnectionString* contains a valid Analysis Services connection string pointing to the server with the Chapter18 database, that the *TextBox* control *txtMDX* contains the MDX query text to be executed, and that a *WebBrowser* control named *wbrMain* is available to display the HTML results.

Listing 19-2 Executing MDX Queries with XMLA

```
// XMLA:
Microsoft.AnalysisServices.Xmla.XmlaClient xmlac = new
  Microsoft.AnalysisServices.Xmla.XmlaClient();
```

```
// System.Xml:
XslCompiledTransform xslCellSetTable = new XslCompiledTransform();
XmlTextWriter xtwCellSetTable = new XmlTextWriter(Path.GetFullPath(".") +
 "\\Execute.htm", null);
XmlDocument xdcResults = new XmlDocument();

string command = "<Statement>" + txtMDX.Text + "</Statement>";
string properties = "<PropertyList>" +
                    "   <Catalog>Chapter18</Catalog>" +
                    "</PropertyList>";
string results;

try
{
    // Load the stylesheet:
    xslCellSetTable.Load(Path.GetFullPath(".") + "\\xamd.xsl");

    // Fetch the XML into a string:
    xmlac.Connect(ConnectionString);
    xmlac.Execute(command, properties, out results, false, true);

    // Load the XML text into an XmlDocument
    xdcResults.LoadXml(results);

    // Strip off the outer <return> tag (which the stylesheet is not expecting):
    xdcResults.LoadXml(xdcResults.FirstChild.InnerXml);

    // Transform the XML to an HTML file:
    xslCellSetTable.Transform(xdcResults, xtwCellSetTable);

    // Close XmlTextWriter:
    xtwCellSetTable.Close();

    // Display generated HTML file in the WebBrowser control:
    wbrMain.Navigate(Path.GetFullPath(".") + "\\Execute.htm");
}

catch (Exception ex)
{
    MessageBox.Show(ex.Message);
}

finally
{
    // Close the connection:
    xmlac.Disconnect();
}
```

Notice that the *XmlaClient* object has an *Execute* method that accepts XML strings identical to the contents of the *<Command>* and *<Properties>* child elements of the *<Execute>* element supplied in Management Studio's XMLA Query window. The results are assigned to a third string argument. The last two arguments are Booleans of relatively little importance in this case.

Once the *Execute* method call is complete and the XML result string has been assigned to the *string* variable *results*, the code simply loads it into an *XmlDocument* object, applies the stylesheet transformation, and dumps the resultant HTML to a file called Execute.htm. The code then displays the file's contents in a *WebBrowser* control. Your results should look similar to those depicted in Figure 19-35.

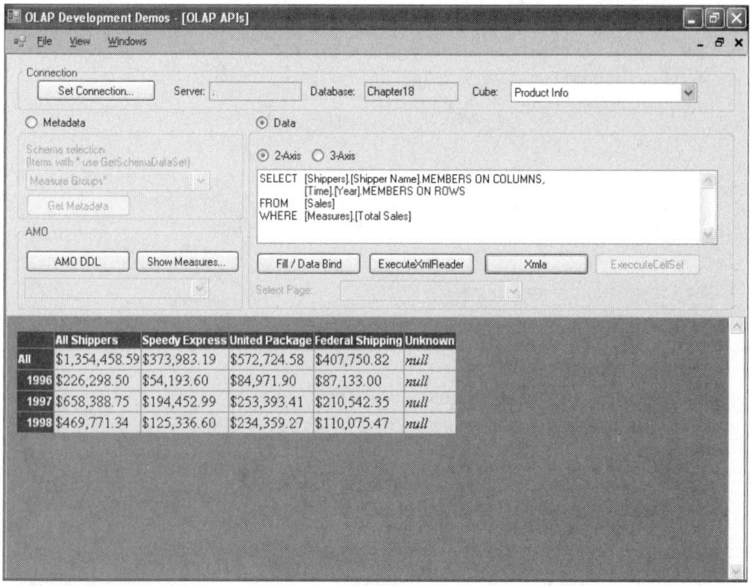

Figure 19-35   HTML-transformed results of an MDX query run via the XMLA *Execute* command

Manipulating XMLA Response Content from ADO MD.NET

In addition to using the stylesheet in conjunction with low-level XMLA coding, you can also use it with ADO MD.NET. That is because the *AdomdCommand* object has an *ExecuteXml-Reader* method that directly returns the XMLA response payload generated when an *AdomdCommand* objects MDX query is executed. So by combining the *ExecuteXmlReader* method and code similar to that in Listing 19-2, the results can once again be displayed as HTML in a *WebBrowser* control.

Sample code for this technique is provided in Listing 19-3 (taken from the *AdomdCommand* *.ExecuteXmlReader* source code region in the form *frmAPIs* in the sample code's Chapter19 Windows Forms application). This code makes the same assumptions as Listing 19-2.

Listing 19-3   Using *ExecuteXmlReader*

```
// ADO MD.NET:
AdomdConnection conXML = new AdomdConnection(ConnectionString);
AdomdCommand comXML = new AdomdCommand(txtMDX.Text, conXML);
```

```
// System.Xml:
XslCompiledTransform xslCellSetTable = new XslCompiledTransform();
XmlTextWriter xtwCellSetTable = new XmlTextWriter(Path.GetFullPath(".") +
 "\\Execute.htm", null);

try
{
   // Open the connection:
   conXML.Open();

   // Load the stylesheet:
   xslCellSetTable.Load(Path.GetFullPath(".") + "\\xamd.xsl");

   // Fetch and transform the XML to an HTML file:
   xslCellSetTable.Transform(comXML.ExecuteXmlReader(), xtwCellSetTable);

   // Close the XmlTextWriter:
   xtwCellSetTable.Close();

   // Display generated HTML file in the WebBrowser control:
   wbrMain.Navigate(Path.GetFullPath(".") + "\\Execute.htm");
}

catch (Exception ex)
{
   MessageBox.Show(ex.Message);
}

finally
{
   // Close the connection:
   conXML.Close();
}
```

For the code in Listing 19-3 to compile properly, the following namespace inclusions must be properly inserted at the top of your source code file:

```
using Microsoft.AnalysisServices.AdomdClient;
using System.Xml;
using System.Xml.Xsl;
using System.IO;
```

Analysis Services CLR Support: Server-Side ADO MD.NET

Our last stop on this tour through various OLAP programming models brings us back to the server itself. That's because, as it turns out, SQL Server 2005 Analysis Services supports a programming model very similar to the SQL CLR programming we discussed in Chapter 3. In the Analysis Services CLR model, you can load .NET assemblies onto your Analysis Services server and call their functions programmatically from ADO MD.NET or XMLA, or manually from Management Studio's MDX Query window or XMLA Query window.

> **Important**   Unlike SQL CLR integration, Analysis Services CLR support is on by default. In fact, it cannot be disabled. However, only users with administrative permissions on the Analysis Services server or database may load CLR assemblies. This contrasts significantly with the SQL CLR feature, which can be made available to non-administrative users but is disabled by default and must be turned on using T-SQL or the SQL Server Surface Area Configuration tool.

Visual Studio offers no project templates for server-side Analysis Services programming and the programming model does not use code attributes, but the CLR support in Analysis Services is similar to, and about as easy as, SQL CLR programming. In Analysis Services, such functions are referred to as *managed stored procedures*.

Managed stored procedures can execute without returning anything or they can act as functions that return values or objects. Although these function-like stored procedures can return scalar values, they will typically return and/or accept MDX entities such as tuples, sets, and expressions. This is made possible through the use of the *Microsoft.AnalysisServices .AdomdServer* assembly, which includes definitions for these types and for special builder objects used to create some of them.

> **Note**   Managed stored procedures can also be used for data mining tasks and can execute and return result sets from DMX prediction queries. We provide an example of such a managed stored procedure at the end of Chapter 20.

Writing Managed Stored Procedure Code

You can start writing Analysis Services managed stored procedures simply by creating a Class Library project in Visual Studio 2005 and setting a reference to the *Microsoft.AnalysisServices .AdomdServer* library. Then you simply add the following *using* statement at the top of a C# class file:

```
using Microsoft.AnalysisServices.AdomdServer;
```

and you're ready to write your first managed stored procedure.

For example, the code in Listing 19-4 (taken from Books Online and found in the file StoredProcedures.cs in the Chapter19AdomdServer Class Library project in the sample code) implements a CLR function that accepts an *AdomdServer.Set* object and a filter expression (as a string), and then returns a subset of that set containing just the tuples that meet the filter condition.

Listing 19-4   CLR Function *FilterSet*

```
public Set FilterSet(Set set, string filterExpression)
{
    Expression expr = new Expression(filterExpression);
    SetBuilder resultSetBuilder = new SetBuilder();
```

```
    foreach (Tuple tuple in set)
    {
        if ((bool)(expr.Calculate(tuple)))
            resultSetBuilder.Add(tuple);
    }
    return resultSetBuilder.ToSet();
}
```

Notice the use of the *Set*, *Expression*, and *SetBuilder* objects for typing the function's parameters, return type, and variables, and notice the *Tuple* object for the controlling variable within the *foreach* loop. A string containing the MDX expression we want to use is passed to the *Expression* object's constructor. From there, the *Expression* object's *Calculate* method is used to test whether each tuple in the passed-in set meets the filter condition; if it does, the code adds the tuple to the *SetBuilder* object's internal collection via its *Add* method. Finally, the *SetBuilder* object's *ToSet* method is used to generate the *Set* object that is the function's return value.

Once the assembly is compiled and loaded into your database, you can call the *FilterSet* expression from an MDX query as if it were part of the MDX language itself.

Loading the Assembly

To load an assembly, first right-click the Assemblies node underneath your Analysis Services server in Object Explorer and choose New Assembly (Figure 19-36).

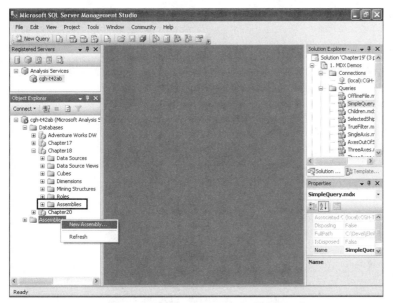

Figure 19-36   The New Assembly menu option for the Object Explorer's window's server Assemblies node, with the *Chapter18* database's own Assemblies node highlighted

The Register Server Assembly dialog box opens (Figure 19-37).

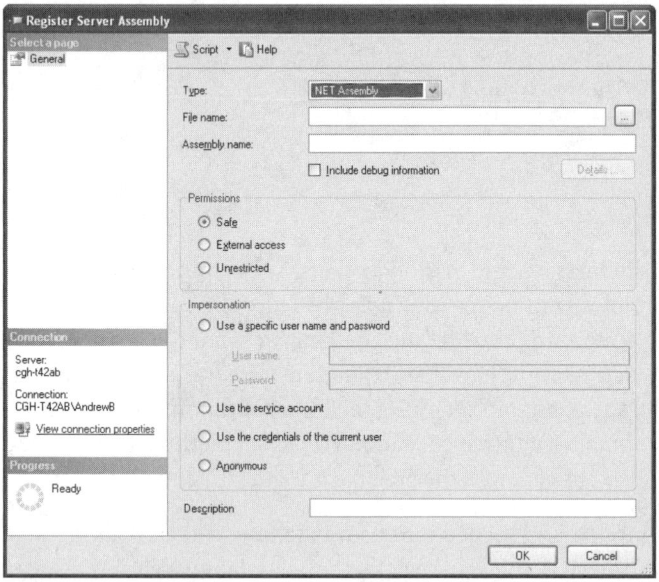

Figure 19-37   The Register Server Assembly dialog box in Management Studio

Select .NET Assembly from the Type drop-down list, and then enter the full path to your assembly in the File Name text box or click the ellipsis (...) button to the right of the text box to specify the assembly through a standard File Open dialog box.

> **Tip**   You can also add assemblies to individual databases rather than to the server as a whole. The procedure is identical except for one difference: Rather than right-clicking your *server's* Assemblies child node, you right-click the Assemblies child node belonging to a specific *database* (highlighted in Figure 19-36). The Register Database Assembly dialog box will appear instead of the Register Server Assembly dialog box. The two dialog boxes are identical except for their names.

By default, a "friendly name" is generated for your assembly in the Assembly Name text box. This name will be identical to the file name of your assembly, minus the .dll extension. You can change this to any name you like, but you must remember it because you will need to use it when you call any of the assembly functions from MDX. If you want to debug your assembly, select the Include Debug Information check box. We will provide full details on debugging server-side managed code shortly.

As with SQL CLR assemblies, you can assign the assembly any of three permission sets: *Safe* (the default), *External Access*, or *Unrestricted* (equivalent to the *Unsafe* permission set for SQL CLR assemblies). You can also set the impersonation technique used by the assembly. Options here include specifying a particular account; using the service account; and impersonating the current user, the anonymous user, or an Analysis Services–defined default. The

Impersonation setting is pertinent only when you select the *External Access* or *Unrestricted* permission set because the *Safe* permission set does not grant access to resources outside of Analysis Services, making specific account permissions irrelevant.

After you have specified your assembly's type, file name, "friendly name," debug information option, permission set, and impersonation mode, click the OK button and the assembly will be permanently loaded (unless you later delete it). Functions within the assembly are now callable using the naming convention *AssemblyName.FullClassName.FunctionName*, where *AssemblyName* is the assembly's "friendly name," *FullClassName* is the fully-namespace-qualified name of the class in which your function is defined, and *FunctionName* is the name of your function.

More Info   You can also load Database-level assemblies by adding them to Analysis Services projects in Visual Studio. Right-click on the Assemblies node in Visual Studio's Solution Explorer window and choose New Assembly Reference... from the shortcut menu to invoke the Add Reference dialog box, where you can add one or more assemblies to your project. After you add an assembly, you can change its friendly name, permission set, impersonation mode, and description via the Properties window. Once the project is deployed, the assembly will be physically loaded into the database on the server.

Calling Managed Code from MDX

Calling your function from a query is easy. For example, the following MDX code (which can be found in the FilterSet.mdx file in the CLR Demos project in the sample code's SSMS solution) uses the *FilterSet* function we just created in a query against the Chapter18 database:

```
SELECT Chapter19AdomdServer.Chapter19AdomdServer.StoredProcedures.FilterSet(Shippers.
[Shipper Name].MEMBERS, "[Shipper Name].CurrentMember.Name < 'U'") ON COLUMNS,
    Time.Year.MEMBERS ON ROWS
FROM Sales
WHERE Measures.[Total Sales]
```

You can execute this query from your own application (using ADO MD.NET or XMLA), a Management Studio MDX Query window, or an XMLA Query window (if the query is embedded in the appropriate XML stream). Regardless of the method you use, the query should yield the following results:

	All Shippers	Speedy Express	Federal Shipping
All	$1,354,458.59	$373,983.19	$407,750.82
1996	$226,298.50	$54,193.60	$87,133.00
1997	$658,388.75	$194,452.99	$210,542.35
1998	$469,771.34	$125,336.60	$110,075.47

Notice that the set we submitted to the *FilterSet* function is *Shippers.[Shipper Name].MEM-BERS*, the MDX expression passed is *[Shipper Name].CurrentMember.Name < 'U'*, and the resultant filtered set becomes our query's *ON COLUMNS* expression. The result is that only shippers beginning with a letter that comes before U in the alphabet appear across the columns axis (which means that United Package and the *Unknown* members are skipped).

Debugging Server-Side Managed Code

There is no project type for Analysis Services assemblies, so Visual Studio has no innate awareness of them, but it is still possible to debug your .NET code running in Analysis Services databases. To do so, choose Attach To Process from the Debug menu in Visual Studio to open the Attach To Process dialog box (Figure 19-38).

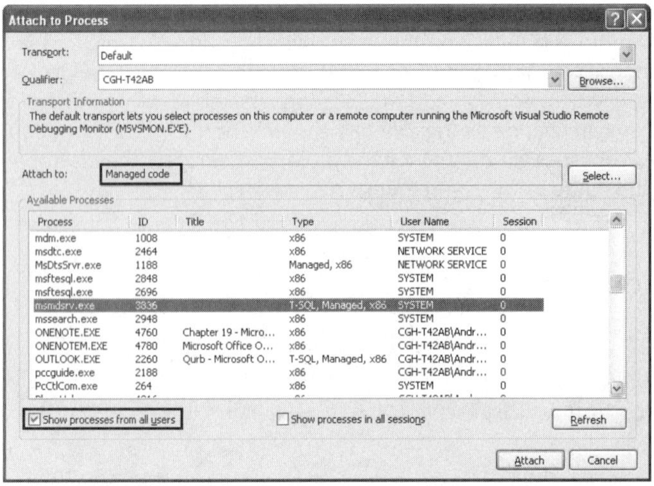

Figure 19-38   The Attach To Process dialog box in Visual Studio

Select the Show Processes From All Users check box in the lower left of the dialog box, and then select the msmdsrv.exe process in the Available Processes list box. The string "Managed Code" should appear in the (grayed out) Attach To text box; if not, click the Select... button to the right and select the Debug These Code Types option button and the Managed check box in the Select Code Type dialog box (Figure 19-39) and click OK.

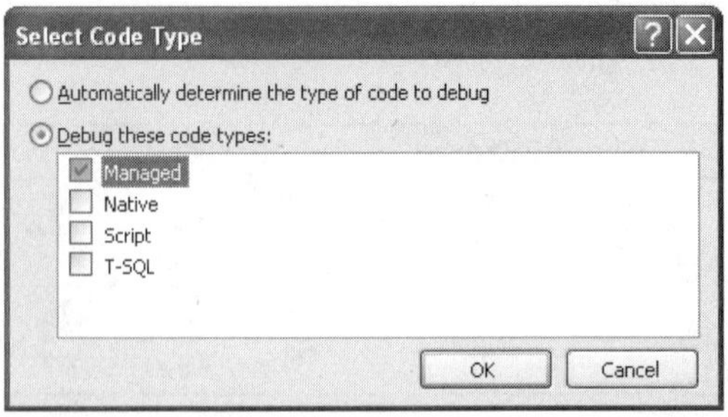

Figure 19-39   The Select Code Type dialog box

> **Note**   The next time you open the Attach To Process dialog box, the Show Processes From All Users check box should be selected by default. Also, when the msmdsrv.exe process is selected, "Managed Code" should appear in the Attach To text box without requiring you to use the Select Code Type dialog box again.

In the Attach To Process dialog box, click the Attach button to place Visual Studio in Debugging mode. You can now set breakpoints in your code, which will be hit whenever the CLR code is called from an MDX query, whether it is run from other .NET code or from an MDX Query window or XMLA Query window in SQL Server Management Studio. To test this, set a breakpoint in the first line of code in the *FilterSet* function, return to Management Studio, and re-execute the previous MDX query. You will hit your breakpoint and have full access to the Visual Studio debugging tools, including the Locals window and expression visualizers (Figure 19-40).

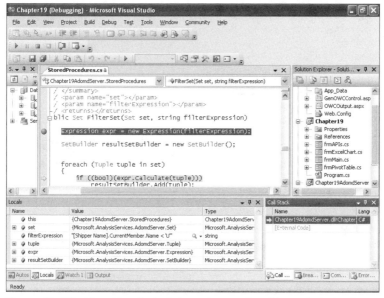

Figure 19-40   Visual Studio in Debugging mode, with Analysis Services CLR stored procedure source code being traced

Void Functions

You can also create *void* functions (*Subs* in Visual Basic) that perform various actions and do not return data. Typically, such functions use AMO to perform various data definition tasks, including creating a new database and processing a cube. By combining AMO with the *AdomdServer* library's *Context* object (similar in concept to the SQL CLR SqlContext object), you can create DDL stored procedures that run in the context of the connection you've already established. For example, start by inserting the following namespace code at the top of a class file:

```
using Microsoft.AnalysisServices;
using Microsoft.AnalysisServices.AdomdServer;
```

Then use the code in Listing 19-5 (adapted from one of our initial AMO examples) to implement a stored procedure that creates a new database called NewDatabase on the currently connected server. (The code in Listing 19-5 can be found in the source code file StoredProcedures.cs in the Chapter19AdomdServer Class Library project in the sample code.)

Listing 19-5 Server-Side AMO

```
public void CreateNewDB()
{
    Server s = new Server();
    s.Connect("Data Source=" + Context.CurrentServerID + ";Initial Catalog=" +
    Context.CurrentDatabaseName);
    //s.Connect("*");
    Database dbNew = new Database("NewDatabase");
    s.Databases.Add(dbNew);
    dbNew.Update();
    s.Disconnect();
}
```

Notice the use of the *Context* object's *CurrentServerId* and *CurrentDatabaseName* properties to build the context-sensitive connection string used in the AMO Server object's *Connect* method. It is also permissible to reference a context connection using a connection string of "*", as is done in the commented-out line of code.

Void functions are executed using the special MDX *CALL* command rather than the *SELECT* command. So, to call the previous stored procedure, you would use the following MDX code:

```
CALL Chapter19AdomdServer.Chapter19AdomdServer.StoredProcedures.CreateNewDB();
```

Try executing the previous command from Management Studio (by simply opening the file CLR-DDL.mdx from the CLR Demos project and executing it), right-click on your server's Databases node in the Object Explorer window, choose Refresh from the shortcut menu, and then expand the node (if necessary). You should see a NewDatabase node appear; you might want to delete it after completing this test.

Result Set–Returning Functions

Although you should not think of Analysis Services managed stored procedures as being *designed* to return result sets, it is in fact possible to return tabular results sets from them, in the form of *AdomdServer.AdomdDataReader* or *System.Data.DataTable objects*. For example, the code in Listing 19-6 (also found in StoredProcedures.cs) implements a CLR stored procedure that returns a simple two-column, two-row result set:

Listing 19-6   Returning a *DataTable*

```
public System.Data.DataTable GetDataTable()
{
   System.Data.DataTable dt = new System.Data.DataTable();
   dt.Columns.Add("ID", typeof(int));
   dt.Columns.Add("Name", typeof(string));

   object[] row = new object[2];

   row[0] = 1;
   row[1] = "Andrew";
   dt.Rows.Add(row);

   row[0] = 2;
   row[1] = "Steve";
   dt.Rows.Add(row);

   return dt;
}
```

When called with the following MDX command (found in GetDataTable.mdx), the code in Listing 19-6 returns the tabular result set shown following the command.

```
CALL Chapter19AdomdServer.Chapter19AdomdServer.StoredProcedures.GetDataTable();
```

ID	Name
1	Andrew
2	Steve

This example is trivial, but the ability to return result sets can indeed be helpful. You can, for example, use actual ADO.NET code to return data from an SQL Server relational database based on input values from a passed MDX set.

Mixing Client and Server to Return Flattened Cell Sets   Unlike with SQL CLR programming, you will typically *not* use the ADO MD.NET *client* library (*AdomdClient*) in your server-side code; instead, you'll use the *AdomdServer* library in server-side programming, as it replicates most *AdomdClient* objects. However, if you want your stored procedure to return data from an MDX query (for example, as an *AdomdDataReader*), you *must* use client-side ADO MD.NET (*AdomdClient*) objects in your stored procedure. This is illustrated in Listing 19-7 (also found in StoredProcedures.cs).

Listing 19-7   Returning a *DataReader*

```
public Microsoft.AnalysisServices.AdomdClient.AdomdDataReader
 GetDataClient()
{
   Microsoft.AnalysisServices.AdomdClient.AdomdConnection conContext = new
      Microsoft.AnalysisServices.AdomdClient.AdomdConnection("data source=" +
      Context.CurrentServerID + ";initial catalog=" +
      Context.CurrentDatabaseName);
   Microsoft.AnalysisServices.AdomdClient.AdomdCommand comContext = new
      Microsoft.AnalysisServices.AdomdClient.AdomdCommand("SELECT
      Shippers.[Shipper Name].MEMBERS ON COLUMNS, Time.Year.MEMBERS ON ROWS
      FROM Sales WHERE Measures.[Total Sales]", conContext);
   conContext.Open();
   try
   {
      return comContext.ExecuteReader();
   }
   catch
   {
      return null;
   }
}
```

When this code is called with the following MDX query (found in GetDataClient.mdx), it yields the tabular results shown following the query.

```
CALL Chapter19AdomdServer.Chapter19AdomdServer.StoredProcedures.GetDataClient()
```

[Time].[Year].[Year].[MEMBER_CAPTION]	[Shippers].[Shipper Name].[All Shippers]	[Shippers].[Shipper Name].&[1]	[Shippers].[Shipper Name].&[2]	[Shippers].[Shipper Name].&[3]	[Shippers].[Shipper Name].[All Shippers].UNKNOWN-MEMBER
	1354458.59	373983.19	572724.58	407750.82	
1996	226298.5	54193.6	84971.9	87133	
1997	658388.75	194452.99	253393.41	210542.35	
1998	469771.34	125336.6	234359.27	110075.47	

The stored procedure shown will execute properly only if the assembly containing it is assigned *Unrestricted* permissions. This is because the *AdomdClient* assembly is not callable from partially trusted callers, and only assemblies with the *Unrestricted* permission set have full trust. You should therefore use this technique only as a last resort, when MDX queries cannot be executed from the calling application (for whatever reason). The scenarios for creating (flattened) cell set–returning stored procedures are thus limited, but the possibility is nonetheless intriguing.

Analysis Services CLR features are at least as compelling as, if not more so than, the SQL CLR functionality offered in SQL Server relational databases. They extend the capabilities of MDX, add easy-to-use DDL commands, provide end-to-end debugging, and serve as a unifying environment for ADO MD.NET, AMO, ADO.NET, and mainstream .NET Framework programming.

Summary

This chapter has covered extensive ground. You've learned how to use Excel PivotTables and charts from a variety of environments, including Excel itself, to build compelling front ends for your OLAP cubes. Also, by learning a small subset of the MDX query language, you learned how to use the MDX Query window in SQL Server Management Studio to query your cubes more precisely than you can with PivotTables and charts.

You've seen how to apply your MDX knowledge programmatically by using ADO MD.NET and how to get detailed metadata and perform numerous DDL tasks with AMO. You learned how both libraries provide façades around XMLA, and you learned how to use XMLA directly, from the XMLA Query window in Management Studio and in code via *Microsoft.AnalysisServices .Xmla*, as well as through ADO MD.NET. Finally, you saw how to use many of these technologies on the server via the Analysis Services support for CLR assemblies, including full debugging support in Visual Studio.

Microsoft's OLAP platform is not only powerful and feature-rich, but it is also highly programmable. This developer-friendly approach is a hallmark of Microsoft technologies and is what will ultimately drive Analysis Services to near-certain dominance in the business intelligence market.

Chapter 20

Extending Your Database System with Data Mining

—Elsie Pan

The data mining component of SQL Server Analysis Services (SSAS) is an unsung yet intensely compelling product. The 2005 data mining release improves on its predecessor in a number of areas, including ease of use, feature richness, sophistication of client tools, and programmability. It allows developers, even those with no previous data mining experience, to integrate data mining into applications quickly and effectively. It makes the data mining component in SQL Server 2000 look like a bare-bones, proof-of-concept product by comparison.

> **Note** Some of the terms introduced here might be new to you. Rest assured that they will be explained thoroughly over the course of the chapter.

The number of data mining algorithms has been extended significantly. Whereas the 2000 version offers only two algorithms (Clustering and Decision Trees), SSAS in SQL Server 2005 offers those two plus seven new ones (Naïve Bayes, Association Rules, Sequence Clustering, Linear Regression, Logistic Regression, Neural Nets and Time Series). A Mining Model Wizard guides you through the choice of inputs and outputs for the models, abstracting much of the complexity of the algorithms. At the same time, several algorithm parameters are exposed, allowing more advanced users to tweak the models by changing parameter values from their specified defaults.

Tools for browsing the models have also been extended significantly. Multiple viewers are available for most mining models, thereby offering different perspectives on the results of the models. Furthermore, you can embed these viewers in applications, allowing developers to take advantage of a full suite of visualization tools in custom applications.

Mining structures, a new entity in SSAS databases, contain a common column set configuration that can be used by multiple models within the structure. This setup enables you to easily create several related mining models in one place and to process those models with a single pass through the data. Each constituent model can be built using a different algorithm or the same algorithm with different parameters. Better yet, new "lift" charts allow you to graph the relative accuracy of all your models for both predictable columns and specific values of those columns.

Why Mine Your Data?

The ability of businesses to gather and store data has increased exponentially over the past 30 years. Organizations are increasingly building data mining into their business analysis strategies because it offers powerful tools for detecting critical patterns within vast (and usually growing) stores of available data. For example, customer service organizations can identify peak calling hours and schedule staff work hours accordingly. Retail companies can better understand which products are selling well in different geographic regions and can optimize their supply chains in response. Food service companies can observe which perishable food products might spoil before being used and therefore arrange for later deliveries. And clinical medical data can be analyzed to determine demographic factors (such as age, gender, and ethnicity) that might be associated with treatment side effects or reduced treatment effectiveness.

In short, data mining is becoming a key step on the path from business data to business knowledge. Data mining helps you act on your data rather than just maintain it. Figure 20-1 depicts the components of a fully developed data mining infrastructure and the members of the Microsoft business intelligence (BI) "stack" that comprise each of these components.

Let's discuss these components a little bit. Most data mining processes start with raw data, most likely from a conventional, relational online transaction processing (OLTP) system. Typically, the data used for data mining projects has not been collected explicitly for the purpose of mining–instead, it has been collected during the normal course of business.

Next comes the arduous task of cleaning and transforming the data so it is in a state suitable for analysis. This is the extract, transform, and load (ETL) step, where you can bring together data from multiple systems into a single data warehouse. Next, you create a task-driven or content-driven data mart for the specific data analysis task at hand. This is the data to be mined. Figure 20-1 shows two possible paths to the data mart from your OLTP data: a route through a data warehouse and a direct route, in which you forgo the creation of a data warehouse. Either way, SQL Server Integration Services (SSIS) can get you there. SSIS offers a complete toolset for extracting data from source systems, manipulating the data into a format suitable for mining, and saving the data into a data warehouse or data mart.

Using SSAS, you can explore and mine your data. The results of the data mining are presented in reports and charts. Business users can then draw new knowledge from the analyses.

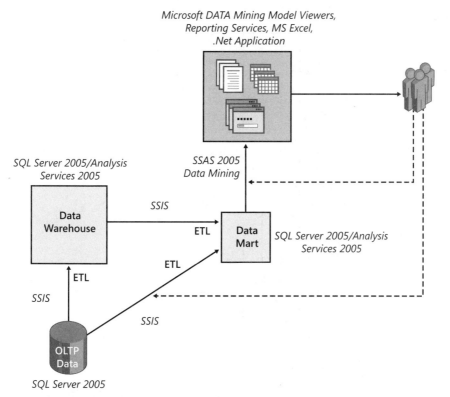

Figure 20-1 A fully developed data mining infrastructure using tools from the Microsoft BI "stack"

Two feedback loops are depicted in Figure 20-1. The feedback loop to the ETL step represents the use of data mining for data validation. By identifying typical data patterns, data mining can help identify data anomalies that can be addressed as part of the ETL step. This helps reduce the noise in the data, which in turn improves the quality of analyses based on that data. The feedback loop to the data mining step represents the iterative nature of data mining. Data mining is most effective at generating business knowledge when it is performed as an iterative process. The results from a mining model can be used to refine the analysis population included in the data mart or to tweak the parameters used to estimate a model.

Most important, data mining is a business-driven task. It is commonly defined as the process of finding useful relationships and patterns in large data sets. The relationships and patterns are useful only to the extent that they address a business problem. Some additional examples of business tasks accomplished using data mining include product recommendations or cross-selling, targeted mailing campaigns, fraud detection, customer profiling, forecasting, and data validation. The business task at hand determines the data mining algorithm used. Figure 20-2 shows some common business tasks and the mining algorithms in SSAS that are most appropriate for performing each task.

Algorithm Matrix

	Cross-Selling	Targeted Mailing	Fraud Detection	Customer Profiling	Forecasting	Data Validation
Association Rules	✔					
Clustering		✔	✔	✔		✔
Decision Trees		✔		✔		
Linear Regression				✔		
Logistic Regression				✔		
Naïve Bayes		✔		✔		
Neural Nets				✔		
Sequence Clustering				✔		
Time Series					✔	

Figure 20-2   The algorithm matrix shows appropriate mining model algorithms for some common business problems.

In his book *Business @ the Speed of Thought,* Bill Gates writes, "The greatest value of data mining will be to help companies determine the right products to build and the right way to price them." The companies that can best determine the "right products" and "right price" will be the companies that can best identify their most likely customers and understand the buying habits of those customers. The power of SSAS is that it makes that kind of advanced data mining functionality easily accessible. The tight integration of SSAS components with the more traditional database components in SQL Server 2005 makes data mining available as a natural extension of any database system.

A Statistics Refresher

This chapter does not assume in-depth knowledge of statistics, so here are definitions for some basic statistical terms used in the chapter. To get more complete definitions, you can conduct a simple Web search.

- **Mean**   More commonly referred to as "average." It is the sum of observed values divided by the count of observations.

- **Median**   The middle value of a set of numbers. Half the numbers in a set have a value greater than the median, and half the numbers have a value less than the median.

- **Standard deviation**   A measure of the dispersion in the data. Specifically, the standard deviation measures how spread-out the data values are from the mean.

- **Range**   The difference between the smallest and largest value in a data set.

- **Distribution**   The array of values observed for a particular attribute in your data. Data distributions can often be usefully depicted using histograms or pie charts.

- **Continuous data**   Data whose possible set of values is not countable. Examples are height and age; the more precisely these are measured, the more possible values exist. For example, we are all aging at every fraction of a second.

- **Discrete data**   Data whose values are isolated points or whose possible set of values is countable. Examples are country of residence or marital status. (Data that is continuous can be "discretized" by grouping the possible values into sets. For example, age is continuous but can be discretized by creating groupings such as "Younger than 21," "Age 21 through 50," and "Over 50.")

Getting Started

Now that you are fired up to mine your data, how do you get started building mining models and using them in your applications? This chapter shows you, by using an example of a customer profitability analysis using the AdventureWorksDW sample database that comes with SQL Server 2005. We will use SSIS to build a small data mart and a new SSAS database with mining models based on the data and then use scripts that extend the model and query its content.

Building on the model and scripts, we'll create sample Windows Forms and ASP.NET code that embeds similar querying functionality and create a Reporting Services project against the models. We'll also load a managed assembly onto the server that implements a data mining query stored procedure, and we'll perform data mining queries by using XML for Analysis (XMLA). Let's start by going over the steps required to create a data mining project.

Preparing Your Source Data

The AdventureWorksDW sample database is a dimensional database with a subset of the data from the normalized OLTP AdventureWorks sample database. As a reminder, Adventure Works is a fictional bicycle manufacturing company that sells to wholesale customers as well as individual Web customers. Detailed demographic data is available for the individual customers, including income, marital status, number of children, and home ownership. In addition, because the data warehouse is built from a relational database containing data from a transactional order system, it includes detailed data on the buying behavior of customers: customer tenure, number of products purchased, "recency" of last purchase, types of products purchased, and so on. We want to use this wealth of data to discover detailed information about the customers.

Because we are using SQL Server 2005, we can take advantage of its Transact-SQL (T-SQL) enhancements and run a query using the new *NTILE()* function, as shown in Listing 20-1.

Listing 20-1   Using the *NTILE()* function to analyze data

```
USE AdventureWorksDW
GO

SELECT
   count(*) AS NumCustomers
   ,Quartile
   ,min(TotalProfit) AS MinQuartileProfit
   ,max(TotalProfit) AS MaxQuartileProfit
   ,sum(TotalProfit) AS SumQuartileProfit
FROM (SELECT
         Customerkey
         ,ntile(4) OVER(ORDER BY TotalProfit DESC) AS Quartile
         ,TotalProfit
      FROM (SELECT
               Customerkey
               ,sum(SalesAmount)-sum(TotalProductCost) AS TotalProfit
            FROM FactInternetSales
            GROUP BY customerkey) AS c) AS q
GROUP BY Quartile
ORDER BY Quartile
COMPUTE sum(sum(TotalProfit))
GO
```

The query returns the following results:

```
NumCustomers Quartile MinQuartileProfit MaxQuartileProfit SumQuartileProfit
------------ -------- ----------------- ----------------- -----------------
4621         1        1077.4324         5273.81           9149434.8261
4621         2        156.2055          1077.4324         2608879.4859
4621         3        26.4672           156.1322          251766.6393
4621         4        1.4335            26.4672           70802.6937
   sum
--------------------
12080883.645
```

You can see that 25 percent of the customers (Quartile 1) are generating 75 percent of the profit ($9,149,435 divided by $12,080,884 equals 0.757). Who are these customers? Do the high-profit customers fit a certain demographic profile? If so, we could design advertising campaigns geared toward those customers. Or do the customers exhibit certain buying behaviors? Can those high-profit-yielding behaviors be encouraged among more customers? We can use data mining to answer these questions.

To start, run, in order, vProfitability.sql, vCustomerProfitability.sql, and vCustomerPurchases.sql, the three SQL scripts included in the Chapter20SQL project of the SQL Server Management Studio solution included with this chapter's sample code. The scripts add three views to the AdventureWorksDW database: vProfitability, vCustomerProfitability, and vCustomerPurchases. The vCustomerProfitability and vCustomerPurchases views will be the basis of the mining models we create in this chapter. The vCustomerProfitability view has one row for each customer and includes demographic data and summary data about each customer's buying behavior. The vCustomerPurchases view has one row per line item for every customer order in the database. vProfitability has one row per customer purchase. The profit associated with each customer purchase is calculated in this view. The view is referenced by vCustomerProfitability. vProfitability is not referenced directly by any code in this chapter. It is used to simplify the definition of the vCustomerProfitability view.

Creating Training and Test Samples

A data mining project typically has separate samples for training (building) and testing the mining models. Testing the accuracy of a mining model with a sample other than the one on which the model was trained guards against tailoring the model too much to the particular data you have at hand. After all, the true value of data mining lies in how well you can apply the model to new data, not in how well the model tells you about what has already happened.

In Chapter 16, you learned about transforming your data using SQL Server Integration Services (SSIS). The SSIS Percentage Sampling Data Flow transformation task makes it easy to create training and test samples for your data mining projects. Let's build an SSIS project that puts this transformation task to work for us.

1. In Visual Studio, choose New, Project from the File menu.

2. In the New Project dialog box, select Business Intelligence Projects from the Project Types tree view on the left and select Integration Services Project from the Templates pane on the right.

3. Name your project **Chapter20SSIS**, type a path for your project, and type **Chapter20** as your solution name. (Figure 20-3 shows the completed dialog box.)

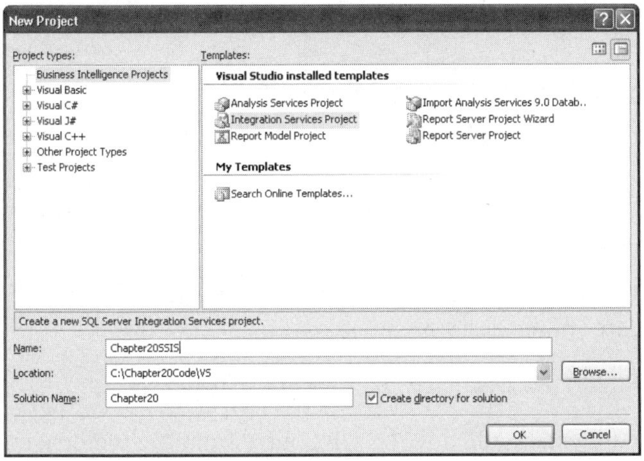

Figure 20-3   The New Project dialog box for an SSIS project

4. Click OK, and your project will be created.

    By default, an empty package called Package.dtsx is created under the SSIS Packages node of your project.

5. In Solution Explorer, right-click Package.dtsx, choose Rename, and rename the default package **CreateDataSamples.dtsx**. When asked whether you want to rename the package object, click Yes.

We want to create training and test samples of customers in the AdventureWorksDW database. This is a SQL Server database, so the first thing you should add to your SSIS package is a connection to it:

1. Right-click in the Connection Managers area at the bottom of the designer window, and then choose New OLE DB Connection.

2. In the Connection Manager dialog box (Figure 20-4), select Native OLE DB\SQL Native Client from the Provider drop-down list. Configure the connection to point to the AdventureWorksDW database on your SQL Server 2005 server.

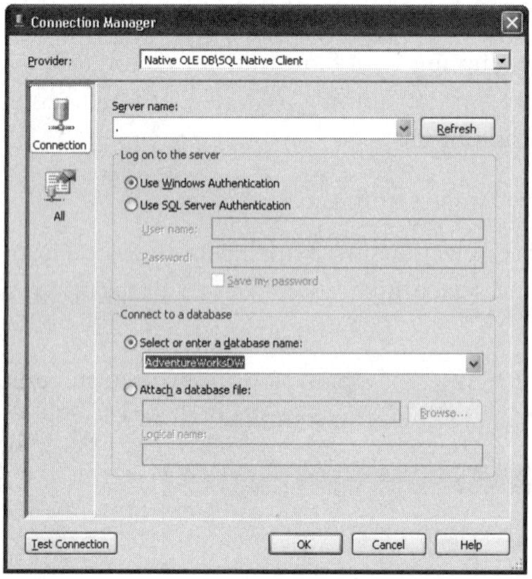

Figure 20-4 The Connection Manager dialog box with the SQL Native Client Provider selected

3. In the dialog box, test your connection to verify that your connection settings are valid, and then click OK.

4. Add a Data Flow Task to the package by dragging one from the Visual Studio toolbox onto the main area of the designer surface.

We now need to configure the Data Flow Task we just added:

1. Click the Data Flow tab. Add an OLE DB Source from the toolbox, and then double-click it.

2. In the OLE DB Source Editor dialog box, set OLE DB connection manager to *ServerName*.AdventureWorksDW (where *ServerName* is the name of the server your Connection Manager is pointing to—for example, LocalHost).

3. Set Data access mode to Table or View, and set Name Of Table Or View to [dbo] .[vCustomerProfitability]. (Figure 20-5 shows the specified Connection Manager property settings.)

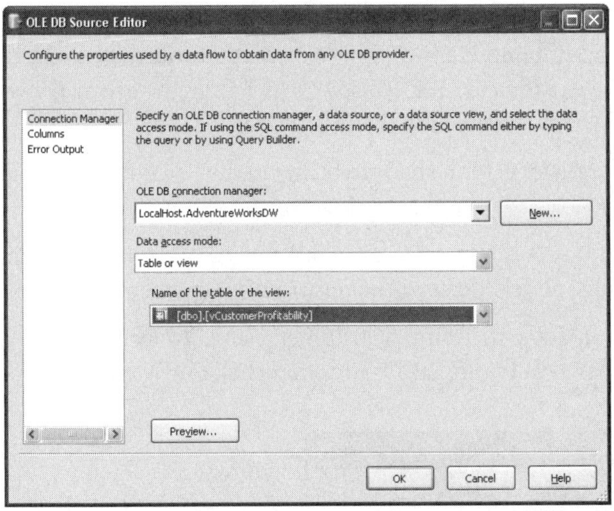

Figure 20-5   The Connection Manager properties in the OLE DB Source Editor dialog box

4. Select Columns from the list box on the left of the dialog box; all columns should be selected, as shown in Figure 20-6.

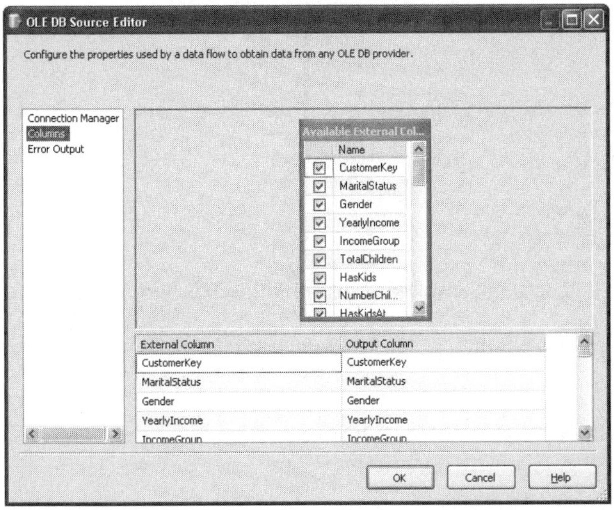

Figure 20-6   The Columns properties in the OLE DB Source Editor dialog box

5. Click OK to save your settings and close the OLE DB Source Editor dialog box.

6. Rename the OLE DB source to **Customers** by setting the Name property in the Properties window or by right-clicking the OLE DB Source shape and choosing Rename.

Now that we have specified our source data, we need to configure things so that we use just a portion of the data. We do this by adding a Percentage Sampling Transformation to the Data Flow Task. The Percentage Sampling Transformation accepts one Data Flow Source as an input and outputs two Data Flow Destination objects.

1. Drag a Percentage Sampling Transformation from the Toolbox onto the designer surface and then click the Customers OLE DB source and drag the green arrow on it over to the newly added shape, connecting the two shapes.

2. Double-click the transformation shape to bring up the Percentage Sampling Transformation Editor dialog box.

3. Set Percentage Of Rows to 70 to create a sample of 70 percent of customers with which to train our mining models (leaving the remaining 30 percent usable for testing).

4. Set Sample Output Name to TrainingCustomers, set Unselected Output Name to TestCustomers (as shown in Figure 20-7), and then click OK.

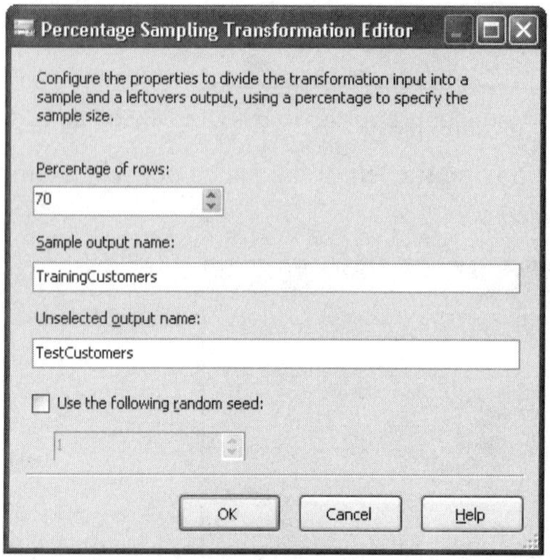

Figure 20-7   The Percentage Sampling Transformation Editor dialog box

To finish building our SSIS package, we'll add two OLE DB Destination objects to the Data Flow Task:

1. Drag two OLE DB Destination objects from the Data Flow Destinations tab of the Toolbox window to the designer surface. Change the names of the destinations to **TrainingCustomers** and **TestCustomers**.

2. Click the Percentage Sampling Transformation shape and drag its green arrow over to the TrainingCustomers shape.

3. In the Input Output Selection dialog box, select TrainingCustomers as the Output, and then click OK.

(In this context, "Output" refers to the output from the random sampling.) You should see a green arrow, labeled TrainingCustomers, connecting the Percentage Sampling Task to the TrainingCustomers destination.

4. Click the Percentage Sampling Transformation shape again and drag the new green arrow over to the TestCustomers destination.

    You will see a green arrow labeled TestCustomers connecting the Percentage Sampling Task to the TestCustomers destination (and no dialog box will appear).

    The red *X*'s on the Data Flow Destination objects indicate that you are not quite finished—you need to configure the destination objects (in other words, you must specify where to store the results of the random sampling).

5. Double-click the TrainingCustomers destination object. Set OLE DB connection manager to *ServerName*.AdventureWorksDW, and leave Data access mode set to Table or view - fast load.

6. For Name of the table or view, click the New button and verify that the *CREATE TABLE* statement creates a table called TrainingCustomers with all the columns from the vCustomerProfitability view. Click OK.

7. Click Mappings in the left-hand list box and verify that all columns are connected between the source and destination. Click OK.

    Follow the same steps to configure the TestCustomers destination shape, verifying that TestCustomers is created by the *CREATE TABLE* statement.

    When you are finished, the Data Flow Task designer should appear as shown in Figure 20-8.

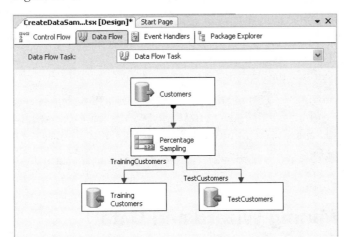

Figure 20-8   Data Flow Task for creating training and testing data tables

8. To execute the package, click the Start Debugging toolbar button (the one with the green "play" icon) or, alternatively, choose Start Debugging from the Debug menu or press the F5 key.

As you will recall from Chapter 16, this causes SSIS to enter Debugging mode. Although there are several ways to execute your SSIS package, you should execute the package you have created only once; otherwise, you will end up with duplicated data in the TrainingCustomers and TestCustomers tables. In practice, you will likely have a step in the package to truncate the data in the two tables before the Percentage Sampling Task; or, if you want to create multiple training and test sets, you can horizontally partition the data in your training and test tables by adding a column to the tables to indicate the sampling round from which the data was generated.

9. After the package has executed successfully, stop debugging mode by clicking the Stop Debugging toolbar button, choosing Stop Debugging from the Debug menu, or pressing Shift+F5. (Alternatively, you can click the "Package execution completed..." hyperlink at the bottom of the SSIS Package designer.)

Your training and test samples have been created. You are now ready to design, process, and test your first mining models.

Adding an SSAS Project

With our SSIS project built, we are ready to create an SSAS project (and database) that will contain our mining models. We'll add the new project to our existing solution.

1. In Visual Studio, choose Add, New Project from the File menu.

2. In the Add New Project dialog box, select the Analysis Services Project template, name the project **Chapter20**, and then click OK.

As with our cube-containing SSAS projects and databases in Chapters 17 and 18, we must define a data source and a data source view in this project.

1. Right-click the Data Sources node in Solution Explorer and then select Choose New Data Source. This brings up the Data Source Wizard. Click Next and then New to bring up the Connection Manager dialog box.

2. Specify your provider (.NET Providers or SqlClient Data Provider), server (the local SQL Server instance on which the AdventureWorksDW database exists), any logon credentials, and the database (AdventureWorksDW). Click OK to dismiss the dialog box.

3. Back in the Data Source Wizard, click Next, supply a name for the data source, and then click Finish.

Using the Data Mining Wizard and Data Mining Designer

Start by adding to your project a data source view (DSV) called CustomerProfitability that contains the vCustomerProfitability view.

> **Important**   Normally, instead of using the vCustomerProfitability view in the DSV, you would use the TrainingCustomers and TestCustomers tables that were created by the SSIS package. Then you would use TrainingCustomers to train your mining models. If we were to use the TrainingCustomers table now, however, the results of the mining models would be not quite the same as those shown in the figures. The Percentage Sampling Task generates *random* samples, making the results slightly different from those presented in this chapter. Using vCustomerProfitability, which includes all customers, makes the examples in this chapter completely reproducible.

For the customer profitability analysis, we want to find out the common characteristics of high-profit and low-profit customers. To do this, we must add a calculated column to our DSV that defines "high profit." We don't want to store this in our database because it is a definition specific to the analysis we are doing.

To create a calculated column in the DSV, take the following steps:

1. Right-click the vCustomerProfitability view on the DSV design tab and choose New Named Calculation.

2. In the Named Calculation dialog box, give your named calculation the name **Profit-Category**, enter the description **High-profit customers in the top quartile of profit**, and type the following in the Expression box:

```
CASE
    WHEN Profit>1077 THEN 'High'
    ELSE 'Low'
END
```

   This creates two categories of customers: the "High" category for customers in the top quartile of profit amounts and the "Low" category for all other customers.

3. Click OK. You will see your newly created column in the DSV with a calculator icon to the left of it.

Now we'll browse the data within the DSV:

1. Right-click vCustomerProfitability and choose Explore Data. The Data Explorer window opens.

   You can choose to view either the top x rows in your table or a random sample of x rows from your table. (The value of x is configurable.) By default, the Data Explorer window shows data for the top 5000 rows in your data source (the exact meaning of "top" will vary, depending on how the data is sorted in your table).

2. To change this default, click the Sampling Options button (the one with the properties icon) in the upper-right corner of the window. This opens the Data Exploration Options dialog box.

3. Click the Random Sample option button, leaving the Sample Count at 5000, and click OK.

4. To implement this configuration change and see the data for your random sample of records from vCustomerProfitability, you must refresh the data. To do so, click the Resample Data button (the one with the refresh icon) in the upper-right corner of the Data Explorer window.

    Now scroll to the rightmost column of the table. You will see the named calculation you just created. It will look no different from any other column of your table.

Using the other tabs in the Data Explorer window, you can create PivotTables and charts or simple data distribution charts. To use the distribution chart feature, follow these steps:

1. Click the Chart tab.

    By default, column charts are displayed for a subset of the columns in your DSV. You can click anywhere on the drop-down control at the top of the window to modify the view to display charts for any combination of columns from your table.

2. Select the ProfitCategory column from the drop-down list, and either press ENTER or click the Chart tab—or click somewhere in the chart area—to dismiss the column list. A column chart for Profit Category should appear alongside the other charts.

3. You can change the chart type to a (horizontal) bar chart or pie chart. To change your column charts to pie charts, click the pie chart button in the upper-left corner of the Data Explorer window, or right-click a blank area of the chart and choose Pie Chart. Figure 20-9 shows pie charts of several customer characteristics.

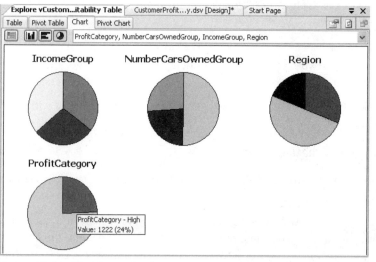

Figure 20-9   The Chart tab of the Data Explorer window allows you to see how your data is distributed.

You can see details about the data represented by a particular item on the Chart tab by hovering the mouse pointer over the item. For example, hovering over a pie slice shows you the count and percentage of records that are represented by that slice (as shown in Figure 20-9).

Data Explorer allows you to see the distribution of your data quickly and easily without your needing to write a single line of code. This can be useful during the startup phase of your data mining project, before any models have been created.

Creating a Mining Structure

Mining models in SSAS are contained within *mining structures*. A mining structure consists of a subset of columns from your DSV and one or more mining models that use the columns. The content type of each column is set separately by the mining model—for each mining model in your mining structure, you specify whether the column is a key, an input, or a predictable column. (We'll discuss the content types in more detail later.)

Because you can also indicate that a column in the structure should be ignored for a particular mining model, you can conceivably have two mining models within the same structure that do not share any input or predictable columns. But it makes more sense to group, under the same structure, mining models that answer the same business question and that have some commonality in columns from your DSV. This is because mining models created within the same structure can be compared using the Mining Accuracy Chart functionality of SSAS, which we will examine shortly. Furthermore, mining models that share a structure are processed in parallel, with a single pass through the data.

Getting back to our data mining goals, we want to know whether particular characteristics or buying behaviors can help us predict who the high-profit customers are. We also want to cluster customers according to their demographic characteristics and buying behaviors. To that end, we will use the Data Mining Editor in Visual Studio to create a mining structure with models that use the Clustering, Decision Tree, and Naïve Bayes algorithms. (Later we will discuss how each of these algorithms works, how they differ from each other, and their appropriate use for specific prediction scenarios.)

Creating a Mining Model

To create the initial mining model, follow these steps:

1. Right-click the Mining Structures node in Solution Explorer and choose New Mining Structure. This starts the Mining Structure Wizard.

2. On the Welcome page, click Next.

3. On the Select the Definition Method page, select From Existing Relational Database or Data Warehouse and then click Next.

4. On the Select the Data Mining Technique page, select a data mining technique for your initial mining model, which you must configure when you create a mining structure. After the mining structure is created, you can add additional mining models to that structure. Select Microsoft Clustering from the drop-down list and then click Next.

5. On the Select Data Source View page, select the DSV that you created earlier and then click Next.

6. On the Specify Table Types page, you will see vCustomerProfitability from your DSV along with check boxes for specifying the table type. Select the Case check box next to vCustomerProfitability. Click Next.

Tables for Mining Models

SSAS has two types of tables for use in mining models: case tables and nested tables. Every mining structure must have a case table. Simply put, the case table defines the entities to be analyzed for your mining model. In the customer profitability analysis, the basic unit of analysis is the customer; therefore, we will define vCustomerProfitability, which has one row per customer, as the case table. Nested tables are used to provide additional detail about your cases. Not every mining structure will have a nested table. For now, our mining structure will have only a case table. Later in the chapter, we will extend the profitability models by including the types of purchases customers made. We will do that using a nested table.

---

7. On the Specify The Training Data page, you will see a list of all the columns in your case table. To the right of each column is a set of three check boxes for specifying whether each column is a Key, Input, or Predictable column in your model, as shown in Figure 20-10.

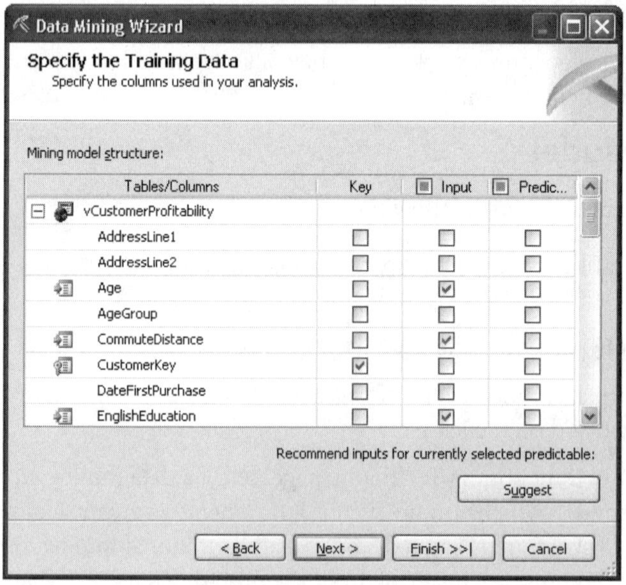

Figure 20-10 The Data Mining Wizard's Specify The Training Data page

The Key column uniquely identifies each record in your case table. Input columns form the basis on which data pattern discoveries are made, whether they be descriptive or predictive patterns. For example, the clustering algorithm creates clusters based on the values of the input columns. The Decision Trees algorithm decides tree splits based on how well the values of an input column predict a particular outcome.

Predictive and Descriptive Mining Models

From a technical standpoint, marking a column as predictable means that it can be selected from the model in a DMX prediction query. (We'll discuss prediction queries in greater detail later in the chapter.) This is true of the predictable columns in any mining model, even those that do not have prediction as a goal. This definition doesn't really convey what predictable columns are for. For a common-sense definition, we need to distinguish between *predictive* and *descriptive* mining models.

Predictive mining models are designed to forecast (predict) the value of their predictable columns. For descriptive mining models, predicted columns have a technical usage, and that usage varies. In a clustering model, input columns are used to determine the clusters. Selecting only the Predict check box for a column means that the column will not be used to determine the clusters; however, including the column as a predictable column in the model allows you to view its distribution within each cluster and compare its distribution across clusters after the model has been processed.

---

8. Back on the Specify the Training Data page, select CustomerKey as the Key column of your case table and select the Input check box for the following columns: Age, CommuteDistance, EnglishEducation, Gender, HasKidsAtHome, IncomeGroup, IsCarOwner, IsHomeOwner, IsNewCustomer, MaritalStatus, NumProdGroup, RecencyGroup, and Region.

9. Select the Predict check box for the ProfitCategory column, and then click Next.

10. On the Specify Columns' Data Type and Content page, click Detect.

This forces SSAS to determine whether your input and predictable columns are discrete (categorical) or continuous. You can also modify the content and data type by clicking in the cell and selecting the type from the drop-down list that appears, as shown in Figure 20-11.

11. Verify that the content type is continuous for the Age column, key for the CustomerKey column, and discrete for all other columns. Click Next.

12. Name the mining structure **CustomerProfitCategory** and the mining model **CustomerProfitCategory_CL** and then click Finish.

This brings you to the Mining Structure tab of the data mining structure designer, as shown in Figure 20-12.

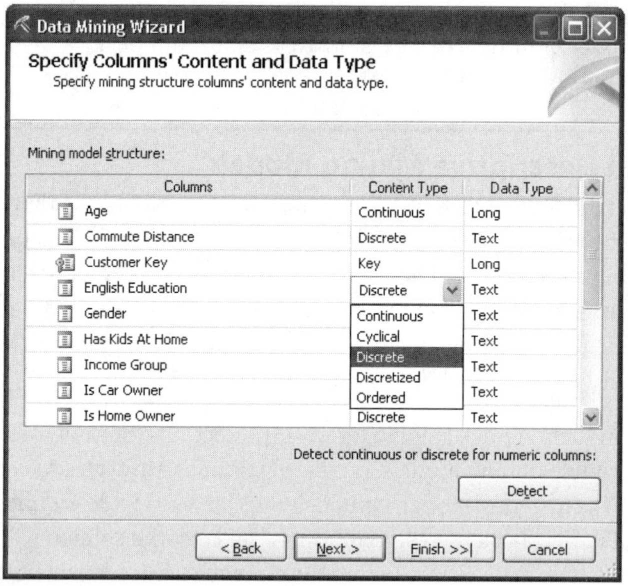

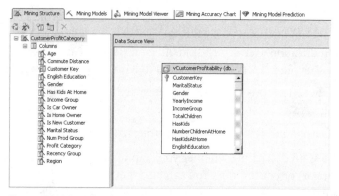

Figure 20-11   Content and data types of columns are specified at the mining structure level in the Data Mining Wizard.

Figure 20-12   The data mining structure designer's Mining Structure tab shows the columns in the mining structure.

The left pane of the tab contains a treeview display of our mining structure. From here, you can add and delete columns and nested tables by using the tab's toolbar or by right-clicking anywhere in the treeview pane (on the left) and selecting options from the context menu. The Data Source View pane (on the right) allows you to explore and edit the DSV.

Editing and Adding Mining Models

With your mining structure and first mining model created, you are ready to create additional models within the structure. On the Mining Models tab of the data mining structure designer, you can view the definition of your mining model, as shown in Figure 20-13. You will see the columns in your mining structure configured according to the choices you previously made for how those columns should be used in your clustering model.

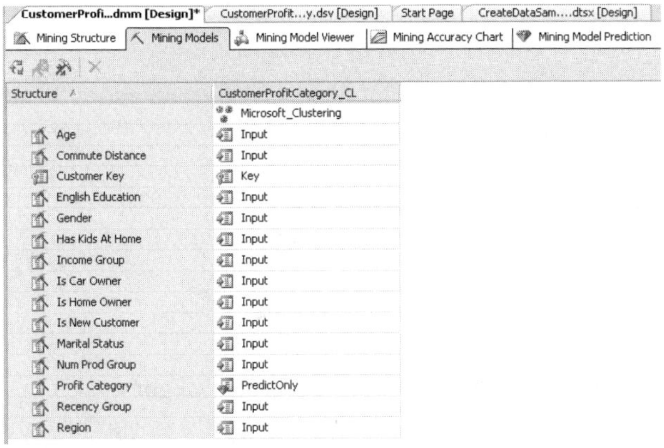

Figure 20-13   On the Mining Model tab, you can see how the mining structure columns are used in each mining model.

Editing a Mining Model

You can also edit the definition of your mining model from the Mining Model tab. Profit Category is specified as a PredictOnly column in the mining model. We want to change the usage type from PredictOnly to Predict. To edit column usage, take these steps:

1. On the Mining Models tab of the data mining structure designer, click the cell next to Profit Category.

2. In the drop-down list that appears, change the column usage to Predict, as shown in Figure 20-14.

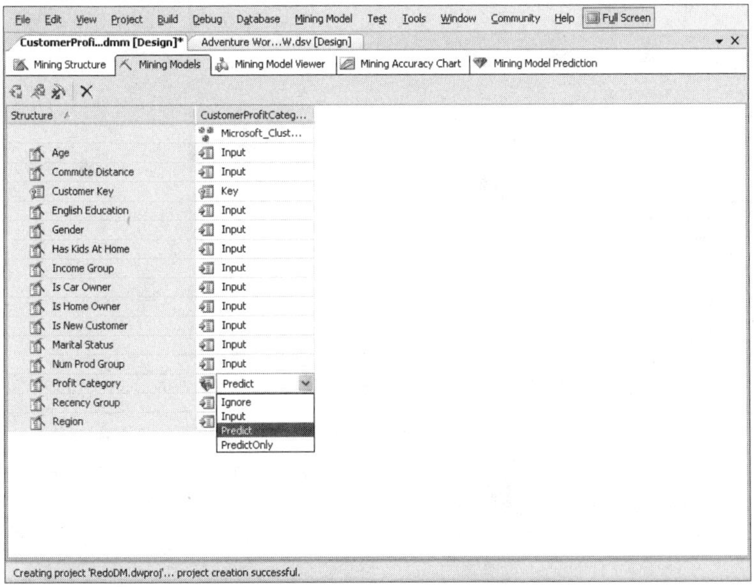

Figure 20-14   Clicking a cell next to a column to change its usage in a mining model

Changing the column usage from PredictOnly to Predict allows customer profit category to be a factor in how the clusters are determined, and not just a descriptive characteristic analyzed after the fact.

Adding a Mining Model

By default, the Microsoft Clustering algorithm creates 10 clusters from your training data. As a thoughtful data analyst, you might be concerned that users will have trouble grasping the nuances of the differences in so many clusters. You might therefore want to create a second clustering model that segments your customers into only five clusters. To do this, follow these steps:

1. Right-click anywhere on the Mining Models tab and then choose New Mining Model.

2. In the New Mining Model dialog box, type **CustomerProfitCategory_CL5** in the Model Name text box and then select Microsoft Clustering from the Algorithm Name drop-down list. Click OK. A new mining model is added to the right of the existing model.

3. To change the number of clusters created, from 10 to 5, right-click the CustomerProfit Category_CL5 column header or any of its column cells and then choose Set Algorithm Parameters.

4. In the Algorithm Parameters dialog box that appears (Figure 20-15), you can set algorithm parameters that are specific to the selected mining model.

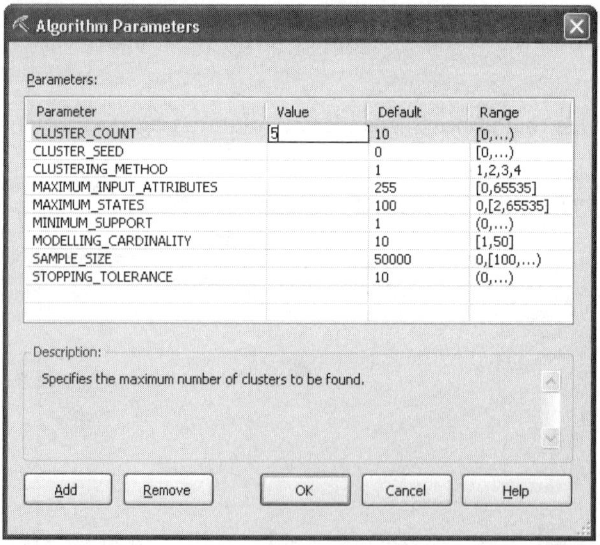

Figure 20-15   The Algorithm Parameters dialog box for a Microsoft Clustering model

This can be a bit perplexing at first because the designers abstract much of the complexity of data mining through their UI and wizards. Meanwhile, the dialog box cracks open the black box and allows you to fine-tune your model. Click the various parameters in the parameter list and review the descriptions in the Description area below.

5. When you're done exploring the parameters, click the cell at the intersection of the CLUSTER_COUNT row and the Value column, type **5**, and then click OK.

Adding a Model That Uses a Different Algorithm

We now have two clustering models in our mining structure. To validate the accuracy of one model in a mining structure, it is often useful to create an additional model using a different algorithm. We'll add a new model using the Decision Trees algorithm. This can be done with surprisingly little effort:

1. Right-click anywhere on the Mining Models tab and choose New Mining Model.

2. In the New Mining Model dialog box, name your model **CustomerProfitCategory_DT**, select the Decision Trees algorithm (it should be selected by default), and then click OK.

   The CustomerProfitCategory_DT model appears to the right of the existing clustering models with the same columns and usage.

Changing Column Usage

Adding the model is helpful, but it would be even better if we could use it to predict the number of products people buy (in addition to predicting profit category). To change the column usage for NumProductGroup in the CustomerProfitCategory_DT mining model, click the cell corresponding to the NumProductGroup under CustomerProfitCategory_DT and select Predict from the drop-down list. By setting the content type of *both* the Profit-Category and the NumProdGroup variables to Predict, we are allowing each to be an input in the decision tree of the other. If we had instead set the content type of the Num-ProdGroup to PredictOnly, the number of products purchased would not be a factor in creating the ProfitCategory decision tree—that is, the number of products purchased would not be considered in the splits of the ProfitCategory tree.

> **More Info** *Splits* are the branches at each node of a decision tree. Each node of a decision tree represents a subset of the population. This subset is characterized by the parentage of the node. Splits at each node are determined by identifying the input characteristic by which the distribution of the predicted variable differs most for the subset defined at that node. When the distribution of the predicted variable at a node does not vary significantly by any input characteristic, there are no further splits and the branch ends. A node from which there are no splits is referred to as a *leaf*.

Mining Models and Data Types

Let's continue building our mining structure by adding another model, this time using the Naïve Bayes algorithm:

1. Right-click the CustomerProfitCategory_CL model, and choose New Mining Model.

2. Name your model **CustomerProfitCategory_NB**, select the Naïve Bayes algorithm, and click OK.

A message box will appear explaining that the Age column will be ignored because the Naïve Bayes algorithm does not support working with continuous columns. Click Yes. Notice that the content type for the Age column is set to Ignore, the content type for the NumProd column is set to Input, and the content type for the ProfitCategory column is set to Predict. For this model, we want to predict only ProfitCategory, so no content type modifications are necessary.

> **Important**   Because we created the Naïve Bayes model by right-clicking the CustomerProfit-Category_CL model and choosing New Mining Model, the CustomerProfitCategory_CL content type settings were used in the new model, making ProfitCategory the only predicted column. Had we instead right-clicked the CustomerProfitCategory_DT model and chosen New Mining Model, that model's content type settings would have been used, and NumProd, in addition to Profit-Category, would have been a predicted column.

We mentioned earlier that age is ignored in the Naïve Bayes model because it is a continuous variable. If age is a significant determinant of whether a customer is a high-profit or low-profit customer, the Naïve Bayes model will appear to perform worse than other models where age is included. Therefore, we want to include at least some indication of age in the Naïve Bayes model. To do that, we must add a "discretized" version of the age column to our mining structure and include it in our Naïve Bayes model.

The Mining Models tab supports the deletion of columns from a mining structure, but to *add* a column to the structure, we need to go back to the Mining Structure tab.

1. On the Mining Structure tab, right-click the tree view and choose Add A Column.

2. In the Select a Column dialog box (Figure 20-16), select the AgeGroup column in the Source Column list and then click OK to add AgeGroup to the mining structure.

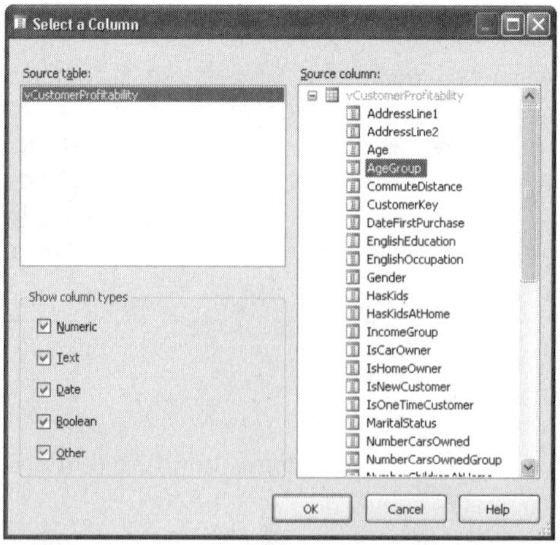

Figure 20-16   The Select a Column dialog box for adding a column to your mining structure

> **Note**   The AgeGroup column in vCustomerProfitability categorizes customers into groups such as "Under 30," "Age 30 through 35," and "Age 36 through 45" by using a *CASE* statement. SSAS also has a column content type called "discretized" that can be used to categorize a continuous attribute. A discussion of this functionality is beyond the scope of this chapter, but you can read more about it by searching on "discretization" in Books Online.

3. Return to the Mining Models tab. You will see that AgeGroup appears in the mining structure, although its usage is set to Ignore in all of the defined models. To include it in the Naïve Bayes model, click in the cell corresponding to the AgeGroup column under the Naïve Bayes model and change the usage to Input. Your Mining Models tab should appear as shown in Figure 20-17.

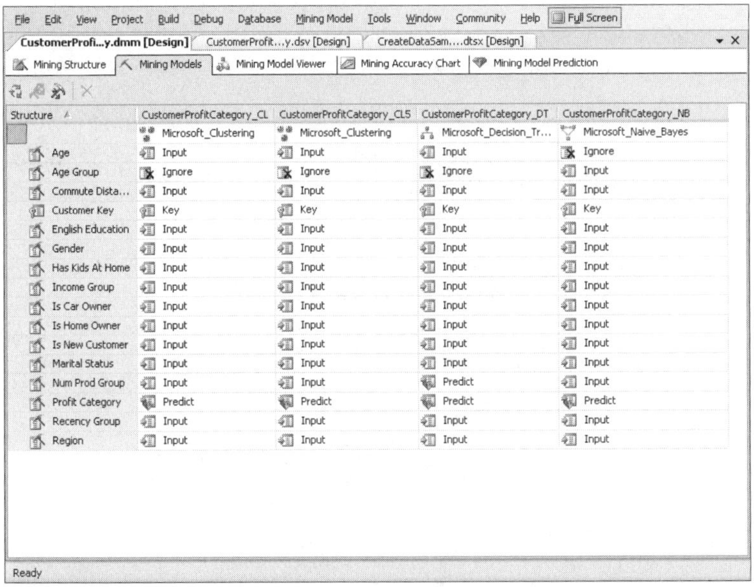

Figure 20-17   A mining structure with several mining models and a "discretized" Age Group column

Deploying and Processing Data Mining Objects

We have done a good bit of work already, having defined a mining structure with several mining models. We are almost ready to view and query the models, but we must first deploy and process the SSAS database that contains them. We can deploy the database and process the mining models in a single step by choosing the Start Debugging command from the Debug menu, clicking the Start Debugging (play) toolbar button, or pressing the F5 key.

Caution The Visual Studio solution included with this chapter's sample code is configured so that the Start Debugging toolbar options and menu commands will *not* automatically deploy the Chapter20 SSAS project (or the Chapter20Reports project we will discuss later). We took this precaution to keep you from unwittingly deploying the database when debugging the Windows Forms and ASP.NET client applications included in the same solution. If you are working with the sample code and want to deploy the SSAS database and process its mining models, simply right-click the Chapter20 project node in Solution Explorer and choose the Deploy command.

Deployment and processing might take several minutes. You can monitor deployment and processing progress in the Deployment Progress window, which by default appears as a docked window in the lower-right corner of Visual Studio when you start the deployment. If the Deployment Progress window is not visible, you can show it by choosing Show Deployment Progress from the View menu or by right-clicking the project node and choosing Show Deployment Progress in Solution Explorer.

It is easiest to monitor the progress of the deployment and processing of your mining structure and models by undocking the Deployment Progress window and resizing it to a relatively large size. Figure 20-18 shows the Deployment Progress window for a successfully deployed and processed SSAS project.

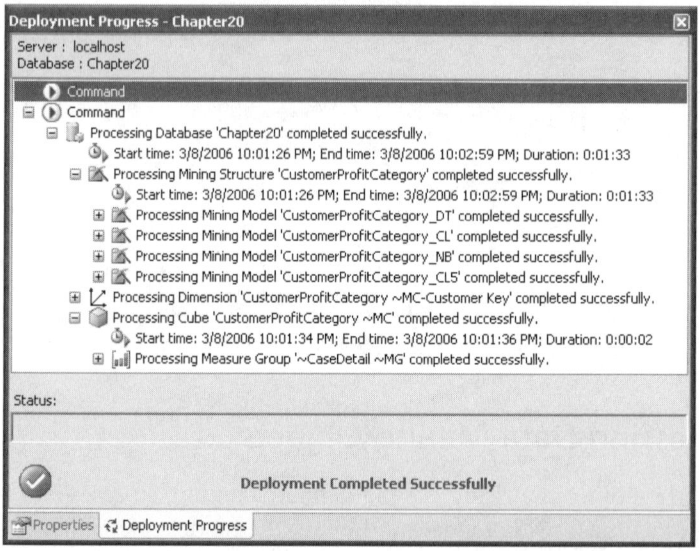

Figure 20-18 The Deployment Progress window after a successful deployment

Tip The easiest way to undock the Deployment Progress window is to double-click its title bar. You can redock it after processing has completed by double-clicking the title bar a second time. This avoids the sometimes confusing drag-and-drop procedure for undocking and redocking the window.

Caution   If you encounter processing errors indicating that columns of your data source do not exist, you might need to change the impersonation information of the data source in your SSAS project. To do this, double-click the data source node under the Data Sources node in Solution Explorer, click the Impersonation Information tab, and select an appropriate user. During development, you can select the Use The Service Account option button. Before deploying the database and mining models to production, however, you should select a specific user account with the appropriate rights.

After the initial deployment of the SSAS database, you can process mining models without deploying the database. To process all the mining models within a structure, choose Process Mining Structure and All Models from the Mining Model menu. To process a single model in a mining structure, select the model on the Mining Models tab and then choose Process Model from the Mining Model menu. Both the Process Mining Structure and All Models command and the Process Model command are also available from each model's shortcut menu on the Mining Models tab and from the two leftmost buttons on that tab's toolbar.

Viewing Mining Models

SSAS provides algorithm-specific mining model viewers within Visual Studio Analysis Services projects (and in SQL Server Management Studio—more on that later) that greatly ease the otherwise daunting task of interpreting a model's contents, observed patterns, and correlations. The visualization tools provided by the viewers thus make data mining accessible to a larger audience than do traditional data mining products.

Take, for example, clustering, which is used to create subsets (clusters) of your data that share common characteristics. Imagine trying to digest the implications of a clustering model with 10 customer clusters defined on 8, 10, or 12 characteristics. How would you figure out the identifying characteristics of each cluster? How could you determine whether the resulting clusters are similar or dissimilar? The Microsoft Cluster Viewer makes it extremely easy to answer such questions. We'll see how next.

Using the Cluster Viewer

After you have deployed and processed all of the mining models in the CustomerProfitCategory mining structure, you will be brought to the Mining Model Viewer tab. If it's not already selected, choose CustomerProfitCategory_CL from the Mining Model drop-down list. Then choose Microsoft Cluster Viewer from the Viewer drop-down list. The Cluster Viewer offers four ways to view the results of a clustering model: Cluster Diagram, Cluster Profiles, Cluster Characteristics, and Cluster Discrimination. A separate tab is provided for each of these visualization tools.

Cluster Diagram   The Cluster Diagram tab of the Cluster Viewer contains a diagram in which each "bubble" represents a cluster from the model. The cluster diagram uses color to indicate data density: the darker the bubble, the more records that cluster contains. You control the actual variable and value indicated by the shading by using the Shading

Variable and State drop-down lists; you can select any input or predictable column. For example, if you select ProfitCategory from the Shading Variable drop-down list and select High from the State drop-down list, the diagram will configure itself so that darker clusters contain a greater number of high-profit customers relative to lighter ones. This is shown in Figure 20-19.

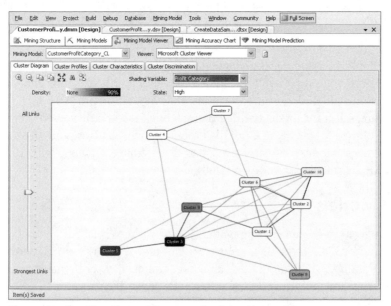

Figure 20-19   The Cluster Diagram tab of the Cluster Viewer

Note   The cluster numbers you see should match those described in the chapter text and figures. There is, however, some inherent randomness in how the Microsoft Clustering algorithm determines the clusters, and this might cause your numbering to differ from the numbering seen in the text and the figures. Even if your exact cluster numbers differ, you should still see the qualitative results described in the text.

The darkest bubbles are 3, 5, and 9—these are the clusters with a relatively large concentration of high-profit customers. Hovering the mouse pointer over a cluster displays the exact percentage of customers in that cluster who are in the high-profit category. Now select Income-Group from the Shading Variable drop-down list and select High from the State drop-down list. The clusters 9, 6, and 3 should now be the darkest bubbles. Select IsCarOwner from the Shading Variable drop-down list and N from the State drop-down list. The darkest clusters should now be 8, 7, and 5.

By examining the cluster characteristics in this manner, we can assign more meaningful names to the clusters. You can rename a cluster by right-clicking the cluster in the diagram and choosing Rename. For example, you can right-click cluster 3 and rename it "High Profit,

High Income, Car Owner" and then right-click cluster 5 and rename it "High Profit, Lower Income, Less Likely Car Owner."

The clusters are arranged in the diagram according to their similarity. The shorter and darker the line connecting the bubbles, the more similar the clusters. By default, all links are shown in the diagram. By using the slider to the left of the diagram, you can remove weaker links and identify which clusters are the most similar.

Cluster Profiles   The Cluster Profiles tab, shown in Figure 20-20, displays the distribution of input and predictable variables for each customer cluster and for the entire population of customers. This tab is particularly useful for getting an overall picture of the clusters created by the mining model. Using the cluster profiles, you can easily compare attributes across clusters and analyze cluster attributes relative to the model's full data population.

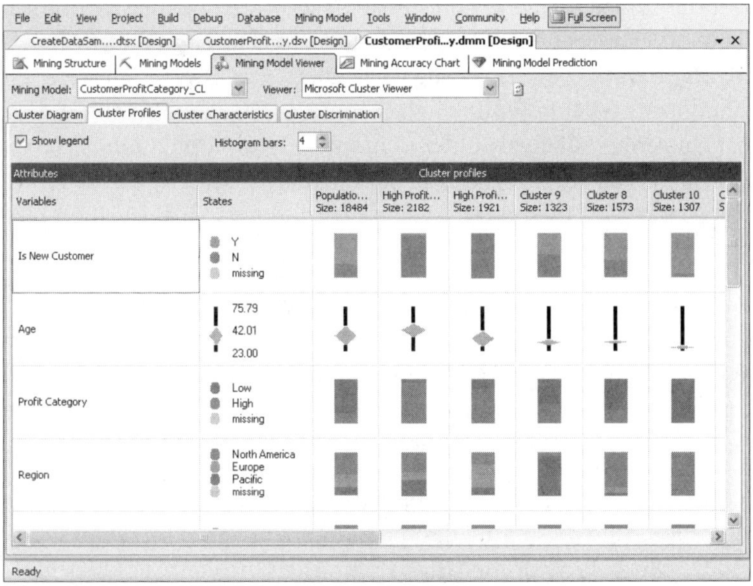

Figure 20-20   The Cluster Profile tab of the Cluster Viewer

The distribution of discrete attributes is shown using a colored bar. By default, the Cluster Profile tab shows the four most common categories in the population with all others grouped into a fifth category. You can change the number of categories by increasing or decreasing the number in the Histogram Bars text box. Go to the row showing the IncomeGroup attribute and then scroll to the right to see how the distribution of IncomeGroup varies across the clusters. Compare the histogram bar between the population "High Profit, High Income, Car Owner" and "High Profit, Lower Income, Less Likely Car Owner" clusters. (You might need to click the Refresh Viewer Content button at the top of the Mining Model Viewer tab in order to see the new names of your clusters.) The histogram bar for the population is divided into three relatively equal segments because the population has relatively equal numbers of customers in the high, moderate, and low income groups. In contrast, the High Income segment of the histogram bar for the "High Profit, High Income, Car Owner" cluster is larger than the other income segments for that cluster because it has relatively more customers that are in the High Income group. The High Income segment of the histogram bar for the "High Profit, Lower Income, Less Likely Car Owner" cluster is virtually indiscernible. If you hover your mouse pointer over the histogram bar, however, you can see that the High Income segment comprises 0.5 percent of the bar.

The distribution of continuous characteristics is shown using a bar and diamond chart. Go to the row showing the age attribute. The black bar represents the range of ages in the cluster, with the median age at the midpoint of the bar. The midpoint of the diamond represents the average age of the customers in the cluster. The standard deviation (a statistical measure of how spread-out the data is) of age for the cluster is indicated by the size of the diamond. Compare the diamond chart between the population and the "High Profit, High Income, Car Owner" and "High Profit, Lower Income, Less Likely Car Owner" clusters. The higher and flatter diamond for the "High Profit, High Income, Car Owner" cluster indicates that customers in that cluster are relatively older than in the total population and that the age variation in the cluster is less than in the total population. You can hover the mouse pointer over the diamond chart to see the precise average age and standard deviation represented by the chart.

By default, the cluster characteristics are shown alphabetically from top to bottom. Locate the cluster you renamed "High Profit, High Income, Car Owner" and click its column heading. The cluster attributes will be reordered according to the characteristics that most differentiate it from the total population. Click the cluster you renamed "High Profit, Lower Income, Less Likely Car Owner" to see how the order of the characteristics changes.

Initially, clusters are ordered by size from left to right. You can change the order of the clusters by dragging and dropping clusters to the desired location. Figure 20-20 shows the cluster attributes ordered by importance for the "High Profit, High Income, Car Owner" cluster and the clusters ordered by percentage of customers in the high-profit category.

Cluster Characteristics   The Cluster Characteristics tab lets you examine the attributes of a particular cluster. By default, attributes for the model's entire data population are shown. To see the attributes of a particular cluster instead, you can select one from the Cluster drop-down list. For example, if you select the "High Profit, High Income, Car Owner" cluster, the attributes will be reordered according to probability that they appear in that cluster, as shown in Figure 20-21.

The attribute with the highest probability in this cluster is that of *not* being a new customer—in other words, there is a 95 percent chance that a customer in this cluster is not a new customer.

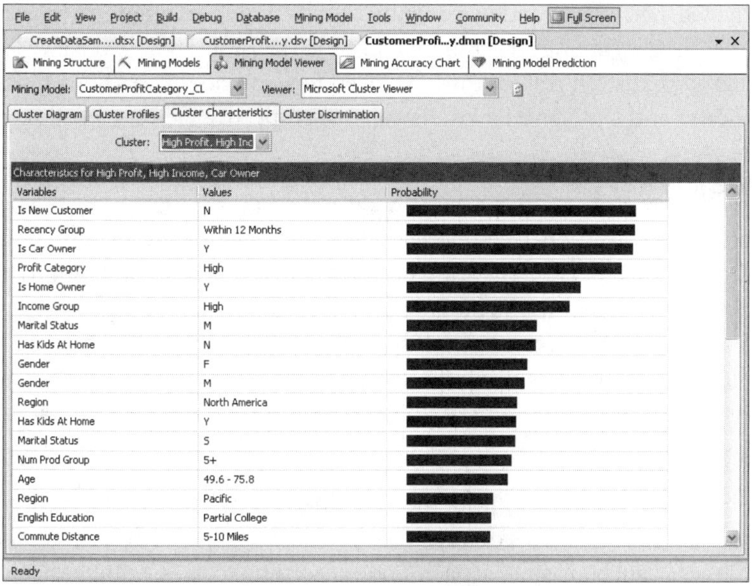

Figure 20-21   The Cluster Characteristics tab of the Cluster Viewer

Cluster Discrimination   The Cluster Discrimination tab is most useful for comparing two clusters and understanding what most distinguishes them. Select "High Profit, High Income, Car Owner" from the Cluster 1 drop-down list and "High Profit, Lower Income, Less Likely Car Owner" from the Cluster 2 drop-down list. The attributes that are most important in differentiating the two clusters are shown by order of importance. A bar indicates the cluster in which you are more likely to find the particular attribute, and the size of the bar indicates the importance of the attribute. As you can see from Figure 20-22, the two most important distinguishing attributes of the selected clusters are the high-income and low-income groups.

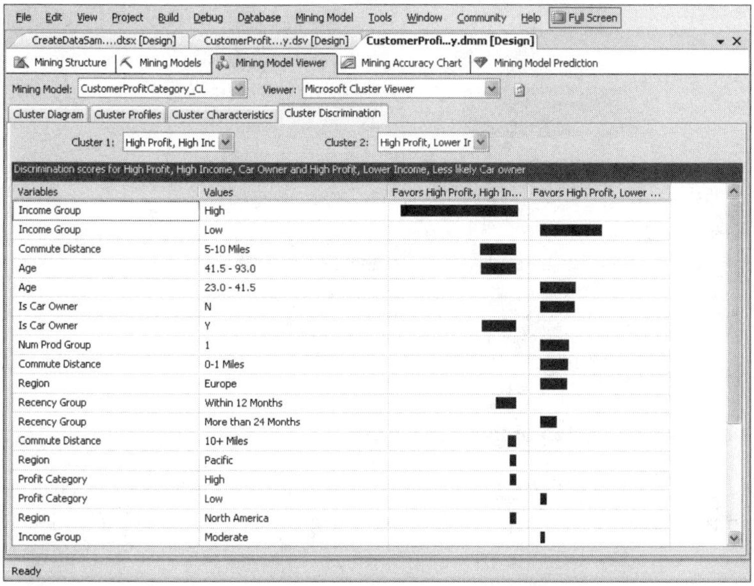

Figure 20-22   The Cluster Discrimination tab of the Cluster Viewer

We've covered the Cluster Viewer and its constituent tabs in depth, but don't forget that we have mining models in our mining structure that use the Decision Trees and Naïve Bayes algorithms rather than the Clustering algorithm. We need to also understand how to use the Microsoft Tree Viewer and the Naïve Bayes Viewer—the respective viewers for these models.

Using the Tree Viewer

To view the results of the Decision Trees model, select CustomerProfitCategory_DT from the Mining Model drop-down list. This will bring up the Microsoft Tree Viewer. The Tree Viewer offers two views of the results from the model estimation: a decision tree and a dependency network view. A separate tree is created for each predictable variable in the decision tree view. You can select the tree to view using the Tree drop-down list. In our model, we have two trees, one for predicting customer profitability and one for predicting the number of products purchased.

Decision Tree   Select ProfitCategory from the Tree drop-down list to reveal the tree for that variable. The Tree Viewer provides a sideways view of a decision tree with the root node at the far left. Decision trees branch, or split, at each node according to the attribute that is most important for determining the predictable column at that node. By inference, this means that the first split shown from the root All node is the most important characteristic for determining the profitability of a customer. As shown in Figure 20-23, the first split in the ProfitCategory tree is premised on whether the customer is a new customer.

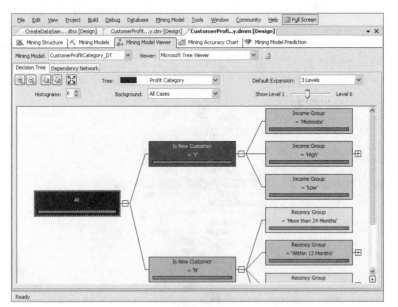

Figure 20-23   The Decision Tree tab of the Tree Viewer

The Tree Viewer shows a bar chart of the ProfitCategory at each node of the tree and uses the background shading of a node to indicate the concentration of cases in that node. By default, the shading of the tree nodes indicates the percentage of the population at that node. The shading is controlled by the selection in the Background drop-down list, where you can select a specific value for the ProfitCategory variable instead of the entire population. If the predictable variable is continuous rather than discrete, there will be a diamond chart in each node of the tree indicating the mean, median, standard deviation, and range of the predictable variable.

By default, up to three levels of the tree are shown. You can change the default by using the Default Expansion drop-down list. A change here changes the default for *all* decision trees viewed in the structure. To view more levels for the tree without changing the default, use the Level slider or expand individual branches of a tree by clicking the plus sign at the branch's node. A node with no plus sign is a leaf node, which means it has no child branches and therefore cannot be expanded. Branches end when there are no remaining input attributes that help determine the value of the predictable variable at that node. The length of various branches in the tree varies because they are data dependent.

Dependency Network   The Dependency Network tab for the CustomerProfitCategory_DT model is shown in Figure 20-24. Each bubble in the dependency network represents a predictable variable or an attribute that determined a split in the decision tree for a predictable variable. Arrows connecting the attributes indicate the direction of the relationship between the variables. An arrow *to* an attribute indicates that it is predicted, and an arrow *from* an attribute indicates that it is a predictor. The double-headed arrow connecting ProfitCategory and NumProdGroup indicates that they predict each other—each splits a node in the decision tree of the other. If we had set the usage type of each of these variables to PredictOnly or Input rather than Predict, we would not have been able to make this observation.

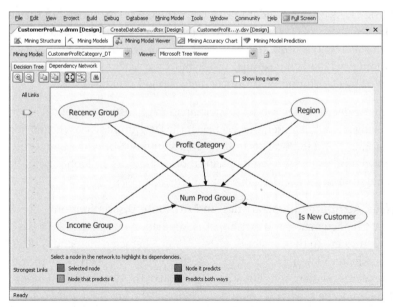

Figure 20-24   The Dependency Network tab of the Tree Viewer

Click ProfitCategory. This activates color coding, as described in the legend below the dependency network, to indicate whether an attribute predicts, or is predicted by, ProfitCategory.

The slider to the left of the dependency network allows you to filter out all but the strongest links between variables. If you move the slider to the bottom, you will see that the strongest predictor of ProfitCategory is whether the customer is new. Slowly move the slider up. The next bubble to become reddish-orange is Recency Group; this means that the recentness of the last purchase is the second most important predictor of customer profitability after whether the customer is new.

Now move the slider back to the bottom and click NumProdGroup. The color coding now shows the predictors of that variable instead of ProfitCategory. Even though no predictors are colored, you can move the slider up slowly and see that the first bubble to become pink is ProfitCategory, revealing that the most important determinant of the number of products purchased is the profitability of the customer.

Using the Naïve Bayes Viewer

We have yet to view our Naïve Bayes model. To do so, simply select CustomerProfitCategory_ NB from the Mining Model drop-down list, bringing up the Naïve Bayes Viewer. The viewer has four tabs: Dependency Network, Attribute Profiles, Attribute Characteristics, and Attribute Discrimination. Our experience with the Cluster Viewer and Tree Viewer will serve us well here because we have encountered slightly different versions of all four of these tabs in those two viewers.

Dependency Network   The Dependency Network tab of the Naïve Bayes Viewer looks and works the same way as the Dependency Network tab of the Tree Viewer, but it reveals slightly different conclusions. As before, a slider to the left of the tab filters out all but the strongest determining characteristics of customer profitability. If you move the slider all the way to the bottom and then slowly move it up, you will see that according to the Naïve Bayes model, the most important predictors of customer profitability are whether the customer is a new customer, followed by the number of products the customer purchased.

This differs from the decision tree model's determination of customer profit. That model suggests that after being a new customer, the recency of the last purchase was the most important predictor of customer profitability. This underscores an important point: even though the viewers for the two models use the same visualization technique, each one uses a different algorithm and might indicate slightly different conclusions.

Attribute Profiles, Attribute Characteristics, and Attribute Discrimination   The Attribute Profiles, Attribute Characteristics, and Attribute Discrimination tabs of the Naïve Bayes Viewer are functionally equivalent to the Cluster Profiles, Cluster Characteristics, and Cluster Discrimination tabs of the Cluster Viewer. However, instead of allowing a comparison of the distribution of input attributes across *clusters,* they allow a comparison of the distribution of input attributes across distinct values of the predicted column—in our case, the ProfitCategory column.

Click the Attribute Profiles tab and then select the Low profit group. As shown in Figure 20-25, according to our Naïve Bayes model, the most important characteristics for predicting whether a customer is a low-profit customer are whether the person is a new customer, the number of products purchased, and the region.

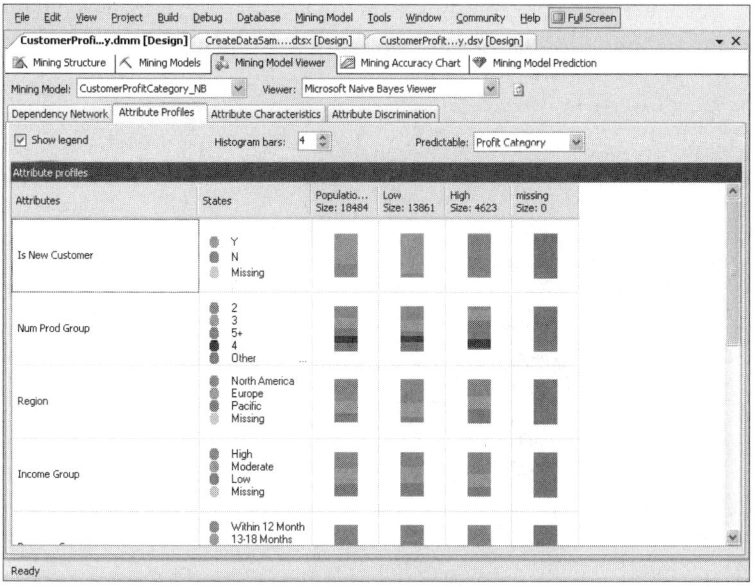

Figure 20-25   The Attribute Profiles tab of the Naïve Bayes Viewer

Validating and Comparing Mining Models

We have processed the mining models and analyzed their predictive contents, which, though similar, are not identical. Although it is easy to conclude that being a long-time customer is an important determinant of customer profitability, the models differ somewhat in their conclusions about which other customer characteristics or buying behaviors are important indicators of profitability. Given these differences, how can you determine which of these secondary predictions are correct? You can do so by using the data mining structure designer's built-in "lift charts" and classification matrix facilities, which make it easy to validate the relative accuracy of various mining models in your mining structure and compare their predictive ability.

Click the Mining Accuracy Chart tab. It has three subtabs—Column Mapping, Lift Chart, and Classification Matrix—which you can use to compare the accuracy of your models based on supplied test data.

> **More Info**   A mining model should be validated using a test data set that is different from the data set used to train the mining model. Earlier in the chapter, we created an Integration Services package with a percentage sampling task to break our customer database into a training and test set. In practice, we would have used the TrainingCustomers data to train the mining models and the TestCustomers data to test the models. As before, for reasons of consistency, we will continue to use vCustomerProfitability, this time as our test data. Using the full sample of customers in AdventureWorksDW ensures that the results presented in this chapter are reproducible. If we were to use a random sample in the examples, it would be possible to reproduce results similar to those presented, but it wouldn't be possible to reproduce equivalent results on demand.

We need to tell SSAS how to map the columns from the test set (vCustomerProfitability in our example) to the mining models. The correct mappings are shown in Figure 20-26.

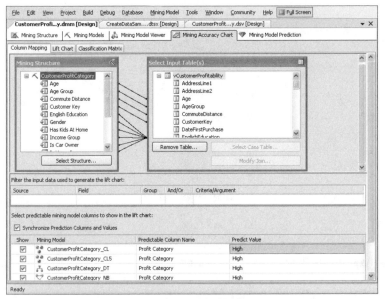

Figure 20-26   The Column Mapping tab of the Microsoft Mining Accuracy Chart designer

The Column Mapping tab has three sections. In the top section, you specify the table that has the test data set and how the columns of the test data set will map to the columns of your mining models. In the middle section, you can specify filters, if any, for your test data. This is useful if you want to test the accuracy of your mining models for a particular subset of data. Lastly, you specify the models, predictable columns, and predictable column values from which lift charts and classification matrices will be created.

Starting at the top section of the tab, verify that the CustomerProfitCategory mining structure is selected in the Mining Structure mini-window on the left side. If it is not, click the Select Structure button in the Mining Structure mini-window, select the CustomerProfitCategory mining structure, and click OK. In the Select Input Table(s) mini-window farther to the right, click the Select Case Table button to specify the test set. In the resulting Select Table dialog box, select vCustomerProfitability and click OK.

Columns in the input table will be mapped to columns in the mining structure that have the same name. To fine-tune these mappings, right-click anywhere on the Column Mapping tab and choose Modify Connections (or choose Modify Connections from the Mining Model menu, which is available only when the Column Mapping tab is active and when you have clicked it). This brings up the Modify Connections dialog box, which allows editing of the mappings between the mining structure and the input table. Click a cell below the Table Column header in the dialog box to reveal a drop-down list of all the columns in the input table. You can change a default mapping, if necessary, by clicking a cell and selecting the desired column from the drop-down list. The proper settings for our mining structure and test data table are (partially) shown in Figure 20-27. After you verify that the mappings are correct, click OK.

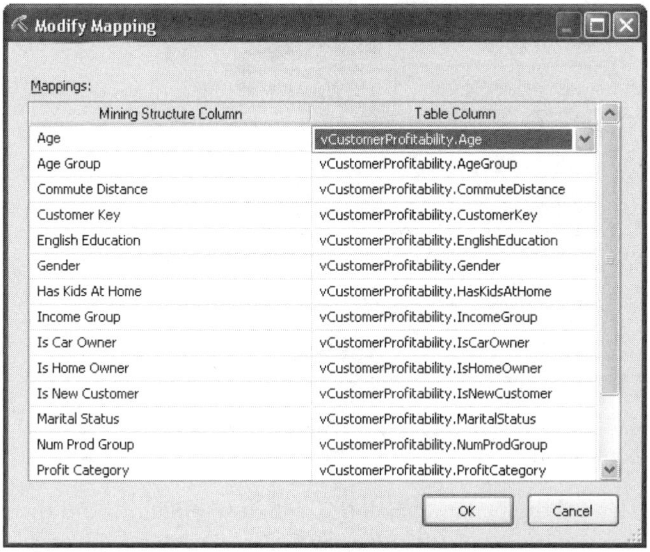

Figure 20-27 The Modify Mapping dialog box, where you map columns from the test data set to mining model columns

> **More Info** The Column Mapping tab's input filtering grid (in the center pane, below the column mappings) allows you to create a *WHERE* clause for your input table. This is useful if you are interested in testing the mining model for only a particular subset of the test data. For example, to test the model for customers in North America only, you can select vCustomer-Profitability as the Source, select Region as the Field, and type = '**North America**' as the Criteria/Argument.

You can create two types of lift charts on the Mining Accuracy Chart tab, one of which allows you to specify the state of the predictable column. (The other type of lift chart does not allow you to do this.) If you specify the state of the predictable column, the lift chart shows how well each model predicts that particular state. If you do not specify the state of the predictable column, the chart shows the relative accuracy of the models in predicting the column value overall.

By default, all mining models in the mining structure are selected, and no state is specified for the predictable column. Click any cell in the Predict Value column of the grid in the bottom pane of the Column Mapping tab, select the High option from the drop-down list that appears, and then click the Lift Chart tab. After the chart has finished loading, make sure the Lift Chart option is selected from the Chart Type drop-down list. The result, which compares how well each mining model predicts high-profit customers, is shown in Figure 20-28.

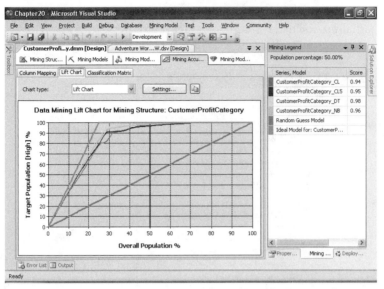

Figure 20-28   A lift chart comparing models of customer profitability

The x-axis of the lift chart shows the percentage of the overall population, and the y-axis shows the percentage of the population that is high profit. Recall that we defined high-profit customers as those in the top quartile of customers. In an ideal model, in which you can predict perfectly who the high-profit customers are, you need to look at only 25 percent of the overall population to identify 100 percent of the high-profit customers. The ideal model is represented by the salmon-colored line in the figure. Note how it hits the top of the chart at the 25-percent mark along the x-axis. The cornflower blue line in the figure represents random guessing. By randomly guessing, you would need to look at 100 percent of the overall population to identify 100 percent of the high-profit customers. The mining models are an improvement over random guessing; the decision tree model (represented by the mustard-colored line) is the most accurate, followed by the Naïve Bayes model (represented by the light blue line). The colors of lines may differ in your version of the graph, but the results will be the same.

Nested Tables

Nested tables are perhaps one of the most confusing features of SSAS data mining. Once you understand them, however, they will likely become an integral component of your data mining toolset. Nested tables allow you to include transactional data in your mining models *without* changing your data structure.

For example, suppose we want to include data about the *types* of products customers bought in our profitability analysis. Adventure Works sells four categories of products: bikes, clothing, accessories, and components. What kinds of products do the high-profit customers buy? Are bike buyers high-profit customers? What about clothing, accessory, or component buyers?

Although we could add four new columns to the case table to flag the types of products a customer bought, what if Adventure Works later decided to sell 10 categories of products? Or what if we want to know whether particular *models* of bikes, of which there are 50, predict profitability? Adding distinct columns to our case table for each of these values would clearly be inefficient, both in terms of storage for the case table and the ETL work needed to build it. Nested tables eliminate these inefficiencies, allowing you to leave intact the transactional data's existing structure.

To understand this a little better in the context of the mining structure and models we've built so far, let's look at the create statement for the vCustomerPurchases view shown in Listing 20-2.

Listing 20-2   A view with transaction data

```
CREATE VIEW [dbo].[vCustomerPurchases]
AS
SELECT
  f.SalesOrderNumber
  ,f.SalesOrderLineNumber
  ,f.CustomerKey
  ,t.FullDateAlternateKey
  ,pc.EnglishProductCategoryName AS ProductCategory
  ,psc.EnglishProductSubcategoryName AS ProductSubcategory
  ,isnull(p.[ModelName], p.[EnglishProductName]) AS [Model]
  ,f.OrderQuantity
  ,Row_Number ( ) OVER (
    Partition BY f.CustomerKey
    ORDER BY t.FullDateAlternateKey, f.SalesOrderLineNumber)
  AS PurchaseSequence
FROM [dbo].[FactInternetSales] AS f
INNER JOIN dbo.dimProduct AS p
ON f.ProductKey = p.ProductKey
INNER JOIN dbo.dimProductSubCategory AS psc
ON p.ProductSubCategoryKey = psc.ProductSubcategoryKey
INNER JOIN dbo.dimProductCategory AS pc
ON psc.ProductCategoryKey = pc.ProductCategoryKey
INNER JOIN dbo.dimTime AS t
ON f.OrderDateKey = t.TimeKey
```

The view is constructed with a simple *SELECT* statement from the fact table with a join to a few dimension tables to pick up product names and product categories. (We'll discuss the PurchaseSequence column, which uses the new T-SQL *Row_Number()* function, in the next section.)

Table 20-1 shows customer attributes along with transactional data about customer purchases. Suppose we want to identify Melvin as an Accessory Buyer and Jennifer as both a Bike Buyer and an Accessory Buyer in our mining models without explicitly adding the attributes "Bike Buyer" and "Accessory Buyer" to our customer profile data (which in our analysis comes from vCustomerProfitability). Adding the transactional data (in our analysis, vCustomerPurchases) as a nested table to the mining structure will do the trick.

Table 20-1 Nested Data

CustKey	Name	Profit	Gender	Income Group	Customer Purchases		
					Product Category	Product Name	Seq
11580	Melvin	Low	M	Low	Accessories	Sport-100 Helmet, Blue	1
11036	Jennifer	Low	F	Moderate	Bikes	Mountain-200 Silver, 46	1
					Accessories	Sport-100 Helmet, Black	2
11376	Lance	Low	M	Moderate	Clothing	Half-Finger Gloves, M	1
					Clothing	Short-Sleeve Classic Jersey, M	2
11136	Brianna	High	F	Moderate	Bikes	Mountain-200 Black, 38	1
					Accessories	Fender Set, Mountain	2
					Clothing	Classic Vest, M	3

To use vCustomerPurchases as nested table in our mining structure, we must first add it to our DSV:

1. Double-click AdventureWorks DW.dsv in Solution Explorer to bring it up in the data source view designer.

2. Click the Add/Remove Objects toolbar button (first from the left), right-click the designer window and choose Add/Remove Tables, or choose Add/Remove Tables from the Data Source View menu. Any of these three actions opens the Add/Remove Tables dialog box.

3. Locate vCustomerPurchases in the Available Objects list, move it to the Included Objects list, and then click OK.

4. To complete our DSV changes, we must establish the relationship between vCustomerPurchases and vCustomerProfitability. Click the CustomerKey column in vCustomerPurchases and drag it onto the CustomerKey column in vCustomerProfitability.

5. Save your changes. The data source view designer should appear as shown in Figure 20-29.

6. Back in the Mining Structure designer, click the Mining Structure tab.

7. Locate, but do not click, the Add A Mining Structure Nested Table Column toolbar button (fourth from the left).

    Note the term "nested table column." SSAS considers the nested *table* to be an additional *column* in the mining structure—that is, it considers it to be a *column* that has a "data type" of *table*.

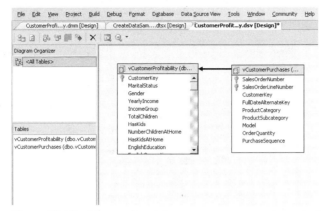

Figure 20-29   Transactional data on customer purchases in the DSV will be used as the source table for a nested table in the mining model.

> **Note**   In keeping with the SSAS mapping of nested tables to a special "data type" of table, note that in Table 20-1 we portrayed vCustomerPurchases as just another customer attribute (albeit a hierarchical one), along with Profit, Gender, and Income Group. We did this because we knew we would use vCustomerPurchases as a nested table column.

8. Click the Add A Mining Structure Nested Table Column toolbar button. This brings up the Select A Nested Table Key Column dialog box.

9. Determining the key of a nested table can be counterintuitive initially; your first instinct might be to select CustomerKey, SalesOrderNumber, or a combination of SalesOrder-Number and SalesOrderLineItem as the nested table key. In fact, none of these is an appropriate key for the nested table.

    When you specify a column as the nested table key column, the distinct values in that column become usable attributes in your mining model. As such, the correct key for the nested table in this scenario is ProductCategory, which has the possible values "Bike," "Clothing," and "Accessory."

    Select vCustomerPurchases from the Nested Table list, and then select ProductCategory from the Source Column list. Click OK.

    As you will see after we modify and process the mining models, selecting ProductCategory as the nested table key column adds attributes such as vCustomerPurchases(Bike) and vCustomerPurchases(Clothing) to our mining models.

    Notice that the nested table has been added to the mining structure tree view as a column of the CustomerProfitCategory structure (appearing with the name "v Customer Purchases"). Unlike other columns in the mining structure, it has a plus sign next to it.

10. Click the plus sign to expand the table. Now expand the columns of the nested table. The mining structure tab will appear as shown in Figure 20-30.

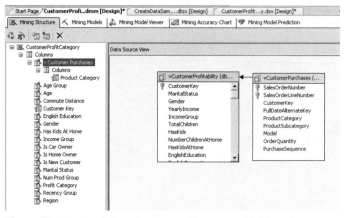

Figure 20-30   A mining structure with a nested table column

When you add new columns to an existing mining structure, they will by default be ignored by existing mining models. Therefore, you must specify the usage of the new columns in the models where you want to include them:

1. Click the Mining Models tab and then click the plus sign next to v Customer Purchases. You will see a new row for the Product Category child column, which is also ignored by all models.

2. Click the cell corresponding to the intersection of the v Customer Purchases column (the "parent" row) and the CustomerProfitCategory_CL model.

3. Click the drop-down arrow in the cell to view the entries in the drop-down list, and select Input. The setting for the Product Category child column is automatically changed from Ignore to Key.

4. Repeat the process for each of the other mining models in the structure. Afterwards, the Mining Models tab should appear as shown in Figure 20-31.

Deploy and process your mining models. This might take several minutes. When processing is complete, click the Mining Model Viewer tab.

Click the Cluster Diagram tab of the CustomerProfitCategory_CL5 model (the model with five clusters). Using the Shading Variable drop-down list (note the three variables that correspond to product category), change the shading variable to v Customer Purchases(Bikes). In the State drop-down list, the two possible states of the variable are Existing and Missing. If the Bikes key exists in the nested table, the customer is a bike buyer; if the Bikes key is missing, the customer is not a bike buyer. Select Existing.

Take note of Cluster 1 and Cluster 5, which have the highest concentration of bike buyers. Change the shading variable to Is New Customer, and select the Y state. Cluster 5 has more new customers than Cluster 1. Change the shading variable to ProfitCategory, select the High state, and note that the two clusters with the highest concentration of bike buyers also have the highest concentration of high-profit customers.

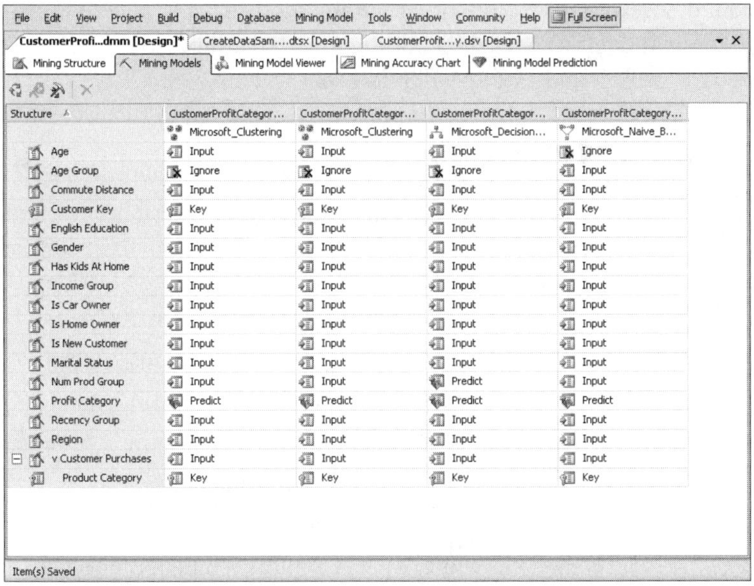

Figure 20-31 Mining models in a mining structure with a nested table column

Figure 20-32 compares the five clusters on the Cluster Profiles tab. When the key of a nested table column is included in a mining model, the distinct values found in the key column form the basis of existence attributes that are used to train the mining model. The value of the key column represented by the existence attribute is shown in parentheses after the nested table column name. Cluster 1 and Cluster 5 have a markedly higher proportion of bike buyers than do the other clusters. The proportion of accessory and clothing buyers is similar across all clusters.

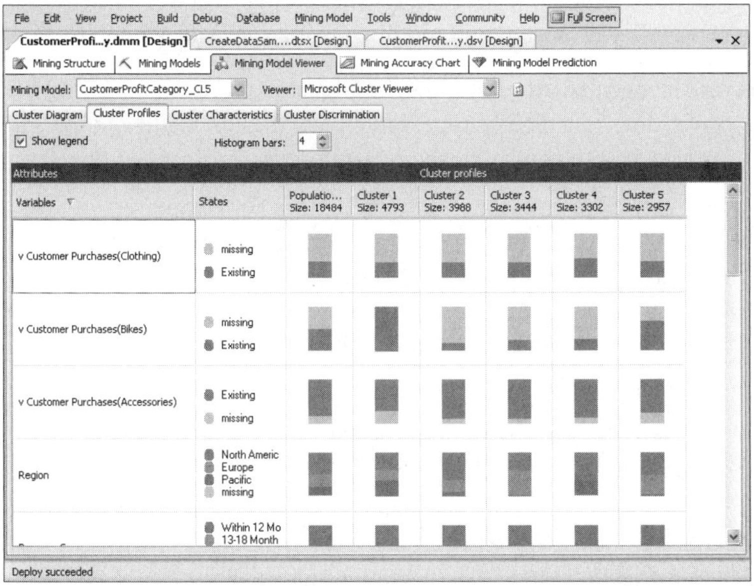

Figure 20-32 Viewing the results of a mining model that includes a nested table column input

Use the mining model viewers to explore other mining models. Take note of the input attributes added to the models as a result of adding the nested table to the models. Close the project and exit Visual Studio.

Using Data Mining Extensions

So far in this chapter, you have seen how to use the data structure designer within Visual Studio to create, train, and view mining models. Now we will see how to use SQL Data Mining Extensions (DMX) to do those same tasks. DMX is an extension to the SQL language for creating and working with data mining models in SSAS.

As with conventional SQL, DMX has two kinds of statements: data definition language (DDL) statements and data manipulation language (DML) statements. DDL statements are used to create mining structures and models. DML statements are used to train, browse, and predict using mining models.

It is true that you can avoid writing DDL queries in DMX by using the SSAS designers. It is also true that DML prediction queries (which we will explore a bit later in the chapter) in DMX can be autogenerated using those tools. But as with relational databases, it is better not to completely rely on tools when a powerful, declarative language is available to perform these same tasks. We will now cover writing DMX code to add a mining model to an existing mining structure, create and train sequence clustering and association rules models, and perform prediction queries against trained mining models.

Data Mining Modeling Using DMX

DMX can be used to create, modify, and train the same mining structures and models as those created using the Data Mining Wizard and modified using the Data Mining Designer:

1. In SQL Server Management Studio, show the Object Explorer window if is not visible. If your SSAS server does not already appear in Object Explorer, add a connection to it using the Connect drop-down list or the corresponding toolbar button.

2. Drill down on the Databases node and then the node for Chapter20, our sample database. Notice that Object Explorer provides a dedicated node for mining structures. Drill down on the Mining Structures node and verify that you can see a node for Customer-ProfitCategory, our mining structure. Drill down on this node and then drill down farther on its child Mining Models node and verify that nodes appear for each of the four models we created previously.

3. Click the Analysis Services DMX Query button on Management Studio's SQL Server Analysis Services Editors toolbar (the fourth button from the left).

    After you work through the Connect to Analysis Services dialog box, a special query window will open in which you can execute DMX statements. Much like the Multi-dimensional Expressions (MDX) query window, which in its Tools pane lists cubes, dimensions, measures, and MDX functions, the DMX query window has a Tools pane containing a drop-down list of all models in the database (for all mining structures), a

Metadata tab that lists all columns in the currently selected model, and a Functions tab that lists DMX functions. In addition, Template Explorer offers a number of DMX query templates. (Template Explorer will be discussed in detail later.)

4. For this chapter, we will review the code in several DMX scripts, contained in the Chapter20DMX project, belonging to Management Studio's sample code solution Chapter20.smsssln. Double-click the Chapter20.smsssln file from Windows Explorer. Doing so will open the sample solution in SQL Server Management Studio. Next, open the first five script files in the project (the five top-most scripts in Solution Explorer under the Queries node within the Chapter20DMX project). Your Management Studio environment should appear similar to that shown in Figure 20-33.

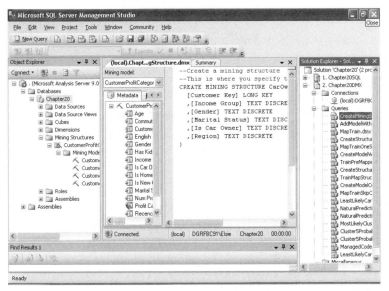

Figure 20-33   SQL Server Management Studio with a DMX query window open

Using DMX, you can either create a mining structure and then add a mining model to it, or you can create a mining structure and a model in a single step. The scripts CreateMiningStructure.dmx, AddModelWithDrillthrough.dmx, and MapTrain.dmx, respectively, show how to create a mining structure, add a mining model to the structure, and process the model. The scripts CreateStructureAndModel.dmx and MapTrainOneStep.dmx show how to create a mining structure and model in one step and then process the structure and model.

Why would you bother running three scripts when you could do the same work using two? To begin with, you might want to create a mining structure that supports many models, where each model will use only a subset of the columns in the structure. The columns defined in the mining structure form the domain of columns from which you can choose to build your individual mining models. But creating a mining structure and model in one step forces the structure and the model to share a set of columns.

Another reason for using separate DMX statements for creating mining structures and models is simply to get a deeper understanding of how SSAS thinks of mining structures and models.

The simplest form of the *CREATE MINING STRUCTURE* statement is as follows:

```
CREATE MINING STRUCTURE <structure>
(
    <column name> <data type> <content type>
)
```

You must specify a name for the mining structure and define the columns for the structure. For each column in the mining structure, you must specify a column name, the data type of the column (for example, Text or Long), and the content type of the column (Key, Continuous, or Discrete). An example of a simple *CREATE MINING STRUCTURE* statement is given in the CreateMiningStructure.dmx script. Open it and follow these steps:

1. Click the Execute toolbar button or shortcut menu command, choose Execute from the Query menu, or press F5 or CTRL+E. You should see a message saying that the execution is complete, and the status bar in the lower-left corner of the query window should indicate that the query executed successfully.

2. Go to the Chapter20 database node in Object Browser and refresh its Mining Structures node by using the Refresh command on its shortcut menu. You should see the CarOwner _DMX structure you just created. Expand the structure, and you will see a Mining Models node indented beneath it. If you expand that node, you will discover that it is empty; this is because the mining structure does not have any mining models associated with it yet.

   To add a mining model to an existing mining structure, you must use an *ALTER MINING STRUCTURE* statement with an *ADD MINING MODEL* clause. Let's take a look at a simple form of the statement:

```
ALTER MINING STRUCTURE <structure>
ADD MINING MODEL <model>(
   <column name>  [<prediction>]
)
USING <algorithm> [(<parameter list>)] [WITH DRILLTHROUGH]
```

   The script AddModelWithDrillthrough.dmx gives a specific example of an *ALTER MINING STRUCTURE* statement:

```
ALTER MINING STRUCTURE CarOwner_DMX
ADD MINING MODEL CarOwner_DT(
   [Customer Key]
   ,[Income Group]
   ,[Gender]
   ,[Marital Status]
   ,[Is Car Owner] PREDICT
   ,[Region]
) USING Microsoft_Decision_Trees WITH DRILLTHROUGH
```

This example adds a Decision Trees model for predicting car ownership to the mining structure. Note that the column list for the mining structure specifies the data type and content type for the columns. The data type and content type of columns are common among all the mining models that are part of the same mining structure. In contrast, column usage is model specific. Column usage—whether the column is an input column or predictable column—is specified in the mining model column list. By default, the columns are input columns; therefore, you need to identify only the columns that are predictable. In the example, the [Is Car Owner] column is marked as a predictable column because we want to use the Decision Trees algorithm to predict car ownership. Let's continue the example.

3. Execute the query.

4. Refresh and expand the Mining Models node below the CarOwner_DMX mining structure node. You should see the CarOwner_DT model. Right-click the model and choose Browse. You will receive an error message saying that the model must be processed. Right-click the model in Object Browser and choose Process.

5. In the Process Mining Model dialog box, click OK. You will see an error message similar to that shown in Figure 20-34.

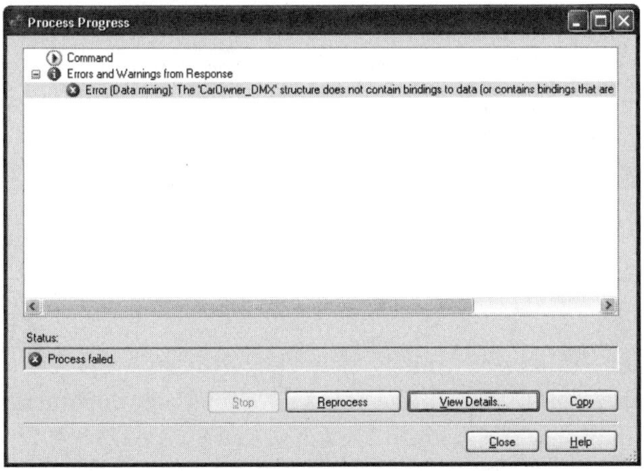

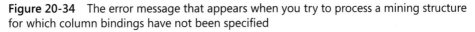

Figure 20-34 The error message that appears when you try to process a mining structure for which column bindings have not been specified

This error message appears because SSAS does not know the source data for the mining structure. So far, all we have done is specify some column names in a mining structure and model—there has been no mention of the source of the data for the structure or model. Binding the columns of a mining structure to data is done using an *INSERT INTO* DMX statement. Here is a simple form of the statement:

```
INSERT INTO MINING STRUCTURE <structure> (
  <mining structure columns>
)
OPENQUERY(<named datasource>, <query syntax>)
```

To run your own *INSERT INTO* query, close the error message and the Process Mining Model dialog box. Close the empty viewer window and open the DMX script file Map-Train.dmx by double-clicking its node in Solution Explorer. An example of an *INSERT INTO* statement to bind data columns to the columns is contained in the script:

```
INSERT INTO CarOwner_DMX(
  [Customer Key]
  ,[Income Group]
  ,[Gender]
  ,[Marital Status]
  ,[Is Car Owner]
  ,[Region]
)
OPENQUERY([Adventure Works DW],
  'SELECT
    CustomerKey
    ,IncomeGroup
    ,Gender
    ,MaritalStatus
    ,IsCarOwner
    ,Region
    FROM AdventureWorksDW.dbo.vCustomerProfitability'
)
```

The column list consists of the columns that were specified in the *CREATE MINING STRUCTURE* statement. The named data source was defined in the SSAS database—in our case, [Adventure Works DW]. Our data source is a SQL Server database, so the code within the *OPENQUERY* expression is actually a Transact-SQL (T-SQL) statement.

To continue with the example:

6. Execute the script. The statement binds the mining structure columns and processes the mining model.

7. Go back to the Object Browser window, right-click the CarOwner_DT model's node, and choose Browse. This brings up the Tree Viewer in a new document window. The Tree Viewer is identical to the one you used in Visual Studio.

8. Right-click a node of the decision tree and choose Drill Through. This brings back the rows from vCustomerProfitability that belong to the node that was right-clicked. (The drill-through feature was enabled by the *WITH DRILLTHROUGH* clause that we specified in the script AddModelWithDrillthrough.dmx.)

9. Close the viewer window and any open DMX Query windows.

Moving on, let's explore how to create a mining structure and model in one step. We do so by specifying the column name, data type, content type, and usage in the column list:

```
CREATE MINING MODEL <model>(
  <column name> <data type> <Content Type> [<prediction>]
)
USING <algorithm> [(<parameter list>)] [WITH DRILLTHROUGH]
```

The DMX code in CreateStructureAndModel.dmx is an example of this statement:

```
CREATE MINING MODEL CarOwner_DT_OneStep(
  [Customer Key] LONG KEY
  ,[Income Group] TEXT DISCRETE
  ,[Gender] TEXT DISCRETE
  ,[Marital Status] TEXT DISCRETE
  ,[Is Car Owner] TEXT DISCRETE PREDICT
  ,[Region] TEXT DISCRETE
) USING Microsoft_Decision_Trees WITH DRILLTHROUGH
```

Take these steps next:

1. Execute the query and then refresh the Mining Structures node in the Object Explorer window. You should see a new node for a structure with the name CarOwner_DT _OneStep_Structure. SSAS appends the *Structure* suffix to the name specified in the *CREATE MINING MODEL* statement in order to distinguish the mining structure from the mining model.

2. Expand the structure's node and then its child mining models node. You should see the CarOwner_DT_OneStep model; this model and its parent structure were created by the single DMX statement.

3. Open and execute the script MapTrainOneStep.dmx to process the CarOwner_DMX model. Browse it if you want, and then close the viewer and all open DMX Query windows.

Here's the DMX code from the MapTrainOneStep.dmx script:

```
INSERT INTO CarOwner_DT_OneStep(
  [Customer Key]
  ,[Income Group]
  ,[Gender]
  ,[Marital Status]
  ,[Is Car Owner]
  ,[Region]
)
OPENQUERY([Adventure Works DW],
  'SELECT
    CustomerKey
    ,IncomeGroup
    ,Gender
    ,MaritalStatus
    ,IsCarOwner
    ,Region
  FROM AdventureWorksDW.dbo.vCustomerProfitability'
)
```

This query is similar to the query in MapTrain.dmx, which was used to process the CarOwner_DMX mining structure. In MapTrain.dmx, a mining *structure* was specified in the *INSERT INTO* statement; the DMX code in MapTrainOneStep.dmx specifies a mining *model*. Specifying a mining model in the *INSERT INTO* DMX statement processes that specific mining model. Specifying a mining structure in the statement processes the mining structure and all of the models in that structure. The mining structure we created has only one mining model, so the result is the same regardless of whether we specify the structure or the model.

DMX statements for creating and processing mining models with nested tables are slightly more complex than for models without nested tables. As mentioned in the previous section, SSAS views a nested table as a column; it is a column with a "data type" of table. The concept of a nested table being a "column" is confusing. The concept becomes more clear, however, when you consider DMX statements that create mining structures and models that, in turn, use nested tables. Here is the syntax for adding a mining model that uses a nested table to an existing mining structure:

```
ALTER MINING STRUCTURE <structure>
ADD MINING MODEL <model>(
  <column name>  [<prediction>],
  <table name> [<prediction>] (
    <column name>  [<prediction>]
  )
)
USING <algorithm> [(<parameter list>)] [WITH DRILLTHROUGH]
```

An example of adding a mining model with a nested table is shown in the CreateModelWith-NestedTable.dmx script file:

```
ALTER MINING STRUCTURE CustomerProfitCategory
ADD MINING MODEL ProductBuyer_DT(
  [Customer Key]
  ,[Age]
  ,[Commute Distance]
  ,[English Education]
  ,[Gender]
  ,[Income Group]
  ,[Is Car Owner]
  ,[Region]
  ,[v Customer Purchases] PREDICT
    (
      [Product Category]
    )
) USING Microsoft_Decision_Trees
```

CreateModelWithNestedTable.dmx adds a decision tree model–for predicting the category of products that customers buy–to the CustomerProfitCategory mining structure that we created with the Mining Model designer earlier in the chapter.

1. Execute CreateModelWithNestedTable.dmx and then check that the ProductBuyer_DT model was added to the mining structure in Object Browser.

2. Right-click the model and choose Browse. You will receive an error message saying that you cannot browse the model until it has been processed.

3. To fix the problem, execute the DMX code in the script file TrainPreMapped.dmx. This query provides an example of using the *INSERT INTO* statement to process a mining model when the column bindings for the structure have already been defined:

```
INSERT INTO ProductBuyer_DT
```

The CustomerProfitCategory structure was defined using the Data Mining designer. When you create a structure using this designer, you select columns from your data source view for the structure; the mining structure columns are bound to the source data at that time. When the mining structure columns are already bound to the source data, the DMX statement to process the model is very simple:

```
INSERT INTO <model>
```

4. After you execute TrainPreMapped.dmx, go back to Object Browser. Right-click the ProductBuyer_DT model in the CustomerProfitCategory structure, and choose Browse. This time the Tree Viewer appears with no error messages.

5. Use the viewer to explore the model. The model predicts whether customers are bike buyers, accessory buyers, or clothing buyers. Figure 20-35 shows the dependency network tab for the model.

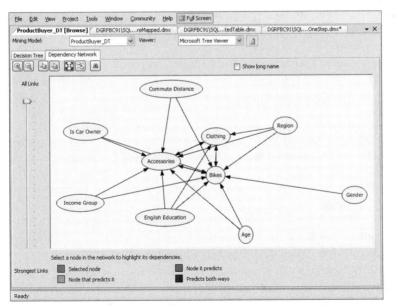

Figure 20-35   Browsing a decision tree mining model using the Tree Viewer in Management Studio

The query in the file CreateStructureWithNestedTable.dmx creates a mining structure and model that uses the Association Rules algorithm to predict the bundles of products customers have purchased:

```
CREATE MINING MODEL PurchaseAssociations(
  [Customer Key] LONG KEY
  ,[Customer Purchases] TABLE PREDICT
    (
      [Product Subcategory] TEXT KEY
    )
) USING Microsoft_Association_Rules
```

The Association Rules algorithm is used to find combinations of items that frequently occur together. The most common application of the Association Rules algorithm is in market-basket analysis. By understanding the bundles of products that customers have purchased, you can make recommendations for future purchases.

The script file TrainMapStructureWithNestedTable.dmx contains code that shows how to bind the columns of a mining structure that has a nested table to source data. The source query that specifies the columns from the source data to map to the mining structure columns uses the *SHAPE* command. At its simplest, the *SHAPE* command takes the following form:

```
SHAPE {<parent table query>}
APPEND ({ <nested table query> }
    RELATE <master column> TO <child column>)
        AS <nested table column name>
```

The *SHAPE* command, originally added to SQL to support ActiveX Data Objects (ADO) hierarchical (or "shaped") *RecordSet* objects, lets you combine data from multiple *SELECT* statements into a single hierarchical result set (a result set with an embedded table).

> **More Info**   For detailed information on the *SHAPE* command and the MSDataShape OLE DB provider, see Microsoft Knowledge Base article Q189657 at *http://support.microsoft.com/kb/q189657*.

A result set with an embedded table is precisely what a mining structure with a nested table column requires. Use of the *SHAPE* command with DMX requires that the parent table query and nested table query each be ordered by the column that relates the parent table to the nested table. For the query in TrainMapStructureWithNestedTable.dmx, this is the Customer-Key column. The query combines the use of the DMX *INSERT INTO* command and the SQL *SHAPE* command to bind the columns in a mining structure with a nested table.

Here is the generalized form for such queries:

```
INSERT INTO MINING STRUCTURE <structure> (
  <mining structure column> | [SKIP],
  <nested table> (
    <nested table column> | [SKIP]
  )
)
SHAPE {<parent table query>}
APPEND ({ <child table query> }
    RELATE <parent column> TO <child column>)
        AS <nested table column name>
```

The actual code from TrainMapStructureWithNestedTable.dmx is as follows:

```
INSERT INTO PurchaseAssociations(
  [Customer Key]
  ,[Customer Purchases]
    (
      SKIP
      ,[Product Subcategory]
    )
)
SHAPE{
  OPENQUERY([Adventure Works DW],
    'SELECT CustomerKey
    FROM AdventureWorksDW.dbo.vCustomerProfitability
    ORDER BY CustomerKey')
  }
APPEND ({
  OPENQUERY([Adventure Works DW],
    'SELECT CustomerKey, ProductSubcategory
    FROM AdventureWorksDW.dbo.vCustomerPurchases
    ORDER BY CustomerKey'
)}
RELATE CustomerKey TO CustomerKey) AS CustomerPurchases
```

The mining structure columns specified in the *INSERT INTO* clause of TrainMapStructure-WithNestedTable.dmx are the structure's column names. The column list after the *INSERT INTO* clause uses the column names with the spaces—these are the names that were specified in the *CREATE MINING MODEL* statement. (Note that the ordinal position of the columns in the list corresponds to the columns returned by the source data query, which in this case is the result set returned by the *SHAPE* command and its *APPEND* and *RELATE* clauses.) If the source data query returns columns that are not required by the mining model, you must use the *SKIP* keyword to indicate that the column should be skipped.

The query in TrainMapStructureWithNestedTable.dmx skips the CustomerKey column from the child table query. You are required to include the column that relates the child (nested) table to the parent table in the parent and child table queries. Both the parent table query and the child table queries in TrainMapStructureWithNestedTable.dmx select the CustomerKey column; however, the [Customer Key] column appears only once in the mining structure. Therefore, you must use the *SKIP* keyword to skip the CustomerKey column for the nested table.

Execute CreateStructureWithNestedTable.dmx followed by TrainMapStructureWithNested-Table.dmx, and explore the PurchaseAssociation model by right-clicking its node in the Object Browser window and choosing Browse.

The queries in the script files CreateModelCustomClusterCount.dmx and MapTrainSkip-Columns.dmx together provide another example of using DMX to create a mining model with a nested table and then binding its structure to the source data. CreateModelCustomCluster-Count.dmx creates a mining structure with a clustering sequence mining model:

```
CREATE MINING MODEL PurchaseSequence(
  [Customer Key] LONG KEY
  ,[Profit] LONG CONTINUOUS
  ,[Income Group] TEXT DISCRETE
  ,[Customer Purchases] TABLE
    (
      [Purchase Sequence] LONG KEY SEQUENCE
      ,[Product Subcategory] TEXT DISCRETE PREDICT
    )
) USING Microsoft_Sequence_Clustering (Cluster_Count = 0)
```

In the Clustering Sequence algorithm, not only are the combinations of items frequently occurring together of interest, but the order in which they occur is of interest. In our example, the model clusters customers according to the sequence of the product subcategory of their purchases. The model sets the *Cluster_Count* parameter of the algorithm to 0. This has the effect of forcing SSAS to determine the optimal number of clusters to create. By default, the algorithm creates 10 clusters. Execute the queries in CreateModelCustomClusterCount.dmx and MapTrainSkipColumns.dmx, in order, and then browse the model using the Cluster Viewer.

Data Mining Predictions Using DMX

DMX is a powerful tool for mining structure and mining model DDL queries, but you can also use it to write what are arguably data mining's most valuable asset: prediction queries. The next six DMX script files in the Chapter20DMX project provide examples of such prediction queries. Using special DMX prediction functions, you can apply the results from data patterns discovered by your mining models to new data.

The basic format of a prediction query is as follows:

```
SELECT <select expression list>
FROM <model>
PREDICTION JOIN
<source data query>
ON <join mapping list>
```

For specific queries, replace *<model>* with the mining model on which you want to base the query predictions and replace *<source data query>* with the data to which you want to apply the prediction. Often you will replace *<source data query>* with an *OPENQUERY* statement similar to those used in the *SELECT INTO DMX* modeling statements for binding the data mining columns to the source data. You can replace *<select expression>* with any combination of columns returned in the source data query, predictable columns from the mining model, and DMX prediction functions that return a column of data, including a nested table column. Replace *<join mapping list>* with the column mapping between the source data and the input columns of the mining model. The LeastLikelyCar.dmx script contains the following code:

```
SELECT TOP 250
   t.FirstName
   ,t.LastName
   ,t.Phone
   ,PredictProbability([Is Car Owner],'N') AS ProbNotCarOwner
FROM CarOwner_DT
PREDICTION JOIN
OPENQUERY([Adventure Works DW],
   'SELECT
      c.FirstName
      ,c.LastName
      ,tc.*
   FROM vCustomerProfitability tc
   INNER JOIN dimCustomer c
   ON tc.CustomerKey = c.CustomerKey')
AS t
ON t.Gender = CarOwner_DT.Gender AND
   t.IncomeGroup = CarOwner_dt.[Income Group] AND
   t.MaritalStatus = CarOwner_dt.[Marital Status] AND
   t.Region = CarOwner_dt.Region
ORDER BY PredictProbability([Is Car Owner],'N') DESC
```

By using the *TOP* and *ORDER BY* clauses supported by DMX, the query returns the names and phone numbers of the 250 people in vCustomerProfitability who are least likely to own a car according to the CarOwner_DT decision trees mining model we created earlier. The query uses the *PredictProbability()* function, which takes two arguments: a predictable column from the mining model and a specified value for the column. The function returns the probability of not owning a car, as predicted by the CarOwner_DT model.

Execute the query, and you'll see that the 250 customers least likely to own a car all have a 78-percent probability of not owning a car. The CarOwner_DT model predicts car ownership based on gender, income group, marital status, and region. Many customers in the database will have the same values for those characteristics. Customers who share a characteristic that is important for determining car ownership will have the same predicted probability of owning a car. To see the next-highest probability of not owning a car, try selecting a larger number of customers, say, the "TOP 1250."

When the column names in the model and the source data query are the same, DMX allows the use of a *NATURAL PREDICTION JOIN*. When you use a *NATURAL PREDICTION JOIN*, you do not have to specify an *ON* clause for the prediction query. SSAS joins the model and source data based on column names. The script file NaturalPredictionJoin.dmx provides a simple example:

```
SELECT TOP 250
   t.FirstName
   ,t.LastName
   ,t.Phone
   ,PredictProbability([Is Car Owner],'N') AS ProbNotCarOwner
FROM CarOwner_DT
NATURAL PREDICTION JOIN
OPENQUERY([Adventure Works DW],
   'SELECT
      c.FirstName
      ,c.LastName
      ,tc.Phone
      ,tc.Gender
      ,tc.IncomeGroup AS [Income Group]
      ,tc.MaritalStatus AS [Marital Status]
      ,tc.Region
   FROM vCustomerProfitability tc
   INNER JOIN dimCustomer c
   ON tc.CustomerKey = c.CustomerKey')
AS t
ORDER BY PredictProbability([Is Car Owner],'N') DESC
```

Execute the query in NaturalPredictionJoin.dmx and verify that the results are the same as for LeastLikelyCar.dmx.

To be considered a match by the *NATURAL PREDICTION JOIN*, the names in the model and source data query must be identical. If the source data query does not have a column with a name identical to that of an input column, no error message is returned; instead, SSAS makes the prediction based on the columns for which matches *are* found. The query in NaturalPredictionJoinMissingMappings.dmx does not alias the column names in the source data query to match the names from the mining model.

```
SELECT TOP 250
   t.FirstName
   ,t.LastName
   ,t.Phone
   ,PredictProbability([Is Car Owner],'N') AS ProbNotCarOwner
FROM CarOwner_DT
NATURAL PREDICTION JOIN
OPENQUERY([Adventure Works DW],
   'SELECT
      c.FirstName
      ,c.LastName
```

```
    ,tc.Phone
    ,tc.Gender
    ,tc.IncomeGroup
    ,tc.MaritalStatus
    ,tc.Region
  FROM vCustomerProfitability tc
  INNER JOIN dimCustomer c
  ON tc.CustomerKey = c.CustomerKey')
AS t
ORDER BY PredictProbability([Is Car Owner],'N') DESC
```

In this query, the prediction is made based only on columns in which there is an exact match in the name (Gender and Region, in this case). Execute the script file NaturalPredictionJoin-MissingMappings.dmx and note how the results of the statement in it differ from those of the previous two.

When the model has a nested table column, the queries are slightly more complex but have the same basic structure of joining a data mining model with source data and specifying the mapping of the source data columns to the input columns of the mining model. The complexity of the query comes primarily in the source data query. The query must return a result set with an embedded table column. As you will recall from the DMX modeling statements we looked at earlier, this is done using the *SHAPE* command.

MostLikelyCluster5.dmx provides an example of a DMX prediction query using a model with a nested table column:

```
SELECT TOP 250
   t.FirstName
  ,t.LastName
  ,t.Profit
  ,ClusterProbability('Cluster 5') AS ProbCluster5
FROM CustomerProfitCategory_CL5
PREDICTION JOIN
SHAPE {
  OPENQUERY([Adventure Works DW],
    'SELECT
       c.FirstName
      ,c.LastName
      ,tc.*
    FROM vCustomerProfitability tc
    INNER JOIN dimCustomer c
    ON tc.CustomerKey = c.CustomerKey
    ORDER BY tc.CustomerKey'
  )
}
APPEND({
  OPENQUERY([Adventure Works DW],
    'SELECT
       CustomerKey
      ,ProductCategory
```

```
    FROM vCustomerPurchases
    ORDER BY CustomerKey'
  )}
  RELATE CustomerKey TO CustomerKey)
    AS PurchaseCategory
 AS t
 ON t.Age = CustomerProfitCategory_CL5.Age AND
   t.CommuteDistance = CustomerProfitCategory_CL5.[Commute Distance] AND
   t.EnglishEducation = CustomerProfitCategory_CL5.[English Education] AND
   t.Gender = CustomerProfitCategory_CL5.Gender AND
   t.HasKidsAtHome = CustomerProfitCategory_CL5.[Has Kids At Home] AND
   t.IncomeGroup = CustomerProfitCategory_CL5.[Income Group] AND
   t.IsCarOwner = CustomerProfitCategory_CL5.[Is Car Owner] AND
   t.IsHomeOwner = CustomerProfitCategory_CL5.[Is Home Owner] AND
   t.IsNewCustomer = CustomerProfitCategory_CL5.[Is New Customer] AND
   t.MaritalStatus = CustomerProfitCategory_CL5.[Marital Status] AND
   t.NumProdGroup = CustomerProfitCategory_CL5.[Num Prod Group] AND
   t.RecencyGroup = CustomerProfitCategory_CL5.[Recency Group] AND
   t.Region = CustomerProfitCategory_CL5.Region AND
   t.PurchaseCategory.ProductCategory =
     CustomerProfitCategory_CL5.[v Customer Purchases].[Product Category]
 ORDER BY ClusterProbability('Cluster 5') DESC
```

The query uses the CustomerProfitCategory_CL5 clustering mining model to predict the probability that a customer will be in cluster 5—this is the cluster with a relatively high concentration of high-profit customers, some of whom are likely to be new customers.

We are interested in customers who are likely to be in this cluster because we'd like to keep them as customers. The above query returns a list of customers, including the dollar profit amount generated from each customer and the probability that the customer is in cluster 5. Execute the query; a portion of the result set returned by the query is shown in Figure 20-36.

FirstName	LastName	Profit	ProbCluster5
Rosa	Ma	455.9126	1
Kari	Ramos	419.8279	1
Tasha	Goel	14.8862	1
Nelson	Serrano	629.9777	1
Fernando	Long	13.7595	1
Cassie	Xu	618.48	1
Carly	Deng	640.3837	1
Jerry	Xu	638.0549	1
Albert	Rubio	311.5603	0.99989465509...
Nicolas	Xie	932.7811	0.99988891855...
Christy	Zeng	48.3709	0.99988628174...
Erika	Sanz	25.0274	0.99988548363...

Figure 20-36   The results of a DMX prediction query

The query uses the *ClusterProbability()* prediction function, which takes a specific cluster as an argument and returns the probability that the input record belongs to the specified cluster.

You can also return a (nested) table column in a *SELECT* statement. For example, the clustering algorithm supports the use of the *PredictHistogram()* function with a clustering column argument. This returns a table column with the predicted probability of each record in the result set being in each cluster. This is illustrated in the query in script file Cluster5ProbabilityDist.dmx:

```
SELECT TOP 250
  t.FirstName
  ,t.LastName
  ,t.Profit
  ,Cluster()
  ,PredictHistogram(Cluster())
FROM CustomerProfitCategory_CL5
PREDICTION JOIN
SHAPE {
  OpenQuery([Adventure Works DW],
    'SELECT
      c.FirstName
      ,c.LastName
      ,tc.*
    FROM vCustomerProfitability tc
    INNER JOIN dimCustomer c
    ON tc.CustomerKey = c.CustomerKey
    ORDER BY   tc.CustomerKey'
  )
}
APPEND({
  OPENQUERY([Adventure Works DW],
    'SELECT
      CustomerKey
      ,ProductCategory
    FROM vCustomerPurchases
    ORDER BY CustomerKey'
  )}
  RELATE CustomerKey To CustomerKey)
  AS PurchaseCategory
AS t
ON t.Age = CustomerProfitCategory_CL5.Age AND
  t.CommuteDistance = CustomerProfitCategory_CL5.[Commute Distance] AND
  t.EnglishEducation = CustomerProfitCategory_CL5.[English Education] AND
  t.Gender = CustomerProfitCategory_CL5.Gender AND
  t.HasKidsAtHome = CustomerProfitCategory_CL5.[Has Kids At Home] AND
  t.IncomeGroup = CustomerProfitCategory_CL5.[Income Group] AND
  t.IsCarOwner = CustomerProfitCategory_CL5.[Is Car Owner] AND
  t.IsHomeOwner = CustomerProfitCategory_CL5.[Is Home Owner] AND
  t.IsNewCustomer = CustomerProfitCategory_CL5.[Is New Customer] AND
  t.MaritalStatus = CustomerProfitCategory_CL5.[Marital Status] AND
  t.NumProdGroup = CustomerProfitCategory_CL5.[Num Prod Group] AND
  t.RecencyGroup = CustomerProfitCategory_CL5.[Recency Group] AND
  t.Region = CustomerProfitCategory_CL5.Region AND
  t.PurchaseCategory.ProductCategory =
    CustomerProfitCategory_CL5.[v Customer Purchases].[Product Category]
```

Execute the query to see how SQL Server Management Studio handles nested tables. You will notice that each cell of the predicted cluster histogram column (the last one) has a plus sign. Click one of them to expand the nested table for its row. The result will appear as shown in Figure 20-37. For example, Aimee He has a 76-percent probability of being in cluster 5 and a 24-percent probability of being in cluster 1.

FirstName	LastName	Profit	$CLUSTER	Expression		
Cheryl	Diaz	3452.7854	Cluster 1	⊞ Expression		
Aimee	He	3496.171	Cluster 5	⊟ Expression		
				$CLUSTER	$DISTANCE	$PROBABILITY
				Cluster 5	0.24116990600...	0.75883009399...
				Cluster 1	0.75883009399...	0.24116990600...
				Cluster 3	1	0
				Cluster 4	1	0
				Cluster 2	1	0
Cedric	Ma	122.7269	Cluster 4	⊞ Expression		
Chad	Kumar	3465.7352	Cluster 1	⊞ Expression		

Figure 20-37 A DMX query result with a nested table column

The results from a query with a nested table column are rich and interesting but might be difficult for many applications to manipulate. To address this concern, DMX has a *FLATTENED* keyword that allows you to return the nested table column within a nonhierarchical result set, even while using the *SHAPE* command to obtain the nested data. The query in the script file Cluster5ProbabilityDistFlattened.dmx returns almost the same result as that in Cluster5ProbabilityDist.dmx, except that it uses the *FLATTENED* keyword to return a nonhierarchical result set. It also specifies that the top 1250 records should be returned instead of the top 250. Each row in the nonflattened result set has an equivalent five rows (one for each segment of the histogram) in the flattened result set; therefore, to see the same data we have to request five times the number of records as before:

```
SELECT FLATTENED TOP 1250
   t.FirstName
   ,t.LastName
   ,t.Profit
   ,ClusterProbability()
   ,PredictHistogram(Cluster())
FROM CustomerProfitCategory_CL5
PREDICTION JOIN
SHAPE {
  OpenQuery([Adventure Works DW],
     'SELECT
        c.FirstName
        ,c.LastName
        ,tc.*
     FROM vCustomerProfitability tc
     INNER JOIN dimCustomer c
     ON tc.CustomerKey = c.CustomerKey
     ORDER BY   tc.CustomerKey'
  )
}
```

```
APPEND({
  OPENQUERY([Adventure Works DW],
    'SELECT
      CustomerKey
      ,ProductCategory
    FROM     vCustomerPurchases
    ORDER BY CustomerKey'
  )}
  RELATE CustomerKey To CustomerKey)
    AS PurchaseCategory
AS t
ON t.Age = CustomerProfitCategory_CL5.Age AND
  t.CommuteDistance = CustomerProfitCategory_CL5.[Commute Distance] AND
  t.EnglishEducation = CustomerProfitCategory_CL5.[English Education] AND
  t.Gender = CustomerProfitCategory_CL5.Gender AND
  t.HasKidsAtHome = CustomerProfitCategory_CL5.[Has Kids At Home] AND
  t.IncomeGroup = CustomerProfitCategory_CL5.[Income Group] AND
  t.IsCarOwner = CustomerProfitCategory_CL5.[Is Car Owner] AND
  t.IsHomeOwner = CustomerProfitCategory_CL5.[Is Home Owner] AND
  t.IsNewCustomer = CustomerProfitCategory_CL5.[Is New Customer] AND
  t.MaritalStatus = CustomerProfitCategory_CL5.[Marital Status] AND
  t.NumProdGroup = CustomerProfitCategory_CL5.[Num Prod Group] AND
  t.RecencyGroup = CustomerProfitCategory_CL5.[Recency Group] AND
  t.Region = CustomerProfitCategory_CL5.Region AND
  t.PurchaseCategory.ProductCategory =
    CustomerProfitCategory_CL5.[v Customer Purchases].[Product Category]
```

Execute the query; the results should appear as in Figure 20-38. Each column of the nested table now appears as a column of the parent table. The values in the non-table columns of the parent table are now repeated for each row of the nested table. It is important to realize that this flattened view of the nested table's columns is a perfectly valid view of the data, given that the nested table is itself considered a column of its parent.

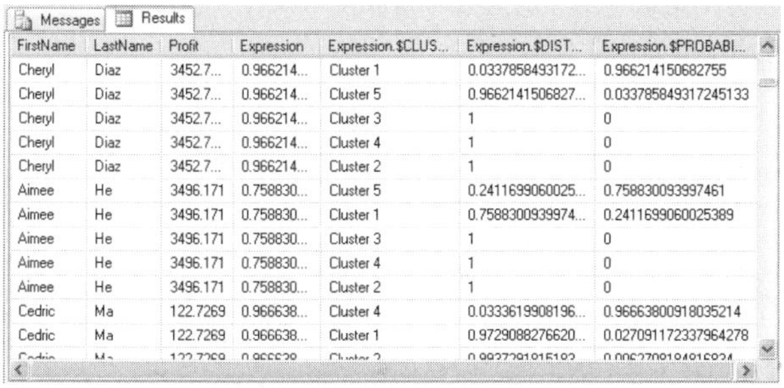

FirstName	LastName	Profit	Expression	Expression.$CLUS...	Expression.$DIST...	Expression.$PROBABI...
Cheryl	Diaz	3452.7...	0.966214...	Cluster 1	0.0337858493172...	0.966214150682755
Cheryl	Diaz	3452.7...	0.966214...	Cluster 5	0.9662141506827...	0.033785849317245133
Cheryl	Diaz	3452.7...	0.966214...	Cluster 3	1	0
Cheryl	Diaz	3452.7...	0.966214...	Cluster 4	1	0
Cheryl	Diaz	3452.7...	0.966214...	Cluster 2	1	0
Aimee	He	3496.171	0.758830...	Cluster 5	0.2411699060025...	0.758830093997461
Aimee	He	3496.171	0.758830...	Cluster 1	0.7588300939974...	0.2411699060025389
Aimee	He	3496.171	0.758830...	Cluster 3	1	0
Aimee	He	3496.171	0.758830...	Cluster 4	1	0
Aimee	He	3496.171	0.758830...	Cluster 2	1	0
Cedric	Ma	122.7269	0.966638...	Cluster 4	0.0333619908196...	0.96663800918035214
Cedric	Ma	122.7269	0.966638...	Cluster 1	0.9729088276620...	0.027091172337964278

Figure 20-38 A DMX query result with a flattened table column

DMX Templates

Management Studio offers templates for writing DMX queries. To see the templates, choose View, Template Explorer in Management Studio. By default, SQL templates are shown. Click the Analysis Server button on the Template Explorer toolbar (the middle button, with the cube icon) to bring up a tree view of the Analysis Services Templates. Expand the DMX node to see the DMX templates. The Template Explorer with the tree view of DMX templates is shown in Figure 20-39.

Figure 20-39   Template Explorer in SSMS

SSAS offers templates for three types of DMX statements: Model Content, Model Management, and Prediction Queries. Under the Model Content node, you can find templates for writing queries to return metadata about your mining models (essentially the same information presented by the viewer controls, but without the visualizations). Under the Model Management node are templates for writing queries to create and train mining models, such as the ones we wrote earlier. Under the Prediction Queries node are templates for writing prediction queries. The templates provide a boilerplate for writing some of the most common DMX queries and are a time-saving alternative to writing queries from scratch.

Data Mining Applied

You might be wondering why we had an entire chapter devoted to OLAP application development and only a single chapter for data mining overall. SSAS data mining is no less programmable than OLAP, and although SSAS data mining can sometimes be more straightforward than OLAP development, for the most part the two are comparable in complexity.

Then again, data mining development *is* different from OLAP programming. To start with, data mining queries are typically not drilldown-oriented, making Excel PivotTables far less compelling as a front-end development tool. On the other hand, the model content browsers available in Visual Studio and SQL Server Management Studio are available to developers as Windows Forms controls, and building on that visualization programmability, the data mining team at Microsoft has also included sample code that implements a few of those browsers as ASP.NET server controls. Browsing models from within your applications using these controls is important and merits discussion.

But what about executing prediction queries and presenting the results? What about running DML statements in DMX programmatically? What about server-side stored procedures? Or management tasks against your databases, mining structures, and mining models? Why doesn't this plethora of topics merit another chapter? The reason is that what you learned in Chapter 19 about OLAP API programming gives you almost all the skills necessary to do high-powered data mining development.

Whether it be ADO MD.NET, AMO, or XMLA used programmatically or from Management Studio, virtually everything you've learned in the context of OLAP cubes works with SSAS data mining models. This is true for both client-side development and managed code running on the server. In fact, you can easily create stored procedures that execute DMX prediction queries and return result sets to the client, and you can do so without using the *AdomdClient* library and without granting the assembly Unrestricted permissions.

In this final section of the chapter, we will provide a few applied examples of using model content browser controls and *AdomdClient* code in both Windows Forms and ASP.NET 2.0 environments. We'll also show you how easy it is to create a server-side stored procedure that executes a DMX prediction query and returns the results, and an XMLA query that does like-wise. We'll finish up by showing you how to take advantage of the direct support for data mining prediction queries provided by SQL Server Reporting Services.

Data Mining and API Programming

As we just said, ADO MD.NET provides full support for data mining. This is true on the meta-data side as well as the query side. For example, the *AdomdConnection* object has both a *MiningStructures* and a *MiningModels* collection. Each member of the *MiningStructures* collection has its own *MiningModels* collection as well. The *MiningModel* object also has a *Parent* property pointing back to the *MiningStructure* object that contains it. This flexibility in the ADO MD.NET object model allows your code to browse the models in a database as a flat database-wide collection or through the hierarchical collection of structures and models. The *MiningModel* object also contains an *Algorithm* property and an *Attributes* collection, allowing you to determine programmatically the input and predictable columns in a model and the algorithmic context in which they are used.

Using the WinForms Model Content Browser Controls

One really good application of all of this metadata is to provide an interface where users can select a model and display its contents in the appropriate content browser control, in effect providing much of the same functionality that SQL Server Management Studio provides via its Object Explorer window and the Browse shortcut menu command, but without requiring users to install and use Management Studio itself.

You can get to the content browser controls in a couple of ways: if you have Management Studio installed on your machine, the controls are already there—you simply set a reference to the Microsoft.AnalysisServices.Viewers.DLL assembly, which by default is installed in the

C:\Program Files\Microsoft Visual Studio 8\Common7\IDE\PrivateAssemblies folder. If your development machine does not have Management Studio installed, you can download the controls from the SQL Server 2005 "feature pack" page at *microsoft.com*.

> **More Info**   At the time of this book's publication, the SQL Server 2005 feature pack page was located at *http://www.microsoft.com/downloads/details.aspx?familyid=d09c1d60-a13c-4479-9b91-9e8b9d835cdc&displaylang=en*. An Internet shortcut to this URL, which will save you the trouble of typing it in manually, is provided with the sample code. If the link is broken when you attempt to navigate to it, try performing a Web search on "Feature Pack for Microsoft SQL Server 2005" or "Analysis Services 2005 Data Mining Viewer Controls."
>
> Each component of the feature pack is available as a separately downloadable file; the content model viewer controls require first downloading and installing the Analysis Services 9.0 OLE DB Provider, which is also part of the feature pack.

After installing the controls, if necessary, you might want to add them to the Visual Studio Toolbox. To do so, use the Browse button in the Choose Toolbox Items dialog box in Visual Studio (discussed in more detail in Chapter 19) and select the controls' assembly. Each of the constituent controls will be selected, and you can just click OK to add them to the Toolbox.

Using the controls is a snap; simply drag one onto a form and then set its *ConnectionString* and *MiningModelName* properties through the Visual Studio Properties window or in code (making sure the algorithm of the model you specify matches the viewer type you selected from the Toolbox). The controls use OLE DB, so make sure the *ConnectionString* value you assign includes the clause "*Provider=MSOLAP.3;*" in addition to *Data Source* and *Initial Catalog* clauses. Then all you do is call the *LoadViewerData* method on the control, passing *null* as the required parameter value. The following three lines of code show how to do this, assuming that *objViewer* is an instance of one of the viewer controls, that *strConnectionString* contains an ADO MD.NET–compliant connection string (specifying *Data Source* and *Initial Catalog*) as its value, and that *cboMiningModels* is a *ComboBox* control containing a list of mining models on the server, with one having been selected by the user:

```
objViewer.ConnectionString = "Provider=MSOLAP.3;" + strConnectionString;
objViewer.MiningModelName = cboMiningModels.Text;
objViewer.LoadViewerData(null);
```

The Visual Studio sample solution provided with this chapter includes a Windows Forms project called Chapter20WinClient.

> **Important**   Make certain that all assembly references in the Chapter20WinClient project are valid before proceeding. If warning icons appear next to any references, delete them and add them back manually through the .NET tab or Browse tab of the Visual Studio Add Reference dialog box.

The Chapter20WinClient project includes a multiple-document interface (MDI) child form called *frmModelViewer* (file name DMMViewerDemo.cs) that allows the user to specify a server, database, and model to view and then displays the model's content in the appropriate viewer control type. Rather than using a control created at design time, before it executes the code shown previously, the code in the form declares *objViewer* as type *Microsoft.AnalysisServices .Viewers.MiningModelViewerControl* (the class from which each viewer control inherits) and then assigns a new instance of the appropriate algorithm-specific viewer type to that variable, based on the *Algorithm* property of the selected *MiningModel* object. It then adds the object to the form's *Controls* collection and sizes, positions, and anchors it within the form.

The UI of the form lets the user click a Show Databases button after specifying a server, the *Click* event handler for which opens an *AdomdConnection* to the server and retrieves a Schema *DataSet* containing all of the catalogs (databases) on the server, which it uses to populate a *ComboBox* control. Here's a simplified version of that code, in which *txtServer* is a *TextBox* control containing the server name, and *cboCatalogs* is the target *ComboBox* control:

```
AdomdConnection conn = new AdomdConnection("Data Source=" +
  txtServer.Text);
conn.Open();
foreach (DataRow dr in conn.GetSchemaDataSet(AdomdSchemaGuid.Catalogs,
  null).Tables[0].Rows)
{
    cboCatalogs.Items.Add((string)dr[0]);
}
conn.Close();
```

Notice that only a *Data Source* clause, and not an *Initial Catalog* clause, is supplied in the connection string. We need server-level information only, so this is sufficient.

When the user makes a selection from *cboCatalogs*, the code fetches a list of, and populates a *ComboBox* control with, names of all the models belonging to the selected database. Here's a simplified version of that code (with *cboMiningModels* as the target *ComboBox*):

```
strConnectionString = "Data Source=" + txtServer.Text + ";Initial Catalog="
  + cboCatalogs.Text;
AdomdConnection conn = new AdomdConnection(strConnectionString);
conn.Open();
foreach (MiningModel mm in conn.MiningModels)
{
    cboMiningModels.Items.Add(mm.Name);
}
conn.Close();
```

As soon as a model is selected from *cboMiningModels*, the code that instantiates a viewer control and connects it to a specific model can be executed.

Executing Prediction Queries with ADO MD.NET

The programming techniques we have explored so far are fairly straightforward, but executing prediction queries is even easier. In Chapter 19, you learned that you can use the ADO MD.NET *AdomdCommand* and *AdomdDataAdapter* objects to execute MDX queries and return flattened result sets in the form of an *AdomdDataReader* or a *DataSet/DataTable*. Similarly, you can use them to execute DMX prediction queries and return their result sets in tabular form. The following code, a simplified version of the code in the Chapter20WinClient project's form *frmDMXAdHoc* (file name DMXAdHoc.cs), executes a DMX query, retrieves the results as a *DataTable*, and then binds the *DataTable* to *dgvResults* (a *DataGridView* control):

```
AdomdConnection conn = new AdomdConnection("Data Source=" + txtServer.Text
  + ";Initial Catalog=" + cboCatalogs.Text);
AdomdCommand cmd = new AdomdCommand(txtQuery.Text, conn);
AdomdDataAdapter da = new AdomdDataAdapter(cmd);
DataTable dt = new DataTable();
da.Fill(dt);
dgvResults.DataSource = dt;
```

In the code, *txtServer* and *cboCatalogs* are equivalent to their namesakes in the form *frmModelViewer* (discussed previously), and *txtQuery* is a multiline *TextBox* control containing the DMX query.

Note that *frmDMXAdHoc* is functionally equivalent to Management Studio's DMX window. This means that almost all of the DMX prediction queries in the sample code's Management Studio project can be run from this form (and even the comments can be left in the query text). One exception is that the code will not properly handle result sets with nested columns (such as the one in Cluster5ProbabilityDist.dmx); be sure to use the *FLATTENED* keyword to avoid this problem (as was done in Cluster5ProbabilityDistFlattened.dmx).

Model Content Queries

Other DMX query types can be handled by the ADO MD code used in the viewer in *frmDMXAdHoc*. For example, each of the DML queries in the sample code's Management Studio project can be executed in the form. However, none of these returns any data, and it would be more reasonable to run them using the *AdomdCommand* object's *ExecuteNonQuery* method. Finally, model content queries (which we briefly discussed earlier in the context of DMX templates) can be executed as well. For example, the following query returns textual information about the CustomerProfitCategory_CL clustering model:

```
SELECT NODE_CAPTION, NODE_DESCRIPTION, NODE_PROBABILITY
FROM   [CustomerProfitCategory_CL].CONTENT
```

This query can be run from a DMX Query window in Management Studio or from *frmDMX-AdHoc* in Chapter20WinClient. (Try it and see.) The content data in text form is much less elegant than the visualization of that data, but its programmatic use is intriguing. Your application could, for example, query the model in advance, learn of certain patterns by parsing the NODE_DESCRPTION column, and then execute predictive business logic upon entry of new data.

ADO MD.NET and ASP.NET

Most of what we've covered so far in the context of Windows Forms development can be implemented similarly in ASP.NET. The Web site Chapter20WebClient, which is included with the sample code's Visual Studio solution, shows an example of how to code an ASP.NET equivalent of Chapter20WinClient. The model content viewers must be handled in a different way from their Windows Forms counterparts (as we will discuss shortly). However, the execution of DMX queries is handled in much the same way as shown previously.

For example, you can populate a *GridView* control called *gvResults* with the non-hierarchical results of a DMX query, as follows:

```
AdomdConnection conn = new AdomdConnection("Data Source=" + txtServer.Text
 + ";Initial Catalog=" + ddlCatalogs.Text);
AdomdCommand cmd = new AdomdCommand(txtQuery.Text, conn);
AdomdDataAdapter da = new AdomdDataAdapter(cmd);
DataTable dt = new DataTable();
da.Fill(dt);
gvResults.DataSource = dt;
gvResults.DataBind();
```

In this snippet (which is a simplified version of the code on the DMXAdHoc.aspx page in the Chapter20WebClient application), *ddlCatalogs* is an ASP.NET *DropDownList* control containing a list of the databases on the server whose name is specified in the *TextBox* control *txtServer*. This code is strikingly similar to its Windows Forms equivalent and is just as versatile at handling DMX queries.

Using the Data Mining Web Controls

It's good to know that DMX querying can be handled much the same way in an ASP.NET application and in Windows Forms, but what about the visualization of model content? The content viewer controls are designed for the Windows Forms environment, so we can't use them in an ASP.NET application. However, Microsoft provides sample .NET code that implements dynamic Hypertext Markup Language (DHTML) versions of the Cluster, Naïve Bayes, and Decision Trees viewers as ASP.NET server controls. Specifically, the Cluster/Attribute Characteristics and Cluster/Attribute Discrimination tabs of the Cluster and Naïve Bayes viewers and the Decision Tree tab of the Tree Viewer are implemented. This means that only certain models can be browsed and only certain views of those models are possible.

Although they provide only a subset of the functionality supplied by the Windows Forms controls, these ASP.NET components are still extremely helpful, especially given the reach of the Internet and the Web. However, these controls are provided as sample code only and are therefore a little harder to use in your applications than their Windows Forms equivalents.

You can obtain the source code for the controls (in the form of a C# class library project) by installing the Microsoft SQL Server 2005 Samples. (The setup package for these samples is available in the Documentation and Tutorials\Samples submenu of the SQL Server 2005 main menu group on the Windows Start menu. The installer places the Visual Studio source code for the controls, by default, in the folder C:\Program Files\Microsoft SQL Server\90\Samples\Analysis Services\DataMining\Data Mining Web Controls. If you open the WebControls.sln solution file in that folder and build the project, you can reference the generated assembly in an ASP.NET Web site in Visual Studio and add the three viewer controls to the Visual Studio Toolbox window.

You can use the controls by placing them on a Web form and setting their *Server*, *Database*, and *Model* properties, each of which is string-typed, and store or return the name of an SSAS server, database, and mining model whose content you want to display. As an alternative to assigning values to the *Server* and *Database* properties, you can create an *OleDbConnection* object, connect it to a specific SSAS database, and then assign it to the controls' *Connection* property.

The Tree Viewer has a *ViewType* property that you must set to one of two enumerated constants: *Tree* or *NodeDetails*. If you set it to *Tree*, you must also set the *TargetTree* property to the name of a predictable column contained in the mining model. If you set it to *NodeDetails*, you must set the *TargetNode* property to a specific node in the decision tree. The Naïve Bayes and Cluster viewer controls both feature a *ViewerMode* property that also must be set to one of two enumerated constants: *Discrimination* or *Characteristics*, depending on the functionality of the tab of the Windows Forms viewers you want to duplicate.

> **More Info**   See this chapter's sample code for more details on using the ASP.NET viewer controls. The Chapter20WebClient application implements certain complex handling, the discussion of which is beyond the scope of this chapter. For example, each viewer is wrapped as an ASP.NET user control to aid in the ability to refresh the viewers with new model content at run time.

Developing Managed Stored Procedures

Applying your OLAP development skills to data mining doesn't end with ADO MD.NET on the client; you can use the *AdomdServer* library to execute server-side DMX prediction or content queries and return the results. For example, Listing 20-3 provides all the code necessary to implement a server-side version of the prediction query in the LeastLikelyCar.dmx Management Studio script covered earlier.

Listing 20-3   Using AdomdServer for DMX queries

```
using System;
using System.Data;
using Microsoft.AnalysisServices.AdomdServer;

namespace Chapter20ServerAssembly
{
    public class StoredProcedures
    {
        public DataTable GetData()
        {
            DataTable dt = new System.Data.DataTable();
            dt.Columns.Add("FirstName", typeof(string));
            dt.Columns.Add("LastName", typeof(string));
            dt.Columns.Add("Phone", typeof(string));
            dt.Columns.Add("ProbNotCarOwner", typeof(double));

            object[] row = new object[4];

            AdomdCommand comContext = new AdomdCommand("SELECT TOP 250 t.FirstName,
t.LastName, t.Phone, PredictProbability([Is Car Owner],'N') AS ProbNotCarOwner
FROM  CarOwner_DT PREDICTION JOIN OPENQUERY([Adventure Works DW],
'SELECT c.FirstName,c.LastName,tc.* FROM vCustomerProfitability tc INNER JOIN
dimCustomer c ON tc.CustomerKey = c.CustomerKey') AS t ON t.Gender = CarOwner_DT.Gender
AND t.IncomeGroup = CarOwner_dt.[Income Group] AND t.MaritalStatus =
CarOwner_dt.[Marital Status] AND t.Region = CarOwner_dt.Region ORDER BY
PredictProbability([Is Car Owner],'N') DESC");
            try
            {
                AdomdDataReader dr = comContext.ExecuteReader();
                while (dr.Read())
                {
                    row[0] = dr[0];
                    row[1] = dr[1];
                    row[2] = dr[2];
                    row[3] = dr[3];
                    dt.Rows.Add(row);
                }
                dr.Close();
                return dt;
            }
            catch
            {
                return null;
            }
        }
    }
}
```

Although it is not possible to execute an MDX query using *AdomdServer*, it is permissible to execute a DMX query. In the case of this stored procedure, we simply create the *Adomd-Server.AdomdCommand* object *comContext*, passing the DMX query to its constructor.

We make sure to type the function as returning a *DataTable*, and we populate a local *DataTable* variable with the contents of an *AdomdDataReader*. The latter is obtained by calling the *comContext* object's *ExecuteReader* method. As with the managed code in Chapter 19, there is no need to explicitly create a connection to execute this query—it implicitly uses the connection in whose context the code is called.

The code in Listing 20-3 is taken from the Class Library project Chapter20ServerAssembly in the sample code's Visual Studio solution. This project can be built and deployed to the Chapter20 database (using the techniques discussed in Chapter 19 for deploying managed assemblies). When deploying the assembly, you should assign it ExternalAccess permissions; assigning it Unrestricted permissions is not necessary, and assigning it Safe permissions will prevent the DMX query from executing and returning data properly.

Once deployed, the stored procedure can be called using the following DMX code:

```
CALL
Chapter20ServerAssembly.Chapter20ServerAssembly.StoredProcedures.GetData()
```

This query can be executed in a SQL Server Management Studio DMX Query window (it is contained in the Management Studio project script ManagedCode.dmx) or in the Chapter20WinClient and Chapter20WebClient applications. If the code were more complex, you would perhaps want to debug it; you could do so by using exactly the same technique described in Chapter 19 (by attaching the Visual Studio debugger to the SSAS process).

Keep in mind that your stored procedures can also execute DDL queries using DMX (by using the *AdomdCommand* object's *ExecuteNonQuery* method) or perform administrative or DDL tasks using AMO. The AMO *Database* object contains a *MiningStructures* collection, each member of which contains its own *MiningModels* collection. The AMO *MiningStructure* and *MiningModel* objects have an array of properties, methods, and child objects that are useful for performing any number of administrative or DDL tasks against your mining structures and models.

XMLA and Data Mining

To round off our coverage of data mining development and how it compares with OLAP development, it is important to mention that XMLA can be used for all data mining tasks, including execution of a DMX query (of any type) or the scripted creation of objects. As with OLAP objects, you can right-click a mining structure or model in Management Studio's Object Explorer window and choose Script Mining Structure As (or Script Mining Model As) to generate an XMLA script for its creation, deletion, or alteration. Similarly, you can use the View Code option from the Solution Explorer window in Visual Studio on a mining structure in an SSAS project to reveal the XMLA script that will be executed to deploy that mining structure to the server.

As a quick example, the following query (contained in LeastLikelyCar.xmla in the Management Studio sample solution) executes the same DMX query contained in LeastLikelyCar.dmx and retrieves the result as XML:

```
<Execute xmlns="urn:schemas-microsoft-com:xml-analysis">
  <Command>
    <Statement>
     SELECT   TOP 250 t.FirstName, t.LastName, t.Phone,
              PredictProbability([Is Car Owner],'N') AS ProbNotCarOwner
     FROM    CarOwner_DT
     PREDICTION JOIN
       OPENQUERY([Adventure Works DW],
        'SELECT c.FirstName,c.LastName,tc.*
        FROM    vCustomerProfitability tc
         INNER JOIN dimCustomer c ON tc.CustomerKey = c.CustomerKey')
        AS t
        ON t.Gender = CarOwner_DT.Gender AND
           t.IncomeGroup = CarOwner_dt.[Income Group] AND
           t.MaritalStatus = CarOwner_dt.[Marital Status] AND
           t.Region = CarOwner_dt.Region
       ORDER BY PredictProbability([Is Car Owner],'N') DESC
    </Statement>
  </Command>
  <Properties>
    <PropertyList>
      <Catalog>Chapter20</Catalog>
    </PropertyList>
  </Properties>
</Execute>
```

Notice that the structure of the query is virtually identical to the XMLA script QueryCube-Chapter18.xmla from Chapter 19. The only differences are the change in database name within the *<Catalog>* tags and the replacement of an MDX query with a DMX query.

Unlike QueryCubeChapter18.xmla, however, this query returns its XML data using a very straightforward schema. Here's an excerpt from the response stream:

```
<return xmlns="urn:schemas-microsoft-com:xml-analysis">
  <root xmlns="urn:schemas-microsoft-com:xml-analysis:rowset" xmlns:xsi="http://
www.w3.org/2001/XMLSchema-instance" xmlns:xsd="http://www.w3.org/2001/XMLSchema">
    <xsd:schema…
    </xsd:schema>
    <row>
      <FirstName>Gerald</FirstName>
      <LastName>Moreno</LastName>
      <Phone>1 (11) 500 555-0189</Phone>
      <ProbNotCarOwner>7.808883911907428E-1</ProbNotCarOwner>
    </row>
    <row>
      <FirstName>Erick</FirstName>
      <LastName>Fernandez</LastName>
```

```
      <Phone>1 (11) 500 555-0117</Phone>
      <ProbNotCarOwner>7.808883911907428E-1</ProbNotCarOwner>
   </row>
   <row>
     <FirstName>Alisha</FirstName>
     <LastName>Nath</LastName>
     <Phone>1 (11) 500 555-0173</Phone>
     <ProbNotCarOwner>7.808883911907428E-1</ProbNotCarOwner>
   </row>
 ...
  </root>
 </return>
```

Because the schema differs so radically from the OLAP/multidimensional schema we studied in Chapter 19, the XSL stylesheet we discussed in that chapter is of no use to us for the tabular result sets returned by DMX queries. However, the tabular schema is so transparent that it can be easily parsed using various objects in the .NET *System.Xml* namespace or using a simple XSL stylesheet of your own creation.

Before closing this chapter, let's finish up our tour of application-level data mining techniques with a look at the data mining–specific functionality in SQL Reporting Services.

Data Mining and Reporting Services

Once you have designed and trained your mining models, it's easy to display the results in a Reporting Services report. DMX, although powerful, does lack some basic query functionality that might be desirable for showing data mining results. The ability to write DMX code to aggregate or group results is notably lacking. Because you can specify an SSAS data source in Reporting Services, you can leverage the reporting functionality, including subtotaling and grouping, built into Reporting Services for displaying the results of your mining models.

1. Return to Visual Studio and create a new Reporting Services project by choosing File, New, Project or File, Add, New Project.

2. In the New Project or Add New Project dialog box that appears, select Business Intelligence Projects from the Project Types tree view on the left, and select Report Server Project from the Visual Studio Installed Templates list on the right. Name the project **Chapter20Reports** and then click OK.

3. You should see a node labeled Chapter20Reports in Solution Explorer. Right-click the Reports node below the Chapter20Reports node, and choose Add, New Item. (Alternatively, you can choose Project, Add New Item or press CTRL+SHIFT+A.)

4. In the Add New Item dialog box, select Report from the set of Visual Studio Installed Templates. Change the name of the report to **Classification Matrix** and click Add. Your Visual Studio window should appear similar to Figure 20-40.

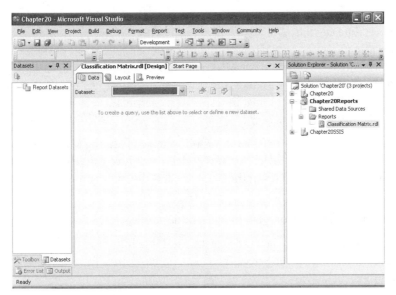

Figure 20-40   The Report Designer for a new report

5.   On the Data tab, select <New Dataset...> from the Dataset drop-down list.

6.   In the Data Source dialog box, select Microsoft SQL Server Analysis Services from the Type drop-down list and then click the Edit button.

7.   In the Connection Properties dialog box, set the Server Name to the name of your SSAS server, and then select the Chapter20 database from the Select or Enter a Database Name drop-down list. Click OK.

8.   Back in the Select the Data Source screen, change the Name to **CustomerProfitMining**; the settings should now appear similar to those in Figure 20-41.

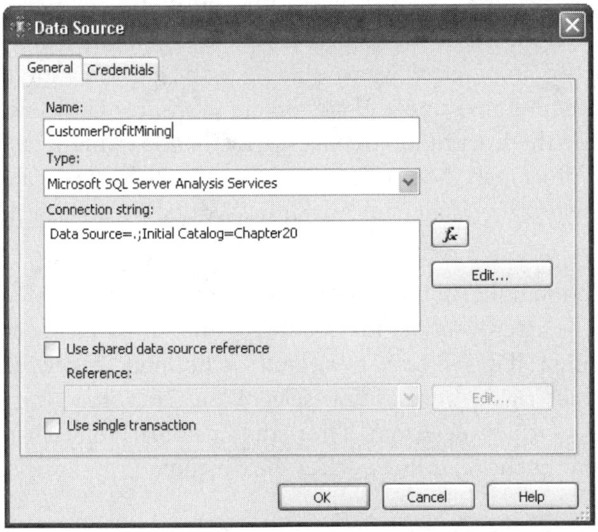

Figure 20-41   The Data Source dialog box with an SSAS database specified as the source

9. Click OK to create the data source. You will see the DMX Prediction Query designer render on the Data tab. When you specify an SSAS database as the source for your report, Reporting Services provides a special Analysis Services query designer, which can help you design MDX (OLAP) or DMX (data mining) queries. Because our database has a mining structure and no cubes, the designer defaults to its DMX mode. (Clicking the Command Type MDX toolbar button—the fifth from the left—would allow us to switch to the MDX designer instead.)

10. On the left of the Data tab is a mini-window labeled Mining Model; click its Select Model button to display the Select Mining Model dialog box. This dialog box displays a tree view of mining structures in the database and the mining models within each.

11. Expand the CustomerProfitCategory mining structure's node, select the CustomerProfitCategory_DT model's node, and click OK.

12. Back on the Data tab, click the Select Case Table button in the Select Input Table mini-window to bring up the Select Table dialog box. Select the vCustomerProfitability view and then click OK.

13. Back in the Select Input Table mini-window, click the Select Nested Table button, select the vCustomerPurchases view in the Select Table dialog box, and then click OK once more.

14. Right-click the Data tab's designer surface and then choose Modify Connections. In the resulting Modify Mappings dialog box, verify that the mappings between the mining model and the case and nested tables are correct and then click OK. (The Customer Key mining model column will be unmapped and should be left as such.)

We are going to create a report that shows a classification matrix for the CustomerProfitCategory_DT model. The classification matrix shows the actual profit category of customers and the profit category predicted by the Decision Trees model, along with a count of the customers. By looking at the count of cases where the actual category differs from the predicted category, you can get a sense of how well the model predicts profit. In practice, we would create the classification matrix using a test set, such as the random sample of customers in the TestCustomers table, which we populated using the Integration Services percentage sampling task earlier in the chapter. As stated previously, however, we will use vCustomerProfitability, which has the full set of individual customers in AdventureWorksDW, so that the results are reproducible.

15. In the grid in the bottom half of the Design tab, select vCustomerProfitability from the drop-down list in the first row under the Source column. In the Field column, select the CustomerKey column. (If it is selected by default, do nothing.) In the second row, select vCustomerProfitability again, but this time select ProfitCategory as the field. The predicted profit category will be determined from the CustomerProfitCategory_DT mining model; therefore, in the third grid row, select the CustomerProfitCategory_DT mining

model as the source, set Profit Category as the field, and then set its alias to Predicted Profit Category. The Data tab should appear as shown in Figure 20-42.

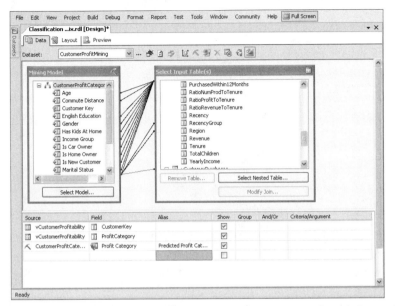

Figure 20-42   The DMX query designer with the Report Designer's Data tab

16.   To see the actual DMX query generated by the designer, you can deselect the Design Mode toolbar button (first from the right) or right-click anywhere on the Data tab and choose Query. The DMX query generated by the designer will appear at the bottom of the Data tab. You should recognize it as a DMX prediction query—not too dissimilar from ones we wrote in the previous section. In fact, you could paste this query into an empty DMX Query window in SQL Server Management Studio and execute it there. You could also do the reverse—create a report based on the results of one of the prediction queries from the Management Studio Chapter20DMX project by copying the DMX statement directly into the Data tab.

We are now ready to design the layout of the report.

17.   Click the Layout tab. Drag a table item from the Toolbox onto the Layout pane. Right-click the leftmost cell in the Detail row, and choose Properties. Change the Name of the text box to **CustomerKey**, and select =Fields!CustomerKey.Value from the Value drop-down list. Click OK.

18.   Follow the same steps to add the ProfitCategory field to the middle column of the detail row and the Predicted_Profit_Category field to the right column of the detail row, naming the text boxes ProfitCategory and PredictedProfitCategory, respectively. Figure 20-43 shows the General tab of the Textbox Properties dialog box for the ProfitCategory field.

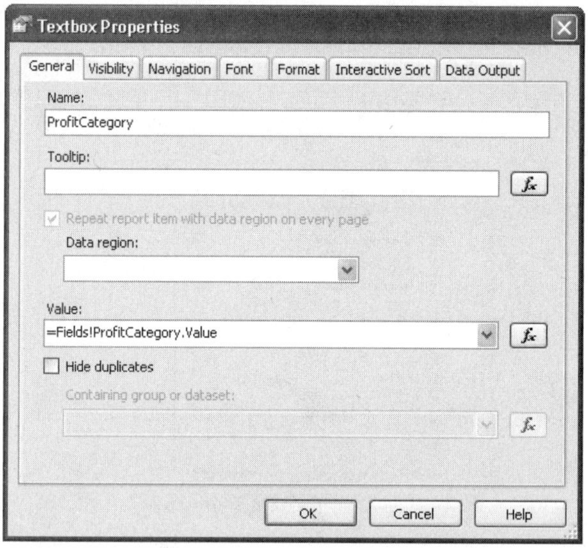

Figure 20-43   The Textbox Properties dialog box

19.   In the Header row, type **Customer Key**, **Profit Category**, and **Predicted Profit Category** above each of the corresponding cells of the Detail row. Format the background color of the Header row and then left-align all cells in the table. When you are finished, the Layout tab should appear similar to Figure 20-44.

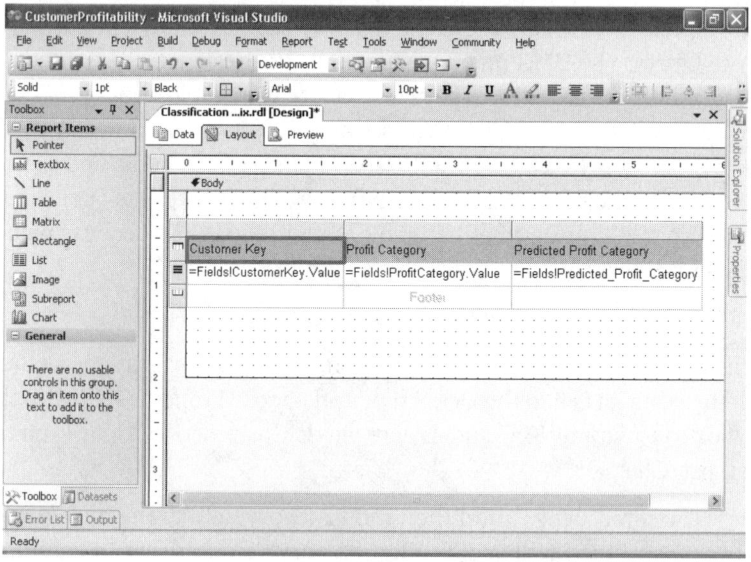

Figure 20-44   The Layout tab of the Report Designer with a Table item

20.   Click the Preview tab to preview the report. The report lists each customer in vCustomerProfitability along with the customer key, the actual profit category of the customer, and the predicted profit category of the customer.

In its current form, the report is long and unwieldy. To change this, we must group and summarize the records in the table.

21. Go back to the Layout tab. Right-click the gray row header to the left of the Customer-Key field on the Detail row and then choose Insert Group.

22. On the General tab of the Grouping And Sorting Properties dialog box, select =Fields!ProfitCategory.Value in the first row and =Fields!Predicted_Profit_Category.Value in the second row of the Expression grid in the Group On section. Click OK.

23. Back on the Layout tab, you will see two rows added to the table: one above the Detail row and one below the Detail row. Delete the row that was added below the Detail row. (Select its row header and press the DELETE key, or right-click the row header and choose Delete Rows.) Next, right-click the middle cell below the Profit Category heading and then choose Properties. Change the name of the text box to **ProfitCategoryGroup** and then select =Fields!ProfitCategory.Value from the Value drop-down list. Click OK.

24. Repeat the previous step for the cell below the Predicted Profit Category heading, naming the text box **PredictedProfitCategoryGroup** and selecting =Fields!Customer_Profit_Category.Value from the Value drop-down list.

    Finally, we want to add a summary measure of the records to the table.

25. Right-click the gray column header of the Predicted Profit Category column and then choose Insert Column To The Right. Give the new column a header of **Count** and then type **=CountRows()** in the cell under the header.

26. Change the background color of the group header row so that it can be easily identified in the report. Add a Textbox item (from the Toolbox) above the Table object in the report, and enter the text **Classification Matrix**. Stretch the text box to the full width of the report, center-align it, and format its font and color settings so that the report appears similar to Figure 20-45.

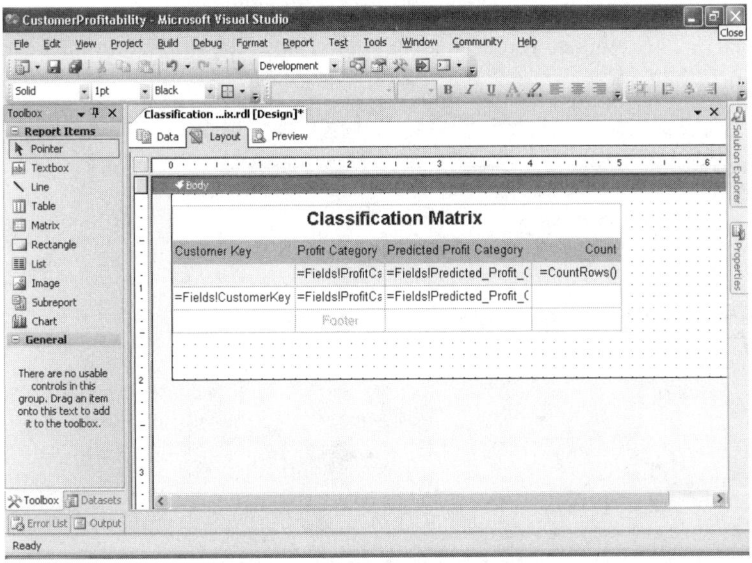

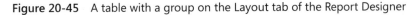

Figure 20-45   A table with a group on the Layout tab of the Report Designer

27. Click the Preview tab. Page through the report. The report is still unwieldy and shows all the data rows. Inserting the group simply reordered the detail rows in the table and added a row before each possible actual and predicted profit category value pair. To fix the report so that it displays a simple classification matrix without the customer details, we must hide the detail rows.

28. Go back to the Layout tab, right-click the detail row header, and then choose Properties. Expand the Visibility property in the Properties window by clicking its plus sign (+) icon. Set the Hidden property to True and the ToggleItem property to ProfitCategory-Group. The properties should be set as shown in Figure 20-46.

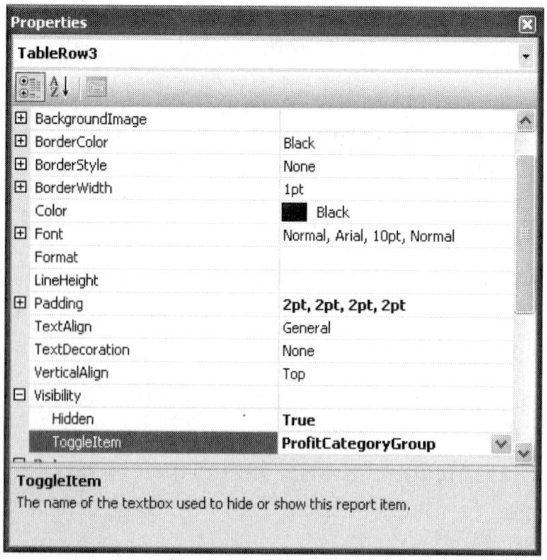

Figure 20-46   Setting the Visibility properties of a table row

29. Click the Preview tab. You now have your simple classification matrix, as shown in Figure 20-47.

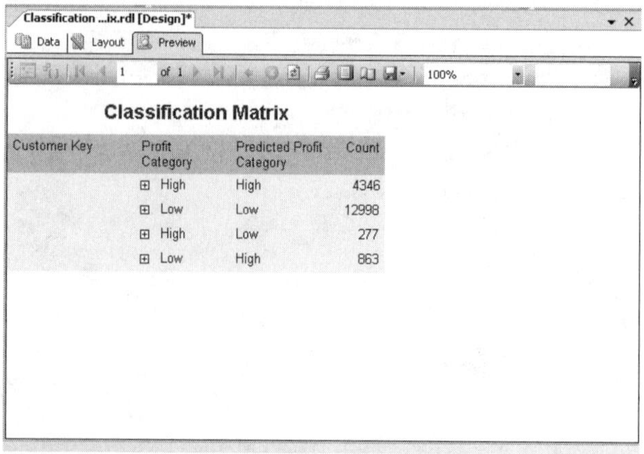

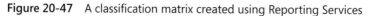

Figure 20-47   A classification matrix created using Reporting Services

The classification matrix shows that your Decision Tree model of customer profitability performs pretty well. The first two rows of the classification matrix, where the predicted profit category is equal to the actual profit category, represent the cases in which the Decision Tree model got it right. Out of 18,484 customers (the sum of the Count column), the model correctly predicted the profit category for 17,344 customers (4,346 plus 12,998). Click any profit category's plus sign to toggle between showing and hiding the detail rows. For details on deploying this report to a server and incorporating it into an application, see Chapter 21.

Summary

SQL Server Analysis Services 2005 offers a complete toolset for a data mining solution. This chapter has introduced you to these tools and their many uses, from creating random samples to presenting the results in a custom application for business users. You've seen how to use the percentage sampling task in SSIS to create random samples for training and testing your mining models. You were introduced to the Data Mining Wizard, which guides you through the creation of a mining structure and mining model. You saw how to add and edit mining models, including how to tweak algorithm parameters, from the Mining Models tab of the Mining Structure designer.

You browsed the results of several mining models using Microsoft's mining model viewers. Several viewers are provided for each algorithm, allowing you to analyze the results from different perspectives. You created a lift chart for comparing the performance of different models.

In a brief introduction to DMX, you saw how to use the DMX query language to do the very same kinds of tasks that you did using the Data Mining Wizard. You then saw how to apply your DMX knowledge programmatically using the development tools you learned in the context of OLAP cubes. As you saw in this chapter, ADO MD.NET provides full support for data mining, and you can easily embed the powerful mining model viewers into a customer application. You also saw how to take advantage of the direct support for data mining prediction queries provided by SQL Server Reporting Services.

As with the Microsoft OLAP platform, the data mining component of SSAS is distinguished by its ease of use and high degree of programmability. The additions made to the data mining component with the 2005 release put Microsoft squarely among the top business intelligence solution providers.

Chapter 21

Reporting Services

–Bill Wolff

SQL Server Reporting Services is a set of technologies that provide development, management, and display of rich data-driven reports. It includes tools for professional report design, ad hoc queries, and secure administration. Programmatic interfaces–including SOAP-based Web services, URL addressing, Windows Management Instrumentation (WMI)–and extensibility classes give developers excellent flexibility in report management.

Report definitions are stored in an XML dialect, published to an SQL database, and managed through a Web interface. A Windows service handles report processing that separates data retrieval from report rendering. This allows a single report to be displayed in a variety of output formats to multiple users. On-demand report delivery and scheduled e-mail or file-based subscriptions enable timely report viewing.

Business reporting needs are satisfied out of the box with little or no programming. The Report Designer tool creates professional layouts through a series of wizards and design surfaces. Ad hoc reports are created with templates and models in the Report Builder tool. Developers can embed Reporting Services in custom applications using Web service rendering or the *ReportViewer* control. Web parts are included that help Microsoft SharePoint users integrate reports into portal applications. The programmatic interfaces and Report Definition Language (RDL) file format are well documented, allowing developers and third-party vendors to create complementary tools and services.

Reporting Services was first released in 2004 as an add-on to the SQL Server 2000 family of products. This technology has been widely adopted and appears in many popular Microsoft applications, including Microsoft Operations Manager, Microsoft Data Protection Manager, Microsoft Dynamics, and others. The SQL Server 2005 suite fully integrates Reporting Services into all aspects of configuration, development, security, and management.

The report life cycle starts with a report definition combining data queries and page layout. Completed report designs are stored in an XML dialect and published to the report server through a Web service interface. Users display report output through a browser interface, e-mail, or file share. Reports are organized in a folder hierarchy and are secured using a Web interface or Web services. Report server configuration, monitoring, and management are controlled with Microsoft Management Console (MMC) applications, WMI interfaces, and log files. We'll cover each of these areas, starting with report definition and design.

Report Definition and Design

Reporting Services includes a professional report design tool called Report Designer that is hosted in Visual Studio 2005 or SQL Server Business Intelligence Development Studio. Report Designer provides rich graphical query tools, report layout design surfaces, and a built-in report viewer. This tool is geared to programmers and skilled reporters.

Business analysts and users can make their own reports using a client-side ClickOnce application called Report Builder. Data models hide the underlying tables and joins so reporting becomes a drag-and-drop affair. Report Builder definitions use the same format as Report Designer and can be used as a starting point for more complex reports.

Hardcore programmers and third-party vendors can embrace the Reporting Services architecture, XML file structures, and SDK tools to create their own report development suite. Microsoft and many independent software vendors (ISVs) are integrating Reporting Services into their products.

All these tools combine some data source query capability with report layout and design. In some shops, these tasks might be performed by separate individuals or teams. Report Designer can be used in this environment, but doing layout and design in one setting is more common. We will first investigate data sources and then explain how the two main reporting tools use them in the design process.

Data Sources

Data sources can be specific to a single report or shared across multiple reports. Reports can contain one data source or many. Specific data sources are defined in the RDL file for that report. Shared data sources are stored in a separate file structure in the development environment and on the report server.

The three primary sources for report data are relational tables, multidimensional cubes, and hierarchical XML structures. Each has syntax and graphical tools that enable quick and efficient selection, ordering, and grouping of data. You can combine all three data types in one report, but each must expose a tabular dataset. The resulting datasets appear in Datasets Explorer next to the toolbox, as shown in Figure 21-1. They are used to supply data to report controls and parameters lists.

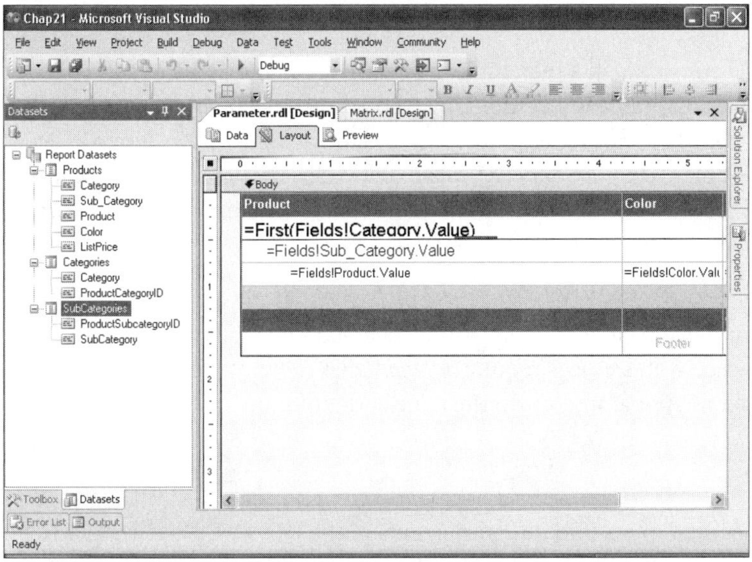

Figure 21-1   Datasets Explorer with three datasets and associated fields

Datasets include a list of fields that appear under them in Datasets Explorer. Fields can be mapped directly to a query column or a calculation. Calculations can be simple concatenations or complex mathematics. You can change the field names to make them more readable to the report developer.

Relational Data Sources

The most common data source is the relational table based on SQL query text or a stored procedure. The data connection information specifies a server, database name, and credentials. The specifics depend on the type of database. Reporting Services supports SQL Server, Analysis Services, Object Linking and Embedding Database (OLE DB), Open Database Connectivity (ODBC), and Oracle. Underlying OLE DB and ODBC drivers provide connectivity to a wide range of data sources. If your data source is not covered by this list, consider writing a custom data processing extension to gather the data and package it in the format required by Reporting Services interfaces.

Multidimensional Data Sources

Analysis Services cubes and data mining predictions are the second source of report data. You can use Multidimensional Expressions (MDX) to slice and dice summarized data from processed cubes. Data Mining Prediction (DMX) queries use advanced analytics to produce data by probability. Any multidimensional query must produce a flattened tabular dataset. This appears in Datasets Explorer, just like a relational query. (See Chapters 19 and 20 for details on MDX and DMX query syntax.)

XML Data Sources

XML documents store data in a hierarchical format. Reporting Services can connect to a Web service, a Web-based application, a well-formed document available through a URL address, or an embedded XML. It cannot use native XML data types stored in the SQL Server 2005 database engine unless they are exposed through a Web service or Web application. Note that only integrated security and anonymous authentication are supported. You cannot pass credentials to a Web service.

The XML query syntax uses XPath and can optionally include a namespace-independent element name. Where an element name is not specified, the first available leaf node collection of elements is used. Web services require a *SoapAction* element with at least one method. Add any required SOAP parameters to the dataset definition.

Report Layouts

You place datasets and fields into design elements in the Report Designer toolbox. Several controls display data: table, matrix, list, and chart. Each control can have one data region. The data region is associated with one dataset. Some reports have only one data region and data control. More complex reports mix these elements in any combination to create free-form content.

Table Control

Table controls display data in a row-and-column format. The column count and order are static. The number of rows depends on the record count returned by the underlying dataset. You can use grouping and sorting options to create banded reports. Each band can have its own row header and footer. An example of a table control is shown in Figure 21-2.

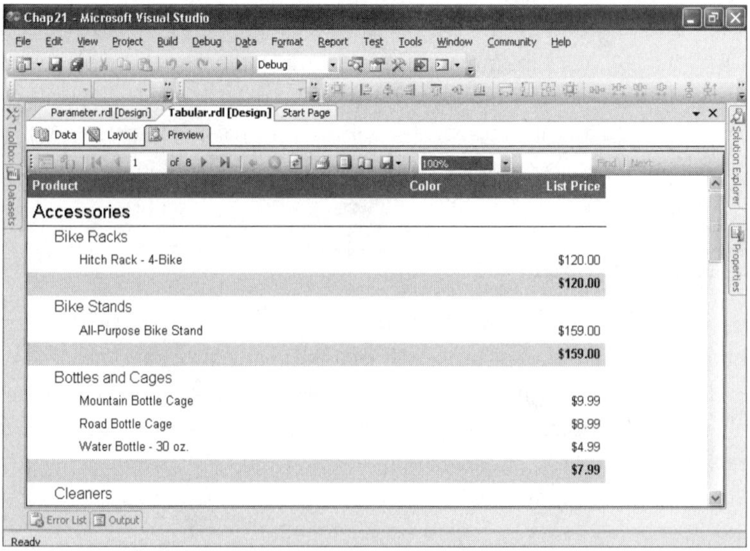

Figure 21-2   *Table* control with groups and subtotals in the preview pane

Table cells contain text box controls by default. You can change this to another type of control, such as an image. You can merge cells to create more interesting layouts or add detail rows to display multiple rows of data for each dataset row.

You add subtotals by inserting text box controls to group header or footer rows. An aggregate expression tallies the data for the associated group using a formula like this one:

```
=Avg(Fields!ListPrice.Value)
```

Matrix Control

Matrix controls summarize data, as shown in Figure 21-3. They are often referred to as *crosstabs*. The rows and columns expand to accommodate the summarized data. A matrix contains four cells by default. The upper-left cell is called the corner and is typically used to display a label. The upper-right cell is the column header. The lower-left cell is the row header. You can use multiple grouping levels for the rows and columns to create a rich, interactive report. The columns expand to the right depending on the number of values in the dataset group. The rows expand downward as each page fills.

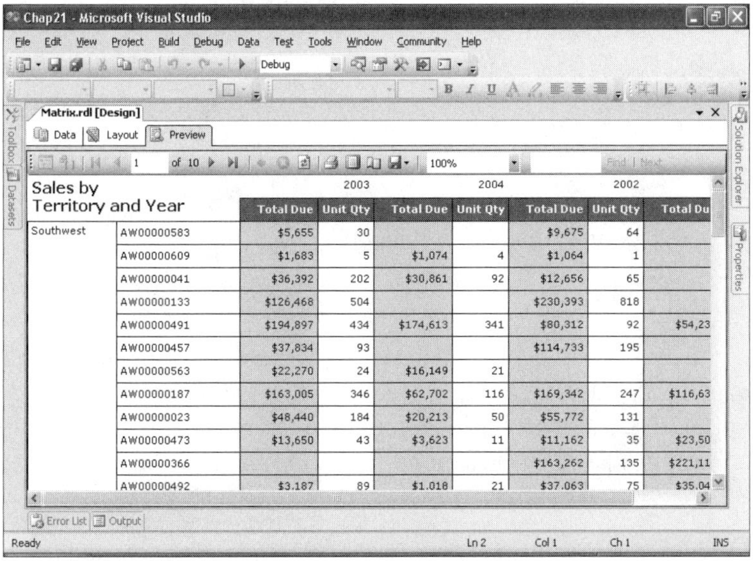

Figure 21-3   *Matrix* control with expanded columns and rows in the preview pane

The detail cells store one or more aggregate values. The summary value is calculated for the intersection of each row and column. If there are multiple aggregates, each appears in a separate column.

Matrix data regions work well with Analysis Services cube data. The cubes already have aggregate totals, so there is little query work for the data engine to process. You can add drill-down capabilities to make this even more interesting (as explained shortly).

List Control

Lists provide free-form arrangement of discrete controls. Each dataset row is rendered according to the layout defined in the list definition. Lists can include text boxes, images, tables, matrixes, charts, subreports, or other lists. The nesting feature allows virtually unlimited design flexibility. The layout view of a free-form report appears in Figure 21-4.

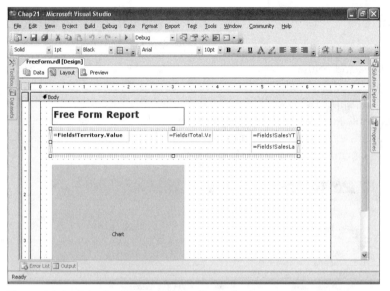

Figure 21-4   Free-form report with a list and subreport

Chart Control

Charts display a graphical representation of a dataset, as shown in Figure 21-5. Chart types include pie, bar, line, and 3-D charts. Charts have areas that are similar to tabular groups. Value series are displayed as a single-line point or bar for each data element. If groups are defined, a line or bar is displayed for each group. The value series can be optionally described in the legend.

The chart tool included with Reporting Services is from Dundas Software and has a good set of basic features. For more demanding output, Dundas and other third parties offer richer charts that are compatible with Reporting Services.

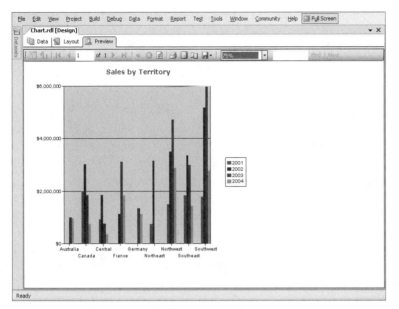

Figure 21-5   *Chart* control in the preview pane

Subreport Control

Many reporting chores are repetitive. Once a good matrix or chart is working, you can easily insert it into other, more complex reports. A subreport owns datasets and layout controls. Each time a subreport is rendered, the underlying queries execute and the content is rendered. The result is passed back to the parent report, which inserts the content into the finished report. Figure 21-5 shows a sample subreport. The subreport is rendered inside of the parent report in Figure 21-6.

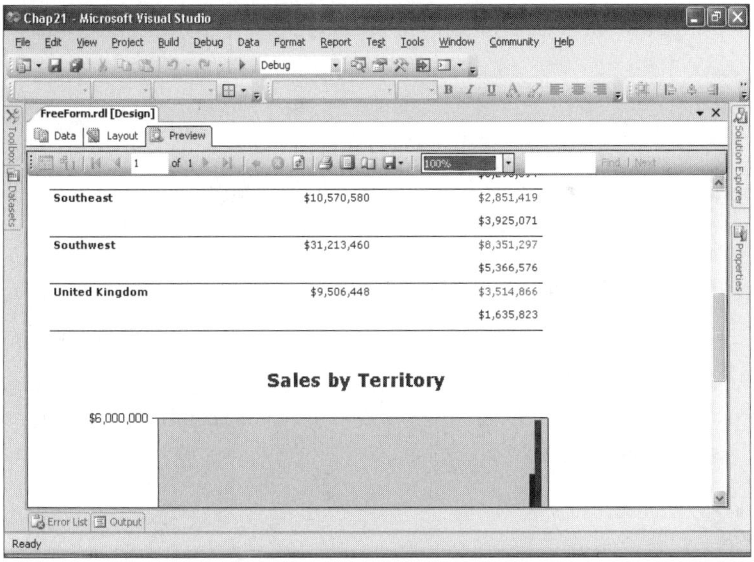

Figure 21-6   Free-form report with rendered subreport in the preview pane

A library of smaller report parts can be extremely useful. You can add these parts to the report server and link them to larger master reports. If you never want to run the smaller parts on their own, you can hide them from view but still call them into action for a larger master report. Hiding report parts is covered later in the chapter.

Rendering and Pagination

The task of placing the data onto pages is carried out by the rendering engine. This is a two-step process. The report datasets are filled based on the query definition and optional parameters. Sometimes the data is cached and therefore retrieved quickly. If no cached copy exists, the query is run and all rows are returned before rendering continues. The resulting data is stored in temporary tables while the engine attempts to fill each data region control. The report and page headers are rendered according to their visibility. As each record is added, the engine checks for the height and width of the new data. A row that fits is added to the current page. If the row exceeds the page height, a new page is triggered and the footer is applied. This process continues until all datasets and controls are rendered. Because data regions can nest, this process can take some time and can result in hundreds or thousands of pages.

The actual rendering occurs whenever report output is requested. Several presentation formats are detailed later in this chapter. The pagination results might differ if the report is rendered once in HTML and again in PDF. Some output formats support a limited set of features, so portions of a report might not render at all (as explained in more detail later).

Reports can include headers and footers that run along the top and bottom of the page, respectively. They can include page numbers, text, images, and other design controls. Data regions cannot be placed into headers and footers. If you want dataset fields in headers and footers, you must write an expression that references the intended field.

Multiple-column output is supported in PDF and TIFF output mode. The designer displays only a single column, but rendered reports will snake data across multiple columns.

Report Designer

Report Designer has a rich set of features that will satisfy report professionals and programmers. Reports can be simple or complex, highly structured or free form, static or interactive. You have complete control over layout, formatting, formulas, and pagination.

Business Intelligence Development Studio

Report Designer is installed as part of Business Intelligence Development Studio (BI Development Studio), which comes standard with SQL Server 2005. BI Development Studio is really a slimmed-down version of Visual Studio. If you install Visual Studio 2005 on the same machine as BI Development Studio, you can access the reporting tools from the menu of either product.

Reports are stored inside project templates. When you create a new project in Visual Studio or BI Development Studio, select the Business Intelligence Project category in the New Project dialog box, as shown in Figure 21-7. Three of the six installed templates are used for reporting purposes. The Report Server Project opens an empty project template. The Report Server Project Wizard guides you through the creation of a single report while creating the necessary project files behind the scenes. The Report Model Project is used for reporting models (as discussed later in this chapter).

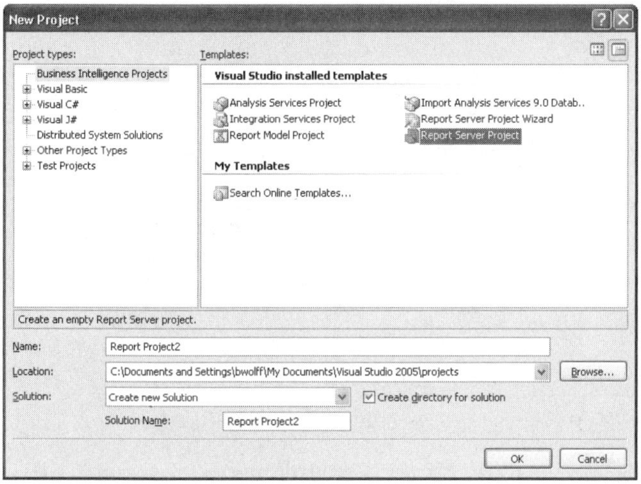

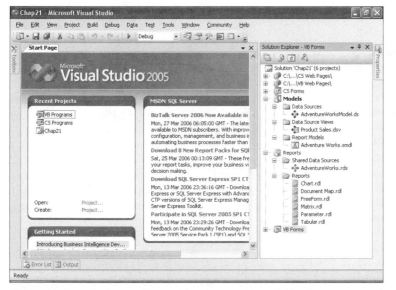

Figure 21-7 New Report Projects in BI Development Studio or Visual Studio

Report projects contain two folders. The Shared Data Sources folder holds the database connection information for the project. The Report folder contains reports (Figure 21-8).

Figure 21-8 Solution Explorer with Report and Model Projects

You cannot create nested folders for categorization. Instead, you must create separate report projects and have each project deploy the completed reports to a specific folder on the report server. This creates the desired categorization and keeps the reports segmented enough that multiple developers can work simultaneously. You can set the deployment target folder in the Reports Properties Pages dialog box (Figure 21-9). You can set the target server, data source folder, and report folder. There are separate properties for each Configuration target. You can change the target server or folders based on the target environment.

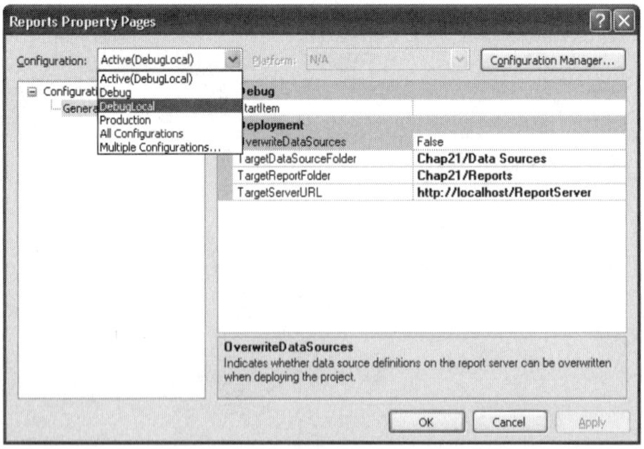

Figure 21-9   Report Properties Pages dialog box with configuration options

Shared data sources can be specific to the working environment—for example, development, test, and production. As reports are promoted from one environment to the next, these named data sources can be pointed to entirely different database resources. You can create new data sources or add existing ones already saved to disk. They are stored in RDS files that have a simple XML format. Data sources have a name, connection properties, and credentials, as shown in Figure 21-10 and Figure 21-11. Credentials options include integrated, user specified, prompted, or none. Server stored credentials are encrypted using key technology.

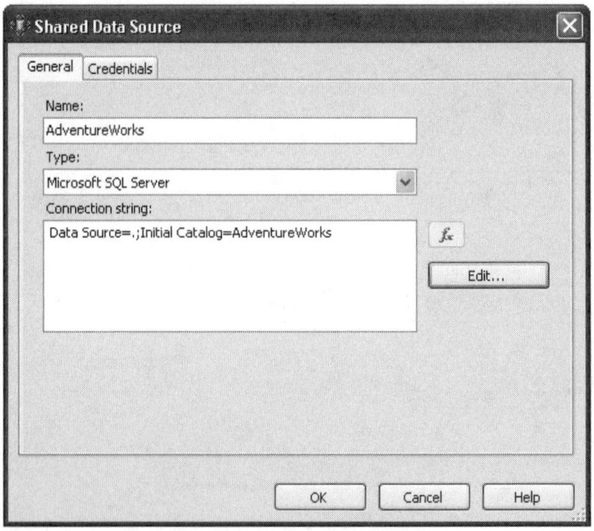

Figure 21-10   Shared Data Source dialog box with SQL Server connection type

Figure 21-11   Data source connection properties for SQL Server with credential details

Be careful when you deploy project data sources. An overwrite option on the Report Properties pages indicates whether to replace the data source. This defaults to false because the credentials used by a developer might differ from those used in testing or production. The first time a report project deploys, the data source is copied to the report server. After that, the administrator can change the server-based credentials to satisfy the user population. Subsequent deployment of report versions do not overwrite this data source unless you change the default.

Reports are added to the Report folder. You can make new report items using a wizard or a blank report. You can add existing report items stored on disk as an RDL file. You can also import reports from Microsoft Access. In this case, most data source, query, and report layout information is translated into RDL and stored in the report folder.

Report names must be unique within a project. As long as each project deploys to a unique folder on the report server, it is possible to have the same report name several places on a server. Keep this in mind when you define naming standards for your reporting infrastructure.

Once a new report is created or an existing report loaded, the report displays in a tab in BI Development Studio or Visual Studio. The left side of the screen has a series of tabbed tools. One is called Datasets, and it contains the datasets and fields associated with the report. The second is the toolbox, which contains the data region and graphic controls used in report layout. On the right side of the screen is the typical Solution Explorer with a hierarchical view of report files and the Properties window for inspecting report and control details.

The center panel has three subtabs called Data, Layout, and Preview. The Data view is used to create and manage datasets. The Layout view is a design surface used to create and style report elements. The Preview tab has complete rendering engine capability and can display reports that work exactly like the report server. This is made possible by using the same .NET DLL on the server that is used in development. The viewer includes a toolbar with pagination controls, export capability, print/preview, and zooming.

Query Builder

The Data subtab for a report definition manages datasets. You can edit existing datasets or add new ones using the Dataset drop-down list at the top left of the dialog box. Each dataset has a name, data source, and other information specific to the command type and selected data source type.

SQL relational data sources support text and stored procedure command types. The query string can be edited or pasted directly into the Dataset Query page. It is often easier to leave the query field blank and use the built-in query editors. There is a text-based editor (Figure 21-12) with a result window in the bottom pane. Click the Run button (exclamation point) on the toolbar to see the results of a query.

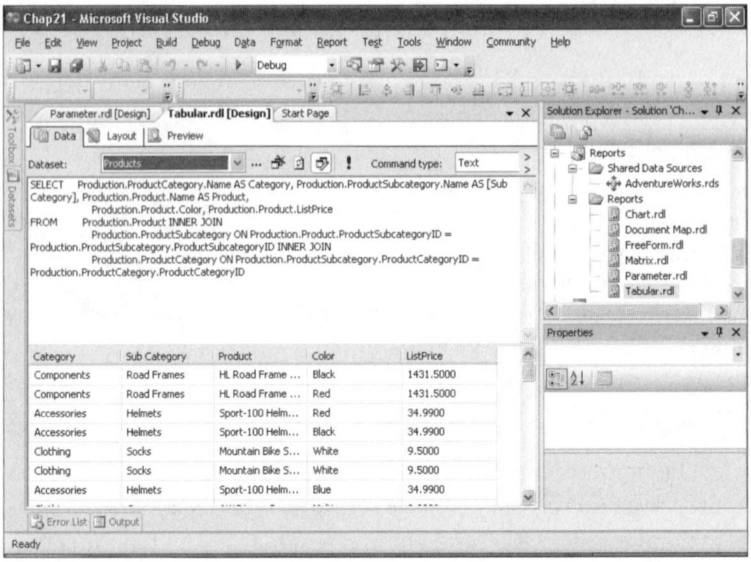

Figure 21-12   Text-based query designer

The Generic Query Designer button toggles from text to graphical mode for a relational dataset. This editor, shown in Figure 21-13, will be familiar to anyone who has worked with Microsoft database products over the years, including Microsoft Access and previous versions of SQL Server. The top pane has the table diagram. Use the Add Table button to add more tables. The second pane is the column grid. You can specify columns, aliases, sorting, and filter criteria. The third pane is the SQL statement. You can paste working statements into this area and have the table diagram and column panes fill automatically. There is no color coding or IntelliSense in the statement editor. This pane has a properties dialog box where you can modify the statement with options such as distinct values and top rows. Finally, the bottom pane displays the results in response to the *Execute SQL* command. Any of the four panes can be toggled on and off to improve readability.

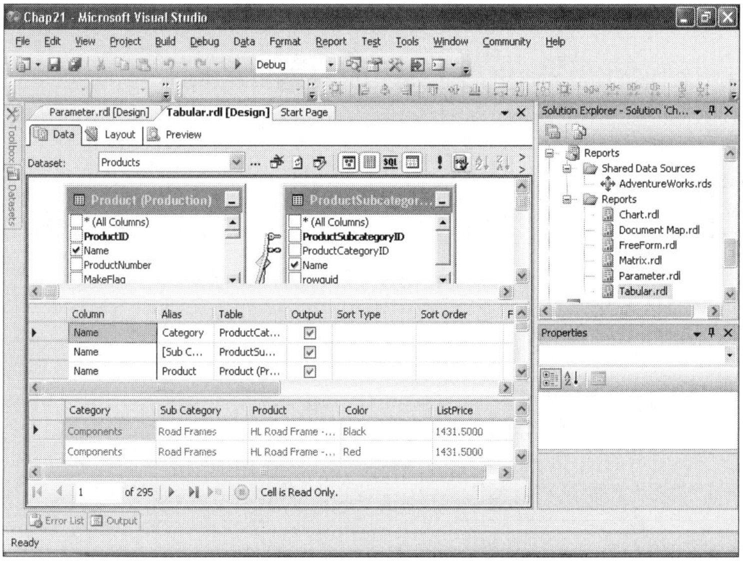

Figure 21-13 Graphical query designer

Some queries will include optional parameters. The syntax for these depends on the data source type. SQL Server uses the *@parameter* syntax. It is easiest to enter these into the filter column of the grid pane. When the query is executed, a dialog box appears asking for the parameter values, as shown in Figure 21-14. Enter a known value or select from the drop-down list. Dataset parameters will appear in the report layout pane dialog boxes and the preview pane toolbar.

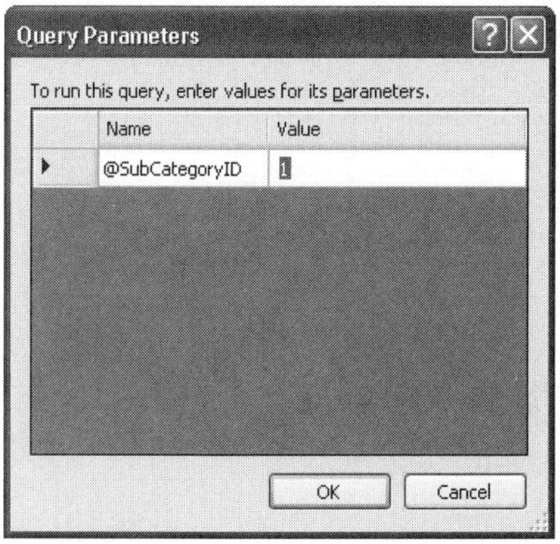

Figure 21-14 Query Parameters dialog box

The query editor also supports stored procedures. You can enter the name of the stored procedure directly into the text window. When you run the procedure, any required parameters appear in the prompt dialog box. Use the Generic Query Designer toolbar button to toggle into graphical mode. A drop-down list displays all the available stored procedures based on the target database name (catalog) specified in the data source.

Analysis Server MDX/DMX and XML datasets provide only the text editing pane. Consider using other query tools to perfect your query statements and then paste them into this query editor.

Report Layout

The Layout subtab of a report definition has a design surface that aids in visually creating report elements. The interface is typical of popular form creation programs such as Microsoft Visual Basic and Access. The sample Chap21 solution includes a Reports project with six sample reports.

Design Surface   New reports start with a blank canvas. Select report control objects from the toolbox, as shown in Figure 21-15, and drag them onto the design surface.

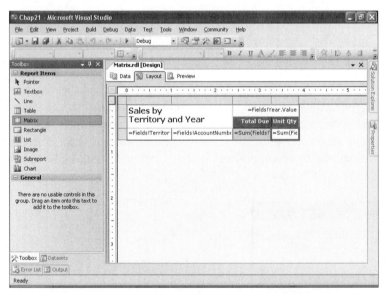

Figure 21-15   Report Designer toolbox

There are nine built-in controls, four of them representing data regions. Custom controls require custom report processing extensions. Third parties are busy developing add-ons to meet this need.

Each object has a unique set of properties that appear in the Properties window. Use the shortcut menu to select the Properties option. This opens a dialog box specific to that control type. It is often easier to complete this dialog box than to scroll through the Properties window. Simpler objects such as the text box have shortcut menu shortcuts for setting the value expression.

The Properties dialog boxes share General, Visibility, Navigation, Filter, Sorting, and Data Output tabs. The General tab has name, ToolTip, and dataset options, as well as page break and header/footer options. On the Visibility tab, you indicate whether the control should be rendered. This is interesting because you can build data-driven expressions that determine visibility. You can , for instance, display a graphic only if sales have exceeded some threshold. On the Navigation tab, you associate fields or expressions with document maps and book-marks (as explained shortly). On the Sorting tab, you specify the order of detail rows. You can use filters to limit the number of rows displayed—this can be different from the underlying data source. You can combine filters and expressions to create some interesting effects. The Data Output tab is primarily for custom XML output.

The *Table* object in the Tabular.rdl sample adds a Group tab to the Properties dialog box. Each group has its own Page Break, Header/Footer, Visibility, Sorting, and Filtering settings. The *Table* control layout is shown in Figure 21-16.

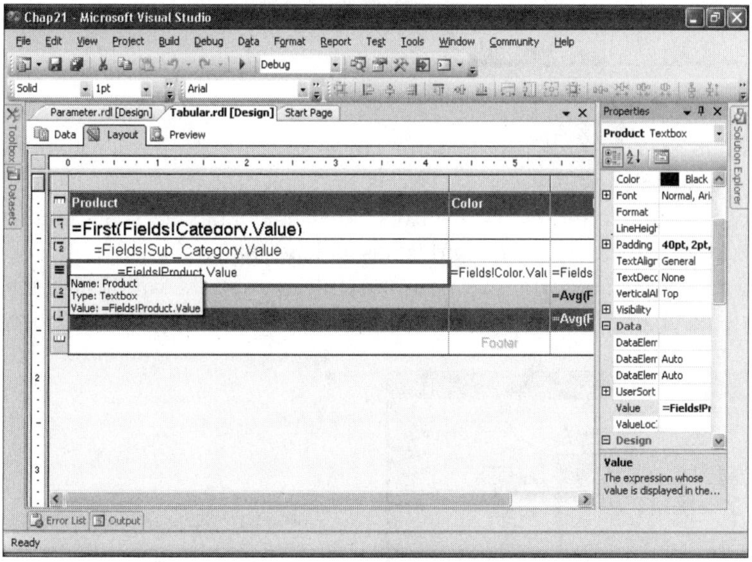

Figure 21-16 *Table* control in the layout pane

Graphical icons represent the various groups and regions in a table. Click on the row or column to set properties specific to that area. Right-click the left table column to insert or delete rows or groups. You can see the rendered tabular report in the preview pane in Figure 21-2, shown earlier.

The *Matrix* control in the Matrix.rdl sample also has a Groups tab, but it has no Sorting tab because the data is summarized and there are no detail rows. The Groups tab has both row and column groups with a defined order. This helps you create drill-down and nesting effects. Note that Sorting is an option within each group. The *Matrix* layout is shown in Figure 21-17. (You can see the rendered matrix report in the preview pane in Figure 21-3, shown earlier.)

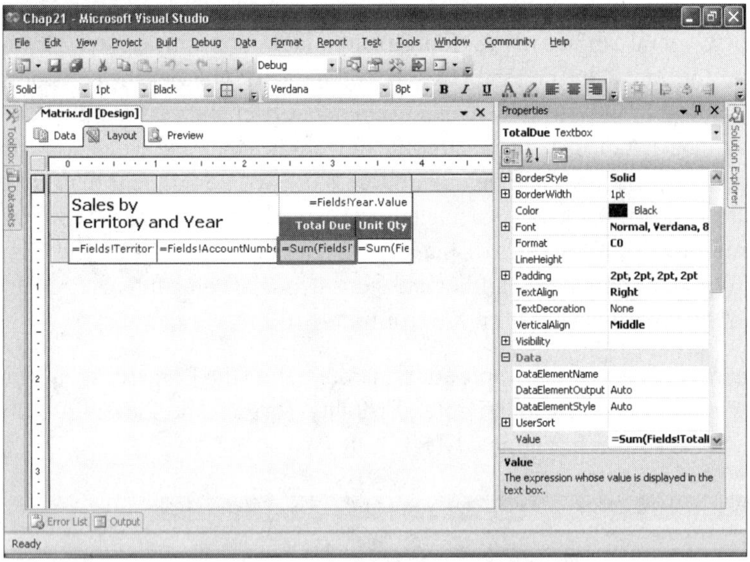

Figure 21-17   *Matrix* control in the layout pane

The *Chart* control in the Chart.rdl sample in the layout pane has property pages to set chart type, Data series, X and Y axes, Legend, 3D Effects, and Filters (Figure 21-18). Data series are similar to groups in the *table* and *matrix* controls. The General tab has style buttons for controlling border and fill colors. Series and labels all have font and style format options. If you prefer, you can use the Properties window and drill through the various categories. (You can see the rendered chart report in the preview pane in Figure 21-5, shown earlier.)

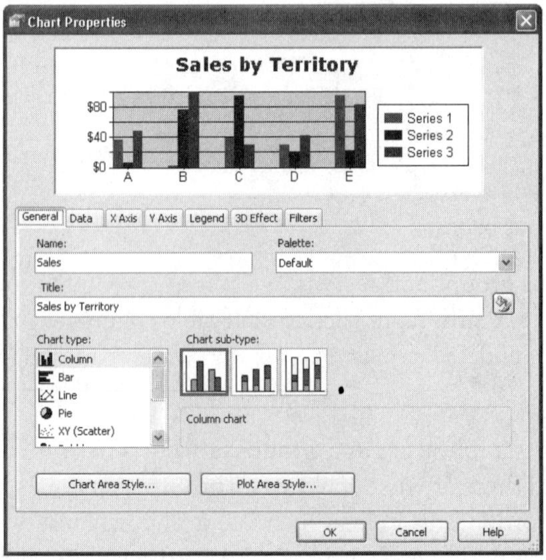

Figure 21-18   *Chart* control properties in the layout pane

The *List* control appears in the FreeForm.rdl sample. A list has no groups. Use the Edit Details Group button on the general Property tab to see Filtering and Sorting options for the underlying data. The *List* data region control is a container that holds other controls. Our example uses a few text boxes and a line to build a layout that repeats for each detail row.

FreeForm.rdl also contains a *Subreport* control. Subreports have an optional Parameters tab in the Properties dialog box where you can connect the parent report to a child using data-driven values in an expression. Select the required parameters from the drop-down list, and set the value to some expression. You can see a rendered *Subreport* and list in Figure 21-4, shown earlier.

Expression Editor

The Expression Editor can create formulas for data display and formatting options. Most of the properties available for report objects have an *<Expression...>* option in the drop-down list. The Edit Expression dialog box has a color-coded syntax editor with Undo and Paste buttons. It also supports IntelliSense, so functions display parameter options as you type.

The *Treeview* control on the left has a list of syntax categories. Select one of these to fill the center list of syntax options. The description on the right panel explains how to use each feature. Double-click the item in the center panel to have it pasted into the expression. This approach is very useful for dataset fields and report parameters. The Constants category is specific to the property being edited and will show numbers, colors, or other appropriate values.

The example expression in Figure 21-19 sets the text color based on the value of two other fields.

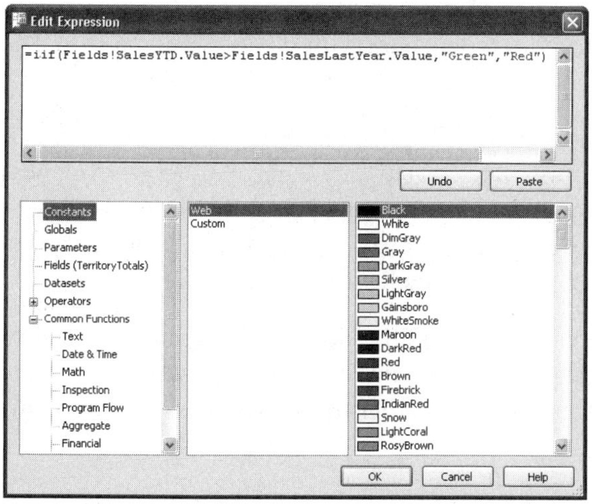

Figure 21-19   Expression Editor with a simple formatting statement

Code and Custom Assemblies

The Expression Editor can reference .NET code that is stored with the report definition or in a custom assembly installed on the developer machine and report server. Use the Report Properties dialog box to find the Code and References tabs.

The Code page presents a simple text editor where you can add multiple instance-based methods written in Visual Basic. There is no color coding or IntelliSense. Consider writing the methods in a regular Visual Basic project and pasting the code into this window. To access the code in an expression, use the Code class as follows:

```
=Code.MyConvert(Fields!Price.Value)
```

You can write custom assemblies in any .NET language that uses static or instance methods. The calling syntax is different with a static member:

```
=MyNameSpace.MyClass.MyStaticMethod(Fields!Price.Value)
```

Make sure the assembly is loaded to the Reporting Services bin folder or the global assembly cache (GAC). Note that custom assemblies are loaded once for each development session and changes do not appear until Visual Studio is restarted.

Interactivity

The Reporting Service delivers static and interactive reports. Much of the interactivity comes from the use of query and report parameters. These values are known only by the end user running the report. Parameters can also be supplied from a table when you run subscriptions (as described later in this chapter).

Parameters and Filters   Most parameters are based on data source query input values. The exact syntax needed to create a parameter depends on the data source type. In SQL Server, the parameters start with the @ symbol.

The Chap21 solution has a report sample called Parameter.rdl that includes several query parameters. In this case, three datasets are created. The Category query lists all possible categories. The SubCategory dataset has a Filter expression that asks for the CategoryID. When you run this query on the Data tab, you are prompted for a CategoryID value. The third dataset is Product, which also has a filter asking for a SubCategoryID.

When this report is run on the Preview tab, a drop-down list is created for each parameter. You must specify a category before the dependent SubCategory list is enabled and filled. These parameters dynamically build on each other through expressions (as shown in Figure 21-20).

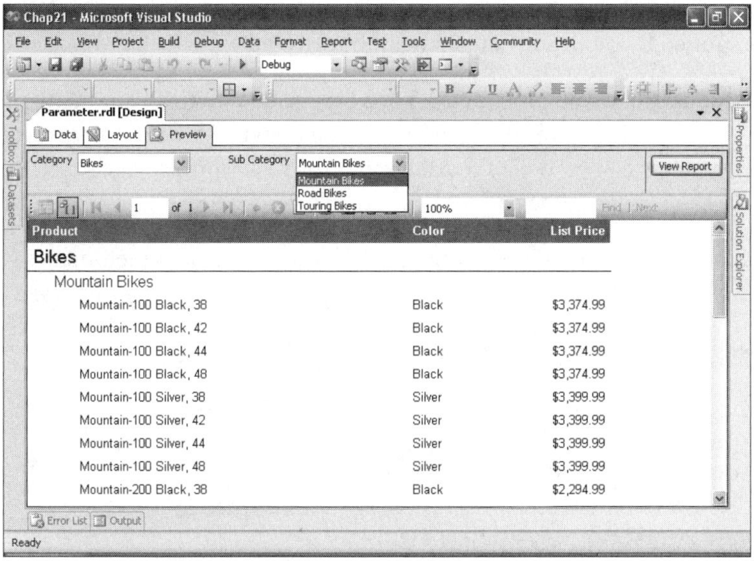

Figure 21-20   Dynamic parameters selected in the preview pane

On the Layout tab, use the Report menu or right-click on the design surface to show the Report Parameters menu option (Figure 21-21).

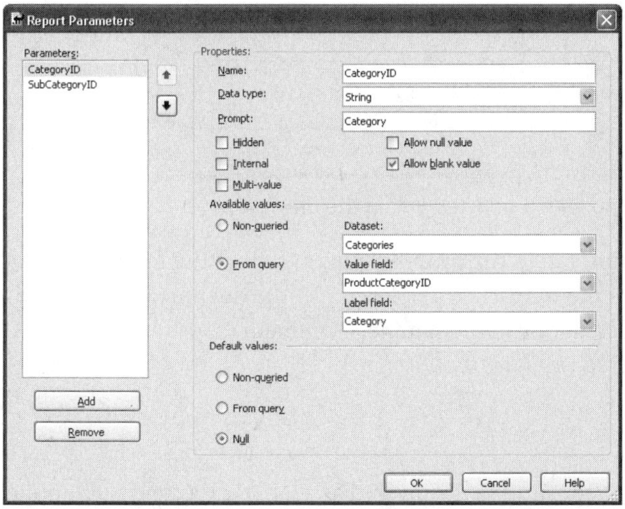

Figure 21-21   Report parameters generated automatically from query parameters

Notice that each dataset with a parameter creates a matching *Report* parameter. For each parameter, you can specify the name, data type, and prompt. If you need to associate data values with a parameter, these can be hardcoded or derived from a query. Default values can also be defined in this dialog box. The extra datasets in this report are used to fill the report parameter from a query. The order of the parameters is important because, in this example, a CategoryID is required before a SubCategory can be selected.

This is just one example of adding interactivity to a report. Parameters have many purposes in advanced report building. They can appear in titles, headers, expressions, and other calculations. Reports with parameters can be linked to each other to create sophisticated drill-down reporting.

Document Maps Another interesting interactive feature is the document map, which you can see on the left side of the rendered DocumentMap.rdl report sample (Figure 21-22).

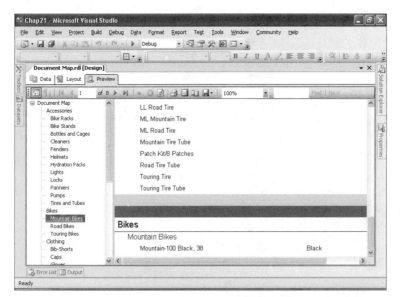

Figure 21-22 Document Map with a selected link in the preview pane

Each control has a Navigation tab in the property pages. Setting the Document Map entry to a field or expression causes the map to be displayed. Set the document map to a different grouping level to get the nested look in the sample. Document maps render in HTML, XLS (as a cover worksheet), and PDFs (as a document map).

Report Builder

Report Builder is an ad hoc reporting tool delivered as a .NET 2.0 ClickOnce application that a user downloads from the report server. Predesigned report templates are used as a design surface, with drag-and-drop placeholders for data. The data is presented as a report model with predefined relationships and column attributes. Users can sort, group, filter, chart, and summarize (with limited support for formatting and formulas).

Ad Hoc Reporting

Report Builder is designed for non-technical business users who understand the data but not how to use SQL statements to build complex queries. All reporting must be done through report models that mask the underlying table relationships. Ad hoc reporting is the primary benefit of this tool. You can save the reports to the report server or to a local file. Both locations allow re-editing of the report definition. Once a report is modified by another tool (such as Report Designer), Report Builder can no longer open it.

After the tool downloads, the user is asked to select a report model. The list will include all models on the report server for which the user has permissions. The user must also select a template: table, matrix, or chart. There is no free-form reporting or list capability. The templates are restricted so that only a small subset of formatting properties are available. There are no expressions, code windows, or wizards. The user picks fields from the report model and drops them into labeled locations on the template. The result is a basic but useful report layout like the matrix shown in Figure 21-23.

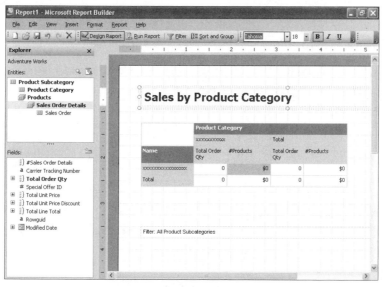

Figure 21-23   Report Builder in Design Report mode with a matrix template

Report Builder offers clever client-side sorting and filtering tools. The filter clause appears on the bottom of each report, which is very handy. The completed report can be run directly in Report Builder, as shown in Figure 21-24.

Report Builder has limited appeal to professional designers. Savvy business professionals already familiar with reporting capabilities in Microsoft Excel and Access will be more comfortable with those tools. You can use Report Builder to start a simple report that will be finished by a professional. (The tool would save little overall development time.)

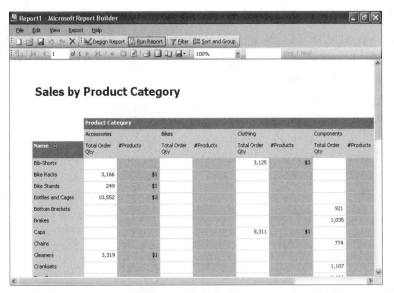

Figure 21-24   Report Builder in Run Report mode with a matrix report

Predefined Report Models

Report Builder relies on report models published to the report server. Models are a semantic description of business data. This means that the table and field names might be different from the underlying data. The real value of this is that it allows business users to work with familiar terms. Models also hide the relationships and joins required for complex relational queries.

Report models have their own project type in Visual Studio. The Chap21 solution includes a project called Models that contains a single model. The project has three folders. The Data Sources folder stores the pointer to a data connection. It uses a slightly different dialog box (Figure 21-25).

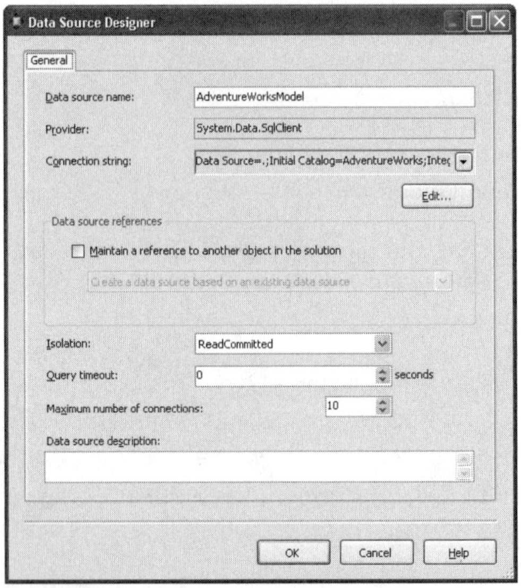

Figure 21-25   Report Model Data Source Designer dialog box

Data sources also use a slightly different dialog box for data connections (Figure 21-26).

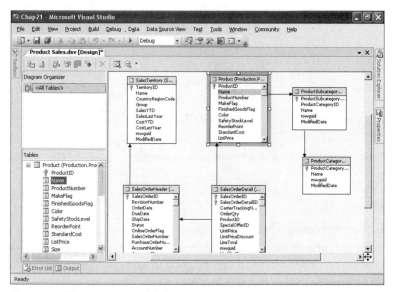

Figure 21-26   Report Model Data Source Connection Manager dialog box

Once the data source is set, you can create a data source view, which is basically a subset of the tables and columns available in the underlying data source. One project can have many data source views. Data source views have a graphical relationship editor (Figure 21-27).

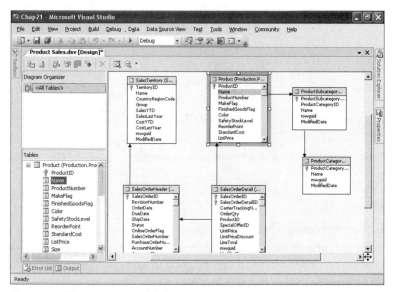

Figure 21-27   Report model data source view

There can be multiple diagrams in the Diagram organizer on the left side of the designer. Table relationships are shown in the center panel. You can create logical keys and relationships even if the underlying data does not define primary and foreign keys. This is useful when you report from legacy systems in which database changes are not possible.

Report models are created from a data source view. One project can have many models. The models sift through the data by doing repetitive queries, and they determine the cardinality and constraints of the data to create a map of possible entities and attributes tuned to the data. For instance, numeric columns have a predefined total, minimum, maximum, and average. The business user can later pick these logical fields directly without knowing SQL query syntax. Other column types, such as dates, automatically create fragments such as month, quarter, and year. Model designers can tweak and customize the entities and attributes to create a more meaningful description of the data. The finished report model has attributes and roles, as shown in Figure 21-28.

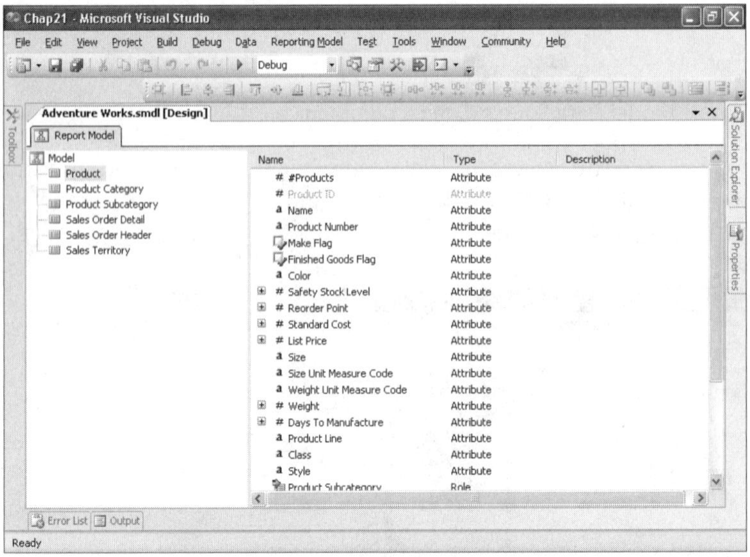

Figure 21-28 Completed report model with attributes and roles

Keep in mind that this is not an Analysis Services cube that calculates and stores aggregate values. Instead, it is a map that a business user can use when building a report definition.

Completed models are deployed to the report server. Report Manager and SQL Management Studio include tools that automatically generate models based on data source schemas. You cannot edit field or table names, but this is a quick way to get started with models. In Report Manager, open the properties page for a data source and click the Generate Model button.

The Reporting Services models are stored in an XML file with the Semantic Model Definition Language (SMDL) extensions. They do not use Universal Modeling Language (UML)—they have their own syntax and personality.

Report Definition Language

The report definition file format is an XML grammar controlled by an XML Schema Definition (XSD) and namespace that serve as the blueprint for a report. Use the Visual Studio Solution Explorer to view code for a report definition, or open the RDL file in any XML editor.

The root of the XML document is the *<Report>* element. There are nested sections for *<DataSources>*, *<Body>*, and *<DataSets>*. Each *<DataSets>* section has a *<Query>* element and a *<Fields>* collection. *<Body>* has a *<ReportItems>* collection containing *<Table>*, *<Matrix>*, *<List>*, or *<Chart>* elements. Each of these elements has child elements that define the numerous settings and properties required to render a report.

The XML is well documented and easy to generate using some clever XML coding techniques. Because so many graphical tools (such as Report Designer and Report Builder) already produce well-formed file definitions, there is little reason to programmatically generate your own XML for anything other than a coding exercise.

Report Management

Completed report definitions are loaded to a report server, where they can be accessed and subscribed to. The process of loading the report is referred to as *publishing*. The report is parsed and stored in an SQL database partially compiled, somewhat like a Transact-SQL (T-SQL) stored procedure. The report appears in a folder hierarchy similar to filespecs in Windows Explorer. Each folder and report has properties and settings that determine visibility, access, data source, and execution capabilities. Several tools are available for organizing and managing the published reports. These include the Web-based Report Manager, the Visual Studio–based SQL Management Studio, and Web service and WMI programmatic interfaces.

Publishing

Popular report authoring and development tools have built-in publishing methods. Some are geared to developers, some to end users, and others to system administrators. Pay careful attention because the terminology used in each tool is quite different!

Report Designer uses the Deploy menu option in the Solution Explorer folder tree. Select Deploy on the project name to publish all data sources and reports in the project to a target report server folder specified in the project properties. You can also deploy a single report file. Once deployed, the server copy cannot be edited directly. Instead, edit your local copy and redeploy.

Report Builder has a business user slant and uses the term *Save* instead of *Deploy*. It also lets you open a report directly from a report server or file location, as long as the report definition was created in Report Builder. The edited report can be saved to a report server folder or a file location.

Report Manager administrators can select the Upload File button on the toolbar. Select the Browse button to open a file dialog box. The report name is specified with an Overwrite check box. An existing report has a General property page with Edit and Update links. The Update link loads an RDL file to an existing report name. The Edit link lets you save the RDL for editing in another tool (such as Report Designer).

SQL Server Management Studio can connect to an instance of Reporting Services. The folder hierarchy appears in Object Explorer. Right-click any folder and select Import File to get a dialog box prompting for the report name and file location. Right-click an existing report object to get options for editing, viewing, replacing, and scripting a report definition. The latter option is interesting because Visual Basic code is created that includes the entire report definition and all associated settings. This is a good tip for anyone interested in using the Reporting Services object library to manage report definitions.

Finally, programmers can use the Web service interface to load and manipulate report definition settings.

Report Manager

Report Manager is the Web-based report content manager that by default registers a virtual directory called http://someservername/reports. It uses ASP.NET 2.0 Web pages to present tabbed views of folders and rendered reports. Administrators have extra tabs for manipulating object properties.

This tool was developed using the Web service interface that installs at another virtual directory called http://someservername/reportserver. You can use this Web site as the main interface for all reporting functions, but it is actually intended as a demonstration of what can be programmatically accomplished using the Web service foundation and architecture. The ASP.NET pages are available for editing, but most of the work is done by controls and code-behind. The documentation recommends that you not make any changes because service packs and future versions might overwrite your work. You can edit the CSS style sheets to change fonts and colors. You can also change the main title in the Settings page, as shown in Figure 21-29.

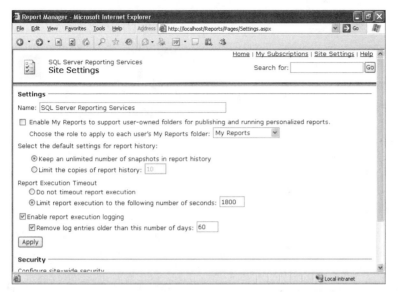

Figure 21-29   Report Manager site settings

Report Manager offers simple and straightforward navigation. The title and folder name appear in the upper-left corner. Below that is a set of breadcrumbs that help you move through the folder hierarchy. The next level has a set of tabs that will vary depending on user roles and permissions. The toolbar below that has buttons for adding new objects to the current folder. Again, only users with elevated roles have these options. The button on the far right of the toolbar shows and hides object details. This is useful for seeing hidden objects, owners, and timestamps. The details view also provides a check box for item deletion (Figure 21-30).

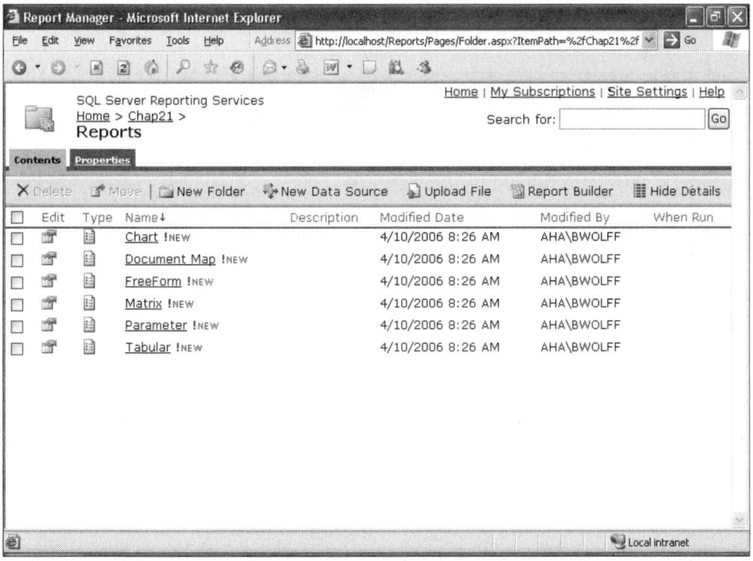

Figure 21-30   Report Manager folder namespace with the details view

The upper-right corner has menu links for Subscriptions, Settings, and Help. The Settings page (Figure 21-29) has a text box for the descriptive server name, the My Reports option, timeout values, and logging options. Below that is a security and job scheduling section where you can manage permissions.

A search option is also available in the upper-right corner on each page. Use this to find an object by name or description. This option can be quite helpful on a fully loaded report server with hundreds or thousands of items.

Report Manager Objects

Each object in Report Manager has a set of properties and additional tabs as needed. The main object types are folders, reports, data sources, and models.

Folders   You use folders to organize and categorize reports. The breadcrumb navigation and descriptions help guide you to the report you need. Each folder in a report server has a property page. Using the property page, you can set the name and description of the folder, and you can restrict access to particular security roles through the Security tab. Buttons on the General tab handle deleting and moving folders. You can use the details view to delete or move report items.

The Security tab lists the applicable group or users with their assigned roles. Most security is inherited from the parent folder. It you select the Edit Item Security toolbar button, you are warned that inheritance will be affected. You can then add new role assignments so that only specific users or groups can view or edit folder items. At any time, you can use the Revert To Parent Security toolbar button to put inheritance back. This security approach applies to all object types.

Reports   Reports are published RDL files that have General, Parameters, Data Sources, Execution, History, and Security tabs, as shown in Figure 21-31.

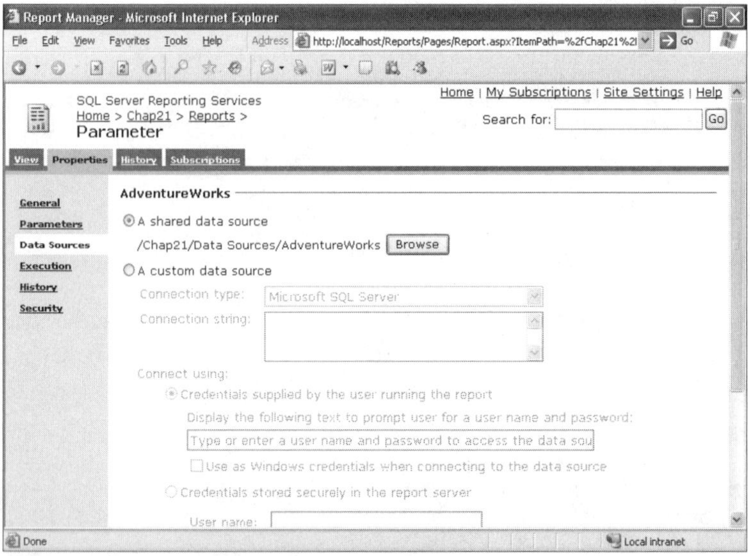

Figure 21-31   Report Manager property pages

The General tab supports name and description editing. It includes links for editing and updating the RDL file and buttons for moving and deleting.

The Data Source tab toggles between shared and custom data source information. Shared data sources store server connection and credential information centrally, so many reports can benefit from one definition. You can set shared data sources using a graphical selection tool (Figure 21-32). (We'll discuss custom credentials shortly.)

Figure 21-32   Report Manager's Shared Data Source Selection tool

On the Execution tab, you can control caching, snapshots, and timeout values. Caching can greatly reduce report query impact on the target data source. You can cache on an expiration time period or a shared or custom schedule. If you have data that changes only once a week, consider creating a schedule that caches the data weekly. All report requests during the week will come directly from cached data stored in the ReportServerTempDB database. Reports will appear faster, and other database processing will continue at a faster clip. Snapshots are similar to caching, but they make a point-in-time copy of the data that is stored indefinitely. You can use a snapshot weeks or months later to get a report using data saved at that point in time. This method is more efficient than archiving a report in a certain output format because the user can specify the desired output format and the exact snapshot dataset to render.

On the History tab, you can control snapshot aging and schedules and also determine manual history creation. The History tab for the report will then display records of snapshots created and reports rendered. Note that both history and snapshots are dependent on cached credentials (as you'll see shortly).

The Security tab for a report works exactly like folder security (explained earlier).

Reports have two additional tab pages on the horizontal menu. History displays a list of snapshot and report execution records. The Subscriptions tab lists all subscriptions for this report and allows you to create new subscriptions (as covered in more detail shortly).

Data Sources   Data sources are published RDS files that contain shared data connection information and associated credentials. It is useful to store all data sources in a separate folder. The Visual Studio project properties enable this (as explained earlier). You can upload data sources or create new ones from scratch. Existing data sources have General and Security tabs on their property pages.

The General tab lets you edit the name and description and offers a hide option. The Connection Type and String options define the target data server. The Connect Using section covers the credential details. User credentials can appear in a prompt when the report runs, be stored securely on the server using key encryption, be integrated with Windows (typically via Active Directory), or be left blank. Note that some useful features such as history and snapshots require stored credentials.

The Security tab for a report works exactly the same as for folder security (explained earlier).

Data sources have two additional tab pages on the horizontal menu. The Dependent Items page displays a list of all reports that use this data source. The Subscriptions page lists all subscriptions that rely on this source.

Models   Report models, stored as SMDL files, are custom built in a Visual Studio project or generated from a data source. It is better to keep all models in a separate folder. The model property page has General, Data Source, and Security tabs.

The General tab allows editing of the name, description, and hide option. It offers links for editing and updating the SMDL file and includes Move and Delete buttons.

The Data Source tab has only a Shared Data Source option. You cannot specify custom credentials.

The Security tab for a report works exactly the same as for folder security (explained earlier).

An additional page on the horizontal menu for Dependent Items lists any reports built with this model. Models are primarily used in Report Builder, so this is a good place to see how the models are being used and who is using them.

Resources   You can load other resources into the report server. When you select the Upload File toolbar button, the Choose File dialog box defaults to Any File Type. It is common to load images (such as JPEG or GIF) that are shared by several reports. This is more efficient than storing images in the RDL file, but it does make them less portable. Another popular resource is an XSLT file that processes an XML output format to render a new XML dialect or custom XHTML. You can also load text files or plain HTML for documentation and training purposes.

My Reports

My Reports is a special feature that is enabled on the Site Settings page. It automatically creates a folder for each user that has a role and permissions on the server. End users can create their own reports and control access without having broad permissions on production folders. This is a good solution in situations where business analysts are empowered with tools such as Report Designer or Report Builder.

The feature creates a hidden folder called Users under the Home level. Administrators can browse the folders to monitor user activity. Each user has a folder with his or her user name. The folder appears to users as My Reports. This works well if users are already comfortable with the My Documents or My Pictures folders in Windows Explorer.

Security

Security is configured on the Site Settings page, which offers three links to security-related tasks.

Site Wide Security maps a Windows user or group to a defined role. The role has a detailed list of tasks that can be enabled for fine-grained control. By default, only system administrators have access. All others must be assigned a role.

Item-level roles package several discrete security tasks into a named entity, which can then be assigned to a user at the item (report, folder, data source, or model) level. Five roles are built in, and you can add as many others as you like. Browser is the most common role; it allows a user to view and render reports. The Content Manager role can manage (administrate) objects on the report server.

System-level roles include Administrator and User. You can associate a user or group with such a role if they will be working with reports in most folders of the report server. Keep in mind that all folder and object permissions are inherited: If users have the System User role, they can get to any report in any folder. To keep someone out of a folder, you must override the inherited permissions and set specific users and group roles for that object. The role assignments for the home folder are shown in Figure 21-33.

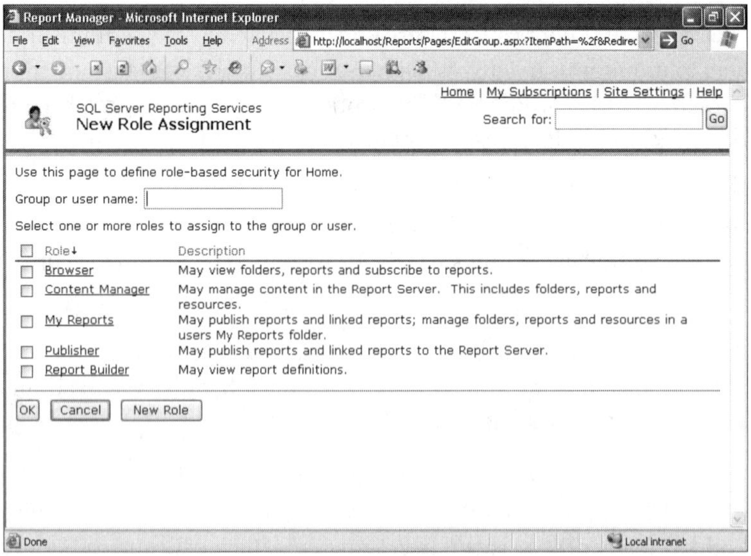

Figure 21-33 Report Manager role assignment for a home folder

Schedules

One other area of interest in Site Settings are Schedules and Jobs. You can use shared schedules for report caching, snapshots, and subscriptions. Rather than enter time and date particulars for each report, you can simply define a shared schedule with a meaningful name and then link this schedule to the target objects. Note that schedules have start and stop dates, so you can be very particular about when things happen.

The Jobs link at the bottom of the Site Settings page is a simple monitoring tool for report-related job activity. Any in-progress report or subscription appears here if it has been running for at least 30 seconds. This is the place to cancel long-running reporting jobs.

SQL Server Management Studio

SQL Server Management Studio can open a connection to Reporting Services. You can manage the folder namespace and all objects as shown in Figure 21-34.

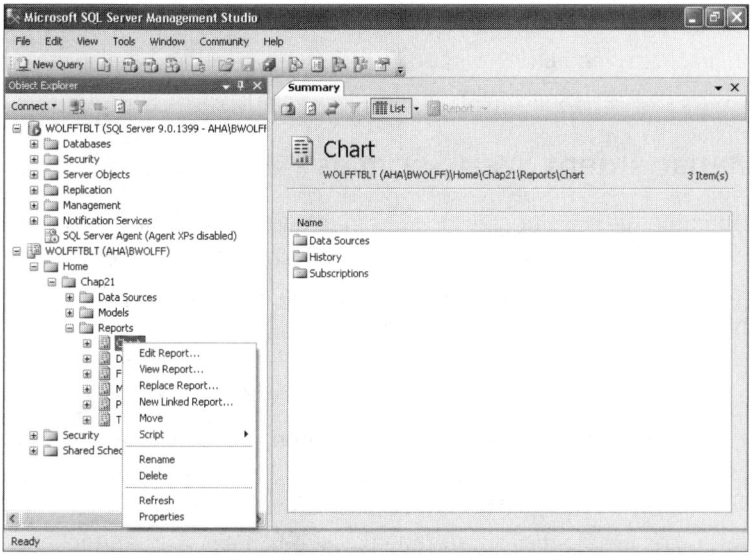

Figure 21-34 SQL Server Management Studio with report options

The nodes of Object Explorer represent the report server folder namespace and the built-in Security and Shared Schedules folders. Each object has a unique icon and shortcut menu. Use the right-click shortcut menus to access node-specific options. The dialog boxes mimic all the functionality of Report Manager in a simple interface. System administrators will be very comfortable with this productive approach.

Reporting Services Scripts (RSS, not to be confused with Really Simple Syndication) is a feature unique to Management Studio. Select a data source, model, or report object and use the shortcut menu to generate a script to a file, the clipboard, or a query window. Save the generated RSS file for use with the command-line utilities mentioned in the next section. You can also paste the resulting code into a Visual Basic project to save precious development time. Unfortunately, you cannot script folders, roles, or schedules.

Command-Line Utilities

Three command-line utilities are included for maintenance and batch operations. The script host, Rs.exe, runs batch scripts in RSS format that copy content between servers, publish reports, adjust item properties, and more. The configuration tool Rsconfig.exe stores encrypted data connection credentials in the RSReportServer.config file. The key management utility, Rskeymgmt.exe, manages symmetric keys used to encrypt report data. It also creates key sets used in large multi-server scale-out deployments.

Programming: Management Web Services

The Chap21 solution in the code samples includes C# and Visual Basic projects that interact with Reporting Services. The CS Forms project has two forms, called Service.cs and Render.cs, that enumerate folders and report items using the Web service interface. You must add a Web reference to this WSDL:

http://localhost/reportserver/reportservice2005.asmx?wsdl

You then create an instance of the *ReportServer* object. Numerous objects and methods expose the management and rendering functionality of the server. In our two examples, the *ReportingService2005* object is queried with the *ListChildren* method to get a list of items at a specific folder level. The item names are stored in a list box in Service.cs and in a tree view in Render.cs. The latter has logic to iterate multiple folder levels.

This is just one example of the Reporting Services Web service power. You can create tools that modify properties, manage schedules, create snapshots, and render reports. Note that Report Manager is actually written using this functionality. This technique is explained further later in the chapter.

Report Access and Delivery

Several methods are available for delivering reports to users on demand or by subscription. Most popular is the Report Manager interface described earlier. You can embed reports in SharePoint Portal using the included Web parts. Direct browser access is handled by URL parameters. There is also a *ReportViewer* control that programmers can embed in ASP.NET or Windows Forms applications.

Delivery on Demand

Reports are available on demand through Report Manager and direct URL browser Web connections.

Report Manager

The basic navigation concepts for Report Manager were described earlier. Users navigate the folder namespace hierarchy or use the search prompt to find the desired report. Folder and report items are presented as single-click hyperlinks. Clicking a report runs the report with a control toolbar at the top of the page. The toolbar has buttons for paging, zooming, search, export, refresh, and printing, as shown in Figure 21-35.

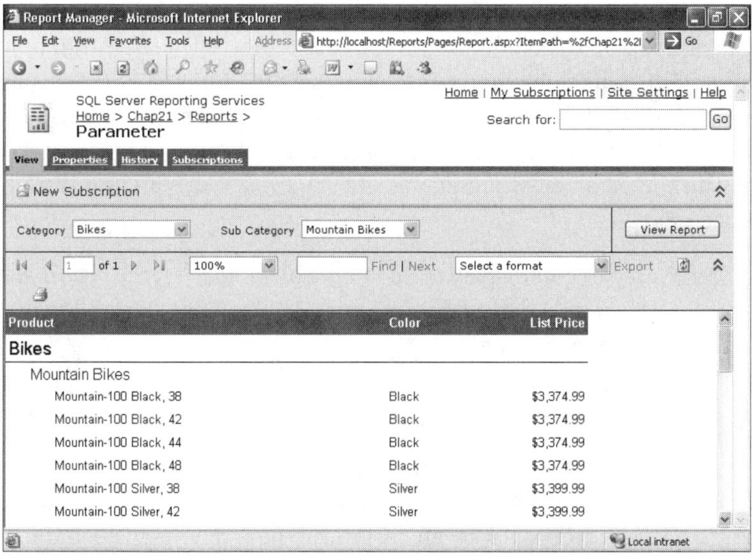

Figure 21-35   *ReportViewer* in Report Manager

The search text box accepts a string. Entering the string enables the Find and Next links, which help you search larger reports for a particular phrase.

The Print button loads a print preview ActiveX control that downloads from the report server. You can set device properties, adjust margins, and select page ranges.

If the report requires parameters, a text box or drop-down list is included on the toolbar for each parameter. Fill in the details or select from the list. Click the View Report button to render the report and see the Report Viewer toolbar. Some parameters are dependent on each other, as described earlier. In this case, selecting from one list fills the next.

The Select A Format drop-down list works in conjunction with the Export link to render reports in a variety of presentation formats. The output options are discussed later in the "Presentation Formats" section. Custom formats are possible using the rendering extensions discussed later in the section titled "Rendering Extensions."

SharePoint Web Parts

Two SharePoint Web parts are included that enable folder navigation and report viewing. These work with SharePoint Services or Portal Server. The Web parts must be installed on the SharePoint server using the Stsadm.exe utility. Report Manager must be installed and operational because the Report Viewer Web part makes URL calls directly to this site. If SharePoint and Reporting Services live on the same machine, the Reporting Services virtual directories must be excluded from SharePoint Services.

You add the Web parts to a SharePoint page. You can use Report Viewer by itself or in tandem with Report Explorer. In standalone mode, the report server address and report path are entered in the Web part's Properties dialog box. You cannot enter required parameters. The report runs automatically when the page is displayed and prompts you for the parameters. If you want a page with the parameters preset, use a PageViewer Web part and the URL access approach described next.

The Report Explorer Web part can display the contents of a folder on the report server. You can select a report and have it linked to a Report Viewer Web part for display. Report Explorer also has links for subscription management.

Browser URL Access

Instead of navigating Report Manager, it might be preferable to display a report directly in a browser window. This technique allows integration with existing Web sites and forms applications using a browser control. You can customize the report viewing and navigation experience by including parameters in the URL phrase. You can also pass report and query parameters in this fashion. The URL phrase is often used in a Web page hyperlink that opens in a new target window or iframe.

Two sets of parameters are used to control navigation and viewing options. The viewer commands are prefixed with *rc:* and include Toolbar, Parameters, DocMap, Zoom, Find, Paging, and Stylesheets. The report server commands are prefixed with *rs:* and include Format, Language, and Snapshot. Samples of the URL syntax are shown in the URL Access programming sample.

ReportViewer Control

The *ReportViewer* control is part of the .NET Framework 2.0. It works in Windows Forms, as shown in Figure 21-36, and Web pages, as shown in Figure 21-37.

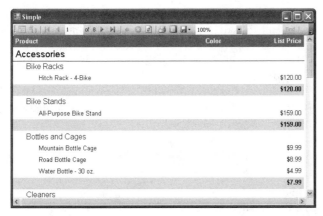

Figure 21-36   *ReportViewer* control in a Windows Forms application

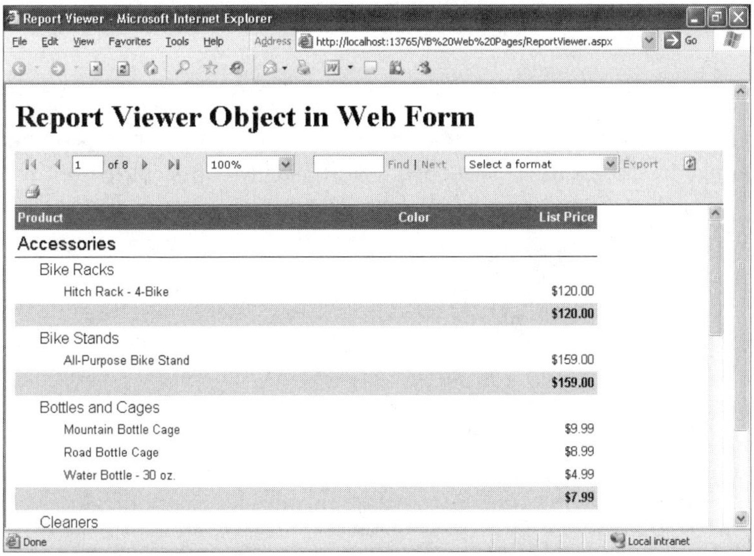

Figure 21-37   *ReportViewer* control in an ASP.NET Web page

You can configure *ReportViewer* to render a report locally or from a report server. Both use the same basic rendering technology. The local client-based rendering relies on an RDLC file included in the project. The report server method requires a report server URL and a report path. Properties are set to configure toolbar, navigation, and output options. This control is provided royalty free and is a great addition to any polished .NET application. Report Viewer code samples are described later in the chapter.

Subscriptions

You can automate report delivery through subscription services. You can link or attach a report to an e-mail message or save it to a file share. You create subscriptions on the Subscription tab of a report; they are summarized in the My Subscriptions link at the top of each Report Manager page. Note that all subscriptions require cached credentials in the report data source.

Once this requirement is met, the New Subscription button on the Subscription tab opens a page that prompts for the delivery method. Report Server File Share is one option. If e-mail settings are configured for the report server, the second option is Report Server E-Mail. Custom delivery extensions are described at the end of this chapter. They appear as additional delivery methods.

Subscriptions must have a schedule. You can manually create a schedule for the report or use a shared schedule maintained by an administrator in the Site Settings area. A schedule can specify running once or repeating hourly, daily, weekly, or monthly. Select the desired days and time. Start and end dates limit the lifetime.

Subscriptions are dependent on the SQL Reporting Services Windows service and the SQL Server Agent service. Both must be running to successfully complete your subscription.

E-Mail

The e-mail delivery method creates a single e-mail message with a report link or an attached file. Links are more efficient for internal reporting and usually connect the user directly to Report Manager. Attachments are appropriate for external mailings, typically in PDF or XLS format. You can specify the To, Cc, Bcc, Subject, Priority, and Body (comment). You are prompted for any required parameters at the bottom of the form. Formatting support is limited. Highly stylized messages require a custom delivery extension. The same is true for multiple file attachments per message.

Shared Folder

The folder delivery method creates a single file for each report. You enter the path and select a report format. Credentials are required for access to the file share. Options for overwrite and file versioning are available.

Data-Driven Subscriptions

Data-driven subscriptions can generate e-mails or shared folder files. The required settings are provided by a database query. You can use a subscription-specific or shared data source to host a query that returns one row for each report that you want to generate. The columns include names such as To, Cc, Bcc, Subject, filename, path, render_format, and values for required report parameters. You map these directly to the required settings.

This method provides a lot of flexibility for customized report distribution. You can create a sales report for hundreds or thousands of employees or customers that is then tailored to specific regions or product areas. This is also a good way to maintain archived reports to satisfy retention policies.

Presentation Formats

Report output can be produced in a variety of Web-, page-, and desktop-compatible formats. You cannot edit these files using the Reporting Services tools, but third-party products are available to fit this need. Each format has specific options and properties that configure the rendering extension. The same extensions are used on the report server, the Report Designer environment, and the *ReportViewer* control.

HTML

HTML is the default rendering extension. It produces UTF-8 encoded pages or fragments. Standard HTML 4.0 is produced by Report Manager, SharePoint Web parts, and direct URL access. HTML 3.2 is possible only through URL addressing with the rs:Format=HTML3.2 option. MHTML is also available through URL addressing and the Export option in Report Manager. This format, referred to as Web Archive, combines the graphics and report data into a single file.

All report data regions are rendered as tables. Charts become images. Style properties turn into CSS style tags. Report-level items such as headers and footers become HTML *<DIV>* tags.

Excel

The Excel rendering extension creates BIFF files that are compatible with Excel 97 and later. Each page in the report generates a worksheet in the Excel file, as shown in Figure 21-38. The data is stored in tabular format with nesting. Some colors are not supported, so substitutions are made. Limitations exist for worksheet, row, cell, and column sizes, so very large reports can be problematic. Charts turn into pictures and are not editable Excel chart objects. Document maps are rendered as the first worksheet with links to other data sheets.

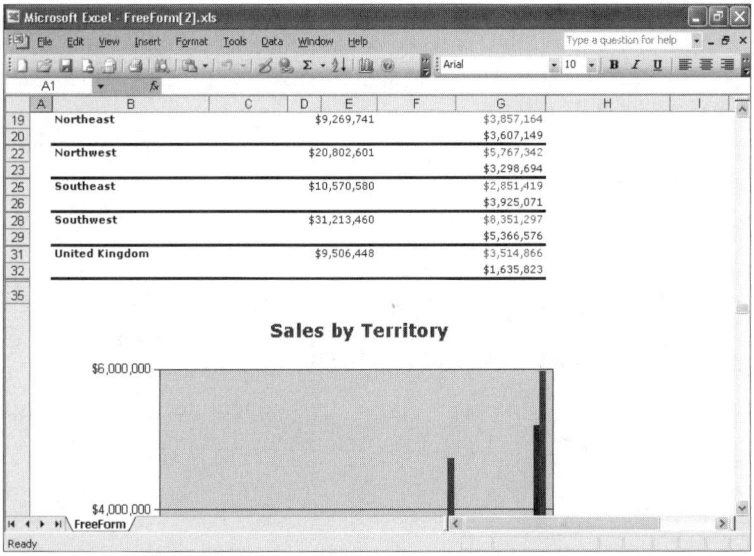

Figure 21-38   Report output in Excel format

PDF

The PDF rendering extension produces PDF 1.3–compatible output, as shown in Figure 21-39. These files are suitable for viewers such as Adobe Acrobat. Bookmarks are supported and turn into PDF bookmarks. Avoid drillthrough links—use hyperlinks instead. Make sure that all fonts necessary to view the report are installed on the report server as well as on the target clients.

Sales by Territory and Year		2003		2004	2002
		Total Due	Unit Qty	Total Due	Unit Qty	Total Due
Southwest	AW00000583	$5,655	30			$9,675
	AW00000609	$1,683	5	$1,074	4	$1,064
	AW00000041	$36,392	202	$30,861	92	$12,656
	AW00000133	$126,468	504			$230,393
	AW00000491	$194,697	434	$174,613	341	$80,312
	AW00000457	$37,634	93			$114,733
	AW00000563	$22,270	24	$16,149	21	
	AW00000187	$163,005	346	$62,702	116	$169,342
	AW00000023	$48,440	184	$20,213	50	$55,772
	AW00000473	$13,650	43	$3,623	11	$11,162
	AW00000366					$163,262
	AW00000492	$3,187	89	$1,018	21	$37,063
	AW00000403	$137,887	226			$212,107
	AW00000648	$162,715	288	$97,970	142	$233,269
	AW00000167	$314,023	589	$70,592	179	$357,057

Figure 21-39   Report output in PDF format

TIFF

The Image rendering extension creates a bitmap or metafile. The default format is TIFF, which stores multiple pages in a single file. Other available formats include valid GDI+ variants: GIF, JPEG, PNG, BMP, and EMF. Size, resolution, and image format are configurable. Items are rendered in the order that they appear in the report definition. You can control this by setting the *zindex* property of select objects.

CSV

The Comma-Separated Value (CSV) rendering extension produces plain-text files with no character formatting or graphics. This is useful for importing into other applications, such as spreadsheets and databases. The first row contains field names by default. All data regions are output with a column for each data element. This extension ignores such items as headers, footers, images, and ActiveX controls. Field, record, qualifier, and header settings are configurable.

XML

The XML rendering extension creates XML documents that are specific to the source report. Layout and images are ignored. XML is useful in application integration scenarios. The top-level element in XML is Report. Each data region creates an element. The elements and attributes are generated in the order that they appear in the report definition, as shown in Figure 21-40. Data types are notated in the included schema. You can set element names by using the *DataElementName* property of individual objects in Report Designer or by using raw RDL.

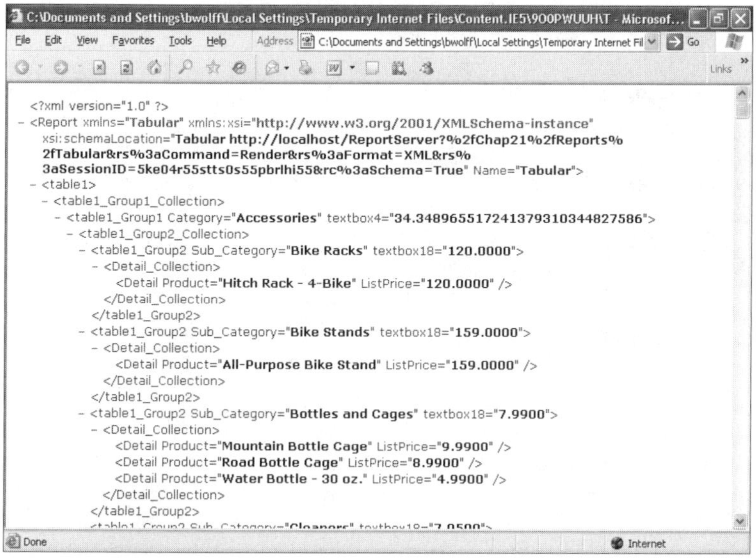

Figure 21-40   Report output in XML format when viewed in Internet Explorer

The rendered XML can be transformed using an XSLT document that you specify in URL addressing. This is a creative and efficient way to produce custom output formats. The result can be a more complex XML document, XHTML, or plain text. Note that each report creates unique XML output, so the XSLT transforms are specific to that report.

Programming: Rendering

The code samples for this chapter include several examples that demonstrate report output. One uses ASP.NET Web pages to host links and iframes for URL access. Another incorporates the *ReportViewer* control in both ASP.NET pages and Windows Forms. The third is a useful utility that combines Web service functionality with rendering to create a report file generation factory.

Parameterized URL Access

One project in the Chap21 solution, CS Web Pages, includes a URLAccess.ASPX page that demonstrates URL access, as shown in Figure 21-41.

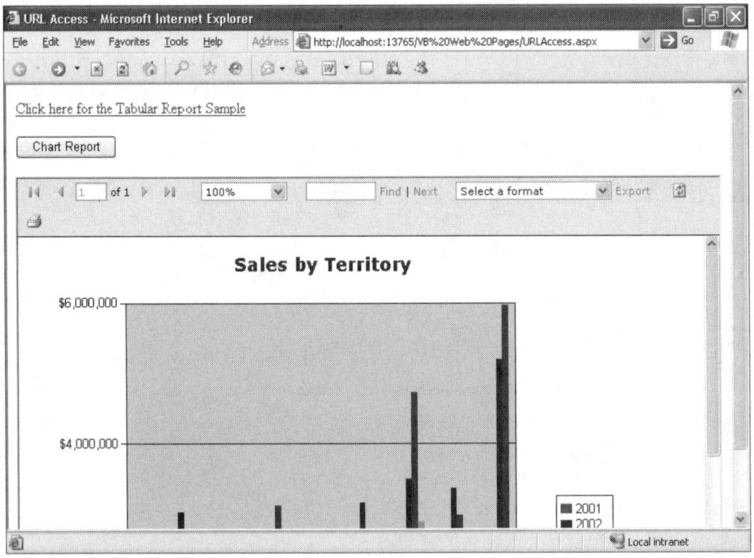

Figure 21-41   URL access inside a Web Page using an IFrame tag

In design view, you see a hyperlink (<A> tag) that opens a new page with the Tabular report. The URL phrase is shown here:

http://localhost/reportserver?/Chap21/reports/Tabular&rs:Command:Render

In this example, *localhost* is the server name and *reportserver* indicates the Web service virtual directory. The path and report are the first URL parameters. The *rs:Command* parameter instructs report server to render the report. Several *rs:* and *rc:* parameter options were described earlier.

The Chart Report button on the Web page has an *onclick* event handler that sets the *src* property of an iframe. This causes the chart sample to appear on demand.

ReportViewer Examples

The *ReportViewer* control is part of the .NET Framework 2.0. You can use it in ASP.NET pages as well as Windows Forms, as shown earlier in Figures 21-36 and 21-37. The ASP.NET project called CS Web Pages has a page called ReportViewer.aspx that embeds this control. The properties of the control have a *ProcessingMode* that defaults to *Local.* Choose Remote, and use the *Smart Tag* control to set the Report Server URL and Report Path. The Toolbar category in the Properties window has options that control the toolbar display. No code is needed for the report to display at runtime.

The project CS Forms has a form called Simple.cs. This form embeds a *ReportViewer* control with the *Dock* property set to *fill*. You use the *Smart Tag* control or Properties windows to adjust the settings. Notice that the report properties are identical in the Web and form versions. Adding this control to the form automatically generates the necessary lines of code:

```
private void Simple_Load(object sender, EventArgs e)
{
    this.reportViewer1.RefreshReport();
}
```

Another sample form, called Service.cs, uses the report server Web service to enumerate folder and report names in a list box. Selecting a list item triggers the *SelectedIndexChanged* event, which sets the *ReportViewer ReportPath* property and calls *RefreshReport*, as shown in the following code block:

```
namespace CS_Forms
{
    public partial class Service : Form
    {
        ReportingService2005 rptSrvr = new ReportingService2005();
        CatalogItem[] catItem;

        public Service()
        {
            InitializeComponent();
        }

        private void Service_Load(object sender, EventArgs e)
        {
        rptSrvr.Credentials = System.Net.CredentialCache.DefaultCredentials;
        rptSrvr.Url = "http://localhost/reportserver/reportservice2005.asmx";

        catItem = rptSrvr.ListChildren("/Chap21/reports", true);

        foreach (CatalogItem item in catItem)
            {
              ListBox1.Items.Add(item.Name);
            }
        }

        private void ListBox1_SelectedIndexChanged(object sender, EventArgs e)
        {
            ReportViewer1.ServerReport.ReportPath = catItem[ListBox1.SelectedIndex].Path;
            ReportViewer1.RefreshReport();
        }

    }
}
```

Rendering Factory

The report server Web service can render reports in several output formats. A CS Forms project called Render.cs combines the folder navigation methods with a *Treeview* control to display the folder hierarchy. Select a report from the /Chap21/Reports folder. The option button in the middle of the form determines the output format. Enter a file name, and use *FolderBrowserDialog* to select a target file folder. The Generate button renders the report using the Web service and redirects the byte stream to the target file. This utility can quickly generate sample output for testing purposes. The code can easily be edited to automate other report generation tasks.

Report Server Architecture

Reporting Services combines a mix of Microsoft technologies to create a scalable server-based reporting architecture. You can view this as a middle-tier server in your enterprise planning scenarios. It is one part Web server and one part database server, with a dash of .NET managed code to bring all the pieces together. Using Visual Studio as the base development platform is somewhat challenging for a business user but very comfortable for the seasoned developer. Business-savvy users are better suited using the report model and Report Builder tools, which are also built into the .NET Framework.

Internet Information Services

The Web server portion of Reporting Services requires Microsoft Internet Information Services (IIS). You will experience significantly improved performance using IIS 6.0, which is included in Windows Server 2003. You gain even more substantial improvements using the 64-bit version of Windows Server and SQL Server. Configure the server to support ASP.NET 2.0. (This happens automatically during installation.) Two virtual directories are created in the same application pool (Figure 21-42).

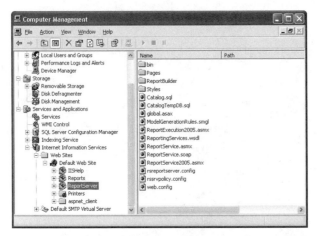

Figure 21-42   IIS virtual directories for Reporting Services

It is a good practice to keep the Reporting Services directories in a separate pool on IIS 6.0 so that they can be stopped and started without affecting other Web sites on the host machine. One of the virtual directories is the Report Manager application, which is written using the same API and Web service capabilities available to custom developers. The second Web site is the Web service interface, where all the heavy lifting occurs. Encrypting report delivery with SSL is optional but highly recommended if your reports have sensitive data. Keep in mind that SSL has a slight performance impact.

Both virtual directories point to folders under the Reporting Services installation. Note that these live on the C drive by default. Some enterprises have policies that require all applications to be installed on drives other than the root. Reports are actually stored in a database, so these folders do not grow much in size other than their error logs.

You can change the virtual directory names and target site by using the Reporting Services Configuration tool. The default names are Reports for Report Manager and ReportServer for Web services.

SQL Server Databases

Reporting Services creates two SQL databases. One stores reports, report models, shared data sources, resources, and metadata managed by the server. It is called ReportServer by default but can be changed using the Reporting Services Configuration tool. Use this technique to move reporting from one server to another, repoint a test instance to production, or have multiple servers share one database for a scale-out cluster. The other database is called ReportServerTempDB; it stores temporary tables and data snapshots. This database can grow significantly with heavy use and should be closely monitored.

Note that the table structure in these databases can change over time, so writing directly to the tables is not recommended. Use the SOAP Web services and rendering extensions instead.

Windows Services

A single Windows service called SQL Server Reporting Services runs unattended on the report server. It is responsible for managing, scheduling, executing, rendering, delivering, and granting access to reports. It should be set to run automatically at startup and restart automatically on failure. The service can run under the local system account or a domain-level account.

Subscriptions rely on the SQL Server Agent scheduled jobs function. The reporting service polls the metadata tables in the database periodically to determine whether a report job is ready to run. The job is actually entered into SQL Server Agent and set to run at a scheduled time. If one of the services fails, subscriptions might not complete. Make sure that both services are running if you depend on the subscription feature.

All the SQL Server services are monitored and managed through SQL Server Configuration Manager. You can get to this through the SQL Server menus or the Computer Management console (Figure 21-43).

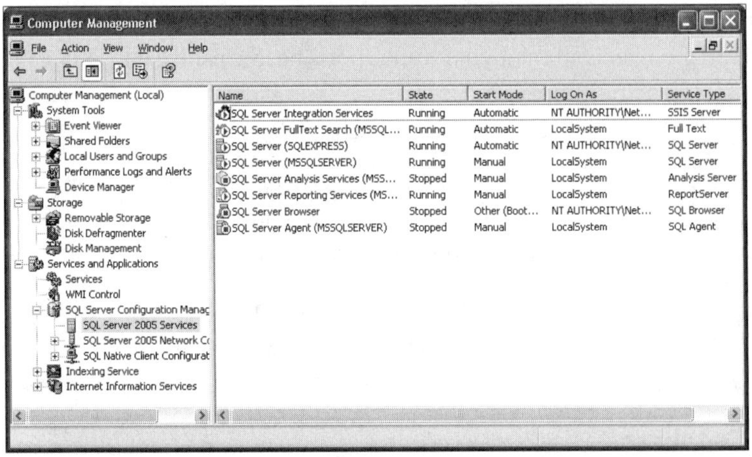

Figure 21-43   Windows Services in Computer Management console

Events and Logs

The Windows application log contains information about general events. Look for the Report Server, Report Manager, and Scheduling and Delivery Processor event sources. The Performance log has counters to track number of reports and other metrics. Use the RS Web Service counters to monitor report server performance, and use the RS Windows Service counters to track monitored operations and report delivery.

The report server trace logs are text files stored in the Reporting Services installation LogFiles folder. There are four types of files:

- ReportServerService_<timestamp>.log traces worker threads.

- ReportServerService_main_<timestamp>.log traces management threads.

- ReportServerWebApp_<timestamp>.log details Report Manager tasks.

- ReportServer_<timestamp>.log traces Web service calls.

You can customize the tracing details in the report server configuration files. These files are very detailed and not easy to read, but they do contain the information needed to debug or troubleshoot execution and security issues.

Numerous files in the SQL database store information about report execution and delivery. You can extract this information into a table format that is easy to query and report. Use the supplied extract packages and sample reports in the Report Samples.

Deployment Modes

The Reporting Services architecture can support small workgroups or large enterprise accounts. A single server can run the reporting engine and a copy of SQL Server that houses the reporting databases. You can split these over two servers by using a remote instance of SQL Server for the database portion. You might do this for disk space, memory, or processor usage reasons.

Combining Reporting Services with Windows SharePoint Services or SharePoint Portal Server is popular. If both exist on the same server, install Reporting Services with the Files Only option. You must run the SharePoint STSADM configuration utility to exclude the Reporting Services virtual directories. This prevents security and ISAPI filter issues. Use the Reporting Services Configuration tool to complete the settings for the report services and databases. Make sure the SharePoint and Reporting Services virtual directories run in different application pools on IIS 6.0 or later.

SQL Server Enterprise Edition and Developer Edition support a scale-out deployment model. Multiple report servers rely on a shared database instance on a local or remote SQL Server. For optimum redundancy, run the SQL instance on a Windows Server failover cluster.

Internet facing scenarios are also supported with some custom configuration. Installing the report server and Report Manager outside the firewall allows full use of reporting features. There is no built-in forms-based authentication, so you must develop a custom security processing extension. A more secure approach is to have Report Manager live outside the firewall but keep Reporting Services inside the firewall. This mode does not support report drillthrough, e-mail subscription links, or Report Builder.

Note that an SQL Server license is required for all computers running Reporting Services. If the database, services, and Report Manager are split over three machines, three licenses are required.

Extensibility

Reporting Services is designed for extensibility. You can use the .NET Framework to build fully trusted managed code assemblies that provide delivery, data processing, rendering, and security capabilities. Report Service is typically managed by using the full-featured SOAP-based Web service interface. For even more detail, consider using the WMI provider.

Delivery Extensions

Reporting Services includes delivery extensions for SMTP e-mail and network file shares. These are closely tied to subscriptions. When a user subscribes to a report or runs a data-driven subscription, notifications are generated and a delivery extension is called with the parameters set in the subscription. The delivery extension is responsible for rendering reports and sending the data through some communications channel. The rendering logic and delivery mechanism are completely controlled by the extension developer. An XML configuration file defines the extension components on the report server and Report Manager. Your .NET assemblies are installed in the reportserver\bin folder.

Data Processing Extensions

Reporting Services data processing extensions retrieve data from a connected source. The built-in extensions connect to SQL Server, OLE DB, ODBC, and Oracle. This covers a large percentage of the available data sources in any organization. Some custom applications might require data sources not handled by OLE DB and ODBC. These might include scientific or industrial devices, older computing systems, or proprietary technology. There are well-defined interfaces that must be coded in a managed code assembly. The required classes include *connection*, *command*, and *datareader*. The latter fills a dataset that is consumed by the rendering engine. The XML configuration file is deployed to the report server and Report Designer in BI Development Studio or Visual Studio.

Rendering Extensions

Reporting Services rendering extensions create device-specific layout information from a report definition. The built-in extensions include various HTML flavors, Excel, PDF, TIFF, CSV, and XML, as described earlier. Consider using variations of these built-in extensions or XSLT transforms to create proprietary output. If your needs are more specific, you can use a well-known set of interfaces called the Rendering Object Model, which provides a collection of classes to an extension developer. Managed code iterates through these classes to produce an output stream suitable for the target device. Deploy the completed assembly to the report-server/bin folder and create an entry in the XML configuration files.

Security Extensions

Reporting Services security extensions authenticate and authorize users and groups for report administration and delivery. The built-in extensions work with basic Windows security providers such as Active Directory. Consider writing a managed code extension for forms-based external Web site access or integration with existing security providers. Implement the *LogonUser* and *CheckAccess* methods based on the well-known interfaces.

WMI Provider

The Windows Management Instrumentation (WMI) interfaces are the bedrock of the Microsoft Dynamic Systems Initiative suite of products that includes Operations Manager and Systems Management Server. Reporting Services supports numerous WMI classes that allow discovery, control, activation, and monitoring of Reporting Server instances. These classes are defined in the *root\Microsoft\SqlServer\ReportingServices\v8* namespace.

Report Integration

Reporting Services is a powerful platform for report creation, delivery, and management. As this technology matures, numerous ISVs are integrating reports into their custom products. The SOAP-based Web service, open RDL and RDS file formats, extension classes, and WMI support make a wonderful foundation for the skilled developer.

Microsoft is a leading implementer in this field. It offers reporting links to many of its popular application products. Among the more popular ones are the Web parts designed for the SharePoint portal suite. They make customized Web-based report delivery a snap. Other prominent products that use the full Reporting Services feature set include Microsoft Operations Manager (MOM), Data Protection Manager, and some Dynamics offerings. A new Systems Center Reporting release combines Analysis Services cubes with Reporting Services to create a comprehensive suite of infrastructure management reports. It marries the log and metric data from MOM with the inventory and deployment details of Systems Management Server. This is an excellent example of the evolutionary integration work done by Microsoft product developers.

Summary

SQL Server Reporting Services provides a wealth of features and benefits for both developers and end users. You can report on data from the most popular sources, build rich layouts with little or no programming, add interactive features such as parameters and document maps, and produce output in a variety of useful formats. Reporting Services understands XML for input and output and uses it internally to store well-documented report definitions. The management tools help categorize and organize reports in a folder structure driven by role-based security. The middle-tier architecture is built on the fast and reliable SQL Server, IIS, ASP.NET, and .NET Framework foundation. If there is any reporting need not covered out of the box, the Web service framework and extensibility platform provide exceptional flexibility. You can confidently rely on SQL Server Reporting Services for all your reporting needs.

Index

Symbol
<> (bracketed parameter declaration tags), 162

A
Access Query Designer, 158
AccessMode method, 232
Accumulate method, 74, 77
ACID properties, 330, 332
AcquireConnections method, 233
Action property
  database backup, 183
  database restore, 187
  log file backup, 185
  log file restore, 187
actions, 645–648
  defined, 645
  executing via schema DataSet objects, 714–716
  testing, 647
Active Server Pages (ASP), 218
ActiveX controls, PivotTable/ChartSpace controls as, 686
ActiveX Data Objects (ADO), 218
ActiveX Task, 238
ADDLOCAL parameters, SQL Express and, 143–145
AddModelWithDrillthrough.dmx, 783, 784, 786
AddToWhereClause method, 320
ADO (ActiveX Data Objects), 218
ADO MD, 576, 706
ADO MD.NET, 576, 691, 706–718
  Analysis Services CLR support, 729
  data mining support, 801
  DMX prediction queries, 804
  library, 707
  XMLA, 728
AdomdCommand object, 707, 708
  DMX prediction queries, 804
  XMLA, 728
AdomdCommand.ExecuteCellSet method, 707
AdomdConnection object, 707, 803
  cube metadata, 711
  data mining, 801
AdomdDataAdapter object, 707
  DMX queries, 804
  MDX queries, 708
AdomdServer namespace, DMX queries and, 806–808
ADO.NET, 219
  isolation levels, 341, 346
  local transactions, 338–340
  query notification, 387, 388
  version 2.0, 219, 231–242

Adventure Works Cycles, 312, 319
AdventureSales sample application, 312–328
AdventureWorks database, 745
  CTEs, 14
  downloading, 157
  Native XML Web Services, 319
AdventureWorks sample cube, 601, 603
AdventureWorksSalesTeam security group, 317
Agent service, security and, 211
aggregate expressions, 31
aggregate functions, 36
Aggregate property, 621
Aggregate transform, 212
AggregateFunction property, 621
aggregation design, 651
All member, changing, 606
AllowDBNull property, 224
AllowPropertyToolbox property, 685
ALL_RESULTS value, 306, 310
ALTER DATABASE statement, 390
ALTER ENDPOINT statement, 305, 309
ALTER MINING STRUCTURE statement, 784
ALTER permission, 310
ALTER scripts, CLR entities and, 88
ALTER SERVICE MASTER KEY REGENERATE DDL
    statement, 207
ALTER TABLE statement, 336
AMO (Analysis Management Objects), 691, 716–718
AMO library, 716
AMs (anchor members), 16–18
Analysis Management Objects (AMO), 691, 716–718
Analysis Manager, 579
Analysis Servers, registering in Management Studio, 12
Analysis Services, 573, 644
  CLR support, 692, 729–739
  new features, 601–603
  Reporting Services, 821
Analysis Services designer, 579
Analysis Services event provider, 395, 398
Analyze Query in Database Engine Tuning Advisor option,
    150
anchor members (AMs), 16–18
Anchor property, 685
APIs (application programming interfaces), 371
applications
  backup-and-restore, 182–188
  ClickOnce deployment, 157–171
  client, 310–311, 319–324
  dashboard, 633
  debugging, 259–297

X

About the Authors

Andrew J. Brust is Chief, New Technology at twentysix New York, a Microsoft Gold Certified Partner specializing in business intelligence, enterprise integration, and .NET application development. Andrew is a Microsoft Regional Director for New York/New Jersey, a Visual Basic MVP, a member of Microsoft's Business Intelligence Partner Advisory Council, a Conference Chair for VSLive!, and a Vice Chair of the New York Software Industry Association.

© 2006 Jay Brady

Stephen Forte is Chief Technology Officer and cofounder of Corzen, Inc., a Manhattan-based provider of online market research data for Wall Street firms. Stephen is also the Microsoft Regional Director for the New York Metro region as well as an MVP and INETA speaker. He speaks regularly at industry conferences around the world, including Tech Ed and North Africa Developers Conference. He is the author of several books on application and database development. Prior to joining Corzen, Stephen served as CTO of Zagat Survey in New York City and also was cofounder and CTO of the New York–based software consulting firm The Aurora Development Group. He currently is the comoderator and founder of the NYC .NET Developer User Group.

Contributing Authors

Kent Brown is the manager of the Enterprise Integration practice at twentysix New York (*www.26NY.com*), a Microsoft Gold Certified Partner.

Kent has 17 years of experience in software development in the pharmaceutical, financial services, insurance, legal, and manufacturing industries. He has authored over 12 articles, primarily on enterprise integration technologies—service-oriented architecture (SOA), Microsoft BizTalk, and SOAP. He has been involved with Microsoft .NET since its early beta, and he spoke at VSLive! 2001 on .NET Remoting. He often plays a mentoring role, providing training, design, and team leadership to help teams establish correct architecture and best practices around new technologies (such as object-oriented programming in .NET and SOA).

Kent is the founder and leader of the New Jersey .NET Architecture and Development User Group (*www.njevbug.org*). He is also a leader of the NYC Connected Systems User Group (*www.nyccsug.org*).

Sergei Ivanov is a self-taught programmer who currently works as a software development lead at Microsoft. He started at Microsoft as a Volt contractor in 1998. For the past eight years, he has been on development teams for Windows 2000, Windows XP, SQL Server, and Office RTC. His current project is unannounced. Before joining Microsoft, Sergei was part of several research and development organizations in Europe. As a student at University of Paderborn in Germany, he wrote Windows front ends for the MuPAD computer algebra system and a V-Cam 2D and 3D plotting tool. In 1996, he wrote the first implementation of Public-Key Cryptography Standard #12 in collaboration with RSA, Netscape, and Microsoft, kick-starting adoption of the standard by the Netscape Navigator and Microsoft Internet Explorer browsers.

Ted Lee is currently a development lead at Microsoft on the SQL Server Integration Services team and has worked as a software design engineer on both Data Transformation Services (DTS) and SQL Server Integration Services. When not at work, he enjoys hiking and other outdoor activities in the Seattle area with his wife, Adrienne, and their German shepherd dog, Tausha.

Sahil Malik is a Microsoft MVP (C#), INETA speaker, author of a best-selling ADO.NET 2.0 book, ADO.NET trainer for Keystonelearning.com, and a telerik evangelist. He also works as a consultant, trainer, and mentor in various Microsoft technologies. He frequently speaks at local usergroup meetings and industry events on a variety of .NET-related topics. Sahil can be reached at *www.winsmarts.com*.

Elsie Pan is a senior database developer at twentysix New York (*www.26NY.com*), with many years of experience implementing data warehouse and OLAP solutions for financial institutions. She also has more than 10 years of experience in statistical modeling and data analysis. Prior to joining twentysix New York, Elsie earned a master's degree in economics from Princeton University and worked in the public policy research arena.

Patrick O'Toole is a Visual Studio .NET programmer with 20 years of programming experience. A programmer by day and a writer by night, he has published technical articles online and in *Advisor Guide to Microsoft Visual Basic .NET* magazine. In addition, his screenplays have been pitched to and well received by Hollywood production companies. He currently works for Mercom Systems, Inc., in New Jersey, where his primary focus is developing new applications with AJAX technologies. Past projects have included a content management system and Web site for Zagat Survey, LLC. He resides in northern New Jersey with his wife, two step-daughters, two cats, and three dogs.

Rob Walters is a program manager on the Microsoft SQL Server Security team. Before moving to the security team, Rob worked on SQL Server Express Edition. He has written numerous articles on SQL Server 2005 and is a contributing author to *Pro SQL Server 2005* (Apress, Inc. 2005).

Bill Wolff is an independent consultant, trainer, and architect specializing in Microsoft development technologies. His company, Agility Systems, is based in the Philadelphia area. He ran the consulting firm Wolff Data Systems for 15 years and directed armies of consultants in the dot-com world. Bill is founder and president of the philly.net user group; is an INETA board member and vice president of its speakers' bureau; and is involved in several other user communities. Bill was a contributing author of several books and articles and currently writes for *.NET Developer's Journal*. His certifications include trainer, systems engineer, developer, and Microsoft MVP for Visual Basic .NET.

William H. Zack is a consultant, architect, administrator, developer, systems integrator, and author of several computer books and white papers, including the book *Windows 2000 and Mainframe Integration* and the "Host Integration Server 2005 Reviewers Guide" and "Enterprise Single Sign-On" white papers featured on *www.microsoft.com*.

William is co-moderator of the NYC .NET Developers Group, founder and past president of the New York Enterprise Windows User Group, and the founder and past president of several other computer user groups. He is also the founder and president of the New York chapter of the International Association of Software Architects (IASA) and a member of the IASA board of directors.

He is currently employed as a solutions architect in the Financial Services Group of Microsoft Consulting.

What do you think of this book? We want to hear from you!

Do you have a few minutes to participate in a brief online survey? Microsoft is interested in hearing your feedback about this publication so that we can continually improve our books and learning resources for you.

To participate in our survey, please visit:
www.microsoft.com/learning/booksurvey

And enter this book's ISBN, 0-7356-1923-9. As a thank-you to survey participants in the United States and Canada, each month we'll randomly select five respondents to win one of five $100 gift certificates from a leading online merchant.* At the conclusion of the survey, you can enter the drawing by providing your e-mail address, which will be used for prize notification *only*.

Thanks in advance for your input. Your opinion counts!

Sincerely,

Microsoft Learning

Microsoft | Learning

Learn More. Go Further.